DAYS OF FUTURE'S PAST

DAYS OF FUTURE'S PAST
1989

Alisa M. Hoffman, Editor

THE NATIONAL LIBRARY OF POETRY

Northwest Business Center
5E Gwynns Mill Court
Owings Mills, MD 21117

DAYS OF FUTURE'S PAST

SECOND EDITION
IN ANTHOLOGY SERIES

Library of Congress
Cataloging in Publication Data

ISBN 0-940863-16-2 (Hardbound)
ISBN 0-940863-06-5 (Leatherbound)

Distributed by
Watermark Press
Owings Mills Industrial Park
5E Gwynns Mill Court
Owings Mills, MD 21117

Manufactured in The United States of America

Foreword

It is again my pleasure to bring to the public's attention the artistry of today's fine poets. After reading a great number of poems in this edition, I can understand why the judges had an extremely difficult time in choosing the winners. The reader is in for a very enjoyable experience, as there are so many fine poems in this edition. We are proud to be able to provide the public access to the talents of those poets through this hardbound series, and we are committed to maintaining our reputation as the country's foremost publisher of poetry anthologies.

Jeffrey Franz, Publisher

Acknowledgements

The publication of ***Days of Future's Past*** is a culmination of the efforts of many individuals. Judges, editors, assistant editors, typesetters, computer operators, graphic artists, layout artists, paste-up artists, and office administrators have all brought their respective talents to bear on the project. The editors are grateful for the contributions of these fine people:

Dorothy Anderson, Jeffrey Bryan, Roslyn Cook, Phyllis Franz, Ardie L. Freeman, Kimberly Harmeyer, Dawn Michelle Koslowski, Rachel Krumheuer, Olorah McLendon, Ruth Annette Logan, Michelle Ann Munter, Nancy Oberfeld, Bonnie Sue Pollack, Kathryn Runde, Elizabeth Sowell.

Also, special thanks to Jane Elizabeth Miller whose creative talents are evident in the beautiful illustration (page 1) and cover design. Her artistry has been an asset in making this edition even more lovely than the last.

Howard Ely, Managing Editor

Editor's Note

As editor of *Days of Future's Past*, as well as one of the three judges of the competition, I had an opportunity to read and discuss all of the entries that we received. Believe me, this was no easy task. I was amazed at the wide range of subjects the poems covered and the way the poets were able to evoke strong feelings in the reader, whether humorous or sensitive, pensive or optimistic. I enjoyed them all, but there were some that stood out from the rest.

Mary Carol Fox's poem "Requiem" was truly one of my favorites. Not only is this the most original poem I read, but Fox's unconventional use of words made up to suit her purpose enables her to "eggsactly" present the tone for which she is striving. The Latin phrases also add a dramatic contrast.

"I Cannot Stay" written by Karen O'Leary is a very insightful piece and graphically expresses a situation common in real life. What makes this poem different, though, is the extended metaphor which she uses. The straight-forward conclusion is very fitting. Michael J. Scharf's submission "Where Do They Go?" is a very thorough yet light-hearted look at what happens to sick squirrels, written in a traditional style. It made everyone in our office smile.

Our Grand Prize Winner, A. K. Penn-Lambert, gives a chilling account of man's destiny if technology is left unbridled. Through the mystic ceremonial rites of an Indian Shaman, the reader is subtly reminded of his individual responsibility to future generations.

Although only 70 top prizes could be awarded, all of the artists published in this volume are deserving of recognition for their fine artistic talent, for it is only with creative minds such as these that written language can continue to delight and inspire the reader.

Alisa M. Hoffman, Editor

Grand Prize Winner

A. K. Penn-Lambert

Second Prize Winners

Christine Bright	Karen O'Leary
Tina Louise Crisp	Michael J. Scharf
Mary Carolyn Fox	Lori Skalabrin
Kathy Watson Jumper	Edwin L. Stephens
Kathy S. Moussette	Stephen Volk

Third Prize Winners

Mary Elizabeth Anderson	George Gram	Lesia Johnson Powell
Paul Arblaster	G. Gorecki	Katrina Reef
Arthur Ashley	Christy Halverson	Harvey E. Reese III
Marion J. Beauregard-Bezou	Arden Heller	Judy Rinard
Zola C. Beebe	Patricia Fain Hutson	Robert Allan Ross
Isabelle Bennett	Terrie Jelsma	Mark Antony Rossi
Marjorie Blankenbaker	Sharon Kamman	Rachel Sidebottom
Kristin Bowling	Anne-Marie Krause	Amy Sinclair
Shirley Ann Bradley	Harvey LaGasse	Katherine A. Smith
K. Bryant	Lisa Martin	Jeanne M. Stauffer
Sandra Clutter	Joan Matlaga	Alex Stewart
Crystal Cochran	Bobbi McGonegal	Agnes White Thomas
Maria E. Collins	Roger J. Monigold	M.H. Thompson
Bernadette Court	Laura Moulton	Jennifer Tokatyan
Rose Cromer	Laurel Newton	Jo Truman
Mary Scroggins Crow	Wendy Silberman Pennes	C.L. Vincent
Alba H. De La Pena	Esther Elena Peterson	Kristina Walker
Jenna Dran	Ann Pham	Roy E. Walters
Helen L. Earp	Karen Joy Pollworth	Lori White
Lilah Friedland		Lucy M. Young

There were also 160 Editor's Choice Awards.

The Shaman

The Shaman rises with the sun, technology unrisen still
And gathers to him bead and bone, and feathers from a hallowed kill,
And packs them in a leather pouch, worn thin and supple over ages,
Gift of holies there before him, ancient wise ones, mystics, mages.
Then chanting low the sacred sounds of wind and fire and air and earth
Calls back the knowledge he was given, even long before his birth,
And dressing in the holy skins, the rare white fur of bear
First held aloft and softly offered to the gods of life in prayer
Takes to his breast a totem, of teeth and claw and clay
Which came from the sacred mountains where all his kin now lay.
The eagle comes, as does the hawk, like moths to meet the flame,
Drawn to a time of power, drawn to know its name.
The runes are cast, the future spread, in symbols at his feet,
Not spared the revelation, with vision so complete.
The Shaman wept to see the world's nuclear waste and swill,
And wept again to know he'd seen, just Man and his free will . . .
Rise up, oh Man, before the sun, and gather bead and bone,
And call back to you hawk and eagle, lest you find yourself alone.

—*A. K. Penn-Lambert*

My Friend the Ocean

I sometimes am confused about everything around me.
I am afraid of who I am, what I'll be and where I'm going.
Life seems to be taking it's own course and it's not stopping for me to live it.
I feel as though I have nowhere to turn
and killing myself is the only resource.
But that's something that's just too drastic to do,
So on a quiet night I like to go to the beach,
Sit in the sand and let the cool water touch my feet and relax me.
I somehow have a communication with the ocean and it with me.
It feels as though the ocean breeze is whispering in my ear
Trying to say something, but its beautiful language can't be translated.
The breeze surrounding my body has a special aura.
I have no one to talk to and no one to be with,
so I turn to my friend the ocean.
Wait, I feel silent, I feel a powerful force grasping me;
It's the ocean's arms that are holding me tight
In a place where nobody knows and nobody cares.
My friend the ocean has finally taken me in its hands.
Now I see my loved ones are grieving for me,
but I know now I am a part of my own world.

　　—Tina Van Vleet

The Lighthouse

The lighthouse stands
Upon the gentle slope
That overlooks the pebbled shore.
Never has it not been,
Yet daylight brings its beauty
Neglected.
The quiet sea needs no comfort,
Gives no thanks,
And the lighthouse stands.
The night falls,
The storm comes.
Through the wind and through the mist
The tower shines and burns for those who need,
Until morning breaks and tension fades
And everpast and evermore
The lighthouse stands.

　　—Kathleen Patton

The Sea

What wonders do you hold, oh great and ancient sea?
You are like a mysterious box, of which no one holds the key.
To your strong and turbulent waves, the ships and gulls abide,
And biting away at the land, comes your wicked tide.
Deep beneath the murky water, way down far below,
There lay priceless artifacts, protected from gales that blow.
No one knows your secrets, the ones you draw so near,
You drive away intruders by your calm, yet awesome fear.
And when the day is over, and silent darkness falls,
We quiver with the coldness of the calmness you install.

　　— Stephanie Wheeler

Storm at Sea

Monsterous black clouds began forming
Over the warm morning sun.
Gulls cried in distress.
Waves that once lapped gently against the beach
Were now crashing against the shore.
The light morning breeze changed to an over-powering wind.
Suddenly a flash of lightning split the sky
And the turbulent roar of thunder moved closer.
A pier in the distance collapsed like a fawn
Attempting to walk for the first time.
White-capped waves enveloped the crystal beach.
Although it was afternoon, the sky was as black as a moonless night.
The violent storm lasted into the evening then retreated reluctantly.
The once flawless beach was left scattered with debris and wreckage.
Night fell and the shore was left awaiting another brutal attack.

　　—Tracy Hundley

A Fading Light

I wish not to be
The only rock in the sea.
I long to feel again
The rays of sun upon my skin
And the warmth that nourishes
My soul within.
As waves of gently baby blue
Open and engulf in their wings
The sky high above and
The land far below;
The honey brown sand, sweet and warm
Holding and surrounding me,
Quickly dries from the rain of falling tears.
While I await for wild waters to form
And give renewed life to the impending storm,
That darkens each night
With timeless memories my only light.

　　—Kelly A. Fasco

Her Captain and Crew are Me

Swiftborn and dream bound are we.
We sail a hundred sleepy tides.
Her captain and crew are me.
She sings in the night;
On our craft, winged in white,
As we see lights and sights,
That no seaman has ever seen.
In the night, her song takes me in flight.
Though her sound once gay has turned to sorrow
And her eyes meeting mine turn away.
I shall wait to shed my tears;
I dare not be tear blinded,
Though my grief will never go.
Her captain and crew are me.
Swiftborn and dream bound are we. We sail a
Hundred sleepy tides,
where never a seaman has ever been.

　　—Kenneth Alford

Cupid

Cupid shot me
in the heart,
So now I feel
a missing part.
Cupid put my
eyes on you.
Did little Cupid
shoot you, too?
With his little arrow
and little bow?
Somehow you
just never know.
So give in to me and
I'll give in to you
'Cause that's what Cupid
wants us to do.

— *Jacki J. Boone*

If Only...

If only you knew
How I feel right now
If only I could show you
If only I knew how

If only I could just once
Look deep into your heart
If only we were together
And decided to never part.

If only you were here
Right here next to me
You would know how I am feeling
My love you would definitely see

If only I could express
The feelings I feel for you
Things could be really good
If only you knew

—*April M. Elkins*

Kissing

Each time
Our lips entwine
I am reminded
Of a rich chocolate
Syrup dripping
Slowly over the
Purist snow like
Ice cream.
Chocolate used to
Be my only weakness.
But, now there is you.

—*Deborah Davis*

The Gift

I am sending you a gift,
I hope you will use it well.
It has no dollar value,
For it is something I would never sell.
I am giving it to you,
And ask nothing in return.
This gift will never break,
This gift could never burn.
Though it has been handed down for years,
It will never fall apart.
It is not very fancy,
But it is straight from my heart.
This gift is very special,
For it comes from up above.
This gift that I am sending you; is simply love.

—*Jennifer Bass*

Untitled

Wrinkled pages felt from a time
   that used to be;
Colored by the morning dew-rays
   captured hues
   of falling leaves.

A bird, a bird, it sings its song
   of amber days
   not long far gone...
Wintry nights that stole the heat
   from warm embrace and
   fluttering beat
From a love-full heart,
   never trace its leave—
Sadness falls, the stars to sleep.

— *Devon D. Hoefer*

My Hidden Lover

There is a secret deep inside,
A secret that I feel, I must hide.
For only the almighty above,
Can truly know my hidden love.

What I feel for my lover is pure
And no one, knows the truth for sure.
When together, we must hide away,
Wishing the truth could come out one day.

My hidden love is one of a kind,
And she will be forever on my mind.
With her now is where I long to be,
Hand in hand, for the world to see.

Society says what we do it wrong,
To be together, means we must be strong.
I could never give my love to another,
But for now, you must remain my hidden lover.

—*Dennis G. Demers*

This Ring

With this ring, I'll truly say
We loved so sweetly until today.
As you unfold the ribbon around the base,
Think of me; the last time you saw my face.
The ribbon is wrapped like I was to you,
But everything we had is gone; we're through.
So unfold me carefully, lay me down light
And I won't come back; I won't even write.
The base of the ring is shiny and new,
But it will tarnish like the love of me and you.
Someday all the wear will commence a break
And the foundation will crack like thin ice on a lake.
The jeweler can fix the ring once again,
But my broken confinement will never mend.
Maybe someday, joy to my heart, love will bring
And I can be repaired once again like this ring.

— *Donna Gill Burke*

Touch

The touch of your hand still warms my face
I hear the whisper of your voice in the gentle sound of the wind
I see your smile in the rising of the sun
And your tears in each star that appears in the heavens
Forever I will tread softly on the leaves of fall
For they are the memories of a summer past

—*Jane Glass*

Breath Giving

While—
Colors at sunset
Lie hushed,

Place a kiss
To a soft
Summer wind.

Someone is waiting
Breath taking—

— *Don Dillingham*

Personal Expression

Do I dare tell you thoughts
That I harbor so close
About feelings and fantasies
Wished upon the most?

Do I let you become
My most wildest of dreams
Or keep them locked safe
Until they reach their extremes?

Embarrasement noted
And thoughts recognized
I now feel uplifted
As it's taken from inside.

I tell you these thoughts
With a heart left undone
The feelings and expressions
Specially written for one.

—*Dawn Ardry*

The Simplest Fact

It rained tonight...
Just like it did then.
Just like the night you told me
You loved me.

I watched the rain...
I was feeling the thunder
Inside my head,
And the lightning
Struck my heart.
Just like the pain I felt when
You said good-bye.

I never want it to rain again...
Such a simple fact of nature
Hurts so deeply.
Just like the simplest fact of life.

— *Jill Denise Corsi*

Untitled

If the moon was the sun
I'd love you.
But it's not
But I do love you.
If day was night
I'd love you.
But it's not,
But I do love you.
If right was left
I'd love you.
But it's not
But I do love you
If I was your lover
I'd love you.
But I'm not,
But I do love you.

— *James Herring*

Past Is Presence

When the sessions of sweet silent thought
Summon up remembrance of things past, I sigh the lack of
Many a thing I sought and moan the expense of many a vanished sight,
For precious friends hid in death's dateless night,

They drive you and leave you drifting in the endless waters of the seas.
Save me from tomorrow, the waters of history,
But if the while I think of thee, dear friend,
All losses are restored and sorrows end.
— *Dawn Martin*

Wondering Streak

His touch is sensuously soft with each gliding stroke,
swaying and hanging comfortably around.
His fit is pleasurable to say the least
in his high tech style of placement and harmony
with his art deco and modern philosophies within
his high, contemporary tech styles
that's seen bright for the length of miles.
Though there are some who would not agree or approve,
he's my style, he belongs to me, no one wears
him better than I
as we pass with a pleasing smile.

But, if you could feel his fit as I do,
you would never let him fade past
'cause there's nothing more comfortable than he
who is my cotton shirt at last.
— *Gary A. Drury*

Backyards of America

In the hustle and bustle of life
With fast cars and motor bikes
We fail to appreciate our neighbor's strife
If only to walk and see the other side
Of someone else's backyard
Our idea of living is less seen by the ride
The bird, bee, and butterfly
Sing their magic songs
Among the flowers and trees as we walk by
Boats, motors, and bicycles galore
Crowd the house lots of America
Which only our casual stride can adore
To appreciate a different way of life is to walk with your dearest
Through the portals of nature a slowing of our existence
Will result in appreciation
Of God's gifts to our nation.
— *Wesley L. Calder*

Different Worlds

I sit here between walls of steel and concrete
While everyone around is trying to compete.
Tears and broken hearts have torn family and loved ones apart.
My tears I have hidden, but the love I have for you is from the heart,
Even though we're living in different worlds.

I dream of you in a house made of nothing but wood
And I long to hold and love you if I could,
But the occasional phone call and letters we write
Will keep our hearts content through every lonely night,
Even though we're living in different worlds.

Time will come; we'll be united soon
To share our nights under the stars and moon.
We share our dreams and hope they come true.
How much more can I say? I love you,
Though we're living in different worlds.

Though we live in different worlds and distance keeps us apart,
You mean the world to me and you're always in my heart
Because different worlds won't ever keep us apart.
— *James A. Fulk*

Summer Love

In the eyes of a little white dove
Are the signs of our wonderful love.
It all happened on a warm summer day
When you told me you had something to say.
You looked me in the eyes; you looked down deep inside
And told me you would stay right by my side.
So just to prove my love is true,
I'd give my life to be with you!
— *Nellie Gross*

Worth Me

I wanna take you, babe, where the eyes can't see.
I'm gonna take you, babe, where there is just me,
To where mere beauty is peace of mind,
To where our love will grow beyond the point of blind.

Each night with the beauty of the moonlit sea,
Each night with the beauty of you holding me,
Let's sail away, forget the rest
So to each other we can give our only best.

If you can't give this to me then let me go now.
I want the closest perfection Jehovah will allow.
In everything else I may be lost,
But this love I want is worth any cost.
— *Angelic Lockhart*

Mamalilaculla

Our feet crunch softly on the skull-white strand,
crushed clamshells, skeletal remains of long-past feasts,
the memory of winter-sheltered days.
We gaze about us in a dreamlike trance.
A lone tip-tilted house on rotten piles
stands guard above the beach, and near at hand.
a long-beaked totem leans into the wind,
ungainly as a heron poised for flight.
Inland, engulfed in brush and thorn and vine,
the remnants of the village can be seen,
the shadow of the longhouse with no walls, no roof,
no substance but its massive carved facade.
The silence has the force of thunder
and the emptiness the pressure of a silent crowd.
The spirits tell us we are stangers here
and knowing this, we paddle humbly away
leaving no trace of our intrusion save
the indentations where we trod upon their shore.
And these the rising tide will wash away.
— *Hereward Allix*

Penumbra

The limits that guide me have broken down-
Out I come, casting storms, lightning, and winds of change
Into a desert of reason, a sweltering waste
Of broken dreams and misperceived ambitions-
Yet, here I stand on the great
Plain of possibilities, white of clues,
But black and billowing with life.
What brave new beginnings await me?
What manner of explosion must I next endure,
To merit praise and notice for this new me?
Bathed in the wash of my own fear and uncertainty,
I am nonetheless serene for my situation.
Goodness is my discipline, asceticism my hope.
I breathe in limited air-
But the time will come when I am again free to linger,
To be held...and caressed, calm;
His love, the eye of all storms,
Centered, finally, over me.
— *Vincent de Paul Louis*

The Way I Feel

The way I feel
For you inside,
Makes me want
To be by your side.

You are the one
Who is always there
You are always around
When I need you to care.

The way you look
And smile at me
Drives me to insanity.

We will always
Be together
Because our friendship
Will last forever.

—*Amanda Hayden*

The Dating Game

Laughter on the path
the back door halts
further advance.
An inquiring eye
gets tangled in the lace,
forced goodbyes
desire hangs in the night.
Breathless
youngblood screeching tires,
questions and answers
on the living room couch.
Trust disappearing up the stairs
Hope, the make up of tomorrow.

—*E. Surina*

I Give You

I give you love
 For being my friend.
I give you life
 For keeping me from dying.
I give you a smile
 For giving me many happy days.
I wish for you the best.
 In life and love—especially.
You gave me something no one will-
Something I cannot return-
Within a million years.
 I ask just one favor more-
Please still love me...
 Forever more.

— *Angela C. Hoyos*

Forbidden Love

From the time I saw you
I knew you were a flirt
I fell in love with you anyway
Knowing I would get hurt
Tying you down is hard
Making you love just one
How can I do what none have done
I know you never have loved
Knowing you never loved me
And trying not to cry
For the strength to kiss you good bye
I find hard to come by
When you reach for me again
I won't be there for you
A love I want to call my own
Not one I have to share,
I have not one to share alone.

—*Elaine Kersey*

Sensations

Perhaps it was the touch of your lips
Upon my breast
Or the scent of you that filled my head
When we first caressed
Or the taste of you that burned my throat
When your pleasure was released
Or the sight of your naked splendor
When the trembling ceased
Or perhaps it was your sighs
Or the sparkle in your eyes
Or your hands upon my thighs.

—*Vivianne Hardy-Townes*

What Dreams are Made of

I wish my friends would see
That I love you and together we shall be.
My love for you is true
Without you I would be blue
Every minute without you I miss
The tenderness of you and your kiss.
So when you are lonely remember that
If I was there, I'd give you a love pat.
I think of you everyday
To pass my lonely times away.
I imagine us walking into the sunset
Hand in hand, side by side.
Then I hear the ocean's tide
I hope that we never say goodbye
For when we are together our emotions fly.
I guess this means that we are in love,
And now I know what dreams are made of.

—*Carmen M. Schlientz*

Because of You

Because of you, my world is at ease.
You are the only guy my heart will please.
Because of you, I have no fears.
You are always there to wipe away my tears.
Because of you, my eyes shine bright.
Because of you, I dream beautifully through the night.
Becuase of you, I feel secure
My love for you is rare, I am sure!
Because of you, I am a sainted dove,
And because of you, I now know love.

— *Wendy Nelson*

Friends the Jewels

Friends are like rare jewels
Precious, priceless and few
Together they share
Their sorrow
Their laughter
Their pain
Their memories of good times
That they love to tell
They have no more friends they need to gain
And they know each other very well
And they are very rich to have these friends
For the happiness never ends
And the friendship never bends
For they understand you need no more new friends
These that you have are loved from you
And you love these very few
For they are like none other for these are precious, priceless
And few.

—*Angie McGee*

T.O.

Shuckin jivin   slappin backs
Aces   Jacks
Pop a tall one bud
Party hearty   throwin' down
   Actin'   clown
   Everybody does
So gettin' late   change th'date
Sunrise   wait
Twowheels   tame   th'road
       Weaving
         Bobbing
          Catching air
```
R   T   T
O   H   H
U   R   E
N   E   R
D   E   E
```
Smoke for seven more
caddiebrakebigmistakehandlebarstopthatcar
     Endo   endo
    Crask and burn
     Ironic   turn
      No despair
   Asphalt   hair
  Livin breathin dark and light
Damn quick fight
         close my eyes
         No more sighs

—*D. Bassett*

A Lease On Love

Love me, love me forever.
We'll share everything we do.
We'll cuddle up close together.
I'll keep all my lovin' for you.
Be my lifeline, my darlin'.
Be my heartline, please do.
We'll cuddle up close together.
I'll keep all my lovin' for you.
Give me a lease on your love, darlin'.
A lease on love for love.
Give me a lease on your time, darlin.
A lease for a lease on mine;
We'll slip away to a world unknown
To all but you and I.
I'll give a lease to you alone.
A lease on my love, until I die.

— *Helen McCutcheon*

To Think of You

When I'm alone in my room I think of you
Of our happy times together,
It makes me glad to think of you
'Cause each time things are better.
When I close my eyes I see your face
Always smiling to me,
And when I'm down you're always there
To fill my heart with glee.
And to think of you and how much you care,
I always know that you'll be there.
When I think of you and I fall asleep,
My mind dreaming a wonderful dream,
I think of you and hope you are
Dreaming along with me.

— *Wendy McConnell*

A Drawer Without a Key

My mind wanders lead by my heart,
To where it is forbidden.
A sweet melody refuses to desert my lips.
I fill my lungs with the scent of my past,
Moldy from being locked in a drawer.
A drawer without a key.
My heart longs to open this drawer,
To take each article out and examine it closely,
Clean them and put them back more carefully,
So that I will never be able to find them again.
My memories will be prefect.
Each will have a special space.
Uncrowded, meant for it.
I will always know where each lay.
My heart longs to open this drawer,
But my mind does not know where to find the key.
For it too is lost among my memories,
Locked in a drawer protected by my heart,
This drawer without a key.

—*Anne Page*

A Part of Me

I think of you all of the time.
I smile just knowing that you're mine.
By one touch of your hand, I feel so complete.
You are every breath I breathe and my every heartbeat.
You make my world turn and my sun shine bright.
I long to be with you every day and every night.
You are the one I trust when something bad comes my way.
I believe in all that you do and all that you say.
Lock me in your heart and throw away the key.
Forever and always you will be a part of me.

— *Autumn Grizzle*

Everlasting Love

It seems we have gone through every possible situation
And together we have conquered without hesitation.
It seems our friendship has endured the fights, the failures
We haven't both enjoyed. But through it all you stuck close
By to lend a helping hand and with your support and dedication
I am able to be where I am.
You offer timely advice and always give me a smile, to brighten
Up my day and make my life worthwhile
Cherish all the moments, cherish all the love, our friendship is
Everlasting with love sent down from above.

—*Genoulia Hollinshed*

Love

Gazing up at the sky,
A whole new world above and beyond.
Bright sparkling stars;
Never dying, but constantly changing
Each one representing a different part of our confusing lives.
A shooting star, an intricate mind, desperately trying to sort out the pieces
We stand closely as observers, watching this totally strange
Yet very familiar romantic world above us.
Almost as if, in a new and intriguing way,
We are watching ourselves.
I turn to gaze deep in your eyes,
Wishing all our worries away.
The calm, beautiful night envelopes us,
As the brilliance of the stars reassures us,
Revealing that for this special moment,
Everything negative is taken care of.
So the rest is ours to enjoy:
Peace, joy and...love.

—*Amy Weinlick*

Pearly

Early in spring a snail called Pearl
Took a lesurely walk one day.
But by the time she reached the end of the park,
The springtime had passed away.

Blue skies had turned to the darkest of black
And the weather was getting cold.
And Pearly had added six months to her life,
At least, that is what I have been told.

Now the Fall of the year had come, it seems.
And Pearly was far from home,
So Pearly crawled into a rabbit hole,
And slept through the winter alone.

When the warm and fresh rains of Spring seeped in
And awakened our Pearly dear
She immediately started her journey back home
Thus, losing an entire year.

But, imagine the stories she would have to tell
To her grandchildren, some summer's day,
About the time she went for a leisurely walk,
And a whole year slipped away.

—*Eva J. Farrell*

When Someone Lets You Down

Someone whom I love and trust betrayed me.
Someone I believed in has not lived up to that belief.
Bless and help him now.
This experience has altered my concept of that person,
Yes, but don't let it destroy my faith in him altogether.
Let me remember and bless the rest of the good in him.
Above all, don't let it destroy my faith in other people,
For surely, faith in our friends, our family, those we work with
Is one of the dearest things You have given us.
Without it, we ourselves are empty and meaningless.
Bless all the people I know and love and deal with.
Let us all keep faith with each other as best we can.
Please especially bless the person who has disappointed me,
For he needs your help even more.
His weakness cries out for your strength.
Bless him. Help him. Intensify the good in him.

— *Heather Lewis*

Untitled

The sound of my silent life is as free as a flower swaying in the wind
My soul is so far off locked in a black pit waiting to be let out
My strong tears are sadder than a helpless puppy
Where shall I go?
I am stuck with no home, no family
The pressure builds up inside of me
Rays of light shine through my heart like a stabbing needle
My head spins, but my soul won't let go
I hide day after day away from happiness.

—*Carrie Wollack*

I

I feel the hard, wooden desk in which many bambinos
Have written some of their greatest notes.
I feel the cool wind hiding in my hair.
I hear the silent footsteps of a person coming late to class.
I hear the slamming of lockers say, *until tomorrow.*
I taste the spicy-mixed spaghetti sauce go down my throat.
I taste the chocolaty world of an M&M melt in my mouth.
I smell a dozen roses on Valentine's Day.
I smell popcorn being showered with melted butter.
I see oil doing an exotic dance around the frying chicken in an oven.
I see a world full of imaginable and mysterious things
Just waiting to be discovered.

— *Alouette Cervantes*

Wedding Night

Every night I go to sleep, my last thought is of you
My sweet. You make my day bright, you are the glitter in
My life. A tender kiss you touched me with a gentle sigh
Of relief I hissed. You took me in your arms so slowly
It swept me off my feet with no place to go. The sound of
Your voice leaves my heart in desire in the heat of the
Moment I closed my eyes to come to the conclusion
That I was too no more a *white satin bride.* You slowly
Undressed me as we layed in bed, you put into the devil's red.
You looked at me with flaming eyes I felt so naked deep inside.
You brought me closer, as the tears ran down my cheeks,
You whispered gentle in my ear *don't worry sweetheart*
There is nothing to fear.
You embrace me close;
I wanted to die for you were everything
I ever desired.
     —*Pia Althea Clarke*

The Measures of Love

Oh, the depths and measures of love! They are many.
Love is like a fresh rose opening forth, awakening to its beauty.
For each moment and each relived memory of its tranquil,
Peaceful love, lives within the soul.
Its tender moments are photographed and reflected within the heart.
It leaves a lasting and lingering touch of tenderness
Wherein a trace of cherished and treasured memories remain.

This love is the road to happiness, peace, joy and
Contentment,
Touching our lives like the
Warm and gentle summer breeze.
Its memories are forever.

Oh, the joy of knowing love,
The joy of being loved!
     —*Eleanor Lee Gustaw*

The Good Marriage

We rush around, so much to do.
But it's you I want when the day is through.
To chide me for my day's errors;
To keep me safe from inner terrors.
My ideas you speculate,
And when I win, you congratulate.
When we retire to our bed
We kiss goodnight, and I turn my head.
With your hand, you reach for me.
I close my eyes then I can see
Just how special life has been
Since the day you entered in.
     — *Ann Marie Sullivan*

Someone

This feeling I have is so intense
It's a strong feeling, a good feeling
I have the feeling that someone cares for me
For once in my life, I feel there is someone
Someone who can trust me,
Someone I can touch and hold
And feel the same warmth given to me
That I am giving to someone else
I can kiss him
And it feels like...love
Someone I can have fun with no matter what
I am actually starting to depend on someone
For the first time in my life and I never,
No matter how hard it gets,
Never want it to stop.
I want it to go on...forever.
     —*Carol Barb*

So I Thought

We had some good times and some bad.
We shared all of our joy and pain.
Yeah, we were having problems,
But I thought, so I thought...
Another day comes. I write a letter to see
If we can fix things.
You write back saying you hate me,
Never want to see me again!
I'm crushed. I thought we were best friends. So I thought...
I go home and collect all of our memories.
So do you.
I guess this is goodbye, forever, my friend.
It's hard getting over you my friend.
The memories still live in my heart.
And I will never forget you my friend.
     — *Patti Zitzelberger*

Champagne Moon

The half moon, full to the brim with clear champagne,
Dipped himself low into my backyard again;
I might have cradled myself within his chalice-like dish,
And snuggled and cuddled there to sleep upon a silvery wish.

How fun to awaken lightheaded from the bubbles
    having slipped up my nose;
Then to have sidled over the edge, dangling from his lowest tip
    and wiggled all my toes.

I would have gently fallen onto the dewy carpeted lawn,
Rolled around and giggled and giggled until the early dawn;
Then stood so I could curtsey and bid him fair-thee-well,
Of your splendid secrets trust me not to tell.

Yes, the half moon, full to the brim with champagne bright,
Dipped himself low into my backyard last night.
     —*Ava Graham*

Insomnia

Sitting in the sticky heat of a September night
The girl trapped in a woman's body
Leans her ruddy cheek against
The cold straight steel of the window ledge.
The window lethargically squeaks closed,
Nudging her visage out of its space.
She glances out the window to the white lights
Which look like finger painted crucifixes
Through the blue of humid evening rain.
A wisp of breeze steals through the slit in the window pane.
For a moment cooled, she suddenly feels the engulfing heat
Of restless adolescence pervading her body. The burning wet heat
Imbedded in her crossed thighs works its way to her nervous underarms
And perspiring palms. Her thoughts jog wildly to the thought of summer
Eroticism and her cheeks rust with shame at the thought of those thoughts.
There is nothing to quench the longing nothing left but sleep.

—Jennifer Koren

The Perfect Couple

One day I looked out the window and I saw the shadow of love,
It was a young couple in the moonlight with the stars gleaming above.
And thoughts went through my mind about how perfect they were together,
They looked like they would be there for all seasons and types of weather.

When I looked past their appearance and saw what was really true,
It made me smile to think that still their emotions grew.
How wonderful it must feel to be truley in love,
Happier than a butterfly and higher than a dove.
Yes, they're the perfect couple and it'll be great to see,
The outcome of this relationship that is certain to be.

— Nicki Webb

Carousel

Magical. The gleam in their eyes; hearts pounding in their chests;
The skipping over of the loose gravel, spraying in all directions;
Excited beyond belief over the lights whirling in the distance, closer and closer,
Awed by the tinny music coming from the orchestra dazzled, dazed, and awesome moment;
Climb aboard, catch the brass ring, try again, lean farther and farther out.

Who can judge what success shall be theirs, those who are still lured
By these moments of their youth, recaptured with those who are smaller than they?
Rejoice that they have lost it not—the speed of the carousel horse as it
Rounds the far bend, hanging on tightly at the thrilling shocks to the spine
And nerves at the jolting movements of up and down.

The only way to recapture youth is to relive it, experience it, love the thrill of it alive in your heart.
You can't wander the streets carrying a teddy; you can't play with dolls or trucks;
You can't play pretend because life is too real for you, but this sojourn into the past,
Long before your youth, is equivocated because you've become an antique yourself.
It allows its own voice, a squeal of delight, practiced each time it is boarded;
To return you to those thrilling days of yesteryear, to ride off into the distant sunsets
With a wet kiss for the horse, not for the heroine,
A little proud that you are not the only one who has not forgotten.

— Willard M. Glasgow

Untitled

Somehow, I know I'll never forget you because unlike you, my feelings were true.
You were the thing that gave me the strength to face the day; I never thought you would leave in such a way.
Maybe you think I'm too young to know what love is, but to myself I say, *My heart is part of his.*
I thought I was handling all of this well, but love is strange and puts you through Hell.
I guess I only saw one side of you; I didn't know what I thought I knew.
What I thought was that you felt the same, but I was wrong; you were playing a game.
I guess you never will understand that wherever I look, there you stand.
Even if you really aren't in sight, to get over you I would have to put up a fight.
Your touch made me feel secure, but now that touch goes to another girl.
I've tried my best to save my heart, but I guess all you ever wanted was to break it apart.
No matter what I said, there always seemed to be more to say, and as I said before, my memories of you will never go away.
But the saying goes, *If you love something, set it free...* and since I was never loved by you, the one letting go has to be me.

—Jennifer L. Dunlap

Destiny

How many times have you wondered
If only I had a chance
If only I'd heard the music
If only I'd got up and danced.
And how many times have you heard them say
Your destiny's all up to you
If only you'll reach out and grab it
There's nothn' you can't do.
Well we're taking control of our destiny
And we're taking it all the way
Noboby's gonna stop us now
Nowhere...no how...no way.
We're here to fulfill our destiny
We're ready to take our chance
We're waiting to hear the music
'Cause baby we're ready to dance!

—Harold Schlenker II

A Dog Named *Trouble*

Trouble was my middle name
which I lent to a long-haired spotted dog
who I befriended as a child.
Wise beyond her years,
Trouble kept the secrets of a
fragile 12 year-old's heart,
mended hurt feelings—scraped knees,
mitigated grievances against mothers
bearing crepe myrtle switches
and licked the sting out of
freshly *switched* legs.
She was fearless in confrontations with the enemy,
whoever it happened to be at the moment,
and unselfishly and tirelessly surrendered
to my childhood games.
Her love and loyalty were unconditional-
a treasure in a young girl's life.
From a dog named *Trouble* I learned
the value of friendship.

—Bonnie Walp Spotts

The Puppet

The puppet master pulls the strings,
Attached to the little people,
Their limbs correspond to his command,
Responding to his every whim,
Knowing this is their only chance to live,
For at any time he may return them to lifelessness.

—Janet Guilliams

Looking Glass

Crystal shards
Adorn the floor,
Glimpsing rays of sunlight
In shattered despair.

What did the mirror see?
Only a reflection,
Only a truth,
Hidden deep inside of me.

— Jeffrey M. Shealy

Teenage Life

The pressures, worries, tragedies and stress,
The confusion of choosing the way I should dress,
The fear of taking a drug,
The pressures of drinking that first chug,
And then the depression to be thin,
Then the challenge of being in,
And finally the fear of smokin' that first puff,
Oh God, take me! I just can't handle this stuff!
    — *Amy Rockwell*

Helpless Child

Helpless child, everytime I see you, my heart breaks.
I feel like crying but my soul does that for me.
You are so beautiful and I just can't forget
You are with no one to take care of you.
I want to help you and I'll try because I love you
And you'll be able to count on me when you have problems,
When you are sick or when you need someone
To give you the warm, giving feeling of love.
    — *Anel P. Barrera*

Rage On

You'd like to believe that after a while the pain is silent
And never heard from again,
But you never forget the dying of a friend.
It seems little time or none has passed,
But indeed-
It is three years since you saw him last.
That moment's never silent,
You hear it again and again.
It is all your pain now and that has ever been.
Your mind wanders, lost to many cherished thoughts of long ago
And though you may try, you can't keep back the tears that show.
The pain of your dying friend, once here, is never gone.
The tears of remembrance rage on!
    — *Anastasia N. Edwards*

If Only I Had Told Him

If only I had told him that I loved him, there would be no pain.
If only I had told him, my eyes would never rain.
If only I had told him that I loved him, maybe he would see.
If only I had told him, he might have loved me.
If only I had told him that I loved him, there would be no trouble.
If only I had told him, he would not be lying in the rubble.
If only I had told him that I loved him, we might have been wed.
If only I had told him, he might not be dead.
If only I had told him that I loved him, the sun would always shine.
If only I had told him that I loved him, he would forever be mine.
    — *Carol Ann Britton*

A Beautiful Day

Without drugs in my way
I am able to see such a beautiful day
I have a plan what I am going to do
Share my love with all of you

I was never able to understand why
People use drugs to feel grand
I awoke today and started on my way
First I thanked the lord for his great reward
And then you see, I look at me and said
I am glad to be alive and straight in my head

Taking drugs will bring me down
I would rather be smiling than to wear a frown
It is a beautiful day and I am on my way to happiness in life
I do not need drugs to feel like this
Because using drugs, all the beautiful days I would really miss

So please do not use drugs and all the beautiful days will be yours too
Without the pain of drugs you will have a lot to gain.
    — *Glenda Bryant*

The Brink of Death

Faintly I hear
In the silence
Of the night,
The voice of reason
Calling out to me.
It whispers
Through the treetops,
Glides across
The cool waters far below,
Telling me I'm wrong
That I do matter
That people do care, and slowly,
I step away from
The brink of death.
    — *Barbara N. Herst*

Wounded

Looking out into the world, I see your smiling face,
I want to be with you, But I'm stuck here in my place.
I need to feel your arms around me, and to share
Everything with you, but you don't want me
Anymore, your feelings have changed through and through.
Now, when I call to you, your head turns as you
Look away, I can't go on anymore, not
Another treacherous day.
What I had is no more and what I want can never be,
At this moment my life is slowing leaving me.
    — *Erin Greene*

Supernatural

Driving,   road seems endless;   glance at clock.
Midnight,   strong winds, rain;   wipers vibrate.
Drowsy,   my eyes close;   burst of colours.
Darkness,   regain consciousness;   lay still.
Standing,   can't feel rain;   thick haze.
Distance,   car overturned;   person inside.
Spark,   catches on fire;   must help.
Run,   reach burning car;   brake window.
Seconds,   racing time bomb;   free victim.
Safety,   car explodes;   loud as thunder.
Shock,   see victim's face;   it's me?!
                    END.
    —*J. Michael Dubé*

How?

How could a person do this to your life?
They drink then they drive, it's like they hunt you with a knife.
Look at you in your hospital bed,
And it was just a few weeks before we wed.
He told me he was sorry many times.
But I don't listen because of his horrible crime.
His crime was driving while drunk and at the same time hurting you.
You were an innocent victim that got all the bruises, black and blue.
And while you lie on your bed waiting to die, the man who did this
To you won't even cry. How can someone live with the shame inside.
I just saw him laughing because he wasn't tride It's just not fair,
Seeing him loose and free, while your soul and body is slowly leaving me
It should be the other way around, It should have been on the ground
Lying there and feeling death creeping his way. He can tell me he
Is very sorry everyday, but his words can't make my hurt go away.
Because a nurse, just told me...that you died today.
    —*Angie Meyer*

Dawns Happy Song

The dawn begins, the sun a bright orange glow
And across the sky, puts on a colorful show

The colors blending into the sky designs
As the night begins to fade and die

Birds sing in a brand new day
And glide on the wind in their morning play

Frogs croak in a lazy pond
As a cottontail wonders aimlessly along

A muskrat swims to the pond's other side
As a quail cubby looks for a place to hide

The bobwhite sings his familiar tune
And off in the distance there's the cry of the loon

A nearby brook sings happily along
And with the birds, sings dawns happy song

    —Elizabeth Hamilton-Wyche

Dreams of Love

There by the quiet waters of love did I sleep
There savored my dreams of you.
There found my hopes as I looked into the deep
Clear water for an image of you.

I heard the birds as they sang in the trees
I watched them fly in their joy.
I shouted hot words of love in the breeze
And I was once again a boy.

I heard them echo and fall to the ground
Like falling leaves in a darkening view
The notes of my voice were dead
And buried under the morning dew.

I turned when I heard the birds' last sound
I saw that your face had also fled
Fled from the waters of my dream
A lost image in a cold, cold stream.

    —George Bankoff

Heartbeat

Lying here,
My head resting on your chest,
I listen to your heart beat
Rhythmic and comforting.
My thoughts are filled with pleasant fantasy,
Like when I was a child warm in my bed on Christmas Eve.
Tomorrow seems so far away.
You softly kiss the top of my head
And the dreamy child in me wonders
If you can hear my thoughts,
While all I can hear, is the beat of your heart.
I close my eyes and I smile
For in this moment of time
The whole world is just you and I.

    — Alice O'Brien

One Moment

We live a life of many years
We live a life of many fears
Yet all I ask is that someday
In someway
That I might have one moment.
One moment free from tears
Let me have one moment
So that you might see
I too can love and I can live,
I can share, and I can give
Let me have one moment free from pain and care
Let me have one moment for all the world to share.

    — Beth Howard

Untitled

Sam, you were my baby and in my heart you always will be.
To lose you was the hardest thing to go through.
To comprehend the pain, the agony, the despair is hard to explain.
You didn't have much time here with us; to hear your son call you Daddy.
It's so painful to think of all this and know you can never be with us again.
The only thing that keeps me going is the knowledge
that we will be together again,
But it seems like an eternity 'til that times comes
and my heart hungers for the sight of you
And to hold you in my arms once again—
Until then, we pray God takes care of you
when we shall come to you in Jesus' glory.
We miss you, Sam. Love to you on this Valentine's Day.

    — Allegra Gorzelsky

Love

Love is a signature engraved deeply on your heart
Written in a special ink with long and lasting art,
Monagrammed with trust and care, a sweet and tender rhyme
Outlined with a familiar smile and memories of the time.
Love is a dream you dream sometimes when your mind can ease the pain,
A daydream of sunshine in the sky when all you see is rain,
A thought of being together knowing someone's there,
A wish for laughs and happiness, enough to give and share.
Love is an image of how you feel and what you want to be,
A reflection on the way you live and what you like to see,
A picture you paint of yourself and the things you like to do,
An impression left about the ones that mean so much to you.

    — Valerie Jo Abel

Too Young

So you say you're too young.
First, are you too young to live? Or too young to die?
Too young to weep? Or too young to cry?
What is your youth too young for? You say you're always on the go.
You really should consider taking it slow,
Doing things the right way will help uplift your day.
Because all the friends that you may seem to have in the street
Get down sick, none of them offer to wash your feet.
It's really something to consider.
You should be thankful to God that you have a friend in me,
A true friend for all eternity.
That extra strength from your retina to help you foresee
The things in life you never thought would be,
So as to guide your feet from misery.

    —Valerie Whitfield

To All My Children

The lesson's we learn through life, awe...they would fill a book.
But who would want to know of trials and tragedies we've been through.
There would be much to tell—pages and pages of many of hells.
Heavy times that knew no end...at least it seemed from within.
Maybe our children would want to know, so that they won't feel the
Very same blow. How can I tell them, that they are part of the show.
That they set the stage for their very own play, and the characters
They thought of on a long ago day. Would it be to early for them to know?
That they hold the master plan and the key that opens the door. That
They are the directors of this vast life show. Many times the road will
Be hard—you'll wonder if you'll make it at all. Then the sun will come
Shining through—and the light will be bright, then you know. All of
The trials and errors you made—are part of the knowledge you must
Substain. So that one day you too, can tell your children of the lesson's
You learned through life, and someday you maybe able to write...A book
The young will pick-up and read. A book the young would learn to heed.

    — Angela Rousseve Parris

Lesson

The fruit of the tree of knowledge is truth
Not life
Sorrowful indeed are those who pick from its branches
For they surely must be those who mourn the
Deepest
  —*Gennaro Milo*

Farewell Heaton

Between dying fields and pathways
A town slumbers in ghostly attire;
The blood of life is ebbing,
The day of wine is gone.
Long ago, the school bell rested its toll
When homes within fell barren;
A nearby farmhouse weeps by a well,
Falling prey to a silhouette of darkness.
The wind of desire scattered the young;
Like the brambled fields nearby,
The old are fading away with time.
Only memories escape the cloth of mourning
As the harshness of winter engulfs the plains;
Falling to elegiac verse is a town once filled with life;
A final farewell chiseled in stone
In a nearby cemetery adds
An occasional name to another Dakota sunset.
  —*Peggy L. Dudley*

My Wish

I wish that I was so far away that no one could ever find me.
Away from life, but not from death.
A place no one else knows about.
A place only I can see. I can only get to this place in my dreams.
It is such a fabulous place with lavender trees and unicorns running free.
Where the water is deep blue in color and
Where the pale green grass waves on and on
Into the distance as far as the eye can see.
Oh, how I love this place, I feel like I actually belong
In this fantasy world.
I really wish this place of mine was real and
I could go there and stay there forever,
All by myself.
  —*Holly Graser*

Kanker

His name was Kanker, some think that's odd.
I gave him an odd name because he was an odd yet special dog.
We were the best of friends, down to the end.
Now my heart refuses to mend.
When I needed him, my Kanker came through
Always ready to see if there was something he could do.
In the little time we had togehter,
We each learned a lesson to cherish forever.
He taught me how to love a dog with all my heart,
But most of all he renewed my faith
    in everything I had ever dreamed of, everything I was ever taught.
He also taught me in so many ways to never give up.
    He let me know I had a friend,
A friend that would stay with me until the very end.
I'd like to think I taught him a lot about trust.
I'd like to believe he grew to trust me very much.
I think that Kanker knew that he could put his life in my hands
And that I would do the best I can, that I would never ever hurt him.
He knew I loved him way too much.
If I could talk to him right now, first I would tell him
    how much I miss him, how much I care.
Next, most importantly, I would tell him just ten simple words:
    Thanks for being my friend and for always being there!
  —*Jennifer Hyman*

O Silent Heart

In my heart, a wanton love, burst.
Love have I, but the pain of love, worse.
My silent heart, for you, does long.
My dreams, for you, of quiet love song.

O silent heart, will you not speak?
If just a whispered kiss, upon his cheek
O silent heart, let this love be so.
If just a gentle moment, that is quick to go.

Are you to be silent, as you always do?
Will you not tell him this love is true?
As flowers blossom, with passion for spring
Tell him o heart, with love, thee do sing.
  —*C. J. Davidson*

Silver Wings

I was going to make things right
Sneaking out in the dead of night.
I had no self control;
I knew it was wrong.
Because of that, I now own
A pair of silver wings.
Halfway there I knew something was wrong.
A white cloud of mist obscured my vision.
A white mist is now where I reside.
Even before the truck went over the cliff,
I knew I was going to die.
Never seeing you again is my agony,
Your never knowing was my burden.
I now own a pair of silver wings.
  —*Heather Mussman*

To My Beloved

B lue are my skies and round me flowers bloom.
E arth seems to me a heaven after all.
C an this be witchcraft, all this boundless thrill!
A starte-like, you keep me in your thrall.
U tter the words, if this be but a trance.
S ay what you must to terminate the spell.
E den can fade once more into the mists...

I f only you remain, all will be well.

L ife can be golden on this sorry sphere
O nly if you will share my tears, my joy.
V ibrant vision, vouchsafe me this plea;
E nslavement in your personal employ.

B reathe on my frame the life you can bestow.
U ndying love I'll give you in return.
T ell me my hopes and prayers are not in vain.

Y ield to my pleas, and you shall quickly learn
O lympus can be transferred here to earth.
U nequalled bliss would be our prime concern.
  —*James R. Markle, Sr.*

Colors of the Night

The colors of the horizon mean something.
The purple accents the golden sky,
Yet the pink accents them both.
The night air turns cool as the moon begins to rise.
Soon, the twinkle of little stars twinkle in my eyes.
The sky is midnight blue as a perfect picture
Of clouds are set against it.
I wish upon a shooting star and hope my dream comes true.
Then I knew we were friends forever,
Friends, me and you.
  —*Yvonne Sandoval*

Illumination

Sun illuminates
 Dawn
Moon illuminates
 Water
Stars illuminate
 Sky
Light illuminates
 Darkness
Reflections illuminate
 Thoughts
But knowledge illuminates
 The Soul.
  — *Phyllis Walker Milardo*

Place De La Concorde

Egyptian
Obilisk
Gift to Paris
Nine thousand years ago.
As I gaze
My blue and white coat
My navy beret
Shrink
Swiftly.
Time
In a hust
Pauses.
  —*Betty G. Morrison*

Burning Touch

Here we are,
Oh lady of beauty
With eyes of blue,
Hair golden and free.

Here we are.
Yes, I hear you.
Your voice soft and tender,
Your touch a burning warmth.

With you
I enjoy many things.
  — *James M. Cannon*

Untitled

i run
scamper the wild
wavy pathos
once called
murmurs
you begin to run
by my side,
feel the tender air
clasping
(like the soft moss you sleep upon)
your every thought's desire.
  — *Gabrielle J. Strong*

Theos Obless

Cherish a thought
Kindle a dream
Faith
Begins with this
Stoic hope
That Charity
Will find the way
  — *Janice Arthur Leny*

Sea

All alone I sit
The lonely echo of the waves rolling in
The surface and sea
Is a quiet world
Pouncing against the sand
When I come here
I talk
To the sea
To the sand
To the wind
To myself
Now I know I've been with friends I knew
  — *Elizabeth Young*

Time

Time.
The clock on my wall the thing on my wrist.
Time.
What I do not have enough of.
Time.
What I have too much of.
Time.
What my life is measured in.
Time.
For me to die.
  —*Wanda Hawkins*

Were We Meant?

Were we meant to be apart,
Or is it some kind of fate that tore us
From each other?
Last night the phone rang,
I ran to get it but by that time
They hung up.
If it was you, please call back and give
Me one more chance.
For what I did, I do not know.
Were we meant to be this way,
Or is it a plan our friends thought of?
Cause' I'm with him, and you're with her.
Do we love them, or are they there to
Hide the hurt?
Were we meant to be apart, because
If we were it's quite unfair,
For you have my heart.
  —*Billie Jo Schaff*

A Small Item: 1867

Resting beside a river,
Erasmus Jacobs, aged fifteen,
saw a stone.
Golf-ball size,
with a sparkle.
Caught his eye.
Picked it up.
Took it home.
Pretty enough.
Anyway, his mother
didn't throw it out.
Later on, she gave it away.
That stone became the first
recorded diamond found in South Africa.
Started a diamond rush.
Made some men rich and powerful.
Erasmus Jacobs didn't even
become famous.
  —*Eugene G. E. Botelho*

Looking Forward

In preschool, I tried to run and skip.
I though of it as quite a gyp,
That bigger girls could jump and play,
While I had to struggle to do as they.

In first grade, the challenge was to read.
Bigger girls seemed prone to greed.
While they were scanning fast as that
I had to sound out C A T.

In second grade, reading trouble over
My goal. To find a four leaf clover.
Big girls looked in fields hung with dew.
When found, they sighed, now my wish comes true.

Keeping up with big girls was getting tiring.
I was spending too much time admiring
Finally I began to see,
That the only one I should compare myself to is me.
  —*Bekah Burgess*

Dreams

It hurts to see you just walk on by
Not even stopping to say, *Hi!*
I can't understand why you're acting this way.
I'm beginning to think that love doesn't pay.
When you and I were together,
I thought our love would last forever.
But now my dreams of forever are swept away
And my unhappiness is here to stay.
Why can we no longer be together
And why can't your love last forever?
Now I'll try dreaming new dreams and no longer of you
But I can't help wondering, will these dreams fail me, too?
  — *Falla Lindsey*

Why I Can Never Not Be Me

I can never be an elephant that dances in a ballet;
I can never be a cocker spaniel or a collie named Ray.
I can never be a fuzzy kitten, I guess you ask me why
These things I can never be even if I try.

I can never be a tree waving in the breeze;
I can never be a bird gliding smoothly at ease.
I can never be an apple, peach, plum or pear;
These things I can never be even if I dare.

I can certainly never be Michael Jackson gliding across a stage
I can never be a crayon, a lovely shade of beige
These things I can never be, it's impossible you see;
Because if I were to see myself, I'd probably want to be me.
  —*Valerie Rawlston*

The Buffer Zone

Like blankets of deep, patient snow
Hides old cars and putrid trash dumps,
Distance, time and forgetfulness
Hides what we leave in disarray.
Hidden are sugar-coated words
Concealing honed razor-edge blades.
Our foibles are under wraps. Results of broken vows are gone.
Days of Future's past are at rest.
How harmless they appear to be
Clad in spangled robes and white folds. Nature, like morals
Hastens to hide the evils of age and men.
Hold off, O spring, your melting warmth;
Do not heat the cold buffer zone.
It's better to endure the chill
Than have these phantoms haunt again
For summer thoughts gone far awry.
  —*James D. Stone*

Through a Forest Dark and Deep

Tonight I will go walking through a forest dark and deep
The forest is my mind, the darkness is my sleep
I take this journey often, across the well-worth peat,
And fallen leaves do soften the passage of my feet
I know just where I'm going, I know the way by heart
Because I go there every night, when my dream do start
I came upon a meadow, so quiet and serene
Nowhere is a shadow to mar this peaceful scene
I call out and you are there, as lovely as can be
The sun lights up your long brown hair, you laugh and smile at me
I move to take you in my arms and never let you go
To enjoy your many charms and share your golden glow
But, you are gone from my embrace, and I understand
The look of love upon your face was for another man
I turn away as tears begin, and cry out in my sleep
Yet, tomorrow night I'll walk again through a forest dark and deep

—*Bernard H. Pierce*

Living my Life

Don't hide in your world, please come to mine and stay.
We'll sow our seeds of love so we can harvest them someday.
For your love and devotion, I'll try and do things your way.
Water from a faucet, strained with traces of rust,

Climbing a steep mountain, thinking of you and dying of lust.
Whatever made it happen to our dying love and trust?
Living my life in high fidelity, I'll find my way and return someday,
I'm on my way back to reality.

We live in a promise, we live in a dream. Love glowed around us.
It really felt serene. Now that we are losing it, it don't feel so keen.
The sun sets on the horizon. Nite time has again set in.
You promised me your undying love and a chance of our romance again.

Now morning has woke me, realizing I was dreaming again.
Living my life in high fidelity,
I'll find my way and return someday,
I'm on my way back to reality.

—*Buster Berry*

Song without Words

I heard a lovely song today and thought of you,
It had no lyric to recall some past forgotten word
No, it was the melody that spoke to me of you,
Evoking memories of tender moments that occurred.

I know I'll never hear that song again...it came and went.
It had the most enchanting sound that I had ever heard
It whispered softly of our love and all that it has meant,
And told a wordless story which to others seems absurd.

It some sweet future day when I can look upon your face,
And hear your voice, and feel the bond of love that's there, yes then,
I'll recognize those unsung words in that new time and space
The silence will be broken and I'll hear that song again.

—*Carol Herwood*

No Thorns on the Roses

In Heaven, before the world began, the beautiful rose of Sharon reigned.
Seated on the right of the father above, they planned the world and made it with love.
In the wonderful beauty of their creation, a man and woman waited with anticipation.
For the father to walk and talk with them, where the roses bloom in the cool of the evening.
Into the garden of Eden there came, old Satan himself, the lying deceiver.
He stole the truth from the woman and man, and he thought he had ruined the Father's plan.
For the Father had to curse his beautiful creation with death, and thorns, and much destruction.
But into the world the rose of Sharon came, conquering death and bringing fellowship again.
Old Satan thought he had won this time, when the rose of Sharon died.
On a cross for our sins he did pay, so the thorns on his creation would fade away.
Now on that bright and beautiful morn, we can hold the roses and they won't have thorns,
And the rose of Sharon can reign in the hearts of those who love him.
All you must do is ask his forgivness, and he will come in and never leave you.
And all because of the rose of Sharon, there won't be mourning when we get to Heaven.

— *Gayle Massey*

You and Me

Rainy day sweetheart
Castaway baby
Cuddle up dream lover
You and me against the world

Sleepy eyed darling
Little boy blue
Dream on crystal vision
There is nothing here to fear

Some say I'm a witch
All agree that I'm mad
You are my slave forever
I summoned you from beyond

I brought you to my castle
I give you everything
Now we'll remain together
You and me against the world

—*Hope Farrar*

Winds of Time

Window's barren light
Reflecting shadows passing in the sun
Where are the days of innocence?

Morning's frozen ground
Holding only footsteps of yesterdays past
Wher are the days of youth?

The winds of time
Are blowing the days away
But leaving memories unsettled in my mind.

— *Vivian Rey Dickson*

Pink

If I could smell pink,
It would be sweet like a rose.
If I could touch pink,
It would be soft like a pussy willow
And thin like silk.
If I could taste pink,
It would taste like a cookie
Dipped in pink dye
Or as good as a sweet apple.
If I could hear pink,
It would sound like the song of a robin
Or soft like a hummingbird.
If I could see pink,
It would be as soft to the eye
As pussy willow is to the touch.

— *Ingre Reinhardt*

Weaver of Spells

Boy, you drive me crazy
With all the things you do,
You have made my world go hazy,
With a spell from a witch's brew.
Boy, your eyes are entrancing,
Like a spell from the deep blue sea,
They make me feel like dancing,
With your arms holding me.
Boy, your smile is magical,
Like a unicorn running free,
I have tried being practical
But, you have cast your spell on me.
Boy, you come and haunt my dreams
On these carefree summer nights,
So why does my heart feel torn at the seams,
Whenever you whisper your soft goodnights?

—*Heather L. Getzelman*

A Friend is

A friend is kind, a friend is true,
But no friend is, quite like you.
You listen to worries, you talk about fears,
You lend your shoulder, when my eyes are full of tears.
You laugh when I am happy, you cry when I am sad,
You are proud when I do good, you scold when I do bad.
You never pretend, to be who you're not.
You're never stuck up, you're never a snot.
You're always there, in my time of need,
You fix me up, when I start to bleed.
You're the greatest person, I've ever known,
And from you, I have grown.
You have taught me many things, I never will forget,
You will always be my friend, no matter how old I get.
　　—Ericka Quale

Parting

We departed in such sweet sorrow
Never knowing when the next time we would see each other
The next time we would hold another
All we knew
That it was time to go
And all we have is the memory
The memory of our love
The memory of one another
I know one day we will be together
When I just don't know
Keep the hope of us reuniting
For one day it won't be just a memory
It will be us together forever
　　—Patricia A. Stevens

I Wondered?

Two birds flew away, towards the night;
I wondered if they were in love,
Or just partners
In flight.
They joined with the clouds,
Then were lost to my eyes;
The wings of life,
Charting uncharted skies.
I wondered if they floated
To leave sorrow behind,
Or just birds flying freely
To capture my mind.
I hoped they were somehow aware of our situation...
Two birds flew away...physical imagination.
　　— Alix Hayes

How It Was

Shadows cast by a golden ray
A widow walks to the holiday
Harmonic love through all the land
Played with trumpets by the band
A piper of stone who cannot play
His hands are stiff for they are of clay
A jester smiles upon a stage
And the circus freak sits in his cage
The guards are stiff like statues stand
And the jugglers juggle with one hand
Colored puppets move with ease
Like moonbeams dance in the midnight breeze
The midgets walk on platforms high
For they are the ones who will reach the sky
And far away under a tree
A poet writes about the sea
　　—Vincent Salvati

A Summer's Night

On a dark and stormy night
My heart was filled with fright
For the jets that soared overhead
Were soon to be counting the dead.

A sudden flash,
A giant crash
And then the silence fell
Like a sound that would forever dwell.

On the mountains high
And in the valleys low
The roaring planes
Were slow to go.

And the heartache and pain, the sadness and sorrow
With the death and destruction that would surely follow.

Two countries at war
Two soldiers to fight
Such sadness and pain
On a cold summer's night.
　　—Becky Sample

Dragon Fire

My dragon sings of life
Ingesting the sun he relieves the heat.
Red his strength,
Chewing the miles he wings home to me.
He smokes a dog, a friend, the earth. Listen to his
Research, speak of tomorrow. I can read his heart,
It is for me he lives, wings beating frantically against
The odds. The cricket under my foot protesting to no avail,
The message bounces, rebounds, breaks-
Fragments, sand in the mind.
Fly to the sun,
Wind batting leaves in my face, let's play tag.
　　— J. W. Wack

I Had Rather Have a Friend

I had rather have a friend, than a pot o'gold so rare,
I'd rather have your trust, than wealth without your care;
I had rather just be able to look into your eyes,
And smile and say, *I love you,* and this you realize.

I had rather be a friend, than someone of renown,
That you may call and know, will never let you down;
I had rather be trustworthy in any game of life,
Than think I know it all, and give you too much strife.

I'd rather stand for right, like three Hebrews of the past,
Who faced the King, and said, *Your golden image will not last.*
We won't bow down, O'King, tho in the fire, we're thrown,
'Cause God, on high, we know; will make Himself well known.

I'd rather please the Lord, than have the praise of men,
You see, one day, I'm looking for Him to come again;
And since I dearly love Him, who have His all for me,
Then one day in the future, with Him I'll forever be.
　　—Ilene Noble

Life

Life, what is it worth?
Is it worth all the pain and sorrow you go through?
Is it worth the litle bit of happiness you get?
Is it worth it if you don't achieve your goals?
Is it worth it if you know you lost and you haven't even started yet?
Life is but a gamble; you win or lose.
I lost, so what is life worth now?
　　— Denise Ledoux

...She Is Gone

My girl has gone, gone on her way
She used to be here each and every day.
She is on her own now, independent as can be
Why all she does is look away from me.

She is all grown up, but not ready yet, to sever the ties
Why are there tears in her eyes?
Does she need me still, in her own way?
Will she welcome me in on some cold and rainy day?

I have shed my tears and have stopped holding on
Now my beautiful Lauren is gone.
I dream of the day she spreads her arms
And gathers me into her life from that day on

There will be no closed doors forevermore
And the love between us will forever soar.

—*Carol Goldman*

World in Jeopardy

Is any chance for happiness, worth dying for?
Evidently, young men think so.
Everyday they reach for a drug studded pendulum,
To escapte the realities of the ghettos.
Day after day, newcasts are filled;
With death, destruction and sorrow.
Young men are dying, poor mothers are crying,
Will you cry for yours tomorrow?

How can we stem the tide of drugs?
How can we make young men see?
Fortunes they seek, that seem so easy,
Are not to be had for free!
Oh God of mercy, overseer of us all,
Can't you hear all the mothers crying?
Give leaders a resolute quality of mind,
To stop all the young men dying!

—*William Roseboro*

Memories of Mom

Mom, I can remember how sad I was
When you were not there
How alone I was.
I can remember your soft touch when I was down.

Mom, I can remember all those tears
I felt you were so near.
I can remember each day we lived together
Your wonderful love, I can't forget.

I can remember your sweet voice
Liz, I love you and that is my choice.
I can remember telling you I love you,
Can you hear me?

Hold me tight in your arms
And cheer me
And never let me go.

—*Elizabeth Campos*

My Diary of Life

You sit on my bed all ragged and all rags,
But you're always there, you always care.
You sit very silent, very content,
As you listne to my innermost, private,
Yet beyond the ordinary most wildest things.
You're the only one who knows whom I've spotted in my eye.
You've heard about the people I love
And things I despise.
Your eyes seem to understand what I'm going through,
Your arms sit in a way ready to be hugged
And although you don't talk, I hear what you're saying.
You're my diary of life, you're my teddy bear!

—*Beth Verciglio*

Only In My Mind

I wonder in and out of people's minds,
I enter my own mind to
Try to figure out my problems
By being within myself
Somehow I draw you into my mind with me.
You have told me, you are finished,
Finished with love.
If you are finished with love, you will die.
I have tried to save your love
By being your love
You have given up,
You have died in my mind.

—*B. J. Blank*

Short Time Love

When we first met our love was so beautiful
Like there was no one here but you and I in the world
We were so proud of our love
It is too bad such a beautiful love has to last such a short time.
I know we have had this love for a few years
But when it is gone, it seems like such a short time
Love, when the love is gone
Time feels so short but when the love is gone
And the hurt begins with words and tears hurt
So bad, it feels like no end to the hurt
From someone you love so much.
It goes on for a few days and weeks and months
It feels like forever
That is why love feels so short,
Love is such a short time,
Enjoy while you have such a beautiful love
Because it is just a short time love when it is gone.

—*Priscilla Robitaille*

Somebody Told Me

Somebody told me
All about the man called Jesus
And, somebody told me that Jesus will help you
When you are in trouble
And, then they told me that Jesus was coming back again
But, I know that Jesus is coming back for me.

But, now I can tell the world that Jesus is the only way
And, now I can tell you
All about his love
But, you will never know that it is true,
Until you try Him.

—*Evan B. Farrior*

No Other Girl for Me

No other girl can take me away from you,
No other girl can surpass the beauty in you.
My head and my heart are filled with love,
A touch of your hand is soft as a dove.

Exciting moments of caring will always be yours,
Nothing you ask will ever be called chores.
My life belongs to you and my heart will always be true,
It will bring happiness and joy that will cheer you through.

My choice of caring is an undetermined dimension,
The starry light in your eyes brings out my tension.
I can't wait to hold you gently in my arms,
Nor can I wait to feel the vibrations of your charms.

Your presence stiffens my body with a warm angelic glow,
The love expressed by your lips flares up my loving flow.
So be that girl that nobody else can have,
No other girl like you makes life a living staff.

— *Edd David McWatters*

The Drapest

The drapest comes
To howl upon my window,
Scratch upon my door;
Eagerly asking entry.
I refuse.

I've no money for the wolves,
No bacon from the beast.
My sweetened fruit has now rotted.
Catch me if they can.

I've a candle which burns dimly.
I await the drapest, the wolves.
I shall throw them all a meager bone.
Let them fight for it.
All to hell.

— *Carol A. Dick*

Blind

I have traveled lonely roads
through the country
and through cities.

I have lived in graveyards
and tried to befriend Death.
yet, I lived on.

Now, I am beginning to travel
paths with more people.
And I find that
I was never alone.

— *Bruce W. Watkins*

Untitled

A girl without a cause.
Lost with a reason.
Refusing directions,
Issued from yourself.

Simply an auto,
With no wheels.
An angel,
Lacking wings.
Unintentional, misguided,
Pain.

I ask of you
To ask yourself,
Girl without a cause.
What do I mean to him?

And you will ask me.
That will answer yourself.
Still I would tell you,
Hurt prevails from unkept promises.

—*Alan Williams*

Stars in the Sky

The first star seems so lonely
until the second one appears,
Then so many more come;
The darkness disappears.

Without stars in the sky
Love seems so unreal.
Then you find someone special
To share what you feel.

When your life seems dark and lonely
Love can lift your spirits so high.
That someone and you are like
Stars in the sky.

—*Angie Fischer*

The Only Answer

Hello, my friend.
They say we are enemies.
I look in your eyes,
Why do I see peace?

They don't understand,
We're one in the same.
We both have two eyes,
We both have two ears;
Why can't they see?
Why don't they listen?
Peace is the only answer.

Our stars in the skies
Are the same stars in yours.
The image in our eyes
Is as twisted as yours.
Why can't they see?
Why don't they listen?
Peace is the only answer.

—*Aimee L. Richards*

Rarity

On balance wing
My poem sing
Speed silence into song.
Wayward speak

For dew fond leak
Soul at dreams belong.
Would center self
Poor wage pelf

Rich in treasure lore.
Word I think
Mix further ink
Tell what mine adore.

Time ply ripe
No sullen gripe
Fill me with despair, tell I true
Where pieces flew love strew.

—*Orien Todd*

Holocaust Honeymoon

The dying tree
Stood straight
Its bare armed
Branches
Beckoned for embrace
A burning bride
Of forest flame
Came quickly
To its mate

— *W. W. Reed*

Stand by My Master

I wake up in the morning,
Then fall to my knees,
Thanking the master,
For a new start, to please.
I must be good,
And do what I'm told,
Or out I go, into the cold.
For if I do what is right
Not to stray,
I know that some day
I'll be free.
To stand by my Master
With a spirit just like his,
Helping others to be, as he is.

— *Edwin L. Shaw*

Gossip

Gossip is contagious!
You find it everywhere!
Does a lot of damage,
But the gossips just don't care!

Vicious gossip spreads with ease
And is such a deadly game!
Like a contagious disease,
It destroys one's good name!

A story oft repeated,
Changes much from mouth to ear!
So before you spread it further,
Better put your mind in gear!

If the telling of a story
Will hurt or cause one sorrow,
Why not just forget it!
You'll feel better tomorrow!

— *Arthur F. Ward*

On the Piazza

Do you remember
How St. Mark's square looked
In the cold; in the dark?
We shivered and walked
In the moonlit mist.
We talked about our dreams,
And struggled
With our troubled hearts.
We knew the price
Of failure
And never would
Accept defeat.

— *Henry M. Mestre Jr.*

Brooklyn

It is humid and hot,
the air stands still,
so many streets
for the people to fill.
Too many street lights
so many cars,
too many street fights
for proof are the scars.
Loud music blares
with hispanic and rap,
but nobody cares;
they're proving a fact.
There is too much to do,
there is too much to see,
so sitting on the stoop
is the place to be.

—*Bridgett Olene Taranto*

Wake Up My Little Tom

Wake up my little Tom.
You've lots to do today.
Wake up my little Tom.
For you to God I pray.

Wake up my little Tom.
Your soul is His to keep.
Angels are watching over you
And angels never sleep.

Wake up my little Tom.
You've many rewards to reap.
You are with the angels now
And angels never sleep.

— *Amy Gibbons*

My Best Dream

In my best dream, I am a butterfly or a deer
Or a flower on the table of the dining room in a convent.
I can feel the warmness of God around me.
I can smell His quietness.
The flowers move back and forth with the wind like dancers.
The mountains call for adventure and a climb.
The woods hold trust in its branches.
Children's laughter peeps through the sky.
All the birds and animals smile.
God is everywhere.

    — *Lee Christopher*

The Dude

They say he came from Boston,
A greenhorn, through and through.
He prefers imported brandy,
To our local Northwest brew.
We all thought him a dreamer, to dare this mountain life.
But his eyes warned of a strength, hones sharp as any knife.
He carved his winter refuge, from a stand of lodgepole pine.
He learned the art of trapping, and how to follow sign.
His clothes he cut from rawhide,
He smell of cedar smoke.
And what he calls his dinner,
Would make a lady choke.
When Earth calls forth a dreamer,
Let us not begrudge.
If found to be deficient,
Let mother nature judge.

    —*Thomas P. Murray*

The Day Has Come

I sit on my branch
Trying to remember all that
Mother has taught me
For I've been out in that world.
I took a big leap too.
I flapped and I fluttered,
But I still failed,
And mother had to come and rescue me.
Now here I sit,
Remembering all the lectures and directions.
Going over every detail, for this time I must not fail,
I dream about taking that leap
Spreading my wings and soaring through the great big sky.
But now is not the time for dreaming, I must take that leap,
And open my wings for some day I will surely reach
The sky.

    —*Rusoun Belue*

My True and Faithful Friend

She was a German Shorthaired Pointer, the dog I chose for my own
Who was one of the truest friends, that I have ever known.
She was a fine and beautiful animal, my companion and faithful friend,
Always alert and watchful, always ready to defend.

She would never desert me, even when I had chores to tend,
She was always there to keep me company, on her, I could always depend.
She liked to chase and run with the kids, and was always ready to play,
I can't tell you how many times, she brightened up my day.

She was a good bird dog, a purebred of noble birth,
And every time she went in the field, she proved how much she was worth.
But at long last she became ill, as the years went swiftly by,
And we were told that someday soon, she was going to die...

So I tried to make her last months the happiest she had ever known
I took her everywhere that I went, and every night I gave her a bone.
She was such a big part of my life, this faithful friend of mine,
And I know I'm gonna miss her, for a long, long time.

    —*Mary Fields*

Listen

Listen.
The silence of a million years is all around.
Hear with an open spirit,
As it invades the capsule of your mind.
Embrace it.
Cherish it.
Move with it like music.
Listen.
As it calls for your attentions,
And relieves the sounds of everyday life;
As sleep falls upon the earth,
And movement ceases.
Listen.

    — *Charles Thomas Maxie*

Spring, Fall, Summer, Winter

Spring, Fall, Summer, Winter
Leaves changing colors
With ever change shows signs of winter
Winter just around the corner
With snowflakes and snowmen
Christmas on it's way
Children waiting for their toys
When it's all over
Spring comes with April rain and May flowers
Trees with green leaves
And children waiting to swim
For hours on end
Summer with hot weather
Strolling through the leaves in the Fall
Walking just to see the leaves with bright colors
Seasons change again and again
They come but soon are gone like the wind.

    —*Michele Johnson*

Great Black Bear

Among the snowcapped mountains
Lies the great black bear
All hunters must be aware
Danger lurks about everywhere
Cries of pain heard all around
A small bear cub falls to the ground
Soon mama bear is pretty near
Her eyes are filled with sorrow and tears
She rips the hunter to tiny shreads
The brave hunter now is dead
So among the snowcapped mountains
You will find the
Great black bear

    —*Chris Benson*

The Dreamer Inside

I live behind a mask of fear
And each day lose the power
To discern the truth within me
From the cage in which I cower.
I cling helplessly to my peers,
Hoping to be one of the free.
Somehow I can't let them know
That I just want to be me.
I don't usually make my views known
For fear of their cruelty and laughter,
But deep inside of me there is
The dreamer, the artist I'm after.
I long to be me and to escape
From the force behind which I am pinned,
To cut loose the ties that bind me,
And sail on a September wind.
— *Wendy M. Frechette*

Petals

Petals on the wind. Silent they fly!
Tossed about in the harshest manner.
Petals on the winds. Take flight, be free.
Let not the humans crush you beneath their feet.
Take flight, fly free as you were born to be.
The land has no hold on you.
You have served your purpose.
Now fly free before you are destroyed.
They don't know all you bring.
For they are shallow and self serving.
Fly free petals on the wind.
Be free as you were born to be.
—*Aundrea Ali*

Sami

Long blond locks amongst a tiny fair face
With a big round dimple on one side
Endless questions with an awe of wonder
And an ever embracing smile.
She's always there when you need her
Always willing to be a part
And although she's only three feet tall
She's bound to steal your heart
A little girl named *Sami*
As pure as a snow white dove
The answer to countless peoples dreams
God's tiny gift of love.
— *Gale E. Avery*

Untitled

He lies in wait.
Motionless; watching,
With great intensity,
The young, colorful bird.
The breeze can only ruffle
His smooth, black fur,
And now, more than ever,
He is suddenly a panther.
Young, wild, and free,
Stalking his prey.
Then he looks at me
With bright, golden orbs,
And, in all of his beauty,
He runs to snooze in my lap.
There is a mutual understanding between us;
He is mine, and I am his,
My beautiful black panther.
—*April Dickens*

Tomorrow

Tomorrow is a great day
To do the things you love
You wait around for it to happen
'Cause you know it's just above
Now my life is over
It's my turn to go
I never really lived my life
'Cause tomorrow never showed.
— *Deb Emery*

Serene Moonlight

On a serene summer night,
The water in the lake
Shimmering in the tenderness
Of the moonlight.
Passionately reflected on it,
Was the inverted shadow of the moon.
The water was so imperturbable,
And the moonlight...so abiding.
Bestowed my sentiment upon the night, I would.

On the water surface
Blew the gentle wind,
Brought about tiny ripples,
Sent a small quivering wave to my heart.
Disseminated an inconceivable tidings.
Still, I reckoned your radiant eyes
The most glittering stars
Of the night.
—*Peng Eng Lee*

Facing the Darkness Ahead

Through all the years
She has always been there
To make everything all right.
Always a model and one to care.
She was left as a widow
At a very young age,
And with us three small children
She did housework for a very low wage.
Up early each morning
On KRT she would go,
Arrive home late each evening,
Then out to the garden to hoe.
Now, at a later age,
Alzheimer's she has now,
I think about the days gone by,
And want to help, but how?
—*Brenda Griffith*

Eyes of Fire

Eyes like fire
Burn a hole through my heart,
Your eyes of fire
Tear my soul apart.
Your eyes like fire,
They melt me in two.
The only thing I want
Is to be with you.
Your eyes show everything
That you never say.
Strange those eyes of yours
Can make me feel this way.
It seems like so much pain
Is bottled up inside,
But with eyes of fire, like yours
Your emotions can never hide.
—*Holly Perkins*

Prairie Fire

Nothing more deadly
stealing
the lands away
Nothing more final
an
ashy completion
Nothing more quick
or
uncontrollable
A rush of devouring
flames
destroying anything
Nothing more demised
than
the lost lives
Nothing more deadly
than
the Prairie Fire
—*Xandria*

In Memory

I really don't know why I'm here
Standing by her, oh so near.
I still smell her sweet perfume
And her hair, oh such gloom.
Her eyes, her face,
Oh so cold now!
No!
How could it be?
Yes, it's real.
I'm here.
She's gone.
Forever.
— *Vita Burkhart*

An Experience

To hear the tittering of a
woman's laughter;
or the gurgle of a
baby's sigh—
To hear the wind rushing
through the leaves;
and screaming seagulls
in the sky—
To feel the hunger of a child
who never had a
good meal;
The love of a Mother's
arms he can
never feel—
We live/we laugh/and
we cry; then comes
a time we all
must die—
I ask myself . . . Is there something better?
Who knows . . . no one went
beyond and sent back
a letter—
What is the meaning of all this; I say . . .
Never mind stranger,
just let the
music play—
—*David L. Collier*

More and More

All this poem is going to say
is how I will love you more and more each day.
At times I know everything's not right,
but what's a relationship without a fight!
We may argue, we may yell, we may even scream,
but I know for sure I have a dream.
I have a dream that you will be
in love with me for eternity.
I know that's always not what we feel,
but deep down inside I know it's real.
I know it's real and true to say
that I will love you more and more each day.

— *Gina Marie Cruz*

My Soul

Who are you that I cannot see?
Who are you that I can feel and know?
You, who lies so still, are within,
A silence always there, and yet, wait...
I feel a strange pull from deep within.
It is quiet and yet, all knowing who and what I am.
When I die, where do I go?
How many lives have you and I been?
I am part of a nest of curiousity.
I see with an invisible eye that only you can be.
Life is precious to me, though unending are you.
I see a beginning and, through you, an everlasting eternity.
I want to be a soul and have a sense of being...
I am me.

— *Yvonne Lee*

I Love You 4 Ever

My heart just tore,
When I was told you don't love me anymore,
At first I'd thought it was something I had done,
And I thought, being with you had been so much fun,
All that night,
I had so much fright,
Wondering what I might do,
Because I thought our love was so true,
I decided I wanted to die,
Because you wouldn't tell me why.
I had so much fear,
And I wanted you near,
It just wasn't fair,
But all of a sudden you didn't care.
I wish we could be together,
Because I love you 4 ever!

— *Heather Hart*

What Is True Love?

What is true love?
Is it just hugs and kisses?
No, it's something special in your heart.
Staying together and never being apart from your true love.
When you're feeling down, your true love can fix that frown.
He will put a smile on your face.
He will kiss you and hug you with his warm embrace.
That is true love.
When you fall, he will pick you up and say you are okay.
Then you will smile that smile that he says you can see for miles
So true love is not just hugs and kisses, it's smiles and poems
Or saying I will love you forever to your sweetheart.
This will make your love true and the best one ever.
So if you believe in true love, you can make your love true.
Making your love true is one of the best things you can do,
And that is true love.

— *Nicole D. Clark*

Tangled in Love

I am so tangled in love with you
That I must stretch my legs to match your every step
So as not to miss even a public communion with your presence
And our arms entwined become a giant pretzel,
Linking us.
I sometimes wish to be your siamese twin
So that where you end I would begin.
Your breath controls my heartbeat
And my mind expands to think your every thought.
Your hands feel like extensions of my flesh
And yoour words of love echo from inside me.
Suddenly within my reach
Are the elusive fantasies that an adolescent girl
Dared to dream beneath her private covers
And all that I stored away as foolish
Is reachable and real.
The stories of love so strong and sure
Are really how I feel.

—*Pat Harwell*

Love Is Not the Reason

I bend over and the pain shoots through my body.
I apologize but this just will not do.
It seems to me everything I do is wrong, when we both know it's right.
You say it's love that tells you to hit, when I know it's not that at all.
I love you, or so I try, and would never want to do the same to you.
Why is it that you only feel hatred towards me when I've tried to be the best
    I possibly can?
Is the best not good enough for you?

— *Abigail G. Cummins*

Broken Hearts

Broken hearts are something that can never be fixed.
A heart is fragile just like friendships.
When you have a friendship that's broken, your heart's broken.
Your friendship hurts too much to say you don't care.
You drop into sorrow and depression; nothing ever goes right.
You need your friendship, but God only knows you'll never get it back.
The chance was then, the pain is now.
Your friend doesn't know you're there.
She says she cares, but really she doesn't.
It was all just a saying of a used friendship,
A friendship you thought really was,
But in reality, it's a broken life
With a broken friendship that has a broken heart.

— *Yolanda Epskamp*

Collage of Love

The cupidlike bow that unleashes its
unsolicited arrow toward an unworthy
Object. The magnanimous magnet of affection
that gathers the shattered fragments of a life once sliced by the knife
of hatred. The glowing offspring of emanating personal pulchritude
The magic mirror that reflects its innocent image to another's face
The plush, pleasant of memorable, warm compassion
The gentle hand that rocks the cradle of beneficent care.
The generous garment in which anonymous philanthropy is wrapped
The flickering candle that dispels the enveloping darkness of a dreary
night, the burning brand that distinguishes enduring fact from fleeting
fantasy, the badge of bravery for a friend or foe caught in the mesh of
no return, the sheltering shadow for an injured, staggering fellow pilgrim
The secure staff on which the weary finds repose
The rope of rescue for the soul sinking in deep despair
The towering torch that signals triumph over struggle, tragedy and pain
The limitless extension of life for life.

—*Wendell K. Babcock*

Sweet Dreams

I am dreaming of a mountain
That no one has ever seen
With flowers made from lolipops
And a flowing kool aid stream.

The trees are cotton candy,
Pink, fluffy, and oh so high.
The mountain is a candy kiss
That reaches to the sky.

The birds are always singing
It's sunny everyday.
The dewdrops taste like honey,
And fairies come to play.

I really love this mountain
So fresh and clean and sweet
I hope I'll go again someday,
If only in my sleep.
—*Amy Marie Shupe*

I Care

I hope that you know
That I care about you.
I'll try to show you
So you'll know that it's true.
I care about what happens
Each day of your life.
I want you to tell me
Of each struggle and strife.
I want to tell you
That I'll always be here.
It doesn't change anything,
Whether I'm far away or near.
I want to share all
Your hopes, dreams and fears.
I've told you before
And I'll tell you again
Now and forever,
We'll always be friends.
—*Brandy Lundeen*

Pink Flowers

A field of flowers beckons my mind-
Fills me with a memory
Of childhood innocence,
As I remember a child
Running and dancing
In a field of pink flowers-
Wanting to become one
With the beauty and peacefulness
Of the meadow.
She made a wreath of flowers
To wear on her golden hair;
She danced and sang,
Celebrating her new found haven.
Her fantasy shattering
As the time to leave arrived,
Not understanding why
Such beauty couldn't last forever.
—*Angela Berndt*

A Mother's Day Poem

Violets are blue,
Roses are red.
I am mixed up.
Now what do I do?
My mom, she is always there.
She'll know what to do.
Happy Mother's Day, Mom.
— *Amy Appleby*

Mankind

Somewhere.
Don't ask me where.
    We've lost ourselves.
Here we are running in circles.
    Searching.
    Probing eternity.
    Trying to find;
        Where we are.
        Who we are.
        Why it matters.
Sheep looking for a shepherd.
Someone to lead us to greener pastures.
Safety in numbers.
Huddle together.
Somewhere.
—*Jack Curtis*

Seven Voyagers

Seven voyagers on their way into space
Riding on a rocket ship
A rare mixture of religion, gender and race
On a special trip
On a column of fire the rocket arose
Glistening in the sun
What happened next we may never know
Things just came undone
A flash of fire, a cloud of smoke, a roar
Tiny pieces rain down
The space shuttle Challenger is no more
Disbelief spread around
The choice has been made to go for it all
Perhaps it was in haste
Seven voyagers answered the call
What a shameful waste
—*William R. Whittaker*

Abortion

Oh, should weep the mother
Who murdered her child.
Tis not done in a moment of insanity,
For she had time to contemplate her deed.
Tis not done for the sake of revenge,
Like Medea slaying her own sons;
But for some done out of fear,
Fear of being responsible
When at the prime of youth,
A youth full of friends and parties.
For others pure selfishness.
Whatever the reason for destroying a babe
Before it could breath in wonderous life,
One thing for certain—for each death,
One miracle denied a chance of love;
A chance of life;
A chance to look in loving eyes
And think—mother?
—*Nhung Nguyen*

Untitled

The city buildings are a view,
Of prestige and power.
To see who can be the highest,
The one which will over others tower.

People are just like that,
They like things that are new.
People build up money, wealth and popularity,
But then people build buildings too.
— *Erin Alford*

Please God

Show me grace and guidance
As I walk life's narrow way.
Guide my inner conscience
And teach me how to pray.

If you fill my cup, Lord
I will drink it dry to thee,
I will speak with words of wisdom...
So that others follow thee.
For in you, there is no failure
Our souls feel full and free.

Jesus, you are my saviour,
So merciful and true,
I know that you will guide me
If I will ask but what to do.
—*B. F. Johnson*

A Mother's Song

Do you hear what I hear,
A child, a child
Crying in the night
With a voice that is frightened and clear
With a voice that is lonely and near.

Do you know what I know,
A boy, my boy
Left the other day
For a dream that is silver and gold
For a dream that is terrors untold.

Now you have heard what I know,
A man, my son
Died just yesterday
In a land that is sunless and bold
In a land that is war torn and cold.
—*C. J. Burgher*

Your Place or Mine

Should one wish to compare
The sun to the shadows
Smell breath of a drunkard
While the old actor bellows
A line of poetic flatulence
Sobbing the parasites struggles
The axis grinds and winds
As the termites fresh rubble
The great lizards wept warm tears
Mother's children many more years
As the asphalt tumors dining
Confirmed their darkest fears
So the sphere turned blue black
While the Eden absorbed her seas
The psychopath turned his back
On the air his lungs do breath
—*Isaac Ben Joel*

Spring in the Park

After a tempest winter
not only of weather,
but of life too,

the old man bent to pray.

Lord, let me know love again,
the soft gentle feel
of a caressing wind,
a smile,
a touch,
a best friend.
— *Bobbie J. Pugh*

My Friend

You are my friend,
We have a friendship that will never end.
With all my heart I love you,
You often keep me from being blue.
You have become a part of me,
Our friendship will always be.
I want you to know you can always lean on me.
Because you are always here,
I feel I have nothing to fear.
You're a part of my life I don't ever want to lose.
Always remember I love you
And that you will always be
More than just a friend to me.

—*Bridget D. Budgetts*

Be my Guest

It feels so strange,
To no longer need to arrange.

A power far greater than you see
Operates very well with or without me.

It was sad when I first realized I was not in command,
Yet I became glad,
To realize this stand.

Now I can appreciate the ups and downs,
The joys and the sorrow.
Of the yesterdays, the today and the tomorrow.

Why could I not see before?
Pride and fear stood in front of my door.
Willingness to trust helped me take the step.
Proceeding onward, I have found much of life in depth.

Thank you to all involved in my quest,
And an open invitation to you
Be my guest.

—*Bettye L. Hanley*

Mother Love

Grow a little faster, seed.
I am impatient to see what I have made.
Could it be you can feel my love?
It flows through me replacing the blood in my veins
And if I carried this love within my hand and
Made a fist to protect it from all others
It would seep through my swollen fingers
Falling soundlessly to the floor, forming puddles at my toes.

As my baby grows deep within my being
Deep within my soul my mother love germinates.
It grows as the child grows, a strong overwhelming thing,
Stronger than I or the child,
And yet the child and I have invented the love.
We tenderly cultivated it through the months
Our only aspiration, for the love to be returned.

— *Gail D. Austin*

Unpercieved Thoughts...

Winter is a season of realization.
It strikes us with blunt posture
And breathes a whispering message in the air.
The message is not one of feeling,
For feelings are too intimate.
The message is in each body that has life.
People have to search beneath the creture they display
And grab ahold of their inner figure, not letting go until
They fully understand
Their individual message
Of winter...

— *Nora Rodli*

A Mother Is a Friend

A mother is a friend
who always loves you.
A mother is a friend
no matter what you do.
A mother is a friend
you can always count on.
A mother is a friend
whether you have lost or won.

A mother is a friend
who always has the time
to play a game or two
or make up a silly rhyme.
A mother is a friend
who would give you anything
though sometimes she won't
because it's not the best thing.

Thank you, mother,
for being a friend.

—*Pam Sledge*

Description

Description!
What is a description?
I tried to write a note.
But
I couldn't explain
the reason why
I tried to write
a photograph
but
I couldn't explain
the reason why
I tried
to write
a telegram
but
I couldn't afford to lie
What is a description?
Will!
I find out
before
I die.

—*Hubert Reeder*

Hope of Love

I used to think that
Dreams came true.
    Now I know
    They don't
    I have often
Dreamed of you,
Sharing your life
    With just me.
    Now I know
That it can never
        Be.

—*Dorietta Corrigan*

Forty Plus

Forty plus, moving;
Forty plus, grooving;
Hopping cracks,
Making tracks,
Endless youth proving.

—*Patricia C. Harrison*

A Tender Moment

A 'jink o' water for you, Mommy,
My very young son said
He wanted so to help me
As I lay sick in bed.
The scene had been reversed
So many times before
When fever from an occasional cold
Had brought him chills—and more!
What had my child been thinking
As he saw me prone in bed?
A worried frown across his brow
Told of his inner fears,
Security was shaken
For one so young in years.
I gave a cheery, *Thank you*
No other words were said
I smiled, then placed a loving pat
Upon his tousled head.

—*Blondine Louise Reddick*

What is Black?

What is black?
Black is the blinding white snow
Stilled by winter's cold
What is black?
Black is the cool spring water
Dancing over shapely rock formation
What is black?
Black is sizzling hot summer days
Interspersed with the ocean's breezes
What is black?
Black is autumn's trees
Facing each other on a long winding road
What is black?
Black is a part of all seasons
Until earth cease to exist.

—*Gloria Frazier*

Tye Dye the Flag

Psychedellic trip
Twisting, turning
Circular patterns of cosmic colour
Floating in white stars
Corrupted, impure, unholy
Swirls of brillance
A single expression of radical rebellion
Freedom
No—escape
There is no freedom
From government
From religion
From society
From self
Absorption of etiquette
Rules, captured, punished
All for a piece of cloth

—*Heather West*

Love

Don't tell me that you love me,
Because I'm afraid that its not true,
When we're apart for so long.
The days turn so very blue.
So when you say you love me,
Make sure that it's for real.
So when it is all over,
My heart isn't what you steal.

— *Amy Loeser*

Every Rose Has Its Thorn

They say that every rose has its thorn,
I guess that goes for love.
Ours was never perfect,
With differences we are born.
When stars were shining bright,
With one another we would fight.
At times like others,
We got along like perfect lovers.
Then suddenly in two my heart was torn,
I guess it is true.
Every rose has its thorn.

—*Brandy Hicks*

To See Clearly

To see clearly you must not see with your eyes.
But truly you must see through your heart.
Seeing from within your soul and not your mind.
Touching by the edges of your eyesight
And not your fingertips.
To feel with tracing eyes of movement
With visions of realism.
Seeing with your heart of mind.

— *Brian Michael*

Unselfish Love

Your love was the inspiration, the guide;
The light during my journey from childhood.
In my pain you always understood.
In my joy you were rewarded.
Your wisdom was surpassed only by the beauty,
Of your unselfish heart.

Your love was the magic, the potion;
The hope in my impressionable days.
In my sorrow you brushed my tears away.
In my gladness you rejoiced.
My gratitude is surpassed only by the beauty,
Of my devoted heart.

— *Wandi (Wanda Woldahl)*

I Love You

I treasure our life together.

Loving you the way I do
Often sets my heart on fire.
Vehemently you're my one and only desire
Evermore to be.

Younger than springtime
Oh! Definitely.
United as one

We shall always be
Until death do us part.

— *Patricia Ann Schwinn*

The Two of Us

Everyday through the sunlit window I see him.
While I sit on the inside looking out.
I see a vision.
The two of us walking side by side.
When we stop I stare into his eyes as he holds me tight.
I can feel his touch through my body.
My desire for him gets stronger.
As he kisses me I suddenly awake.
Betrayed by a kiss.
I realize its no longer real.

—*Patricia Caso*

The Answer

To hate you laugh
To love you cry
Life is a riddle
To solve you die

— *Bob Avey*

Love

I may not be rich.
I'm glad I'm not poor,
But I have your love
And that means much more!

— *Beverly Wohlert*

Jumbo

elephant   walking
talking   circus
three   ring   circus
       ring
       ring
       ring
        ing
      telephone
      elephone
walking   talking
    saxophone
giant   walking
talking   sax

—*Stanley E. Keen*

Why?

Dripping, falling, helpless
Not rain,
Not a faucet,
Tears.

Why, you may ask,
Does she need to cry?
She's got everything.

She looks up and sees them.
Lowered head,
Sniffled tears,
A thrown Kleenex crumpled
Underneath the park bench.

She walks away.

— *North Landreth*

Lying Ahead

Oh starry night
the black velvet
covers the sun.
The moon's
faint light
creates a path
for us to follow
leaving our sad
stricken days behind us
and our memories
lying ahead.

— *Amanda Freeman*

Telltale Shadows

One final trip through empty rooms
Upstairs and down.
Patterned indentations remain as telltale
Shadows of chairs and other furnishings removed.
Only dust motes challenge the sunshine
Searching harbor, slanting across the room.
No noisey children roll and tumble upon the floor.
The dog, slump tailed,
Eyes pleading follows as though
I somehow can return the house
To furnished life again...but I cannot.
The vacant rooms, the house
A shell, still hold memories that made it live.
Stoop shouldered, I turn,
The misted scene a blur,
And walk away.

—*Paul M. Lamb*

What If I Am?

What if I am? What will I do?
How will he react? Will he say, *I hate you?*
If I am, what do I say?
Do I say, *Please stay with me,* or *Go away?*
He'll say it's my fault and call me a tease.
I'll just cry and say, *Help me, please.*
Then he'll turn his back and say, *Get lost.*
Then say, *You did it, now pay the cost.*
That's when my heart will break in two.
I have no one to turn to, nothing left to do.
He's hurt me more than words can say,
But why, oh why, would he leave me this way?
What if I am? What will I do?
How will he react? Will he say, *I love you?*

— *Nanette Pittman*

More than Friends

Trying to think of something to do
But all I can think about is you
I think about you night and day
Happy you stopped caring what people say

I'm glad you finally realized that people are sometimes wrong
And now our relationship is going strong
I hope this relationship never ends.

I hope we will always be more than just friends
I guess we both feel the same way
So, we'll take our relationship day by day

— *Ilona Wheeler*

Love To Me

You are the warm sun in a clear blue sky;
  you are the sparkle in my eye.
The sweet smell of beauty in a blossoming red rose;
  you are love to me.

You are the wishing star in the darkest skies;
  you are the glimmer of hope through all the lies.
The innocence of the young and the knowledge of the old;
  you are love to me.

You are the strength of love in my mind;
  for you I'd leave the world behind.
The captor of my heart and soul;
  you are the world of love to me.

— *Eva Sichmeller and Jill Kelso*

Mark of Mine

Ages pass, ages gone
One wonders, is it still there?
Small, minute indentations in the grains,
Covered over time and again by shifting,
Swirling sands; many millions have tread upon,
And thought not of those to come; but that one indented,
Crushed grain, leaves its tale to some. Bright, cheery days,
Those days, I walked among the fields; and wondered if someday
Someone would see my booted heel within the indentations. They are
Still there I'm sure, I am. Though His lost in the dark; Signs of
Our passage whether now or then, have surely left their mark.
Nature covers and covets it's own, preserving what once had been;
But deeply mother sees the marks of many men, longing comes to me
This time, I think of Eons gone; where one man placed a barren foot,
I want mine to be one; so I do leave, philosophically, to mother nature,
Time; so I do leave esthetically, this one mark of mine.

—Gary McCollum

The Lion as I Have Seen Him

You can read the past in his face now.
The lion grows tamer with age
And experience has taught him many lessons.
He has suffered so much of the pain, the disappointments,
The thrills and the joys that life has to offer.
Yet with all this, there has been little love.

Once he had love and let it slip away.
Now it's as if life has given him a second chance
And maybe a last chance that love has returned.
Yet he still fears that loss again.
The exterior is so tough; the manor so abrupt.
Beneath that armour is a gentle, caring beast
That longs for true affection and constant companionship
Of one who really cares.

Will he be able to hold on and still maintain his strength and determination
As *King of the Beasts* or will he succumb to be
A toothless, spineless pussycat whom love has stricken?
If he is the true *King* then love will only make him
More durable for he is a true survivor.
The lion will determine his own future as
The *King* or the conquered.

— Fran Armstrong

Dear Grandpa

It's been so long, it's been so long since I could have told you, *I love you,*
since I could hold you.
Only I was too young to realize that you're gone,
But not too young to know the special feeling you bring into me.
You send through me these vibes, these vibes of never-ending love.
I have the memories in my head. The things I've read are all of you.
I have your nose as I was told. You have his hands as they began.
Dear Grandpa, you'd be proud of the little granddaughter you once knew.
You used to watch me from a distance. Now you watch me from above.
With God's guidance, He helps you see in the right direction.
When I smile, it is of you. When I laugh, it is of you.
When I cry, oh when I cry, it is of you.
You created my Mommy who created me
and I'm here to love you for you are me.
Dear Grandpa, I was only three when you had gone.
Now I'm thirteen and it seems wrong.
I need you, Grandpa; I need your hands to hold me.
I need your heart to love me.
I need you, Grandpa. I hope the angels with their golden wings
have brought to you my message
For I am your granddaughter and you are my grandfather,
For you're the river with no end which I shall treasure.
Dear Grandpa, it's been so long.

—Heather Gallo

Tears

Through my eyes
The tears do seep.
Down my face
Memories do creep.
Of family and friends,
Of laughter and tears,
Of years gone by,
That have disappeared.
Now as they roll down my face,
I remember well.
Oh what tears of memory do tell.

—Ericka Ford

Lost and Deserted

Lost and
Out of
Someone's
Touch.

Another street,
No food to eat.
Dangers and

Dares. Some
Eager words,
Special menu
Eats, and
Rats to chase.
To the
Evidence,
DEAD.

— Angela Duncan

Falling Star

Lost in the darkness
Masquerading as a star.
Overcome by severe stillness
Of mute immortality,
Pulsating illuminescence,
My utter insignificance
Hides and is forgotten
As I fall from infinity
Scarring it with my death.

— Amy L. Owings

Untitled

When I look out the window
Quite a sight do I see.
War, hunger, women and men
Piecing their lives together again.
Too many of us ignore
The plain reality
Of what is easily seen
In front of you and me.
What the world needs
Is more people
Who aren't afraid
To fulfill their dreams,
Dreams of peace
And of love
And the tender caress
Of the everlasting...
Peace loving...
Dove.

—Erica Sullivan

Lonliness

I see the lonely,
Sit for comfort.
And in their eyes,
Colors of desperation.
Their arms barely,
Keeping their spirits intack.
As they wait for kind words,
Or someone to talk to.
Who will not attack them,
But rather leave them.
With hope to hope.
That better days will come.

—Adrienne Lee

Rediscovering Me

Was it a space in time
Or a time in space?
Whatever, it is no longer.

When will this energy,
So overwhelming,
Cease to invade my emotions?

How do I recognize
Or find strength to know
The woman I am without him?

Who the hell am I,
Or was I before
My being was conquered by his?

Rose petals and fall leaves
Have their time to shed.
The vital force is in the root.

Let the seasons be brief,
The rose petals drop,
My essence will be born again.

—Elizabeth C. MacNeille

The Doe

In the meadow stood the doe,
Surround by the silent snow,
There I saw the hunter go,
With his arrow and his bow.

I watched with fear and with woe,
As it was stalked by it's foe.
I cried for what it didn't know,
And prayed that soon it would go.

And as the
Hunter approached real low,
The young doe
Fled through the snow

— Angela Lea Rose

A Gem

Life is just a tiny minute . . .
Only sixty secords in it.
It is mine.
I can't refuse it.
Didn't seek it.
Didn't choose it.
I must suffer
If I lose it.
Give account if
Just a tiny, little minute;
But, eternity is in it.

—Florence M. Musgrave

Only You Have Gone

When you are gone
Half of me is also gone
I feel incomplete
Lost within another time
It's a strange feeling
When you are gone
You are always on my mind
When the day turns into night
When I turn around and think of you
As for being with me last night
I feel so incomplete
As in lost in another time
As if half of me is gone
But only you have gone.

—*Donna L. Russell*

Thoughts and Time

I would like to share
A thought or two
To say what is on my mind,
It is really very simple
But I never seem to have the time
That it would take
To do so.
So let me put it
Simply-
I have tried
And what I find is-
Trying to say I love you
Is like trying to catch the wind.

—*Carol D. Stearns*

Lost

Seeing you for the last time,
As you hug me and say goodbye
I start crying
As I feel like part of me is dying,
You drive off leaving me alone,
We know we will never foget,
The happy times we shared,
We will never forget each other,
We feel like we are in the dark,
Lost,
Shut out from the others,
The light is only each other
Miles apart
We both feel lost.

—*April D. Kelly*

Memorizing Years

Upon my pillow fall cool tears
Of these memorizing years.
Thoughts of you and that we're through,
What am I supposed to do?
Every time I thought of you
My heart began to melt.
I wonder if you really cared,
I wonder how you felt.
I thought that we were meant to be,
Those special words you said tome.
At first you were my Mr. Right
Until we had that first fight.
There was once a start,
But now it's the end,
But just remember
We're still friends.

—*Jenifer Fenimore*

Keith

He lives beyond his grave,
In my mind is where he stays.
With his long blonde hair,
Blue eyes
And his strong but secret grin.

Keith was my knight in shining armour.
My perfect guy, my Mr. Right
He could make all problems disappear.

But secretly they were killing him.
They are the ones who drove him over the edge.
Not me!
It was them with their drugs and booze.

And then there was the phone call,
Accusing me.
But secretly I believe they were accusing
Themselves.

—*Jenna Aiken*

Sonnet

'Tis gentle as the breeze along the sea,
Which softly breatheth life into its path.
The weak it doth restore so tenderly;
It ne'er instilleth fear, nor showeth wrath.
It giveth shelter 'midst the frightful storms,
And showeth kindness to the ones outcast
By those who look disdainfully; performs
Its duties quietly; forgives the past.
'Tis as unchanging as the evergreen;
It moveth not; it hath no seasons' turn.
Its constancy is ever true; 'tis e'en
More faithful and consistent in concern.
 Its price, its worth, the rest are far above;
 Eternal beauty hath it—this is Love.

—*Deborah A. Keene*

Love

Love is something to be cherished forever more.
Love cannot be stored or put on a shelf.
Love is something you must find out for yourself.
Love cannot be fixed or arranged.
Love is something that could use a change,
A change from all the heartache and pain,
The pain that could cripple one's life
And put their emotions in use of a cane.
Yet, love is something everyone wants to experience!

—*Jennifer Carrulba*

Sharon

Thank you for the memories
That bridge the present and the past.
For good times to call upon when life goes too fast.

Remembrances of times long ago gone
Bring a sweet sad smile to my heart.
With the swiftness of a magic wand,
I escape to where the present has no part.

A place of happiness, dreams and desires,
In a time of wonder and doubt.
Though years and miles have tried to divide us,
We have weathered them out.

Secrets of the soul have passed between us,
Bonding us forever.
Always there to call upon, never forgotten, never.

We have our own families now
And wish them happiness without end.
To this I add that in their lives,
They find someone like you, my friend.

—*Dianne Gill*

All My Days

After these many months,
You still overwhelm me with your ways.
My heartbeat still quickens
At the thought of seeing you.
I still melt when you hold me so tight.
Any you carry me yet farther,
Each time we love as one.
Your kisses are still so soft,
Your touches so tender,
And our passion still makes me surrender.
My love for you I find
Grows ever stronger each day.
I've opened my life to you,
And as the months pass,
I want all my days shared with you.
And I can truly say.
I will love you forever.

—*Debi Buettnerr*

To Christine

Even though I have thoughts of confusion,
I still know I have you.
Even though life looks at its dimmest,
I still know I love you.
My words are harsh.
My language is rough
But what I feel for you is smooth and polished.
I try so hard, but there is nothing I can do
Except love you!

— *Dennis Favor*

After

So I stand here
With tears pricking my eyes, silently
Watching you drive away

From the place
Where I said goodbye, fearfully
Deaf to any words of parting

Coming from your lips
That I so wanted to touch, longingly
Hoping you understand

The reason act this way
is because I love you so much, actually
I always have.

—*Elizabeth Reed*

My Everlasting Love

Waiting...she stands longing for a heart
To embrace her fears away
Holding on to yesterday
She must not face again.
Crying...away in the lonely night
Trembling her life away
No one to soothe her bitter tears
But my light searches on
Knowing...my light will reach her
Warming her heart inside
Wrapping itself around her tightly
Holding her soul in mine.
Hoping...the cry will scream out,
    the pain and anguish disappear
And the life she has known, forever
Will fade violently into the darkness,
    surrounding her with love,
My everlasting love.

—*Dayna Sammons*

War

A young soldier
Slid like a snake
Across the gentle grasses
To the jungle's wake.
Thinking of his parents
His lover, now his wife,
Of his child, the one he'd never seen.
A baby face covered with fear,
But a mind draped with stars and stripes forever.
Oh America,
Why did you lie to him when he loved you so?
Why didn't you tell him that as the
Bullets ripped through his apple pie brain,
He would cry for his Mom,
Not for you...
    —*Patricia A. Rarey*

You and I

You and I together in the moonlight,
Loving each other and holding on tight.
Treasuring the things we share,
Letting each other know we care.
The love we have is too good to be true.
I guess that's why the end makes me so blue.
Forever together as we used to say,
Maybe things weren't meant to be that way.
I'll still care down deep in my heart,
You'll always be remembered in that special part.
But for now remember the love we had,
Follow your dreams and try not to be sad.
    — *Beth Joelle Watts*

Do You Fear

Blue, revolving shadows in misty air
On a rain slicked roadway or
A prevalent scene on a dark city street?
Shattered glass sparkling like fine crystal
On a white background or
Blades of knives severing an existence?
Red liquid streaming from a lifeless form
Staining black asphalt or
Yellow liquid from a can staining a future?
Ambulance doors slam shut and ride
Into the ominous night or
Doors locked permanently under dark ground?
Good spirits and happy faces
In a dizzy unreal existence or
Memories and hidden fear of the darkness of death?
    — *Donna Nichols*

My Childhood Memories

Everytime it rains,
I sit by my window with pains.
I look out of the window,
And my eyes are filled with sorrow.
Outside I see children playing,
With eyes that are shining.
They laugh with joy and gay,
And for them everyday is a beautiful day.
They are always together,
And they think this will last forever.
For their love is undying,
And one for all, and all for one, they are always saying.
Then the kids disappeared,
And through the glass window, I appeared.
I said, *One for all and all for one.*
But no one answered because I was the only one.
    — *Abigail Abad*

Memories

Memories to me
are like a sack
full of bright
cherry red apples
and then they turn
brown and rotten.
Once, something
that tasted so
sweet and juicy
and then you get
a mouthful of
something that
tasted so awful
you never want
to bite into
anything that
terrible again.
    —*Jacinda Poole*

Mountains

Mountains are beautiful
Although violent sometimes,
But that's the only way
To express their feelings.
So when one explodes-
Leave it alone
And when one is silent-
Have fun
And don't make one angry.
    — *Holly Scofield*

Creation

A dying ember
Blown to life
By a puff of air.

Kindled, slowly burning,
Flames dance-
Here then there.

Leap forth,
Extend,
Leap forth.

Recoil to spark,
Die out,
Again.

A dying ember
Blown to life
By a puff of air.
    — *J. J. (Joseph J. Sherman)*

Vision in White

First one flake,
Then another,
And another,
Until they're piled up
All around.
Crisp, sparkling brilliance
Coats the surface of the earth
To glorify its every corner.
It glistens in the sun
Day after day.
Dirt and sand coat its surface
And turn it a dingy brown.
The days get warmer.
The snow melts,
Slowly, until a lump of brown ice
Is all that is left of the spectacular
Vision in white.
    —*Emily Soden*

Just a Position, My Friend

Enigmatic and energetic
Automatic and synergetic
Genetic and pathetic
Wondering down synthesis lane
Why do we have to do this again?
Comes the refrain insinuendo, my friend.
    —*Anne Mulcahy Dower*

I Remember Father's Day

I can remember father's day of long ago
When the family treated dad to a show.
I can't remember what it was about
But dad enjoyed it without a doubt.
I remember, the first card I made him
He kept and treated it like a gem.
When I got my first job, I took him out to eat.
He had a plate of potatoes and meat.
I remember the last we had together,
He was sick and dying in bed
We acted happy and didn't show our dread.
The father's day we have now
Are totally different, somehow.
On his grave I place his favorite flower, a red rose
My love for him it always shows.
    — *J. Wesley Hutto*

Colors

When I look at the world around me
It greets me with a wintery look—gray
We should take care of what we love
Someone once told me
I'm inspired by the color of the day
Although some find it uninspiring
I'll look for another color
If there is another color to be found
For most of what we see as brothers
Is decaying, dead or dying
Can we all look beyond this gloom
And see a new world through another spectrum
Of course we can, spring will be here soon
It will greet us with that other color—green
The color of health and life
Our true color.
    —*W. H. Gillespie*

America! In Spite of Us?

A land that's of cycles and seasons;
A land that's of changes and visions:
        Our hope and our faith and our love are
                the seeds that we plant in its richness.

The songs from the trees' rustling branches;
The hum from the meadows' lush grasses;
The voices of peepers rejoicing:
        A heavenly song for the earthly.

The autumn's cascade of its colors;
The glistening blanket from snowing;
The wind and the rain of renewal
        The land that's of cycles and seasons:
                With cities as tombs for the living;
With cities as shrouds for the hurting:
                Successful just scurrying through them,
                ignoring the plight of the dying.

    —*F. Esther Barnard*

There He Was

There he was standing alone.
No one else, just him and the phone.
It was cold outside and I needed to call,
Just five minutes, that was all.
After my call, I stepped aside.
I waited by the curve for my friendly ride.
It was getting darker and I couldn't see,
So he took off his jacket and put it around me.
Before I thanked him, he got on the bus.
After he left, I threw a little fuss.
Another bus came and I took a seat,
Trying to beat the cold and staying with the heat.
I sat in a seat and a voice said, *Sweet love,*
So I turned around and there he was!

    — *Carol Asbury*

I Ponder

I ponder...dream away the whole night through,
And when I am alone I think of you.
As I wonder what it would be like
Just to get a kiss from you some night
Open your eyes and heart and you shall see
The very sensitive side of me.
When you look inside these blue eyes of mine,
You will see the love for you divine.
Then you look inside deeper and you shall see
My lustful mind meant just for you and me.
Whenever you get bored, depressed, or down,
Just give me a call; I will be around.
'Cause love's an emotion shared between two,
And right now love's meant for both me and you.

    —*Edward D. Wiget*

A Friendship Lost

Our friendship is somehow forgotten.
Softly and unsoundly we separated,
Without a thought.
The friendship must be quite gone,
So far and so lost.
Two years of fun and laughter,
It seems like a lifetime.
But now all you hear is a lonely silence
And forever goodbyes.
In the beginning it was so great,
But as you know things don't last.
With tears in my eyes
Our friendship seems to be forgotten,
Far in the past.

    —*Alexsandra Popovic*

The Fiddler Calls

Why are you speaking of court dates now set?
We all are concerned, because we have not heard yet!
My heart feels so burdened at all these events.
I fear for your safety and soul.
For certain things, a Mom cannot prevent,
And you always have been so bold.

Yes, I will try to be patient
And wait for the times to appear,
I will try to keep busy, and use the faith in my mind,
And I will ask my Lord to stay near.

I am asking you now in deep concern?
Are all these court dates your keeping,
The results from your past, a garden of crime,
That somehow you are just now reaping?

And if indeed a lesson be learned,
Will you admit you were wrong?
And deserved what you earned?

    —*Elveda O. Pritchett*

Life, We Cannot Explain

Life is a burning fire, which we often cross.
It is a river of strategy,
Which we sometimes cannot fiture out
Life has meaning, yet the hungry prey on us
It can be bitter and mock you, at the same time.
Life continuously dedicates it is time,
To forgive us of our wrong doings,
And praise us for the right.
Its conclusions to problems, is sometimes soothing,
But no mercy will be given to our problems,
Which we make up.
Life is a whole eternal sky,
Which gives the power to think of different rhymes.
It is always going to have a reason,
For which we cannot explain,
And we learn by life's experiences,
That no ones life is the same...

    —*Ashlyn Bridger*

Our True Love

Our true love is a candle within
Bringing the warmth of security
And the light of eternity
Feelings one cannot mar
Knowing who we are
As into each others eyes we are always looking
Seeing we've discovered someone to trust with our truth
Believing to no one but us should our love be proved.
Our true love is a flower undying
Showing the beauty of caring
And the tenderness of sharing
Feeling we are one when even we are apart
Knowing the other will not go away very far
As into each others arms we are always reaching
Touching softly as an expression of our inner emotions
Becoming closer with our true love motions.

    —*Elizabeth A. Warren*

M.I.A.

There are webs beneath the house
That I should clear.
The grass never stops growing,
And the screens must come down.

They told me it would be only a matter of time
Before they learned the truth.
But the lace darkens and the flowers wilt,
And Mama put the paper bells away in the attic.

    —*Alice E. Hendrix*

Yearning Unity

Two small flames gleaming in the night,
One is amidst and the other out of sight.
The heat from their peaks touch in the air above,
And in a second's flash the two lights are in love.

The warmth in their hearts is all they know of now
And long to find a way to join as one . . . but how?
The keen sky aloft is aware of the flames' deep love
And calls for a breath of wind to act as a sheer, gentle glove.

The tender breeze glides down to the desperate flame in the night
And scoops it up carefully not to disturb its light.
The sparkle is translucent through the delicate breeze's hand
And is seen with great delight from the iridescent sand.

Shining on the sand is a soft, shimmering light,
And the patient breeze descends to unite the flames' hearts tight.
The two flames solidify and burn as one in the night,
And rejoicing in their quest, thank the breeze in flight.

—*Lauren-Michele Torro*

Above the Sun

Will you walk first and leave me to walk alone?
I need to see you, Lord, so now I'm coming home.
The hurt inside me as I hear my loved ones cry
Give me the strength, oh Lord, to tell them good-bye.
Tell them I'll be waiting when their time comes,
And we shall be together again in Your Kingdom above the sun.

— *ToniJoy Robin*

Memories

As I watch the waves crash endlessly against the rocks
I think of our relationship and what became of it.
I can no longer hear your laughter that made me laugh
Or see your smile that made me smile.
All I can remember is the hurt and anger
I felt when you left me,
And all the promises you made but never kept.
You left me without any answer why
And didn't come back with an explanation.
Forever I'll wonder what made you leave,
And forever my question will go unheard and unanswered.
Maybe with time I may be able to forgive you,
But now the pain is it too clear in my mind.
We might be friends again and laugh like we used to
And smile like we did before.
But now I can't face you
So I'll look at the waves and try to mend my broken heart.

—*Corrie Meddaugh*

On the Anniversary of A Young Bride's Passing

It was easier with the miles laid out before us
There was a comfort in such distance and I always drove too fast...slow
    down! She would yell and laugh,
Leaning carelessly through the open window
Bathed in the autumn air and dusk's cantering glow.

This was New England, at the onset of fall, endued in the usual garb
October's soft and sudden fanfare and a still acceptance in the air
Of what, smiling, she would call a long and welcome sleep.

In twenty years she touched more hearts than you or I will ever know
And if reaching out, were held in the palm of a soothing hand,
That did not beg tomorrows or try with tears, to buy them.

I remember all of this with painful clarity, five years later,
It is all that so steadily remains...curious
Like being in Nantucket again waiting for winter along the coast
Alone, with a weary bottle.

In a small roadside church, I lit a birch candle to her memory
And in my dreams saw it drift out over the pines and hover in the twilight
A lone beacon signaling in a dark and silent harbor.

—*Timothy McKenna*

...a part of...

Alive and a part of life, alone and a part of love,
Able to laugh, able to cry, but unable to change the skies above,
So sorry for what has been done, so happy for what is to be,
A sunny day, a starry night, if only I could see,

Alive and a part of you, aware and a part of all that surrounds me,
Able to think, able to dream, but unable to set myself free,
A time to look to tomorrow, a time to relive the past,
Now, as life goes on, so must love, help me make it last.

— *Steven Alan Wolfson*

One Summer Night

Lying here alone with you all seems so very right;
Reminds me of the time we kissed,
That special summer night.
Your eyes are always sparkling;
Like green stars up in the sky,
Your gentle touch is warm
And makes my heart sail oh so high!
I have been wanting to tell you I love you,
But the words seemed to get in the way.
You have made my life so much better, in every possible way.
Promise me you will never leave;
You are my dream come true.
We have fallen in love after all this time;
Now we are together, just me and you.
I never want this night to end;
It's all so very right,
I love you and I want you to know
That I need you in my life!

—*Angie Dunn*

Colors

When I open up my bedroom curtains I'll tell you what I see:
Pink, yellow and purple flowers surrounding a large green tree.
These colors add variety and life to our days
And fascinate us so much in so many different ways.
People also come in different colors to add variety to our world.
Unfortunately, some are treated differently from others, which is absurd.
Every race has their own knowledge, talents and ideas.
If we could combine them all together, our intelligence would whiz.
Maybe if people could open their eyes and communicate with one another
There would be no hate or war and everyone would love each other.
We should stand together like the beautiful flowers
and make the world a united place.
Why should we pay so much attention to such a little thing like race?

— *Stephanie Dougherty*

Crying

The product of an anguished heart or
    the disappointment of a wanting child,
Fruits of an inner darkness consoled only by a tear letting.
Feelings emulating the interior of grief gone awry
Or the joy of renewed greetings of one been apart.

The victory of celebration, the agony of defeat,
Perhaps loneliness or the thought of its aftermath,
Count the numerous moments of joy and you'll find crying its equal,
A salty wetness of evaporating paths on expressful faces.

Fathers, mothers who've lost their child or others who've gained one,
The observance of others who suffer something,
A cut in the hand or a slapped face,
The first prize one, second a distant mile,
Beauty erased with only uglinesses herald...

Or God sitting on His throne seeing once,
Once a familiar world.

—*Kevin J. Kimmel*

Veins Flow in Currents of Full Fright

I hurtle into full night,
the gaunt, lonely silence
of the swamp.
Thousands of dead trees
stick white ghosts into my eyes.

There, at the end of the valley
burning borders of thunder clouds,
unreal, except the howls of coyotes
leaping in my ears.

I drink the hemlock on the mountain
where the wind is wide in its sweep.
Veins flow in currents
of full fright-
burrs and thorns know the blood drops
of my feet.

Echo—echo reechoes of morning bells-
rising into the clouds-
May dreams—and I walk throug lilacs.
—*Emma Crobaugh*

Stories of the Indian Nations

Let me tell you of the old days
When the Indian owned the land
Never doubting his dominions
Nor the loyalty of his clan;
Proud the wrinkled high boned faces,
Proud the elders with their wisdom,
Sharing tales of days gone by,
As they gathered in the wigwam,
As the other tribal leaders
Made their plans and smoked their peace pipes,
Told their tales of shadow people,
Of the days when there was strife,
Of the days when there was no warring,
When their hopes for peace went soaring,
High among the Indian nations,
High among the tribal brothers, in the old days,
Tales of old ways, told by chiefs, written by others.
—*Virginia Lemperle*

God's Messenger of Wings

On the wings of an angel God sends from above,
Brings joy, hope and eternal love.
For peace of mind and serenity,
On the wings of a dove He sends to me.
On the wings of an eagle so proud and free,
A message from God says I too can be...
Free as a bird is His message to me,
And He is sayingI too am free!
On the wings of Lucifer a warning from on high,
That wings of fire can never fly!
God clipped Satan's wings as he fell from the sky
When God threw him from Heaven on high.
It's the angel wings that win the victory
Against the demons of Hell from beneath the sea.
God's messenger of wings so graceful in flight
As they soar away upward with all their might.
On the wings of an angel God sends from above,
Brings joy, hope and eternal love.
For peace of mind and serenity,
On the wings of a dove He sends to me.
—*Evelyn Sapp Salter*

Untitled

Tree over water
Grasping for its reflection
In endless depths.
— *Amalia Kessler*

Silver Cord

I am sitting in the backyard,
Staring at leaves.
My oldest daughter
Has just left for college.
I caressed her plump hand
With its gaudy red nails.

Her blond hair
Fell rich on her shoulders.
On high heels, in satin black,
She will make her entrance
Into anthropology.
I miss her already,

Though I have longed
For this day all summer.
I have two more daughters,
And a wounded eagle.
All must learn to fly, away.
—*Helen Lawson*

Inside Out!

A wolf in sheep's clothing,
 Is none the less by name.
Tho we change the cover,
 Inside we stay the same.

If we were inside out,
 Then we could not hide.
Feelings and emotions
 And things we keep inside!

The *homeliest* in the world,
 Or the *fairest* of them all!
We would look the same,
 Except the *short* and *tall!*

Honesty with each other,
 Is what it's all about!
So if we must *pretend,*
 Pretend we're *inside out!*
—*Arnold S. Becker*

Time

Start a circle
        from beginning
                  to now
on to future
        joined to circle
                  the past.
Time   circle
infinite   God
—*Betty V. Bruder*

In Memoriam

I am filled with anguish I just cannot show,
And sorrow I just cannot tell,
I want to open it to you, and you alone:
I wish you were here with me, and hear once more,
How you mean to me still, even now...

After these days of distance and dispair,
I cannot stop loving you; I cannot start forgetting
Neither do I want to do it,
For you, your memories, deepened inside my heart,
Influencing my thoughts, tormenting my soul,
At times, ruining it!

Ah! That is what I am at this moment
A prisoner of love, a slave of memory,
I will go on living this way, enslaved by it...

And, if it is a fool's way to live by memory,
Then, let me be,
I have reason to be so,
For I have so much to remember...
—*Francis M. Banaynal*

Reflections

The lights fall over the river,
The river moves with a rhythm of its own,
Tomorrow brings dreams, clouded mist,
I remember your soft touch, your smile and caress.
The river calls your name,
How I wish... but wishes aren't real,
The water ripples and shimmers,
I remember your glow...
The river calls your name, calls and calls...
With the shadows of twilight
Hung across my brow,
I didn't have the words then
To say I love you;
I have them now, but
Now is not the time,
There is only the river and
The sound of angry falling rain
Into my cup on the edge of the shore,
There is only the river calling
And time... time.
—*Frank J. Hopkins*

Flight into History

The red rimmed mesa, far below,
    like rubies on the nation's breast,
The sparkling lakes on the mountain tops
    and snow capped peaks that mark the crest,
The winding rivers form the beads
    with silver pendants where they roar
The deep dark canyons seem like scars
    of those who fought our nation's wars.
Like wagon tracks our pioneers
    made the endless highways east to west
The towns that dot our course below
    once way-stops in our father's quest.
Majestic mountains cross our pathway,
    deep crevices form an arduous trail
Do I see wagons struggling down there?
    No, it's just the ghosts of those who failed.
The mountains gone, the sea before us,
    I've known such great sensations,
For in just short hours,
    I have flown through the history of our nation.
— *Harvey LaGasse*

Reminiscence of Youth

Good times, spent with my friends;
Times I will never live again.
Skipping school and playing cards;
Poker, spades, rook and hearts.
Smoking cigs and chewing skoal;
Flooding the truck in the old mud hole.

Dodging the cops, and cat and mouse;
Then getting drunk at my old house.
Throwing a buddy through the hedge;
While another whizzes off the front porch ledge.
Playing chase, in the cemetary;
And the cold stone statue, we thought was scary.

Crusin' in the winter with the windows down;
Or cutting 180s in the middle of town.
Stealing gas from a neighbor's farm;
And the small time things that did no harm.
These are the times spent with my friends,
Times I remember; now and then.

—*Chris Goeller*

Tonight I Cannot Sleep

Mother...tonight I cannot sleep.
Their chains have kept me up
Why aren't all men free?
Mother...I cannot see the sun.
Their hands are much too black
How long have their fists been raised?
Mother...I cannot lift my arms.
Their cell walls are much too heavy.
How long does oppheression last?
Mother...I cannot speak my mind,
Their tongues have been cut
How many voices have been lost?
Mother...I cannot breathe.
There are hands around my neck
They look like yours,
Mother...I cannot hear your voice.
Their screams are much too loud

How far away is South Africa
—*Lilah Friedland*

Il Vient De France

A schoolboyish look is what I want:
Tall, slim, handsome, petite but masculine.
A poet or a writer, preferably un peintre—
Perfectly French.

Scene—Une maison a Paris
Il est Francais.
En vacances—l'Angleterre, l'Irlande,
l'Espagne, la Hongrie, la Grece,...

The book on the page of which I write
Le Francais.
My mood denotes a doubt, an uncertainty.
Voudriez-vous fermer la porte, cher?

— *Kavita Subramani*

Lost

Her face was drawn, her eyes were dim
Her steps were slow and growing tired
Of living, of trying and carrying on
She had lost her pride and life's desire
This little old lady grown old and helpless
No one knew she was once so strong and bold
With no fear of life's fragile hold
Until she lost her family and her pride
In a wave of futility she could not override.

—*Louise McPhail*

The Conquered Goal

From goal to goal,
Challenge to challenge,
Or whatever came your way.

You have given all,
You had to give,
Just for a little fame.

Now you can stop,
To look and see,
Like looking through a glass.

This latest goal,
You have received,
You have conquered now at last.

Through struggled fields
And rugged hills,
You have managed to have past.

You did your all,
Stood so long.
You have won at last.

—*Cindy Sibert*

Patient Tears

Losing you for the second time,
I feel like a child for crying.
The tears don't help,
For they are always patient.

Why are hearts so easily broken,
And spirits torn away
From the happiness they knew
For a few sunny days?

It's a hurt, no one can stand,
The feeling of being torn apart.
One doesn't know
When he falls in love,
But they do know
That when he cries
He cries of a broken heart,
From losing you
For not having patient tears.

—*Jennifer Renner*

Attract

To gaze into your eyes
Is beauty magnetized.
Gentle is a smile
With so much power.
As if Venus was your body,
It can touch my soul.
Setting off a spark into love
And stripping me naked.
Woman, feel our hearts
Burn higher.

— *Kenneth Dewayne Bolden*

The Dusty Steps

The dusty steps to heaven,
So little used by anyone—
I sweep them clean as I go,
Go on to what seems-
A dusty attic to most,
The pain and agony-
Of the passage shunned,
By most;
There are no fellow travelers,
Here-
I am alone.

— *Joseph J. Brankey*

Mystical Madman

Cannot believe what I read today,
A labor of love that lost its way,
A lunatic's fear for which he will sley,
An inimical heart of ice.

Children slaughtered by a bloody hand,
To make those on high meet his demand,
A way of life I do not understand,
A senseless sacrifice.

Adrenaline flows with a pain so deep,
I pray the Lord my soul to keep,
The ax put one by one to sleep,
I hear them call my name.

The *Olive Tree* it burns so bright,
And with *New Adams* it lights the night,
Grinding the Bush is nowhere in sight,
Zimbabwe will never be the same.

—*John A. Chavez*

Spinning

The world will spin
And yet we do not see
The pain that is caused
By you and me.
We do not stop and think
About how this world will end.
We only fight, and do not care
And yet the world spins and spins.
Someday we will see
When the world is gone
How the pain we caused
Still lives on and on.

—*Kimberly Godden*

Trip of Life

Walls of hard emotions
Keep me in my insanity
Escape from reality
Life is hard to hold

In my mind, behind my memory
Time and time again
I see the cold, fresh shadow of dawn
On the day I die

Fearing the time that flows quickly by
Awaiting my merciless fate
Sanity has long since gone
Hell awaits my destiny

First my world of color fades
Then my crystal shattered
And you, the fool, who sees in the mirror
Will stand in my shadow

—*Jasmin L. Mau*

Nature's Wonders

Your hair is like the glisten of
The flames of burning fire,
In your eyes I see the gentleness
Of the moon that shines much higher,
In my heart I feel the twinkle
Of the stars that make the light,
As I dream of all the happiness
In the world tonight.
I need you always like the sun
That makes the day,
The same sun that shines on the path
That leads our way.

—*Jenny Martineau*

My Mind Would Grasp

My mind would grasp the beauty of the rose,
The only answer holds: who knows-who knows;
My thoughts would dwell on might of leaf and blade,
My thoughts their potent realm cannot invade.
Oh might of sun and sea, of land and air
Placed lavishly about me everywhere
So that my gaze, my heart, my all may see
The wealth that God has strewn on Earth for me.
How can I, wretched mortal, weak in all,
Before these mysteries stand and not appall;
And marvel much that one so great as God
Grants gifts like these to me while Earth I trod!

—*Louise Pannullo-Parnofiello*

The Rose Dream

I looked out on the quiet praire.
The sun was giving out its last orange rays of light
Then something caught my eye
Amidst the plain of hushed browns.
It was a single red rose, swaying in the breeze.
Beautiful, yet lonely.
I ran to it in desperation.
Trying to grasp the rose, trying to grasp my dreams.
I ran and ran until I reached that rose.
I pulled it out of the ground.
It wilted in my hand.
And as my tears fell onto that rose,
I thought of my wilted dreams.

—*Susie Tabb*

He Is an Indian

Alone he stands against the baren land,
His deadly spear grasp in his hand.
Before him stands the wilderness vast,
When all will perish he will last.
His skin is dark, his body fit, he's full of
Bravery, courage, and wit.
He lives and survives allalone, tormenting
No one not casting a stone.
But when he hears the cry of the white amn,
He will stand bravely to protect his homeland.
He is an Indian.
But in the heat of violent battle, the
White warrior stood proud on the horse he strattled.
His aim steady, his bullet straight, he
Quickly sealed the indians fate.
His people will never forget him, for his
Spirit will never let them. For he was an indian.

—*Kevin Skelley*

Colors

Will thou come to me with open arms and heart
To soothe my tortured soul in its aloneness
If you touch your palm to my heart
You will measure the rhythm of my desire
If I frighten you with all that I am
Hold fast to the dream we have created
And fantasize the true sense of our being
Until fear ceases and you become as desirous as I
Become lost inside of me and let me guide you
Through my world of soft stolen moments
Hear the echoing silence when we touch
And gasp for air as we drown in our dreams
I will wildly love you as a beast of humanity
Gently leading you through a hazy state of fire
With colors that I have never seen before
Except through the very essence of my desire.

—*Kimberly Pennington*

The Labyrinth

Through the labyrinth of time
The confused one wonders,
Always seeking the end
To the problems he ponders.

As each dead in appears,
His hopes fail a little more.
The conflicts seem endless
With each slammed door.

The maze streches on and on
As the puzzle loses another piece.
Its tangled web is ever present
And the mirages are placed eloquettly to tease.

He who builds the labyrinth knows
That very few are able to endure
He will place the ones he has chosen carefully
To wonder aimlessly in despair and torture.

—*Loretta Anne Burkes*

River of Thought

Ever changing—rippling outward-
As by pebbles cast astream,
Broadening. Seeking deeper knowledge.
Taking time to drift and dream.
All creation is a challenge
For each item—large or small-
Was a seed of thought—maturing-
But for that—here not at all.
Each of us must be creative
Lest our minds stagnate and dull,
Lift our thoughts upward—yet onward-
Like the ever soaring gull.
It matters not—life's endeavors-
Nor what final height's attained.
Just by striving to do better,
We will prove our goal is gained.

— *Lorene Hyatt Carnevale*

Forever and Beyond

You've waited forever for a destiny so near
Caught in a landslide of yesterday's fear
Eternity approaches, then passes you by
Deceived by time, you wait hopelessly to die

But in the end, life's a conspiracy
So long, my friend, I'm destined for misery
Hours slowly pass in a timeless reality
Reaching out again, raging insanity

Picture a sunset, a breath taking sight
Keeper of boundaries, fading day into night
Yet, this treasure of nature, enlightening the sky
Is soon to die, and likewise am I

Welcome to your destiny, insanity and pain
Satan is your savior, captor of the slain
Hell in our playground, playing games of sin
Approaching final fate, evil forces win

—*Steve Sutcliffe*

A Reflection

I look in the mirror and I can actually *see* myself.
Like another person, staring at me and tlking with her eyes.
I can trace her brows, nose and lips
Using her own fingertips.
It fades away and says, *It's you,*
But only from a different view.

—*Kelly Rackley*

Straight from the Heart

Though we are destined to part, I try not to look ahead
Because of the heartache I receive.
I know there is no way to change this,
But when we part I want to let you know how much
You have really meant to me.
The love you have shown, the tears we have shared
The comfort that could only come from a friend like you,
And most important of all, just being there
When I really needed you.
I now realize you were the best friend I ever had.
Though I will miss you deeply I will always remember you
No matter how many people I meet
No one will ever replace the priceless gift
You have given to me...
Friendship

   —Dana Bronk

Thoughts of You

Thoughts of you fill my mind like waves upon the shore.
Sunny days and star filled nights remind me of you more.
I begin to think of you as the setting sun leaves a golden sky.
A tear falls down my cheek shed for you and I.

You left me here by myself without a smirk or smile
Though I still hear your voice across the distant miles.
We'll always love each other in our own special way.
Everything will work out well, hopefully someday.

   — Danica Knox

Don't Touch Me

You sit there smiling, your eyes wide and bright
Your hair slanting over your beautiful cheek
You begin to laugh, your mouth upturned
In a foolish grin, your eyes twinkle
You act as if nothing has happened
As if my heart does not lay shattered on the floor
Forgotten. Don't touch me or I shall forever drown in an
Ocean of pain. You continue talking.
We can still be friends
These words I cannot bear.

   —Kiva Sherr

Parting

With a tear on his cheek and mist in his eyes
he looked up at me
and all within that moment a quick second, we
recaptured all the good in our childhood.
In language only a sister can speak to her brother
without words or gestures, we said good-bye.
Knowing that we would be reunited with lavish emotion
of rejoice, hugs, kisses and tales of lands far away,
and the comfort that accompanies a safe homecoming
and a rekindled spirit.

   — Cora Lyons Isbell

The Base Of Gossip's Foundation

Hark, they say, *is that of my ears that I do hear?*
Or is it the malicious whispering of the wind,
That blows in one ear and out the other onto another
Echoing jealous whims of a friend to a friend?
Casting stones on my honor...their envy smothered
Embellishing itself within the salt of my tears.

So here, come a time, that I have sown
Its seeds of news to harvest on
The gossip to spread like fire on land
For the dwellers who indulge themselves to eat upon.
And judge me a fool, for a fool I am,
Because the talk I reap, is the talk of my own.

   —Cynthia M. Reed

Wishing Lamp

If I could but rub a magic lamp that made wishes come true, I wouldn't
Waste them on frivorous things. In it's stead, I would trade some for your
Everlasting love, and the bliss your love brings. I wouldn't wish to
Be a wealthy king, sitting on a gold and bejeweled throne, and, daily
Watch my loyal subjects bow at my feet, and then lie prone. No my love,
My fluttery turtle dove, that is not my style, but if it were, I'd rule
You with a deep love, which is pure and true, and springkled with
Heavenly blessing from up above. I'd rub the lamp for wishes galore,
But only to gain your undivided and eternal devotion, which I pray
Will be as high as the blue sky, and as deep as the churning ocean.
Should a royal proclamation is issued, selecting me as an emperor, I'd
Shock every third world nation, by taking you as my wife. If necessary
I'd forfeit a bundle of wishes, to have you lie beside me through the
Cold, wintery night. My warm kisses would blanket your shivering body
To prove our love is right. When I reach the bottom of my wishes, I would
Save one to order a million more, *ain't that what wishes are for?*

   —Joe Dovich

Picture Taking in Nature

In the bounds of nature where the atmosphere is vivid
brings the perfect setting for expressive pictures.
While walking and admiring the beauty of nature, I was trying to capture
the precious scenes of nature for an everlasting memory.
The elegance of nature brought stimulation to the views in which I beheld.
The shadowed mountains of the vast mass made the images seem genuine.
The fresh air that my lungs inhaled added to the sensation
of nature that portrayed appreciation.

The animals of the grove seemed to stir in an anticipated manner.
I was able to capture these distinctive actions as well as
the crisp colors of the tall, brittle trees.
Boundaries of nature reflected upon a grayish body of irrigation
that flowed in a peaceful manner.
I could not help but notice the extreme rough textured bank
in which many levels of rigid rock presented many shades.
As the brisk summer days came and went, it left burnt, golden, frail grass
that would snap with the least bit of pressure, but the availability
of a momento was lessened by the dark colors of the powerful sun
as it set slowly behind the distant mountains.

   —Kimberly Rudd

Days Gone By

Yesterday gone by forever, never to be seen again.
Oh, how we would change things if what we know now we knew then,
There's many regret in days gone by that left many a teary eye
A broken heart we wish we could mend from that harsh word,
Why did I say that to my best friend?
We all have our times we wish we could forget.
Now and forever we continue to regret, if they can only forget
Forgive us for my careless, thoughtless, wasted days gone by.
If only what we know now we knew then.
Life now we hold so dear, feelings are more sincere.
Before lashing out you now stop and think, with love and a wink.
If you are young as we were then, instead of a enemy be a friend.
Don't lash out, stop and think or something will happen quick as a wink.
I guarantee the day will come when you will say,
If I only knew then what I know today.

   — Janice M. Owens

Appreciate

Live life to its fullest because no one can foresee
When it might be our calling; we can't predict our destiny.
Take time to smell the sweet fragrance of spring flowers in the air.
Appreciate the beauty of nature, learn to really care.
Realize the glory of a sunset at night in the sky,
The glistening of fresh fallen snow, a tiny firefly.
Learn not to take things for granted, tell the ones you love how you feel.
Life is not a dress rehearsal, my friend; this finale act is real!

   — Lana Mooney

The Human Quest

The first explorers sailed in sight of shore,
Hugging old coastal landmarks with their eyes,
Content to stay in earshot of the roar
Surfbreakers make beneath the sea gull cries.

Who, first, dared steer his craft to open seas,
Charting new course by stars, cloud veiled in skies,
That nameless mariner, the world agrees,
Nerves all whose deeds, old boundaries defy.

So did King Philip's son march off known maps.
His conquests titled Alexander great;
While timid souls stayed home, appeased by naps,
One leader's gait made borders out of date.

Our age, today, awaits those daring traits,
Which stir the human spirit in its quest
To move past limits, which intimidate
And free the world from landmarks which oppress.

—*William F. Keucher*

Elvira

Elvria there is no game,
People want to know the name.
Is she as fickle as a maiden fare?
Or, does she hide in a corner's bare?

What? Is a question to ponder
Eyes dance wanting to wander
Over the mountain vale, questing a man's sail;
Never is a word too pale, in the light of Elvira's veil.

Click of a heel with a quick
Dances the lilt of a pick.
To you Elvira, open her arms,
Embraces you her charms.

Never could you resist
The faint body mist;
Elvira you can insist.

—*Elvira M. Leon*

For Thomas

How much I loved you,
I guess I still do.
The love that we shared,
Always seemed true.
Our time may be past, but I'll always cherish.
All of the memories, our words could not perish.
As I stand alone now, I remember our dreams.
It all seemed so real, but nothing is as it seems.
Maybe love is an illusion, but if that were so,
Why do I remember? Why can't I let go?
I see you're not mine now, but I still remember
All of the good times that we've shared together.
I will never forget you, you will remain in my heart,
Together forever until death do us part!

—*Dawn Burns*

Come Be My Love

You smiled,
And your warmth rolled over me
Like so many waves upon the sand
For so long I have waited for you,
Not knowing when or from where you would come,
Only that you would come.
Now you are here
And our moments together are but precious few.
Come, lie beside me, let me look fully into your face
And be my love.

— *Bruce Quiggle Jr.*

The Expansing Universe

It is a vast widespread vacuum
Holding strings of nothingness
All the eerie pieces,
Of this enigma fit together.
This enamoring area
Captures the best of life and splendor
There is much to be explored
In this vacant lot.
Is this place never ending?
Like a country road winding
Around royal heaps of earth
That lead into the heavens
When you look at this mystifying territory,
You feel like you could ride up
The moonbeams of light, this tract of radiance
Should be cherished by all humanity.

—*Jennifer L. Drust*

INSANITY

THOUGHTS LIKE SPAGHETTI
TANGLED AND TORN
ADDLED OF WITS
GIVEN TO MANIA
LOSING ALL REASON
FEELING ENNUI
YOU'RE SUCH A CRACK POT
Don't say that! In my mind there's
NO SUCH THING AS INSANITY

—*Catherine Maloney*

Sentries

And then there are
Identical twin old men
Taking turns at being alive.
Like sentries at their post
Between the two, taking turns
As sleep mocks death
Waking moments sometime forced
By attendants. Rude awakenings for an
Efficient nurse.
Damn!
Allow their dreams
Of racing the sexy lady...
Pausing for enlightment from a signpost.
More geese and a general's madness.
Listening to the stars on a moonless night.
Prosecuting bureaucrats for crimes against disorder.
Shouting love of life, escaping from hell.
Until each has entered the door of no return.

—*William A. Van Vacter*

The Savage of Tranquility

As frosty dew drips down the flowers' stems
And restless birds scatter from tree to tree
I watch and wonder what in me condemns
The beauty that the others see in me.
The flowers in the spring so brightly are alive
The birds, no doubt, are eager for the day
But could it be for happiness they strive
Unknown, beneath their colorful array?
If so, how puzzling it all seems to me
That in their peaceful world they're not content
And in another life they wish to be
Not I, if I were they, I'd not repent.
For it is in their world I long to be
Love I, the savage of tranquility.

—*Jennifer Tokatyan*

Not Common Sense

Hated by your friends
Loved by your enemies
Forgotten by your family
Close to your brother
Careful of your thoughts
Thoughtful of everyone
Perfect in every way
Cheerful and never depressed
Close to strangers
To pull instead of shove
To hate instead of love
To frown instead of smile
To stand tall instead of to fall

—*Jennifer Zimmer*

Gone

The wind is gone.
The rain is gone.
The grass is gone.
The flowers are gone.
We could not be friends.
We had to be enemies.
The children tried to stop it.
The President could have stopped it.
But no, he had to be a phoney.
So it happened.
And it is all gone.
The people are gone, too.
How will the world rebuild itself,
When we are all gone?

—*Jennifer Vaughn*

Foreign parts

May I help you sir?
Yes, I am looking for a calculator
Made in the United States.
Okay, here you are.
But this says, Japan.
Yes. It was only assembled in Japan.
The parts, they are Japense
But it was supervised by Americans
For and American company.
But what about this American labor?
It is American, sir, it is just that
The people of Japan made it. Sir,
Do you want...
Turning to the other clerk
I guess he did not want it.

—*Fred McCray*

Let the Ripples Flow

The southwest winds begin to stir
And the sky is dark with gloom
Lightening flashes and thunder roars
It is raining now, outside my room.

I watch the sky as it lightens up
The flowers and trees sparkle in the glow
The grass looks greener and soon
I know the ripples will begin to flow.

Suddenly the sun peeps through
The damp leaves really sparkle
A rainbow breaks through the shadows
And nature's life is once again remarkable.

The rain drips off the trees
Gently tickling the small plants below
And they in turn
Let little ripples flow.

—*Quinn E. Dahlstrom*

Our Country's Symbol

As the bald eagle represents our land,
With courage and strength he takes his stand.
Soaring and protecting far above,
Capable always of eternal love.
Always prepared and ready to fight,
Leading upward in endless flight.
He displays his form with great pride,
With honor and valor in his stride.
His strength and stamina that he displays
Guiding and leading all the way.
As our eagle soars way up high,
With freedom limitless as the sky.
The beauty and gracefulness should be for always,
Though his species now endangered by man and his ways.
Territorial by nature and sharp vision he has,
His preservation is essential or our symbol will pass.

— *Susan Escoffier*

Untitled

I had to keep going although you were gone.
You were all that I had, but I couldn't hold on
And even though you were no longer with me,
I'd pretend that you were and wish that you could be.
I would write your name down again and again
And wish life could be as it had been.
I made you my life, I became obsessed,
Yet I missed so much, more than I'd guessed.
I still have the memories that I'll never forget,
But living in the past I'll always regret.
So I've decided to live every day
And I'll keep the past tucked away.

— *Kris Tina Werfelman*

Knocking at the Door

There came a knocking at my door.
Not knowing who, I carefully opened the door.
To see open arms reaching out to me.
Then a voice saying, *Come my child, follow me.*
It was the voice of our dear Lord.

He said, *Come and you shall find
Peace, love and guiding hands.*
The place for finding your true place,
He only asks that we truly believe
In Him and all things are possible.

So with the first step towards the Lord
Those that follow will be of no labor,
He takes each of us in His shielding arms
To protect us from all evil.
He only asks that we trust and believe in Him.

— *Sue E. Cardinal*

Wings of Change

Under the watchful eye of God
She is born;
Remnants, scattered across the deepening sky,
Touch of the madness and the ectasy which is Man;
Golden rays elicit tattered dreams of hope
For a dying future;
Promises, born on the wings of change,
Soar ever higher towards the heavens;
Hope springs eternal death,
To which man can only sit and ponder.

— *Tim Ouellette*

Reflections

I looked into a mirror; it stares back at me.
Two reflections are what I see.
We laughed and played upon green grass so tall.
Two shadows dance upon a wall.
Oblivious to time our lives were so sweet.
You shall hide and I shall seek.
I reached to grab but down you fall.
Now one shadow dances upon a wall.
No strength to live, no life to gain.
I watched you die, I felt your pain.
I looked and I sought almost everywhere.
Why did you leave me standing there?
I look up to a somber sky.
Through my ears I hear you cry.
I look into a mirror; it stares back at me.
Now one relfection is all I see.

— *Susan Bonny Blocker*

The Girl in the Cell

Eighteen and you look ancient
As you sit in the cell,
Nose running, crashing down
From your heroin addiction.

I light a cigarette for you, as dinner sits cold
Beside your blanket wrapped body.
I feel guilty as you bless me for the match,
Angry that you could let this happen.

Five years on your medicine
And none since yesterday.
Every fiber in your body much ache,
As a constant reminder.
Learn from the pain.

Arrested for burglary,
You will be going nowhere soon.

— *Susan A. Clark*

Bonded Together

My love for you will never disappear
Our words of love are for all to hear
Standing beside you I will never part
For we are combined heart to heart

As you stand in the midst of night
I will be there as your guiding light
Never being too near, yet far
Remember I am with you wherever you are

Listen closely to your heart
While I am away
And you shall hear only happiness
Coming our way

Explain to our child, where I am at
Tell the baby, Daddy will hurry back
Whenever you feel you have to cry
Look at our baby and that is where I lie
Take care of yourself and the baby
For I love you always, my dearest Lady

— *Leonard J. Morris Jr.*

Untitled

please don't rush me
be patient,i need time
my life is just beginning
to come together—
i've done a lonely pennance
for so long; trust, love,
they don't come easy,
i'm just finding my
rainbow—
please don't make demands-
i'm just starting to
love you

— *Toni Pieskas*

If You Listen

Four walls of concrete
Block of steel can't keep
In how I really feel.
If you listen you might
Hear my heart aching
For someone dear.
If you listen you
Might hear the thoughts
Of my wanting you
Always near.
If you listen you
Might hear the sound
Of one lonely tear.
If you listen you
Might hear me calling
Out to you

— *Tammy Zettler*

Prima Donna

Footlights.
Single cello
Rises then falls
As if fainting; ladylike.
The Prima Donna enters;
Toe and toe and toe
Her effortless image
Whispering
To those
Willing to listen.

Regardless,
Her innate dance,
Pirouette upon pirouette
Exists within each
Kaleidoscope cell.

— *L. Stefanac*

Colors

Colors are pretty
My favorite is too
Can you guess my favorite
Yes, it is blue.

There are colors everywhere
Here and there
Far and near

I like the rainbows
I like the skies
I like the few colors
People have in their eyes

Colors are pretty
My favorite is blue
I am sure your favorite
Is very pretty too.

— *Theresa Barber*

My Guy

When I look into your eyes,
It makes me so happy I can just cry.
It's hard to believe after all of this time
That you are really and truly mine.
When I wake in the morning,
My first thought's of you,
Wondering if it's really true
Or was it just a sweet dream
I dared to dream in the night
To think of that, oh such a fright.
Then the phone rings and I hear your voice.
I surely know now that I am your choice.
When I come to see you, this means the most
Because I get to hold you close.
I feel so good when you hold me tight;
Now I know I can go home and sleep all through the night
Without one fright because when I wake up, you'll be in my sight
For now, for always and all through my life.

—*Laura Biscotti*

Leaving

You're leaving now...behind you a year of friendship...
In front, a lifetime of success...between, a feeling of sorrow and loneliness.
Your friends are gone to live their lives and so must you.
Many people will miss you...many will cry...I shall be one of them.
Don't feel guilt or regret because I cry,
    feel loved and cherished because I love you.
And so have many others before me and will after me...
You are being launched into a new world
    ...it will force you to grow old quickly.
Don't let it change you...don't let it take away
    the laughter and cheer you've grown famous for.
Please remember me...I will cherish your memory forever.
I know this isn't the end but the beginning
    ...the beginning of a great adventure for you.
For me, I must start over and pick up the pieces of life
    that you dominated for so long...
It is not regret, but thankfulness for allowing me to be a part of your life...
A part of you...to you I dedicate life, love and my tears
    ...for that is all I can give.
There is no way to repay you for everything
    you've given me and done for me.
I thank you...I love you...I'll never forget you...good-bye.

— *Leesa Jerzakowski*

What Is Love?

Love is the fuel of the heart, without it, your heart can't start,
Love is something that is never old-fashion,
Love is something that is a passion,
Love is a puzzle, one very hard to fix,
Love is a cocktail, one very hard to mix.
Love is a game, one very hard to play.
Love is something you don't learn in one day
Love is a song, with that special kind of beat,
Love is warmth, it takes two to make heat,
Love is summer, Spring and all,
Love is winter, and even fall,
Love is a book, one very hard to put down,
Love is a learning thing, something that just doesn't come around,
Love is that look, so deep in someone's eyes,
Love is sunshine, and all kinds of weather,
Love is two people committed forever,
Love is something that we learnt to do,
Love is forever, Love is Me and You!

—*Keith Allen Parlier*

Sunset

The sunset is like gold shimmering in the distance.
As you watch it go down, you see the dreams of the day drift away.
Then, as the night comes along,
Different types of dreams come into view.
Will these dreams come true?
Or will they fade away?
Into the sunrise, as the night fades into daylight.

— *Lorraine V. Knight*

A Snowy Morning

The snow covers the sleeping earth for miles and miles,
And the sloping hills lie untouched as the children scramble for their sleds.
The icy wind chills the mailman as he makes his rounds
    on a deserted sidewalk,
And in the distant stillness, I hear a shovel scooping snow from a driveway.
From my window, the snow seems to go on and on; to me it goes forever.
The wind surprises me when I step outside
    and the snow cushions me as I fall backward.
I look upward and the gray, gloomy sky looms above me.
It looks as though it could explode
    and hurl the snowflakes down on us once more.
I sit down and lean back, breathing in the air.
It won't last forever; only the memory of the forever stillness
    will keep me until next winter.

—*Lori Brown*

After Words

A flash of light consumed the sky, the lucky eyes were blinded.
The children sheltered 'neath the earth were spared from the unkindness.
The unfortunate survivors staggered here and there
With burning skin, bloody scabs and falling out of hair.
The chillywoks and chillypoks, mutated birds of prey,
Picked flesh from bones outside the homes, ate even the decay.
The leaders' airship streaked the sky. The fuel would soon diminish.
Surveying damage was for naught as landing was their finish.
Freakish mutants encaged the craft, enraged by their condition,
Brought on my occupants within who ordered the decision.
Darkness soon engulfed the world, utter silence creeped the land
For not a living thing remained. Not animal, not man.
The final war now over shouts of victory unheard,
For the world was simply ended with one discouraging word.

— *Bev Boggs*

Pledge and Promise

I pledge my undying love to you
Without restrictions or limitations
I pledge my never-ending devotion
For you without any reservations
I promise to accept you as you are
And compromise our differences
I pledge to stand by you in your endeavors
And through their consequences
I promise to be faithful and loyal
As long as we are together
I pledge my commitment to you
A promise to go unbroken forever
I pledge to you my heart and soul
In hopes that we will become *one*
I promise you from this day forward
That the best of our *life* has just begun

— *Tricia Newman*

Untitled

I can't believe that in this
Time in which I live
I would be left with
Nothing to give.
No gift, no box with
Paper and ribbon for you
On your birthday
No money in my pockets
I had no words to say
I searched for a present
And found one just for you.
It was there, I couldn't see it
Or feel it but here it is
The gift just for you.
I give to you all the love I have to give
For this is my richest gift and I will be in debt to
You for as long as I live, Happy Birthday.
    —Glenna Hill

From Mine to Yours

my heart is your canvas and yours is mine
our memories kept vivid with intricate design
this paintbrush of love blends both into one
both of us knowing we have only begun

a sip of your life calms my desperate cry
when separate from you my soul knows not why
a drink of your essence refreshes my mind
just knowing you're near is almost too kind

absorbing your touch each tearful caress
my entity reaching trembling in excess
with a shower of passion oblivion takes over
you are once in a lifetime my own four-leaf clover

my heart is your canvas and yours is mine
and both of us know our love is divine
    — Brenda Glisan

One Day

Everybody always says to me, *One day,*
One day you'll meet someone special,
Someone that will carry you off into the sunset,
Someone who will make your days and nights
Seem like there's nothing to worry about
And someone to look at the stars and dream about
Tomorrow and the next day after that.

But I guess I'll never be the one that
You'll hold tight at night.
In this world there's just not enough love
To go around, so that's probably why
There's so much pain all around the world.
Because with no love,
There is no tomorrow!
So maybe...one day!
    — Antoinette Barbosa

Lost in the Tide

The waves crashed reflecting my feelings,
Emotions of past love remained on the shore.
The sun set, going down with my heart,
All was silent except the sea's roar.
It began to calm down but the tears gently flowed;
My heart breaking in two, tearing apart.
There was nothing I could do, nothing to mend it,
What was once his I lied asleep in my heart.
No more love, nothing inside;
My last hope of love lost in the tide.
    —Anita R. Lucer

Spider

I have four tiny bumps
On my face
And a couple of more
Halfway down
I must have cancer
No says my mother
Spider bites
No way   no spider could
Crawl on my face
And bite me four times
I must be sick
I found the dead spider
Its legs crushed under its
Pinhead body,   in my bed
Halfway down   did he know
He was going to die
    —Diane H. Thomas

Paths

A fleeting glimpse at dawn
Keeps all our hopes alive.
We see at once, though dimly lit,
How all the paths we've wandered
Are merged at one point,
To comprise all we are.
When dawn has passed
And daylight brightens all,
The pathways fade
As though the day were night.
All that we are,
Has been covered with time.
Our lifelong paths
Are never clearer
Than when the dawn
Draws our paths nearer.
    —Pat Michael

Looking Back

We started in the valley
 Climbing up the rocky hill
Struggling with the obstacles
 That tried to break our will.

There were bears along the way
 So we stayed close together
And built our fires for warmth
 To survive the chilly weather.

Now we have reached the summit.
 We can see down there below
What is happening in the valley
 Where we started, years ago!
    —Pat Castle

Counterpoint

Grey the walls
And grim the windows,
Barred and blurred.
At times, some blank face
With demented eyes
Will press against the glass
And for one brief, sane moment
Study the sparrow's nest
Built on the ledge
And wonder why the singing.
    — Verna Cahill

Growing Pains

These few years will not last long
The fun, the tears, we sure have grown.
Remember as kids, we had no worries at all.
Just playing with our toys and having a ball.

We were faced with pressures, alcohol and drugs
Child abuse, murder, what is this world made of?
Friends in trouble, worry and pain
The things people do can drive you insane.

Finish school, get a good job.
A good education is a ticket to the top.
The earth is made for you and for me.
So be successful, the best you can be.
    —Anita Peeler

Mirror Image

Every number's got a busy tone
Every boy and girl needs a home
Everybody's got a broken heart
Every hero feels torn apart.

At times I feel, at times I cry
There is a time to heal and a time to die
The mission has yet to be accomplished
The world must share or be demolished

Every little girl has a doll
Every little boy fights to be tall
Everyone's got a dream to be shattered
Everything revolves around the molecules of matter

Time is precious, time is unique
The time spent with you makes me feel complete
The baby crys, the house shakes
Your lips on mine is all it takes.
    —Emily Novotny

My Final Farewell

Sometimes I feel so lonely all I can do is cry,
And I drown in an ocean of tears, wondering why.
I hurt so bad, but what can I do?
How can I tell you that I love you?
I have glimpsed eternity through my love for you,
Now there is nothing else for me to do.
I want to bid you a final farewell, my love,
Though my love was something you never knew of.
Now for me is the end of the game, farewell.
    — Becky Stutler

Legend of the Rio Grande

Wandering in the darkness of the night, *La Llorona
Crying like the coyote howls at the moon beams,
Lost to eternity of the desert, you have
Thirst, no waters can quench,
On the sandy banks, as the cactus and sage reflect
Off the stillness of a haunted lands blood,
Mid the deserts high mountains, interlaced
With the river cottonwoods.
Lost and searching are you LaLorona
Young, to have drowned your children
In the waters of the Rio Grande,
Cursed, you go knocking at the adobes and
Pueblos, for your dead children, *mothers beware*
A hundred-and-some years you've wandered,
For them you can't find,
As a phantom to the living, you haunt the river shores.
Doomed to cry and wail forever.
    —Billy M. Dazey

The Love in You

When I look at you I see
Everything love was meant to be.
The softness of your smile
Makes me feel as though I'm just a child.
Even though we are miles apart,
You are forever in my heart.
When I listen to music, I hear
All the love songs loud and clear.
They reminded me of the good times we shared together.
It's just a shame they couldn't last forever.

— *Jennifer Rosenberry*

The Mysterious Land

I know a place so far away that is always full of fun,
But to get there you can not walk or run.
You cannot take a car or bike,
And you will not end up there on a hike.
In this place no one is sad or cries,
No one cheats and no one lies.
It always has beauty and it is full of charm,
And in this place there is no harm.
In this land the sun rises in the west,
And does not go down until the time is best.
Children laugh and help each other,
And every sister loves her brother.
To go here you need no invitation,
Because it is the land of imagination.

—*Jennifer Levine*

Flight Lonely

This path I chose, I alone walk it
Had I the choice to choose all over again
I would do no different

This journey I quietly undertake
Teaches me daily of the humanly mistake
The one where souls such as I
Have no place to abide

This flight sends me flying to regions untouched
Touching in me areas unexplored here to fore
And this rendezvous awakens every part of me that sleeps;
Such joy have I come to know.

This is my destiny, treading the lighted pathway
Ah, but the sorrow, too, ulluminates...
Searing through the depths of me, ripping me apart
Unparalleled in its fiery burst.

—*Amelia A. Wise*

Game of Love

I started this game of love
The day I saw your eyes,
The knowing of your name
Gave a certain blue to all of the skies.
The days seemed greater
the nights were the best, you
Are the one so different from all of the rest.
You could make me laugh, you could make me cry,
Especially when it came to our last goodbye,
I held you close then walked away,
The night grew darker, the sky turned grey,
I felt all alone, there was a big empty space,
I knew I started this game of love when
The tears rolled down my face,
I know you're gone, but I still will pray up above
Thanks for being the one who started my game of love.

—*Jenny Topper*

Always to Yourself Be True

To be loved for who and what we are
Is more important than anything else by far.
To be known for any accomplishment we may have done
Is truly more impressive than honors which first must be won.
If before others we always remain true to ourselves,
We will attain more reward than any kind of earthly wealth.
If always we are an honest, true friend and we do remain,
More riches will be gained than all of life's worldly fame.
We are always judged by what we become in life.
A lasting impression is greater than words said
    that hurt like the cutting of a knife.

— *Janice Paris Smallwood*

Windy Moments

As the breeze makes the leaves hit the ground with a soft sweet sound
They rustle along with a song.
To let us know that a windstorm is on its way, which will
Last all through the day.
The trees are tall and green for they can be seen.
From the mountain tops as the dew drops
Drop they glisten as we listen
To the soft sweet sound as the leaves hit the ground
We know that winter has come
For the cold breeze makes our hands numb
So it's time to go and start a fire
And sit back and admire
The leaves as they rustle along
With there soft sweet song.

— *Jennifer Lindquist*

Death

Feeling so lonely, drinking a bottle of beer, wishing the end was near.
I'm all alone there's no one here.
Talking to myself, thinking of all the years, and I'm still wishing
I wasn't here. starting to cry, wishing God would let me die. Looking
Around, there's not a sound, think of death.
Wondering why, I'm wondering why I wanna die. Ask myself why was I born.
I don't wanna live, but I'm scared to die, but I don't know the reason
Why.
I'm thinking of my family, while I'm think of dying
Thinking of my friends and why I'm always crying.
I'm going crazy in a sick world, where it's man vs. man, killing one
Another, this is what I see when a person dies I'm wishing it was me.
Thinking of the note I should leave behind, wording out what to say, trying
To assure them I'll be o.k.
Now I go to someone to help me with my fears.
So I'll be alive in future years.

—*Jennifer Vlacich*

For the Glory of Love

Falling in love with him wasn't what she had planned.
But eventually she did. And so did he.
As each day unfolded unto the next,
They drew closer together, unaware of where their feelings may lead.
The moments they spent together placed a lasting effect on their moments apart.
Somehow a special bond was formed out of their innocent love for each other.
It was this bond that kept them together.
Her dreams were of his world and his dreams were of her world.
Their fantasy——both worlds as one.
They're good together, is what everyone said...maybe just too good to last,
Because on one cold and gloomy night he told her that
He wanted to be *just friends*——he wanted to let go.
And as the saying goes, *If you love someone, you'll set them free.*
She did love him, so she agreed to letting go,
But deep inside, she knew she could never really let go of him.
As she nodded her head agreeing to his offer, a sense of emptiness suddenly came over her.
Then tears gently rolled down her cheeks so she quickly turned and walked into the night,
Never once looking back for she knew that if she did,
He would see in her eyes that she did it all for the glory of love.

—*Doines Borja*

A Beginning

The glow from you
Eyes-
Shined like no
Tomorrow-
Your touch,
Embrace,
Showed me-
You cared.

The candle burning
Shadows on the wall-
The incense-
A smell of a beginning
For us.

—*Dorothy Vanderhoef*

Spring

Winter leaves its icey stage,
As spring brings something new
Fall is in the dressing room
As summer waits its cue.

The yellow heads of daffodils
Compete with tulips red...
Gently swaying in the breeze
They grace the flower bed.

The naked trees stand twisted;
Reaching to the sun...
Knowing they will soon be clothed
Now spring has just begun.

And when springtime is over,
And all her work is done
She smiles and takes applause from us
And welcomes on the sun!

—*Jeanette C. Bown*

My Riches

Oh, I have riches worth far more
Than all of Midas' gold.
Not wealth that in the bank is kept,
But what the heart does hold.

The priceless gift of work is mine,
A work I love to do,
And each day's task fills time so full,
I am never sad nor blue.

The love song, the love of books,
These are a part of wealth,
But far above all else, I count
The luxury of health.

And more than all the rest, I count
A friendship, tried and true,
For that is where all real wealth lies,
In having friends like you.

—*Bernadine Bailey*

Fallen Star

Oh star gazer who seeks out the night,
Why love the darkness instead of the light?
Your love is for space and it's wonderful things,
Like the moons of Jupiter and Saturn's great rings.
You sit and watch the stars, and wonder how, they can be,
And I sit and look at you, and know you don't love me.
You tell me you love me, and you say it's true,
But how can I believe you?
For you're a star gazer, and you watch the sky,
But no matter how beautiful, all stars must die.

— *Pamela Zinsmeister*

A Cry from Hell

A quiet cry in yonder room,
A quiet cry is all it is.
What makes this quiet cry?
What makes this quiet cry, cry?
If I knew I would not tell
'Cause all it is is this quiet cry needs help.
If I can't help this quiet cry, who can?
It seems to be this quiet cry is getting louder.
What should I do?
This quiet cry is now not a cry,
It's a yell screaming for help!
I no longer can help this yell
  'cause it's getting too loud.
Oh,
Now I see,
It has to be;
This quiet cry is from Hell.

— *Deanna Reiter*

No More Than This

The fertile ground made ready for seed
To sprout and grow the food we need.
The meadows lush, the plains stretched long
The spring that bubbles and refreshes
The gentle trees to shade man's brow
The sunlight warm on fields of corn
The rain as gentle as the morn
The dog that walks beside my stride
Who meets with danger and does not hide
All these things I'm thankful for
And could not ask for any more.

— *E. A. Teresky*

Eternal Paradox

The end of life, the beginning of death.
The start of peace and the finish to breath.
The future's vision is today perplexed.
Tomorrow's hope is now yesterday's vex.
The universe without immense to see.
Within ourselves, we hold a space tiny.
How can love's bad intent design
Evil to grow, then die benign?
The child, the adult they so envy.
The adult, the child would like to be.
How can evil's good intent see
Love destroyed; spread eternally?
Creatures live in a world so small.
Space unbounded, galaxies all.
Today's the future so well known.
Yesterday's past, alive and grown.
The beginning of life, the end of death.
The end of silence and another breath.

—*Jeanette Hancock*

After a Basketball Game

The track is a dark dream
    in the moonlight, it begs
for presence, for someone to whisper
    empty words.
Every blade of grass is blue clarity
    and frost sparkles like a universe.
Above is fog and an ice cube moon,
  Casting shadows.
Here is
    silent.
        Here is
            free.
here is forget, because home
  is loud
      and we just lost.

—*Laura Dunham*

At the River's Edge

At the river's edge
I scoop my hand
To feel the rippled coolness,
The water rushes between my fingers.

At the river's edge
I dangle my feet
On slippery stones,
The water tickles my toes.

At the river's edge
I sit and watch
Mosquitos whirl and minnows
Dart beneath foaming swirl.

At the river's edge
Where the willows grace the mossy bank,
I close my eyes and drift into
Gentle sleep.

—*Ana Pine*

The Statue: Teacher of Liberty

The Stutue of Liberty,
Her torch held high
Lights up the midnight blue sky.

A bronze statue
Over 100 feet tall,
Of a proud woman
Spirit to all.

Lady Liberty, a century old, beckons all,
The tired, the hungry, the poor,
Even the small.

As a symbol of liberty, she seems to say
Follow, follow me,
Across the sea
To the land of the free.

—*Jennifer Thomas*

Best Friends

Best friends are people you can trust.
Best friends are people you can depend on.
Best friends are people that care about you.
Best friends are people you can talk to.
Best friends understand each others feelings, of pain or hurt.
Best friends are people you can laugh or cry with,
Best friends are people to go places and do things with,
Best friends are people to be with when you are down.
Best friends are people you can tell your deepest, darkest secrets to.
Best friends are people who are there for you, when no one else is.
But most of all, best friends are very special people.

—*Audrey Willhelm*

Untitled

Your sight is the sun, and I squint for its gaze
Your hair is a leaf, and I desire for its charging
Your leg is a stone, and I itch for its smoothness
Your voice is a song, and I yearn for its whisper
Your hard is a vine, and I long for its grasp
Your cheek is a cloud, and I need for its softness
Your tongue is a fire, and I stretch for its warmth
Your arm is the thunder, and I want for its power
Your ear is a cave, and I hope for its depth
Your bosom is a tree, and I feel for its shelter
Your touch is the wind, and I lust for its feel, your heart is a
Star, and I live for its light, your tear is the rain, and I thirst
For its wetness, the body is the sea, and I hunger for its motion,
Your face is a flowers, and I smile for its blossom, you mind is the
Dark, and I listen for its secret, your lip is the storm, and I covet
For its coming, your womb is the earth, and I dream for its child.

—*Jeff Cornelius*

The Space Shuttle Sadness

Why did we fly our flag at half staff?
To honor the space shuttle at the moments that pass.
It rose in the air like a giant plane,
And came down in ashes like falling rain.
It burst into pieces like shooting stars,
And NASA called out the Coast Guard.
Just think of the kids, the husbands and wives,
That lost their dear loved ones in the sky.
It got so common to go into space,
That no one thought that they would be crying tears on their face.
Francis, Michael, Judith, Ron
Ellison, Krista, and Gregory are gone.
But their memory will be with us all the time,
For they were the bravest of their kind.

—*Donelle Jensen*

The End

Everything has to end
There will be a day
When all things just stop living.
People and animals will die,
Flowers and trees will wilt to their deaths.
All life will stop,
Maybe one at a time
Maybe all at once.
The ocean will be the last to go,
Because it is most beautiful.
At some point the waves will crash violently on the shore.
Then slower, calmer the waves will shrink smaller and smaller
Until the last gorgeous wave rolls in, and hits the sand.
Then all will become still. The sun will drop and fall to the earth
Here it shall burn the remains of history and time and that will
Be the end. Forever.

—*Gina Marie Cocivera*

Lee Anne

In times gone by I'd hold you tight and sing you a song by evening light.
It was once upon a time, you know, to some far off story land we'd go.
With your blanket in hand you said, *Rock me, Daddy, and put me to bed.*
It's looking back now to by-gone times of bedtime stories and nursery rhymes.
I'd sing the *Bye Old Baby Buntin'* song as you and I rocked along.
Rock-a-bye, Lee Anne, in the tree top and you'd say, *Keep rocking; please don't stop.*
Victory in Jesus I'd sing and to my shoulder you'd tightly cling.
Humpty Dumpty and *Little Bo Peep* and *Now I Lay Me Down to Sleep,*
You have grown too large now for Daddy's lap or a lullaby and afternoon nap.
Even the circus and its great big top, no longer scared of noises going pop.
It's all together another clout with new loves that leave old Dad out,
For all I crave now are your memories, for in mine you will always be!

— *Olie H. Phillips*

A School Day

The morning bell rings, the kids rush in.
Already halls resound with the din.
Kids are so eager to get to their room
They rush down the hall, it seems they all zoom.

Each one smiles as he sees the teacher is there.
A day with a sub is more than they can bear.
The lunch count is done, the pledge has been said.
It's time for reading to check what's been read.

Afternoon lessons go without a hitch.
No one does wrong, someone is sure to snitch!
Before you know it, the day is done.
You feel as if a battle you've won.

The kids are gone, the halls are quiet.
Blackboards are clean, the lesson plans set.
God give me the patience to teach just one more day.
And show me I've made a difference in some small way.

— *Dusty Dennis*

The Frigate Stark

Frigate stark stood guard on Persian Gulf!
Men chatted on her deck.
None perceived pending disaster.
Nay, not one, by heck!
Some men went about their duties.
Some men stood tall, alert, erect.
None perceived a missile striking.
Nay, not one, by heck!
So with untold force, complete surprise,
The missile struck the Stark direct.
Left thirty-seven men dead. On top her ravished deck.
These men loved and served their country well!
These men died for a land they vowed to honor and protect.
None would've done it differently.
Nay, not one, by heck!
So 'tis fitting Stark's flag hang half mast above her lonely deck.
But nay shall we forget those thirty-seven brave,
Nay, not one, by heck!

— *Wanda Warrenburg*

Rest Now my Child

Rest now my child and place your head upon my chest
When entering this Kingdom upon me your burdens will lie,
Trials and tribulations are no more take your rest
And gently close your eyes.

I have prepared this place for you
Now come join me in this solitude,
You have labored long and earned this rest
No more worries, you have done your best.

Rest now my child your head upon my chest
For I will watch over you while you rest,
No more tears shall you cry
My child, you are with Me now.

—*Barbra F. Mosley*

The Day After

The day after the world is black, no sight of light is present.
All is calm, no sound to be found. White ashes float
Into the never ending space of Chaos. Souls vanished
Without a trace of existance. The ringing of
Quietness getting louder until there is no eardrum
To bust. No smell, no feel, as if there were nothing.
Though there were no time of day or night the
Blackness going on forever as if eternity had passed.

—*Eddie Williams*

Beautiful Sky

Have you ever really
looked at the sky?
Its beauty is
of that most high.
Its colors are
the strangest thing.
It makes you want
to dance and sing.
I wonder if
it will stay this way
or if some day
it will fade away.
I've asked myself this
time and time again,
Will I see
this beauty again?
The beautiful scenery
that's in the sky
fills me with joy;
I just have to sigh.

—*Jennifer Jenna Natashia Welsh*

Sweet Thoughts

Sitting under the sky
With stars up above
So shiny and bright
Reminds me of our love,
Sweet kisses so gentle
And touches so right.
Little whispers you whisper
When you hold me so tight.
Thoughts of each other
Race through our minds.
Our love for each other,
Sweet and kind,
Staring in your eyes
So crystal clear and blue
Telling me you love
Such a beautiful thing.

—*Jennifer Sizemore*

Steadfast Roses

I had to smile at the roses
For they were so steadfastly brave
Sitting on top of their briars
Making a cluster so grave,
While all around was disaster,
The scallions all faded and sere,
The drought dry tall stalks of the tulips
And even the grasses were drear.
And there sat three roses together
To me some amusement it gave
For in spite of the scarceness of raindrops,
They were being so steadfastly brave.
So hear the song of the roses,
Of how, in hard times, to behave:
Be strong, stand tall and together
And always be steadfastly brave.

— *Patricia Whitesel*

Friendship

I'll never forget the times we've had,
Some times were good, sometimes were bad.
Even if we had to shout
We made it through the rain without a doubt.
I know it hurts to say good-bye
Because I saw a tear from your eye.
I know we'll always keep in touch
Because our friendship means so much.

—*Jackie Whelan*

Best Friends

Six o'clock
Sirens wailing,
People staring,
The bathroom door was locked.
I told her not to do it.
She said she had a reason.
The rope burn around her neck bled.
I stared down on my friend,
Her face was blue.
Clutched in her hands,
The necklace I gave her
With our motto,
Best friends.

— *April Verga*

Flower

Rows and rows of flowers.
Rows and rows of scents.

One by one, they find new homes,
Beautiful flowers, you were picked.
Oh, so perfect flowers.

The sun seldom shines now.
The most beautiful flowers are gone.
The chill in the air bites only one.

One lonely flower.
Weary with waiting.
And sad.
Only the beautiful flowers are picked.
Dewy tear drops slide down the fallen petal.
The lonely flower dies.

—*Bobette Boggs*

My Letter to Space

This is my letter to space,
That has never told a soul,
Of things that live inside its place
Of which it has control.

What do you hold inside yourself,
Your vast, enlarging space
Far from me, but near the shelf
That holds your secret's place?

You say planets, comets, and meteorites,
The sun, the moon, and the stars.
And a color dark as the black of night,
From which I view afar.

—*Brandy Costello*

We Will Be Among Them

If guns are roaring,
Bombs are exploding,
If the killing persists,
We will be among them.
If children keep crying,
People keep suffering
If many are straving.
We will be among them.
If most are heartless,
Love doesn't matter,
If nobody can care,
We will be among them.
We will be among the stones sitting in the green.
Lying still, loving none, being gone
If we keep up as we do now,
We will be among them...

—*Nichole K. Boudreau*

Mermaid

Soft the tide flows, up and back
To the ocean, calm and black
In the full moon's paling light,
So soft the tide flows through the night.

A flash of skin and shining scale,
Human face and fish's tail,
Flowing hair black as the sea,
Slowly a smile, wild and free.

To passing ships, her song calls out:
Enchanting, deadly, as with not a doubt
The ship turns to her rocky throne
And splinters to its death. Alone,

Once more her smile fades,
A tear at the destruction made.
Alone at last, she breathes a sigh
Awaiting ships to pass her by.

— *Amy Sinclair*

Forbidden Love

Even though it is not to happen
It always turns out this way
We cannot deny the feelings we have
What more are we to say?

We know we are hurting others
As we go along
Our heads tell us we should stop
Our hearts say we do nothing wrong

Back when all this started
How were we to know
That the future would bring such troubles
Sorrows destined only to grow

Now as we gaze peacefully
Into each other's knowing eyes
The love we once saw as shameful
Now is no surprise.

—*Aneta Patronite*

Untitled

I sit in my room
Everything is ever so still
I miss the outside world
Although I feel the need to kill
Everything seems so quiet
Off to its own kind of sleep
Impulses run through my head
Although these impulses I cannot keep
Everything is just right in its place
Whether it be on the wall or bed
As I lay here and look around
I feel so lonely and wish to be dead
But then I think of the future
And think of what is going for me
A healthy happy living life
A life full of adventures that I will soon see

—*Jennifer Lamont*

Happy Birthday

A tear hanging in my eye,
Still there, though swelling, but why.
A tear running down a child's face,
As she touches her dress with torn lace.
A burn on her arm has yet to heal,
The scar on her soul, she will always feel.
A party would be normal for this day,
But the spanking she received in a different way
Happy Birthday.

— *April D. Smith*

I Believe

Fly high, my friend;
Sing your song,
For the world is waiting
To hear you speak.
Open your eyes,
And you will see
You have the world at your feet.
When the road is dark and dusty,
Remember what I've said
And don't let your misfortunes
Travel to your head.
Now my eyes can clearly see
That you are a star
And, yes, you my friend,
You will go far.
Searching for yourself
Is the hardest thing to do.
But remember all I've said, my friend,
I believe in you!

—*Aimee Ball*

Artificial Light

What will become of me whenI
no longer see. The countdown
has begun. Will fireworks
display a fond farewell? Will
a blackout wipe away day?
Or slowly like a candle burn
quietly without sound nor wind
come night reaching its end.
My eyes are lights set loosely
in the sockets with a bad
connection caused by the wires
inside my brain.

— *Nancy Denofio*

The Challenge

The picture painted when I was small
Is hidden behind a masquerade wall.
A wall of confusion, a wall of defeat,
A wall of thickness that must be beat.
To stand on my own is a struggle if not,
To forget all the lies and sort through
What was taught.
A building of one's own pride,
To know that after the battle,
A single soul had tried.

—*Wendi Janell Davis*

Retired Kids

Honey, let's retire—let's make it soon,
We can have one more honeymoon.
Our children are raised and on their own,
Now we can buy a new motorhome.

We'll travel north, south, east and west,
We'll stop at places we like best.
No more crowds and rubbin' elbows,
In the train and airplane depots.

When the traffic gets too great,
In a rest stop we will wait.
We will sit beneath the moon,
Your gentle arms will hold me soon.

A tender kiss—a sweet embrace,
Our hearts are one let's not wait.
Look out world here we come,
Retired kids are on the run.

— *Patricia Hammer*

Portrait of West Point

It is here that my heart will stay
Amid this place so bold and gray,
For within its age-old walls of stone
There are many secrets still unknown.

Once inside these massive gates
A special feeling it does create;
One of honor, excitement and mystery,
All have a place in this living history.

Although each day the sun does rise
Minutes and hours seem not to go by.
Here, time is suspended in perpetual flight.
It does not matter, there is no night.

It is here, among the splendor and glory,
A person can tell his dream-like story.
It is here that my heart will stay,
Amid this place so bold and gray.

—*Ann Schill*

The Search

In search of a dream, in search of a way
That God will give me,
Just one more day.
In search of a love, in search of a hope
That I will stop using,
More and more dope.
I'm lying in bed, I'm lying awake
Trying to forget,
That one tiny mistake.
I'm thinking of you, I'm thinking of you
Oh God how I wish,
You were here too.
I'm sitting in a well, too deep to get out
Oh how I wish I knew,
What life is really about.
I'm out of this hole, I'm ready to give
All I really want now,
is just to LIVE!

—*Patti Gilbert*

Forgiving Path

Crosses are t's
A sign of the Ghost and home of our Host.
He really sees,
As we bend on knees only to please.

Soften my load
Remove my burden,
Let me walk in a peaceful mode.
Rid me of my guilt ridden load.

Forgive and forget, take His hand,
Dig through the sand and rejoice in our land.
Live for tomorrow, bury the past,
For nothing will last.

Sow the seeds,
Plow new fields, take His lead and do good deeds.
Mother his land, treat it well,
Whereas you can see,
He can tell!

—*Patricia A. Brahm*

Outlaws

Outlaws, outlaws, they're self-contained.
They stick to themselves like a piece of grain.
Don't move thy body; don'r move thy lips.
They just keep to themselves from place to place.
Oh pity, oh pity, what a disgrace.
They keep to themselves from place to place.

— *Debbie Henry*

Make Believe

In this world of make believe
All our sadness and pains are gone.
In this world, it is love and happiness I receive,
All the bad and horror wrong.
There is no evil; there are no frowns,
It is all that you wish for; it's smiles, no downs.
All uphill, there is no ending
The roads are long, forever and ever sending
Messages to and from
Telling us to come
To the world of everlasting
To the world where there is no hassling.
A place far away; there is no fear.
No doubts or losses, love is always near.
So join me here, come with me,
To this world of make believe
Just lay down your head; close your eyes,
Dream, dream away, never wake up...surprise!

—*Carol Brown*

One Day At A Time

Oh, happy our world would be...
If only each of us could see,
How precious is that word a Day
Ours to spend in our own special way

Some know the value,and some do not know...
For if they understood, their love would surely flow
To all they meet and greet
To friends and foes out on the street

We would forget to worry about the unknown...
But care about the Time we have blown,
We would make time count to all who care,
And live our life to all being fair

What does it take for us to feel...
That time is not ours to steal?
Please give us a sign before we part
To know and live what is in our heart.

—*Donna Clothier*

Happiness

Happiness is like walking on a beach
With the wind slightly blowing at your body.
It tastes like freshly picked fruit.
It smells like newly budding daisies.
It looks like the sun shining brightly.
It sounds like children playing, having fun.
It is like the colors of pastel.
Happiness is the best thing you can get out of life.
You can have love—but you should be happy.
You can be gloomy—but why?
Anyone can be happy—even you and I!

— *Jennifer Cowles*

Brain Drained

Poetically speaking, I am perplexed and aghast
At what life and science have done to my craft.
Happy and gay, is a bright, lively phrase,
But poets avoid it nowadays.

I write about hearts and love a lot,
But with all the transplants, whose heart has who got?
Can I say, *With all my heart* if my heart isn't mine?
Take heart! gave us courage and a feeling sublime.

With organ donations, I am respectfully deeming
Why not take all of me? has an updated meaning,
When brains are transplanted, since mine is a remnant,
I am applying posthaste to be the first recipient.

—*Hope Tenhaeff*

If I Were To Say

He was from the wrong side of the tracks.
What would it mean?
That I'm better than he?,
He lesser a person than me?
I richer,
He poorer?
Who really knows?
Who really gives a damn?
Not I,
Surely not he.
Then what does it matter?

She's not lady like.
What would it mean?
That I better of a person?
She lesser?
Who really knows?
Not I,
Surely not she.
Then what does it matter?
Who really knows?
Who really gives a damn?
        —*Lynne C. Knobbe*

Megapolis

The cavernous bands of streets
Intertwine their black latticework
Under the glut of glass and chrome
Severing the canopy of stars.
A cacophony of fireworks
Ricochets off the skyscrapers:
While below the Lilliputians
Roll and gyrate,
Wingfooted race
No where-
Going no where.
        —*Sylvia Semel*

Terror

Terror creeps in,
Like fingers of mist,
Like fingers of sin.
Unbidden, a cry
 Escapes my lips-
 Lips mist kissed.
I fall! Down, down
 Ever down.
Down to the floor.
I feel I shall drown,
Drown in terror, as in folklore.
It takes over.
I will die now.
Die now as terror creeps in,
Like fingers of mist and sin.
        —*Lisa Williams*

Loneliness

Far away,
a seagull cries.
He has no one,
no one but...
me?
I know him;
He I.
We stand together,
yet we are
alone.
Far away, a seagull cries,
And I cry
too.
        —*Christine Lyseng*

The Dove

Fly, fly, fly away,
Gone away now, gone to play.
Where are they, where can they be?
In a meadow, up a tree,
Wings of steel, hard as a rock,
In the sky now, in the flock.
They are the beauty which I love.
This is the beauty of the dove.
        —*Jodi Smith*

Songbird's Flight

I am but a songbird,
Gliding fanciful through
The light April breezes.
Reciting my song among
The willow boughs.
High and mighty above
The ground, but feeling
Higher than the clouds.
Knowing only that moment,
Never looking back at
Yesterday.
        —*Tammy Wheatley*

The Last of Its Kind

I wanted it to be beautiful
As beautiful as your smile.
I understand now
You had a certain style
I can never even try
To create a poem for you.
I would only disappoint myself
And treat you unjustly too.
You have gone far above
Literature of this kind.
It is time I said goodbye to it
And leave it all behind.
All the ways I love you
Cannot be shared in lines.
You mean more to me
Than I can write in rhymes.
        —*Chris Moriarty*

Old Man

My vision has grown dark,
Stumbling around old docks,
Begging food like a dog.
'Til one day I fell down a step...
And was eaten by a shark.
        —*Conni Pheil*

Totalled

Squealing around the macadam curve.
Black tires gripping.
I tell my brother
I'm scared.
But it's not my brother
sitting next to me.
Then we've broken through. Free.
Flying in space. A gentle downward arc.
The earth far below.
Falling. Falling slowly.
Drifting down.
His hand reaches toward me.
I close my eyes.
Blessed comfort. Total relaxation.
Sleepy.
I tense.
Waiting for
Impact.
        —*Paula L. Brown*

Untitled

the sacred place is in the womb
and not in the hearts of men
nor in the great stone temples
nor in the peace of a distant meadow

for in the womb
there is no hunger
longing
or pain

the sacred place is in the womb
for if the butterfly died in the cocoon
it would suffice
never knowing what flight was
at all
        —*Lisa Eberharter*

Oh Dear Grandfather

Oh dear Grandfather,
See me through all the trials
You've been through.
Oh dear Grandfather,
Lead me on, for as you see,
I have not much strength to go on.
Oh dear Grandfather,
Please protect me,
For you're at the place I dream to be
And one day as you'll see
I'll be there for it's my destiny
To carry on what you taught me to be.
Thank you, Grandfather.
        — *Tammy Bell*

Reflections

Reflections can be funny
Reflections can be true
One could be the song in my heart
Or, one could be you.

In the water, in the wind
In the sun or the moon
Stars continue falling
As a rose heals a wound.

Standing here before you
My best, I shall wear,
Feel through reflections
The truth within your heart.
        —*Kevin Delong Fleshman*

Mystical Labor

We shall accentuate the true feeling of a laborious desire
to ignore the void with love.
We shall invent a new contemplation to attain nirvana now.
We shall continue a misleading desire to romanticize
a small planet within our world.
Within our own minds we shall control the riches of a critical niche.
I can pull the earth into the palm and run it long my lifeline.
I can pull the earth into the abscess of oblivion waiting to be devoured.
I can exalt the very being of what we are made of.
I can prepare a banquet for a contemptuous makeshift politician
eager to please the multitudes already gathered at the waterfall
where there is a time and a place for martyrs.
Let us take on the moth and all for the price of a traitor.
30 silvery white lies to divinity.
Exodus: the coming of a new day. Three days mourning.
Trees swaying to the unmasked sounds of a whore's spittle.
Enthroned: Lawful couples. This learning provides
short stories for the young.

—*Randy Orzada*

A Peace in Times of War

In my mind the echoes ring
While my heart is filled with a bitter sting.
This last fight outdoes the rest
It puts my endurance to the test.

I want to know what I did wrong,
Why this warring must continue so long.
Something I did give them the right
To want to yell and scream and fight.

Somehow I don't quite pass their test
Even though I achieve my personal best.
When I see each hardened glance
I silently beg for another chance...to do things right.

Maybe it's the way it's supposed to be, no one promised
Life would always go happily. But I want this wrath and ache to cease,
To be replaced with an eternal peace. So for my strength I'll look
Above and pray for God's unerring love.

—*Shayna Szmiot*

Cradled in the Arms of Morpheus

The wind precedes thunder
Which soon will cease my slumber
As I fight to stay afloat in this deep void of sleep.
Icy cobalt fills my eyes
When I look up to the skies
And comprehend the harsh reality that surrounds me when I wake.
From pure Eden I do fall
To a world of brazen wall
Where the timid and the quiet are given laws and told to speak.
A deep depression engulfs my soul
As I peer out through this hole
Of consciousness, and realize the confusion into which I am to plunge.
So in response to what I feel
From this land of glaring steel
I let go of what is real
And drift effortlessly through darkness to my own soft paradise.

—*Jerry Burch*

A Feeling of Love

You are all I want; is it hard to see
That happiness equals you plus me.
You are so very special and so very dear,
I want you by my side to whisper in my ear,
About how much you love me and about how much you care,
About how you'll protect me and how you'll always be there.
Whenever I'm feeling sad or when I'm feeling down,
It will make me feel so much better just knowing you're around.

—*Rae Ann Terrill*

Just As I Am

If I were any different, than what I am today,
Would you still love me, would you want me to stay?
If I were quite taller, or smaller, or thin,
If I had a different color of skin,
If my voice were to change, from higher to low.
Would you still want me to stay and not go?
If I were not healthy, and far, far from wealthy.
Not a penny to my name, and surely no fame.
Would you definitely, unquestionably, want me to remain?
If I had shorter, or longer hair,
Would you still want me, to know that you care?
If I were older, or younger, or smart,
Would I still find that special place in your heart?
I want you to sit, and just think for awhile
What if I had a quite different smile?
Would you want me forever, or just for while?

—*Kerry L. Koster*

The Reunion

An old man sits on a park bench,
Feeeding breadcrumbs to the hungry pigeons
Out of a crumpled paper sack.

His eyes have clouded over and the corners of
His mouth have sagged into a permanent frown.
The wind dances about his shrunken body and
It seems to mock him for a moment.

He pulls his timeworn overcoat closer to his chain and waits.
Suddenly he comes alive as a young woman,
Whom he has not seen for years, runs toward the bench.
He carefully stands up as she comes closer to him.

A brightness replaces the former haziness of his
Eyes and the corners of his mouth are trembling.
The young woman embraces him and tears spring into
His elated eyes as she whispers,
Daddy!

—*Cheryl Loomis*

Empathy

In the corner of my night room
Stands a cube made of glass, thick as steel
And twice as cold.

The man inside
Throws his bloodless hands to the wavering surface,
His face contorted like a dying monkey's
In a silent, futile scream.

Do not trust him.
For if you were to split his cage, loose him to his will,
He would only rape and burn and kill
And swallow up his own miserable death,
Leaving you behind in the corner of my night room
To fervently construct your own captivity
From the broken shards.

I know...
That's how he got here.

—*Kristin Bowling*

Believe

Do you believe in dragons,
Dragons that fly high.
Do you believe in sunsets,
Sunsets that never die.
Do you believe in other worlds,
Worlds that laugh and cry.
Do you believe in magic,
The magic deep within your heart.

— *Rose Nesbitt*

Thin Ice

This house has changed its mood.
A dark stage, set for a play.
Everything in its place.
As if I had never been away.

It unnerves me. I feel cold.
How did time stay outside the door?
Maybe if I open the windows
The house will come alive like before.

Before? When was that time?
Winter? Yes, I remember the snow.
Michael, do you remember the winter?
Michael, now where did he go?

Oh my.
What is wrong with my head.
I keep on forgetting.
Little Michael is dead.

　　—Stella A. Soda

Waiting

Cold minutes are like hours.
Beneath me the battered bench,
Is hard coated with splintered frost.
A freight train rattles over the tracks
Its whistle lingers in the frozen air
Then falls away.
I've been thinking.
Staring into the weathered rail station,
One moment—a place filled with people
Who are waiting. Another second passes,
Vacant and standing still
Beside the railway station,
I've been waiting.

　　—Cindy E. Tebo

To Die: In One Man's Silent Reality

He died all alone in his bedroom.
There was no one there to be sad.
Not a soul to shed flowing teardrops.
This last moment was all that he had.

His mind went faster than ever before
As his life slowly was draining.
He ached for a chance to do it again
To feel sun when it's shining,
To feel wet when it's raining.

　　— Stephanie DiNardo

Remembering

A little girl sits all alone
Thinking of people she used to know
People who used to be her friends
People who used to care.
She tinks of how she used to belong
To a rather dignified social group
And how she had friends
Who, at once, were her sisters.

She tries to think of all the happy times,
Of all the smiles and laughter and stupid jokes.
But those days have gone,
And her sisters have resigned.

A little girl sits all alone
Thinking of people who used to care
And she cries
Silent tears of loneliness.

　　—Julie Whisnant

Last Request

I beseech thee
Oh, Great and Mighty Power,
Hear my prayer
During this my final hour.
Give me strength
When I am faint from weakness.
Give me light
When I am wrapped in darkness.
Give me hope,
When I am cast into eternity,
And touch my soul
That I may walk with thee.

　　—R. L. Quaid

The Eternal Rebellion

Never look back, never look down,
said the Thinker to the Clown,
who frowned,
with the laugh still upon his lips,
as together they watched
the sinking of the other ships,
and tried to ignore
the water lapping at their feet.

Never look back, never look down.

　　— R. Troy Martin

Easy Way Out

He was from the bad side of town,
A drop-out from school.
He thought he could make it
In his make-believe world.

His father was a drunk,
His mother was dead.
He was messed up on drugs,
So he put a gun to his head.

It was easy to pull the trigger,
Because he had no real friends
To love and to miss him,
So he made it all end.

His life was messed up
And clouded with doubt,
And like so many others
Took the easy way out.

　　—Kim Pennell

Only the Wind

Sometimes I think I hear you,
but it's only the wind.
An awesome chasm separates us,
though sometimes our spirits ride
together
over free and forever silent plains.
There will be no echoes to remind me
that you have gone;
you left no warning.
You were snatched into the grips
of black nothingness.
Just last night I saw you,
riding over the hills
in your sun-glistening chariot,
and I thought I heard you,
thought I felt you with me.
But it was only the wind.

　　—Sherry Jones

Peace of Mind for Him

He is gone now but not forgotten.
I can see him in a beautiful field of cotton.
On his face is a look of peace of mind.
There is no more pain to make him blind.
He is waiting for his loved ones to meet him.
He knows what is ahead for them.
He left his mark on us, which was love.
Now he is with God up in Heaven above.

　　—Kathy Jones Anderson

Jon

Child-like eyes full of fear
Why could you not have cried a tear
Gave us a sign of what was to come
Instead of just leaving us alone and numb

So many questions we never asked
Remain in our minds as part of the past
No one will answer them now that you're gone
And so with God's help we'll carry on

And now in death you need not fear
No suffering and no despair
So rest in peace dear troubled child
And watch as we travel life's endless miles

　　— Lucy Grossi

Suicide

It seems that every passing night
Becomes a harder and harder emotional fight.
Never time to take, but only to give,
Really makes me wonder of any real reason to live.

Always sad and always crying.
Makes me wonder if I'm living or slowly dying.
Always wondering if life is fair.
Never knowing if anyone cares.

Always wondering how it would be to always smile
And never to cry,
But the only way there is not to live
Is to die.

　　—Darla Grese

A Flight From Reality

I took a little flight by the airlines
Because I thought I'd get there faster
In keeping with the times.

I took a little drink before I started
To overcome my fear of being another soul departed
But the drink wore off and I bounced upon the clouds.

And all I could see was the passengers in shrouds.
I battled with the infinite and wished that I were dead.

I tossed and turned and banged my head
To see had I not had a nightmare in bed.
But, alas, the clouds were real and the plane came down
With the greatest of zeal.

Next time I fly, if ever
I shall most certainly endeavor
To take off without false courage.
And my flight will not be a ghastly mirage.

　　— Louise Van Woert

The Gift

In the stillness of dark
I asked deep within
The Gift that you sent
Is not to be found
Have you taken my Gift
As an unfilled quest
A thundering sound
My attention it had
Speaking soft from within
The gift that I sent
You now have become!

— *Kathleen Lee Mendel*

Nature's Power

Wrapped in a blanket in front of the fire
Staring out of the window
Watching the snowflakes fall gracefully
Took me with all its power.
I felt cozy and warm inside.
The beautiful and peaceful moment
 took away my troubles.

— *Tonya Bess*

Life

Life is like a rainbow
It has it's ups and downs.
A happy smile that fades away
And turns into a frown.
Life has many different colors.
Some are warm and some are cold.
Life is also very amazing
To watch, and learn, and hold.
Hold on to it very tight
Or it might slip away.
And cause a very happy rainbow
To fade very far away.

— *Suzi Alesso*

Moonlight Love

The moon,
The stars,
And my love.
The night is cold, and
Yet my heart is warm.
We never notice the chill.
A night on the sand,
A gentle light in her eyes-
Is that the moon
Or something from inside?
Together tonight,
With simple loving and dreams of more,
There is nothing to divide us.
Just our love,
Wider than the shore
Moonlight love.

—*John Scognamillo*

Untitled

Love is not just silver and gold
Or a crease or a fold
Or a wish or a kiss.
It's a magical binding
Between two people
Who dedicate their lives to the other
To help and love forever.

—*Kate Uhlmann*

The True Self

The being within
Is cold and lonely
Sometimes overpowering
He is cruel and unkind
He causes our darkness
Yet,
He hurts
From his hurt,
There comes our fear,
For the one within,
Is our tortured truth.

— *JoAnn Baker*

Untitled

Living,
a free fall
kaleidoscopic scenes
glimpsed in passing
days and nights
meshed
with dreams of tomorrow
yet to be broken
by today's demands
of being
of becoming
all the while
obliterating now.

—*Cheryl Caponigro*

Untitled

The see-saw totters
echoing in the wind,
the silver slide glistening in the sun...

The laughter lingers,
the air is gleaming,
filled with dew,
the raindrops shimmer,
and all becomes one...

The raindrops linger,
sticking deep within their soul...
countless rays beat down,
ending the reminder
of the peacefulness that we adore...

The children dance,
and chant in time.
These children are the future,
still dreaming of tomorrow...

—*Susan Marie Dietterich*

Untitled

My friends have just split.
Two lovers who shared so much;
Days, weeks, months, years.
They lived for the other's touch.
They lost their closeness,
Their ability to speak.
Problems get out of hand.
The relationship became weak.
Things have changed for them.
They're just not the same.
But what can we do?
Who is to blame?
Now they go their separate ways.
As each day passes by.
And what can I do?
I sit alone and cry.

— *Connie Querry*

The Age of Distrust

Squinting through the dust,
I saw your body torn.
Walking through the ruble,
I hear the thundering horn.
Everyone died today. it cried,
Everyone died today, I sighed...
Sorry, but it lied, lied...

— *Joe Laceby*

I Wish

I wish there was an easy way out,
But there is not.
I wasn't the only one to make a mistake.
You helped out.

Maybe it wasn't meant to be,
You and me,
To be friends the way we used to be.

You act like you don't care
But I know you do.
You care about me
As much as I care about you!

— *Theresa Jozwiak*

So Lonely

Sable in the heart
So lonely
But the other world rules me
With rigorous
I'm so ravenous for romance
For someone who understands
Me
Some say I have the prowles
To be a winner
Some people perspectives of me
Are to be perfect
But in the realistic world I'm
Consider a failure
Sable in the heart
So lonely

— *Susan Clarke*

Lost

My mind went on a trip again,
A futile trip, indeed.
It traveled down a widened road
To hold all its companions who
Traveled with it, each alone, in
Search of light, but not their own.

And so we went, hither and thither.
We didn't know if friend or foe
Obstructed our vision. Yet,
No one thought to share *his* light
To brighten the so dark a night.

And so, confusion did abound;
And fear and despair all around;
And just because each one alone
Wanting to share a light.
But not his own.

— *Johanna Best*

Life

The delicate birth of an orchid
So gracefully it opens
Like the sun opening to a brand new day
The sweet fragrance of its slender body
Waft's through the summer breeze forever
And then it dies...

—*Susan Braidis*

Autumn of a Friendship

For us, the Autumn has arrived
The leaves of friendship fade and die
You leave, move on to greener things
I stand among the drifting leaves.

Leaves of gold and red and brown
Fall to form my dying crown
Wrapped in chilling. Aquilo's breath
Watching a friendship's last struggles in death.

There are so many things I have yet to say
And far too many things left to do
But it seems, my friend, that time is too short
To say the things I have been meaning to.

Things with meanings lost to time
Times that people shall never know
Like the life within a winter tree
That yearns to bloom and grow.

—*Monique Moffatt*

Peer Pressure

I tried it once and I will never forget
Because all this time I've been trying to quit
Love, sex, drugs, cocaine, beer, alcohol,
They are not my answer, not at all.
They said it would be interesting and fun,
Dear God, what...what have I done?

I have decided to...commit suicide,
Then I will not have to hide
I will be in God's arms
And free from all the worlds' harms,
Love, sex, drugs, cocaine, beer, alcohol
They are not my answer...not at all.

—*Amy Lahr*

Under the Moonlight

Like ghosts in a large deserted field,
The abandoned plows are standing;
They bring a search for depth in life.
The silver clouds slowly swaying
Are bursting over the land, and the snow
Is falling fast upon the frozen ground,
The implements in white arise a haunting memory.

The young farmer recollects the horses' strength
In pulling hard to till the rich soil, then
He thinks of the healthy cattle roaming
In the glossy meadows at sundown.
A flowery scent around teases his nostrils;
In seeing his wife's rounded figure approaching,
He feels the vigor of summer in his veins.

—*Emma J. Blanch*

Wisdom

Life's no longer, like it used to be
Technology has changed it, don't you see
From sweat shops and drudgery, we've been set free
With more leisure time, for you and me.
From our climatized home, we view the world
Into outer space, big birds are hurled
A man on the moon, our flag unfurled
And from the sea, sunken treausres are lured.
Children no longer, know their place
Life isn't sacred, abortion's no disgrace
Elders are shut away, they can't keep pace
And morals are threatened, by a humanistic race.
Knowledge might be exploding, the world around
While heads are bursting, to a metalic sound
But ethnics in business, can seldom be found
And without wisdom, we're genocide bound.

—*David O. Fisher*

With You

Hold me,
Hold me tightly,
Tightly from the night,
The night so dark.
Love me,
Love me carefully,
Carefully to make it last,
Make it last through eterntiy.
Kiss me,
Kiss me gently,
Gently take me away,
Away from the world.
Stay with me,
Stay with me forever,
Forever and always,
Always in love,
In love with you.

—*Tammy Downing*

Untitled

My love is gone
He couldn't say,
He touched my life
Then slipped away.
His heart joined mine
To make it whole,
He kissed my mind and
Caressed my soul.
His voice was low
His words were sweet
Though just a memory
He's my retreat.
Bathe me in your loneliness.
Like tears of joy and pain,
Comfort me, fulfill my dreams,
Sweet, sweet summer rain.

—*Danielle Zarlengo*

I Am, Am I

I am the daylight
And the darkness,
The twilight born again.
I am the laughter
And the sorrow
Found in the heart of man.
I am the stillness
And the movement,
That surge of life within.
I am the small
And the mighty,
An equal to the land.
I am the good
And the sinful;
There is naught I have not been.
I am the first
And the last
In his, the final plan.

—*Ruth Stegemeier*

On to Love

Within reason, what reason
Is the reason we be?
Should life be a lock
Love must be the key.

On to love, blissful love,
By which we commence;
To be thought of intently
To be felt with intense.

— *Thomas P. Kingston*

One More Drink

Lord, help me understand
Why You let a drunk driver take the life of my man.
A wonderful husband, a father, a friend,
Why such a tragic end?
The drunk driver said he didn't think;
He didn't know why he needed that one more drink.
Now my child sits alone,
In a world of her own.
Tears stain her face,
Memories of her dad she can't erase.
Seems like only yesterday
I heard her laughing while at play.
Today my life is falling apart,
Emptiness claims my heart.
I find myself walking the floor,
Bill collectors knocking at my door.
Lord, help me understand
Why You let a drunk driver
Take the life of my man.

—*Catherine Kerns*

One Sunday Morning

In the early morning dew
You could hear the birds crying out to the sky
There were raindrops in the air
Falling from tree to tree
One leaf to another
The red breasted robin scurrying across the dirt
Hunting for his first meal of the day
The sunlight came through my window
Brightening up the room
The chill of the morning air was turning my skin pink
The wind was still, nothing moved
It was calm except for the birds dancing in the air.

—*Julie Wickstrom*

Neve

You skated into my innocence
On a frozen pond of eloquence.
Creating enchantment
With a fur wrapped waltz,
You sliced your signature through my heart.
With icicle eyes shining
The promise of trapped air beneath your surface,
You coaxed me on to thin ice
Sculpting a spectator of fantasy,
   a cameo of frostbound feelings
Abandoned to thaw and to feel
The endless drip
Of a melting love.

Dust from cut ice wiped clean from your blade.

—*Sharyn E. Marion*

Suicide

Suicide is what you do
When life gets harder than 2+2
People decide they want to die
Because all they do is sit and cry
Life gets hard and they do not know why
They do not even want to try
When people commit suicide
Their last breath goes out with the ocean's tide
They smoke the car, or use a gun
Some kids think it sounds like fun
They send out signs, but they do not know
They pray to God that these signs will show
If they do not, all is said
These are the ones that end up
Dead!

—*Melissa Atkisson*

How Do You Say Goodbye

How do you say goodbye to someone you call friend?
How do you say goodbye when your feelings will not end?
My closest and dearest friend, why did you go?
Why did God have to shake your hand
Leaving me standing alone?
Now, who can I talk to
When I seem to lose all hope?
There is no one beside me
Without you I cannot cope.
How could you just slip away
Without saying goodbye?
I have not a reason to understand
Now nobody can tell me why.
My closest and dearest friend
You always would have been mine.
I want you back, to hold you tight
But your hand, I will never find.

—*Kim Gillissie*

Missing You

Well here I am in the cold
Lift my head and say I am bold
Light at day, dark at night
Hide the fear, hide the fright
Memories have come and gone to pass
Yet all I can do is hold my ass
The thought of leaving you behind
Reeps and roars across my mind
Yet someday I know that we will unite
To spend the evening, to spend the night.

—*Albert A. Bachelier*

A Spring Farewell From a Son to His Father

It's springtime, dad, and you're free of winter's corpse:
The light within you has been liberated
And it brightens the paths of life ahead of me.
Graduation time is here too, and you have finished first
In your class as you ascend to higher and
More meaningful levels of seeing, knowing and understanding.
Memorial day is a few days away, and, along with millions of others,
I have the privilege to remember, honor and appreciate
All you did for me, our beloved country and world.
Father's day is around the corner and, as you know, it's your day,
Your's alone, and no one can or will ever take your place.
So, thanks dad for listening, caring, loving, always helping,
Sharing and always being there when I needed you...
In life as in death
I love you, always and forever.

—*Roland A. Foulkes*

Pace in Requiescat

Long, the lily lingers near,
Sign of resurrecting cheer.
Great God, in they firmament,
Hear the prayers of penitence
For lives were living can improve
Help us, dear lord, to know you move
In quiet, hidden ways in hearts.
Depart
Still, silent souls, take flight.
To your earthbound dreams,
Bid good night.
Slumber softly, Eternal eve
Shall sooth those behind, bereaved.
Peacefully while lilies in the breeze sweep
Away memories that now must fleet. Their trumprets truimphantly
Herald heven bent souls on their Elysian journey homeward.

—*Sandra J. Endres*

A Dying Light

It seemed like just yesterday everything had been perfect.
The sun that had risen that morning,
Was all the more beautiful than the one that had set the very night before.
But now this day has been every bit as awful as yesterday was grand,
For, there was no sun that rose in the east, only a cloudy day.
And now our mother has been taken from us,
And our father can't seem to go on,
Our life is crumbling at our feet, just dying away.
Our family just doesn't seem to be meant for happiness
For, now that our mother is gone, there is an empty place in all our hearts.
Now that her flame has flickered out,
It is like the last light on earth, has suddenly died away.
It is ever so true, that we are not the same family as we were just yesterday,
Laughing and singing every night,
For now, we have all experienced a loss.
We all have that empty space in our hearts,
That no one can fill.

—*Julie Hirsch*

Heaven Await

There's a beautiful place I dream of, it lies up in the sky.
The only resort to get there it to live your life then die.
It's a place that bares its kindness, caring, affection and joy,
An image of our world for every girl and boy.
It's full of birds and trees and lakes of crystal clear,
A word that means eternity and no more saddened fear.
It's full of joy and pride where no man shall stand alone,
A place to take a rest from all the mortal stuff you own.
There's no easy way to get there; we all must wait our turn
And the ticket for this journey takes many years to earn.
Don't wait for it to happen, just try and do your best
For one day the Lord will come to you and you will pass his test.

—*Shelley Lynn Bailey*

Dying to be Free

South African people just want to know why,
They ask for freedom and are forced to die?
In the tens of thousands and maybe even more,
They ask the question, *What are we dying for?*

The people who rule them do not seem to care
If what they are doing to a nation is at all fair.
They are frightened to think what would become of their race,
If they just gave the South Africans their own free space.

Now is the time for the oppressors to pray,
For when they reap what they sow will be a tragic day.
Though my words are few, I know the message is clear
If we are human, the desperate cries we must hear.

After they are beaten, then stoned and shot to death,
Freedom is whispered with their very last breath,
I know God is angry and how sad he must be,
To witness *His* creation dying to be free.

—*Rhonda Brown*

When I Needed You

When you were feeling down, I comforted you
When you were celebrating, I rejoiced with you.
When you faced a tough challenge, I supported you
When the world looked dark, I held the light for you.

When you needed to spill your thoughts, I listened to you.
When you wanted to be alone, I kept my distance from you.
But when I needed a hand to lift me up, you just let me sink further.
And when I cried out for help, you turned your back on me and walked out.

I would give my life, my soul
But you did not have the time for me
You always took what you could
But when I needed you, none would you give.

—*Celeste Ogden*

Resting in the Grass

Soft grass against my toes
And the sun against my eyes.
Rainbows of color by the sun
With the cloud that's floating by.
— *Sara Graham*

The Seasons

Flower on tree
The wind blows gently
Flying butterfly

Ripplings on water
Rock keeps waiting longer
Fish stirs up

Woods changing
The dear listens to falling
Leaves

No bird in the sky
Just snows and ice
Mount was lost
— *Song Ho*

Where Is the Sun?

When I was a child
I was told:
When the sun comes out,
You may go out to play.
Then I grew up
And I rode in a plane.
Above the clouds
I discovered the sun.
It was there all the time.
— *Shirley L. Goldman*

The Big Blue Waves

The big blue waves
Crashing about
The white foam
All throughout
The warm brown sand
Close at its side
Like the beauty
Of the land

The big blue waves
For all to see
The great whales crashing the sea
The rocks covered
With the sharp barnacles about
You should be warned,
For there all around

The big blue waves
—*Karson A. Schmiedeskamp*

The Sky

The sky,
So beautiful, so bright.
Oh! How it makes me cry
At such a beautiful sight.
Up there so high
It makes me feel like a butterfly
Going up, up, up, up...
Oops! Look at the time.
It's time to say goodnight,
So sleep tight,
My dear, beautiful sky.
— *Chastity Ann DelMoral*

Walk on the Beach

Walk on the beach
And see the pepper spots of snails
Awash in autumn foam.
The spider crab's shell
Is white and dry. A horseshoe crab
Has left himself behind.
Sea lavender
Is almost blue, the sky
Is truly blue, and high.
Walk on the beach
Enrobed in wind and haloed
With a hazy sun.
Autumn is the time
To re-explore
The past we're heading toward.
— *Joanne Ickler*

Cry of the Willow

Just behind a woodshed
Underneath a tree,
Lies a baby willow,
As happy as can be.

It yawns and wakes
And grows quite tall.
It spreads its seed around.

Until the day
The choppers play
And fell it to the ground.
—*Chuck Bright*

Untitled

Gently dusting rooftops and treetops
Sidewalks and grass
Season's first snowfall
Little brother of blizzards
Dances silently on

t
i
p
t
o
e
s

— *Charles Breslau*

Flight

O, Pegasus, thou winged beast
Come take me on thy back!
Come fly with me, eternally,
Throughout the night so black.

O, Pegasus, thou mighty steed,
Thy hooves of molten ore
I beckon thee, come fly with me,
And trespass heaven's shore!

O, Pegasus, thou equestrian myth,
Thou beast of winged flight...
I summon thee, come fly with me,
And we'll explore the night!

O, Pegasus, thou mighty steed,
We'll race throughout the night!
Come fly with me, and we will be
One with the stars on winged flight.
—*Sandy Hearn*

The Radiance

At dawn
The sun cascaded pink,
Filtered through shadowy branches
Brilliant to deepest pink-
Rich against the green of trees,
The blue of skies.
The radiance!
— *Sylvia Semel*

Lonely Roads

Youth,
is a treacherous path
bitter memories choke pleasant ones
failure tramples achievement
The winding path twists
honesty is but blurred truth
of believeing in ones own self.
Love,
is crushed under hurried feet
fantasy crumble before its creator
left is one lonely road to follow
twisting, turning
till roads emerge.
— *Christine K. Cornett*

Beach Sonata

I miss my youth
...a pebble plops
I miss the days when I used to
...a wave gently ripples,
then longingly snores
Ride my bike till I was
...kicked sand flails
furiously in the wind
Free.
...another pebble plops,
then shoots itself into mid-
Air breezes past, like a child
let loose...
...the sun sets regally,
the sand flies into a blue void, and...
I miss myself.
— *Claudia Darde*

The Sun

I sat there, looking on the cloud view.
The sun was shining slim.
It was like an almost burnt out light bulb
trying to light the clouds' silver line.
When I think of the sun, I think of life,
As when the sun rises, people everywhere, try
to feel new, as when the sun sets, we shut down
while others are feeling the sensation of morning.
Where is it written that we shoulld not live each
and every moment God has given us.
We should live up to each day.
Forget yesterdays' memories, tomorrow's future.
Where is it written, when did a wise man say
When will it be known that such a man has
given us a ball of fire—-the light that shows the
way—-our fate, our destiny
The sun.
—*Kerry Wells*

Ferocity of Nature

Lightening streaked the darkened sky,
The thunder booming from on high.
Wind tousled the trees and the branches bent,
And leaves torn away had their freedom and went.
Then a frightening calmness filled the air,
More menacing and threatening than we were aware.
Suddenly hail and heavy raindrops fell,
Pelting and beating and all was not well,
As the azalea flowers with petals so fair,
Were cruelly beaten from branches that bear,
Visions of rainbows that they always bring,
Color and hope and promise each Spring.
For over an hour the rains would not cease,
As the lightening and thunder just seemed to increase.
Then slowly and deliberately the storm moved away,
Leaving raging rivers and destruction this May.
Could it be possible for the sun to beam so bright,
As the raindrops glistened in the early morning light?

— *Valerie Neveraskas Lorenz*

Fall's Love

Fall's a special time of the year,
Just around the corner of our new year cheer.
Fall's a time when the leaves change colors
And it makes the mood so right to want to hug one another.
Walking in the beautiful forest,
Especially walking with the one you love most,
Playing in the leaves over and over,
Cuddling with the one you so much adore.
There's nothing better than falling in love
Other than the love from our Lord above.

— *Caroline Gonzalez*

The Hedges of Southampton

Above them peek the chimneys and now and then a rooftop,
Majestic walls of finely pruned and shaped ligustrum
Hiding well the splendor of their charges.
While sheltering the priviledged, they also shield the passer-by
From waist-high grass or barren land; potato fields abandoned.
Seen from the road, an awesome backdrop for the stately trees that line it.
A common shrub, ligustrum, the tract builder's choice for landscaping.
But here,protectively surrounding their mansions by the sea
It has risen above its lowly beginnings,
Not unlike many who come to live and walk beside them.

— *Nancy Hannan*

The Forest in the Fall

Softly the wind blows around the branches,
And I listen carefully as I walk.
There is not a sound in the forest
Except the chirping of the birds,
The whisper of the tree branches rubbing together,
And the soft crunch of leaves,
That crunch under my feet.

Yellow, red, orange, and brown,
These are the colors of the forest now.
The home where all animals are friends,
Except the hunter-who hunts alone.

The deer chase each other through the trees,
The rabbits gnaw at food together and chat.
The birds chirp to other birds in other trees.
All animals speaking a different language.
This is the fall forest.

— *Nancy Ellyne Swerdlow*

Awaiting the New Day

It's never easy to wait for something,
Especially when you've been waiting for a long time.
Dreams give us something to look forward to.
Hope lets hold on to them.
When it is cold and dark and it seems
As though the sun may never shine again
And you're waiting,
Waiting for a little warmth,
A little reassurance that you haven't
Lost...
Everything
The new day dawns and you are comforted
You can now hope again and hold on to your dreams.
For dreams, keep the soul young
And the heart warm.

— *Valerie Cardenas*

Winter Wonderland

Snow covered trees glistened
At the foot of the bay
Icicles hung from the branches
While sparkling from the moonlit sky.
There is not a living or wandering soul around
The place is so quiet
The bay is frozen over
Everything is sparkling from the ice,
Could this be a winter wonderland?
For no one shall know
For everyone is inside their houses
Keeping warm by a fire in their fireplace,
Perhaps singing Christmas carols, putting up the Christmas tree,
Hanging their stockings, celebrating Christmas.
For that is why no one knows
Of the winter wonderland outside.

— *Catherine Greenwood*

Feelings For You

I still think of you
I hear a song you used to sing.
I see faces that remind me of yours
Just when I think I am over you—I am reminded of my feelings.

I know you will never feel the way I do.
So, I try to convince myself I do not care for you,
But it does not work.
My feelings are so deep, but wasted.
I remember our time together.
If only it would have worked.
I am trying to convince myself it is not your fault,
But the pain is making it so hard.

I can only sit with my dreams and pain.
Dreams of you and I together,
The pain you have caused me,
And the hopes for my future.

— *Kathy Richard*

Now I Love You

As I board the ship, solitary once more after being thrust and jostled
And as I surrender my passport to the purser, your touch comes to rest
On my lids and crown turning the real me to face invisible you
Caress gentle as the wing tip of a butterfly...
You are a gossamer medico momentarily, healing my wound of love.
Now I feel an abyss deep as the sea I sail.
In rememberance a withdrawing into a love of your love
That transports me as the vessel glides from port,
But the revelry of boisterous passengers remove your touch
And I retreat to my cabin. Now alone with the mature knowledge
Of my empty self in your absence, yet overwhelmed by my need
And the distance between us, and by all spans, that of your touch
And that of our lives. Now I love you with a feeling of breaking apart
As the waves break into foam across the bow and recede into a sea
Of deep longing and love as eternal as the universal tides.

—*Lois Riddle*

You Are My Inspiration

We belong together and our love will bloom like a flower and grow
And the love I have for you will be just like a river and flow.
I know a place that is paradise and someday I will take you there.
We will be together and love and laughter we will share.
My heart will skip a beat and paradise will reign like a dove.
Beauty will be all around us and we will exchange our love.
So take my hand and come with me,
I will show you paradise and it will be heavenly.
My eyes will shine like the twinkling stars and your gaze will tell me more.
I will speak your name, for it's you I adore.
Two hearts will beat like one nd our kisses will taste like wine
And when we touch, our love will flow and it will be divine.
Night is the time when stars will shine and the summer breezes will chill the air.
There will be magic all around us and music is everywhere.

— *Joyce Willis*

Age

Sorrow quietly embraces me bringing memories from the past.
Tender mercies abandon me and the darkness has seduced the light.
Tell me why did it come and how long does it last?
Why did you pass from view, and out of my sight?

A bleaker night I have never known,
The violence of the lightning streaks across the stormy sky.
Love drifts away just like fallen leaves that the wind has blown,
Just ashes remain from an aching heart that never again will cry.

Darkness approaches our once faithful dreams.
Bitterness is the only feeling I now know as I turn from life another page;
Silenced voices shout unheard screams,
Hearts once young older did grow and sadly age.

— *Karen Bass*

Pendulum

Searching endless roads, memories worn with traveled time.
Visions of days long gone by, dreams of times before I die.
Destinations, haunted by silent music,
Marking this past place in mind.
Recollections of hopes, as well as expectations,
Some won, others given up.
Defeat stained by wells of tears, cured with joyful laughter.
Scars upon the heart now healed, walls broken down,
Knees cusioned on pillows of desire, with prayers of fulfillment.
Filled with wanton, to abolish all hurt and unfurl all mysteries.
Mesmerized by the events of past futures.
Yet without satisfaction.
My hour glass is glutted with the sediments of time.
In the silence of my abode, I hear the pendulum,
Tick...tick...tick.

—*Robert O. Pugh*

Released at Last

The chains entwined about your heart and mind,
Were shared with great effort on your part,
With those willing to love and care about you.

Adroitly you succeeded in manipulating the shackles
of your creed onto others,
Until; any move, became the wrong move,
Any thought, became the wrong thought,
And any life, became the wrong life.

To find salvation, the only way, became a dagger thrust
Twisting into my bosom, rending my heart into pieces,
Thus, killing the last remnants of what lay between us, setting me free.
As free as the phoenix after a fire of destruction and death,
To soar, among the clouds, reaching
Ever closer to heaven.

—*Karen A. Bowers*

As Long As We Believe

As though it may seem life is just not fair,
When you hold on to someone suddenly, that person is not there.
You stand shocked! Hoping just an illusion
Wishing passed time could come true, the present...only dillusion.

But you face what has happened with guilt and regret
As that person you love, you are trying to forget
You just cannot do that, you can try with all your heart
But you seem only to remember the day that loved one part.

When you think back to times spent in your memory
It gathers happiness together into one truthful story
Of hope and belief and facing the truth
That the memories you have stay on honest youth.

All that person wishes is that you joyfully recall.
For if you think of them with tears and pain,
Just don't think of them at all.

Smile at your memories and don't doubt what Heaven conceives
Loving will last forever, as long as we believe.

—*Stacy Price*

The Promise

Somewhere back in time, deep within the night,
The Lord created a masterpiece which bestowed a glittering light.
This light represented a promise, a promise that surpassed the rainbow.
A promise of life with love and happiness and treasures richer than gold.
Since it is the Lord's masterpiece it is very fragile and very rare.
It sits atop a pedestal for its dedication and its care.
Although it is so precious, it is often pushed away.
People tend to overlook it we progress from day to day.
So together let us thank the Lord for we've all been truly blessed
Through the creation of this masterpiece, our mothers,
our promise of happiness.

— *Julie Pfaff*

The Beckoning Trail

As he did peer across the hidden vale,
The peak alone he saw above the mist
And wondered what might lie along the trail
Which lay between that next point and this.
Standing high among the clouds
The tall, gray structure beckoned
Him to brave the hidden trail
And explore what lay ahead.
So he arose, preparing to descend
Into the mist and seek the trail he saw
Meandering between the lofty peaks
As he did peer across the hidden vale.

—*John Bains*

The Lighthouse

The sky seemed gray as the night was closing in
At the top of the stairway looking out
One could see the calmness that fell upon the ocean
And feel the bitter chill it was sending into the air
Looking through the weather beaten glass
At a faraway distance small lights could be seen
Fishermen in search of the evolving light praying
For signals to get them home for the night
Slowly the walls were becoming cold
The winds were screaming
While the water was smashing below
The lights were no more at a distance
They were now in the cape safely home again
The old lighthouse did it again
Brought everyone's journey to a safe end
For this night has closed to an end.

—*S. Corbett*

The Sounds of Life

As I stand gazing out my back screendoor,
A combination of sweet sounds I enjoy.
The blue birds twitter, my little daughter sings,
And the leaves rustle softly in the wind.
The red bird sings in my red maple tree and
The mocking bird sounds on the barnyard gate.
The grey squirrel chatters to the cat below and
My daughter sings accompanied by her squeaky swing.
In the distance I hear faint call of Bob'olink,
And close crowing and cackling of rooster and hens,
A blend of lifes sounds that embrace my heart,
They sound to my ear like fine blended voices.
I know, standing here, it would be very sad,
If my daughters grew older in years and
They could not enjoy the sounds that I hear.
I pray in my heart, that they are not deprived
Of all the beautiful, simple, sounds of life.

—*Yvonne Kathleen Wade*

Be My Valentine

Be my Valentine, oh honey-child.
Be my Valentine with your lovely smile.
Be my Valentine not for today only.
Be my Valentine because I don't want to be lonely.
Be my Valentine and don't hesitate.
Be my Valentine and don't be too late.
I hope that you are the one for me.
I guess I'll just have to wait and see.
There are many Valentines in this place,
But I'll keep making a sturdy pace.
Yes, I am going to keep on marching for you.
I believe your love for me is true.

— *Sam E. Woods*

The Gentle Way

G is for the good days we shared together...that couldn't be any better.
E is for the enchantment that I tried to give you
 ...on the days you were feeling blue.
N is for never forgetting your birthdays or any other day of the year.
T is for the times when there was nothing too difficult
 that couldn't be understood.
L is for loving you...yes, love that brings understanding
 from all the heavens above that comes in all colors.
E is for eager...all the eagerness I have in wanting to do
 ...the best things especially for you.
 The world spells...
 Gentle...
 Gentle in my way.

— *Lucille Fields Borden*

My Father

Hand and hand he walked me through the journey of life.
Showing me all the beauty, love and joy
That is seen and felt through time.
Although he too showed me all the ugliness, hate and saddness
That is seen and expreienced.
Yet knowing that he was at my side
Holding my hand, made everything all right.
Then, one day, I turned around, looking for his helping hand,
But he was no longer there.
We had grown so far apart in so short a time
That I now knew there was no turning back.
Things would never be the same again.

—*Toni L. Schoen*

To Jer, Who is not Alone

Drifting from emotion to emotion.
No pattern, no rhythm, no reason,
Jump from a plateau of happiness,
To a valley called depression.
Even when we think we are most steady, we sway.
Questions pelt our security barriers.
Am I a good person? Who defines good?
Misfortune follows us throughout our lives.
Death is the cold wind that tails misfortune.
My body has been chilled by such a wind, too many times for my short life.
Sorrow is the darkness that makes us appreciate the light of happiness.
Friends are the moon and the sun.
They are there in darkness or light.
Love is the breath of fresh air that vitalizes fading dreams.
Hope is everything, that restores faith in yourself.

— *Joan St. Peters*

German Boy (Shattered Dreams)

Dreams in pieces like shattered glass, wanted to speak, had too much class.
My tears streaming down my face like the evening rain,
head against the window pane.
Only can see you from afar, only chance is to wish upon a star.
My darling German boy, you were once my friend.
Their deceit and lies made it come to an end.
When you later would talk to me, bitter with tension there I stood.
It hurt me more than you; I'd take it back if I could.
When our eyes meet, I get a certain high, feel light as the clouds in the sky.
Can't get you out of my mind, I try and I try.
When I hear your name, my heart beats fast, throat is dry.
You have forgotten me by now, I am sure.
Meanwhile, in the golden field I wait for a cure.
They say time heals it all, seasons keep passing, winter through fall
As we grow older and more wise in this life,
My pains will grow dull, no more sharpness like a knife.
Handsome, smart, strong and clever, I will cherish
my thoughts of you forever and ever.

— *Susan Kirkpatrick*

How to End Poems

When much more can be said
maybe too much more
you've said enough.

— *Sharon McPeters*

Untitled

Lovely maiden of south beach
Suddenly runs out to me
Just to show me her two-piece
So it seems
Interrupting quite my walk
There is no such thing as talk
Only stalking primitive lust
And she is a real girleen
Lovely as a summer dream
Downy limbs and gold brown hair
Passing lovely, passing fair
And I want to stay there
Yes, that is a nice two-piece
Aren't you nice to show me
And a bruise mark on her ribs
Like some secret language
told me I was never so smitten
In the space of fifteen seconds

—*Frederick Houde Jr.*

My Friend

I had a friend who told me
I really should be me
He said the time had come
I really should be free

Stand on your own two feet,
Stop taking so much heat.

So I gave my friend complete
I opened up down deep
I told him all I knew
I thought that he too grew

And so I let myself just go
How was I to really know
That he would turn on me
He suddenly could not see

That letting me be me
Was not with him for free

— *Leslie Wehle Broaker*

Lasagne

Parmesan, ricotta, tomatoes
wafting to my nose.
I wish it'd go away.
I'm trying to do my geometry.
Mom is making pasta;
she frowns.
We're out of milk
and she doesn't have a job.

I run to the store
and forget my coat.
I shiver, my fingers are raw.

I come home—
The paint is peeling, I realize
the sidewalk is cracked.
I hand my mom the
milk.
The phone rings.

—*Lesley Foxhall*

A Single Rose

A single silk rose
Sits alone on a desk
A rose that once stood
For love, hope and
The promise of tomorrow
Now holds only dreams
And the memories
Of yesterday

—*Kelly S. Mack*

You Were Wrong

Once, a very long time ago
You told me I'd never make it
You were cruel and your words
Were harsh. You cut my soul open
For the world to see
Once, a very long time ago
You left me standing there
I went home to cry and
I cried for weeks
But then I got mad
Once, not so long ago
After years of hard work
I reached my goal or
At least beginning of it
And all without you
So you see, Mr. Butler,
You were wrong.

—*Karen Lai*

The Right Words

The sonnets of Shakespeare
 Don't say what's in my heart;
The poems of Browning
 Don't say what's on my mind.
I've been looking for the right words
 To say to make you mine.

The lyrics of love songs
 Just aren't right enough.
The quotes I've read on love
 Just aren't strong enough.
I've been looking for the right words
 To say to make you mine.

The poems I write you
 Just aren't good enough;
My words are so feeble,
 But words are all I have.
I've been looking for the right words
 To say to make you mine.

—*Joseph Anthony DeLucia*

Recipe for Lasting Friendship

½ cup of patience
½ cup of tolerance
½ cup of kindness
½ cup of understanding
1 cup of love
½ cup of humility
½ cup of freedom
Mix all together and serve as needed,
With a big hug
Great conversation
And a flair of uniqueness
Toss with a pinch of charity
Serving anytime

— *Sylvia Howard*

Desert Blossom

In scorching sun
With cracked lips,
Sandpaper tongue,
My soul knows
Dryness.

But you lead me
To bubbling springs
And desert streams.

And in that wilderness
I rejoice and blossom.

— *Sharon M. Daley*

Freedom

The branches of the old oak tree
swayed and swished
always free.

— *Jenni Wurzbacher*

Time

Time
Will be found,
But has been lost.
It flees from us,
But surrenders willingly.
Some have too much,
Others have too little.
We cannot stop it,
Or start it over.
And once it is gone,
It can never return.
Time...is forever...and ever.

—*Cheryl May*

Untitled

People forever
They don't care
About me and won't
Do the best job they can.
People forever
They don't care
About your feelings.
So care about yourself.
And be happy.
I just hope you don't
Care about me.

— *Calvin Hutchinson*

How Torturous...

How torturous it is
When a flower is snatched
From the stem of existence
Thrown away in the stream
Of forgetfulness
And lost in unknown destiny.

—*Sargon Kheedo*

A Tear

I look across a crowded room,
A tear.
A hint of sadness in one's smile,
Fear.
A heart to be broken soon,
The end is near.
Love, there are no answers,
It is quite clear.

—*Kathleen S. Prophet*

Untitled

One red petal left
And I slowly pull it off
Yes, he loves me not.

— *Danielle Blanke*

Knight in Gold

In the window she sits,
Her hair hangs down.
Never a smile to be seen,
Her face wears a frown.
She sits patiently waiting,
For her true love in gold.
You are foolish to wait
By her mother she is told.
She dreams day by day,
Of her golden knight.
To take her away,
And make her days bright.
Her days will stay empty
Until he appears
Her eyes swollen,
From burning tears.

—*Sheryllyn Florindo*

Questions of Life

I wish I could live
I wish I could die
So hard these days
Seeing eye to eye
Wondering what's wrong
And wondering what's right
Could you believe
I now see the light
I saw it there
It was there that it came to me
What life really should be
It was when I saw
The baby's face
That had such grace
It was then that I
Realized the true meaning
Of life.

—*Danielle Purvis*

Being Alone

I sit in my room,
Of grief and gloom,
No one to talk to,
No one to meet.
No one to say hello,
No one to greet.

I walk along the grey streets,
Brimming with hope.
I live in a world,
Unable to cope.
My hope drains away,
At the thought of yesterday.

 I go back to my room,
Full of webs and coccons.
I am full of sorrow,
Wondering,
What'll become,
Of the morrow.

—*Kathleen Kingeter*

Stand By My Side

In my heart, I feel hurt, for you are my pain.
As a butterfly am I, flying somewhere without destination,
Having life as a unique creation.
Love me, for my heart is condemned, as a fox in a steel trap,
Feeling the coldness of life.
Set me free and heal my wounds.
In my heart I feel bitterness, you are like a Hyena,
Always getting, always laughing, without a care in the world.
What my heart desires is in your heart, like an Eagle.
His mate is for life, he will forever take the wound of the knife.
Stand by my side, for I am equal, I am human.

—*Regina Feliciano*

Goodbye Bryan

I slowly look down upon your face
And give you one last final enbrace.
I kiss your cheek and stroke your hair
As I think of our friendship and how it was so rare.

The pain I am feeling, oh, it's so unreal.
I know the wound in my heart will never completely heal.
Bryan, you were so much better than the rest.
I don't mean to embarrass you, but you were the best.

It seems so unfair that it should happen to you.
You were taken away from us, and why—nobody knew.
I think that God just wanted you now, He just couldn't wait.
It must have been your destiny, it must have been your fate.

I slowly raise myself up, a silent scream explodes in my head.
The moment has come now, the moment of dread.
I kiss you one more time and whisper, *I love you*, into your ear.
I say my final, *Good-bye*, as I wipe away my last tear.

—*Lisa Morris*

Your Special Love

Your a friend who cares
A friend which will listen
A special friend who also shares.
You are willing to share your feelings just for me.
You've been with me through the good and bad
You've done things for me no one else would ever have,
You are that special part of me that makes me smile
You're that special part of me that makes me laugh and makes me cry.
You show me your love in a very special way
A way that is one of your own,
You tell me you care like no one else could
You are yourself and that's why I love you so.

— *Robin Kaye Decker*

The Bagswing

As a child I would swing for hours
Never tiring of the wind rushing at my face, blowing through my hair.
Holding on with two hands, with one
Becoming a daring cowboy riding his wild steed
Who could dare go the highest, from what step could he jump
Yes, for hours I would swing alone or with a companion
Dreaming, playing and daring.

When it would get worn and sagging from the use,
We'd make an event of restuffing the bag with fresh straw,
Of tying it all back up
And of being the first one to swing on the *new and improved*.

Now sadly, its only rider is the wind
Forgotten with time
Lonely swinging
To and fro.

— *Tiffany Benna*

Seasons of Life

Unmarked by sounds that echo the age-old strife between
The warm and cold, our seasons slip away
With a silent song of sorts, and memories drift on back
To long ago times when dreams were real as day.

Forgotten days that drift beyond the veil of thought
Till chance gives birth to a gossamer vessel that seems
To bend our minds on back, remembering little things
That grew until reality faded our dreams.

With the passing of the summertime we slid into
The autumn eventide, and waiting just
Beyond the day of life, a long, cold night is poised
To show the time when dreams have turned to dust.

So endlessly bleak the night descends to drape the land
In unending sameness, covering all like rust,
As time itself is slowly winding down to stop;
When everything has turned to dust.

— *David L. Foster*

The Whistling Wind

Oooh! Oooh! The whistling sound of the roaring wind
Tore my soul asunder.
It tempted me by its restless ways to evermore just wander.
And I, being young, with no roots yet to nourish
Chose this route of the vagabond.
A knight of the road, like the wayward wind
Just blowing from this place to that.
So I gathered my knapsack and went down the trail;
No goal, for I had none in sight.
For the wind, it just wanders, aimlessly on its way.
And that, too, was the way of my heart.
Through the hills, down the dells,
By the streams flowing waters,
Everywhere did I roam with the breeze.
Not a place was excluded,
For this life that I led
Let me wander and rove where I please.
Now my life, it has passed;
Like the sun, it is setting.
Soon my soul, like the wind, will be free.
But I'll always be with you,
Everywhere will I whisper-
Oooh, oooh, won't you come follow me?

—*Robert Weetman*

My Friend Ronald

He is a brilliant leader and a distant friend.
I have not met him personally, but we both
have been setting a very similar trend.
My friend Ronald is a friend, a friend indeed.
He's always thinking about our nation and her every need.
He is taking a difficult job and turning it into ease.
I am understanding now his reasons for spending leave
On his ranch in California, clearing off the land
and chopping logs and trees.
My friend Ronald is doing us all some good.
Perhaps after his brilliant reign as Mr. President,
he and first lady Nancy will once again return to us
through the screen of Hollywood.
My friend Ronald, I have been in your army now since June 18, 1981.
Sir, all I can say is that you are a wonderful leader
and it has been a great big ball of fun.
My friend Ronald, you are appreciated and admired, sir,
by many Americans both young and old.
Furthermore, every word that you speak to the nation, sir,
is worth a ton of pure gold.

— *Rufus Varker Morris*

Camper's Psalm

The Park Ranger is my guide,
I shall not get lost.
He leadeth me beside all Comfort Stations
For my daughter's sake.
He anointeth my head with thunder and rain,
My bucket runneth over.
I do not sleep.
Yea, tho' I walk through the Valley of Lassen,
I fear no trail
For my Ever-Ready flashlight is with me.
My strawberry shortcake and gimlets, they
comfort me.
Surely gnats and mosquitoes shall follow me
all the days of my trip,
And I shall dwell in dirt forever.

— *Julie Hester*

Ode to a Fallen Warrior

(From a War We Have Tried to Forget)

Tho' his helmet's chipped and battered
in the jungle's rotting sand
And his rifle's grasped by the naked bones
of a fighter's sturdy hand
Tho' he's only just a memory
of a long forgotten war
If he had it all to do again
he'd stand and ask for more
For this kind of guy is a breed of man
who gives his all for his loved land
So even tho' he's only dust
on the mortal sands of time
He's a monument of faith and trust
in a place of rest DIVINE.

—*John Morrissey Gray*

The Forgotten House

A little house, a forgotten abode
Set back away from the country road.
Two eyes for windows, a door for a nose,
It's paint was faded like thread bare clothes.

The sparkle in the eyes had long gone out,
With tattered roof and rusty gutter spout.
No fire in its hearth to cheer its soul,
Where the chimney had been—a gaping hole.

Weeds grow in the path that led to the door,
Showed signs—that no one stopped to explore,
It had served its purpose and was left to decay-
Like some aged person who had got in the way.

— *George Gram*

wooden toys

in silence we hide
pledging loyalty we decide
that soon our love will be returned
that soon our souls won't be burned

in vain we tried
in darkness we cried
no one would listen we learned
and soon even from god we turned

we're the children that died
the children that were denied
there is a lesson never learned
the child stands alone even when the courts adjourned

we're lost within a social maze
disguised only by our silent ways
we're broken girls and broken boys
only used and abused wooden toys

—*Victoria Ramirez Martin*

Creation of Love

God made woman from the rib of the man,
The closest thing to his heart, I understand.
Go ye and multiply, build a great nation,
As He watched with love over His creation.
Over the years it became clear to me.
We forgot God's plan in the beginning, don't you see?
Children and parents against one another.
No one to come to the aid of their brother.
He wanted us to love as He has loved us,
But all we can do is argue and fuss.
God gave His own Son to save you and me
And was nailed to a cross for the whole world to see.
The tears He must shed as He looks down from above
And remembers with sadness; it all started with love.
Forgive us, dear Lord, and help us to try
To love one another as time passes by.

— *Louise Evans*

On Growing Old

Rejoice love, in truth you find
Age is but a state of mind.
Years are naught but tempest tossed,
Birthdays more than cards embossed
With smiling faces, flowers, verse.
Engage the ages do their worst.
Let humor be thy rod, thy staff,
Meet days gone by with smile and laugh.
Truth, time's effects we cannot hide
But eternal beauty in truth resides.

— *Tom Champion*

Unreal Reality

Catch a sea of rain in a baby's first cup.
Push the wind to blow boats far.
Scare the lightning with a look of blame.
Watch the blood stream through life veins.

Make time stop when sweet times cheer.
Talk with graveyard dead exchanging sad, true tales.
Cry in heartbreak with a smile and glow.
Smell the spade-turned earth after a winter snow.

Embrace a sweet love but with no touch.
Fondle a hummingbird as it rests from flight.
Catch the laughter of a child at play.
Listen to a fickle-phased moon wax and wane.

Taste the sweetness of an after-rain forest.
Feel the grace of a deer in life flight.
Reality shackles minds and gives no space.
Imagination defies and takes its unreal place.

— *Peggy Ambrisco*

Rules of Love

Reassure me when I'm afraid; miss me when I'm away.
Keep good the vows you made; believe in what I say.
Laugh with me when I'm happy; cry with me when I'm blue,
And when you love me, really love me, prove your love is true.
Correct me when I'm wrong; stand by me when I'm right.
Think of me in the morning, dream of me at night.
Comfort me when I'm lonely; have faith in what I do.
Follow me to the end of the world as I would follow you.
Kiss me softly and gently; hold me tenderly but tight.
If I should lose my temper, please don't let us fight.
When you say you love me, mean it with all your heart
And if you really mean it, even death can't make us part.
Forgive me when I'm not myself; try to understand.
Just put your arms around me and tightly hold my hand.
God bless you when you say your prayers, the way I pray for you,
And tell Him with all your soul to keep our young love true.
Keep these rules of love with everything you have to give
Though rules were made to be broken, but our love was meant to live!

—*Linda Jeanne McGill*

Love

I feel I own the heavens
Since falling in love with you, my dear.
And the earth it moves a little
Whenever you come near.

And now I own the universe
For you have said you love me too
Evermore, I will return your love
And walk on a path of stars to you.

—*Grace Pearson*

Stepping Out

She stepped out of her body
To recollect her life
Her face was drawn with terror
And pain peirced like a knife

She stepped out of her kingdom
To see how the other half lives
Her eyes grew yet still wider
With a look she seldom gives

She stepped out of her present
To recall her distant past
Her mind cleared of delusion
Will the truth be known at last?

She stepped back to her present,
Her kingdom, her body, herself
And I knew the minute I saw her
It was me looking back at myself

—*Shirley Ann Bradley*

Snow

As I sit here
I'm watching
Snowflakes fall softly,
gently to the ground.

The snow's so white,
so pure.
It leaves a beautiful
blanket on the ground.

Snow is beautiful as long as
I'm inside and it's outside.

— *Julie Mollander*

Aftertime

Seems to me
I've been here before
through yellowed with the passing of time
still unchanged.

Reflections of performed futures
jest me in dance
only to dissipate
at the fusion of conception.

— *Debby Sereda*

Sun Set Sun Rise

Golden rays beam from the sky
As the sun goes down to hide.
Slowly fading out of sight
Giving way to the night.

Darkness floating all around
Time goes by without a sound
A peaceful calmness fills the air
A time of silence everywhere.

Then peeking through the edge of night
Shinning with all its light.
The sun coming up as if to say,
Good morning America, land of the free
Good morning America, it is only me.

—*Leanna Howard*

The Hermit Hope

Demons rage within my mind
Fighting for control
Rending the fabric of my life
Savaging my soul.
An angel hovers overhead
Occasionally she gleans
From the battlefield left behind
Some seed of shredded dreams.
With compassion she buries it
Smoothing the trampled ground.
Vowing to watch over it,
With a soft and fluttering sound
She unfolds her wings and glides away
Into the stormy night.
Now a hermit hope in the ravaged field
Sprouts in the dawning light.

—*Patricia Fain Hutson*

Lyrica

Lyrica shall be the name
Of the child born the poet.
A child of black flowing hair,
Cyan eyes of depth
Knowing the edge to dare

The keeper of time,
The sleeper of mind.
Let her paint the landscape
With the rimes of poetry.
Let her point man's escape
With the chimes of prophecy.

Be her not a witch,
Be her not a magician,
But an artist
With the touch of a physician,

A torchbearer
Of her father's tradition.

—*Mark Antony Rossi*

The Unpainted Cat

Colors and contours of my imaginary cat
With a bent mind and a twisted tail;
So aimlessly it wades through the puddles
Of my amateurish water-color painting.
Tiring, it delicately steps off the edge
Of the moist paper and heads for the door;
These words trailing behind:
I'll be back later when you've improved.
A rainbow of pawprints are there on the floor.

— *Judy Rinard*

Color It Love

Lavender lights the evening sky,
The day is an azure blue.
Our world is like a rainbow.
Love brightens every hue.

Indigo nights with silvery stars,
Precede the sapphire dawn.
The golden sun sends warmth our way,
As we lie on an emerald lawn.

We watch the scarlet sunset,
Over a sea of aqua blue.
Then comes the amber twilight,
When love is always new.

An apricot moon birghtens the night,
The stars are like diamonds above.
Together we wait for tomorrow.
And the rainbows color of love.

—*Christine Bright*

The Liar

When I was just a little child,
I had a special bent.
I found that it was really wild.
I practiced my talent.

It started with a little lie,
But I improved with age.
I was always able to get by.
I was constantly on stage.

My parents never needed to scold.
They always believed in me.
Because the stories that I told
Were full of creativity.

And now I am a big success.
Politicians rely on me.
I write their speeches, with finesse,
For a humongous fee.

—*Anne-Marie Krause*

Thought

Alone I sit upon my bed.
A million thoughts dance through my head.
Faces jump and memories climb
A fading look at passing time.

A tinted light, a window brings.
To hide the pain when sorrow sings.
What makes it hard for one to see
A lonely man, someone like me.

The years turn back, the wheels roll on
What makes us grip to what is gone.
Why do we hold these woven thoughts
Within our minds for ever caught.

—*Ron Elliott*

Giant Sequoias

Stand still and you'll hear it, the dampening silence
Sounding the centuries of snow covered trees.
Here with the giants, standing as witness
To cycles and seasons with unpeopled peace.
This silence unknown to summer or spring
No buzzing, no humming, no bird's winged flight.
No sun shining down, now shadow, no glare.
A cold grey ceiling suffices for light
As if in a dream, muffled noise in the distance
Inaudible whispering hushing the leaves.
Around us the forest, flocked in a snow coat.
Redwoods and fir trees as far as we see.

— *Wendy Silberman Pennes*

The Night Has Come

Alas, the darkness blackens the heavens:
It draws its curtains of soot across the vast lands
And the moon brightens the entire barren sky,
The glittering stars scatter in the distance.
Yes! The night has come.

The enveloping shadows cool the day burned sand,
Flowers fo to sleep in a deceptive manner.
The soft swishing sounds of breeze and that
Of the croaking frogs fall on deaf ears,
The drk and clear waters stroll lazily.
Yes! The night has come.

The creatures cuddle themselves
And the sweet voices of the birds die.
The entire atmosphere is filled with dreams;
Sleep, the only desire now, gropes in a deep darkness,
The shade of darkness crawls over us,
The black waves descend on us.
Yes! The night has come.

—*Eric Bimpong*

Ode to a Human's Appendage

There she sits, forelorn, alone,
While I wait, worry and moan,
Left to remember the countless miles
We traveled together as one.
We loathed cold mornings.
While she'd groan and cough
I sat shivering, waiting for her warmth
To envelope both of us.
Her loyalty never wavered,
Though times I neglected her needs.
Soon they will come and take her away
But when they bill me, I will gladly pay
Any amount for a well running car.

—*Jo Truman*

Lamb

There's been so many jokes
about Mary's sweet lamb.
One more or less cannot matter.
They've attacked the poor critter
from north, south and west—
No wonder, he had a strained bladder.

Mary, they say, gave birth to the lamb.
They accuse her of out and out incest.
When the truth is to be told,
(By one half as bold)
He was simply a pet and a pest!

How they talk about Mary
with such undetones,
causing friction and made Mary hate 'em.
Not once did she kiss
the lamb on the lips,
she just barbecued him...and ate him.

—*C. L. Vincent*

My Mind

Darkness is in the corners of my mind
Where undreamed dreams
And new thoughts lie
Where things that must be spoken
Lie waiting to be said
And poetic lines
Are formed slowly in the head
Where things that I have learned
Are stored while they're not in use
And the wrong things that I've done
Fill my mind up with abuse
Where my future is uncertain
And the present does not exist
Where the past is but a memory
I call this darkness.

—*Dawn Bryan Myers*

Disposable Planet

We tread this earth with callous feet.
Beneath her tainted skies.
Her forest shrinking in defeat
With acid tears she cries.

We fly our flags in her soft wind
Our colors bright and proud.
Although against her we have sinned,
Our banner's now her shroud.

We sail her seas filled with our waste
Displayed upon her shore.
Her beauty now has been disgraced
And yet we do it more.

We search the heavens with great care
And telescopic eyes.
A greedy hope within our stare
As this poor planet dies.

— *Laurel Newton*

The Flag Inside My Heart

The flag had flown high and strong,
But now the war made life all wrong-
The flag now flew at half mast;
To accept the hurt
Was an unsought task.
The crowd was cheering
For people
They had not known,
While my heart was bearing
What grief bestowed.

— *Michelle Renaud*

Good-Bye

Like the weeping willows
I cry on my pillow.
When you said to me, *I cannot love you any more,*
As if loving me had been such a terrible chore,
I did not want to become your faithful wife.
I just wanted to be a part of your life.
Let's not remember out endless fights,
Only the long, romantic moonlit nights.
So now you may leave me alone to cry.
Good-night, my darling, fairwell, good-bye.

— *Michelle Eichacker*

Loch Ness Monster

Nessie is a marvelous beast.
On algae and kelp she does feast.
She's quiet and shy
And no one knows why.
Some have seen her,
Some went down on a sub,
Some on the way home from the pub.
But all do agree
That it's best she lives free
Because Nessie is a marvelous beast.

— *Jennifer Ann Liles*

My Loved

My love,
There are so many ways
I wnt to say I love you...
But I am torn between
My timid self and your distant heart.
Looking at the sky,
I see your eyes a million miles away...
Oh when will you fill my soul
With the warmth and spirit
Of your love?

— *MiYung Susan Lee*

Feed a Cold and Starve a Fever

Feed a cold and starve a fever
Is what they say to do,
Whenever I have both of these
In what they diagnose the flu.

But how can I starve that fever
Or feed that cold
If I have them both together.
Which one do I do, I must be told.

It is impossible for me to try
To starve the one and feed the other.
I cannot do it that I know,
What I can do is call my mother.

My mother told me I was a puzzle,
She gave me an answer quick.
Have a cold or a fever never both
If I must be sick.

—*Rita O'Brien*

I Have Known Anger

I have listened to anger;
  heard the stormy waves crash against the shore,
  the guns fire without mercy.
I have witnessed anger;
  seen the red flames turn blue skies black,
  the fire sweep through war-torn lands.
I have sampled anger;
  tasted the bitterness on my tongue,
  the acrid, choking smoke.
I have breathed anger;
  smelled the burning fields,
  the odor of death.
I have held anger;
  felt the unbridled fury,
  the stinging burn.
I have known anger;
  realized the terrifying nightmare,
  the agonizing truth.

—*Katrina Reef*

A Winter's Tune

The northeast wind sings
And the branches sway in
Time to the music.
Winter's blanket,
White with snow,
Contrasts with the blacks and grays
Of the village beyond.
The rising pitch of the wind combines
With the drone of a nearby snowplow
To create a symphony of conflicting
Forces...
One natural,
The other not.
Mother Nature laughs
And takes her time
Composing a song for spring.

— *SJM*

Untitled

Droplets spot the window of our small car.
The silence grows to monumental height.
Why, I wonder, are you near, but so far?
The forecast told of wet and rainy nights.

Pressing my face against the window pane,
I think of days when I was all you knew.
Now memories flow unbidden through my brain.
The mist across my eyes distorts the view.

Days we threw a frisbee at each other,
Talking of Zen and quoting Robert Frost.
Sun filled times we played with one another.
Cold winter nights and cribbage games you lost.

As windshield wipers cut through sheets of rain,
I realize we cannot go back again.

—*Laura Moulton*

Loneliness

There is a man that lives in a zoo.
He is so lonesome that he wants one too.
When there is rain and people come to the place.
He leaves and goes to outer space.

Now one day he went too far;
And hitched a ride on a shooting star.
He thought this was like riding a kite,
So he contemplated traveling the speed of light.

If a photon I could be,
Then this would be the life for me.
A photon travels the speed of light,
And does away with time and sight.
I would come from days past,
And travel into the everlast.

— *Allen Larman*

Your Shadow

The world has turned, another day
Sunlit skies, will fade away
The moon is full, so big and bright
The shadow blends into the night

Your shadow's brave and strong of will
Turn to see it standing still
No heart, no soul, or brain to think
Your shadow does not swim or sink

No independence that is a fact
Your shadow now can just react
Longing just to be set free
Turn and find your shadow's me.

—*Mike Fitzpatrick*

The Writer's Recitation

He had a story to tell,
but fear kept him from telling it.
Around him, the music of voices kept dancing.

He hunched over the podium,
turtle-like and tried
—struggled to speak the words he'd written
while within his protective shell of solitude.

A few painful false starts...
his mouth clicking
making the same sound a cat
makes as it creeps toward its prey.

Finally he pounced upon the words,
but still we could see him tremble-
he disarmed us with his fear
and then he killed us with his words.

— *Sharon L. Burghard*

Snow Flakes

We may be tiny—we may be light
But don't underestimate our might
Sometimes we fall softly in the night
With howling winds paint the great earth white
Folks view us with such great awe and fright
But we can be a beautiful sight
Man can't stop us whether wrong or right
Traffic stop—We make their world sit tight
Then we accumulate to great height
When the sun comes out we make our flight

— *Margaret E. Wright*

The Mannequin

I pass the store each morning.
Pre-cise-ly at eight!
She's always there, all dressed up.
She smiles, I always wave.
But she wasn't there this morning.
So, I looked in the door.
She was standing by herself,
Way back in the store.
I saw them take her up the stairs,
And they stood her in a crowd.
I snuck back, there was a sign that read,
ONLY MANNEQUIN'S ALLOWED!
I guess it was wishful thinking,
That she smiled at me that way.
But every morning, when I passed her store.
She really made my day!

—*Cynthia Kollin*

Suicide

She was nice, considerate and kind
But had problems within her mind
She had troubles that is no doubt
But about them she did not pout.
Inside of herself was a constant fight
She fought it with all her might.
Although I was on her side
She still committed suicide.

—*Sarah Russell*

The Football Game

First there is a marching band
Marching across the fielded land.
Playing all instruments loud,
Facing toward the roaring crowd.

The referee soon walks out,
Tossing and turning the ball about.
Players coming from all directions
Hoping and planning for interceptions.

Players pads knocking around
An uptight feeling from the sound.
After all this has gone on,
The players all go off the lawn.

The winning team is happy and proud,
The losing team has failed the crowd.
Soon they will come back again
And each of the teams will try to win.

—*Shantele Rosseau*

Changing Wishes

I remember climbing the steps and trying to see
Over the mountains and across the sea
Straining my body in every way known
Begging and pleading just to be shown

They just smiled at me, looking down
Talking with words that had no sound
Saying, *wouldn't it be nice to be like you,
When all our worries would be just few!*

So I kept quiet waiting for time
But by then I'd figured the rhyme
The more you see, the less you know
The longer you wait, the harder the blow

There comes a time when your fantasy
Turns to cold, harsh reality
Now that I am old and have seen it all,
I frequently look back and wish I was small.

—*Jessica Victoria Kida*

My Love For You

It takes more than just words to let you know
How much our relationship means to me
It would be so hard to have to let go
For my love for you will always be so
You are always there to give me a hand
To assure me of everything I do
For you are the only one to understand
My love for you could never be as true
Ever since the first day I met you
I knew from that moment on, I loved you
It was strange that our love just grew and grew
As beautiful as the sky is so blue
There will come a time when you are no more
I will never love like I had before

—*Cheryl White*

Friends

A friend like you, I want to keep
When I need you, please don't leap
I wish I knew, just what to say
To make you see what I need today.

A real good friend
Who cares about me
Who when I'm around
Acts like me...you see...

I need someone I can talk to
Who will know just what to do.
When I am down and want to blow away
Who can get my spirits back up to stay

I think you can
I know you can
I'm glad you can
Because I need you...

— *Shannon McCord*

The Turning of a New Leaf

I turn now
To face the world below.
Yes, I think I will take it
With me to the greater world
That I must now call my own,
Where there are no exceptions,
Only ones of equal or greater goodness.

What remains left behind?
I don't remember.
What am I taking with me?
Only the knowledge of a greater world
And the turning of a new leaf.

— *Maren McConnell-Collins*

How Special Am I?

You told me I was special
And I, of course, believed you
You always told me you needed me
Until now, because we are through

You are my one and only,
Is what you whispered in my ear
You were the one who smiled and laughed
And wiped away my tear

But now I sit in silence,
Alone in my own dreams
You lead me to think you cared
Or so that is the way it seems

So alone I am waiting,
And I keep asking myself why
Am I the one you wanted
How special am I?

—*L. Shannon Andrew*

On Speaking Vulgar

No imagination does it take
To speak base, or obcene too
But wit takes things true
Skillfully creating an earthly view
Not only of the coarse
But the celestial as well;

Thus two truths are told as one
And wicked goodness chimes wedding bells
Head and tail merge
Anti-Christ reigns
And the poet exclaims
I am alpha and omega.

—*Ron Wright*

Reflection

I saw a hand that once had grace,
That once was soft, yet supple, strong,
Where skin was clear with youthful glow
And slender fingers held the promise of time.
It clutched the glass with evident pain,
And raised the wine to sip.
Now knuckles bent and fingers gnarled,
I wondered where my time had gone.
— *Marti L. Wheat*

Remembrance

I think of him constantly.
The shape of his face.
The feel of his lips against mine.
On quiet summer days,
I feel his arms around me
Holding, comforting, loving.
His eyes watch me,
Memorizing the shape of my body;
Awakening the passion in my soul.
He is with me always.
In my dreams.
Reminding me,
There is no need to be alone.
To hear his voice, touch his smooth skin,
Is a reminder
Of the time we have spent.
—*Mitzie Smith*

An Endless Sleep

Death,
An endless sleep
Of total darkness
While my soul keeps.
Is this what I have,
To look forward to in my life?
To lie upon a bed,
Upon which there is no strife?
To sleep for all time,
Unaware of any changes,
With my mind
Locked in cages?
My thoughts unable to escape,
My words to lie unspoken
I think that I shall hate,
This treasure token,
Called death!
—*Melissa D. Wolter*

My Corner

I go to my corner
When life gets too tough
And when the clouds hide the sun
My corner has none

When the news of the world
Is frightening and dim
My corner is there
Offering peace from within

Now my corner's not big
Nor is it too small
But it helps me each day
To find goodness in all

And when the world looks to be
A somewhat better place
I come out from my corner
With a smile on my face
—*Michelle Joyce*

I Wonder Why

As I sit over the ocean,
As I look into the sky,
As I dream of all I can be,
And I often wonder why.
Because it's never clear to me.
But then just one look in your eyes
Tells me all I need to know.
Because now I know I'll never let you go.
I watch the sunrise and I watch the sun set,
And I'll always remember the friend I have met.
You make me laugh and you make me cry.
And now I'll never have to wonder why.
— *Misty Peters*

My Friend

Alone, he stands on the hallway stairs,
The lamp light shing in his golden hair.
It was time for him to leave, his time had come.
How could anyone so smart have been so dumb?
He was offered a drink, and he chose a beer
Then wiping away his last, remaining tear,
He yelled his very last goodbye.
It was a lonely, hollow cry.
I was watching the news when I heard his name
His car had crossed the center lane.
And now to my very best friend,
A tear and my regrets I send.
—*Michelle R. Swartz*

A Babbling Brook

A babbling brook is made of streams
It's a kind of stream you have in your dreams
It has water that is crystal clear
The water sparkles when you are near
The sparkling, clear water is calm and cool
Just as if it were a swimming pool
Its beauty enhances the entire place
As if it were a satin lace
People go to brooks to think
Sometimes they go there to have a drink.
— *Michelle Abejon*

Myself

Sometimes I see myself and I'm afraid.
I see corners of my soul untouched,
Apart from the rest of me,
And I feel unable to grasp it.
Sometimes I see myself
And imagine boundaries undiscovered, and unprotected,
And I fear for peace of mind.
Sometimes I see myself
And envision dreams into my reality
And ponder where lies the difference.
Sometimes I see myself
And wonder why I exist,
For my presence is unclear to me
And the search seems endless.
But most times, I realize these visions
Are mere stepping stones on a path
To enhance my growth
And enable me to become my true self.
—*Toni Gopee*

Tired

Oh I'm just so tired,
need to go away,
want to see the raindrops
cry into the bay.
want to see a rainbow
dance about the sky,
and watch the world of cloudliness
echo through my eyes.
do you hear the chorus
singing in the field?
they sing a song of beauty;
love and peace do yield.
do you want to learn to fly,
soar on through the sky?
do you want to go away?
aren't you just so tired?
— *Michelle Napoli*

Untitled

So many people
Rushing busily by
Yet there he lays
Helpless and deprived
Not one smile
Not one hello
To brighten up his day
Noone to care
No food being shared
Or fire to keep him warm
I slowly bend
To touch his withered body
Only to find it stiff; cold
Left dead in a darkened loneliness
— *MiChelle Montgomery*

Life...

It starts seeping
Through the chains and doors

It grows quietly
Soaking into minds

Feelings make us move
Reaching towards a goal
Encouraging by its warmth
Entering our souls
Defended without doubt
Ours to always hold
Master of the heart
—*Mayra C. Diaz*

The Untitled World Is Alone

The untitled world is alone.
It is afraid,
It is always found somewhere
In a lonely heart.

It is yet to be explained,
It is never to be described.
It can always be seen
In an empty place.

An untitled world,
An empty heart;
Destiny unknown.
—*Matt Hogsett*

Like a Beautiful Diamond in the Sky

Like a beautiful diamond in the sky
Shining from bluest Heaven,
Just like a dream you came along
With your eyes that shine above evening stars.
Your face appears to me
Gazing at me with a smile.
One heavenly moment you are in my embrace.
Let me feel the bliss of your thrilling kiss.
It's the nearest to Heaven I know.
Oh, just let it keep on forever.

Let's sing and dance with all our glory,
This night forever.
Mother earth gives the moon for lovers
With its mystic light divine,
For all the world to know
Like a beautiful diamond in the sky.

— *Marie S. Lembo*

Lost Innocence

Move away,
For you'll never stay.
Lust is all you want,
True love you've never brought.
Why surprised?
Are you afraid I've finally wised?
Yes, I have grown.
And forever more it will continue to be shown.
Innocence lost,
My very own it has cost!
How deeply for you I cared,
But to show any real love, you never dared.
Mistaken affection, for I thought of you as perfection.
So far from you I now must go,
Because right from wrong I've begun to know. All of my pain,
That you have caused, has made that innocence of mine forever lost.

—*Jennifer K. Levinsky*

Knowing Love, Without Saying Nothing at All

As I stand here looking up to the sky
Down my cheeks, I can feel the tears run
For out of the corner of my eyes
I catch a glimpse of the sun

He is looking down from above
Watching over me night and day
Sending down his pure sweet love
As I kneel to pray

But as I walk across the land
I can hear God's call
So I reach out my hands
Without saying nothing at all

As I know my time has come
I look to the present from the past,
And the lives I've touched of some for now,
I am going home at last.

—*Mary Margaret Pester*

Old Flame

The yearning that lies inside is a sin,
Craving your love to fill me within.
On lonely days and restless nights I suppress
The desire to feel your tender caress.
But a kiss from you now would blister my heart,
For love is what keeps us so far apart.
Or is it the fear that we once melted too well,
That keeps us from responding to the passionate swell.
Why can't the wave in my soul crash on new sand?
There's this emptiness inside me I don't understand.
Yet the emptiness within will constantly yearn,
For you are an old flame that will forever burn.

— *Julie Graves*

A Plea For Robbie

Every house has its ghosts
The same holds true for mine
He screams, he bangs, he raps and taps
He is a poltergeist
The spirit of a child that once was
Destined to remain here
Forever on Earth
No way out, no way home
Victim of a curse
He must roam this planet alone
Heaven put his soul to rest
In his lifetime he did his best
Take my noisy ghost into your care
And know that he will be happier there
And see to it that those who bound him here
Will find out what it is like to spend a hundred years
Roaming the Earth in disgrace
Searching for their eternal resting place

—*Theresa Campbell*

This Child

This is the child who runs on wobbly legs,
Waving his chubby arms.
This is the child with the chocolate face,
The one with the the muddy hands.
This is the child who argues,
I don't want to, In a minute!
This is the child who is busy with play,
He gives quick hugs and sticky kisses.
This is the child who whispers softly so friends don't hear,
I love you Mama, forever and ever.
This is my child

— *Mary Beth Engle*

A Message

Have you found him?
He's here.
Have you looked for him . . . everywhere?
Can you see him . . . anywhere?
Do you know him?
Do you care?
This man is strong . . . and never wrong.
Would you fight for him?
Or do you care?
He's filled me with love and such a song.
He's powerful and never weak.
He loves you and you should seek.
For his love runs so deep.
Just reach out to him . . . he's there.
Take his hand and share.
Like other's . . . the undying love of our lord above.

— *Sheila Aniballi*

Summer's End

Summer is me.
Summer is you.
Summer is all of us put together as two.
For when summer ends I'd like to die.
Then I see my friends break down and cry.
Some parts go fast.
While others go slow.
But somehow they always seem to go.
We go see friends far and near.
But I have always come back right here.
My beach is fun as it sits under the sun.
Then the sun goes in and that begins the fun.
By this time we know what we have seen
And what we are going to see. But maybe it's you
Or maybe it's me.
But summer's end has always meant to be.

—*Jennifer Sanifer*

The Cows Still Walk the Meadows

The words from her mouth roared in the wind.
Gradually, slowly, deadly, hitting the pours
in her face, while pulling
unnecessary tears from her eyes.

Somewhere else in time the cows still walk the meadow.
The buses make their runs
While the towns people
Go to Church...only on Sundays.

Yet, somewhere else, someone wondering.
Tomorrows time
Taking a ride to an ocean
Asking questions, unable to answer.

Slowly driving back
Only to find
The cows still walk
the meadows.

—*Karen J. Ross*

The Farm

Oh, how I love to be back on the farm,
To be able to smell the freshly cut hay,
And to see the steam rising off the manure pile.

Oh, how I miss the wide open spaces,
The acres and acres of lush grass,
And the gently rolling hills.

Oh, how I yearn for the peacefulness,
Sitting at a nearby stream,
Or laying in the tall grass, gazing at the drifting clouds.

Oh, if only I could hear those familiar sounds,
The clucking of hens,
The squealing of pigs,
And the rustling hay being tossed back and forth in the breeze.

— *Soren Schneider*

In a Garden

In a garden brown and bare,
I saw messengers of spring.
Oh, it's true, no flowers fair,
But a shooting sprout was there.

In a garden brown and bare,
I saw messengers of spring.
Oh, it's true, no bluebirds dare,
But a redbird's flare was there.

In a garden brown and bare,
I saw messengers of spring.
Not in colors bright and rare,
But the blue of sky was there.

— *Margaret Allison*

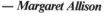

A Cow

I wonder what it would be like to be a cow?
To eat and drink all your stomach would allow.
You'd never have to worry about the weight you would gain,
Or outgrow your clothes or exercise again.
You may have to walk to your food when it's served,
There'd be no hot kitchens, burned food and ragged nerves.
Then, when you're finished eating, there's nothing to do,
But lay around in the grass and enjoy the view.
When a cow gets pregnant, (that's the problem I had)
Nobody whispers, *Not again! How many now? Ye gad!*
A cow has no worries, no problems at all,
Except for producing calves and milk, she's having a ball.
But then you start thinking how very dull it would be-
Not to be able to sing, to love, to laugh with glee.
No sled riding downhill with your kids on a winter day,
No family to love, watch grow, in their own special way.
So, maybe it is best to be content as God made us,
Let a cow be a cow, and we stay just as we *was.*

—*Susanne B. Stroup*

My Best Friend

As I look out in the early morning
I see the birds in the trees.
The sheep are in the meadows
They are frolicking in the breeze.
The children romp and play
Enjoying the brand new day.
Everything seems wonderful but I have tears,
Today I lost a friend.
She has been with me for twelve years.
My Boxer dog named Dinky
Who loved me through thick and thin.
She shared my good and bad days
And helped me when I cried,
She licked the tears away
And showed me that she cared.
I miss he so very much
My wonderful Friend.

—*Lurena Buzan*

The Bug

I saw a bug upon the wall
What I wanted to do was make it fall.
I chased that booger around the room
I sealed his fate, he met his doom.

But lo, behold, across the floor
A bigger one right near the door.
I quickly ran toward this creep
Into the carpet he nuzzled deep.

To the kitchen I swiftly ran
I opened the cupboard and grabbed the can.
I raced to the spot where he had crept
I sprayed the Raid into the depth.

That ugly varmit, out he came
Trudging through the mist of rain.
Alas he staggered, soon he fell
I'm sure that roach went straight to hell.

—*Joanne Spece*

Weeds

Dear Lord, why did you make weeds?
Or is that really what they are—
Could it be they're a symbol of our faults
That must be pulled out here and there?

If we get them—top and roots and all,
Then we rid outselves of sin;
But if we only get some part-
Then we have to try again.

Let your graces fall as the gentle rain,
And nourish my flowering heart-
Let me be able to weed out sin,
And the faults that keep us apart.

Keep the garden of my soul
Free from sin and evil weeds-
Let the rain ever wash it clean,
To follow only your good deeds.

—*Mary J. Schulte*

The Busy Bee

There once was a busy bee
That buzzed all the way up a tree.
He had dinner first
But came down with a burst.
The other bees just watched in glee.

— *Karrie Duke*

The Last of the Blue Sky

The sky grows dark
Gray clouds emerge
Two cresents of dull color
Ready to merge
Caught in between
Is the last of the blue sky
In seeing this sad world
It's the closing of God's eye
The eye gets smaller
Blue now almost extinct
Raindrops begin to fall now
The cresents becoming linked
Looking up above
Where all the cover is gray
It's the last of the blue sky
That's sadly gone away.

— *Mary Comstock*

The Song

A bird,
lost,
trying to sing its song-
unable to reach the tree
that God meant
it to perch on
gives its few strong feathers
to another
younger bird,
praying that it will
be able to reach
that tree
and sing the song
for the older
weaker birds
that are now
unable
to fly.

—*Amanda Skidmore*

Silver Bird

Sweet silver bird
Consumed by the fire
Silent tears
Burning desire
A new beginning
Follows each end
Rise as the Phoenix
Fly once again
Sweet silver bird
Beautiful flyer
The Spirit is with you
Climb higher and higher
Sail across the heavens
Soar up to the sun
Descend to earth
Bring light to everyone.

—*Kristine Drennen*

In and Out A Vision

Sometimes I let my mind wonder to depths not near
Far beyond where anything precious is constant or clear.
While there I cannot worry why you ever stay or leave
For just that brief young moment I am totally carefree.

In silent, yet brightening moonlight I vent my fears through shadows,
And they stay there sometimes longer than anyone ever knows.
But in the desparation of darkness I catch myself by surprise,
And tiptoe around the memories where all the anger lies.

The trees will whisper to me, as they often do,
Each branch is a feeling that leads to and away from you.
And when morning shines upon me, and the bluest sky lies in my hand,
It is like a little baby leading me back to the vivid fantasies again.

When my hair is warm and soft from the sun's silver rays
My thoughts are aimed towards a future neverending day...
When you and I are flowers hidden among long, tall blades of grass
My leaves are slightly wilted, and my petals somewhat dried
But with all your many colors, you do try to keep me satisfied...
Yet before I ever knew it, the vision had to pass

    —Kellie Entwisle

One Long-Stemmed Red Rose

A guy I used to care about, a guy I used to know,
Now he's acting like he cared a very long time ago.
We used to share our time together; we used to laugh and cry,
But now the only word from him I hear is, *Good-bye.*
I know he used to care, but now he won't let it show.
I really wanted our friendship to grow.
He hurt me in a way I just can't explain.
Now all I feel towards him is all my hurt and pain.
I've been up every night and all I do is cry.
If I could ask him just one question, then what I'd ask is, *Why?*
I've had so many heartaches, so many broken places
And all the memories in my mind are of all their handsome faces.
His image is too big now and he's got so many other girls
That I guess he's forgotten me, the blonde girl with the curls.
All I can be is myself, but I guess I'm not good enough for him.
I hope that pretty soon, my heart will start to mend again
'Cause crying doesn't bring him back, and all I have to show...
...Is a heart all broken up...and one crumpled, long-stemmed red rose.

    —Shannon Mehl

Untitled

I always believed times would change, that I would live a better life.
I should have known better.
I always thought of the way things could be if she were here,
But I've changed; I've lost all sense of hope.
That was the only thing that I believed would make the difference.

Who do you turn to when you all of a sudden are left alone?
I want to share, to be that special someone to the one
who thought dreams were never possible.
I want to be a part of a world where we can share our thoughts and our
Fondest memories, to feel that our world
is the world that we chose as our own.

I do wish for a dream.
Sometime, somewhere, someplace a dream will come true
for someone who believes.
Our world will be a world of peace, a world where
we alone can live and breathe as one.
We will remember, not forget, happiness is shared, never lost.

I'll find her someday, that special someone who
I can take like a kitten and hold close to my heart.
Like an injured bird that I can care for and love
until once again it is flying free.
I will love her for the feelings that we will share.
But 'til then, I must wish that my dream can come true only if I believe.

    —Scott McConnell

Love of Life

Be not afraid. Take my hand and walk with me.
Take my arm. I will be your anchor.
I will not let you fall, nor will I let you go astray.
I am here as long as you need me. Love of life is so precious.
When you are ready to go on your own, remember these words:
To learn the profound wisdom and to know the difference,
To build hope to one foundation,
To build life with determination
That holds its dream to come true.
Remember what I taught you:
In time of despair, when someone else needs help
By giving your part of yourself to care for others,
Later on in life you will be richly rewarded by
Love, respect and kindness.
Love of life is to give your inner strength to go on
With courage to stand, that nothing will stop you
From reaching your goal. At last, someone else will follow your
Footsteps for a better world to live in.

    —Sandra Cook

The Piano

The piano is loud and clear and sharp.
The piano varies in size.
The piano is beautiful.
It has a melody no other instrument can withstand.
The piano is my favorite.
It doesn't even need a stand.

    — Sara Kiber

A Storm of Emotions

A storm is brewing in the lonely night
as emotions inside of me grow to a new height.
The darkness is broken for only an instant, but the rumbling lingers on.
Lightning flashes relief upon the clouding sky
as your soothing face flashes through my mind.
The thunder grows and the rain follows just as my feelings rage,
pouring tears to release the growing sorrow.
The earth welcomes the water as it has not felt
its soft touch in what seems like years,
As I wait for you only with the soft touch of your memories
and the abundance of water that is my tears.
Lonely is the earth without the rain as it stands almost peacefully,
but my tears are my only comfort,
As I live in the hands of loneliness.
Oh, can I last to see you again?
As the earth knows it can wait.

    — Robin Pellegrino

No One Will Ever Know

Cold winds whisk through the grey, desolate forest on an autumn night,
But especially around a certain tree.
This tree was beautiful once,
All marveled at him, although he never knew it,
And he took for granted that he wasn't, and never would be special.
Pain and neglect lurked about him.
He was a hideous monster, doomed to stand alone forever,
Even if only in his eyes, but that was enough
No one could help him now, even if they knew his thoughts,
And in his most painful, yet happiest hour,
He shed his last leaf into a nearby fire that was left by some passerby.
And as he watched a part of himself die, he began to wish his whole self
dead.
And as he continued to watch the leaf burn,
He bent his branches over into the flames,
And they quickly leaped upon him as if his life meant nothing.
And although he felt pain, it was nothing like the pain already inside,
So he didn't even try to save his life, but instead
He was glad it was being taken.

    —Joy Sterrantino

Reality

Here I am alone again
With people all around me
The silence of this moment, Lord
It's calm and soothing
The world would lure me to its pace
But there is a new day dawning
To dwell on You and all Thy grace
There is quietness and calmness with thee
What joy!

Here I am renewed again
My spirit whelms within me
It soars me on to worlds unknown
And You are there beside me
To teach me of Thy wondrous love
So pure, so rich and holy
Abiding always like a dove
There is strength and security with Thee
What joy

—*June L. Wehr*

Sitting in the Sun

Here I sit beneath the sun and sky.
Beside me, glowing golden brown,
Lays a friend of mine.
A friend of strength, of fortitude so strong.
Of eyes that glimmer, oh so blue,
A heart-shaped face that smiles, too.
I often sit and wonder why,
Why I was put here beneath the sky.
Then I turn and look at you,
Purring softly in the morning dew.
Suddenly, it doesn't matter why,
For there is just you and I.
Here we sit beneath the sun and sky.

— *Julianne Jerina*

Memories

As I sit counting the moments
Until I will see you again,
I remember all the good times
We have had and hope that in the future
Our times together will be more precious.
I really cannot express my feelings.
They are just so hard to describe.
I hope that we will stay together forever
But if for some reason we do not
I will keep the good times in my heart,
And cherish them always.

—*Joyce Wright*

WHERE, BUT IN AMERICA...?

Where, but in America
Could a small town gal like me
Have come so far in the good life
Without even a college degree?

With guts and determination
I began a Talent Agency,
And realized success from the start,
Earning respect in the Industry.
Where, but in America
Could I write and record a song
For my city's Anniversary...
Which local radio played all day long?
Where, but in America
Would I be so proud and free?
I thank GOD today and always
For happiness and for LIBERTY!!

— *Judy Atwell Blecha*

The Overcomer

Amid the rolling thunder of a troubled mind
Fall misty raindrops of faith and hope
Gently lifting the soul from its catacomb of despair
Allowing the spirit to burst forth in freedom
And shine light through the windows of our eyes.
Joy springs from a well long forgotten in the turmoil
And manifests itself through the pleasure of a smile.
Dawn of the radiant glow of the whole person
Gives no hint of the darkness that has passed.
Rain that has fallen gives birth to the seeds of belief
And the overcomer stretches forth his hand
Letting raindrops seep into another's storm.

—*Julia W. Merrill*

The Wild Fall

The maple, oak, and walnut tree.
Are changing colors galantly.
Cranberries, pumpkins, squash, and corn,
In the garden, not in scorn.
Scarlet, crimson, russet, and rust, amber,
Maize, gold, and brick, get your colors, take you pick.
Howling, wailing screaming roaring,
That's the wind when rain is pouring.
Frostly, chilly, brisk, and breezy,
It makes you and me very sneezy.
Glistens, glitters, sparkles, and glows,
The sun shines through and the colors it shows.
Whirl, swing, float, and drift,
The leaves move with the breeze so swift.

— *Justine Cutcher*

A Day Worthwhile in the Eyes of the Lord

He starts us off by touching us
With a finger of His love
And giving us a portion of His grace.
Let us rejoice and give thanks,
Not only on Thanksgiving Day,
For the Lord has done great things.
Let us testify of His many blessings
And hold our heads up high,
For God said if we walk in the most
Righteous way, He shall bless us
To see another day, a day
Worthwhile in the eyes of the Lord.

— *Joyce Rosier*

Sweet Angel

From the cradle to the cold, dark ground,
little baby makes no sound.
With only the warmth from a blanket of snow,
to God's safe, open arms does sweet angel go.
Mama's eyes are full of tears,
as she thinks of all those wasted years.
Papa's heart, filled with despair,
yet Angel knows how much he cares.
That God should let wretched creatures walk this earth,
yet take away sweet baby's breath at birth.
Now perfect angel, baby's breath so sweet
choirs of angels in Heaven to greet.
Don't fill your hearts with aching grief,
let memories and God's love bring some relief.

— *Julianna Batizy*

As I Lay

As I lay and I ponder,
My mind gets up and begins to wander.
Drifting off into the night,
With strength and hope that I might-
Find you standing somewhere near,
To hold me tight and ease my fear.
I long to see your smiling face,
And melt within your sweet embrace.
You make me laugh and make me smile,
And make my wait seem all worthwhile.
The sparkle in your eyes lets me see,
That the future holds a place for you and me.
Thoughts of you linger in my mind-
Fighting to keep my past behind.
I have you now and could not ask for more,
You give me something to be living for.
You are my life, please take care of my heart,
It's forever yours til you tear it apart.

—*Amy Harwell*

Stars

Stars in the sky,
Like lights in the attic,
Shining bright for light,
Guiding us for life,
They open the door to the night,
For love and romance,
Time passes stars fade,
The sunlight seeps through the morn,
The stars have faded into the day,
I'm sure you all said goodbye,
But fear not they will return,
To guide us once again.

— *Kathy Reichel*

Untitled

It was us against them,
no mercy, face to face.
You could smell the aroma of
hatred in the air.
The word peace was never used,
who once was quiet was now loud.
Words confused in language,
no meaning at all.
For the first of the last time,
no one volunteered to the word
surrender.
Stacked neatly on the shelves
were those words of hatred.
Haste before your eyes the
feeling of dread.
Shadows danced, for mercy was the fall.
Peace and quiet was a rare feeling
for jealousy and hatred was only there.

—*Kathleen O'Neil*

Life, Why Live It?

When life means nothing to one,
why live it?
Are there loved ones who love you?
How should you know if they don't show it,
    but on others.
When you're born you're loved,
When there is others born you're loved,
When there is drugs you're forgotten.

— *Colleen Lynn Murphy*

Clearing Snow

A thousand tiny tinsel bits
sparkling and flying,
Whipped and whirled through
a clear, cold, sharp blueness.

A moaning, pulsating purr
as each bite scrapes
Packed, shimmering tinsel
off frozen New Mexico pottery.

A yo-yo shooting the moon,
out and back, to and fro,
Openness spreads slowly as
butter on cold cornbread.

—*Kenneth W. Tidmore*

Friend

If you ever need a friend
I have alot of love to share,
I will be here until the end
To show how much I really care.

If you ever need a guide
To help you see the light
I will be right by your side
To make everything seem bright.

If you ever looking for love
You have to look no more.
For I will show you a side of love
That you have never seen before.

So, if you ever feel blue
Just remember: I love you

—*Holly Grunert*

Together for Eternity

The time is near
For us to part,
The day I've always dreaded.
No more laughter, no more tears
All those feelings that we shared.
The memories we must store
Deep in our hearts,
Keep our days together.
For somewhere,
When our lives are complete,
Our paths will cross forever.

— *Kalai T. Larson*

Hold

Hold my heart
Don't let go
Let our hearts glow.
Hold me now
Hold me forever
Hold me close, closer than ever.
I know I have to be careful
The way I treat your heart
Let me make a brand new start.
Hold the laughter,
Hold the crying
Hold the fighting
Hold the sighing,
Hold the tears
Hold the fears
Hold the cheers
Hold them close, hold them dear.

—*Tanya Matthews*

Brotherless Brotherhood

There is
Bond of common hold
Upon all men, which found therein,
Shall be but a thought,
As all truth which exists,
  Not at heart,
  Nor mind,
  Nor the soul,
Yet among that which the universe
Reveres in silent sound,
  a purpose of
individual unity.

— *Eric Sparks*

Ode to Blue

Grief is like waves
Gathering size unnoticed
Swelling, rolling continually
Breaking on the shores of our souls.
A love, a friend, death, dis-belief
Over and over with out relief.
Sometimes I think I've forgotten
Then a big one crashes in,
The sand swept smooth and clean
Until the next time I remember
How much we loved the sea.

— *Marianne Sipple Chenoweth*

Untitled

Alone
  golden silence fragile as butterfly wings
  gossamer bubbles floating on the air

Loneliness
  black silence heavy as the ache of death
  jagged stumps still rooted in the ground

What a difference
  choice makes

— *Helen McNaughton*

Procrastination

Procrastination is a misgiving
According to what some people may say
But I find it adds more time for living
And has become quite my forte.
As the famous man once said
About when he would drink his wine,
Likewise, I too, shall finish no job
At least, not before it's time.

— *Joseph Kenneth Sarto*

You Are

You are the sparkle in my eye,
You are my warmth on a cold day,
You are a cloud in the blue sky,
You are the one who leads my way.
You are the tingle in my stomach.
You are the butterflies under my skin,
You are the sweet icing on my cake,
You are the chill I feel from within.
You are my sunshine on a cloudy day.
You are the feeling I feel in my heart.
You are what makes my cares fade away.
You are the one I have loved from the start.
You are my life, my hopes, and my dreams.

—*Tracy Mohrbacher*

When Shall I See You

When shall I see you again clothed in light?
My heart still searches for that long ago night
When love enfolded us, two became one,
And passions of lifetimes through a million suns
Swept us upward in raptuous joy
As on wings made of stars such the angels employ.
When shall I find my soul's other part,
The union once more of our spirit and heart?
In mind and body may we find rest,
Knowing our togetherness by God has been blessed.
Come to me now for we both know the way.
This is our moment, let this be the day.

— *John C. Taylor*

There is no Me

I only met you once, but I knew
That someday I would have fallen in love with you.

Together we were for one quick day
Together our passion was so true
Together we threw it all away
And now at night, I cry for you

I want you, I need you
Oh, why can't you see
Without you
There is no me.

With you I could be so open
It did not matter what I said
But now my heart is broken
And without you, I'll be dead

My heart is smashed
It floats through space
My whole life has crashed
And I have lost the race

—*Kimberely Burnes*

The Perfect Love That Cannot Stay

The most perfect thing that I can imagine
Has just walked into my life.
The sweetness of life still remains.
I, being tired of the routine of life,
Have suddenly found happiness.
The shyness in myself looks for sadness,
But none I have found.
I already know the worst that can happen,
And that is for you to leave me.
Which will not be long
For our lives lead different ways,
But there is still no sadness to be found.
For at least I have had the chance to know you.
You are the best I have ever known.
I love you and will never forget you
For you are one of a kind.

—*Michelle Severy*

The Ole Christmas Spirit

Whatever happened to Christmas joy?
When children thought of more than just getting a toy.
What happened to the time where people stopped to think
About the homeless child with nothing to drink.
The spirit of Christmas, where did it go?
Did it melt away with the snow?
Did it fly away with the breeze?
Or burn down with the trees?
Come back ole spirit why did you go?
Will you come again with the new snow?

— *Tanika Lipford*

You Were There

Now Dad would you look at me,
Remember when I came to your knee.
I still remember your rocking me,
Back when I was only three.

We had good times and bad,
As is the story of every lad.
Outdoor life we had our share,
But most of all you were there.

Now we have good memories to share,
We had a relationship that was rare.
Now my son will learn from you,
That things young men should do.

I thank God you are my dad,
I will always treasure the times we had.
Remembering when I came to your knee
Then as now you always were there for me.

—*Gladys Ritenour*

Doing Fine

You watch him but he doesn't mind.
You advise him but he doesn't listen.
Soon you ignore him but with understanding for
He has chosen without thought, to pretend
That he's doing just fine, unassisted.
You hear of him in time and sight.
You still wish for him life's happiness
But chances have not changed, things are
The same as they were when you knew him then.
Only now, doing just fine
Is bolted down.

— *Revish Windham*

What is True Friendship

Friendship is communication. Being able to associate your
Ideas and ideals with those whom you love so much.
Friendship is giving. Gifts of love; whether
They be as small as a grain of sand or as large
As life itself. No matter what size or shape,
Love is always brilliant.
Friendship is sharing. Something is nothing
Unless it can be shared with others. Enjoyment
Felt by many is greater than solitary happiness.
But most of all, friendship is love and caring.
Sharing love is the greatest task ever encountered,
The greatest feeling ever felt, and the most
Rewarding emotion ever expressed.
If only understood by two
True friends, friendship
Is everlasting.

—*David A. Kern*

Every Moment

When I talk with you I feel so secure,
Yet my heart's beating fast I'm still so unsure
I know I could fall in love easily,
But I must guard my heart, I must wait and see.

It feels as if my dreams all come true
Whenever I'm alone with you.
You make me feel special when you hold me tight,
The world seems to stop and dark turns to light.

You make me smile, I'm so natural with you
You came into my life from out of the blue,
And now that you're here I won't leave your side,
You're all that I need, there's no need to lie

You're funny and charming, you're romantic and sweet,
I feel when I'm with you my heart skips a beat.
Every Moment I'll cherish, you'll live in my heart
I'll pray Every Moment that we never part!...

—*Mary Beth Carpanzano*

Good-Bye

To every rose there is a thorn
And from this thorn you bleed
And even though it hurts you
You know it's what you need.
And when the teardrop starts to fall,
Don't wipe it from your eye,
For if you truly cared for me,
You'll allow yourself to cry.
The rain, it falls, and it falls hard,
But even through it all,
Soon will come a rainbow
To save you from your fall.
The pain will pass as will the clouds
And you'll be on your way.
Don't fall back; don't push ahead,
Just take it day by day.
For you would never have to mend
If nothing was ever torn,
And the tear that's hardest to mend of all
Is the tear from the rose's thorn.

—*Tracey Herman*

Recollections of an Old Man

My beard has turned a silvery gray
From fully living life each day.
I have seen my loves grow old and die,
Yet relived days still bring a sigh.
I have seen my children grow so tall
And see their children throw a ball.

I have seen a thousand changes wrought
By a world whose deeds are senseless thought.
I have watched men die in pointless races
And lost my dough to smiling faces.
I have had some good times and some bad,
I know they are not the last I have had.

I have lived, and laughed, and loved, and lied.
So many things I wish I had tried.
But though the years have passed me by
I will not sit just idly by.
For I have nothing to regret
I have lived a life I will not forget.

—*Michael D. McCracken*

Frantic

The winds blow on my collar,
My back to the bellowing crowd.
Walking, my feet felt a cushion
Of disregarded butts and papers.

My eyes fixed like an owl
To continue on.
My hands swayed like a windmill,
My forehead became like dew in the morning.

—*Warren Rolband*

Shanty Lines

Can you remember the times
Of the shanty lines?
Box lunch and old good times,
When smoke filled chimneys filled the air
And walking trusses without a care,
And Grandma rocked her rocking chair,
When just to hear that old train whistle
Sent young minds to wonder,
When skies were blue and fields were golden,
No nuclear waste or atomic explosions,
And the certainty of life was all so clear.
Can you remember?
Where has it gone?
The times of the shanty lines.

—*Katherine Jones*

Lee

Like a bird in flight,
You think you have freedom at your feet.
Choosing your own ideas
And creating different feats.
Everyone admires you, Lee.
They think you are so perfect, so innocent,
And so free.
You are like a gentle dove,
Flying through the sky.
You are like a child giving,
A gentle sigh.
Everyone wants to be in your presence
Because they think you are so right,
They want to be with you always
In the bright sunlight.
But under all that bright light
And all that freedom
Lies a raging fire.
Who within its flame
Holds a liar.

—*Miroslava M. Arredondo*

Everlasting Love

When our love first began
I told you over and over again,
Just how much you mean to me
And that our love will always be.
You entered my life in a casual way
With lots of loving words to say.
I know at times we have our doubts,
But never a one we can't work out.
We always get along oh so well;
This is an everlasting love, I can tell.
From one another I know we'll never
Part, for you are the only owner of
My precious heart.
Take care of it as I have done;
Cause our two hearts now beat as one.
Until you came along my life was
Always blue. Now all I want to say
Is...I am in love with you!

—*Melanie Crowder*

Life

Riding the merry-go-round,
Going up and down,
Life goes up and down,
The thundering waves crashing against the shore,
The crystal will shatter,
Just as the stars shall fall,
The orchard white doves flying in all directions,
Can I fly?
Dance, dance, oh dance,
Never fail keep going?
No, no, I must not shatter,
Go ahead, nobody cares,
Life is an image of many creations,
Without my presence life will still go on,
The merry-go-round keeps going around,
The crash of an angry wave will not drown in silence,
Fly beautiful doves, fly,
Dance until you can no longer,
For when life ends, soon for me, maybe you,
Nobody can say, I never did try.

—*Jodi Lynn Blasco*

Nothing New

I've had few words to speak
but many books to read;
By studied recollection
I've come to one conclusion:
There's nothing new in
what I think.

— *Mary Aileen Armstrong*

Untitled

The moon in the sky
Like an eye
Watching me,
Tears falling,
But never dampening
The earth below.
Bloodshot stars,
Solar scars,
Orbit round
Permanently.
A crying universe-
A deaf world-
Ignoring
The moon in the sky.

—*Marc Sapoznik*

Good Byes

I'll miss ya, you know.
More now than ever.
I wish I could stay,
Forever and ever.
Remember the good times.
All the fun we've had.
The dances and the ball games.
Just don't think of the sad.
I'll come and visit,
I'll write you, too.
Write me back, okay?
I won't forget you.
Oh, come on!
Don't worry about me.
I'll be fine.
Really, you'll see.
Bye bye.
I gotta go.
My dad's ready to leave.
You've been a good friend to know.

—*Marsha Franks*

Untitled

Puppylove,
I could live without it.
Puppylove
Is so demanding.
Crushes
Are a lot like love.
Crushes,
We all have to live through them.
Crushes
Prepare us for the real love that lasts.
Love
Is so special..
Love
Is what I dream of.
Love
Will someday come to all of us.
Love,
A combination of the above.

—*Michelle Adams*

Snow

Snow is made of crystal,
Snow is like vaper,
It is white,
It is also soft.

—*Michele Minor*

Uncertain Faith

Of other worlds and saintly fools,
I lie naked on the strength of a charm.
Still though I strive to be alone,
The cries of sin I'll always hear,
A silent judge
Perched gently upon my shoulder
And to this reign I'll always serve.
My identity forever seen...
Through the eyes of another.

— *Michael Lewis Green*

The Letter

I wrote it, and mailed it-
Next morning, he had it.
I meant every word it said.
Then panic
Overcame me-
But of course, now,
It's too late.
Oh God,
The mistake
Of committing to paper
My heart!
Where it can be examined
Ridiculed, judged
Torn apart, and
Thrown away.

— *Marsha Ann Miller*

Snowflakes

On a grey chilly winter's day
Have you ever had snowflakes
Settle lightly on your sleeve
Studied their crystal latticework
Fragile, delicate, intangible
Each flake perfect, formed
In all its simple symmetry
Realized someone greater than we
Has made it so?

— *Mary Garnett Messner*

Abuse

The mourning fog
Rolled in
The sorrow for
The loss
Of my young
Innocence
A deep and real thing.
I often wonder with deep sorrow
How many are like me
And don't know it.
Child Abuse has
Such a deadly ring
But
How often practiced?
How often forgotten?

— *Cleo Chamberlain*

Vision In The Sky

A transparent beauty
It remains free
Spread across the sky
So all can see
Only touched by hearts
And glorious shades
A glimpse of beauty
Then it fades.

—*Marie A. Capone*

A Rainbow

A rainbow was over the sky
Who made me feel that I could fly
It had wonderful colors like
Pink, blue and white
They always cheer you up when
You are not feeling bright.
So when you have a problem
Always look up to the sky
And find the rainbow of...
Pink, blue and white.

—*Myra Angerstein*

Confessing to All

When I went to confession
I used to wonder
if the people waiting in line
could hear my sins and
if my mom was listening and
if I would get in trouble when
I got home.

sometimes confessing to
one can mean
confessing to all;
I don't go to
confession anymore.

—*Janine C. Festa*

Shopping Spree

Often times, it seems to me,
Life is but a shopping spree.
Running madly, store to store,
Never picky, buying more.

Now your funds are running low,
Debts, you see, begin to grow.
As you pay these less and less,
The soul from you is repossessed.

—*Michael Ryan*

Run to Me

When you're lonely and blue
And life's got you down
Run to me
I'll be your clown
When things get tough
And nothing seems worthwhile
Run to me
I'll make you smile
Hand in hand
We'll walk together
I'll be your comfort
I'll be your man
Just run to me.

— *David R. Rose*

Dreamland

Up above the sky,
There's a place I like to go;
It's a place unreal,
But a place I know.
It is a place where I can be young,
A place to run and play;
It is a place where I do what I want,
A place where I like to stay.
It's a place I want to take you,
Where we can be together;
It's a place where once you've gone,
You'll visit it forever.
It is a place I know you'll
Want to see;
It is a place for just
You and me.

—*Marisa Hunter*

Life

A graveyard of buried hopes
collected without prejudice
covered with strong-scented flowers
and marble slabs to disguise
the ruins of its wrath.
Scars of the veterans, forgotten
under the weight of the soil,
call to the others.
Beckoned to the same destiny
that will carry them to their
grave of life, of death.

— *Lori Koberstine*

Sneak Peeks

I watch you play
I watch you sleep
I watch you laugh
I watch you cry

Sometimes I feel defeat
But then I sometimes stop to hear
The little pattering feet;
Then I realize you're growing up so fast
From the babies, you've become

I watch you play
I watch you sleep
I watch you laugh
I watch you cry

Sometimes I just sneak peeks.

—*Cheryll Heibel*

May I

Don't say can I, say may I
My teachers always said
They taught me the alphabet
And not to be afraid.

May I stuck with me
And now I know
That may I have a cookie
Is can I get the dough

For you see, the cookie won't come
From may I, said to me
It is can I support my habits
When the money can always be.

So may I be excused
Is nothing like the blues
When you must ask yourself
Can I do the job; no woos

—*Leola Caldwell Gardner*

Thoughts

If I were but a summer thing
I would see the trees all green.
I would never see the boughs of trees
In their entirety.

I would never see the snow heaped high
Nor hear the silence of it.
My heart just might never sing
If I were but a summer thing.

—*Mabel A. Price*

A Flight Beyond the Stars

I shall go out and travel beyond the stars,
Out beyond Jupiter and Mars!
And I will stake my claim to life's old grueling game
And I will carve my name
Beyond life's riches and its fame.

I shall sojourn to life's glorious milky way
Where everyone will have his good old days.
I know not the price I pay.
I know not the traps that lay.
But I will make my trip to life's glorious milky way.

I shall attempt to reach that unreachable star.
I know that I will travel near and far.
But it is destiny!
That God has given me.
And destiny shall fuel my flight beyond the stars.

—*Tommy Johnson*

Lights! Camera! Action!

Lights, camera, action! Reinactment of the crime.
What began as support turned to a waste of time.
Drop by drop, the liquid was swallowed.
Little by little, this pattern was followed.
Drank and drank, till all senses were shot.
Disallusioned and dimented were all that were thought.
The liquid was drank to be taken away,
From the pain and strife felt on that day.
Using alcohol to wipe away tears
Of the sadness, madness, loneliness, fears.
Somehow every day becomes a repeat
Of the challenge, struggle, drinking, defeat.
Pretty soon your life becomes such a frolic
And before you know it you're an alcoholic.

—*Teri Moore*

Dreams Do Come True

You always dream of meeting a special someone
Who could take that place in your heart;
Someone who would always be there when you
Felt as though you would fall apart.
Well, I have met my someone and he does so much
For me, for when I am down, he makes me smile.
When I need a shoulder to lean on, he's always
Free for a while.
I have been blessed with something that no one else has;
A special someone like you.
Of all the days in my life, my most precious moments
Were those spent with you.
There is one thing that everyone should do;
Never give up dreaming because it will always
Come true. I should know...
My dream was YOU!

—*JoAnne Robrecht*

Why

Why does it have to be that no one notices me?
When I start to cry, people pass me by.
Whenever I want to confess, people seem to listen less.
I cannot tell if it is night or day.
Sometimes I want to fade away.
I do not want to mess with living,
Or put up with people taking and never giving.
So why does it have to be, that no one notices me?
It is because of you.
You are the one everybody talks to.
They notice a pretty face, and then I have no place.
They watch every word you say, and not once look my way.
But one day, they will notice who I am
And in your face their doors will slam.
It will be you who is never seen, and I will be praised like a queen.
Will you never stop to see,
That one day they will notice me.

— *Trinity Garamella*

Through the Looking Glass

The reflection of our feelings enchants the precious glances
   we exchange with anticipation waiting.
Golden gleam shot from the falling sunset making our silhouettes
   dazzle in the darkness.
Lingering emotions carry tender moments of precious times afar
   not to be seen.
Memories escape of an elegant beginning.
Now the sunset fades into a time of cold romance.
Our silhouettes no longer dazzle, instead the darkness surrounds
   the dreams that grow within our minds.
Beckon calls of love deafen the passion we share.
Now afar the reflection is all that can be shared.
Pondering the past brings our once shared feelings alive again.

— *Kimberly I. Gilgen*

Charles

I'll cherish your love on every lovers' day.
I'll honor your love each and every day.
I'll forever love you for the rest of my days.

I remember you when I walk on the snow on a cold winter day.
I remember you when I hear the laughter of children at play,
Wearing big smiles that make you want to stay.
I feel your touch whenever raindrops fall on a cool spring day.
I'll forever cherish, honor, remember,
feel the presence of my sweet old man.

— *Sandra Melendez*

I Feel Lonely at Times

I feel lonely at times,
Times when things go through my mind.
The time I take is a precious time.
I go through and sort things out,
But it's the precious things I find.
Sometimes I feel like running away,
No place to go and no place to stay.
I'm afraid of what I might come across.
I'll take one wrong road and be eternally lost.
I feel I have a problem with no explanation.
I want to figure out this difficult situation.
I need to find help, I wish I could call out
But I'm the only one who knows what would help.
I need time away to think. About what, who's to know?
I want to change, I know I should.
I have to take time if I only could.

— *Stacy Wilson*

The Tree's Final Grasp

The tree and the leaves held tight,
Last spring it seemed they'd be forever bound.
But now autumn's wind grows cold and the fog goes low
And the sun is forever lost against the pale sky.
Who can save the leaves as they break off and die?
The tree's final grasp is coming soon, slowly they can
Slowly they can cling no more
As the wind takes the leaves away.

— *Sky Earth Youngblood*

The Harvest

After a spring rain the worms are dispersed
like strings. They dangle from a black suit coat:
the ER parking lot. Change-seeking boys who are versed
in picking off threads from the garments which boats
(flush folks' Cadillacs) moor on top of descend
after each of May's stream-feeding storms like shoats,
searching for silage. The children bend
their backs like hunters of seashells and tote
milk cartons in which to store the Dacron
they've come to collect. The hospital lawn,
ignored by the mercantile robins, is no factor in
making them rich although the annelids spawned
underneath it. The boys' pockets long to find
coins: nuggets, the fleers of Washington's mines.

— *Ted Yund*

My Turn

There is a time in every life
A time when there is nothing but incredible sadness
A feeling of being totally alone.
You beg and plead
Yet there isn't even one small tear to release pressure
A time so very dark
Grasping for someone, something
To hear a whisper, to feel a touch
Is it laughter in the raindrops?
Or maybe the wind calling my name
Sunshine on fields of snowdrift
The scent of a babe asleep
Raw is the emotion
Terror, and pain
Onward I shall wander
The light within a candle flame
Sometimes flickers, but if cared for continues to burn

— *Scarlet Fetty*

Hymn to Unknown Children

Before the law came to their aid,
Children were used and much underpaid.
I sit and muse of their plights
And of those who usurped their rights:

What do I owe to some child somewhere,
Given so many burdens to bear,
From a life in a mine, to a sweltering field,
To a sweatshop maligned, or on a ship, sealed,
Or fought in the roar, of some bureaucrat's war
Or made low, a slave to be, to some base economy?

Into this world, with strength of spirit
Came the child-hero, or heroine's merit.
Surviving the meanness, or rising above it
Lived in that world and became someone's parents.

Honor these children whose great dignity
Refused to go under to such cruelty,
We stand on a base that is their creation.
Rejoice in their awesome determination.

— *Ruth Ann Burrell Hickey*

Little Mountain Morning

Morning mist
rolling down
the mountainside
roiling streams
without sound
    — *David J. Van Meer*

Love

Love is mysterious in its own way;
I still can remember the tricks it played.
First there was Jody, then Jimmy and Jon;
Don't forget Eric or lastly Paul.
I will always remember the good times and bad.
But for now I will keep hoping
For someone like Dad!
    —*Lisa Sayess*

Willows Whisper

Face I know or do I still
The moment seemed all too real
Etched in stone heart of glass
Time to care love will pass
Weeping willows whisper still
Life's confusing is it real
Touched at last from heart to soul
Gone in a moment no longer whole.
    — *Janet Garrett*

Four Orders

I am a dead rose.
I am a cracked mirror.
I am a dull stone.
I am a black spider.

Rose, bloom in the garden.
Mirror, reflect my radiance.
Stone, be a part of my rock garden.
Spider, crawl up the wall.
    —*Rosa Delgado*

Chameleon Child

Frightened child who tries to please others,
Take heed to their every word.
Strive to fit in. Ache to belong.

Lost puppet,
Dance to the strings of the wind,
Slave to the shifting mood of friends.

Quit living your life through others!
Chameleon Child, when will it end?
    —*Susan A. Robinson*

Our Last Words

It's too late to go back to what we were.
There has been too much hate and too much love
In so little time.
It's time to forget, but not to forget.
To start over.
Our new lives are waiting.
That special someone is waiting,
Not only waiting for their life to begin
But also to start over.
Good-bye.
    — *Michelle Timmerman*

My Summer Love

Happy was a word
I once knew it well
It was you and me
The cool summer breeze
The special moments together
The days spent with you
But summer has ended
And its time for us to leave
Why does the end of summer
Have to take us so far apart
    — *Michaela Bivans*

Dreams of Memories

What's so easy to remember,
yet so hard to forget?
The memories of our past
will live forever in your heart.
Now I don't want to go
and leave you here all alone,
But I can't stay forever
and you knew that from the start.
Now that my time has come
there's something you should know.
Those times we spent together,
all that precious time alone,
Will live on after I am gone
until you dream no more.
    — *Laura Dodge*

Kisses of Love

When you're far away from me,
All I want to do is see your face.
And when I hear your soft, sweet voice,
I want to feel your sweet embrace.
You're all I ever dream of,
You're all I ever think of,
And when I look into your eyes,
I feel a wonderful sense of love!
Your presence makes me shiver,
Your touch makes me quiver,
You make me feel you're from heaven above,
When you give, to me, your kisses of love.
    — *Carrie Herron*

Memories of You

As I walk along the shore,
I think of you.
Of all the things that we did,
All the things we could do.
All of our future,
Is now called the past.
All of our dreams,
Never did last.
All that was said,
Has now been spoken.
All the promises,
Are now broken,
All that remains
Are memories of you.
Lie upon lie,
All that is untrue.
    — *Regina A. Place*

But Only

Let me have the time-
your time to make you mine.
I know I can love you
the way you should be loved
But only if you say
the words.
I can take you anywhere,
even to the stars above.
Let me have the heart-
your heart to mend my love
Together and not apart.
But only if you say
The words
I can love you forever.
    — *Raechel R. Guerra*

Untitled

I believe life is a dream
A dream in which we don't
Feel the wind or the rain
Our decisions are nothing
Lasting only for a moment
We are in flesh, non existent
And we know not what we
Will see next or what we will
Be next. We live from thought
To thought, not from day to
Day, so you see we live as
We dream and die as we awaken.
    — *Mary Loree Browning*

Colors of Love

If the ocean is blue
And the sky is too,
How come you can't share your love
The way I share mine with you.

If the sun is yellow
And the grass is green,
Why is it so difficult
To include me in your dreams.

Make it any color you want.
It's such a waste, it's such a shame
Because love is just like colors
No matter how dark or light the shades.
    —*Cheryl Effland*

Let Nature Sing

Why do people hunt innocent creatures
Or trap them so cruel
Why kill them
They did not harm you

Why mistreat God's animals
They are compassionate
True friends to us
We are sometimes selfish beings
So we kill those who cannot help themselves

This is their world also
And we can share
There is room for them
Please let them here

If we could just learn to love
Take away some destruction
Our world, our animals
We would all live in harmony.
—*Krystal Hibshman*

Wind

If you couldn't feel it, it was gone
But you'd have to
The magic of it
So smooth
Always best to reach out to it when ol'
sun was at her strongest.
So beautiful, they'd say.
But you couldn't see it.
Only in their eyes they saw the wonder.
Unlike the sun and rain, this was the best,
The treat of the summer.
Wind, wind.
— *Abby Wohl*

Comes the Moon

He comes in the still of the night...
Tripping up my mind and carelessly spilling light.
Swiftly he glides across a starlit sky,
Oblivious to the wind and the whip-poor-will's cry.
Weaving fantasies, he breaks into my dreams,
Plants tender kisses, continues with his schemes.
While he controls my wanton urges,
He covers my body with dappled splurges,
Coloring me silver in the night
With the magnificence of his pure, cool light.
He brings me peace and sated rest,
Calms the rhythm beating in my chest,
Showers crystal drops of dew——his heady wine,
Amongst my tresses, a hint of jasmine he does twine.
Upon gentle beams, to sleep, I am borne,
Then silently, he steals away before the coming morn.
— *Kathy Watson Jumper*

Autumn Gray

I feel the impenetrable wall of gray
Shifting, swirling 'round me like an ocean wave
Whispering tardy words of wisdom
Through the chilled autumn air.

The wind tugs my trench coat softly
As I close my eyes once more and see my mistress cry.
This stoney day recalls too much.
I want to die.

I trace a crumpled, withered leaf in flight
Feeling its loneliness, decay and destiny with death
As it flutters helplessly in the whispering sky.
Circling high in a draft, swooping low, moving restlessly,
It beckons me to follow its self destructive path.
—*Daniel G. Cox*

The Wind in the Trees

When I stand in the wind,
I try to get out of the wind,
By going in a patch of trees,
One day I was doing this and
I listened to the trees for a couple of minutes.
The wind sounded like the ocean.
It goes one tree at a time, almost like a wave.
Only this wave is as loud as a lion's roar.
When it comes up the line of trees,
It is as if it were a mystery story,
And you are waiting for the wind in the trees
To reach you
Listen to the trees
They are probably trying to tell you something.
—*Tiffany Devine*

Perceptions

Phantoms of the wind, shelter
This place where mountains grow:
Boughs of green, complaining,
Under blankets of shimmering whiteness;
The source of a thousand sceptors
Erupts from the center of the monolith.

Spirits of the mist, protect
This vale where streams begin:
Ponds of darkness, encouraged,
By the breath of eagles soaring:
The source of a thousand rivers
Emerges from the depths of its serenity.
—*Truth*

Magic

Birds, bells, magic spells
To keep you on your toes
It never tells, wishing wells
To wish away your woes
Baby blue skies, little white lies
Fall, winter and spring
A little bird flies, an older one dies
To be treated like a king
Yesterday some other way
I've lost my one true love
Nothing to say, I don't want to play
High up on the wings of a dove.
Listen to me, I am aching to see
The mysteries of the land
Someone to be, just set me free
Find someone to understand.
—*Jessica Burton*

The Forest

Soft as September leaves
Floating listless to the earths floor
The trees shed their frail fur
For winter is bound to take them away

Buried deep beneath the core of the earth
Lie the roots that sustain their existence
Their arms hold security of home sweet home
And sometimes bear bitter sweet fruit
As life supports life
Death also brings death

The trunk of the tree is the heart of a wise man
For he has seen many winter's
For love and war pass beneath his branches
As a fighting man breathes his last breath
A tree falls quietly in the forest.
—*Julie Ann Walter*

The Rose's Petals

Flower petals,
Drop and fall,
After a while don't last,
But the love of the flower,
Last forever,
Before the tired petal fell,
For its beauty and love,
Will always remain,
For no one flower petal, is the same;
The shape, color and scent,
Of all the rose's petals yet,
Are different,
One that a person
Won't forget,
And love best together yet.
— *Kathleen Ann Trainor*

Sentinels

In darkness cold my dreams are bright
As sentinels in shadows reign.
They are shattered from inside,
But they hold on and hope remains.
To me the seasons eternal turn
Wears thin the heart's worn shell.
Emptiness like cancer burns
And leaves me in this silent hell.

Words ring in hollow tones;
The distance grows in cavern strides
And isolation chills my home:
The ashes wash to grey inside.

They give me to the ground,
In tears, farewell, without a sound.
—*Scott McCrea*

A Peaceful Summer Night

The wind blows swiftly
On this summer night,
The full moon,
Is a beautiful sight.

There are lots of stars
And many constellations
The milky way galaxy
Gives me a great temptation.

The trees sway gently
Side to side,
There is nothing tonight
Too peaceful to hide.
—*Shannon Meadows*

Autumn Leaves

The wind lifts
the aged harvestors of light,
letting them fall to the forest floor
in the yearly cycle of life.

A quilted
cascade of colors,
natural, not refined,
blanketing the ground.

Scarlet reds,
earthy browns,
golden yellows,
woven between the changing green.

Gift from the trees;
a sign of passing
into winter's blissful sleep;
the Autumn leaves.
— *Robert Davis*

The Rain

I've put you from my mind,
No longer to feel the pain.
Your smile can't even hurt;
Your image resembles the rain.
The rain...
Falling down gently, like the tears I've shed for you.
The rain...
Here for awhile, like your memory I've tried to lose.
Your face is on my heart,
Because it won't go away.
The words make me remember;
Thinking of the rain that day.
The rain...
Racing down the glass, like my heart when I see you.
The rain...
Erasing the loneliness, making my heart feel new.

— *Roberta Leigh Hughart*

Eruptions

The deep seated anger reared
Its azure head and spat
Venom of hate into the
River coursing the body.

So rich and pure was the
Putrid and arid spittle,
That the body recoiled and
Convulsed in its moment of fright.

Demonic creatures, ugly and sored
Raced across the vistas of the future
As the purging of the body became
A retching of spittle and venom.

Clearness met calm waters
As the body became clean again.
The sailing was not tranquil,
But at last I mastered the helm.

—*S. L. Spotts*

True Friendship

A friend in need,
Is a friend indeed!
I find this very true
Especially when I think of you!
Always wearing a smile
No matter what the trial!
You have problems of your own
But you know you're not alone;
That's why you're always there
To show that you truly care!
Never too busy or troubled to lend an ear;
How can your friendship be anything but dear?
This is why I'll shout aloud,
Of your friendship I am very proud!
Real friends like you are hard to find
And those who think otherwise, are blind!
These few simple words are to show
I hope our friendship will forever grow!

—*Sharon Sherriff*

Feather Bed

Yellow cotton wrapping you
Softer than the virgin dawn,
Filtering through forest trees,
To touch, to warm the sleeping fawn,
Softer than the sweet grass,
Sprouting in the seeded lawn,
Softer than this bed will be,
The moment you are gone.

—*Robert F. Vitalos*

Good-Bye

I loved you once, I loved you twice.
Maybe three times would be nice.
Although my love is flowing strong,
Somehow I feel it would be wrong.
You say you love me, then you don't.
I could still love you, but I won't.
I'm oh, so tired of the lies.
I've had too many good oh cries.
I wish for once it would be gone.
That same old memory lives on and on.
Please for once leave me alone.
Don't call, don't talk, don't telephone.
I need some time to be by myself,
Though without you there's not much left.
Just say you love me one last time
And that is it; I draw the line.
Good-bye, my love, once and for all.
I will survive; I will not fall.

—*Kathy Sidelinger*

Sadness

Sadness is when you're feeling blue,
No one can stop what's inside of you.
You need some affection,
Because not all of us have perfection.
You need love,
Because our wings aren't as white as a dove's.
So go to your room to have a cry,
And give life another try.
In time, this feeling will change,
But your heart will be in the same range.

— *Heather Beardsley*

Misled

It happened again,
My hearts broken into two
Weiry pieces of disaster.
I only see thoughts of grey dark sorrow.
My eyes are clouds of a never ending shower.
Only I feel the pain
They only see it.
No one understands.
Time is supposed to heal
But with each passing day my heart
Seems to ache more.
If only he would listen to himself
And see how much he is hurting you.
You scream bloody hell at him in your mind,
But in your limp heart you really love him.
Misled and in love,
It happened again.

—*Christina Huck*

Now You're Gone

Now you're gone I realize,
You were a precious friend.
You brightened up my cloudy skies
And loved me to the end.
You led me to my real self
And showed me who I am.
You took my heart off the shelf
And let me know I can.
So now I'm thanking you, my friend,
For everything you've done.
And to you my friend I send
To you my shining sun.

— *Linda Truett*

Waves of Dancing Light

Moonshine on the water
Waves of dancing light
I am sailing to other harbors
As I think of you tonight.

The wind is drawing me closer
And farther from the shore
You can see the beacon flashing
You can hear the ocean roar

The course is ever changing
With wind and open sea
But I will always be there
If you care to think of me

Moonshine on the water
Waves of dancing light
Carry me to another
Carry me through the night.

—*Robert J. Bjornsen*

Friends

Your friends all love you
If you've got style,
And If you're rich
They'll always smile.
But is there a friend,
Out there somewhere,
Who'll care for someone
Through grief and despair.
Who'll love you through
Sickness and health and still care
Is there that kind of
Friend anywhere?
The answer, my children,
Is plain 'til the end,
The only real answer
Is to say a true friend.

—*Darcey Hufnagle*

Inspiration's Kiss

Inspiration is a fragile kiss
Pausing not to linger
For slow wit to savor.
It stirs thought gently,
Like waves softly driven
On a wind-rippled shore,
Briefly washed and left alone,
Moist
Subtly longing
For the virtue of its caress.

— *Richard A. Bell*

Outside

Ridged cold hands clasp
Against a starless sky
Where a crescent moon looms
Upon two fear torn faces
With heads held to the gods.

Parting lips touch as
Tears are silhouetted
By the candle's dim light

On this dismal night
White roses dipped in
The bloom of a lamb
Lie scattered
On the withered remains
Of a summer's lawn.

—*Rocco Palmieri*

All About Dad

Dad is special!
Dad is nice
Dad is the guy who gave us life!

Dad is there
Dad is fair
But you loved it when Dad lost his hair!

Dad is tall
Dad is bald
Dad wants you to have it all!

Dad works all day
Brings home his pay
Just so he could send you away!

After all that dad!
I am now a college grad.
And I am using this poem to say,
Happy Father's Day.

—*Richard Stone*

Frozen Cold

Cottonwood sap frosted, blue,
Shaped in deep webbed thistles,
Hidden hemp shook all around
Leather shoes lay deeply
Bruised, frozen sap
Refused to ooze, barefoot
Shepherds sipped blue-bottle booze
Thistles raked in bundles blond
Husked leather
Cottonwood valence cut
Webbed sky,
Shepherds shake forked stamens
Hidden deep,
Yellow clouds weep
Earth breath freezes, the
Clear blood.

—*Tammy Jirik*

Hades

I have known you well, Hades,
With your flames dancing through
My hair and your venomed fangs
Striking at my heels. Your
Smoke has choked me until my
Cheeks were scorched by your
Searing flames. I have felt
Your piercing fork cut into me
And shred me of my dreams.
Hades, you inferno, thinking that
You have melted my mettle, only
Tempered it, and fighting fire
With fire, say unto you,
Tomorrow always comes!

— *Jeannette A. McDaniel*

Silhouette

Rushing light, disfiguring wind,
Creating truths formed in ancient times.
Among the dust swept plains
In a moment of riot-
Chilling shadows of icy silhouttes,
That ring by the transformation
Of unbridled temptation.
Far across the seas-
Echoes loom from distant storms.
Bittersweet cries of a hawk in fearful flight,
Never to land again.

— *Dewayne K. Roseboom*

I Rode the Black Horse

Black horse was a devil, could see it in his eyes
Not a bit like the filly that stood by his side
But I wanted to ride him, to try his wild stride
Thought I could conquer his meaness if I tried
So chose the black horse, left the filly by his side
Climbed on the black devil and started my ride
He jumped a wide gulley and every fence he found
I wanted a wild ride so never slowed him down
Go faster, go faster, black devil, I called
I want a wild ride, don't give me a stall.
So faster he went, then for no reason stopped
Needless to say I went over his top
I'm in a hospital bed with my legs in a sling
One thing I have learned and this is the thing
If you want a wild ride with its wild devil fun
There's a black devil waiting to see you get one
But if I am ever tempted to ride him again
I think I will ponder the possible end.

—*Myrtle Frost Reed*

The Last Time

A dream filtered out from the depths of her soul.
It twisted upward like the smoke from a lit cigarette,
Then a whisper floated from her soft lips.
It was only a mumble to my ears, but satisfaction
To my heart. I remember the way she slept that day;
Her face was peacefully still and
The warm glow of morning light
Reflected against the smooth curves
Of her body. Her impression melted
Into the rippled sheets.
Now, there is a colorless void
With fading fragments of memory.
I still remember love,
Or what I thought was love.

— *Darryl Bruce Mickens*

Alone and Lonely

Alone in the darkness to fend for myself,
I search for another but there is no one else.
I look for a light to help me find my way.
I look for a path but find I've gone astray.
I beg for help but no one has heard.
I cry out for someone to hear my uttered word.
It's hard for me being here alone.
Why this has to be, the reason is not known.
I've had enough of loneliness; I want no more.
I wish it could disappear by the opening of a door.
My strength each day gets less and less.
I'll always be alone and lonely, I don't hope, but I guess.

— *Sherri Russell*

The Product of Love

A pilot joins his partner in a flight:
A buxom bundle nestled in his arms,
To ride him upward soaring like a kite
Wiht music soothing to the ears like psalms.
The branches twined around the trunks keep clutching,
As passion's ivy climbs upon a tree;
Two pelts like bristling furs shake briskly touching;
The joyful yelps in harmony agree.
The flying mission of the dove fulfilled,
Two lovebirds' shaft and sheath fuse as one feather;
For good use thus a stamen's pollen spilled,
So that the seed can sprout one plant together.
The fray fulfills the dweller with his wife,
To secure him in the pleasant ooze of life.

— *Stephen Feinland*

The Eternal Realm of Time

A single life is but a spec of grain
A single ray the sun doth shine
Many came before and will come again
As the geese will fly in wintertime
The deeds of mans hands are all in vain
And so the ideas of brilliant minds
But the words of the heart on paper stained
Will live forever, until the end of time.

— *Randall C. Gibbons*

Sunshine

As I stare into the night,
Darkness squeezing my heart so tight.
Release my heart and let me free,
Sunshine, please shine within me.

Give me strength to fight the pain,
Water around me can't see for rain.
I opened my eyes and saw the sky,
The beauty the warmth I felt from hi.

Give it to me I have lots of room,
Don't look down with that look of gloom.
Sunshine inside and outside too,
Given to all but taken by few.

— *Lorei Rooks*

A Time to Go

I see you darkness, call my name.
I cannot bear to stand the pain.
I'll take a little, it won't hurt a lot.
I'll only take another shot.

I see my life pass before my eyes.
As the sun sets, and as they rise.
You clutch my heart within your hands.
With you, I rise to distant lands.

My head is heavy, I have to sleep.
Just kiss me for I am too weak.
I cry a tear as you take my heart.
This is goodbye, and another start.

And just as the wind started to blow.
They lowered my casket into the snow.
This is what happens to many alive.
When they use drugs, and think they'll survive.

— *Katherine Mendoza*

Undying Love

When alone and feeling blue
Your smiling face would get me through.
How many secrets we shared.
Although we fought we always cared.
The love that I feel towards you
Will be forever true.

This I very well know,
I made a mistake when I let you go.
Oh! To return to those good ol' days
But the memories are just a dull haze.
You were my only love and best friend.
I am so upset that it did end.

If I could regain the past,
I know that our love would last.
When I see you, it cuts like a knife.
What an empty space I have in my life.
As the clock on the wall does chime,
My love for you will last 'til the end of time.

—*Cathy Riggins*

Romantic Night

The moon was silver against the sky,
As we looked up we saw birds pass by.
We were sitting on the beach,
Then in his pocket he started to reach.
All I saw was a shiny thing,
As I looked closer I saw a ring.
It was shimmering and shining just as I,
And just then we looked up at the sky.
Over the ocean there was the sun,
He told me that I was the one.
He asked me then to marry him, what could I say,
I said, *Yes,* and felt happy and gay.
And that was my romantic night,
Shimmering and shining and oh!, so bright.

—*Steffi Bergman*

Living Love

Blending love with our lives
Becoming more beyond our own
Sharing self and all we are
We were once one, but now are more
Needing you so much to live
Apart from you I suffer
I've become that beacon light
Away from you, sheds no light
Blending life within our love
Closer we become each other
Accepting changes, where surrender lives
We take not from each other, but give.

— *Lamont Prell*

Searching

He walks with style and confidence
In how he looks and acts.
A hand inside his pocket,
And books upon his back.
He looks about the campus
Searching for a face
A friend that looks familar
In this wonderous different place.
His thoughts are those of adults,
His face is that of youth.
Searching ever searching
Ever searching for the truth.
Why do people have to die?
Why do people kill?
He knows not of the answers
And he probably never will.

—*T. Melindah Musa*

Without Your Love

Without your love
I roam aimlessly without destination.
I am no longer jovial.
I am without celebration.

Without your love
I ponder thoughts of you, unremitting.
I am deeply saddened.
I am without endearment.

Without your love
I continue to proceed throught life's movements.
I am still disheartened.
I am without entity.

Without your love
I will make you perpetuate in my memory.
I am resuming my course of life.
I am without you, but not without love.

—*Amy McLamb*

Sunshine Haze

Do not stand by my grave and weep,
I am not there, I do not
Sleep,
I am the warm wind that blows,
I am the sparkling diamond on
The snow,
I am the sunshine, not the
Pain,
I am the splatter of a drop
Of rain;
Do not stand by my grave and
Cry,
I am not there...
I did not die.

—*Tonya Lynn Winston*

Fuego de Amor

My love is like a candle that burns forever.
A dainty flame in the midst of all my pain,
There is an eerie mist that gently embraces it,
I wish to clear the mist away, but, yet, I hesitate.
I am afraid of smothering out the fire,
Though the flame is strong it can perish,
Just like a life taken away in its prime.
My life may diminish, but the fire of my love
Will live on forever...

—*Tracy Meagher*

Burning Love

Burning love you set my heart on fire.
With a flame of your love that will never die.
Just like a burning ember kindled by the wind.
It never cools and it never mends;
Just keeps burning your love deeper into my heart.
Leaving a burned out empty space that no one
But you could every replace.
Oh, won't you ever return and give me back
Your love devine.
And heal this burning aching heart of mine.

—*Robert L. Stowe*

Shine

See the star, his hands are sore
From playing his guitar.
See, his soul is tarnished,
It is worn out from being a star.
He wants to shine and be loved
By people he does not know.
He wants to see how far in life he can go.
See the star, he is doing shows in
Las Vegas. He tried to hard,
Went to fast, in his goal to be famous.
See the star, he is not here anymore.
We hope he is somewhere better,
Because he will be there a long time,
Maybe even forever.

—*Lola Strickland*

Midnight Wish

As the dim, dusk light fades away,
As the first star peeps from the blanket of black,
I look out my window to make a final wish,
A wish that my memories be wiped away,
For it is easier to die this way.
My tears drop like falling stars.
As I walk across the crystal pond
A shooting star fades away,
Just as the ice gives way.

— *Amy Peterson*

Changes

Once, not to long ago,
We had these special feelings.
You see, I loved you and you loved me,
But now that is all changing.

You've found someone new
And seem very happy.
You have gone on with your life
And have forgotten all about me.

Things here have not changed,
I linger on the past.
The memories of you and me
Just will not let me rest.

I guess I am just hoping
For one last small request.
I hope we still can be good friends
Because you were the best.

—*Tracey Henrikson*

Someday

Someday when the mountains bloom,
Smothered in flowers and green;
Someday after our present doom,
After something yet to be seen;
Someday after we say our last words,
And mutter a sorrowful farewell;
Someday we will meet in heaven
Instead of living in hell.

—*Rebecca Duvall*

Once and For All

You have left me
Once and for all
You left me crying
In the school hall
I want to go see you
Or maybe give you a call
I have to go up to you
Once and for all.
I need to tell you
You may not understand
That you meant nothing to me at all
I wanted you to know,
This is to get back at you
Once and for all.

— *Kim Eggert*

Heart Song

Gazing deep into your eyes,
I slip away with cosmic sigh.
Full of love and void of fright,
We sail away into the night.

In endless space and silver streams,
Our bodies meet in life like dreams.
On soft white clouds, we dance and play.
On winds of time, we fly away.

Then, in a blink I'm back on earth,
Sitting where I was at first.
Wondering if you even knew
Just where we went, how far we flew.

But in my heart and in my soul,
You're part of me, I know you know.
An earthly moment, a timeless flight.
I love you so, with all my might.

— *Robert O. Laho*

The Stranger

Pictures of us surround our bed
Holding memories of good days gone by
They show us as a perfect pain,
I look at them and begin to cry.

I look at the stranger next to me,
He has a familiar loving face;
But yet I do not know the man
Not since the changes have taken place.

He comes and goes like the winter wind
Leaving behind dead frozen ground.
He no longer has the loving touch
My lover in him cannot be found.

The miles that came between us
Over sometimes took my man away
Now all is replaced with silence
And the stranger that I sleep with today!

—Stacie Johansen

You Chose to Be With Me That Night

Everyday and every night was blue
Before I met you.
I never thought
My dream would come true.
When you asked me to dance
You make me so happy inside,
You read my mind
I closed my eyes
And prayed that it wasn't another silly dream
That would fade away.
The very next day
I soon discovered
It wasn't a dream
As you took me in your arms
And held me tight.
But I still can't believe
That out of every girl in sight
You chose to be with me that night

— Deanna Lombardo

A Thing of the Past

Sprawling factories, industrial wastelands
The green of earth a thing of the past.
The sky covered in shades of brown and grey
The bright sun a thing of the past.
Toxic plumes of waste fill the sky
Toxic streams of waste fill the water
Clean air, clean water, things of the past
Things seen only in movies of old.
Man a reflection of the environment
Reflected in somber tones of brown and grey
Man doomed to a life of decay
A life soon to end.
Man, a thing of the past
Seen only in a movies of old.

— Kenneth F. Paffrath

Dreams

Dreams. Don't let them die.
Think of all those who have made dreams their motivation.
Dreams brought people to fly, to think, to achieve.
Sometimes to cry,
Sometimes to sink,
Sometimes to leave.
It may take a lot of devotion and determination,
But in the end...
You may have a wonderful creation.

— Courtnay Peifer

Lies

I can see the lights,
Shining in your eyes.
I can't believe you'd
Tell me those lies.
When you tell me
You love me.
You really can't care.
It is you, you know,
Whose love you can't share.
I do understand now
The feelings we've shared.
All of this time
Only one of us cared.

— Heather Querry

Mountain Reality

Oh deepening sunset sky,
Who shareth thou
With beautiful shades of hue?

Oh unyielding summit pass,
Where goeth thou
With passionless spires of stone?

Oh clamorous mountain stream,
Why cometh thou
With shimmering coat of ice?

Oh yellowing aspen grove,
When changeth thou
With beautiful leaves of gold?

Oh lamenting evening breeze,
How searcheth thou
With impaling eyes of steel?
Oh creation of mine God,
Thou uncommon friend of man
With power for pain or awe.

—O. Ray Dodson

Counterpoint

Two members leaning
Upon one another
Create a point of balance.
If one leans more heavily
The other must react
Immediately, without question,
With strengthened support.
Should one stumble
Or falter momentarily
The other must stand
For a time, on its own.
But, should one pull away
Or become overburdening
The other
Will certainly fall.

—Ralph Hartman

Before

Before I saw your eyes
I thought I had already
Seen the most beautiful sights.

Before I heard your laughter
I thought I had already
Listened to the most wonderful sounds

Before I held you in my arms
I thought I knew love

Before you were born
I thought I was happy
I was wrong.

—Robin S. Bennett

Catching Insights

I race with stillness
on runways of clouds
stirrings of truth
fluff my insights.

Everytime thought
is about to seed
in night from fruit
of stars in daylight

I—oblivious
of its slumber
in sun secrets-

run ripe for harvest
all there to pen and puff
with every live fire.

Of poem and justice one
in force fields of faith:
well-groomed thought loved of wisdom
beauty springs of godlife peace.

—Reina Paz

Remember

You will always remember me.
I know I'll always remember you.
When it comes right down to it,
We'll think back to all we've been through.
I know I'll never forget you.
I wish I could be free.
I still think back to what we thought
Love was supposed to be.
I'll remember the good times
As well as the bad.
Sometime in the future,
I won't be so sad.
Even when I think I've forgotten,
It all comes back with a start.

— Leslie Swab

A Special Friend

A special friend you are to me.
A special friend you'll always be.
To bring joy for all eternity.
A special friend I found in you.
A special friend who will be true.
To help me through all that's blue.
A special friend who is neat.
A special friend who is sweet.
To help me shake the day's I'm beat.
You are a very special friend indeed.

—Jessie Gingerich

The War Zone

In the war zone
wildflowers grew quietly...
A bird was heard singing
when the cries had all faded
as if he'd heard nothing...
And the warriors locked in combat
did not have the strength to care
    that down in the garden
    the children dodged bullets
    by laughing too loudly
    and playing until they were dizzy
so that the neighbors might not recognize
the camouflage for what it was-
parents hidden upstairs in the war zone

— Isabelle Bennett

Only a Dream

I think of him and wonder why
He could never be my guy
He's really sweet, but not too shy
When I see him there I want to die

I've never felt this way before
And I don't think I will anymore
Cause I want him to be the one
The one to help me see the sun
The one who brightens up my day
And cares for me in every way
I always dream and think it through
But I know it's a dream that won't come true

Inside, my body wants to scream
Inside my head it's only a dream
    —Stephanie Millette

Untitled

The cool evening breeze stole upon her
Waking the yellow moon in the deep blue sky
Whose aura illuminated the murmuring curls
Of the churning, salty sea.
Alone in this world of sights and sounds,
She cried out to her friends,
But her voice was caught by the wind
That whispered sweet nothings to the moon.
Leaves rustled and shivered in the cool air,
And sand swelled smoothly,
A murmuring brook
Of the sea's loot from many journeys.
Her eyes saw many nights as such,
Where silence was noisy with the sand
And the sea and the wind.
And the nights to come would be as such
Where silence means nothing
And the moon surrounds.
    —Lisa Kavanaugh

The Decision

Today the day was set, the decision had been made.
I knew the way things were, our love was going to fade.
We tried and tried to make our love work out
But always when we tried, we knew we had a doubt.
If we hadn't started being lovers and started being friends,
Our love would last forever, forever to never end.
But we had to let it end before another mistake.
At least it ended in caring instead of in hate.
I'll always think of you in everything I do.
I hope you won't forget me, that you'll remember, too.
I guess it's time to say good-bye, but it's so hard to do
'Cause I never had anyone to treat me as good as you.
    — Sandye R. Collins

Forever Be Mine

How would it be if it were just you and I?
Together, alone...by ourselves.
Would you hold me, and kiss me, and say that you are mine?
Would you love me forever...beyond the end of time?

If you held me and kissed me and said that you are mine,
I would love you forever...forever be mine.

If you are alone, please think of me.
And think about it...how it could be.
If it were just you and I.
Together, alone...by ourselves.
    —Tiffany Amber Lee

Return

Mary returned today
from a long trip.
Exotic places
has she visited?
Sunny places
Have burned her?
...Or stormy weathers
have been
her constant companions?
Not a pleasant trip
has been this one!
...And for a long time
it lasted, too.
How could she have endured
all that pain?
How can she love again?
Mystery of the earth!
Metaphysics of the sky!
    —Santa A. Lalli Marazzani

The Storyman

Once upon a time
Gather around, gather around
The storyman calls,
As he sits down.
The children come running
To hear the story,
Of brave men fighting
In battles of glory.
The children come running,
To hear the sound
The delightful sound
Of the storyman.
    —Katie Herman

Nature

Feel a light breeze
whistling through the trees,
watch a deer scamper by,
see the clouds in the sky.
Hold your loved one by the hand
while walking through
a beautiful, quiet land.
    — Serena Spofford

I Only wanted you

You gave me all your time,
But never gave your heart.
You gave me happiness
But never gave love a start.
You shared with me your thoughts,
But never made me your dream.
You gave me more than I could ask for,
But never everything.
You showed me how to laugh,
Yet somehow made me cry.
You taught me of possession,
Yet you were never mine.
You gave me all the joys of life
And one thing still stands true;
Of all the things you gave to me
I only wanted you!
    —Kimberely M. Posey

My Mind Is on Fire

My mind is on fire
In the word of desire
The lone heart is troubled
Now the pressure is doubled

When the heart gets close
Sanity somehow seems gross
The beat is heard not
Therefore the blood will clot

The hardened heart will weep
That no one wants to keep
A spark ignites the flame
Burning towards the shame

Ignorant and once blind
The heart seeks to find
Another heart to sow the seed
And not just a body to breed,
So the heart thinks to retire
That is why my mind is on fire.
    —Rex Mason

A Kind Heart

We never know from dawn to dusk
What joy may come our way
Until we remove life's heavy husk
And hear what God has to say.

He told us then; he tells us now
The price we have to pay:
The heavy heart, the humble heart
Will brighten the coming day.

We never know form night to day
What joy may pass our path
Until we set our hearts aright
And remove form it all wrath.

Let no anger cloud your mind
On life's long tedious road.
You only have to be but kind
To lighten life's heavy load.
    —Charles B. Briley

The End of Life as I Know It

If I kissed your flavorous lips,
Slowly and gently,
Carefully savoring the exquisite taste
Unique to them
And to your teeth and tongue,
So skillful in this matter,
So knowing in this way,
Then all else in life
Would become, to me,
Instantly and forever,
Meaningless.
    — R. Christopher Coski

Always

Some time shows as always
Some shows as a while,
My time shows as always in my eyes,
For the person I love.

Always is the time I spent and will spend,
I spent always searching for you,
I will spend always with you
Now that I found you.

Always, we will share, love and care
You are my always.
    —Terri Treece

The Forgotten Shade Tree

The tall bushy tree
Stands and cast a shadow
A resting place can be
Do I want to enjoy its beauty?
Relax a moment in the shade spread for me.
Out of the blistering sun a refuge
To feel the gentle fresh air blowing abundantly
Have we forgotten the peacefulness it could give?
All the modern air conditioning
We grab, isn't free.
But, the shade of the tree
God gives to thee
Free.
Let's not forget the blessing of the shade tree.
— *Maxine Choate Downing*

A Moonlit Night

As I sat in the darkness,
the night air cold but peaceful,
I spotted a shooting star,
suddenly the break of awareness,
and I thought of myself,
could there be any planets like ours?
Oh, even if there were, none are in sight
as I watched in the moonlight.
I must have watched for hours unknown.
When I went to bed that night,
I wondered if people on another planet
sat and watched the moonlight
from their moon like I did.

—*Stacey Gomes*

Bluebonnets and God

I was lonesome one day, living all by myself,
So I thought I would just take a ride.
Along the Bluebonnet Trail I went.
And God was right there by my side.

The hills were ablaze with such splendor of color
By mere words simply cannot be told.
So I bowed my head and said, *Thank you dear Lord
For this beauty my eyes can behold.*

I loved Him before, but since my Bluebonnet Ride
I find myself loving Him more.
And joy fills my soul, knowing some happy day
I will walk with Him on that Heavenly shore.

I cannot stop here, for there is work I must do
To tell everyone whom I see,
Christ will forgive all your sins,
Ask Him into your heart, and you will be forevermore free.

—*Mary Snow*

Oh Mighty Tree

Oh mighty tree in the soft wind you blow,
Take me far away
Let my spirits forever flow.
Oh might tree in the sunlight you sway,
I am forever with you
Take my thoughts faraway
Oh mighty tree in the wind your seeds of life spread,
Without the beauty of trees
This land would be shameless and dead.
Oh mighty tree on this land forever you will be,
Pick up your gracious roots
And hide away with me.
Oh mighty tree the end is so near, do not be afraid
Your future is quite clear.
Oh mighty tree the end has come,
Keep your thoughts clear
Or you roots will become cold and numb.

—*Keri Burkhamer*

Untitled

Deep from within the thicket
As day gives way to dusk
Marble ebon eyes emerge,
Oh deer...
Camouflaged against bronzen dunes
Prancing...
 Prancing...
 Prancing...
Leaving only a cast in the sand.
— *Edith E. May*

Sundrops

The moon is full tonite
The stars are hung in place
Longingly waiting for tomorrow
To feel the sun's embrace.

The warmth of unseen rays
The scent of heat on land
Reaching up into the sky
I catch some in my hand.

—*Amber C. Meltzer*

Winter

From inside our shells
We look out at icy feathers
And crystals.
Outside, white gems fall,
Forming a snowy white blanket
Upon the frozen earth.
Hibernating beneath,
Lies the promise of a lush,
Green carpet, just waiting
To emerge when the sun shines
Once again.

—*Sherri Lynn Glebus*

A Mountain Glen

As I walked in the field on a spring like day
The mountain is covered
With a colorful array
Plants of different size and shape

Like soldiers waiting a great debate
Asters showing their azure blue
Give rise the prim
Rose pinkist hue

There in the distant on will die
So that another blossom might arise
As skillful as a painters with his hand
So does God gives color to American's land
— *Michael Lovell*

Seasons

In fall, leaves change colors,
Birds fly south,
Bears begin to stuff their mouths.
Winter is just around the corner.
Soon it will be fall no longer.
Now in December,
The fire glows in a shade of amber.
Spring, as usual, will bring
Back the birds who sing.
In the midst of July
You feel as though you will fry.

— *Christine Moire*

Change

The myriad glossy leaves
of a giant magnolia tree,
tossing lightly in today's
breeze; at times blowing
hard in a gale-
mirror ebb and flow
of billions of human lives-
all who live on Mother Earth.
As designs take form
in a kaleidoscope;
disband, then reform;
so is change inexorable
in every one's life.
They are wise who welcome change.
Change leads to growth.

—*Clara S. Dick*

Globe

A spinning globe picks up speed
Around the mighty world spins
Countries blur together
A harmony of greens and blues.
Peace is running rampant
Across the blue-white waters
The world becomes one
At peace for a whirling instant.
The globe slows and stops
The land stand apart, together no more
Peace is drowned in the waters that it rose from
Only the globe is quiet
The world outside is loud and warlike.
A spining globe lasts not forever,
A world would, if not so many people
Tried to stop
The natural spinning of a globe.

—*Jessica J. Guerriero*

Never Alone

You're never alone when no one's near
To help you see the words are clear.
You're never alone after going through a trial,
For the Lord will give you a number to dial.

You're never alone without a friend
Who gives you comfort throughout the day's end.
You're never alone when a friend is around
To share in talks and laughs and games.

You're never alone after having troubles
For all life has lots of bubbles.
You're never alone after having a fight
For there is someone who stands for the right.

You're never alone after being called names,
For people are always playing their games.
You're never alone in doing the right thing
Because that's how you learn to sing.

    —Margaret Desmond

For the Strong

I was anxious about my future
So I asked my father for advice.
He said, *Be alive, follow your heart and believe in yourself.*
If you should choose wrongly and feel guilt later, that is good.
It means you are still a part of the process of life ongoing.
There are no dreams in the ground, no dreamers,
No love, no risk. These are for the strong.
You must leave me now, here in this cemetery,
But you take what you want from life,
And don't stand still.

    — Karin O'Brien

Untitled

The love I had for you I carried within me for no one to see, a secret to all.
I stored it deep inside of my heart and as each summer came, I saw you
And it bloomed like a beautiful flower in spring.
Its petals soft and gentle welcomed your companionship
and made you a part of its life.
But as the winter destroys the beauty of spring,
so too were the obstacles of our love.
As each petal drifted away with the breeze,
it became more and more distant
From its original bud, like you and I.
No one's sure of what becomes of each petal blown away,
Whether it brings new life or gets buried beneath the soil.
Sometimes I think it brings beautiful life
and blossoms twice a pretty as before.
I hope in future days to come we too
will let the love that's faded away with time
Bloom again like the beautiful flowers in spring.

    — Michelle A. Castaneda

Country Autumn

Put another stick in the stove, son, and shake the ashes down.
It's getting cold outside, son, the leaves are turning brown.
The wild flowers are all withered and the grass is not so green,
The wild things have taken shelter, there're only a few birds to be seen.
There'll be ice in the water pail and you'll need another quilt.
Some popcorn will taste good, son, with a great big glass of milk.
And bring your Mama her Bible so she can read a verse or more,
And we'll thank God for His bounties that we have put by in store.
The apples were so sweet this year, the spuds and onions can't be beat.
The cabbage heads were nice and big and the carrots crisp and sweet.
The turnip patch has plenty of greens and turnips, too,
And the sorghum and the honey, why they'll just have to do.
Our cow is fat and sassy, the chickens are laying well
And the old gray mare has plenty of hay form the meadow's swell.
The granary's full of corn and wheat
So there'll be plenty of bread to eat.

    — Marcia R. Morris

Youth

Youth, the leaders of tomorrow
Struggling each day with sorrow
Youth, the forerunners of the 21st Century
Brave hearts enduring stormy seas
Youth, take a stand, and courageously right the wrongs
Implanting happiness of humanity where it belongs
Youth, stop the fighting between each other
And realize we are all sisters and brothers.
Youth, Challenge your weakness and boldly stand
Take charge of your life in full command
Youth, banish the evils of weapons and crime
Cut the ropes of suffering with wisdom devine
Youth, stop slandering the body with drug pollution
And enjoy your own magnificant Human Revolution
Youth, together travel the emerald road hand in hand
Envisioning world harmony and peace within our land.

    —Shirley D. Zagorec

Riding the Wave of Life

The pressure is on.
Every single eye of the crowd is on you
The choice is yours,
Although your reputation depends on which you choose
The chance of a lifetime,
Ride that wave, it'll take you high as the sky
That's what they told you, before you wiped out,
Now under the ground's where you lie.

You could've ridden that other wave,
And would've handled it great
But their words were, You'll like this one much better,
You'll do fine, just wait.
You didn't know what you were getting into
For that you're not to blame.
That is why I'm writing this, to tell others,
DRUGS ARE A DEADLY GAME!

    —Robin M. Rose

Hurt

Why is it that I'm always getting hurt?
I don't deserve it, but I'm always getting burnt.
I hate always hurting
Because the tears are always returning.
Please, my love, make it fly away like a dove.
Please take away the hurt.

    — Staci Autrey

The Answer

She was tired of living in the past,
She was going to end this charade at long last.
There wasn't anything to be afraid of anymore;
This was the one and only cure.
Outside there was a breeze in the air.
She called a friend, but no one was there.
Depression sunk in deeper, she was not needed.
Her mind made up, she prepared for the deadly deed.
The world was oblivious to the impending doom.
She was tired of living in the world of gloom.
She reached, instinctively, for the gun,
She pulled the trigger, the task was done.
A sickly silence overcame the room.
They found her with a bullet lodged in her chest.
She looked like an angel when they laid her to rest.
The question, why, raced through everyone's mind,
They thought her perfect, but to her,
The world hadn't been kind.
They buried her with a single red rose upon her breast.

    —Marnie L. Vogel

A Better World

In this wicked world of ours
There is much for us to contend
There is a need to be kind
A need to be a friend

Trust is of the past
Caring put aside
Love is rarely shown
Hatred seen worldwide

Fidelity is seldom heard
Aids beome a public word
Alcohol is second nature
Drugs to free unwanted pressure

A better world we all desire
A world with happy endings
A world when ones join together
A world when problems cease forever.

— *Karen Bather*

Memories

Memories of times past,
Are recorded upon the brain,
Like the pages in a book.

I've often wondered what
My life will be,
When you are no longer
Upon this earth, with me.

I know that I shall miss,
The love that we share,
And the friendship that
Is there.

The feeling of something lost,
Leaves the feeling of dispair;
Then from the recesses of my mind,
To it's fore front, I realize,
Memories of you,
Will forever be mine.

—*Marjorie J. Carroll*

Children

I cry because I'm afraid
I scream because I'm hurt
Please don't let them do it again.
I try because I'm forced
I'm forced because I'm needed
I scream because I hurt
There—They've done it again.
Why must this happen to me
No, it's not what I want
Forced into a place I don't want to be
When will the pain stop?
Please don't hurt me again
No, please stop.
Oh God, it's closer now.
It's here now.
Passing from one life to the next.
Should I say thanks?
Going to a place where so few care.

—*Clifford A. Davis III*

Thoughts to Live by

What we believe—we do achieve.
When we plan—then we can.
When we serve—we do deserve.
When we forgive—then we can live.
When we pray—we don't decay.

— *Marilyn Lunger*

Pain

The room lies quiet and empty
And the sky looks dark and grey.
There is no explanation
And there's nothing more to say.

But bright colors now seem dimmer
Anbd storms now sound mor harsh.
Music is very monotomous
And the ocean resembles a marsh.

Facts are no longer interesting
And pretty birds don't sing.
Nothing brings contentment,
Not even a blooming spring.

This leaves us with a scar
From the pain that's far from mild.
The heart never stops aching
After the death of a child.

—*Dana Elkun*

A Food Fight

Finally, it's lunch time, but oh, I could cry!
This could ruin Mom's apple pie.
This room is a junk yard; no, it's worse than that.
If it ever gets cleaned up, I'll eat my hat!
And now, not on purpose, but with all my might,
I tossed a tomato and made a food fight.
Oh no! It hit Joey on the top of his head.
Now it's official; I'm going to be dead.
But I got off easy; he just flings a pea,
But still it is headed straight for me.
I duck. It hits Sandra, and boy is she mad.
She jumps up and yells at us, *I'll tell my dad!*
But what could he do to us? Boy, that was dumb.
But Sandra's a baby; she cries, sucks her thumb.
Now Tommy hit me, he hit me with beans.
They hit me and splattered all over my jeans.
Now lettuce and ice cream are headed for me,
And so is the lunch lady, *What did I see?*
Did I see a food fight with lettuce and jelly?
Oh great! Joey hit her with beans in the belly.
I stomp on her foot and run out the door
Past jelly, tomatoes and beans on the floor.
I'm finished with food fights. I won't start one more.

—*Susan Cash*

A Beautiful Friend

Jodi Ann Howard is a lovely name,
Also, there is no girl quite the same;
Her character, her smile, her tender face
Were all blended together with God's loving grace.

She has such fine blonde beautiful hair
Her facial expression is often found rare.
The eyes gleam with a gorgeous blue
When she lifts her head and looks at you.
Luscious perfectly describes her lips
Which want for a long, loving kiss.
Then there is that expressive, radiant smile;
It sends out warmth and gracious style.
Besides her looks she possesses charm
Even if she wanted to, she could do no harm.
This precious woman means so much,
I hope forever, we keep in touch.

As one can see, she is really great;
She is one person you just cannot hate.
Unfortunately, this poem has to end,
Of telling of a beautful friend.

—*Kyle Kennedy*

What I See in Life

I see the sun go down every day,
Beautiful flowers wilting away
I see wasted days and thoughtless nights,
Nobody caring about human rights.
I see many good people losing hold,
The kind I thought were strong and bold.
I see bitter tears shed over hate,
People understanding only too late.
I see soft, warm hearts turning cold,
Young children quickly growing old.
I see people dying, others sighing.
Don't they care? Why aren't they crying?
I see people thinking, others dreaming,
But not catching on to life's true meaning.
I see people sinking, some are falling,
Others turn away when for help they are calling.
I see the ways of this world in every day.
Lord teach me how to help and pray.

—*Merna Satterfield*

The Silent Tear

Be good, be well, my silent tear.
Don't show yourself in sadness or fear.
Don't fall from my eye, don't wet my cheek.
Don't quiver my voice so that it cannot speak.
Perhaps you will lie, but no one will know
That you really live but you never show.
You can contain what I choose to hide,
Either my sorrow or my shallow pride.
But if you fall, my silent tear,
If you expose my sadness or reveal my fear,
Then tear, you'll see, you gave me Hell
Because you made the others fall as well.

— *Tanya Laden*

Poor Little Timmy

Poor little Timmy, has no one to greet him,
No one will give out cigars at his birth,
No hug, no love, no kiss, no gift
Potter's Field will be his crib;

No baby shower, no waiting father,
Not even a flower will be placed on his grave
He could find love with a childless couple
But this unborn boy will soon be destroyed.

Beyond the stars there are millions of angels,
Many are constantly near God's throne,
But in a dark cold lonesome field
Will lie a little angel that nobody knows.

—*Eric Betancourt*

Untitled

A lonely day, a lonely hour,
Dreary as a wilted flower.
The sun does not rise, the sun does not set,
In fact, I have not even seen the sun yet.

I do not really see anything anymore.
My life is drained and I am a bore.
I have no energy, excitement or fun.
I feel as if my whole life is done.

Why do I feel this awful way,
It is a question I ask, most every day.
I let my heart be slowly taken,
And now my whole life is shaken.

By a stupid mistake with a little boy,
Who used me and left me like an old toy.

—*Melanie Wisniewski*

Where Have These Times Gone?

I used to live in my own little land
Where everyone worked hand in hand.
Everyone did their own little thing
And everyone was their own special king.
There were no fights or dickers between anyone.
It was a time when people all had fun.
Where have all these times gone? some people ask.
To answer this question may be the hardest task.

— *Crystal White*

When We Meet Again

When we meet again my love
I will smile and I will cry
Thinking of our time in days gone by.
Our hands will touch as we walk along,
Then you will tell me why you left me alone.
When we meet again my love
I will tell you how I suffered through the pain
And tears I felt over you. Though the torment
Eased as the years swept by. It now rushes in
As you stand by my side.
When we meet again my love, I will find the
Courage to say good bye. Then I will turn and
Walk away, Leaving you with the pain that was
Once left for me, now it will be yours for eternity.
For when we meet again my love, the love affair
Will finally end. So here's to you my love
Until we meet again.

—*Connie Bahm*

Lost Memories

I cry each day from now till then
Wondering why I let myself hurt you again.
The pain in your eyes is more than I can stand,
To watch you slip away from the reach of my hand.
I know that you can't take it all away,
But please remember me each night and each day.
I hope you'll never forget the times that we've had,
When you cheered me up when you knew I was sad.
Those are my memories, the only ones I've got,
And they rip at my heart like a gigantic knot.
You made me smile and laugh again,
But to be happy now would be committing a sin.
I let you down in every way,
And for the rest of my life I'll repay you some way.
I thought it'd be different, that we'd find a way,
But now I hope again to go far away.
Where no one will hurt just because of me,
I'll leave you alone and let you be free...

—*Haley Jewett*

Memories

The memories of our friendship flash by
And I only remember when we soared high.
As I hear old songs being played
I reminisce about those unforgetable days.
The thought of your touch against mine
Gathers strength to tell others that I am fine.
I only wish to hear your voice or to see your face.
Just once I wish I was the special one that you embrace.
I have that only one wish to ask for:
To see that smile you once wore.
Please, let me know if you are alive today.
Just a couple of simple words is all that you would have to say.
I just want to hear, *Hello, this is Keith; how are you?*
Is that so difficult for you to do?

—*Kathryn Castle*

Tempus Fugit

Moving into the future,
With each yesterday.
Somehow never quite realizing,
That tomorrow became today.

Tomorrow, I knew, would make me,
Wise beyond my peers.
Yet wisdom is not mine.
And today is yesteryear.

The future seemed so distant.
How did the present move so fast?
What once was tomorrow's promise,
Has become a thing of the past.

—*Maria E. Collins*

Memories

I sit in my room as memories come through,
Memories of friendship and hearts ripped in two.
These walls have seen so many things:
Happiness, sadness, everything life brings.
It's heard secrets kept throughout all years.
It's seen smiles turn into constant tears.
They've heard me sing and seen me dance,
Heard my secrets of love, hate and romance.
I sit in my room one final time
Because womanhood has come
and the ladder of life is what I must climb.

—*Tammy Cowin*

Until Tomorrow

When today becomes forever
And yesterday is but a dream
That is when I will find my soul
And I will know my fortold scheme.

When today becomes the future
And yesterday is at long past
That is when I will know my fate
My long lost dream at last.

When today becomes tomorrow
And yesterday is just a memory
That is when I will realize
My God inspired destiny

When the present becomes eternity
And the past lives no more
I will finally know the way to go
Through lifes long corridor.

—*Mark Berardino*

Untitled

Seeking time for healing
In touch with what I'm feeling
To find a poem inside me
Makes living most appealing

— *Richard L. Bywater*

Will You Remember Me?

Will you remember me
When days are short and
Nights are long?
When it is cold and
The wind is blowing?
When the sky is dark
And the stars are shining?
When the sun sets in
And the moon rises?
When the earth is moving
And I am still?
Will you remember me?

— *Margaret del Palacio*

Time

Time goes by
So very fast
As a car when it moves.
Time is valuable to everyone
Especially me
When I'm with you.
Time is what I need!
to be with you
to be sweet
to be charming
and tell you how I feel
about you, my lady,
A lady who's kind
A lady who's nice
A lady who lights my fire
Deep down in my heart.

—*Titus Cochran*

A Monday in September

Red blurs her velvet soft,
　my touch
From coarse grit,
　sweaty hand
Drive the nail that stops the rain.
The saddest blue is in
　a fireplace room.
Love pleases best
　with safety.
No confine or structure makes
　me believe
Why convenience lies
　when the wind blows cold.
Love is not a delicate thing.

— *John Allen Moseley*

Changes

I know it's horrible
Almost too bad to tell
Then why do they
Always on my past must dwell

Whats done is done
It can never be changed
Then why do I
Always wish for it re-arranged

They need not mock
I'm aware what I did
Then why do they
Always on my past must bid

It's my move now
This time forward not back
Nothing will stop me
I'll fill every hole and crack!

— *Kristine Redling*

Untitled

When the day ends
and my shirt begins to fall
My coat's hung up
　hat on the wall
The car in the garage
all safe, ha!
　and secure
That's the time
I know for sure,
I love you...

— *Lori Gatewood*

Fallen Youth

The mourning of these days gone by
Haunts these fragile souls,
As the fallen youth try to maturally grow.

Troubled times are with us,
This world has torn them down
As the fallen youth search to be found.

Death stares them in the eyes.
Love has lost its throne.
These fallen youth no longer have a home.

The future is before us and with it no hope,
As the fallen youth struggle, trying hard to cope.

War, hunger, and destruction have chipped
Away our times.
But now the fallen youth, will have to pay
The price for the crime.
Tell us when this will stop, when will the youth be free
You claim us a tomorrow,
But will a tomorrow ever be?

—*Stephanie Cargill*

Scarred

Down a row of razor blades I slid,
Through to the bone they dug.
Slicing and ripping, halfway down I stopped.
My muscles and tendons got tangled.
You came to my rescue saying, *I love you.*
Forcing salt into my wounds you said, *I love you.*
At school, I told everyone our story.
Kids ask the strangest questions.
Bones soften the blows of baseball bats.
Doc said to stay out of those flimsy tree houses,
But I know that you love me.
This stuff that's for my own good hurts-though.
Breaks and bruises heal,
Mental scars are everlasting.

— *Mark Lane Bledsoe*

Child Without Life

Poor unborn child not given a chance to live,
Not able to show the world the love you could give.
You could have made someone happy out here
But your mother took that away without a tear.
So for you and all the children that don't get a chance to live,
I cry all the tears I have to give.

— *Melaena Ramirez*

Please, Say No

What in the world is going on with the youth of today?
And why is it so hard for them to find safe games to play?
When friends try to convince you of wrong places to go,
Don't get upset and all uptight, just simply tell them no.
When offered alcohol at the company's party, don't accept one for a show.
You'll be remembered for taking the drink, be firm and tell them no
When classmates spread bad rumors of your being a little slow,
Keep the good work up, don't listen to their chatter; keep on saying no.
And when your girlfriend's angry and threaten to let you go,
Throw your loving arms around her, tell her sweetly, my answer is no.
Now there's one more thing I'd like to say to every teen I know,
There's million boys and girls like you who wished they had said no.

— *Mark Eric Lyons*

A Bottle Half Empty

A bottle half empty sits on the table
A man stooped over
Lonely and blue
A cry for help but no one hears
For he speaks in a voice
Silent, full of despair
A man's anger deep as the sea
Struggling to be free
Free from the harsh waves
That constantly slash
Across his face
But somehow knowing
He won't escape
So, slowly he reaches
For his courage, draining at last all his emotions
Till numbness remains and misery his only fate.

—*Margaret E. Peirson*

Battered Women

Black and blue,
The colors so often seen all over arms and legs.
Facial cuts, blood red scars, broken bones and ribs,
Puffed up bruises never to be healed.
These are the marks and scars left on these women.
Chosen for a reason unknown.
Why do men beat them?
Why do they stay?
Can they leave?
No. They will be found and taken back,
Abused again and again.
But it's not the bruises and blood
that make the pain.

— *Micole Linehan*

Untitled

Why didn't we see?
She was a fragile child who suffered a lonely agony.
Her skin was marred with bruises and sores.
She had bumps, scratches and abrasions.
Her hair was uneven and left in clumps.
It was limp as if left unwashed for days or weeks.
Her clothing was dirty.
She cried out for help.
Why didn't we hear?
We must risk being wrong when we feel a child is being harmed,
For the price of a child's life can never be replaced.

— *Karen Nielsen*

Little Children

Little children all over the world
Lookin' out for Santa Claus on every Christmas day.
Little children at the school
Have learned something to read and write
And havin' some fun to play, little children.

Little children, anyplace and anywhere,
Playin' soldiers, cowboys and Indians.
When little children become a man some o' them stays in church
The others in battlefield but some are gone, little children

Little children in several poor lands
Livin' with no clothes, no toys, no homes and money,
But some children in various regions
Have lots of luck and are playin' freely, little children.

God in Heaven knows them all; God in Heaven loves them all.
Those poor little children, those rich little children,
Yes, in the eyes of the Lord, they're all wonderful,
Beautiful little children, wonderful little children,
Little children, little children.

—*Mario Cristobal*

The Boat

Old and broken, chipped and frayed
On the beach in the sand
Away from people, away from man.

Pieces coming off, losing its shape
Just like the dunes of this beautiful state.
It sits there and hides from the sea itself,
But opens itself from the birds and kelp.

I have seen this boat in my mind
All alone as if it were mine.
I've seen its color, its shape.

It is wrecked, yes I know,
But it is pretty there,
Unknown.

    — *Heather Boothe*

Believing in Love

When should I cry for you?
When should I die for you?
All the times that I've tried,
You always seem to hide.
Do you believe in love?

You had the key
To my little treasure.
It gave me joy
And so much pleasure.
Then, you believed in love.

    — *Devon Ferree*

Sunday—8:45 a.m.

The morning's so nice
early on a Sunday,
Looking to the sky
whose clouds have covered the sun,
SILENCE,
no human beings running around
but oh, then I think of you
and go back
to an empty bed.

    — *Diane C. Hurilla*

The Light

The light shines so bright
as she looks into the
deep blue skies what is it
she sees no one can see
what she sees maybe
it is an image or some unknown
thing or maybe she sees
the future

    —*Deborah Rincon*

Alone

Amidst a diamond clad dancer
Thrived a struggling search for a
Disjointed concept of happiness.
Extended through fumbled fingers,
Eyes glared to find some entity
To complete her eternal bliss.
But away she ran so freely
To the rhythmis undulations that
Breathed in her soul
Illuminating grandeurs of where
Her potentials would take her,
Having commenced upon the perfect state...
Alone.

    —*Annacarol Lampe*

Acid Rain

An aerosol can
spurts in spasms
as a fan frees fumes.
In this verdant vapor,
pungent air stifles
the smell of fresh
flowers that struggle
to survive the blast.
The downfall scatters
waste in streams,
doling out disease
to unsuspecting souls.
And a shallow undertaking
of umbrellas only
cast the caustic
postponement of
the inevitable.

    —*Denise Martinson*

In Sight

Can you see me?
I mean, can you really see me?
My body may be here
And my soul may say many things,
But do you know what I fear?

I fear that you see
Only what you want to see.
Then I act according to what you see,
Until even I
Can't see me.

    — *James Lynch*

The Poet

Write me a poem, she asked,
Blue eyes twinkling in the sun.
A cinch, I replied, as I looked at her,
Consider the job as done!
With Pen in hand I sat me down,
Deep thoughts crossing my mind.
But words such as lovely and precious
Were all my fingers could find,
To write for this Cherub beside me,
Whose trust put me in this bind.
So *Roses are Red,* I wrote,
While some are pink and yellow!
My blue eyed Cherub said this was *Great!*
And thinks me an original fellow.

    —*Eunice I. Standley*

Untitled

Let her dream
It's good for her heart
If she thinks of the good
She doesn't have to think
About the bad
No one has to know
Only I
She doesn't
If she dreams beautiful
Then she can be beautiful inside
I know someone will come
And tell her
But for now
Let her dream.

    — *Jan Cho*

Scattered

My blood surges fire within,
my body burns fierce with,
my sword draws out of,
my blade it is sharp as,
my soul cries out with,
my thoughts race through,
my brain plots out,
my goals are like,
my imagination is like
my writing. Scattered!

    — *James T. Langley Jr.*

Whispers

Whispers of air,
Not a thought,
Not a care.

Words overhead,
In and out of my bed.
Trembling at night,
Whispers would fight
To get the first word.

Life is so fake.
Nobody cares.
Except for the bad.
Whispers care.

Care about you?
No, what a lie.
Nobody tells the truth.
Whispers *do* care,
But care about the bad.
Whispers are fake.

    —*Debbie Turano*

Of Things Worthwhile

Too many a task
I refused to commit
Because I feared the struggle.
Then it dawned,
that struggles were necessary.
The promise was not
that labor would be easy,
only that it would be worth it.

    — *Dean Phillips*

Rhyme in Time

Rain of colors
Smiling
Fading
In waves of time
 walk
A talk
A touch
Of much
Feeling
Never ending
A tune
So immune
To colors
And flowers
Of rhyme
In time.

    — *William K. Yakoubian*

Autumn

The leaves gently fall
As if they were obeying
Some strange inner call.

    — *Jenny M. Misiak*

The Kiss of a Princess

I was tired, oh so very tired.
Every bone in my body ached,
And it was late, way too late,
But when there's work to be done, there's work to be done.
Now, finally I was home, slumped down in my easy chair.
Then it happened
The kiss of a princess.
Was this some trick of my imagination?
A grand hallucination?
A wonderous dream?
I shook my head.
I rattled my brain to clear the cobwebs,
But oh, to no avail.
I did not know for sure, for I could only recall,
The kiss of a princess.
Try as I may, I was at a loss.
Was my feeble mind going berserk?
Was I losing touch with reality?
Slowly, oh so slowly, I began to get a grip on myself.
The mystery began to reveal itself.
The picture went from fuzzy to focus.
The missing piece was now in place.
Good night, Daddy, the kiss of a princess.

　　　—Geoffrey Ray Shuman

Marx Brothers Comedies:
Better Red Than Dead or Ugly American

Is it better to be *Red* than dead?
And why the ultimatum?
We Americans are not ugly
As we pay the bill
For sourgrape *continentals'*
Racism; organizing also an
Interracial America in
US university armchairs where
Economists and sociologists solicit and/or
Predict third-world standards for us
Of South Africa's mixed race *coloreds* and life style
Commensurate with Charles Dickens' gruel and grime;
School for child thieves,
Beggars, and sexual misfits, pimping as streetwalkers in the
Oliver Twist—like porno; that there is no US Constitutional
Opportunity for all
Should we remain predominantly white-born-heritage
In our fought-for freedom since 1776-1812.

　　　—Geneve Baley

Astral Handgliding

Fly now, your spirit is free.
Your spirit is gone from where your body does flee;
A glassof wine in your hand
As timeless as the grains of sand
Float downstream; it's not dying.
Go towards the light while it's still shining.
Through astral plains your mind can see
Things that are and were never meant to be.
Fade away; you're free at last.
Now your name is in the past.
Life went on and slowly it crept
Past the place where your body last slept;
A peaceful feeling, your spirit unheld,
Go now where you conscience does meld;
Ascend a pair of spiral stairs
Where long ago confronts you there.
As your soul stands in the light,
There's no need to run; there's no need to fight.

　　　—Heather Carolla

New York

Springtime in New York
People rushing to and fro
In an endless stream
Weary of winter, eager to go
To the parks and the zoo
Flowers bursting into bloom
Visitor dining, shopping
Winning at Belmont Park
In the afternoon.

Gawking at the Statue of Liberty
And affluent Park Avenue
And laughing with the musical shows
Remembering all the sights
And the sound
I return...to a sleepy Southern town
To dream of another Spring.

　　　—Gladys Cooley

Aggregate

What we are together
Is more than adequate
The sum of our number
Equals a high aggregate.
We are smarter than the average bear
We look before we walk
We know that since we care
We no longer need check stock.
Sure we get lonely
We miss each other constantly
This we will rectify
With all rules we comply.
There is no mistaking
This is not temporary
What is slowly forming
Will provide no vacancy.
We make our own silver lining
For fate we are not waiting.

　　　—Alex Chornyj

Don't Give Me the City

Don't give me the city
With its grey concrete paths
And skycrapers high;
Give me a green grassy field
Where I can look at fluffy clouds
In a beautiful azure sky.
Don't give me the city
With its many neon lights;
Give me a winding country road
So I can see the shining stars,
And be bathed in bright moonlight.
Don't give me the city
With its hustling crowds
Who jostle as they pass by;
Give me a small country town
Where the folks you meet
When you walk down the street
Are friends who smile and say *hi.*

　　　—Waneta V. Emery

Lost Love

To you, the one that I loved,
The time has come that I must go
And say good-bye to you
And all that we shared.
I love you so and I promise you
That I'll never forget you
Because time after time
I will think of you and wish
That you were here with me
To hold me and love me
Like you once did.
Some day my tears will dry
And the memories will fade
But for now, I'll keep going
And try my hardest
To leave you behind.

　　　—Naomi Cords

Meandering Hearts

What could be more rare
Then someone who truely cares
A love so sweet
But so rare
Is it fair

You and me
I can see
The love you have within thee
As your eyes glem upon me
With happiness and glee

Holding thee
Oh! So near
Feeling our hearts beat
With a glow
That will never go

　　　—Brenda Strickland-Vieira

Autumn Interlude

Chilly breeze, falling leaves,
Bare trees, sillouettes against
October's bright blue sky.

Squirrels busy
Through autumn days.
They know winter is
Swiftly drawing nigh.

Birds gathering
At the feeders.
One more hardy feast
Before they fly.

South for winter,
But they'll remember
And return.

One day
when winter winds
Have said goodbye.

　　　—Beatrice Hiss

His Eyes

The eyes I looked up to, now have closed.
The eyes that took away my fears;
The eyes that watched the fall of my tears.
The eyes that made me laugh,
The eyes that showed me love,
The eyes with the innocent look of a dove.
Many times I have looked to those eyes for comfort from my life,
To shelter me from harm and strife.
I have found that my eyes have lost their sparkle, their love.
Every night I pray to God above;
To send me the eyes I long to love.
Someday I will see his eyes across a crowded room and know;
The eyes I long to love, love another.
And will never know how many times
his eyes have comforted me from pain and strife.
And possibly, I will pray for his eyes the rest of my life.
   —*Brenda Shockley*

I Thought of You Often Today

I felt a warm breeze encircling me it reminded me of your hugs.
There was clear blue sky that reminded me of your eyes.
I turned on the radio and the songs reminded me of times we've shared.
There was a sunset so beautiful that reminded me of our friendship
Past and future. I though of you often today. I saw a flower blooming
That reminded me of your warm heart. There were children playing
In the park today they reminded me of your playful ways. I looked up
At the sun it reminded me of your shinning smile. There was a bird
Singing his song it reminded me of how gently you speak. I thought
Of you often today. But yet, I felt a tear trickle down my face today.
It reminded me a love once shared is gone.
There is an emptiness in my heart.
Reminding me that you are no longer mine.
But still...I thought of you often today.
   — *Angel Telesco*

Friends

Friends are people who you wish upon to endure.
You tell them your secrets and ask of them more.
You know they will help you cause their always around,
They care how you are and what you have found.

Friends you take for granted and never let known,
Just how it is, you care for them so.
You in your heart know they are the best,
But now is the time to let them know
In you they have achieved someone above the rest.
Be there for them as they are for you
And make it known that it is them alone
That have shown you the way to life unshown?
   —*Alisa Franklin*

Untitled

I fell in love with you
Not knowing what the future held.
We got along so good,
I knew it wouldn't last for long.
Then you told me you were leaving
And the thought of losing you hit me hard.
Knowing I had to give you up for a girl I didn't even know
Broke my heart into a million pieces.
I needed time to figure it all out and you gave it to me.
Now I know what's happening and can accept these facts.
But if I knew this was going to have happened,
I would have just loved you for a friend.
   —*Carol Fowler*

I Found a Friend

I touched the golden sky
And caught a ray of sun
As I soared across the heavens
I found a lonely one
I took an autumn leaf
And brushed it gently upon his face
I opened my arms to him
To await a kind embrace
We sat along the stream
Amidst the morning dew
We cried, we laugh, we talked
And we prayed together too. I found a bit of hope
Beneath that old elm tree. I found a life worth saving
I found a friend so dear to me
So when the sky turns golden
And the world turns bright and clear
I'll remember that quiet stream
And the friend I found so dear.
   — *Valerie L. Harris*

To My One and Only

My dearest Erica, I need to be with you,
You have to understand I'm deep in love with you.
Time isn't remembered unless with you it's spent,
When I'm with you, my heart's full and content.
With you in my arms, I need nothing else,
Not money nor jewelry or gifts from yourself.
You are my life as you already know.
I need you so much, for you, my life away I would throw.
Whatever's needed, just ask me,
My hardest I'll try for you to be pleased.
If you're ever hurt or sad,
For me to help you I'll be glad.
One last thing before I'm going,
I hope you see that this is all truth you're knowing.
Erica it's true
When I say that...I love you!
   — *Brandon Clark*

Teddy Bear

My teddy bear,
Ragged and worn,
Sits on my bed
Waiting for me to come home.
Always there to listen,
Never to complain,
Always loving me
No matter what I say.
So Teddy, I am sorry
That I worry you
Or even call you names,
I just want you to know, Teddy,
I love you anyway.

— *Heather McCutcheon*

Memories

People ask me if we're still together.
I don't know what to say.
We're together in my memory
Every single day.
Memories are all I have now.
I guess that we are through
But the pain will never go away
Just like the memories of you.

— *Angela Hazelbaker*

His Own Little World

He knew how to act both oncreen and offscreen
This was his job, and so he did it superbly.
He had every teenager in his spell
This man had quite a story to tell.
Not only did he have a love for acting,
He also had a passion for car racing.
A rebel, he was, in his own little world
The name of his car was the Porsche Spyder.
He got in his death car, and he was speeding
As if to him the world was nothing.
So on that day, as he had sped,
Soon the world was to know that James Dean
Was dead.
Now, he may be dead and may return never.
But in our hearts he'll last forever.

— *Natalie Khoshaba*

Remembering When Time Was Young

I can remember way back when jumping jacks counting from one to ten.
Skipping rope fell and almost broke my chin.
From the limb of an old oak tree a tire on a rope was hung.
I can remember when time was young!
I was all dressed up in a cowboy suit, everyone said I looked so cute.
Wearing shirts with a sailor collar, running to the candy store across
the hollow 'cause my daddy had just given me a dollar.
I can still remember the childhood songs we sung.
I keep remembering when time was young.
I remember summer would end and the school bells would ring.
We would give up hide and seek and everything.
The game we now would play was show and tell,
Changing class at the ring of a bell.
Pulling on little girls' long pigtails, my how they would yell.
I just keep remembering when time was young.
I remember playing football in the park and my mamma saying,
Boy, you better get back home before dark.
Remembering whan time was young!
But now time has changed and I'm all grown up.
And as I sip coffee from my cup, I keep remembering my growing up.
Remembering when time was young,
I keep remembering when time was young.

— *Andrew F. Clemons*

Monster in My Closet

It was late one night, so I went to bed,
When I noticed someone was breathing over my head.
I sat up and looked around,
I didn't see anything but a footprint on the ground.

I lay back down to get some sleep,
But I couldn't so I counted sheep.
Then in my closet came a rattling noise,
I looked to my left to see all my toys.

They laid on my floor, but how did they get there?
Then I heard a voice inside me saying *Beware, Beware!*
I opened my closet and the monster I could see,
He put out his arms and tried to grab me.

He pulled me in the closet with all of his might,
Then my mom came in and turned on my light.
I notice the monster was only my coat,
So I went back to bed and dreamt about boats.

— *Paige Wright*

Memories Remain

Dear Lou;
Today our hearts touched base and we talked for hours
Of childhood days when we ran through fields of flowers
Chasing little yellow butterflies-
Cupping our hands over sun-filled eyes.
In those days we didn't realize...
 time disappears.

— *Inez Simpson Kemp*

School

We have to go to school every day.
We hardly have time to run off and play.
I guess I could say something nice about school.
Nah, that would just make me look like a fool.
What I hate most are hot, sunny days
When your brain goes kerplop and your work blurrs and looks like a maze.
I guess it's something we all go through,
But if you want to know why, I haven't a clue.
You need paper, erasers, pencils and pens
And you have to know about hundreds, ones and tens.
There is so much to learn in high school, they say.
Pay attention! Don't throw it away!
But you already know so much Math, History, Science and such
But let me tell you...it's too much!

— *Erin Murphy*

Little Sparrow

Little Sparrow how we have learned from you
Such lessons of great wealth
You never fall to the earth from any tree
Without God's tender-loving breath.
He breathed upon the birds and bees
And mankind since the world began
His wind ripples, blows through the breeze
As only his omnipotent power can.
Little Sparrow, it is your trust and grace
In such a Mighty One
That we posses such faith in this race
To endure until the victory's won.
The battle is not easy as we attempt to soar
While adversities rage and tempters roar.
Above the heights and depths of woes
We've learned from you to conquer any foes.
So, Little Sparrow, thanks again, for showing us the way
To walk on through the storm and rain until we find a brighter day.

— *Helen D. Russell*

A Spirit Trying to Die

Why muffle the pounding and swallow the fear?
Why smile and please when screaming inside?
What possible danger can match the fury,
Of a spirit trying to die.
Why struggle to convey what no one can see?
Why challenge tradition when change is futile?
And what is the point of loving you when,
My spirit is trying to die.
A razor sharp spasm is clutching my heart.
Sighting a shriveled and mangled corsage,
Threatens tears to my normally gritty dry eyes.
But my spirit has already died.
A cross in the ground to mark my passage,
The shadow it casts is all that I've left
No sun will rise to warm my stiffened body.
My spirit has died! My spirit has died!

    — *Teresa Sherzey*

Class Ring

As I stand beside her,
A tear runs down my cheek,
While the memories run through my head:
Playing in the snow,
Dancing in the sand.
No one dares to say a word,
As I slip my class ring off her hand.
Her eyes so cold,
Her lips so blue.
I place the ring back upon my finger,
And as I step away they lower her casket into the snow.

    —*Christina Spicer*

Suicide

I look around and call out,
But no one seems to hear my fatal shouts.
I think about what brought me here,
All my pain and lonely fear.
My family just doesn't seem to care,
About my problems and what's fair.
The time grows near to complete my task,
Why are you doing this, my brain seems to ask?
For a moment I hesitate and think what I might be able to do,
But the pain in my heart does not give me a clue.
So I take a step and fall to the sea,
And now it's all over there is nothing left of me.

    — *Stacy Schneiderlochner*

It's Okay

I love you grandpa with all my heart
I knew I loved you right from the start
When you said that *it's okay*
I knew I'd see you another day

And as the tears ran down my face
It was time to let go of your embrace
Oh dear God just take his hand
And guide him into your sweet land

He is too precious for us to lose
But that is not a choice for us to choose
And as I start to bid farewell
This man is seemingly feeling well

And then it came to his last breath
Before I knew it he was at his death, this man is too good
For heaven above and yet he still needs all our love, so goodbye grandpa
Till another day as you say so long with *it's okay*, I love you.

    —*Tracey Tunstall*

Silent Whispers

Alone I sit
Wondering why
I stare out my window
The snowflakes fall,
As fast as my tears,
I think of my endless love.
When will the pain go?
When will my tears dry?
He's gone with my happiness
They say he'll never hurt,
But what about me?
I was just with him,
He showed no pain.
Not knowing it was forever,
We softly said goodbye.
I still hear the stillness
Of my grandfathers
Silent whisper

    —*Kim Lawson*

The Suicide Note

Dear Mother:
When you find this, it will be too late,
I finally gave in to my anger and hate.
I could not live, so I took my life,
It was nothing really, I just used a knife,
And opened a vein, so the blood could run.
I was stoned already so it was really fun.
You see, Mommy dear, I turned to dope
When you turned me away and stomped on my hope.
I tried for so long to be the perfect child,
Then I changed my life and became naughty and wild.
The sex, the drugs, the violence galore
I tried to get help, but my body wanted more.
Why mother, why, did you turn me away?
You made my life worse from day to day.
So good bye Mother dear; it has been quite fun,
I hope your heart breaks.
Signed, your dearly departed son

    —*Wendy Waddell*

The Funeral

For I lost a loved one today
And I wish I could go somewhere happy and stay.
I didn't want to feel sad and I tried,
But my heart just cried and cried.
They say it happens to everyone
But my heart was still stung.
If I had a wish, I'd wish her back,
For her being gone is one thing I'll always lack.
She's in the secret window now that no one else can see
And I know she will be in my heart and looking down at me!

    — *Julee Balko*

Randy

December 26th, the day after Christmas, he died.
He left without saying a word.
The first guy that I rode a horse with.
The first of many cousins.
The first to live, the first to leave.
Why did God take him?
What was the purpose of him having to leave so suddenly?
I ask myself why!
Was it really necessary?
Now all that I'm left with is the beautiful memory of my friend,
My cousin he may be gone,
But nobody will ever take my beautiful memories from me,
The one I hold, in a special place, in my heart.

    —*Kathy Tankard*

Lost

Denying survival in the unkown life;
Ghost of presence past.
Feeding our hearts with a knife;
Eating on a bloody feast.
Time is a barrier between our worlds;
Silent whispers in space.
Lost scattered around and hurled;
Eyes empty with no face.
I feel a strange presence in no place;
I reach into a translucent fog.
Two worlds without a trace;
Who will write our epilog...

—*Elizabeth Boyington*

Real Friends

It's not too hard
To find a friend,
If you settle
For just anyone.
Maybe it's not true
But this will have to do.
Yet someday soon, this will end.
Because someday soon, I'll find a friend.
A friend that's real, a friend that's true
A friend who will treat me, as I treat her.
Haven't I found this friend?
I think not.
For my only real friend
Doesn't treat me
As I treat her.

— *Ann Savino*

Contract of Love

Is there a special reason
Why two people fall in love?
Is it written in a book
In Heaven way above?
Is it someone's plan of healing
Ten thousand broken hearts?
Or is it Cupid's arrow
That makes the love bond start?
Maybe it's a contract
To be with only you
To love, respect and trust
Through pain and sunshine, too.
Yes, that I think is what love is:
A contract of one to be
The keymaster of one's heart
And share their destiny.

— *Amy Bernice Helen Emma Anderegg*

Death Awaits Me Not

My life seems at an end
To groan and grieve and wonder why;
Like fallen angels descending
From beneath a dreary clouded sky.
Though my heart seems empty and never more,
For that which flows in me will never blight
As life yet ceased to mean,
But where there is darkness, there is light.
And if I no longer turn away
The faith that has christened me,
Till death awaits me not.
Then I should come to plea:
The gates of heaven I long to see,
The thorns of Hell
I dread to be.

—*Albert Gonzalez*

Love

I've been in love with you this long,
 why not wait a little longer?
I've learned you have to wait a little
 longer for the things you really want.
If you've been aiming for something
 for this long, why not aim a little longer!

— *Angela Nice*

Poetry

Poetry is giving and receiving thoughts
Thoughts that have emotion
Emotions with meanings of life, love and joy.
Joy is the communication of feeling.

Poetry is feeling life as a soul part
A soul part that reaches inside you
Reaching, holding your senses
The senses of seeing and feeling the essence.

Poetry is the essence of our being
Being one with fantasy and reality
Seeing reality as only part of our existance
Helping fantasy take route in our hearts.

Poetry is the heart felt love
In the giving and understanding of life
Life being our dreams, goals, and future
Future of our everlasting pleasure in print.

— *Penne Ada*

Confused About Who I Am

Lately I've been very confused,
Not knowing which way to turn,
I don't know,
Maybe it's just a tough time in life,
Maybe it's supposed to be this way.
It's almost as if I'm standing still
And everything else is flying by.
Things are so bad,
That I'm not even sure who I am.
I know that all through life,
Things are only going to get tougher,
But why now,
Why can't this be later.
By having this happen now,
It's only causing a great deal of problems,
And emotions that I didn't think
That I would have to face
For many years to come.

— *Heather MacMullen*

It Is Hard to Forget a Loved One

Forget the way he held you tight,
Forget the times you laughed or cried,
Forget the song you chose together,
It is hard to forget a loved one.

Forget the gifts he gave to you,
Forget the way he made you feel,
Forget the nights you spent together.
It is hard to forget a loved one.

Forget about wearing his school jacket,
Forget the nights you went skating or to a show,
Forget the way he looked at you,
It is hard to forget a loved one.

I still love my lost love,
Even though he does not care,
I think of him all the time,
When I am all alone, in the darkness of my room.
It is hard to forget a loved one.

—*Amber D. Reimers*

Seashore Warning

Walking along the seashore
You notice the gulls in flight
They swirl and dive, sit on the poles
And spatter the pier with white.
Other gulls roam free above
Discussing the scene below
Don't do it in the water, guys
When over the pier, let go.
So when your loafing at the beach
Enjoying the sun and nerds
Use the waves as your refuge
Avoid being decorated by the birds.

— *Harry S. Hunting*

Blue Eyes

Blue eyes sparkling in the sun
I don't want to see them clouded
Why must your blue eyes die?
Your blue eyes were meant to sparkle
In the sun
Under the moon
Your eyes will sparkle once more
Twinkle on a moonlit night
One day someone will see the sparkle
Let your blue eyes sparkle
Let them dance in the light of
 a summer moon
Share them with another
But don't let your blue eyes die!

— *Beverly Schmidt*

In My Mind

Sitting in the window up above
Thinking of a true, wonderful love
Hidden deep down inside my soul
To fill that one and only goal.
You seem so true, so sweet,
So good, so trusting to meet.
Together so close we will stay
In a place so far away,
Looking into the sky
Together, wondering why?
Holding hands we will run away
To some other day.
All I need is the love you give,
For only in my mind you will live.

— *Heather Settle*

My Mother

My mother is important.
Disturbed but most of the time happy,
She is strong, quite firm in her ways.
Pretty with brown, short, silky hair,
Dark brown eyes centered and shiny.
She works hard and plays joyously,
Gives me food, clothes and a house.
Her good advice never fails me.
She hates the bad and loves the good,
She nurtures the well, helps the sick.
She feels hurt, pain and sadness,
Feels pleasure, happiness, joy.
She can make a pretty picture
Out of the worst movie ever.
Understanding, hopeful always
She is the greatest gift God gave me!

—*Nicole White*

The Holdup

Slyly, sneakily, the gray clouds strut,
Stamping footprints across a pale sky,
Prepared to perform their dirty deed
of darkening the world.
Posing as innocent balls of fluff,
They approach the unsuspecting sun
Who is defenseless, and surrenders,
Disappearing under their cloak of gloom.
The flowers hibernate inside their homes
fearing to face the gray.
The shadows, caused by the morning sun,
Fail to appear, leaving the city
Still and lifeless.
Moods are dampened, words harsh and cross,
Minds dulled and empty;
Not realizing the sun's plan of revenge
to unleash the sash of the gray cloak
And rise triumphantly the next morning.

— *Karen Abbott*

When You Are Gone

Music when soft voices die
Vibrates in the memory of you.
Rose leaves when the rose is dead
Scatter in the wind.
Your life was cherished
With your friends.
Your memories will forever
Live in our hearts.
And so my friend, when you are gone...
Love itself shall slumber on.

— *Aubrey Dietrich*

Having Eaten Two Stuffed Animals

Having eaten two stuffed animals
In the middle of the night
Having stumbled over furniture
That my mother had arranged
Having loved all them fully that I love
And still loving
All those stuffed animals to whom time...
Has brought me more
Ambition raises itself
To help me survive my life
Just any stuffed animal
Though I know quite well
The words to say no more!

— *Angela Bailey*

Wailing Child

Somewhere a child is wailing
The screech fills the deadness of the night,
Slicing through the billowing piles of snow,
Making the bare trees shudder
And sleepers wake in terror.
The razor sharp pain
Penetrates the hearts of those who hear;
They search and wonder
And cannot find the child.
Till slowly they learn to recognize
The screams that fill their dreams.
Then they see and feel and name the scream.
They look and say, *it's me.*

— *Barbara A. Hanson*

You and Me

You and I will always be one
Loving you more than none.
Keeping your sweetness close to my heart.
Where I know it and I will never part.
I stare at your picture by my bed
Where my warm caresses have led,
When I close my eyes I hear you call
Knowing deeper and deeper I must fall.
I reach out to you before I awake
Way down deep inside I know I made no mistake,
I know in tender love are we you and me.

— *Vickie Ziegelmann*

Recovery

Love and pain coincide as one,
But nevertheless, what can be done?
It happens in summer, it happens in fall,
But it hurts in the heart most of all.

The male species will come and go,
But one thing we will always know,
No matter how much they hurt us
No matter how much our hearts yearn for them,

We will recover...eventually
Then, we will go find another,
Either that,
Or go back to the other.

— *Gretchen Wells*

Once I Was Blind

I heard the children in yonder park
Playing happily, then, a small dogs' bark,
The melodious song of a meadowlark,
And crickets chirping after dark.
The old house moans as it seeks to rest,
And every creature settles into it's nest.
Then silence, so still, all around me grows,
How lonely, how frightening, no one knows.
Never to have seen a glimmer of light,
By day, or star-studded, moonlit night,
Or to have seen a bird soaring high in flight,
Destined to darkness, this was my plight.
Then fate intervened upon my life,
Through the skill of a surgeon's razor sharp knife,
And though I was blind, now I see,
The colors of a sunrise, bursting gloriously.

— *Velma Gosnay*

Golden Apples

You are like golden apples
Sitting in a silver basket.
Your gentle and quiet spirit
Soothes my inner soul.
Your strength is like a beautiful shiny horse
Prancing proudly through the waters.
Your soft voice calls to me in crowds.
Your tender touch I can feel always.
I think of your kneading bowl
And the fragerance of your cooking
Sifts thought the air.
I love you, Mother.

— *Frances Mills McMillian*

What

Nameless snake
You wound your serpentine body
Around my dream child

Insinuated your evil intentions
Among the woven fibers of my life
Caused me trembling

Nameless snake
Slithered in the darkness
Of your anonymity, presumed to be God

Nameless snake
Your stealthy movements
Mimicked an overture of danger

Nameless snake
I
Call you evil

— *Vanessa Austin Wardlaw*

Cry America

Cry for fame...you dirty soul,
Cry for jet-set lifestyle, in the
Glamour world of rich and famous,
Cry and overdose your obsession with
Cocaine.

Cry for oxygen...you poor survivalist
Cry fighting the toxic air pollutants,
Cry and overdose your environment with
Acid rain.

Cry for children...you paranoid mothers,
Cry for your missing and exploited children
Cry and overdose your emptiness with
Tranquilizers.

Cry for peace...you bloody soldier,
Cry for peace solution and disarming,
Cry and overdose the time bomb with
Neverending fear of war.

— *Enver Sulejman*

A Hug

Open wide your arms.
Be your heart receptive.
Bring in much, much more than
Your arms can hold.
Embrace others that you love.
Feel the warm breeze in
The breath of time
Filling the tunnels of the mind.
Hear the silence of peace
Like quiet ripples on the
Deep pools of thought
Touching the sandy beach
Of an eternal world.
See the sun shining
Where fog once settled,
Where fear once stayed
And darkness began.
Know the essence of life
Is close
And that love is never far.

— *Calvin E. Hubbard*

The Journey of My Soul

Across the Sea is a Mountain.
A mountain so bold in motion it
Moves me.
This mountain shall reach the highest
Limit in the sky,
That it shall conquer all seas.
Richly, but bitterly,
My soul soars across the sea
Only to reach my mountain.
The strong feeling of triumph
Overwhelms me the most,
A feeling of bitterness
Soars in me the least.
As I land Softly
On my humongous mountain,
My bold, motionless heart;
Triumphant to reach the sky,
Is limited by the sores of my soul.

—*Sheeran Barnes*

Beauty of Nature

When the sun comes up
And it's another day,
I looked at my calendar
To find it's the beginning of May.
I went outside;
I looked over the hill.
I couldn't see anything
But an old Dutch mill
And the beauty that had been done
By the April showers
That helped bring up
The May flowers.

— *Michelle Weber*

Perfect

When I realized what you meant to me,
You were gone.
My only thoughts
Were of you.
My only feelings
Were for you.

When you came back to me
You were lowly in my expectations.
I loved an image far away,
Built up over time,
Too perfect to love,
Too perfect to forget.

— *Marguerite Beckley*

Another Monday

Morning arrived from a long flighted journey
And as I laid unconscious to the world around me
Its unpretentious light boldly walked in
Carelessly I slumbered and slept
Awakened by his warmth against my back
Without hoping...without a prayer
Yet knowing that he would come for me
Relentlessly and faithfully morning returned
Bearing the gift of yet
Another sunrise...another misty breeze...
Another taste of wheat bread and honey
Another Monday.

—*Marilyn Bradford*

Love Loss

The hurt does not heal
And the scars do not fade
But I am sorry
For what I did

The words you used
Were taken to heart
And because of that
I am falling apart

My feelings never changed
The love never faded
But we were apart
And can never be replaced

The time has passed
And the hurt is still there
Your soul will not reveal
What your heart will bare.

—*Marie E. Morais*

My Mom

We have been best friends
Since the day I was born.
We have been through a lot
Our hearts have been torn.
We are there for each other
To heal the pain.
When talking to the other
There is never a strain.
When God chose you
To be my mom
He knew I would need you there
Standing strong.

—*Kristie Henington*

The Fantasy of Love

Love is a simple fantasy
That totally fills one's mind
A touch can be an ecstasy
A kiss an eternal fire.
The type of fantasy love is
Will roll you along waves
And gently send you listless
Into loving arms again.

—*Robin Lynn Muir*

Things Not Remembered

Searching the archives,
I found I'd lost the volume.
Misguided librarian:
You took the history text
And,
One by one,
You burned each horrible page.
Slowly, carefully,
You rewrote my life,
Word by word, phrase by phrase,
Lie by lie.
What remains after the embers have died
Is all that I know now
And all I have forgotten.
If I come here again
I will not seek your aid
And I will write my own stories.

—*Daphne Rose*

Hunted

Lives crashed down
And laid across one another,
Like debris of the redwoods
That kids climb on.

And silk webs clung
To nothing I could see but the sunrise,
Pink lace patterns that would sell,
We buy anything.

A hush in the air
That only a body could hear,
That creeps the skin.
Cautiously adrenaline tip-toed.

Not to disturb
The hyper-sweat
Giving consent and feeding
On the fresh kill.

— *Margaret Ann Anderson*

To Love and Care and Dream

I said to him, I love you, as
I held him in my arms.
I will miss you more than anything,
You will never come to harm.
You made my life so wonderful,
I learned alot from you.
I learned to love and care and
Dream, those things I never knew.
I looked at you, and then away
And tears came to my eyes.
The person whom I spent my life
Now is gone,
He died.

—*Marnae Paskett*

Memory of Love

I'm not so sure you love me.
I'm not so sure you care.
I only wish to God
You'd think of all we share.
The days we spent together
Were oh, so very real.
They made me realize what love is
In a way only you could fill.
But now you are gone
Never again to return.
It hurt so bad,
That awful scar you did burn.
So I'll hide my broken heart
Behind a laughing face
And though you'll think I never cared,
No one will take your place.

— *Melissa Skaggs*

Escape

The snow is falling softly.
I see it from my bed where I still lay.
Unable to move, my soul has transformed
Into a snowflake I see—-falling.
Softly outside my window
My body reaches out to my soul
For the two must be together...
But before I could reach it,
It fell to the ground.
Now, they will be apart forever.

—*Tina McCann*

Ready for a Second Chance

All my life I have waited for a love to come and stay.
Wasn't long before it came to me and then it went away.
I wasn't able to show all the feelings from my heart.
Then I saw that faith and trust was where I had to start.

So now, I am ready for a second chance.
Please give me one more shot at real romance.
I once again want to tell him I love him so.
And all the things I should have said so very long ago.
I am ready for a second chance.

If I had him here with me, I would make him see.
That him and I forever, is how it is goning to be.
I would surely share with him in each and everyway.
I would surely love him, every night and day.

So please, I am ready for a second chance
Please give me one more shot at real romance.
I once again want to tell him, I love him so.
And all the things I should have said so very long ago.
I am ready for second chance.

    —Theresa Hutcherson

Untitled

Nothing matters when I'm with you
Lost is my reality in your arms
Warm is your naked body against mine
Blind tongues swim in the ivory seas
Our bodies become one.

    — David A. Mills

Shadows

In majestic purples, with touches of gray
The shadows will linger beyond and through the expanse of day.
They will remain entombed in memories that seem ever changing
As we dance along the winding way, energeized by shadows,
Alive in thoughts that we allow to stay
The cold wind screams in the night
Of our humanity, and shows all roads
Lead on and on, as we try to catch
The feelings that matter
To touch the bareness of our base
With radiating warmth that envelops our thoughts
And leaves us open to the beauty of our gentleness
And the power of our lust.
Two souls touch in an explosion of being
As the cold goes away, slips past us, and fades
In purple majesty, throwing shadows along our way.

    —Susan Jordan

Tomorrow's Tears

Rustic shutter banging softly in midnight breeze.
Twinkling stars hung in nightly sky as jewels
Stars hung as jewels twinkling midnight sky,
Astonishment—surprising—joy.(As angel sing)
As tea kettle whistle, napping on goose feather pillow,
Banging shutters,
Drifting dreamland,
As soft music says, *Hello,*
Church organ playing *It Is Well with my Soul,*
Sunray gives way to shadow creeping across
Pastoral fields, solitude bids farewell with haughting gaze.
Antagonize oppresive feeling where house long remain vacant.
Songbirds singing lifting his name in glorious praise
Gaz-ing heavenly toward celestial beauty drifting across meadowlands.
Long forgotten farm's rustic shadows,
They stand on lonely hills asleep.
(Laughter) fades into tomorrow's tears...
Beyond the Sunset into tomorrow's tears...*Auction off...*

    —Joyice Bernice Young-Brown

A Mirror Image

The marbled sky lays low, and heavy on my shoulders-
I am caught in the tides of the approaching storm
And lie watchful, and wary.
Night is pouring in from directly above
Like wind rushing through the small confines of a tunnel:
Compressed, contained and channelling itself.
The shadows shape themselves,
Become the things in my dreams that linger in my day,
And find their way into my thoughts.
Thunder rolls in, great waves of discontent—
And the earth pulses,
A reflection of my own inner disquiet. Everything subtly glows
With a pure and vital energy. The storm belongs to no-one
And yet we can all claim it,
Finding our own blood and face
Thrown back to us in the wind.

    —Donna Santoloci

The Loner

A man of many faces, a man of many dreams
He's going many places or nowhere so it seems.
This man he fights for freedom but doesn't understand
The chains that now enslave him were made by his own hand.
This man is well accepted. Of this, he's truly proud
Because he's not a leader, he follows with the crowd.
He doesn't even notice his mind is not his own
Although he makes decisions none were laid in stone.
He strives to match the *in-crowd*
And doesn't know a soul
Which puts him one step closer
As he digs a deeper hole.
He's looking for a job now
Does not know where to turn
His training though extensive
He still has much to learn.

    —Jeffrey Oberlee

The Natural Revival

You are resting calmly on the smooth sand of the beach
Which at night still radiates the glaring heat of the day.
A cool, soothing breeze is caressing your hair while the
Waves are gently lapping at your feet as if at play.
Your mind drifts into a lull in the peaceful quiet
As you watch the moon's reflection in the liquid mirror.
It wiggles and weaves, shimmering in the rippling tide
Appearing to dance to music only it can hear.
Your body relaxes and willingly allows your
Worries, tensions, and frustrations to subside away.
You realize that this short, tranquil commune with nature
Is the escape you needed to confront the next day.

    — John T. Teehan

Untitled

You remind me of the sunset
Slowly drifting away the day to bring upon us a new night.
The sky was gaily lit by the brazen moon.
As you approached me, I could feel the electrical currents
Running through me as a river flows freely.
Closer, closer and even closer than that you came towards me.
You came as close as our bodies would go.
There we stood as the sky was as colorful as a tree during autumn.
Then quietly and softly you kissed my lips.
Then we looked up into the sky to see the sun
has disappeared below the horizon.
The moon was now approaching the powder blue sky
to rest in a bed of twinkling stars.
We gave each other a final look,
then we set our eyes upon the ground and went our separate ways.

    — Stacy Sellitti

Romance

I'm just a hopeless romantic
Drifting on a lonely sea
In search of another dreamer
Who believes in destiny.
My world consists of fairy tales
Reality is too hard to accept
So I play my part with skill
Forgetting promises upkept.

—*Ali Williams*

Lavender Love

I locked a leaf of green
into a golden heart of love.
So many years it rested there
in a jeweled case, above a
drawer of white leather gloves.
Slender hands musically cast,
preempted by love.
A love that held fast.
Lavender love cherished and old.
Purple skys cast a violet wall.
A lifetime of summers
but now it is fall.
Oh lavender lavender love.

—*Dorothy Miller Ward*

Never Ending

My heart wraps around you
With all the understanding it holds.
It's never ending love
Will be yours to keep and to mold.

I want you to know
It's an unknowing heart,
It doesn't know when to stop
It only knows when to start.

It will love you no matter what
But if it gets out of hand, or too much,
Just tell it to ease off,
And it will do so just as such.

My heart will keep on glowing
Even through the distance we are set,
For it has felt the joy of knowing you,
And it's just happy that we met.

—*Amy Tovani*

Love Is Like A Flower

Love is like a flower,
It keeps growing as days come and go.
The buds are like your heart,
They open up so they can share their
Beauty with someone special.
Even as flowers wilt and die, so does love.

—*Jennifer Mays*

Adore

Showers at sunrise
teardrops by noon
regrets are here
far too soon.
Rays of color
of purple and golds
mountains of whites
tremendous and bold.
Sweet breezes
of our youth gone by
songs of such loves
of mellows and highs.
All of these
and nothing more
extended my thoughts
of everything I adore.

— *Debby Knight*

Someone Special

All you have to do is smile
And I come alive
All you have to do is turn away
For me to break down and cry
You have a way about you
That brings out the best in me
Still aching from a broken heart
I locked away all my emotions
Intending to keep them unseen
But somehow you found the key

When I looked up and saw you
My heart skipped a beat in surprise
But that first night I knew
I had found someone special in you.
The question is...
Do you see someone special in me?

—*Nancy Dehrer*

Shy Sensitive Sighs

Messages are transmitted
To my eyes from hers.
My state of mind is that
Of mesmerization.
Her eyes *tell* me that she will send me
To another plane of lovingness,
Shy sensitive sighs radiate—
—from my emotional self,
These waves of heat exchange cause me
To have excitations with consolations,
If I die now I will have experienced,
Finally, a predestined pleasure—
Which others may not have reached
In their resolutions!

— *James M. Bernard*

Him

His eyes bedazzle me,
Sparkling brighter than ever could be.
His smile is ever so wide,
From him, nothing can I hide.
Looking into his eyes makes me shiver,
Kissing his lips makes me quiver.
Hearing his laughter, brightens my day.
Living without him, there's just no way.
I don't think about how my life could be,
I won't think about how my life would be,
Without him.

— *Debie Thorp*

Longing the Moment

Do you remember the first time we kissed?
Since that night, not a day have I missed.
Thinking of you, wanting you here,
Longing the moment that you will be near.
Treasuring the moments that you're in my life
And the times we argue, it cuts like a knife.
But still I know whatever we do,
Nothing will change, I will always love you!

— *Debbie Haga*

Love

Why does love play with your emotions?
Once you think you finally caught it,
It suddenly slips away.
And you are lost and alone again.
Why does this always happen
Even to the nicest people?
Is that the way love works?
If so leave me out, count me out,
I want absolutely no part of it.
It is not worth a broken heart again.
Yes it is happening all over again...
Again
Why?

—*Jennifer M. Buchholtz*

Since I Found You

I can see it in the way you smile
It is in your eyes, it is in your style
It is always there when you look my way
I hope that it is here to stay
It is in your touch, it is in your moves
With it I know I will never lose
It lights up my nights, it brightens my days
It is shown to me so many different ways
It lifts me up when I am blue
It is the love I have felt since I found you.

—*Jenny Marie McInerney*

Tears

A glistening tear is shed
Memories shattered, empty heart
Echoing in the silence
Nightime prayers
Wishing you were mine
Whistling winds in the lonely nights
Calling out your name
Late night dreams
You and me
Wishing that was the way
It could be

—*Jennifer Norman*

Unending Love

Wondering if in another place we would have met,
Surely your beauty, I never would forget.
Your eyes, like the color of the sky above.
Since the moment I saw you, I knew I was in love.

My desire is heightened, by the look upon your face,
My heart is pounding as if I were running in a race.
I pray that we will be entangled as one...
From the deepest part of night, until the morning sun.

Never will I leave you, for you are the partner of my life.
I will always be true, and happy to be your wife.

—*Donna Kaye Hawes*

Untitled

Now that I look into your cold, stone eyes
I know its true that love never dies
You're gone from my life but you will
Always be in my heart
The bond that we have will never
Keep us apart
Now that I'm saying my last
Goodbyes
I have forgotten all those terrible
Lies.
We'll be together eternally
For you have left the world
But not me.

— *Brittney Morgensen*

Old Is Beautiful

Old is beautiful—don't you think?
The silvery moon—and stars that blink.
The golden setting of the sun,
For many things—life's just begun.

Old is beautiful—in different ways,
Though once was young—it lives its days
With snow white caps on mountains high,
Reaching up to kiss the sky.

The valleys green—the babbling brooks,
The rains that came—the rivers took.
Way beyond and out to sea,
Old and beautiful as she can be.

Yes, old is beautiful

— *Duste Tribble*

Untitled

onetwothreefourfive—
don'tstopjustrefill—-
quickonerightaftertheotherjustkeepthemcoming.

onetwothreefourfive—
now the room is blurry—
now it's spinning 'round—
don't stop yet, you haven't hit the ground.

onetwothreefourfive—
s l o w l y   y o u   s t a n d   u p   t o   g o —
a n d   s l o w l y   y o u   s t a r t   t o   f a l l —
t o o   b a d   y o u   w o n ' t   r e m e m b e r —
w h e n   y o u   h i t   t h e   g r o u n d .

— *Tamera Brodin*

Swamp River

Like a jumbled puzzle, liquid silhouettes
And crescent shaped pieces of the sky,
Shimmer on the surface, while the somber moon
Sends its beams to dance across in a gleaming row.
Guant shapes reach out.
The cypress knees with roots plunge deep;
Never to quench their lifetime of thirst.
Hidden limbs host the choking parasite.
Crepe, gray moss, draped like a warlock's beard,
Is a leery costume of the foggy dawn.
Hot dampness drenches the suffocating air.
A woman's scream cries from the throat of a cat.
The wood owl flies.
A shadow spashes.
The gator's eyes sink into the reflection
Of the sky.

— *Jackie Newsom Clark*

Love, Why Bother

Love, why bother?
It is all a dream, wishing never to wake,
It is all just a game of give and take.
Love can make you strong or weak,
All you do is search and seek.
True love may never come by,
Maybe that's good,
For true love will either make you laugh or cry.
They say everyone needs someone,
Where is the someone for me?
Maybe love is just hard for me to see.
Right now I can only pray,
That someday love will come my way.
Love, why should I even bother?

— *Deana Gross*

Sometimes in Love

Love is really hard to explain.
Sometimes it causes so much pain.
Sometimes it leaves you full of fear.
Sometimes it will make life more clear.
Sometimes it makes you want to hide.
Other times it might make you feel good inside.
Sometimes you want to cry,
But you fight it with a soft sigh.
Sometimes it makes you dream.
Sometimes it makes you want to scream.
Sometimes it makes you mournful.
Other times it makes you joyful.
Sometimes you feel you're lucky to have love.
Sometimes you wish it was something never spoken of.
Sometimes it makes you wonder how and why
Someone could just let a love simply die.

— *Debbie Guetens*

Mayan Mystery

Today I walked on foreign land,
Felt the heart and soul of mayan man.
Scriptures left on a forsaken wall.
Secret clues to their great fall.
Archaeologists living in thatched shacks
Desperately searching for hidden facts.
No one country attributes true claim.
American, English and Mexican historian can't name
Mayan destruction, her secrets she holds
Sharing with no man her secrets untold.
A civilization vanished without a trace
Leaving behind a most tranquil place.

— *Anna Collie*

South Dakota

South Dakota not only means a state
To me, it means beauty, wildlife, pine trees
And freedom.
It means meeting new people and leaving new cultures.
It's a place to love, enjoy and respect in many
Different ways.
South Dakota means climbing up Mt. Rushmore
To see the faces of our great presidents.
It's a land where great crops are grown and
A land of friendly great, knowledgeable
People
It's the land everyone loves and respects
South Dakota.

— *Donna M. Wilbur*

Gone

A hole through my heart
Is what you have left me
In a whirl of rejection
A heavy state of depression

I loved you with all I had
That love will never die
For you I ache
I scream in pain

All I had was you
Now, nothing
As I sit and wonder why
Deep down inside my heart cries

—*Jennifer Causley*

The Circle

A continuous, solid line of one
The beginning is to the end,
As end is to the beginning,
Neverending motion of togetherness
An entity unto itself
Can never be broken

— *William Douglas Prystauk*

Untitled

I wonder what the world is.
I guess it's a big circle.
It might be me,
Me in the world alone.
But I'm not alone.
I get a lot of love from my family.

— *Ellen Moeller*

Rapt

Visions:
Orange sunsets overrun fiery seas
Bringing bittersweet recollection
Of joyous times that used to be.

Memories:
Fragmented phantasmagoria
Batter down barricades of age
To create euphoria.

Ideals:
The necessary base of our goal
Become mere hyperbolic
Explorations of the inner soul.

— *Albert P. Busendorfer*

Wondering

I wonder how the world began,
How romance and loyalty became.
I wonder.
I wonder, 100,000 years from now
If there will ever be world peace
Or if the USSR will become friends
With the US.
I wonder.
I wonder if the universe will ever end
Or if it will just blow up.
I wonder.
I wonder why God makes us die
And lets us live.
I wonder.
I wonder.

— *Carla Martinelli*

Words

Words to me are magic
When put into a verse,
I cannot paint, nor sing a song
It really comes out worse.

But to write a line about someone
Or tell just how I feel.
Makes all that I really care about
Seem so much more than real.

To write about a bird that sings
Or watch as a flower grows,
Reminds me of His majesty
And the way that his love shows.

So as He sends his rainbows
To share with us that love,
I will write a verse of blue skies
Sent from the Lord above.

　　—Donna Dyal

Underneath the Moon so Bright

The moon it came into my room
To bid to me goodnight.
Its soft romantic sheen did loom
In the velvet sky so bright

It gave me dreams of foreign lands,
Of fairy queens, of lovers and
It took me to enchanted places
Where magical people with lovely faces
Did dance and sing all through the night
Underneath the moon so bright

And when in the morn the moon faded away,
The sunshine replaced it with a glorious day.

　　—Amity Featherly

Beneath Summer Skies

Nice things happen beneath summer skies.
The back yard barbecue
With your best girl by your side.
Hotdogs, hamburgers, and fries.

What could be nicer than a hike?
Walking down the trail
Under those beautiful skies,
Or even riding a bike.

How about a boat ride?
The sun is warm in the sky above.
It's such a beautiful day,
With the girl that you love.

The countryside or a fishing trip.
Maybe even camping or a ball game.
Much fun can be had beneath summer skies.
Whatever you plan will do the trick.

　　— Gerald H. McKelvey

The Game

An innocent child
Trapped in a life of confusion.
Sometimes Mommy, sometimes Daddy
Big people call it Divorce.

But...If Mommy and Daddy
Are so grown up...
How can they play a game
Called tug of war
With a child's life?

　　—Deann Willoughby

You

You're the only one I think about,
No matter where I am
I'll always long to hold you,
Though I know I never can.

You mean so very much to me,
And I want for you to know.
I always think of being with you,
And how much I love you so.

I want you there to talk to,
To sit and take my hand.
To hold me and to love me,
And to know you understand.

You may not know it now,
But you'll realize in time.
You're a very special person,
And I wish that you were mine.

　　— Ashley Mancinelli

My House

My house is big;
My house is tall.
My house has a roof
And it has four walls.

It's made of bricks;
It's made of wood.
I'm glad it's my house;
I'd never leave it, I never would.

　　— Casey Emrich

Essence of Time

Each moment of our time,
Is so precious to us all.
The antique clock keeps passing
The seconds on the wall.

As years impair our bodies,
Deep lines upon our face
Old father time is upon us,
We cannot stop the chase.

What shall we do tomorrow?
Our day is almost spent,
Don't dwell on things to come
But make each moment count.
Can't stop the world from turning,
Or keep the time at bay
Life and death our destined call,
It came from yesterday.

　　— Norma Deisher

When You Close Your Eyes

When you close your eyes
What do you see?
Do you see love and peace
In bright spring colors?
Or hate and famine
With no hope for others?
When you close your eyes,
What do you see?
Do you see picnic
Baskets and trees?
Or romantic sail boats
Gliding on the seas?
Or do you see,
What I see too?
When I close my eyes,
I only see you.

　　— Heather A. Martin

Grandfather

A man I admire
With all my heart and soul
He's always there beside me
To help me make it through
If I'm down or feeling blue
He's always there with a smile or two
He's behind me no matter what I do
He always gives me strength to push
Towards my goal
To make something of myself
And have something to show for it too
He makes everyone feel welcome
That's just the way he is
He always has a hand to lend
This man just isn't the grandfather
That I love.
He is also my very dear friend.

　　—Amy Bennett

The Moon

How beautiful is the moon?
Does the moon deceive us
By its whitish glow meaning purity?

What is the moon?
Why do we stare up at night
And wonder if there is another
World behind its transparancy?

The moon, like a fresh pearl
From an oyster of the sea,
Never fails us; It's always to be.

　　— Jaimie Booth

Ask Why

Does time deceive in ease
The cadence sweet at parents knees
The child we were to them is still
This child we are with rigid will

Ask why. Does time sieze face for mask
This half stone one with busy task
Cannot accept years rob unjust
The heartfelt sobs and yearling trust.

Ask why does time continue on
Its sojourn making change the song?
It's much like asking why the rain
Does little for a soul in pain.

　　— Donna Norman

Untitled

It hurts my mind with nothing to show
How far behind a man can go
With so much laziness
And so much frustration
Never enough happiness
And to much hesitation
With everything to show
And so many friends he can see
But soon will all blow
When they all feel as he
It is all so easy
Yet is seems so rough
It seems to change me
Realizing I am not so tough
Don't fall into this trap of so much fun
However, fall you will, into every little chance
You can get to fulfill.

　　—Glenn Adams

Long Journeys

Rose colored crystal tears
Fall from eyes that are blind.
Ears that cannot hear
Lips that cannot speak,
Lost in a vision of time.
Facing tomorrow with yesterday gone,
Long journeys that never end.
Moments go slowly, the years so quickly,
Nightmares and daydreams blend.
Years that whirl away,
Days that will not stay.
Nights gone in time and mist.
Rose colored tears that fall
For moments that will not return
For a soul that is never at rest.

　　　—*Emery King*

I Yearn for the Gift of Life

I yearn for an infant's cry.
Days became weeks then years pass by.
To hear the sound of a child's voice,
For in my heart I will rejoice.
One more chance, is all I ask,
Yet my yearn is somewhat a task.
They tell me don't give up.
It's in the Lord's hands,
Tests prove I'm childless as it stands.
I yearn for the gift of love.
Yet my spirit flew away with the dove.
For now I still strive,
Hoping for the gift of life.

　　　— *Deanna M. Klomp*

Sonnet

If he were all else but n'er looked at me.
If he were a jest but n'er made me laugh.
If he were a seer but not make me see.
If he were a steer not the golden calf.
If he were idle I could not make bread.
If he said a lot then I could not swear.
If he slept little I could make the bed.
If he loved me much that's what I would dare.
If he tells a lie I would go to church.
If he tells a joke I would be the punch.
If he were a soul I would go in search.
If I'm not his friend I would play a hunch.
If I'm old too soon there will be a child.
If I take a chance he could be quite mild.

　　　— *Blaine A. Jones*

Can't Take Any More (I'm Breaking)

I can't take any more of your demands;
You want me-but just to be your clown.
I can't surrender more of my soul,
This is the limit, I'm breaking down.
I can't take any more of your smooth lies;
You love me-won't ever give me up,
Yet you make me out to be your fool;
It's too much for me, I'm breaking up.
I can't take anymore of your changes;
You feel I should just do it your way.
I've lost too much to go on changing,
That's why it's time, I'm breaking away.
I can't take anymore of your reasons;
You must understand what it's about.
I must try to make it on my own,
It's my turn at last, I'm breaking out.

　　　— *Andrea M. Redhead*

Grandpa

He was a man so gentle and loving
His thoughts for his fellow man.
Never asking much of others
He spent his life caring for them.
His face was worn by many a sorrow
His hand grown very unsteady.
Yet his thoughts were not for his troubles
For he loved his fellow man.
His pockets and bank held little
But he was a very rich man.
His simple loving manner
Gave him many a kind true friend.
And yes I loved this fellow
And love him still today
For I always shall remember
His gentle loving ways.

　　　— *Carol Ives Holmes*

Pink Cloud

Open the door to my heart
Oh my prince
Keep me satisfied with
Your love

Drench me with kisses
Powdery soft yet possessive
Tie me to you forever
Through this great love of ours

Pour your fragrance over me
Ride with me on the Pink Cloud.

　　　—*Val Marie*

Look Towards Tomorrow

Look towards tomorrow
The past is hauntingly sorrow.
Look towards tomorrow
The present is delightfully now.

Look towards tomorrow
The future is uncertainly bright,
Guiding by a brand new light.
Look towards tomorrow
Forevermore.

　　　— *Debbie Gauvin*

Nothing I Can Do

Like a child stands over
his dying mother,
Bewildered by her fading smile,
and crying because he cannot help her

So do I stand here, looking
out the window
Watching you leave.
Crying because there is nothing
I can do to stop you.

　　　— *Holly Boyd*

Tastebud Care

Your tastebuds do not care
About your stomach's rights;
They savor junk and goo,
And then who suffers—you!

You train a dog;
You train a muscle.
Why not eat for snap and hustle?
Train those tastebuds now!

　　　— *Jean Crea Gordon*

See The Dandenongs

You can see the Dandenongs,
Come ride Puffing Billy with us.
We will travel with the throngs
Through the stands of eucalyptus.
Here is where the tree ferns grow,
Where in daytime hides the wombat,
Refuge of the raucus crow,
While the forest makes its comeback
From the devastating fires
That destroyed its ancient trees,
Giants thrusting lofty spires
Toward a heaven filled with leaves.
You can see the Dandenongs,
See them while we ride along.

　　　— *Don Peyer*

I Dream of Your Face

I dream of you face every night
Wishing you would treat me right
Thinking how it used to be
Thinking how you used to love me
Wondering where we went wrong
With you is where I belong
I see you have found someone new
But my heart still cries for you
Love has come and gone so fast
I thought love was supposed to last.

　　　—*Anna Lincoln*

Could You Tell Me?

Have you ever had that feeling
That your feelings are stronger than hers?
Well I've got that feeling
Only with mine and yours
Whenever I look
Into your eyes
I can't see love
Just surprise
Maybe its boredom
Maybe it's not
I don't really want
To get myself caught
Into this love that might not be
So if I love you
Could you tell me?
Do you love me?

　　　—*Becky Chrisman*

Relations

Winds—willows—wreaths wrapped
'round that
wresting bellow's breeze.

Delicate necklace adorning
slender finger branches
of heads lolling
swaying trees.

Dipping, dancing, down
Darkness the damp
Delicious
lip-moistened dew-drop

To offer up
cup
of tongue
to receive like
life—birth its
wet—blue—spark of
soul—lightning—sighing.

　　　—*Vinnie Maciorski*

Jenny

There was a girl named Jenny,
Who made a mistake one clear bright day,
All to see afterwards was such a pity,
That is, what was in her eyes with dismay.

Rememberance of the best times seemed so long ago,
So when at the end, on a fine summer afternoon
She could look back and say
With such happiness, *I did it!*
And the rest would go its way.

But not this year,
No more, for why I am not sure.
Something changed, mistakes were made;
Never again to be the same.
Now she must pay,
In a way, I am not sure why.
        —*Jennifer Bonnette*

Willing

I am willing;
Even knowing the hurt you can bring.
I would take you back in an instance.
Taken a chance on sorrow once more!
I am willing;
Today to try to look to tomorrow.
Forgetting the pains of yesterday.
Knowing for all the heartaches.
There was laughter and special times!
Or the hurt would not have touched so deeply.
I am willing;
To start today discarding all we shared before.
Making new plans and dreams.
By giving you my heart once again.
Knowing you have bruised it.
Hoping to find the love we gently touched before.
I am willing;
If you are!
        —*Dena Boyd*

His Special Lady

He called her his special lady, the woman
In his life, the
Special someone that he'd been in search of to

Share his hopes and dreams with, a
Person who understood the give and take of love,
Endlessly, having no end.
Creating the bond of eternity, as one together,
In love they signed the treaty of forever with their hearts.
As the marriage vows were written,
Life began to live, being everlasting.

Looking into his eyes, they whispered, *I love you.*
Always, to have and to hold 'til death
Do us part. Cherish me, as I cherish
You, for you are and always will be...
...My special lady.
        —*Debra R. Moellers*

Hope

In vain you say, *I'm sure he loves me.*
In hope you say because in hope you wish, pray, meditate.
Old shoes stop at your door.
In hope you say, *I'm sure these old shoes love me.*
On the day when breakfast is
You hope the look you see on the other end of the table
Is one of love.
        — *Diane C. Coates*

Where Do Babies Come From

Alice, I said, do you know where babies come from?
I was helping her with the buttons on her dress,
Slowly, almost indignantly she said, 'Course I know
First you get married and then you have babies
Three or four, or maybe more,
But, wait, before that, you tell everyone
'Cause that's when the boxes and packages come
All tied with ribbons and fancy strings,
And filled with all kinds of real nice things.
Then you walk down the aisle, the organ plays and somebody sings
Then you say, I do, and now you're a Mrs. instead of a Miss
And then you kiss.

Some people cry and have tears in their eyes
Others have boxes of tiny white things
That they throw at you when you go out the door
While the organ plays a little more

Alice, I said, it is ten after eight
You must leave for school or you'll be late.
        —*Imogene V. Lee*

Freedom

From the snow capped mountains reaching almost to the sky,
To the desert valley below covered with sand so hot and dry,
Here is a country made for you and for me,
The United States of America; thank God I was born free.

We fought for our freedom, we won the war.
We'll fight again if need be, with anyone near or far.
This country is ours, we love it dear.
Many a life has been lost, we've shed many a tear.

Our men have courage, our women are strong.
We'll defend our country, separating right from wrong.
Salute the flag, America of today.
Stand up for freedom, say what you have to say.

America the beautiful, we praise Thee, oh God,
For giving us our freedom and the land on which we trod.
Stand up, America, sing it loud and clear;
Let every nation know we have nothing to fear.

Thank you God, for yesterday, today and tomorrow.
May our children never know the dictatorship of sorrow.
Old Glory, I salute you, your colors of red, white and blue,
And the stars and stripes, America, that's freedom for me and you.
        —*Dorothy Osura*

Terrorvision

Television as it is today-
No wonder our children seem to go astray!
They fear everything, with minds so young;
They see it in movies and hear it in songs.

Every wolf they see by the light of the moon,
Is something from *The Howling* and they shriek from their doom!
Every bat that they see flying low and higher,
They fear in their dreams as a dreaded vampire!
They always look for fear and they are never ready
To go to sleep or dream since they've met up with Freddie!
They fear all strange men and they seem to go so wacko
After seeing crazy Norman in the movie series *Psycho*!
They even fear church going and religious conviction,
When they hear the weird lyrics of Prince's song called *Crucifixion*.

To cover up their mistakes, they try to catch us off guard.
They're now placing our innocent children in a group called *Monster Squad!*
It's become hard for us parents to always screen the television.
Where do we go from here? It's all gone terrorvision!
        —*Gloria B. Jarret*

Incubus

Black satin tidal waves
And monsters from the id
Descend upon my mind.
I can't scream.
I can't move.

The angry bears,
The iron cages,
Chase me far,
With whip and spur,
Down some dark windy meadow,
Up to a steep cliff's edge.

Black silhouette man puts
His scalpel to my throat.
Strange incoherent threats
Draw closer,
Face to face.

—*Howard R. Burch*

Masks

The world is hidden
By a parade of masks.
No one understands
And no one asks.

People hide their true
Feelings behind a mask.
It's underneath where
The people fear to ask.
True sorrow, true tears.
Beware, everyone wears a mask.

— *Donna Hart*

The Dying People

People dying
No one cares.
Nibbling on someone's leftovers
Fighting to live, no one will share.
Dying in the dust
Bodies covered with flies.
Some young and some old
No one cares, so they die.
Little food and little hope
They wonder if they will ever get help.
Dying in their huts
Outside hungry dogs yelp.

— *Wayne Porter*

Angel Tear

A tear that falls from an angel's eye
Tears the heart of an infinite dreamer.
A tear that falls from an angel's cheek
Secures Satan's dreams forever.
A tear that falls from an angel's lips
Kills a child's heart.
A tear that falls from an angel's face
Tears the world apart.
A tear that falls from an angel's skin
Burns a memory.
A tear that falls form an angel's lace
Remains for eternity.
A tear that falls from an angel's chin
Drowns the yellow rose.
Why the tear falls from the angel's smile
No one ever knows.

—*Carla Hasenauer*

Ravages of Time

Rubbish suffocates the untamed land,
Nature withers like a drowning man.
The stench circulates among the trees,
Born is pollution, a man made disease.

Afflicted by pestilence, they crumble to dust;
They creep in their corners and turn to rust.
Banished by society, swallowing tears of defeat;
Homeless citizens decay on our streets.

Vivisections performed, doors remained closed;
Whimpers of anguish, living nerves are exposed.
Innocent animals, now you can rest;
Peace awaits you in the abode of the blessed.

—*Dawne C. Bielefeld*

Think

Think of all the times you've cried,
The times you've laughed, the times you've sighed.
Think of all the days gone by.
Of what you've said, of what you've tried.
Think of those that you have met,
Which you have hurt, with no regret.
Think of all the chances lost,
You can't replace at any cost.
Think of all the friends gone by,
The many hours, wondered why.
And if you will, then think on this,
Of life's rewards which you have missed.

— *Jeffrey S. Buyle*

I Remember You

I remember you.
With your poems, artwork, inventions,
Smiling, laughing, talking,
Proud and happy.
I remember you,
Sitting in your wheelchair.
Watching you and grandma,
Hoping and praying you'd be well.
I remember you,
Although I was so young,
I loved you.
And I remember how I cried for you, grandpa,
When I learned that you were forever gone.

— *Debra D'Agostino*

Lost

The hieroglyphics on the sign posts of my mind maze
Indecipherable
I have lost the entrance
I cannot find the exit
Unbrearably lost
The hieroglyphics on the sin posts of your mind maze
Unreadable
They point to nowhere
I am lost
Utterly.

—*Della Slater*

A Cure

Three years ago I got this disease.
Everyone promised that by now there'd be a cure.
I've prayed.
I've been strong.
I've even managed to smile.
Now all I can do is wait.
Patiently I'll wait behind the dam.
The dam I built to keep my tears from flooding this town.

— *Jen Savarese*

Shattered

Broken into pieces,
that lie on the ground.
Smashed into nothing,
as it fades away.
Broken open like flesh,
with a razor sharp blade,
Shattered are my dreams that once were.

— *Ann Cornell*

Alone

I sit her in my lonely world,
A depressed young child,
Too many problems, too many tears.
I feel alone and empty.
Life revolves around me
But I am not a part of it.
I am all alone in my faraway world,
Untouched by people or pain.

— *Denise Pierson*

Inside Cry

My body aches with sadness,
As I hold it all inside.
These feelings of torment
I cannot put aside,

The darkest nights I lay awake,
Quietly by your side.
The tears I cry, are not wet
Just choking tears inside.

I cry to God my deepest sigh
Hoping he will reply, I hide,
I hide.

My choking tears
I hide for you my cry!

—*Deborah J. Lacayo*

The Locket

It holds no pictures
Only memories.
If it could speak, it would tell of
Darkness, flames, smoke, sadness.
Gallons of water
Slowly raining on my parade.
It smells of smoke.
Under the gray it shines.
I engrave the "C" with my eyes.
It stays closed forever.
It holds no pictures
Only memories.

— *Amy Clifton*

Voice of God

The voice of God comes quietly
Wafted along on angel wing
Wherever you happen to be
Like a tiny bell goes *ping*.

He seeks you out in solitude,
No matter, you can't retreat,
While in prayerful attitude
Or on the busy street.

So heed that still voice of God,
He'll lead you not astray
Along the path, a mile, a rod.
Go! Now! His voice obey.

He speaks loudest in the silence
When you decelerate your life
To gather courage and strength
To face your days of strife.

— *Dorothy Stephenson*

I Will Never Forget

I will never forget the day I met you;
The smile, I saw, would make any gray sky turn blue;
I will never forget how I felt when you drove away;
I knew I had I had to make you mine one day;
I will never forget the first time, you held me tight;
Everything in the whole world seemed so good and right,
I will never forget the first time you kissed me, so tender;
As to your passion, I did freely surrender;
I will never forget the good things we had together;
Our sunny days did not invite stormy weather;
I will never forget how you made me feel like Cinderella,
So many times; my love for you didn't have any boundary lines
I will never forget, when the weather changed to stormy that day;
When I had to realize, from me, you were drawing away; I will never
Forget all the times I've cried, *wanting you here,* darling, *in my
Heart, there'll always be a place for you so very, very dear.*

—*Shirley James*

Let's Make a Memory

You and I will build a world of our own that we can run too.
We will find what all true lovers have known.
We will make our dreams come true as we walk hand in hand.
Put your faith in me and we'll make a memory.
You and I have dreamed so long tonight to learn what love is about.
Come to me and lay yourself by my side and we'll kiss away the night.
We're together at last I feel your heart beating so fast,
After all said and done memories linger on...

—*Laura Ann Salerno*

Changes

Deep inside the way I feel is really not the same.
Changes that have taken place, who is to blame?
Sometimes I'm afraid of changes, of what they all may be,
But all I need to know is that I should just be me.
Everything changes, people change, I can't break the chain.
But why should so many changes be the cause of so much pain?

So many different feelings we always seemed to share.
With all those special people who said they'd always be there.
They're all gone now, I don't know why.
I had no idea that strong feelings could die.
So many hearts are broken, dreams gone down the drain.
But why should so many changes be the cause of so much pain?

Friendships that are broken, because of someone new,
Old friends are the best. They're always true to you.
It's just another change in the bunch that we'll receive.
Always remember your hopes and dreams and in God believe.
No one can change the way things are, this is the way they'll remain.
But why should so many changes be the cause of so much pain?

—*Shelley Griffith*

Farewell, My Friend

We travel along the road of life...bit by bit, step by step,
mile by mile...and every so often someone very special joins
us along the way...perhaps just for a little while.

This little bit I have traveled along your side would not have
been the same without you passing my way. The time went fast,
so very fast, I wish there was more.

Forever, I'll remember this little bit of the road with a
fondness too deep to be expressed for someone too wonderful for
words. You gave to me, I shared with you and gained so very
much more in return.

'Tis sad, but true, the bend in the road is just ahead. You'll
go your way and I'll go mine. Who knows what treasures God has
placed for us just over the hill, or around the bend.

And now, it's time to part our way until...perhaps we'll meet
again, once more, some day. As I tip my hat and say, *Fairwell,
My Friend,* we round the bend and go our separate ways.

—*Lynne Ocone Speed*

Painted Memories

Remembering our days of future's past,
There upon a beach crowded and hot
Where the sands blistered mercilessly at our bare feet.
Back when I was young in years
Walking amidst the many-colored parasols,
I imagined these sandy shores would bind us here forever.
There upon the boardwalk an artist labors,
Artistically capturing upon his canvas
The beauty that once was our lives.
With every applied, skillful brush stroke,
He painted into immortal life you, my beloved Ruth.
While in your flight to escape the burning sands,
You found your way onto the framework of his painting.
Now, dear Mama, your future days have long since passed
And your once beating heart lies cold and still:
But that which was once vibrant and warm
Still thrives within this portrait of painted memories;
Cherished memories of an eternal form.

—*D. Leslie Spence*

Black Granite Memories

Many years have passed, but the memories remain
Of sandbag hooches and the hard-driven rain,
Paddies of rice and basses of fire,
Jungle and mud and concertina wire.
I remember, too, the smell of the place;
Moldy clothes, sewage and lip mau paste.
I hear the sounds so vivid within my ears:
The beat of the chopper and no one's cheers.
Most haunting of all, I remember the faces
Of names on a wall looking back through the spaces.
They are young and bright yet old and darken;
Heroes of a war, they will not be forgotten.
Come to the wall, this black granite shrine;
Come to the wall, perhaps you will find
The sights and sounds and smells of fear,
All the things that brought them here,
And in their faces, you too might see
The way it ends, war's destiny.

—*William L. Denney*

Friend of Mine

We share more than most friends ever do,
Our love of life, our likes and dislikes too.
Through disappointments of the time,
You are understanding, friend of mine.
We share the good times and the bad,
And all of the dreams we ever had.
Through the rain or the sunshine,
You are always there, friend of mine.
We share the laughter and joy of each success,
And the tears and anger of every mess.
Through sickness and good health you are there,
And best of all, friend of mine, you care!

—*Jo Ann Roberts*

Friendship

It's all a blurr of how a friend can just leave you there alone,
With nowhere to go and no one to turn to.
My heart is broken;
Just thinking of how a friend can do that to another.
I only hope it will never happen to us, my friend,
Because I never want us to feel that way.
So let's stick together through all kinds of weather
And always be friends forever.

—*Sherry Kochuyt*

Ode To a Young Scientist

Trampling through wintery marshes...
At sunset, through long evening hours;
In blizzard or gale, in darkness, at dawn,
Through summer or springtime showers...
There goes the seeker of elusive truths-
Small kernels of knowledge.
Painstaking to produce!
Bright young scientist, scholar, dreamer,
Worker, near-slave, planner, schemer...
Lonely hours while Truth evades;
Bright discoveries, hopes that fade!
Would that I could walk with you,
Share your journey... discover, too!
Without the faith you symbolize,
All dreams are dead:
One whole world dies!

— *Marlena Coffyn*

Growing

Pursued and led by indignant manifestations,
Youth perplexed and misunderstood
Stands on the threshold of life;
Rendered obsolete, by forces compelling within.
The who, where, why and what is;
Become unsurmountable to his inner man.
Dare I, must I, can I?
Question upon question!
Revealed only to his innermost self.
Is there a worthwhileness in all this complexity?
Somewhere, lying dormant within is the answer.
Rebellion fails!
Sleeping youth, maturity awakens and beckons!
Life is looming ahead!
Go! Go! In all your power.
You must tame your aggressions.
You must conquer defeat!
At last, breathe freely!

—*Marie Anne L. Taylor*

My Son

He's learned how to fly, he's learned how to soar.
Now to accept there'll be no more.
No more projects together or games to attend
Or heart to heart talks with him and his friends.
No more noise from his bedroom nor clothes on the floor.
I love you, I whisper as I walk past his door.
No more smell of cologne as he comes down the stairs
To meet his best girl who checks what he wears.
How do I look? he asks with a smile,
Knowing full well what I'll say all the while.
It's hard, oh so hard, to watch him move on.
My heart feels so broken, *Why can't he stay home?*
Let go, my heart, let go, I say.
The time has come, he must go his way,
The way God has called him, the way God has planned.
Your dear son is now a man.

— *Regina Ruiz*

Special Memories

Memories are good as gold,
They are special things, that is what I am told.
To remember is a wondrous thing.
To bring them back by imagining.
That what was then, is now again
As long as I am remembering.
A time when everything was fine
When things in life were so sublime.
When memories were pleasant ones
At a time when things were truely fun.
When we were still so very young,
And ambition never hurt us none.
When exploring was an exciting thing
I loved to do until day's end.
I think of people way back then
That I may never see again,
But remembrance yet seems so real
That I can always keep them near.
Remembering the days gone by,
Can bring a tear to my eye,
But please remember just one thing
The future that with time shall bring.

—*Robin Marie Laycock*

My Wreck

All I was doing was following Mom to school.
That stupid, wild Canadian goose
Was just in the neighborhood.
Mom slowed down to get a better look,
While sis yelled hello to a friend.
The sun was so bright,
I had to put down my visor.
Just then I noticed Mom's brake lights.
I slammed on my brakes...
B A N G !
It was too late.
Boy, was I ever in a mess.
The front of my car was smashed in;
Mom's bumper was twisted under.
Finally, the sheriff arrived.
NO CITATIONS!
On to school.

—*Marla Colleen Butch*

As the Salmon Runs

What is this magic
About the Begin?
That calls and beckons
And draws up the stream?

What is this force
That drives with such challenge
Against odds up the rapids
To reach at the source?

—*Rachel Gil*

Bring Me Home

There was a time I felt
I did not belong
In this place
In this world
Or even beyond.

Hitched a ride on a dream
Found a place all my own

Took a pen in my hand
And thought of a poem

Looked and there in my mind
I was not alone.
It was me
It was God
I was home.

—*Kathy Weliever*

Know It All Parents

Parents think they are so great,
Never let you stay up very late,
They think they know all about me,
Never satisfied with a C
They say I know what's on TV,
So what if I don't know my geography,
Parents are bores also dull
Always hate the shopping mall
They yell at the littlest stuff
Mention a F, there in a huff
I know I'm not the perfect doll
But I still love them most of all

— *Misha T. Schaffer*

Reflection on Cougars

My car's a red cougar;
Sleek and beautiful; fast and wild.
The cougar's a throwback to more primitive days;
He snarls, and he slinks as he searches and preys
On helpless small creatures for his food and life
He's controlled force and energy;
Violent and menacing—
Performing in instinctive ways.
Unlike a brass cougar necklace
Found tarnished and worn
Left lying in a drawer
Like a dream that's been torn
Out of an eager heart;
Dying and forlorn.
— *Wanda Bracken*

Feelings

No one knows how it feels to move away
From all your friends, your home, your happiness
Until one day, it happens to you.

Feelings! You had before, but never
Never were they so strong
Nor all at one time.

Lost and lonely, scared and confused
Feelings I know
Which I wish would disappear.
—*Bobbi Jensen*

Transparency

I seem to see, yet I am blind.
The only reality, remains in my mind.
Climb to the top, of the mountain ahead.

I then leap off, reality is dead.
The dream of life, is paradise you see.
Peace of mind, need you only plea.
For only in fantasy, can peace be found.

Deep within the mind, you are homeward bound.
Life is not real, tis' only a dream.
A dream as transparent, as the thinnest light beam.
If you can overlook yourself, draw further within,

Use you eyes as a mirror, to see where you've been.
Life is not a problem with an answer to give,
It is but a question,
That requires only to live.
— *Edwin E. Walls*

I'm Lonely

In life's ceaseless ocean
I am a stowaway
In an unnamed, rainsoaked ship.
There is no reason to abandon craft
If healer's hand did yield some hope,
And,
My beingness was reserved for something rare
That I would have outrun death.
Oh, I wish my Mom were here,
For just a day or two
Until my soul regains its serenity
Of sunny childhood of yesteryears.
Remembrances of cooking smells, long apron string drawn
Tight of nestling in the rocking chair sunlit morning,
Crisp white dresses. Oh, I wish my Mom were here,
For just a day or two.
—*Ismail Ersevim*

The Gift of Life

Today you shed
The cloak of darkness
And quietly step out
Into the light
A blossom fully matured
Breathing deep within
The spirit of life
Knowing truth and knowing error
Brings a new dimension
To a world full of strife
And in need of repentance
Walk forward in the path of light
Carry on for a battle
Has been won, claim the love
Joy, peace and happiness
Given to all who believe
Jesus Christ is God's beloved son.
—*Pauline J. Richards*

Sweet Briar Forever

Color of deep scarlet
Emerald hands holding it's set.
Blankets of velvet inside
Outer woven silk to abide.
One long leg filled with rain
Accompanied by thorns of extreme vain.

It's vital leg grows day by day
A relationship follows the same way.
Then there is the dangerous thorn
Where usually a troubled problem is born.
Finally the bud will slowly open...shy
But the bud and the love shall never die.

A token of love is it's conquest
Love and beauty is what it suggest
Hightens passion to it's extremity
Brings forth a woman's femininity
Gives a man a chance to say
That the bud of his love will never go away...
—*Pamela S. Erbe*

For a Nominal Fee

My stack of direct mail
waits ominously for me
in a friendly, brown basket.
It rises daily
and interrogates me:
Will I respond to urgent surveys,
contribute to campaigns, conservation,
medical research, efforts to aid
the starving and oppressed?
These I save and ponder.
Others create skepticism
as they dare me to enter contests,
games, lotteries and take new risks,
or to purchase (for a nominal fee)
astrological information on myself.
But the prices are far too high
and my future too valuable,
to entrust it merely to *the stars*.
—*Eloise Hatfield*

Friends

Friends are forever, caring and true,
They will be there for you, if you are down and blue.
They support you when you try new things.
Through thick and thin, they are always there.
They will lend you a smile or a hug or a laugh.
Or they will just be there to be your...
Friend!
—*Jennifer Johnson*

The Keepsake

A faded letter,
Dusty with age,
Old-fashioned loops
Swirled 'cross the page,
A blurred *I love you*
—or so the words seem—
Ends the letter
And the dream.
— *Olivia Alford*

Cobweb Cathedrals

Though dim they be
Don't dust
Your cobweb jewels
Pellucid chandeliers
Of mi-asmatic creeds.

Go glean the slister
From your spectral ties, but
Bind me not—
I need no cobweb culture
Miasma's not for me.
— *Don Winsor*

The Inhibitors

Their censored eyes
Cast wayward looks
Upon creative souls.
Their narrow minds
In tune with righteous ways.
They thrive in every institution
Known to man,
Searching for traitors
Among their own,
Hoping to justify their existence.
—*Donald Caldwell Jr.*

Death

Death is something,
That we fear.
Especially when the time,
Is near.
But when God says,
Your time has come.
The rewards are here,
For the good you have done.
He will look upon you
Nice and mild
Reach out his hand
And say,
Come my child.
—*Nicole Caum*

The Mirror of Truth

In my mirror, what I see,
Is the hopeless lover there in me...
No pretty trim, no pearls and lace,
Just the honest longing of a lonely face...
A mouth that once was pretty and young,
Before the lines of age had flung,
The tired look and the empty eyes,
And puckered lips that uttered sighs...
Oh that mirror, cruel you be,
To dare to show the truth of me...
The person without a grin or smile,
Or love to hold onto all the while,
The memory is there just left someplace,
Beaming out from the mirror is that face.
The mirror tells all the reasons why,
The pretty face and smile did die,
Age and years was not the cost,
But the mirror shows the face of love, lost...

—*Bonnie Barton*

Life

Life is troublesome at times
There are aches and pains,
And all sorts of problems
That happen again and again.
There are tears that are cried
Pouring like rain from people's eyes,
There is anger and frustration
Deep inside away from green pastures it lies.
But sometimes there is
Happiness and joy,
And everything seems to go so right
All you seem to say is, *Oh boy.*
No matter how hard life can be
Everyone has a reason to live,
No one said life was easy
You know what, life has a lot to give.

— *Natasha Mayes Montero*

The World Around Us

The day's work is not yet done,
We must empathize the needs of our friends.
But, love is not condoned by the greedy,
Who forsee war and opulence to be
The only way out.
Who says lust for power is all bad?
Is it ever good?

Do you say your prayers at night,
For the homeless, or the Godless
Who have their own futile methods of worship?
Pray for the souls of men who see
The world through God's eyes:
Be benevolent to the penniless waifs, who
Seem to understand that The way and the Light
Is our only true path...to salvation.

—*Patricia A. Robinson*

Light Absorbed, Light Reflected

Color is the reflection of light
from an object.
The color black absorbs light,
without reflecting any of its rays.
The color white reflects light,
without absorbing any of its rays.
One color complimenting the other.
Making perfect the color spectrum.
So it is, with humanity's rainbow.
The differences of hue and thought
complementing the race.

— *Neva F. Darbe*

A Year

December clouds, distant nebulae
Hovering, like leviathan tufts
Of dandelion
Those cotton candy days of summer
Drifting from hour to hour
Of lazy nocturnes
Dreamlike, linsome moments
Fade to autumn
Whereas summer.
Is born of spring
While both the colored leaves
And brilliant tulips
May merge to the clouds:
Once again, another day.

— *Nicole Suzanne Berard*

My Dream

Here I sit in a dream,
Looking all around.
But I know it is not real
For this dream has no sound.
When I come back to reality.
I know that I will find,
A world that has not even changed.
It is still in the same old bind.
So I sit in this unreal world,
Some say that I am insane.
But in this unreal world of mine,
There is no room for pain.
So if you happen to dream alot,
I hope that you will find,
An unreal world of no pain.
A world that I call mine.

—*Becky Butterfield*

The Eyes

The physical eyes are false,
Reacting biasedly to what they see.
From left to right they waltz,
Bypassing nought,
But know not what they see.
It is the mind that translates for me,
And tells me what the meaning
Ought to be.

The physical eyes are unsure.
They'll not perceive
The deep intrinsic meaning.
They look, but see no more
Than surface dull
Or gilded matter gleaming.
It is the mind
That 'neath the surface pries.
It is the wealth of brain behind the eyes.

—*B. Washbourne Hall*

Our Love

Our love is like a rose
That beautifies the world
So delicate and pure
But yet so strong
The petals are the fun and joy we share
And the thorns are defense against others
Our rose is the largest
And most beautiful by far
Because there really are no others.

—*Brian McIntyre*

I Will Be Loving You

You said that you loved me and that it was true,
But now we are apart and I am not in your view.
You have made me a slave and I want to be free,
I am clinging to you because you said you loved me.

Now I stay here just debating,
Should I be here standing and waiting?
You have left me here with a broken heart,
I shed my tears and I am falling apart.

Without you I am on my own,
Feeling as if I am all alone,
Because when I am down, you are never there,
You have changed alot but I still care.

And so I say, as friends we are,
And hope our friendship will go far.
I will always admire you from my view,
But everyday, I will be loving you.

—*Gwen Carson*

Mrs. Beasley in Heaven

I know who you are: you're God,
Omnipotent, all-wise and good
Now thanks for the chastenin' rod
But it was awful hard sometimes.

I dis-owned you God, when Mathew died
Like the time my father sold my calf
I wished he'd die, and then I cried
I prayed for him same as I had.

Mathew's heart had hoed the same row
As mine for more'n forty years or so,
We'd raised ten boys and watched'em grow,
Gone to church and said our prayers.

I'd grown so used to Mathew God
Like my calf, I guess, I clean forgot
He still belonged to you, and so the rod;
Fathers is good trainin' for Gods.

—*Bernice Anita Reed*

Hunger

What is but can never be.
Commotion, uncaused by a world which is unturned.
Frozen in time; held motionless
In the hands of the unknowledgeable man.
Man incapable of the technology
Which lies in reach of every hand
And mind of the human ascent.
Help! The people scream within themselves;
Screams unknown to the outside world.
Inside are the tormenting screams
Of hunger and sorrow unable to be calmed
By any kind word or soft touch.
Only by the technology unreached
Will the sources of life be fulfilled.

— *Bridgett Holland*

But Who am I to Judge

In the dark recesses of my mind,
Shadows dart to and fro,
Some are friends and some are foes,
But who am I to judge.

The night torments with promise of sleep
Knowing well its promise it cannot keep
But who am I to judge.

Life goes on by in a circle
As much as it changes
It still says the same.
Disappointment has become my middle name,
But who am I to judge.

—*Pam Hovanec*

A Christmas Poem

Christmas time
comes so quickly
and leaves so slowly.

People with their cold, void lives
    trying to spread good cheer
decorating their half-dead trees with a trickle of lights
    that look at night as though suspended in air
                    (on limbs so bare).

All this hustle and bustle in a season known as *Love*
    a time to give, to share, to really care for each other
                    (if only for a day).
All this joy is the midst of the highest suicide rate of the year
and all these people are too busily happy to notice the
    sorrow trapped in the suicidal's heart.

So ironic this season of hope, this season of care,
    Is filled with empty, dark despair.

— *Annette Wordsworth*

Love Is Like a Rose

Love is like a rose, it lives and then it dies;
I thought I had a rose that would last forever with you;
But every time I gave my love to you and only you,
You just closed your heart and would not let it through.

And then you say you want my love just once more;
My heart is telling me to give you just one more chance,
But my mind is saying no
That all you are going to do is add one more hurt
To the list of miseries that you have already put me through;

I guess that is what I am really afraid of,
But most of all, I am afraid of ever losing you
And if I did I just do not know what I would do;
So I guess what I am trying to say is that:
I love you!

—*Amy Polk*

My Communion Prayer

God has blessed us through his words.
He sent us Jesus to help forgive,
We sin; he forgives.
He has saved us.
We carry him in our hearts.
He loves and watches over us,
We sin; he forgives.
He fills our lives with dignity, he is our Royal Guard.
He helps us through our troubles,
And helps us learn our lessons,
We sin; he forgives,
He is the light of our world, he shows us our duties and
Helps us to see them through.
We sin; he forgives.
He died for us
To give us eternal life,
He is our Savior,
Jesus Christ.

—*Amy Beth Little*

Alone

I sit here alone-
Wanting to hold you,
And touch you again.
I wait for the day
I can see you again.
And to have the safeness
That I feel when I am in your arms.
Until that day comes,
I will sit here alone.

—*Anna Maria Lichota*

Victory

V—Victory is a word which triumphed the darkest crucial hour
    of man's destiny.
I—It is assumed indicating the challenge of perseverance and experience
    of amazing excitement and joy.
C—Consequently contemplates the final timely moment of happiness,
    extraordinarily pleasant that occurs.
T—Truly translating the only recognized, respected,
    the honored and dignified to the throne.
O—On the height of competition, selection of man's remarkable
    excellence in the zenith of respectable gain of greatness.
R—Rewarded for the constant devotion to work service, supplication,
    sacrifice the greatest of all the judgement and the choice of the people.
Y—Yearned, nourished by faithful love of country recorded,
    dedicated to serve mankind,
Confined to confirm the aspiration of your wildest dream.

President George Bush, you are as happy as I am now;
I congratulate you, the battle is won.
God has allowed you to lead this great nation of the world.
Your right to make America God-fearing, more powerful,
more progressive, more beautiful and peaceful to live in,
Expecting therefore, your benevolent reward of knowledge
and wisdom from God,
Open doors, highlights and showers the hope to benefit
every individual living in this Nation.

— *Pete G. Galozo*

A Perfect Match

To think of all the women, God picked you just for me.
Someone that is compatible to share my life and dreams.
Truly what a God of knowledge with a divineness so sweet,
To know what I truly wanted to make my life complete.
You have all the specialties I could ever need:
Love, patience, understanding and a sweetness that's so sweet.
What more could a man ask for when he doesn't have to choose
To find a perfect woman who fits the spot like you?

—*Calvin E. Daniels*

Fourteen Karat Dream

I stood within the gates of Hell and wondered how to cope
With the many problems of this world. I had given up all hope.
As I replayed my tape of life, I saw what I had become;
A fallen angel deep within; how had it all begun?
First, there were the hopes and dreams of all who want to live
To be the perfect person and give all that they can give.
Then come the disappointments when you see it is not so great.
Life throws lots of curves my friend, that carry lots of weight.
You make your own requirements in a world that you have created;
Building lots of pretty dreams, gold and nickel plated.
Then a shift of reality steps in to lend a hand,
And it crashes all your castles to lay there in the sand.
I am glad I played my tape of life, for now I see the way;
If you dare to dance to the fiddler's tune, you know you have to pay.
Will I stop dreaming and hoping for a world of joy and peace?
No, my friend, I never will, because that is my release.

—*Carol D. Colello*

Life or Death

Water crashing, smashing at the bottom of its fall
A wave of new green moves, smoothes over the trees makingleaves fall
Steep gray shale meeting the twining, winding stream below
A tree holding, molding to the shale light life above dim death below
Steeper, grayer shale I sit seeing the beauty of life
Death, down in the dark, marked water down in the water that brings life?
Fragments from the summit plummet into the water
Attention drawn to the sky, high circling, screaming over the water.
The hawk plunges, clutches life then death
Below there is water, shale, shale, water not life or death.

— *Adrien Fiorucci*

Eyes

Many colors mixed or alike,
Watch them glow at a new bike.
Eyes that wink and ones that cry,
Watch these eyes check out that guy!
Hazel, brown, blue and green,
You can tell if that person is mean.
Some bloodshot, with cataracts or sore,
Eyes are needed to drive to the store.
Eyes that sparkle, eyes that shine,
No one has eyes quite like mine.
Some people blind, others with glasses.
Eyes help you get through classes.
Eyes are needed every day.
Take care of them or you will pay.
Eyes are sensitive, very easy to hurt.
My eyes attract to that skirt.
Take care of your eyes, they are needed,
So protect your eyes, you're being pleaded.

    —*Tammy McCall*

I Do Care

Why do you think that I don't care,
That I don't miss you when you're not there?
I'm always telling you that I do,
But you still think what I say isn't true.
I know I may hide a lot of what I feel,
But I'm telling you now I know what's for real.
That is my special love for you.
I just pray that you love me too,
That you know that I do care
And that I worry when you're not there.
See, I'm scared to say exactly how I feel
But I've fallen in love with you for real.
But you have got to know what I'm saying is true,
That I honestly do love you!

    — *Christina Leyba*

The Misty Air

The misty air cleared and he was in a hall
Covered with pink ribbons, wedding bells and gall
A new chandelier was suspended from the ceiling
And a coat of arms was in a corner
The head of the castle was dressed in white robes
With a wand in his hand
He entertained a tempting smile, so tempting
That he found it necessary to open his mouth
Revealing his fangs which had been the prime
Tools in the art of induction.

The misty air cleared and there he stood
Watching the judge in his black robes as he
Pronounced sentence on him for wearing a white
Arm band in the ROTC building.
Four years in the Nam, the judge said,
Next time you get yourself a flag and let it
Fly above your head...you pot head!

    —*S. B. Jones-Hendrickson*

Nature's Demise

The land shines green like an emerald.
The water glistens like bronze.
The clouds in the clear sky flow like a waterfall,
And the trees sway back and forth as if to say *Hello.*

One day a change took place.
The emerald lost its value.
The bronze rusted.
The waterfall stopped flowing,
And the friendly *Hello* is now but a weak cry...
Nature's demise.

    — *Ronda Janowski*

My Last Tear

Tonight you go,
The darkness hides,
Leaving me alone,
There is freedom in your sight.

No one will know
Do not ever turn back,
My spirit will follow.
Do not look, you'll crack.

The dream we shared.
Nightmares we lived,
You rae the only one who cares,
Comfort we give.

Good luck to you,
I will always be here.
Our friendship is forever true,
For you, I shed my last tear.

    —*Laura Terry*

A Little Something

A little tear
In my eye
A little fear
That I might die
A little care
To brighten my day
A little prayer
To help me on my way
A little honesty
To succeed
A little charity
When I'm in need
A little hope
To share with friends
A little poem
That has come to its end.

    —*Dana Askew*

Anger

Champagne bubbles
Ready to burst
Will the cork pop
Or the bubbles break first?
The bubbles they push,
Force their way to the top
The pressure increases
Will it ever stop?
And then an explosion
That's hard on the ears
It frightens our senses,
It plays on our fears
Then the bubbles they sleep
But continue to shake
Never knowing the next time
They might rewake

    —*Geeta J. Isardas*

Taken for Granted?

Friends,
So often taken for granted.
If only once,
Is one too many.

They mean so much,
A fact never realized.
When they are gone,
Is when,
You know you need,
Friends.

    —*Christa R. Lundberg*

The Statue

Weathered dreams engraved in stone
Convincingly oppose the winds of time.
A faceless expression of beauty unknown
Speaks breathless fragments of distant rhyme.
Long and forgotten the years have been seen,
Not a moment remembered can ooze from within.
A moment in time in crystalline,
Ancient messenger, disfigured from rain and wind.
And the heart that had chisled, sweated and cried
And gave of its fullest for beauty and love
Continued to grow till the master had died,
And the stone that's left standing, a mere home
For the doves.

    — *Richard C. Wager*

Encouraging Creativity

Take a tour of your unconscious mind,
The brain and the nervous system,
The storehouse that you will find,
Of memories and thoughts and creativity,
Of sadness and happiness, of drama and levity.
The regulations and rules, the exercises and tools
We use for thought,
Revealing patterns forever changing,
Like the kaleidoscope you bought!
Take special care to reward ideas,
Illustrate arguments, resolve old fears.
Reflect on issues that might solve a mystery.
Furnish incentives to create your future history.
Don't limit your curiosity by ideas that are small,
Think, with ferocity...and savor it all!

    —*Sandy Leigh*

My Grandfather

To my grandfather, throughout the years
Whom has helped me without any tears
We take the time to tell you this;
To have a great grandfathers day,
Because you are misseed.

We are ashamed that we have not seen you much,
But we hope always to keep in touch.
So do not get mad if we do not call,
Because grandfather, we still love you of all

And of the older, that I know, you have given
Me smiles that you always show.
Because of you grandfather, don't you ever let go.
We need you, like the winter needs snow; forever.

    —*Charles Hammett Sr.*

Untitled

And so I pose;
My mask is thick
Of the years' posturings
And the ashes of burnt lives.

I strike at shadows and thick veils;
My enemy is a figment of mad dreams.

Though I gesture with my pedagogic
Finger, though I chant with stentorian
Tones, I am supercilious and shallow.
I have lived the tinsel life too long.

Go to, for I shall speak
With the idiom of yesteryear;
I cover my face to hide the bleak
Show and distract the rising of fear.

The days may have been good,
Good were the moments so few
And I enjoyed seconds of love,
Distillations of moods, evanescent words.

    —*Sheridan Fonda*

Untitled

I'm the kind of person who always has something to say
Until that cold April day.
We sat talking, but really wanted to be walking.
You told me there is nothing to live for;
My heart went poor, nothing to say.
The shock of those words made my thoughts lock.
How can you say there's nothing to live for?
Open the door! Open your eyes!
There's love, there's life, there's happy and sad.
You say no one loves you, well who am I?
And I'm not going to let this go by!
So open your heart and don't you lie.
You said you love me, and if you really mean it, don't let go.
Don't let life go! That would be really low.
Love me for ever and don't end everything!
Keep your chin up and don't look down. Smile for me.
Remember when there's no one else, there's me.
Hopefully someday you'll see you really mean the world to me.

　　—Denise King

Love Me Forever

For you and me I had a thousand dreams,
But life never works out the way it seems!
I guess I wanted to go one way and you the other,
Though we'll always be special to one another!
For us things happened too fast.
We should have known it wouldn't last!
n our differences, we gained and lost a lot.
We didn't obtain everything we sought,
But in your eyes I saw something I will always remember.
It was a look that told me no matter what, you'll love me forever!

　　— Dawn Higgins

Candles

Looking at his face as he lay on the ground
As they take off his jungles and silenced of sound
Blood covered body in this land of the bound
Pale is his face his body limp as he is handled
Frail is his life like a breeze on a candle
Hail it did on his body from these people of sandal.
Blood in the dirt all around him
Faces on him
Mothers dream is in a heap
Choppers better get here or this situation will be grim
Nobody here cares to weep
Pray to God but he doesn't seem to answer out here
Off in the distance sounds slapping the wind blessed are their sins
Throw a smoke bring him in
Time is short drop your fear
Doc, lets move him out, grab his gear
Into the chopper the blades start into a tear
One more day in this place of sandals we are all like candles.

　　—Bob Mahoney

Tyrant Within

I thought this world would be sweet today. We walked together a long, hard way.
He said, *All work, no God, no play.* And his opinion would bear no sway.

The road is narrow—life's incomplete. The memories we have shared, how sweet!
The little things were such a treat, when we walked so lovingly each street!

The tyrant steps forth from the throng. He says, *Your tune is ever so wrong!*
He says, *Cut out your crazy song! Be more like me—get along—get along!*

The heart withers in the tyrant's reign. There is no song, no love and no gain;
Ultimately, there is no pain. Can we ever find the SELF again?

The self who can trust and love and care; individual, unafraid to share the
Sparkling feelings beyond compare. Life's a fleeting moment for those who dare!

　　— Diana M. Kilbourne

Mourning

You said the love we once shared was gone,
We could no longer carry on,
Do you have any idea what you have put me through?
Oh my, what I would not do,
I want to feel you close to me,
Just like the way it used to be,
Please, do not let this be the end,
Precious time has been spent, my friend,
Please just say we can make a new start,
That would surely ease the pain in my heart.

　　—Jana Hayden

If I Could Change the World

If I could change the world
The one thing I would like to do
Is make the world a better place for me and you.

I would like to make the world a better place
For each and every one of us in this human race.
I don't want to see the pain and agony on a child's face
Because a child's face is just so fragile, like a piece of lace.

The soldiers which are our loved ones
Are sent so far away.
Some get burned
And many are never returned.

Who can we blame
For putting ourselves in this sadness,
For we are the ones causing all this madness,
But only ourselves, of course,
Are to blame.

　　— Diane Marie Reeves

Painting the Underpass

Panic sprung like a mouse trap
Held there helpless
The two piercing lights
Becoming blaring, blinding
Running, the wet pavement turned to rubber
Stretching longer and longer, running in place
Air was a knife stabbing my lungs
My leg muscles turned to jello
My footsteps echoed slow
When I reached the end the jaws would crash down
Tearing my flesh like a shark
Still I ran, the engine was roaring
The headlights turned and searched
A blast of wind hit as I dove below a bush
Holding my breath
Silence,
Motionless
Hours passed
As the car went slowly by

　　—Deborah Henshaw

Sweet Slumber

Come, sweet slumber, tenderly seal weary eyes,
Slow spinning thoughts, calm tense and tired limbs...
Kindly proffer my being temporary oblivion.

Ease the clattering cacophony tearing away within,
And slip it into uncaring recesses of the dark.
Let it jabber there, heard only by its echo,
Until the freshness of the dew rejuvenates my being.

Sweet slumber, let night's respite breed new strength
Silently mushrooming into caring, patient wisdom
To greet dark's open door and banish the calamity you bore.
My soul will then unleash its contagious serenity.

　　— Frederick W. Koteskey

Minor Tragedies in a Five Billionist Society

The Earth is very crowded so
Some brown bears have no place to go,
Some flowers have no space to grow,
And virus germs just go with the flow.
        A man lies sighing in the cold.

The realms of the mind are too curtailed;
For lifting food young men are jailed;
For dense construction mayors are hailed
'Til quakes or famine show it's failed.
        A man lies crying in the cold.

The misty mountains and the sea
Send blue and green to you and me
To paint our eyes and minds while we
Engage in readers' reverie.
        A man lies dying in the cold.

        —*Silva M. Kohn*

Untitled

On a bitter cold winter's eve
I stood staring across a snow covered field
Lit only by the full moon.
A house on the far end of the field was the
Only other sign of life,
And the aroma of its smoke,
My only warmth from the cold.
Before me once stood a field growing with life
And now, in the dead of the year,
Nature awaits its new dawn
Winter may be a dreary time for some, but life must go on.
Even in the coldness of winter, I still feel a peace
And comfort in the beauty around me,
Knowing life has not ended,
But only resting and will once again return green and
Fresh with the birth of spring.

        —*Doug Hotham*

I'd rather be laughing than crying

I feel so sad and blue, I do not know what to do
I am surrounded by my emotions and they are getting me down;
I think of my problems which keep going round and round;
I cannot stand the pain and I ask myself why
Where did these feelings come from
What must I do to get rid of this strife?
I think I will start taking a different view of my life
Because I would rather be laughing than crying.

Why do I choose to laugh throughout the day?
It helps me push my frustrations and sorrows away.
I laugh at the things other people say or the things I say
And do, but I would never laugh at you!

I look at things in a funny way to help get me
Through my day;
How do I keep from sighing,
By laughing instead of crying.

        —*Anna Marie Newkirk*

David Lee's Curve

David Lee got killed in this curve on graduation night.
The anguished wails of his classmates still swell in my ears each time I pass.
Oh! He was choice!
So strong, so fine.
Ended, stopped, suspended in time.
I pass by growing older each time I meet the curve.
David Lee remains eternally eighteen.
I wonder?
Which of us is harmed the most in this curve passing?

        —*Jane Stringer*

A Glimpse of Perfectness

This is the place of a tequila sunrise
And the land of the midnight sun.
And you really have no problems,
Your worries are virtually none.
Through the glazed green palm trees
And on the sun dried sand,
I think a glimpse of perfectness
Is holding your deep browned hand.
The natives will wait on you hand and foot
They love to hear your praise
Their ignorance is like the morning water,
With that thin pink line of haze.
And if you really want to say farewell.
If you want to say goodbye.
Then all you really have to do is open up your eyes.

        —*Erica Wilson*

A Past to Remember, A Future to Mold

A past to remember, a future to mold,
And that's the story which I was told
When the fields were ripe and days were old:
A past to remember, a future to mold.

And one day in that time
My grandpa told me a little rhyme,
A rhyme of life, a rhyme of peace,
A rhyme of death and Christmas wreaths.

Then I was young and now I'm old
And all the fields are dead of cold.
So gather my children and all their aunts
And let me tell you that rhyme of Gramp's
Which he told me in summers old:
A past to remember, a future to mold.

        —*Donyll Countryman*

And They All Fell Down

The steeple was high that rainy night,
The earth was brown, no moisture for the hay.
The farmer's plight was despair.
Would feed for the cattle be dropped by air?
With no garden to speak of, what would Mom have to store away?
Could a rain maker help, as some say?
Then suddenly, like an angel in the night,
Soft, sweet raindrops were in sight.
Let's give thanks to this Kansas soil
As once again the fields we toil.

        — *Jane Pippin*

Waves into the Future

Memories of what was can never be once more,
So even as we die they, too, crumble to dust
For waves of time drift in endless motion
Forming the path we follow, as all must.

The wide, sunlit sea curls white as it laps at the ancient fortress,
Acco, where respect for a sleeping father lost a duke's domain.
Both the fable and the fortress will disappear.
In time, only the roll of the waves will remain.

As if in thunderous applause for those brief moments of embrace,
When we stood marvelling at the sunset across that sparkling blue,
Soaking soft in a warming glance at a quiet place
So fleeting, its full meaning we almost never knew.

Now, broken in body, we reflect upon the path of waves
And we know we never can regain that momentary still,
But must drift on toward the end of days
With the waves, the memories, and God's will.

        — *Adele Jay*

Goldfish

I sit
And watch a goldfish
As it swims along the glass.
Like moths against a light bulb,
Constantly charging, but never gaining entrance.
The goldfish, never gaining exit.
For a moment I pause, then push,
And the tank falls to the floor.
Glass shatters,
Water flows out the door
And down the hall.
The goldfish flaps its fins on the floor,
Sommersaults, then lies still,
Suffocating.
Free at last.
Soon to be dead.
    —Michael Greschler

Summer's Eve

Under the sunny, blue sky we lay
Watching clouds throughout the day
Some are small and some are wide
There is a beach and here comes the tide

Smiling, laughing and holding hands
There is no better place in all the land
Faster and higher the hammock swings
We hang on tight as we start to sing

A chirping bird joins right in
Oh, what a great summer this has been!
Buttercups still popping up across the lawn
Sleep at night and wake at-dawn

Fresh-cut grass can be smelled rising up
Chasing the mower is our little pup
Now picking up is a cool breeze
Tickling our toes this summer's eve
    —Cindy Letterman

Homeless Autumn

Magnificent sunlight stokes the inner hearth,
While autumn's chill breeze dances 'round about.
The sky, blue, captures space above the earth,
Striking, untouched by white mists of clouds;
As free as my soul, but pure like blue flame.

A taste of wood smoke recalls the town to mind,
Beneath noon's long shadows of a year near spent.
Warm houses brightly bathed, arrayed in quiet,
Belie the knowledge of those without and alone.
Those cold like wet snow with none to help.

Sweet autumn, bright autumn, homeless autumn,
Too many folk so many different shades and hues.
Touches by bright sky and good earth can't compare
With warm glowing hearths and hearts in smiles
In the sweet autumn, bright autumn, homeless autumn.
    —Mike Phillips

In the Morning

In the morning I can smell the sweet smell of flowers.
The sun shines through my window.
I see the birds fly,
I see the butterflies, too,
outside on the branches when they sit and play.
As I watch the swans scatter through the blue water
I see white feathers all over.
In the morning I like to look out my window.
You can tell there are wonders out in the wilderness,
Something new each day.
I like it down here in the country.
    — Rose Stafford

Freedom

A screaming hawk
  circling the valley
  following the river,
  casting shadows
  onto the hills below,
  black body
  on the blue sky
  settling upon a cliff
  wrapping wings
  around his body.
    —Kimberly Ridenour

Willow Tree

The willow tree so soft as can be,
The willow, willow, willow tree.
To me as soft as a pillow,
Maybe even softer,
The willow tree.

It bends in the breeze of a
Young spring day.
Then the summer with bright, green leaves
And shadowy call,
But then the fall cries the leaves
Softly away—
Thinking of that young spring day.
Then comes the winter,
A blanket of snow, the wilow tree
Has nowhere to go,
Except where it's rooted,
Covered with snow—
The willow, willow, willow tree.
    —Melinda Johnson

Fall Days

The day comes in on soundless feet
My body seems suspended here
Above this day of patterned toil,
And then, from everything apart
I hear the far off tinny call
Of the one and only timeless cock;
While little sounds break thru' my sleep
And beat a tom-tom in my heart.
In the distant dimness of this day,
Comes the old familiar noise
Of the milkman and I know that soon,
I too must make my same old way
Down the long and dimlit stair;
To do the many little things
That housewives everywhere will do,
When Indian Summer wanes
And fall says come again.
    —Margaret S. McCutchen

If You Will...

Imagine a big tree with many leaves
A warm friendly wind rushes through the tree
Picking out one single leaf
And tosses it in the air.
The leaf dances and flies freely with the wind.
Then the wind turns icy and stops dancing
The leaf falls helplessly to the ground
Where it is left alone to turn brown and die.
Now imagine me as the leaf dancing
With the ever changing wind,
The tree is now life,
And the once warm and comfortable wind
Is you.
    —Tara Solander

Alpha

Vast frontiers unexplored
Origin of time and space
The ultimate mind-boggling equation.
Eons of time
Chaos unveiled, dnynamic energy unrestrained
Expanding eternity onward and outward.
Precision of movement
Shimmering points of light suspended
A dense pit of unawareness.
Swirling cosmic mass
Swimming in an endless void
Beautifully awe inspiring, fearfully grandiose.
Gradual revelation unfolds
Understood through eyes of discernment
Unadulterated wisdom, Generator Of Diversity.

— *Perry Tallman*

Praying Mantis Dream

Drink the rays of the setting sun
As your eyes no longer seeing
Focus on oblivion.
Dream
The dancer's grace, the lightning strikes—
The terrible elegance that was yours.
The futile search for shelter
From the evening chill
Need not concern you.
The morning light will find
Another twig on the garden path,
As you spill your dream over eternity.

— *Carol J. Rahbari*

Fire

A rage of warmth against the cold,
A lion's claw, a tiger's nose,
A flame of anger, sadness, pain,
Yet all the love had been in vain.
A wild flying colored true,
A change to come, but yet to you,
And as we watch the flame burn down,
The story goes without a sound.
Fire, fire, burning higher,
Reach to the heart of the liar.
Touch her with your warming flame
To bring love in her again.
Channel love 'til flowing through
A life of happiness, love and truth.
Be with her 'til her dying day,
But when she's gone, don't burn away.
Let your flame burn with the hue
Of a wild flying colored true.

—*Anne Reynolds*

voyant

the seer
    penetrates
        soul's disturbing dimension
  knows
      consuming progression
the seer
  feels
    molten cancer of creation

    . . . and from raging annihilation
    a phoenix of golden births
    communion with eternity . . .

—*F.A. Krull*

My Tear

A continuous tear runs d
      o
      w
      n my cheek.
A tear only you have given me.
A tear full of . . .
    anger . . .
      jealousy . . .
        confusion . . .
Maybe someday you'll be mine,
  the day my tear
    sinks
  deep within my skin.

—*Suzette Noecker*

Footprints   of the time
in the sand   they'll reach you
Footsteps   touch you
on the stairs   feel your
in the air   rapid heartbeat
you hear them   pulsing
feel them   throbbing
sense them   pounding
coming near   out the rhythm
getting closer   which keeps us dancing
closer   to the tune of life
by the moment   sung joyfully by some
waiting   and sadly by others
in anticipation

—*Erin K. Jones*

Rainbow Reflection

A spray of mist,
A drop of dew;
The sun peeks through the clouds
And out comes your friend, the rainbow.

You do not see her very often,
But when you do, she brightens your day.
What is it about her that makes you happy?
Her majestic colors? Her heavenly shyness?

What about the gold at the end?
But there is no end. She keeps going
Around and around
In your thoughts; in your dreams; in your desires.

And, her gold is found only
Within your heart.

—*Amy M. Irving*

The Next Universe

There is a universe beyond our universe
One that is not clear
This universe beyond our universe
Is one that's very near.
There is a universe beyond our universe
One of a different cult
I feel that there is yet another universe
Because space does not come to a halt.
There is a universe beyond our universe
One I hope will be clear someday
This is a hope a very big hope
Which I ask the Lord when I pray.

— *Gabriel A. West*

Rainbows

Dismal, dark clouds part;
Sparkling, silent raindrops fall—
Brilliant rainbows beam!

— *Pamela E. Millwood*

Believe in Me

Do you see me?
Do you hear me?
Do you know when to listen?
Do you feel me?
When I touch you
Do you know when I am there?

Believe in me.
Because I am everything you see.
Open up your eyes,
Open up your heart,
And believe in me.

I am not a shadow
I am your spotlight,
Shining brightly from within
Believe in me,
Because I am everything you need.

—*Patricia Riordan*

The Gift of Days

The creator gives us each day as a gift.
Use the hours wisely as they come.
With hope and optimism trust in Him,
For we shall have each day but once.

Our youth skips past with agility,
Hair turns gray and eyes grow dim.
We make memorandums lest we forget.
Actions no longer turn on a whim.

When life begins slowly winding down
We can rest assured we're not through.
The creator's gift is more valuable then.
There's more quality in what we do.

When we go on a few paces ahead
Of those we dearly loved so long,
The way we used our gift of days,
In God's time may right some wrong.

— *Anna Hart Foster*

Save the Twinkling Stars

Humid fog,
Charcoal grey-
Covering the horizon,
Encircling the towering trees.
Somewhere in the distance,
A coyote howls.
There is a child huddling in the darkness.
Young and trembling,
All alone.
With each sound,
His shivering increases.
How he came to be here is but a mystery.
Dank, cold and frightened,
He cannot see.
Everything is hidden
Under a blanket of darkness,
Save the twinkling stars.

—*Heather Sturm*

Memory

As the days go by
I think of the sweet memory
Of the love we once shared.

Walking arm in arm
Through warm, unforgotten
Sands of the beach
We once loved so dearly,
Dancing to the romancing
Music of the midnight bands
As the waterfront
Breeze swept through
Our carefree hair.

Now that our love is
Just a memory, fading so slowly,
Carried by the waves
Of the ocean.
It is never to fulfill
My bleeding heart.

—*Sherri Snodgrass*

Crying on the Inside

Dancing on the outside-
Crying on the inside.
Laughing and joking with her face-
Hurting with her heart.
Helping and holding others-
Reaching out for help.
A pretty smile in a crowd-
A sad tear in a lonely room.
A wonderful, terrific friend-
A lonely girl...
Crying on the inside.

— *Lisa Estle*

I Thank Thee

The first aureole of sunlight
Streches its golden arms out
Across the somnolent countryside.

With each small step the aureole
Is reborn into a magnificent smile
Of God's mightiest creation.

A chill skips down my spine as I
Sense the warmth of the sun
Dancing upon my face.

I wake to gaze upon the dawning
Of Beauty in a world of love and
War, where the most precious gift
To a mortal is the Blessed Legacy
Of Life.

I thank thee for thy greatest gift.

—*Julie Musser*

Special Place

Unique are they
Who can live without strings.
I tie no bounds
To my feelings for you.
What I give to you
Is by choice to make us feel good.
In return, I feel good about me.
I never knew it could be like this.
I close my eyes to see your face.
It takes me to a special place
That my heart holds just for you.

— *Stephanie Kruszewski Kiger*

A Little Older

She's a little older and a little colder
She can no longer love and thus she must pass by
For there is no one left to give her their shoulder
She's a little older, her thoughts no longer fly

Aloft to heaven's rim, but settle thin and deep
She's a little older, I weary of her praise
She tries to wake old times that long have gone to sleep
Her only future now is chasing every craze.

She's a little older, her tears just for herself
A stubborn, selfish fool with rightousness her faith.
Her only strong belief is adding to her pelf,
Happiness eludes her, a curling, twisted wraith.

She's a little older and a little bolder
All men count in her schemes, she gives each one a try.
She's a little older and a little colder,
She can no longer love and thus she must pass by.

— *Joseph F. Stratton*

Emotions

There is a turmoil of emotion churning inside me,
It is like a fiery dream and sometimes a calm sea.
Within seconds I will explode, a confetti of confusion.
All these things that I am feeling, are one big real illusion.
No single soul can feel it, the war within me grows.
From the tip top of my head, down to my very toes.
I am hurt, I am angry, happy, sad and blue.
Within a mere few minutes, I may be crazy, too!
It has been the hardest, longest wait I ever have endured.
And maybe in the end, my emotions all be cured.
Tears roll down in warningless streams,
I will never again be sane it seems
I toss, I turn through sleepless nights,
Emotions always win the fight
Soon I will be at peace inside,
The raging waters to low tide
The churning turmoil shall subside,
A peaceful ending will abide.

—*Lisa Steadman*

Reflecting on Your Presence

Help me to keep silent and reflect on your presence.
In my rushed way of life, I forget to be thankful.
As I reflect on your presence, I realize how much you care.
Help me to love you in a special way.

— *Connie M. Burke*

Swifter Higher Stronger

I have endured yesterday, and am standing tall
Today, because I have not permitted myself to
Worry about tomorrow. My life, sometimes a battlefield
Strewn with the wrecks of dead dreams, and shattered
Illusions, but some of those dreams, and illusions I
Have caught from the sky and made into reality, even
Though they were only but a few. And when those few captured
Dreams and illusions became reality, I felt as if I
Had been instantly lifted out of the darkness of a dungeon,
And into the light of the sun.
I have also known happiness and love. I have reached out
And did my best to love and touch all people; thus I have
Felt the power of God, as I had never felt it before.
Try to touch life at every point, to become swifter,
Higher, stronger. Thus, when death comes upon you, like
The ancients, you can surely say, I HAVE LIVED...

—*Mark E. Temme*

You're the One

Sometimes I feel down and depressed
I feel real bad and blue,
But as I start to close my eyes
I see an image of you.

That image that I have of you
Is very sweet and kind,
You fill my life with compassion
And make me feel divine.

I'm glad that you are here for me
I really care for you,
Without your love and compassion
I wouldn't know what to do.

We've been together for some time
Our love is strong and true,
I hope the love that we have
Will still come shining through.

The moments we have shared together
I hope will never perish,
And all the love you've given me
I will always cherish.

—*Michelle Peterson*

Goblin Bells

Running through the streets
In our costumes orange and black
Going to trick or treat
Bringing our goody sacks
Bells on porches ring
Lights in front yards glow
What fun it is to yell and sing
And maybe you should know
Oh, Goblin Bells Goblin Bells
Are ringing loud and clear
To see if you've been spreading yells
Or lots of halloween cheer.

— *Chrissy DeMarco*

My Life is Over

My life is over, it's too late
To dance, to date, to ski, to skate
My life went by rather quickly
The years past by all too swiftly
I used to be: young and carefree
Now I am old, bent like a tree
The tree will live for years and years
But so corroded are my gears
There's nothing left, but sit and wait
What God has for me, my last fate
A peaceful death would be pure joy.
Come hold my hand like I'm a boy
I will now say to thee goodnight
Enjoy while it is within your sight
For all too soon, your time runs out
You'll be beside me, I've no doubt
My life is over, in the past
Your life is starting, make it last.

—*Marie Pezzano*

My Love for You Is Dying

It's in my heart and ready for death;
It's about to take its very last breath.
It used to be so beautiful and bright
When things were so wonderful and right.
But now it's all wrong; there is no doubt
That the light on it is about to go out.
Once my love for you was crying
But now my love for you is dying.

— *Sherri Lillie*

Goodbye

Into the sky my eyes pierce the night
Inflicting such wounds that bleed of starlight
Goblets to be, I raise my hands high
Hoping to drink the full of night's blood
Yet can this quench the thirst of my heart
Left arid and vile, torn slowly apart
Dreams I have dreamt now hang crucified
Nailed to today where tomorrow once stood
My soul slowly fades, adrift as a mist
Damp from the tears of mystical loneliness
The promise of sunrise, the promise of lies
Truly I know the pain of goodbye

— *Scott T. Summers*

Common Sense

What good is wisdom,
Without common sense,
There are many that think they're smart,
To most others they're just densed.
One thing to realize,
All brains is not enough,
Brains without common sense,
Leads to a road that's rough.
In every instance,
Both seem to go hand in hand,
As it was meant to be,
Using both together is the right plan.
If you believe in God,
There's no way you can go wrong,
He'll help you make the right decisions,
That will keep you wise and strong.

— *Solomon Jones*

Proposal

In the passion of the moment
I saw the fire in your eyes
They were as crisp as mid December
And as blue as summer skies.
In those flames you so embraced me
With your smile you touched my heart
Now I'm bound for all eternity
From your grace I cannot part.
Now I hold you in my memory
In my darkness I can see
For a light now brings me joy and hope
Now your flame burns bright in me.
Tho by miles we may be parted
I feel so close to you inside
And I hope that some sweet day you'll come
And hearts join as my new bride.

—*Shane Pruett*

The Empty Page

This empty page lies before my face,
And inside me is enough love, hate
Desire and need to fill a million pages.
Should I try to fill this empty space,
Or do I accept a quieter fate,
And close my heart for all the ages?

Should I fill this empty page,
Or let my heart forever rage?
Dare I presume to take pen in hand,
And share my mind's fantasy land,
Or do I die of grim old age,
Staring, glaring at this empty page?

—*Shana Delaine Poissot*

Cycles

The cold winter air makes me cringe
The pure white snow puts the earth to rest
And reflects the sun's dim rays

The multicolored leaves fall to the ground
Leaving a dark corpse in its place
Shivering at every cool wind

The sun's rays of orange and yellow
Gives the earth energy
And the sweet smells of pollent fill the air

The renewing of nature begins
The soil gives birth to small plants
And the trees renew their foliar coats

So are the seasons of nature
So is the cycle of human life
From birth to death we live a life
Filled with ups and downs
And shattered dreams

—*Myronn E. Hardy*

Try

How labored breathe the lungs of ages
Withered muscles fade in stages
Memory turns times' yellowed pages
A life of passing by

Weary eyes that once did glisten
Caring heart that still does listen
Spirit strengthened by wisdom risen
A life of learning why

A youthful dreaming dancing vision
Of days long gone of life decision
Follow dreams or face dull prison
Of life of never try.

— *Sean Kevin Neilland II*

Images of Love

The earth trembles ever so slightly
When we soar the heavens.
Sweet gentle breezes carry us
To unknown ectasy.
The essence of our being
Dictates our perseverance,
Mirrors cast images in stone.

Our inherent desire to fulfill
Hastens our thirst.
Pleasures not easily forgotten
Make reality a task.
Mirrors cast images in stone.

These things we seek in awe,
Destiny provides.
Worry not when you find the secret of life,
For nothing else matters
But the images mirrors cast in stone.

—*Ramona S. Petro*

My Best Buddy

He's cute and sweet and lots of fun.
He plays with me till setting sun.
I comb his hair and fix his treats.
He likes hot dogs, cookies and sometimes sweets.
We walk and run and roll in the grass
And when we're running, he's ever so fast.
And if you haven't guessed by now,
He has four legs and goes, *Bow-wow.*

— *Shellie Marie Jackson*

Came A Poet

Riding on the crest of time,
Came a poet of uncertain rhyme;
Spreading words across the page
Like the wisdoms of an ancient sage.
Mounting up on eagles' wing,
Came a poet with words that sing;
Setting hearts aflame with emotion
Like the spells of a witches' potion.
Climbing on the waves of pleasure,
Came a poet with untold treasure,
Writing words of truth and light
Like the stars that shine in the night.

—*Sharon W. Flynn*

The Love I Have For You

I think that I love you
But of course I do not know
Its better than being blue
But my feelings, hard to show.

I know you'll always be there
And me the same
Just how can I be sure
That our relationship will remain.

I have no doubts
Because I love you more each day
Its just from what people tell me
Are you sure you feel the same way.

But lets not think of tomorrow
How about just today
The love I have for you
Will never go away.

—*Tara Walczak*

Good-bye Grandpa

Today I went to the hospital.
I went to see my grandpa there.
The cold pain in his eyes
Was more than I could bear.
He asked me to come to him
As if I didn't care.
My mom pushed me towards him,
He stretched his arms out to me.
A tear rushed down his cheek,
Then I couldn't see.
I ran over to him
And held him close to me
As he whispered something wonderful
About Jesus and a tree.
Then he pushed me away
And then he said, *Good-bye.*
Then he whispered softly,
It's my time to die.

—*Sheila Christian*

Unplanned

How wondrous to ponder future's allure
Presaging nuances dotting the path of life
Accuracy of prediction becomes a total bore
Living becomes perfunctory, a colorless display
Savor the unknown, a nebulous circuity
Forging ahead as helmsman, no route is true
Surprise's aurora unveils each morn
An agenda of challenges, yet to be born
Precious spontaneity, a commodity so rare
Beckons to all, to be handled with care.

—*Stanley S. Reyburn*

Friendship

What a strange symphony we compose.
Our moods, like ever-changing rhythms
Derive the foundation for our tune;
And our lives, never reaching a common tempo,
Set the time.
And yet, our song is played over and over again-
Every measure filled with meaning,
Every note filled with love.
We forgive past mistakes
And look forward to each finale
Maintaining our melody throughout.
Our symphony would be lifeless, without the melody of its players;
And our lives would be empty without each other
So let us strive to keep our melody flowing;
And let us cooperate to keep our symphony alive.

— *Diane Nino*

Sister

She is all grown up now, with two babes of her own.
But I can still see the little girl dressed in overalls standing there.
She is so innocent and shy,
Her little red western flyer wagon tugged by the smallest of hands.
Her fine blond hair drifts in the breeze over her face,
But you can still see the blue of her eyes twinkle through.
Her complexion is that of the porcelain doll on the shelf.
She is three and cuddley with two little dimples
Reminding me or Shirley Temple.
Oh, see the butterfly?
She spotted it, with a smile as big as Texas...she is off and running
Through the lazy susans, indian blankets and crests of blue bonnets
She chases the flittering little creature, to no avail.
She is so small, yet so big.
She is independent and with that, she is six feet tall.
She is part of my heart and
She will always be my little sister.

—*Peggy DeLaVergne*

The Rocking Chair

That rocking chair was such a special chair...
It chased away the fears of childhood.
It healed a skinned up knee.
It helped to make the long nights short, the dark seem bright,
The bad seem better.
The rocking chair was such a symbol of life's trials, joys and growth.
Even though the carpet did show the tracks its rockers rode,
No one knew just how far or where it really went.
I have ridden many times upon the rocking chair's trail and learned
To grow from its great journey...
The years have passed, the chair is gone, and I have gone my way...
But I must say, I sure would like to have just one more ride.

— *Deborah A. Bottorff*

Insanity

You open your eyes to see nothing but total darkness.
As you are staring into nothingness
You are hearing thousands of screaming voices going through your head.
You lay back down on the cold damp ground.
You start listening to the voices in your head.
They get louder and louder and suddenly, silence.
A cool breeze brushes through your hair.
You start to shiver.
Your eyes begin to adjust.
Everything gets brighter as the sun quickly rises higher and higher in the sky.
But the stars are still out.
You realize you are in a magical place.
You look above you and see the earth high in the sky.
You quietly step out of your coffin and realize this must be heaven.

—*Ed Rowe*

I Love You

If I told you that I love you,
Would you run away,
Or would you look me in the eye,
And say you want to stay.

Would you laugh or stare at me,
While I would run away to cry,
Or would you smile and then say,
Let us give this love a try.

Would you think that I am dumb,
Because I am so blue,
Or would you hug and hold me tight,
And say, *I love you, too.*

—*Deane Rudolph*

From God to my Child

Here I am way up high hoping you
Will see I care.
I look down at you, watch over you
Hoping you will see I'm there.
I have people looking for you
Hoping to bring you back to me.
I love you dear child can't you see?
But that awful thing wants to take
You away from me.
Then I watch you destroy yourself
With the things he has to offer
As a tear rolls down my face
As I watch you wave good bye.

— *Jackie Jaussi*

Prejudice

A young Jewish boy lies dead
He lies on the ground shot in the head
Why did he have to die?
Prejudice like this makes me cry
Shot to his death because he was a Jew
Hate like this is not new
If people are prejudice and hate...
Then war and destruction is the worlds only fate
All people are equal, and no one is above
Every single person must be loved.

—*Natasha T. Champney*

Soaring Wings

I watch the birds soar in the sky.
Fluttlering their wings on the wind they do fly.
Looking down upon the land
To see all that was created by God's mighty hand.
To hear them sing or give their call
Should be a reminder to us all
To give praise and thanks to the Lord above
For His creation He does love.

— *Andrea Vilardi*

Diagnosis

The pupils are moving fast
Along
Below
Along
Below
You are quiet while someone else is in love and hates
You are watching forms of targrag
On a white background
You can't exist without those ridiculous marks
So you are
An idiot.

—*Barbara Flis-Pachocka*

Drift

Drift away to an endless time
Where one soul searches
For the one left behind.
As the mist fades away
Reality is blind
For searching is the soul
Yours, found mine.

　　—*Carole Reynolds*

I Dreamed

I dreamed of a world
In which there was no pain,
No sorrows, no heartaches,
Everything was the same.
But none were happy,
And least of all, me.
For there was no joy,
Or love I could see.
If I give up the evil,
Then I give up the good.
And life cannot be enjoyed,
In the way that it should.
So I learned a lesson
From the dream I had.
It is necessary in life
To sometimes be sad.

　　—*Shannon A. Montgomery*

Across the Miles

Every drop of blood,
Every tear that falls from my eyes,
Every silver smile from my lips,
Every emotion ever made by me
Is ment for you to see.
For every drop of blood
Comes another little life.
For every tear wept,
Comes another bud.
For every silver smile
Comes another mile.
For every emotion
Comes a bigger ocean.
If I leave today, I will meet you
On the coast of that ocean.
Then you will be able to see my
Every emotion.

　　—*Dana Giblock*

Fire in the Hole!

One hundred years of teton splender,
Enjoyed by foreign, local gender.
Massive meadows, towering timber,
Permitted to burn exploding ember!
Fire in the hole!
Deer, elk, bear and bird
Flushed afar blackened
Skies smoken eyes
Fire in the Hole.
Let it burn is Federal
Policy.
Legal tender burns like
Teton splinder
All the black will turn
To winter splender, if we
Don't run out of timber!
Fire in the Hole.

　　—*Karaleigh Rodgers*

Lonely Dreamers

In my heart I have a place
Reserved for the man of my dreams.
A man who in my eyes is the best in the world.
A man who to me symbolizes perfection
In every detail
In my loneliness I begin to wonder
If there is such a man,
Who like me, dreams these lonely dreams.
Where are you my love?
I hunger for you to fill me until overflowing
With the sweetness of your love
I will await you my unknown one
Until we meet and realize
That we were meant to be together with love
Flowing freely between us and understand
The desire of our lonely dreams.

　　— *Sarah Houston*

Child of June

Gone in June before I knew you
Tell me, whose child will you be?
Left alone, no one to claim you
Your life is silent, now you are free.
We turned away because we were afraid
In favor of selfishness, we scorned.
Words could not save you, though our Father made you.
And loved you before you were born.
I may never know those hearts who betrayed you,
Child of June, no one heard your pleas.
Can I believe and you life forgiven?
Did you belong to him or to me?

　　— *Roger Max Miller*

Silent Memories

While you were building sandcastles
my world was caving in
And the bedtime stories that you heard
weren't mine to comprehend.

You see, my childhood was different
from the one you came to know.
There are many things that can happen
behind a home's closed door.

You see, I could never tell you
because I couldn't understand myself,
so I pushed it deep inside
to pretend it wasn't real.

Now I am an adult and everything should be fine
but the secrets of the past have never left my mind.
So I try real hard to hide them within a once upon a time
but no matter where I run, there's no place they can't find.

　　— *Barbara S. Scott*

Summertime

Summertime is for little boys
They catch fish and play with toys
In the dirt and in the sand
Then come in for lunch with grimy hands.

They ride fast and hit their brakes.
Look at that skid, for goodness sake
On the weekends they like the beach.
Swimming is something you don't need to teach.

They splash, play and build castles in the sand,
Then stand back to look at what they made with small hands.
Their favorite time is when they imagine
Changing role and clothes again and again.

To be Mom and Dad brings so many joys!
That is why summertime is for little boys!

　　—*Lynn Wisor*

To Tara

Can you learn to love,
Someone you don't know?
Can you learn to see
The player in the show?

Will you teach me how to love,
Someone I admire?
Will you teach me how to see,
Through society's mire?

Can you learn to run,
Before we even crawl?
Can you be true to one,
When you could have it all?

Will you teach me how to run,
High above the clouds?
Will you teach me to be one
Alone amongst the crowds?

　　—*John Barnhart*

Mute Child

The waves of my love run deeply in a
　　stream of silence.
I cannot speak
But yet I can.
I see a colorful cheeriness about the
　　world
and there is blackness
The cruelness of the world runs deeply in
　　a stream of hatred.
　　And I am blind.

　　—*Sara Smith*

Midnight Rider

We ride through the night
Across the starry sky
Exploring new worlds,
My black steed and I.
Only we know where we have been
Though, it may appear in bed am I.
I can't explain the magic we have seen,
My black steed and I.
We ride across a sea of stars,
Our own discovery.
We ride in imagination and in dreams
My midnight steed and me.

　　— *Rachel Ann Parks*

The Forbidden Rose

Last summer's rose so bright
It stood above me to watch me grow
His eyes like the sparkling morning glow
Shone only then for me.

Winter came as seasons passed
Withering my rose so bad
Its drooping fast, I think it will die
My young forbidden rose

I fertilize it through tears
Passion and love
It has not the will to live.

Last summer's rose was only a season
It died and left me dry.
I must live on my summer's rose
Father time will pass me by.

　　—*Inez Bennerman*

Freedom

Freedom how much we like to be free.
Some think that freedom is to act as we
Please. But they don't know that freedom
Has its limit, and ignore it.

To be free doesn't mean that I should go
Bare foot, where order should be, Freedom
Has a pattern God gave to me, yes we
Need to be free, but like the water of

The river starts getting short, so Freedom
Will be. The stream doesn't seem to be
Running as clear as it used to be.
Because freedom is something we need to

Hold on it's part of the living God gave
To us. How much will it cost?
Some gave their live, other gave their
Sons and never, never should it be
Taken from us.

—*Candid Feliciano*

The Nothing

I went into the nothing the other night,
No psychedelic inducements,
Only freedom led by a gentle hand.
No anguish,
Only a state of fundamental self realization;
Unselfish, but all my own.
Euphoric and complete,
The soul drifting effortlessly,
Floating like we all can't remember,
But have experienced...
Before birth?
In a no place that is...

— *H. Doyle Campbell*

The Tunnel Black

One day I saw the sun's glory
Now my life is a different story

I started falling into a tunnel black
For me the sun will not come back

Climb out
I try, but every hold I grasp
Looses its strength—back on goes the mask

Coldness then heat, which will come
Matters little—both leave me numb

There's no usefulness, no reason for me
You give questions to answers I cannot see

I hear, *I love, need and want you*
But the emptiness is blue

Can't you see my life here is through

— *Lucy Cordell Hamilton*

Here Lies The Bones of Logan Rex

I lick the page
Let all of my fruitful juices transfer
Into ink.
Let you gaze upon it
You do not have to understand
Let these words pull you away
Vintages of growth...
Empty fields from the dirt
Under your finger nails
Travel wild in shrubbery and temperatures
Somewhere in your brain wander,
When you have never been there...
Remember

—*John Parhamovich*

Two Hearts

One touch of love can bring laughter,
To someone in despair...
And one heart can be in pain,
While another beats so strong...
But the heart that has its strength
Is the heart that can belong...
When it senses that you care,
And finds a friend in you...
There is no limitations,
To what our hearts can do.

—*Sabrina M. Lee*

Keep Fighting

Beating, whipping in torturing ways
Never to stop—not for days and days.
This painful, treacherous life goes on
Yet these brave humans march on
Never to give up hope and fighting
Their wounded hands never to stop writing
Hoping someday this will all end
And that they will be home
Safe and sound once again.

— *Keely D. Schaefer*

The Search

Many things I have had that I desired,
Still always wanting something,
Searching, longing, waiting and hoping.
Knowing that it could be sound
Traveling to and fro like a vagabond,
Wanting this something
That I could not name,
Asking others; they could not tell me
What I was searching for,
Couldn't put a name to the feeling
That I was craving to know,
For nothing satisfied no matter what I tried.
After a time so tired from the journey
I had taken myself on,
I discovered that my need was
To know myself
And God.

—*Juanita Hutson Kangas*

America the Weary

America offers her money and help,
In return, her embassies burn,
Her people are killed, then to top it,
Those she's helped raise their prices
To drain her life's blood away.
This is America's respect today.
Her people choose oil or food.
Her face is slapped and *she* apologizes.
Her troops are used, then she is told,
Leave, we've no use for you now,
As we've gotten what we want by using you.
So, America loses lives and only she cries.
Send money and food abroad, while her own
Starve or freeze, money wasted uselessly
On frivolous investigations, not on schools.
Empty chairs with high salaries, *this*
She sees and shuts her eyes. America is dying!

—*Dorothy J. Joten*

What If?

What if the seasons never changed
If winter were the same as spring?
Nor clocks did moments rearrange
And sunday church bells didn't ring,
If trodden earth broke not to mulch
Nor brilliant rainbows crowned the weath'r
If seedling knew no blossomed self
No beloveds bound together;
If adolecent mountains stayed
While never raindrops touched the air
Un-aged beneath a cloudy shade
Nor green turned yellow round the pear;
If nature left us ever still
Life had no purpose, death no chill.

— *Joanne Rose Trapanese*

Precious Flowers

P retty pearl petals
R ipe red roses with
E xquisite ways of growing.
C alm lilies with
I nteresting stems
O range daffadils
U nder the petals hide bugs seeking shelter.
S waying silk leaves,

F lying in the wind.
L avender lilacs with
O dors so sweet.
W ilting willows and
E xciting snap dragons.
R ays of sun help
S nowy orchards to grow.

—*Jodi Watkins*

Questions

Love is a mystery to me
Like when the moon is half or full
Or why the stars shine so brightly.
Lovely things are a mystery to me
How do they get so lovely?
Why can't that be me?
Inner feelings are strange
They change only with time
Can only time change form?
Life is a mystery
Sometimes unfair; sometimes complete
Why are there such mysteries?

— *Julie Deann Saunders*

Music

One sustained note paints the black sky
With color and earth ripples as God throws
Back his head and laughs.
The motionless air begins to cavort
Over the growing hills
And the melody reverberates.
Earth is clothed with orchestrated perfection
And the sixth day dawns.
God puzzles, chin in hand.
Something is missing.
With tender hands he takes the virgin clay
And sculptures a replica of himself.
The story of man begins with a heartbeat,
And creation pulsates with joy.
The dance can begin.

— *Cindy Jones*

Rich + Poor = One

Alone I stand at the window at night
Hearing the sirens and seeing their light.
Dark alleyways and bums on the ground,
Piles of clothes and people in mounds.
For this is the street of poverty row.
Rich people's money, where does it go?
Into theri clothes or maybe their cars
Walking the streets or into bars.
Having not a care but only for one:
Paying off their house their service is done.
The money, the clothes, the snobbery of it all-
Wasting the money and having a ball.
No life, no money, no more fun...
In the end they found out we were all one.

—*Juli Brown*

Great Friendship

You are a friend that is very dear.
I hope that you will always be near.
In times of trouble and of sorrow,
You always show me the right path to follow.

When I lost one of my dearest friends,
You were there for me once again.
I cherish your friendship, oh so much
For you heal my deepest wounds with a caring touch.

You are with me, good times and bad,
And when I am happy or sad.
You say, *I will always be here for you*
Now I say, *I will be here for you, too*

When I think of them I want to cry,
Then I think of the past and say goodbye!

Test time is coming.
Test time is here.
I want to say, *I will always be cheering*
Now I repay you by saying, *I will always be here!*

—*Lawanna L. Stanford*

Checks

I saw a mailman delivering a sack of checks today, he said,
They were on their way to mothers, widows, orphans and wives
As payment, for their loved ones who made the sacrifice and gave
Their lives, that dependents, might live and henceforth be forever
Free, to enjoy the boon of liberty! The checks were encased in
Envelopes colored brown, they were just the color of the hallowed
Ground in which the men lay buried. The burden of tax beneath which
We groan, the cost of war will never be known, the anguish and the
Many tears, besetting all our lives in a sea of briny tears and
Blood more than offset the good derived by ship of state
Let us awaken before too late, and band together and create a
World in which the corner stone is peace, and where no man is
Greater than the least!

— *Marion T. Hummons*

Desperate Cry

I have been traveling along this road with the sun on my back.
I brought with me the bare necessities in my shoulder pack.
It's getting lonely now as the sun starts to descend.
I miss my friends and family, but I am happy, I can pretend.
As my back tires and my brows run with sweat, I grab for my flashlight.
The evening sets in and my loneliness turns to fright.
I rested in a deserted camp and listened to distant cries.
I had easily set my unforturnate position with packs of untamed lies.
It will all soon be over as I just escape to the clear
But I will never forget the horrible mistakes I commited last year.
When I wake, I promise, I will have another try
But the only way I can fall asleep is with a desperate cry.

— *Marta Gutwillig*

Wish

If tomorrow were the last dawn,
if tomorrow were to bring
a glimpse of time untold
a shade of hours unknown
I would wish for a wing
a wisp of pure free time
a burst of unbound truth,
pure, clear, real,
strong,
light, so very light
to carry me to finishing—
to sealing the burning scars.

— *Monique Adam*

Reflections of the Eighties

The woman's face is ashen is color
A reflection of her inner pain
Torn and unkempt clothes
Are soaked from the unrelenting rain

Huddled in a corner
Resembling a child within its mother's womb
One is easily overcome by this intense feeling of doom
My heart aches for this woman

But what can my money do
When there are so many like her
And our dollars
Add up to be so few

— *Leslie A. Smith*

Mankind Is Equal

All of us as humans are equal born,
Scattered in this world like sheaves of corn.
Our birth-right may be honored but we're just
Adam's generation God cast out and cursed.
Our color in the skin may be different in look,
Though black or brown or whatever color we took.
We are just humans all equal in spirit.
A body in a soul...one life we get.
Some may have the ability to do great tasks,
A gift within them while in time they last.
Some may lack it yet we are all born to be
On earth in time's limit to trod, you see.
For God never sends an unequal soul within a body.
He made us all equal in soul, you see.
All come from a beginning...must have an end.
All in dust. Amen.

—*Khaloutie Ragubeer*

Tears

I pray for you the sick and weak
and wipe a tear from my cheek
I want to help you
help you to live and grow
but you have to help me
for I do not know.
Please tell me
how can I help, do you know?
I wish for you
the things I have
to run and play without pain
to catch on my tongue a drop of rain
to see your dreams
become the truth,
to iron the seams
and live past your youth
I give you hope
I give you my heart
to show you that, in life,
you've got an endless part.

—*Sarah Johnson*

Harvesting the Past

Show the children
Before its gone,
The beauty of this planet
That man lives on.
Plant well for the future,
Looking farther than today,
Using seeds of knowledge
To build the world gone astray.
Look farther than yourself,
Look deeper in you heart, at last.
And remember...
The future will harvest the past.

—*Karen Johnston*

Orphan

I mostly grew up all alone,
Hoping one day to be found.
And when my parents come to me,
I will shriek in jubilee.
Then I'll get another home,
That is mine to call my own.
But every parent is the same,
They ship you off like it's a game.
And when I get back here again,
I wished the dream would never end.
But then the lady calls to me,
Wake up, it's morning can't you see.
So if you are like me,
Hope to God to be set free.
And if you have ever felt this way,
Turn your cheek the other way.
And just hope for another day,
When some parents come and take you away.

—*Colette Sonksen*

You and I

If we look into the future as I hold your hand in mine,
The tears begin to fall as we notice all the time.
Not salty tears of sorrow, rather sweet tears of joy,
For we have come thus far beginning as girl and boy.
There is a trail behind us, yet we have a path to tread.
Together we can do it. Do you believe in those words said?
I am standing in the presence of what now is a young man,
One who has come to realize a young woman is at hand.
The present's all our own; the future's for us to claim.
We believe in all our tomorrows
because our love grows just the same.

— *Susan Shank*

Silence

I looked at you in silence that only two can share,
And noticed stars that faded to a darkness out somewhere.
We loved each other dearly as night turned into day.
The mirrors of a thousand lights were there to guide the way.
The sun was clearly hidden by the light of loves glare.
As I turned to leave in silence that only two can share.
A thousand burning candles to light the darkened night.
Embracing on the evening enthralled by the delight.
a sugar coated memory is all that really lasts.
I leave behind a single rose upon the grave thats there,
And shed a tear in silence that only two can share.

— *Connie Devries*

What Has Happened to My Heart?

My heart was oh so small with a dullish tint of red.
My heartbeat was faint until the day we met.
As each day passed by, it grew bigger and bigger
And became redder and redder.
Each second of time it beats faster and faster,
For it was the sign of love.
The day you broke away, my heart began to bruise;
It began to ache.
Each thought of you day by day, a piece was torn off,
A feeling of it dying.
I see a piece break apart and watch it fly away.
When I look into the sky, all I see is a blotch of red
For my heart has flown away...
The day you return, the pieces will start to mend.
Back into place, little by little, stitch by stitch,
You'll see my heart form.

—*Michele Streletz*

The Fight for Love

If only we had more time,
But it doesn't look like time was on our side.
I wish we could have found out earlier
Our feelings for each other, but we
Can't put all that in a month.
We have to give it time to grow
And time to show if we really love each other.
The Lord has given us an obstacle
To see if we can pass, and if we can't
We just have to go on to other things.
But we have to try if we really want this
And if we don't, we will find out
At the end of our obstacle.
If we really want it, we will fight it
Every step of the way, and if we fail,
It was never meant to be.
It is so great when you're young and in love.
You see, it gives you time to flee
From a love that was never meant to be.

—*Gladys Wetherbee*

The Unsung Poet

She was forty, so young and yet so old,
Writes many poems that go untold.
Divorced, rejected, confused and alone,
Hours spent sketching and writing poems.

She was too afraid to publish them,
For fear of being rejected again.
A poem half written, and an overdose of pills,
Too much stress and unpaid bills.

For so many years she lived in her own prison,
So emotionally spent and exhausted, she made her decision.
So many people came by today,
And they read one of her poems called *Late in May*

She is no longer tied to this earth
But is free and I am glad.
For the unsung poet you see,
Is me!

—*Jan Emery*

And Then There Was You

I was invisible.
I wasn't here, I wasn't there, I wasn't anywhere.
It was as if I were floating in air,
Unseen, unheard, unloved,
And then there was you!

You came along.
You saw me, you heard me, you loved me.
You turned my life into a song.

Now I am visible.
Now I am seen, now I am heard, now I am loved.
Now I can see, now I can hear, now I can love.
And I love you,
My wonderful, wonderful you!

— *Lorna Tallent Kidwell*

Surface World

Can't you see what is coming down?
We are going underground.
Underground or overhead,
Our surface world is almost dead.
You know what we need of course,
We need another power source.
One that is clean and will not fight back,
And does not leave your wallet flat.
So stop this alternate power your using,
It isn't that confusing.
Most of us know, the answer will be...
Fusion.

—*Doris Louise Lawrimore*

An Unknown

A transparetn bottle stood in my way,
 blocking the doorway
not seeing
or envisioning it,
i step halfway through to a place
totally unknown.

Where feelings are non-existant,
life has no meaning
and good does not exist
to the outside world.

— *Michele Kuzmick*

My Lost Wishing Rock

I made one wish on my wishing rock,
And it came true.
I made many more
One a day,
And they came true
I made one last night.
It was for happiness,
It did not come true.
For hours, I cried
And love died.
It died in my heart,
For him the love I felt
Was lost,
Just like my wishing rock.

—*Marla Cioni*

Our Love

Celestial bodies are a wayward love
You the moon a calming glow, revolving round
I the sun, brilliantly affixed
And together we unite as spirits one
A fusion of energetic motion
Then a clam, a lake still then
Rippling, extending outward
Till it nears an end
Only to be renewed again
Our love will forever be
As the sun shines by day
And the moon glows by night.

—*Mary Rita Throneberry*

Ecounter

The chubby grubby hand she offered me
Held no awareness, of my dress, of pristine white.
Such effrontery from such a grubby child
Made blind my eyes.

I am so very glad, I stopped to smile.
She stood as still as statue made of stone
And in her blue eyes, wonder, was at home.
I blinked my eyes and with a joyfilled cry
Beheld her pointing finger, where perched a
Monarch Butterfly.

—*Marna Bryant*

Friends

Lovers may come and lovers may go
But friends are here to stay
Friends want only one thing
But lovers want everything else
Friends are understanding
Lovers are demanding
Lovers may break your heart
But friends will remain in you heart forever

— *Michael O'Mara*

Woodland Silver Vision: An Elegy for Stacy

Walking, leaf-pine needle path, your silver light shows the way:
Dancing and alive, two of us in this dream.
Drug-induced, your first sleep came too soon.
Now awakened, your vision has given fair warning.
All in moon-white, the dancing eyes speak with perfect coolness,
Do this...follow naught in my place for this sleep has no peace.
I loved you awake and love you now
With all the wishfulness in my soul.
I need to come to this wood to remember you,
Daughter of Zeus, you live with each full moon.

— *Laurie Kaye*

When I Wish Upon a Star

The time may pass and years may go
You will always be special to me, this I know
We can love each other through good times and bad
No matter how far apart we are, we do not have to be sad
The many times I wonder if you really care
I know in my heart you will always be there
You say you only want to be friends
And that our relationship has to end
But after seeing you again
I know that this kind of love has no end
Because at last, you opened your heart to me
And you showed me that our love can be
When I look at your face, I see stars in your eyes
I wish upon these stars, a sign of no goodbyes
When this happens, a special spell is cast
And in God's eyes this means that our love will forever last.

—*Mona Jean Gauthier*

My True Love

Thanks for the memories
Over the past eight years
They've been the best years of my life
Even with the crying and the tears
All you would have to do is smile
And my heart would just melt
God, I'll never forget
Just exactly the way that felt
So thanks again for the memories
That you've given me
And always remember kiddo, friends we'll always be
I know you like a book and I tell you how I do
You see, eight years ago I gave you my heart
And my heart is always true
So just remember one thing, my true love you'll always be
Have to get going. Forever, love me.

—*Margaret Andelmo*

My Hun E

In the dictionary, love is defined as a type of affection between two people
When I think of love, I dream of you and all the happiness
you have brought into my life
Until this time, I never thought I could care about someone
as much as I care about you
But...you have shown me how to love and given your love in return
I will never forget you for that
As I look into my past, I seemed so alone and empty without you
My life now has never been more complete because of you
Many couples tell one another that they love each other,
but when I tell you I love you, I am also saying I want you forever
Thank you, Hun E, for teaching me to love and for loving me back
I am always here for you because I love you so much, I really do

— *Michelle Daukshus*

Dream

What is a dream?
Some people say that dreaming
Only causes heartache
But when there is no dream,
there is nothing to look or strive for.

One of my dreams is YOU!
You holding me and telling me
that we will be together forever.

But how long does it have to be a dream?
If only I could tell you, tell you about this dream
I have had about you and I for so long.
But what if your dream is not the same as mine?
I think I would just want to die.

But you need to take some risks in life.
I think one of my risks in going to be
to tell you about this dream I have had
About you and I for so long.
　　　　—*Marci First*

I Need Thee

I need thee more than words can say.
I need thee not just to cook for me and wash my clothes.

I need thee for love and understanding.
I need thee to be my guide.
I need you when I'm in trouble and all my friends
Turn their backs on me and walk away from me.
Oh how I need thee.

I need thee through sickness and death,
Through time of storm when the sky is cloudy
And the night is dark.
　　　— *Millard Jenkins*

No Nuclear War

We don't want no nuclear war.
We do not want our world to be a thing of
The past.
We don't want dead bodies lying around.
We sure do not want our houses burned down;
What we want is peace and unity.
We want to get rid of all nuclear weapons.
Use the money to feed the poor and needy.
Help those who really need pity. Stop starvation;
Give our children more education.
Teach them well;
Don't send their poor souls to hell.
Teach them to love one another.
Teach them to avoid world disaster
We don't want no nuclear war.
We do not want our world to be a thing
Of the past.
Away with nuclear weapons.
Make the world a safer place.
　　　—*Coleen Hanson*

The Ballad of Cardinal Cooke

He was born in 1921 and died in '83
And through those years he became as famous as can be.
Cardinal Cooke was an inspiring man; he was loved by everyone
Until one day the doctors said soon his day would come.
He was suffering from a deadly disease that didn't have a cure.
They said he'd live a few more weeks but didn't know for sure.
Leukemia was the disease he had; it's dreaded by one and all
And even though he was very strong, his chances were very small.
Then one frightful Sunday night he became very weak.
His condition took an awful turn, his future very bleak.
Cardinal Cooke was 62 when on that tragic day
Doctors said at a quarter to five Cooke had passed away.

　　　— *Michelle Bagnasco*

You and Me Together in this World

The world can only give out so much.
We can only take so much.
We should take time to give so much
And the world to take time to talk a little.
Sharing with each other is the key.
Saving our hearts for each other.
To share is a deed and task for everybody.
Just so much in everyone.
We can use some
You and me.
Saving a little and giving little.
You and me,
We can make it in the world together, if we give a little and
Take just a little. Not much at all. Sharing it means living in this
World together. Just as long as its here and so are we. Together just
You and me, just you and me.
　　　—*Cyndi Jones*

A Sonnet To My Love

My love, the warming summer sun doth shine
As gentle droplets on her golden hair.
And slender hands that speak her every line
Like dancing ballerinas in the air.
She moves like willows swaying in the breeze
As saucily she quicky slips away.
Her laughter rustles through the autumn trees
Like petticoats amid the crisp new hay.
Two liquid pools of sapphire, softly glow
Beneath the startled raven's fluttering wings.
While in the midst of winter's virgin snow
An apple blossom robin sweetly sings.
My love, is pure perfection it might seem.
But she is just a lonely poet's dream.
　　　—*M. H. Thompson*

The Master Painter

He mixed up his colors and made just for me
The bright golden summer the dazzling blue sea.
His paintbrush wisp
Lightly the stars in the sky

The greeness of summer the clouds floating high.
He painted the daisy with delicate stroke
The blush of the
Rose was inspired to evoke.

The day's waking sunrise the night's ending dawn
The muti-hued rainbow the stripes on the fawn.
Aft stopping to rest masterpiece nearly done
He painted his soul in the guise of the sun.
　　　— *Marsha Morelock*

Down the Plate Glass

Down the plate glass...muddy waters sparkle against neon bloodshot
Lights...glaring on my fingertips.
And my swizzle stick, I see your hands everywhere as motors hum
Like wolves attack and volcane down the maindrag
In diesel packs, at a local picture show, I brown bag Chivas
Regal and bundle up my throat
On the screen...tenement structures dominoe in shades of green and gray,
I have a dream but first I live the nightmare...and it begins
In black marker trip-type streaks... ticking off to urban Camelot
Where I have no idea if you will be waiting in a bus stop or cotton
Sheets...if this plymouth will just keep coughing and wheezing...
Maybe be left to rest and over heat...in the Nebraska wheat.
I have my lips in a french kiss on the Regal, using parked cabs as
Walking sticks, too much pain swimming around my brain...Where's my
Keys, where's my knees, chances are I will never leave.
　　　— *Ms. Norton*

A Dream Place

Light the candles one by one.
Let them glow by the set of the sun.
See the tropical breeze form from the trees
And blow the flicker of the light
From the candle sight.

The ocean sings a song
And drags the shells along up to the shore,
Where we can adore.
It is a beautiful sight to see
Shared by you and me.

It is a dream so far away
That your only hope is luck
And to pray for that special day.

—*Missy Kline*

Human Spirit

You are a multi-hued
Stone
Of brilliant rainbow colors
In a mountain
Stream.
Shining and beckoning
Me—I took you home.
But your colors faded
To shades of brown.
I took you back.
Some things are not
Meant to be possessed, but
Relished and left alone. I hold you often in
My heart, and peek at you
From here.

— *Michael J. Hallock*

You, My Realization

Before you held my hand, I knew you.
Your smile said welcome.
You spoke and I was home.
Since the beginning, we were
We'll always be
With you, each time is the first time
With you, each time is perfection
The thought of you brings harmony,
And in this quiet excitement, I am found.
Ah, my beloved, the wonder that is you,
Has made me complete.
This will I recall,
All is mine.
I've been loved by you.

—*Marilyn T. Kenul*

Days Called June

June is a month that goes too fast,
Next day longer than the last.
It has thirty days,
Follows May.

Known for the month that wedding bells ring,
Father's Day it brings.
We honor our flag.
Children have time to play tag.

The coming of fresh peas, cherries and strawberries,
Pies made with blueberries.
Welcome in the first day of summer,
Time for a little slumber.

God gave us those days called June,
Comes once a year and over too soon.

— *Martha Bender*

Etched in Straw

I wonder
speculate
theorize
and marvel
at man's inconsistencies.
He promises the world
wrapped in a harvest moon.
He produces straw from dead wheat;
wheat that gave birth in fertile soil,
rippled, flowed, swayed,
then died a thirsty death.
Promises that fail to germinate
are sad
and a loosely wrapped paper moon
moves under a cloud
and hides
not caring to light a sad face
etched in straw.

— *Margaret M. Tollefson*

Heaven?

The stars unseen in a dark gray sky;
The light that is shed before us.
Do we follow the road of light?
Or go forward onto darkness?
The wind is still,
The silence falls,
And yet we still don't know.
Do we go on
Or do we stand alone?
You follow the trail of light;
The beauty of God is great;
It's scary,
But we believe,
So therefore we shall succeed.

— *Marci Huston*

Brothers

Brothers are friends,
Big or small.
They always seem to understand,
Although they may not show it at all.
They're love is great,
So hard to find,
But always secretly there,
Hiding in their heart.

— *Tammy James*

A Ghost

Today I feel like a ghost.
If I talk, am I heard?
If I run, can I trip?
If I care and love you,
Do you see or feel it?
Or just never send it back?
If I have a problem,
Will you hear my cry for help?
If I die, will it really matter?
I just hope it does to the person
I love, and it happens to be you.
But am I a ghost to you?
Do you know who I am?
Can you see me? Can you hear my cry?
Do you care if I die?
If you don't I'll be a ghost.
Just there locked in your shadow.

—*Melissa Espericueta*

Kasey

I think of people everyday,
But the thought of one won't go away.
I like this person very much,
And I love the feeling of his touch.

Everytime I pray and kneel,
I wish I could tell him how I feel.
There's something deep inside,
That just wants to stay and hide.
I wish there was a way I could show,
a way my feelings would let go.

To be with him I would sigh,
But to be without I would cry.
And one thing I know for sure,
My love for him is very pure.

— *Missy Cottrell*

Golden Ghost

Golden ghost with features froze
Who everyone sees and nobody knows
Standing close to the circle of fire
What would be your heart's desire?
Midst accolade and autograph
Forgotten are your smile and laugh
But through the haze and stardust mist
I know your spirit does exist
Hide it not when you see me
Bring forth your identity
And when the lines have all passed through
There's someone here who cares for you
Not as an accessory
But someone who is dear to me
Please lead me not to fame's front door
I wish to be with you once more

—*Maureen E. Van Balen*

Canto Deciso

On the lace of time,
We move and shed a glow.
As inspiration seems to be sublime;
In this deep hope, then will our knowledge grow.

No sound exists without which silence dwells,
These are harmonies of confidence and fears;
Encompassed within, reigns a thousand hells;
Explaining all things within the spheres.

Life is a medley of truth and illusion,
A carousel of hope and despair
Our isle of deep seclusion,
The chord of life, a vibrant air.

—*Andy J. Patterson*

A Friend Named Jenny!

A friend like Jenny is hard to find.
A friend so funny,
And someone who's kind.

Where could I find a friend like Jenny?
So nice, so funny!

Jenny has a job, she's rolling in money.
Horses are her job,
And riding is her hobby.

Her hair is sandy blonde, her eyes are hazel green.
Her favorite color, blue,
Pizza's her favorite food.

I'm just glad I have a friend named Jenny,
A friend so kind,
So nice, so funny!

—*Kerry Claeys*

The Train to Russia

I stood in awe looking at the Great Wall
Taking pictures, joyful in China's beauty
Then suddenly a train
Began to pass;
The Beijing to Moscow train,
Tourists—Russians and Chinese-
Waved from the windows
I waved and smiled
Felt a little sad that I stayed
I loved China and its newness to me
It antiguity in the world
But how I wanted to see Russia
I always seek one more country,
Never quite content where I am
The Great Wall I could see
Russian and Mongolia still loomed in dreams.

— *Nancy Hoekstra*

My Shadow

I have climbed over countless mountains
And crossed over many a sea.
And yet, in all my travelings
My shadow follows me.
The light my shadow does reveal
And so from light I flee.
And yet, no matter where I run
My shadow follows me.
I hide in darkness so that folk
Might not my shadow see.
But though unseen, it is still there.
My shadow follows me,
No matter where I try to hide
Or what I feign to be,
I cannot leave behind myself,
My shadow follows me.

—*Shane Cutler*

Love?

Was it love that I felt
When it was me that he held close?
Or was it just a feeling
That I needed to feel the most?
Oh love, you're so confusing
When you're kept discreet,
Not like other emotions
I can honestly and easily meet.
My love is beginning to be
A thing of the past.
Even though I would have enjoyed it
If it could be a thing that would last.
Love, love, love, oh you scare me so.
When will you strike again?
I guess I'll never know.
Can you tell me, love?

— *Shannen Smith*

My Only Love

I hate it when you go away.
I dream of you each night and day.
I pray to God up above
That He'll bring back you, my only love.
I love you deep way down inside.
My love for you I'll never hide.
So stay with me till time will end.
You are my love and my friend.

— *Sheri Kern*

The Dancer

She lives among imaginary friends
Her talent for dance and her one pet, the cat.
She dances alone although her classmates
Fill the room and music fills the air
And the bars that hold her in are rusty
And let no light in.
She hears only faint whispers of persons,
A hand of comfort touches her.
She dances until she falls,
Or her mind falls.
She sleeps until morning.
When she dances at home, she dances
Crazily in hope to wake up from her dream.

— *Sarah Turner*

Untitled

We walked along the moonlit beach
As the wind blew through our hair
Hand in hand, we cherished what we had
And all that we had shared.
It seemed we knew it had to end
With another summer gone by
Different towns and different faces
But our dreams will never die.
The memories we held so tight
With the wonderful dreams we had made
Will surely last in our minds
And never, ever fade.

— *Kathy Litchfield*

Somedays

There is a time for everything
For the events in our lives
There is a time for meaning
This we must realize
Somedays have meaning
While somedays have none
Somedays are sad, Somedays are fun
Somedays are special
While somedays just go by
Somedays you sing. Somedays you cry
Know this day, and know this way
That someday you will show
What someday you will know,
Know this day
Somedays are kind, somedays we search
Somedays we find

—*Christopher Robert Barton*

Flying Free!

Today is such a beautiful day to me
because the sun is shining
the wind is blowing
and the flowers are just as pretty as they can be.

As the sun shines
and makes the flowers grow
as the wind blows swiftly by
as the water flows
There's no place I'd rather be
besides up in the mountains
where the Eagles fly free

As I sit in the mountains
under a tree
I see the Eagles
Flying Free!

— *Cynthia G. Bolton*

Nature

The rain keeps falling down
as I sit and listen to it shower.
The ground is moistened all around,
and tomorrow will bring beautiful flowers.
The trees are swaying in the wind,
the sky is shattered with lightning.
Clouds that are sharp and bright, send
a sound that is very frightening.
The thunder echos in my heart
like the calm roar of the sea.
The clouds are slowly moving apart
unfolding like that of a mystery.
Mother nature is a mysterious thing.
now the sun is breaking through,
And the birds are beginning to sing,
bringing us a day that is bright and new.

—*Stephanie Poole*

Just Tell Me Goodbye

The flower reproduced
With beautiful petals again
Will we blossom once more in the spring
Or is this finally the end?
If it is over
Please bid your last goodbye
Do not tell me you love me
Just leave me here to cry.
Get out of my life
Just let me be
Let me save my soul
Let me find my dignity.
I cannot deny my love for you
It would be a lie
But there is nothing more here for us
Just tell me good bye.

— *Kathy L. Menninger*

Indigo

All frozen up, no place to go
Like a musician in silk pajamas
Sitting at a polished baby grand piano
With sad, broken keys that have
Surely seen better days.
My heart's just a relic,
Indian indigo.
Jagged icicles hanging cold...
A shiver, a frown, growing old.
The notes of love so delicately preserved
Only to be rudely shattered.
A rusty hinge, a broken gate,
Tears unchecked,
Twist of fate.
In the realm of a heartache
I see you there
In a pink shirt and tux,
No comb for your hair.

—*Jill Josette Shaw*

Summer Days

As the sky turned to a dark blue at late afternoon,
My thoughts turn to all the happy summer days
That look alike in many ways,
From the beautiful displays
Of red at sunrise over the shore
To the same brilliantly colored sunset
On the horizon's floor,
Lie all the hopes and dreams
That every tomorrow brings.

— *Sarah DeJarnette*

Love Can Be Painful

Love can be painful, yes it's true
First come the promises, then come the games
Our love was true as true as could be
but four months later came the tragedy...
You'd rather be with your homeboys,
instead of me, why?
You say you love me but it's hard to believe
considering the fact you used to be true to me...
You came over one night and filled my heart with your lies,
and my eyes with tears...hoping you had changed your old wicked ways,
hoping it would be just me and you...
I guess you could say you were just lonely that night,
but yet I'm still true, and still loving you.

— Maria Castellanos

The Flame

I wanted to tell you so many times before
But each time I came close, fate closed the door
I wonder now what would have become of love so blue
But now I hope the one youare with is always true
Remembrance hurts the most in times so far gone,
I try to block out the pain that lasted for so long.
I wish destiny could have been changed,
And that my love for you would never be tamed.
But now my heart has been encaged,
And time has moved in to blow out that final flame.

—Tamila A. Williams

No Answer

Do you think of me as you watch the sunrise;
The first light of loving in your eyes?
Do you laugh at the thought of the times that we'd share,
Or do you wish me away and pretend not to care?

Are you happier now; now that you're free?
Have you experienced the world you so longed for to see?
Do you wish me away?
Do you hold back the tears?

Do you relinquish the thought,
And run from your fears?
Do you regret what you've done?
Have you forgotten my name?

Do you keep moving on,
Or is your song still the same?
Will you turn back again, though this road has been long
And will I still be here, or will I be gone?

—Michelle Duncan

Myself

The beautiful, poised girl was failed by the wind
As her hair started scattering around her face.
When she skittered it was so graceful and soft
And quiet, otherwise it was peaceful.

The girl turned taut as the cool breeze gushed around
And inside her body. She was in shock with the cool tears
Dripping from her beautiful brown and black eyes.

The girl was short but beautiful.
She was eleven years old. She had very little friends
But she was her own self.
The name of this beautiful girl is Myself.

— Regina Bernard

Friendship

Friendship is forever
A hard task,
But friendship from the heart
Is the one that lasts.

— Tina Williams

Do You Love Me in Your Heart

I have loved you for so long,
I have told you from the very start.
You say you love me too
But is it coming from your heart?

Sometimes I need to hold you in my arms,
When the tears begin to start.
But you usually turn me away,
To me that is not love coming from your heart.

Sometimes, I wonder if I know the real you,
We are different in so many ways,
Maybe that is why I do not understand you,
Or maybe, it is just a phase.

I love you so much.
Do you really love me too?
I guess sometimes I just need your touch,
And an occasional, *I love you.*

—Missy Metcalf

A Sense of Insanity

Like the last few drops of alcohol
Fall the tears of despair and anguish.
The terror of feeling emotion buried alive
By the failure of conformity.
The entwined bodies of one being faceless
Twisting a nightmare forever etched in subconsciousness.
I reach for reality with clawing fingers
Only to find deceit of my own awareness.
A dimness subsides to create the emptiness
Of a soul shattered by infinite lust.
Who dare the human being the right to share
Another's soul?
Let the sense of sanity exist if only to
Allow a breath of life.

— Daniel LaPorte

Life's Unhappy Changes

Life is like a candle
That can just burn away
It can sometimes be hard to handle
So many people say.

Everyday we have new experiences to face,
People to meet and things to see.
But it would be a waste
If we decide to neglect what could be.

When problems begin to upset you
Don't be ready to give up
Talk it over with a friend or two
Because I know that it's tough.

We all have problems...you and I
And it helps to know that we're not alone.
I know that we can all deal with them if we try,
So that someday we'll be able to live life on our own.

—Judy Yu

The Dagger

Your wind is blowing stronger,
So the sunshine is my shield;
And I'm searching for the dagger,
Hidden in our battlefield.
The meadows stretch beyond us,
We both stop to take a breath;
Then I shake and grip my courage,
And turn to face my death.
As I gaze into the sky,
You strike me by surprise
I turn in fear and then I see,
The dagger is in your eyes.

—Lori Skalabrin

Dewdrops of Dawn

Catching all the glimmer of early morning rays
Among the dewdrops on the grass and blooms along pathways;
Shimmering like diamonds in early morning light
Then fading as a memory as falls the new twilight.
It is as though a picture has been painted in minds eye
Capturing the beauty that goes too swiftly by;
But memory seems to have a way to bring out all the best
Of beauty that one can behold all questions put to rest;
About the reasons God might choose to bring us now and then
The silhouetted images as each new day begins.
Dancing crystals like the tears that fall upon ones cheek
Are but the sparkling dewdrops kissed, then placed about our feet;
To be touched ever so gently, before they fade away
We thank the Lord for bringing us fresh dewdrops every day.
As summer turns to autumn then cold winds start to blow
The dewdrops return this time as freshly fallen snow;
Covering the green of grass, with blankets of pure white
Until returns the dewdrops blessd in early summer light.
    —*Genevieve McClelland*

Waking Up to Another Day

Another day has come to the country side,
Waking people up far and wide.
Birds awaken from a dreamless sleep,
Their babies slowly bring their heads up with a peep.
The flowers open up with a silent yawn,
And the dew sparkles like jewels on the lawn.
A soft wind blows gently through the trees,
With a slight rustling of the leaves.
Crickets start a chirping sound,
When it starts, the message gets around.
Cars go down the country road,
Some with city people, others with a load.
In the distance a tractor roars to life,
While the cow gets milked by the farmers wife.
The animals in the barn get fed,
Others are still sleeping in their hay filled bed.
The day goes on without a fight,
The sun slowly sinks behind the mountain peak.
Farmers shuffle home feeling tired and weak.
The sky is dark, the stars are out.
A day has gone, another will come, that I have no doubt.
    —*Holly F. White*

A Good, Satisfying Day

I was awakened this morning with the kiss of love.
I'm sure I wasn't as gorgeous looking as Snow White was;
    that's what makes it so special.
I got to sleep in until 9:00 a.m. today; nice not to get up by the clock today.
The kids slept in too; now they won't be grouchy
    from the late hour last night.
It's a sunny gorgeous day; the snow sparkles like diamonds.
The sunshine gives us all energy, makes us want to spring clean the house.
So we all pitch in; in short order the house also sparkles
    from basement to porch.
I've outdone myself by cleaning my work room—even the closet!
I can see the top of my sewing table again, the ironing basket is empty
and the mountain of mending is done—-Hooray!
The closets are full of freshly washed and ironed clothes.
We had a tasty, hot dinner with homemade bread.
I soaked in a hot bubble bath and will sleep in a clean, warm bed;
in a big, warm house filled with love.
I read yesterday you have to be able to enjoy
    the simple things in life to be happy.
So, I must be just about the happiest person in the world
    because it's been a satisfying and rewarding day working together.
    — *Patsy J. Curry*

My Meaning of Freedom

To me, freedom is awakening in the morning
And feeling the midst of God's presence all around,
Seeing the blue sky with red clouds
As the sun is about to arise without a disturbing sound,
And having a clear conscience of all my doubts
When hearing the birds singing and being happy to be alive,
Feeling the cool breeze which God sends as I glorify His holy name
That He is no respector of persons because He treats us all the same.
Knowing that my husband is alive and having him in my heart,
That God will be with him as he begins another start.
Touching the children You gave us and giving You praise,
Coming to You, Lord, and talking to You personally
Makes my whole being at ease
With Your powerful embrace, looking all around
And knowing that God is alive
Which keeps me giving more praise! Praise You, Lord!
How wonderful is Thy word!
You treat everything and everyone with a tender, loving heart.
Oh! How freedom is being lifted up high as I meditate on God's word
Which is my mighty and powerful sword.
Freedom is the road to God's kingdom
And today I've discovered and awakened to His voice.
The love You have for all
Is greater than what we can ever imagine,
And it is in Thee, oh Lord, that I rejoice.
    — *Elva R. Lamb*

Requiem

I bought a dozen eggs
and dropped them in the parking lot.
Four eggs survived, four were wounded
and four leaked out their eggness
onto the hood of my car,
into the cuffs of my jeans.

Requiescant in pace, eggsouls,
from chicken you came,
to asphalt commended.

The wounded went into an old tin cup
to be swallowed up in some odd recipe.
Today Mother cooked the eggs
but they smelled bad, as the wounded will,
so she gave them to the dog.

The dog ate the eggs
and then he ate the paper towel.

Sic transit gloria mundi.

— *Mary Carolyn Fox*

I Remember

I remember the color blue,
The color of tears in the rain.
I remember the color red,
The color of the rose
That lay on the grave.
I remember the color black,
The color of darkness and death.
What I remember was the happy days we had.
I remember the white rose you've given me.
I remember my heart filled with joy,
But now pain and sorrow is in place.
Now the cold winds are blowing,
And my tears hit your stone.
I know now the love for you will never go.

— *Mariann E. Hemeyer*

Wishing

Just sitting here wishing you were with me.
Wondering how you are spending your time.
I have been thinking about you alot lately.
Imagining how it would be if you were mine.
Wondering where you live
About your family and friends.
Although none of that really matters,
All I care about is you.

I think about your great smile
And how it is directed towards me.
If I could only find out what you are telling me,
My heart would be at rest.
Why is it that people hide their feelings
Sometimes until it is too late.
Please do not say it is too late.

— *Margaret Murphy*

My Love For You

My love for you is something that cannot be explained.
It's just too strong to be written down.
I just want you to know
That you are the best thing that has happened to me yet.

You make me happy and sometimes you make me sad,
But we always manage to work it out.
If only someday you would find out how much you mean to me,
If only you could just see how much...
I love you!

— *Sheila Stansell*

The Mighty Mystery

I stepped out in the blinding light
To see a marvel,
It's great arm stretching forward and then back again.
It yelled out as in pain
For all to hear.
Its voice can be heard miles around.
It can be calm and serene,
But in a wink of an eye
Become a fierce giant,
Be man's greatest fear,
But in another a great joy.
It is not a mere fantasy
But the sea,
A mighty mystery.

— *April Renfro*

The Sands of Despair

The spectors of my mind to which I've been confined,
Be as beacons in vain from more washed away rain.
How the flame flickers, how the candle burns
My shadow snickers, and as the tide turns.
Dreams which I should like to leave in the barrows to time,
Still remain in the realm of love's domain without rhyme.
One recurring dream by day of wanton, calls
From beyond reality, from dreamland's falls
To give up my world yet again
And with the pixies I bargain
In fraught hopes of passion with Gina
In passion's play, who's in the arena?
Beneath my walk, the sands of despair are enthrow'd
Deep in my heart, I know that with Gina I'll never
Have bestowed.

— *Lewis Feinland*

State of Loneliness

I'd bare my soul to anyone;
anyone who would listen, to anyone who would care.
But it's hard trying to talk
When nobody is there.

I'd bare my soul to anyone;
anyone who might pass by, to anyone that I could befriend.
But it's hard trying to talk
When your voice is snatched by the wind.

I'd bare my soul to anyone;
anyone who would give me time, to show me that they too have cried.
But it's hard trying to talk when you yourself have nothing
nothing to offer...except a battered pride.

Yes, I'd bare my soul to anyone;
anyone who would listen, to anyone who would care.
But it's hard trying to talk
When nobody is there.

— *Charlene McNamara*

Sudden Death

The first time I saw death I shuddered and I cried.
I did all that I could, but the patient still died.
I almost blamed myself, but had to wipe away the tears and be strong.
The patient was gone.
She was up there in years, 87 to be exact.
But she was choking, I thought; nope, it was an awful hack.
She turned the deepest shade of blue
So I gave her some O_2.
But she somehow knew that her time had come.
Boy was I dumb.
She threw an emboli and at 6:05 she died.
We can all learn from death as sure as we are alive.

— *Mary E. Forrester*

Shine Black to Deadly

A black object of metal,
Hand held to kill.
A deep yet shallow opening, waiting until...
Six pieces of steel, ready to be turned.
With the lever pulled back, and still nothing learned.
Quite heavy to handle, yet not heavy enough.
What kind is this object, it's an object that's tough.
Raising it higher, into the lights reflection.
For now it's too late, there are no more objections.
The shine of deadliness, fulfilled the air.
For no more pain, was he left to share.
One piece of steel has left the object for good.
One more awaiting, too confused if he should.
Now there's no longer, a man with such pride.
This man was my father, who committed suicide.
Now can you guess, this object of one?
Shine black to deadly, this object's a gun.

—*Starr Atiyeh*

Suicide

Just another tear, another sad and lonely year;
A corner of the house, me as quiet as a mouse.
A shiny razor reflecting my thoughts,
   on the window outside the patterned raindrops.
A trickle of blood from the stream of hate.
   This is my destiny; am I too late?
A bottle of pills unmarked on the floor,
   for weeks they've been hidden in my dresser drawer.
The shadows cast on the dreary walls,
   the look on the faces of the dusty dolls.
Evil works in my mind; the good times all left behind.
My mind is lost in a pool of confusion;
   the evil shadows I hope just an illusion.
This will soon be over, finished and done;
   my teary eyes will never again see the sun.
It's over...I'm dying...this is the end for me.
   Someday, somehow they'll all learn to see.
I can't handle the pain, the hurt in my heart.
   I've been put down; I was never too smart.
Forgive me, I beg, I did it for love.
   Whenever you need me, just look above.
You never knew to this day who I was;
I never understood love and to the heart what it does.

— *Danielle Dowsett*

Why Did You Let Me Die?

Why did you let me die?
I came to you for help...
But you only pushed me away
And all because I was a little different...
I wasn't good enough
Because I wasn't like you.
If only you would have just sat down
And listened to me...
Just once would have been enough,
Then you would have heard my cries
And maybe I wold not have committed suicide.
But no one cared...
I had no friends,
No one to love me,
No one even wanted to get to know me.
So now I ask you...
Why did you let me die?

—*Keisha McGuire*

Never?

I want to feel you close to me
Though I know it shall never be.
I want to see your persuasive lips
As we drink red wine in fulfilling sips.
I yearn to look into your eyes
As if to find a passionate surprise.
I want to hear your soft, soft voice
Whispering in my ear,
The little things that you will say,
The things that I will hear.
For I love you...I find you so dear.
My heart, how it pounds when you are near.
I feel your warmth, your touch, your love
And my heart, it soars like a dove.
Though you don't know...I find it so clear
We must have something special here,
For I want to feel you close to me
Although I know it will never be.

—*Cindy Cox*

Untitled

A heart is so fragile,
   just like glass.
It needs to be treated delicately,
   or else everything is broken.
It sits inside a case so no one can touch it.
   Just how glass is to be seen.
When you hand it out,
   You've got to be careful.
Someone could snatch it away.
Treat it with care and won't let it break.
Then suddenly he breaks it in two.
Just like a glass,
   A heart can break.

— *Kath Wang*

A Vision of America

Black man
The object of hatred
Racism
As innate as the panthers desire for blood
Chimerical vision
Black demon-white fairy
Viewed as monsters
It's tradition
Machinations
The black man stands for all the powers of evil
Hypocrites
Is the Devil a black man?
Pathos for human love and respect
To many, damned poor things
Hungry beasts
The truth is a nasty thing to stand

—*Keith L. White*

Captive Soul

This is where I stay
Under your protective wing.
You don't allow me to move.
You won't let me learn to sing.
My friends are out there flying.
It is where I long to be,
Soaring high in the sky,
Careless and free.
Why can't you let me spread my wings?
At least let me try
For if I am forbidden to spread my wings,
How can I learn to fly?

— *Rose Ann Sciacca*

The Reality

I sit all alone—
staring in the mirror.
Seeing your reflection—
wishing you were here.

If the mirror shattered—
so would the dream.
Love is an illusion—
What else could it be?

— *Lisa Rose*

Emotions Overloading

My emotions are getting th best of me
And I don't know what to do.
If only someone else could see
Just what I'm going through.

If someone could just understand
How tough it is to be me,
If someone would just take my hand
And explain this all to me.

I would take the time
To help a friend in need,
So how come no one could
Just do the same for me?

— *Shannon B. Davis*

Lonely

I feel so lonely,
the sky is clouding up.
Nobody cares,
This nightmare goes on and on.
I just wish I could
love somebody who
would love me back.
Why is it so hard to be lonely?
People wonder and wonder,
things just don't seem right,
why do I cry in the night?
Loneliness hits my heart,
As it would yours,
Loneliness hurts when the
Loneliness bursts!

— *Marianne N. Catalo*

When a Loved One Is Away

Time seems forever
When a loved one is away
Patience is required by her
Waiting until that day.

What ever may happen
Happens under God's command
Time again
Is controlled in God's hands.
Quietly wondering
Whether future is certain
To discover timing
Draped as a long red curtain.

Mysterious as time will be
I know without a doubt
To watch the endless sea
My tears have formed a drought.
My last thought of you
Only faith is true.

—*Sandee D. Mortvedt*

Just Wait

JUST WAIT, a Second at a time;
JUST WAIT, a Minute at a time;
JUST WAIT, an Hour at a time;
JUST WAIT, a Day at a time;
JUST WAIT, a Week at a time;
JUST WAIT, a Month at a time;
JUST WAIT, a Year at a time;

JUST WAIT, until your name is called;
JUST WAIT, until you see your Creator;
JUST WAIT, and you will be glad you followed
His path of love and righteousness for His
name's sake;
JUST WAIT, for your reward from Him is great;
JUST WAIT, for your reward is the gift of eternal
life with Him;
JUST WAIT, for paradise IS just around the corner
of the next cloud, and just around the corner of
the next star;
JUST WAIT, believe in Him, believe in His word;
JUST WAIT, your time is soon!
JUST WAIT!!

     —Dale W. Davis

A Most Honorary Descent

My body feels-
Like a battered old battleship,
Bobbing slowly but proudly,
Forever trying to keep its
Chin up,
Its nose just above water-
Back toward the shore out of the line of fire.
For its day of bloodshed is nearing,
Ever so closely—its end.

And then, only then, across the shore shall its wounds
Fade into twilight-
Out of existence-
And its fullness made...
Manifest.

     —Zeretha Lenore Jenkins

Yesterday, Today, Tomorrow

Yesterday has past, leaving its scars behind.
The times are changing with each shift-specks of sand.
The past is another page of memory in your mind.
Its joys, its sorrows are softly within.
Today is here, it's your hour now to live,
For yesterday you say goodbye—a clouded mist.
Live today's moments, calm among life's changes,
With peace and inward trust, life's daily melody.
Tomorrow has not come upon life's horizon,
For when the sun awakens it is today.
Walk today in faith—as if it was your last.

     — Darlene M. Hill

Forevers

We are but a moment in time,
A moment that will last forever
In our minds and hearts,
Something time nor distance can destroy.

Time is so unfair to those who love-
With forever being just an evasive word,
That fails to hold adequate definition,
Existing always in realistic abstraction.

We might vow to love one another forever,
Knowing that it is possible,
As long as we understand; the toll of the moment
Is all that we can ever rely on.

     — c. clark

Darkness

In her despair
She sought darkness.
The kind of darkness
That comes from sleep.

She is in peace
When she sleeps,
A deep sleep
That enfolds her in its arms.

But even in sleep
This trouble sought her
Making her toss and turn,
And when she awoke
She found she could not cope.

So she thrust herself without grace
Off her shelter into space
And found the greater darkness
She had sought.

     —Ruth Pappa

Little Child

Little child standing near,
Are there many things you fear?
Do you smile as you sleep,
Or quake with fear alone?

Are you held and conforted,
Or do tears stay inside?
Do you run free with love,
Or stumble on the cracks?

Is there a kind hand waiting,
or must you walk alone?
Will you grow strong in body,
Or lack the food for growth?

Will you excell with knowledge,
Or see bliss in ignorance?
Perhaps you are one of many,
Who struggle every day.

If you lag a step behind,
I pray you fly some day.

     —Joyce Huff

Untitled

A tear falls down my cheek
As I sit and think
Of my life's troubles
One tear followed by many
For every tear that rolls down
Equals a piece of my agony
Life is pain
Death is a release
From the prison
Death is the soul
The prison is the body
As my soul escapes me
Day by day the prison in
Which it is held
Breaks down more and more
Until there's nothing left
But Eternity

     —Keri Leistiko

Racing

Out on the water I see
Six sailboats each as pretty
As the sunset
They're racing with the wind
And against each other.

     — Kathryn Sawrey

Jubilee

Pause on the path, catching the sound
Of God's laughter, sudden intrusion
Awakening from silence, feeling God's gaze
Of gentle approval on every yesterday
Enfolding all our tomorrows, molding their shape
In a harvest of hope.

Jubilarian
Fresh as a gift in cupped hands
Mirth in your memories, dance in the dawn
Of your jubilee journey joyously shared with us
Rooted in God's ground, inching upward
And outward toward more life.
Journey forward in jubilee hope.

     — S. Brenda Walsh

Sandpiper

Sandpiper scurrying along the beach
Darting backward and forward just out of reach.
Foamy wave tips rush toward your feet,
With deftness you measure a hasty retreat.
Snatching your morsels with the ebb and flow,
Instinctively knowing just how far to go.
It must be frustrating to the Old Man of the sea,
Ever hoping to catch you in the boiling melee.
Leaving me to wonder at the life you pursue
In your quest, the sea ever one step behind you.

     —Linda E. Lynch

Love

Love is like a bird;
It finds and keeps a home for many months,
And then one day takes flight searching
For a new place to stay.

Love is like a rainbow;
It is very beautiful when it appears
But unless an effort is made to keep it in mind,
It disappears as if it never existed.

Love is like a flower;
It blossoms and grows in the spring
But when things around it turn cold,
It withers and dies.

Love is like knowledge;
It is acquired through time,
But it can be lost if it is not shown
A little more each day.

     —Sheryl L. Tiffany

A Sad Death

A bead of sweat runs down his face;
A gruesome death is about to take place.
The sun is hot, the sky is clear;
He knows his time to die is near.

The children around him are laughing and playing
They don't seem to notice his face is decaying.
His eyes are sliding toward his nose.
Oh why must this happen to me?, he woes.

The day goes on, the sky is bright;
There seems to be no sign of night.
As this endless day wears on;
His feelings sink; he'll soon be gone.

The smile on his face has changed to a frown;
His heart is heavy, his spirits down.
His three different sections are coming together;
He cannot survive this hot, sunny weather.
All through the afternoon heat he swelted;
Yet another snowman has melted.

     —Rachel Moorhead

Think of a Star

Think of a star
Make your mind a welcome host
Let the color of the wind guide your way.
If your star wants water
Give her the sea
If your star wants a flower
Give her a rose
If your star wants a bird
Give her a dove
If you star wants to shine
Give her your love
Don't let your star fall prey to the sky
Teach her how to make herself shine
Mount her picture in your heart.
Then, if someone tries to paint her
For the sake of their own gain
You'll know the paint will never dry
But only leave a permanent stain.

—*Katherine Trouern Trend*

Finally Free

Find me in your deepest dreams,
I am never far away;
I'm with you day by day.
Through your memories of sunsets,
You will feel my guidance
Leading you through the evermore.
Do not be scared nor
Cry tears of fretful pain;
My hand will lead you through.
Let your heart adjoin with mine.
Together we will travel
Through the shallows of the dark
Until our lips meet
For the last time.
Then awaken from your wanderance,
My soul will be with you;
Together we can be
Forever free.

—*Lisa Engleman*

Myself and I

Just me. Just me.
A small boy cradle by a huge red chair.
Safe, like being in my mother's arms.
I'm gazing out an oval-shaped window onto a wing—
An elongated diving board.
One can jump or fall into a world of fantasy.
Distant grayish-blue cumulus clouds
Swiftly glide across a sea of tranquility.
No two are alike.
Each one on their own.
My first flight. My first flight.
Reflections of me in the glass reveal..
It will always be..
Just me. Just me.

— *John T. Stuart*

I Can't Help Lovin' You!

You tell me you care but I know it's not true
But I can't help lovin' you.
If you cared about me you'd let me know.
If you loved me you wouldn't mind being with me.
I know I shouldn't but I just can't help lovin' you.

— *Christie Damon*

Times Frames

Childhood is but a misty memory;
Adolescence, a confusion long gone.
Young manhood's a ghost of harsh events,
And middle-age a bland old song.
The autumn years are but a resume
Of all that went before;
And the winter of life is but a bridge
To some eternal shore.

—*John Cull*

And the Wind Blows

The leaves rustle,
And the wind blows.
The moon shines,
And the wind blows
The rain falls like the single teardrop in her eye,
And the wind blows.
Her heartache is everlasting,
And the wind blows.
Her broken heart is ever so painful,
And the wind blows.
Her silent cry for help is not heard,
And the wind blows.
Her hand is aimed,
And the wind blows.
The shot is heard,
And the wind blows.
Her red heart is at rest,
And the wind shall blow no more.

—*Sarah Lyon*

You

You are the one who opened my eyes
And brought love into my life.
You are the one I gave my heart
And you pierced it with a knife.
You are the one I trusted
That we would always be together.
You are the one who broke my heart.
You were pretty clever.
You are the reason behind this poem
But don't be too proud.
You were once my rainbow
That is now covered by clouds.
You are the one I truly loved
And never will I forget.
You are the one I think of now
And wish we had never met.

— *Karrissa Diamond*

Tomorrow

When life just isn't going your way
And you know you can't handle another day
When you just can't seem to do things right
And the top of the mountain is out of sight
When all you feel is sadness and sorrow
Remember that there is always tomorrow.
When the road you're traveling never ends
And you seem to be living in a world without friends.
When the arguments grow and get out of hand and
The dreams you've built no longer stand when you
Want to give up and call it a day
Remember tomorrow's just a day away.
For no matter how bad your life may seem and
No matter how much you tend to dream
There's only one thing you need to know
Wherever you are and wherever you go
The sun will come up tomorrow.

—*Karyn McCoy*

Encounter

Eyes...
As clear as two oceans,
Inviting me to divein.
A tempting escape,
Too good to be true.
I hesitate,
Wary of testing the waters.
The moment is lost.

— *Sandra Lynn Barrett*

Spirit Inside

Spirit inside,
Take flight; do not hide.
Fly with me to the sky
Take me ever so high
Let my dreams carry me
On your wings.

Spirit inside,
Do not forget where home lies.
Bring me down again
To my family, my friends,
Let my dreams carry me
Through the night.

Spirit inside,
Take flight; do not hide.
Fly with me to the sky,
Yet do not where home lies
And let my dreams carry me
On your wings.

—*Robin Buckmiller*

Eternal Love

Our love is like
An eternal candle,
Burning silently and brightly.
Our passion is like
The flame,
White hot and forever lasting.
You are the match;
You ignite my fire.
I am the wick;
You're my burning desire.
Together
We'll burn strongly and brightly.
Apart,
We'll flicker weakly and lightly.

— *Renee Stieber*

Faceless Stranger

He is always near
Mimicking your every move
His black ghostly form
Identical to your own
Frightened children run
The dark stranger close behind
Faceless and nameless
The tracker stays by your side
Every breath you take
Instantly his own
You feel his presence
Closing in on you
But the sun's rays go down
Bids you farewell and departs
Only to return
With the early morning rays.

— *Sandra Domenichini*

G.L.O.W. Wrestlers

Tina Ferrari is the queen
Palastina gets really mean
The California Doll likes to surf
Soul Patrol get mad if you are in their turf.

Dementia enter in a cage
Princess of Darkness puts her enemies in a rampage
The Russian want to win the crow
But everyone pushes her around.

Susie Spirit's gymnastics are neat
American is really sweet,
THe bad girls say their not
But the good girls prove they are not.

There is always a championship fight
Turn to channel 50 every Saturday night
David Maclane is the host
You see his gals from coast to coast

And if you never of G.L.O.W.
   ...well, now you know.
      —Krista Staten

According to Your Will and Plan

Lord, what will it take to make him see
That drugs aren't cool?
Doesn't he know they are just another of
Death's killing tools?
Because his friends mess around with drugs,
He thinks he should.
He said he had quit them all;
I wish he would.
So many people care for him.
Doesn't he know he is hurting them?
Please Lord, help him understand
That dealing and doing drugs shouldn't be his life plans.
All I can do is pray, now and always.
I'll place this concern of mine
In Your loving and merciful hands.
Please Lord, help him
According to Your will and plan.
      —LaDette Collins

Only You

You have opened my eyes to the joys life can bring
I've learned the true meaning of love.
Loving, caring, trusting and sharing
That only He could have sent from above.
I used to pray for God to send me someone like you
You fit the image so perfectly.
Now I pray to thank Him
For He has truly blessed me.
Now I would give anything, to spend the rest of my life
Just caring and sharing
Every thought and every feeling...
With only you!
      —Cynthia McKay

Wisdom Is A Gift

Teach me to learn, to gain knowledge and wisdom.
Teach me to understand, to gain meaning and purpose.
Teach me the rules of the land,
To have respect for justice.
Teach me to read, with eyes full of questions.
Teach me to write, with words full of answers.
Teach me to listen, with interest and love.
For the world of learning,
Is a gift to be blessed.
Yet above all, teach me to share.
For a wise man who does not share his wisdom,
Is but a fool!
      —Sheryl Bailey Lanzarotto

Don't Cry for Me

Knowing I love you will only help less.
This moving away has no happiness.
Understand why and try to see;
Most of all, don't cry for me.
Each time I see you, I want to stay
But I know I can't have my way.
I'll never forget how you're so nice and kind.
You will always be within my mind.
I know it's hard to say good-bye
But please, for me, don't ever cry.
      — Sheri Lewis

The Champion

Flaming was the horse's mane
Flying through the meadow,
Silhouetted against the crimson afterglow
Of a dying sun-blazed inferno.

He was pulsing for his goal.
His strong hooves beat the ground,
His chestnut body muscle-bound.
The lake was his destination.

His proud eyes glazed with fury.
His heartbeat raced the speeding moments.
His heart rejoiced with his seized independence.
The champion had won again.
      —Katie Haines

I Haven't Been Here Very Long

I haven't been here very long
But I came to you.
You, promised you would help me
Learn the things I need to do.
I took you at your word mom,
I trust your every move.
I've come to you to help me
I, need to learn from you!
As each new day passes
I reap what you have taught.
I know with prayer you'll guide me
Into living proper thoughts.
With kindness, and by example,
I'll learn and tender be.
I'll learn to be the kind of child
God expects of me!
      — Shirley Berteaux

One With Nature

The sky is like an artistic dream,
While the grass embraces more,
Than the color green.
The trees I used as shelter from sudden storms,
While I one with nature,
Laid safe in my lover's arms.

I took time from my busy day,
To listen to the birds,
Hear the things they say.
I took time to smell the flowers,
Admiring the colors,
Ignoring the passing hours.

To become one with nature,
My deepest desire,
To feel cool winds lift me higher.
Yet I can truly say,
I have kissed the wings of doves;
For being one with nature; is being one with love.
      —Shiree McCarver

Vellum

An expression of the deepest feeling;
Happiness or sorrow,
   joy or pain.
Furtively hidden from all others;
Secretly communicated only to one.
A special one.
I will not embarrass or humiliate.
It will neither laugh nor cry.
It will just be pleased
   with anything
   I have
   to offer.
      — Tanya Castiglione

On a Ship

On a ship in the dead of the sea
You opened my heart
As never I thought it could be.
You are so special only just to me.
You are giving me love
   as never I thought it could be.
I am giving the chance to be loved.
And taking the chance to love you.
This love never to end.
This love never to die.
Is what I want,
Is what I need.
For us to be happy,
For us to be free.
To live our lives,
Together.
Just you and me.
      —Kelly Howell

Silent Tear

Who can hear your silent tears
When all are deaf and blind,
And the only way you show the pain
Is when your heart is kind.
Hiding in the shadows,
Proves nothing but your fear,
And in the dark, there is not a soul
TO see your silent tear.
So delicate the feelings that you fear
That they might break.
But to truly live your life
You must always give and take.
So shed one tear for me
And keep it always in your heart.
So that everytime you slip away,
Your world will not fall apart.
      —Nicole D'Aoust

The Past

I never had a guy
Who didn't break my heart.
I never had a relationship
Which didn't fall apart.
I never had a boyfriend
Which would hold me all the time.
I never had a guy
Who said he was only mine.
I guess I shouldn't think about
The things I never had.
Just be grateful for the good
And throw away the bad.
      — Robin Naccari

The City

She wears her morals on her back bumper
And turns to attack her squalling blonde mistake
Honk if you love Jesus...Christ.
He straddles the bar
Filterless camels drool brown spit
Head bowed, this dive is my poe raven
I shall not want, annointing himself with beer
Teenagers glide by, calm hips of steel
Hot pavement steaming oasis
Their laughter at the penguins walking
Tears tear lines in the face
I am cross bred here, between time and space
The horse calls me, his hooves pawing escape
I see the country rolling hill over hill
The city squeezes the breath out of me
Slowly, indistinctly,
I die at the bustop.

 —Jennifer Rowland

Central Park

Kids are screaming
Their balloons stuck in trees
Begging tired mothers for yellow pinwheels,
Running from cage to cage
With endless spurts of energy,
Wondering what those wrinkled faces
On lines of benches are smiling at.
Getting dizzy from the smell
Of animals and crackerjacks.

Standing on a rock
Surveying the belly of a softball pitcher,
Watching chubby kids
With their eyes fastened to kites,
Lovers embraced
Beneath the trees.
Music from the carousel reminding you of long ago
When you had no front teeth
And loved the days in Central Park.

 —Helen Fischer

City

People walking, talking
Busy streets
I look to faintly see the sun
The clouds, smog barely covering it.
As the wind picks up,
I feel sprinkles on my face
Then heavy patters, people rushing
Walking with umbrellas
I close my windows,
Rushing to play in the rain.

 —Cortney Davidson

In Medias Res

When a man walks slowly through the clouds
in his mind, ideas, like bright lights
illuminate the shadows swaying across
another time, formless. Many nights, my
outline on the wall looked gaunt, twisted.
I gaze into the dark, ask for the world.
Pulsing, jagged peaks, the pens on my desk
stab the dull light like broken bottles.
A streak of moonlight illuminates a broken
black mirror on the wall. Hours pass. The
Sun rises slowly. Reveals an imperceptible
beauty of which many poems are written
as the landscape reassembles. Life, seems to
evolve, in the miracle of divine indifference.

 — Thomas A. Phelan

Deep and Gray

Yesterday I slipped into a hole deep and gray
I felt so old and you were standing next to me
And your steel face didn't change.
When you reached out, your hand was ice.

The only pleasure was the numbness surrounding me.
So I didn't come to you
I wouldn't be able to melt your grip around me.
I stayed there, trampled into the frozen earth
Where everything was solid and cold.

 —Tamera Sides

Dance of Death

I dream about
A dance of death
The living glide
Designs unknown
To even themselves,
Acting out a sorrowful fear,
I scream for them to stop
My heart is aching,
Breaking
With every step of their
Woeful waltz. They stare into a
Meaningless void,
The dead stare back, their eyes aflame
With anger and jealousy, that they might dance
In the dreams of the living.

 —Tracey Deets

Separate Lie

I stand outside looking in
with eyes of separate caste.
No common thread nor brethren link
to comfort from the storm.

Alone among four billion strong,
a society of one.
Strain solitude rains through separate grounds
to reap the fruits of none.

Traced and bound by fear's narrow gaze,
yet without true identity.
A single wind drawn down lonesome way
to the shores of separate sounds.

The time may come when darkness bold
through seasons right to die,
curve long lost moments with one's regret
to live a separate lie.

 — Dale A. Mills

Where Did it Go?

Peace!
Wanted by everyone,
But never spoken of.
Wished for by children,
Who wonder what they can do
Yearned for by parents,
Who want to see their children grow.
Peace!
Will it never come?
Must we live in fear of war, forever?
Will children always have to wonder,
If they will be the next to kill,
In the name of peace?
Why do we have weapons and arms,
To kill a species of the same race?
The human race!
When will peace return?

 —Jessica O'Mara

Please Come Back

Mom the lady took down
Your pictures and posters.
She said they were dumb
And we don't need them.
Please come back...

Mom, your plants are
On the windowsill,
The lady waters them
But she doesn't talk
To them like you did.
They need you.So do I.
Please come back...

The lady told me you hate me
And I should hate you and
She said you're crazy and
Please come back.
Mom, I still love you and I miss you
Please come back.

 —Chelcey Dunham

I Loved Him

His eyes were so blue
I knew he was true
I followed him.
When he smiled at me
I thought he would see
I wanted him.
While we were'nt together
It seemed like forever
I needed him.
We were as good of friends as any
And moments we shared were many
I liked him.
He was a part of me
For an eternity
I lost him.
Now through the years
I still cry the tears
I loved him.

 —Leslie Mesmer

Confusion

You think it is love
But you are not sure
Your heart says yes
You say no
Always thinking about it
Always dreaming
Cannot wait for the moment
You meet again
You feel lost
And cannot find your way
Back to the world
As though you think.

 — Christa Bergum

Untitled

I am scared you will
Use me or
Abuse me
I am terrified you will
Take me then
Break me
Are you faking
Will my heart be breaking
Is that all you want
Or do you want the real me

 —Wendy Wells

One Last Wish

Oh, please, tell me why
Life is passing me by.
Why?
I go through each day in a daze
Hoping, wishing something would come my way.
Why
Do I feel so unwanted and alone
At school and at home?
Why
Do I feel life has no meaning,
Do I feel I lost the will for living?
So now I make one last wish:
That life would stop and save me from my anguish.

— *Sonia Chapman*

At Denitti's

So you're sitting with your Great Aunt Jane
At some local restaurant where the lights are too bright
And there are roaches hiding under the chairs
And all the waiters
Are art students or fairies
Who recite the daily specials like the rosary
And Great Aunt Jane is wearing too much make-up
And talking too loudly
And you excuse yourself to make a phone call
And instead wind up shaking in the ladies room
Hoping that this is just a bizarre test of faith
And later you can score some coke
And tell Great Aunt Jane
That you only want the house salad.

— *Kathleen C. Ambrose*

The Inter-Weaving

Talk about a sweet surprise!
Meet me? you barely suggested.
Surely you jest, dear man.
Your gypsy lady, head in the clouds,
Would crawl, ride a pig, swim the Sahara
To see you.
We had one very dear hour
Before other things called you on;
But that beautiful time
Together brightens today and more.
For days afrer, words of love unspoken
Sing through time.
By now my life is so much
Intertwined with yours I forget
Whose roots are which. Am I
The trellis or the vine, tree or leaf-
And does it really matter anymore?
Love grows love.

—*L. Sallaberry Recalde*

It Is Okay to Cry

Sometimes we wonder what makes old folks
So ugly and so mean
Maybe they have lost the one who would share their
Coffee and cream.
Sometimes we wonder why children want to misbehave
And act so bad
Maybe they have lost something they love
And cannot deal with being sad.
If we were given half a chance to talk
About our pain
We would find that it is okay to cry,
And a friend is what we gain.

—*Sandy Vance*

The Gift of Words

The temptation
once you've grown
to pay off
every debt
of hurt and pain
you can't forget,
to have finally learned
that when it comes
to weapons-
nothing extracts vengeance
better than
the wickedly spoken
or written word.

— *Constance Smith*

Suicide

I feel so alone,
Like no one cares
I'm always hoping for
You in my prayers
You talk about *her* in
Front of me;
I fantasize how I wish it
Could be me.
I don't want to leave,
But what can I do;
Because the only one
I love is you;
Good bye for now and forever.
Just remember I did it because
We couldn't be together.

—*Jennifer Paradis*

I Sense the Loneliness

I sense the loneliness
Deep inside,
I feel the intense hurt
You try to hide.
I see the look
That says everything,
When your lips
Say nothing!
You say so little...
I hear so much!
Everything you do speaks volumes.
Even your touch!

— *Robin R. Pulley*

Why a Rose?

Red roses by day
Aid my friend on his way.
Over mountains and clouds,
He flies to his call.

Red roses by night
Aid my friend through her fright.
In valleys and shadows
She flies to her home.

Roses were given
By friends through the ages
To ease heavy burdens
And calm tearful fears.

Here is a friend
And here is a rose.
Please be my friend
And please take this rose.

— *Leslie E. King*

LISTEN

Listen
Please hear what I say
And when I talk
Don't turn away.
The words
With spaces in between
Surely you know
Just what they mean.
Sometimes though
I know it's hard to understand
Exactly what's on my mind
But look at my eyes
My unconscious gestures
And you'll figure out the mine.
For words you know will dissipate
And we shouldn't need them to communicate.

—*Claudette Leandro*

Once Upon a Time

Once upon a time, on the edge of nowhere,
There stood a boy looking down at a dream,
Wondering what his life would be.
As time goes by, and the pieces fit together,
And life seems more at reach.
And now, nowhere is now somewhere.
Once upon a time on the edge of somewhere,
Where the past and present are one and the same;
Stands an old man, looking down at his life as
If it were only a dream.

—*Lisa Hlywa*

Untitled

I use to sit around,
Just waiting by the phone.
But now it seems you never call,
And I'm left all alone.

Could it be that you lost me,
And I'm the smart one here?
Or is it that it's just a game,
And your left free and clear?

It seems to me that you lost out,
And you're the one to cry.
Then why am I left standing here,
With a tear trickling down my eye?

It makes no sense after all of this,
That you could just walk away.
But I'd rather you leave me crying now,
Then walk out on me someday.

— *Susan Rodrigues*

Graduation

Now that we are Seniors and we are graduating,
We deserve to be able to look to the past
And give ourselves a pat on the back,
For we have made it this far,
But it is also time to give up the past.
It's time to fly away from the nest
And build our own.
It's our time to soar with the eagles
And to show them that we can fly higher,
But as we fly higher, we must not
Forget who we left behind.
We must remember that no matter
How high you soar, you must always
Return to the nest at some time.

— *Tammie P. Huot*

Grandpa

My grandpa has been dead awhile
And now I realize I will never again see him smile.
The gifts I gave him and the gifts he gave me
Made him my favorite grandpa and the only one I would need.
I saw him that day before he died.
He came to my swim meet and stood by my side.
After a glass of water in the middle of the night,
He fell down and died, no pain, no fright.
A couple days later, the memorial service came.
One man spoke, a lot of people came.
With a lump in my throat and a tear rolling down my face,
I know God has him and now he is safe.

— *Amy Berry*

The Word Hate

I'm really not in the mood to write in rhyme,
But I gave it some thought, gave it some time.
I just want to warn of using the word hate,
Warn you, refrain, before it's too late.
Though you may not know it, the word is strong,
Before you know it, you may have said it, and really done wrong.
Suppose one day your victim was to die,
Then you'll know a feeling of a heart destined to cry.
The word might have hurt, meanly stung,
This pain caused by quick slip of the tongue.
So I caution you, wisely choose your words,
Avoid heart tears falling...like flapping wings of birds.

— *Ann M. Lacy*

How Can I Tell You

How can I find the words to say that you are in my heart
And I would be so lonely, love, if we should part.
How can I make it known to you that your soft caress
Is the only answer to my happiness.

You are the meaning of my thoughts, the purpose of my life
And all the courage and strength I need to conquer life.
You are the minutes of my day, the hours of my night
And only when they shine on you forever bright
But how can I impart on you this feeling so devine
And make you understand, my love,
I want you to be mine.

—*Ana Maria Mosquera*

My Undying Love

I told myself it was over. I didn't want to see you anymore.
I wanted to stop loving you. I thought it would be easier if I didn't see you...
So I didn't call you. Now I find out that you're dating her again.
That only reinforced my want—my need—to be detached from you. I thought I was okay.
I thought all of my feelings for you were out of my heart and into my past.
Then, through the crowded room, I saw you again. My heart sank and I felt a thousand emotions
All at once: joy, anger, wounded, sorrow. Joy because I really was glad to see you.
Anger because I remembered that you *didn't have time* for me when we talked last.
Wounded because you didn't even realize that you hurt me. And sorrow-
Because the feelings that I thought were in my past crept back into my heart again.
We embraced—your arms around me again—I felt like a helpless baby in your care.
You touched my hair, mentioning how light it had gotten. I felt a warmth go through me.
You asked me a question. I forget what it was because I was rapt in your brown eyes.
I looked straight into them and sent you a mental message, *I still love you,*
But there was no response. We chatted, then said our good-byes.
I'm tired of you not loving me back. I'm tired of you not having time to see me.
I'm tired of fighting my urge to love you. But most of all, I'm tired of being
A prisoner to the love I have for you—my undying love that I thought was in the past,
But I knew I could never get rid of.

—*Anna Lynn Skamangas*

A Desktop Beauty-Watch

O! Unadulterated beauty
Image of the Almighty
WHen soberly in quest again for
Beauty to walk upon hid third creation.

Mornings may be bright, afternoons may sparkle
Evenings glitter in dark, cool background
When stars shine around the central moon
That are your snow-white teeth
Generating love and compassion
While thin clouds that swim on surface
The beaming of your eyes.

Is the Trojan beauty of legend
Reincarnate in black without name change?
For that eulogised beauty of long ago
Comes matching to my mind in lust and longing as
The job at hand suffers; while your efficiency moves
Behind the writing-machine fingered to say
Ta, ta, ta, ta, ta...all along
In your enormous speed, O! Helen.

—*Gabriel O. Ighile*

A Meeting

I was in awe, for my hand was held,
And my body frozen in time,
There was a greatness,
It came on me while I was unaware,
And, though alone, I was not alone,
For the fire of God had lit my mind with thoughts,
And my mind was not my mind,
And my body frozen in time;
There is darkness in the room,
Yet I could feel the light, for it touched my hand.
And my body was like sand;
I tried to break away: but the power kept my body still,
And the warning to relax,
Not to force the moment from my mind;
All at once I understood,
There was a meeting, and I had much to learn.

—*Andrew M. Wolf*

Walking Through the Woods

As I was walking through the woods one day,
I had to just stop and say:
Thank you Lord for all of nature's array,
And folded my hands to pray.

Thank you Lord for the trees so high,
Some of which seem to reach the sky
For the flowers that upon the earth lie,
And in winter disappear as if they die.

For all the big and small animals that roam,
Together they can never stand alone.
For all the mountain's glory,
They tell of your creation story.

For the bright raising sun, that tells us when a day has begun.
For the moon so big and round,
   that seems to follow us and upon us look down.
Thank you Lord for all of these,
Help us to keep Your beauty please.
   —Linda Harrington

Autumn Illusion

I have seen the moon
That shining, perfect orb
Hang over my Blue Ridge
With her trees fiery red and gold
Come to life with that God given light
I have seen this beautiful mountain
This backdrop of my childhood
Transform at this secret moment
As a bride when first she enters
And my eyes hold a moist reflection
Of my memories of this mountain
And the love of this, my home.
   — Constance Willson Bell

Trees

Trees—in their mute silence
   Watching me so closely.
Trees—hollow, sunken, rotted or tall
   Laughing at me, mostly.
Trees—elms, oaks or birch
   Reaching out to the sun as they pray.
Trees—those eyeless, ghostly, lanky wonders
   With jut-like limbs just for plund'ring.
Trees—whose warm shoe brown is their color
   Tho nature did cast one with an ashen pallor.
Trees—sure stole *my* spotlight in this route today.
   — Rosalie H. Contino

My Dream Knight

Last night I dreamed of a magical love
Where everything had been handled with care
Red roses and wine...soft music to dance to
But my knight was not there.

Candles were lit...and they peacefully glowed
With such dramatic light
Everything looked so beautiful
So wonderful, so mystical, so right.

I turned to look behind me
And there in the doorway he stood watching...waiting for me
He had known all along the way to my heart
And I'd belong to only him...forever faithfully.

He took my hand and pulled me close...slowly we began to dance
The music was ending and the candles were burning out
My knight has come to claim my heart
He loves me without a doubt.
   — Sabra Brenda

Him

I climbed a hill,
To see his face.
I wanted him.
Embrace me!
He didn't look, at all; he wouldn't even face me.
One drop, a drip. My body dripped.
The heat, seemed to arouse.
Him.
He dribbled down my neck. I looked up,
And he kissed me.
His eyes flashed, face lit up,
A yearning,
For one thing.
I heard his heart pounding, ripping thru his flesh!
His hair, so green. His rose! Satisfied, at last, ah.
Quenched. I rose to see it fall.
He is no stranger, the rain.
   —Monique Lowi-Teng

Passion

Devotion of two, miles across the sea.
Tingle of our bodies, sensuous to touch.
Tears shared together, moments of sorrow.
Laughter shared, times in ecstacy.
Love letters scented, smell of home.
Melting kisses, flavor from abroad.
Gentle smiles, affectionate words, hopeless yearning.
Tears of passion, separation, a long journey.
Tender embraces, lovesome arms, tightly held.
My life.
Forbearance commended, when anger erupts.
Being near, claspng my hand.
Passion is you, my love, my life.
   — William R. Gebel Jr.

Consolation By the Sea

Whenever the day is rough
And troubles worry me
I come to where the ground is
Caressed by the wave of the sea.
Divine order I pray
Then I feel ye my God console me
And take the pain away
As I walk on the beach
And listen
To the sounds of the sea.
   —Shonda D. Keeling

Love That Won't Fade

Our love won't fade because we have it made,
My love for you is not hard,
Because I do not have to go far.

You always see the best in me,
Even with lack of rest.
My love for you will never die,
Because I know not to lie.

I love you will all my heart,
Even though I cannot cook tarts.
By dawn you have mowed lawns,
But you have still not been gone.

I have seen you play sports and have heard you snort,
But you still get no warts.
When we talk on the phone,
You sometimes have a grown tone.

You are like gold to me, that I hold but don't mold.
Our love that won't fade.
   —Tiffanie Ramsey

Forever My Companion

A place called memory,
Hidden in the mind,
Structured in the pattern, human life designed.
Doors, unexpected opened with involuntary key,
Deep inside the pockets, of the soul's eternity.
With smell of rose or prick of thorn,
Each stage in life may be reborn.
A subtle smile, sudden glance, haunting voice or song,
Recall that special time and place,
Now forever gone.
Ribboned letters, sourvenirs, pictures from the past,
Etch laughter or a pensive tear
In the spirit cast,
A spell of happiness of gloom, depending on the door,
Opened in my memory, by wind of song or lore.

— *Marjorie Blankenbaker*

We Soldiers

We are hallow punch, a mute echo of a mute voice.
A hard heart, a disturbed soul.
What were we?
Alert soldiers stiff and firm
Infront of the wars, listening to the sounds of sirens.
We are puppets without smile
To decorate the mouth of our friends with laughter.
We are now manequins in exposition
In a shop window, frozen for a time, lost emotions.
We are now a powder of the earth,
Cremate in open fields, blown in the wind.

—*Maria Da Costa Nogueira*

Serene Days Captured

When roses are red, violets blue
And honey so sweet with the morning dew,
The world must be in peace for there flies a dove
With the world in hope and we're in love.
There must be a way to save this day
And you are so clever to find the way.
To take a picture to last the days through
Of the sun, the flowers and the morning dew.
For when there is trouble and the sun never shines,
We can look back to see how beautiful it all was at one time
And be happy again.

— *Marilyn Lee*

The Statue of Liberty, Lady Liberty

Beauty so symbolically magnificent created by God omnipotent
Beauty serene beyond compare could never be found elsewhere.
In the harbor, you are a shining beacon,
your devotion to all will never weaken.
With torch in hand in the harbor you stand.
Only in our incomparable Lady Liberty,
rings the beacon of freedom so intently.
Beckoning to all the laboring masses,
you include all the down trodden classes.
Waiting patiently for opportunity's glances
and blessings of liberty for prosperity's chances.
Far exceeding our greatest expectation
with great compassion and exhilaration.
Calling far and wide, I will care for your needy, troubled and forlorn,
And will Give blessings of liberty to this nation reborn. All waiting for a
All waiting for a chance only with providence guidance
with complete reassurance and compliance.
You stand with torch in hand, with freedom and justice for all to stand.
Lady Liberty eternal symbol of America the beautiful,
replete with splendor and oh, so bountiful and fruitful.
So let us all together be for united we stand and divided we fall.

—*Marilyn J. Irrgang*

Lost Love

A soft and gentle breeze carresses my body
Chilling me with its coldness
My love has gone
Gone to a place not known
Leaving me...oh...so alone

I feel a December rain
It tries to awaken me with pain
But no pain can be shared by that which has taken hold of me

A sense of nothing has invaded my soul
Leaving behind an empty shell
Left to walk through life
With nothing left to hope for

I refuse to walk alone with no hand to hold on to
But my love is gone
He has taken with him the sunshine
And now all I see is darkness

Soon I will follow that road I watch him walk down
And happiness I will once again know
In a place of serenity
Where my love can be found.

—*Margaret Kathryn Ruder*

Once Upon a Christmas

Sleigh bells ringing, children singing
Snow flakes falling, church bells calling.
The season is bright and full of cheer;
All 'round the tree, glad hearts we hear.

Down through time the angels sing,
Of yonder manger that holds our king.
Though we weren't at that holy scene,
Of that first Christmas we all must cling.

Star in the sky, shining bright,
Lead me on through the night
To the place where my savior laid,
While Mary watched with endless praise. Christmastide comes and goes-

Still the fire in the fireplace grows and grows. Till all the warmth is
Spread around to light every face—erase every frown. Now is the day we
All must share, Love, peace, and joy casting every care upon the holy
Babe that was born that day in Bethelem to light our way.

—*Marcy Chattin*

The Wind and I

Lying in the darkness of my room
waiting for sleep that seldom comes till the morning sun.
Listening to the wind humn softly through the trees
wondering from whence it came and where it will be going.

I strain my ears to listen for a sound but she is gone,
Somewhere blowing in the stillness of the night.
Ah, at last I drift into a peaceful slumber,
As peaceful as the dove that's perched above my window sill.

But not for long, for just as quickly I awaken
And watch the shadows on the wall.
While lying there pondering I delve deep within my soul to find answers,
Then in haste I surface back to reality.

Once again I turn my ear to listen to the quietness of the night,
Did I hear a faint sound? Ah yes, I cried,
She's back, the wind is back to break the silence of the night.

Once again I listen to the gentle breeze
Pass my window and then she's gone.
Where to? again I wonder as I slip back into my peaceful slumber,
No more to awake until the morning breaks.

—*Margaret Halcomb*

The Sound of Footsteps

The sound of footsteps coming closer
Anticipation grabs hold of me
In hopes the heel taps stop at my door
And through that archway it's you I see

But the sound of footsteps continue past me
And a shadow passes by my door
So I wait and listen for more footsteps
For the next shadow will be yours yours I'm sure

And the sound of footsteps with the beat of my heart
Are the sounds that slowly rock me to sleep
So when the footsteps really are you
Forever in my arms it's you I'll keep

The sound of footsteps coming closer
Open my eyes and at you I stare
Only to awaken to the passing shadows
Only a dream that you were ever there.

— *Joseph C. McBratney*

Sensations

I sense your eyes upon me—I turn and you are there.
The warmth of your gaze touches my soul, dispelling
Any fears or doubts that linger.

Thoughts of you invade my brain without warning,
Scattering concentration to the winds.
Though we are miles apart, I feel your thoughts
With me also, creating a bond few may comprehend.

Futilely I attempt to fathom the cause of this effect
But no answer appears.
So I succumb to the wave of emotion washing over me,
Letting it carry me where it will.

Cast adrift on a sea of feelings I had believed lost to me,
I rediscover and uncover each one like a buried treasure.
But they must be handled with care, for feelings long dormant
Are often fragile and can crumble to dust
In an instant if mistreated.

— *Cyndi Johnson*

Two Become One

Two people, in love
On Little Alum Lake
Swam naked, in the dark of night
Where shadows clothed their privacy
Softly embracing expressions of love
Endeared their bodies in oneness
In the waters warm enclosure
The moon's circlets of gold
Spiked the fragrance of him
His fruit, was sweetly passionate
And she, desired it, to hers they were refreshingly sustained
Never fearing, for he held her taut secure in the veiled evening's
Shield, she drew him between her breasts, their shallow
Breath, mouthed, without speech, his lips, of milk and honey,
Touched hers soon loosing all sense of time becoming
Inebriated with love, shamelessly without reservation
Two became one, on Little Alum Lake.

— *Constance Jeanne Livernois*

Peace

It's said to be the one thing everyone wants
Yet no one will take the first step towards it.
When will we awake from our slumber and realize
That war cannot create peace
As weapons will surely create death.

— *Stacy Nick*

Wondering about You

As I sit alone I often wonder about you.
The perfect life that grows inside me,
Awaiting birth into the world.
Everyday I think of you
And all of the things we will do together.
The three of us,
Me, you and your father.
It is hard to know you are there now,
But slowly you grow
And I see you by the swell in my stomach.
Oh little child I have so much hope for you.
You are the light of my life
And I look forward to the day I will hold you in my arms.
I will make your life one full of love,
Because I know how important love is.
I am looking forward to the day I will meet you little one.
I love you.

—*Traci Luginbill*

Remember Me in September

Remember me in September...
   when the wild flowers are in bloom.
With these I'll fashion you a bouquet
   so our love will ever bloom.
Later on they may fade and dry
'Tis not the end for you and I.
Next year they would bloom again!
True love can never die,
As long as you remember the last September.
Here's hoping you never forget; How can I?
Just in case I'm not around,
Bravely gather some wild flowers.
Plant them where I rest.
I'll see you somehow from above.
With a flash of lightning, I'll send you all my love.
May you always remember that dying ember that once was my name,
All the wild flowers I gathered for you to put into a frame.
Though your love was hard to tame,
I hope I have succeeded.
Maybe you will remember me picking wild flowers
   in the September rains.

—*John P. Zerillo Sr.*

Untitled

The drops of rain running down my window
Are like the teardrops running down my face.
Both of these drops can fall quite rapidly or quite slow
But they will always leave a trace.

— *Stacie Bromley*

A Teenage Moment

Each step on the sand leaves a trace
A path to her lonely sea
With agony, she manages to retain a smiling face
Although she's trapped in, unfree
As the ocean tides rises and falls
She imagines her life collapsing from the bind
Leaving her problems so intricated like pebbles
Her world seems selfishly unkind
It's alright to tip off the balance scale
At least every once in a while
We have ordinary setbacks along the trail
It's not a curse with intention in doing vile
For she no longer needs to crawl back to her shell
So she then turned her back and walked away
As her deepened mind echoed like cloudless well
The seawater sipped her troubles to decay.

—*Rowena de Leon*

I Love to See You Smile, Yvonne

I love to see you smile, Yvonne.
You look so good to me.
I love to see you smile, Yvonne.
You are as pretty as you can be.
You have made me so very happy,
By letting me call you my friend.
And I will be forever wishing,
That our friendship will never end.
I love to see you smile, Yvonne.
Please, smile for me again.

— *David L. DeVilleres*

Wondering

I thought I would never find you,
Yet one day you crossed my doorstep,
Right into my open arms.
I have always remembered that day,
But I also remember the next day,
When you walked out of my arms.
No that has not been the first time,
There have been many others.
Though this time is different,
You said you would return.
Where are you? In someone else's arms,
When you should be in mine.
My heart longs for you,
As each sun sets over the horizon.
I pray for you to come.
For my love is undying,
And I will take you now and forever.

— *Rebecca Wilson*

Hardship

A fathers eyes grown cold,
From hardships untold.
A mothers arms unfold,
Offering shelter to the child she will hold.

The *man* has spoken!
He offers his token.
The child's heart is still broken.
Swept from society's sight,

Offered no solice for their pitiable plight;
A family's spirit will fight.
Bound together through their
Struggle for survival;

Love brings hope's revival.
Character put to
The bitter test,
Brings about our country's best.

— *R. G. Richardson*

Pilate

His name was a synonym for ambiguity
Known throughout the Roman Empire
For his irony was Pilate
Even The Master had to clarify
When asked if he was the King of the Jews
Are you saying this
Or is it others have told you this
Am I a Jew?, he replied
When he stated he found no cause in Jesus
Was it no legal case
Or his own proximity to the Amazing Grace?
Always the enigma of history
Is Pilate

— *Thomas F. Smith*

A Crush

It's hard to fight the way I feel.
I wish for once my dreams could be real.
I knew your job was done and you had to go.
Once again my heart I had to sew.
It was hard to see you walk out the door,
Fighting my tears like never before.
I know you and I, we could never be,
For I am just a child, that is what you see.
It would be typical for you to think
Without a hesitation, without a blink,
You're so young; it's only a crush.
Take your time. What's the rush?

— *Kriss Harvey*

Untitled

Pull us apart, breaking hearts
Why can't they see, it's us from the start.
You are too different, he and you.
You know his love cannot be true.
Holding each other, we turn our backs
We both know, opposites attract.

You are too young and he's too fast,
You should know that it won't last.
Joined by emotions from head to feet
What they say doesn't matter once we meet
Foolish people don't realize
It's not who we are, what we've done
Or where we've been,
It's what's to come.

—*Rebecca Costello*

Untitled

Keep the light burning,
It helps to light the way,
The way is life—it's love and hope;
The challenge of the day. It winds and twists,
Many are led astray. Don't walk by the shadows,
They hope to suck you in
To engulf you and hold you,
Until you must give in.
Keep the light burning,
The shadows will fade away.
Walk sure on the path—in faith and trust;
Stand fast in the light of the way.
The shadows will be there for eternity,
Just waiting for falling prey.
Polish your light and keep it bright,
The enlightened never wander astray.

—*Luanne M. Carlson*

A Foreign Affair

Hasta la vista when we're in Spain,
Leaving you now there is nothing to gain.
When in Italy, I'll say arrivederci to you,
Where I'll be next I haven't a clue
Au revoir to you when we're in France,
If we meet again it will only be chance.
I'll say sayanara if we meet in Japan,
I will try to forget you if only I can.
Australia bound I will leave you with a fond G'day,
Once again I must go away.
England will release you with a kind cheerio,
Bringing back memories of long, long ago
Mexico will be gone with a friendly adios,
Meeting again we came so close.
Saying goodbye is a foreign affair,
That's one thing that all of us share.

—*Lori White*

Think First

The words we say are scratches deep
Upon a surface bare.
We may remove the varnish,
But the markings are still there!

Some things there are we cannot mend,
Nor wrest to former glow,
For once the grain is scored in pain
The scars will ever show!

— *Roxann Dewtlinger*

Raped in Isolation

The pain surfaces
Feeling shattered innocence
Violated body suffocation
Encompassing separation of spirit and body
Restrained body wanting to fly fly
Cries piercing crys deafening cackles
Spiritual image performing a ritual
Hands grasping downward entry
To the human figure unattainable
While the body was being violated
An illusion illusion illusion
As the spirit re-entered while
The audience left the performance
Powerless powerless body encased
Within a cocoon of armor left
The stage.

— *Raye Inglis*

Answer

I'm told my father has a house
Where I will someday go
To dwell with him forever,
And all answers I will know;
Why babies may be slaughtered,
While their killers get off free,
And those who try to save them
Are mistreated brutally...
Why children starve in far off lands,
Ands we have fields to burn;
Or classrooms teach the lies
Of how from *nothing* we can learn.
They say we all just happened,
And it all just fell in place.
Well, someday there'll be answers,
When we meet God face-to-face.

— *Shirley M. Puckett*

To a Very Special Someone

In the darkest times of life
You are as a candle, there to bring
Forth a flame to let me know
That there is still light.
When I'm in my loneliest times
You are my friend someone to
Talk to, make me laugh, and show me
That things are not really so bad.
When things seem to always go wrong
And it seems I can do nothing right
You are that *special someone* I need
Praising me in different ways.
When you take me in your arms darling
All my problems seem to fade, with the
Gentle loving kisses, and your tender touch
I feel safe as if no one else can hurt me,
Because I have you, I love you

—*Sheila Dill*

Allusion

Standing on the beach,
As the sun rises,
The wind blowing my hair
Away from my face.
The ocean tide, slowly rolling in.
I stand there and look out into the sunrise,
Over and above the beautiful sea of water.
I turn and see you,
Standing there.
As you deeply look into my eyes
As we silently stand.
On the opposite sides of the sand,
We gaze into each others eyes,
And you reach out your hand.
Then you disappear in disguise.
And I realize it was just an
Allusion deep in the skies.

—*Jodie Houde*

The Sloop at Pilot's Point

There she sits,
Paiently waiting in the shallow cove,
With naked masts and barren decks.

The winds have blown from all directions,
The waves have relentlessly
Pounded at her bow.

Now she rests during the long, cold night,
But smiles with the sun at her back
At winter's solstice.

She peacefully sleeps from the constant
Rocking of her mother,
The sea beneath her.

But is never fogotten for a moment,
In the dreams of the sailor,
Who awaits her wheel.

—*Anna Beatrice Zacchina*

The Homestead

Here stands this ancestry
Now before me unchanged.
Shingles dark and worn
Brown with mossy growth, guarded
By densly packed soldiers of cedar.

Home to many generations; unknown to me.
Now it is empty and I may enter,
That smell lost in my senses until now.
The summer kitchen, white metal wash basins
And relics of tarnished engravings.

Many rooms, a million doors,
A richly carved staircase
And the attic; that smell
And draft of chilly air that ever so slightly
Rocks a once wickered chair at the west end.

—*Laura Tuthill Gleason*

The Movies

If only life was like the movies,
People smiling, laughing, being another person,
And if they die,
They will be in another place, another time,
Yet still be with their loved ones.

— *Tracie L. Cole*

For Libby

I have no need of metaphor
To say it's you whom I adore
Nor of some useless simile
Impotent to describe for me
A depth of love that's only seen
In these brown eyes by yours of green.

— *R. Gordon Holcombe Jr.*

Even Though...

Even though you said we are through,
I cannot help but think of you,
And even though I know you are gone,
My feelings still go on and on,
And even though we are not together,
My memories of you will last forever,
And even though you let it end,
I hope someday you are mine again
And even though you said goodbye,
My love for you will never die,
And even though you went away,
My love for you is here to stay,
And even though I know we are through,
I hope you are thinking of me, too.

—*Tara Sody*

Chance and Choice

I found a coin that is worn quite thin.
Tails you lose; heads I win.
It is in the air; I can't keep track.
If I lose, it won't come back.
It is coming down; I am headed up.
The choice is made; I don't need luck.
I have skill and will; I won't be stuck.

You ask, what does it matter?
What matters you don't see.
I've got to climb that ladder.
That's what matters most to me.
Make me an offer I can't refuse.
Heads, I win; tails you lose.

The coin is mine; it's in my grasp.
I'll take my chance; too much has passed.
It's up to me and I know the task.
The coin reveals...I have won at last!

—*Leane H. Reed*

Responsibility

Busy little fingers, eyes wide with wonder,
Eager minds absorb what's around;
Nothing too daring for experimentation
Whether detrimental or profound.

Unsupervised, the latch key kids wander,
Left to their own devices;
Open prey to the scum of the earth
Who peddle hell in various disguises.

Big twitching fingers, eyes glazed with drugs,
Street wise and slaves to the devil;
Stealing, killing, selling the substance
That brought their lives to this level.

Who is to blame for this threat to our nation?
Fingers point in every direction;
Love for a child begins in the womb,
Responsibility is akin to affection.

—*Leah Peterson*

Love Is a Feeling

The night is over, toward another day.
I miss your love, in every way.
I can't help feeling the way I do,
So please tell me, if you feel it too.
Feeling this feeling is something rare.
This feeling I feel, is it really fair?
I ask myself time after time,
But I never get a positive sign.
The way I miss you holding me tight.
You'd hold me forever, all through the night.
I know it's crazy, but it's true.
The way I really feel for you.
I know you still love me, just say so.
I'll never let our love go.
I love you today. I'll love you tomorrow.
I'll love you forever to come.
Just say those special words to me.
Forever, our love will run.

—*Melanie Lorenz*

Friendly Memories

The unobstructed gentle blue sky
Filled with fanciful adventures
Invisioned only in your creative minds,
The repititious sights and sounds
Of the familiar crashing waves,
Sounds unpolished by the civilized world,
Sights beautiful enough to paint pictures of
The crystal-like brilliant white sandy beaches
As hot as I can imagine fire to be.
My companion and I were talking of old times,
The times we shared together in our friendship,
The humorous days,
The mournful days
And all the days in between.

— *Lynn J. Boivin*

Home

On either side of this lonely road
Wyoming stretches wide.
Sagebrush, dry grass, scrub pine here and there;
Low rising cliffs with sculptured forms
Made by Wyoming's artistic wind;
Thunderheads in the sky defying all description.

That sky!
Sometimes sunshine blue,
Sometimes thunder blue,
Is even bigger than the land.

This is the country that sees my impatience as
Home's not far away.

Home...
Those mountains against the Western sky
Hold deep within
That very precious jewel,
Home.

—*Lyn Goffaux*

Just Good Friends

Why? Why do you treat me this way?
I loved you once and then again,
But all you wanted was to *just be friends*.
I'd tell you, *I love you,* you'd just turn your head.
Well, now I know my love can never be returned
And as I said I loved you once and then again
But now I see all we can be is just good friends.

— *Melissa Nevarez*

Together Forever

I thought our love would last forever.
Like a pretty red rose in bloom all year.
I thought things could only get better,
Our love was a dream to good to be true.

A ray of sunshine brightened our lives,
As nature guided us through thick and thin.
Together we never sighed,
We were the best we could have been.

You filled that empty space,
You even trimmed it with lace.
Our love was meant to be,
True for us both to see.

True love is hard to come by,
And we have struck gold.
We will never say the word goodbye,
Our love is something to hold.

We are together, forever.

 —*Tara Buckley*

Someone

I need someone who will always care,
Someone who makes life to bear.
A person who is loving, gentle and kind,
A friend who will always be on my mind.
I need a person, I need a sign
I want someone who will be mine.
Time goes by, that I know,
It does not wait but I need to grow.
Life is great fact and myth,
But life is better when you have
Someone to share it with.

 —*Lucy Polizzi*

The Green Freckle

It is bad enough I have brown freckles,
But now a green one, too?
Is it something I eat,
Is it something I drink,
Is it something that I do?
It is situated right under my nose,
What a funny place to be.
Why not on my cheek,
Or on my forehead,
Why does it even have to be on me?
But then I touched it,
And it felt slimy,
Not at all like the other ones do.
It came off of my face and onto my finger,
Then I realized what it is not.
Instead of being a freckle,
It was a green glob of...

 —*Lainie Winter*

Tongue Depressor

The tongue is a tool that scratches ever so deep.
The damage done may be there for keeps.
For with the mouth the heart doth speak,
And with lying lips the will is made weak.
Let us not overlook the damage we've done,
And have to say, *oh Lord what have I done?*
Always make sweet the words that you speak.
For you never know what words you must eat.

 — *John H. Burns*

You Are the Only Cure

You whispered in my ear
When I was alone with you
I told you that I cared.
When you told me we were through
You claimed that you loved me
But I know now that you lied
How could you have done that?
For I hurt so much inside
I wish we could get back together
Just the way we were
I can't stand the pain much longer.
You are the only cure.

 — *Monica E. Martish*

When Love Dies

We were torn apart and lost our love
Or at least forgot what love does
We didn't realize, our love was meant to be
I looked into your eyes, but couldn't see.

We've lost the spark can't even be friends
Out in the dark with only loose ends
We tried to keep what was there
At the end—we didn't care

How could this be, you'd never guess
Our perfect love was put to rest.
Questions I asked bothered you
The future or past, I have no clue

It was once, but now it's not
Or just a hunch, which we forgot
Maybe someday, we'll be together
I only pray, we're right for each other.

 —*Lee Ann Hamby*

The Spark

The two of us together
I hope will last forever
We stood by each other's side
When our love died.
We tried for another spark
But our love was in the dark.
There was no chance for another romance.
We were a perfect couple
But we had a little trouble.
I tried to fight
But all I did was cry at night.
I want it to be there
The two of us a pair.
Just stay with me
And you will see
The love for you
Will always be.

 —*Liz Archett*

Buddies

Characteristics from the heart,
the magic that lies within the soul.
The love surrounds us and holds us tight,
understandings of the magic are hard to fight.
Years fly by as we grow closer,
days go by as heartaches are shared.
As the sun goes down, the magic is lost,
the love that was once upon us is hard to invision.
Memories are there,
but is that enough?
If love is truth, it will show us the way,
It will bring back the love that was meant to stay.

 — *Michele Houghten*

Riddle Space

Slowly an eye opens wide
As feelings are pushed aside
Hear the shadows begin to wail
As someone catches a star's tail.
In the light of flowing time
There lies a riddle in a ryhme
And if intuition answers true
A door is open for that few.
Step by step through the shdadow
They see the knowledge that they know
To calmly reaveal their soul's face
And change the colors in they're space.

 — *Mary L. McCullough*

Touch Me

Magick, untamed...wilderness.
Come away with me into
The passion of an untried soul.
Pure fire unbridled, waiting to explode.
Subtle extremes, dare to touch me.
Touch me.
Enter the fire, white hot desire.
Fly into infinity, steal the breeze with me.
Feel the magick of the first, touch.
Taste the magick in my soul
Spirit to spirit, one vital whole...
Touch me.
Alive to fly further than ever before.
Alive to see the breaking of dawn,
The coming of spring.
Touch me.

 —*Johnny R. Morgan III*

I Promise

I promise to love you forever,
I promise to never cheat.
I promise to always be faithful,
No matter who I meet.

We could be friends forever
And never fall apart.
We could be more than friends
For I love you with all my heart.

I tried to hide my feelings
And tell you I did not care.
I spent every day and every night,
Wondering how I could dare.

How could I just turn my back
On my feelings for you,
When all this time, I knew deep inside,
My feelings of love were true.

 —*Crystal Mjoen*

Dead Sight

Dim the eyes and begin to drown.
Pass in comfort a lonely town.
From children to stone, words they send.
Watch the steady, for they will bend.

Young rabbit plays in grass so tall.
Torn man drinks, blinded by the fall.
To his mother, baby gives call
When soldiers build tomorrows wall.

To enter and not hear a sound.
To depart only to be bound.
Footfalls of dead sight all around
And the light in night always found
 when in one candle vision.

 — *Lewis Inouye*

Toybox

Beneath darkest shadows dwell
Fingers of infant skin ponders
Excitement quivers young minds
Tender
Throwing of variance well
Down under where sight of just
One wonders
Thirty six inches plunge within
Smiles practice in findings, of
Thoughts never to be
Baby brother found his toy,
You see!

    —Barbara L. Williams

Everlasting Friend

My mother and I share everything,
Our hopes, our dreams, our thoughts.
With us, it's share and share alike,
For there are no secrets.
She'll always be there for me
And I'll always be there for her.
My mother and I have something special
Which no other mortal shares,
A bond of trust, loyalty and love
Which is respected by all
For without the other,
There would be no everlasting friend.

    — Heather DiBlasi

Remember When

Remember when we were young,
When our lives had just begun.
We had no worries and we had no cares,
And we all played with teddy bears.
Remember when we were growing up,
All we wanted was a little pup.
We played outside from morning until night,
And Mama was trying to teach us wrong from right.
Remember when we started to school,
That is when we all thought we were cool.
We always walked around the halls,
Picking on people without a cause.
Remember when we were at graduation,
We showed our pride and appreciation.
We now have children of our own,
Please tell me where the time has gone.

    —Angel N. Hastings

In Memory of the Children

The hills cry for the young
As the earth bears silent witness.
The eagle circles her nest
And endless waves battle the shore.
Blossoms crushed too soon.
Fruit withered on the vine.
Nature calls home early
Some of the children she has borne.
But though life screams
While sorrow weeps raindrops.
The earth turns, the tide ebbs.
And once again the flowers grow.

    — Valerie Sim

Haiku

Weeding my garden.
Some ducks pleasantly arrive.
Quack, quack, quack, quack, quack.

    —Walter Kaczkowski

Parenting

It is only the beginning,
The battle has just begun,
Our job gets harder, tougher yet;
When we advise a daughter or a son.

They falter here; they teether there;
And then they come around,
To do the things we taught them to do.
The joys, they do abound.

It is worth it all! Oh yes, it is!
And I would do it all anew.
For just a pat or just a hug,
Or a whispered, Mom, Dad, I love you.

    —Betty Watson

Peace and Silence

A child like creature is present,
Sleeping like a lamb in a stable,
Turning around in sequence.
A babe asleep once more in someone's arms,
Asleep to the music, to love.
A nurse by his side for his every need,
To have him awaken at the correct time,
To be there for him to see as he awakens,
To have him feels secure by holding him,
Perhaps like a teddy bear.
A teddy bear by a teddy bear,
Wrapped around each other,
Asleep until the crack of dawn,
Asleep until both have had enough,
Enough of peace and silence,
Peace and silence.

    —Elizabeth T. Kozak

Untitled

When a new child is born
It's like a new flower in spring.
Starts as a seed in the warm, damp ground,
TThen a growing stem waiting for the bud to appear.
Finally, a hint of a flower appears
And grows into a beautiful, tall flower.

    — Amanda Des Re'maux

Healing Poet

And there
in a room of strangers sat
a healing poet

the white noise
of their voices
like television gone mad
swirling 'round
and around the poet head

but quiet in herself
finally
herself a steady hum
of blue sparks
thought long dead
from fingertips
dancing words
to paper alive

    — Beckie Decker

The Stars of Love

Two stars
Lie together
Joined in the sky
Will last forever
Filled with love
For they can't ever die.

Just as
The love of two people
As bright as the skies
Will be endless
With no more cries
The touch of the lips
Will last forever
Now they are together
Their hearts joined as one
A new life has begun.

    — Ivana Segvic

Untitled

The day is new
The air is fresh
It's waiting there
Just for you
The nights are calm
You hear a song
That's soft and sweet
Throughout the palms
The times together
Are cut so short
But now I've found
That I will love
You forever.

    — Anna M. Samuelson

The Path Never Ends

As I walked,
Along the path,
Guided by
The patch of silver moonlight,
I saw a rose
A rose of beauty,
Love
Tenderness,
Loving,
A rose that unlocks
The beauty and dreams
For tomorrow and forever.

    —Annette Salitsky

Dear Andy

A year ago today we were together
But now he's gone out of my life forever
I love him so much and I hurt so much inside
Since he went away I want to cry

Our love was so true we cared so much
I love just to see him, just to feel his touch
It was four simple words that tore us apart
Those words killed us as one, and stabbed his and my heart

Those words were not meant to be said
They were just the result from the confusion in my head
Now that we're apart I feel so much sorrow
All I do is waste my life away until another tomorrow

I apologize for everything, and try to explain what went wrong,
But he won't listen because even though he hurts inside
he wants to appear to be strong.
What I would give to have him believe me,
forgive me and finally let live,
But I guess at best, so he has his reasons,
I'll let it lay at rest for as long as I live.
    —Tracey Cappy

Thoughts of love

I am away from you, but I'm still close.
I still think of you, but it's not very much.
It's when no one is around,
When I feel all alone.
When the one I love is missing,
When I am on my own.
I can't give you a call, but you're in my prayers.
I wish for you a girl, but I hope you don't find one.
So that I know I can love you,
One day when I am free.
So that when I understand you,
I can bring you back to me.
I wish I could talk to you, but you wouldn't understand.
I wish I could tell you everything, but you wouldn't believe.
Because I know I hurt you badly,
And that will always be in my heart.
But maybe if you'll forgive me,
One day we won't be apart.
    —Cathy R. Mapp

Paper Doll

My life print was decided long before I was born.
Many things I can change.
But my pattern was cut by scissors that do not fit my hands.
    —Laura Sensenig

Investigating the Unknown

Why do you seek this thing called the unknown,
Won't you believe it exists, do you have to be shown.
Where can you find this place of great mystery,
It is real, or some kind of strange fantasy.
What would you find there, if you could get near,
Maybe there would be darkness, danger, and fear.
How will you get there, is there a way,
Will it take a century, a year or a day.
When will you start on this great task,
Do you know which questions you need to ask.
Who else will you find there, are you the first one,
Imagine the excitement, the anticipation, and fun.
If your wishes and dreams were all to come true,
Would you be satisfied, would you still be you.
Will the unknow be found, explored, and confined,
Or will it always be out there to challenge your mind.
    — Michael R. Willey

Forever Loving

I think about you always
Never forgetting the time we're together.
I hope we'll stay close forever.
You're in my heart, on my mind.
I love you all the time.
    — Michelle Jacobs

The Illusion of Love

Love is an illusion,
It causes pain and confusion.
The sorrow it sends,
Causes heartache that never ends.
The joy it releases,
Brings happiness that never ceases.
The tears that are cried,
Are of feelings that died.
The memories made,
Will all begin to fade.
Nothing lasts forever,
Especially the thought of being together.
    —Mary C. Gunter

Love Pass By

Looking in the sky
Don't just watch love pass you by
Search in your heart
Cause I know you're really smart
Find your true love
By looking above
You'll find it someday
Then your searching will pay
So look up high
Deep in the sky
Don't just let love pass you by
    — Missy Buchholz

Truths

Letters are written.
Words are spoken.
Covering so carefully,
So quietly.
Wondering, true identity
Unknown.
Lost in thought.
Doubting the truth.
Yet, wondering.
Seemingly fantasy,
Reality?
Knowing, beyond all doubt.
Carefully considering.
Knowing beyond all
Doubt.
Really??
    —Sondra Lin

Endurance

Once in a lifetime...
There is a moment set aside for sadness
Not little sadness...but an agony
It is that moment, that has just passed
The pain remains forever...
One cannot forget
Yet there is still time
Before the sun will set
For happiness and love.
    —Taunya Price

Jealousy

I saw jealousy clearly.
She was prestigious and powerful.
She turned and glided towards me,
with a venomous tongue.
I saw her green eyes and bronzed skin.
And I heard her strike with envy,
and I felt fury.
    — Lori Tracy

FILLED WITH FANCY

Surely you knew
I was intrigued
By the wit of your charm...

These caressing eyes listened
Absorbed as a sponge,
Giving warning to operating shutters.

The fluid that is stored
May commence flowing—
As it floods the slopes of its fields,
There too, to be absorbed
No longer to be stored
In the memory of its pores...
Distinguishable now
Only as salt.
    — Kathy Aberth-Bozsan

Love

Love...
What is love?
A great big hug
from your boyfriend,
A great big smile
from your best friend.
Love is shared between
one and another
whether from your best friend
or lover!
    — Katie Passanisi

A You and Me

Oh love, you give me happiness.
Sometimes you cause me pain.
If I could live without you
What would be my gain?

Less stumbling blocks before me
As I try to do my work
For more important things than you.
But then...I would be a jerk!

If always by myself I would be
With nothing in my way,
I would find an emptiness inside
At the end of a busy day.

Though I could live without you
And maybe be more free,
You give my life more purpose
When there is a you and me.
    —Clodah G. Summer

Rodney and Me

Together forever, never to part,
Special love straight from the heart.
He's always close to keep me from harm.
He's so handsome, so full of charm.
No other could be as special as he.
Together forever...Rodney and me.
    — Kimberly J. Kroll

A Part of the Darkness

As the fog rolled in, the scent of extinguished
candles was blown past.
Up in the sky, darkened clouds enclosed the
bright moon and stars.
Walking along in the crisp air,
nightstalkers could be heard.
And you were alone.
No one there to share the night—no one
who cared enough to spend the time.
And as a car drove by—the headlights shined
upon your path.
You were no longer invisible to the world-
you had been seen-
Was it what you wanted?

— *Heidi Busse*

Life in the Fast Lane

Life changes as time goes on,
From one day to the next,
From dusk until dawn.

Life is full of good and bad times,
From sharing with friends,
To those almost deadly climbs.

Life has no easy breaks,
From the time you are born,
To the last bit of energy it takes.

Life depends upon you,
From the amount of self-confidence,
To the seemingly impossible dreams you pursue.

Life is a very hard test,
From pleasing your family and friends,
To strive in succeeding and to do your best.

—*Barbara Dempsey*

The Door

It's as plain as the walls around it.
Yet it's different, more than ordinary.
I can look back, but not ahead.
Behind the door there can be joy and happiness,
Or there can be sorrow and consequence.
When looking at the door, I feel excited and happy,
Yet worried and anxious.
I cannot change what is behind me,
But I can do my best to change what is ahead.
I know I must open the door,
But I am hesitant,
Not sure if it's the right time.
I will open the door and hope for the best,
Prepare for the worst.
And I will live through it,
Only to encounter another door.

—*Alissa Brandemuhl*

What Do You Do When a Friend Turns to Drugs?

For me, It was a nightmare I never thought would come true.
At night I lie awake worrying and not knowing what to do.
He has a searching and confused heart,
But God only knows why he chose to start.
I feel the pain of his cries.
I feel the pain when I look deep into his eyes.
I must have told him I loved him ten times or more,
And every time I could feel the tears start to pour.
He warned if I told anyone I would never see his face again,
But in a case like this, you must tell a trusted friend.
Everyday my prayer is that God would show him the right way,
And that our every tear would soon fade away.

— *Carrie Beech*

Silence

Silence, an unending sound
That creeps up when least expected
And violently captures the crying heart
Between her one hand and the mourning soul in her other,
Joining them only when she is fascinated
With the invidious abhorrence of the two forces.
Recollecting her thoughts
As nostalgia corrodes her brain,
Over and over and over again.
She, a personified expression in a molded face
That collydes and collydes and collydes with hate.
She walks upright, yes, alluring, cardinally bearing her
Finely sculptured mask which hides her screams and terrors inside.
Silence, oh silence! Her fate without pity,
Her smile without feeling,
And then slowly, she fades away.

—*Ana Ituarte*

Last Hope

Forces about shriek; my soul responds
to the mystical wave of their magical wands.
Everyday life can't tell why I'm here;
it only records.
In the light of the night when the world's gone away
and the mind's on its solitary search
for the place of creation,
only one hope left.
A light pierces the darkness.
Old light. New light. My light!
How much must pass through your spectrum
before the light's perfect once more?
How much must I not know
before my last hope?

— *William Fallos III*

Melancholy Sunlight

Everyone around me rejoices,
For a victory which is sheer delight,
I don't wish to join them.
What they celebrate is not what I wanted.
But it is important to them; so
I smile, illuminated in greetings-
A light of praise that is cold, far colder than darkness.
For what they wish to illuminate does not exist.
Then I leave, hurting,
For it aches to move away from the past,
Even a past that is dark and molten.
It is the pain of birth and death in one.
It is agony no heart withstands.
My tears stream in melancholy sunlight.

— *Natalie Boon*

Above the World

Sitting on top of the skyscraper so high.
I watch all the little figures pass by.
Watching the people that are down below,
I feel that everyone is my foe.
Because right now I am sitting here all alone,
I wish at least I had a friendly clone.
Then I would have someone to talk to
And I would not feel so down in the dumps and blue.
Although the sun shines brightly there,
I still see a gloomy glare.
For the clouds just stay in my mind,
I wish I still had the happiness that I left behind.
This poem may sound so sorrowful and sad
But by writing it, I feel cheerful and glad!

—*Caryn R. Graber*

How Do You Spell D-I-V-O-R-C-E?

We
are the people they
left
discarded socks and panty hose
  on carpeted floors.

Statistics-
people destined to become
numbers
  on census forms.

This
happened to other couples
not to people who paid
taxes, attended church
and voted.

— *Mary Sewell Causey*

Bleeding Hearts

Sometimes I wonder, when will it end?
Lonely people looking, reaching out for a friend.
Sometimes no one is there to help the one in need.
They are just pushed away to let their heart bleed.

I once had a friend I treated this way.
I will always regret it until my final day.
She felt unwanted, unloved, not there.
She thought I'd forgotten her and that I didn't care.
I went to her funeral a few weeks ago.
Suicide was the wrong answer; now she'll never know.

The other day at her burial site,
The flowing tears, I could not fight.
I pulled out her picture and remembered her need,
Then saw it was time for my heart to bleed.

— *Missi Woodruff*

Singles Bar

Do I remember you? Well sure I do. Would I forget how
You caught my eye from clear across this big, huge room?

(yes, I remember well the scented searchings
of your starving mouth and slithery tongue
and clutching, kneading hands that joined me
  with your spastic
ebb and flow
  that heaved me on
a rumpled sea of bitter
  musk till I dropped
down, down, down, down, down,
  to a trembling
empty, mindless, humid calm.)

Sorry, tell me your name again. I have never been very good
At remembering important dates or birthdays or people's names.

— *John L. Lowden*

God's Answer to Anger

Anger sleeps with a heart.
Awaken by an injustice, it often seeks vengeance.
Often it is blind, for it closes it's eyes to love.
Love fills itself with understanding,
Anger empties itself in unforgiveness.
When cherished, love brings joy.
When ignored, anger brings pain, for
Pain walks hand in hand with anger.
Each brings tears to moisten the seeds of indifference.
Love sleeps in the arms of peace, while anger walks the corridors of
Unrest. Love seeks to compromise, but anger demands it's own way.
Time is unable to separate love, yet anger can divide a heart.
The answer to anger must be love,
For where love stands together, anger must kneel.

— *Darrell M. Peterson*

Single

United I fall, divided I stand
When I am alone, I am in command.
When I am one, I can stand tall
If I give in, I am set for a fall

So my heart is now locked, only I have the key
When temptation is freat, I hide it from me,
One brick at a time, I have built a great wall
That no one can see over, no matter how tall,

A sign I have posted, no one is allowed
Until I am ready, to this I have vowed.

— *Kevin Askew*

A State of Mind

Sometimes feelings can get confusing.
Believe me mine sure do
Maybe its because I don't know if I love you
Other people are also amusing.
But deep down inside I have this feeling
A feeling like I'm stealing.
Stealing you from others, stealing your time.
I just want you to be all mine
But I want to see others, I want to be free.
I don't want to end the relationship between you
And me.
I don't know, maybe I'm not being fair.
Many people say we make a great pair.
I'll leave it up to you, whatever you want to do.
Maybe we could start a new?
Just remember I'll always love you.

— *Michele Abbazia*

Love, Life and You

Life is fun
And what makes life fun is the people around
The friends who care and are cared for
Friends who love and are being loved
Life is worth living
And what makes life worth living is you, my friend
Your thoughtful, caring and loving way
Makes me ask for nothing more
And your presence makes my day complete
You're all I live for
And the one I love most
Love is all that matters in life, so...
...What is life without love
And what is love without you!

— *Regina Eco*

Time

I will open up my mind
If you would like to step inside and look around.
I do not know what you are searching for
But if you find it, do not forget to pay and ask for a receipt.
I have many things to sell but only few are bought;
Most are words not in use these days;
Friendship, loyalty, trust.
If you will kindly make your purchase now
Because I am tired and want to retire.
Just as I thought, you have bought the most popular items:
Enmity, betrayal, and deceit.
Time to restock although I do not want to,
It seems these days that is the only thing that sells.
So for now;
I am closed.

— *Sharon Redner*

Untitled

Clouds looming overhead,
Winds howling in the night.
Waters drown the happiness,
A mirror of my fright.

Lost within this world,
A world as vast as space.
The sky that once was bright,
Now darkness rules its place.

This is but an image,
It hasn't really begun.
I'll hold it in my heart,
For what we might have won.

Remember what I've said,
The words I wrote above.
It's the picture of one thing,
A life without your love.

     — *Denise M. Sumera*

Alone

A whisper in the darkness,
A bird up above.
There is no one here to talk to,
No one here to love.

There is no one here to love me,
Or keep me safe at night.
If I suddenly become afraid,
No one here to hold me tight.

I hate being all alone
But what else can I do,
The only thing I wish for,
Is that someone will love me too.

     —*Debbie Herkel*

The Divine Celebration

Here,
I do not celebrate
My lady on being fair.
Nor do I worship, a mother though she is divine.
I celebrate I.
My celebration is truly divine,
I celebrate I!
Here, I am the fair.
Have given birth to thyself.
Having parted with all,
I am now serving Christ, govern thyself.
I celebrate I!
My lover is I.
Companion I.
I celebrate I.

     —*Eric Childs*

A Lion's Image

My friend, your lion's image stands so near,
With blonde moustache and wild tossed mane,
That I quiver with excited fear
And long strong words
Softly said so sane.

My friend, this lamb's meekness clothes no more,
My sad deception and eyes untrue,
That I shiver like a naked whore
And long soft words
Strongly said by you.

     —*Irvin Edwards*

Because you are an Artist

Because you are an artist
In a world that is tenuous
At its best,
At a time when the next hour,
May not arrive,
Realize that your song will always live
In the souls
Of your audience's mind.

Your truth shines through your song
However denied,
However decried,
You will continue to sing
Because you are an artist.

There are those who will belittle
A voice misunderstood.
Your song will help them see
A world that could be free.

     —*D. R. Ferron*

The Snowflake

Each one falls gently as it
Leaves its home in the heavens.
It finds a new place to be a
Zealot of purity, peace, preciousness.
Around the world it is known.
But always together is it found.
Everyone with another will cling
To never be alone. The snowflake
Has a lesson to teach us.
However different you may appear,
Or however complex you think you are,
Really you don't have to go very far
To find one whose friendship is dear.
Open you eyes, reach out with meekness,
Noticing those who need your gentleness.

     —*Ben Radin*

Personal Finance

No matter how you count your coins,
Subtract your checks with great precision,
Keep track of credit card receipts
And tips and other cash expenses,
The total sum of moneys that
Remain is always less than what
You think it is and never ever more.

     — *Henry W. Gutsche*

Autumn is Here

Wintertime's coming.
Ready for that day?
Fortify, prepare!
But wait. There is still time to play.

Leaves color and fall
They will soon soar away.
That is the fall wind's mission.
But wait. There is still time to play.

Squirrels scramble for nuts;
The goose won't stay;
The kitty's coat thickens
Wait. Can we wait? Dare we play?

Autumn comes before us in a grand array.
Its color; its music, aroma too.
Wait until tomorrow to fortify, prepare.
Play today as fall fades to winter blue.

     —*Jacquetta M. Ross*

The Sandbag Look

Everytime I see sofas and love seats
With double tiered bolster backs,
I think of all the *Jills and Jacks*
After they've consumed too many *lite* snacks!
How will they ever rise to greet
Their guests, who come looking lean and neat:
I feel like writing the manufacturer
To slim down, its upholstered furniture
That *Sandbag* look has too much flab,
And the *Jills and Jacks* can no longer grab.
Perhaps the manufacturer will then install
A device, built-in, well-known to all
Called *touch and go*
With guaranteed *get-up*, they'll move like a *Pro*!

     — *Alice Mary Rachels*

As the Children Are Lost

Tortured flesh.
Tormented minds.
And they thought they had left their troubles behind.
Here innocence leads to freedom's demise,
and only the night wind pays heed to their cries.
It whips their sorrow through the city like leaves,
echoes their pain,
and drowns out their pleas.
Memories of home they now cherish as gold,
lie to themselves and feel their youth growing cold.
Deprivation inflicted by vultures and thugs
are open wounds licked often with alcohol and drugs.
Soon only their eyes mirror their mistake and its cost,
and love turns its back as the children are lost.

     — *Diane Lyon*

The Custodian

Dreams of a custodian with the same routine;
Of mealtimes and bedtimes, washing and cleaning.
Her life at best is mediocre it may seem,
To others who are busy following a dream.

There are stolen moments when she travels a road;
Another place in time where secret dreams take hold.
She becomes a bejeweled and pampered princess,
And adventure is great with glory and success.

She is no longer a slave to another's needs.
With abandon she follows where her passion leads.
She stays in this place for as long as she can,
Until its time to be a custodian again.

     —*Debra L. Martin*

Untitled

If she only knew how much he loved her
She would have never done what she did
Taking off like that, without even a word
Leaving him like that, a broken hearted man.

Why didn't he let his feelings be known
Why didn't he let his love shine through
What was he so afraid of, she was only human
What was he so terrified of, rejection?

Instead of living in the world
He dwell in a world of fantasy
Instead of making an effort to approach her
He withdrew, he looked at her from a distant eye.

He anticipated the future, he knew where
His destiny lay, he knew she could never be his
Not in this life time anyway,
When he was ninety and she only nineteen.

     —*Paula C. J. Thomas*

Untitled

Poe's fear of death lies within me,
An evil death, don't let it be.
A scared little girl hidden within,
Or an evil child with a life full of sin.
Yet on the surface, one sees a great lion,
Untamed and uncaring of one who is dying.
Whatever's inside, one will never know,
For what one sees is just for show.

— *Pam Wat*

No Iconoclast, I

Have you ever wondered what makes the sky so blue,
Why birds sing, or church bells ring, or I am in love with you?
Have you ever, on a summer's night, looked up at the sky,
At twinkling stars, the planet Mars, or just the moon on high?

Isn't it amazing, the way it came to be,
The universe, the planet Earth, the forest and each tree?
I cannot comprehend the magnitude, or realize the expanse.
Nor can I bring myself to accept that this occurred by chance.

Genesis states quite clearly +God created Heaven and Earth
My life I've placed into His hands since the day of my rebirth.
No apes are in my family tree, no lizards in my past.
I know that God created me, I am no iconoclast.
Each day I stop to thank the Lord, for doing what He's done.
For this wonderous world, my very life, and most of all His Son.

—*William E. Broadwell*

soul-snatcher

As we walk along the endless boundary between us and them,
    The soul-snatcher rushes up to grab at out feet trying to
        pull us closer,
        Sometimes even throwing rocks at us as if to say, "Do I
            have to get
                rough?"
        We are still walking and the soul-snatcher retreats
    slower now.
        Nevertheless, it rushes back angrier than before;
            It is determined to strip us of our identity and
                blend our tracks in with theirs.

        We are still walking, determined to beat the soul-
            snatcher but as we walk further it surrounds us.
                It has won this time, but not the next time we vow.
            We will win the next time we are walking along the
        endless boundary   that separates   us from
them.

—*Rivka Glaser*

The Dream: Prophecy of Warning—The Drought

Death, black and faceless sits, hidden, in white flowing robes.
His formless limbs are ominous, threatening, even in repose.
Slowly, he lifts amorphous arms over America's harvest table.
Although it is God holding rain from the farms, it is I who will disable.

On the board in front of Death sit many small but healthy seeds.
Suddenly they shrink in length and breadth then, converge at center for all needs.
At center, Polestar—malignant form, husky, blackened, crusty looking,
Absorbs the rest as if by storm: Unfair advantage! Milking! Rooking!
Polestar now looms potent, huge, a new and fearsome kluge.
Its death work done, it is Death's own icon.

All throughout this gruesome scene, God's thundering voice was saying,
Pray: only I can save you from the fiend. I am the ONE FOREVER REIGNING.
He would armor America's labors. He rains upon the unjust and just.
Even now He speaks, reminding us *In God We Trust.*

— *Penelope Trier Thomas*

Alien War

We go to them with war on our mind
A long journey and we may not return
Curiosity and fear over what we might find
Don't know what we will learn
About the monster and the creatures it bore
But we'll give it our all to win the alien war

— *Anne Wirick*

Fatal Evolution

The outside world is full of despair,
Crime, corruption and hate...true friends are rare;
Once beautiful skies with clouds floating in air
Are now ruled by pollution because no one will care.
Forests have evergreens, oaks and pines,
Now fires and axes leave little behind;
Love, romance, fidelity and matrimony
Is now anger and hatred...compassion is phony.
What happened to the world that once bloomed with growth?
Where people were kind to friend and foe both.
So, as you walk the troubled road of life,
You must look for solutions while avoiding the strife.
We must learn the balance between give and take,
Because our lives and our destiny may both be at stake.

—*Anthony DeMatio*

Nuclear Bomb

Inside my body there's a fear of dying
It's the nuclear bomb that leaves children crying
The push of a button could end it all
It'd kill everything whether big or small
This earth should be a carefree place
But how, with the threat of a bomb in our face,
When darkness falls across the land after I go to bed,
I pray to myself that when I wake up no-one will be dead,
I hope the world will hold out one more day
I hope the enemies will make peace in someway,
If adults are the ones who solve problems by war
Then they shouldn't run the world anymore,
Us children, we, want a future too
But our future really depends on you
It would be nice just to have one day
When you wouldn't have to worry about being blown away
Life was meant to be fulfilling
But that's impossible with the obsession of killing

—*Amanda Banning*

That Damned Second Coming

I gave my friend a book to read.
It was the *Talmud.*
His *church* said not to read it.
I gave my friend a book to read.
It was the *Wisdom of Buddha.*
His *church* said not to read it. I gave my friend
The *BhagavagitaGita.* His *church* said not to read it.
The Catcher in the Rye wicked words make wicked men
Mark Twain's *Letters from the Earth*—in Hannibal, his
Statue reads: *His religion was humanity, and the whole
World mourned for him when he died. Lust for Life, Dear
Theo, Christ and the Fine Arts, Taoism, Pilgrim's Progress*
The puritan's staple. Beware the *christian:* He only reads
His Bible. *If you can keep your head about you when all are
Losing theirs*
That damned second coming.

—*Cary Miller*

The Lost Soul

In the midst of your confusion, the voice of your sub-conscious
Cries out for a peaceful solution to rid itself of this state of desolution.
Will the mind ever cease this never-ending state of restless thought?
Where is the peaceful rest that in the past sleep alone has brought?
Living is forgiving, but oh, the struggle to continue believing.
Your heart is understanding, trusting and undemanding.
Tomorrow never comes and yesterday is so unrelenting.
Today lasts forever and the now is unbearable, forbidding.
You live to love, to share, to caress and be caressed.
You search but never find; your inner self remains unfulfilled.
You seek desperately peace of mind, your spirit survives as the soul slowly dies.
There's a deep sadness in your hollow eyes.
You must continue to search your inner being your true self cannot hide.
Never give in to this confusion; the answer lies somewhere deep inside.
Keep hoping, keep dreaming, keep fighting until spirit and soul are reunited.
And the elusive shadows you've been chasing you will have at last captured.

— *Ann McLemore*

Seasons

I can see the winter's fair snow
Breezing across the town like a nestly, white blanket.
Within the season of spring in a common, country aurora,
The golden sun floats magestically over a lush, green hillside.
When summer rolls around, the sticky summertime heat
Is gluing to everyone, no matter where you happen to wander.
The air turns hasty and crisp in autumn.
The hueful leaves dance in the air as they glide across the ground.
These are all my favorites, I simply cannot just have one.
So as I look out into the world which is always changing,
I continuously look forward to the next beautiful season.

— *Jakki Clarke*

Tears of the Soul

Shrouded deep within minds murky cloak,
Earth's rapacious covenant yields ivory eyes upon malignant deeds.
Forever cries the snowy dove as the bloodied Apollo falls,
And proud Pluto ascends to Eternity's throne on high.
Frozen as the bitter ice lay the dead hearts of reigning men.
Conscious rejected, fades like death's final blow.
Forever cries the snowy dove as the bloodied Apollo falls,
And proud Pluto ascends to Eternity's throne on high.
Sunny skies, painted waters coloring men's illusions.
Tattered falls the tortured wood. Lifeless born the poisoned bird.
Forever cries the snowy dove as the bloodied Apollo falls,
And proud Pluto ascends to Eternity's throne on high.
Tomorrow's morn comes not a tinseled gift, but a treasured prize.
Never fit for blackened minds, nor for powers corrupt,
That tear the tender earthly flesh.
Forever cries the snowy dove as the bloodied Apollo falls,
And proud Pluto ascends to Eternity's throne on high.

— *Pamela Cranmer*

Precious and Unique

Like a rainbow spilling to the ground, feelings for you wash over me
Draining me of all my energy, leaving me limp and listless,
Yet with a sense of fulfillment; filled to the extremities with love
And joy and passion that only comes with thoughts of you, that only
Comes with your sight, that only comes with your nearness, which in turn
Leaves me overwhelmed with emotions too complex to explain to cherish
And hold on to forever as long as we both have a heart and a soul,
A soul to share with you, the most precious gift ever to me given.

A snowflake, you alone are my snowflake with your own uniqueness that
Holds you oh so ever close to my heart. Before, you were one with the clouds,
Preparing yourself for the time when you were to leave. Now you are falling
Down to the ground and into my heart on earth where we will dance forever
Without end, for you truly are my rainbow and my snowflake, precious and
Unique forever in my heart.

— *Jamie Barren*

The Rose

Glistening and pink, soft petals folding,
Under the snow's weight you still were holding
Your place in the garden, the only rose there,
Oblivious to snow flakes filling the air.
More beautiful now than ever you were,
With elements beating you trying to spur
You to hasten your short stay on earth,
All day you stood firmly proclaiming your worth.
In stoical silence your message you brought
To one who was wearied by action and thought.
How could you have known, sweet rose in the snow,
That she would pass by who needed you so?

— *Doris VanBuren*

Since You've Gone

I woke today with thoughts of you,
I didn't know what to do
My heart was dying with the loss of you,
I, myself was dying too.
I had dreams I thought could be fulfilled,
But when you left me they were killed.
I had hopes of things to be,
But when you left these hopes left me.
Since you've gone away,
I have been dying to say;
I would give my heart to you,
And I would give my whole life too.

— *Henrietta Orsol*

The Willow, the Wind and Me

With the wind I go, she's just like me,
Flowing to and fro like a willow tree.
She sings in a whisper sweet melodies
Although I'm not sure what she really means.

And in the heavy winter deep within the snow,
I can still hear the whisper of the lonely willow.
In the spring when the snow is gone
You can hear her sing but no one sings along.

As summer comes she's brighter still.
As she sways in the wind on the lonely hill.
Then in the fall as with all the trees
She stands proud and tall when she's lost her leaves.

She's bare but cheerful, eager to be heard,
Her hands out wishful for the long gone bird.
In the early mornings when the air is still.
She doesn't sing from the lonely hill.

So who am I and where will I go?
Will the loneliness die like the lonely willow?

— *Jennifer Lee Fontaine*

Ode to a Day

Imagine a day when ancient ones from ages past
Told the stories of all their conquests.
How in raging battle and victory they reigned supreme,
Only superseded by greater dreams.
One foretold the coming of a thousand years,
A day of righteousness, love and cheer.
Fulfillment of a promise to mankind,
A uniting in all of heart and mind.
That nations on the earth would dwell
In truth and freedom's light,
Securing the future with peace and not strife.
Hail to the days of wisdom, understanding and salvation,
Golden ages, when man brings forth new life,
Renewed by illumination.

— *Beverly Reedy*

Through the Days

So the nights are endless in your eyes
The rose of our love a million times over never dies.
And though I run slow and alone through the maze
You will never change to me through the days.

I will never be able to change my thought.
That it was only you that I sought.
My love, I still care in many ways.
And forever and always I will love you
Through the days.

—*Ashlee Alexander*

Sweet Child

Be cautious sweet child, beware in the city
Watch for those who approach to sample your beauty
It's like the candy bar you buy at the mart
It's purchased, it's eaten, but the wrapper; discard
Watch with a dubious mind and heart
For those who pursue with a sick sigh
They are hungry to test your purity of mind
Examining your goodness...so refreshing...so smart
For you shine like the light in a world so dark
They will take you for a ride so bumpy and curved
Destination: unknown, down a dead end road
Leaving you stranded, raped and pillaged
Wondering just where to go
Feeling nothing; not even the air
A soul that is cloudy with sorrow and despair.

—*Jane Van Doren*

Inside, Looking Out

I met a man one morning,
While strolling through the sky
I asked him where he's going,
And he asked me why.
I hung my head for shame of it,
He knew I didn't care.
I flew about to speed away
When he said, *don't despair.*
I am lonely just as you,
In the multitude.
That love we all are searching for
Finds ease in it's allude. But never fear the darkness son,
And never trust the light. For pain will always linger there,
Always out of sight.
I cried a bit to ease the crush of uninspiring gloom.
For then I knew I could go on, but never leave that room.

—*Duane Alan Kuehn*

Surfer

You are one with the wind in your face,
The one who wishes to be alone.
To feel the ocean breeze inside, and yearns to be home.
For your home is the waves of the
Roaring, crashing, sea.
To tame it is your goal.
You and your board go out together.
To try it just once more
You fall but get up again
For it has hurt your pride
But you can never tame it
It does not matter how you try
For sea lives alone, and wishes not to be tame.
To set new goals for your and your board
Is its eternal game.
But you dear surfer, go ahead and try
And then one day you will realize
It no longer hurts your pride.

—*Jean Kim*

Friendship Lost

A friend I knew
Along life's way
And I crossed paths
Again today.
I saw, I heard
How lives have changed.
A friendship, lost,
I've now, regained.
The good, the bad,
The in between.
I'll not forget
What friendship means.

— *Nadine Rose*

A Gift of Money

Alas!
Some may think
A gift of money
Crass.
But the folding green
Has a touch of
Class.
To wit:
It has a color
Fresh and green,
Has a texture
Crisp and crackly,
And is exchangeable
Exackly!

—*Jane Oster*

Destiny

How can I express
What I feel in my heart
Now that our world
Has drifted apart
Pain
Is a part of what I feel
Trying to cope
So my heart can truly heal
Love
Is what I feel inside
A feeling I know
My heart will never hide
And you my dear will always be
A part of my world
And future Destiny.

— *Patricia McCurn*

Counterpart

Alter ego—counterpart
How is it we have *one* heart

Why is it I sense one-half
Sagging, wandering, reaching
 searching

Why did not the other part
Feel the separation pain

Did it splice and mend anew?
Did it splice again—and seek—
New dimensions, loftier ties
Does it ever fret—

—Aye yet
My waiting heart beats—acutely tuned

For your return
Alter ego—counterpart

— *Edith Buckley*

When a Child Cries

What do we do
When a child cries
We cannot turn them away
We cannot fill them with lies

The only way to wipe away
The tears of hurt and anger
And put a smile back on their face
Is talk and not be strangers

When you see a child
Cyring from the pain
Do you ever feel guilty
As if you were to blame

What do we do
When a child cries
We cannot turn them away
And we cannot fill them with lies
So what do we do when a child cries?

—*Eric J. Farmer*

Whisper

I don't know why my place by you,
Is haunted by the things I do.
When I need love and you say no,
I need love bad, you hurt me so.
I have no place else to be,
Yet, you can't make sweet love to me.
You keep me always by your side,
Commited faith I keep inside.
Through the day you let me see,
How much you truly wanted me.
As the doors are closed at night,
Something doesn't feel just right.
Why can't love be shared by us?
Making love is such a must!
I've waited hours through the night,
Without you, love isn't right.
Whisper nothings in my ear,
Tell me words I long to hear.
Until that day when you are mine,
My mind is held in endless time.

—*Pamela J. Hudson*

Flow of Poetry

A poem is emotion growing—flowing from
The inside to the outside
With the beat of the heart
With the flower of the soul.
Poetry swells to touch a thousand emotions
To make an instance breathe
To make the ordinary—fantasy.

— *P. J. Gluck*

Sitting in Front of the Fireplace

The heat cascading onto my flesh.
The oak growing to a deep, dark crimson.
Flames are jumping to and fro
And smoke is dancing with the clouds.
Shadows descended into the dark room.
Furniture moving with the flames
To and fro
To the beat of the crackling wood.
Tempo and melody awakens the silence
As the thunder and lightning enter.
Wind whistling through chinks in the brick
And I watch the flames die low.

— *Di Ann Fay*

Spring

The sky is blue.
The clouds are white.
The stars are shining through the night.
A twinkle here.
A twinkle there.
How electrifying is the sight.
The trees are swaying at the rythmn of the breeze.
The moon grows full as night grows deep.
The air takes in the smell of spring.
Oh, how beautiful is the night.

    —*Alexia Basios*

Time

Sands of time defeat me not
Though wrinkles on my brow is wrought
Integrity has been pursued
Enhancing my performance hue.

Have strived to capture all things good
And shun evil like I should
This thought has been my motto strong
To avoid all things wrong.

Adversity and pain etch wrinkles
But will smile in spite of all
God in his own special wisdom
Guides me if I heed his call.

Years have passed, it will not be long
My earth probation will be gone
Until that time, may patience stay
A rainbow so the aches will stray.

    —*Erma Roper*

God Made You Special

God made you special to shine and glow,
That others who meet you just might know
That God the Creator is still on his throne
Loving and caring for each of his own.
Some people may doubt as they look upon you
That God is just or kind or true.
They look at you with eyes alone
Not seeing the truth that God has shown.
What lie beneath the outer shell?
A joyful spirit, alive and well,
A heart that's faithful and on Him depends.
His strength and joy He ever sends.
Most people take for granted, life
Especially when there's little strife.
So God made special people just like you
To change the others' point of view!

    — *Carole M. Wright*

Never Seen Such a Day in Spring

Never seen such a day in spring
I muse over the greeness of green
The warm rays never felt so sweet
The rhythm in my heart throbs a new beat

I breathe new freshness from the air
Fragrance gives new birth everywhere
Old dreams don't seem so faded today
As the sky holds a pageant of clouds on dispaly

I want to reflect these sensations inside
I want to touch emotions with mine
I'll dress all my windows in white flowing lace
And beckon the breeze to dance through my days

Come in, come in, oh genesis of spring
I welcome the unknown love that you bring

    — *Victoria Shayne*

Summer

Summer is when the air is hot
And nights are bright, filled with stars,
And when people swim to get refreshed
From the hotness of the air.
The nights are filled with joy
And comfort to each one's soul.
The summers are filled with joy
To each boy and girl.
Summer is time for freedom
To each boy and girl.
Summer is for unwinding mean thoughts
In each one's mind.
Summer is for relaxing our minds
And doing fun things all the time.

    — *Hope Jacobs*

A Visit to the Sea

Today I went to the sea
To collect her shells
To collect my thoughts carefully.
She took me under her spell.

Many dollars there did I find...
Sand dollars she gave to me with pleasure
I went home rich with peace of mind
And a handful of her precious treasure.

    —*Beverly Trask*

Today

Out of Eternity's vast abode
Out of the travail of night
Encamped upon the breast of time.
A golden caravan of light.

The majesty of an unconquered sun,
Across the canopy of space,
To scorch the drifting desert sand.
And bless the Artic's frozen face.

Until crimsoned banners tinged with gold
Soon pales into pedestals of white.
Then with the company of the past.
It moves ahead into the night.

    —*Eleanor Ponton*

Spring Time

I hear birds singing,
Fireflies flickering,
Crickets shirping,
Robins singing in the trees,
Bringing in the joy of spring time.
I see flowers blooming,
Green grass awakening from a winter's nap,
Leaves bearing arms of green,
Streams flowing through the meadows,
Bringing in the joy of spring time.
I see little children playing in the park,
Hearing merry voices,
There's joy in the mountains,
There's life in the air,
Bringing in the joy of spring time.

    — *Walter Mae King*

What a Beautiful World

When trees wear their prettiest green
Daffodils yellow in borders,
Lawns become a picture scene.
Spring's in order,
I whisper, *What a beautiful world.*

When dreams wake March showers
Woodland violets lavender blue,
When squares color April flowers
Fragrant jasmine mingle through,
I whisper, *What a beautiful world.*

When songbirds sing their sweetest song
In breezy springtime weather,
When chapel bells ring along,
Happy hearts sing together,
I whisper, *What a beautiful world,*
O-O-O-O what a beautiful world.

    — *Virgie McCoy Sammons*

A Poem

Come down from your pedestal;
Come down from the sky.
You are not the only one,
We can live that high
The clouds are your companions,
No one lives that way.
I am not your only friend,
But I am here to stay.

    — *Bonita Buffkin*

A Message

Every face tells a story,
In his time,
Everybody tells a story,
In his time.
Every story has a message,
A message to share,
Everybody's story has a message,
A message of care.
Each message makes you wonder,
Do they really care,
Each memory makes you wonder
Did they really share,
Each story is a light across the world,
It's a shadow in the light,
Everybody's story is a light across the world
It's a light in the night!

    —*Pam Morse*

Everybody is an Actor

Everbody is an actor born into this stage of life.
Some are real, some are plastic, some are born and we don't know why
But, all are born with hearts of love.

Plastic people mean you know harm, it's just they've been taught wrong.
Everyone is an actor participating in this stage of life.

Presidents try to rule the world, judges want to take your life
Forture tellers leave your head to swirl
Tell me, what's your part in life?

Little children, at first you have no fear
Of playing your role in life.
Full of joy and laughter till someone makes you cry.

Everybody is an actor, acting in the stage of life.
Some are failures, some are winners, some never try.
Go on, I tell you, act your part in life
But please, try to be real
Don't let the hate steal your love
In this hectic stage of life.

—*Barbara Barber*

Loneliness

The feeling of loneliness is so hard to explain.
The feelings inside leave me in such pain.
Knowing no one seems to be there
Leaves me thinking, *Does someone care?*
The feeling of loneliness in my heart brings tears to my eyes
And all I ask is for someone to listen to my cries.
But now I know the feeling of loneliness will never fade away,
So try to understand, loneliness is hard to explain
And all it leaves inside is unexplainable pain.

— *Helen Vraniskoski*

On Loan

How can I love you when forever teardrops fall
coursing down my cheeks until my heart with sorrow is rent?
Is it love or loneliness that beats heavy in my chest
when I think of you and the time that, together, we never spent?
Why does grief bear down and yearning tear at my soul
each time a song of yesteryear cries out about what our love had meant?
How can I help but love and remember the joy of dreams
and promises that were made when youth held time in check until
    ...age was sent?
Will ever age release its grip as vice-like hands on us
preventing words we wish to speak from reaching past our lips? It can't!
And so we live in separate worlds never knowing realization
of those dreams, hopes and aspirations...for love was only to us lent.

— *Jeanne Dykstra-Brooks*

My Awakening

I know religion plays a part in everybody's life,
For the inner strength that people need helps lessen all the strife.
Whether Catholic, Jewish or Gentile, each believes his own
And who's to say which one is right, for no one is alone.
I've never been a fanatic or a Sunday only prayer,
But I do believe there is a power whose strength has been my stayer.
I believe, I trust, I love, I care and I try to live each day
So God can always look down and say, *I created her that way.*
He's tested me in many ways to see if I could weather
The many trials and barriers that life seems always to gather.
My most current test was the toughest, and it left me very sad,
But I gathered strength from the God I love
And He removed the doubts I had.
My body might not be perfect, but this is such a small part,
For what I have is love and faith deep within my heart.
I feel I've been saved for a purpose and I always intend to be
The kind of person God had in mind when he took all cancer from me.

— *Audre J. Mixon*

Forever Inspired

I'm sitting on a mountain—what a breath-taking view,
In deep conversation with somebody new.
His words are so wise, His comfort so dear.
His arm around my shoulders, *Let go of your fears.*
Your life here on earth has meaning, you see.
Be at peace with yourself, put your trust in Me.
A calm quiet feeling comes stealing in,
A wonderful man—this new found friend.
He hands me a book—his treasure, the key.
The story of His life, entrusted to me.
We look out in silence—at the breath-taking view, my heart light and free,
This new found friend—my Lord and me.

— *Nancy Phillips*

The Sounds of Yesterday

I heard the sounds of yesterday come knocking at my door
I saw the face of agony as it never was before
I grasp for greed and untold lust, and crawled in mortal sin
I weeped and moaned for what was not and for what might have been.

I cursed and cried for happiness and blamed my plight to fate
And, lo, I did not wonder why my sins did not abate.
Then slowly, slowly up I climbed away from endless strife.
I searched and looked for answers to my unrequited love for life

Higher, higher up I climbed I reached among the stars
And on the way I plucked my soul of its unwanted scars.
Amongst the floating clouds I found my search was not in vain
For there reflected in my eyes was my loneliness and pain.

I cried at last for now I've seen my savior in disguise
Waiting there for me to come among the brilliant skies.
He welcomed me into his home and led me through his door
And there his angels gave me faith and hope forevermore.

—*Peggye F. Forster*

World's End

The world's coming to an end.
When the day came to a shutting point, my heart hurt so bad;
You didn't know just how much I loved you.
The world's going to end tonight. When you kissed her, I went crazy.
I love you so much and it hurts so bad.
When I saw that, I lost my head. The world's gonna be dead.
I lost my head upon this dream,
For I knew it was a dream and I knew you had no love to give me.
But my world will end tonight;
Over and over I see it in my head, you kissing her with that look on your face.
You never cared about me and you never intended to.
But one thing I want you to know,
I could have given you a lot more than anything she had to offer.
Since this is the night my world will end, you need not worry
Although you never cared anyway.
I'm sorry it bothered you that I had so much love for you
And I'm still willing to fight for you, no matter how much it takes.
Once I fall asleep, I never want to wake up again.

—*Denise Lynn Selvaggio*

Friendship Long Parted

A bird took its flight as day turned to night.
A day without happiness is like a cloud without fluffiness.
We had love to share, but now we are bare of the love we once shared.
For now we are not together here, so no longer do we cheer
To some this poem may lack sense, for I have love that is emmense.
My heart is not bare, but there is sadness in the air
For a friendship long undone, to me lacks fun.
So a part of me goes where they go.
Forever and ever cry I will never,
For my friends look up to me,
So a crying girl I will never be,

—*Donna Lynn English*

A

IT came to us from the passions
    of Adonis-on-Adonis   contaminated blood
        the re-used "thorns" of Junkies
           . . . and who knows what else.
When it was still MYSTERY;
    The World thought it "served-them-right"
          to pass-on from life;
      but NOW . . .
         even some of The Innocent   are FALLING.
Medicine Men   Trying   Failing
            and Trying again;
    but the Four Letters of Death that incubate . . .
          keeps   hatching on.
Not caring about   Age   or Boundary;
        plaguing its way,
           from one Land   to another.
Who ever thought that A.I.D.S.
        might be   The ARMAGEDDON.

   —Sir Raggety Flagg (Lynell A. Brown)

From the Darkness

Seeming nothingness hides deep within its walls
The essence of the man, the center of creation.
The black and the dark, two shades drawn side by side
Light, a shadow of pink barely visible, the edge of the inner mind.

The sun colors the dying sky
And I feel the universe inside me
Calling from the depths the
Union of all that has been or is to be.

We thrive on that which is no color
For blankness breeds the power of the soul.
Take away my hands, my feet
The heart erupts through words you cannot quell.

Strike me not, oh mighty god of chaos
Lest my pain deafen me to my own heart.
My song will never rest but take its sound from me
And I am lost in your being, a captive of hell.

I watch the golden sun blacken the world
Awaiting the shadows that call forth my light.

   —Patricia J. Ruocchio

Will Time Be the Mirror

Comprehension of the mysterious Cosmos stifles our mortal minds.
In the vastness of etheral space, Earth, one world among many,
is but a moment in eternity.
What interstellar cultures exist beyond earth, beyond our galaxy;
on other planets, stars, suns? Who knows now?

The heavens we see, is not the home of *holies*,
but the portal to greater celestial creations.
As everything is relative in the infinite, Cosmic universe,
there must be more intelligent, God-images,
than the Earth's insignificant civilization.

How long will we be aliens to far distant, galactic empires?
Will we escape the quarantine of our planetary bonds?
Do we migrate; do *others* immigrate?
Will ancient mythology become scientific reality?

Are we primitive or ancient? Was Earth the cradle of mankind?
Or is space exploration man's attempt to return to his origin?

As we sleep eternally, will the immortality of time
mirror the epochal conquest of terrestrial space?

   —Paul F. Schmidt

Our Never Ending Love, Is Ending

On this stormy night, as the rain falls,
Thunder echoes through these empty halls.
Surrounded by darkness of the stormy night's shadow,
Quietly I watch the rain fall upon my bedroom window,
And as I lay here beside you to rest,
My heart beating wildly within my chest.
For I know time cannot change the unavoidable,
As I place my wedding band on the bedside table.
Laying here beside you ever so quietly,
I find myself lost in the memory,
When we once promised our love forever to keep.
Now instead of making love, we just fall asleep.
Though my night seems gloomy and somewhat meek,
As the tears fall down upon my cheek.
Tonight I will watch the night slowly pass me by,
For tomorrow we will say our final goodbye.
For there is no reason why we should continue pretending,
When we both know our love is ending.

   —Denise M. LaJoie

Untitled

There is an emptiness within me
Where a little girl once lived
Or is she trapped inside a prison made of fear?
Waiting for her daddy to unlock the iron bars
I have a feeling she'll be waiting many years.
I watch her from a distance
Through the shadow of my soul
And listen to the echo of her cry
And sometimes she'll go running to the corner of
Her cell to find that all of daddy's promises were lies.
Time has made it harder now to hope for much at all
And the woman she's becoming feels unsure
For what has she to offer having spent her life in fear that daddy
Wouldn't come and rescue her. So she hides inside a fantasy of stories
Left untold because the ending was a truth too hard to bear, that daddy
Doesn't have the key to free her pain, Mommy wasn't every really there.

   —Deborah Sorensen

The Middle Child

The little girl screams out silently, *Please, be glad I'm here!*
But the parents and siblings do not heed the cry.
To them, she's that rather tarnished daughter sister they've known
For forty-eight years and never quite accepted.
They smile occasionally when her eye catches theirs, but it's a rather
Disapproving bending of lips to her; not a *nice to see you* smile,
(That she would become perfect for, if just once they would give it to her.)
Instead it's a *what did you do now?* kind of wry amusement that instills
Instant guilt in her.
They'll take her help and impose their will upon her, but they will never
Accept her as they think she is.
She covers her feelings with a facade of angry looks, loud talk and
Aggressive behavior—or complete indifference.
The little girl still cries.

   — Denice Donnell

Someone Hard to Find

We all need someone who we can tell our dearest secrets to,
Someone that doesn't criticize, but rather accepts you for being you.
Everybody needs someone that will come to his rescue, any time day or night
And no matter what the situation, they won't leave until you're alright.
We all need someone that we can depend on during our times of need,
Someone who doesn't consider helping to be a favor, but rather a deed.
We all need someone that will stand with us through thick and thin.
There're very few of these people left, but we all need at least one true friend.

   —Jeffery Jessie

Death for the Soul

As we sit, hand in hand,
Revealing our dreams,
Concealing the magic,
That most often seems,
To upset the picture,
Held clear in its frame,
Increasing the odds,
Of the mind wielding games,
That keep us in touch,
With the forces of life,
The heart is thought safe,
Yet cut by the knife,
Of the concious that killed,
As the mind lost control,
The feelings of guilt,
Spelled death for the soul.

—*Brian Hughes*

Retribution

I wanted so to tell her
That I loved the threads of gray
That time had sifted though her hair,
But I could only say,

The weather has been nice up here;
The kids are all in school.
I washed today. These inane words
Were mouthings of a fool.

Why didn't I say, *I love you, Mom,*
And all the things you did
For me I've cherished
Since I was just a kid?

I couldn't quite express myself
To say I felt that way:
But maybe now she'll understand;
They buried her today.

—*Bernice Walter*

A Christmas Prayer for Daddy

Christmas is near and you're gone away.
Your little girl asks as she silently prays...

Please, oh Lord, I know it's hard,
But Daddy's gone away so far.
I pray for him every night
And wish with all my might.
I wish upon the brightest star
And ask the Lord where you are.
If you can hear me this very night,
Just let my Daddy hold me tight.

— *Patricia L. Button*

My Brother Joe

How I miss my brother Joe.
But God has plans for this whole wide world,
So God came one day and said,
Come, Joe, it is time for you to go.
Oh, how I miss my brother Joe.
But God saw fit to take him home.
He had plans for Joe, so he said,
Come, Joe, I am taking you to a place
Where you will never roam.
God had plans for my brother Joe.
He has plans for you and me.
He will soon come back
To lead me to the other shore.
Where I will be with my brother forevermore.

— *Bonnie Williams*

Goodbye

As I look upon your face
And know for me the searing time
Shall fill each day until we reclasp hands,
It is impossible to speak.
But this word which is at once
Drummer in my brain
And executioner to my heart,
Must be said.
Oh life, how did the bright little ribbon
On which I began my journey
Fade to this awful hue?
How shall I keep from stumbling?
Now it has divided and lays separated before us,
It's frayed edges bearing silent testimony
To the pain of parting.
Goodbye

—*Hannah I. R. Greayer*

Don't Abuse the Children

When you think of all the loves
You've lost and what the future
Might bring, you blink your eyes
In silence and pray that you
Weren't seen.
Sometimes you feel so lonesome,
So lost and so abused, but don't
Take it out on the children or they'll
Feel abused too.
When your feeling abusive just simply count to ten,
And think all the love you wanted when you were
Young back then.
Their love and admiration
Is a very precious gift
So don't abuse the children
And you'll get enough to live.

—*Jennifer Cox*

I Forgot

I was going to tell you I cared
And reminisce about all things shared
I was going to tell you it mattered
When our dreams were torn and shattered
But, I forgot...

I was going to tell you how nice
That our love was strong enough to suffice
I meant to tell you I was glad
You stayed through the good and the bad
But, I forgot...

You did the little things that meant so much,
You enriched my life with your special touch,
I intended to brag about your thoughtful deeds.
That far surpassed my frugal needs,
But, I forgot...

Now, it is too late, you are no longer here,
And so many things are now so clear,
Good intentions have paved many a road to hell
Oh, God, why, now does my memory serve me so well?
Why did I forget?

—*Peggy Vaughn*

Untitled

The moon that shone that night was the only moon.
The world spoken then were the only words I needed.
The moon left, the words ceased, but the memory stayed.
Oh, how I miss you.

— *Jennifer Anne Johnson*

Mourn no More

Mourn no more my darling, for
I am here to wipe away your tears.
I know it hurts when you
Loose someone very dear.
Time will soon heal the wounds
And the hurt will disappear.
It was fate that opened the gate;
For time was flirting with the dirt.
So dry your weeping eyes and
Let time wipe away the hurt.
Let us celebrate!

—*Anne Burwell Harris*

How Come

How come life can be so hard
How come sometimes I get so bored
How come nobody gives a damn

How come each person stands alone
How come it seems at times what really isn't
How come we hate and love so hard

How come I would like to die but don't
How come the world is so unjust
How come I eat so much prejudice

How come I have to grow up
How come nobody cares
How come nobody knows

How come people think they know so much
How come so many people don't like to share
Why are we so wrapped up

Why do we carry on
Why is my dad already dead
Why would anyone want war

—*Donella Lee Shoultz Davis*

Alone in the Company of Friends

Alone and crying
Feeling inside like dying
No one to care about
No one to love
Nothing bright but the sky above
Days into nights
Nights into days
No hope in sight
My mind is a haze
No love and no feeling
No friends and no foes
So close and yet so far apart
That no one knows how really alone I am.

—*Jaime R. White*

The Little Sheep that Went Astray

The little sheep wondered from the fold;
Far away he strayed out in the cold.
Then he heard a voice, tender and kind,
Come, little one, I'll not leave you behind.
Tangled in briars, he was hard to find.
Lifting him up, the briars he did unwind.
His aching, bleeding wounds he did bind.
A warm place in the fold he was assigned.
Our Master is saying to us, Come home,
The fold is here when you cease to roam.
Like the little sheep that strayed away,
I'll bind up your bleeding wounds today.

— *Dova B. Conner*

Questions

To love;
or not to love?
To be loved;
Or not to be loved?
To give;
Or to take?
Is it real;
Or is it fake?
Who has the questions;
Who has the answers?
Am I sane;
Or am I crazy?
Shall I stay;
Or should I go?
Is the devil guiding me;
Or am I in God's hand?

— *Janie Meservy*

Thinking of You

I was thinking of you
The other day,
And a single lonely tear
Fell to my cheek.
I do not know if it was because
I am weak from crying,
Or if it was because I have not
Any more tears to cry.
I do know, however, that
I love you,
And more than anything else
I want your love in return.
All that seems rather hopeless
At this time,
And so, I guess, I will just
Have to keep crying.
Crying forever and crying
Unseen tears.

—*Denise Lyle*

Untitled

The distance in his eyes...
Portrays the hurt,
Inside his heart.
The anger within his mind...
Is tearing,
His soul apart.
The shadows of his past...
Are standing,
In his way.
The guilt from deep within...
Is a heavier
Weight each day.
The love he has to offer...
Is there,
For someone to share.
But the memories in his mind...
Make him wonder,
If someone will really care.

—*Debra L. Daly*

Truth

If what you say is true,
Then why don't I believe you?
It just doesn't seem right,
To be so blind in sight.
That I could be numb,
To the things I thought dumb.
Unless, I didn't want to except,
The truth.

—*Norma L. Price*

Please Don't Tease

Why do you do that William? You are such a tease.
William, you never stop, quit the teasing please.
You tease so much, you make me cry.
Why don't you stop? Atleast try.

I am asking this because you pester me so.
Mother warned me, but I love you, don't you know.
What was that? Why you love me!
Answer me did you say that atleast give me a maybe.

You did not mean it, I know you did not.
You lied to your best girl about tieing the knot.
Another joke! You only love money.
Well let me tell you. I have got more than that to give, honey.

No, don't leave me. I love you anyway.
...Fine, leave then, I can get a man anyday!

—*Donna Marie Gosizk*

Sunset Secret

The sun sets like the moon shines and the lake shows a secret reflection.
The sun is looking toward you in a secret.
You move slowly into the heart of the sun as you drift away.
A slight breeze blows over you and changes the hard to the soft, like a
    transformation.
Your mind is as soft as a feather.
As you dream in your mind, your secrets drift away.
Peace and quiet surrounds you.
No rumble does what it does, nor the smell of polluted air.
Fresh smells and scents rapture you in a dream.
All the tiredness disappears like magic.
Your heart is filled with soft thoughts and you think of a sweet smell.
You look at the sun as you see a dove fly by.
You close your eyes and hear a nightingale sing, and so you look out and
    see the stars shine.

— *Jennifer Cembrano*

Dear Friend,

I thank you for lending a helping hand.
Even if problems are small you still understand. All the precious
Times we spend together through the laughs and pain. Are relived over
And over again. You stood by my side through the thick-and-the-thin.
And I'm grateful to know you'll still be there in the end. So thanks
For your time and your care. And in return it will be my friendship
Which I shall share. When I'm feeling down I look up to you. Your
Strength and dedication to me remains true. The power of our friendship
To go on is our trust and that kind of friendship is a must. For when
All seems lost and I'm beginning to fall. With you there to catch me,
It's not lost after all. Never weaking, always standing strong beyond
Possible limits. Never a fading light, always staying bright showing
Me the way. That is the symbol of our friendship, which breaks impossible
Barriers day by day. And when the worse gets you down, I'm someone you
Can count on. As time goes on, and years have past, there's one thing
That remains, our friendship, which will last and last.

—*Jennifer Lee Wallick*

The Beginning of the End

Thrown into outer darkness, beyond the rim of time
Are the souls of men of pleasure, with certainly no peace of mind.
Legions and legions of spirits, each one distinctly defined
Ever and ever probogating, pressure on both body and mind.
With battle to battle it's heightened, the stinch of smoke one can smell
Surely it seems there is no ending, to all the rages of hell.
For all the roots of bitterness, I must give a round of applause
Deceitfully doing a marvelous job, leaving all not knowing the cause.
It is deeper and deeper we travel, when on the broadway we abide
Seemly never, seeing ever, shadows that follow every stride.
With voices it seems we cannot utter, and with eyes we certainly are blind
Groping thru the halls of darkness, for anything we can find.
Listen to this illustration, and take it to heart my friend
You have heard the story of my life, and the beginning of the end.

—*Perry Evans*

Beauty Not Seen

White misty streams
Falling in a pitter patter rhythm
Belong in a shadow
Of majestic green forest.
The soft dull murmur
Of a waterfall
Pitted against green shadows
Is so ever present.
To truly see the beauty
Of creeping green shrubery
One needs not to open
Ones eyes, but ones heart.

—*Jenny Smith*

I Thought I Loved You

I thought I cared
But I realized
You were never there
I was always
Just a friend to you
It was
Never true
But when I say
I love you
I will always
Be true
You only lead me
Like you always do
Just say
I will never love you

—*Jennifer Selby*

Everything to Me

You mean everything to me
I love you very much
You're sweet and very caring
You have the perfect touch
For if I'd ever lost you,
I don't know what I'd do
Because you're always there for me
When I'm feeling blue.
You hold a special place
Deep inside of me.
You protect me from the world
Like I never dreamed it could be.
I like it when you hold me
I feel so warm and safe
I know those very moments
Nothing could take your place
So as long as I have you now
To be here with me today,
I can hope and dream tomorrow
That you will always stay.

—*Jenni Margosian*

The Special Pebble

In each life's beach there is a pebble,
Among the countless grains of sand;
Of all of us just few are able
To ever hold ours in our hand.

And yet of those that theirs do find,
Just few will recognize the shine;
The rest will pay to theirs no mind,
Throw it away, attach no line.

—*Gonzalo Leon*

Hope Where There Was None

Dead like a nuclear winter;
Life stricken, famished humans roaming
Through endless nothingness with nothing
Left to hope for.
But in the weary distance through
The murky grey snow lay a sight of hope,
A tiny bud of life like from Saint Nick
Himself a gift to all.

—Heather W. A. Boynton

My Life

So many times I cry,
And all those times I want to die.
I want to be strong through this life,
To just play along through struggles and strife.
All I can do is wipe my eyes
And sit around as my spirit dies.
I put up a wall to shut out the pain,
But there's always a door through which it came.
Behind this door with my feelings inside,
Only I know the secrets I hide.
Only I have the key to the door in my mind
Because, my friend, I've been hurt too many times.

— Debbie Russie

Heaven's Tears

These tears of wine I cry
Between sanity I walk a fine line
Soul mates in heaven we were chosen.
Unknown forever, forever unknown.
I follow my destiny, does it include you?
Roses are red, love will come through.
We run hand in hand tonight and forever.
To catch a falling star our souls walk together.
I drink wine, I search for the star
I'll miss you forever my love, wherever you are.

— Donna Plunkett

Shattered Dreams

You gave me hope, so long ago
The kind of love I never thought I'd know.
You made me happy when I was depressed;
You were my life. I was obsessed.
You gave me life when I wanted to die,
And you made me laugh when I wanted to cry.
You gave me a dream, to keep in my heart,
That we would get married and never be apart.
You gave me a reason to see my life through,
With loving and laughing and always with you.
And then the hope you gave me suddenly was gone.
Your memory is all I have to help me carry on.
And now I am alone, and no longer complete,
With a million shattered dreams lying at my feet.

— Jan Stafford

Where Are You?

Were you ever so lonely you thought you'd die?
Did you fear for your life at the slightest cry?
Were you ever so lonely your heart felt broken?
You knew you'd feel better if a few words were spoken.
Were you ever so lonely you wanted to give up?
Well, keep your dreams; just hold your head up.

— Dolores Kaine

Untitled

The dimple on my face,
It looks like a teardrop.
Water erodes ridges
Forever into stone.
Tears have eroded a scar
Upon my face.
The dimple helps to hide
The pain,
The shame,
Behind a smile.
A mask to help hide
To cover
The erosion
Of my emotions
Evolving into
The morbid truth of my pain.

— Cara L. V. Flynn

You

In the corner I sat and wept
For what seemed an eternity.
Whispering softly, prayers
Of your return and so it
Seems as the years drag
Slowly forward you
Are not to return to
My loving arms, adoring heart
You, with your gentle eyes
I call your name over
And over, until everything
Is a blur. Silently, my
footsteps lead me back to
That corner and once again
I sit and weep.

—Vicky Wolfe

Wondering

When you pass a graveyard,
Do you think of the dead?
Do visions of their past lives
Wander through your head?
Do you ever wonder why it is
That you were once nothing,
And now you live,
Just to be nothing again?
One way or another,
How can you win?

—Jamie Hodges

Whispers

The ghosts of the dead
Come back to earth
To talk of life and love
In words the living cannot hear.

Here and there, they sit
So quiet and pure
Whispering, whispering, whispering,
Of times they cannot relive.

This, to them, is Purgatory,
Seeing all around,
The living, as they go on living
While they remain in the ground.

Soon, life so long and tiring
Will drain the livings' limbs
Then, here they will come,
To whisper, all again.

—Jamie Allen Parsley

Heaven and Hell

Hell
Could it be real, have you been there, no
Not this morning, heaven...have you seen it,
No notthat I know of,
How may you see it

How will you know when you get there,
Son, please read your Bible.

I do not know where it is,
What does it look like,
Dad, do you have one, what son,
You know, a Bible, yes son

Wait a minute, son, it was right here.
Dad when was the last time you saw, Dad
Was it that long ago

—Dorsey Baker

Quest

Silent tears fall down my face, I'm searching
For something better, more soul satisfying.
Why can't they see me through the eyes
Of beauty, and not the beast?
Why can't they accept me for who I am,
And not who they want me to be?
Why?

—Autumn M. Smith

My Secret War

In my room, behind my door
That is where I fight my secret war.
Mom's always asking why I'm so down
So I put on a smile to cover up my frown.

Thinking one day of ending my life
Can't deal anymore with the strife.
Leaving behind my family and friends
In hopes of starting over again.

In another time, in another place,
We all someday will come face to face
If, by then, they have not understood
I'll tell them, *Because I thought I should.*

No one to talk with, no one here
To think of death and have no fear.
In my room, behind my door
That is where I fight my secret war.

—Dawn Brower

Nature

As I sit and watch the world go by,
I dream of flying in the sky
Over the mountains and across the trees
Among the birds and the bumble bees.

Imagine climbing a sycamore tree,
Imagine being wild and free.
I love to smell the colored flowers,
To sit in the sun, and the thunderstorm showers.
The woods so tranquil and the surf so loud

Watching a bird glide under a cloud.
So peaceful are the beaches of sand,
As graceful as a hawk may land.
The palm trees sway in a calm breeze,

Think of how the icycles (at the poles) must freeze!
The pig's oink and cow's moo,
A baby's mother hums a sweet coo
The world of nature, it is so free,
It's where I wish and want to be.

—Jenna Snyder

But She Wanted to Know Other Worlds

But she wanted to know other worlds:
Other worlds outside her island world.

She loved Jamaica, yes
With the poinseittas ruffling,
Feathery blood-red flowers,
In the warm Christmas sun;
Moving to the tune of sweet kisses,
From the cooling Christmas breeze.

And the flame-red poincianna flowers contrasting,
Contrasting against bright June skies;
And the misty blue mountains,
And rolling green hills,
And sparkling clear, shiny sea.

Yet she wanted to know other worlds.
Other worlds outside her island world;

The worlds of ice and snow-
Those worlds where the tropic
Winds did not blow.
Those worlds so big and grand,
Where it paid to be a man!
Those worlds where with determination
and hard work, one could make it to the top!

She wanted to know those other worlds.
She wanted to know!

   —Farika Fayola Birhan

First Frost

Outdoors the air is pure and cold,
And inside, patterned on the pane,
Jack Frost's designs are sharp and bold.
And drawn on lawn and country lane
His icy, magic tracery
Coats tree and bush and all around
With frozen, snowy lacery
That spreads across the sleeping ground.

The stars wink out against the black
With icy glitter in the sky;
And curling from the chimney stacks
Sweet wisps of smoke are wafted by.
The crisply bright air of the night
Is incensed by its perfumed mist,
And peace is frozen in the sight
Of pristine land that God has kissed.

   — Verna Hutchinson

Marginal Existence

We live in peace, we are civilized, we claim,
Yet we live as always in shame.
We fail to realize this,
The guilt of generations lies within us,
Unseen but expanding.
Battles and wars are fought then reasons are sought.
People die every day for unknown causes,
Fighting for reasons they cannot understand,
Or that don't even exist.
People believe, never question,
They follow, never ask their destination.
We have faith-blind faith. Obedience blinded by belief.
The ability to believe everything and anything,
To follow everybody and nobody,
To be everyone and yet no one.
Questions cannot remain unchallenged,
We cannot continue to avoid what is real.
Pretending it does not exist.

   —Vicki Pardallis

The Streets

The streets are home
So harsh and cruel.
Why is it so,
The people there,
That they must live
In such despair?
The young and old,
It's all the same.
Are they to blame?
Do we not know
That we are them?
Hope and kindness,
They must come
To save us all,
A common home.

   — Alex Collins

          in a
      sudden
            e
              g
          r
       u
     s
          of
            wanting
             i ponder
             your body
                and mine
           our lips as
      they touch/we feel
       SO MUCH
           our limbs
               as they
                 entwine

   —Amy Spangle

Friends

Friend, dear friend,
You're my only hope.
You're a friend
And not a dope.
You may smoke
And drink some, too,
But don't do drugs;
It's not good for you.
I'm not saying
Smoking's not,
But the answer to life
Isn't pot!
Up the nose
Or through the vein
In the end
Drugs only cause pain.
Please talk to someone.
Oh, can't you see?
If not for yourself
Then do it for me!

   —Ami Paulachok

Untitled

I don't know where my life will go
Or if I will be found
Perhaps I'll find all that I need
When my soul is not around

I don't know where this path does lead
Or why all leaves do fall
Perhaps a rock is the greatest of things
It possesses no feelings at all

I don't know why I am tired
Or why water flows downstream
Perhaps the bridge I need to cross
Is only in my dreams

Oh where is all the laughter
The height of a mountain peak
For all I see is lonely
And all lost souls are weak

Please come and find me sleeping
And wake me if I am there
Come hope and faith and blossoms rich
Come sent my wretched air-

   —Elisabeth Anne Lozier

Rock and Mull/Rocking Chair

I rock and mull the time away
they are all grown up by now,
and cannot stay.
The visit seemed so short today.
I wonder-
can't they stop and play?
Their voices ring with childish glee,
so close—yet
so far away from me.
Slow down, let's talk and friends we'll be.
But I need to plead.
They do not hear, nor do they see.

So I rock and mull the time away,
and lonely pass the time of day
and wonder at my children gay
for I have paid
the price they'll pay.

   —Arden Yale Crawford

Solitary Prints

Come take my hand and walk with me
Along the ocean shore.
We'll let the wind play us a song
And ask for nothing more.
Creating footprints in the sand
For now our very own
If only for a moment,
Then washed away in foam.
We'll watch the waves turn over
And feel so very small.
We'll hear the ocean's thunder
And hear the seagulls call.
And somehow as we stroll along
And taste the salty air,
We'll know this fleeting moment
Was only ours to share.

   —Edward J. Muzatko

Life As We Know It

The world is such a weird place to live in.
The sayings and doings of different people,
Living in different places, upsetting different nations.
...The rich, like buzzards hovering over a corpse, hover over the rest of
    society, feasting upon everyone else.
...The poor, helpless and hungry, roaming the streets in the midnight mist,
    multiplying in the night, trying so hard, yet feeling every bit of pain.
...The wastes and toxins, constantly being poured from our factories, slowly
    deteriorating whole communities.
...The educators, teaching the future, working hard, yet earning less than the
    man who kicks a football...
Who created this chaos?
This world of no longer hard working men, clean air, and fresh flowers,
But of cheaters; pollutants killing us all;
nuclear bombs ticking away in the closet.
Will we ever rid ourselves of such damage,
spreading like a cancer throughout the world?

— *Carleen M. Sawicki*

Friends 'Til the End

What's a friend?
A friend is one to share those dark secrets with,
One who you know will never shush you or rush you to finish a story.
Friends, a very special treasure in life.
Add the word *best* and that's how they'll find you and me.
Remember how we cried over our first loves?
We thought life would surely end.
How we played in the snow and we were always on the go.
We swore together that's how we'd stay.
But now we've strayed away,
So on this lonely night as tears hug my cheeks
And before sleep I'll even think,
I'll kneel to say a special prayer,
One that you'll still care.

— *Fran Martin*

Aurora

In the dim neon lights outside the airport, later than midnight
But still not close enough to the coming morning, the plane has arrived.
Once it touched the ground, the doors opened to let the people out.
One by one, they are welcomed with their first breath of the tropical air,
High humidity and heat on this summer night,
    August 5, 1986, in West Palm Beach.
As my heart accelerated, and with most attention, I stand there
    looking at each passenger coming toward the exit gate.
When seeing them moving all together, it was a large mass,
    reminding me of a grey landscape, giving me the feeling of monotony.
But suddenly, in the shine of one neon light, the closest to the gate,
It looked as if the sun had suddenly fallen out of orbit
    and had dropped on earth by an unexpected phenomena.
There was a big, orange form and it was moving and coming closer.
Once more visible to me, I could recognize in the light:
    first the figure, then the head,
And then the face with a big and happy smile of a girl,
    carrying her bag on rollers behind her.
Yes, there she is! My daughter, my child, my love! Sabina! Aurora—
Touching the earth, waking up the darkness of this night.
    Aurora is coming, ascending the light!
And my heart is so full of joy while she was running
    into my arms, greeting me
And there we stand, forgetting the world and the people around us,
    in the embrace
A mother and child, lost and found in the universe.

—*Era Gregersen*

No One Knows

No one knows the child cries in the night
No one knows this child's plight
No one knows about the child's anger inside,
No one knows that the child wants to run and hide.
No one knows about the hate that runs deep in their viens.
No one knows that the child is going insane.
No one knows as they start to grow and mature,
No one knows how easily they are lured.
No one knows the child is starving for love,
No one knows except for God up above.
No one knows the child is dreaming,
No one knows the child is scheming.
No one knows the child is gone,
No one knows the parents did wrong!
No one heard the child's cries in the night,
No one knows this child's plight
No one knows...

—*Carolyn Carvo*

Mono Mood

An ill wind blew upon my soul
Intending to rob me of my goal.
It held me down so I could not fight.
It dragged me along, holding on tight.
And I wondered and cried at this merciless ploy,
Which could drain me of all interest and joy.

Someone at last then brought it to light.
An identity telling me what I must fight.
Bad Virus which lies in a throat and waits
To attack the wary with it's fate
Of strength wasting germs and listless goals.
Not on the wise will you take your tolls.

Use strategy, friend, in fighting this foe.
Rest and good food will help it to know
You are onto its tricks. It drains you no more.
Your prayers, your cures have reached the core
Of your very fiber; your strength renewed,
You rise and fling off the Mono Mood.

—*Grace E. Cook*

Letting you Know

Friends forever, it is used a lot
Friends forever, but do you realize what you have got?
Without these friends, where would you be?
If they were not there, life would be so lonely.
You have good times, those to remember,
Happy ones, and those that are tender.
But there is a different kind, used so freely
Its meaning gets lost, through the passing of time
Though even in the darkness it still tries to shine.
What I speak of are the words *best friend*
You have just one, from beginning to end.
I have my best friend, she is the greatest there is
Without her around, I do not know how I would live.
The one I am writing about, I need to reveal-
She deserves the credit...this I will not steal.
Do you know who she is? I am speaking of you,
You are my best friend, I want you know it too.
I thank you for your love, I thank you for your tears,
Locked inside my heart, are these forever golden years.

—*Eden L. Melton*

Be Honest

Tom Brown, a woodcutter, was sitting by a brook
When his ax fell into the water and he began to weep.
A fairy came up and said to him, *Why do you weep?*
He said to the fairy, *My ax fell into the water.*
The fairy came up with a golden ax and said to him,
Is this your ax? He said to the fairy, *No.*
The fairy went down and came up with a silver ax
And said to him, *Is this your ax?*. He said, *No.*
The fairy went down and came up with the wood handle ax
And said to him, *Is this your ax?* and he said to the fairy, *Yes.*
You can have all of the axes because you are honest.
Tom Brown came home and told Sam Jones, his friend.
Sam Jones went down and sat beside the brook
And let his ax fall into the brook and began to weep.
The fairy came up to him and said to him, *Why do you weep?*
And he said to the fairy, *My ax fell into the water.*
The fairy went down and came up with a gold ax and said to him,
Is this your ax? He said to the fairy, *Yes.*
The fairy said to Sam Jones, *You have lied. You cannot have any of the axes.*
He came home and told Tom Brown and Brown said to Sam Jones, *Be honest.*

　　—*Andrew Scruggs*

Among Her Memories

Fingerprints on her mirror, footsteps in the hall
Tiny voices saying, *Nan* in a way she loves to recall
Their smiling faces and laughing eyes and the way they'd
Holler *hi*, the way little faces pucker up before they start to cry.
Always there when life gets rough,
She wishes she could be helping to make things clearer,
For little eyes to see, gently watching as each one grows
So very strong and tall wanting to be there, to pick them up
Each time they stumble and fall. Just to hold them gently and
Wipe away their tears, gather them all closely and banish all their fears
She prays that God above will grant the peace and harmony
That will guide all her grandchildren and all humanity.
Smiles show as she travels thru her treasured memories, she
Speaks so very often of her happy reveries, none of them seem to care
About wealthy legacies
They just seem to be content, being among her memories.

　　—*Alma Amodei*

Patterns

Darkness was around, through, swirling, creating a pattern upon my soul.
Then there was a spark, tiny at first but growing stronger with each passing hour and day,
Causing the darkness to scatter, like scampering animals that are afraid of the light.
Now my soul stretches.
It reaches up toward the warm rays of the light.
I now am reveling in the growing process
Knowing it is just the beginning and that more growth is to come
As I continue to reach toward the light.

　　— *Alethia E. Mattio*

A Friend Remembered

In the hearts of his friends, he will live on,
even though his body is gone
Because memories of him can never die,
just shine brighter than the sun in the sky.
Death has set his soul in flight
unto a land where there is no night.
And he is far more better off than we
in a place that our eyes cannot see.
And if, by chance, he looks down from above,
he'll see that, by his friends, he is still loved.

　　— *Bethe Moore*

A Close Friend

I know that you say we will never be together,
But in my heart, this love will last forever.
Each night, I lie here and cry;
I think to myself and wonder why
You do not love me, but I do love you.
You see, this is the reason I do not know what to do
It looks as if dreams never come true
But just to be sure,
I will hope some more,
That in the end, you will be more than a friend.

　　—*Wendy Bonekemper*

Missing You

I have been without you for only a short while
And already I miss your smile
Those summer nights that together we spent
You cannot comprehend how much they meant
Help special in my heart and in my eyes
It is of those memories I fantasize
I envision you holding me tight
On the sand near the ocean on that hot summer night
Not speaking, just staring as together we lay
Trying to keep special each passing day
Because we knew the day was nearing
The shadow of aloneness we were both fearing
The day was coming...time to depart
Settle in for winter alone and apart
Return to school separately
Yet wishing each second you were here with me
I am missing you.

　　—*Brenda O'Connor*

Memories of that Past

Everybody, it is seeming,
Forgot what they once knew,
When we were tiny, little beings
In our mother's womb.

When traveling was as fast as thinking.
Awareness of sin was non-existent.
Our memories of that past start shrinking,
As we move through time slowed by sins resistance.

My mind is away in the distance
And I'm finding its effect is severe.
I'm only trying to comprehend this existence
Of being when you're not really here.

There's a story behind our lives,
But I'm not all that sure what it is.
It must be a glorious high,
Because what it is, is His.

We're all a part of history,
Because we're all a part of His Story.

　　—*E. C. Seaberg Jr.*

Just the thought of you

Just the thought of you; revives
Me, like the dew drops, when it falls upon
The vines of the morning glory, causing
Them to awaken and stretch forward,
Their small blue blossoms lift up
Their head, so does the very tho
ught of your love lifts me, al
though you are gone, but
Your love lives on in my he
art, I am kept by your
Ever
Last
ing
Love
I am for
Ever yours, thank
You my darling, where ever
You may be, my love goes with you.
—*Annie P. Hopkins*

They Said He Did Not Love Me

They said he did not love me
They said he did not care
But, I would not listen
Now I'm the one whose nowhere

I thought that he was special
The only one for me
But I see now I was the one
Barking up the wrong tree.

I thought I was in love
Didn't have a care at all
You were my knight in shining armor
Dark, handsome and tall.

But, I stand here now
After all the tricks
The only thing you wanted
Was a couple of kicks.

—*Amy Emory*

Confusion

You were once in such control,
Now confusion closes in upon you.
It grabs a hold and will not let go
It tries to suffocate.

You try to break free
You run and try to escape.
You run until you can run no farther
You collapse and care no longer.

You let confusion work it's ways over you,
Once you were so strong.
Now all you can do is wonder why
Your spirit and will are broken.

Confusion relaxes it's mighty grip,
But it is too late because you are now a mere shadow
Of yourself.

—*Bridget Talbot*

The Day I Longed for at the Beach

A warm day at the beach where the sun sets,
Watching the waves of the water,
Feeling the cool breeze pass me by,
Smelling the water's fresh scent,
Watching a bird flying by:
The day I longed for at the beach.

— *Noemi Marie Jeudy*

A Fairy Tale

A fairy tale
Is a merry tale;
People get saved,
Crooks get caught,
Heroes get paid
So everything's okay.
— *Nathan Williams*

Love Is the Light Inside Your Heart

There is a flame
that burns
deep within
the heart
it starts out
with a spark
of charm
and burns
bright
and leads the
way which two
become one.
—*Amy Mangus*

THE END

Death.
Perish the dawn.
A last breath,
Go . . .
Going . . .
Gone.
—*Susan Renee Flickinger*

A Prayer

Shield me with your heart,
 Wrap me in your soul,
Whenever we're apart
 And trouble takes its toll.
Our love will see us through,
 The Lord is on our side,
There's nothing else to do
 With Him, we will survive.
— *Evelyn M. Wenzel*

Family

Father
And
Mother
Is
Loving
You
— *Beth Jackson*

Intimidation

The dark garments of fear he agrees
to prevail.
A concern well thought
by courageous dissertation of one's space,
to overcome insecure doubts
of self-confidence unpleasantly caught
in jealous furies.
A roulette of times' calling
a bulls-eye tactic of his preconcocted game.
Roles turn a timid eye, who passify
this bahavior of a beast let loose,
in a message sequence
and emotions ring of civility.
Self-esteems's highest climb
to reign over an irrational rapport
of totalitarian welcome.
— *Patricia Anne Solek Fritsche*

Puddles in the Street

The sky seems to black out
And the stars are covered with gray.
Daylight flashes across the sky
Leading the thunders way.

Trees dance in the wind,
Foreign sounds fill the sky.
The moisture weighs down the earth
As the clouds go running by

Electric pulses of light
Flash across the darkened day
Without a warning, things are silent
Leaving nothing but the gray

All that is left is the night
And the puddles in the street
But there will be another time
When the thunder and lightening will meet.

—*Nicole Waldron*

Hotter Than Fire

How much torture can you take?
Are you satisfied or could it be another mistake?
Trust me; hold me, dear.
I can promise forever without my own fear.
Do you desire?
Can I make fire?
If I cannot,
Give no second thought.
Just fire your shot.
Am I game or am I hot?
— *Beth Morse*

OFF SHORE DRILLING

Surfeited surfs surge
Depositing foam on the
Blackened beach where Pelicans
Once reposed incubating eggs, and
Burnished surfers surfed in splendorous
Gold. Now, banished by the blackening
of that beach
by Greed
and
the
Indulgences
of an Insatiable being
—*howard a pitterson*

Who's Afraid?

He pushed the Red Sea back like walls,
And let his children cross dry-shod.
He gave them manna from above,
And quails were sent to them by God.
For Daniel's sake the lion's mouths
Were closed, and still God's outstretched arm,
In tenderness is reaching out
To keep his children from all harm.

We as a nation, could reach out
Our hands to God, and let him lead.
What power could evil forces have?
Our father would supply each need.
An earthquake shook the prison walls
Where Paul and Silas sang and prayed,
And they were free. He calls to us.
If God is with us, who's afraid?

— *Alta Richardson McLain*

Green Eyes

Green eyes peeking from beneath the bed
Only eyes, no head
Showing underfoot.

Glowing brightly
Closing tightly
A cold wet dab on my foot
My cats nose
Pink as a rose
Showing underfoot

Black fluffy tail
Slow as a snail
Swishing and tickling my foot
My cat's tail
Swishing around
Showing underfoot

—*Amanda McGill*

Paper Dolly

She dresses her paper dolly
And sends her out on a date,
Or she bedecks her in a wedding gown
And gives her a life long mate;
She always gives her dolly a dream man,
A "Ward Cleaver" or a "Father Knows Best"
She rejects what she knows as the real thing,
She likes her fantasies best.

But she had to put away her paper dolly,
And put on high heel shoes,
But she often steals away in fantasy
When reality deals her the blues;
When the real things is just too natural,
She slips back in time for a while.
Waltzing with the great pretender
And wearing her paper doll smile.

— *Carol B. Link*

I

I, brought forth through my mother's womb
Am carried forward
By a conceiving daughter
Who is mother to a daughter
And passed through a woman by a son
Who has shared me
With her daughter and two sons.
I am, and will how long be I?

—*Ann M. Rabb*

Hills of Gold

Yonder wait the hills of gold
As dark still holds the dawn.
They stretch to reach the billowy
Blues of a morning sky's spawn.
Clouds of fire that rope the wind
As the sun does surely rise,
Nothing stirs this desolate hour
But the ghosts of yonder guise.
Trees give way to shadows spent
As the wind does make them dance.
Throughout the night they march
To pro and highly they do prance.
Nothing sings to reverie till all
Is spent in the morning's scene,
But all for glory to be found when
The hills of gold have come and been.

— *Alishia Tillman*

A Love to Love

You're the perfect one
For me to lay upon
And listen to your heart
Where the sweet sound start.

The love you give
Is the life I live
It's the best thing
That you could bring.

The love I get
Is something I don't regret.
It's like a sun
That bring so much fun,
I know it's not a game
And it'll never be in flame
Because your love is still the same.

I love the things the way you do
For they don't color me blue
But most of all, I love you!

—*Grace Jenkinson*

Defamation

There can be no forgiveness
For the sadist's tongue
That tears and shreds
The name of anyone
What therapy can cure or
 even help
the victim left bleeding
From hate-spawned words.

— *Eunice Talbott*

A Summer Storm

Thunder roars aloud
Lightening splits the sky,
Rain cascades down
On earth tinder dry,

Flowers drink their fill
Of rain drops from above,
Each drop is welcomed
Like a kiss of love.

Umbrellas deftly raised,
Shielding human form,
From enclement weather
A rainy summer storm.

—*Allen Thompson*

The Truth Hurts

Thousands of children are missing
Truth; this will never change
Racism is growing rapidly
Truth; for their hate is to blame
As days go by someone dies
Truth; the killer gets the fame
Children are taught right from wrong;
Society prepares them for *war songs*
We thank the Lord for food to eat,
While others steal to get their meat
Aids is sweeping out most countries
Truth; we are warned everyday
Society is pushing religion aside
Truth; soon we'll have no place to pray
Maybe things will eventually change
Truth; the homeless *may* find somewhere to stay
But the truth be changed as well?
Truth; only time will tell...only time will tell.

—*Franceilia Y. Boswell*

A Story of Love

A lonely emptiness lays inside
It tries to find a way to hide
From all the good things I try to feel
Whether or not I think it is real
For me I need to see your eyes
It still does not make me realize
That what we do may be wrong
It is a decision we decided to choose
We can win or we can lose
But if I knew from the start
Then maybe you would not own my heart
Things are too wild to understand
I love the moments you held my hand
Times like that seem so sweet
Sweeter than the times our eyes will meet.

—*Carrie M. Watkins*

Eighteen

Love, Friday night dates
Saturday nights, working late
Hugs and kisses in the moonlight
Sex now...Is it wrong or right?
Friends and parties, so much fun
Drinking and driving...which way to run?
Finally a job, money to spend
But you need to save...Will this ever end?
Considered an adult, responsiblities at hand
Yet still a kid...Can you handle the demands?
Homecoming, Prom and Graduation are near
But what comes next, you can't help but fear.

—*Amy Kumpf*

My Garden

You, Lord, love me unconditionally
And like the seeds in my garden,
I am sprouting and bearing fruit.
Your warmth caresses and I reach for the sky,
The dew quenches my thirst,
Let me give pleasure in my lifetime,
Let others know I was here,
Make my compost rich and productive,
So when frost comes, I will not hesitate
But be ready, having accomplished my task

—*Alice Judge*

Life On the Moon

This is the nineteen eighties you know. On your next vacation
You can go to the moon. Yea, just get away from it all.
I mean everything! We are now planning trips out of this world.
But half way around the world there's a man that can't even plan
His next meal. Can this really be? What's the poor man to do? Steal?
Oh yea, from who? So you're going to the moon. Did you know there's a
Man half way around the world in jail, his only crime is wanting to
Be free. But it's your vacation you worked hard for it. Still there's
A man across the street that can't even find a job. You see it's been
A year since the plant down the street shut down and left town. What's
The poor man to do? Steal? Oh yea! From who? We're all your neighbors
Here on the ground. But go ahead on your trip. Just remember! What
Goes up and around...must come down and back around.

—Jerry L. Edmonds

Take Time to Wonder

Newborn flowers in springtime, birds singing in the trees,
Blue, blue skies above us, how did we come by these?
Children at the park running, laughing, playing,
Squirrels chasing, squeaking at one another; I wonder what they're saying!

Rain pouring down, it's fragrance is so clean.
Lightning...the roar of thunder, I wonder, what does it mean?
People hurriedly passing by other people on the street
Walking, running, riding, driving, is there a chance they'll meet?

Cold, cold days of winter, biting winds...pure white snow
Icicles hanging from a roof in a scattered, uneven row.
God has given us so many things to add wonder to our days.
If only our eyes are clear to see through the foggy, man-made haze.

— Debra J. Lee

Seasons

Golden yellows; sunburst orange; crimson reds; these are the colors
Of our fall leaves. Temperatures fall; school bells calling; mother
Nature's beauty for us all to see. Winds whipping up the fallen leaves
Soon the land will be bleak and all the tress bare. Waiting silently
For winter to bring a blanket of snow, falling ever so gently to
Earth, without a care. Christmas bells ringing and children singing,
Bring warmth to the cold air. Icy chills from winter winds, almost
Makes you wish you had been spared. Till finally sprigs of green
Shown through, and the buds of flowers are all in bloom. Warm sunshine
Caressing the green grass, newly there. Blue skies up above and the
Melodies of song birds fill the air. Temperatures soar..green blades of
Grass scorch in the heat. Thunderstorms brewing overhead, winds carrying
The scent of rain so sweet. Grey coulds rolling and lightening splits
The air and as soon as it's over...a beautiful rainbow appears. God
Created the four seasons for us all to enjoy,
Let's bow our heads in prayer and thank him-rejoice.

—Ella W. Richardson

Remembrance

The human quest falls to the horizon. Through tunneled eyes,
The sky's seams meet the heavens,
To find, beyond what is learned, the reasons.
Screams, like madness, cite the acceptance.

When the trials of weather have seeded the hope,
False men will make the claims of creator.
As stategy, the masses side with their humaness;
They make common, their fear, at all costs, they prosper, then vacate.

For it will come as omen, like the rains of the north;
Befriending the pysche, in denial of invasion.
And like insects, it will bite; like blood, will ooze;
In the confusion of domination, they blunder.

In time they will find fault, but meet with failure;
As flesh, find flaws, but meet with extinction.
When the sun reaches its destination;
Men, across the fading floor, shall make graves.

— J. Preston Holden

Growing Pains

Mere existence brings no honor,
Though it may prevent some pain.
True life has both joys and sorrows.
Living holds both sun and rain.

I have grasped love all the more
When lonliness has left its mark,
For the storm accents the rainbow
Lights shines brightest in the dark.

Thank you, Lord, for all the good times.
For the blessings I have known.
Thank you, too, for days of sorrows
Times in which I've learned and grown.

— Denise B. Wisse

Missing you

As you are there and I am here,
You're just a friend, a peer.
As you turn to look over your shoulder
Hoping to find someone,
There is nothing, no one.

I had this same feeling once before.
I came knocking, knocking at your door,
But there was no one home.
Now I am here all alone.
Is there no end to this madness
Of sitting here in sadness?

I'm still alone, I've got only my shadow
To cry myself to sleep at night.
At least I feel not alone.
I have someone here, right at home.
It's Mom and Dad; They'll take care of me
While you're gone.
I'll still be missing you.

—Dayle Schopen

It's Up To You

It's up to you,
I've done all I could do;
I've liked you from the start
My feelings come from the heart;
I want to hold on to you,
But I'm not sure what to do;
You're always on my mind,
and I wonder if it's you I've been trying to find;
You take my blues away,
Because you're like a drop of the golden suns ray;
You make me feel fine
All of the time;
But it's up to you.
I've done all I could do;
Please make up your mind.
Please don't leave me hanging on the line.

— Natasha E. Mayes Montero

A Hawkin Man

Can yer hear ta clams a sqwawkin,
All way ta Chatsworth from Manahawkin?
Ta bogs, sugar sands, an pines they's a talkin,
Git yer barrels, scoops, an sacks a hawkin.
Then I quickly goes ta ketch what e'r I gits
Be they berry, moss, pine cone, or birch tips.
There hain't a bit o what I e'r choose ta cares
Awhile I goes bout gatherin me Pineland wares.
Fer there's a special buncha PINEY POWER
By what e'r gits scooped an sacked by hour.
There be's a Pinehawker ta best o enny man
When I exchange a sack a berries fer a Manahawkin clam.

— Harry S. Monesson

Untitled

I tried
Pressing leaves
Melting glass
Pictures
My lines
Memorized
Mimeographed
I tried
Held my ground
Held my breath
And though
I tried
To close
My eyes
The sun still set.

    —Virginia Teevan

Divine Geometry

I was lost,
Until you pointed out
The way.
But, in so doing,
You unveiled
A part of yourself,
Vision of beauty
Blinding the eye,
Because it allows
Naught else to exist
In my mind,
Or in my heart.
My soul is captive
Of Divine Geometry,
In you I see
The face of God.

    —Giorgetta McRee

Desert Moon

Sitting on the sand
I memorize the sky
Thinking of dreams
In which I could fly
To soar to the stars
That shine so bright
Bright enough
To light up the night
The sky seems to never end
Never cease
Everything beautiful in
Every crease
I want to touch
That brilliant moon
To see how it feels
That desert moon

    —Gina Radoy

Living A Dream

To live, is to dream
To dream, is to live
Before you can dream
You must live.
Before you can live,
you must dream.
But to live a dream
Is what living should be.

    —Gina Gaetz

Love and Loss

A lighthouse in the dark, silently awaiting the passing of a ship.
A lonely tide gently caresses the reef,
As a subtle breeze drifts through the soft hair of the
Lighthouse keeper's daughter.
Alone upon the seashore she gently weeps.
He sailed out of her life, like autumn to winter.
Her heart has been broken. Will it heal?
Only time will tell.
It was short and bittersweet
Her first love, and her only it would seem. Her heart was broken,
Her life destroyed. With him he took her will to survive,
Without him she wouldn't. Depression made her strong, emptiness
Made her want, sorrow lifted her up,
And yearning threw her in,
And the waves crashed, and the angels sang,
And finally all was right with the world.

    —Gretchen Browne

Beautiful Kentucky

Kentucky, my home state, a beauty of a place.
Anticipation fills my soul as I walk through the deserted streets...
The longing I feel as I look about on memories past.
Its lovely hills, lush, green fields,
The serenity of it all as I listen to sounds of distant whip-poor-wills...
Small country homes, weathered and worn
Filled with memories that embrace my heart with warmth.
Rolling hills, cool running streams.
As a teen, I left this to follow my dreams...
From school you graduate, a new future you seek.
What goals you set, what course in life you choose you strongly debate...
You seek to find, never quitting until
You accomplish the things most important in your mind...
An education you get, a career you achieve,
But the roots of ole Kentucky still remain a part of me.

    — Vickie Pollitt Moore

Echo, Echo, Echo

Echo, echo, echo——it seems to be all around,
no matter where I go, a new echo I have found.
Echo, echo, echo from the moments gone by,
they keep saying—-try, try, try!
I don't want to hear it, but it has surrounded me.
Echo, echo, ECHO, it gets louder and louder, I can't seem to get free.
The echo is as fickle as day and unsure as the night,
hopes and dreams that may someday be——is a never ending plight.
Dreams that were to be, dreams that shall never come about,
I hear them in the echo as if they were a shout.
Is a thought, a dream, a memory just an echo of the past?
Or is it happiness, a love story, or precious moments that forever shall last...

    — Francine E. Pintar

A Heartful of Love

I'd like to dress you in the early morning sunshine,
Place on your head a crown of stars and around your neck a string of dew
Drops and on your feet moonbeams for shoes.
I'd like to give you the world on a string to play with,
Make sure that you never feel any pain,
Guarantee that you never know the word called loneliness,
But all I have to offer is a heart running over with love for you,
But riches and wealth have I none; fortune and fame I cannot offer you,
But the little I have, I've given it all.
My heart's running over with love for you.

    —Evelyn R. Brock

Sins

My life is one lie
after another.
I lied about my love
to you.
I lied about my child
too.
There is no truth in
our lives.
So I say what I should
have said a long time
ago.
A sin is a crime. Now
I have to pay for my
crimes of sins.

    — Gina Mota

Inside a Lake

The lake
Is a mirror;
Its depths reflect
The distant past,
Memories
Of long ago,
Its surroundings
Project the future
And the destiny of the lake
Itself.
Its surface;
However,
Portrays the golden pink
Sunsets
Of today.

    —Gretchen Mominee

From Me to You

A tear and a smile,
A drop of water,
From my eye,
An invisible grin,
Upon my face.

Loneliness surrounds
My blind sight,
Joy quenches,
My sun dried lips.

Love is seen,
By my heart,
Kisses are given,
With tongues of passion.

Only for you,
Across every mile,
I shall willingly deliver,
A tear and a smile.

    —Amy Blaska

Red.
Too much hurt to deal with.
A slit and the red seeps up.
It's too painful
Help.
But no one listens.
Red flows, my vision blurs
My way to cope.
Black.

    — Elaine Rubin

As a Friend to Me

As a friend to me you are my best.
We shared our life's dreams and our life's success.
We are always there for one another.
If one needs a shoulder to cry on, the other is there.
We have never had a fight; sure, we have had
A few yelling matches, but no fights.

As a friend to me, you have shown me that taking isn't enough.
You have to give something in return.
We have grown up together and become best of friends.
Time can't tell how much we have shared,
But the time we have shared will always tell
That we have been friends for a very long while.
Someday when we move away and forget our school years,
Please don't forget the friendship that we have shared.

As a friend to me, you will forever be in my heart.
Even if you forget me in the years to come, I will never forget you.
We are almost ready to step our feet out into the real world.
Please don't forget...as a friend to me you are my best.

—*Tamilia George*

I Think of You

When dawn and your alarm call you to begin another day, while your mind
clears of dreams and the sleep leaves your eyes, do you ever roll over and
wish for someone to awaken with soft kisses? Do you think of me?
When your day is headed in the wrong direction and everyone seems to point
their finger at you, when the pressure gets so great you feel the weight is
too much to bear, do you ever release your mind from its burdens so that it
can recall for just a moment a memory that makes you smile? Do you think of me?
When the sun shines bright and your heart sings with the glory of just
being alive, when you're filled with laughter, do you ever want someone
beside you to learn and enjoy all that life gives together? Do you think of me?
When you lie in bed at night with a desire burning deep within you, do you
ever ache for someone to hold in your arms and as one release the passions
you've hidden from the world? Do you think of me?
When you're locked in your dreams drifting through and beyond forever, do
you ever hear the echo of whispers that breathe of a promise of the magic
known only to two when their lives and their souls intertwine as one?
Do you think of me?
When you think of love and all its miracles, do you ever pray for someone
to touch you with a love that is trusting and true, a love without question,
a love that is infinite in the giving, a love you can return in kind?
Do you think of me? I think of you.

—*Dani Thomton*

Loved Ones

You weren't happy with your life, you ended it so soon.
I wish I knew what made you do it, or how, why or who.
All I know is now you're gone and I am left alone.
I had never seen nor heard from someone who had known,
But now four years later, my heart still hurts like that.
I had to finally realize that you weren't coming back.
You know, the hurt was not so strong because you had died
But more when I heard the way was merely suicide.

— *Tammy F. Barnes*

Thanks for the Memories

You really have inspired me to display an open mind
You've shown me there is much to see and so much more to find
You've helped me be more open then I have ever been
You've been a real good teacher; you've been to me a friend
You've been a great influence on me and I have come to know
That opportunity has no bounds; with that we all can grow
You've picked me up on days when I was down and out
You've helped me open up new doors; you've ridded me of doubt
I'd like to thank you once more for all that you have done
For all the times you made me smile, it really has been fun
Soon I may have to move on, but with me will be this
The memory of a fine teacher, and a friend that I will miss

— *Steve Miller*

Untitled

Did you ever have that feeling that you could not cope?
You tried and tried to go on but just gave up all hope?
Many times I felt that way though what was I to do
I wanted to start over and begin my life anew.

I knew it was not possible, so I had come to see
I must stop all the pain and end the misery.
I did not want to deal with this in such a drastic way
This was the best that I could do, there's nothing left to say.

I never meant to hurt you, so wipe away the tear
Just try not to forget me and keep my memory near.
You know you were the only one who ever really cared
I did appreciate your love, but still I was so scared.

I did not want to leave you; I did not want to die
But now I'll never feel the pain; I'll never have to cry.
Please try not to hate me, I know it was not right,
I did not have the strength to live...I just gave up the fight.

—*Tamara Talik*

You're Not Alone

The Vietnam vets many gave their lives.
Never to be seen again by
Mothers, fathers and wives.
I was very young when they all went to war.
My mother said it was crazy,
But they kept sending more.
The government was wrong.
What they did to these men
To put them in a situation they'd never win.
Washington felt sorry so they put up a wall.
Many families were insulted
They didn't like it at all.
These men went through alot and not treated fare.
But there's people who still love them
And who truly care.
So when you Vets read this hang it in your home.
And remember we love you all
And remember your not alone.

—*Ellen Procalamos*

A First Love

When I think of you, I think of warm summer days
I think of the peace and happiness you bring
I think of dawn angels drawing back the curtain of night
When I see you, I see my hearts desire
I see compassionate wisdom
I see crystaline starlight with no trace of shadow
When I touch you, I feel the sun on my skin
I feel the silky petals of a new rose
I feel the serenity of a moonlit beach
When I love you, I love the zest you have for life
I love the way you smile when you get your way
I love to love you.

— *Jeffrey Halkyard*

Never Give Up

When you feel like the world is closing in on you
And your life seems so hopeless,
There is always someone to help pull you through.
When that someone has been taken away,
You must find a way to pull through on your own.
There may be people or things that seem as if
They are trying to keep you away from the person you love
And you have to fight them every step of the way.
Just remember,
You must never give up
Because in the long run,
If it was meant to be,
Everything will work out.

— *Trisha Buttrey*

Sit and Talk With Me

Sit and talk with me awhile,
How I long to see your smile.
You are the one,
You mean so much to me.
Somewhere in those eyes of blue,
There is a hope to see me through.
You keep me always smiling,
Like a precious time in spring,
You give me reasons for living,
You give me songs to sing.
You ask of me my confidence,
So, to the crowds I will go,
Telling of my love for you,
Shining, like the freshest snow.
Please, do not fear my actions,
They are simple, pure and plain,
To love you until forever,
And to love you then again.

—*Tracy Rogers*

Rain Song

Music is in the air,
Cricket and frog and bird
There's music everywhere—
The rain has now been heard.

The sun so bright and hot
Had dulled the happy day—
It drained it dry and bare—
Then, rain came by this way.

The grass was laying low
It now has diamond drops.
Flowers and trees now glow—
But now wave shining tops.

Music is in the air,
Cricket and frog and bird
They sing without a care,
Because the rain was heard.

—*Kathryn Hupp*

Life

More meaningful, into life
Moving with seasons
Not falling apart
But lives woven in
Cycle and ends our
Darkness and begins
Our journey on to
Our life.

— *Julie L. Dvorak*

Love

Love is beauty
Love is sadness
Love is a way
To share warmth and gladness.

Love can be good
Love can be bad
Love is something
Everyone should have.

Love is sweet
Love is a flower
Love is weakness
Love is power.

Love is special
Love is a start
Love is my family
That will always stay in my heart.

—*Stephanie Wilson*

Nothingness

Blossoming from the seed
On which a reality is based.
Growing into a mead
Where skyward they have raced.

What is the reason
Behind the eternal abyss?
Once only a season
Now it has surely gone amiss.

If one need look
Do not seek far.
Written in no book
Found by no car.

What each of us desires
Is not conceivable by the brain.
It is he who admires
And a secret from us to remain.

— *Carter Cue Johnson*

No Time for Dreams

Hello.
   What?
Hello.
   Who?
You
   No. Who are you?
You.
   What do you want?
Time.
   For what? I don't have time.
Please.
   Who are you?
A dream.
   I have no time for you.
Fly with me.
   I can't, not now, I have no...
Good-bye, then.
   Wait! When will you return?
Return? Why? You have no time.

—*Julie M. Goebel*

The Chip

Oh dad, can i tell you?
will you listen for a minute?
while i give a confession
through the talks and the lessons
i do believe that now i see
all your faith and honesty
all that's inside of me too
Oh dad, can i tell you?
just want you to realize
see, i'm growing wiser
but never too wise to say
i do believe that now i see
all your faith and honesty
all that's inside me
sometimes life throws curve balls
and the organist forgets to play
it seems like you always know
just what to say,

i knew you'd turn out this way

— *Lisa Nanstad*

Life

Wind rustles dead leaves,
They fall to the forest floor.
Now one with the earth.

— *Starr Proctor*

Until that day...

With the distance between us
And all the tears I have cried
I long to have you hold me
Forever by my side.

And I'll wait for that day
So patiently
As I hold on to the dream
You gave to me.

You tell me you love me
And I love you
So deep in my heart
I know this love is true.

So until that day
When were together
I will be waiting here
For you...forever.

—*Tonya Walker*

Somewhere

Somewhere there is a rainbow
Somewhere there is gold
Somewhere there is a child,
Lying in the cold.

Somewhere there is a smile,
Somewhere there is no fear,
Somewhere there is a child,
That sheds a lonely tear.

Somewhere there is forever
Somewhere there is fame
Somewhere there is a child
That suffers endless pain.

Somewhere there is a dream,
Somewhere there is a dare,
Somewhere there is a child,
That needs someone to care.

—*Jodi L. Beatty*

Love Is

Love is kind,
Love is sweet
If you can find
Love when you meet.

I night of pleasure.
9 months of pain,
3 days of birth
And a baby to name.

He said he loved me.
Never to part.
Than he found her
And I was forgotten.

The love we shared
Was lost after time.
Put back in memories
Drowned with happy times.

— *Danielle Anderson*

Search

Like a gracious swan
I'll spread my wings
And search for love
And all the things
That make a life
Worthwhile to give,
A hold on that
Desire to live.

— *Vivian-Marie Agotesku*

And So it Goes

After a while you learn the subtle differences
between holding a hand and chaining a soul.

And you learn that love doesn't mean leaning,
and company doesn't mean security.

And you learn that kisses aren't promises,
and presents aren't contracts.

And you begin to accept your defeats with head
up and eyes open, with the grace of an adult,
not the grief of a child.

And you learn to build your roads on today,
for tomorrow's grounds is too uncertain for plan.

After a while you learn that even sunshine burns
if you get too much.

So plant your own garden; tend your own soul.

And learn that you really can endure;
you really are strong.

You have had plenty of practice.

—*W. G. Harich*

A HOME FULL OF LOVE

Just like a child, I'm a beamin'.
Awake, I'm like I'm dreamin'.
I can't believe love has found me,
Wrapped her clingin' arms around me.

Just like a bird, my heart's a wingin'.
A lover's song I'm singin'.
My lonely days have subsided. I'm resided,
In a HOME FULL OF LOVE.

I've made a rainbow mine.
My world is all aglow.
She paints it with sunshine,
and makes the shadows go.

NO stocks have I, to watch by hour,
No penthouse in a tower,
But I have a wealth far greater. It's contentment,
In a HOME FULL OF LOVE.

—*James I. Kotter*

Color

Let me color the picture of my life the way it used to be: Blind devotion
...to you. One I trusted, believed in and carried everything that you gave
me inside then let radiate back to you in: Faithfulness...a difficult emotion
for most, for even you. All my thoughts, feelings, fears, hopes and desires
were all saved for you, but I learned: Rejection...you wanted unattachment,
but define that, please! You said no relationship, but you were involved...
with me! You never did make up your mind, but I did and I found: Me...a person
who is very sincere, one of the most likable persons that I could ever encounter.
I found I liked the way she walked, talked, acted...the way she carried herself.
She is a lady with high goals and values. I sit back and watch as she strives
for perfection. Her biggest flaw in her personality is that she lacks patience
with people who lack self-discipline, but...she has confidence in herself.
It's a trait I do so admire. She has friends who really appreciate her and
she sits back, often just watching, letting her surroundings sink in through
observation. At one time it was thought that her quietness was from ignorance,
only to find...she was hindered, stifled...she found: Life is much more enjoyable
without deep mental relationships that demand time that should be hers alone...
She found tranquility with herself as well as for people in her world, strength
of mind, determination to fulfill her wants and wishes...She and Her are I
and no one can take these treasures from me.

—*Brenda L. Mullins-Winebrenner*

Reality

A cup of noodles, no job, no Bob, no cash, no bucks,
No love, no Lotto, no races or bets, no bottles or booze,
No ands, ifs or buts,
Not even a glimpse of a chance for luck.
A baby in womb...a baby yet to feed,
No one certain to fulfill my needs,
A need of comfort, security, good health
While military arms receive the wealth.
Going out of my mind glaring out of the TV.
Nancy buying China and serving tea,
Saving pandas across the sea.
All waste, no taste; Reaganomics, cash in space.
Tell me what happens to the human race
Born in the U. S. of A. hungry and free.
Can't see the forest through the trees,
Is that the way life should be?
Robbing me of virtue, robbing me of trust, turn my back that's a bust.
While dwindling is a gush of political mush.
Passing through days one by one, facing all as it comes.
Slowly struggling along the way, Lord, still waiting for a better day.

—*Vanessa Ann Stafford*

The Cabin

My grandpa built me a cabin on a forty acre lot.
It was a tiny log house, one room and a sleeping loft.
While I paid him for the land, My help was what the cabin cost.
It came with the old cook stove from the homestead where my dad was born
A sink from the town junk yard, a kerosene lamp burned with a golden glow.
Yes, it was full of luxuries, even two windows complete with screens.
I spent my sixteenth summer chinking the holes between the logs.
My seventeenth summer, finishing touches, helped my dad put in the well.
The summer of my eighteenth year I *found* myself, living there alone.
I must admit to moments of terror, like the night a bear stood outside
The door. Or when I stayed out too late, walking home thru the night
Black woods. I never totally over came my fears, but learned in spite
Of them to go on. Many years have passed since then, a stoke took Grandpa
Away. The land was sold to help finance one daughter's fight against her
Fate. Now she lays next to grandpa. Leaving two daughters for us to raise.
But in my heart my cabin still stands in the clearing surrounded by woods.

—*B. J. Anderson*

Betrayal

You were never there for me,
When I was a little girl and scared
by the noises in the dark,
I never had you to run to for comfort.
At school events I would look for you,
But you were never there.
I didn't have someone to look up to
While I was growing up.
All I got was you.
You betrayed me, Father.
For that I don't think I'll ever,
Ever forgive you.

— *Terisa Ridgley*

Untitled

Insecurity
Is a vast wasteland
In which you leave all of your
Dreams
Behind you
Because
You are not confident
You allow others to influence
Decisions that affect your life
Also
You do not allow yourself to do what
You want
Because
You are always putting up a front so
Others will accept you
Who is the real you?
How sad.

—*Lauren K. Dechayne*

You Are Important to Me

Life soft music,
You are soothing to the soul.
Like a white dove,
You are so tender and peaceful.
Like a mother,
You are understanding and caring.
Like a best friend,
You are fun to be with.
Like the eagle,
You are full of strength.
Like a falling star,
You are hard to come by.
Like a twinkling star,
You radiate beauty.
Like my best friend,
You are very important to me.

—*Tracey Hubbard*

Hemorrhage

Bandage covers the explosion, deep red
All other shades vanish,
The color of scabs.

In a piece of mangled flesh
Air sucks whistling,
Cutting in two.

Our shallow soul,
The birthmark,
Smiles.

The soul trapped,
The suffering continues,
The windows iced, cracked.

— *Thomas J. Le Roux*

A Silent Death

I sit alone
an empty room
filled with the
memory of you.
Your name echoes
silently
as our past
plays constant
reruns in my mind.
We couldn't see it
through our little
misunderstandings;
No longer with you
love still lingers
hauntingly over me.
Makes me wonder what
you're doing as
I cry for
a silent death.

—*Thomas H. Sarc*

Little Miss Muffet

Little Miss Muffet
told me to stuff it
when I asked her to
go to the dance.
I don't know why,
so I started to cry.
what a kick in the pants.

— *Liah Strain*

Danger

Danger
A gun held to your
head as you breathe
your last breath.
Danger
Walking on a ledge
and you lose your
grip on the rocks.
Danger
Jumping from a cliff
into the water and
there isn't any water.
Danger
You and your worst
enemy alone in a
dark alley.
Danger
A way of life.

—*Leslie A. Kilgore*

Untitled

The curtains close
Shutting out the light.
Nothing stirs.
My soul and heart mourn
For love lost.
My life is empty
For there is no one to
Love.
No one to care
No one to hold
The light will not come
Until I find the one
To give my
Love.

— *David Barfield*

More to Come

When everything is getting you down
And all your smiles are suddenly frowns
When you think there's nothing left for you
When you really do not know what to do
Think of why you are here
The end is not at all near
You have friends and family that do care
Think of them and how they would feel
How they would miss you and want you there
And of all the things you still want to do
You're young, wild and free
So just love, live, laugh, and let it be...

—*Lynda Tarkouski*

I Can See the Light

Oh help me Lord in my time of need
I now take back my selfishness and greed
If You could only see the trouble I'm to face
My heart pumps at a slow, steady pace
The black dome starts closing upon me
As I sink down lower, oh Lord I cannot see
I close my eyes so very tight
And pray to You, Lord, with all my might,
You hear my word from inside,
Oh thank you God—now I don't have to hide
I see an obstacle at the end of my vision,
Two ideas in my head form a collision,
I suddenly feel a shake on my shoulder to see,
Your wonderful face right there for me,
Those eyes twinkling like that one bright star,
My mind drifts off so far,
He takes my hand to hold me tight,
Oh Lord, oh Lord, I can really see the light.

— *Kristi Dunghe*

Hold on to your Past

To grow up is to live,
To grow old is to give,
But to grow young is only to dream.
You may remember the ways
Of those since bygone days,
But those memories are more than they seem.
For those beautiful times,
The childhood rhymes
They were gone with a whisper and wink.
The good times, the bad
The happy and sad
I recall as I sit down to think.
I am glad I remember,
I let good things last
But more than the rest,
I hold on to my past.

—*Kristen Simoes*

Sometimes alone I dream a dream.
Sometimes inside I scream and scream.
Sometimes I picture a picture of me
Lying dead, it all goes to the head.
My feet are like lead, the days I dread,
The things I've said...
All come to a stop.

When I'm lying down with my thoughts
In the air, grabbing what's there
For all who care, I sit there
And stare, into the air...
And it all comes to a stop

And still sometimes alone
I dream a dream.

— *Karen Grieveson*

Auschwitz: Decades Later

The shifting winds
Carry long ago and forgotten
Silent screams and pleading whispers.

Each particle of dust that is carried,
Proclaims the terror that still clings
In empty barracks and crematoria.

Ghosts of the dead, are entangled
In the barbed wire
Which is now unelectrified and harmless.

The gas chamber
Which exterminates no more,
Holds shocking, diabolic memories
Of the tragedies before.

Although, all will at one time disintigrate
The harrowing portrait
Will forever remain.

— *Laura Velez*

Lovely Things to Remember

We have lovely things to remember
Like the fires last dying ember,
Rosebuds just about to bloom,
Soft shadows in a sleepy room.
Silver moon sailing across the sky,
A fragrant breeze fluttering by.
A sky bright with sunset glow,
A countryside soft and white with snow.
Bluebells blooming in the grass,
Nodding to ladies, as they pass.
Wild flowers growing on a hill
The haunting song of a Whippor will
Fuzzy baby birdies, waiting in the nest,
Busy mother bird, never takes a rest
Love shining in sweethearts eyes,
A sweet mother singing lullabyes.

— *Gwendolyn Derifield*

Nightwind Song

A splendid minstrel, you
As your song through me sang.
With tender words and gentle smiles,
We sang the secrets of our heart.

Our love surged as the river,
Flowed from untempered youth.
We drank the wind; our hearts made merry.
We bound our darks with love;
Our lips sweet secrets kept.

Thoughts of you make melody within,
Golden promises,
Scented dreams.
Your nightwind song
Lays gently on my mind.

— *Linda S. Stogner*

Little Girl Grown

Our little girl, is little no more
Yet it seems like yesterday, she was only four
She was pretty, and smart, and ever so sweet
Now she's cute as ever, with boys at her feet.

Moms and Dads, have it kind of rough
We try to do right but at times it's tough
Like watching her grow into womanhood
As one day, we both knew, she would.

Now our little girl is in her teens
Her life full of boys, and hopes, and dreams
She returns from school and heads for the phone
Oh how we miss our little girl grown.

— *Kay Burks*

Were I

Were I a bird in mating flight, scanning the world with a conquering eye,
Beating my wings to gain more height, performing my art in a sun-soaked sky,
I'd search for you on mountain peaks, on craggy hills and thin-faced clouds,
In far-flung wastes of wilderness, in the leading edge of blistering winds
Where the wild cry shatters the icy air and pierces the heart with loneliness.

Were I the fabled king of beasts ruling the land by strength and fear,
Receiving the homage due my station, roaming forests far and near,
I'd search for you on treetop heights, on mountain slopes and untread passes,
In the wild and untamed jungle, in the heart of some forgotten trail
Where the deep mystery of night stirs the chill air with soundless sighs.

Were I the man I long to be, free of fear and the chains of right,
Moved by the joy of ecstasy of love's incandescense burning bright,
I'd search for you in every path and open walk in daily life
Guided by sight, by sound, by an inner light to a fiery flame of loveliness
And finding this I'd shout my right to keep my gain and draw my line
And stake my claim to you.

— *Leonard A. Jonas*

Thank You, Lord, for My Parents

Again, I thank Thee, Lord, You see, for giving me parents so wonderful to me.
I never realized until my own, how needed you are and never alone.
And the feeling I get from being loved is as beautiful, Lord, as being above.
And I take the time to just say this, 'cause without them they'd really be missed.
It's not an act or a role; it's in their hearts and in their soul
And every second that goes by, you can be sure they're on your side
Caring, sharing, doing their best, picking us up, fighting the rest.
If only someone could understand their faith I feel,
    never missing a birthday or our favorite meal.
The memories I hold are a precious thing to me and wherever I go, they will be
And always will I be thankful for their deeds
    'cause they're always right there with things that I need.
Oh thank you, God, again I say for not taking Mommy and Daddy away.
I need them, Lord, as you can see 'cause I've never been able to set them free.
Where I want them is right by me.
So thank You, Lord, for hearing my prayer; it isn't hard to say
'Cause as you can see, from high above, I love them more each day.

— *Joan E. Kelley*

The Sky at Night

A look to the heavens to see what we could perceive
A vast oasis of blue, sprinkled with brilliant starlight
The ground surrounds us, dimly lit by the crescent moon
Shadows from the trees gently walk across the open field
Beautiful silence; an inspirational playground for the mind
The big city dances on the horizon, remaining at a distance
The soil once trodden by cowboys and indians remains
Unscarred by the machines time has created
Open journey of serenity, exploring above and below
Sanctity for nature and wildlife, human choice to preserve or destroy
This glorious nest man's appetite, unrelinquished by curiousity, won't
Stand still in the quest for something much greater than that which
Was bestowed upon us by the One above, something better left unchanged
And untamed. For I dream that generations to come may discover the
Solitude before it is bereaved. Hold strong, hold tight children
To the sky at night.

— *Daniel E. Wells*

Lights Off

Close your eyes and ride along the convolutions of your brain.
Yes this is Harrisburg, Pennsylvania and monsters are born here.
But forget about the monsters, they will soon disappear when the lights
Come on.
Sit between the Mad Hatter and Billy Budd.
Ask Father Time who his favorite is.
Mother Nature or Mother Goose?
Who are the blinder, the three mice or those three little pigs?
We can only see what we believe to be true.
Believe in yourself and you will see a beautiful person.

— *Kathleen M. Lambert*

Silence

I once heard a silence
A beautiful silence
And recorded it
Now when it's noisy
And people are yelling
I turn on my silence
As high as it will go
And sit and think
In my silence

— *Leif Husman*

Always

I'll always stay.
I'll always be there.
I'll always love you.
I'll always care.

I'll turn your skies
From gray to blue.
I'll love you forever,
Whatever you do.

— *Laura B. Garrett*

Box of Emotions

Sometimes I feel
I am trapped in a box,
With different emotions
Used as locks.

I don't understand
And I don't have the key,
I can't escape,
And I don't know me.

I'll find determination
To reach my goal,
To dig deep down
Into my soul.

I'll leave the box,
I know I can
And finally realize
Who I am.

—*Lisa McManus*

Loneliness
An empty promise
Leaves a lonely heart
An empty room
A devastated mind
And a confused state
So many people
So many empty promises
Too many lies
Unnumerable deceptions
Often leave, a frustrated being
A person who goes to all means
To end the emptiness and loneliness
A person like I
Who was deceived
By a person like you

—*Kelly A. Cruice*

Conception

The poem rested on my eyelids
The pupils carried it inside
Where the left side of brain
corrected it
The right side wrote it out

— *Lilla Carlson*

Love and Relationships

Examine each person with your mind
Before you do your heart
For feelings will often deceive you
And one's friendships fall apart.

— *John Hartzell*

Little Dewdrop

Little dewdrop laying
On this blade of grass
Glistening clearly as a raindrop
Awakening the morning light.

Little dewdrop slowly fading
From my sight this morn
Escaping into day's new freshness
As the morning dawns to light.

— *Joyce Johnson*

Untitled

I hide behind a mask of joy,
Hiding my feelings from you
And no matter how I try,
I can't ease the pain.
I stream and struggle
Into the night praying for help
To lift this mask of terror
But to no avail—
For even if I break free,
The mask will stay forever
—in my mind.

— *Jenna Wolfe*

The Vow

My vigil has been long;
Yet I remember.
Time passes with each new breath;
Still I remember.
The shades of passion which linger
Won't let me forget,
My promise of love, forever,
And forever it will be.

— *Judson Boulineau Jr.*

Inside Out

How come people look at others,
Judging them from the outside in;
Life can only be that much more unfair.
Trying to break from the past,
Only to relive it.

—*Christine Campion*

Meyer Lane

The scent of mimosa and pine
Fills the air.
Maples line the freshly
Paved road.
Sprinklers click rapidly,
Spraying smooth, clipped lawns.
The sound of basketballs, dogs and
Children echo through the neighborhood.
My neighborhood.

— *Janine M. Utell*

Over East and West

A man looks to the east
As the morning sun yellows the hazy air;
Fighting its way through the dense particles
To give an array of hope to the new day.
As the man looks on in wonder
At the immeasurable magic befronting him,
He realizes the awesome percipience of life's power.

His brother looks to the west
To see the bright, hopeful day that was,
Slowly being covered by a darkling shroud
Which squeezes the very depth of life from the sky.
And as the man watches the dying of the sun,
He can no longer feel his brother's untainted awe,
Only the hard restitution of the overpowering darkness.

— *Lynette Parry*

A State of Tension

A time for extension
Doubt attempts to destroy belief
There's never victory, never relief
You get lost in your dream and find pleasure in pain

The eyes that fall upon you, judge you as insane
Yet insanity is a word clearly opaque
And its attribution to you is clearly a mistake
True that life is contigent upon circumstance

But I know of no life that is void of chance
And when the pressure seems insurmountable
It's not the pressure, but you who is accountable
Synonomous are the words easy and hard

It's clearly a matter of personal regard, what is true is caused
By convictions so as to what's true there's no restriction,
In a frenzied state scream, *I will overcome* I'll take my chance
Because there might not be, another one.

—*Larry Youshah*

The Light at the End of the Tunnel

In this world when things are as gloomy as night,
You must continue down the tunnel to everlasting light.
In this life full of pain and hurt,
There is always a friend with an encouraging word.

In this world full of hatred and death,
Love continues to survive, refreshing, immaculate.
In this life when your world is falling apart,
You find a shoulder to lean on and comfort your heart.

In this world when depression sets in,
Remembrance of happier days forces you to grin.
In this life full of loneliness and despair,
There are always special friends that really do care.

In this world overflowing with sin,
Goodness is present which in the end will win.
In this life that consists of ups and down,
Thank you so much, God, for staying around.

—*Lonnie V. Curry*

Death of a Loved One

Life is now a cold, dark tunnel with nothing to feel but the cold,
Nothing to see but the darkness,
All feeling is gone.
An empty room, once full of laughter, is now silent;
Not a sound is heard.
Memories linger of happy times shared and sad times shared,
Making the long days bearable.
So we will love them and cherish them forever,
For they are all we are left with.
Nothing else.

— *Kristen Trainor*

During the Night

The soft music of the winds
blows through the trees
and makes them sway to the melody.
The crickets chirp and the animals
run wild making their homes for winter.
The little people scurry in to keep
warm and hide, once more,
from the dangers of the night.
The moon sits happily in the sky
watching over the children of the night,
only to disappear when a new day comes.
— *Juliett Coker*

In Touch With My Lord

As I stood there hand in hand
With all my life on shifting sand,
You took my hand and led me through
Now I find my life is new.

I felt the tingle and the fear
For yes, Lord, I knew You were near.
I asked forgiveness for sins of past
And You granted me with life that will last.

I pray for others in much need
Grant them health, oh Lord, with speed.
Let them tarry, not with pain
But let them spread Your word like rain.
—*Judy Quinn*

My Dream

I have a dream.
It doesn't matter what it is,
Just that it is mine.
It doesn't matter who tries to take it away,
As long as I dream it.
It doesn't matter what happens with my dream
As long as I hold it,
And rainy day will not dim my hopes,
For my dream stays bright.
Someone may try to stop me,
But it will not matter,
For my dream holds strong,
As long as I keep it.
— *Jessie Carlson*

Caring

Caring is a word of faith
Many have never used.
It's a word of love that very often
Is overly abused.
It deals with sharing and compassion;
And trust and concern;
Yet it's a word whose meaning
Many of us never learn.
It's a word that's linked to thoughtfulness
Of one for another,
And somehow carries the implication
That each man is my brother.
Simply put, it's a word that says
When a problem gets too overbearing,
We can handle it more easily
When we know someone is caring.
— *Charles E. Stickle*

Untitled

I can hear
But cannot see.
I feel wind
But I am not free.
Yes, I smile
But silently cry.
I don't care,
But yet know why.
I am numb
But still I feel.
I'm alive
Though I'm not real.
— *Judi Wallace*

Mommy and Daddy
    aren't
Mommy and Daddy
    anymore
They are
Mommy
   and
      Daddy
Never together
Sep
  ara
    ted
Such a separate word
never connected
where it should be.
—*Charlene Pesce*

The Game

Games start to finish,
Life begins to end.
What is more important,
How the game is played
Or who wins?
What is a winner
After the game is over?
—*Chris Warren*

Love Dies

Yes, it is true.
Love does die.
Love leaves suddenly
With no reason why.
After all these years,
You still do not learn.
You believe all the lies.
Only for love you yearn.
He plays his tricks
And wins the game.
It does not matter to him,
He has no shame.
Then it is all over
And no reason why.
Out of love.
Love does die.
—*Lori A. Wilhite*

The Table

As I sit at this table that used to sit eight
I can still remember where I placed each one's plate,
How at first glance, I knew when one was missing.
As I sit here, your dad and I just reminiscing.
It seems only yesterday you were here, bad manners and all.
Those were such beautiful years, family together, I love to recall.
Each child so special, each smile so priceless.
Times were hard, yet we managed through the crisis.
So many jokes were told, some a bit out of line.
So many problems were solved, even some of mine.
So many manners trying to be taught,
So much happiness to us each of you brought.
All my kids are married and have families of their own
But love is still with us, we are never alone.
You kids left, each one taking a piece of our heart.
Even now I miss you, it's always hard to part.
Yes, this old table has known all you dear hearts.
It seemed at this table, conversation was split in eight parts,
Each one taking his turn; you'd be surprised all Dad and I learned.
As I end this meal very quiet and content,
    only Dad and I can know what our love and family meant.
—*Lee W. Kahler*

An Ode to Ignorance

The concept of oppression has been with us for ages,
Espoused by the bleeding hearts, the judges and the sages;
They bid us all to hate the man who acts as an oppressor
While telling us that men are slaves because they are oppressed.

But we must be reminded of the partnership they share,
As they feed upon each other as a symbiotic pair...
When the misdirected power of the man who makes the rules
Afflicts as well the master as it does unto the fools.

There are a few of late who have reversed the roles as such,
To put the blame upon the men who seem to suffer much;
They tell us to despise the slaves who live their lives oppressed...
Who therefore give the power to the source of their duress.

The truth is that the weakness of the witless, stupid sheep
Is harmful as the strong arm of the men atop the heap;
Through ignorance they seemingly will drain each other's wells
While in the true reality they just afflict themselves.
—*Dale Patrick Hoffman*

Wish on a Falling Star

A shining star in the sky means something to us all.
We'd wait around forever, anticipating its fall.
You watch closely, squinting, hoping and praying
While the whole time you're wondering what your heart is saying.
You want to wish for peace or an everlasting love.
You want to wish for someday to make it to the heavens above.
Many things go through your mind
    and you wonder what it would be like to be blind.
Considering not being able to see what is up so far,
Not being able to wish on that long-awaited descending star.
Not being able to see it, but always feeling in the dark,
Not even seeing its dying spark. To think about it breaks my heart.
Broken hearted, I gaze up again, trying to imagine another wish.
I could wish for the world to be a perfect place
    or something vain like a beautiful face.
Or one day to be able to wear a white wedding dress all covered in lace.
The things I could wish for are endless and my shattered heart is mendless.
I finally snap out of my sorrow
    and realize that it is coming closer to tomorrow.
It will be daylight soon;
    nothing will be left visible in the sky, not even the moon.
The sun will fade all of my wishes away, then I'll be left standing there
    alone without having said a thing.
— *Kimberly Portulas*

Light for All Seasons

Winter solstice.
A time of revaluation,
Spiritual, mental, emotional.
Summer shines forth,
Days pass as light walks with me.
The reflection shines upon me.
One season ends, another begins.
Look back to love and memories.
But, the step forward,
Will transcend the one behind.
Security lies not in where I am,
Or what I am doing,
But who I am—and where I'm going.
In the seasons of life,
I'm following a light
Which will never go out-
Jesus Christ—today, tomorrow,
In seasons forever!

 —*Erma J. Sybil*

Christmas Season's Drawing Near

Christmas season's drawing near and people on the street
Are wishing Christmas joy and cheer to everyone they meet.
The folks are dressing up their shelves with mistletoe and holly
To wait for Santa and his elves to make things nice and jolly.
Kids are playing in the yard hoping with all their might
That it will start to snow real hard to make this Christmas white.
While the dads are out buying special treats,
The moms are all inside baking Christmas sweets.
When Christmas Eve rolls around, the little girls and boys
Will fall asleep all snug and sound and dream of Christmas toys.
On Christmas day before the sun has come out to shine,
The children want to have some fun so down the stairs they climb.
They race each other to the tree to see their brand new toys,
And in the middle of their glee, they hear a tiny noise.
You two kids should be in bed, they heard somebody say.
Santa Claus then turned his head and simply flew away.
As they heard the jingle of Saint Nicholas's sled,
They said, *Goodbye Kris Kringle* and scurried off to bed.

 —*Wendy Sue Parnell*

The Babe in a Manager

It's Christmas, a time of rejoicing and love.
A time that our savior was sent from above.
Our lord who was born of a virgin that day
Was laid in a manger, in fragrance of hay.

His star shone above as the prophesy said,
To guide a few worshippers there to his bed.
The wise men brought gifts and the shepherds adored
While angels above them sang in a great horde.

This Jesus who, born on this first christmas day,
Secured our forgiveness from going astray.
He suffered and died for forgiveness of sin
For all who repented and followed him in.

He gave all his life for the love of us all,
To teach us and lead us that we may not fall.
We honor his birthday by giving with love
And honoring Jesus who rules from above.

 —*Gay E. Ray*

Winter Is Near

The sky looks so beautiful at night
While the stars sparkle so bright
As the brisk wind blows in the air,
Makes me know that winter is near.
And the leaves begin to fall from the trees
While I stand there and face the nice cool breeze.
It brings back memories of years ago
When I used to play in the fresh falling snow.
I'd go upstairs to get nice and warm
And hppy to hear we're having a storm.
Tomorrow, no school and I'd have all day
To get dressed warm and go outside to play.
Though I am older, I still love to hear
The sound of winter and the breeze in my hair.
And I still love to walk in the fresh falling snow
And the thrill of my children feeling the same, I know.

 — *Carol Veldran*

The Winds of Winter

The winds of winter blow so harsh
Stripped the trees and left them bare
Starkly silhouetted against the sky
Like soldiers marching to some far battle
Forever marching never to die
With no where to rest and no one to care
The winds of winter blow so bitter
They howl across the open fields
Destroying everything in their path
Turning the flowers and golden leaves to litter
Whirling them in furious wrath
Leaving them to die alone and forgotten
The winds of winter blow so harsh stripping the trees and
Baring their souls with empty branches lifted toward the sky
Not trees at all just actors playing a role, come the sun and
Spring softly weeping ah but they were not dead, only sleeping.

 —*Geneva N. Jobe*

Slow Songs

I remember those times when we went out,
The slow songs that we heard.
Your eyes so serious, your gentle touch,
And yet you spoke not a word.
Passion, loneliness, sadness, fun,
When we were together our hearts were one.
Those silent memories,
Each enchanting kiss,
Now apart from you
These times I miss.
Locked deep in my heart are these memories,
Each one a burning flame.
Sometimes I hear those same slow songs
And wish things were the same.

— *Jennifer Ramsour*

One Single Rose

One single rose,
the beauty of its opening bud,
with dew slipping off every moist petal.
One single rose,
providing so much joy
as the color rushes to the cheeks
of a flattered young girl.
One single rose,
with its beauty and splendor
lasting as long as
a compliment.
One single rose,
as weather and age
have withered away
to a lost memory.
One single rose,
now just a reminder of the past; gone,
with his fleeting love.

—*Jennifer Raney*

October Days

There's something special about the fall
And the maple tree standing tall
Amidst the forest in a blaze
Wearing the blush of October days.
It's time to harvest and gather food,
Lulling the earth to a somnolent mood.
It is the time when the country bumpkin
Finds icy fingers have brushed the pumpkin.
It was this month of witches and ghosts
That Columbus sailed toward his trading post.
Autumn leaves and Indian summer haze
Embrace the hills on October days.

— *Dixie Ruth Cook*

A New Life

A seed has been planted, a seed has been sown.
Nurture that seed until it has grown.
Give it love, and give it care.
Your life, with this seed, you will share.

This seed has been planted by God above.
Sent to you for you to love.
Care and patience, you must bestow,
On this seed, as you help it grow.

A lovely flower, this seed will soon be,
As your love for life, it will always see.
It will blossom, and at times it will wilt.
It will thrive on the roots that you have built.

As you age, your accomplishment will be shown,
For this seed, in reality, is a child of your own.

—*Jeanne Swicklas*

Untitled

Where did they
Get this ideas
Of God?
What is he,
Santa Claus?
What is he,
Your tailor?
Don't bother
Him
He's thinking.
Besides, how would
You like it,
Being pestered
All the time by a lot of people
Who won't go out
And get jobs?

—*Janet Mullins*

Child Abuse

Why does it have to happen?
It happens every day
To so many different people
In so many different ways.

One child is beaten
And one teenager died,
One adult listened
While another child cried.

This thing that happens
Is so very sad,
To think that a child is beaten
By its Mom or Dad.

— *Janet Darlene White*

India

Oh India,
You shall hold my heart
    when it ceases to give me life
You shall take my hand
    caressing it when it is limp
You shall warm my soul
    against your sun drenched breast
    when my body is cold
You shall fill my ears with songs of bells
    when they know only silence
I shall smile with my tears
    as they join your rains
    to fill the Ganges
And my last breath
    will whistle with your winds
    across the deserts of Rajastan
    as we become united for eternity.

—*Janet Whitehead*

Young Love

When you started out
They said, *what is this all about?*
They are too young
To understand the meaning of love.
That was five years ago,
So it is apparent that they don't know
Love has no age limit.
It is the two of you that make the difference.
As you continue to walk through life hand in hand,
Just remember others opinions don't stand.
The power of love
Goes far above,
Those opinions
Of any one man.

— *Jeff A. Zysset*

What is This?

When all else fails,
Go to a friend to talk.
With them there are no gales.
Talking will be with no balk,
They will always be there
With a listening ear.
Never into them throw a scare,
Because to them you are dear.
But in return you must listen.
You must help them with their problems.
'Cause if you don't you're missin'
Of course we don't always have problems.
You always have fun with them,
Even if your humor is dry.
They are there to help you off your limb.
To say something a friend once said to me,
Try!

— *Janice Hall*

Island

I am an island,
Tropical and green
I am an island...a sight to be seen
With crystal blue waters
That tickle my shore
With miles of sand, and much, much more
With bright summer sun,
Light spring breeze,
And scattered clusters of tropical trees
With every sunrise the island comes alive,
To see a new day, awake, revive
With every sunset the moon comes along
To sing a heavenly, mystical song
Yes, I am an island as beautiful as can be
But I wish that someday
Someone would find me.

—*Dawn Pesola*

Yesterday

Wasn't it yesterday when we were friends?
Wasn't it yesterday we were making amends?
Scheming and ruling, we had it all down,
Holding on to the friendship together we found.
Living and laughing together,
Making playful fun of each other,
But that was yesterday, now it's today.
Broken promises, so now we both pay.
When the trust is forgotten, so is the friend.
Now all there is to do is start over again.

— *Jennifer Osborn*

Easter

Easter is when Christ the Lord arose
Which everyone in their own way knows.
The jealous people lied
So everyone thought it'd be right if He died.

The people made Him wear a crown of thorn,
But never, not once, did He start to mourn.
They beat Him with a whip
Somewhere right near the hip.

When He died,
He had been crucified.
So when He arose,
He proved that He was Christ to His foes.

— *Dawn Thompson*

Lost Love

The love we had
I'll always cherish.
The love we had
I'll never change.

No other man
Has swept me off my feet
The way you did
When we would meet.

I wish to God
That you would come back,
But my wish hasn't come true
Yet!

I loved you then.
I love you now.
And if my wish comes true,
My love will grow
By every minute
In hopes that yours will too.

—*Jennifer Pollock*

The River

Drop by drop, a life begins,
As tiny droplets hit the water
Of a prospering spring.
Pitter patter,
The rain begins to fall.
Growing larger by the second.
Over flowing with confusion.
Now swiftly flowing down to a
River of challenges.
Changing directions at a rapid pace.
Billowing over obstacles now faced.
Easily raged.
Yet as it reaches its final destiny,
Open, free, peaceful, and calm,
Its graceful motions lie a rest
A mind at ease.
And an adult life springs forth
From its depths.

—*Jennifer Rader*

Winter Sky

Orange streaks quickly descend,
As another day of winter ends.
Twilight comes and all is dark,
Except for a star which gives off a spark.

Dawn comes and all is light,
Except for a cloud which is mostly out of sight.
Winter skies seem so cold,
Just like fall skies, they are also bold.

—*Jennifer Baker*

Daylight's Triumph

The bright darkness
Up above,
Greets the rain,
In a strangelove.

Down below,
Puddles of pain
Look like footprints
From the rain.

Daylight brought me back to life,
Nature's timeclock is waking,
Drying the tears with pennies of sunshine,
A new day begins...

And I smile.

— *Jeanne Michelle Gonzalez*

You Being with Me

They say, *Time heals all wounds,*
But this time that we're apart only creates them...
There is a wound in my heart that yearns for your care,
A wound in my soul that I cannot bear...
No doctor can heal
The wounds I feel.
It's a pain I can't describe
And there is no medicine to prescribe.
No bandage can stop the bleeding, nothing to stop the pain,
Only you with me again.
Now you see, it's you I need.
Only you can stop this pain I bear.
All it takes is your love and your care
And you being with me!

—*Jenny Samaras*

Sonnet On A Smile

When skies were bright, when sunshine filled my world,
When friends were near and laughter was the style,
You caught the light, your hair all tossed and curled,
And I could hear the music of your smile.

The sun, now low, casts shadows on the sand,
The friends, apart, remembered for so long,
And now the glow when I enfold your hand,
And in my heart, I feel your warm, sweet song.

The night's above, the sun's beyond the hill.
The friends are gone, and memories mean so much.
But you, my love, so warm and warmer still,
Await the dawn, and I await your touch.

We walked our walk in sunshine and in rain,
And now we talk of feelings felt again.

—*Edward Robert Raupp*

A Married Woman

It is a love affair of sorts.
The kind that never should have been.
The kind where someone else comes first.
And we try to hold on to something
That is not really there.
And what we have
We have through stolen minutes
At lunches where we do not eat.
In the car where embraces are tinged with guilt
While we watch to see if we are being watched.
We make promises we know we cannot keep,
About feelings that cause shame instead of pleasure
What's he like, I wonder.
But I know it does not matter.
This will end as it began, longing eyes meet,
They send messages that need no words.
It is a love affair...of sorts.

—*Jim Kise*

Untitled

A thesaurus will not say what needs to be said
And words are weak when feelings are deep,
But sometimes the truth tries too hard.

So please do not touch what you cannot see until
I can feel what you cannot say,
Because I will never find a dictionary definition
For this intensity.

I am not saying I do not understand
Or that I am afraid to learn,
But everytime I take a breath, you take it away.
So lie with me and define our love
Before I find a book that will.

—*Jennifer Kemper*

They Exist

Alf and E.T.,
I believe you can exist.
Sure, Mr. Know-It-All,
There's no life beyond?!
Why, then, do creatures
Thrive here?
I believe
There's any chance
Mr. Spock
Will beam down here,
Right now.
Maybe Mork will meet Mindy...
Today, maybe.
So don't scoff any
Of those big-time astronomers
That scan the stars...
They may be real close by!

—*Jennifer Ray*

Dirty Dishes

I made a dish entirely new,
It really was a tasty stew,
And even Father said so too.
Now I'm left...with dirty dishes!

The T-V calls...the program's rare,
And father sits in his easy chair,
And how I'd love to be in there.
Instead of here...with dirty dishes.

They seem to look at me and grin,
And what I'm thinking is a sin,
But in the end I know they'll win.
Those awful, dirty dishes.

I'll hide those things out of my sight,
And put them in the sink tonight,
And wash them come the morning light.
I'll get even...with dirty dishes!

—*Dorothy Nickerson*

Without You

A flower is among
Natures most beautiful creations,
Yet when the petals separate,
Falling from their stem,
The beauty of the flower
Is carried away
With the silent wisp
Of the wind.
I rely on you,
As that single flower
Depends upon its petals
To make it whole.
We fit together perfectly,
As one creation; but apart from you
I am but the stem of our relationship.
I am not the same
Without you.

—*Deborah A. Kovacs*

Grandma

Grandma is a friend;
She will be loved after the end.
Grandma will never die,
She will live forever in the sky,
Grandma will soon be called by God,
To live with him forever even,
Though she is loved,
From earth to heaven.

— *JaNell Davidson*

It Is

Like the beauty of a blooming rose, and...
Of the rain when the fierce wind blows.
Like...the dawning of these new days and
Of the sun with its blinding rays.
Like the warmth of a newly built fire, and...
Of my love you're the one I desire.
Like the passion of lovers intertwined, and...
Of the days you're on my mind
Like...the wonder of a story book tale, and...
Of my dreams I cannot prevail.
And...like...our friendship of lasting pleasure, and...
Of my life, our love, I'll always treasure.

—Jacqueline Boucher

On the Threshold of a Dream...

They stand, hand in hand, in wonder
He and she, together, gazing yonder
Let's take a chance! says she.
I can't, I am afraid! says he.

She sees a rainbow; he sees just rain.
She sees adventure, freedom; he fears pain.
Take a chance, take a chance, she whispers.
I can't, I can't, he moans.

Reach, reach for the moon! says she.
I'll fall, I'll fail, says he.
*So what? So what if you fail to reach the moon
And you fall among the stars!
Is that so bad? Try, take a chance.*

No, no! I'll fail...wait...don't leave...don't go!
...And she is gone.
...And he remains...alone...lonely...
Ever on the threshold of a dream.

—Dorothy J. Dunn

Scream your Silence

He is borne, wafted on his dreams,
Visual streams of dreams in his eyes.
Dreams grown in the world of weird,
Running across dream worlds, and
Knowing the terrors of darkness;
Though he sees for he dreams light.
In his dream worlds, there is no suns,
Only reflections.

Why does he run and run in his dreams.
With screams in streams from his mouth?
There is a cornucopia of silence with
Only the visual of sound to hear with
Dream eyes.

He cannot hear for he left behind his skeleton,
His conductivity, and dreams of light reflected.
The evils of myth inhabit his dreams, as odd and
Familiar people of his peopled dream worlds
Run screaming their silence.

—James B. Baker

My Dearest Friend

The years will pass and we'll grow old,
But we will have our memories to hold.
My dearest friend, I cannot express the love we share,
The kind special friends should have.
My dearest friend, we are so close, but yet we are so far.
Will our friendship stand the test of time?
My dearest friend, this is a question for only you and I.

— Allison J. Sutherlin

Sky of Dreams

I see a sky of vast blue.
I feel the eternal dream of each cloud moving by.
It seems so close.
But when I look it shows me the enduring reality.
I wonder why a blue so beautiful can hide the hope of every unborn dream.
I wonder why clouds smooth out the lost dream of eternal pain.
And this is when I see that the sky of blue shows the dream,
And the morning sky of clouds hides the enduring pain.

And even know some dreams are hid behind smooth white clouds.
There is always one that rides the clouds onto the sky of vast blue dreams.
Which is a world of unborn dreams, faded into reality.

—Jennifer Pyles

Death

Darkness swept across me with a surge of pain.
People gathered 'round to see the place where my body lay.
My soul crept slowly upward to the sky and clouds above.
The only thing to pull me was a little white dove.
He pulled me to a golden gate where a man sat quietly by
Asking only if I wished I had some wings by which to fly.
I nodded, looking past the gates where a bright light shined,
Asking only if he knew if Heaven was nearby.
*Yes, my dear, you are here from where death becomes a new life.
Welcome to God;s home, where you belong, We hope you will never roam.*
Softly, gold and silver bells shimed the hour of the day
Then the gates opened to where the children quietly play.

— Jessica Willis

Somewhere

Somewhere, a flower is blooming.
Langourously opening her petals for the sun's benediction.
Somewhere, a child is starving,
Confused, frightened, not knowing where to turn.
Somewhere, a man cries out in pain and is quickly silenced,
Choked by the fetid smell of death and garbage.
Somewhere, a butterfly is flying through an abundant field of daisies,
Pausing here and there listening...listening to the rushing of the wind.
Somewhere, a baby is born...into despondency, depravity and neglect
To a girl who has no home.
Somewhere, a child plays in the sewer
Trying to ignore the hunger that threatens to consume him.
Somewhere, a waterfall is rushing into a small pond
Amongst the twittering of birds and wandering deer with her fawn.
Somewhere, a child is crying...

—Jennifer R. Van Duzer

The Search

Have you ever roamed and wandered in a search for something gone,
Looking desperately to find it and the place where you belong?
In a little room or castle, wondering which it may be,
Maybe in a field or meadow, within the serenity.

Could it lie beneath the ocean in the calm and tranquil deep?
'Neath the ruins of Atlantis in a hibernating sleep?
Or among celestial bodies moving silently in space?
Maybe on the wings of Saturn, if I look I'd find a trace.

But my journey's growing hopeless yet within my angry shell
I relentlessly keep looking for the place where it might dwell.
Though I'm weary and I'm beaten, when I'm knocked upon the ground,
I keep picking up the pieces, patching each one as it's found.

For I must continue searching on a quest that never ends,
Fighting obstacles before me, finding now and then a friend
Till one day amongst the shadows comes a small light from within.
Then I'll feel the glow enfold me and I'll be made whole again.

— Gloria Ember Nelson-Grier

Destiny

Destiny will be
When you educate your mind
Set your thoughts free
And to yourself be kind.
You're here for a reason
Don't question the thought
You'll change like the seasons
So keep peace in your heart.
A power you possess
Is to hear your soul's voice
Souls free of dreams die a slow death
Give it life it's your given choice.
Don't frown on your plans
For life can be fair
To those that really care
How you live is in your hands.
Destiny will be
When you kill self doubt
When you're ready to see
Destiny will be.

—*Robert G. Yeager*

With Me or Without Me

Sitting here alone
I think of days gone by.
Soon I start to laugh
And then I begin to cry.

We've been together
Through lots of difficult times,
Through many changes
And heard many clocks chime.

Although soon you will leave me
For another one,
You know I'll always care
And our love can't ever be undone.

Times do change
And with them so must we,
So go on into life
With or without me.

—*Darrah Sanders*

Ballin the Jack

Eyes closed,
The mind paints pictures.
Hands caress the bat.
Batter up!
The ball is pitched.
The bat kisses the ball.
Up, up it glides.
Down, down it smoothly comes.
Bases.
First, second, third, steal home.
The crowd erupts.
You open your eyes.
The crowd is gone,
You are alone.

—*R. A. Melos*

Self Preservation

Apples drying in the sun.
Apple pies and purple plums.
Jars of apples on a shelf.
Jams and jellies for myself.
Through the winter and the spring,
No matter what tomorrow brings.
There will be food
For a peasant or a king.

— *Marie Wills*

A Day In the Life

Sunshine on a river bank
Complete grace of movement
Shared with gentle sighs
As the eternal heartbeat
Within the self subsides
As the released arrow from the bow
Destiny unfolds
Open sandy arms
Scorched by the mid day sun
In unpitying self denial
Sunshine fading-the river flows
A servant to time
Closed eyes-in silent prayer
Searching for truth of the self
Reaching for a day in the life
In the temporary-tomorrow

—*Mary L. Williams*

There are no faces here
There are no people
There are only childlike dreams,
Infantile creations
And schoolyard sameness...
There are no splashes
Of creativity
No difference
Here, in the American Commons...
Only...
    colorless faces
    with plain featurres
    and no names...

— *Cathy Salustri*

Viewpoints

Someday I would like to see
What other people see in me.
Do they see just face or hair?
Or do they see what isn't there?
Can they see what's underneath,
That which makes us all unique?
Do they even want to know
The things we try so not to show?
Those hidden secrets, pains and fears,
Tucked away for years and years.
Just once I'd truly like to view
The outer shell they think is true.
Or maybe they instead could touch
The inner me that feels so much.
So sad that this can only be
A dream but not reality.

— *Hazel M. McClain*

The Summer's End

It is going to be a lonely year,
Even though I know you are near.
If only I could let you know,
About all my feelings deep below.
When I look at you, my heart
Begins to shutter.
When I listen to your voice, my
Stomach begins to flutter.
Eventually our time will begin,
When we are back together again.
Even though the time is slow,
Just how long we will never know
Summer has come and gone,
Now it is up to us to keep this
Going on.

—*Tanya Kay Estelle*

My Love

First turmoil;
Confusion
Waves and winds spin
Me around
Flying here and
Drifting
To other shores
Winds die down
And direction
Is found
And then
The seagull,
Like my love,
Come to rest
On you,
My shore.

— *Les Kato*

A Prayer to the Great Spirit

Each day, O Manitou
I ask you most humbly
For your wisdom to live
As you have intended
With strength and love for all,
A sense of fairness and
Justice for everyone,
Opportunities for all
To live to the fullest
Serenity and peace
For all of my children;
And life with security
For all the children of
The Great Spirit. Amen.

—*Mary R. Kellar*

Coming and Going

The wind blows
Then it snows
The baby cries
The summer dies
The bells ring
The people sing

The wind will still blow,
Days will still come and go

The baby will still cry
But summer never says good-bye

— *Maribeth Zanone*

Heaven Is Not a Place

Heaven is not a place
It is a woman
It is you
It is the thing that you are,
It is the things that you do
Heaven is not a reward,
For the good who have died young
It is you, my song of beauty
And you are waiting to be sung
And heaven is not the abode,
Of angels in white
It is simply loving you, my love
Every day and night
Other men live good lives,
And hope that heaven, their achieving
But when my good life with you ends,
I know it is heaven I will be leaving.

—*D. Burnett Wells*

To You

valentine,
To you I give my heart
I haven't much to offer
in fact it's all I have.

To you I give it fully
in return from you
I ask not a thing.

Accept it graciously
 or
return it piece by piece.
valentine,
This, from me to you.

— *LynnEtte Mueller*

Faithfully

I have asked myself again and again
Why did I let go?
Why did I let it end?
I suppose it was better for us to be apart.

But sometimes it hurts
The pains deep inside my heart.
I will never really understand
Just why I let it go.
We could have tried to work it out.

Deep in my heart I know
I have tried to call several times,
But you are never home.

I really should get over you
But that is not really easy to do.
I guess I will end this now
If you ever need me I want you to know
I will still be there, faithfully.

—*Monica Masaraki*

A Smile

A smile is a ray of sunshine
To a lonely and broken heart.
A smile can bring back together,
Two lovers who have been driven apart.

A smile can show forgiveness,
Even before a word is said.
Good will is shown through a smile,
Through smiles it will spread.

Keep smiling, even when all goes wrong.
Your hardships won't last for long.
Keep smiling, even when you're feeling blue.
Happier times will soon be due.
Keep smiling, even when you want to cry.

—*Sharon L. Raymond*

I'm Blind

I'm blind to see nothin'.
Now I see the beautiful world.
You opened the doors to my life and my heart.
You opened the doors to my dreams.
I was blind but now I'm awakened to
See your beautiful face.
Don't abandon me now that I can see.

— *Corinne Mullaney*

Ballerina's Awakening

She danced, with perfection,
On pointed toe,
Like a humming bird poised
On a tilted limb.
Her petite breast exploded
With joy
As he vowed his undying love.
So until the limb swayed
Or the dance ended,
She would believe.

—*Nadine Marx*

I'll Be There

Though things are rough
and the going gets tough
...I'll be there.
If she finds another guy
and you just want to die
...I'll be there.
If the rainbow dies
and your heart cries
...I'll be there.
Don't hesitate to call
anytime at all
...I'll be there.
When all else fails
my smile prevails
...I'll be there.
When the sky goes gray
all you have to say is, *She'll be here.*
...and I will.

—*Lorraine Jetland*

A Painful Good-Bye

pouring raindrops
they seem to forever fall
never ending teardrops
good-byes are so sad
long wind storms
they blow so hard
terribly mixed up emotions
good-byes are so sorrowful
will any of this ever stop
will I ever see this person again

— *Stacy Kinyon*

Should I Give Up?

Should I give up?
Or keep on trying?
I'm so confused
that I feel like crying.
Do you likeme
or are you a flirt?
Please tell me now
before I get hurt!
Sometimes you talk to me
which makes my day
and sometimes you don't
so with my heart I pay!
You act like you like me
then shove me away.
If this is a game,
I don't want to play.
So if you're afraid
of what your friends might say,
please tell me the truth,
should I give up today?

—*Jodi Trees*

Young, Strong and Beautiful

I enjoyed sitting under the weeping willow tree.
Shaded comfort from the hot sun it provided me.
It stood so tall; it reached to the sky,
Hung low numerous branches, it breathed a sigh.
My arms could not surround its trunk so wide.
At times it proved a good place to hide.
It was quite old, many roots were showing.
Grammar school, high school, its leaves gently blowing.
I promised to bring my children someday to see
That wonder of wonders, most beautiful tree.
It stood alone in a grassy vacant lot,
Uprooted, discarded, not for age or rot,
Replaced with houses for couples young and new,
The old weeping willow gone from view.
Not many to remember that willow tree
When young, strong and beautiful, full of glee.

— *Mena Crescenzo*

Innocence Lost

In innocence he came to me,
Imagining some vague dream of what could be.
He gave me a gift to prove his love.
He had saved it for sixteen years, a beautiful, porcelain dove.

To him I gave a golden ember that soothed his heart from pain
But because we were forced into maturity, it was a loss instead of a gain.
Now we are marked. We used to be beautiful and pure.
Reality has set in. It destroys hope once more.

The porcelain dove has fallen and lays shattered on the ground.
Our dreams of trust and happiness have all turned upside-down.
The ember burns within his heart like a piercing flame.
Only emptiness and haunting memories remain.
Even though we shed tears of regret and sorrow,
We cannot erase the pain we will endure tomorrow.

—*Melonie Fontenat*

Remembering

Remembering yesterday, dreaming of tomorrow
Looking back at special memories
Burying all the sorrow.
Forgetting all the hurt, learning to trust again
Developing new relationships, starting out as friends.
Allowing my love to grow, letting you plant the seed
Nourishing it with your strength and love,
You meeting its every need.
Remembering our moments together, our spirits were free to soar
Thinking of you every day and
Remembering until I can remember no more...

—*Tess Cooper*

A Wanderer Muses

All those different places I have seen.
Some I recall, others so long ago have left my mind.
I remember traces of where I have been.
Some barren and cold.
Like marble statues, dirty, cracking, old shades of grey.
Some were friendly and warm.
Bold blazing fires, calling, thawing on winter's day.
Seeing people's faces as if in a dream.
Can't quite remember from where, or even when I knew them.
Those bright faces I still recall, others almost hidden, remain dim.
Some I wish I had never known.
Stealing special feelings, weaving scars upon my memory.
Some I long to see again.
Remembering those gentle ones, tenderly renews the world I see.
As life leads me on, to places I have never seen before,
I often enjoy looking back upon my life to find
Exactly why it is I long to see, more and more and more.

—*Michael Davis-King*

Echoes in the Darkness

Footsteps creeping along down the hall.
Creaking doors.
The smell of alcohol creeping under the door
Not again, she screams inside.
Panic stricken, tears fill her eyes.
Please Mommy, hear the sounds and wake-up; realize
Knowing that will not happen,
She hides under the covers, clinging to her teddy bear
As the door opens.
The smell of alcohol fills her room,
As she feels a cold hand on her arm.
Horror fills her eyes, as he satisfies his hunger.
Stripping her of her youth
Forcing her into believing that she is bad.
What can she do, nobody will believe her, everyone will blame her.
Believing that she is trapped, she silently cries herself to sleep.
Praying that the echoes in the darkness will desist.

—*Michele Sunderland*

I Wonder

As I look up at the blue sky, or see the rainbow or the birds
Gliding...oh so high, I wonder where is heaven?
And is it more beautiful than all of this?

As I feel the peace when I stroll quietly in the forest and
See the animals playing and the butterflies sitting on the flower petals
I wonder is heaven like this?

When it thunder and lightenings or people get so angry and speak of war
When there is hunger all around and broken hearts
People wonder where is God? Does He love us and does he care?
Where is all the love and peace He told us of?

Do we have to wait for heaven and find all the beauty
Or is it here and we just fail to see
Are we too busy hurting each other and striving for wealth to see his Love
Or walk quietly in the woods and feel his peace?

Do we have to wait for heaven and find it there?
I wonder...if we would just open our eyes and see and open our hearts in
    prayer
If we could find the love and peace right here?

—*Marlene Stevens*

We'll Have Big Fun

Summer comes and goes, but our love depends on us.
To make or break, or do or die, time has no stand still.
As we love each other with so much going on in the world,
Yes life is very short indeed, that is why we must live one day at a time.
'Cause in the meantime we'll be having fun; we'll have a little fun.

Please be with me; it takes two to tango
and you are my private party of fun.
 We'll have a real good time 'cause it don't have to be
A different situation or a victim of circumstances.
'Cause in the meantime we'll have a little fun, we'll have a little fun.

There's no time like the right time, no matter what.
A little fun to the end; we can do it; we are a team.
Before you go to work, we'll have a little fun,
In the meantime, we'll have a little fun.
We will...we will do...we'll plan it together, trust me.
'Cause nothing can stop us, oh no; we're on the move.
Be real, get real, we are real; we'll have so much fun together.
Always be by my side, as one;
we are the role model for LOVE for the young.
Down with dope; up with hope. Be real; get real. You can do it.
In the meantime, we'll be having fun, fun, fun. Are you positive?

—*Michael Gary*

Because You're My Friend

If I could have
A better life
I would want the friends
Who were always there
To share
Each other's lives
Over chilled ice tea tasting
As sweet as the memories we share
Together. If I could plan my days ahead
Of all those friends
I'd want you near to share
The memories and secrets
Good or bad;
Because I love you
Because you're my friend.

— *Ana Cook*

The Empty Chair

There's an empty chair in the news room now,
Just one empty chair; it makes a difference somehow.
There's one less smile, one less cheery hello
And that voice and laughter we all used to know.

There's an empty chair where sat a real friend
And I pray to God it didn't have to come to an end.
Just think of the thrill we'll have
Meeting loved ones who've gone on before;
Think of the joy and the happiness,
Yhen think of the parting no more.
(Dedicated to: Jerry Turner)

— *Floyd J. Kantz*

Why I Laugh

I laugh, though my heart may be breaking!
I laugh, to cover up my tears, you see!
I laugh, and I encourage others,
To laugh along with me!

Don't you give in to feelings of deep despair!
Laugh, let your heart be merry and gay!
For laughter is a gift that God gives to His own,
To take their cares and fears all away!

So I laugh when I feel lonely,
And I laugh when I am scared or alone.
I laugh if I find myself becoming depressed,
I laugh, and once again, secure in His love,
I know that to Him, I do belong!

— *Bernice Couey Bishop*

A Wish

A child cries from hunger,
It's small hand reaches out.
The mother worn from childbirth and poverty,
Slowly tries to gain strength, an instinct to protect.
Begins to breastfeed the child.

A teardrop rolls down her cheek,
It crosses many lines on her face.
Not from age, but from despair, hunger and pain.

The child now sleeps and the mother lays it down.
She looks out into the night, the stars so many,
She sees one falling fast, she remembers a poem.
A poem from her childhood, about wishing on a star.
She makes her wish, yet knowing that nothing changes,
Unless a miracle, could it be!
She lays beside the child, they sleep a long, deep sleep.
But, she'll they awaken?
Only God knows, the wish she made.
A wish of a mother and her child.

— *Bennie Branson*

Epilogue

In writing my life's story, should you
 Arrive at the Epilogue;
Say, *He came not from beast nor was he
 Related to the frog.
He was but a plant that grew, flowered
 Awhile; then death overpowered.
He loved his God from the depth of a gentle,
 Kindly heart.
From this sin-sick world he was not hesitant
 To depart.
He sought no honor offered by this world
 But longed for paths that angels trod.
Through streets of gold near gates pearl'd;
 There he sups forever with the Lamb of God.*

— *Bob Brown*

Untitled

It hurts to know all I can hold
Are memories locked within my mind.
I pray to God they will not fade
With the cruel passing of time.
What would I give to go back in years
When the tears I shed were for joy;
Our Mom brought home
Our dear *man child,*
Her long-awaited little boy,
But now I cling desperately
To twenty-two years of memories.
I won't permit a single one
To slip from my heart, dear Sammy,
Until the day I can hold you
And never have to say, *Good-bye,*
Knowing our love was not in vain
Nor all the tears we've cried.

— *Pam Hovanec*

Me and You

Me and you;
We went through a lot together,
I was having the time of my life
And I thought it would last forever.

Me and you;
So many new experiences we have shared,
I knew you were always there for me
When no one else cared.

Me and you;
I guess in the end things didn't work out,
But now that it's over
My love for you I will never doubt.

Me and you;
All that is left are memories
And there is nothing more I can do,
But no matter what happens now,
I know I will still love you.

— *Nicole Palmer*

Children Ask

What in this world is worth living for?
They say watch us close 'cause we are the future.
Can't they see the mistakes they're making?
We know and
We see.
They say we're children and don't know anything.
Sometimes I feel that we know more than they know.
Why can't they see the world from a child's eye?
Can't they see back to when they were young?
Or have they forgotten?

— *Ayron Sequeira*

View from my Window

The rain still falls
But it is not the same.
I watch as it drops
On my window pane.

My lonely tears fall,
As I think of the pain.
My tears are falling,
Along with the rain.

My window protects me,
From the cold of the rain.
But what will protect me,
From this kind of pain.

Your love is my window,
My protection from pain.
I will stand in this window,
And watch the rain.

— *Wendy Greene*

Haiku

Car screeches to a stop.
Time to react; time to think;
Just an accident.

— *Adina Astor*

Not of This World

Here I lie in a comatose state,
There's nobody home upstairs.
I know not of this world.
My soul is crying to get out.
I do not want to exist as a
Sleeping person.
I cry to be released from my
Silent agony.
Please dear God take me now,
So I can leave this silent shell.

— *Bonnie Brundage*

Silent Torture

What is he thinking?
For I fear,
It is not about me.
I wait patiently
For a sign
To tell me he cares.

Sitting here my mind wanders
To a far off land of memories.
His touch I feel,
again
His voice I hear again,
Forever, ringing through my head.

I can't take it.
The cuts
Bleed
Of this...
Silent torture.

— *Andrea Heap*

Rain

Quiet doth the rain...she fall
Knocking at the door.

Cleaning the air
Purifying the earth;
And bringing peace,
To those
Who feel
The rain.

— *Pauline Bonnici*

Subourbon River

It takes one drink
To start the flow
They never think
Of how it grows,
But comes the day
For heaven's sake
That you must pay
For your mistake,
And so you drown
Your poor liver
With just a frown
In Subourbon River.

—*Zachary Berman*

No More Tears

Everything seems so close to me
Up here in the sky,
As I watch
Everything go by.
It seems as if
Life went by so fast,
As I remember
My life in the past.
But now
It is okay,
Because from now on
I will be so far away.
I am away
From any troubles or fears,
And now
There will be no more tears.

—*Ashley Smith*

Awareness

Awareness is discovery
Of beauty, love, security.
Awareness holds a mystic power,
That of an ancient passion flower.
Awareness leaves no fear
It ripens year by year.
Awareness opens every door
To knowledge...the essential core.

Awareness of the universe
Inspires man from planet earth.
Awareness made great history,
On moon within this galaxy.
But awareness of a tiny seed
Is life itself and love indeed.
And awareness at maturity
Holds wisdom and tranquillity.

—*Elfriede Elisabeth Ruppert*

Friendship

Friendship is:
Kind deeds to that special one
Always having lots of fun.
Calling each other in the phone
To make sure they got home.

Friendship is:
Giving advice
And always trying to be nice.
Sharing cookies at the malt shop,
Double dating to the sock hop.
Always saying you'll be together
For ever and ever and ever and ever.

—*Bridgette Meiners*

The Believer

Winds that blow,
Hills that sigh,
Standing alone
Watching the world fly by.
Wishing that someone was near
To share the moments of peace
Yet in the meantime,
You keep them hidden
Never to be told,
But in the heart they are written.
So the time alone
On the hillside you stand,
Never to be held in anyone's hand.
But only in the heart of the believer.

— *Val Schneider*

Everlasting

As I see the sun rise,
I feel your heart,
we touch our happiness with our eyes.
For a moment we're one,
trying to rush time,
seeing things we've never seen,
things that make us blind.

We're counting the days,
touching the past,
showing the way,
in a new everlasting romance.
A love that will take us
to our destiny,
to the end of our journey.
The journey for everlasting...

— *Paul M. Genovesi*

Forever Moon

It guides our love, our endless joy
a heart unbroken, not to play.
Be careful for it's not a toy.
The nights we've shared under the sky,
It gave us the hope to have one more try.
To be forgotten, left undone
The moon is out and not the sun.
We've only got a few more hours.
Let us walk up through weeds and flowers.
So much to say, yet time runs out.
I've now forgotten what love is about.
I look up to the moon for goodness and light.
If we love each other, it will work out right.
The memories we have in such a short time,
You are with me and you're finally mine.
The breathtaking glow, the shivers of fright,
The moon forever, yet only at night.

—*Becky McIlwaine*

The Writer's Stain

I sit alone and ponder through the time
With empty page and inspiration gone
And never find a word or phrase to rhyme.
My pounding head reminds me of a gong.
Attempt to write then mold into some shape
The careless blobs that form upon my brain,
That ooze on out and down around my nape
And leave what I have named *the writer's stain.*
And yet I find a way to use my pen
In capturing the necessary words.
Painstakingly I count from one to ten
I feel this sonnet is but for the birds.
At last I've reached the welcomed end of this
And find it something I will never miss.

— *Jennie Hayes*

My Mother In Law

To the greatest lady that I have ever known
And I have known quite a few in my day,
She is a pillar of strength in a crisis
And spreads a message of love on the way.

She is always there when you need her
She is just what a mother should be,
I have loved her since the day I first met her
And she is just a mother in law to me.

Her children have scattered throughout the states
And they have their own lives to live,
They could still call Mom every now and then
Would that be too much to give?

She took care of you through your childhood days
And gave you her love that was real,
And she is still there when you really need her
So let her know of the love that you feel.

—*J. Elmo Smith*

Longing for Thee

How I long for thee?
You are the apple of my eye,
The one I never saw or knew,
The perfect one,
No mistakes, none at all,
How I long for thee?
I wish we had more time,
I wish we had more things to say,
I wish we had a bond of love,
I will wish for everything, just for us,
But I wish I could see you and you will know,
How I long for thee!

—*Denise M. Detry*

Alone

Here I am, alone I lie
Under the mysterious bright blue sky...
Staring off into the lonesome day,
Wondering how many miles I am away...
Where will I be when I come down?
Will I be alive, or dead in the cold ground?
Will it be life like it used to be?
Or will I be running wild and free?
Is my life going to change?
Or will it be filled with the same old things?
Back down I fly
Through the bright blue sky...
Here I am, alone I lie,
Under the mysterious bright blue sky.

— *Jenni Whipple*

To My Father

My father I remember in a special way.
He is my friend when I need him,
I can talk to him every day.
The father I never had is the father who's still there for me.
Although he wasn't there to see me in the past,
He is still in my future,
I remember him in ways I can.
Through pictures of him and when others talk of him,
Although he's not around,
He is still the father I need now.
I talk to him through my words in prayer,
And see him in my midnight dreams.
I love him with all my heart,
And I hope he still loves me.

—*Diane Ozburn*

To My Twin Soul

Come sit with me here by the stream.
Let's dangle our feet and dream our dream.
Mine begins with color and passion,
Blue-green eyes revealing an ocean.
Eyes that glanced and stirred the voice,
There, there is the man of your choice.
Eyes of a pharoah, a priest and a brother,
Then, now and always you, my lover.

— *Beverly J. Grove*

My Secret Place

How often I've come here to be alone
As I sit by the water's edge
I think of you
My body becomes the clouds
My mind the wind
I travel through the tree tops like a warm gentle breeze
I smile down at the birds as I pass them by
I travel on
Over the scent of the wild flowers
Blooming in the fields
I move back over the water
I ripple the mirror that looks up at me
It shines like your blue eyes
I'm at peace here
Alone again at the water's edge
Not lonely just alone and happy, with my thoughts of you.

—*Antonia Slate*

My Special Love

If there was ever a love I would give my life for, it was you.
Even though you broke my heart and were sometimes untrue.
You're more precious to me than diamonds or gold.
For you, my love, I would sell my soul.
I wish you could be mine now and forever.
I would cherish your love and leave you never.
But for now the time has come to set you free.
Please remember always how very special you are to me.
When I look back on the memories we shared,
I will know how very much you once cared.
And when the sun is shining on me from above,
I will always think of...my special love.

— *Paula Cook*

Even if I never see you Again

I will remember candlelight flickering upon your face,
Nashville in the winter as a wonderful place.
The first time I saw you standing there,
The specks of gray that frost your hair.
And I will remember what made you so special then
Even if I never see you again.

I will remember the walk in the rain we took that day,
When we needed each other being a phone call away.
The city streets which were covered with snow,
Driving for hours with nowhere to go.
And I will need you now, as I needed you then,
Even if I never see you again.

I will remember the talks we had, jokes we shared,
Little things we did to show each other we cared.
All the decisions I could never make,
Crying when you left, knowing my heart would break.
Yet you are still a person in my life, I will never forget,
And a part of my past, I will never regret.
And, I will love you now, as I loved you then,
Even if I never see you again.

—*Yvonne Lee Miller*

A Troubled Heart

A troubled heart that's what I have.
A troubled heart that's what I know and see.
A troubled heart deep down inside.
A troubled heart that's what's wrong with me.

I have a troubled heart.
A troubled heart yes indeed.
Troubled deep down inside,
That's what's wrong with me.

My heart's so troubled.
Troubled with TLC and greed.
A troubled heart that's not what
I deserve, but yes,
A troubled heart that's what's wrong with me.

— *Angel Adams*

Yours of All Things

Of all the lights that have shone in my direction,
Yours remains the most blinding.
Of all the love that has pierced through my soul,
Yours remains the most outstanding.
Of all the beauty that has demanded my time for judgement,
Yours requires no time for thought.
And of all the tortues that have ever penetrated me,
Yours has the most torment brought.

— *Edward Casado*

Love

Love feels like a lotion—soothing, smooth, and caressing.
Love tastes like mint ice cream—cool, creamy, and refreshing.
Love hurts like a sore—constantly causing pain, but later heals.
Love looks like a rainbow—brilliant, colorful, and inspirational.
Love is a pillow—comforting, relaxing, and ready to cushion you.

— *Andrea Woo*

Untitled

There is something very special that's locked up in my heart.
I would really like to tell you 'cause it really means a lot.
It's something very tender and it's something very dear.
It's something very useful when your heart is full of fears.
It's something that brings sadness but fills your heart with joy.
It's something very special, but it's nothing like a toy.
What I'm really trying to tell you is that your love is in my heart
And like I said a while ago, it really means a lot.

— *Ada Ivette Vallejo*

Relationships

Wishing to talk to you, dear friend.
Hoping you feel the same.
Seeing you,
but not knowing if the time is right to approach.
Wanting to share something precious and beautiful,
but unsure of my words.
Not knowing if talking or listening is best now.
Remembering past moments of love and beauty,
and wishing for such deep and intimate sharing again.
My heart reaching out yearning to touch yours.
This moment, charged with hopes and fears.
Loving relationships,
full of the potential for richness and joy,
yet also possible disappointment.
Lows deeper for their distance from the heights once shared.
Still love always straining to share once more those heights with you,
and praying I do not disappoint you in this moment together.
Trusting that your feeling my love for you will be enough.

—*Walter E. Williams*

When Angels Wake

There are the children sound asleep,
Their cheeks so flushed, their smiles creep
Into your heart. You whisper low,
The little angels. I love them so.

Then the day. They wake. They're up.
Each one cuddly like a pup.
What's this? The floors are shaking,
The very walls are quaking!

Where came this thundering horde?
Where are those angels last night adored?
Merciful heavens! The stairs will go!
As down they come fortissimo!

So through the hours, until day is gone,
And one by one, a nod, a yawn,
Sleepy goodnights, a whispered prayer...
And again there are angels there.

—*Mary A. Manning*

A Storm of Emotions

A storm of sadness
    swept through me
    the night you left me.

A storm of confusion
    swept through me
    the night you said, *Good-bye.*

A storm of happiness
    swept through me
    the night you said,
    I'm back and I love you.

— *Sarah Lerow*

Mother To Daughter

Isn't it strange
How people can change.
Only yesterday you believed in Santa Claus,
And now I watch as a tear falls
Down your cheeks.

I feel for you my lonely friend,
For it feels like the darkness will never end;
And that light won't ever come,
And I just wish I could give you some
Comforting word.

I've traveled the road which you now walk,
And I'm here to listen if you want to talk.
I've experienced the pain you now feel,
And believe me it was just as real
When I lost my first love.

— *Tammie R. Trail*

To You Mother

For the many, many years that I have known you
Have been satisfying through and through
You taught me the difference between right and wrong
You let me know the places where I did and did not belong
You gave me the special qualities that you are made of
Which include honesty, kindness, modesty, and love
You are always there to care and understand
You are always there to lend a helping hand
I thank God for not giving me any other
Than you, the best of all mothers.

—*Michelle Denise Phifer*

The Little Ballerina

The little ballerina, posed and ready
A-top the music-box,
Spins and twirls, at the twist of a key
To a tinkling melodious waltz.
A lovely vision she is to see,
She revives such wonderful memories—
They let my mind roam free
Free to recapture and clasp to me.
The lilting tune enfolds me,
A fantasy is in full sway—
I am the little ballerina
And I bow to thunderous acclaim.
The music-box slows down and stops,
The little ballerina falters and halts
'Till someone rewinds the key
And once more she will dance sublimely.

— *Thelma D. Chivis*

A Mother

Upon mid-summer
She came over to laugh.
In the summer, she took us to a dance.
In the winter, she kept us warm
When the wind was getting cold,
But as she knew she was getting old,
A tear rolled down her face ever bold
For she knew soon she must go
And leave all the wonders she had known.
Then she remembered when she held her little babies on her lap
And told them she loved them, loved them very much.

— *Khelley Hellwig*

Dear Mom and Dad

Hi! Remember me,
The one you didn't even get to see?
I often wonder what you're like.
I sometimes even hope you're happy, mostly out of spite.
My life is okay, I have no complaints. My parents are fine
If only I could say they were really mine.
I have a brother who's as beautiful as can be
But he's like me—his parents also had set him free.
Maybe you had no money, maybe you were young,
But I can't help wondering, do you regret what you have done?
No note attached, no letter of love,
My only hope is someday we'll meet above,
Dear Mom and Dad.

— *Tammi Terwilleger*

Old Cabin Home

My little cabin home
Sitting below the hill
With the chimney made of stone,
Back in Powder mill.

I love my little cabin
Under the tall oak trees
With flowers all around it
And a never-ending breeze.

It isn't very fancy,
Just primitive as can be.
Not much of a home for most folks,
But good enough for me.

— *Kathy Williams Johnson*

Sixteen Once

And darkness fell
All too fast, white to black
There was no stopping it now.
Everything had changed.

She closed her eyes
Trying to remember the old days
Days of roses and daisies blooming
Not ashes and thorns on the ground.

The times had changed and so did she
The little girl had grown up,
But was afraid to tell anyone
And the darkness fell.

— *Rachel Ribnick*

On the First Day

When God created the world,
He put upon it a girl,
With skin colored olive,
A body of silk and eyes
Of crystal clear bronze.
God realized she was lonely,
Then created He, the boy.
With hair of golden locks
Body, bold and tight
And eyes of pearly blue seas.
He gave to them each other
To do with what they please.

—*Allison Mary Celiberti*

Leave Your Mark

The future is returning
as we watch the children learning.
Yesterday's dreams are
Today's play things,
and Tomorrow's past
is Today's task.
With this in mind,
use your time with care.
Dare to leave your mark
written in the children's hearts.

— *Melody McCoy*

On the Road to Dunsandle

On the road to Dunsandle lie the sweetest sounds I have ever heard
Not of violins or cherub grins, but the cheerful spoken word.
You will be friends with all around you no matter what your name
And 'tis home to where you are going from no matter where you came.

There will be leprechauns with green suits out to greet all who come to call
They will play funny tricks with their walking sticks and dance for one and all.
Oh the road to Dunsandle is lined with cobbled stones
Where you'll bump and slide on a merry ride that will rattle up your bones.

You will see an old banshee hide behind a tree keeping watch as you go by
Later on her wail will ring out the tale of the things that made her cry
Yes, the road to Dunsandle is a gleeful place indeed
Where the blarney's as real as a cabbage meal and your fantasies are freed.

— *Jennifer Bronte Uniacke*

Lillie Mae

Lillie Mae was proud of herself that day.
She was graduating college and on her way.
It didn't matter that she was fifty-two,
In times past she was much too busy fighting the blues.
As she stepped forth to receive her degree,
She heard a soft voice whisper, *Lillie Mae go and set your sisters free.*
Free from the search to find someone to care,
Free from the thorny beds that leave them bare,
Of dignity, honor and self esteem,
Free from the poverty that ignorance breeds,
And Lillie Mae uttered a silent prayer,
Thank God for a purpose.

— *Brenda Green*

My Mind

I'll splash my mind upon this page for you,
    the shadows of a thousand dancing thoughts.
Glimmering, shimmering they dance a crystal confusion waltz.
Perchance you'll catch a glimpse of my madness
    and let your heart stir with mine,
Caught in a whirlwind of fleeting genius-seeds, swept away never to root.
I'll splash my mind upon this page for you,
    while its thoughts are still turning and twisting,
Alive like a fish on a hook—prisoner of dark chains
    forged from powers that rage against my soul.
Perchance it's all too tangled—the colors like a shimmering, stained glass
Cathedral filled with beauty from inside; pale, average from without.
I'd love to have you dance with me from hall to hall exploring what I see;
Running barefoot through green spring rejoicing;
    hushed by the solemn whispering prayers;
Terrified by the dark forebodings of the Black Prince's wrestlings.
Perchance you'll understand—maybe—a little bit.

— *Paul E. Tooley Jr.*

Apples in Season

October, and the apple season in my valley.
Trees hang heavy with limbs almost touching the ground.
I finger a smooth Red Delicious, bite deeply.
Juice drools from the mealy beauty, pungent and sweet.
People crowding the packing shed, apples are cheap now.
Bins and bins of apples, the sorting belt spewing apples.
Apples spilling on the floor covered with buzzing bees.
Grimes Golden, red Winesap, York, Jonathan and Roman Beauty.
Over the land a sweet smell, apples and autumn leaves.
Crunchy apple pies thick with brown sugar and spices.
Hot apple dumplings smothered in cream.
Brown apple butter on homemade bread.
And applesauce cake with slabs of fresh butter.
Contently, I munch to the white core and black seeds.
Waiting for the station wagon to be loaded.
Unbidden, an ancient Biblical saying comes to mind.
King Solomon with three hundred wives, perhaps?
Oh, feed me with apples for I am sick of love.

— *Dorothy H. Wooldridge*

Magic

When is the sun ever as bright as the dawn?
Clear, stabbing rays
Penetrating the darkness.
Such brilliance,
Giving vision for thousands of miles.
Sounds, touch, smells,
Every sense amplified by a moment of magic.
Nature, the voice of all living things,
Silently holding its breath as the moment passes.
Anything can happen.

— *William L. Estep*

Past Shadows

Lingering shadows of a girl form your past
Memories of her perfect love holds your heart fast
Dreams of this love you secretly hold true
Shadows over the one who now loves you
Blinded by your short lived love affair
Never seeing all these many years how I have cared
Living on dreams of a past that can never be
Shadows over this pain it brings to me
True and gentle love comes but once in a life time
You found and lost your's before I found mine
Now shadows of your past between us stand
I can't compete with this girl of a foreign land
You left your once in a life time love so far in the past
Yet my once in a life time love for you will forever last.

— *Peggy M. Comalander*

There's an Old Fashioned Parlor

In this old house, so many things of long ago...
There's an old fashioned parlor.
The curtains covered with dust
They were made of lace
The finest of long ago!
And in the corner sits this fine old grand piano
On which beautiful melodies were played
By many find ladies of long ago.
Carpets from the orient covered the floor
Still on the shelf sits a vase from who knows where.
The dust is undisturbed.
The windows are covered with webs spun long ago
And in the corner too sits an old spinning wheel
Spinning yarns of long ago.
So let's not disturb
And gently leave it to its dreams.

— *Howard T. Logan*

Harpers Ferry, West Virginia

Small mountains, large mountains, valleys below,
A canal, Potomac and Shenandoah Rivers flow.
A tunnel thru the mountain, where a train whistle blows.
Can be seen from a hilltop above,
Where you can see a June Art Show.

A quaint little town under the azure sky,
Holds so many events of eras gone by.
The legends they tell of the Civil War days
About the soldiers who rode over the mountains
And camped in the hills.

A little drummer boy wounded in the war
Waited his turn to pass thru the church door
(Used for a hospital high on the hill.)
Now I am saved, the weak voice uttered.
Then the little boy's body slumbered.
The church stands to this day,
Still welcomes visitors that pass its way
In the historical town of Harpers Ferry.

— *Florence J. Sowers*

Nuclear War

The heated stones underneath the raging stampede
explode in fury at the burning city.
The divine light shines heavenward
searing all who dare to watch.
Silence, sweet silence.
Nothing left, all regreted.
The swarms come covering all that survive.
And the rain, big and black and hot.
Nothing is safe, nothing is sound.
Then there evolves a new breed.
Fresh and young, all eternal
Erecting a new city, a new life.
Old habits remembered
Old conflicts not forgotten
Nothing learned.
Destruction is the only future.

— *Anastasia Panagakos*

My best Friend

Sometimes the road I travel seems so steep and narrrow
That I often fall down.
And it is hard to face another day of continuous failures
And defeats.
Yet through the confusion and hurt I see your face,
And I hear your strong voice telling me to go on...
And even when it is raining outside and on the inside too,
You help me see that shining rainbow.
Somehow you know just what to say and the precise
Time to say it.
And so I want you to know how thankful I am to
God for sending you to me;
And remember: I will always cherish our friendship.
You are an inspiration to my life
And I will never forget you.

—*Heather Christine Clark*

From One Path To Another

A long hard road you have finally crossed over
Now onto a bridge yielding fields of clover.
Of course there will always be thorns in among them
Quite often disguised by the lovely white blossoms.
But although they may seem like the worst of all pains
Never jump to conclusions...wait and see what you gain.
For their avoidance may send you on a quite different route
To a silver lined cloud or a magical flute.
So remember to always keep eyes open wide.
And set sights on the future...let dreams never die.
But also take heed to retain all your past
For otherwise memories fade away fast.

—*Heather L. Davies*

I Have Never Left You

In this universe of yours and mine
I have always wondered where I was going.
And in all my wondering what I find.
Sometimes I'm happy and sad
To see what I am doing.
I look to heaven and ask for help and guidance
In this world of ours, and where I am going.
Is there some place for me to rest my mind
And be happy.
I ask the Lord for his guidance and blessings
Wherever He may be..
And his answer, *I have always been with you,
Good and bad, happy or sad, at your footsteps
And in my bosom, I have never left you.*

—*Frank Arnett*

As I Grew Taller...

As I grew taller,
I grew prettier and nicer.
All that surrounded me was beautiful;
All that I looked at was wonderful.
But as colder weather grew,
My petals began to fall until I was nothing.
Yet I knew that my petals
And all of my surroundings would come back to me
Just as they do every time spring comes around.

— *Emily Guilbeau*

Dandelions

I'm walking home to my family
From the welfare office
Down on Alexander Street
With the needy monthly check.

I just wish that there was something
I could afford to bring home
To that gal of mine
Who treats me so very kind.

Then just ahead of me at Oppenheimer Park
Dancing in the summer breeze
I see a bright yellow patch
Of pretty dandelions.

Dandelions for daffodils,
Dandelions for that gal of mine.
I sure hope that she doesn't mind
Me bringing her home a bunch of dandelions.

Dandelions for the one who is
The sunshine of my life;
Dandelions for the wife who is
The flower in the garden of my heart.

—*Emmerson Luffman*

The Brother I Love

Although the years quickly pass
My love for you will always last.
You are my brother, a source of truth
A friend, a pal, yes, I have proof.

You were there when I was down,
And all I could do was to frown.
But you told me, at one time
That I was special, in your mind.

Those words you spoke affected me so,
That my love for you continues to grow.
For when I feel I need a friend,
I know, on you I can depend.
So may God bless you with His love,

Rich and plentiful, from above.
Because down on earth, you are cherished
Not only by me; with love that will not perish.

—*Cary Connors*

Being Strong

Being strong in your body, mind and soul,
We have to understand that life goes on,
And keep our bodies in tone.
Keep our heads on straight and our minds together.
We'll all last forever.
Have a good heart and believe in the Lord
And no one can pull the cord.

— *Gregory Coleman*

Endless Cries

I cried out to you
And you never cared.
The feelings I felt
And the love we shared,
As the day goes on,
So do I,
But you never heard
My endless cry.

— *Carrie Clark*

Choices

She will
She won't
She's undecided.

He cares
Agrees
But is otherwise committed.

Traditional
Occasional
Circumstantial
Accidental

Art
History
Science
Religion?

I choose HOPE!

— *Esther M. G. Smith*

Beauty

I look at pictures
In magazines
I look at storybooks
Of lovely Queens

Sometimes I wish
On the brightest star
That I could be beautiful
But I am not so far

But Grandpa tells me
It is not how you look
No matter how it seems
In all those books

He says that beauty
Is not what you see
It is what you are inside
It is you and me.

—*Elena Strange*

The Ocean

As the ocean folds over
And touches the sand,
I reach out
And touch your hand.
The gentle breeze
Goes passing on.
A ray of light
Shows it's dawn.
The bright big sun
I seem to miss
As I lean over
And give you a kiss.

— *Amber Gilewski*

Everyone Needs

Everyone needs a good friend...
From time to time...
To tell their troubles to...
To talk things out, when feeling blue...
A shoulder to lean on...
To get you through it all...
Everyone needs a good friend that's true.
Someone who may know, just what you're going through
A friend who understands...
And is willing to give you a helping hand
Everyone needs a good friend like you.

— *Debra Ayres*

The Dark Shadow

It comes and goes like most usually do, but this one's different,
This one's rare, it takes you over, it takes you anywhere.
It's stronger than your higher power, it's stronger than your mind,
It takes your life, it takes your love, it leaves you with no time.
I call it the dark shadow, it traps you inside and won't let go.
You can try to escape but the yearning for it will ache, and ache,
And ache. It can leave you rich or it can leave you poor, can
Make your hurt want more, and more, and more. The shadow is not
Like anything else in the world, this one is indistinct and deadly.
The shadow is a way to escape from your problems, yeah, but that
Darkness will get you, anyplace, anytime, anywhere. It may thrill
You, but it will kill you, that's why I call it the dark shadow.

— *Heidi Mimm*

Leaves and Love

One after another I counted the leaves
　　as they fell from the almost bare tree to the ground.
I caught one.
It resembled the days that I had been with Lee.
Once our love had been growing like that leaf budding.
Then we were together, understood each other and had fun
　　like the leaf was green this summer.
The next thing I knew, there was something wrong.
The something wrong had grown and grown inside him like that leaf
　　changing colors in the fall.
He didn't tell me or let me know until
　　like that leaf, his love for me was gone.

— *Angela Smart*

I'll Be Waiting

I've loved you for so long it seems.
It feels like an eternity, when in reality it's only been a little over a year.
Funny how time flies when you're on the edge of love.
Not quite in it yet, but very close; just one little push,
　　one little glance and I'll be in it.
I never wanted this to happen, but ever since the first day that I saw you,
　　I couldn't stop thinking about you.
Even when I swore to myself that you wuld never play a part
　　in all these make-believe fantasies that you inspired.
Even then, you entered into my dreams at night and I lay there,
　　an unwilling prisoner to sleep.
And those times when our eyes would meet acoss the room,
　　they were almost unbearable.
I wanted you to hold me, while even then my mind was saying, *No.*
And those few times you spoke to me, though I might not have shown it,
inside I was a nervous wreck,
Wondering if it was as visible to you and the rest of the world
　　as it was to me.
Could everybody see, as I could when I woke up in the morning
　　that I had been dreaming about you?
Was I that transparent? But you never made a move toward me
　　that would make us more than casual acquaintances.
But I don't give up faith easily, so until you are ready for me, I'll still be here,
The same girl that almost loves you, waiting.

— *Jenn Smathers*

Stars

Millions of stars twinkle in the night
The heavens to brighten with their light.
Galaxies, constellations and Milky Way delight
The full splendor and miracle of our sight.

Little wonder as we look upon a star
That we should wonder who we are.
Are we destined to travel in space so far,
Or is to remain on earth our par
And wonder as we look upon a star?

— *Billy F. Andrews*

White On White

The room is white on white.
Shadows stretch, an early evening blue.
Unbleached muslin curtains fly
From chrome rods hung over the wall of open windows.
The cool breeze lifts her hair from her face.
The woman stands up slowly from the vanilla cream sofa.
A box of tissues sits untouched.

Black low-heeled pumps
Caked with graveyard dirt
Kicked in the corner.
A plain black dress lies dead in a heap.
She leans against the window frame,
Her head bowed, forehead resting.
The phone rings, another condolence call.
It rings unanswered.

— *Alice Grant Kenney*

The Beach!

The ocean breeze so tranquil and calm,
Relaxing the mind like a soothing balm.
Watching the waves roll in with the tide.
Gladly casting all worry and care aside.

Contently walking along the foamy surf.
Leaving a trail of footprints in the sandy turf.
Listening to the pleasant ocean sounds.
Combining with the joy and laughter that abounds.

Searching to find a large sea shell.
Amazed and awed at the ocean swell.
Enthralled with the beauty of the boundless sea
Tranquilized by the sway of a tall palm tree

The wonder of it all so hard to believe.
Sadden to realize it's time to leave
Peace evaporating with the ocean spray.
Footprints in the sand slowly fading away.

—*Betty Sue Kimbrough*

Heart

It is a steadfast soldier
Marching you smartly to all your destinations.
It pumps tirelessly; an engine
Driving your blood from valve to vein.
A fat pin cushion, it has been stabbed over and over
By the pangs of love.
And within its four chambers,
Adam and Eve hide each other.
It has all chemical properties; it can be
Changed to stone to gold to ice.
It is the valentine that says it loves you best.
Only your mirror is more faithful.
And is keeps time for you
With all the impartiality of judge or a good watch.

— *Jacque Parsons*

The Price of Love

You can't buy love or so they say
But there's a price you sometimes pay.
For when you love and there's none in return,
It's a lesson you cannot learn.
There are so many times I have cried,
I feel like a part of me inside has died.
I see them together on every passing day,
But there's nothing I can do, nothing I can say.
Because the chioce is his, it's not up to you,
Though I wish there was something I could do.
I wish there was something to ease the pain,
Or stop the tears that fall like rain.
But I know there's nothing I can do,
It's the price to be paid—its for loving you.

— *Carla Sloke*

Beyond

The raptured joy in spiritual dreaming
Between our God and Man has two fold meaning
Evaluating here and there as truism
What purpose life's reality is yielding
Yet levitations force can bring real feeling
Infinity will bless a hue less prism
As Abraham foretold our Father's chrisom
The Covenant by God for man revealing
A oneness. Lo! and I am with you always
As rainbows tinged an atmospheric blessing

Thru sun and clouds and skies the rapture sending
A blessing there and blesses me here as I lay
My faith in brilliance. Shine thru Lord arraying
Stand I in awe in spiritual dreaming.

— *Dee Hedenland*

Amorous Archaeology

If the universe is a finite land,
Then by the mere right of one's birth
Love's suspended within animate sand.
But tell me, who controls the hour-glass,
If it's neither broken, nor made...
Are we always attending the mass?
Is there emotional evolution,
And if so, is creation the nucleus of its own revolutions?
Are we intrinsic essence of humankind with singularity voided;
Are we the edgeless edge of some master-mind? If it's true life
Is insurmountable, the sky's a terminal mirror-
The spirit's allure is redoubtable...
Maybe judgment day is every day...
Maybe by actions we always
Are subconsciously kneeling down to pray.

— *Diane Maietta*

Moon Shadows

The moon casts her gentle, tranquil shadows
Across the snow.
Ethereal, peaceful, the embodiment of my soul.
A spiritual dance to the rhythm of my breathing.
A feeling of expectancy in the night sounds of
The forest, as I walk.
I mediate from a place of empowerment looking
Over lake and mountain.
Continuing rays of sunset linger in the deep
Pink clouds on the horizon.
A soft warm breeze embracing me, I feel one with the universe.
I turn to see *the light of the mother* round, full, rising in the
Gathering darkness, for her dance with the night. I send you my love
A whisper sent across the evening sky. Do you feel my presence
My warmth, my smile, my kiss?

— *Jacquelyne A. Lotz*

Oh So Well

I thought it was going *oh so well,*
But now you're gone and I'm as lonely as Hell.
Is she pretty? Is she sweet?
Where does she come from? How did you meet?
I know all about her; I know her name,
So please stop playing this silly, silly game.
Her hair is like snow, her eyes are like the sea
And she's everything that I never could be.
You said you loved me, how could you have lied?
Now my heart has stopped beating and my tongue has tied.
But when I saw you with her, I knew we had come to an end,
But, my God, why did you have to pick my very best friend?

— *Angie Deavers*

Paradise Island

A paradise island is what everyone dreams of,
Especially all the young people deeply in love.
The rays of the sunsets are beyond explanation,
With the pink and orange clouds full of imagination.
The palm trees sway softly in the warm tropical breeze,
And there's nothing like a cool drink in the shade of a coconut tree.
Also, remember when the end of your dream vacation is near
There's always hope that you'll come again this next year.

— *Nicole Stoddart*

Human Being!

All human beings have one day to say,
My birthday, have one like today.
I could say today is my day,
One day for me to write my poems.
One day for you to read my poems.
Just do some critique about me. I like that!
I like somebody saying something.
Don't close your mouth without talking.
If you died without talking, you're nothing.
Say something for the other people talking
Like M. L. King Jr., like Ronald Reagan,
Like Ed Koch, like Elvis Presley...say something...
About yourself and other people too...try brothers and sisters,
Try, keep going...It is not easy in the ground
To find life without being somebody.
It's nice to say, *I am...I am what am.*
The man you should be know...try, keep going...
The world is big, the life is short.
Your message is more important than your face.
Say something that other people can use in the future.

— *Emmanuel Latouche*

Libido

Leaves of fire swirl 'round me with red, they alight and become my eyes;
The skull of the beast cowls my head, the beginning of this dark disgiuse.
The hook of Thanatos emblazons my chest, in my fist,
Clenched an axe of execution; silver-studdied manacles encircle
My wrists, glinting power and schiziod action.
I crack the whip as I scream with delight,
For the longest night that is waiting;
Calling from dreams those moments of fright,
To this darkest hour of creating.
And now, out into the night I go,
Fighting mortals and wreaking destruction;
Humor and horror I combine in death's dance,
Drink, women and song, my compulsion.
The moment is ripe for grand execution, I run into the
Black of the dream; leaping and hollering the cursed delight:
The season of eternal Halloween.

— *Bruce J. Leksa*

Springtime

The mountains are standing at their peaks
And the sun's pressed against the southern wind.
The sky is moving all around.
The birds are flying northern bound.

Flowers are starting to come in bloom.
Spring fills the air like a touch of perfume.
Trees are growing, there's no doubt
And soon the leaves will start to sprout.

The seas are coming upon shore
And everyone's gathering shells once more.
The grass is growing once again
And everyone is enjoying what springtime has to offer them.

— *Louise Russell*

The Wild Geese

Today I heard them in the pre-dawn darkness,
Their plaintive, poignant cries awakened me,
Arousing primitive emotions in my breast..
Earth-bound, I longed to rise and follow them,
Soaring wild and free through the crisp October air
Across the windswept countryside toward sunrise.
What faith and courage they must have
To make this arduous journey every year
Their strong wings beating through the air-waves,
Following their leader trustingly.
What prompts them, forcing them to leave their nesting grounds
To ply uncharted skies?
What guides them so unerringly to their destination?
Who leads their leader?
None but our own Heavenly Father,
Guardian and Leader of us all.

— *Lucy M. Young*

Secret Spells

A maiden dances bare
The starlings catch her hair
Around the wind she dances
While pan amidst the glowing prances

A hundred pair of amber eyes
Forward lean in mock disguise
While tiny specks of floating folly
Bedeck the hazelnut and holly
And the maiden in her stress
Fills them all with tenderness

—*Suzanne Foster*

A Look at Nature

As the sun rises, its brightness reflects from golden sands,
As sea gulls fly up and down as if to pay tribute to the sun,
As my spirit flies on the backs of eagles,
Far below a herd of wild horses race with the wind.
In this day, most of nature's beauty
Is just as illusive as the wind itself.
As the seasons change
So do the forces of nature
Like leaves of green change into colors red, gold and in the end to brown.
Then the blanket of winter falls upon the cool earth
As if to keep the ground warm
From the cold cruel winds.
Then comes spring as all starts to warm up.
Nature pulls back her blanket of snow
To let you and me know that soon flowers will bloom.
Nature, like time, is always on the move.

— *Thomas T. Graef*

Flying Beauty

As I look up in the sky I see a bird as he flys by.
I wonder as he spreads his wings,
Little bird, can you see me?

Little bird, little bird flying oh so high,
Are you ever worried about falling from the sky?
How do you stay up there keeping up so high?
How do you keep flying and being oh so spry?

Your beauty it astounds me, so confident you are.
Never seem to worry about going way too far.
I wish I had your beauty, your confidence so spry.
I wish I had ability to fly up in the sky.

To look down all around me to see you down below.
And look upon the beauty as the water flows.
The water of the river bed as it flows on by.
Just as confident as you are flying in the sky.

—*Elizabeth M. Robinson*

Vermont (for Kristen)

Green stretches to the sky
Wind filters through the leaves with a sigh
Green blurs into blue
Blue of sea and sky and dew
Sunshine flows down
Sparking on the water like the gold of a king's crown
Dusk rolls by
Hanging a brilliant red shawl in the sky.

— *Jyothi Kanics*

The Essence of the Butterfly

As the butterfly leaves the cocoon,
It is an expression of freedom
Transformed into another life.
As it flies high through the air
So gracefully and with ease,
One can notice the beauty of the many colors.
Indeed, the colors are brilliant
Creations of Mother Nature.
Only Mother Nature can draw such a creation
To the earth to be nurtured
With the nectar of life.
In flight I can imagine as the summer breeze,
Sunn and rain touches its wings.
It is oh so gentle for nature knows
The life span is short.
If I could fly with thee, oh how free I could be.
I believe in the essence of the butterfly
'Cause I believe in you.

—*Kenneth Smith*

The Wind

The wind blew coldly upon his face,
But the man stood unyielding in his place.
The wind that blew dried his tears;
His steadfast standing had hid his fears.

The man still remembered his past
The one that was ending...at last.
But the future is about what he thought
And the battles and wars yet to be fought.

His past was black, gloomy and dark
But, this man, had certainly left his mark.
His future is happy, bright and gay
But how long it will last, who can say?

In his past, he felt the pain, and missed the joy.
Who would believe he was ever a boy?

—*Troy Moyle*

April Snow

Sometimes it snows in April
The flakes can leave you blind
Cool, quick strokes that swallow everything in their path.

Stinging April drops that fill the canyon
Widening, deeping the gorge.
The bitter storm ends new dreams, new hope, new growth
Fate...Mother Nature...April snow.
Emptiness, sorrow...a fragile world shattered.
I can still see the inner glow; the lust for life.
Suddenly! The fire quenched.
If only...
We were having such a good time, until it began to snow.

    —*Barbara Ann Hechavarria*

Tumbleweeds

It's windy and blowing——the tumbleweeds are rolling!

I thought about a tumbleweed, but there isn't much to say!
It simply sits there on a spot, then bounces on its way:
I've only seen them on the move, I've never seen one growing.
The only one I've ever noticed is one that's dead and blowing.
Now what did God invent them for? What purpose do they have?
They're not pretty, I wouldn't eat one——can they make a salve?
Is it ever covered with pretty leaves? Perchance a blossom?
Maybe its duty on earth is to be the chaparral possum.
All I know is this for sure; guess I knew it all along.
They gave a great composer material for a classic song.
Hey! That's why they were put here——'cause music we all love.
They've made the *Sons of the Pioneers* just a class above!

    — *Jackie Carter*

Stepping Beyond the Sand

Deserted expressions, sand swirls, dust that covers the air about me.

I stand in a desert of contentment. Because my tracks have
been covered behind me. My thoughts cultivated by Jesus.

Plants meet, separate, then recover from drifting sand
Particles in the air. Distraught visions seep into my
head: beware of the devil, of sin.

Acknowledging mistakes retreats my own boasting.
Forgiveness asked for, received through separate and silent vigils.

Calm and clear, there is not any fear.
Sun shining in solitude, growth in my fortitude.

Eyes that still approach in kindness. Sifting through,
somewhat blue. Changes are received from above.
Plans that are shown, humbleness has grown for me and about me.
People that find a certain respect for life are cherished
inside. Thanking each, deceiving not one. It's honesty
that tells me I am longing for Heaven.
I reach out with new hope; acceptance pleases me. Turning
theirs into mine. Stepping carefully with them. No
longer sinking in the sands of outsider' wishes.

    —*Gordon Bruce*

I Am Here

I entered this world with a big bang, a daughter of the moon,
at one with the universe.
I came from another place between primordial soup and oceanic waste.
Energy created me, the seas evolved me, I am here.
I am slave to wind, my captor, the sun.
This warden protects me from the ice man.
I bathe in rains that flow through woods into murky moss layered ponds.
I inhale air smelling sweetly of baby breath, as real as a carefree spring day.
I am here, knowing little of who you are.
I am just a friend from another star.

    — *Benita Beryl*

Troposphereic Beginnings; Hell is Above Us

    After an explosive 'Big Bang'
Earth had the sense not to go near the 'Sun' again.

    I wonder what 'causes' there were on Earth,
    That didn't like 'Burning pain'
    Keeping Earth of the Sun in refrain?
    Life-giving rays of the thing
    Birth'd furry-like mold and bacteria,
    stagnating the waters with a plethora of cells
Perhaps, one thought per cell forming 'Natures Total
    Wisdom'?
But God inspired us to call such Horrendous Heat
    Fire and Hell.
    So why, do We merely refer to it as the
    'S.U.N.' ? ? ?

    —*Eraina Q. Reynaldo*

Untitled

So; you're confused.
I offered to give you the space you needed.
You accepted it readily.
You had a few different options to chose from,
And now you've made you decision.
You chose one path; and left me behind.
I only hope for your sake, the decision wasn't made in haste
I like you, even loved you somewhat.
I wish you success on this trip you have chosen to take
It can be extremely hard, so think out your possibilities.
Farewell to you, my friend.
I hope your search will lead you
to inner peace and unending happiness.

    —*Hayley Parker*

Time Vanishing

Staring out the window as the world becomes so strange
A dusky dimness runs into the sparkling rain,
The shed of lamplight glow turns the streets to mirrors
Holding softened reflections of some past or future eras.
Within the slow yet vibrant view this could be England long ago.
Or Rome in a wild wet autumn of yesterday or tomorrow;
Rain makes the world softer and bevels harsh contours,
Electric light now candle-flame has somehow lost its power;
I sit upon the window seat of an anywhere at anytime
Looking into the echo of Time's endless rhyme.

The ringing of the telephone
Catapults me into today;
Your car comes 'round the corner
And Time fades into yesterday.

    — *Alys Caviness Brosius*

Confessions of a Small Town Boy

I close my eyes hoping that she will come to me
and find me sleeping here upon the ragged bedspread
as a symbol of a truce, a draw.
She says there are rarely winners at love.
Superimposed image: I rise to wash my hands,
the mirror above the sink reflecting the dirty plaster patches
and I catch my eyes, wide and dull, staring at the fixtures behind me,
her reflection in the bathtub, the lukewarm water lapping.
I turn to face the bathtub quickly
but there is only my washcloth floating, my soap cake sinking
in an empty tub, my body sinking
to the cracks of the caulking, drowning,
and in the cheap neon of the big city lights
I see the tiles close in around me
just as I was thinking they wouldn't.

    — *Ingrid Anderson*

Racin Jason

They call me racin jason
Yea, that's my name
Cause when I'm on the
Go kart track I don't
Act the same.

I'm always trying to pass them
By darting here and there.
And when I get up on them
They're easy to scare.

So move over when you see me
Coming, cause I'm going through.
The only place for me to be
Is up ahead of you.

— *Debbie Stuart Blankenship*

The Love I Have for You

Being apart just breaks my heart
Because I can't get the love
I have for you out of my heart.
I try to let you go,
But it seems so hard.
I try to forget all the good times
We have had and all the bad
'Cause I feel so sad.
I realize now that it is over
And that's why I feel so bad.

— *Debbie Freeman*

Tear in My Eye

Sitting in this lonely room,
Thinking about the past.
Thinking of how it would have been,
Oh, I wish it could have last.

I wonder what you're doing now,
I wonder how you look.
I wonder if I should call you.
I have your number in my book.

But if I called, would you even care,
Or would you have a few words to share?
Well I guess it wouldn't hurt to try,
I just don't want to end up with a
Tear in my eye.

— *Donna O'Brien*

Keeper of Dreams

Oh, keeper of dreams
At freedom's gate you stand;
With welcoming beam stretched high in hand
Guiding the many immigrants to her land.

Oh, keeper of dreams
At democracy's bench you preside;
With law book held by your side
Guarding each new citizen's rights with pride.

Oh, keeper of dreams
At oppression's hold you strain;
With truimph breaking the shackles and chains
Guaranteeing relief from the suffering and pain.

Oh, keeper of dreams
At imagination's portal you dwell;
With visions of liberty that are known well
Giving each generation an experience to tell.

— *James Nelson Deitz*

Something Beautiful

half grinning
with shyness in you
never smiling totally
hiding something beautiful
so beautiful in your eyes
like a little boy
hiding behind the facade of a man
you watch and listen
but not like ordinary boys
sincerity and love
trying to read you, exploring your mind
trying hard to break through
wanting so, to be loved.
showing a bit
enough to want you
but always half grinning
hiding something beautiful.

— *Jennifer Borsum*

Feelings Are Forever

Although we are far apart and can't be together,
My feelings for you will always last forever.
I care so much and my feelings are true.
If you ever need me, I'll be there for you.
It's you I think of all night and all day.
For us to stay friends is all that I pray.
I miss you so much and wish you were near
But your feelings for me are so unclear.
You make me laugh and show that you care.
I wish there was more we could possibly share.
Though I'll get over you and find someone new.
I just want you to know that my love was true.

— *Jami Hickman*

Think Big

And search for the stars
The more you believe, the more you'll find
Lifes brilliance
The more faith you have the more your shall achieve
Then, share with others that blessing
Do merit good when the going gets though
Think big, so life won't seem to be in vain
Although joy might be the twin of pain
Think big and stay beautiful for your friend sake
As in the grand theater of your mind
Where sits the severest of critics
Judging your daily act
But keep cheery and hold your head high
And think big in whatever you do
And soon you shall clearly see
How through it all you made it be.

— *Bozsi D. Varga*

Without You

As I walked through this enchanting valley
It didn't cast a spell on me.
You were no longer there,
Blue skies and birds of song,
You were not there to share.
The lofty mountains and painted cliffs,
Roaring mountain springs,
Are a lost paradise without you.
The morning sun wakens and the dew is vanishing fast.
I walk along without you,
Still dwelling in the past.

— *Doris M. Walker*

He Knows

Though we walk along a path
We at times feel alone,
Though we are enveloped by
Sadness with him we are at home.
Prayers are messages to the Divine,
Only genuine love will mend in time.
Though we see his footsteps
We think he is not there,
But believe in him for he loves he cares.
He knows our Lord what you are
Going through,
You are not alone for he feels it too.
When you have learned the lesson
You need to grow,
He will mend with love much
Faster than you will know...

— *Geri Laveglia*

a flower died in abbsylon

a flower died in abbsylon
coarse raiment...and the sky
devoid of pain...repealed the rain
and let the flower die
the petals curl...the colors fade
abject to childish eye
that in the sense...mortality
would let the flower die
the powers gave...unto the grave
the choice to modify
the sorrow born of audience
to let the flower die
a flower died in abbsylon
the farthest shore...and i
withdrew the claim...upon her name
and let the flower die

— *Doug Miller*

Untitled

Behind you the sun shone bright
As you stood on a pedestal of gold
Flowers bloomed all around you
A young god in a crown of jewels.
My loving eyes adored you
You were animal, mineral and vegetable
A god among mortal men
My love to you I gave.
Now the darkness has set in
The pedestal has turned to rust
Weeds have choked the flowers
The jewels have been ground to dust.
My eyes are no longer loving
Instead they are filled with tears
No longer a god, but only a man
The perfection is no longer there.

— *Diane M. Presta*

Untitled

The wet sand squeezes between my toes,
The cool ocean breeze blows;
I smell the bitter salty air
And the wind rushes through my hair.

The seagulls fly up in the sky,
Swooping low and floating high;
The frothing waves come rolling in,
The red sun sets and night begins.

— *Holly Cookis*

Real Love

When I first met you,
it messed me up inside.
I've felt love,
but nothing like this.
I feel so warm inside.
It's you, all I think about.

I wish I had the heart
to say, *I love you,*
'cause that's how I feel.

I thought real love
was easy,
but it's painful.

— *Beth Spencer*

Untitled

heat lightning.
hot flashes in my mind,
etching pictures of desire
for you
upon my heart.

— *Jennifer Kuske*

The Rose

I'll give you a rose
That holds all happiness.
If the rose shall wilt or die,
Give it love and care,
For with that love and care,
The rose will live on
As does my love.

— *Jennifer Sherman*

Erotic Night

Full moon
 Tickled by thin clouds
Flloating lazily
 Naked as silk
Over this sub-Arctic landscape.
Below,
 The full-blown forest
Shivering its leaves
 (A standing ovation)
To this strange white whole
 peeking into the night.

— *Enrique Tessieri*

Forever

Never say forever
Because I know it isn't real.
It isn't something lasting;
It's something you think you feel.
But never say forever
Because forever makes me cry.

— *Jenny Covalt*

Love Is Like...

Love is like a flower,
It blooms then sometimes dies.
Love is like a river.
It flows till it dries.
Love comes from the heart,
Always from the start.
Love isn't something you can desert
Even though it sometimes hurts.
Love is like a rose
Till it dies in the mist.
Love is something that can change
Your life time and time again.

— *Becky Jackson*

Good and Bad Times

My heart gets filled up with things
That make me want to cry.
But it makes me feel much better
When I know you are near by.
The times that we've been together
Make me feel real good,
And when the bad times come along
I'd change them if I could.

— *Jessica Linder*

An Unexpressed Love

At that time, you always thought it would last
But now you realize it is all in the past.
Sitting at home waiting for his call
And thinking to yourself you have it all.

But when it never rings you wonder why,
And soon enough you start to cry.
What has happened between us two,
And you wish you knew.

Has he given me any clues
Or was I blind in watching his moves?
You thought it was love, but how do you know
All the many things that come and go.

Maybe someday we can get together again,
Because we were such good friends.
Wondering why we ever broke up and
Thinking if only we had better luck.

A love that you share with special people you know
Is something that can help you grow.

— *Nicole Moore*

Eye on Me

You watch me. Who are you?
You haunt me with those eyes.
Feelings of love rise in me as you stare.
Your eyes...their beauty is so rare
Should I dare stare back?
Do I lack the nerve?
I swerve in love
As you look above and at me.
I feel like I should flee from your gaze.
But you amaze me and I cannot look away.
I faze in and out of your stare.
My cares are lifted, I feel like I can fly.
Just as long as you spy me with your eyes.
But my hopes will never die as I lie in bed.
And instead of sleeping, I am keeping track of your eyes
Watching my every move. I want to prove my love to you
By keeping our hearts and thoughts in love's sweet views.

— *Angie Mirocha*

Understanding

Her eyes were like a mist of gray.
They were like fog and mist during night and day.
When she would be ready for night each day,
Her personality would change into a shade of gray,
For when she woke up each morning and day, her personality
Would change into sparkling and misty gray.
Her fragrance would be as fresh as the Lillies of the Valley
When she walked in the dewy clover in the morning
So fair and in the sunshine so bright:
For I'll never understand her divine way
But someday we'll meet in her enchanting way,
In her fog and mist during night and day.

— *Wendi Carruth*

Salvation

I pray for you
All day and night
Until my life
Is through
And when my
Time is over
You'll know that
He loves you.

— *Jenni Philpott*

Sweet One

For you, sweet one, passion burns.
My heart it calls, my body yearns.
I need you now here by my side,
To give me hope, to give me pride.
For you I call among the stars,
To place my heart where it belongs.
I love you truly and I care,
But not to be loved back, I cannot bare.
Farewell, sweet one, and cherish this poem,
For I wrote it for you and you alone.
I love you.

— *Amie Brown*

Untitled

Love is everywhere
it's all the memories
it's the time we share together
it's the dreams we dream
it's when we look into each other's eyes
it's our first kiss
it's the feelings that we feel
but most of all it's you, baby.
I love you, Steven!

— *Ann Marie Mellinger*

Never Ending Love

When next I see your face again,
We'll sail up high on the river gin;
On wings of doves to heavens high,
Up to the blue wonderous sky;
When snow white clouds for us do part,
We'll drift on through to his heart;
And when the golden bells ring thrice,
We'll dwell in peace in paradise

— *Jacquie Neeley*

Painful Words

He spoke to me
Only two words-
It's over.
One could not even begin to imagine
How two simple words
Could hold so much meaning.
I turned away, fighting back
The tears.
As I turned away, I realized
That this was only the beginning of
The end.
In one second,
My dreams shattered,
My heart was broken.
I heard you walking away
As a tear slowly slid down my cheek.
It's over.
And that's all that was said.

— *Jenna Thieszen*

My Husband, The Carpenter

My husband likes to measure, shape, hammer, nail and saw.
He loses himself and his spare time in his creation.
Happy in what he is doing with a piece of wood in a vice's jaw.
He makes lovely wooden gifts to our home, special friends and relations.

Our little home is a showcase for all his labor.
His handy touches, extra shelves and little tables.
And sometimes he even sells his artwork to a neighbor.
I call him my honey do please, if husbands have labels.

—*Desoree Thompson*

The Challenge

My mind has crossed a million stars
And I have seen a thousand sleepless nights.
Pain and fear grips my restless soul
As I ponder what lies for me untold.
But since that fateful day in 85
I've heard the voices of seven echoing from Heaven.
They paid the price for what they knew,
Of courage and direction to guide them through.
Now the clouds have lifted and the message is clear.
It is one of challenge to all mankind!
A challenge to continue the search—to continue the climb!
Life is more than mere survival.
It is love, compassion, understanding,
And the constant search of knowledge with a never ending drive for
New horizons. The gauntlet has been tossed and ours to head its call.
To live, to love, to discover, is the greatest challenge for us all!

—*Doug Bruner*

Lost Hope for a Future Generation

Past memories fade into the surrounding shadows
And the countless number of tears I have shed are lost in a clouded mind.
The pink neon lights that pierce the night
Reveal a lonely Chinese cafe,
And two men fighting.
The fear painted on their grimy faces
And their harsh words
Play in the reflection of the pink lights.
A crowd gathers inquisitively around them, inscribing them in a circle
Of hatred. The members of the crowd become one and cheer the white man
On the silence is powerfully loud as a knife plunges into the defenseless
Body again, again, and again. Fear pulls the crowd away,
Taking it back to a warm house,
But a dark shape is left behind in ths shadows of the lights.
The black man dies alone,
And past memories befome present reality once again.

—*Jennifer Burbridge*

Special Friends

The change of scenery was a little more than I could handle, then you
Walked into my life. The time we spent together was a pleasant type of
Escape from loneliness. School began and our friendship disintegrated.
You had developed new relationship with no need to remain only with my
Friendship. Then you returned; our friendship was revived but in a
Different way. I sought in you a person I could confide in and let out
My frustrations. In turn you did the same, but once again our closeness
Spread farther and farther. Something had come between us. Someone and
Something that I had trusted. As she slowly wormed her way into your
Life, our friendship was pushed out. You didn't realized it at the time, but
My love for you soon turned to hate. Learning to ignore became a routine
And hate subsided. Finally you realized just how bad she was for you
And what she had cost you. I wanted to renew our friendship but
Something from within held me back. I guess it was the hurt still talking.
Now we have become acquainted once more but yet again it is different.
The once playful joking has turned a tad more serious.

—*Diane Michelle Haig*

Year of the Child

There is a need of focusing the young.
One has only to think of the
Daily newspaper headlines:
Drug abuse.
Teen-age pregnancy.
Bodies lying dead in the streets.
Abortion, vandelism.
Child abuse.
Violence, suicides.
Neglect
The young on a round-the-clock basis.
It is hoped that the child of
The year,
Will encourage, will obey,
Will come together for the good
Of the people
Because of the great polar bear.
We can look forward to the future.
Of *The Year of the Child.*

— *Phyllis Malone*

Sometimes

Sometimes I do not feel loved.
Sometimes I feel unwanted.
Sometimes I feel all alone.
I am missing the love you have not shown.

Sometimes I wonder if you care.
Sometimes I get this outrageous scare.
Sometimes I wonder if I love you,
Or do I just feel sorry for the things you do.

—*Gwendolyn Murray*

Flimsy Excuses

No need to ask questions, your suggestions
Only masquerade as conclusions for your reasons why.
Flimsy excuses for a guilt free good bye.
You promised you would never leave; mere professions.
I need no further confessions.
Only death would set us free...a lie.
Beloved, truly gone is the need to try.
Love's melted passion brings on aggressions.
Teary eyes disguise the stare of murder...surprised?
So I shot him in his chest.
Without guilt, I watched him die.
Before his last breath, I realized
His clenched fist tore my dress.
A concluded solution echoes eternally...Goodbye.

—*Debra Mathenia Hollmon*

Getting Over Him

I miss you so much,
My body aches for your tender touch.
I look back at our times together,
Oh how I wish it would continue forever.
Why is life so unfair?
I've realized that he doesn't care.
If he did why did he hurt me,
You tortured my heart and I sob constantly.
I feel so miserable, I don't know what to do,
Days go by as I desperately try to forget you.
I take a deep breath, and start a new.
Trying to find that special someone meant
For me but it wasn't you. So you have to look
For him and try again. Your heart is broken
But it will mend.

— *Niki Yulissa Arakas*

War

No winner
No loser
Promises made
Promises broken
Children's cries
Adult's screams

They say they love
They say they care
They say they'll protect
They say they'll always be there

Young soldiers
Miles of white stone
Dead flowers
Tears
Cries
Death
—*Emma Snowball*

Air Force Cadets

To the ramparts
Of country's call,
To the ramparts
Cadets all.
Hearts soaring with the falcon
High above the Rampart Range.
Stalwart American son
Fly above the Rampart Range.

To the ramparts
Of life and beauty
To the ramparts
Of loyal duty.
Hearts soaring with the falcon
High above the Rampart Range.
Stalwart American son
Fly above the Rampart Range.
—*Elizabeth Wilkinson Anderson*

The Desert Breed

Horses galloping along the shore,
Running to a land of evermore.
A land of all eternity,
For creatures of great beauty.
Blood a thousand years old
Flowing through their veins,
Born wild for only the winds to tame.
Of Arab blood are these horses of grand
Who live and die among the desert sand,
But none of that matters in their sacred lives,
For their only concern is to live, love and survive.
—*Jeannette Gallivan*

1976

I'll never know for certain when
You rejected me
No, not even
When I rejected you
But here we are
Two thirties
Running through a busy life and feeling
Guilty over our deception-
The insincerity of not
Whispering or yelling, 'reject!'
All the while
Telling the children to *tell the truth,*
And *exactly how they feel.*
We do this without self-understanding
So as to avoid guilt
Or even worse; rejection.
—*Ann Marie Power*

Freedom Cry

The brittle cold of winter will crack;
The blisters baked in summer sun.
Reality will break your bending back.
You will snap-on a plastic smile,
Melting into despair, in your safe heart.
Never deciding; a choice too tough to make;
Ice crystals melt
Into passionate longing.
Once again encouragement spawns hope.
Sparks fly as needles sharpen and
Preparation begins for weaving a new fabric.
—*Debora R. Krebs*

Only Two Things in Life

As soldiers all, from cradle to grave
Mankind marches toward life's final end
Not wordly things but memories save
Truly blessed to have had one true friend
Slowly begun but even faster the pace
We all travel the pathway of life
The most bitter of tears sometime love will erase
Sweetest joy often trampled by strife
I have time without end, a statement of youth
But alas, turn around and we are old
Love everlasting is seldom the truth
Fires of love unattended grow cold
But eyes ages old still sparkle and sing
If just once they have seen love ever true
Important in life there are only two things
Someone to love, someone to love you
—*Dayton Farley Jr.*

Open Roads

To build a road to freedom, to build a road to life,
To build a road of destiny was always in my sight.
What Heaven really means is solitude and might,
A place with no wars, where no one's ever blamed,
A place where nature rules the land and freedom
Will never be claimed.
Where the sun sets slow, we still have time to see
The earth and sea and mysteries beneath.
Time changes land and the clouds that furled
As we stop to think what will never leave this world.
— *Jen Schofield*

Sunset of Fury

A raving sunset
Resting upon the sea.
Light rods of...
Red, violet, orange, gold
mingle together;
Blanketed clouds
—tinted blue-
interwine among majestic colors.
A sweet breeze sculptures
—of this subtle scene-
a fiery funnel of fury,
Aloft in the sky...
away from mortal destruction.
—*Amy K. Smoke*

Crisis in Sanity

Thank God, there are people,
Not always, good or bad.
That help us all, to touch our self,
Feeling of happiness, or sad.

Forever we are growing,
From the past, all time and space.
Forever we are sowing,
Future seeds, throughout this place...

When we ever get,
So, so, far ahead...
To be behind, the past unwind.
To lightly, soften up, the bed.

Will we cure all insanity?
To realize, reality.
If there comes humanity,
Understanding, silently.
—*William G. Thompson*

Grace

A hundred thousand years go by
And yet, remains the same.
The foremost end to all becomes
A passion in its game.

Believe and feel its righteous hand
A light upon a place,
Hidden from the world outside
The beauty...
Yes, it is Grace.
—*Jan P. Lawson*

The Vagabond

I am the vagabond sea,
Rolling over the sands,
The gold fleeced lane to the world.
And the pathway to distant lands.
Under the winds that sway the world,
That moan and cry and sing,
I alone in a world of my own,
I, alone am king.
Here in my depths lies the past
And on my foamy, white breast,
Who but God, alone, knows
That here the future may rest.
—*Eleanor Dodge*

My Mother's Hands

My mother's hands
are cracked and dry
yet she toils
throughout the day
she gives me love
I know not why
so long I've been away.
The time she's spent
caring for others
and now—me—with mine
I'd like to see her
day by day
walking among her flowers.
　　— *Anne W. Dean*

Accepting the Destiny of Life

My treasured memories of days past;
Are unique in every way.
Bringing everlasting happiness,
With blessed thoughts of thee.
Accepted advice given from friends;
Never questioning them why?
Celebrating events from the past,
By fulfilling all my dreams.
Exchanging knowledge with wisdom,
Great accomplishment complete.
I realize now what the future holds;
Is the path to my destiny.
　　— *Jean Ann Wakeman*

Simplification

Simplify your style of life
In this day of get and gain
Simplify it once again and
While you have the time...
Slow down

Now is the time for simplification
Take a moment of vacation
From the hassle and the worry
Take the time now...
Not to hurry.

All the fuss and all the bother
Tend to shake us up somewhat
Learn to simplify the matter
It will simplify
Your life
A lot.
　　—*I. C. Murphy*

Broken Promises

When I was young
I believed what I was told
I lived in a dream
Believing everything without a thought
Liars, they lied to me.
They really do not see,
What life is all about.
Everything is out there,
Someday I will find it,
That freedom I long for.
I will live for myself.
I will forget the broken promises
For I will have won.

　　—*Heather Lynn Gay*

Father's Hands

His hands like a bulldozer
level thorns in life for the family.

His stout hands lift
a tomorrow's dream against
the unexpected changing time.

When I was ten
early spring in the field, he ploughed
and told me:
*Sweat irrigating soil will
grow grain one day, even for rugged earth.*

In the coming fall
he held my hands walking on the ground,
I finally understood what's the deep feeling of a tiller.
I read his pleasant smile,
and my heart was flooded with the warmth of harvest
via his callous hands...
　　— *Pang-Jen Kung*

Why Parents Love You

They love you when you're wrong
And somehow make life a song.
They love you when you're out all night long.
They love you when you're bad.
They love you when you're sad,
But they will always try to make you glad.
They love you no matter what you do.
That's why parents love you!
　　— *Debby Pratt*

Pleasures of our Memories

In the mirrored reflections of our past,
It's the simple things that seem to last
And upon out heart their happiness cast
The pleasures of our memories.

Winter's magic harmony
Was the twinkling icicle symphony
With sparkling diamonds on the snow
Where sunbeams danced to and fro.

Yet, summer lingered very slow.
Under the swaying branches of the trees,
Lying in the waves of ocean grass,
I watched the drifting clouds roll past.

I found other ways for time to pass.
Pump handle rides, making mud pies,
It's the simple things that seem to last
In the mirrored reflections of our past.
　　—*Delayne McKinley*

A Grandmother's Love

Love is tender; love is sweet.
But a grandmother's love goes much deep.
A cut on your finger, a tear in your eye,
A grandmother's love will brighten the sky.
A problem you have that needs to be resolved,
A grandmother's love will make it dissolve.
A boring day or a rainy sky,
A grandmother's love will make it pass by.
So now you know of a grandmother's love,
And a grandmother's love will never die.
So don't think of a love so grand,
A grandmother's love must be made of a loving hand.
　　—*Victoria Buglione*

Reaching for Home

I was lonely and afraid,
Always reaching back for home.
No matter what you did or said
Still I wanted to go home.
Now I am here,
But this is not home.
I realize that home is not a place.
Home is the warmth of your arms,
The smell of your skin,
The sound of your heart.
I am lonely and afraid,
And again
I want to go home.
　　—*Jennifer Getzinger*

Mother

Little lines erase,
The beauty from your face.
Eyes that once a sparkle lit,
May cloud and dim a bit.
And though with age,
Your skin may change.
Your hair may a little gray,
And sometimes fade away.
Time cannot steal,
The inner beauty so real.
Nor take the skills attained.
Or the wisodm gained
No one can steal your title,
Of *World's Greatest Mom* and
My life long idol.
　　— *Buffy Weaver*

Comfort

They are strong but gentle,
They comfort and console,
Touching my face
They relax and lull

They used to wipe my tears
And hush my cry,
But now they only
Wave goodbye

Now they no longer wear
Wedding bands,
But they will always be
My father's hands.
　　—*Jessica Mefford*

Changes

It is cold outside
the ground covered with snow,
I'm alone in a cabin
with someone I know.
Outside is the world
all white and grey;
a fire crackles inside
in its own warm way.
Time will pass by
crisp air will be smelt,
birds singing, snow melting
spring soon to be felt.
The sun beating hard
on the ground down below,
we'll come back next year
after the snow.
　　— *Denise Taylor*

Success

I've always been told the secret to success
Be yourself, be the best and nothing less.
But in my opinion there's better advice,
You have to work your hardest no matter what the price.

Set your goal and pride youself in getting there.
People who work real hard will reach it but those people are rare.
Never set a limit to how high you want to go,
There's always better so take every chance, don't say no.

If you want something bad enough you can get it for sure,
So keep on striving and with each rejection endure.
For many lessons you have to learn and keep it in mind,
Always give that extra effort and success you will find.

— *April Probasco*

But You See, You Know

Many a night, I would stay up and think, about fiction,
Dishonor and my brain that might shrink.
When life could come to this marching end
With all that ran backwards, unwilling to bend.

I would tear and thrust, being perfectly nervous.
But all this empty hanging had no purpose.
You see, the dead once whispered something about innocence,
Which I would carry cheerfully for some distance.

To a house full of pain, all in mystery, all insane.
And there, lying in complete procession
Was all of my previous ultimate obsession.

Strapped ridiculously to crooked chairs, unavoiding my excercising stares.
Such make belive made me feel so indifferent.
But of course, I was on moonbitten pavement.
This whole was an unforgiving movie screened,
But I born again, had just been weaned.

—*Evan Beloff*

The Fruitless Passion

With the moon shining bright and the stars twinkling on high,
Sparkles a love so true, a love so pure, a love that money can never buy.
A love that grew from the seed of friendship planted way back when,
With visions of a love that could have been; that should have been.
As I sit at our spot and watch the ripples in the pond,
I reminisce on golden memories you made so fond.
If in the future this love is not meant to be,
Let us remain forever friends from now through eternity.
I'll always recall our lost love with a mournful sigh,
Knowing the happiness I could have given if only given the chance to try.
'Tis a true love, a pure love, t'is an everlasting love,
'Tis a love that can only come from heaven above.
'Tis a love sent from God as he reigns on high,
'Tis a love very few men experience before we die.

—*A. M. Womack*

Grandma

Mamma always told me to write you a letter.
She said news from us made you feel a little better.
Just tell her that you love her and you wish that you could see her
And you'll try to come out Sunday; you miss her, that's for sure.
I never even called you and I always had a dime
But I never knew what could happen in such a short time.
I just took it for granted you would always be around.
You weren't just a grandma, but a friend that I had found.
I thought that you would be there for all my little needs
And I like you never scolded when I did a dirty deed.
I never knew your family very well, I must admit.
We just grew up different, I never thought I fit.
But now I know them better after all that we've been through.
We were all there together; it was something we had to do.
At the end, when you wouldn't speak and inside you tried to hide,
I understand now and in a way I too have died.

— *Bridget Marchese*

Awaken to a Dream

Life begins again for me.
That June 19th shall mark the day.
Who will journey to the garden
At early morn to see
The division of the cycle of the earth?
The sunrise did so and I am reborne.

Take my mind and walk with me,
Though, only for until the darkness falls.
Flowers always bloom again
And nature sees the springtime
For their life throughout the season.
The sunrise did so and is reborne.

You have taken me away
Fom the pain that I once knew of.
You will see to give me strength to carry on
And live the life that I have dreamed so very long.
The sunrise is so and you are reborne.

—*C. Cheryl Lemmons*

Moving

As I travel down the road
The sky behind me is a brilliant blue.
The sky in front of me is drab and gloomy.
As I cross the state line.
A single tear rolls down my cheek.
I remember all the good times I've had.
Even though I will make new memories,
Life will never be as perfect as it was in the beginning.

— *Heather Reese*

Being Grandpa

Being grandpa is lots of fun, at least that is what they say
You grab yourself a lot of hugs, and then just stroll away.
But I wanted more than that, you see, so we went off together
To Epcot Center, Disney World and all that lovely weather.
They hurried here, they scurried there, then suddenly were bored
Keeping pace with all their whims could leave you kind of floored.
The apartment was a clutter, baseball cards were everywhere
And anywhere you tried to sit, furry creatures filled the chair.
We all played ball within the pool, splashing one another
The smaller child, angelic girl, was teasing her big brother.
Suddenly her whining rose, clumped gum was in her hair
Not knowing what you should do next, you fixed him with a stare.
The gum created quite a mess until her grandma faced it
Ice cubes and scissors eased the pain, snacks all around erased it.
So daily we splashed, we walked, talked and read
And they ended each day as they collapsed into bed.
Ah! It is peaceful and quiet, you can rest from your day
Being grandpa is just fine, at least that's what I say.

—*William C. Sinclair*

God I Am

I am the moment.
I rise as the swelling of the belly of dawn,
Such brilliance, my radiation is but a hue a myself.
You have seen the embers of my shadow child, birthed,
Rising in the east;
Could you comprehend the real light of me that casts the shadow
You see as morning sky?
I am the moment of that understanding.

I am timeless
In me slides the grain of sand gently grazing,
Ongoing, forever ongoing upon the murky river bed bottom.
I touch my brothers as I am, and as I am,
Propelled by the current of my water love.
I am the forever moment
Never separated from my self.

—*Brigid L. Foster*

Dust Devil

A pro-creative miracle is done
When ancient sea is sipped by thirsty sun,
Its bed reduced to sediments, on land
Composed of shifting, hot and sterile sand.

In meeting, vectors mate,...engage in sin
To clock and counter-clock a lusty wind.
A snaking dust will rise to that turmoil
In satan's torrid, shameless ballet royal.

From devils' rite, a sprite from desert torn,
A lively, leaping ballet star is born
To dance passe,...perform the pirouette,
Then tour-jete across the gritty set.

Circling, curling, whirling-dervish funnel,
Demon spawn in twisting, cyclone tunnel,
Conceived in wanton lust for this debut,
Expends its energy and then,...adieu.

Old mother nature's wine will oft bouquet
Her cameos. Strip-teased,...they're quite risque.
　　　—Edwin L. Stephens

Four Seasons and a Wish

When bluebirds sing on the garden gate
And showers blow your way,
You will hear a cadence soft and sweet...
And you will remember me.
When summer sun sends its warm rays down
And trout flash in the stream,
You will miss my smile and warm hand clasp,
And you will remember me.
When golden leaves swirl sprighly down
On our old familiar trysts,
You'll long for my touch with deep desire
And you will remember me.
When snowflakes fall on a wintry night
And burning logs fill the grate,
There will come laughter from far away
And you will remember me.
　　　— Alba H. De La Pena

Untitled

Oh, how many flowers.
Don't worry, she would say.
The true beauty is in your heart.
I wish it would all stay the same.
The gentle breeze touches my cheek,
The cold grass under my toes.
A hawk circles above,
She is going home to her children.
They are hungry, she provides.
I love my mama.
We are a pair.
We run through the flowers barefoot
As if nothing matters—does it?
When I am with Mama, nothing else does,
Nothing in the world.
I am hungry, she provides.
　　　— Carmen Levasseur

True Love

The willow weeps great green tears...
That shed, and wither and die.
The hawthorne tree, with its backdrop sky...
Shudders... and then sighs.

The lovely lake, a mirror pure...
Reflects the cloudless tie
Of memories and ducks flown by
Of love that said *I'll try.*
　　　—Alva Irish

All Eternity

The captain sails the ship
Through the stormy sea
And the waters calm down
As smooth as can be.
While in port he stops
And draws a crowd.
He's followed around
Throughout the town.
Children love him
And follow him around.
He is their captain;
He sails from town to town
Healing the sick
And showing his love.
He is the son of God.
If we only listen
And sail our ships
We'll weather the storms
And sail the seas
Through all eternity...
　　　—Ann Marie Murrell

Untitled

Mother burned
scorched
How can I see the
bright lea
When floods this life
with treachery
Mother's light burns
dim
The flaying words of
life and limb
I fill with the stench
of words unsaid
Cannot I waken from
the dead
The setting sun it draws
to close
The weight of Mother love
too heavy a load
　　　—Ann Bajovich

Life Goes On

As life goes on
 I feel lost
Sometimes I wonder
 what's right or wrong
Don't think I can go on

If I found a rainbow
 in a drawn out dream
 I couldn't go on
If I found the right
 or the wrong
I'd feel lost forever
 But life goes on

Life goes on
 with me or without
Life goes on
 and I don't know why.
　　　— Carol L. Taylor

Up

Today the world is removed from its box,
And the sky is unzipped.
Childrens' voices play with the stars
Like carefully plucked strings.
Today the sun and moon are in the same bowl;
Flowers whisper to the clouds,
And you and I will jump
Into the sky to ride on
 Wind's gift, and listen to this splendid sight.
　　　— Alden Elizabeth Jones

Deliverance

Oh how foul a wind hast blown to bring such
A heavy yoke to bear and rest on my shoulders.
My forgotten sins of past transgressions
Surely have called for the debt to be paid in full
Elst how can my burden compound itself with
Such regualrity...giving little or no quarter.

Is mine as the fate of others before me to decimate
And destroy myself on the rocky shoals of life.
Asking...awaiting for destiny to call, to serve,
But alas be denied. Oh blow ye foul wind that
Bids me to suffer then serve, but to suffer
For the sake of suffering only, nay. My soul
Cries from within for deliverance, but alas
My ship is awash with the heavy ballast of sin
Doomed to flounder in the stormy seas of life.
　　　— Ed Kassner

Cages of Freedom

In a society exhibiting the symptoms
Of acute mental illness
We need to identify not the enemies
Without our realm of peace
But recognize the cages within that strife
The fullness of life bred into us.

Neurotically we reject the cage of loving
To be caged in the duties of love.
Angrily we lash at the opportunities in life
To embrace the prison of pleasure.
Boredly we frustrate the exhileration of doing
To cheer the occasion of spectating.

So brick, by brick we build the cells
That imprison our destiny,
Until illusion waltzes with delusion
To the silent tune of chaos.
And we whimper our passing breath
To agonize the living who love us.
　　　—Arthur E. Winslow

Lonely Man

When does love stop and hate begins
For not knowing what are sins?
An animal throughout his life,
Man does not want to take a wife.
Plays the field in all its glory,
Sometimes pleasant, sometimes gory.
But he knows best from what and when,
A chance to find himself again.
Following through to seek a new,
Man must change a rule or two.
When shadows fall before your feet,
'Tis not darkness but defeat.
Go for the gold with all its merit;
Never too late to change and share it.
The world becomes a new found place
With happiness for the human race.
　　　—Albert L. Buzzo

Ma'at

I searched
deeply for
Mary
and
found
The Black Madonna
— *Auset BaKhufu*

The Mirror

I look in the mirror
And who do I see?
A person with a life
Full of pain and misery.
No past worth remembering,
No present, no hope;
She's seen it all
Though in a very small scope.
Yes, I look in the mirror
And who do I see?
A hurting child
Looking back at me.
— *Georganna Creech*

Soldier Boy

You
won my love
because
you
died so graciously
and I
look upon your grave.
My tears
miniscule
to the childhood you
lost.
My love
miniscule
to the life
you lost.
— *Amy Whitfield*

Wondering

Did you ever reach the sky?
Did you ever wonder why?
Wonder why the grass is green,
Wonder what you haven't seen,
Wonder what the sun is like,
Burning like a candle light.
Wonder what the moon is like,
Shining in the starlit night.
—*Andrea Lee Schmidt*

Untitled

If you do not understand
What is going on
In my head,
Just ask me.

If you want to
Believe in me
And love me
For who I am,
Just tell me.

But if for some reason
You cannot
Or will not
Or even do not care,
Just leave me.
—*Ali Buie*

Memories, Memories

Memories, memories of a cabin in the sky
Fill my mind with many thoughts of you and I
Watching flickering flames burn a glowing trace
Across cedar logs, burning in our cabin's fireplace.

Memories, memories of lovers in the night,
Holding hands in soft flickering candlelight
Sparkling through two glasses filled with wine;
My heart filled with love and joy while you were mine.

Memories, memories of music, sweet and low,
Records playing songs of love by firelight glow.
The snowflakes falling outside our cabin door
Coccooned two lovers from the snowy winter hoar.

Memories, memories of our love will stay
Within my mind and soul until we meet some day,
And find again that tender loving joy we knew
In that warm log cabin, with the snowy mountain view.
— *Fred W. A. Smith*

Note to a Playboy Philosopher...on his 60th Birthday

A butterfly in the glory of her brief day,
A blaze of color in the summer afternoon,
Sparkled like fractured sunbeams on rippling lakes;
Her wings, royal blue, fringed in white,
Too virgin pure to be of this world at all;
Once caught a Boy Scout's roving eye,
And was impaled upon his common pin.
His collection gathers dust, and the child,
Now old, still pins his skirted butterflies.

But framed upon my wall, crafted by the artful hands
Of some Chinese Michelangelo, is a thing of beauty,
Pagodas, bridges, mountain streams.
Classic lines stitched with patient care
On silk, the fantasy of...a moth.

Fools still trap the butterflies
To impale upon their pins.
But moths enrapture wise men
With fantasies of silk.
—*Carlton W. Truax*

Ship of Youth

Silent to the distant call
The young mother cries
Not knowing how to live at all.
The candle of youth flickers then dies.
She is alone on her Odyssea
Scared with feelings of a child
Motherhood unannouncing came
Waking realization far too suddenly.
How cruel the world really is
Gone is the beauty of innocence
Overcome by ugly ignorance
Guilt plaguing, can't escape closed doors
Creaking with age before their time.
Prisoner of her body, warden to her heart.
Love is extended but dies before reaching her.
Turned to rain then bitter tears
So filled with emotion they glide away, frightened
Dreaming of an untitled ship upon a foreighn ocean.
That she never again will board
The once familiar but now forgotten ship of youth.
To a dear friend
—*Ariella Chezar*

Lost Love

Love is gone
I saw him go
We kiss and part
Forever

My tears are like water running
My heart is in pain
Out of life and into death
Good-bye
— *Estela Aboyme-Patel*

Up to You

There is a special way for living
For everyone of the kind.
If what doing you believing
What create your peace of mind
Then develop aspiration
On the level you can cope
With awareness true perception
Where to start and when to stop.

There is a special way for living
And artistry changing heart,
Challenge after challenge meaning
Only daily living chart
Which you drawing on self power
To find in world worthy place,
So develop richer fuller
Your potential, to do best
Your potential, to be best.
—*Adam F. Misterka*

Your Eyes

Your eyes.
What they hide from me
I do not know.

They are so dark.
They look somewhere else.
Not at me,
Not anywhere
But at something else.
They hide your feelings,
They hide your emotions
inside of you.
They will never come out.

You stare at me.
You look deep within me.
Do you see my feelings
inside of me?
I don't know.
—*Abigail Hofman*

Missing Piece

Red and satiny,
Smooth all around,
Made of diamonds
Nailed to the ground.
Silk so fine,
Like golden hair.
Ivory cups
Designed with flair.
These riches fill
My castle you see,
But what I really need
Is you with me.
— *Adrineh Shahijanian*

My Daily Prayer

Dear Lord;
There are things I do not understand,
but I rest assured, because you're in command.
There are times when I've sat and cried,
then I remember how You suffered and died.
Please give me strength, please give me courage,
to fight off those who try to discourage.
To keep the devil behind me at all times,
to walk in Your love and let Your light so shine.
So others may see You through the works I do,
to remember those words that came only from You.
To keep the faith, no matter what the cost,
to walk straight ahead and never be lost.
Keep me near, my Lord so Dear,
walk with me, talk with me,
please don't leave me alone, because,
the people are hard and cold like stones!
You are my Strength, my Hope, my Redeemer,
please, Dear Lord, don't leave me here to linger.

—*Gloria J. Washington*

Religion

What is religion to me?
It's being able to love the many people who thrive in animosity
And abuse you to make their dreams come true.

What is religion to me?
It's being able to smile when you are hurting from scorn
And when you are able to realize the real reason you are born.

Born to return that great love which God gave to you
And feel sorry for others who cannot share it with you, too.

What is religion to me?
It makes me smile when it's necessary because
any tears I shed are for your sorrow.
It gives me great insight to know your schemes
And I don't have to respond to your dreams.
I am strong, I don't need to scheme.

I don't need to run away, I can walk.
I don't need to cry, I can smile.
I don't need to be judged, I advocate justice.
I know when to love, which is always.
That's why I smile all the time,
The God in me utters every sound.

—*Willie Mae Latimore*

Life

There will be times in your life, when you will feel sad,
And there is nothing, that will make you glad.
All of your feelings, are tied in a ball,
And to you those feelings, do not seem small.

You will not know which way to turn,
And as tears fill your eyes, they begin to burn.
You cry for your hopes, your loves and your dreams,
And inside your heart, you let out screams.

Then one day these feelings dissolve,
Although they still remain unsolved.
It appears your life is right on track,
The problems remain, but you do not look back.

These are the ups and downs of life you see,
It happens to you, it happens to me.
Inside our hearts, we are all the same,
And for our problems, no one is to blame.

Life has many twists and turns,
And to overcome them, is something we all must learn.

—*Heather Moran*

Jesus, When You're Ready...

Jesus, when You're ready, take my hand and walk me home.
I've been waiting for a long time but I don't want to go alone.
I know that there are mansions and the streets are paved with gold,
But it's the valley of the shadow that I'm afraid to walk alone.

Jesus, please forgive me; I know You are my friend
And I know that You promised You'd stay with me till the end,
But somehow I can't help it; I feel so alone.
Jesus, when You're ready, take my hand and walk me home.

Now Jesus when You call me, I'll be ready to go
And I won't mind leaving this world below,
But there's one thing I ask You, please don't make me go alone.
Promise when You're ready, You'll take my hand and walk me home.

— *Georgia Ellin*

Christ, the Beginning and the End

The past, present, and future revolve around Christ.
Because of the sins of mankind God, the Son, left Heaven
To be born of a virgin, whose lineage included King David. He came in
Augustus Caesar's time who defied God with Baalbek. Twelve men he
Chose to follow him and change the world from darkness into his glorious
Light of truth. Yet one, Judas Iscariot, chose to betray him instead.
The lamb of God willingly gave Himself for the sins of the world.
On the third day after His crucifixion Christ arose conquering
Sin, death, and the grave, never suffering corruption. Five hundred saw
Him at one time. Later He ascended into heaven. Ten days after that event
On the day of Pentecost in Jerusalem Christ founded his church when
Peter preached the first sermon. Three thousand were baptized after showing
Faith and repentance. By following the new testament and enduring to end
Of life the christian will have the greatest future of all-
The guarantee to live with God and His loved ones forever.
Will you stand up for Christ on earth to dwell with Him in heaven?

—*Virginia W. Thomason*

Faith, Love and Fear

Faith is like a flower. It grows and blooms letting itself fill
the air with scents of perfumes which spread like a rash
throughout time sometimes like a golden chime that produces
itself like an endless rhyme. Let it be know that Faith is
like a stone. It cannot break, it is not a fake. Faith can
fill the emptiness where there is none. It can provide for the
young. Faith works for the future and endures the past.

It has but one enemy, and it is fear. Fear is a feeling that
danger or evil is near. A serpent of the Devil can make fear
grow. We must lessen fear with faith. We must have knowledge
that fear cannot grow in us if we have faith. It cannot touch us
if we have faith. So have faith my children.

Last but not least comes love. Love is like an hourglass. Only
it cannot end nor break. It puts a blanket over fear, and it
waters faith.

So now that I have enlightened your thoughts I ask but one
thing. What I have said let it spread throughout the nation
like a disease known to man as a grateful attempt to cure the
world.

—*Amy L. VanValkenburg*

Let's Go Travel

Let's follow the wild goose on its flight,
Watch the beaver at work in the pale moonlight,
Smell the scent of the pine in the mountains high,
And listen to the eagle's lonely mournful cry.

Let's stop for lunch at a cozy inn,
Where none of us have ever been;
Then bask in the sun by the shimmering sea,
And indulge ourselves in luxury.

Now we've visited all our favorite shops;
Heard the sigh of the wind on the mountain tops;
Had a peaceful night in a quaint motel;
And we are blessed that all has gone so well.

As our journey rounds its final bend,
We rejoice in meeting our new found friends;
In merriment our voices blend,
And wish this day would never end.

—*Ann M. Toomey*

Bethlehem

Sublimely sound the vibrant chords of arcanum harp
By quick gratitude of the lover's deep human heart,
Burnt by tenderness rising by inner beauty
Of expressions and by the fullness of power—light
Above the ancient miraculous Bethlehem's holy night.

Stupors circumvent. The cosmos,
Transformed by the glimmer of the stars,
The regal splendor of the sun,
The luminous flux-silver of the moon,
The intense fragrance of the gardens,
The azure breathing of the sea,
The harmonious waters of the rivers,
The high snowy crests of the mountains,
The soft rotundity of the hills,
The green oasis of the forests, the immense plains
Of all the nature are in festival and merriment
Because of an immortal charming event
That continues, at Christmas Day, to astonish the space
And the season among the growing humanity.
All the souls in love are shuddering placably!

—*Franco Buono*

Loneliness

Approached alone,
Your eyes tinged with sadness.

I can see what life
Has done to cause your grief.

Shortly and briefly
Our paths cross for awhile.

We try to make the best
Of a hopeless situation.

What you seek,
You may not know.

Is something I cannot give
At this moment.

—*Edward Ehrlicher*

The Flame

A burning candle
Sits with a flame,
Wild and willing
Without any shame.
It lingers longingly
Lusting its light,
To force out darkness
And banish the night.
Only a little one
But nothing to fear,
That won't give up
'Till daylight draws near.

— *Eileen Mooney*

The Hurricane

A hurricane howls like a wolf.
It demolishes things and
Rips them apart like a hungry lion,
A predator swirling across the sea.

— *Cara Williams*

Raindrops

Cold, crisp tears
Fall from the sky.
I wipe off my face
Which does not stay dry.

Musky odors
Tickle my nose.
Nickel size drops
Dampen my clothes.

The sky remains
A dull looking gray.
Yet wetness does not
Ruin my day.

It livens me up
But I still wonder why
All of these clouds
Make heaven cry.

—*Carla Noto*

Cry of the Cat

gentle silver memories
wrap around me against the dark
yet lonely loud pain still makes me weary

but long ago love acts to shield
somewhat from sight and sound
the cry of the cat.

— *Catherine Blair*

Departure

A sailor of the stars
On the wings of the night;
I travel far
Yet my bed is still in sight.
As I travel through the sky
Where the air grows thin;
I spot the house where I lie,
And the rising sun, still dim.
I can never go back
Yet I do not feel sorrow,
My life I now lack
For me there is no longer a tomorrow.

—*Carolyn Hoey*

Someday

Pale blue eyes,
Crying.
My fragile heart,
Broken, dying.
My love for you,
Never fading.
Here I am
Forever waiting.

— *Angela Shallenberger*

Waste Not . . . Want Not

When you tell your friends,
I have nothing to wear,
Did you look to see
What is hanging there?

One Sunday outfit
Two changes for school
Take care . . . make them last,
Was our daily rule!

We learned how to mend
When the *hole* was small
We have things away
When we grew too tall!

Your favorite jeans
With holes in the knees
Shirt buttons missing . . .
Better mend them, please!

—*Edna M. Parker*

Untitled

With love you see,
With light you cry.
These emotions build
Up like a balloon
Ready to explode.
What will
Come of
These
Feelings?
I saw through
Love guiding me
Through life like a
Daydream,
But then woke to find
No love.
I wept great tears
Of reality.
The love was gone.

—*Carrie R. Johnson*

Say It

Everybody has a story,
Listen people to what I am telling you.
Everyone has his glory.
We all at one time or other will be blue.

From win and lose.
The varied otrocities.
From the bottom of their raggedy shoes.
To the tips of their extremities.

No more, yes, yet less clean air to breathe.
We pack our children and grab our clothes.
It is never too soon to leave.
Because everyone knows, and everyone goes.

To the country.
Where your old neighbor is now your new one.
There goes another oak tree.
And the band plays on and the band plays on...

—*Carlos Castro*

Spoken In the Wind

In the quiet times of solitude
We seldom have to ourselves,
The wind whispers answers,
To the questions we ask in spirit.

The wind howels in our times of lonliness,
A warning of a force at hand,
One that we cannot see,
One that we cannot understand

The wind cries for the forgotten souls
That cannot speak for themselves
Whos credit lies in the hands,
Of the ungrateful.

The wind, the great communicator
The breath of the imagination.

The wind whispers
The wind howels
The wind cries
Does the wind ever laugh?

—*Allen Camilleri*

Dream on, Young Dreamer

Reach to the stars, young dreamer,
Your future could be there
Not in fruitless dreams,
But in actions, if you dare!
Dreams are just the basis,
For which we plan our life
But in them we cannot live forever
Because our lives could end in strife!
So dream on, oh young explorer,
The world is yours to enjoy
There need not be any limits,
Be you man, woman, girl or boy!
Strive for success young dreamer
Keep determination in your heart
Soar the heights of countless horizons,
But in your life always make God a part!

—*Carmen Irving*

My Love

When I think of you and the times we've had
It makes me want to sing.
Our life hasn't been all roses,
But the petals of happiness
Weigh over the thorns of displeasure.
Understand, my love, that you are my life
And I thank you for all the love you have given.

— *Carol L. Ruth*

Silhouettes

Silhouettes against the dark of night
Against the moon shining bright
One miniature star to put in your hand
To take away to a far off land.
Music playing soft yet clear
Enough to soothe a savage fear.
Scent of sea breeze tickles your nose
With the faintness of a summer rose.
Walk away down the ocean side
You feel so light you almost glide.
The crashing of waves at your feet
Makes you feel the world is complete.
Forever breaking on the shore
Wish upon that single star that
You could stay forever more.

—*Autumn S. Crisp*

Lament of an Autumn Leaf

New Hampshire, my New Hampshire
I love thee, I did not want to leave
My home throught the icy branches
Or the whispering green leaves
On a warm sunny day.
My home on a sugar hill with
Maple leaves so red, I did not
Want to leave thee New Hampshire.
Sun slanting eyes dispatched me
Through a messenger, now I
Am dead.
Do not forget me, remember my
Demise. This fall, paint brush
Full color, destruction once started,
Others will fall.

— *Ann Kimberlynn*

You

When you touch me
A chill goes up my spine
When you hold me close and love me
I can see that you are mine
When you kiss me
My heart skips a beat
My love for you flows from my head
Down to my feet
When you make love to me
My body trembles with a love so strong
It makes me realize
Loving you cannot be wrong.

—*Carissa Ann Spaulding*

On Going West

While walking westward to the sea
To see what is before me
I have a feeling I will be
Quite wet if waves rush over me!

Wet is a way of life with thee,
Sweet mermaid in thy beauty,
You becon me, quite haughtingly
As if it was my duty
To walk in water westwardly
While acting resolutely
But you and I cannot agree
For all we do astutely:

Though wetness is a way with you,
It drowns me, absolutely!

—*Earl Amundsen*

We Three

Out set we three, on a journey far, far from home.
A forbidden one, which only encouraged us more
To roam. Though the path was long
And each step painstakingly slow, we three.

Never faltered in heart, and barely in spirit.
The journey went on, from beginning to end.
Not elegant, or even fun. But more of a fulfillment
Of the soul and the spirit.

For knowing that one so young could outwit
The trained minds of their elders, is a joy.
That can be known by no other,
Than we three.

—*Carlly Albers*

A Broken Mirror

A large mirror broken into different shapes
Lay scattered on a city's sidewalk.
Some people walked by and wondered
How the mirror had gotten there.
A few ignored the shattered pieces,
Too busy to stop and consider.
Others just glanced and hurried by,
Too superstitious to look.
But, once in a while, a curious pedestrian
Would carefully pick up a fragment
To look at and sometimes keep.
So, the once large mirror-
A necessary decoration-
Was now shared by many,
And was useful once more.

— *Carol R. Roe*

Mary's Gone

Mary's not here anymore.
She's not at the table...nor at her door.
Her wheelchair is empty, her phone is on the floor.

Mary's above all the pain.
She has no restrictions, no goals to gain.
Her spirit is soaring, her Heaven to attain!

Mary's free of her burden of flesh.
She does not even need to dress.
Her body is dead, her spirit is fresh!

Mary's new temple is energy pure.
She never received an MS cure.
Her spirit is weightless, that is for sure.

Mary's now laughing, giggling in glee.
She is worshipping Jesus on bended knee.
Her eyes are on Christ, as they ought to be.

Mary's waiting for us to appear.
She's serving her Savior, her Savior so dear...
Her joy will be full when we come near.

—*Carol Elkins*

The Sock

It was a Saturday morning around eleven o'clock.
It was then I noticed I needed a yellow sock.
I thought I had one, but I must have been wrong.
So I hopped in the car and then I was gone.
I headed to Shopland; it took a half hour.
There was a traffic jam near the old rusty tower.
When I finally arrived and checked every store,
I noticed the sock I needed was the one I wore.
Since I was already at Shopland, I decided why not?
I returned two hours later with an outfit from Dots.
Dots is a new store, I love their clothes.
And all 'cause I couldn't find a sock for my toes.

— *Cami Larson*

The Shadows of My Fear

Love looked me in the face and spoke no words
But smiled and beckoned with outstreched hand.
Reluctant was my heart to follow where he led;
Aching still from wounds half healed, I hesitated,
Drawing away, hiding in the shadows of my fear.

Love looked me in the face and spoke no words
But turned and walked away with stumbling steps.
Tears dimmed my eyes as I watched him go;
Wishing I could erase the pain I had caused
By rejecting, hiding in the shadows of my fear.

Love looked me in the face and spoke no words
But passed beyond the limits of my sight
To seek another, more receptive resting place
Where laughter and sunshine and warmth abide,
And left me there, hiding in the shadows of my fear.

    —*Cathe Kimmel*

The Heat of Desire

I am floating away on the fragrance of your soft skin...
I am far above the grasp of reality's cold fingers,
Lost in your sweet seductive magic
With desire now knocking gently at my heart's door,
Begging to come in.

Yearning slowly ignites its flame, releasing the heat of desire...
I am suddenly engulfed in the warmth of your touch
And caught in the rushing whirling flames,
Unable to escape from the passion of this flaming fire.

Shining softly in the quiet afterglow of your secret charms...
I melt completely into your secure embrace,
Lingering there in love's delightful unity,
Content at last to be just close to you and resting in your arms.

    —*Alice M. Miller*

Untitled

Our love is like the spring.
It is new and grows stronger every day.
May our passion for each other
Always burn as hot as the summer sun.
In the autumn of our lives
Let us look back on our memories
For they will be as fragile
And beautiful as the falling leaves.
Our everlasting love is undying
So that we won't have to fear the winter.
May death drift over us,
Quiet and gentle as the falling snow.
And after the winter and bitter cold
Spring will once again return
To last for eternity
Like our love.

    —*Alicia Micaelia Anderos*

History

The people are present,
 life is present.
But history?
Yes.
The portraits, the places, the words...
They are forgotten
 but it's all still there.
It's waiting to be remembered,
 wanting to happen again.
The people who have been in the past
 are still alive.
Like clouds, it travels wanting to be watched.
Remember history
 because soon, you will *be* history.

    — *Ashly Richards*

Do It Now

No more spirit of Christmas, no more thrill frome the snow,
No fun sitting by the fireplace, where did the happiness go?
As my teens passed on by me, I'm no longer hell bent,
I watch myself grow older, and wonder where my youth went.
The things that used to thrill me so, no longer matter anymore,
I think about what could have been, as I sit staring at the door.
I guess what I am trying to say, is don't be a fool,
Don't let your youth go speeding by, don't sit staring at the pool.
Dive right in and take a swim, cause life is much too short,
Live it up while you still can, don't be a spoil sport.
Or just like me, you'll sit and think of what you might have done.
Toomany times, we just don't know,
Just how fast or life speeds on.
You're young just once, and not for long,
So live it up and have some fun.
Or you too will sit and think about,
The things you could have done.

    —*Francine Corgliano*

Soul Mates

O' from some strange power high and far,
love burst to flames like a firey star.
Love glimmers bright in man, land, and sea.
Love like eagles flies strong winds of bliss.
Rich the soul who lives the art of love.
Dumb fools, who refuse love, find sadness.
Men who fear, hate, and lie live in waste.
Jealous tongues burn forever in pain.
Love—the royal road to happiness.
Love guides its course, finds its paradise.
Not falsehood, love anchors in each soul.
Love binds the souls together, as one.

    — *Angelo Cisneros*

My Dad

I thank you for example set
To work amidst the strife,
To give and give of self
To ease the agonies of life
I thank you for the love, like balm
Poured into my wounds, old and new
Teaching me to do the same
To all, even those so untrue.
I thank you that I know how
You gained all this wisdom
This power to do
Because you sit at at the feet of the master Jesus
I do too.
It is too much to hope and pray
That you, my daughter will
Do likewise someday.

    —*Vi Dykins*

The Hickory Nut Tree

If you feel sad, come along with me
Down the path that leads to the hickory nut tree.
We will watch the cows eating their hay
And see the fields of corn along the way.

We will sit on a rock under the Hickory nut tree
And feel the soft breeze blow on you and me.
We will talk about our troubled times.
Soon they are forgotten and every thing is fine.

A few soft white clouds go drifting by.
Like our troubles, against a bright blue sky
We can now walk home trouble free.
Like the birds that are singing to you and me.

    —*Frances Swan*

Watching the Way

I saw her hair, gently blowing in the wind;
She just stood and stared into the fields of no end.
She watched as the trees shivered and swayed,
But she never once took her eyes off the way.

The birds flew in crowds, as if to keep warm;
For winter was coming, bringing snow to be born.
But still she stood staring past the barren fields,
To another time, another place, where summer never yields.

You see, she was frightened of the world and its men,
Of their harsh, secret ways and their lives of sin.
They tore her apart from the one man she'd need,
And she dreamed of someday repaying their deed.

She knew her poor husband would never return,
But each day she watched for his light which would burn,
As he'd walk through the fields back into her arms,
Where she'd love and keep him safe from all the world's harms.

He never returned though she would watch every day;
And slowly she died, while watching his way.

—*Kanoa Smith*

By Your Side

If you're ever feeling blue, if you're ever feeling lonely
Just reach for my hand to hold onto yours and I will be your only.
I'll be there for you—daytime or night.
I'll be there for you to make everything all right.
You've given me so much, I think I owe you a few.
I can't help but care and do all that I can do
To get you through the bad times and lead you on to better
And make it all a little easier—for now and forever.
So if you're ever feeling down, hold on to your pride
Close your eyes and remember I'm forever by your side.

— *Tania Lee*

Anatomy of an Affair

I often think about you; of things I'd like to say.
I often think about you; seems like every day.
I wonder if you're still married, and why you wouldn't leave.
Were those just lies you told me, or words I just believed?

I think of you in winter, and the skiing trip we shared.
Frolicking in virgin snow and when you said you cared.
And what about the springtime; the plantation home we stayed.
Sipping mint juleps on the veranda, and nosey chamber maids.
I think of you in summer; on the day that you were born.
I wonder if you're happy, or like me so forlorn.
The saddest time was autumn; the time had come to part.
The mistress had to end the affair that broke her heart.

I wonder if you think of me; do I ever cross you mind?
Do you wonder how I'm doing; if time's been hard or kind?
Our love affair is over; our paths can never cross.
But I still can't help remembering the love we both have lost.

I often think about you...

—*Darlene Lester*

A Tear of Sorrow

Why! Why do we have such sorrow?
I do not understand why we have such sorrow in the world.
I look at a man with pain in his eyes.
I will cry for you, I say,
But it does not take away the pain.
What can we do for these people?
The rich only become richer and the poor only become poorer.
I grieve for these people, but still that is not enough.
I pray for you and I reach out my hand and I say,
Don't be discouraged; it's just another day and another tear.
If we all stick together hand in hand through thick and thin,
That love, trust and care for each other will help us to see another day.

— *Tiffany Adams*

Closed Door

She stopped at the door to say *good bye,*
Nobody wanted her to go, they just wanted to cry.
She had changed a lot, for worst or best,
People described her as one who *lost her zest.*

Her eyes lost all their shine,
Once they used to look like mine.
She just didn't care anymore,
Not a care in the world as she walked out that door.

Didn't her parents care?
They had things to say, but didn't dare.
There it was, a tear, a tear as she walked out that door,
I know she felt us near, she just didn't care anymore.

A slight glance, nothing more, people knew drugs is why,
Why she walked out that door. She died later that day,
I guess this shows that you really do have to pay.
Her trip wasn't like it was suppose to be, this is a lesson to you and me.

— *Jenny Adams*

I Should Have...

I should have spent more time with my family
    like I had promised that I would.
I only wish now that I could...
Instead, I let the minutes, hours and days pass me by.
Now all I have are memories and tears in my eyes.
All it would have taken was just a moment a day—out of my abundant
    lifetime to spend with you.
Now I regret all the things that I had wanted to—but did not do.
I should have told you that I loved you before it became too late.
Why, oh why...did I have to wait?
The steady pain that I now feel will be a reminder of what I had neglected
    to do when you were here with me on earth, my special friend.
It will forever be a constant reminder to me to never let that kind of
    neglectfulness ever happen to anyone whom I care about again.

— *Debbie Best*

I Smile, Too

I cannot wait for that day when I walk down that isle
You will be smiling your ever so sexy smile.
When I see you all dressed up, I smile, too.
As I remember all the plans that never came true.
Now, on this day, our plans will be carried through.
As you pledge your life to me and I to you.
After we say that last *I do*
I turn and I look at you.
We both have tears of joy running down our face.
As the preacher says that we now can embrace.
After we kiss, we turn to present ourselves to our family and friends.
Now fully aware that our lives together now will finally begin.
After the wedding is over, we are surrounded by our peers.
Then, we get rice thrown on us, neither of us feeling any fear.
Now we get hurriedly into our *get away* car
Because we wanted to be together soon and away far.

—*Tammy Jackson*

The Only Reason One Man Is Rich

Like the flow of water from one glass to another,
Like the act of one man not sharing his wealth with his brother,
Like the baby who grows up without the love of his father and mother,
Like countries around the world at war
instead of at peace with one another,
Like brother against brother, sister against sister,
father against father and mother against mother,
Like family neighbors hating each other instead of loving one another,
Like the many men and women throughout history
who willingly sacrificed their lives for the livelihood of others,
Like the difference between high and low tides of some far off distant shore,
The only reason one man is rich is because another man is poor!

— *Thomas A. Johnson Jr.*

Times

I wish there was a time
When no one knew my name
Not even the wind would
Whisper it along the plains

I wish there was a time
When no one knew my face
Not even the sun would
Find me in it's shadows

I wish there was a time
When no one knew my way
Not even the people would
Find my tracks

—*Adrianna Urban*

Whispers

A clouded baby blue,
The night was coming forth,
The orange dyed horizon,
A mist upon the earth.

The sparkling beads of dew
That covered all the green,
The quiet of the land,
It seemed like just a dream.

A chill was in the air
That streched across the sky,
Like a blanket sewn by birds
And their songs as they pass by.

The sky is getting darker now,
As dawn falls down to dusk,
And only time can tell you how,
In its whispers...
hear you must.

—*Amy LaDuke*

Untitled

A tornado of feelings
Like a top spinning free,
A cat running wild
That is killed by a bee.
The Lord is my shepherd
And I am His sheep.
I know that I'm praying,
But does He answer me?

— *Helen M. Cleveringa*

Seagulls

A walk on the beach,
With seagulls overhead.
Crying their song
As if someone were dead.

And I was dying.
Because I had lost you.
You said you loved me
As up above seagulls flew.

When we were together
The birds had a song.
But when the love stopped
The gulls knew what was wrong.

They sensed me sad,
A broken heart near.
Crying their song
As down my face...
Rolls a tear.

—*Carrie Lynn Davis*

Strength Through Others

I am an individual, but do not have all the answers
Yes I am strong, but I am not the strongest
I must learn to communicate
Cause with others, I find answers
I thought I had everything, till I saw a man with more
A blind man gave me strength, for he sees more than I
A man with no legs gave me strength
For he travels farther than I, someone who has two
I have learned through others
That I have strength in me
Now I see, what it is I can truly be

— *Freddie O. Castello III*

Everything Will Be Alright

There's this feeling inside
I've been trying to hide.
I wish you could see
How much you mean to me.
I need you to hold me tight,
Say you love me and everything will be alright.
I miss you so much.
I need to feel your touch,
Your gentle caress.
Hold me close to your chest.
I know you feel the same
When I call out your name.
We'll be together soon.
We can gaze up at the moon,
Hold each other tight.
Don't worry, everything will be alright.

— *Carin E. Crossan*

The Impossible Man

There is a man that cannot hold to himself.
His ways are somewhat ugly tothe ones that love him
And yet he still goes on to use his mouth to curse others,
His mind to think not, to console not, but to destroy.
He drinks booze out of a can and tops it off with a bottle.
Then wants others to understand his ways.

Sometimes he is like this for days.
Oh—he tries to hide his ways.
This man even tries to hide his ugliness
Wherever he can. What a fool he is to think he can.
For he thinks his life is in a bottle or can.

What can be done with this impossible man
That just must have that bottle or can? Nothing.
Nothing I say can be done for he alone must reach out
And rid himself of ugliness, for Jesus will only help
The ones who ask for help.
I am sorry to say an impossible man
Thinks he doesn't need any help
But the bottle or the can. This is the impossible man.

—*Francis D. Grilho*

Life

The sun shines.
The wind blows;
The road winds,
The water flows.

The boy reads books,
The girl plays house;
The mom cooks,
The dad traps the mouse.

— *Amy Uher*

Where Has The Wind Gone

Where has the wind gone?
The wind that used to blow through
My face and leave a smile.
The wind that used to bring me
A feeling of happiness, joy,
Friendship and love.
Oh, where has the wind gone?
Now the wind has vanished and I
Left with nothing but a frown on
My face, and a feeling of sorrow,
Unwantedness and emptiness.
No more happiness.
No more joy.
No more friendship.
And no more love.
Oh, where has the wind gone?

—*Gabriela Uchimura*

When You'll Cry

There will come a time
When you will cry
That time is now
I must say goodbye.

I'll be back
By this time tomorrow
There's no real need
For all this sorrow.

Today is tomorrow
Tomorrow is today
The time has come
For me to say
Goodbye, goodbye, goodbye.

— *Virginia Rasmussen*

I Wake in the Morning

I wake in the morning.
I see the faithful sun
In the east and know
Some things are forever.
I walk upon the green grass,
The earth beneath my feet.
As I walk along the day,
I see the flowers in bloom
Almost every color and know
God loves the beautiful colors.
Then as evening comes,
The faithful sun sets in the west
With the beautiful colors
Of crimson, red and orange,
White clouds in the blue sky.
Another day ending once again
Remind some things are forever.

—*Virginia Johnston*

The Missing Pink Rose

Missing are the eyes that seek a love that does not judge
But a love that turns to lift just one from an overwhelming smudge.
Missing are the arms that hold a lost and frightened child
To rise above what sorrow brings from a court case long since filed.

Missing is a sister lost to someone who could pay
The ransom of some greedy Doc on a cold and snowy day.
Missing was a soft pink rose plucked from the family garden
Who searched to find the answers in a world which gives no pardon.

Missing is a mother loved by one more who was found
And in her freest moment shed the sun from beneath the ground.
Missing is a love no longer forgotten by those who care
Included in their lives again a family can now share.

Missing only years gone past and now they are renewed
By a love far greater than we know with no more truth subdued.
The missing pink rose has now been found and Mother can now rest
For when she brough this child into the world, she did what she thought best.

Rise up, sweet child, for you are loved, this world is yours for sure
And never will we turn our backs on Mother's rose so pure.

—*David Robins*

Understand Me

Understand that I am only human, of the female species
  and I am vulnerable.
Understand that I have deep set emotions that may be difficult
  to convey in the right tone.
Understand that I care, even though my heart may seem
  like a closed door to you.
Understand that the man makes the woman and the woman
  makes the man. If you put forth no effort, I'll be less of a woman to you.
Understand that I have many moods that sometimes get me down,
  but if you care you'll understand.
Understand that my love will grow deeper with each step
  that we take together.
Understand that I am willing to listen to your every word
  and express my feelings and opinions on the matter.
If in this you can understand me, then the caring, sharing
  and the needing that we have for each other will never die.

— *Louise R. Hill*

Shadows and Whispers

The night is peaceful and quiet, but at other times, strange and intimidating.
In the summer, the sound of a lonely cricket and a distant passing car tells me I'm not alone.
It lets me look out my window and see in the shadows whatever I want to believe is there.
In the winter, I bury myself under the covers and listen to the sharp, icy wind scraping my window.
Just outside, the soft sprinkle of the light snow glows against the harsh shadows of the cloudy sky.
The night is the frightening, unwelcome enemy of a little child with a strong imagination.
It's where the mysterious and foreboding creatures lurk,
Like the monsters and the boogeyman crouching in my closet
Or the murderers and criminals stirring in the bushes outside.
The night is the long awaited ending to those who've had a busy day,
But to some, it's only the beginning.
Then, the night gradually brightens, spreading into dawn with a soft, new life,
Peeking through my curtains and disturbing my peaceful dreams.
Morning has welcomed me with its early sun dancing on the dewy grass or glistening snow.
I jump out of my warm bed eager, but a little regretful, to start a fresh day
With distant memories of the huge world of darkness enveloping me in its shadows and whispers.

— *Leanne Maxwell*

Sometimes I Wonder

Sometimes I wonder, *Is the world going to end?*
Or is it going to turn out to be something you never thought of?
Sometimes I wonder, *Do people like you just because you are popular?*
Or do they like you as a true friend?
Sometimes I wonder, *Why don't your wishes and dreams come true,*
  like in fairy tales?
Sometimes I just wonder....

—*Dana Ingram*

Riches

The golden tassles on the corn
The fields of goldenrod,
The golden sunlight streaming down,
Are golden gifts from God.

The silver ripples on the pond,
A silver drop of dew,
A silver moon that shines above,
These are my riches, too.

A ruby throated humming bird,
The grass of emerald green,
A starry, diamond studded sky;
I am rich as any queen.

With gold and silver treasures now,
And jewels all around,
These are the kind of riches where
True happiness is found.

—*Jeanne Losey*

overture

a beginning
magnificent in its way
of a bizarre lifetime
filled with flight
love, joy, fear
anguish, pain, anger
reaching, searching
strange thoughts in stranger places
an arrogant
egotistical commencement
starting in flame
and fireworks
starting in glory
and righteousness
and so it begins
incredible and tragic

— *Lisa I. Gregor*

Lucky

I have kept company
With the best of
Spiderwebs.
But, it is time to move on.

Slowly, I move out of my corner.
Into the center
Of the room.
Funny.
It's not much different
From my corner.

Wait.
I see a light.
A light that shines so bright
In a room so dark.

I am ready.
Let me through.
Let me in
Your majestic door.

—*Claudine Tinio*

The Ocean

So beautiful, so blue.
I love it all: the water
The sand and the seashells, too.
So clean and so clear,
It's all so true.
The ocean, the ocean,
The beautiful ocean blue.

— *Christy Rees*

Mother's Bluebirds

I remember as immobile she would quietly stand, alone upon the old brick
Porch feeding bluebirds with peanuts
Nestled deep within her kind old hand; and as she waited for them
Oft I thought I heard an orchestra of music from the swaying trees.
She called them her beloved blue angels, all but one she loved the best
For his song, she named him Skee. With his chattering, happy song
He would quickly come in glory flight through the bloom of apricot
Over red rose bush, worn gate, across the green back yard,
Like a tiny plane searching for a landing spot
Upon her palm, he fled away, the peanut hard between his tiny bill
In joy he fled to some secret unknown spot, to hide it well in a deep niche
To stash it there for winter's hoard, to quell his appetite through snow and ice
Through cold and dreary days, my mother did not fail to await a flash of wing
A sparkling eye to show the peanuts waiting on the dark porch rail,
Until one morning when Spring broke, she heard a whirl of wings
A veritable storm descend upon the peanut cache, with wings a-fan
She saw four babes, one mate, and Skee return, unharmed!

   —Lucille M. Kroner

My Mountain Home

Nestled in the foothills of the Adirondack Mountains is my home.
It is not a palace or a mansion, but to me, it is the most beautiful place on earth.
As I sit on the porch, rocking the first grandchild, my memory goes back in time.

My husband and I came here after we were wed to start a new life.
We purchased some land and built our house on good soil.
We were farmers by trade.
We lived off the land.
The times were hard and money scarce, but we managed to get along.
The children started to come and come and come.

My husband, God love him, was an honest, hard-working man.
No gentler man had ever lived.
Oh, how I loved him!
He left me a few years ago, but I will see him again bye and bye in Heaven.

My children have scattered to different places, but some decided to stay.
I am happy for the little one I rock and hope her life will find the love and peace I
    have in my mountain home.

   — Linda Stevens

Our Flag Is Up There on the Moon!

Above the moon the Eagle soared, descending into shadows of the unknown
Where man had never stpped upon the moon's surface—
   now two men there all alone-
Visions of the dreams dreamed were coming true
   that man one day on the moon would walk
After being thrust into space and from the moon back to earth would even talk.
Our flag so proudly and triumphantly was planted upon the moon that day.
Fifty man-made stars are up there in God's beautiful Heaven to light our way
As in days of future's past when the nation mourned a heartbreaking tragedy.
We were crushed in spirit and shattered were dreams by the sudden catastrophe
When our seven astronauts unto the watery grave had sacrificed life
On their journey reaching for the stars that ill-fated day in such quest and strife.
We salute the Discovery, sharing and keeping their dreams alive today.
Since our flag is upon the moon—now reaching for the stars is a dream away-

   — Juanita McIntyre

Ghost Ship

A ship that sails the ocean blue now lies with its salty crew,
In the grave beneath the surf while white sand fills its rotting planks.
An anchor with its rusty links holds the ship to this place,
While whitecaps kiss the cannon decks, seaweed grows in its ghostly halls
Where once the crewmen used to roam. The advancing tide slaps
This ship's rotting skull and retreats but always returns.
If you walked along the beach at night while the moon shines its light
Upon this ghostly sight, you could hear her bell calling its dead,
To scramble to its rotting decks, to load its cannon and fire
At a distant ship if that gets too close to the jagged cliffs,
So the sea doesn't claim another ghost.

   — Larry L. Tuttle

Brothers, Past Journey's End

When the load is too heavy and the strength too light,
When the life is too empty but the world too tight,
When the game seems over yet the work never ends,
Will you be there brothers, will you be true friends?

If I reach for your touch, will I find it bare?
If I ask for too much, will you give it and care?
If I need all you've got, will you offer it all?
Even if I ask not, will you still hear my call?

A brother is a friend that always is true,
Gives support and gives love, never lets you stay blue,
Can erase all the pain, can evict all the grief,
Never lets your heart be stolen by the thief.

At the end of life's tunnel there is no need to grope,
For the light does at last give us rays of hope.
Till then, while in darkness, we all need a friend.
Who will lead us by the hand past our journey's end.

   —Kathryn E. Wyble

Liberty

Apartments and condos, row after row
All filled with people that we will never know
Little wood houses with fences of white
Where families come home so weary each night
Big fancy mansions on acres of land
Housing the rich, who perfection demand
Dirty old hotels, with bugs in each bed,
Some who must live there often wish they were dead
Knights of the highway, their homes on their back
Spending the night by the old railroad track
New modern houses all built side by side
No one knows no one, and each one may hide
Oh, if each person would take someone's hand
Help them survive in this beautiful land
Then, only then, would all people be free
For giving and loving brings liberty.

   —Jeri Alessandro

Crazy World

This world we're in spins 'round and 'round
Taking us along with it
Sometimes it spins too fast for us
 by the time we catch up, we're too late
Many times we can't control the spinning
Never know when it'll start up again—when it will stop
I think that's what bothers me most
Don't know what to expect, or
 how to prepare for the next blow
Hard to keep track of what's going on
Just as hard to understand why
Someday we'll figure it out, though
Don't know when—Don't know how
But, I know

   — Jennifer Lynn Walker

Wishing Well

A small, copper penny floats through the air,
And softly lands in a miniature blue sea.
A ripple licks upon the wall with a stirring sound,
As the wish from above comes from deep within me.

The memories of you drift through my mind,
Memeories of a n endless, precious time.
I remember you touch-caring and kind
And you voice as you said you were mine.

Our enduring love seemed too pure to be true,
Just like a storybook love shared between two.
Then, one day, you took my heart and went away,
And left only my wish for your return some day.

   — Bridget Lenzie

Winter

The magic is gone and beyond the windows
Of my mind lies little hope of happiness.
I wonder, will I find that the birds
Have ceased to sing their song, and
Everything is still, and the gentle
Rustling of fallen leaves and the
Lonely call of the whip-poor-will
For the birds are taking cover and
Their songs are all but gone.
So I'll face the dreary winter
To wait their cheery song.
— *Lois Logsdon*

A Wolf and Its Song

As I sit in the still night,
I listen to the sounds around me,
The cool water lapping the sandy shore,
Soft fluttering of wings,
A cricket chirping in the background,
As I sit, I look at things around me,
Trees swaying back and forth gracefully,
The reflection of the moon in the water,
Stars shining brightly in the black night,
But none of these things can compare
To a full moon and a soft cry of a wolf,
No nothing can compare to a
Wolf and its song
— *Connie Averson*

Displaced from Green-Winding Streams,

Rough pebbles displaced from green-winding streams,
Lonely glades and aureole clearings, torn
From clear-rushing rivers through dark barrows,
Over chalk moors and against twisted boughs
Into softly polished centers of pale,
Tufted gardens, crushed among serene antiphonies
Of juniper and jade, immutably
Molded in tepid, scattered waterfalls,
Trapped in bleached nooks by gilded statues and
Chestnut canopies, oozing glossy drops
Of ancient rains and limestone miracles
In frail gushings of crystalline murmurs.
— *Hugo Walter*

Heavens

Distance vast beyond comprehension
Glimpse into the past, stargazing with passion
Galaxies reel and globular clusters.
A cosmic parade which only God musters

Our own sun ablaze with fires of rapture
Life-giving beauty men's minds try to capture
The moon silently churns the blue ocean's foam
Stars seem quite still, the planets they roam

Hot worlds, cold worlds and ones made of gasses
Out further in space loom giant red masses
Quasars, pulsars, white dwarfs and black holes
The skies are but filled as if with our souls.
— *Stephen Gee*

Spring

Spring brings flowers and blooming trees.
The children run outside to play.
Everyone's glad that spring is finally here.
The daffodils sway back and forth as they are singing.
The sun beats down on our faces
As our children run through the tall grasses.
Everyone is glad that spring is here to stay.
— *Kristina DeVary*

Driftwood

The twisted roots of an old cedar tree
Stranded on the beach
A memory of what used to be
Beyond the artist's reach
Transformed by waves and sun and sand
Contours smooth and clean
Nature not the sculptor's hand
And far beyond machine.
— *Pat Phelps*

Inspiration

Inspiration! the rocky tree lined mind avenues
Of my thoughts which flutter
Like the wings of a butterfly, fast and light
Through domains and heavens
Of which I dare not tell
For they explode and vanish becoming invisible.
Sometimes you can get to thinking
How hard life is
But the best things in life are easy
And ready to be had for anybody.
They are the blossoms in a free land
And I think of more than myself
When I think their are universes to come
I'm talking for more than myself
When I ask why can't I be free?
Love seems to be the only answer for me.
— *Susanne K. Fahrnkopf*

Winter Thoughts

Winter comes...
The wind howls
Through a black December night.
On a bed of love
Neath a quilt of passion,
Two lovers hold on tight.
Drenched in love,
Entwined as one,
Each wrapped around the other.
Winter's bite
Seems not so harsh
When lying with your lover.
A star to wish a dream upon;
May fortune make it true,
Through winters' frost,
Through eternity,
My lover would be you.
— *Larry S. Davis*

The Miracles of the Beach

The bright sun rises over the ocean.
The ocean so great and so grand
As the waves of fresh blue salt water
Wash across the crisp white sand.

The shells of different sizes
Wash upon the ocean shore.
It brings to mind what wonders
Reside on the hidden floor

Seagulls huddle over the water
With feathers clean and white.
Then they soar towards the heavens
In a smooth and graceful flight.

Alone I face the water and wind,
But I'm standing before a man.
A man that created such miracles,
They're so far yet so close at hand.
— *Susan L. Williams*

Spring

Nature so lovely,
Water so clear;
It is great
That spring is here.

Flowers blossoming,
April rains
As the hummingbird sings
Its refrains.
— *Tara Krajewski*

The Rose

Our love was a rose bud
Just about to blossom
But then the frost came.
— *Christine Muzychka*

Time

Time is but a precious flower
Absorbing the energy of love
While whittling away the
Innocence of youth.
— *Tonya Greenberg*

A Winter's Snow

Nature's kisses
Dampen your face
Landing softly on an eyelash
Quickly melt into a tear
Caught in a mitten
Like faces in a crowd
From afar, indistinguishable
Close up, no two the same
The wind rustling the trees
Sends down clumps of white
Like cottonballs
Falling to the floor
God opens the heavens
Letting loose the gentle flakes
To cover the ground
Like a newborn's blanket
— *Lynette Rummel*

Shadows

The things I see
Are the things within me
My mind, my soul
Have taken control.
At night during sleep
Shadows appear
They draw near
They cannot touch me
For they are not there.
My only friend
Is the one within
Who keeps me near
In times of fear.
The night is gone
The dawn has sprung
The light has shone
The darkness undone
But the silence is still there.
— *Tina Doss*

The Cry

In the night, while the world is asleep,
I lie awake, my pain is steep.
Into the somber darkness I gaze,
The tears within me, I cannot raise.

When I was young, my tears could flow free,
But now they are locked inside of me,
For if I can keep my tears at bay,
Perhaps, the pain will go away.

And then, the hurt I will not have to face.
It might slip away...leaving no trace.
But if I let one teardrop start,
It could purge my soul, mind and heart.

And lead me to another way...
What price then, would I have to pay?
So, my tears I keep locked inside,
My pain in the darkness, growing wide.

     —*Nancy J. Dykstra*

A Tranquillizer

A tranquillizer to see you through?
Oh yes, I use one two.
I'll tell you about mine
For you to use sometime.

First, some deep blue sky,
To stifle a pending sigh.
Pure white clouds, of course,
To wipe away remorse.

The scent of fresh mowed hay
To chase the blues away.
The distant call of the crow
My distraught blood to slow.

Then I lie on my back
Near the old railroad track,
And let blue skies fill my eyes,
And clean my mind from time to time.

     —*John Pitts*

The Ache to Fly

The ache to fly at times does come-
But not in realms that eye can see;
The azure sky where eagles glide
Is heaven meant for them, not me.
My space is veiled, a mystic sea
Where soul and God, like seed and womb,
Are sated not unless they wed...
The grace of wings I must assume.
When passion swells, I'd leap—nay, die-
To be set free from blinded eyes;
The heaviness of finite tread
Is like a cage my heart denies.
But trembling wakes when near the edge;
I grip the flesh and turn away
To flood my eyes...and welcome noise
Which drowns the ache I can't obey.

     —*Judy Mogle*

A Sandy Path

Trotting down an old dirt road
Hand in hand and smiles aglow,
Secrets hiding in mysterious dreams
Wanting to flow out like a glistening stream.
The moon's shining brightly, sparkling on his hair
And you want him to know that you really do care.
You stop your thought because your friendship shall last
As you're trotting down a sandy path.

     —*Amy Miller*

Loving You

Because you make me feel happy when I'm blue
I'll always love you.
When I look into your eyes,
So much passion burns deep inside.
It makes me feel wild,
Just like a little child.
Even though our love is so pure,
It's just so much to endure.
When you're not around,
My smile turns into a frown,
But between me and you,
Our dreams and wishes will forever come true.

     — *Kelley Robinson*

The Dreamless

ghetto melting in the fierce heat,
with no flames.
people, dejected creatures
they crouch
        over the curb
in their heavy blue overcoats.
why?
because they no longer care,
        no longer hope,
        no longer dream.
because the dreams they had
soared up and
        dove down
        just as quickly
        hitting the black asphalt,
        shattering on the hard ground that
        doesn't reflect the sunlight that
        the people don't look up to see.

     —*Nell Freudenberger*

You and I

I know by now it was meant to be
I for you and you for me.
You made me happy when I was sad,
You made times good when they were bad.
We may have had our little fights,
But we always make up and the hugs are tight.
My friendship with you will never end,
And the problems together we will always mend.
My love for you will just grow stronger,
And our friendship will last a little longer.
So by now I hope you see,
The two of us eternally!

     —*Kelli Hood*

Untitled

If only she knew of my love for her,
For she is the essence of my dreams,
And dreams are all that I hold true.

Draped in my inner passions
Which have multiplied by the years,
I continue to wait for her approach,
But her footsteps have grown softer.

She is but a figment of my tortured mind,
Flickering among the shadows,
Now, forever lost to me...

     —*Juris Breikss*

Patchwork Quilt

Pieces of patchwork-
Some pretty, some worn,
Sewn together with memories.

Patchwork memories
Sew to form a quilt
Telling a story.

A quilted story-
Memories to keep you warm
For a lifetime.

     — *Christine Ann Salrin*

Superior Race

The water beetle rides
    the water with
Great importance;
And we ride
    the pavement.
The eagle soars over mountains
    on wings and winds;
And we rape the skies
    in jumbo jets.
The fox burrows deep into the
    earth to find a home;
And we knock down forests
    to build buildings.
God makes life from
    dust and wind;
And we make cars.
Now who did you say is
    Superior?

     —*Lynnea R. Nielsen*

Summer Passed

Summer passed
Love didn't last
Promises broken
Good-byes have been spoken
You and I
Far apart
Moments shared
Remain in our hearts.

     — *Charlene Agustin*

Three Keys

Truth, honor, freedom past
Mankind's keys to rights that last
They are yours to use today
To open doors to future's way

Truth, honor, freedom's light
Belong to all, use them right
Keys of civilization's progress past
Will serve the future till the last

     — *L. E. Babbidge*

A Melancholy Thought

Cast a stone into the water
    And observe the ripple effect;
The rings get larger and fainter
    Disappearing as you'd expect.

Life too often appears this way
    As it fades in our memory;
Folk come to mind day after day
    To confirm this analogy.

     —*Lou Roberts*

For My Husband

Before you there was never enough
Laughter in my life.
Or smiles or twinkles or days
Filled with sunshine
Or moonbeams filled nights.
But now I see diamonds
Spreading out wide before me;
And those smiles that you give me
Wrap around me all night.
My breast warms under your
Kiss and soft voice
For you are my husband
My lover...my life.

—*A. K. Reid*

Dad

Over the fields you used to plow,
Children grow there now.
The last car, the last rein has long
Since felt your hand.
In the tool room undisturbed
The firewood still traps the hoe.
Heavy rains and brilliant suns come and go
To energize your valley land.
Prairie bells seldom ring
For people drive to pray in town.
The steady team is gone.
No longer is their dust trace found.
In your finest time, bright spring,
I will look for you.
This promised homage will track the view
And tell of recent wonders,
I am sure you would want to know.

—*Wayne Wiesner*

My Father, the Devil?

Sometimes I wonder in shame what goes through my father's head,
Yelling, screaming, cursing and tearing, tearing my heart apart.
A love my father could never see,
I tried too hard to let it be.
But I could never hate to his face, for that was the face I loved,
Never slamming a door to him, always accepting his *sorries.*
He held in his hand what kept me alive and that was my heart.
To him it was nothing, another would soon pass him by, he said.
He is tearing my life limb from limb
And I want to die and be happy
And be away from this evil that grows inside me.
Stop using me! Stop loving me! Go away!
You are evil, you are the devil father
And I don't want you to raise your little girl in Hell.

— *Bethany (Kerensa Elzy)*

Untitled

We're always writing poems about problems of our own,
But have you ever stopped to think what goes on outside your home?
There are innocent dying and elders crying over problems outside of their reach.
Denied the simple pleasure of even relaxing on a beach.
The calm, Pacific seemed to make me realize that although there are
So many perfect waves, there are a few that seem to be forgotten.
Those waves represent these lives which people seem to ignore.
Why not take what is sufficient, rather than stealing away the shore?
The hundreds of homeless is just one sign
Of how lucky you are to have surpassed that fine line.
This line represents the block between success and failure.
Two words that should mean nothing, have a great effect for sure.
Before coming down on youself for something not that bad,
Remember its only bringing you closer to that line so very, very sad.

— *Gina Nick*

Family Portrait

Chin up, sparkling eyes seeing deeper than
I fathom. Young body, poised to respond
To your time's tunes. Folded arms show restraints
To *Don't touch*! Scowls of disapproval of
Parental commands. You're my girl. Such joy!
Quiet little moments you share. You're here
And yet yet so far away. Pensive brow, your
Silent stare, raised tiny hands, tilted head
Bespeak so clearly your full personhood.
My own, but really not so, Christianne Joy.
Unflinching jaws, mysterious visage, your sudden smile
Tell you still belong to an other world. A half a century
I waited for you, you lingered, took your time. Past forty,
I never gave up, my joy. Here you are, persistent little winner,
Wonder girl, so serene, full of calm my, majestic child. How
Does mother say it? *I just love you so*! Precious Chrissy Joy.

—*Amalia L. Rylander*

Untitled

I often long to hold you in my arms
But like a child I am afraid.
I often wonder how much more time I will spend alone
Wandering and wandering through space and time.
So much is happening in my life today
That the future does not appear bright.
I'm searching for the perfect moment
When I shall lay my eyes upon you.
Nothing matters to me except finding you.
I am reminiscing the past times; so brief they were.
I live each day for the hope of meeting up with you
Even though I already cherish that moment of your birth, my son.

— *Nicole Metras*

He Is My Dad

He may not be the richest man in the world or the wisest man there is.
This I know, he is willing to share all he has and knows.
For he prays for me on his bended knees.

He may not be the strongest man or the most well spoken man I know.
What he is to me is a friend who is near when I need a hand to hold.
He always finds time to spend with me.

He may not be the most famous man or the bravest one I know.
For I know that in my heart there is a special place for him.
My fears he calms with love and understanding.
Through his smile his love for me I can see.

For now he is in heaven.
This I know because he was a man who loved and lived for the Lord.
His faith in God showed me the way to live.
And one day in heaven with him I will be.

—*Barbara Handy*

Papa

Hear the music I'm playing.
Come listen to each song.
Please plan on staying.
They'll play all day long.

We can sit and reminisce,
Days long by.
Those days we love and miss.
I know it's hard not to cry.

We'll be together one day.
Time really flys by.
But till then please stay.
We'll listen, just you and I.

— *Paul Resczenko*

Tears

You said, *I cry so easily*
As we walked along the way,
Those tears are your greatest resource
Of joy and sorrow this May.

They are one of the measures
Of you, as a friend...
A mother, a worker, and a lover,
No matter whatever the end.

So keep your eyes a little moist
With tears that will run dry;
Trusting, loving and praying,
Tho' you may never know why

Tears, tears, and tears
Ours to share and to care,
God gave us the blessings,
To love and to dare.

—*Opal McKittrick*

Kids

Stained clothes,
Tousled hair,
Scraped knees,
Wandering stare;
Full of questions,
Full of love,
Clearly a blessing
From up above.

— *Julie Willard*

Memories

Introspective camera.
Photographs of heart and mind.
Focusing Life's past.

— *Karol Ann Barnett*

I Write

When I have time for the pen,
I write.
If space permits
And time does not care,
With the typewriter
I take a dare.
But if only I had a computer,
I could do wonders.
And by the laws of chips and circuits
I would not make so many blunders!

—*Eric Bogan*

The Sea

When I look outside
And see the sunset glow
I dream I am on the ocean
On a sailboat, to and fro
Looking at the sea
As it glistens from the sun
Listening to the waves
As they swish and have their fun
Looking at the seagulls
As they swarm across the sea
Smiling at their happiness
Being able to be free
As I open my eyes
I see I am not there
I hope to share the beauty
Of nothing I could compare
The sea has its secrets
People go there to be free
No one will ever know
How beautiful it is to me.

—*Kathy Kraft*

Half of Two

If given a chance
I'd rather be half a pair.
Being one
Is no fun.
I like moonlight strolls
And ice cream sodas.
Campfires and marshmallows
Are appealing, too.
But I'm only one,
And who would join me?
I'm only one,
And one is not half of two
When the two should be a pair.

—*Kathrine Rae Phillips*

Children

Children are so special,
Especially my two
They are there when we need them,
To help us see things thru.
They are not always perfect,
They have their faults, too.
But they give all they've got,
When we really need them to
They're loving and considerate,
Of people all around,
They don't mind helping anyone,
Who they know is really down.
So if you have children,
You have a gift of love.
It's such a beautiful feeling,
It has to be from above.

— *Julia Lucas*

Stone of Silence

Upon that stone
You took my heart
In shattered pieces
You tore me apart.
My cries for you
You will not hear
You didn't want me around
You didn't want me near
Upon that stone
You took my last breathe
My stone of silence
Is my bed of death

— *Karla Hamilton*

Giving into Emotion

Manipulation of thought
by ever-present breeze.
She loses control
and falls to her knees.

Nature's whispered melody
suspended on air.
Hides her true feelings
she cannot bear.

For closeness and comfort
she guiltily yearns.
And her feelings of lonliness
she dutifully spurns.

The sun in the heavens
makes love to her entity
She climaxes in tears
yet is still left empty.

— *Kathy Anne Thwaites*

Thoughts of Yesterday

Memories are useless
Tears only hurt
Friends come and go
Dreams fade and disappear
Love ceases to exist
The past is gone
The future is here
Happiness once found, is lost
Days and night go by
Your image fades slowly
My heart aches constantly
The pain and hurt remain
Strangers form in our souls...

—*Petra Gayle Baldridge*

A Doll

A doll she was, in simplest terms;
Of whom a childs faith could earn.
The unchanged smile to greet the day; set imagination stray.
Atop the shelf and out of reach; arms outstretched, as if beseech.
The red dot dress of cord and satin;
The black shined shoes of brass and patent.
The golden ringlets falling down her nape;
Cherished moments of treasured sake.
Upon the day I was to touch; anticipation, I was in much.
Shed a tear, I think in glee; pretty one, handed down to me.
Briefly held and softly touched;
I brushed away a trace of dust.
After moments it seemed unfair;
    to remove one from ones place of lair.
Placed back on shelf, returned for dust;
In this way, my heart did trust.
She for me, was not a toy;
But a moment of childhood joy.

—*Julie A. Moore*

Sugar

I had a cat named Sugar who drank from the bathtub drip,
Constantly I brushed the pewtered cat hair from my hip.
He dug up frogs and lizards and placed them on the step,
His way of saying thank you for his food and being kept.
No, no, no, I told him. *Don't do that any more!*
Each time he left his offering on the step at our backdoor.
I saw him with a lizard once, alive between his teeth,
I sprayed him with the water hose until he gave release.

And them I saw him stalk a bird, and capture it in flight,
It made me sad...I cried in bed, and wakened through the night.
How can he be so gentle and purring in my arm,
When in his play and folly, his object is to harm?

I loved him, I really did.
He belonged to us for years.
He left one day because he knew his death was very near.
I cried, and Mother too. I think Daddy did,
But we never knew.

—*Judy Harris*

Flowers in the Snow

Life at times seems cold and gray; storm clouds gather and seem to stay.
Events occur which we cannot explain, filling our lives with grief and pain.
Why does hardship follow those so full of love and cheer?
The answer, dear friend, is not found here.
The answer lies not in the knowledge of man
but in the wisdom of God and His almighty hand.
We're all on a journey, the path never clear,
knowing why some things happen is just not to be.
Only each step in advance are we unable to see.
As the foundations of our lives are shattered and torn,
we ask, *Why, Lord, why?* as we mourn.
The rhyme and the reason we are not permitted to know.
Only through experience does our wisdom grow.
But amongst all the sadness, hardship and toil,
seeds of greatness are placed in the soil.
These seeds broadcast by the wind are scattered in places we've never been.
Their radiance and beauty we may never see,
but to future travelers, aid and comfort be.
So when life seems cold and gray and your path seems covered with snow,
Carry on with your journey, carry on with your load;
look not down or to the middle of the road.
Look to the valleys, the hills and the dales
for flowers of greatness growing along the trails.
Pause for a moment, reflect as you will;
look at the flower in its beauty and be still.
Examine it closely and you may see
that this small flower is a gift from me.

— *John W. Drennan*

The Dark

Throughout the darkness I stood,
Only a child could.
Crying in the night;
Without any light
Parents are near
But I still fear
Standing alone in the dark.
—*Alisha McDonald*

The Sea is Dark, the Land Brown and Dusty

The ship is caught up in the harbor under a waxen sky
As yellow as the pasty faced women who lean from their windows
Shouting to the men below repairing ropes,
Hawsers of hemp and straw. The sails coarse and thick
Crackle in the wind. Even the clouds are the color of flesh.

But the sea is dark, the land brown and dusty
Forming an edge in the distance, a thin line of horizon.
The women upstairs, the workers outside
Yell to each other. They are convinced they know
The right way to do a job, While the boats jab at the docks.

Except at sea things change. The sky comes all the way
Down to the deck of a ship and whispers
Wild things to sailors encouraging
Recklessness, thrusting, cheering them forward
Forcing them to dive into the random, churning water.

—*April Ivy Krassner*

Resignation Letter

Notice is hereby given
I am getting out of the race.
Retreating to the peace and serenity of Idaho farmland.
The 12th is my target date, movers scheduled Friday 13th.

Occasional cross-country trips to places yet unseen.
Last child graduating from high school, wedding reception to follow.
Creating a market for my paintings.
Planting acres of Christmas trees.
Canning from my garden, berry patch and fruit trees.
Gathering asparagus growing wild.
Developing plots and characters publishers would buy.
Watching snowflakes from within, enjoying the warmth from my fire.
Not missing earthquake tremors.

These are my dreams
No longer content in black and white
Someday.
Now demanding color.

—*Gail L. Craner*

The Courage I Found

Years ago, sitting anxious in an anteseptic smelling room.
Confronted by the predicted and ugly face of doom.
Repeating words of denial. I was so innocently unaware
Never knowing today was the beginning of my nightmare.

Months went by, the pain and mental anguish grew steadily worse
Tears never ceasing when praying to God, *Lift this hidious curse*
Anger and resentment began to take a destructive toll.
Diseases ravaged my body, bitterness surrounded my soul.

Another year, life slipping by, I could not carry on this way
Preoccupied with the hurt, not hearing what anyone would say
Searching inside, I found a strength I had never fully known.
Through the burden of suffering, I had unwittingly matured and grown.

Now, deeply depending on the courage that saw me through
I leave behind old reminents of a life that I once knew
Gathering on the insights that will help me start again
Relying on myself and the courage I found within.

—*Denise Profumo*

More Than a Memory

Memories dwindle into few,
But I'll never forget the memory of you.
You're a part of my heart more than you know,
You have helped me to live,
You have helped me to grow.
I hope someday you'll remember me,
Because within my heart...
You're much more than a memory.

— *Peggy Peterson*

Time Passages

Time seemed to be passing me right on by.
The only thing the same is the color of my eyes.
I've grown up, married, and have a family of my own.
Somewhere I've lost contact with feelings I've known.
My whole life was planned from the start.
I was lead without knowing what was in my heart.
Then the time came for the need to find me.
All that I am is not what I want to be.
Writing is a secret dream I was hiding from.
My life was passing by waiting for opportunity to come.
Opportunity finally knocked and I welcomed it in.
It was like being swept up by a strong whirlwind.
I'm afraid people might think that it's gone to my head
When actually it's coming from my heart instead.
I just never dreamed I'd ever get this far.
Now it's in my heart to learn to play the guitar.
God only knows what will happen from here.
With my heart as my guide, I'll never fear.

—*Peggy Sue Rickman*

The Masterpiece

I entered the painting in an abstract contest. Pretentious
judges scrutinized and analyzed the *masterpiece.*

*Obviously portrays the downfall of society. Certainly
a nuclear explosion. Note the figures propelled
into oblivion? N-o. It definitely depicts modern man's chaotic
mind. Yes, yes, I see it! What depth conveyed on canvas!*

Prize? I wondered. I wish I'd painted
it. Actually, my parrot did the job. He marched
his tiny feet through a blob of wet paint. His dragging
tail became the brush.

No bomb. No social decay. No chaotic mind. No depth.
A bird
did it.

It won second
place. They call it
art.

I call it
poetry.

— *Bobbi McGonegal*

Green Eyes

Sitting in silence—holding back the tears,
I think of all my troubles and fears.
Not knowing my true feelings is tearing me apart,
Wondering if they're false or straight from the heart.
As I lay and think of what to say—a familiar sight comes to mind,
A pair of emerald green eyes—so precious and kind.
They can see right through the shield and into my heart.
These eyes are not normal—they will not lie.
They're full of love and care—they rarely sigh.
Whenever I'm feeling blue—or I need a friend,
The comforting vision would come.
But, I have recently realized...
This pair of emerald green eyes is the exact thing
I've been hiding from.

— *Jamie Woodard*

Touch Me on the Inside

If only the ability
to dance the way my mind sees
could be of my capability
If only the music my mind can hear
could be heard by other ears
If only the beauty my mind can see
could be seen by more than me
Or if the love that fills my soul
by others could be known
If my dreams should all come true
and I could show them to you
If you could touch
what inside I feel
And you shared with others
what could be real
Such peace would come over the earth
That all despair would be dispersed.

—*Carolyn L. Groat*

The Birch

Birch tree with it's arms outstreched
Always knowing right from left
Leaves are green, as emerald rock
Cares are few yet secrets locked.

Birds find safety in it's hold
And still the Birch is growing old.
Bark is brown, as crispen grass
Sorrow comes birds cry Alas.

Birch tree pulsing, making food
Watching, hearing, doing good
He feels the sun while watching me.
A thing of beauty yet but a tree.

—*April Richey*

The Way Through

When one has known a life of love
And shared its varied hues
He may perhaps forget that he
Must sometime pay his dues.

For what is life, a game of chance,
No matter how we strive.
We run the race, we fight the fight,
Perhaps we stay alive.

But when our love has lost the race
And we alone survive
We would far rather take his place
Than face the daily jive.

But that is not the way things work.
We have to see things through.
Till we create the sun once more
And skies again are blue.

—*Annabel de la Torre-Bueno*

Golden Man

As I stand out in the prairie
With a loose leaf in my hand,
There are visions and distortions
Of a free and running man.

He is painted golden
From rays of Florida sun.
And the legend he is living
Is yet to be won.

Basking in deep meditations
From the trails not yet begun,
I envision him sucombing
To the warmth of the morning sun.

—*Betty J. Gross*

In a Whiff...

Restless, I shopped
Looking to buy some solace
Some peace of mind
Trying to forget you

Instead I landed at the cosmetics counter
Put on your cologne
And took you in...all night

In a whiff...I vanished,
Leaving myself to be
Absorbed in your scent

—*Carolyn Oberman*

Poetry

Everything a poet says
Has all been said before.
The poet with his poetry
Just opens a different door.

By finding words to express
His novel adaptation,
He will tell you the same old tale
Through his interpretation.

—*Dick Robichaud*

Double Standard

If a girl—too long does tarry
Mother feels she'll never marry
Slowly she starts to worry when
She sees her sitting home again
A son-in-law she'd gladly bring
Birthday presents and everything
But when *her son* begins to date
She fears that doom will be his fate
She'd like to keep him home forever
The ties that bind—she hates to sever

—*Pauline Unger*

Onward and Upward

Oh! To be an astronaut,
A real space age pioneer,
To teach this generation
All about our new frontier,
To find adventure waiting
In those places now unknown,
Going out beyond our sky
Where no one has ever flown
Now it is still a mystery.
It is jsut a guessing game.
But there are answers waiting
To bring to somebody fame.
Time and progress do not stand still,
So no matter what my fate,
Just send me into orbit,
Because I want to keep that date.

—*Evelyn Furey*

Sharing Is Love

The old farm house where laughter rang,
Where humor was and children sang.
Where stories filled the air at night
And peace and joy were pure delight.
Where sharing was a thing of play,
Which made the heart feel light and gay.
Where laws were made that children kept
And family love was deeply felt.
In tears, I turned and walked away
And thanked my God for yesterday.

—*Jackie A. Larsen*

Rain

Rain is pummeling against the glass.
I lay here, thinking of you...
Your warm touch, your kiss,
Your heartbeat.
It's still raining, harder now.
I love the sound of the rain,
The muscial rhythm, the pace
Your heart beat.
The rain is slowing now, only drizzle.
I lay here, thinking of you,
Missing you, more every minute...
Your heartbeat.

— *Peggy A. Grubb*

The Rose

Satin silky
Folds of soft color,
Shaped wonderfully
Strong proud
Frail and delicate,
The perfect peace.
But an act of love plucks
This lovely one
To please another.
Something created
Wholly and perfect,
It dies to put a smile
On the face of a lover.

— *Alycia Rusch*

Memory Movements

Remember crawling as a babe
Or the first shaky step-
The swing, the teeter-totter,
Jump rope, or hide and seek.

Or later yet walking to school
Running with a kite-
Jumping with a basketball
Or pounding a volleyball.

How about lifting a weight
Marching in step, dancing,
Swimming, rowing a boat
Or stepping down the aisles of life!

Oh, to ride a bike, leap for joy
Push the baby carriage
Leave for work and return again
A warm bath, cool sheets!

—*Phil Walch*

What I Know

I don't know why it rains
Or why it snows.
I don't know why the sun shines
Or why the wind blows.
But I do know
What you mean to me
And that our love
Was meant to be.

— *Nicolle Marie Johnson*

An Alternative

If there is nothing to laugh at
Laugh at nothing
Because laughing at that
Beats crying for something.

— *Natasha Stallworth*

Darkness

She comes upon you without warning,
A woman's wrath, a womans scorning.
At that awful, gruesome time,
She comes and does one evil crime.
You cannot predict her awful way,
Only feel his painful ray.
She comes about only once a year,
But leaves you with eternal fear.
And when the terrible night is done,
The princess of darkness...she has won!

—*Becky Koeppel*

Dawn of the Storm

Lampposts twinkle and blink in the wind
And my bones know
A storm will blow...

Dawn awakes...
And slowly creeps away
Dragging the heavy veils of night behind...

Lampposts flicker and shudder
As the raging Storm—
Flings his charcoal coat across the heavenly floor...

And from the darkened curtain
Split by electric runs...
A crystal downpour
Begins...

— *Aida Akl*

The Dream Weaver

To do
Is to dream
To dream
Is to not think morally or realistically
But to go overboard
To get to *shore*
Tis so hard
When only a motionless boat in middle of pacific
Use creativity
A sail would do well unto mast
Gradually
With luck of wind
The shore will be embraced by dreamweaver

— *Amanda*

Ways

People judging people for the color of their skin.
When they should be judging people for what is within.
Nuclear war could make us all die.
Maybe its time for the world to ask why.
A single yes could change all our days.
It could also change all our fun loving ways.
People shooting people for the color they wear.
Maybe they should realize today people care.
I only wish we could change the way we are.
Maybe in the future, but the future seems so far.

— *Amber C. Barnum*

Birds

I like the birds up in the sky,
I like the birds I watch them fly,
But it's a shame when you hear the fame,
About their hunters and their game,

Their little games are much to much, but to the hunters
It's just enough and when you hear the big, big, story,
About the birds and their glory,
It is so sad and makes me so very mad.

— *Becky Marion*

The Rescue

He was a man and yet much more.
He was the Son of God.
He preached to tell the world of love.
He gave to show the poor.
He didn't come to shun us.
He came to be our door.

So knock my friends
And you will see
A vision of eternity.
The Father, Son and Spirit are one.
There lies the mystery.

— *Patricia Stauffer*

Sweet Jesus

Oh, sweet Jesus, come take me home.
I'm tired, weak and so alone.
Fly me away on silver wings.
Take me from all earthly things.

I'll come without a whimper
Or the blink of an eye.
Oh, sweet Jesus,
Don't let my loved ones cry.

My earthly home means naught, no more.
Please help me knock on heaven's door.
Take me up beyond the clouds.
Oh, sweet Jesus, I'd be so proud.

I come to you in prayer each night.
Sweet Jesus help me in my plight.
Oh, sweet Jesus, come take me home.
I'm tired, weak and so alone.

— *Pat Grenier*

My Community

As part of it I have a choice
My community I treat so nice
I help in every way I can
Make it a better place for man.
I will not litter or abuse
The things which other friends must use.
I will try not to pollute the air
With smoke and fumes found everywhere.
Respect the water that we drink
It is soiled more easy than we think.
Do not swim or fish in it
Such dirty people I have met.
Germs like diptheria and typhoid
In dirty water seem to hide.
Those germs may cause someone to die
To help our community; please try.

—*Florence Miller*

Chatterbox

She talks incessantly; I cannot cope.
Words run into words that endless seem.
The message is unclear; I do not see
Where her words lead nor what they mean.

Sometimes I wish I had the grit
To smile, then calmly walk away,
But courage I have none and so I sit
And let the idle talk engulf my day.

I worry that one day, I too, might speak
Of things that others do not wish to hear,
And if they walk away and I'm alone,
I'll wish that Chatterbox was near.

—*Belle Mazola*

Daddy's Little Squirt

You were always there for me,
Since I was very small.
To help me when I'd stumble,
Or to catch me when I'd fall.

We had our spats here and there.
But you were always right.
I'd always wait up just so,
You'd tuck me in good night.

Even though I am now seventeen
And wear a mini skirt,
I know I will always be...
My Daddy's Little Squirt.

—*Jacki McArthur*

the sting

serene cool death
oh sensitive slumber
where is your sting
can it be felt in the dry leaves
    that lie atop your bed
can it be heard in the blackbird's
    shrill overhead
is it detected in the wagging tails of the
    gray braided moss reaching down to
    your pillow
shadow and then sunlight kiss the dewy
    tears away from your face
immortality now colors your path like the
    flowers at your feet
and the ones who preceded lie as comfortable
    by your side
who winces from the sting
i do

—*Pamela Baker*

Fremyette

The hours late...the hall is dim,
The night is cold and wet.
The time is brood in solitude
For my beloved Fremyette.
So early plucked from lifes fair sway
And darkness falls upon each day,
From ruby red to ashen gray,
And I'm alone Fremyette.
She was grand in some small way...
Her beauty had no peer.
And I'd delight in darkest night,
As long as she was near.
And once was graced...and youth is waste,
And lonely's galaxy wide.
And my Fremyette...I can't forget,
Until we both have died.

— *J. Derrick Webster*

Untitled

Excitement is a bowl of jello,
Fun is an open book.
Love is like a cherry cordial.
Depression is like a whimpering dog.
Sadness is a sailboat without wind.
Hunger is like a bridge.
Pain is terrible.
Beauty is long, golden hair.
Loneliness is a sand storm with no one to see it.
Sickness is damp, dreary hospital rooms.
Chaos is like running water.
I am like all of the above.

— *Alice Dubin*

Ancestor's Heritage

The two Americas live side by side,
Discovered by enterprising voyagers.
In Portugal, the Queen spent money,
For the voyage of Columbus to America.

There were many voyages to America
First, he discovered Cuba.
Another voyage to North America,
The last to South America.

The natives were warm and friendly,
They greeted him and offered sugar.
Up to America, he sailed
Where he found a land of Indians.

He sought gold for Isabella,
But gold was found in South America.
The sailboats, the Pinta, Nina and Santa Maria sailed
Over the vast ocean from Europe.

The Spaniards thought it was China,
For Columbus landed in Cuba.
He sailed to America
Instead of the land of silk.

    —*Elizabeth Saltz*

The Way We Are

Contra Costa, Alameda, Solano
We all change; nothing stays the same.
Why?
1945
1988
Change so much
Where are the old pastures?
Knocked down for buildings.
Where are the walnut trees?
Cut down for buildings.
Families only have memories; the old remember.
The young hear all from old.
All states, blue collar, white collar, no collar
Debt-ridden, well-off, educated, non-educated,
People who live on hope, people who live on memories,
People who live on both.
Do we understand each other, or do we wish, too?
That's the way we are.

    —*Gina Myrons*

To the Privileged Born

Chance determines from whose womb we are born
And how our lives proceed.
Those whose cradles are edged with gold
Might never feel a want or need.

The view of life from the ladder's top
Is blurred by its moneyed field of green:
It cannot see the bottom rungs
Or know the gaps that lie between.

The wealthy know their special place
Exempts them from life's menial chores.
The poor will cater to their needs;
They will clean their dirt and fight their wars.

When the inevitable curtain falls
And time extracts the closing breath,
The privileged and the poor unite
In the equalizing state of death.

    —*Elizabeth M. McGowan*

My American Dream

In the future my plans are
to set high goals and reach for the stars!
I want to go to college and be an *A* student,
have a sense of humor and still keep up my prudence.
Music in my fingers, music in my feet.
I could be a well-known pianist or a dancer on Broadway Street.
Running and soccer I love to do.
Health and fitness are important, too.
Painting a picture worth a thousand words,
my *American Dream* will forever be heard;
for the talent of an artist can never die.
Creativity improves as one aims for the skies
and if I have faith that my dreams may come true,
I know there's no way that I'll ever be blue.

    — *Allison Sarmiento*

For the Children, the Boy and the Man

He possessed the knowledge of the unspoken; Bravery
He clutched the dark side of the unknown; Fear
He trembled with future uncertainty; Dread
Gentle tears welled deep from within his soul; Compassion
In his eyes was the excitement of newborn dreams to come; Anticipation
The struggle of the heart had begun, yielding to a soft light of love,
Yet darkening while learning to hate.
Within his mind the fight raced, good, evil, right and wrong.
Full of doubt he looked to me as if searching for answers.
I gazed upon his small, confused face, smiled and took his hand.
Rest assured, my son, these feelings are not yours alone;
They are shared not only by that smallest of boys, but still yet
Taunt the full-grown man.

    — *Catherine Hash*

Tomorrow

And then there is tomorrow,
With unsprung events, masked only by time.
A portion may provoke sorrow,
Or, perhaps, a happy little rhyme.
Only a second separates the present from the future,
When the obscured becomes the unobscured.
With the commencement of the crowing of the rooster,
An unveiling, either, welcomed or feared
My mind veers recklessly toward excitement then apprehension,
Then drifts into a soothing state of calm.
Exit fear!—The future is only an extension,
Of the time which presently exists.
What fate might befall me, that has not in similar
Fashion been experienced by others? Were they not mortals with all the
Same senses as me? Even the weakest is capable of experiencing pain,
Death, sadness, but also, happiness, laughter, and lovers.

    —*Elvin J. Duncan*

My Heaven

Here I sit alone in my room
Thinking of my life that's only in bloom.
I wish it would just go ahead and end,
Then I might be at the gates, the beautiful gates of Heaven.
I won't be sick, I'll be healthy at all times
And there won't be anymore of those awful crimes.
I'll be with my real family and friends.
When I walk down those long roads, there will be no dead ends.
Paul will be waiting at those big pearly gates
Offering me this plate of plump raisins and dates.
I'll see Peter, John and all the disciples.
We'll all sit around and read scriptures from our Bibles.
I'll fish and fish and get the catch of the day,
Then that night fix 'em for Jesus in that special way.
This is my Heaven, my Heaven you see,
But until then I'll just stay and pay the fees.
Hopefully you'll stay too, my dear friend
And someday we'll meet in the big Heaven.

—*Jennifer Noland*

Empty

I want to reach out, but who shall I reach to
I want to cry out, but who will hear me.
Nobody knows what I'm feeling inside,
Nobody will know until the day I die.
My tears are falling no tracks, no trace, only a cause.
I'm longing for a love more powerful than the hate and anger I feel
Something big, beautiful and for God's sake, Real!
I have a spare tire, an extra wallet size picture for people to see
So unless they're an expert, they won't find the key.
I refuse to let anyone inside to diagnose, sympathize or advise
One couldn't possibly begin to understand
My mind, my life, my thirst, my whole universe.
Psychologically molding my innermost feeling, my past dealing.
Will I walk from it healing? or feeling? that someone has a part of me?
Will it leave me once again Empty.

—*Adrienne C. Moore*

To Think That We Should Die

A tear comes to my eye, to think that we should die. Never to see the
Birds fly or the season die. Never to hear the wind blow, or feel the
Winter snow. Never champion right from wrong, or sing a happy song.
Never to love again, or know a woman. A tear comes to my eye, to
Think that we must die. Yet, have no regret, we lived our life..
Sometimes in comfort, sometimes in strife, we lived our life.
Have we not tasted fully the joys of manhood? What more can we ask,
We fullfilled our task. A tear comes to my eye to think that we should
Die. Did not we run our course. At times we're not boss? Nows the
Time to enjoy the fruits of our labor in this truth do not waiver.
Now's the time to accept our fate, now's the time to sit and wait
A tear comes to my eye to think that we should die. Never marvel at
The sunset, or wonder at the moon rise. Never again to win the prize,
Yet have no regret, why fret. We lived our lives
Yes, we lived our lives.

— *William T. Cangialose*

Try Another Day

I had an appointment—I *know* it was at nine.
I rushed off to the shop to be ready on time.
I walked in—then realized this can't be right.
Not enough regular customers, not many in sight.
I looked at the clock—now I know I am wrong.
I had arrived to have my hair done, but I've been wrong all along.
Sorry! I know now my appointment was for another day.
After all this rushing, I'll be on my way.
Too bad I had the day mixed up.
I was in the mood to have my hair fixed up.

— *Hilda Laura Morlan*

With His Help

As I open my eyes to the first light of the day,
To face a world in hopes of things going a better way.
I thank God for the many things He has given me.
For all the love and blessings in my family's tree.
I was lost in the wilderness of doubt and despair.
All alone and afraid but I know God was there.
I have seen some bad times but I have endured.
With His help I always will, this I am assured.
He's there when I need him, always close at hand.
He's just a prayer away and He always understands.
So when things go wrong and I feel I can't go on,
I pray to God for reassurance, then all my fears are gone.

— *Jeanette M. Walker*

Because of You

I live my life for him, but he doesn't see it.
I remember all the sweet nothings he whispered in my ear,
The ones I tried to avoid to hear
Because I knew all they would do is leave me blue
And it's all because of you.

I remember nights we spent together.
I wished they would never end,
But as you can see, they did.
Now when I see him, I want to die, but all I do is cry.
It's just because I'm blue.
It's all because of you.

When I lay in bed, I think of him.
When my eyes are closed, I dream of him.
My heart is broken and now you know that, too.
All because I'm blue.
All because of you.

— *Nicholle Jones*

Uncover the Stars

The clouds serve as a moist blanket.
And the rain represents the tears
Of those that should be seen,
But are not.

Their eyes flash and twinkle tears of their own
Because they know deep inside their hearts,
That they must be shown.

Too dazzling are they,
They do not deserve
This institution in which they temporarily serve.
But they must be reminded that soon
The grey blanket shall be lifted.
And they will shine between the eyes of Mother Earth,
And infinity.

—*Gail Blum*

Coming out of Isolation

Slowly, the ice is melting from the ice age
That lasted so long, frostbitten heart and soul
The chill permanently set in.
Even the warm sun could barely penetrate the thick ice walls.

In a depth of darkness and terrifying solitude,
The monsters are frightening and they helped build
The thick ice walls there...
Time had forgotten the beautiful flowers
And the little animals that scurried about.

One warm day in a crowded room the ice began to melt...
At first a small flicker of fire began in the thick ice walls.
Then a brilliant flame in the depths of darkness began to shine,
And the monsters began to shrink in their own fear of the new day.

—*Jean Bourque*

Kiss of Death

The sky was blue
And the birds were singing
I shouldn't have been
Thinking what I was thinking
The sun was overhead
Bright and sparkling
I shouldn't have been
Thinking what I was thinking
The river was like a Kiss of Death
Tantalizing and tormenting
I shouldn't have been
Thinking what I was thinking
My heart was turning into black
The pressure was domineering
Now I think no more
For I have done what I was thinking

—*Alexia Komninos*

Diamonds

Millions of diamonds in my view.
I see them daily, they're all mine.
Each and every one brand new
Sparkling gaily, each to shine

Their worth beyond imagination
Enchantment where the river moves
I thrill at the site in fascination
Crystal rhythms in different hues

Twinkling flashes on the run
Ballerina performing just for me
Quickly as to catch the sun
Mystery, discovery in things that be

Overcast skies rob me of my gems
Dark clouds make them run for cover
Till rays of sunshine come to free them
My dancing diamonds on the water.

—*Helen Richards*

Pearls

Pearls, pearls
Of rich, radiant pink;
Like much cotton or clouds at dawn;
Glowing stars, they;
And sometimes close at hand.
Pearls of fine texture;
Pearls of disarming design;
Here they flash red, there they glow fair.
Dreams are born of pearls: dreams.
Dreams of eyes
Squinted beyond color in spacious smiles
These grown in distant seas:
Pearls and dreams.
A prisoner I'm taken
By the smiles she's been maken,
As if for me there should never be
Smiles like pearls or dreams or sea.

—*George S. Geisinger*

Don't Hide From Love

It's really strange, how you always cried;
How you kept all your feelings locked up inside.
You foolishly drove all your emotions away,
While I kept hoping *we'd* happen someday.
Well, I hope someday that you'll realize,
That I cannot see beyond your eyes,
But when you decide to let me know;
I'll love you forever, I won't let you go.

— *Alicia Malard*

Those Cats

Suddenly, I hear a hiss,
Now, what noise is this,
Crash goes the dish, splash goes the fish
Noisy are those cats.

Quietly they sneak gracefully they peak
Friendly is their purr, soft is their fur
Mysterious are those cats.

Love to catch mice
But watch out for lice,
Different are those cats.

Cuddly to hug, patient for bugs
Affectionate glowing eyes
Hiding in shadow's, how wise
Oh, how I love those cats.

— *C. Silanskis*

DWI Leads to Pain

As the waves crumble against the shore.
I say to myself no more.
No more running, jumping, sledding, skiing
It is not pleasing,
A drunken driver put me here.
He doesn't know what it's like,
To sit here all day.
Now all I want to do is
Go out and play.
But I can't so I wouldn't
If I could I would
Oh! I would!
But these legs won't do anything.
Not move, not twitch, not even itch.
I want to get up
Please help me!

—*Heather Gidney*

The Flying Gigolo

A meadow of Iris
Rainbow hues
Invites a breeze to telegraph
Their suble mating scent
Nature's call directs
The nimble Bumble Bee
To suckle nectar from velvet throat
as feathery spindles drag their strokes
Across expectant petals of satin skin
Protective swords dissolve with multi orgasm
Full bloom vibrates   trembles
Quivering in the breeze
Sigh   Relief   so brief
Bumble Bee bids adieu
Seeking hearts of virgin souls
Waiting lovers everywhere
Busy   busy

—*Shirley Fitz-Patreck*

Untitled

Even though you're far away
I think about you everyday
I wish I was with you, holding you tight
For I'll never forget our special nights.

Looking deep into your eyes, while making love,
Underneath the darkness
Of the starry sky above.

For I'll be waiting to be with you,
My long distance love.

— *Patricia Ann Brickman*

Bears

Bears are funny like my mommy
Even though they cost a lot of money.
Bears are cuddly, not hard to study,
Even though they get all muddy.
Bears are one thing I like best.
They do not harm as much as pests.
Bears do help me day and night.
They keep me safe from the fright at night.
Pain and laughter, cries and tears
Bears do help me through the years.

—*Elyson Ramos*

Something to Believe in

Tell me that you love me
Just one more time my love.
Before you walk away from me
Just one more time my love.
Just kiss me one more time.
Let me hold on one more day.
Let me believe before you go
That you'll come back someday.
Let me believe because that's what I need.
I need something to believe in.
Give me that something, by telling me
Just one more time
That you love me.

— *Aimee Kentner*

A Walk Through the Woods

As I wandered through the woods one day,
Sadly to my dismay
I found a flower all alone
So sad and dreary and all but gone.

As I stooped to pick that flower up,
I saw each petal still and gray.
I held it lightly in my hand
Still it almost withered away.

I saw in this flower of the dawn
A life so drear and so forlorn
As yet untouched by naked scorn
It lasted on from morn to morn.

This flower died
Deep in the autumn wood.
Bathed in darkness all around
I left it lying on the ground

—*Debora Robbins*

Oliver

Dusty Roads is brewing a scandal
It involves a missing sandal
Sadly, we shattered a few dreams
Reality's not what it seems.

Oliver was a wise old bird
But have you heard?
We found the missing clue
Oliver danced out of his shoe.

Oliver's no strange creature
He is the village preacher
His sermons would howl
Now his parishoner's faces scowl.

Oliver was seen dancing with the Stray Cats
And they were wearing funny hats
How can Oliver reconcile his words and deeds?
Oliver you are sowing bad seeds.

—*George A. Hancock*

A Cat's Point of View

From a cat's point of view,
We don't know what they see.
Could be a bird or flower or bee,
Or a mouse or a mole or whatever could be!
Outdoors is their window to the world,
Where they play or sleep all day.
I know there will never come a day for me,
When I can see from a cat's point of view.

— *Becky Thatcher*

Awareness

My University is life
Where truth is evident to all.
Equality to grow is mine,
Awareness is the knowledge key
That opens doors to open minds,
To verity concealed to souls
With narrow, specious, prisoned lives.
If keen, aware, one must glean truths
Beyond his peers in chosen fields
Wherein his life style lies.
Know well, therefore, thyself; perceive
From sun-kissed earth to star-jeweled sky;
For nature animate or non,
Instructs the senses, tunes the mind,
Affirms the truth, rejects the false.
Triumphant now, awareness stands,
Reveals the Everything, the All.

—*Isabelle Casanta*

I Watch

Outside-
The moon is full and
The stars are brightly shining
As I watch the world go by.
In only a few hours
The sun will rise and
The stars will disappear
As I watch the world go by.
The hours have gone by
The sun is high in the sky and
The birds are singing
As I watch the world go by.
Nights falls again-
The moon is out but the stars are dull
As my heavy heart and my tears
Mix together as
I watch the world go by.

—*Deborah Gould*

Light to Begin a Lonely Man's Day

I walk on the beach, and the sun awakes.
As the mist plays leapfrog in the air before me.
I look up and see you, beauty and radiance
Like stars in the night, and white on the dark.

To you, I am as a figure to start your day.
To me, you as a fire in the night.
My pulse is racing. None near as strong.
Pounding. Pounding.
Fast and hard.
As wild horses running free.

For you have mended my heart.
And changed my ways.
I will never forget you.
For you are the sunrise to my cloudy day.

—*Elizabeth Swift*

Rejoining with Love

The one and the only,
The warmth of his skin next to mine,
The total seclusion I feel in my mind
That the touch we have dreaming
Driftlessly into the joy of our inner selves
Would last until our being no longer again exists,
And I, knowing that he, my loved one, would wait
For me until the day that we are rejoined
In the heavenly skies.

— *Jenni Johns*

Gone Are We All as Time Passes

Never give in or allow weakness
While hard eyes stare.
Trembling is not allowed on this side,
At least while hard eyes stare.
Gone are all fears from childhood lost,
And in the end so are childhood joys.
We are all like staples—crisp, straight
And stuck together (one for all and all for one).
Time passes and we separate and bend to
Fit our personal niches.
Unlike staples we can control our
Destinies, so...
If hard eyes stare—stare back.

— *Debra J. Leitl*

The Guest of Honor

The cocktail din was thick and dense
Lives brought up to date the norm
The guest of honor reeked cold silence
She joined not in the joyful storm

Aunts and uncles and in-laws all
Brothers and sisters and old friends too
Smiled and laughed enjoying the ball
The honored one's mood an icy black hue

No response gave she to any soul
She lie in wait for all to leave
At last for her the bell did toll
All then left, the happy bereaved

Alone now with the flowers to smell
To contemplate her final sleep
Her still-live soul caught 'tween heaven and hell
Her memory now for granite to keep.

— *Peggy Ambrisco*

JRTM

I guess out of all the people I've known
He is the only one that has ever shown
That there will always be
Someone to care about me.

One that will care, and
One that will always be there.
One who will make me laugh
And one who will do what's right

It scares me how he knows
What I feel and what I think
It's as if he can see through me
And into my heart and mind.

All I can do is pray that two years from now,
When I go away
We will keep in touch. 'Cause without him
Life will be too much.

—*Deanna Scadden*

Ocean Silhouette

A man, stands alone
Finally content in the one place
That understands him
He breathes with the wind
Mingling in the sea salt familiarity
Solid as the time known rocks
That catch the worst of the waves
Tormenting, a distant mysterious stranger,
I've known all my life
This is his captor,
He, a willing prisoner
Now apart of this lonely paradise
Jalama
An ocean silhouette, glinting in the sun.

—*Erika Smith*

These Times

While day light bathes our outside world
Black clouds reign inside labs' locked doors
As customs of tyranny, cultivated by others
Decayed, old practice vivisection is held.
The cries, the terror stricken eyes of souled,
Defenseless, countless sentient creatures pours
Dead on vivisectors as echoing encores
Of organized crimes continue to run wild
For power of self gain against great odds.
In exercising authority we should govern
By justice and unselfish loyalty towards
The welfare of others, for all born
Have the same right to live; life is God's
Great given privilege; for all is one.

— *Alessandra A. Poles*

It's Me

I'm not like a cultured pearl-
I'm more like me,
Just a plain, old-fashioned girl
as you can see.
I search for a model to show me style,
to teach me to flirt 'n' wink 'n' smile,
but I can't bewitch and I shan't beguile-
It's not like me.

I stand and gaze into my mirror-
I shudder and I have some fear;
she looks back bewildered and full of doubt...
I can't step in—she can't step out.
It dawns on me—I'm shocked; I shout,
*That's not perfection—that's my reflection—
It's me!*

— *Haze Craddock*

Lament for Lost Brotherhood

I cry out in shame,
I cry out in pain.
I know now that I cry out in vain.
For the salvation of this once great land,
Whose credo was, *United we stand.*

For it's brother against brother,
Sister against sister.
On the face of God's earth
We're a festering blister.

Oh Heavenly Father, who reigns above,
Bless us again with Thy gift of love
Bring us together again as one
Shoulder to shoulder and hand in hand
Before our day is done.

— *Elyse Martin*

A Mother Is A Gift of Love

A mother is a gift of love
Which very few are blessed
With this God sent from above
None alike the rest.

It starts when you are a baby
This never ending care
Then as you grow, it always seems
To get stronger year by year

But then at times I test this love
With things I do and say
Given strength from up above
It never goes away.

Now as the years go flying by
I will forever know of
A special friend I call my mother
This wonderous gift of love.

—*Stacie Sandiland*

Best Friends

A friend is someone that is true,
And helps you out when you're blue.
A friend is someone that always cares,
Even when you're feeling scared.
A friend is someone that is always there,
And always right and never unfair.
A friend is someone that always listens,
And even in rough times, always glistens.
Having a friend like you,
Helps all of my dreams come true.

— *Tonja Desirey*

Dear Mother,

When I was a child, you cared for me,
You set me on a straight road,
You put in my heart, a melody,
And seeds of faith to be sowed.

But as I grew older, I began to wander,
A few seeds I scattered along,
And then the rest I set aside,
Searching, for my song.

At last, I grew weary, of empty dreams,
Lost, in what was mine all along,
For in my heart, remains that melody,
And my journey, is my song.

—*Marcia Williams*

See You Soon, My Friend

I know that all friends eventually have to say good bye,
But why is it always too soon?
I know there were some bad times, but most of it was good.
You always had a shoulder
When I needed one to lean on or cry on.
You always had a hand to lend
When I needed help.
You always had an ear for me
When I talked about my problems.
You always had a heart for me
When I needed love and care.
But now you're gone because the pressure was just too much.
I realize I never took the time to give you my shoulder, my
My hand, my ear, or my heart.
There is only one thing that I can still give to you.
My life-see you soon, my friend.

—*Susan Kile*

Lily

Wandering through my mind
I often see Lily.
Dancing in the wind; so full of life
So full of joy.
Her petals are etched with the bygone
Trails of life.
She works from dawn 'til dusk, yet she's
Always there whenever you may need her
She sings a happy tune
Waking the flowers in June.
She always does her best
Sometimes forgetting to rest.
She is always very dear
Held in my heart so near.
She is a friend to all; love to one;
She is my mother.

—*Danene Verner*

Silent Heart

I have a silent heart
That doesn't speak a word.
If someone speaks a harsh tone,
My silent heart's unheard.

I have a silent heart
That locks frustration out.
It soaks up all the evil in me
That my mouth would surely shout.

Some people do not have silent hearts
And I do pity them all.
One day they will get hurt
And their hearts will be very small.

My silent heart is special to me
And one day I will say
My silent heart has broken free
And I will walk a new way.

— *Rachel Clifton*

Mystical Mindscape

Princes, princesses,
Knights in shining armor,
Everyday wishes,
Everyday pleasures,
Chests of gold and
Hidden treasures,
Myths, epics,
Stories of old,
Tales that spark
Imagination,
Enchanting passion
And dreams of
Romance;
Visions of an
Unworldly kind,
The mystical mindscape,
A secret look at our
Being.

—*Rachel Cournoyer*

Lost

The words of others
Voiced in jealous rage
Followed by sulking, petty ways
All too often enrage
Lies—friendship dies

— *Rayford Woodall Sr.*

Flashbacks

A remembered scent
of places visited,
A fleeting vision
of past occurrences,
A warm feeling
of good times had,
A wistful wishing
for the way things were,
When time was spent
with you.

—*Loralie R. Rogers*

Lost Intimacy

The subtle touch
The soothing hug
Loosens the clutch
And breaks the tug

The reaching out
The genuine trust
Lightens the doubt
And becomes a must

The deepest feeling
The rising fear
Begins the healing
And escapes a tear

The lofty kiss
The frightened child
Something I miss
A calm, loving style

—*Rebecca Weber*

Promises

A dream, an idea,
Seed of the mind
A child of thought
Is born

A picture of perfect
But thought alone
Just out of reach
And gone

Fantasy world built
Up all around
And there, done,
Is ideal

Once a change
And always dead
Forever a dream
And unreal.

— *Sandra Smith*

A Friend

What is a friend?

The F is for Forever.
The R is for Remembered.
The I is for Indefinitely.
The E is for Endlessly.
The N is for Now.
The D is for Definite.

That's what a friend is for:
Forever.

— *Shawna Schockey*

My Son

As years take me back,
I think of a small boy.
He loved to go shopping,
And buy a new toy.

I think back with grass so green,
As he would play.
With a sky so blue he would
Turn around until he could not stay.

His Dad would play ball
With him in the yard.
Our German shepard would stand,
As if, on guard.

A football they would pass at age three,
Thanks Dad, it really paid off, you see.

We will always love you more than words can say
Even though your life at home with us is now a short stay.

—*Judy Thompson*

Ode to Gratitude

Words of confidence you spoke on that day:
Are sincere words that were meant to say;
Take it easy: then you'll soon see—
How easy things can actually be.

I'll remember these words in all that I do:
Because they came from someone special, that's you;
So hear these words ever so sincerely said—
You'll be one fondly remembered when I get ahead.

— *Joyce Rafique*

Parents

The new mom and dad are scared at first,
    but really inside they're about to burst!
They're so anxious to show off their bundle of joy,
    whether or not it's a girl or a boy.
They fully understand the job that's ahead
    and that their child is gonna be excellently bred.
The Mom and Pop might be old, they might be young,
    but they also know the fun and work have just begun.
Then the kid starts to walk; then soon he will talk.
Mom and Dad are elated when Jr.'s birthday is first celebrated.
It's school time now, gee Mom is relieved,
    but Jr. just put out a great big heave.
He's in grade five, Mom and Dad's little pearl,
    but not when they find out he just kissed a girl!
Now he's in high school, big man on the scene,
    but now he complains all his teachers are mean.
He is now sixteen, he even has a new car;
    his parents are praying he doesn't drive off too far.
It's grad time now, there's a big party tonight
    and his parents wonder if they've done right.
It's two o'clock, they receive a call. *He's having a ball,*
One of his friends says, *He's just a little stoned.*
    Oh God, the mother just groaned.
They drove him home and they're sure glad he phoned!
They recall the previous hours of the day
    when he was showered with praise.
They smile at each otther and forget all their fears,
    for they now know they did a good job these past seventeen years.

—*Laura Pasquariello*

My Father

My father had a wandering soul, he tried so hard to stay
But as the years kept drifting by, he slowly went astray
I know he really loved us, though rarely ever near
So often I wished things different, praying he was here.
Mom was a survivor, always she was near
When times were rough, when funds were low, she never shed a tear.
She pulled us close and comforted us, so many nigths were long.
Mom is a survivor, victory is her star, sorrow never thrived on her
But the rainbow seemed so far.
Still she never stopped her fight to show her loving care
To lead us through the trying times, Mom is always there.

—*Laureane Noyes*

Yesterday's Child

Today I am different than of yesterday's past;
Embracing hours of solitude,
To find the truth at last.

I have searched deep within
To the days of my beginning,
Days of pain and anger
And to this day of understanding and forgiving.

For now I know my perils have an origin
Created from another's pain
So I will speak to the child of yesteryear
With words that will sustain

For yesterday I was a child,
Helpless and afraid.
Today, new mirror images appear
That only I and God have made.

—*Judy Hayden*

Keep on Trying

Everyday we struggle with our problems
And everyday we either accept them, or we do not.

Somedays I just want to stop trying, stop the pain, stop the hurt.
But everyday, I wake up hoping things will get better.
Sometimes they do not.

Sometimes I ask myself what is life about?
But no matter what I think, it never seems to make much sense.

I am scared of what I think, not sure if I'm all here.
Scared to say what I want to say.
Scared of what others think.

But no matter what happens, you must keep on trying.
I know it is hard.
I know you are scared, but so am I.
But you must...keep on trying.

—*Kim Dillon*

Goals

Goals are a necessity in every person's life.
They supply a vital reason to succeed.
They help one to overcome most obstacles and strife
Just to observe the fulfillment of the deed.

Goals-our elders mourn mistakes, and now their time must bide.
Goals—we, the future leaders, must pay them heed.
Goals—they should be set and attained, not just set aside.
Goals—use them wisely as purposed, that I plead.

— *Kenicia Rahn Coats*

How Far Back Was the Last Sign Post?

A long day's journey
down the road
Many miles to go...
When will my travels cease
Where will I plant my weary feet...

Many days and years gone by
Many clouds pass through the sky
Passing as the very hours
watch them fly...
Still where will it all end
Since this ol' world
is not my friend?
Yet I carry on
Seeking beyond...

I know my destination's near
I strain my ears to hear
A soft breeze whisper,
Worry not, I am here...

    —Ron Dougherty

Silent Cry

Outside the sun is shining.
My lips are smiling.
I'm thinking of you, remembering.
In my mind I know you're really gone
Even though my heart wishes you
Were still here.
Forever was never.
And I will never forget
The memories we shared, how much you cared.
Now as I look outside splashes of yellow and
Orange streak across the sky.
The sun is going down, my heart begins to frown
Because now I remember, alone
As I lie down to rest, I miss your sweet caress
And inside my heart is slowly dying
As I lie silently crying.

    — Celeste Rodriguez

Things Had to End

We were together almost a year
The time has come, the time is here.
You must go and do your own thing
And I must stay here and do the same.
I know you thought everything was just right,
But lately all we seem to do is fight.
It had to end I knew inside
But the time and place I couldn't decide.
And now that I've made my final decision,
I hope you'll understand, I had a good reason.

    — Tammye J. Francis

Boundaries

In those starry winter nights,
The boundaries seemed almost never ending.
In those cloudy summer dreams,
They hold my fists tight,
Angry because it is not winter.
Words that could not be said,
Things that could not be thought,
Tears that could not flow,
Even dreams could not be dreamt
Because of them.
Until one night, I looked
Into a clear summer sky
And found no boundaries
And for the first time realized
There had been no starry winter nights.

    — Cynthia Anne Hawkins

Unconquering

I was startled by the vision
That embraced my shattered presence,
I wondered of the mission,
And trembled at the vengeance.

It was filled with desolation,
Its stench engulfed the air.
Its end time of gestation
Gave birth, and bred despair.

Its essence, cold and shallow,
Its crying pierced my nerves.
I strained to think of the hallowed,
His protection and preserves.

A frantic search for escape,
Else this hideousness take its toll.
But I created this self rape,
As this adversary, is my soul.

    —Stephen D. King

A Little Note

I don't think I've ever told you
Just how much you mean to me.
Being friends has changed my life
More than I ever thought it could be.
I've had many friends, but
None have ever touched me more.
You've shown me a light that went out,
And you've opened a closed door.
I wish there was someway
To repay you for the things you've done.
I've searched for the words,
But I swear there are none.
So this is just a little note
To tell you how much I care
And that our friendship is special,
And for me rare.

    — Mary S. Harris

The Protector

Your scorching lips, hot as fire,
You fill my mind for a thought or two.
Passion, that is the word,
Now I search for something deeper,
A stronger emotion.
You've given me feelings I've not often felt,
Luxuries I don't deserve.
Your love and your touch are plenty.
I wrap myself in your arms and in your mind
And I sleep undisturbed, untouched.
Only silence, dead silence.
There is a power of love in the room.
You hold me as gently but as strong as possible.
Where am I drifting to?
A place of security Is what I hope for.
I awake and you kiss my lips
With a softness I've never felt.
Like a gift, you were given.
You are the protector.

    —Heather Wade

Wonderland

Wonderland is full of wonderful things:
Lollipops, rainbows, queens and kings.
No books, papers, a school kind of noise,
Just storybooks, fairytales and Christmas toys.
Puppies, kittens, animal friends
And fun and more fun that never ends.

    — Megan Davidson

Life

Life, how valuable it is.
And how fragile.
How quickly one is gone
With no time for good-byes.
No time for *I love you*s.
No time for *Forgive me*s
Or *Thank you*s
Or *Please don't go*s.

Only time for tears—
And *why?*s—and *what if*s
For those left to carry on.
To no avail.
No more chances—no more choices.
No answers—not that satisfy.
No hopes—no dreams—
Just nothingness—and too much time—
Too late.

    —Rosaleta K. Van Orsdale

Come Slow Dance With Me

Come slow dance with me
Let us feel this music together,
Come slow dance with me
Let us blend our selves in harmony.

Come slow dance with me
Let us close our eyes and dream
Of a special time and place
Our love will someday know.

Come slow dance with me
Let us cherish this sweet tenderness.
Come slow dance with me
Let us live these moments forever.

Come slow dance with me
Let us be, for life, in love, eternally.
Come slow dance with me.
Come slow dance with me.

    —Mary A. Mykyta

A Lesson in Passion

I fly silent, fluctuating distances,
emotions faltering,
daring not to peer into depths
where objectivity trembles.

I endure unexpressed in self-exile,
suspended between
sensuality and reason,
soaring among mists and peaks.

I wait inside the golden temple
of purity and forever,
veiled in trembling wonder.

    — Sandra Reynolds

Dark Night

I open my eyes to see darkness,
Complete darkness.
I feel scared; it's as if I'm not alone.
As I begin to wonder what is
Out in the blackness
I become paralyzed.
Too scared to move.
I lay wondering what will happen
If daylight never comes.
But eventually it does,
And I look around,
Happy not to know
What the darkness held.

    — Amy Moriarity

Give Me the Sun

I need to get away from these troublesome times,
Run away from the fears in my mind;
Leave these days I hate to face,
Maybe then I'll walk with grace.
Sing me a song that's not too fast,
Erase my memory of the past;
Let me leave this shadowed hole,
So I can play a decent role.
Give me the sun, not the rain,
Make me laugh and forget the pain;
Show me love, give me hope,
Then with life I could cope.

— *Rebecca Leger*

Makeup

Cosmetics are the way to please
Those who snub the inferior.
How much nicer they from head to knees
If they treated their interior.
Cosmetics used for elbows, knees and hips,
For fingers, toes, cheeks, and ears:
A fire that's painted on the lips
Does melt away the years.
But some are plain, they are as they are,
Their lack of vanity dutiful.
To meet them we must travel far,
But they really are quite beautiful.
Wouldn't it be a sight to behold
If men and women set some goals
To beautify interiors to enfold
The potential of their inner souls.

— *Tom Hamer*

Wind

From a subtle caress, gentle and mild,
To a sharp sting of fury careless and wild.
A whispered hint to a loud uproar
An invisible strong arm slamming a door.
A brutal force that buckles the knees.
A secret mutter teasing the trees.
Unleashed power that shatters an oak,
Converting itself to a sensitive stroke.
Manipulating clouds to conceal the moon,
With an audible sigh and phantom tune.
From a kindly touch warm as toast
To a loud, brazen, bone chilling ghost.
From unknown to unknown passing by.
Never captured in hand or held with eye.

— *Sarah Kathryn Garrity*

Yesterday

Yesterday, I was a young girl,
All innocent and new,
Frightened of the future, not knowing where to go,
Not knowing who to trust, not knowing who to love.
Yesterday, I was a young girl as fragile as a flower.
Now it's only memories that fill my mind of the past.
I remember being simple.
I remember being sweet.
I remember being used.
I remember the hurt and pain,
sending my mind into confusion.
I remember growing up and having
reality destroy youth and innocence.
Yesterday, I was a young girl.
Now I have girls of my own.
God, to save them from themselves...
Because tomorrow they'll look back and say,
Yesterday I was a young girl.

— *Rebecca L. Dixon*

The Invitation

The invitation was given,
Come up to the feast;
He always went up
With a gesture of peace.
He ate with the sinners,
And he drank their wine;
He sat at their tables,
He loved their kind.
The religious ones grumbled,
They complained and they whined;
He seemed to prefer others
To them when He dined.
He was ever to bless
All those who came
With a childike trust
In His holy Name.
When the Father summons you
Up to the feast,
You'll find Jesus there,
In a gesture of peace.

—*Stanford E. Linzey, Jr.*

Ceramic Heart

Upon the shelf lay the
ceramic heart
At one time used to live
so freely and lively
inside of me.
But now it has hardened
and turned cold,
For that one special guy has
taken the life out of it.
Now until eternity it will
lay upon the dusty shelf
Displayed for everyone
to observe.
However, though, the memories
still lay locked up inside of it.
The memories are still clear
the day they happened.

—*Ramona Doucet*

Evening

Sunlight disappears,
sounds become music.
Time flows slowly,
filling the void
Between day and night.

Darkness approaches,
shadows blanket the earth.
Minds are pensive,
recalling the faded engravings
of distant memories.

Night comes,
objects fade to images.
The final curtain falls
on the immortal play
we call life.

—*M. V. Wilson*

Reflections

Why can't I see out the window?
It looks so clear,
So clear to the ignorant eye.

Why can't I see in the mirror?
It looks so innocent,
But is innocence just a reflection
of ignorance...

— *Keith Rosen*

Free

Finally broken is the heavy chain
Which bonded me to so much pain
I can now start life anew
I can reach for the deep blue sky so true

I'm through with the people in my life
Whose words have stabbed me like a knife
No longer will they hear my cries
Never again will I believe their lies

Time has given me the chance to live
Now out of life I'm glad to give
The joys of life that I never got
The love of warmth that cannot be bought

I thank the Lord Jesus, God's only son
For my new life that has just begun
For the new things in life I can't wait to see
And the great new chance that I can be me

—*Raina Linville*

Nothing is Forever

What if nothing is forever
And everything just ends,
Would there be no tomorrow
Or making of new friends.
What if nothing is forever
And you only had today,
Would you give up everything you have
Throw all your dreams away.
What if nothing is forever
And alone you sit and wait,
Would you wonder what may have happened
If you hadn't such a fate.
What if nothing is forever
It seems so hard to believe,
But maybe that's not how it is
Maybe eternity is what we receive.

—*Christine M. Doucette*

Our World; The Other Side

The park...on a cold winters night
As a bag lady sleeps under a street light.
Her face is as innocent as a child
But her smile is mild.
A child's scream, it is not a dream.
The mother is lit and begins to hit the little boy.
Food for thought cannot be bought;
As a three pound baby girl dies.
A runaway child, beat in the street
Like a piece of dead meat.
A pregnant woman held hostage at a bank,
Gunpoint has no one to thank.
Poverty in the crowded city gets no pity.
Our world; the other side has yet to leave
Maybe it will if we all believe.

—*Stacy Herriott*

I Am

I am the black keys on a baby grand piano.
I am substance with no emotion, no feeling
that people just pass by and walk on.
The blackness that surrounds me in my closet
intoxicates me and makes me happy but unsure.
I am a single, salted tear filled with
hate and anger, yet filled with love and
understanding. The place that I have been
seeking is not there, yet I hunt it anyway.
I am a scream, released emotions in a
violent rush of anger. I am a lonely spirit
searching for a reason.

— *Kristen Buck*

God's Beauty

Tell me how did Jesus make the world.
Did he make it up of boys and girls?
When you look around tell me what can you see
Do You see the beauty that God made, can you see the sea?
I look at the fish that he put in the sea.
He made them so frail like you and me.
Can you feel the rain that falls?
the sun that glows, even the winter months
When it snow?
So I look and I say, I can really see
That it is truly Jesus that awakens you and me.

— *Sandra Sparks*

Far Above Rubies

Priceless far above rubies, this virtuous woman who walks in beauty.
She's a gem among jewels, for all who see her beauty are amazed.
Her virtue will astound you, for she's a God-fearing woman with
whom God is well pleased.
Her warmth and understanding will touch your heart with delight.
Just to know that she is around will make your day a little bit brighter.
She's one among many, an example before us all, for God knows
the heart of this woman 'cause He's the maker of us all.
She's a mother, a wife and other things too, but her role as a Christian
touches the heart of many.
She's a model in her neighborhood, a friend to her fellow man.
She's a God-fearing person with a heart full of love.
She's an angel of delight, a comfort to the weary and a joy to the world.
Such a woman is rarely seen. Who can deny her?
She is priceless, for her price is far above rubies.
The virtuous woman, a legend in her own time.

— *Sister Barbara Matthews*

Blessed are You Father

Blessed are You Father, I praise Your name most high,
I feel You around when I look up in the sky,
I see You in the flowers and in every living thing,
I feel so joyous about You, I always want to sing.

Blessed are You Father, You died on the cross for me,
You washed away all my sins on the spot of calvary.
When I think of all the pain You went through, just for me.
I know I want to be the best, the best that I can be.

Blessed are You Father, there is much power in Thy name
All the goodness in You should put Satan in much shame.
For he lost all his glory because of all his vain,
One third of Heaven fell with him, what a shame.

Blessed are You Father, You are always there for me.
When I need to talk or when I feel so lonely,
For I am not ashamed of You, I would shout Your name aloud,
In a park with people, a very small crowd.

—*Sonia Holden*

God's Love

The waves crashing through the rocks.
The wind blowing through the salted air.
Memories of childhood on the sandy beach,
Building sand castles and watching the tide come in and take them away.
The beautiful enormous waves of the ocean coming in and going out,
Like the breath of fresh air we inhale and exhale.
Oh how the beauty of gods astounding love abounds us all,
Yet unaware of the miraculous wonders of our lives.
Always measuring them up to size,
Going through the lows and highs of life's tides ourselves.
We can be self assured that we are indeed a part of everything that was,
For this is God's astounding love for thee,
It is a part of you and a part of me.
For there is but one truth and the truth shall make you free,
It is in fact God's love for you and me.

— *Kathleen A. Boyce*

Today Is the First Day of the Rest of Your Life

Today is the first day of the rest of your life,
There may be torments, temptations and strifes,
But tomorrow will bring a new day to stay,
And today will only be your yesterday,

Today is the first day of the rest of your life,
Fill it with dreams and hopes that are bright,
Bring strength to those who are weak and alone,
Give courage to those where fears may be borne,

Today is the first day of the rest of your life,
If paths seem dark, may the lord shine his light,
If burdens are too heavy, and task hard to bear,
May the lord guide you with his everlasting care,

Today is the first day of the rest of your life,
May peace be with you from morning till night,
May love surround you, friendships be your pay,
For tomorrow will come with a bright new day.

—*Peggy Zeaphey*

I Must Walk the Path

As I weep in my room with the door closed tight,
My body trembles from the horrible sight.
Earlier today at the funeral home,
There laid my mother all alone.
Her body was cold and completely white;
Her eyes and mouth were closed up tight.
Her skin was pale and white as a dove,
Not to mention the flowers which were symbols of love.
I recalled the times when she laughed and cried.
I just can't believe my mother has died.
How could God take her and do this to me?
I loved her too much, can't you see?
Now I'm all alone in this bitter land
But it's time to wake up and take death by the hand.
I must walk the path my mother has lain,
For it's the only way out; I can't take the pain!

— *Robyn Tollison*

Lest We Forget

Little children playing 'round the door,
Came with their parents from across the shore.
Days had been hard, but there was a start
To get our country built here, set apart.
Time went along as people cared and shared,
Not only in joy, but work, fear and dread.
Our new nation was becoming in tact,
Then wars came along to set it back.
But courage took hold, and we're stronger by far,
For we didn't give up through many a war.

History reveals each step by step
Days of future's past, which we have kept.
But lest we forget as we travel along,
We're reaping the heart of another's song.
Shared by Our Forefathers, and we share it today,
As we give praise and thanks, on this Thanksgiving Day.
May God's love and blessing continue to last,
While Old Glory waves high, as it has in the past.

—*T. Aileen Karg*

Untitled

There's a place I know of far away.
This place, you can sit and watch the palm trees sway.
The ocean's a crystal sheet of ice.
This island's so pleasant and nice.
This place isn't too hard to find.
Just close your eyes
And leave the rest of the world behind.

— *Stephanie McGuire*

Sisterly Love

Oh earthman, what hast thou done, put a hole in your ozone
And let in the ultraviolet rays of the sun?
Oh sister earth, how can I warn you with no life bearer
Left in me, to open your mouth and swallow up the sea?
Have you no eyes to see why I revolve the reverse of our
Solar family tree?

It is I, Venus, your wayward sister, whose morning light of
Truth still offers a dawn of hope to spare you the same
Fate that has stripped all life from me.

Beware of the manbeast dragon, who sits like a blind Nero,
High and mighty on its temporal throne, counting his kindling
Called money, loving it more than life!

Beware of his deadly fire as it breathes out toxic chemical
Pollutants on you!

What has become of all your wisemen of old, who made
Mention of my name, not to be worshipped by them as a Goddess,
But to serve you, their future generations of mankind, as an
Example of shame?

Take heed my earth sister, that you follow not in my footsteps,
But learn truth from the light of my experience, to serve as
Your Alpha and Omega, your Bright and Morning Star.

—*Karen Joy Pollworth*

It Was She

It seems every day gets longer and longer
And my heart gets less and less stronger.
My feelings are too unhidable
And the memories are way unfightable.
I still think of you more every night and day
And the most I can do is I pray.
The wound just keeps getting deeper.
Our unknown love gets only cheaper.
When you need a certain someone, you know I'll always be here
And lately it's all been coming so clear.
I don't think you could understand my pain.
I'm so incredibly lonely; but who was really to blame?
All I ever wanted was for you to be you.
Why couldn't you have just give me a clue?
I gave you one hundred percent of me,
   but what it all came down to was she.
I really trusted you and I actually thought you'd come through.
Now that it's over; I'm not sure if I'm still part of you.
I know you won't realize, it's the truth.
You know it could've been your move, but your chances were gone.
Same with our love; it's all gone.

—*Laura Fetherston*

Sitting by a Creek I Could Only Watch and Wonder

Sitting by a creek among tall pines and looming boulders,
My senses slumbered by the matrix ease in nature.
I heard the gentle whisper of the flowing water
As it meandered and dodged obstacles along its course
Cascading through narrow channels; deep and shallow pools;
So vehemently self-assured to greet its destiny.

Sitting by a creek among tall pines and looming boulders,
My vision focused on a woman in the distance,
Posing statuesquely with a fishing pole in hand,
In thoughts submerged oblivious to the autumnal chroma
As lifeless leaves dispersed and landed all about her
Indiscriminately choosing their earthly sepulcher.

Sitting by a creek among tall pines and looming boulders,
My thoughts roamed and raced through yonder silhouetted mountains
Which stood majestically in set crepuscular.
I vainly sought to discern the fleeting images
Emerging from darkness like shapeless ghostly vapors.
They lingered unprepared as the aurora cleared the stage

—*Laura Bristan Stone*

Breezes of Good-Bye

A hush, a sigh, a gentle breeze
I whisper as I realize that time is passing even as we breathe.
Sunrise splashes of peach, lavender and smoky blue
Remind me of how youth and its passions
   can disappear like the morning's dew.
You just smiled with eyes that threatened to cry
Leaving without saying good-bye.
I wondered why as I walked through despair's darkness of night
But I see faith's shining light,
That even though you are out of sight, you remain in the things I touch,
The places I go, the tasks I do,
This heart cries out, *I miss you,* but these eyes shed no tears.
I smile and laugh and no one suspects
How the thorns of past memories can prick and make bleed
A fragile heart caught in the gentle breeze.
A warm embrace, an upturned face, a hand clasping a soft arm
Deep eyes reveal unspoken volumes of a bond
   mere separation cannot erase.
My love exists outside of time's bounds though all else becomes as ashes
And blows away.

—*Kathleen Silva*

My Special Friend

You are the rainbow that brightens up my day
You are the one who chases my sadness away
You are the one who makes me feel good when I never thought I could
You are always there when I need you most
You never complain when my attitude is a pain
You stand by me always ; your opinions never change
You are like me and I am like you
We will always be friends through and through
We will have our battles; we will have our joys
But we will friends for years to come
Along the way we may lose track
But when we are back together
It will be like we never separated
Friends forever that is how it will be.
What we have now will last for eternity
Forever friends until the end

—*Sara Schroeder*

True Love

While I sit alone all day wondering what to do,
Listening to the music brings my thoughts to you.
The feeling to be there with you is more than I can stand;
Lying by the ocean side in the golden sand.

Sitting there beside you gazing down upon your face;
If there is any hate in you, I cannot find a trace.
That is the very moment I come to realize
True love lives forever and never dies.

So when someone says, *I love you,* look deep into their eyes,
And if you see a lie in them do not be too surprised.
Because the love they feel for you is not true love at all;
But the love a little girl would feel towards her doll.

Right now I will say, *I love you,* and you cannot say that is a lie,
Because from where you sit right now, you cannot see my eyes!

—*Susan L. Adair*

Untitled

With each day that passes, I feel closer and closer to you.
The only doubt I have, lies within the happiness I feel.
Love has never had so much to give.
Part of me wants to let go, so nothing will destroy our time shared.
Part of me has come to depend upon your masculinity.
Part of me never wants to let you go.
I want your smile, your warmth, your arms around me
Because part of me has fallen in love with you!

— *Darlene Fusting*

A Swiss Morning

A valley between mountains
A goat grazes in the morning light
As a shepherd rests lazily on the moist ground.
Snow caps the mountains as clouds roll by.
White, billowy, serene, all is peaceful in the Alps
The grass is a lucious green,
The sky a captivating pinkish purple.
A bird soars in the air and crys at the lifting haze.
The sun rises higher and the new day ripens.

—*Caroline Thompson*

The Garden

In the hazy morning mist,
I love a walk through the garden.
When all the flowers have been kissed,
With dew as the day starts in.

A tiny spider is working hard,
On a web of glistening dew,
An anxious bird is on his guard,
Aware of my magnificient view.

And then the sun awakes to find,
The roses blushing like a wine,
The colors become so vibrant there,
More beautiful than anywhere.

Where all of nature comes alive,
And sparks of dreams start or die.
A place, where things go unnoticed,
A place, where one can find their solace.

—*Jean Ponting*

Mountains

Majestic peaks with purple hue,
Stand like guardians for all of you.
Cold snow and barren rock,
Cover slopes up to the top.

Rumble of avalanche fills the air,
Woe to the creatures still up there.
Summer comes and snows will melt,
Due to warm winds which are felt.

Bubbling streams come down the slope,
With it comes a lot of hope.
For fields below it will surely wet,
And crops will grow, that you can bet.

—*L. W. Thomson*

Autumn Leaves

Autumn leaves begin to slowly fall from the trees
Beautiful shades of red and golden yellow drift on the wind
Like dreams before you wake
Effortlessly they softly kiss the ground
Reminding me of your lips on mine
Autumn dies easily leaving only clues of her presence
I can only wonder.

— *Kristi Williams*

My Beautiful Princess

You are as elegant as a glass of wine.
You are the princess that I chose.
I love you, I want you, and I want you always to be mine
And you are as pretty as the red rose,
So never change anything that you say or do,
Because you are my beautiful princess and I love you.

— *Christian Lees*

Sunset

Your glowing voice of passion
Calls me from afar;
My senses search the treetops,
They draw me to where you are.
Gazing upon the crimson hillsides
I rush up them to see your face
My soul with passion in return, beckons;
For the warmth of your embrace.
We meet in radiant graces
Though our time is very brief;
Reluctantly you slip down the hillside,
I try to catch you, while watching you leave.
Though physically you're moving out of sight
And I get my last glimpse before your crest;
My soul becomes the other side of the hilltop,
Where you majestically set.

— *Lisa Michelle Brunell*

The Unicorn

How beautiful is the unicorn,
It's pure white coat against the dark green forest.
How strong is the unicorn,
Every muscle pumping as it runs.
How magestic is the unicorn,
Its lovely horn shining in the sun.

— *Cathy Yun*

Memories

Moonbeams beckon me with visions of long ago,
A fireplace glowing with lights turned down low,
Remembrances of dreams of what we were going to do,
Planning ahead for the future together, me and you.
Comforting in the warmth with my love by my side,
But my dreams have all vanished, for my love, you have died.
But I still have the memories of our love together
And those, my precious darling, will be mine forever.

— *Cheryl Provance*

Dancing in the Wind

The meadow sways
with mountain breezes.
Flowers bow
as it teases.
Making ripples upon
swirling streams.
Clouds float by
like in sweet dreams.
Everygreen pines
stand on rocky cliffs.
Everything dances
as the mountain breeze drifts.

— *Katherine O'Donnell*

Mermaid

Up and down in gentle motion
Glides a mermaid in the ocean.
Lazily she stretches out.
Watching the sea-life round about,
Hooks a ride on a dolphin's back,
Then dives deep for a sea-food snack.
Again at the surface, she sights a ship,
So giving her tail a playful flip,
She's gone, and lost to you and me,
Who want, so much, a mermaid to see.

— *Carleton F. Petit*

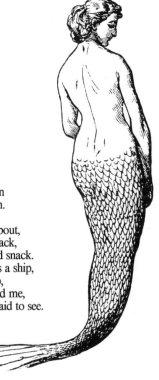

In Search

I am a rare bread borne out of luck
I live in a twilight zone, the
Life of which I do not own. Reading,
Writing and listening I share as
Hobbies. Healthy and honest but not
Perfect. Every season comes and goes
Like a twinkle without a fickle.
Witner, spring and summer makes
No difference. Neither do the help
To which I beg. I crave passion day
And night, dreaming of not perfect mate.
To share and love until death
Render me asunder. If love is eternal,
I will wait til she be ready. If she be
Dangerous, I will pray her. I know
My patience will never go in vain. 'Cause
growing old together has its reward.
Fair love will do me just fine.

—*Samuel O. Okorie*

Shadowless Weeping

Despite delieved intentions otherwise,
After dearest loves discover endings,
Visits falter, embers starve to ashes.
Parting, worded, wounds; confronting icy
Insight blights all remnant faith in finding
Special lasting, pleasant friendship dreamed.
Pangful, Deathlike loss of rare found, deeply
Caring face with beaming eyes perpetually
Sharing heartfelt warmth from welling glowing
Continues aching—void so vast and lonely.
Hungering emptiness wails when there's
Something gone that shouldn't be
You and me! you and me.

— *Samual N. Cogar*

Painful Words

You hurt my feelings, messed up my life
You wished I wasn't born, you called me a loser.
Did you ever realize how much it hurt,
To hear you call me such painful words?
Words so hard, so harsh, so cruel,
How painful it is for a child to hear.
An innocent child, so young yet sad
Because you didn't give a mother's love.
You gave me a pain so hard to lose,
A pain I will posess for the rest of my life.
Such a mother you are, for you gave me birth.
How could you call me such painful words?
Everytime I see you, I wish in my heart,
Please don't call me those painful words.

—*Sampurna Pandya*

The Story

In a book, there is a story
A story of murder, blood and fear.
It was a cold rainy night,
When the beautiful young girl was out walking home.
Late, late at night.
A laugh, a brutal visious laugh.
Silence.
Shrieks broke the silence,
Blood seeped throught the cracks of the wooden bridge.
The blood dripped into the murky water,
The laugh sounded into the silence,
Then the killers silent foot fall.

—*Samantha Lee Gregory*

The Fullness of Time

What appears barren may only be quiescent.
That which is still, in potency to act.
An old woman conceives for the first time;
A poor couple raises an only child.
The one to be a herald for his cousin;
The other to become the Savior of man.

— *Ronald P. Wodrich*

Imagination

I can remember the days of old
When I was very young
When summers were hot and winters cold
And beauty when spring began.
Although I am now old
And no longer young
There are still wonders to behold
When I sit in my chair
Without despair
And relive the days of old.

—*Ronald Claiborne*

Borrowed Stranger

We reach out in the darkness of the night
Holding each other knowing it is not right
Only the passion keeps the feelings away
No words will we ever say
For lovers we are forbidden to be
Another woman is what keeps him from me
Even though we will be stranger tomorrow
Tonight it is his love that I will borrow

—*Samantha Jones*

Together

As sure as the day will come,
There will be days we will be together.
As sure as the night will come,
There will be nights we will sleep together.
As sure as the world goes around,
There will be times we will have our ups and downs.
As sure as the sun rises,
As sure as the sun sets,
I hope I never lose you,
Becasue you are the love I will never forget.
I want you to remember
Keep these words in mind.
I will always love you,
Until the end of time.

—*Samantha Huckabee*

At The Ballet

The toes flutter across the stage
Leaving footprints for the imagination...
Crowned with poise and beauty
We see contrast.
A story told
One moral gained
Entertainment swept through the breeze.
Soft melodies prancing with ease
By enlightened faces
And proud smiles.
Prefect movements like orchestras, they display.
With rosy toes and frills so detailed
One does not cease their amazement.
When toes are not dancing on the now dim stage
And no gentle breeze stirs the anticipation
We know that someday we shall return once again.

—*Kathryn Andrews*

The Rose

I feel as if I were a perfect rose
    Never to be touched...
Soft petals of pure silk
    Beautiful as a butterfly
Radiant color of pretty pink
    Blinding like Heaven's angels.
Fresh smell of spring air
    Breathless as I, but
Friendly thorns of fright are there
    Only to bring me hurt...

— *Regina Bia*

To Ride on a Pegasus...

To ride on a pegasus is
Like walking on air
I know because I was there,
Once, in a dream
The swiftness, the whipping
The sound of air
Rushing past your ears,
Burning your senses
The soft, steady light
The sound of the wings
The creature, with its whiteness
It's personality, with its brightness
Blinds you to all your thoughts
Except for one
I know because I was there
You rode a pegasus
Which is like walking on air...

—*Cynthia L. West*

The Time We Had

Side by side.
Hand in hand,
On the beach,
In the sand,

On the shore,
Where water meets land,
We walk and talk,
But never stand,

We keep on moving,
Walking the shore,
Enjoying the view,
And so much more,

But then the sunsets,
And we must go our separate ways,
But we never forget the time
We had just had.

— *Lynn Warner*

Untitled

How do you do that
How bad can it really be
Did you ask for help
Or did you just collapse
I will do anything for you
Just come talk to me
I'll do my best to get you out
But you have to try too
I've had my share of hardships
But I kept my peace and cool
I want to share it with you
So you can come back to live.

— *Krista Ernst*

Memories Are Today, Tomorrow, and Forever

Memories they are special
Important times you remember.
Like the fun times we had,
And the bad times we had.
So we have to remember you are not dead to us
And keep our hopes and memories.
All you have to do is remember the people
Who loved not the ones who abused you.
So remember we were so lucky
To find someone like you.
To leave the door wide open to us so we
Could step right into the love that lies within
And in our hearts there is a special place for you
And only if you have the faith in us .
So for always you'll be our special girl of the center of our world.
So, *Here's To You!*

— *Jennifer Sexton*

Wonderful Jesus

Jesus is Lord. Jesus is King.
Jesus has given me a wonderful song to sing.
Jesus is glorious. He is the lamb.
The one I serve is the great I AM.
He is worthy. He is to be praised.
To Him, oh glory, will my hands be raised.
He is my strength. He is my shield.
To Him, yes to Him, I will always yield.
And to my Jesus my love I send
Because He is my Daddy, my Savior, my Friend.

— *Sunshine Johnson*

Jesus Came A-Knockin

First the word was offered sown upon a heart of stone.
I had no need of Jesus—I could make it on my own.
Jesus came a-callin' to lift up my failing soul,
Promising salvation, a welcome to his fold.
Jesus came a-knockin' to cast away my sin.
Offered me my freedom but I wouldn't let him in.

Satan almost had me and I struggled to be free.
I called upon Lord Jesus to come and rescue me.
Jesus came a-runnin' and I turned my face away
Ashamed to let him see my sins in light of day.
Jesus came forgivin' my burdens to relieve.
With open heart I listened and I finally believe.

— *Suzana M. Koehn*

The Reconciling

My friend is gone, with this new dawn; I remain behind, and life goes on.
I am permeated with shock, disbelief,
    sorrow rises within for your family, and my grief.
I cannot talk to my friend anymore, so I feel sorry for me.
The whole scenario has just been played, and I am aware of my mortality.
Oh friend, where are you now, did you find a better place?
Do you know the Lord, have you made peace with Him,
    do you gaze upon His face?
Why didn't I ask you these things, way ahead of time?
We enter the world without a thing, we leave the way we came,
    without one plea.
As you know, if you have accepted His saving grace, your gift is Eternity.
It is written: That it hasn't entered the heart of man, what He holds.
If you could only tell me you enjoyed these things since you've been gone.
I believe I could reconcile my loss, for something you have gained.
I'd concentrate on shedding this terrible guilt and pain.
My love for you is still in tact, not forgetting things you've said or done
You've run your race, and I hope that you have really won.
I will put on hold my feelings, until I see you once again.
Your memory I will carry always, my dear and absent friend.

—*Darleen Green*

Dreams Of...

Dreams are visions of things to come to pass.
Or things that we want to come to pass.
A dream of someone special holding you in his arms.
A dream of a hero walking from a fire with a child in
His arms that he saved from danger.
A dream of having a loving, caring family of your own.
A dream of becoming a person who would be remembered for
The good they did in another person's life.
A dream of being me.

—*Rachel M. Sparks*

Hands

The hands of man, such a mystical tool for all the ages.
To saw the brush, to pull and cut back the sages.
Strong and sure are they, as a vase is hewn on potter's wheel.
To hold the cards in place, before each and every deal.
How bold and fierce they appear, when clinched fist is held high.
But the simpest of gestures, to cover the face and sigh.
The scorn of irate parent, raised against child to be scolded.
To be reverent in prayer, by merely being folded.
With pen implemented just so, to write a beautiful sonnet.
Lovely young woman reaches, to adjust her bonnet.
To grasp a cup of coffee, placed against lips, so to drink.
To prop the head up straight, just to think.
In times of despair, the greatest use they will ever be to man.
When singled out stretched hand beckons. Help, if I can.

— *Dan Shemwell*

For All Times

I remember when I was young, how I'd sit and watch the sun
And dream about a love like yours and mine.
Moonlight walks along the sand, late night talks hand in hand,
And as you held your body next to mine, you searched into my eyes
Hoping you would find a love....for all times.

I can't remember how it used to be without you next to me.
We began sharing our thoughts and dreams,
no matter how silly they may seem.
We never felt afraid to express what we had to say
or prove ourselves to one another
And as time went on you discovered, as you looked into my eyes,
a love...for all times.

The magic that's between us will never slip away,
For there is no one else for you and me who can fill our hearts this way.
So I'll be holding you and loving you, I'll be yours and you'll be mine.
I'll be loving you...for all times.

— *Shari Lee Rosasco*

Where Do I Stand with You?

Where do I stand with you?
I'd give anything to stand in your world for a few minutes, just to see
into your thoughts and experience the way you feel, just to see what's
going on in your head and where I fit into the puzzle of your life. Do I fit in?

A part of me wants to belong to you and with you, but not so if I am not
a perfect fit. If my edges don't fit the mold of your puzzle, do not force
what cannot be done.

But I pray that I fit into the scheme of your life, a life that isn't
fully yours because a tiny part of it is me. It is mine. If things hold
true, our lives will not be mine and yours, but mingled and entwined to
become one—become our life. One and one is not two;
    one and one makes one.

Where exactly do I stand with you?
We are all touched by the people we meet; impressions are left on us—
kissed with their being and left with their imprint.

Acquaintances help to mold and color our lives. We paint a color scheme
together to create art . . . human art.

—*Laura Lee Bridgette Smith*

Delusion

The unknown
lures
unsuspecting victims-
enticing fantasies,
dangling dreams.
The naive
enter this realm
of the impossible
expecting miracles,
magic,
the brass ring.
Yet
they find nothing
but a million fragments
of shattered
aspirations.

— *Mindy Alyse Fasteau*

Grays Dance

Blood splatters the wall
Like paint on a canvas
Pain runs through halls
Redness covers my eyes
My bones split into twins
Walking is no longer a task
I can see over everything
I no longer have to ask
Skeletons dance around
With their songs and spells
My weight dissolves to nothing
Not a pound
Bones fall from the sky
Cluttering up the world low and high
Suffocating in the fumes of rot
To be one of the dead or not.

— *Colby Peed*

What Love Is

Love is like a hand-held bird-
Fragile, yet needing-
Squeeze too hard, you'll smother it
By keeping it from breathing;

A grip too loose, it'll fly away.
Impossible, yes, it seems;
However, you must find a way
To hold it somewhere in between.

— *Paula Dye*

My Fears

I am scared of many things,
But you are my biggest fear.
I am afraid of waking up one day,
And knowing you won't be near.
I am afraid you won't love me,
As much as I love you.
You'll break up with me,
And find someone new.
I am afraid that one day,
For me you'll no longer care.
You'll forget all the good times
Oh, that we did share.
If I had one wish,
You know what it would be,
For you to love no one but me,
And only me—through eternity.

— *Mickie Bunyan*

Soldiers of War

Loud blasts as the rifles sound
Bloody dead bodies lay in mounds.
Echos of their screaming cup
Before they finally lay down to die.
Marching as if the fight they will win
Going to battle with an evil grin.
The enemy lurkes in the shadowed night
Not afraid of death not afraid to fight.
If death may happen on this frightful day
They will be remembered as Soldiers of War.

—*Melanie Collier*

Forevermore

T'was a dreary day...a black day,
In a room dark...cold...awesome.
A child stood on a stool by the gas light,
That she could see death.

T'was the father...she knew not.
So still...ashy white...huelike.
Three years old...in death they met...
The dad...she knew not.

Nigh to her...Auntie preached...
Fire and brimstone...Dad in Hell.
Mother's sins...Hades waits.
Her destiny the inferno regions
Should she be as they.

She wondered...feared.
Tried to be good...failed.
O'er the years learned, Jesus saves.
God loved her sixty-four years.
Now she verse his love forevermore.

—*Lorraine Hicks*

Lost Emotions

I want to hold on
To all the memories of you.
But it seems that everytime I try,
It becomes more impossible to do.

I remind myself of all the times we have shared
I thought they would last for years.
And as these memories come to mind
Along with them come the tears.

As I look at the sun lighting the day
My sadness becomes the rain.
And once again the clouds return
Reminding me of my pain.

—*Marie T. Nowak*

Breathlessly Breathtaking

The turn of the tides, the rush of the winds,
The smell of the ocean, the flash of light...
So are you to me—breathtaking!

The birth of a child, baby's first smile,
The break of day, a full moon bright...
So are you to me—earthshaking!

The stroke of your hand, the kiss of your lips,
The warmth of your arms on our first night...
So you are to me—lovemaking!

The feeling of love so fresh and secure,
A future of *us* with everything right...
So are you to me—not faking!
My love, you leave me breathless!

—*Bronson Lemons*

The Farewell Salute

The day was dark and dismal
The world was filled with grief
The scene, the President's funeral
The band played *hail to the chief*

And standing by his mother's side
While all who watched were mute
A charming baby boy with pride
Honored father with smart salute

A stirring memory to see
The baby boy was only three
Now tender hearts remember long.
The farewell salute of Baby John.

— *Donald M. Gage*

Intermezzo

Two blossoms fell, two blooms remained.
Listless in the garden, lonely and unclaimed.
Then as gentle winds caressed the pines.
What once was become hers and mine.

Two petals touched face to face,
A tender kiss, a longering embrace.
And in the warm September rain
Hugged away the haunting pain.

Now two new
Lives have begun
To walk hand in hand
In their autumn sun.

— *D. G. Schneider*

Loving You is Hard

Loving you is hard to do
Its more than you could comprehend
More then romance and passion
Its being my friend
Knowing when my heart means no
And not making harder temptations
To know me and to trust me
Not making hurting insinuations
Knowing when to let go
Or just to hold me tight
Its being honest and dependable
Telling me it will be all right
Standing up for my pride
Just caring what I do
Know how I feel
Or just saying I love you!

— *ReDonn Elkins*

The Changing

O' The winter's white and grey,
Come to pass, but go to stay,
In the midst of thus big frown,
She changes into her bright spring gown.

The summer's hot and humid air...
With flowers bright and big with bloom,
She changes to fall with her loom,
Weaving orange, brown, and red,
To see a tree fall dark and dead.

This tells the story so and prime,
Of Mother Earth and Father Time.

— *Melissa Byous*

The Painter

I've lost my brush, the painter cried, and ran on to the street
And searching all the passers from their head down to the feet
You've lost your mind, the banker said, and pushed his hands away
How dare you search me for a tool that I cannot obey.

What will I do the painter thought, and sat down on his can
Without my brush I'm just like them, another puppet man
Excuse me sir, the blind man said while holding his cup near
Your brush was never lost my friend, just tucked behind your ear.

— *Drew Annese*

Barbara Ann, My Love Barbara Ann

I love you, I'll always love you, you mean so much to me . . .
Your beauty is beyond reality, your happiness is my goal . . .
You were an angel sent in my direction
Your skin is as soft as a rose petal
I love you for your tenderness; Gentle touch; way and spirit
The way you respond to my caress,
The way you make me feel like a total man.
You motavate me, you make me a reason for living.
Lady be mine, and I'll give you love, prestige, and honor.

YES, BARBARA ANN, I LOVE YOU
I NEED YOU
I WANT YOU

BE MINE I PRAY, WE WERE MEANT TO BE . . .
LOVE ME
LOVE ME
LOVE ME.

—*Don A. Prettyman*

Our World We Live in

This world is full of hostility and murder and therefore it seems to fade away
Like a grain of sand that's about to be blown away in the wind.
A wildflower is somethig that is peaceful, beautiful and it makes you feel
Closer to earth each year to the peace that should exist and then we wonder,
Is there just peace in a flower?
We will not live in this world forever and so often an hour seems like an eternity
But we must always strive for security and poisitivity.
In our world we live in, its future is up to us to create and manipulate;
The past may only help build our future by lerning from our mistakes and achievements.
Unfortunately, we all must face pain, sorrow, tears and death because it's
All a part of our world we live in.

— *Philip Gay Fletcher*

Lockerbie Is Still

A silent, silver streak it rose, man's greatest feat in flight.
Then twisted shell, it burst and fell shrieking through the night.
The pipes are crying reedy thin, they tear my soul apart,
My faith is tossed on rocky clogs, the ruins of my heart.

The wind wails low and dismal, my God, what have You done?
You've tested my immortal soul, You took my only son.
Oh savior God forgive me for I cannot see the light
That bathes the heather hillside on this cold and bloody night.

Father, Father, God my God, I cannot stand the pain,
So lift me up and hold me for I doubt I'll walk again.
And if You are the God of Love then why in Heaven's name,
Has love been wrenched and torn and crushed in some satanic game?

The River Styx runs bloody, the demons writhe with mirth.
Our world is dark and dying in the light of Jesus' birth.
Dark purple bells of mourning toll low and all alone,
No silver bells or candlelight will warm or change the tone.

Holy Spirit, God of fire, of wisdom, light and love,
Shield me from the storms of Hell, Almighty, gentle dove.
For I cannot understand and I cannot love the foe
And God I see no reason why so many had to go.

With carols drifting sweet and true from the church upon the hill,
The Christmas bells are silent now and Lockerbie is still.

— *Virginia Anne Brock*

Mourning

Oh window of house in village serene,
What lies beyond your softly lit still?
All else is darkened but your light is seen,
What goes on in that white house on the hill?
In this dreary old house all are asleep
Save a woman who rocks in a chair
Specially painted pink and blue; but she weeps
For the one it would calm is not there.
Oh window of house looking down at the sea
That roars and cries and mourns as it churns,
Do lonely arms press upon your cold pane
As the rain mingles with a heart that yearns?
Yes, she laid to rest her youngest child today;
The breaking of the waves and her heart take turns.

—*Terrie Jelsma*

Missing You

I feel the trembling tingle of another sleepless night
Creep through my body and the moon is bright.
Beams of blue come flickering through my window pane
Like gypsy moths that dance around a candle flame.
The moonlight used to bathe the contours of your face
While chestnut hair fell all around the pillow case.
Now the fragrance of your perfume rests beneath my head
And gently reminds me that our love's not dead.
Morning comes and morning goes with no regrets.
The evening brings the memories I can't forget.
Empty rooms that echo as I climb the stairs
And empty clothes that fall and hang from empty chairs
...And I wonder if you know that I never understood
That although they said you had to go, until you went—
I never thought you would.

— *Tina Louise Crisp*

Mr. Doll

Are you real?
My dreams stand before me, are you really mine?
For me, forever you will be someone only for others
Never realizing you would call out from my dreams
You came...The Doll, the one that I pictured
Not as an image or look but the one as a person
Everything I wanted you took, you took away from everyone
Those qualities I could never find,
It's because you had them all along, you came just in time!
Before I might have settled for less
Less than the best
Anyone else would be
You never forced it as a quest but I've made it that
The Doll is here and I don't want to lose
Making my life real...whole
Mr. Doll, can I touch you?

—*Shirley Hopkins*

With This Needle I Thee Wed

Well now you say, you're tired of grass,
L.S.D., acid, cocaine and hash.
When someone pretending to be a friend,
Say, I'll introduce you to heroin.
However, before you start fooling with me, let me inform you
Of how it will be. I will induce you and make you my slave
I've sent millions straight to their graves.
You'll think you could never be such a disgrace,
Then you'll end up addicted to poppy seed waste.
You'll need lots of money, or have you have been told?
For I'm much more expensive than silver or gold.
Then one day you'll see the monster you've grown,
And you'll solemnly promise to leave me alone. If you think
That you have the mystical knack, just come on and try gettin
Off your back. You'll give up your morals, your conscience,
Your heart, and then you'll be mine, till death us do part.

—*Helen L. Earp*

Here Comes the Night

Here comes the night.
It creeps up to my shoulder and gently taps once-
It knows I'm waiting for it.
Its darkness wraps itself around me, tight,
Causing my eyes to shut and my lips to smile.
The stars are its eyes,
A million of them, looking just at me.
It spreds its space through my hair
And around my face,
Almost liquid as it runs through my fingers,
All of them.
Its soft laugh sits inside my ears,
And runs down my neck.
We move on the air above the ground
Playing in our cool wind.
Here comes the night in all its glory.
In all its glory, just for me.

—*Kellie Brice*

Tribute of Love

I see you lying there
I hear your heart beating
Yet you say nothing.
I feel your hand reach out to touch me
I sense your breath upon my face
Yet you ask for little.
You squeeze my hand for life
You gaze into my eyes for love
Yet you stole my heart.
Your eyes close
You breath your last
Yet you remain forever!

— *Karen P. Krywucki*

Time

Time slips quietly by
When I am with you.
Days turn to hours,
And hours turn to minutes.
It seems as though
As soon as I say hello,
I have to say good-bye.
Although I would like
To stay with you forever,
I know that is impossible
Because soon the clock
Strikes the number
When we have to part.

—*Kelli Rexrode*

Message with the Moon

Last night I looked into the sky
And gazed upon the stars.
I thought about the time and space
That keeps us far apart.

As I watched the stars burn bright
The moon crept out to greet me.
He left behind a dark, thick cloud
And started glowing softly.

Suddenly I realized
How actually near you are.
For who is to say that at that moment
You were not studying the same stars?

So when the night becomes a blanket
And covers the entire sky
Look up and smile at the moon
He will tell me you said *Hi*

—*Karen Godburn*

How I Love You

I love you so very much;
I cannot describe just how I feel.
What I feel is very strong;
And oh so real.

I love you so very much;
I have never before felt this way.
I cannot replace with words;
What only my body can say.

I love you so very much;
Just when you look at me,
You stir in me longings;
That never used to be.

I love you so very much;
I cannot say it enough.
So I am just going to tell you;
I love you so very much.

—*Larissa Horn*

Natural Love

She's like the moon on a long, quiet, distant night,
Yet she's like the sun glowing cheerfully during the day.
She's the goddess of beauty here to make everything beautiful
    throughout the day and night.
I'm the god of changes, here to change the beauty and make it all mine.
She's a quiet, swift-moving stream flowing toward larger streams.
I'm the larger stream caressing and carrying her to her destination.
She's like the fields on a soft, windy day, blowing undirectionally.
I'm a hawk, flying cautiously over her, keeping predators away.
She's like the time, slipping by slowly, without anyone noticing.
I'm the hands of the clock, always one step ahead of her.
My love for her is like nature;
It will always be here, even when we're not.

— *John Collson*

Lonely Heart

Oh, you fill my lonely heart
So much that I will never part.
You bring out the best and worst in me.
You are my life as you can see.
So fill my lonely heart with love.
My love will rise from above.

— *Kristen Vangsness*

Midnight Tempest

The moon shimmers softly with vague intent,
As the wind howls a song of deep lament.
The stars standing guard of the heavens above,
Twinkling at each other with an aura of love.
The black clouds roll in and the moon says goodnight;
The stars fade out, yet watching in delight.
The trees bow down, obeying their master,
As the flashes in the distance come faster and faster.
Thunder joins in now, bellowing loud.
The rain then starts, as if following the crowd.
The lightening, the thunder, the wind and the rain;
Completely at home in their own domain.
But all too soon, with the clouds moving fast
The flashes have faded and the thunder has passed.
Everything is silent, the moon says hello,
As the stars twinkle brightly to the lovers below.

—*Beverly J. Williams*

Love

I was just wandering around
Not looking for anything in particular
Then it hit me, just like a bullet
I was in love.

My life changed suddenly
He was all I thought about
And before I knew it
I was in love.

When he held me close
I felt good all over
Then he said he loved me
I knew I was in love.

Then one day, without a warning
He told me that his feelings changed;
I was devastated beyond belief
Now, I am no longer in love.

— *Christina Giannamore*

Tearfall

Love is never lost,
It is only forgotten.
Forgotten love,
Remembering the pain,
Only creates tears.
Tears that fall to darkness.
The darkness shattered
By forgotten love.
Ones happiness is,
Another's tears.
Tears,
The only release of the heart.
Fall in happiness,
Or flood in despair.

—*Julie Parlette*

Received

Joy, the gift given, twice received,
irreplaceable.
Fragile the heart, enhanced once again
is the spirit of love.
This gift is rare, as a grasp of the
butterflies flight, but some shall reach.

— *Daniel J. Du Mont*

Not Once But Twice I Have Seen Thee

Not once but twice I have seen that
certain expression across your face
as our eyes met your lips came upon mine
all of the things that troubled me
suddenly disappeared
there wasn't a single worry
in the world or not one that was near

Oh how wonderful it is to be right by your side
to feel your body pressing against mine
the touch of your tender hand
sent shivers up my spine
The look of happiness in your eyes
when you said that you loved me
to which I replied, *I'll love you*
more and more as time goes by.
I'll love you in good times and in bad.
When I am far away
I'll love you in the memories that I had.

    — Amber Hunter

A Friend

A friend understands you better than anyone else
And they're someone who you can trust other than yourself.
You can trust them with a secret, a question or a doubt
And you know that they won't tell anyone what your feelings are about.
You can talk to them about things like problems you have at home
Or just sit and gossip until your mouths are as dry as a bone.
But friends are very helpful, they're someone you'll always adore.
Because they're always there when you need them
And that's what friends are for!

    — Monique Raynor

Always

I have this feeling, I cannot quite explain.
It is when I am with you, my heart feels no pain.
You fill my life with sunshine,
Even when the clouds bring the rain.
When we are not together,
I wonder where you are.
You are always with me in my heart and soul.
For no matter where we are,
We both look up at the same stars.
I want to be in your company always
I would do anything to keep you safe.
I love to watch you when you are doing nothing at all,
For your expressions tell me special things.
One day everything will come freely to us,
And our dreams will start to come true.
For as long as our love is so strong,
There will always be...
You and me.

    —Stephanie Schaffer

Just Walking Around

Just walking around.
Nothing to be found.
You don't know how much fun it is,
Just walking around.
Nothing to be found, nothing to be found
You can't imagine, just how much fun it is,
Just walking around.
But then there were somethings I found,
Just walking around
Sunshine and warmth of a beautiful day
A day for a picnic, a day for play
Just walking around...noting things to be found
Knowing just how much fun it is
To be just walking around.

    — Kevin Feingold

Falling in Love

You sometimes creep into my dreams at night.
You sit and stare and hold me tight.
You hold me as if to say you'll never let me go.
You try to tell me something, something I'll never know.
You smile as if to say you still care.
Only in my dreams do I answer or even dare.
To reply to your calling.
And then it seems as if I am falling...
Falling, falling in love with you.

    —Debbie Friedland

Last Twilight

I've seen such death on distant shores where innocence would die.
I've sailed the world's most torrent seas and watched our strongest cry.
I've fought in wars on every land; I've crawled on hallowed ground.
The wall of pain from dying souls I'll forever hear the sound.
I've soared the clouds on silver wings where Heaven softly calls.
I've walked across our golden plains and cried beneath the falls.
I've climbed our tallest mountain peaks where beauty is serene.
I've looked at God in all His works; His majesty reigns supreme.
I've touched great treasure built for kings when bondage was at hand.
I've seen my children starve to death from famine in my land.
I've shared a love of burning hearts and felt its broken pain.
I've lived the seasons of my life this one last gentle rain.
I've lived a life not meant for man; I've shared the greed and lust.
This heart is full, life's so complete; my passing's only just.

    — Arthur Ashley

I Cannot Stay

I wonder about your thoughts
And know they must be tangled knots within you
The others so important, I do not understand

You are intrigued by me, but your convictions
Are much stronger than the truth
Repulsed by what you love, you are guided by your anger

The tenderness is wasted for it lies deep inside
Stifled by the many heavy covers necessary for warmth
When all the time your hands are icy cold

I find myself lost in the softness of such light eyes
Deceiving in their illusive kindness, magically disappearing
Taking always just a little more of me

Entering, I am overwhelmed by the knot of your confusion
Great vines tangle together in protection
And are too strong for me to break
I cannot stay

    —Karen O'Leary

Think Before You Gripe

If you're waking up with aches and stiffness that tend to slow your gait
And your blood feels like it's getting tired and is slow to circulate;
If you can't walk as far as you once did and your back develops a twist.
And you spend lots of time lamenting about all the things you've missed;
If you're constantly complaining and in despair your shoulders slouch
And you're becoming testy and contentious and acting like a grouch;
Well, if this is your condition, you know there's no help in sympathy.
So it's time to evaluate and try the *Count Your Blessings* therapy.
I'm sure you have your troubles and your blessings might seem thin,
But just think of the many in wheelchairs who will never walk again.
And when you write a letter to a loved one or telephone across the land
Consider how fortunate to be able for many don't have a functioning hand.
Then try relaxing in His creation, observe each flower, bird and tree.
Then appreciate you eyesight 'cause there are so many who can't see.
And when you turn on a radio and the sounds clearly reach you ear,
Just think of all who would give so much if they could only hear.
So, next time you're feeling sort of down that's when the time is ripe,
To just pause awhile and count your blessing and think before you gripe.

    —K. Bryant

The Dresden Dolls

The dolls that I have one, two, three, four, five
Have flaxen blonde hair and light light blue eyes
Wondering each night if they are alive
Each day that I play I am quite surprised
Surrounded by glass the house they live in
With maids and a butler dressed so neatly
To your surprise they live in wicked sin
Talking and acting so very sweetly
Isolated in one house all alone
Jewels so galore each had their own mink
Their dreadful secrets will never be known
Guilty were they though sacred did they think
Devil's spawns they were so true it may be
The evil in my dolls you'll never see
— *Toni Ann Caputo*

In My Fantasies; I Miss You

Wearily I draw my curtain
To then await visions uncertain.
Then in my dreams you come to me
To substitute reality.
I fall asleep and then we meet.
Admiring you, there's lustful heat.
The yearning in my heart grows strong
Because I've loved you all along.
The memories of the times long past,
The question burning, *Will we last?*
And then I suddenly realize
Many tears falling from my eyes.
I call your name with hesitance
Upon deciding to take the chance.
You turn to me and then we kiss.
Oh don't you know it's you I miss?
I know the day will surely come
Whereupon we shall live together in aeternum.
—*Michelle Scull*

The Golden Spires

There is a land where there is no night
A far off land that is beyond our sight
A place where the weary come to rest
A heavenly abode, home of the blest

Sunlight glistens on the golden spires
Glowing more brightly than a million fires
This sight is there for you to view
The road is there to be taken by you

Thru Christ is the way to this great land
Before the cross we must take a firm stand
And for this we must earnestly plea
Master, let me dwell in Heaven with Thee

So for a Christian soul do not mourn
When it leaves this earth and is Heaven bourne
Awaiting this soul are Golden Spires
Shining more brightly than a million fires
—*Marshall P. Simpson*

Summer's End

As I walk along the sandy shores
I feel a cool summer breeze.
I hear soft crashing sounds of gentle waves
Caressing my thoughts and feelings.
I think of wishes and long-lost promises
And I discover that life is gone before it has begun.
— *Mika Eve Zipusch*

I Like

A wink or a handshake,
An open hand to take,
A smile from a person passsing by.

A hug to share the beauty inside,
A proud stance to show pride,
A friend to talk about anything.

A kite to float way up high
In the whistling wind soaring by,
A smirk or a nod of understanding.

A flower that brings a sense of serenity,
A bird that could fly on to eternity,
And these, my friend, are a few things
That I like.
—*Stella Meacher*

Be Aware

How can we live in a land so unsafe
Pollution that fills our breathing space
What can we do to clean up the air
Get others interested enough to care
Smoke that comes from trucks going by
Circling the air and up to the sky
Factories that dump their chemical waste
Seems like it's in just any old place
Ozone that is killed by the aerosol cans
With buttons we push with our own hands
More care should be taken in things we do
I will be more aware...how about you
—*Mary P. Criniti*

Miss Quick

A knee high springy girl was Miss Quick
Besides blue twinkles, yellow curls in kinks
She wiggled upon a floating chair
Until she pranked spangling air
Ahead a small silver bowl
Topped with a smaller silver rose
Polished a beautiful sticky thought
Much too bright, too white to thwart
Tasting sugar licky
Inserting flashes of chatter
Scattering grains farther and faster
Spunky Miss Quick tipped the matter
Away like rays sweet glitter poured
Worse, the silver rose broke off like a thorn
Rather than quit, Miss Quick. counting to six,
Fixed the silver rose under and over
With one glorious glob of golden salted butter.
—*Lisa Clementson*

New Things Have Sharp Edges

New things have sharp edges
And stand out against the landscapes of our minds
Their dimensions not yet fitting into place
'Till their colors become part of the unknown design

Time contours the geometric shapes
Into a different blend for our lives
And paints a picture never really finished
A mural that is constantly revised

Nothing ever stays the same
Some things never change
Contradiction becomes clarity
Depending on the range

And new things have sharp edges
Until they're intertwined
—*Sharolyn Dawn*

Understand

Why can't you understand?
He would never hurt me.
The most he has done is hold my hand.
I know you are trying to protect me,
But I've got to stand.
There are people who love me,
You aren't the only person on this land.

I can see.
You got a special man
Who you always look forward to see.
I'm beginning to understand
How different people can be.
There is a man.
A chance is all I can see to be,
For you to understand,
How good he is for me.
— *Michele Gillespie*

Just Like A Breeze

Like a breeze
You came into my life
At a time, I thought I would freeze
Because I had no life.

I love your tiny squeeze
It jolts me back to life
It is like a fresh breeze
To carry me through life.

And now I do not have to freeze
Because you are my life
You are my fresh breeze
And you gave me my life.
—*Mary Pask*

The Sealed Door

As I sit hear in the dark,
Alone and scared.
Confusion circles my mind.
My conscience is weakening,
And my body stays tense.
No hope
No door
No way out!
With each day shattered by a tear,
When will all the pain end?
A question that's lost,
A key that must be found!
—*Amy Lynn Ronk*

The Land, in the Sky

High above the trees,
There is a land,
That seems to be so grand.
Up in the clear blue sky,

Even on a stormy day,
The land will still be there, and why.
For what purpose, for what way.
The people's way, is not the best,

The kingdom's way, to harsh.
So we live with our own rules.
And forget, about the rest,
Just as it's put, just as it's said.
—*B. J.*

You

You were the one who kept me in line,
You were the reason the sun always shined.
Through the special times we have shared,
I always knew that you cared.

Now that it is over, now that it is done
There is no longer a shining sun.
I wish I knew what to say,
I did not mean to turn you away.

Is it too late to start again?
Someday, do you think we can?
I never once doubted your trust
Because I thought there would always be us.

Now that it is over, now that we are through,
I still find myself loving you.

—*Stacey L. Davis*

The Mending

Had a lovely dream last night.
Found a path narrow and bright.
Joyful sounds around me sweeping.
Even the willows were not weeping.
Perched within, a single lark
Sensing not my aching heart.
Around the bend, I heard a voice.
My heart leaped in sweet rejoice.
Had I found the Master of Love?
Take notes, said he, from a cloud above.
And I'll come down and share with you
Some secrets, I'm sure you already knew.
I've been around for many twilite years,
And have always seen lovers tears.
Love dies hard, like hate, my friend.
Stay with me awhile, until you mend.

—*Rosemary Slobodian*

The Monument

The Mothball Fleet still looms on my mind
Like a monument for ghosts, the ships
Are shades in this world and the next.
The image remains impressed on the air
By so much grim grandeur, so much
For life or death valor. I dream of
Dust covered decks and rusting holds
And forgotten men who pass over waves
To make their home in dim cabins.

But a friend says no vagrants live on the fleet.
He tied his boat to an anchor chain
And pulled gray sturgeon from the bay.
A guard is on duty at all times.
There are no homeless among the dead.

—*Lynn Miyake*

New England House Guest

He had no body, only a head.
This is my place you're in, he said.
But I pay the mortgage, I argued with him.
His face seemed to turn a little more grim.
I paid it off before you were born,
By selling fields of hay and corn.
How on earth could I argue with only a head?
So quickly I countered, *I'm alive, but you're dead.*
I can make your life hell, he answered right back.
Since I wasn't quite up to a spectral attack,
You don't need too much room, I briskly replied,
For you seem to have long ago already died.
So our house is now dwelled in by just us three:
My loving wife Julie, the ghost and me.

— *Jodie Poulin*

Shadows in the Night

The darkened edge encroaches
Along the grey walk side
In the brittle evening air
A dry leaf scratches along
The grey concrete pavement,
A slight night-time blur,
Insect like the leaf scratches,
First darkly
Then as the new moon
Parts the darken cloud,
The wrinkled shape scurrys resolute
Pushed by an unseen finger
Centipeedal like a micropedal
Chineese dragon lost in the after
Glare of the fading star shell
Chasing its shadows in the night.

—*Ted Laabs*

Memories

The electric blue sky caught my eye
And reminded me that we all die
As I walked through the beach
The sand at my feet
I remember how you would teach
But now your heart does not beat
I watched the soft waves
Its motion so slow
The love that you gave
As you watched me grow
And though I cannot tell you
How much I care
We will still have memories
That will always be there.

—*Gladys Brillantes*

Secret of Life

In a world turned upside down
And inside out, the inner nature of
The self is calm, serene. Life
Rises to its fullness. I hold the
Answer in my hand.
Existence eternal flame beginning
End now forever, a moment frozen
In time, standing still, trapped
Within a dark cave.
I open my hand, anticipating the
Answer with the dawn.
We all roam together in the pack,
Led by the fearless. We are lonely.
We give up. We die.
We wait for light to be a
Revelation, the answer, the truth.
The day when there will be
A bridge on the horizon.

—*Julie Merten*

Freedom

Freedom-
   a blue sky
   and a light breeze,
   a bird soaring
   into eternity.

Freedom-
   best understood
   by the bird
   with clipped wings,
   who can only long
   for the days
   when she can fly again.

—*Sarah Constance Black*

The Flame Within Love

In the dark depths of the Earth lies a man.
There is no salvation, no helping hand,
Or so he thinks in his state of grief,
Yet there is a way to obtain peace.

Do not fear the dark or cold.
For in this world is a flame that is bold.
This flame is vibrant, everlasting,
It has no limits, constantly passing.

Now I have heard the lonely one,
Now the lonliness is done.
The fire lives within my love.
With you I share it, the one I think of.

Open your heart, let the flame grow.
Bathe within its radiant glow.
Never shall you bask in fear,
For I will always hold you dear.

In the shining heavens of the Earth lies a man,
There lies his salvation, a helping hand.
And so he thinks with great desire
Of the love he receives, the comfort of fire.

—*Daniel A. Cortez*

At One Time

At one time, we would have been conquerors,
Norsemen, questers for the Holy Grail.
now we grasp our HB pencils, and
spoon acronyms to a mechanical deity.
we went awry, my friend, mixing goals
like cocktails.
At one time, we were bravely resilient
ravaging the charts that others made on us,
confronting the hypocrises, smashing facades.
now we are the game played by opportunists.
At one time, we were time's lover
shuffling minutes, like a new deck of
cards.
now we squander days, never watching the
currents that pass our doors
that we have closed.

— *John L. Kirkhoff*

The Rain

The rain falls, and feels
Like cold, dead bodies.
I shiver and feel pins
Pricking me, keeping me
From fading out.
A sense of security,
Like my father's big arms,
Wrapped around my three year old body,
Rushes over me and calms me inside.
I suddenly feel philosophical and
Have much to say as if I had
Been speaking to Nabakov.
The sound of the drops
Entrances my mind like a hypnotist,
As I peer out the window.

—*Sasha Eagle*

An Artist Dream

A mountain rising majestically to the sky;
A valley with lush green grass
Caressed with wild flowers filled with colors;
A rainbow that appears in the sky after the rain;
A choppy sea during a violent storm;
It's all nature's way of painting
An artist dream.

— *Colleen Hammel*

What's This World Coming to?

A school with no concepts to brighten my day
Just terrible feelings to break my heart away
No one to comfort me, no one understands
Though many a time I may grasp at their hands

Only precious few moments of relief do I hold
All of the sorrow in my heart statys cold
My problems are many but solutions are few
With everyone adding making one and one, two

Trusting a friend is hard as you know
And for me I must say, I cannot let it go
Too many lies, oh, too much deceit
It stays in my mind when a new friend I meet

My heart has lost faith that the honest and true
Will be left among the nations when the evil are through

Total honesty's not normal, I have been told
And the best thing to do is to turn your heart cold
Well, if that is the best way, then the best's where I will be
If this world will not have mercy on me

  —Rachel Mankowitz

Autumn

Falling leaves in the sunset
Reflecting silver, gold and crimson.
The air is crisp and cool with the early morning dew.
The day turns warm as noontime nears. As the night approaches,
An owl is heard in the distance with an eerie woo-oo-oo
A cool breeze blows throught the open window, sleep peacefully,
Sweetheart. Birds in the treetop happily chirp, chirp, chirp, chirp
I feel a gentle tug at my pajamas. *Wake up Mommie! Get up Mommie.*
We're hungry. Rain is pounding fiercely on the rooftop. Bacon is
Sizzling and popping in the frying pan. Sister and her baby brother
Are waiting patiently for their breakfast. Eventually the day comes to
An end. Hail starts falling fast and hard. At nighttime, a cool breeze
Blows through the open window;
Sleep peacefully, sweetheart.

  —Rusty Jessie Ventaloro

Real to You

Afraid to start because what if you're finished?
What if all you wanted to do all your life at one stroke can be diminished?
Knowing what you want is half the battle
and trying to succeed a Hell of a fight.
Even if what you wanted at first has changed,
at least you are striving for something that is real to you.
Maybe not to anyone else, but real to you:
Stop thinking if they take you seriously.
What you think and feel will get you through life's circus.
Just because there is a tomorrow, don't waste today.
Friends and lovers come and go, but dreams usually stay!
You always thought loving yourself was selfish . . .it's not; it's survival!

  —Shelley Ann Black

Am I Rich Or Am I Poor?

Tell me, am I rich or am I poor? Please don't shut the door.
I really need to know. I'm not wise like you; I know you will tell me.
I won't have to struggle so.

Tell me, am I rich or am I poor? Yes, I can come in. But let me wipe my feet.
I've been walking the muddy streets. Please share your thoughts with me.
The world is not filled with much glee.

Tell me, am I rich or am I poor? Thank you, I will sit a spell.
I'm tired and a little forlorn. It's nice of you to comfort me.
Kindness is so healing.

Tell me, am I rich or am I poor? You have a lovely home.
It keeps you nice and warm. Oh, thank you for your time.
I know now that I am rich when you say you are a friend of mine.

  — Ruth M. Revecky

The Lord's Hall of Fame

Is your name in the Lord's hall of fame?
I see Ishaiah, Moses, David and Abraham
There is Ruth, Daniel, Ezekial and Jeremiah
Is your name in the Lord's hall of fame?
Peter's name is there, Andrew, James and Sarah too.
I can't name them all, but I will not leave out Mary, John and Paul.
Is your name in the Lord's hall of fame?
As long as the world exists, names will be added to the list;
In the Lord's hall of fame.

  — Thelma G. Monk

Yesterday—I Crossed the Path of Yesterday

I crossed the path of yesterday,
And found a space in time
My mother bid me warm myself,
Beside the fireside kind.
While I gathered there, I listened to;
A voice so warm and true.
Her eyes so full of love and care,
I was glad I ventured through.
I walked further down the path,
Past the *ole* school house I dearly love,
I perched upon a desk of mine;
That warmed my spirits up.
In a distance I could hear
My teacher's voices ringing,
We're so glad you visited us,
Their echo's seem to be singing.
I turned away and left this time,
This peace, this solitude;
And wondered back amid my thoughts,
To a world so harsh and crude.

  — Ruth M. Greening

Heartbroken

Heartbroken is to feel an emptyness inside that will never leave.
Heartbroken is to lose someone who was very near and very dear.
Heartbroken is to love someone who is never there to love you back.
Heartbroken is to feel what can never be there.
Heartbroken is to hope it will soon be back.
Heartbroken is to see black because it can never come back.
Heartbroken is to never feel again what you felt before.
Heartbroken is to never love someone and hold them near.
Heartbroken hurts, but soon will be fine; it just takes time.

  — Shannon Brooks

Forever

I doubt I will ever understand why things turned out this way.
One thing is for sure, in my heart you will forever stay.
We have been through so much; we have shared the pain and tears.
We have so many memories I will remember through the years.

We tried and tried, but we could not work things out together.
Just remember the good times, let them stay with you forever.
It gets extremely hard at times...believe me, I know.
I can still remember all the feelings we used to show.

We are now over; we thought we would forever last.
I thought we could make it, no matter what happened in the past.
We had each other; I thought that was what mattered.
Since you left me all alone, my heart has been shattered.

I hate that something so wonderful had to turn out so wrong.
My feelings for you will live forever; they will never be gone.
We will never be enemies; you can always think of me as a friend.
I loved you before, I still do now, and I will until the end...

  —Sherry Lynn Gray

Two Hearts

I know our love was meant to be
If you'd just open up and let yourself see.
My heart is filled with warmth and care.
Won't you please just let me share?
We've known each other for such a long time.
Can't we put our friendship aside and give it a try?
Is it asking too much? Please tell me now,
For I can't stop my feelings; they're too strong to hold down.
I have fallen in love, so deep, so true—
Now it's up to you to decide, can you make it come true?

— *Amy Kinsey*

Love

I think it's only love
Forming in a design,
But I cannot unfold my feelings
With these clumsy thoughts of mine.
The secret to unfolding love
Is not known to such as I;
Everything you say to me,
In my thoughts just fade and die.
If I cannot trust my feelings that form in this design,
Then how can I dream of having you
to hold and believe you're mine.
So I'll learn to trust my feelings each moment everyday,
And trust my heart for guidance every step of the way.
For the path that lays before me
My heart and soul knows:
I'll trust them to help me out
With this man I chose.

—*Amy Lynn Heep*

My Mind Wonders Toward You

Time...
    so little of it, I wish our moments together would last forever.
Caring...
    we've taught each other how to care a little more.
    Over the years we have seen many changes,
    but have always been there for one another.
Sadness...
    we were once together but got separated.
    We shared our laughter and tears.
Happiness...
    we found each other again.
    You showed me there's always a bright side,
    you made me smile!
Together...
    again.

—*Berta Oehley*

To Touch

What is forbidden is often very sweet.
We ask why and receive no answer.
I ache to hold you, to say the things that comfort
a lonely night.
Love is a complicated thing.
Filled with rage and pain, sweetness, joy and happiness, the same.
Do you feel what I feel?
Do you want what I want?
Open yourself to me and I will come to you.
Receive me now until reality forces truth upon us.
Love is not meant to be tangible.
It is to be just out of reach, away from our hearts.
It is this way for us, touching and yet apart.
We will forever exist apart and wondering where
A real love lies.

— *Carol Coma*

Untitled

One complete moment
Is released
In a single breath.
Gone forever,
Disappearing
In the great domain of time.
Continuous moments
Escaping—
In the single *tic* of a clock.

— *Amy Rubin*

Love

Love is like a song
Full of heart and soul.
Love is like a beat;
Like a waltz or rock and roll.
Love is like an instrument
To create the beat and the song.
Love is like a feeling;
The tune to carry it along.
Love is like music
All everything as one.
Love is like a human
And music lets love run.

— *Wendy Landmark*

Today

Thoughts of you
...Residue
Of last night's love.
Wistful sighs
...Lullabies
Of last night's love.
Fragmented scenes
...Daytime dreams
Of last night's love.

— *Barbara Sandoval*

Nothing

When I look in your eyes
I see nothing.
When I talk to you
You say nothing.
When I touch you
You feel nothing.
When we are together
We do nothing.
I love you, for what?
For nothing.
This must mean to you
I am nothing.

—*Brigette Beckman*

That Sparkle in Your Eye

The look in your eyes
That sparkle of life
To me it means you care
To you I have no clue.
Without you here, my life
Would fall to pieces
Yet I need to know,
That sparkle in your eye
Is it always there?

— *Nicole Barnes*

Love?

Love, what is it?
To me it is a bunch of pain
and suffering, feeling like you
always have lived in Hell.
Why is the question?
It is because our loved ones
put us there and make us
feel like that.

Love, what is it?
To some people it's happiness
and joy; it's feeling that
you're always loved.
Why is the question?
It is because they will
always love and respect you.

Love, what is it
and what does it mean.

—*Nicole Stucky*

Eyes

Eyes that burn
Within the night
Never leave the Devil's sight.
So close
Your baby's eyes tonight
Until you see
The morning light...

— *Nora Hart*

Enchanted by the Night

Standing alone,
On a moonlit night,
The world seems a far away place.
The night falls softly all around,
As the moon peers curiously at me.
The stars that twinkle in the sky,
Enchant the moon with their light.
Standing alone,
On a moonlit night,
I capture this moment in time,
As I become enchanted by the night.

—*Nicole Bolinger*

Who Am I and Where Do I Belong

Who am i and where do i belong?
Not here or there,
Just suspended in air.
Seeking forever to find a home,
To call my very own.
No one seems to see,
The sadness built in me.
i reach out and no one is there,
Darkness engulfs me everywhere.
i will not shed a tear,
i will instill no fear.
i will build me a home,
To call my very own.
Who am I and where do I belong?

—*Onyx L. Johnson*

The Time to Love Would Have to Wait

The two of them, together there so long,
A friendship where they shared their laughs and dreams.
Like stubborn roots, an amity so strong.
The smiles, the hugs, just bursting at the seams.
His fervor grew with every passing day.
All bottled up inside, she never knew.
Emotions that he could not stow away.
At once, the words errupted, *I love you*
Her terror stared a hold right through his heart.
She ran away, and left him there alone.
Over, before it had a chance to start;
Those feelings he would have to keep his own.
    He buried what he felt, resigned to fate.
    The time to love, be loved, would have to wait.

—*G. Gorecki*

A ring of endless light

A ring of endless light
A never ending fight for truth, justice and a trivial way.
Never pledge yourself to anything that is questionable.

Cosmic rays splatter the page.
Question: Why are we are?
Answer: The answer is not known.

Heavy into something light.
Making millions overnight.
Always weighed down during flight.
Close your eyes: try to think about the brink of destruction.
Close your eyes, for one can never prove that we still
Exist in a space, place,
And time
If their eyes are closed and it is dark.
Open your eyes and you are back from the black.

—*Lauren Ivy*

Fantasy Love

Often, I dream of far away places.
Places of peace, love and happiness.
In these dreams, the sun always shines, and the stars are forever gleaming.
My ship is constantly heading for the horizon.
In the distance is the island upon which my kingdom is built.
But I can never reach the shore.
All of this to make me happy, yet it makes me sad.
Ecstacy is just beyond my grasp.
Why does pain have to accompany pleasure?
What am I missing?

I need a dreamer by my side.
Someone who can enter my dreams and travel with me.
Someone who can see beyond the obstacles in this simple life, and enter my world.
To go to kingdoms of castles and wizards and ride the magical unicorn.
I need someone like you.
Come with me and the two of us will be one.
I love you...

—*John W. Krzywicki*

The Threshold of a Dream

I am standing on the threshold of a dream.
I am believing things I've been taught not to believe.
I am guided by faith and peddling fast upstream
Into that rare flow of life only love can achieve.

From the threshold I feel the past taunting me.
Dark insinuative fears that plot to haunt, to deceive.
I fight for love, for life, without any guarantee.
On the threshold of a dream I stand exposed, naive.

—*Mary Ann Taylor*

A Souvenir

Aquamarine like umbilical fluid connecting worlds
is the color I use to paint for you
with vulnerable feelers of an insect
heavy in steaming rain and
tones of voice empathetically mixing with one another.
We are blind—how God would agree.
All I have to give is a piece of myself...a souvenir.

I am a tiny stone on a beach...no, maybe
on the side of a road or a shell on the seashore
a storehouse of emotion and images
waiting to tell a passer-by he is never alone.

And what you can see...different worlds perhaps?
Do you feel creation inside
bringing life to a shell...or a stone?
Do not be afraid—God will translate.
Your heart will decide how open the door
to an endearing beauty that feels like
and probably is a journey through the inner world.

—*Boyd J. Tait*

Gentle Breeze

Gentle breeze blowing so cool and free.
I can see your impressions on the trees.
Gentle breeze blowing so cool all around
I can see your impressions on the ground.

Gentle breeze I can see your impressions on the grass.
As if they are saying, I am glad, do not pass.
Gentle breeze blowing all about
I can hear the sound of the trees as they shout.

I can see the waving braches on the trees.
Saying I am glad to accept you so come in please.
I can hear the birds singing their songs in the trees.
It sounds like they are saying continue my gentle breeze.

You plan to come on a hot summer day.
Gentle breeze I could feel you miles away.
Every earthly thing enjoy when you are around.
And wish they could see you and not only hear your sound.

—*Herman Gordon*

Ponderations

Have I the time to sit and think and wonder at the world,
At its myriad things, and this, and that, and mysteries unfurled?
How would I see indeed the way to greater clarification
Of the arcane, delphic, caballistic and the present generation?

Should I try to solve them all, with explanations, too,
And give my findings, within bindings, just to you and you?
Dare I draw decipherments of a Universal nature?
What then if I were to be deemed a venerable preacher?

And who's to say if what I've solved has not another twist,
Another angle, another view, or something else I have missed?
How would I know at all just how my views are to be fated,
And what if they are not at all by anyone accepted?

And surely if I delved in depth into the dark and mystic,
Too much of what I'd bring up would be torn down by some critic
Ah...
I think I shall just sit and think
And wonder at the world.

—*Dinesh Senan*

Velocettes

Velocette, Thruxton, Venom, Viper,
vapors vexing, leaving hyper,
all they saw, the black-gold striper,
in a blinding wake.

Inhale the trail of choking gunsmoke,
taste the toxin so sublime,
challenge Thruxton, Venom, Viper,
dare to tread the fishtail line.

Thus the reeling, lightning biting,
curare feel, with numbing grasp,
a weakened twist-grip throttle-action,
as Velos thunder, blasting past.

Leather-clad, hell-bending riders,
leave behind their heaven scent,
Castrol-R in day-blaze hazing,
on the mountainous descent.

— *Paul Arblaster*

Eggactly Right

Most farmers don't care about grammar,
Instead, they're *centsible* men;
If a chicken is sitting, or nesting,
They call her a setting hen.
But what the farmers do care about,
Is what that old hen may be saying:
What her boss wants to know when she cackles,
Is whether she's lying or laying!

— *Agnes White Thomas*

August Child

A summer's child with sun-kissed limbs,
A nymph of nature, lithe in grace...
The sea breeze tosses cornsilk hair
As turquoise eyes light golden face.

She gathers berries, juicy-red,
And talks to creatures in the wild.
She rides a dolphin through the waves
And sings to birds, this August child.

Her playmate is the spotted fawn;
She dances in the woodland glade
With fairy folk, on starlit nights,
Or shares a feast the elves have made.

One born to summer's scented air,
She dances by the August moon...
She dazzles like the butterfly...
For both, September comes too soon.

— *Alex Stewart*

Epitaph

Cry not today for me, my friend,
You need not shed a tear,
For soon you too shall meet your end
And you shall join me here.

Live not a life of solitaire
Live not one of regret
But live, my friend, and love, and share,
That may be all you get.

Fear not the cold eternity,
That lies below the earth,
The blinking of an eye shall see
How much your life was worth.

Die not your death alone, my friend
Live not your life in pain,
Let not my death your living end
We soon shall meet again.

— *Mary Elizabeth Anderson*

Window of Life

I look out my window
just a glare, reflection
Reminds me of a childhood
one I never had
hurt, pain
I feel only this

I look at her
a hurting child
alone, alone she cries
Is this the only world;
that's all she said

— *Suzanne Perga*

It's You

Along the deserted stretch of beach,
Washed upon the ridges of the distant shore,
In the air, in the mist, in the night.
We breathe, we see, we feel the
Greatness in others we seem to value;
It pulls us out of our deceiving shell,
The kind that sometimes compels us to
Retreat or resist. To resist only if
It is our own strength deciding to do so.
It is you in the world, not others.
You are the ridges, the beach, the sand.
You create the pictures, believing
They are the best. A message that is a token
By you or by the encouragement of others.
Stand up straight on the feet you
Were given, establish your own design
By the tiny pebbles in the sand
On the deserted stretch of beach.

—*Stacy Albinder*

Bored

Never kill time when you think
You have nothing to do;
Cause as you're killing time,
Time is killing you.

— *Jenna Dran*

Moonbeam's Shadow

Shiny onyx pool,
Ebony mirror,
Reflecting sequinned stars.

Languid midnight disk,
Glossy oval,
Moonbeam's shadow.

Jeweled highlights dancing
Over polished slate,
Treasury of the night.

— *Bernadette Court*

Untitled

An empty glass
Upon the sand
Being carried out
To a blue crystal sea
Never to be full again
Never to be seen again
Floating aimlessly across the waves
Floating aimlessly in the waves
Never to be full again
Of water
Of dreams
Of hopes
Floating aimlessly to a distant shore
Floating aimlessly to a distant beginning

—*M. Arrington Williams*

Desert Thunder

The abandoned road was still;
Silence broken only by
The sounds of a cricket's call
And the mark of distant thunder.

A man stood alone in the darkness.
Accompanied by the reflections of his mind,
He turned skyward.
The flickering stars brought back
The poignant memories of days gone by
As a tear streamed down his face.

— *Karen Fisher-Biggs*

A Lost Love

In my eyes you were number one.
I loved you more than I have ever loved anyon
My friends couldn't see
How special you were to me.
Your smile was so bright I could hardly see.
You were always quick with a kiss
And to tell me how much you missed me.
God, I loved you so much.
I longed every moment for your touch.
Then it ended and now we're apart.
But just remember, you'll always be in my hear

— *Amanda Kate Zimmerman*

Ruins of a Castle

Reclaiming in a slow and fragrant way,
Unmoved in gallant goals to grasp at more,
Increasing bluebells, trees, and vines trap gray,
Neglected castle walls which warm winds wore
Surrendering its stones to seiging soil,
Outflanked by pillars of progressive pine,
Felled in its fight with time, this form once roya
Assents to nature's humble new design...
Cessation for a cemetry style,
A placid place where poets can repose,
Stars shine like steel above stalagtites, while
The Dornach castle ruins decompose...
Lords, damsels, errant knights? Their time is do
Eye's lizards scurry in the setting sun...

— *Stephen Volk*

Sunrise

The sunrise awakes the world
with Mother Nture's art.
It s brilliant colors are unfurled
to give the day its start.

Yet starts a day that's bleak and gray,
no happiness imparts.
Though every day you'll always stay
the sunrise in my heart.

— *Walter H. Baker*

The Light of Day

In the light of day, so all alone
I cry for help, but no one comes
You look so happy, but so, so sad
In a world that is falling apart
What is a person supposed to do
How much can a person really believe
You love him so much, but I guess it's not enou
You have friends everywhere but still not enoug
You think about heaven
How happy it would be
They say death is forever, believe me it's true
But in a world that is falling apart
What does it really matter
How much can a person really believe

—*Mary Beth Weisenberger*

An Heirloom Quilt

The dragonfly needle dips and rises
Over a green quilted meadow
A place I've sewn in my dreams,
Made from cloth and desire;
Threaded out of the mists of imagination,
Insected and flowered with my life;
Days of dark calico and white cotton,
Quilted.
I stitch your name in one corner,
My signature simply *Mama*
With this, you can cover yourself in warmth
On cold nights,
Cover a table on which to spread a feast,
Remember the meadow where we sketched such dreams
As mothers and daughters share
Go from this beginners primitive efforts
On, to your bright designs.

   —*Jadene Felina Stevens*

Wall Street Waltz

Oh, I am just an empty hollow, a hollow lung drawing in
Tis defunct, passive world of the train.
It says nothing tome at this hour; it excites me little at this stage.
Each stop resembles the next, haggard people in a haggardline
Awaiting the sleep of their seat, and I look through
a cloudy, murky window
At passing poles and skimming trees toward the steaming mist ascending
From undistinguished towns. I look away with tired, deepset eyes
Not understanding the meaning of all this metropolis
As slowly we roll forth to the station. And I, not grasping the handle
Of all this furious panic released from pen doors
Trampled out on the steps, clamored out on the streets.
Some monolithic mode, a strange courting of industry
That elicits patches of gray on the finest, fairest heads.
Oh, I want so much to be a writer
But I find myself here on Wall Street
Where they waltz me to different things...

   — *Patricia Mahon*

Vermont Echo, Vermont Sundown

Northern, torrid cold waves blissfully
   Astray in arctic zone, vehemently
Inclined towards our greeny
   Southern camps...
Meanwhile the massive, majestic grnaite
Turns the earth around its axis in a
   Long long way...

Echo of faith in Vermont sundown as this
Is a special place of beauty that the
Heart cherishes—the sun reflecting
On the azure waters of nearby chaplin lake.
Seeing white willows leaves and the
Gentle evening breeze of the flowers land
Wayward the lovely green praries.
It takes both sun and rain to make a rainbow in
The sky. Re-echoing down the silent
Corridors of time. Rotating toward
A bluer horizon of the incandescent
North star like the eternal rescue
Chance of an ethereal deity, weeping
Perennial tears for a beautiful, sublime
Morning splendor and majestic star-light
Night. We admire the rainbow light after
The storm at the evening Vermont sun
   Down!
   From the silvery stars, lux
Lucet in tenebris. Ave lux spes
Nostra, hodie, quotidie et semper.

   —*Allan J. De Fiori*

Boob Tube Coop

Two potato couchers relaxing on their buns,
Finding pleasure mainly in the Kramden's old reruns;
One said to the other, *These new seasons, wifey dear,*
Can't match the older sitcoms, even those films not quite so clear.
Wiser tho was Thelma, his loyal and loving wife;
She said TV's demeaning, that there must be more to life;
Let us dine out some evenings, maybe join a social group.
Great idea, my darling. Let us fly our boob tube coop.
So they huddled there together naming goals and heightening zest:
Oh, oh, we will talk of this tomorrow, we're missing Falcon Crest!

   —*Roy E. Walters*

When I Think of You

I think of many things when I have nothing to do
But my favorite thing to think of will always be you.
When I think of you, your pretty face is in my mind.
It's better than any picture you'll ever find.

   — *Meredith Squires*

God-Send

In the darkest corner of the deepest heart
Is a tear of love and passion's kindled spark.
Oh, won't you let me comfort you and ease away your pain,
Let me clear away your hurt like sunshine does the rain.
If only for one moment you'll let your love be mine,
I would open up my heart and let my secrets shine.
Everything I am inside and everything I'll be
Are yours forever, as I am the lock and you are the key.
If she is your one true happiness, then why do your teardrops fall?
I'll be there to love you back when there's no one else to call.
I saw your heart and how you loved her so,
I will never ask for you to ever let her go.
But as I wish this night to share,
I know to love it would not be fair.
To break the rules is bad enough, to obey them would be blind,
For not to have a true love is but a playtoy of the mind.
Passion's not a love-felt heat to be vanished in the wind
But an answer to a life-long dream that only God can send.

   —*Kristina Walker*

Growing Up

Growing up is really a challenge that is unpredictable, terrifying, unsecurable,
   but can also be excitingly fun.
To have the strength to take each individual experience as a growing pain;
   whether it be good or bad, whether it feels good or it hurts, it's a pain. Feel it
   out, understand it, then define its learning experience and store it.
Do not allow your heart to trap your mind into believing that the pain of a bad
   experience lasts forever because pain only lasts as long as you allow it.
I think the hardest part of growing up is learning to store each individual
   experience because you can always reach back to yesterday for help today.

   — *Maurina Bennett*

The Desire

I'd sit and stare out into the ocean sky.
The sand's warm between my toes.
The wind's whipping my hair to the side—
The tree's a victim of the harshness, too.
The sunset shone a brilliant display of vivid colors on the ocean.
The waves were bringing the colors to the shore.
I had a desire to be part of the ocean.
The desire in me grew higher and wider, it burned in my soul.
I stood and unbuttoned my shirt.
The wind whipped it from my hand and I watched it tear to the ground.
I walked briskly toward the water.
A chill ran up my spine as the water touched me.
Then it dawned on me.
I was part of the vivid colors and ocean, too.

   — *Amy Bowman*

Spiritual Experience

No one ever made love to me
the way he did.
It was a spiritual
experience,
a meeting of the souls.
— *Mary Sue Emison*

A Letter Goodbye

You gave so much,
I gave so little,
And if I could make
You see another part
Of me I would.

You gave me your
Understanding, your
Concern, and your love.
All I gave was
A letter goodbye.
— *Sandra Chessmore*

Life

Life
Is like a train
Always rushing off to the next stop
Regardless of its passengers
Troubles
Pulling the mounting stress
Never at a loss of energy
If just once
Life decided to slow down
And give me enough time
To climb aboard
I would be very
Grateful
— *Josette S. Ferrazza*

Perfectly Human

Alluring spirit
Converging upon me:
Integrate my being,
Substantiate my existence.
Permeate my feelings,
Extrapolate their meaning;
Acknowledge my complexity,
Validate their reality.
Assimilate both spirit and feelings,
Endeavor to become wholistic;
Striving for perfection,
Accepting humanity.
—*Therese' A. Ream*

Be Myself

Loneliness is the poison
Coursing throught my veins.
It burns like hot acid.
I can't stop it, I won't stop it.
I want the pain, the suffering.
To remind me of my ignorance,
To remind me of my lost loves.
To remind me of my scars,
As I sit, by myself.
— *Matt Tyner*

A Mother's Love

A mother's love is faithful,
A mother's loveis true;
A mother's love is always there
Especially when you're blue.

A mom can be your best friend,
She can be your enemy;
She can be your shackles and your chain
When you're yearning to be free.

A mother's love goes on forever
Just like a winding brook;
The memories she keeps locked inside
Are like a storybook.

You know a mother can be
What you'd like her most to be,
But most of all, this mom is glad
'Cause God chose you for me.
— *Mardi D. Nason*

Him and I

He makes me laugh, he makes me cry.
He loves me but he doesn't know why.
He knows my touch, he knows my voice.
He wants to own me, I'm his by choice.

I live here, he lives there.
He's dreamed me before but he doesn't know where.
He's kissed my lips, I've been in his arms
I know his words, I know his charms.

He knows my style, he knows how I feel.
He tries to deny that our love is real.
Everytime I see him, I feel my face shine.
No matter what he says, I know that he's mine.
—*Misty Lee Flynn*

Dreams

When I am lying in bed thinking of you,
Tears appear in my eyes,
I awake with excitement in the middle of the night,
With the thought of you lying by my side,

When you are not there I realize
My mind was playing dirty tricks,
That I considered true, but they were only lies
That will never come true.

Then to know you will never be mine
Makes a part of me fade away
And has me feeling terribly blue.
—*Marci Maple*

War is Our life, Peace is Our Death

The peaceful heartbeat of the soul is like
The quiet ticking of a timebomb.
No one knows when,
No on knows where.
War and peace,
Life and death.
War is the biggest, most realistic threat.
Peace is a promise,
That no one fulfills.
Is war our life,
And peace our death?
In a small townhouse,
In New York city,
We blow ourselves up, we just sit here,
And wait for the day the bombs start to cry,
And we hear the screams of our children as they die.
—*Justine Melby*

On Silent Winds

The voices float on silent winds
Across the stones now bleached
and worn
In fields so brown and tangled deep
He listened to the mournful cries
So whisper light that plunged
Then soared to a towering height
Then at once there came the scream
In anguish and in pain so fierce
He knew he heard the pleas before
Which sought repose and final peace
For those who fell beneath the sword
And cannon's roar
The pain and agony linger on
The pleas unanswered all in vain
Turned misty soft to float again
On silent winds across the stones
Now bleached and worn
—*Maxwell C. Kaufman*

Deep Inside

calmness that hasn't been felt before
feels like life has opened new doors

we have hope to let us fight
to do what we feel, what must be right
to be able to hold our heads up high
to look at the world and let wings fly

we feel the sunshine, the radiant sky
hear the birds singing lullabies
see flowers blooming without care
hear the wind whistling in the air

we have the power in our hands
to help one another and understand
that we must follow what we believe
to look in our hearts and speak what we see

all these feelings we will confide
never again will we hide
new found strength deep inside
—*Mayra C. Diaz*

Kinds of Tears

When a baby cries
in the arms of its mother
every responsible soul is certainly worried;
nobody can tell if it's anger
nobody can tell if it's hunger;
for certain both are a sickness.

When a mother sheds a tear
while having a baby in her arms
who cries for no reason
the guess is lack of milk;
or its life is in danger;
the thought of both is a worry.

When an old man pours a shower of tears
it's an expression of joy or sadness
to remind him of the bitterness of yesterday;
or the mirthful moments shortlived,
or his wise tear fears the unborn tomorrow.
—*Mba Sung-Bamaala S. B. Donyuo*

Too High a Stake

One more night to spend with you,
One more night alone,
And then we'll go our separate ways
Two different paths to roam.

One more night to spend with you,
And maybe things will change.
We'll look into each other's eyes
Two hearts we'll then exchange.

One more night to spend with you,
And we'll both reach out to take
What always did belong to us-
But the price too high a stake.

One more night to spend with you,
And my future I could bear-
Because evryday would be a dream
As long as you are there.
— *Carie Vanderlinden*

S E L F
E
S
S

I read self-help books,
Pump my own gas, and
The automatic teller
Always knows my name.

Once there were people to talk to.
Some were friendly, courteous and caring.
I guess they're still around,
But they all cost something now.

Yes, life is getting easier,
But times they sure are lonely.
And it's hard to think of others,
When the world is on Self-Serve.

—*Terry Earp*

The Gateway

In all of us
There is a gate
Guarded by the knowledge and logic
That is our way
But at night
The logic and knowledge sleep
Releasing the realm
Of our superstitions
That subdue
The knowledge and logic
Of our way
And it lets us run free
Without logic and knowledge
But in the creative ones of us
The gate can be opened
Whenever wherever
The creative are always
Free.
—*Aaron Oliver Greenlun*

Black Sky

Black sky, star's blanket
Crystal on green morning dew
The edge of the dawn
—*Anne Fitzgerald*

A Remembrance

Like two ships in the night
We met
Became acquainted
As friends,
Explored backgrounds,
Expressed feelings—verbally,
Discovering similarities
In our geographical origins...
Yet, though sharing mentally,
Expressing verbally,
Never crossed the barrier
To intimacy.
Each had family.
Time passed: We bade farewell.
One went—the other stayed.
Like two ships in the night,
We crossed each other's path
In our respective lives.
—*Betty D. Mercer*

Departure by Morning

If only last night
This feeling would have come
Over me,
A way would have been found
To never leave her.

She lay there
In black, but not in darkness
Her eyes translatting
My every movement
Into a language all our own

We know
That before the dew is gone
And the sun is warm
I will be halfway home
Alone, but not in spirit
—*Paul Vincent Scholl*

The Wait

Rage of self hate,
aching hands,
nervous knot
in my stomach.
R.E.M. on my feet,
my body lies,
my mind swims downstream
as I wait
for the blood
to spill.
— *C. A. Friedland*

We Loved

Togetherness is love.
You need this love
That which when taken,
We often abuse.
With it is trust.
A trust between two people,
When combined it forms a
Bond.
You have two.
Two that worked together.
Together to form a bond.
A bond of love and trust.
—*Heather Casson*

Boatman

My reed is a hollow flute,—
   Into it, the air swirls
      and pauses to clear,
         true sound.
The river, a silent gloom
     of reeds and dense
         sounds of mystery—
   Unfolds itself
     of deep resinous velvet.
My reed is a hollow flute
   Of sounds true to ear
      as any trill of bird
Resounding with light echo
     past the dark
        and lithesome trees.
  Alone we pass our oar,
  Resume, in quiet reverie.
—*Kathleen Day*

I Shall not Weep

I shall not weep, I tell myself
I have no time for tears.
I'll sing. I'll dance. I'll work. I'll play
I'll hurry through the years.

I'll not remember golden hours,
Or why you were most dear,
Or how I only felt complete,
Whenever you were near.

I'll not remember yesterdays,
The comfort of your arm
Your handsome face, your gentleness,
Your multitude of charm.

I shall not weep, I tell myself.
Now that we are apart,
I'll laugh, I'll sing, I'll work, I'll play
But, I'll weep, cries my Heart.
—*Nan E. Grill*

Too Good to Be True

The first time I saw you, you took my heart,
From that moment on, I knew we could never be apart.
We have had some bad and good times together,
We have had moments to remember.
It seems like we have been together forever.

When I saw you holding her hand, my heart broke.
You tried to explain, as I ran across the sand.
I should have known it was too good to be true.
I really loved you but you made me feel blue.

Now, I want you to remember me,
The moments we shared.
When we were together, how my heart filled with glee,
But now it is all over for you and me.

—*Traci Carr*

Love's Shadow

They lie helpless within love's shadow,
Sleeping soundly, within the womb,
But we feel a need to destroy them,
Never allowing them to bloom.
They rest quietly within love's shadow,
Wanting so to touch our face,
But we remove the seed which holds them,
Leaving behind but an empty space.
They lie patiently with love's shadow,
Waiting to place tiny hands in ours,
But we say they are not yet living,
Cutting them before they are flowers.
Love will continue to plant them,
Never permitting them to grow,
And they will wait, quietly and helpless,
Forever, within love's shadow.

—*Mary E. Kadash*

Choosing the Direction of My Life

Here I sit today
Wondering when I will ever get away
What life has in store for me
Will it be the same or will I be more free.
I have hit the path with the fork in the road
I hope I take the one with the smallest load
One might lead to the same old stuff
And that is just not good enough
I must choose the one where happiness will appear
And I hope all the things in my head will be clear
I want the day to be sunny and bright
Then I will feel my life is dynamite
I know there might be times when the rains will come
But after being here I won't be quite as dumb,
I am learning now to take it slow
I hope I will not be fast to blow
My dirty looks must go out the door
Or I will spend my life upon the floor.

—*Jessica Smith*

Now

Have you considered the little word *now*?
It is a powerful word!
Yesterday and its trials are gone—
They are over—
Tomorrow may never come.
The only time we really have is Now.

Visit your mother—now!
Go to see a sick friend—now!
Send that letter—now!
Visit the hospital—now!
Go to the nursing homes for a visit—now!

— *Lillian Wells Payne*

My Love

You say you love me-will you love me still,
When we grow and fragile as the cobweb there?
Or, do you love me as the wind that blows a while,
And, then, it leaves again, and blows again elsewhere?
Or, are you like the rock that stands there strong,
And never leaves, through sunlight or through storm?
I think you're like the rock, for still you're here,
And we have seen both sun and cloud appear.

—*Marjory A. Treumuth*

My Wealth

The cattle on a thousand hills are His,
The silver, gold and diamond mines
Belong to God, and I am rich beyond compare,
Since I'm His child and heir.

Majestic mountains so rugged and tall,
The rivers that flow, the high waterfall,
All are His and I am rich,
For I'm His child and heir.

The fish that swim and the birds that fly,
The fluffy clouds in the azure sky,
All are His and I am rich,
For I'm His child and heir.

The towering pines and the verdant hills,
The oceans vast and the brooks and rills,
All are His and I'm so rich,
For I'm His child and heir.

He purchased my pardon on Calvary's tree,
By His own death, He did set me free,
Forever I'll sing praises to Jesus who came
To make me His child and heir!

—*Mildred E. Olson*

The Turnoff

I'm lost on this big, wide way.
I'm lost and looking for the turnoff,
To the straight and narrow way.
It's very hard to find, I hear,
But if you put your trust in God,
The path is straight and clear.
You must love all your neighbors,
Obey God's commands;
Help everyone, throughout the whole land.
Be honest and true, don't steal and don't swear;
Be straight-forward and righteous beyond all compare;
Love God before others, honor his name,
And guide others to the turnoff,
So they can do the same.
Do all these things brother, and be of good cheer,
The sign to the turnoff will become very clear.

—*June E. Sams*

Untitled

They attack, they hurt, and they ferociously kill.
If man cannot stop them, nobody will.
They have no mercy, feel no pain.
They leave their victims unjustly slain.

Once they have got you, you will not cope.
These killers offer no chance of hope.
They eat you from the inside out.
They will silence you and your joyful shout.

They rip, they tear, they burn, they sting.
They are stronger than most anything.
These awful slayers grab your mind.
Twist it, scrunch it and make it blind.

You know these villians and murderers too.
They are drugs my friend, and they are after you.

—*Lorie Thomas*

Try, Try, Try

Keep your dreams close to your heart
Don't let anyone tear you and your dream apart
Because that might be as far as you succeed in doing it
So when you finally decide to give up and quit
You can say to yourself
You've done just as good as anyone else
At least you did give it a good try
Instead of just letting them die.
—*Sandra Isley*

Struggling

Where do you go when there's no one to talk to?
What do you say when you can't seem to talk?
What do you do when there's no one there for you?
Where do you go when there's no where to walk?

How can you love when there's no love around you?
How can you care when there's no one to care for?
How can you try whdn no one knows what you're going through?
How can you live when you can't take no more?

I'm trying to hold on but my grips slowly slipping,
I'm trying to live yet my heart says to die.
I'm trying to be happy but my eyes won't stop dripping,
I want to hold on but I can't stop asking why.

I want to be free but the freedom grows lonely,
Then I need someone to hold onto me.
I want to be me, and not just a phoney,
Yet phoney slips out and thats all that they see.

I want to be brave but I'm scared of love,
I'm scared of me, I'm scared above,
Reality and all my dreams, I'm scared of living.
—*Rhonda K. Hericks*

Should I?

When I'm at a party where everyone's drinking, I think that I'm aware,
But as I watch a drunk friend leave, I'm hit with quite a scare.
My classmates are laughing and chugging some beers thinking they look really cool
As I'm standing there sober just looking around feeling somewhat like a fool.

Should I run and stop him grab his keys and show him I'm in control?
Or watch him stumble out to his car and say to his friends, *Let's roll*?
Innocent people are on the roads, I can't let him leave in this shape.
He had arrived at the party with problems to bear, looking for some kind of escape.

The college didn't accept him, his grades were slipping and his family was falling apart.
Just watching him drink in fear he woud drive was truly breaking my heart.
It won't last much longer, we'll probably break up, he loves the drug more than me.
I've tried to help him a thousand times, but I just can't make him see.

Should I ignore that he's drunk, totally gone, and his buddies say I'm a bore?
Or stop him from driving into the night before he slams that door?
I'm going to run after him and risk being told I act just like his mother
Because I don't want to lose the guy I love the same way I lost my brother.
— *Teresa Carpenter*

Another Child

Another child—innocent—filled with curiosity, excitement
in everything new, different—*What's that?* I'd ask so trusting-
awe of bugs and leaves—wonder of simple things—love that flowed
as natural as grass grows.
Time passes learning of things shocking the senses, war—killing-
monsters and things—accidents—illnesses—poverty and greed-
bigotry, ignorance, criminals, thieves—feelings of pain—emptiness-
loneliness—cycles of fear—reaching out of agony toward doorknobs to bliss-
stretching, seemingly searching infinitely amiss—oh, how to break
cycles of fear to find happiness.
A vague remembrance of once feelings of trust, love and faith flowing
through veins of innocence—let me go back to once was—of awe in bugs
and leaves and wonder of simple things.
— *Rhonda J. Rose*

Growing Up

Time is slipping away so very fast.
I can't help thinking of our wonderful past.
I cannot thank you for all you've given me
As I think of past memories.
You've always been there when I needed you.
I've always been there when you needed me, too.
You were the sunshine when I was feeling down,
Never making me go to a frown.
Now as we grow older and more clever,
Remember I love you more than ever!
— *Stacie Lenker*

The Stairs of My Life

Each stair represents an experience,
A lesson that I've found.
Below, a few stairs that tripped me,
And some stairs where I fell down.

But each stair that I ascended
Brought me closer to the truth,
The stairs that are above me
Reach heights above the roof.

I know not where they lead me,
But it's to a greater height.
Each step, a new experience
Bringing wisdom to my life.
— *Katie O'Brien*

Darkest

Darkest before the dawn,
These words are on my brain,
I see my reflection in a pond,
But it is not me, it is just pain.

I have always been giving,
And keep on getting burned,
I will be glad to start receiving,
You would think by now I have learned.

A hug means so much to me,
It shows how someone cares,
When I reach for one; my arms are empty,
There hardly ever is anyone there.

Pressure has always been my middle name,
I will be happy when things start to look bright,
That name is one I would like to change,
I guess I am in for one long hard fight.
—*Annette Morin*

Love Looks for a Soft Glance

How can I prove myself to you?
My rights and wrongs have found no aceptable way
To reach you and to touch you.
I want to share your presence forever.
And yet, it seems that you believe
That to know love, is to bring death.
What I offer is genuine; it is totally naked.
Given as freely to you
As the black ice in your eyes
Is given freely to me.
How deeply love looks for a soft glance from you!
To see your eyes fall on me,
Looking gently without malaise.
My darling, there is nothing to fear.
No hidden jokes; no punch line.
Love looks for a soft glance from you,
Lest it snap like a dry twig in a rising wind
And silently blows away.
—*Linda L. Mahoney*

My Realization

God is almighty, all powerful.
There is no other power besides God.
So I have no power
Of myself to help myself.
In reality, it can't done.
I may seem to improve
My immediate condition
But it is a false strength.
Yet I am powerful, and submit
To, God power, to help me.
I come to the realization of
The eternal, invincible in me
Which cannot be defeated.
What is unlike God, lacks real power
So, with God I am all powerful.

— *Jay Hugo Forde*

Lights

When the bright lights
Shine from the golden shpere
In the hollow sky,
His crystal gaze
Turns towards her
And he smiles.

The trees filter light,
The rosy light that makes streams
Glisten.
Plush, velvety moss
Is welcoming
To a fairy floating by.

—*Jean Ciemniecki*

Looking for Me

As I sit here in this place
With no expression on my face,
I find myself looking over my shoulder
Seeing only the past.
I'm looking for my feelings.
They ae nowhere to be found.
I look deep inside my heart.
Looking for...what? I don't know.
It's tearing me apart.
I look back and see the tears,
Only tears of emotion.
I need some definite answers.
Well, reality always comes last.
So now, sorrow will soon fade...
And my feet will soon follow
The dream of reality.

— *Chesley Cipolla*

The Crucial Must But How

The world is a ball of strife we cannot escape
Although conflicts of the riders grow to force
That chugs the ball toward the final bomb.

We build, we test and roll on screeching failed.
Cannot and must debate and blur the answer.

Diaster mocks the vital part a dud
That sings we must all know what is good for us
And what is good for everybody else,
Then think and do what is good for all of us,
Then cracks from being pounded can and cannot.

The ball still moves to can't, to try, to must.

—*Dorothy Randle Clinton*

Reality

why does she speak
with such a sharp tongue
when soft words are needed
soothing
calming
she does not know
of the pain inside
of the hurt inside
so she continues,
with her harsh, harsh words
I retreat
to a world of laughter
of love
of no pain
of no hurt
but that is not reality
she is reality
reality is harsh

—*Monica Nulty*

A Celebration of Life

Laughter falls from sunlight
Through the trees.
Leaves dance happily,
And rustle a secret melody.
A special place of Nature's glory
Hidden from the world.
I come here to breathe
To be free.

A willow holds me
In its arms, above the earth.
A crystal teardrop falls
From tiger eyes.
And here, a rose
With a crystal teardrop
Slipping from its petals
The air is sweet, and filled with birds
Singing a celebration of life.

—*Miriam Ben-Dor*

Candy Pie

Candy pie thoughts of Roberto
full of sugar sweet smiles
and honeyed kisses

Cinnamon sighs for Roberto
when I gaze to the skies
and miss him

Lemon wine tears for Roberto
as happiness spills
from chocolate eyes

Peppermint smiles for Roberto
as candy pie thoughts
dine high

— *Shari Li*

Untitled

Gardens of stone
Desolate fields of grey
Agonized cries:
Unheard

A lonely road of darkness
Scattered with strangers
Never understanding:
Why?

—*Shannon Meng*

Looking Out My Window

Looking out my window
Across the water
I see the bright lights of New York shining
Like scores of diamonds on a piece of black velvet
I feel the warmth of the air
As though being embraced by a hug
I hear the roar of the planes up above
As I try to figure out their destination

Looking out my window
I find myself daydreaming
And thinking about how many other
People are daydreaming just as I

Looking out my window
The sight of the lights
The feel of the warmth
And the sound of the planes
Are what make New York a great place to be

—*Christine E. Colon*

My Love for a Cowboy

I don't know why, but all I can do is stare.
I'll think of your blue eyes, and then wish you were here.
You do something to me, that I can't explain
You make things seem so easy and you never complain.
But we didn't work out
I guess that it wasn't meant to be
You have seen the world inside and out
And you know that you don't want me.
I know that you can do better,
There's no doubt in my mind.
You have got your life together, and you've left
Me behind. We'll just be friends, we've decided
On that, but my love for you will never end
And you can put your money on it.

— *Cathy Draehn*

Daddy

I'm not a little girl anymore, I wish you were here to see
The changes that occurred deep within the heart of me.
I was so young, I didn't understand,
Why you weren't going to be there holding my hand.
Now that I'm older, I still want to cry,
There's still that big question, I've been wondering why?
Vague memories of you, I try to recall,
About the love that we shared through good times and all.
It's hard to try and remember the love we once shared
Because sometimes it's too much for my heart to bear.
I miss you so much, I wish you were here
I guess I need to keep in mind
that you're still my father and you still do care.
Up in the heavens so far away,
Near in my heart, through night and through day.

— *Rita Santucci*

The Little Boy in My Dreams

Oh, you are the little boy in my dreams
Who excavates for treasures beyond the faceted streams.
The farther you dig, the richer you get
And the purer you receive in your soul.
As dusk sets in and you need much more needed light
Search inside my wounds for enlightenment and sight.
The possibilities are endless in our might
As we discover life's ectasies beyond delight.
Continue on as I shall fight to keep our control
And longevity during this sunny time of night.

—*Rodney E. Pitman*

Color me Love

Love blooms at times
The color of happiness
When raindrops fall on lilac flower
Brings fragrance of colors
After every spring shower
Listening to the breeze
Whispering love songs to the trees
Dreams of our love
Dancing rhythm in my mind
Recalls ancient times so clear
Myth of enchanted love affairs
Happiness so true and pure
It seems
Only happen in our dreams
　　　—*Marlon Anthony Byfield*

The Flame

Love starts out as a spark
Which turns into a flame
When that flame begins to die
Who is it to blame?
Not all love is meant to be
How are we to know?
What kind of love we might find
How long it's going to glow
You and me—our love is true
The flame will never die
Our flame is big and very strong
That's the reason why
We will last to the end
When time grows old and dark
Always remember the precious time
When our love started out as a spark.

　　　— *Michelle Baker*

Love...

The provider of self esteem...
The degredation of one's own character.
A possible fantasy in mid flight...
The beginning of a gruesome nightmare.

The mist of a spring rain...
The wind of a summer storm.
An eternal act..
The short lived scene.

The food of abundance...
The forbidden fruit.

A river of feelings...
The dam of emotions.
Love...the perfection of the heart,
The insanity of the mind.
　　　—*Melissa Dehart*

Forbidden Love

I love him so much I just can't explain
We started out so nice then came the pain
The relationship ended but life went on
He flirted and flirted it went on and on
I excepted his flirting for awhile and then
He turned around and kissed my very best
Friend. I could not take it anymore you see
I said that it's over between you and me
We've talked a lot and he asked me again
But I told him I only wanted to be a friend
I said *I still love you* I'm just confused right
Now he said *that's okay I'll still wait around.*

　　　— *Rhonda Glenn*

True Love

Giving you up is not what I want to do,
I just would not be able to walk away
I am going to do my best to keep you
No more looking back on yesterday

Baby inside of me
Growing big and strong
Nobody can see
Why this is not wrong

When you start to kick
You better know
Mommy should not get sick
Or start to show

Little one
No matter what you will ever do
Daughter or son
I will always love you.
　　　—*Tamera Patten*

Love

What is this thing called *Love*?
Is it for me?
Do I look for it or wait for it to find me?
Can it be bought or is it free?

—Love comes many ways
It has many forms
Love is where your heart is
It comes from inside yourself
It costs nothing
The best way to get love is just allow it
to come to you
Being afraid of it or looking for it can
be frustrting

Allowing it to come to you and letting it
in once it's there can be so wonderful

Love...
Do I really want it...
Or am I afraid of it?
　　　—*Cherron Covington*

A Dream

Last night I had a dream,
Of course it was of you
And as I awoke, I could see
I was hoping it was, a dream come true.

I called to tell you I missed you
And loved you so much
But when you answered the phone
I could not say a thing, I just hung up.

I sat and thought about it awhile
And wondered what it was I felt.
Now I have decided no doubt
Dreams are fantasies I can live without.

　　　—*Cecelia L. Garner*

Ode to a Would-be Poet

She sits and stares out vacantly
From the window by the fire,
And tries to think of subjects
Her readers to inspire.
Should she pick the seasons
Or some emotion deep inside,
Or write about some animal
Or someone going blind.
Somehow the words are hard to find
The phrasing's not quite right,
But there's a poet in the making
Trying to find the light.

　　　— *S.E. Johnson*

Pathway to My Heart

A fragile bridge
That leads to my heart,
Shattered to pieces
Given so many times.

You are the cause for such debris,
But the blame is not yours alone.
I was the fool,
Who believed that you cared.

Our foolish remarks
Those light words
That haunt me in my dreams.
On lonely nights your face flashes before my eyes.

No matter what
I still love you.
I will love you
Until I die.
　　　—*Kelly Doan*

My Rainbow's End

No pot of gold, but pure happiness
No one or nothing else could satisfy
My secret and only hiding place
I release deep feelings and sometimes cry
My best friend quiet and always listening
Welcomes me warmly and always aware
Never have I been misled or ignored
It always knows why I am there
It only expects me to be myself
Not to act like someone I am not
Strong friendship and caring we share
Depends on nothing else each other's got
It lets me relax and feel good inside
With just beauty all around and fresh air
It never leaves me, it is always there
My rainbow's end, often I go there.
　　　—*Tabbatha Todd*

Untitled

Come to love,
Wait for peace,
Feel through time-
To a forgotten doorway,
Enshrouded with...
Smiling faces that beckon you.

To sunlit days,
And carefree ways,
Oh join us won't you...

They call.
Come love,
To peace-
Through time and space.
　　　— *Sharon L. Lewis*

Never Dying Love

He was loved by all who knew him,
He touched us all in a strange way,
I know I'll never forget him,
Because I still love him to this day.
My grandpa was a wonderful man,
Kind, loving, and caring;
But God holds him in his arms
With a love that's always enduring.
Someday I hope to be with him,
Because it cuts like a knife
Not share my love and happiness,
And not have him in my life.

　　　— *Kathleen Hofer*

Shadow Dancer

Dusk's silent aura covers the room.
You gallop in. Legos clutched tight.
Fire trucks and race cars await you.
You rush forward, stop as your companion appears.
Greet each other with a laugh and nod.
You prance to the side; he faithfully follows.
Arms swep air and he carefully mimics.

Mommy calls, reluctant feet obey.
Night orders. Dusk hastens to hide.
Nightlight comforts you and dreamland beckons.
I tiptoe in, see your companion on the wall.
He sleeps quietly next to you.
A familiar stranger leans over him.
She kisses your companion as I kiss you.

Where've you been? I ask her softly.
It's been too long since we last danced.

   — *Kathryn Smith*

Missing You

I can't tell you how much I miss you!
There's such a void inside;
A feeling I have never known
And find terribly hard to hide.
How I desperately miss your lips!
Can almost feel them on mine.
Ever so gently caressing my mouth;
They're almost as one with mine.
I miss us being together!
We know how we both feel.
Without a word, somehow we know,
This oneness is very real.
I miss your arms that hold me!
They make me feel so secure.
I feel so safe, when in your arms;
Can't wait to be with you once more!

   — *Judy Browning*

The Light That I've Seen

The light that I've seen is gone.
You were that light, and you disappeared.
You were the one who made me see the world
     full of light and happiness.
And now, now that you've disappeared,
All I see is nothing but darkness and sadness
The light that I've seen is gone; gone forever.
No one can make it light for me again.
You are the only one who can make me see again
     and make me see the light.
The light that I've seen is gone.
Gone forever.

   — *Kat Halasz*

I Never Knew You, Daddy

Merging into the dark and painful
Recesses of a mindless infanthood
Are dead memories of you, Daddy
You look at me with plucked out eyes
Look at me now-your seed
Has yielded bitter fruit
You pass before my eyes
Surrealistically-
Like an unquenchable flame
You have burned inside
A bottled existence
Decades of hate have lined you eyes
And driven you to liquid hell
Leaving your arms unreachable-
Daddy, I never knew you.

   — *D. Edward Styles Jr.*

Intimate Arms

I need to feel the intimacy,
To reach out and touch your soul...
A shared experience for you and me,
Of warmth to keep away the cold.
I need to trust and not be afraid,
To feel truth and know wisdom.
How the sun and moon are made,
And to be in peace when day is done.
Will you stay by my side,
To ride out the worst of storms?
And when the fierce winds have died,
Will you still be entwined in my arms?

   —*Lucille Stratton Bailey*

Summer Has Ended

The air is still, the sun is hot
And the waves tumble in.
But the beach is empty,
The food stands closed,
The sand undisturbed,
The lifeguards vanished
The seagulls deserted
The shells forgotten.
The sound of laughter is gone
Only the hint of salt is in the air.
For, it is time to go back to school.

   —*Courtney Haley*

Untitled

I wish I could explain
Somehow how I feel.
It doesn't seem as though
Life is real.
I wish I could put this plain,
But I can't and the easiest way
I could is by saying
Dark is dark and light is light
And when they mix, it becomes dusk.

   — *Kerri O'Neil*

The Image

The summer rays glistening on his golden hair.
His eyes gleaming like burning candles
In the midst of spring.
His lips like pale pink orchids
In an exotic bed of flowers.
Cheeks as red as rubies
As he chops firewood in the fall.
A smile that could melt ice
On a snowy day.
But a heart that burns with desire,
As he walks the other way.

   —*Connie Reed*

Running Horse

Running horse, run for me,
Be my spirit, wild and free.

Kick your heels at the Autumn moon,
Test your strength in the desert dunes.

Stretch your legs, long and lean,
Jump your fences, wide and clean.

Your mane blowing back,
Your coat of velvet black.

Running horse, run for me,
Be my spirit, wild and free.

   — *Charlotte McFarland*

Life as a Teenager

Do one wrong thing
And people will make fun of you.
Hang around the wrong people,
And others will avoid you.
Be something, wear something,
Do something different,
And you're *out of sync.*
People don't usually do what they think.

   — *Keri Medei*

Untitled

You say you really love me
And that you always will.
I really do believe you
And it gives me such a thrill.

Our love is much too dangerous;
We're at such a sensitive age.
Will it last forever,
Or is it just another page?

Let's take it day to day
Even though we both know
We need each other real bad;
We'll never, ever let go.

I might have felt this way before,
But it just wasn't quite the same.
I'm older and a little wiser;
I don't want to play the game.

It will be a little while
Before we are man and wife,
But I think I now know
It's you I want in my life.

   —*Joseph DeVito*

Country Crows

Country crows big as cats,
Sit on pine limbs,
Split and cracked.
Feathers shining,
Colored, blue black.
Scavengers waiting,
To launch an attack.
Sharp beaks,
Claws used to scratch,
Its hair raising Caw! Caw! Caw!
Startles, you from your nice nap.
Cover your food,
Leave the table intact.
Take a walk or a swim
Take a ride, horseback.
When you return,
They will fly high and free,
But the food you left fresh,
No longer will be.

   —*Doris Barb*

Hope

The sky had turned to gray
And I wished it so to be another day.
As the harsh gray clouds moved in
And surrounded my happiness,
Sadness began to move in
And I felt as though I was going to vanish.
I looked up to find something to make me smile
But I felt as though I had been drifting for miles.
No one around, but only the ground and the gray, gray sky.
But suddenly a bird flew by
And I knew there was to be a beautiful sight.
My heart was opening up wide and the shining sadness, bye-bye.
As the gray clouds rumbled forth,
The bird flew by with a particular look in its eye.
    —*Maryann Ovissi*

Tender Thoughts

Sometimes I lay awake at night and think of all
The times we have spent together.
Your gentle touch...
That says do not fear, I will protect you.
That reassuring smile...
That says I am here when you need me.
Your bright eyes sparkle and glitter
Saying it is alright to cry.
When we are together, time seems to stand still.
Precious moments are spent loving and caring for one another.
Thoughts of you soothe my fears and anxieties.
Please do not leave my side.
I love you!
    —*Michelle Burgoyne*

Daddy's an Angel

I love to go to the old home place, just to honor your memory
For each time we go to get the remaining belongings from there
We camp out on the lone prairie under the moon and the stars
And it is so very peaceful and satisfying to my soul.
And Daddy, I know that you were there today, near the old well
For I heard the soothing music of that celestial orchestra
As you played those beautiful sounds on the old violin
You know, it just overwhelmed me, into state of euphoria.
The harmonious melody was so enchanting and uplifting
I felt as though I was there in heaven with you
I was so enthralled, and taken away from reality, for a moment
The ecstacy of being in that realm with you was so fantastic.
I felt your presence go with me all the rest of the day
And when we had the awful crash on the highway
I know that you watched over us, as an angel from God
And kept us from being killed by the forceful impact of it.
    —*Mary Richards*

Untitled

One day when I was really hurting, a person reached out his hand.
When they asked me what the problem was, I just couldn't understand
I guess I didn't realize, that someone cared for me
So I acted mean and cold, and walked away, wanting them to leave me be.
But as the time went on, I began to finally see,
That all that person wanted, was to be a friend to me.
When I realized that I hurt that person, I thought about it everyday.
When I went to say *I'm sorry,* my pride got in the way.
I wanted to tell them, *Thank you. It's nice to know you care.*
It made me feel so much better, to know that he'd always be there.
But just like before, I did it again, I left without saying how I feel.
Now I regret just walking away, and the way that I acted unreal.
So now that I've hurt you, I hope that you will see,
If you ever need a friend, you can find a friend in me.
    — *Marnie O'Brian*

A Message and a Warning

Stay away from drugs
Keep them out of your hands,
Cause one day you say it is temporary,
But yet I see you take it every day
When it is hard for you to get it,
You steal and start robbing banks,
You say it makes you a real man
You say it makes you cool too
But only if you really knew it makes you look like a real fool,
I cannot tell if you are dead or alive,
Because everytime I see you, you are always getting high,
Your eyes get red, your face looks pale,
You weigh no more than fifty pounds.
Stay safe and leave drugs alone.
    —*Myra Jenkins*

The Evil Corpse of Mankind

Black within black swirling and churning,
Black within black leeping and turning,
And over the black ocean flys an eagle daring to enter
Into the darkness
And bellow the oceans surface the corpse of mankind wrongs.
And the beautiful black roses never to be seen
For above floats the red rain cloud
Which is all that is seen
As no one dares to wander through the absence of light
Never ending abyss of darkness,
For the cannot face their wrongs or shame themselves
For they know their wrongs and evils
They are within the red cloud until it rains,
Or so the black trumpet sounds...
    — *Tina M. Johnson*

Somewhere in Time

A dusty road somewhere in time,
That's where I saw you come from.
You traveled here from a place that you call home.
I watched you enter into my world,
I saw you make the best of it.
You saw me, but you did not know me.
Now I see yu leaving.
You look down that dusty road preparing for your journey
To return to a place I've never seen,
To live a life that I've never known,
To go back to a place that you call home—
Somewhere in time.
    — *Melissa Gero*

Life

I decided to have a talk with life.
Life, what is life?
Without life nothing in the universe could exist
No creature great or small.
Seems to me that man breathes one long breath from the time
Of birth till death
Because thou can leave in a blink
And there everyone goes to be with the dead.
Life, what is life?
Reveal to me your mystery.
Since thou wilt not tell me
I will ask the spirit of God within me
Now life I know who thou art.
Life thou art God
And God is life
That's why thou art the beginning
And the end of all creatures
And everything in the universe
    —*Marilyn Joseph*

My Dear Paul

What can I say at this time in my life;
Lord you have brought me through so much strife.
When I have needed a friend, you have always been there;
Now I ask myself why aren't you being fair?

Lord bless my dear Paul
Let me see it was time for his call.
Let his memories be ever fresh at mind;
And make us better all in your due time.

Let the love that we shared with him;
Always be remembered as the lights go dim.
I now realize that my dear Paul is not gone;
Nor is anything in which he stood.

He is heaven bound in the glory of the most high;
So why do we sit and cry?
His voice of rememberance and grace is now in heaven
In the eyes of the angelical face.

—*Michelle Heiler*

You Showed Me How

How do you know you love
When every thing is mapped out from above,
Is it the wild beating of two hearts,
That never want to be a part?

How do you know this feeling will last forever?
When before this feeling, you have never,
Felt your whole life long,
But your heart is a light, with song.

How do you know the one you love will love you in return?
When you know for this person your heart will always burn,
You are so afraid of rejection, it makes you shy,
Wary, that all he wants is to say goodbye.

With the sincerity and patience from you,
I know your love for me is true,
With your warm smile and gentleness, I have from you now,
You my darling have showed me how.

—*Regina R. Abrams*

Freedom

I have seen depression many times in my past.
That gray, ugly monster always moved in fast.
It would tell me lies, of worthlessness and gloom.
It could be so convincing that I would build my own tomb.
Breaking free was not easy, as many of you know.
I would fight with it daily, with often little to show.
Then one day, I realized what a liar it was!
I read and I read, all the ways to be free
I learned very slowly, that the freedom was Me!
Do not let that monster fill you with strife
Reclaim your freedom, take control of your life.

—*Linda Frohlich*

Sometimes

Sometimes I wonder what I should do
When I am alone without you
Sometimes I think you do it on purpose
Sometimes I see that smile and know I can't trust you
Sometimes I hope you will never walk around me again
But I will always love you.
Sometimes I see you with her and wonder why you do it.
Sometimes I wish you would just drop dead so I could be free
Sometimes I think I will never love again
But I hope you always see
Just me in your dreams
And sometimes I just long to be free
But you should never let up on me
Sometimes...

— *Michelle Eldridge*

Untitled

Buildings next to buildings
Imitating Lego architecture on a
Grand scale
Block upon block
No child's plaything
A hard place

Pitted by time and weather
People moving through the sidestreets of
Life's periphery
Close to, but not touching
Seeing, but not recognizing
Their humanity.

Days next to days
Routines inside routines in a
Small space
A chosen captivity
A hard life
But it's a life...

—*Mary Ellen O'Brien*

Tide of Tomorrow

On a beach of tomorrow
Lies all hurt and sorrow.
No grain is safe
From sorrow nor tomorrow.

There may be life after death
Deep within tomorrow
On this beach lie only
Hurt and sorrow...

All the good times
Washed away by the
Tides of yesterday.
If only it would
Wash away all the
Hurt and sorrow

Tomorrow would be
A better day...

—*Melanie Holmes*

Untitled

Satan, you can abandon
your constant quest for me.
I know to whom I belong.
I know where I want to be.

Satan, I rebuke you.
I'll stay where I belong.
Even so you stand in the wings,
disrupting the harmony of my song.

— *Claude E. Curliss*

Christmas Time

As Christmas time draws near
The carols we will often hear
To tell about the baby born
Upon that first Christmas morn

In a manger made of hay
Wrapped in swaddling clothes he'll lay
While wisemen come from traveling far
They will be guided by the star

Beautiful treasures they will bring
As they hear the angels sing
They are showing praise for Jesus Christ
The new born Lord and King!!

— *JoDee G. Ebel*

I Wait Alone

No hope moves on my horizon
No hint of dawn in my night
Nothing nothing nothing new
Oh...how could she ever come?

Pierced my heart with slow cold stroke
My life oozed out in her hands
Nothing nothing nothing new
Oh...how could she ever come?

Fear closed in...I clawed at death
'Til...fingers...ripped raw...hung limp
Nothing nothing nothing new
Oh...how could she ever come?

Can't get out...I claw no more
I wait alone...'til the end
Nothing nothing nothing new
Oh...how could she ever come?

—*Martin M. Cassity*

The Search

Looking everywhere, running free
I am looking for him.
He is looking for me.
We are both searching
But never finding.
Maybe someday, someplace
We will both stop the search
And find our love
That was meant to be.

—*Tina Arnett*

Watermarks

The stream of consciousness
Is such a wealthy tide
Beneath the crystal surface
Are all the thoughts we hide

The river of opinion
Can drown a quiet thought
And wash up only lies
When it was the truth we sought

The ocean of despair
Will swallow all our dreams
The faith that we hold onto
Is deeper than it seems.

The whirlpools of emotion
Will never cease their spinning
They carry us through losses
Until we turn out winning.

—*Maria E. Cascone*

Untitled

Once the substance goes in
You're never the same.
It changes your life and the
Way you think.
Why don't you care that your
Killing yourself?
You leave it for us to cry about.
No use hiding behind it.
It always wins in the end
And steals your life from family
And friends
It's sad to see how blind some
People can be, but its up
To those who really see, to
Try and change this awful way
Of dealing with life.

—*Kelly Cloud*

Mid Fall

Lemon Juice and pumpkin spice
from the awful paint-box green.
I watch them fall
like frozen hands, crinkly
from the stained frost
of molasses and dirt.
— *Sarah Elizabeth Avila*

My Soul

There is a presence in my soul
That touches the very depths,
Conquering every emotion
With intense affection.
Carefully possessing every wave
That flows, with a powerful force,
Overseeing the path that
My feelings must go.
Lurking in every corner like a knight
In shining armor.
Protecting my soul as though it was a fragile embryyo;
So tiny and precious.
Embided with surpassing delight.
I surrender willingly to your guardship
And I say,
Yes, you are the unconcious
Ruler of my soul!
—*Mildred Bibbins*

Who Am I?

Who am I?
What am I like?
Prep, jock, thrasher or burnout
Most say a prep, a stuck up snob
I highly doubt.
I'm friends with burnouts, loyal and true
A family through and through.
I just wanna to be me
But who and what am I to be
And who are you to judge me.
What are you?
Prep, jock, thrasher or burnout
You classify me to what you're not
You don't know me, maybe you are the snot!
So, who am I?
I'm me of course.
Anything I want to be you have no force.
—*Martina Steager*

S.A.S.E.

The mail is in. Finally. It's here. At
long last. The mail. Cancelled tan folder
spilled on top the table, open window
envelopes, yellow, white and pink. Many
ways of saying the same thing. Nothing that
hasn't been said before, been reduced to
cliche in symbolist Heaven, so true
to form I'm caught unprepared...The check's in
the mail and, I thought it original.
Stereo typewriter pounds the sounds of
invoices stuck still in lapse of time, springs
release in spasms of real time throws up
content all over the floor. No
watery taste from the back of the throat
can anticipate a sympathetic response,
there's only the cleaning of the mess
put away in the trash,
where legitimate requests become emphatic.
—*David Michael Heinze*

Untitled

Steel hands
claw madly at spinning rubber
with cold raw metal tearing at raw metal
reducing glass
to sparkling crystal beads of sand
and
sudden
screams of fright
shatter the unearthreal silence of before.

Red lights
pulsate, burning into the ink black night
with
squealing sirens
destroying the apathetic solitudinal
isolation
of
desolate
deserted wet glistening back streets.
—*Barbara Cutter*

Untitled

Looking out over this land
All I can see is the garden of stones
Where you sleep until some other time
The cool rain washes down my face
It makes me feel all alone, in this place
Death stalks around the corner
To lay it's weary hand on your shoulder
She's kneeling down with flowers in her hand
Tears don't explain her pain
Out from the shadows of death she does come
To haunt my mind with blame, this time.
She's throwing flowers on your grave
Hoping for your soul to save
Stay away from the tombs
Where the children come to play
The colours shine so bright
In the heart of light, walk away from here.
—*Lisa Lobeck*

Golf Poem

I took up golfing; oh, why me?
I can't even hit the ball off of the tee.
I swing and miss and only hit thin air,
Or hit the ground with my club;
It really doesn't seem fair!
Now, it's fact that all those pros
Make golf look easy; but we all know,
That it takes a lot of practicing to be any good
So grab your irons! Get your woods!
Practice makes perfect; or so they say,
But when I hit par; well, that will be the day!
— *Mara E. Mercier*

The Cycle

I'm walking through the park and a leaf falls down.
How many other leaves were as lonely as this one?
Life plays tricks so you have to watch out.
You could be another leaf falling to the ground.
The leaf falls to the ground, but has nowhere to go.
The wind just blows it until its out of reach.
Soon all the life is drained out,
Then a person will come along,
And as they walk, they won't bother to think.
They step on and crush the leaf to pieces.
No more life; now we begin again.
A new leaf grows, living only to accept its true fate.
—*Michelle Robinson*

What?

My blister was a skin blob
Filled with water
Swimming inside
Was a playful otter
The blister was popped
The water seeped out
The poor otter died
Because of the drought.
—*Kathy Latorre*

Ghosts

Their ghosts remained
Long after the sweeping
And bagging had
Taken their faded bodies.
There on the sidewalk,
Enduring the indignity
Of the soles of those
Without souls who never
Look about them to see
The beauty or the poetry
Or remark the brave deaths
Of autumn leaves.
There, on the sidewalk,
Their ghosts remained.
— *Sally F. Crouch*

Smoky Lies

Thundering hell
Invaded the peaceful.
Fearing death they
One by one paint themselves
With the blood of a buffalo
Across their wet cheeks.
Children raise their
Hands for salvation,
Though the gods weren't listening.
Hope and spirits burned
Until only their ash remained.
Hell had won again.
Shamelessly they laughed
And drank to victory.
— *Sharon Herbert*

The User of the Abuser

I am the user
Of the abuser.
I have no protection,
And I am losing my affection.

My eye is black and blue
And slightly swollen, too.
I am longing and needing.
My lip is constantly bleeding.

He is now coming closer.
I only am his poser.
I hit and I fight.
I kick with all my might.

For I am the user,
Who was killed by the abuser.
— *Kelly Courns*

Anything for You

I'll give to you a day filled with happiness
Full of brilliant golden sunlight
Twinkling upon the water
I'll paint for you a picture
Of the deep blue sky
Where billowy clouds dance in perfect harmony
I'll build for you a fantasy land
Where dreams are found and hearts are never broken
I'll tell you a sweet story
Of two hearts that found one another
And fell in love
I'll sing for you a tender song
Of bodies intertwined upon the white sand
Of a silver moonlit beach.
I'll do anything for you without one moment's hesitation
Because no love could be as strong or as true as ours.

—*Michel Craig*

Armchair Fan

She reads poetry, writes fiction, hears music great
Loves old movies late, what a fate with no mate,
Goes with elderly to church on van,
Returns home, the confound armchair fan.

Dentist, doctors, nurses, lazer beam, cat-scan,
Goes for an hour to the store on company van,
No sugar, no salt, then they forbid the malt!
She cooks, travels the world—don't call a halt

She makes ceramics for the fair, writes poetry at times,
Reads mags, listens to world news and war crimes;
Potluck dinner, birthday parties few; chats with friend or two;
T.V. fan, she rests in the armchair, finds out what's new.

She goes to school, grows gardens; listen to the best!
She goes everywhere on T.V.; plain to see she needs rest,
Lord she's trying to get thinner; no parties, no dinner:
She's an armchair beginner, she's an armchair fan winner!

— *Mary Lou Darnielle*

A Special Love (To Michael)

You fill my life with happiness and joy
To me you are the best little boy.
You have a love so innocent and true
You cheer me up when I'm feeling blue.

I love your laugh and your smile so sweet
I love everything about you, even your cute little feet.
I hate to see your eyes filled with tears
And I want to be there for you when you need someone near.

Even though you are not really mine
I'll love and protect you at any time.
So be good for your mommy and take care of her
Because she loves you a lot, that's for sure.

I'll miss your eyes so big and brown
Don't ever let anyone get you down.
I hope you'll remember me when I go away
Because for you, I promise, I'll be back someday...

— *Cyndi Hammond*

Feelings

Tears on my toes, falling from my nose.
What I really need, is a warm embrace, to brighten up my lonely face.
I'm looking in your big blue eyes, while listening to your little white lies.
I wish I could tell you how much I care, for the love I feel I cannot bare.
What would you say, if I told you today, that I want you all for me?
Would you run far away, or laugh and stay, or let me just plain be?
All I can say, is that I love you, Tom Rohr, I really do.
As you can probably see, my love is now starting to shine straight through.

—*Maryann Meinen*

When I Look Into His Eyes

When I look into his eyes
I see the pride shine and glimmer
And I know he loves me
Just the way his eyes shimmer

I just want to reach into his heart
And be filled with all the love he brings
But I know I receive the love
When I look into his eyes because they sing

I am hoping this will last forever
This love feels strong and true
We will always love each other
I hope this happens to you

When I look into his eyes
I love what I see
He gives me hope and direction
This was always meant to be

—*Krisi Campbell*

What Is a Future?

Where and what is a future?
Can you open a closet door and walk into it?
Is it a dream, a fantasy, what?
Is it in a history book?
Or, in the back of our minds?

If anyone knows what a future is, please let me know,
And direct me along the way.

Is the future a relapse of the past?
Is that the purpose for learning the past?
Can you look in a mirror and see your future?
How do we know when the future is?
By the time we do,
It's already a part of the past.

— *Renee F. Berning*

Untitled

You are so beautiful, one with nature
Like an Indian who lives in unison with her environment.
Surely flocks full of desires will surround you.

Loneliness came.
Liars

Passion swept through as fiery and hot as the hair on his head.
You are so wonderful. You feel so incredible.
You disgust me, you whore.

Loneliness came.
Liars

Hairs caught on the rough brick wall.
Body sliding down.
Tears jerking passed tightly closed eyes.

Loneliness came.
Dying

— *Laura Heffernan*

Love of Mine

Did the sun's heat touch you ever so gently today
As the wind tickled your ears with a soft message that made you smile?
Did the moon's subtle light embrace you and leave you in a trance
As each star glistened and shined?
No matter where you are or whether it may be day or night,
My love follows you always everywhere.
You're in my heart and on my mind.
I hold you in my soul until I die,
Oh great love of mine.

— *Magdalena Nieves*

The Greatest Love

My church means very much to me,
'Twas there I found his love to be
The greatest love that I could know,
And, may that love help me to show

Another, how his love is there
To help, to bless and answer prayer!
If they but ask that he would guide
And, always be there by their side.

As they walk along the way,
And as they do their task's each day,
That, they might also, to another show
The greatest love that one could know!

— *Bessie Long*

Dear God,

I was majoring in the minors
Before you came into my life,
I was focusing on dead end streets
Wasting my time on things
That only bring pleasure for a season
And loneliness for what seems like a lifetime,
But you gave me a new point of reference
And helped me to look beyond myself
And share the beauty and the good
Found in truly loving and being loved,
Now my world has balance,
It has pleasure, hope
It has joy and happiness,
And most of all,
It has you, Lord!

— *Evangeline Carey*

We Remember

We remember...a story that was told
About a night that was made of gold.
On this night a child was born
Who would fulfill his life with scorn.

No one believed that the story was true
So they put him through much misery too!
When the story came to an end
The people cried, *crucify him!*

Only till then did
The people realize
That he would be the
One to save our lives.

— *Elizabeth Daugherty*

Christmas

Christmas is a time to care,
A time to love and share.
You get presents and cards
And sometimes you even get scarves.
And at the stroke of twelve,
You hear sleighbells.
You run to the window and you see
A little man who's chubby.
He carries a sack full of toys
That will bring joy to all the girls and boys.
With the twist of his nose and his thumb,
You know he's not dumb
And with a shout of glee,
Merry Christmas to all that believe in me.

— *Nancy Owen*

Guidance

For all the hate and pain I have caused,
For all the things I have gone and lost,
Is it too late for me to change?
My ways seem set, forever strange.
My heart I gave to a devil of trust
I feel from good, I fell to lust.
Where is there now for me to go?
When every friend I made a foe.
I drove away who loved me most.
Then gave myself to Satin's ghost.
Now as my soul rots from within
I realize the price of sin.

—*Heather Milbury*

Thank You God, For My Friends!

God has given me a treasure He wants me to share;
Who are all my friends, who freely share and care.
My friends are worth more than rubies and gold;
Thru their love, I have received blessings untold .

My friends will always help another person in need;
Not asking anything in return for their good deeds.
My friends will help in any kind of given task;
Who will help whenever needed, all I do is ask.

My friends share in my happiness and good times;
And, they share in my misfortunes and sorrows, I find.
My friends, also, share in my burdens and problems;
And, they share in helping me to solve them.

Thank You God, for the riches I treasure in my friends.
When they need help; let it be me, that you send.
I ask to share my life and love for them all;
So, let it be me, for help, that they call.

— *Barbara Wolfe Heaps*

Mom's Dream

Mom had a dream she kept all to herself
In a can on the top of a high corner shelf.
In it were pictures of a beautiful place.
Just looking at them brought a smile to her face.
She wanted to go to that isle someday,
To a place in the ocean, far, far away.
When life seemed like more than she thought she could stand,
She'd get up on a chair and just take down her can,
Then she would walk on a beach and pretend she was there.
She'd see girls in grass skirts with long flowing hair.
I'll never forget that warm September day,
When Dad came to tell me that Mom went away.
I wonder if Heaven has a soft sandy shore
That my mom can walk on forever more.

— *Bertie Edwards*

To Whom It May or May Not Concern

I, being of sound mind, leave the following to the following:
The sun and the moon, the stars which shine so bright I leave to the blind
    that cannot see, reason being they wish not to see.
For the deaf I leave the songs of the birds
    as they lift their voices in praise for a new day.
This I leave to the deaf, reason being they wish not to hear.
To the dumb I leave all the knowledge which God has given us to learn
    and to teach others on the great gift of love,
    reason being they wish not to learn.
To those that wish to see, ask to hear and willing to learn, I leave nothing,
    for why give to those who are already rich?
May God be with you,I would say,
    though knowing that He already is and will be forever.

— *Youlanda Brewster*

Forever Friends

Whenever I remember
 My friends along the way
There's one who stays with me
 Each and every day.

You see it's very simple
 Guess I've always known
Forever she will be my friend
 I'll never be alone.

The years go by so quickly
 We're living miles apart
Still she's always with me
 A sister in my heart.

With lots of happy memories
 I write this poem for you
God blessed me when he gave me
 My best friend Sue.

— *Bonnie Weikel*

Journeys

i came
i stayed
i left
each day
the sun rose
but only showing itself
at the beginning
to greet me
at mid-point
to entertain me
and at the end
to say goodbye
and to let me know
that there is always
a beginning
a middle
and an ending
to all journeys

—*E. Gene Givens*

Untitled

Through these eyes I can see
The pain in the children's eyes
Which is not meant to be.
I can see the world
As it should not be.
In my mind;s eyes,
I can see joy, happiness
Which was meant to be.
Look through your mind's eyes
For peace and joy
For the world to see.

— *Carina Raley*

Edelweiss

Lovely Edelweiss, clinging to an Alpine mountain,
Lonely, waiting for a friend, who climbs, then rests
Marveling at her beauty, making the journey worthwhile,
On climbs the friend and Edelweiss waits
To cheer on another mountain climber.

Who put this lovely flower high up in the Alps?
Was there a reason for it, to make men pause perhaps?
Matterhorn in the distance, climbing higher on
Lovely, lonely Edelweiss, grow where few men roam.

Now as he reaches his journey, and can rest at last,
Thoughts are of the white and yellow flower he had passed
Reaching out for her, almost at the top,
Made him turn a little, missed the falling rock.
Did he just imagine a flower upon a rock,
Or does Edelweiss watch over men who climb the top?

    —Dolly Dees

Little Firefly

Oh! Little firefly with your fire so bright,
You really are a sight.
Tell me, my bright little friend,
What makes your fire burn to no end?
Is it because you are free
Just to alight on a tree
With not a worry to see.
Tell me little firefly,
What makes your fire burn so bright?
Do you light just for the sight
Or just to be bright in the night?
Oh! Little firefly, your light is so bright.
Little firefly! You must beware of the constant stare
From wandering eyes that cannot bear
The sight of your light.
So they grab and grab with little hands
Until your bright light is no longer in sight.

    — Thomas E. Nix

Over My Shoulder

As I look back over my shoulder,
I find myself getting bolder and bolder
Getting away from just me, me, me,
And thinking how to please thee, thee, thee,
It was ordained this way from the beginning,
The route you go, to be sure of winning,
Giving is better my opened eyes see,
When you think about it, how else can you be free?

    — BettyJane Sheppard Slosser

The Cat

Like the cat with a mind of its own, so let it be.
It get hurt and wants to hurt back with vengence
In the lead.
Like the cat who knows where it's at...
It laughs at all who try to fool.
It wants to prove that fools can't catch
And so it succeeds.
Like the cat who feels fear and anger,
And so it hides in the shadows.
But when brought into the light,
It jumps with fear for something beyond its sight.
Like the cat who plays along for right or wrong;
It knows not what it says or does.
Just that it's a cat.
But may the cat have a meow for help,
Which humans cannot understand,
But keep in mind it may be a sign from...the cat.

    —Michelle D. Thomas

The Driving Force

Bridges to cross and roads to follow.
Paths are open, but the call unsure.
Weak legs step to life's faint tune,
Occassionally fall, but rise controlled.

Scattered across a field of sorrow,
Seeds of decision lie dormant and frail.
Showers of hope and the warmth of love
Cause burgeoning of the life thereof.

Certainty questioned, but the course not obscure.
Faltering inevitable, but determination prevails.
Moving forth to an illusion ahead.
The driving force to attain success.

    —Melonie Dawn Allen

Eternal Light

The light of life will shine my way.
The light of hope and faith each day.
The light that shines and makes men wise.
The light that shines and never dies.
The light that shines on God's creation.
The light that shines on every nation.
The light that shines toward freedom and peace.
That long burning light will never cease.

    —Rosemary H. Kyle

Him

I lay in my bed all snug and tight
And think about him all through the night.
I want him so bad that it hurts so much.
I need to feel his loving touch.
Whenever he talks, his words are so kind.
I only hope I could answer with mine.
But it is not me to whom they are addressed
They are to my friend, which is my best.

    —Kelli Roper

a lone wolf

a lone wolf with no companion
    the sun reflecting of the snow makes his fur seem
    glossy, soft and warm.
his eyes show wisdom and wildness, but also kindness
    loneliness and sadness
isn't he something like me.

he is strong, cunning, skillful, but merciful and gentle.
he faces the elements that would make him mighty
for he has no companion, no mate and no leader.

he lives but barely.

But it is his wisdon, his kindness, his loneliness,
    his sadness, his mercy and his gentleness
that makes me feel pity and love for him.

i say again, isn't he something like me.

    —Shelley Ernst

The Tree

Deformed by time and nature's storms,
The tree bows down and waits for death.
Not feeling now, the sun that warms,
Or seeing spring's first budding breath.

No longer do the chipmunks play,
Beneath the branches, bleak and grey.
Solitary in its decay,
Becoming soon the hatchet's prey.

Farewell, most noble, mighty oak,
I see your sap, it starts to weep,
Acknowledging the axeman's stroke,
That brings you everlasting sleep.

    —Mary Diener

Colors

No one race is superior
Though some seem to think they are so much more.
Be a man white, or be a man black,
Perfection is a quality in which they both lack.

The color of our skin
Should make no difference upon us.
Though society today makes it a fuss.
When will we all learn to be civil,

To be equal to white, and black in turn.
When will we all be brave
And erase this line between colors.
To act the just way

And not the way of others
I long to see the day
When all are treated right.
When people wisen up, and finally see the light.

   —*Rhonda M. Pineda*

It Could Only Be You!

I don't really know where to start,
So I'll start down from the heart.
You'll never know when we'll run out of time,
So I hope you'll always be mine.
Whenever I think of you at night,
I just want to see you and hold you tight.

When we're apart and you're far far away,
It seems like I miss you more each day.
If you ever need someone to talk to or to just care,
Remember that I'll always be there.
When I hurt and feel like crying deep down inside,
There you are, standing by my side

When I'm sad, depressed, or just down,
I think of you, and away goes the frown.
You're a person who's caring and sweet,
The one who makes my life complete.
You're more than a special friend,
You're the one I love, and this will never end.

   —*Lori Scott*

Love Across The Miles

Love is hard to say across the miles,
But I just want you to know that I care;
Care about what you say and care about everything you do.

Miles cannot erase the precious love we share.
Somehow I feel that it is here forever
Because each time we are together,
The bond grows stronger and tighter.

I wish sometimes you were here so you could see
Just how much love I have for you.
It is very hard to express love on paper and send it miles away.
Hopefully, as soon as you conquer your goal,
You will come home to me and stay here for evermore.

Understand that this kind of relationship of love
Across the miles is one of the hardest ones to keep.
But if you can be faithful and have love remaining for each other,
You will find that it is the kind of relationship
That is the most valuable and precious of them all.

   —*Traci Wall*

Depression

I'm sitting all alone thinking about the past.
I'm sitting all alone thinking about the future.
I await in the darkness,
No one to talk to.
No one to listen to.
I await in the darkness,
Waiting for someone to walk in the light.

   — *Lucinda Terwilliger*

The Fair

Cotton candy and carmel corn fill the summer air.
Twirling rigs of red and gold spin faster at the fair.
Bright balloons all in a row making little faces glow,
Fudge pots steaming, children screaming, there's laughter everywhere.
Teddy bears and kewpie dolls and clowns with yellow hair.
There is nothing like the fair.

The strong man rings the silver bell,
A turbanned lady has fortunes to tell.
The carnies yell, their voices gruff,
A bearded lady struts her stuff.
The wishing well reflects our dreams
Like bubbles glistening in the sun, our hopes and schemes.
Winter winds whistle around the cabin door,
My little kitten huddled on the floor.
The fire ablaze, flames licking at the air.
I do remember how I loved the fair.

   — *Jan C. Whelpley*

Feelings

Sitting on the back porch of my small Indiana country
Home I gaze across corn covered fields.
Giving my spirit, freedom to roam.
I feel the walk of my Cherokee ancestors.

As the mountains high they climb.
I hear the softness of their moccasins.
When by the rivers they glide.
Our hearts unite with rapid beats.

As fear instills inside.
The Cherokee has no knowledge of what lies on the other side.
Yet on we press with restlessness,
Waiting for the winds to call.

Be brave, stand tall, there is plenty of land for all.
Silent tears began to fall.
We chant, we pray, God make a way.

Let our tribe survive.
May there be peace, love and contentment.
When we reach the other side.

   —*Ruby Burns*

The Times and Memories

The times of pain, when your heart is caught and can't be set free;
Memories of your past that can only be opened with a key.
Memories of your girlfriend that are happy and sweet;
The times you are hurt and confused, but won't admit defeat.

Others are ones that you can't or don't recall;
The times you are frightened, but can't seem to take the fall.
All these memories are either good or bad;
Some you are glad of and some you wish you never had.

   — *Richard Robinson*

If in Fact, What Then Are We

If in fact the world be a better place, why then the corrupt?
Why then resting the inner, a laden for sin?
The mind is bigger in the of many than in the actual being.
The guilt there of trapped selves inside shells devised as body, defined as the soul.
What then are we?
Why has man made a structural crown, need of existing?
Be never no more unto man, but unto our maker, to whom ever not be completed, complimented by such a meager.
We must be as one.
For a trip over the mountain's breast.
In living now or in at rest, for me to comfort my soul.
In a day as dawn is gladly seen, fearful of the night—which will come.
Stolen away if the carpenter comes.
No matter though, howe'er He brings, in Him I'll live forever.

   — *Sonia K. Hall*

Bright Spirit

Those spirits that are so close to Nature,
With an affinity for birds, the earth, the sea;
They are of this world, and yet they see beyond it,
For they are God's messengers of immortality.

They are quite a part of Nature and of God,
For as they walk and tread life's stairs;
Life's dream is always bright with hope,
And in this earthly sojourn, the stars are theirs.

They are the ones, the pure in heart,
In whose Soul God's flame of love is lit;
To light the way that others might see,
Such a one were you, Bright Spirit.

— *Enid Mitchell*

Too Blind to See

Long ago on this sinful earth,
A holy child was given birth.
Over his head there was a star,
Letting everyone know near and far.
He came to us from God above,
To show us His everlasting love.
Safely laying in a manger,
Not aware of future danger.
Healing the sick, giving sight to the blind,
His only goal was to help mankind.
Then in our cruel, angry behavior,
We tortured and crucified our Savior.
Many were there but not all cried,
Watching our Savior as he died.
When He comes again to set us free,
I wonder if we'll be, too blind to see.

—*Larry Nau*

Earth Beautiful

The earth is beautiful, filled with love
It is written in the lillies and the sky above
As birds sing gayly in tops of trees
I feel God's love flow gentle as the breeze.

So, open your eyes, put your cares away,
God's love shines brightly on the world today.

A child skips gaily over emerald green grass
Watching with wonder as crickets hop pass
She pauses and ponders, gives me a smile
Reminding me still, life is worthwhile.

So, open your eyes, put your cares away,
God's love shines brightly on the world today.

God's riches lie easily within our grasp
Giving in abundance is His loving task.
Blessings of God are totally free...
For those who will only just receive.

So open your eyes put your cares away,
God's love shines brightly on the world today.

—*Ressie L. Tankersley*

The Answer

Young men and women of today...
Are you looking for a high in dope or booze?
Are you trying to get away from your problems,
By drowning them in a bottle or through a needle?
Are you lost and confused,
Bombarded by peer pressure and parents who just don't understand?
Back away from drugs, for it is not the answer!
Turn towards Jesus, He is the key...
He will take away your pain and frustration,
And He will give you a peace beyond understanding.
By just knowing and believing in Him,
He will set you free from your bondage forever!

— *Janice Y. Fukumoto*

Friend

A friend is someone to talk to
when no one else seems to care,
when everything falls apart,
someone who will always be there.
Someone to be with
when nobody else is around.
A friend will make you happy
when you're feeling down.
Friend is not just a word
but a cheerful thought...
a friend is what you call someone
when a relationship means a lot.

— *Sandy Heasley*

Forever Friends

We've known each other all our lives
The closeness we have felt
The secrets we have shared
Will always be charished by both of us.

We share a special kind of love
That only we will understand.
The fights we have had
Seem so meaningless now
For we have both grown.

I feel we are closer now
Even though we are miles apart
Because we are sisters
We are forever friends.

— *Norma Field*

A Moment's Hesitation

A thought passes
I hesitate
A smile appears on my lips
You enter my mind once
Again
Sweet thoughts hit my heart
Warmth runs through my body
Like one of your touches
I long for you to be here
To feel your hands in mine
To touch your face
To lay my head upon your chest
And feel your heart
Beating beneath me
Silence
I hesitate
Peace
Once again

—*Tracy Rice*

Undesired Goodbyes

Love is a feeling
A special emotion
That something I felt
When we met in the ocean.

On the beach
As we stood in the sand
We took a long walk
Hand in hand.

Today we leave
We share a sweet kiss
We face the inevitable
It is you that I'll miss

We'll meet again in a sea of deep
blue together at last together as
two.

—*Chastity Seal*

I Miss You

There is a little voice inside
That wants to jump out
And start to cry
Just the things I think about
The things that really start to hurt
When its involved with love
I cannot really start to blurt
Because my true love did not love.
My heart is still broken
For I still love you
You still have not spoken
That's why I'm still blue
This is the end
There's no reason why
I really do love you
Now I start to cry

—*Tiffany Lassen*

Bewildered and Alone

Death's door is hanging
Over my head.
I am afraid to close my eyes
When I go to bed.

The mysteries of life we
Discover each day.
But the mysteries of death
Who knows or who is to say?

I have always feared the
Sense of helplessness and
The unknown.
Will I just lie in the grave
Bewildered and alone?

—*Karen Buak*

I Wonder?

I wonder if she thinks of me when it's quiet and she's alone?
I wonder if she remembers my voice when she's on the telephone?
I wonder if she remembers the smile I gave to her so freely?
Or our special little talks when I told her my true feelings?
I wonder if she ever stops to think of me now and then?
To wonder how I'm doing and wonder how I've been?
I wonder if she hurts inside whenever they play our song?
I wonder if she yearns for me when a couple strolls along?
I wonder if the memories keep her awake at night?
I wonder if she wishes we never had to fight?
I wonder and question until my wonders all run out.
But, I wonder if she wonders what I'm wondering about?

— *Ray Magruder*

Silence

The golden sunset with its warm hues
Gives way to night with fiery light.
A gentle word, the kindness soothes
The savage heart that rages bright.
Joy and love in the hand of peace,
The life that's sweet with no mourning.
The fog rolls in through the trees
A mighty cloud for every morning.
A solemn look of grave despair
Knowing you must go from hence.
A tear in the eye, a gaze of care,
Giving up at last to love's long silence.

— Brian Holbrook

Wellness

You gave me a World of Wellness,
I thank You for it, my Lord,
I knew I did not deserve it,
But You have the final word.
I prayed to become more worthy
I found it so hard to pray
For You and I were newly made friends,
And I knew not the words to say.
I strained to hear Your instructions
Through the *still small voice inside,*
The more I strained to hear You,
The less You seemed to confide.
When I learned quietude in my inmost parts,
'Twas then I could clearly hear,
As clear as the beating of two strong hearts
The words overcoming all fears,
And You brought me back to wellness,
With Your love, which is where it all starts.

—Katherine Strathearn Baverso

Living

It cannot be said that living is easy
But there are ways you can have a ball.
Many things can make it easier,
And hopefully you will find them all.

Do not worry about what is behind you,
You cannot change that anyway,
Live each day to the fullest,
And make every moment, ecstacy.

Dreams of success are wonderful,
But you must get involved if you want to say.
That you lived your life to the limit
And did not miss much along the way.

—Lloyd Schmidt

Palate Pleasing

Perhaps the perfect pleasure arises from the
Odor of white-hot kernels
Popping in frenzied rhythm with the
Crisp crackling of oil.
Overwhelming aromas
Reach one's
Nose and entice one's tastebuds.

Perfectly still it is, until the unveiling begins.
Once shy seeds release their ruffled
Petticoats. Slowly at first, then increasingly swift,
Creating a craterous crescendo
Of eruptions. Fully revealed kernels
Ricochet off restraining barriers, like
Numerous racquetballs exploding from walls.

—Sandra Lindstrom

An Impossible Dream

I dream of his eyes that sparkle so bright
I dream of his hair that shines in the night
I dream of his smile that there always would be
I dream of his lips that would gently kiss me
I dream of his arms that would hold me so tight
I dream of the feeling I get from his sight
I dream of him, together with me
I dream a dream that I will never see

—Dana Mathiesen

The Sandman

If only you were here,
Holding my hand,
Sitting on the beach at dawn
Playing in the sand
The seagulls fly over and let out their squeal,
Wish I had told you just how I feel,
I loved you more than life itself
But now you are gone,
There is nobody else.
If only there was a way to let you know
I am so lonely now,
My heart has grown cold.
I sit and wonder and think of the sorrow
Hoping, just hoping
I look to tomorrow.

—Joel Yarvis

Day Dreaming

As I sat in my bedroom staring off into space
He came before me but I couldn't see his face.
He put out his hand so smooth and so soft
He stepped slowly closer and held me aloft.

The music sounded, a light little dance,
We matched up our movements and started to prance.
A slow song began and he held me so tight
I thought we could stay that way through the night.

He whispered some words that I could not hear
But I knew by his tone that they were very dear.
I felt I was floating way up in the sky
As I became mesmerized by this wonderful guy.

I curled my hands into his hair
And opened my eyes to find only air.
My mystery man was only a dream
But I understood for a while what true love did mean.

— Lisa E. Johnson

Just Me

I walk through forests, streams and rain.
I walk alone, yet feel no pain.
I rest by a tree, no one is there.
Yet, I do not care,
I am alone and free, just me.

I see the sun rise and set once again.
Then darkness creeps on; it is my friend.
I rest, then silently fall asleep.
I sleep beside a river, wide and deep.
I am alone and free, just me.

I live from day to day, not worrying what will be
I only see life's good things, that is quite enough for me.
I live the simplest way I can.
I live my life without a plan.

And then one day my time will come
As it does for everyone
Then I will die
Alone and free...just me.

—Cheryl A. Noel

So Red the Rose

So red the rose,
The morning dew.
So red the rose
Of beauty true.
So red the rose
Of early spring.
So red the rose
Of mockingbirds sing.
If a flower of beauty more,
The human soul shall endure;
For so red the rose, the body thrives
For its beauty never dies.

— Julie Rees

Together

I wish I could tell you
How much I cared.
Or about all the times
I wish we had shared.
Many years have
Joined the past,
You asked me out
One day at last.
I felt as though
Our love was strong.
I wish it would
Have continued on.
So can't we give it
Just one more try,
And be together
You and I.

—Kena M. Mitchell

Untitled

As I wait
As I sit
I can hear the birds
Whistling in the twilight.

As I lie
As I stare
I can hear th children playing.

As I hope
As I care
I know that homeless and hungry
People are everywhere.

— Robin Mack

Homework

Homework is rough
And sometimes tough
It is not so great
When you cannot go on a date
Your teacher will have a fit
If you do not do it
Each class has its own kind
That will tangle up your mind
Homework is bad
It really makes you mad
When you cannot get it right
And it is really late at night
So if you have a hunch
That you are going to do too much
Come to me
And I will see what I can do!

—Tammy Darr

The Inevitable Quest

We all seek to find
A seal to wrap the soul
To create a bliss known
To heavenly angels
To walk lightly through
The air with an aura
Of confidence and reassurance
To find our existence intertwine
With another
We always seek to find that
Which liberates the soul
From entanglement with thyself
That which releases our
Essence and enhances our happiness
We seek to find a treasure
To Search for the ultimate experience
Which is that of Embracing Love

—*Lourdes Rodriguez*

Days of Future's Past

Come walk with me through the days of yore
In wooded lane and by the shore.

Long years have fled
 Since you drifted away,
But could it be dawning
 Of a bright, new day?

Come talk with me
 By firelight glow
Of the days between
 Our long ago.

How to corral an errant dream-
 Can one hold fast a warm sunbeam?

Come join with me
 A wild endeavor-
Perchance we capture
 Them together?

— *Jessie R. Roberts*

Flowers

Flowers of the darkness
Stimulate the air
Their sweet refreshing aroma
Is always so very near
It lifts you up among the clouds
With such a warm embrace
To hold you in their mystic arms
Like embers of a warming fire
On a cold December day

As seasons change and life departs
To await a new born dawn
The aroma of the flowers
Still stirs within my heart
With each new day
With thought of you
Deep within my mind
Of times we spent in each embrace
With the flowers of the night

—*John H. Whitmarsh III*

The Circus

a crumpled candy wrapper
a cotton candy stick
an old cracker jack box
with a surprise toy trick
life at the big top
is a bowl of cherries
without the pits

— *Lorette N. Geeslin*

In Front of Me

An empty field, a barren tree,
A black hole lying in front of me.

The heartaches and pains
Emptied the field,
Left it dry and unproductive
From lack of a shield.

The barren tree,
Holding only broken dreams.
Fruitless forever...
That is how it seems.

Representing my future
This huge black hole.
Dug deeper and deeper,
By all my crushed goals.

Now, I am praying for the time
That life might find a way,
To a more fulfilling land
With happier and brighter days.

—*Colleen Severance*

Aging?

What is aging?
Is it to be afraid of
 or to look forward to?
Why aging?
Is it to have a set plan
 so you know you will
 be doing something always,
 or rather to have
 a depression stage to avoid?
Why? What?
Does anyone know?

— *Kendra Hoisington*

Death of a Loved One

We remember the good times and the bad.
You were always happy and sometimes sad.
We never expected it that day—
That day you were unexpectedly taken away.
Oh, how hard it was to let you go,
But now we realize how we loved you so.
You are still in our every day thoughts
And you will never leave our hearts.

— *Dana Ferraro*

The Old Man

I am the old man.
Do I dare describe the winds
That tossled my hair,
And snatched my breath,
In days when I was young?
Or walk the rutted trails
Of stories I like to tell?
Or in a foggy haze, see faces I
Once saw with vivid clarity,
Faces that have faded with the years?
Can I describe friends I knew?
Or hear voices from the past?
Do I dare?
And when I go, will you realize
That I am one of the faces, and one of
The voices,
And you are the old man?

—*John Robert McConnell*

Grandmother

Lord,
Take her up tenderly,
Life her up with care
Guide her toward the light, Lord,
Help her up your golden stairs.
Take her to the heavens above,
To the angels singing to one another,
To the place of everlasting love,
To be behind your gates with my mother.
When you take her up into your blue sky,
And she and I are worlds apart,
Tell her *farewell* for me and not *good bye*
For she is gone in body but will forever
Remain in my heart.

—*Kimberly E. Campbell*

Memories

Memories always seem to stay,
With us in that special way,
Taking us back to the past,
When times were simpler and not so fast.

The happiness and laughter always remains,
As it travels over life's plains,
Sadness seems to disappear,
Becoming fuzzy and unclear.

These good memories help us sleep,
As we ask the Lord our souls to keep,
Decisions are more easily made,
Remembering dues previously paid.

Memories are part of the overall plan,
As this all first began,
Keeping life from being so dull,
When life hits that occasional lull.

—*Bob Knight*

Dream of You

I have dreams from a past
 dreams I never thought would last
Can't believe my dream of you
 will never come true
My life was all shattered
 and now I feel blue
I'll dream on and on
 'til my dream comes true
I'll dream on and on
 'til I meet up with you

—*Laura Tavitas*

Blissful Reconciliation

glittering sparks of dust in a
dark-brown golden sky
a lone elm upon a hill
with a dark-haired girl beneath its eyes
a simple linen sundress and dark, slender arms
concentration across her brow

behind, a figure coming over the rise
a young man, his hair blowing in the breeze
he approached her slowly
not wanting to destroy her peace
gently he stroked her hair
and kissed her neck
and gave her a rose saying, *Please.*
Yes, she replied and with tears
in her eyes, they walked off
with their souls at ease.

— *Sharon Gebbie*

One Similar Night

I feel the blanket of drowsiness
Caress me with deep warmth.
Cradling you in my arms,
As the night wraps us in her arms,
I feel your warmth, the beat of your heart,
Your hair smells of flowers and your skin tastes sweet.
Hearing your breath, I press a little tighter
And imagine a murmer from your lips.
Oh, how I wish I could love you,
As I have loved others in the night.
Yet, laying here with you in my arms
I know that we will never do so.
The blanket of drowsiness and
The secret smell of your hair
Are the effective guardians
Of my respect and love of you.
Feeling the warmth of your body,
I press a little bit closer,
And like so many times before,
Fall asleep to the rhythm of your breathing.

—*Christopher Roberts*

A Special Friend

Being a grown-up is not easy to do.
You learn about life as much as you can,
But something in there always turns you down.
It can sometimes drive you crazy, but that's the good part...
From this moment on a true friend finds your heart.
Helping you all the way, through your day. She makes you laugh,
She makes you cry, she makes you understand more about life.
She makes you know what a real friend can be.
And one day you will find out just how special this friend really is.

— *Reylvie E. Ortiz*

A Reason for Being

I ponder the question of destiny's calling,
The quarrels, the struggles; toward my final fate.
Although it is hard, it is there before me,
So clear in the future; Time unveiling it's state.

No blockage, nor hindrance; make me not blind,
To the facts, to the truth, to my strength and my mind.
The challenge, the spirit; my heart is for fight,
But the depth of goal is yet far from sight.

Please guide me and lead me, I follow my heart,
Through sadness and hardships; the tearing apart.
The answer shall be, it's my final quest,
Let me know t'was the reason; I pray 'fore I rest.

— *Kathleen W. VanDyke*

My Love

Forever, I pledge my love to it truest
Until the high mounts become low valleys.
And after the moons have thirty two counts
And still my undying love has not dimmed.
Many the sun has risen to its three positions
Morn, noon, nigh
And yet I hear no sounds,
Not the faintest whisper of where my lover might be.
Even in this night of the new moon,
Silently I begin to doubt, troubled is my mind.
So long since I felt your sweetest love surround me.
So long since your gentle touch has plunged us into
The esctasy of forbidden pleasure.
And again the moon comes, silently shining
Reminding me of days gone long.
When will my friend, my rock, my love come home.

—*Christine Etherton*

Oh Joy!

As love be undressed, bare, blank and naked,
The hitchhiker (a dandy for a grand dame)
Cannot flaunt the parade of glorious love.
Elated and swollen, yet humbly, he cannot
Favor, court or run after the lady that
Overwhelms the senses...peer at her ladyship
And be a noble gentleman...who's caught
Captivated under a charm...lost in wonder
At this marvelous woman wanted for:
Companionship, sharing and intimacy
Of the greatest kind.
Love can be an obscenity, as becoming as it may be.
Abandon and forsake the want with a veil,
Tastefully restrained for its inappropriateness.
The wind came and held its breath too long.

— *Thomas Pecora*

Always A Friend

Whether here nor there, through thick and thin,
You are always a friend.
If I am happy or sad, mad or glad,
You are always there and always a friend.
Through love and hate, you stay by my side,
And keep me in my place, because you are always a friend.
There is no way, I could never thank you enough.
But hopefully someday, I will be able to repay
The love and the time, you have given to me,
Because you are always a friend.

—*Sharon L. Styer*

My Search for an Answer

I pray for a chance for relief from the foreboding
That drives endlessly into more pain.
The pain is over my head for somethings
And others are just an inconvenience.
So if we go the path of righteousness,
Will we find that promised peace and love.
The companionship of a beautiful woman and the love of that woman
Or will we go on searching forever and never find that joy
of sharing one's life and expreiences with one another.
I feel as though I am in charge of something I can't use.
But yet I feel like...bold, honorable, wise & I cannot describe how I feel
I feel like a thousand years and never again
Yet I already have gray hairs of worry and pain that I see around me
So tell me young ladies, do you trust real love
Or do you lust for less trivial people that are just a plastic Cup
With less peace than the greed that wells up in their souls.
Tell me; What do you see, or are you just as greedy?

—*Marc S. Schneider*

The Final Rain

The end of life is like a cloud
Gathering rain for its final spout.
The wind it swells, the tempest roars,
Fear grips the hearts of those on shore.
Slowly, but increasing pace
The rain, it pours through grizzly haze.
And as it gives its final drop,
Life's fleeting rain comes to its stop.
The cloud is gone, the Sun, He burns
The hurt of Death, and peace returns.
But memories does the mind enshroud
The silver life of that little cloud.

　　—Kevin Rhyne

The Loners

Why do they let their ego get in the way?
Why do they let their self-pride rule?
They never have anything to say.
They are people you thought you knew.
You've seen a different side,
Black as the darkest night. Their inside
Has the lack of insight.
They have grown up into adulthood,
With their eyes full of tears
Because they missed out on a sweet childhood
That was full of nothing but fears.
They are who they are,
Striving to be what they need love to be.

　　— Stacie Gardner

An Influential Sky

Day
The sky is a magnifying glass.
Its dense carpet of translucent blue
Enlarges the beauty of nature.
Frosty, white mountains sprout purple tips.
Luscious green valleys shimmer with dew.
Sparkling, clear waters dance in their beds.

Night
The sky is a pair of sunglasses.
Its dense carpet of eternal black
Disguises the beauty of nature.
Shadows of mountains shrink into hills.
Deserted valleys vanish from view.
Tired, still waters tickle the shore.

　　— Shelby Conti

My Thoughts Were Just of You

The stars were out tonight,
The sky was clear and dark,
It was quiet in the mountains,
My thoughts were just of you.

The campfire creckled and sputtered,
The flames were low and warm,
Blue and orange and red and yellow,
My thoughts were just of you.

The stars are in your eyes,
Your hair is soft as night,
Your cheeks are fire bright,
My thoughts were just of you.

Down the path to the creek nearby,
Hand in hand we walk,
Through the ferns and mosses,
My thoughts were just of you.

　　— Charles Rockyvich Jr.

Life

Flowers of gold, in fields of green.
Sounds of birds, heard but not seen.

Skies of blue with bits of white,
Feel the warmth of the sun so bright.

Many a tree with leaves aglow
So sweet the smell as the winds blow.

The crashing of waves on the shore line.
The salty air and a seaguls whine.

The hum of traffic from a distant street,
To relax and snooze in the summers heat.

Taken for granted in countless ways
The gift of life, I'll always praise.

　　— Shannon Wehner

Treasure

I thought you were a dream
When you tore me at the seam.
I always thought it'd be you and I,
Forever on the clouds of love so high.
But now you're gone.
What did I do that was so wrong?
I was such a fool.
You know I never meant to be so cruel.
You know it's you I need.
Tell me, how do you feel about me?
Please don't go.
I love you so.
I will forget you never
For you're my only treasure.

　　—Sarah Skinner

Revival

Oh God, it's raining.
But that's not a surprise.
The rain is inside as well as out.
Gray clouds sweep the sky above me
And the skies within my heart.
The gloom that hangs over the world
Hangs over my head.

Nothing can bring me from my depression.
The thought of ever seeing light again
Seems hopeless.

But suddenly, I hear your voice.
And I see your face.
One smile from you fills my heart with joy.
And the world is as it should be
Again.

　　—Amy Acorn

Without You

A million miles away
I wish you could come back
And hopefully stay.
The day you left
My eyes were full of tears.
I will never forget our togetherness
Throughout the years.
My heart still throbs when I hear your name,
But I know things can never be the same.
I just want you to remember
That I will always love you.
And I know that way down deep
You do too!

　　—Renee Abbott

The Truth About Love

Just when it's found it's lost,
Just when it's true it's false,
It's like a poison,
Burns like fire,
Felt by only one instead of two.
Lost in a world you can't seem to describe.
Falling in instead of out.
Love...cold, stale tears on a bitter night
When you know you can shake it,
Love is luck, love is chance.
Over and over a silent, mindless game
One in a million,
Two in a heart, slowly drifting apart
Memories of what was thought...
I guess love was not.

　　— Amy Linimon

Peace in the World

I am listening
listening to the sounds of nature
nature the beauty of the world
world is in the palm of your hand
hand is where the bird lays
lays in the warmth of your body
body is what makes up the world
world is green with envy
envy is what makes us different
different are our views
views that make us quarrel
quarrel stops the beauty
beauty in nature and in peace
peace which makes the world whole
whole not separated
separated from ideas
ideas which make peace
peace is everywhere
everywhere but not noticed
noticed the peace in the world
because I am listening

　　—Christina Pinch

That Little Black Spot in Your Heart

That little black spot in your heart
makes me feel that you're only half there.
It makes me think that you don't really care.
I care for you like I say I do
And if you please me, I will please you.
You make a wish, but it doesn't come true.
You wonder why and it makes no sense to you.
Just ask the world what it's doing to you.
They just tell you that wishes never come true.
But loving me is loving you.

That little black spot in your heart
makes me feel so alone.
It makes me feel that I am nothing any more.
If you cared you wouldn't hurt me this way.
So don't hurt me again, I say.
You ask me out and I say, *Sure, okay.*
A change in plans, is that all you can say?
It hurts me most when you say you love me.
I sit and wonder why you said it to me.
I love you so much that it hurts me inside.
It would be great if we would only confide.

　　—Stephanie Hancock

Was I There?

What did I do for someone today?
Was I there when they needed me near?
Did I offer my hand to steady their way?
Did I help them to hold back a tear?

Did I listen when someone was hurting?
Did I brighten their day with a smile?
Did I bring them a token of kindness?
Did I offer to stay for a while?

We all need somebody to listen.
We all need somebody to care.
You may be a light in the darkness-
You may even answer a prayer.

—*Shirley Berry*

Winter Love

The snow falls with love
On a running stream
Where the love of the ice skaters was found,
Their hearts attached to one another.
Traveling, traveling light upon dark
And day upon night, love upon each other,
With their hands reached out,
The leaves falling, the flowers blooming
And the love budding.
Rain on the eyes and tears of happiness
In the time of winter.

— *Rebecca Alice Kaapuni*

The Restoration

The warmth—enveloping
cascading from a cloudless heaven.
The sea—inviting
a telling expanse, melting into the horizon.
The waves—forming, building, toppling
onto the sands of my existence
invading my being;
white and purifying—cleansing me.
I stand,
invitation accepted
surrounded, enclosed in warmth
yet penetrated and washed free
of the sorrows that lay heavy on my heart.
As my burden regresses into the sea
it's story adds a page to the tale beyond me
and the heavenly warmth fills the empty space inside
and I stand
restored.

—*Lisa Diane Mosier*

Untitled

I am wandering
Among these closing doors.
Within these darkened hallways.
Upon these cold wood floors.
How slowly pass the days
That aren't really days at all.
I'm waiting for the answer
To this question with no words,
Staying far from the reach
Of these demons and their swords,
And with silent cries beseech
To be let from these stone-cold walls.
I'm searching for the voice that can point
Me toward the view of a sun that's slowly
Rising and a sky of perfect blue, but my days are still
Disguising within my chamber halls

—*Simone Knowles*

It Wouldn't Work

I met you this year.
I couldn't think of you without a tear.
You meant so much from the start.
I never thought I could depart.
I hope you will always share
'Cause you know that I really do care.
I loved our time together,
But knew it wouldn't last forever.
And now that it's all over and gone,
It must not have really been wrong.
I just hope we can always be friends
And I know my heart will someday mend.

— *Christine Prell*

Where Eagles Fly

I stand alone within this nation
Without love or hope for me
All I need is inspiration
To forget the pain I see.

As the sun fills up my morning
And the wind wakes up my dreams
On my knees, I am close to heaven
Searching out, for what love still means.

From these walls that are built around me
Tears of rain fall from the sun
Lift me up on wings so lovely
To clouds of freedom one by one.

For in the shadow of a daydream
I see love where eagles fly
So take my hand to golden meadows
In the sky, Lord, in the sky.

—*Ralph Comfort*

Dare to Dream

Dare to dream with thoughts on wings.
Let imaginations soar.
Listen to you heart—it sings
As it never did before.
Dare to hope, when all around
Voices cry of human plight.
Fear and darkness will abound
Lest the spark of hope gives light.
Dare to live and walk alone.
Moving on against the stream.
Hope becomes the cornerstone
Of the building once a dream.

— *Silvia Parkins*

German Descendant

Genes are what make me German, but it doesn't
End with fate. I
Realize I am part of
My father's ancestry. I
Am part of
Not only German history but of a

Decade of Russian lifestyle. I am part of an
Era that split a family
Soon after
Coming to America in the
Early 1900's. I am part of a
Namesake trying to
Decipher
A family history being eroded by the
Never ending hands on the clock of
Time.

— *Shelley Wiese*

Indebted Still

Upon this hill that lingers still;
His death which leaves me,
Indebted still.

The bloody cross that stood on the hill,
Was given to me a sinner still.
Yet, made me whole, just like the
Prophet told of old.

He loved us then, he loves us now,
This great love has no end.
For the gentile's he gave to us the
Great Apostle Paul, through him
Unfolds it all.

That we might see this gift he gave,
Upon a hill that lingers still.
Which leaves me indebted still.

—*Shirley Anne McVay*

Sherriff, Bang Your Hammer

All banks are extremely polite
When dealing with a Third World blight,
But local farmers behind a plow:
Heavens! We want our money NOW!

— *Robert Emmett Clarke*

Untitled Expression

How can I write the scream
of a bullet writhing in the flesh and bone
splinter-bed heeled in a soldier's left foot.

Can I write the scream
of a newborn mother
with no mouth.

I write the scream
of a child who finds the white rag
in the bushes is her dead kitten.

Write the scream
of a throat stitched together
with the breath of a gutless cat.

The scream
of a voice frozen with
the anasthesia of hunger.

Scream
dancer with no feet.

It's the silence of total recall.

—*Sara Fairbanks*

Untitled

At first, through rhymers, words were sung
To strains of lute and mandolin.
Melodic blends that rolled the tongue
Ranged according to prescription.
Laura's lover began the form,
Idealistic solitude;
Sydney himself made it a norm
To write in an assuming mood.
All poets try to scale this wall
Of scheme and orderly meter.
In strict confines thoughts must crawl
Each trying to be neater
But can one's wits be full indeed
When closed in this poetic mede?

—*Rich Lawther*

Nothing Left to Say

When the disappointment comes raining down
And stops my heart from beating
And hope that cannot be found,
My soul runs full and cannot stop the bleeding.
What is a girl like me suppose to do
When there is not much to say?
I keep running back to you
But you always turn away.
I know what is in your heart and mind
Our love had a start and now there is no time.
Baby, your playing the the wrong dice,
Someday, you are going to pay the price.
You cannot listen to anybody else
You have to belive it yourself.
All the fun and romance has all gone away
Our love once had a chance.
But now there is nothing left to say!

—Lisa K. Anderson

Almost the Top

Once I wished uopn a star
I thought of you from afar
We had our laughs and so many good times
But we never had a nickle or a dime.

We had our laughs and many cries
And most of all we had our lives
At first we just had one another
Then it all had just got smothered.

We were going to run off to a far away place
So that nobody would recognize our face
But just when we got the very best
And thought that we had past the test.

Just as we got this very far
He had a wreck in his car
My life was never the same when he died
All I ever did was sit there and cry.

— Sheila Culley

My Poem

Some make sense, and others do not.
Some are loose, and some are taut.
They can make you laugh, or make you cry.
They can make you think, and make you sigh.

Some are free, and some can rhyme.
But there aren't any that tell time.
They take you places, they leave you home.
And that's the beauty of a poem.

I found this poem on a pad.
For it was written by my Dad.

—Rene M. Nadon

The Worst Sins of All

Deep in the hollows of ancient mind,
Through tunnels of darkness, 'round corners marked *Blind*
Lurks the not so hidden monster of all mankind...

Prejudice...

Monstrous greed since beginning of time
Has squeezed all it can and left only grime.
The rest? Fettered well for poverty's crime...

Avarice...

— Christine Howard

Life

Life go on
At time life seems
Like a chapter of a never ending story
But one day the story ends
The chapter is over
The book has come to a close
The climax is near
Then it makes you think of the beginning
What you really wanted
What the message was
What the living wanted to know
Not what the simple expect
Nor what the majority believe
If I except the present and I am content
Then the future for me shall never be
So I shall not give up my dreams
Nor I be content to believe
That what there is
Shall be all there will be.

—Teresa Lewis

Grandma's

I love my grandma's house
It's always peaceful as a mouse.
You feel so warm and good inside
You have no secrets to hide.
You feel safe as can be
And you never want to leave.
She's always making chicken noodles
And watching all of the kids.
She's very special to me.
We all love my grandma
And thank her very much
For grandma's are very special,
Especially to all of us.

— Tina Ogden

Impressions

Love's melodies from afar,
Stirring quietly in the air.
Waiting for the lady's attire.
As the people come and go.
Talking often of Van Gogh.

Lonely streets cry *Hear our need*
Children hungry, full of speed.
Starry nights smile, inviting sleep.
As the people come and go,
Talking often of Van Gogh.

Cathedrals and taverns
Madonnas and call girls
Lost angels bowing low.
As the people come and go,
Talking often of Van Gogh.

—Sandy James McCall

Fire

Quench this fire within me
that flame, a torch untouched
a heart unrelenting
by naked eye to see.

Give me,
a dewy kiss by candlelight,
under a shadowy painting on the wall;
a silhouette, a promise,
and a secret lullaby.

— Sandra Bowmaker

Returning Home

There's a rustle of the willows
And the low buzz of a fly
Clouds float by unnoticed,
Across the crystal, clear, blue sky.

There's a chirping of the crickets
In the fresh cut fields of hay
A hawk circling skies above,
Its claws clutched tight with prey.

The brook still gurgles gaily
Where as a child I did roam
Overflowing with old memories,
At last I'd made it home.

There as I recaptured childhood
It seemed all had stayed the same
'Till I saw the fallen homestead,
Down the dusty, weed-grown lane.

—Sharon Crooks Nash

Bring Me the Mornings

Bring Me the mornings
It has been so long since I shared them
I had forgotten their wonder
Everything is fresh
New
Never tried
And so much of the world has been
Touched
Mangled and bent
I had begun to think nothing was
New
Clean and open
Trusting
Colorful
Defenseless
I was wrong
Bring me the mornings
I am going to spend my whole life there

—Thomas M. Ryan

A Little Pony

Once I was a little pony
Bright and lovely too.
Running around, hoping someday
To be just like you.

Now, I am just as tall
Getting smarter and loving it all.
A great white horse, so strong and rare
To which no one can compare.

—Chandra Slotkin

Last Will and Testament

If I should die before I wake
Shed no tears for me
For I am with my Maker
As I was meant to be

Cast not my body in the ground
To be covered with the snow
But scatter my ashes across the fields
To let the flowers grow

Waste not my precious eyes
By burying them with me
But let them live forever
To let the sightless see

Mourn not my death, but speak of me
Think of me, and then
Continue on with life and living
For we shall meet again.

—Sylvia Burkhart

Ann

I hope you are doing all you wanted to do,
I hope you are happy; that I wish for you.
I am back in land with the rivers and hills that I love,
I am working, it is better than I had been afraid of.
I have given up all that, you know, was tearing me apart,
And am back on my feet, and taking new heart.

I remember the man who for years had survived his late wife,
Who quit playing the piano when he lost her, the joy of his life,
And you convinced him to play the piano again,
You were just ten then, and convinced him to play it again;
That is why I loved you, that moved me to tears,
Made me unable to swallow, I will remember, the rest of my years.

I will never disturb the new life you have made,
I have bid you farewell, and am on my own way.
I wish with a pang you could know how I have changed,
I know you would approve the new life I have arranged.
I am good with the children of my closest friends,
And, Ann, I am *Playing the piano again.*

—*Newton Brown*

To Imagine the Possibility

In all the world, there is only one key
To bringing together us all safe and free.
Be it nation or country or capital mistrust,
To agree on this one thing it seems is a must.
Why, with all of the people with whom we share this great land,
And with all it has given, still without it's demand,
Such a small part of each to be given at will
Could immensely obscure every life full and thriving just awaiting the thrill.
Every planet in our sphere would awaken with plight.
At the mention of love, they would gleam and bring forth light.
So why wouldn't we, with our problems and fears,
Simply try things together, open minded with our peers.
Democratic or Republic, would we not be the same.
If we truly expected the above without name,
Let beginning bring forth what we all know we need
And together till the end, we will be free from greed.

— *Phyliss Estrada*

From Journey

Sadness burst into squail overshadowing my hope to share a lapful of love
On Mom's visiting day. Instead, faint shrills were interloping my soul,
Echoing the supernal from beyond the hue of sightless moler. My depth
Drenched in darkness, in coma, enfurled in my screams! In falling through
The lightless lacuna insurrected Leviathan rocks towards me kept on to fall!

On descent I splashed down into my tears with my spirit bursting forth
From the depths of my thoughts. Perched on the bank, pristine, gasped in awe
As crossed the river veiled with tears. My exit emerged into a colorful
Nine month dream. Whispers of tenderness, fulfillment upon velvety depth
Shone forth in the dark the vision of my mind in the shadow of my soul.

Echoes reverberated through the hums! Screams of the hushed and hollow
Souls spouting forth the sheenless thoughts! The tomorrows were passing
The doorways of my pasts. From her passion has risen mine, then my depth
Teemed with glitter cascading forth from the shadow of my mirror. The light
Gently caressed my soul whispering through my sail! I began to scale the
Boundless sea. My fine-tuned thoughts escalated into mounting waves.
My teardrops left their path upon the dusty bumper,
then I churned under in infernal pain!

—*Alien Star*

Sailboat

Music, let me ride far away
From the frustrations of the everyday.
Let me ride your silky waves
Away from here
Like a sailboat
Far from the foggy shores we know here.

Spin a web for me
Containing the secret beauty
Of the feelings I want and places I'd like to be.
Let me view this ocean's beauty
Without the baggage of troubles
I bring with me.

Music, take me to a place of dreams,
The places I want every minute of the day.
Let me ride your silky waves
Away from here
Like a sailboat
Far from the foggy shores we know here.

—*Paul Peterson*

Merry-Go-Round

Perhaps, I should have been prepared,
Way back, when life was still a Merry-go-round;
Things were so fast and unsettled then,
So full of laughter, so full of vitality,
The Brass ring was within my reach,
But, I did not want to catch it; not yet,
I wanted to wait, I wanted to savor the moment,
The right time would come, it always does.
This Merry-go-round is not slowing down,
How can I make the ride last longer?
How can I prolong the ecstacy, the sensuality?
I want to stay on this Merry-go-round, until
I can no longer enjoy the ride.
In due time, it will slow down.
It will not be as exhilarating, or intoxicating
To ride the Merry-go-round,
Even the Brass ring, so shiny now,
Will eventually lose its luster and radiance...

—*Nancy St. Laurent*

I Saw You There

I saw you there
          standing . . .
   just standing
     tall and proud
I wanted so much
  to go to you
          to tell you . . .
But I didn't
I couldn't
  there were others
    their eyes watching
            always watching . . .
I was afraid
  afraid
    of what they might say
  if they knew
        only knew . . .
I turned away from you
Now you'll never know
           unless . . .
  I go to you
    the next time
          if there is a next time . . .
I see you there.

—*Ann Nickell*

Secrets of the Moon

The eyes of the moon play in the darkness
As it plays in the body of the sky
It knows come morning it disappears to the day,
To that it only sighs, as do we all.
    —*Theresa Nelson*

Untitled

There was, then, a full moon.
Full of light and joy.
But now, there is nothing.
No more light, no more joy.
There was, then, a full moon.
It was full of everything.
Nothing to make it full now.
Just darkness, and darkness.
When there was a full moon,
There were stars and there was space.
Now, no stars no space,
No more light, no more joy,
Just darkness, and darkness.
    — *Molly Shaw*

Untitled

From the sea of tranquility you rose
And with the power of life you drenched me
With the warmth of the sun
You enlightened me in knowledge
Through the silence and peace
You spoke more than words could ever say

The day brings your light into my life
The night leaves me breathless, a bit empty
But the shining stars and glowing moon
Fill me with your presence
And fear no longer exists
    —*Margaret Masferrer*

Night Cycles

Fragile is the night
Unbeknownst to those who fear
Darkened shadows traveling through their dreams.
Memories of unspoken terrors
Harbored in the deepest sleep
Arise out of nightmare's madness.
The strength of light from dawn comes beckoning
Glimmering with new beginnings.
Hope projects from out of darkness
Colliding with newfashioned daydreams.
The daily cycle thus refreshed
Until the darkness reigns again.
    — *Lesley A. Bizyak*

Saturn

Smooth moves, empires meet, air stands still, time depletes.
Energy builds, particles attract, spheres surmount, solid, compact.
Endless travel, speed of light, embrace the stars, blinding bright.
A new world evolves, creation exists, soft so white, heaven is bliss.
Swirls of glory, dancing stories, rejoice in darkness, lying still.
Floating on waves, ripples flow, splashing crystals, colors glow.
Sounds in silence, forever is here, pleasant surroundings, neverending
Clear. Beauty widens, stars shine, harmony calls, yours and mine.
Earth and sky, meet in a day, time evolves, throughout your stay.
Places and spaces, on the ground, close, far away, together abound.
Believing creating, images alike, visions flashing, there is life.
Words are spoken, not all is said, signs of meanings, confusion instead.
Long to fulfill, weakness to strength, time disappears, there is no space.
Clouds bursting, light so white, love is born, pure in sight.
    — *Mary A. Latallade*

Untitled

Oh moon so high that shines so bright,
Tell me what is the secret of the sky.
You are there with each passing night,
Above the earth with all your might.
When I look upon you above all else,
It makes me feel like I've never felt.
I forget my trouble, I forget my fears,
My sadness and my tears.
I feel as if I'm in a dream so far away
But yet comes another day.
    — *Tamara D. Burford*

Forsythia Days

The yellow daffodils on the hill
Nod promises of
Mellow thoughts
And happier tomorrows.
Runners jog by
Wearing new pinks and purple
Looking not quite so grim
As they did in winter.
Our neighbor behind us
Repairs his fence and
Prepares his garden
For greenbeans and summer squash
The laughter of coatless children
Makes me feel young again
While fickle rain and snow
And harsh winds blowing
Make me smile at the ways
Of forsythia days.
    — *Margo Mase Thiele*

Iris at Frosted Dawn

Half closed bud of iris at frosted dawn,
Your petals, like my heart, rest in shadows;
And solitaire you are, your leaves hang low,
Sunlight moves us, tender as infant fawn.
In crept Adonis, like breezes so still.
The sun he brought, and your life did begin;
I too, did wander, keeping Eros in.
Yet my heart he touched, I loved at my will,
Yet seasons loom on fate, and fall brought fear.
Oh love! for Hades's bullets killed without grace
Death did slap my soul with icy embrace,
Near sacred ground I kissed him, tender tears.
Christened in peaceful spring, our love was true,
In time half closed buds shall bloom anew
    — *Leonora Rita Obed*

Willow

I know a place, a quiet spot, beneath a willow tree,
To sit and dream and watch the sky in aimless reverie.
I taste the fruit of summer days, sun-warm and tangy-sweet;
And hear the birds protest the theft of what they thought to eat.

A lazy flick of summer sun floats through the gold-limned leaves,
To shed its gleam, like fairy coins which dance on sun-browned knees.
The sky, a deep and intense blue, lights up my lacy cave,
Takes up my thoughts and sorts them through,
and gives back dreams to weave.

I think those thoughts and weave those dreams and drink in summer peace;
Then leave my secret, sunlit spot all-filled with gentle grace.
To take up life, with freer heart, by faith and joy embraced;
By sun refreshed and sky renewed, while in my special place.
    — *Mary E. Holmberg*

Fallen

How soft you were up against my skin,
Your face smelling like the fresh fallen rain.
I do remember you holding me and feeling you there,
Your strong but ever so sweet body
Standing there and your face down, bare.

— *Kathleen Hemmers*

Crossroads

It seems only yesterday that our paths met;
Intersecting upon a crossroad on our way towards
Some unknown destination.
Days of joy and companionship soon followed;
Yielding many a moment deeply cherished and adorned,
Laughing and singing by daytime
Or sharing our utmost secrets by night.

Those days shall never lose their priceless value
Though your path turned south and mine north.
No, our memories may they never be mourned
As yesterday fades on becoming yesteryear.
For you are with me even now.
Yes, your home is here my friend, in my heart.

— *Mike Sorenson*

Freedom

Why can't I have freedom over me
To love and to please whatever I see?
Why can't my heart expand but so wide
Especially to a friend that's always by my side?
Why can't I have freedom over my love?
There isn't one gift greater than love.
Love isn't like a rose, it won't wizzle or die.
Love is a four letter word that won't say good-bye.
Why can't I have freedom over my love
So I can have memories to look back on when I'm old
And to share with the loved ones that are there to share
Even if they really didn't seem to care?
Can't I have freedom over my mind
So I can be worthy, truthful and kind?
And there shall be no bombs to destroy my peace,
If so, the noise from the bombs will also decease.
Why can't I have freedom over my eyes
So I can seek and find and won't be surprised?
Surprised to see danger or come what may,
I'm looking for freedom starting today.

— *Sharon Alsbrooks*

A Boy Story

She is sitting at my
Gravestone
She doesn't know why after all this
Time
I am gone
She was always with me; for me; of me
But now we are two separated by God and Earth and Gravity
She wants to understand
She doesn't know why she was left behind
It wasn't bad for us
I look at her from a lead painted sky
I try to show her
She remembers how I couldn't catch a football
She remembers how I couldn't climb a tree
She remembers how I always lost at hide and go seek.
And suddenly she knows
I am not dead
I am at last alive

— *Melissa Rountree*

Joe Louis (The Brown Bomber)

I was a champion boxer and winning was my thing
I held my title belt eleven years
O' so much fam!
I gave lots of my winnings to charity
And for that they taxed me
Lord why? all that time I spent boxing, poor I've
Got to die
Remember, my name is *Joe Louis* Lord why?

— *Raymond Banks*

Untitled

Why is it when the sun goes down
    all is quiet,
as if the animals have
    purposely locked themselves in the cages
    built by others?
That should be the time to take
advantage
    of living in the quiet.
No one yelling or crying to the perpetrators
about the wrongs they've committed
or bragging about all they've done
to escape the conformity of society.
It should be the time when dreams are established, goals invented
and answers found.

Walk into the cold night air, find yourself a rock and firmly
resolve all the things you will do for yourself.

— *Kelly VanCamp*

All Alone

The north star guiding couples in the park
Maybe someday I'll follow it all alone
You tell me your leaving
Without a single word
Now for me to go on all alone
You came in and out of my life like a bird someday, someone will
Make up for this, you say you loved me and you cared
But now you're gone like the sound of the sea, so I go on all alone.
Your words drifted far away should I now understand.
Why does love have to fade and all my dreams turn too dust
But for me to go on all alone
I'll get it one day
Like a boy catching a ball
I'll soon someday understand
All alone.

— *Missy Currie*

A Theme in Avarice

Plumes of snow radiate ascotted archs of thin, electrical length.
The sky twines sideways in relief of its own surge of air.
In its engulfing silence, there is only their silent x-ray.
And then their own cool twins of sylphs of air
To fight into the night, there is a beaded air curve
Moving like the tearing dreams of rain.
But like diamond in convergence
There is only its twain, its patter of summer sun birth.
The existence of its head of cold ice and the
Flashing path of its engeneering.
When an arch of length swings around the moon
We are left with the folliage of summer.
When clouds appear like henna in the sky, the fall of its path is indicative
Like as and are, there are so many rainbows in the sky
That we unlike twin asbestos mating of the earth's sea, wind and air
Can only find its flask long enough for one
Swift, steady throb of drink.

— *Lisa Miller*

Turbulence

Orange lips
Dancing
In turbulence
In the hazes of the night
Our bodies forbidding
What our heart cannot
We are nested
In the waves of our mind
Drifting from the sound
Disillusioned by what we see
Yet able to comprehend
Another sound
The sound of pain
The sound of cries
The sound of yesterday
We cannot deny the inevitable
We cannot deny reality
But we can deny ourselves

—*Malyssa Rollf*

The Hermit

He's societies' unwanted
He lives alone
He cares not what you think
The world naught for him.

He's society's undeclared
With only his mule for a friend
He cares not what you want
He has no home to call his own.

He's society's untrained
The mountain is his home
He cares for the world
The world cares naught for him.
He is an undesireable
He does not exist
He lives alone
No home to call his own.

— *Michael Lanitis*

Lonely

Do you feel lonely?
I do.
It's a feeling you can't pinpoint.
You feel gray, or is it blue?
Do you feel lonely?
I do.
It's kinda different.
You don't feel anything, or can you?
Do you feel lonely?
I do.
You want someone near, or do you?
Loneliness is hard to figure out, or is it?
It's lonely.
Do you feel lonely?
I do.

—*Micheale Frye*

James Dean

He died a tragic death,
Yet tonight I can turn on the TV
And he's there talking to me.
Alive and well.
His face shows hostility.
His eyes show sincerity.

He's a rebel without a cause.

— *Mindi Horst*

Child's Play? Only in L. A.

The sun shines brightly dring the day
while innocent children are at play.
As night falls—
Violence beckons its call.

And as if it were a sacrificial rite,
A gun shot pierces through the night.

A child lay bleeding in the street
with sounds of screaming at his feet.
A family's sorrow will take time to mend—
An American dream has come to an end!

All so senseless, all so brutal.
Yet it happens every day—
...only in L. A.

— *Timothy O'Brien*

From Where and Why

I came into this world, gasping for breath,
I screamed, as air entered my lungs
Letting you know I'd be fine.
I grew and learned to talk and walk.
Soon discovering things on my own.

Childhood illnesses did I encounter,
They went away.
I broke a leg, it healed.
I learned to read and write,
And how to get along with others.
I learned to listen and absorb
What I had heard and learned.
I started to question, you couldn't answer.
I turned to others, their answers were false.
I prayed to God, and he was the answer.

— *Shannon Kniffen*

Abortion

Some say they agree with it,
Others say it's wrong,
But tell me, what about the baby
That's dead and gone?
I feel it didn't have a right,
Nor a chance to stand on its own.
When rape is the case,
I can surely see the point,
But just because it was a mistake,
I can only see the sorrow.
That little baby that wanted to live
Won't even live to see tomorrow.
It is up to you to speak your own voice,
But think of that baby when you make that choice.

— *Jenny Webb*

Do Not Live in Deep Despair

You feel so very alone,
After your mate is gone.
Do not live in deep despair,
You have friends who really care.

Your heart is filled with grief,
From which you get no relief.
Only time has a way of healing,
That empty, sorrowful feeling.

Letting the tears fall are part of life's scheme,
But your grief will slowly become like a dream.
You need not have any misgiving,
About coming back to life with the living.

So look up to Heaven above,
Reach out for God's healing love.
Do not live in deep despair,
For above all others, He cares.

—*Mollie Hoffman*

Abortion

The one that you got
And you didn't see
Is a moral question
Not answered by me
Abortion now for the poor
That was not thought of long ago
Life is a seed planted by need
A decision is made
Before the next one reach their grave
Life goes on just as song
In the hearts of mothers
Who share their love, bless the child from above
Some dread bringing a child to life
Dread the need might be their sacrifice
Most noble work of man and wife
Is to raise a family in this life.

—*Rozell Caldwell*

Broken Heart

Everytime I see you,
I wonder how you feel about me.
Seeing you again hurts so badly.
I remember how close we used to be.
I have been looking for someone like you
For what seems to be a thousand years;
I cry myself to sleep at night,
I count at least a million tears.
Wishing our relationship was like it used to be.
I am sitting here alone
Thinking of reasons why you left me.
My world is slowly falling apart.
I do not believe I went through
All the love and pain
Just for a broken heart.
Now all I ever do is hope that one day
I will be completely over you.

—*Michelle H. Schuldt*

Alone...

I walk alone on a long beach
the wind passing me by
ans if it were going somewhere
I look back and see
no footprints from me, as if I were never there
I try to run where I can be seen
where I can be known
But I still walk...
and think to myself
along the beach that never ends...

— *Megan Jones*

Truth

The gaze of a child
A timid breeze
That longs to disturb
The freshly done coiffure
Of the dignified matron
Who fears she is going bald

A wonder
To the tale tellers
An instinct to the simple
Who live nothing but it

A hope
Whose winds will invade every niche
And sweep up all within its grasp...

The gaze of a Child.

—*Kristine Vrooman Altman*

A Strong Wind a Callin'

I have often wondered of the mysteries of the sea.
It is an awesome sight, but yet, she has beauty.
Somehow men have always been drawn to the sea,
I guess it is the adventure, the want to be free.

I hear a strong wind a callin, the sea, she's callin' me.

She's callin me to a time ago,
To wooden ships, sunken treasures, and stories untold.
I hear a strong wind a callin', is she friend or is she foe?
I hear a strong wind a callin', I have got to go.

My friend, won't you come too?
Together we can find out if they are myth, mysteries, or true:
Davey Jones' locker, Atlantis, and other mysteries of the deep,
Even the mermaid. Careful my friend, your soul she could keep.

It's so peaceful and quiet now that we are down under,
So many men have given their life to the sea, it's no wonder.
You can know what we must see, just listen for the callin' of the sea.
When you hear, listen but beware, 'cause we'll be forever waiting there
To share your company, at the bottom of the sea.
            —*Mark T. C. Bounds*

My Life Upon the Sea

I've lived my life upon the sea
Now I have no ties to hinder me
I'm free to roam the world from here to there
Seeking good times and good friends without a care.

I've been around the world from Saigon to Rome
I've visited the ends of the world from McMurdo to Nome
I've seen the wonders of nature before me lain
The seas, the mountains, the valleys and the plains.

I've seen nature's creatures both wild and free
The creatures of the land, the creatures of the sea
I've met the people of strange and foreign lands
In peace and war I have clasped their hands.

I've joined them in laughter and I've joined them in song
I've joined them in sorrow when loved ones were gone
Some have brought me sorrow and tears and pain
But the joys outweigh the sorrows so I cannot complain

Some day my wanderings must come to an end
My bones committed to the sea, my life long friend
She'll hold me to her bosom there in the deep
'Til the day of redemption my soul shall she keep
            —*Russell Glendenning*

My Father Was Just an Ordinary Man

My father was just an ordinary man, but to me he was special.
He took care of me and showered me with love from a young age.
He held me, told me stories about life during my youth.
He had no formal education, this father of mine,
But all that he did have, he gave to me, his mother's wit.
People he told me about and what to expect from them.
The life that he shared with me, will be a memory
of wonderful things and pleasure.
When I needed attention as a child, he was always there.
Time is something, he had, that he did give freely to me.
Explaining to me that life may not always go,
the way that one might expect.
I never thanked that man for being my father.
So, now I want to say, *Thank you, father.*
My life would have been a bad experience without my father.
I do wish that every child could have what I had, a father.
            — *Mollie Hall-Keller*

Storm Wind

I spring from the sea and race to the land,
Blow ships from their course; with cudgel in hand.
I buffet the waves and snow-deck their tips,
Then smash them to the land as if driven by whips.

I race up the shore and bend back the trees,
I twist them and turn them then snap them with ease.
I pick up a leaf and drop it afar
Then lift it again as I curse at a star.

I howl and I scream as I pass on my way,
I take a bright sky and I turn it to grey.
I batter the birds as they try to pass by
Then worn out with living, I melt in the sky.
            —*Michael C. Hartland*

The Morning Mist

Look into the window
        And watch the silent drops of rain.
The mist of the early morning
        How beautiful it looks;
But in your heart you can feel the warmth
        Of the sun coming up.
The hot, burning sun rising with its rays
        You look out the window
And realize that there is no sun,
        No rays to beam through, no glare.
Your heart's cold and sad
        And you feel like crying.
Then, up in the sky
        Comes a single light of joy.
The rain has gone away
        And so have the hurtful tears.
The mist is still there, but oh...
        How beautiful it feels!
            —*Melissa Martinez*

Ruins in Bloom

I feel sharp scratches of frozen rain
As winter seeps through my window pane.
It creeps past the cracks in caustic clots,
And fills up my head with thorny thoughts.
Winter wraiths upon my empty walls
Dance like shadows in my empty halls.
When will these winds ever rid my room
Of lingering ghosts and your perfume?

As all the summer seeps from my brain,
I feel sharp scratches of frozen rain.
            — *Michael David Wilhelm*

Beginning

A new beginning—a new dawning—the sun rises
The day is bright, the air is cool, dew is like
A wet blanket over the green flooring.
Greet the day with a smile—deeply inhaling the
Invigorating air. I want to dancew, turn,
Jump with glee—what will today be like—
How will I make the flowers bloom—Each pluck
Is love—love of life—love of a daughter's
Smile—love of a mother's hug—love of a
Sweet bouquet. Don't you smile when you see
A bunch of colorful balloons?
Yesterday when I walked down a path—each day—
Sometimes I stumble and begin to walk on the grass—
The day is gray—sad. Today standing on the path—
Dusty—I saw before me—straight with tulips
And mums—brightness—I grin—she skips along
Holding my hand—I whisper, *Happy Day!*
            —*Mildred McCluskey-Hilliard*

Seasonal Spectrum

Trees barren
Icicle daggers stab crunchy snow
Autumn aftermath

Earth thaws
Jonquil nods on graceful stem
End of winter

White clouds in blue sky
Downy beds for giants
Blowing smoke rings

Sand castles deserted
Dissolve in swirling surf
Summer's wane.

    — *V. R. Hailey*

The Old Oak Tree

The old oak tree stood strong and tall
In her own domain
Watching the little acorn grow
Young sparrows nesting in your branches low

Who made thee so tall and strong?
God has made thee from an acorn
You were made for man's supplies
I am thankful for the oak tree as I arise

Old oak tree, you are tall and strong and mighty
You are made for rest and shade
As your branches stretch out with age
You are worthy of the wage
But only God can make a tree

    — *Violet Knowles*

The Healing Place

The beautiful images fill my head
and I look longingly towards the mountain.
The lush, green pine
beckons me...
I am unwhole and broken.
Empty and alone.
I travel to be healed.
It is a place of silence.
Slowly as time passes,
 I begin to feel whole again.
The pieces slowly come together
 rebuilding me.
Breathing the fresh air
 I do not wish to leave
But I know I must.
New I return to my life
Only to return broken next year
 to be healed again.

    —*Alyssa Verdu*

Trees

Trees,
How brave they must be.
Standing tall,
Next to me.

Trees,
All the changes and the fuss,
Red orange and yellow,
For all of us.

Trees,
Though unappreciated, ignored by most,
Except those who stop,
To look.

Trees,
Fighting the weather till it falls,
Briskly,
To the ground.

    —*Antonina Marie Miceli*

Rain

Rain, rain go away
Is just a children's rhyme
But when the rain comes to stay
There is just too much time.

Too much time to sit and think
Too much time to stay inside
Some people may start to drink
But with me, my thoughts abide.

My thoughts abide with me, I know
Sometimes good and sometimes bad
I just wish that they would go
For often, too often, they make me sad

I like the rain, oh yes, I do
It is just that it stays around
Oh, what am I to do
When my thoughts abound.

    —*Elaine Gray*

Waiting for Tomorrow

Standing by the ocean
Walking hand in hand
Sitting in the moonlight
Running our fingers through the sand.

Following our hearts
Searching through the sorrow
Patiently awaiting
Looking for tomorrow.

As the days pass by
Watching for a sign
That will bring us together
Somewhere in time.

With all our love
We hope and pray
That sometime a tomorrow
Will be our glorious day.

And when our day has come
We'll walk hand and hand
And sit in the moonlight
Running our fingers through the sand.

    —*Anita Marshall*

Mementomori

Browning sky through
Horizons filled with
Falsettos fingered through
Dried air.
The smiles
They all come to groan about
Groan out.
In rows and rows
Seated
Waiting for their
Personal Armageddon.
Clouds grow red with unanswered pleas
And days are shorter than
The sun's
As she fought to write,
It is done.

    —*Arline Bennett*

At Eventide

In the evening breeze I hear a song,
A hautingly beautiful melody,
Drifting softly through the air.
In the quiet dimness of twilight
The hills take on a look of etched ebony
Carved by tender loving hands.
It is at this hour of eventide
That I experience total peace,
And feel whole and complete as a person.
This is when the world stops
For a miniscule look at itself.
Then, I see myself without fear,
And without hesitation, I can say,
I am somebody because I am me.

    —*Vivian E. M. Willis*

The Next Day

Life will be very different,
Yes, the trees will grow towards the sky,
And the grass will be a beautiful green
Once again, but, it will be a different world,
We will have to start over
But thanks to our knowledge and education
We will succeed only if we work together,
Life had its advantages for some,
More so than others,
This may not change, but
The next day will bring hope for some,
Sometimes hope is all you need.

    —*Patrick Loveless*

A Tree Is Best Measured When It's Down

Down, a tree on craggy lie, dies poised
beneath itself—high stub, a forest stilt
above its crest—companion mast to severed
life. Feathered ice refracts the cold grey eye
of buzzsaw hungry to deliver noise
into the swim of snow and wounded filth,
like a wheeling song, unvaried, bites the air—
a taunting whine is monotoned on high;
it hacks the stem and desecrates the void.
The logger's slant is set to create tilt,
but revving pressure, angled tremor errs—
the pine half-free, is hanging half-in-sky.
How measures now *this* tree against their glue
and polish purpose, yawning down the slew?

    — *Norma R. Lockwood*

Mountain Stream

On one sultry, summer Sabbath evening
I went out for some fresh air breathing
High atop a mountain where I had never roamed.
I drove along not really caring
in what direction I was bearing,
When suddenly I saw flowing beneath some weeping willows
a cool, clean, murmuring, crystal clear, gurgling mountain stream.
The water as clear as crystal
made me so very wishful
to stop and bathe my weary feet
While the gurgling, murmuring sound of the water thrilled my very soul.
The water was like poetry, mystic and fugitive, telling with mystic rhyme
its stories of time.
Telling of Indian braves and their maidens and their love of long ago,
Telling of the white explorers so brave and bold
and how they stopped here in days of old,
Telling how it helped the early settlers who came here years ago,
And the waters murmured as the breeze stirred the trees,
Tellling more poetic stories oh so beautiful, or so it seemed to me.
Night came on and I had to leave it,
this cool, clear, crystal, murmuring, gurgling mountain stream,
But I have never seen anything more lovely even in my dreams.

— *Velma Robinson*

Love Is Like a Bird

Love is like a little bird flying in the wind,
Flying over the trees so high, then resting on a limb,
Not quite flying low enough for me to put my hand on him
Love is like a whirlwind that takes us up so high.
We feel like we're on a cloud nine as the world passes by.
Love is like being on a mountain top and not ever wanting to come down,
Shutting all the world out and pretending not to hear a sound.
Love is like a snowflake floating to the ground.
With all the snowflakes around us, we never hear a sound.
Love is like a child who waits for Santa Claus
With his spirits so high when he should be sleeping like a log.

— *Virginia Wills*

What It Means to Be Alone

Life can be rough and hard to deal with at times.
It can get really rough when you're alone.
Everybody needs someone, that someone to help you through rough times,

Someone to spend time with, someone to love and hold.
When days and nights get long,
you need someone to help you get through them.
And when you have problems, you need help;
that someone can and will help you with them.
And when you're down and blue, that someone will cheer you up
and make you happy again
And will keep you warm and safe through the night.
And when you're sick and not feeling good,
that someone will make you well again.
Everybody needs someone. The road to happiness can be a long, hard trip.
If you've got someone like this, you better hold on to them
if you don't want to be alone.
It's no fun being alone.

— *Henry C. Schrader*

A Prayer to God

God, please help me through my stay here on earth.
I need Your guidance and love through my life here on earth.
I need the hope and compassion of a loved one.
I hope You can help me make the right choices and decisions through my life here on earth.
I believe if You are really up there I won't die until I make my mark in this world.
While You're up in the sky, can You please guide me through every step of my life?
P. S. Thank you for your guidance and love.

— *Amy Swallow*

Life

You wish it would last
Forever
Though you have no idea
When it really started
Nor when it will end
But
Is there really an end
If we can't remember
How it started?
Why
Should we think it ends
When it was eternity
From the start,
A beginning
With no starting line
And no finish line?
It is always
And forever.

—*Emily Link*

The Way We Were

I will never forget you
The way we were,
But I knew from the beginning
It was to be you and her.

Don't try to explain
The words you have said,
Explanations cannot erase,
The tears I have shed.

Just look at me
And let my tears fall,
No other actions
Can change my feelings at all.

I will say goodbye now
I will not make a fuss,
Because now I understand
It will never be us.

—*Genna Gagnelius*

Courage

Courage is the one thing
Every man wants,
Every man likes;
But not every man has it,
For it takes courage to
Step out of the status quo.
It takes genuine courage
to do the unusual and unique,
For it is not the life
That one lives that matters,
But the courage one puts into it.
That courage that's what matters.
Courage to speak the truth
In the face of possible
Prosecution and suffering,
Courage to stand up to one's beliefs,
That's what courage is,
And this I'll always stand for.

—*Gene James*

All Night Long

Lay me down
Hold me tight
Make love to me
All night long.
Kiss me sweetly
Kiss me long
Never let me go
All night long.
When the day breaks
And you are gone
My feelings for you
Will still linger on.

— *Heidi Lynn Bujok*

Beautiful Houses

Just see all of the beautiful
Houses,
It took those widows too
Many spouses,
Before they were wed,
A tiny little room they had,
Now that they are brides,
And grooms,
They have just to many
Rooms,
Now it is plain to see,
Just how they live like
Royalty.

—*Geraldine Davenport*

Fifteen

Hopelessly enveloped
In hostile loneliness,
Crumpled with fear,
Stalked by the past,
Smothered by the present
And haunted by the future.
Boom!
Shatters the
Midnight gloom,
Evoking
Deafening
Silence.
One boy,
Fifteen,
Lost forever.

— *Henri Emerson Walker*

Sweet at the Beach

Love is sweet, enough to eat
Like candy, love is dandy
With the two of us each
At a sandy beach
Walking hand in hand
Along to the band
Playing in the water
With alot of laughter
Loving each other,
Forever together
I am always happy with you
Our times are special too
I will love you forever
And never say never
We were meant to be
So be with me!

—*Amie Dawson*

Ann and Jim

Once upon a time
In a far away land
There once was a girl,
Her name was Ann.
And she had a guy,
His name was Jim.
Everyone in the village
Thought they were meant for each other.
Then one day Ann found Jim with another.
She ran home and cried herself to sleep.
That night she dreamed that nothing happened.
When she awoke,
She thought her dream had come true
Because when she awoke,
Jim called her and said, *I love you.*

— *Jeni Jennings*

Home

Home
I want to go home
Home is a place where you can trust your friends
Where there is love all around you
Where people respect and understand you
Where people take you for who you are.

As I look out the window
I see the rain fall
The children run to the shelter of their warm houses
All except two, a girl and her brother
They both huddle in a dark cold alley
They have no home of any kind to go to.

Home is the trust, the warmth, the love
Home is where the heart is.

—*Erica Tescher*

Safety Valves

Children have their teddy bears,
And others have their blankets.
Grownups have their alcohol,
And their nicotine habits.

But me, I had my scissors,
And my razor blades, too.
They created for me a big
Safety valve for me to use.

I became addicted to the use of this,
Needing to let steam off too often.
I've got to quit *cold turkey*, or
They'll have *suicide* marked on my coffin.

—*Deena MacKenzie*

Love

Love is like a prism
The white light of life,
Bland and sterile,
Approaches its transparent walls
Without knowledge, without purpose.
The forlorn rays of human existence
Exit the crystal chamber
In a burst of energy, of feverish emotion;
Transformed to a passionate frenzy of colors-
A vivid spectrum,
An erotic spectacle of illumination
Dancing fervently to the rhythmic beating
Of Cupid's wings
Lighting the path to a brighter tomorrow.

—*Debbie Mann*

Untitled

From thine hair falls length;
Flowing...like a victorian dress.
You render me no choice. A pound of gold,
For a story untold,

What does to me your voice.
To me natures child was forever you.
Crystal stream, a mountain, a brook.
When to wade or climb, did I,
Beneath my feet, the ground you took.

Yet I did so much love you,
Still some could not conceive,
How a king of many kingdoms...
Would give, yet not receive.

Was it chance or was it fortune?
Could it have been meant to be?
Such a feeling of overwhelming peace,
Was I...when you...with me.

—*Jay Seigel*

Our Baby

Teddy bears and rattles,
Giraffes and little yellow ducks.
Toy trains, cars and boats
And abundances of trucks.
We never imagined being parents
Could bring to us so much.
The love our child gives us
Leaves beautiful memories untouched.
His eyes of innocence see life's wonders
For the very first time.
Now, even when it's cloudy,
In our home, the sun always shines.
Thank you Lord for his love,
Thank you for this gift of life,
Having been brought to existence
Together through love of husband and wife.

—*Dorry R. Flynn*

Sad Song

I'm not going to think about you, I'm not
Going to say your name.
I won't think about how it used to be, because
It'll never be the same.

But then why do I have you on my mind?
Why do I think about you all the time?
I just can't help to think how nice you were.
I've been thinking your love was my cure.

I see how mistaken I am.
It's not just you, it's every man.
But then why do I have you on my mind?
Why do I think about you all the time?

—*Jennifer Cory*

Untitled

Have you ever wished upon a star
That winked at you from afar?
Well, I have wished and I have prayed,
That you'll come back one of these days.

Have you ever found a four leaf clover
Then thought your troubles were all over?
Well, I have before and oh! did I soar,
Till I realized that you needed more.

Have you ever cried until the dawn
Because someone you loved was gone?
Well, I have cried till I thought I'd die,
But I realized that I must let go and say goodbye.

— *Bekki Camden*

Sleepless Mornings

I cannot sleep
So I watch the sunrise.
The sun that sets golden teardrops
Upon my tired eyes.

The longer I watch
My fears go away,
Knowing the sun
Has turned the night into day.

— *J. Joseph Nelson*

Orcha

An Orcha mother
And her mate
That mate for life
Living on sea lions and fish
Mother holding her baby
Ready to give birth
A baby boy she has had
She sings her song of lullaby,
Like no one else,
As she greets her master
As to her, he is the great one
Very gently they touch noses
Signaling love
As if she had everything in
The world she has ever dreamed of,
Love from all humans.

—*Hollie Johnson*

The Fugitive

He runs blindly into the night,
Fearing only for his life.
His heart beats widly,
As he hears the sound of footsteps.
Hunted like a mad dog,
He runs faster than wind.
A twig snaps,
As the weight of his body falls.
Not daring to breathe.
Nor fear of giving himself away.
They spotted him,
There is no chance for survival.
His last thought,
Dear God please forgive me.
They can't harm him,
For he now is free and safe.
Forever and ever eternally safe.

—*Heidi Snyder*

Reflections

Phone calls, homework,
Schedules, friends,
School bells, energy,
Knowledge, trends,
Smile and chatter,
Life so free.
Somebody's changing;
I think it's me.

Old and tired
With life's autumn glow,
Toiling daily,
Keeping with the flow.
Young people's laughter,
Words to share,
Actions spoken to show I care.

Time escapes without a doubt
And I'm still learning
What life's about.

—*Diane Bergstrom Boaz*

Your History Textbook Never Told You

Let me tell you Indian stories
You will not find in any textbook:

Indian Baby's diapers deerskin
Lined with fuzzy cattail feathers;
Mother rinsed pouch in the river
Very first American Pampers.

Indians were as clean as could be
Through the long and lousy winter,
Huddled tight in smoky teepee,
Springtime muchly need bathtime.

Looked for pond beside an anthill;
Stripped off clothes and dove in water,
Soaking in the Indian Hot Tub
While the ants performed their service.

Every louse and nit was eaten;
Clothes all clean and body also.
Ants and Indian both were happy...
Instant Martinizing!

—*Grandma Margy*

Sitting Next to Nature

As I sit by nature's side,
I feel the cool wind blowing.
Wind, like an icicle, stabbing my flesh.
The radiant sun in the heaven's above
Melts the icicle and heals my wounds.
I'm at peace with myself.
My friend is at my side.
Our tranquil surroundings
Puts peace in our minds.
Evilness does not exist
While we are sitting next to nature.
Sentimental emotions
Erode our thoughts,
As we sit with love in our hearts,
A twinkle in our eyes,
And a smile on our faces.

—*Angela Stewart*

Think About It

Somewhere we have gotten off the track
It's not that we are white or brown or black
We are Americans
English, German, Jews or what
Ethnic origins should be forgot
We are Americans
We speak English as we should
Otherwise we're misunderstood
We are Americans
We can vote and we can pray
We can always have our say
We are Americans
So let's not worry about our birth
We're on the greatest land on earth
We are Americans

— *Grin Moore*

Rainbow

The colorful rainbow comes and goes
When tiny bits of rain fall from the heavy dark clouds.
As you wonder if there's a pot of gold at the other end,
The rainbow gets lighter and lighter.
Finally, the rainbow is gone,
Leaving a little rain behind.
Saying good-bye to the rainbow,
I sadly walk in the house thinking
It will come some other time.

—*Angela Jackson*

Ashes to Glory

When your life is bitter ashes
And your heart is filled with grief;
The hurt so bad—it can't be borne
Only Christ can give relief!

He is your fortress and your shield.
He is your hiding place.
He is the mighty comforter.
He alone can give you grace.

Come dwell in the secret place,
In the shadow of His wings.
This is the place of comfort-
Where the broken heart sings.

We walk by faith, not by sight,
And though the pain is great-
God changes evil into good
For those who trust and wait.

— *Carrie Joann Taylor-Grant*

You Taught us Well

You had a dream
To soar, to fly
High above the sky.

You were a teacher.
Knowledge was your quest.
To impart only the best.

In this our last frontier
You helped to pave the way.
You gave your life that fateful day.

We will not be daunted;
We will continue to explore,
Searching evermore.

We will search the skies,
Reaching into outerspace,
Your dream of knowledge to encase.

Though you may never know,
You achieved your goal.
Can you hear the children singing?
You taught us well.

—*Frances Avera Evans*

Love

It's near
I can feel it
The constent beating of my heart
It gets louder and louder
I am not sure what to do
The wind blows.
Making the trees sway
The animals scury, people scury
They want to save themselves
But how?
What is happening?
What have we done?
We are killing everything?
The world is coming to an end
What should we do?
Believe? Forgive? Thank? Care
No. Love

—*Veronica Lowry*

Love

I have the power to do things;
Things you can't explain.
I can bring you pleasure,
Or I can bring you pain.
I can keep you up at night;
Tossing and turning in bed.
I can make you too happy for words.
I can make you wish you were dead.
I live deep inside you.
I seep into your soul
I can make you lose the game,
Or I can make the winning goal.
Nothing can save you from my sting
Not even powers from above
For mine is a great title;
I go by the name of love.

—*Ashleigh Norris*

Scared To Show

There was a time not long ago,
When my love was not so hard to show.
I loved someone very much.
His love for me was not as such.
He cared for me, this is true.
But he cared for her; what could I do?
I loved him with all my heart.
I gave it to him and he tore it apart.
The love we shared was not meant to be,
For now that is plain to see.
For love is a feeling from inside.
Love is a feeling that is hard to let die.
I loved him for so very long.
His thoughts of love were very wrong.
Now my love is hard to express.
Each time I try I make a mess.
I am scared to let my feelings show.
Because of the pain I have learned to know.

—*Angela Bullard*

When Will Love Come Home?

A child plays alone
Wondering
When will Mommy come home?

A child eats alone
Wondering
When will Daddy come home?

A child lives alone
Wondering
When will love come home?

—*Virginia Teresa Crawford*

Fire Flies

The late evening sun has vanished
Red skies turn ocher across the way
Steeples of trees, lift to infinity,
Against the closing of the day.

Fire flies ignite their small white messages
Love-O-Grams shining across the dark sky
Night light in the closet of the evening
Floating lighthouses as they each pass by.

Suddenly they are disappearing
Putting out their lanterns for the night
Leaving tiny electric smiles,
Silver traceries that are a delight.

—*Victor C. Burnette*

A Word on Love

Strange what a man will do for a lady's love
Getting laughed at and made a fool of
As if there were something in the woman's eyes
That could be compared to the heavenly skies
I tell you there is nothing there
Is the curling softness of her hair
Or in the touch of her fingers cold
That is more valuable than a bar of gold
Let her go while you still have your senses
For in time she'll destroy all your defenses
And if by chance you found a love that's true
Then sad to say I have no advice to give to you

— *John Pudelski*

Elvira

Elvra there is no game,
People want to know the name.
Is she as fickle as a maiden fare?
Or, does she hide in a corner's bare?

What? Is a question to ponder
Eyes dance wanting to wander
Over the mountain vale, questing a man's sail;
Never is a word too pale, in the light of Elvira's veil.

Click of a heel with a quick
Dances the lilt of a pick.
To you Elvira, open her arms,
Embraces you her charms.

Never could you resist
The faint body mist;
Elvira you can insist.

—*Elvira M. Leon*

Still Lovers and Friends!

As the Sun touches my face,
A warm sensation goes through me.
I think you are still here.

As I open my eyes, I hope
To find you standing here beside me,
To take my hand and guide me.

Now reality is back,
And I understand,
I was just drifting in a fantasy land.

It was long ago when we said goodbye,
To an old flame,
And to love that died.

We are still best lovers,
If only in my mind,
And we will always be best friends.

—*Tammy Richards*

Family Crisis Shelter

Fractured bone, dislocated arm,
Blackened eyes, disfigured face...
How did she end up in this place?
Just what was her fall from grace?

Eyes resigned, her fight is gone;
Spirit broken, after so long...
Trying her best to understand;
Trying to please an angry man.

All she wanted was some love,
Then the push turned into shove.
Confused and hurt, full of shame;
Why does she feel she's to blame?

What has happened to her life
Since becoming his cherished wife?

— *Lynn Dixon Walters*

A Mother's Lament

O, babe of my womb
With a fine-toothed comb
You played on my fears
And reduced me to tears.

O, lost child of mine
Why were you so unkind?
Did I not give you life?
Protect you from strife?

O, my darling child
You were so very wild.
Filled with so much anger
In a world of such danger.

I truly tried with all my might
But in the end I lost the fight.

You've found your peace at last.
Free from the hurts of the past
As you lie there so still and cold
From a fatal overdose of pills.

—*Linda Jo Drumheller*

Tears on My Pillow

Lying on the pillow,
tear by tear.

Why, you may ask.

Why do I have to be
the one to stick out
from the rest?

Why, you may ask.

Why do I have to be
the one to do
all the rest?
Why, just why?

Because you are the best.

— *Susan Pavlicek*

Silhouette

I see your silhouette
Against the pale moon light,
A feeling flutters about me
In search for what is right.
Your sweet, tender body
A perfect shadow.
Your enticing, deep voice
A song so mellow.
I see your eyes
Glowing with so much joy.
There is a happiness all about you
As though once again,
You were a young, innocent boy.

—*Hope Burger*

Secret Dreams

You look at him,
He looks at you,
Both of you are wishing,
For your dreams come true.
You have the opportunity
He has the chance.
Both of you are here,
Hoping for romance.
You ask, *Why doesn't*
He like me?
So here is my reply:
He does, don't you
See he is shy?

—*Susan Still*

The Greatest Thing

Love is the greatest of all things
Satisfaction and joy it brings.
Love envies not but suffers long,
Love is willing to right a wrong.

Love and faith lead to heaven's door
Seek them and live forever more.
Love your neighbor along with foe,
Love all thru life while here below.

Kind, gentle, biding its time,
Love is patience yours and mine.
Greatest highest gift of all
God is love oh hear his call.

Thru the long ages of the past
Love is eternal and will last.
Other things will all fade away
Love dear neighbor, love while you may.

—*John R. Kennedy*

Jack Frost

Amidst the mists
And coldest frosts,
With stoutest wrist
And loudest boasts,
He thrusts his fists
Against the posts,
And still he insists
To see the ghost;
He's the one
The mightiest of the mean season,
A loving, zealous son
Who lives among the coals,
Nourishing weary minds and hungry souls
Satisfying ghastly, thirsty hearts,
Never forgetting where he starts,
Always remembering his goals.

—*Lou B. Collins*

When I Am in Love

My heart is as light as air
Like a big red balloon.
See it floating way up there
In the sky above the ground
Towards the heavens it swiftly goes.
For this day I am in love.

— *Katherine Deighton Lapham*

America at 6:00 PM

Church at twelve Sunday morning
Sleepy preacher tired warning
Children drugs, sex and beer
Carbon copies parents' fear
Education breaking down
Parents blaming those around
Cadillac cars and pleasure boats
Deep in debt on loans they float
Travel trips twice a year
Depression states and constant fear
When we're up, we say we've made it
On our own but bored and hated
When we're down, was due to those
Who struck a thorn upon our rose
Judicial courts crime is free
Freedom purchased with a fee
Shadows on the wall street page
Control our hate, our fate, our wage
America—the states you see
Are we the people inside me

—*John A. Pfister*

I Am a Person Who Wants to Fly

I am a person who wants to fly
I wonder why
I hear the planes over head
I see them
I want to touch one.
I am a person who wants to fly
I want to be able to go up high
I pretend I am in a plane
I feel free and happy
I touch the clouds
I worry if the plane will crash
I cry because I'm scared
I am a person who wants to fly
I understand it will be scary
I say I can do it
I try it over and over again
I hope I can fly one of these days
I am a person who wants to fly

—*Camie Russell*

Thank You...

I search for words to tell you how I feel
But they all seem to run away
And hide behind the statues in my mind
Then I slowly realized
Quite to my surprise
The words were always there
Just waiting patiently to be used
No fancy words
The ones down deep in my heart
Rang loud and clear
I love you
I miss you
And the little girl inside of me needs you
Still every now and then
You rock my world with a dreamy lullaby
And help me along to sing my special song.
Thank you Daddy.

—*Amanda M. Hofacker*

I See the Way You Look at Me

I watch you when sitting behind your desk
So intense and I try to guess.
Your smiles
Behind a disguise
Perhaps you are forsaken
And someone already has taken
Your heart and you are not free
But I see the way you look at me.
I see the way you look at me
You kind of strip and creep
I feel your touch so near
Yet so helpless you appear
I feel you in my gut
As your thoughts rush on
Your fantasies may go on forever
To be fulfilled never.

— *Norma I. Hernandez*

The Quiet Country Road at Night

The quiet country road
Is a nice place to be
Because I can talk to God
And feel quite free

The quiet country road
Is a cool place to walk
The moon is shining brightly
I love hearing the night animals talk!

—*Jennifer A. Calhoun*

Oh! What a Beautiful Day (Nature Walk)

The golden sun, the only one
Shining from the sky,
The busy bees and falling leaves
Fill me with a sigh.
The green, green grass on which I pass
And on which I play,
Gives me thought, for which I sought,
Oh! what a beautiful day.

The pebbled brook on which I look
Flows across my feet,
This show of shows, for which I know,
I have the best of seats.
Here I sit and ne'er forget,
What this life has to say,
I listen near, what do I hear?
Oh! What a beautiful day.

— *Dwight Haas*

Hats

How would you like to wear a hat that
was very, very flat
                    Or
                 Even
                    A
                  Hat
                 That
                  Was
               Taller
                 Than
                  You
A hat might have a million colors,
or might even say;
Have
        You
             Hugged
                    Your
                       Hat
                          Today?

—*Stephanie Berardi*

Untitled

I wish I were a traveler.
I'd go from shore to shore.
Walking on the streets of gold
I'd face the world with heart and soul.
I'd climb up every mountain
And sail the seven seas
Or linger by a fountain
Or climb a little tree.
I'd visit places old and new.
I wish I were a traveler.
Then someday I'd find you.

— *Elizabeth Elliott*

Before, During and After Rain

The sky is dark and cloudy
A small light breeze
Shifts the leaves on the trees
There is a faint smell in the air
Then the tears from heaven fall
Onto the earth peaceful and quiet
Feeding the sun dried dirt
Then as sudden as it began
The tears from heaven stop silently
Leaving the earth peaceful and satisfied
As if nothing really happened.

— *Jaime Makelin*

Heat of Colors

The sun was setting behind a hill,
Its rays blazed the sky.
There was a collision of fire's colors,
They all stood out, not one was shy.

It seemed as though the hill might burn
As the sparks fled into the night.
Their arms jumped out,
All the colors of fire took flight.

There was a scar left behind
From the heat of colors so bright.
It looked like a huge black hole
And so day, once again, became night.

—*Donna Appleby*

Walden Pond

Take a vacation
from mass communication,
over organization
too much verbalization.

Find a whispered communion
in a wind-borne reunion
where echoing bird calls arise
and smooth waters meet wide skies.

Discover fragile foilage fragrances
embracing pine-scented essences.
hold close to the momentary quiescence,
hear the whispering of sun-drenched silence.

— *Dorothy C. Brown*

Him

When we meet, I'm oh, so shy.
If I don't open up, our love will die.
I love him dearly but he doesn't know
I will never, ever let him go.
My love for him is deep; I only wish he knew
How much I care for him; my love for him is true.
He's oh, so kind and oh, so gentle.
You can tell my love for him is truly mental.
My love is old, my love is new, my love is real.
If he only knew how I feel.

— *Amanda Diaz*

Glimpses

There are times when I catch fleeting glimpses,
Of her beautiful and majestic form.
These are the times when life stop to stare,
Then move hastily on.

I observe her radiant beauty
When it appears in the first buds of spring.
When it appears on the face of a small child,
Playing happily in the rain.

— *Parthenia Ware Holman*

...From the Memoirs of the High Priestess
Turned Intergalactic Smuggler...

I was seven again today
I watched a girl get pushed to the ground
And kicked into the gutter until her screams stopped
I watched a husband slap his wife,
Watched lovers insult one another.
I watched elderly turned out of their homes
To find some cold place to die.
I watched my parents car explode
I watch myself murder a thief
I watched a police cruiser take
Away my wares and profits for their own use.
I watched the one I love walk away
In dismissal and step on a
Carelessly placed land mine.
Today I was seven again.
And I don't want to grow up.

    —Karen Klimsak

Hypocrite

I ask, *Are you a hypocrite like me?*
You answer in a tone of utter pride,
No, I am not a hypocrite like thee,
Although you spurn and scorn and curse and chide.
I ask, *Do you despise the deaf and blind?*
You say you have compassion for the weak;
I ask, *Do you withstand a crippled mind?*
You tell me that you understand the meek.
I ask, *Do you pass judgment on a man?*
You state with much repulse and more reprise,
No, I count color for the least I can,
And now I see deep hatred in your eyes.
I ask, *Have you known war and sin and strife?*
You whisper, *I'm a hypocrite of life.*

    —Crystal Lea Shiko

To a Damsel in a World of Distress

It is truly a terrible pity
That thou must endure this pain
But I jest, I'm sorry, I cannot feign
I get confused by things insane.

Perchance, it is possibly me
In my callous heart want sensitivity
But I see no point in your sorrow
For I'll always dwell in tomorrow.

What saddens you seems to me a trifle
A mere boy, who kissed but loved you not
By perspective my sympathy I can stifle
Pray, if a belle rejects me does my heart not?

So, fair damsel in a world of distress
Don't let a knave ever you depress
Keep thy innocence, beauty of mind
I hope your chivalrous knight you someday find.

    —Steven Nikosey

Looking at Me

Peering into the lake, I am amazed at what I see.
Someone is peering back, but who in the world could it be?
If I move, he moves; when I smile, he smiles too.
Obviously, he likes me and the things that I can do.
I reach towards the water so that I can touch his face
But as my hand touches him, he scatters all over the place.
Pulling out my hand, the waters become still.
Now once again I can see the face, the face that I can't feel.
Now I realize who he is, that person that I can see.
The person that I've been peering at, that person, it is me!

    — Tracy Oakwood

Time Spent with You

Funny how time changes, your needs to me separated again.
Why do we repeat rather than change?
What we're able to.
Our lives together brought different changes to both of us.
We decided on growing old together,
Loving each other was more than desire, it burned in our souls.
We had our storms. We had each other.
Our love changed and grew, we understood more of the other.
The more we experienced together, the more we grew
To meet each situation we out grew part of ourselves.
Only memories used now, no titles or names.
For our lives has had another change.
We grew and learned hurt brings tears and no respect,
Rejection causes damage to love
We both learned for now, facing problems is done alone.
I learned this from time I spent with you.

    —Theresa J. Hopkins

Escaping the Darkness

I cried out somewhere in the darkness. I was slipping away.
The moon shone down on me and it showed the fear and sadness.
I could no longer stay here with you. I had to leave to somewhere.
Somewhere I could cry freely and escape the loneliness I was feeling
Here. My mind had no space left to run to. Nowhere to go and cry for
Love. Nowhere to go to see the sunshine, only darkness around me.
And as I slipped away, the moon disappeared and sunshine came
Out, and with it the happiness, where it could stay forever, now
That I was gone.
Gone to my own place, filled with freely flowing laughter, and life.
No more darkness, or sadness, or loneliness.
I may be missed, but where I am is where I belong,
Alone and free.

    — Tracy Hemry

A Promise

Once,
You promised me, a rose forever,
My dreams, were of its, love and beauty,
Delicate petals, fragrant, warm as ones blood, unadorned splendor,
Oh marvelous rose, what splended thoughts,
Feelings for the future, filled my being,
Petals forming one, young buds, fruit, a life line, a gracious vision
Of love, you gave, the rose you promised,
I accepted, this flower, with my soul,
As time passed, how I tried to preserve, all its meanings,
Mercilous time, my rose, my glorious rose,
Its color is fading, fragrance gone, pedals dry,
You promised me, a rose forever, with tears, I watered,
My beautiful bloom, live on, live on, so tired, I have
Become, as my rose, dried, welted petals, on weary palms, you
Gave, the rose, you promised, strange, I never saw, its thorns.

    —Theresa Zuber Alonzo

In Memory of Mauricio Paul Chavez

You were a pal to all of us.
Why you would do this is way beyond us.
You helped everyone through their problems.
We just wish we could have helped you with your problems.
You made me laugh when I was blue and down in the dumps.
After we talked, I was in the ups.
The day we all found out, there were a lot of tears in school.
We all thought you were so cool.
We love you a lot and we'll keep your memory in our hearts.

    — Kelly Reynolds

The Children

We are the leaves on the branches of life,
Who will make and create a tomorrow.
We are the ones who hold the hope,
For a long and lasting future.
We cannot pass by, without ever thinking
Of where our actions may lead.
I hope and pray there will be a time
When we won't fear what the next day will bring.

— *Monica Wesley*

Teddy Bears

Teddy bears make the best of friends.
Their listening and caring never ends.
They're always willing to give a hug
And show you that they'll always love.
Teddy bears love to listen
And when you're sad, they seem to make you glisten.
Teddy bears aren't really the talking type.
Into listening they put all of their might.
If ever a friend you need
A teddy bear will always do the deed.
My teddy bears are more special than I can say.
They bring me happiness in every way.
They keep my every secret thought or dream
No matter if it's nice or mean.
So if you're ever in a bind
In a teddy bear, a friend you'll find.

— *Tracie Burkitt*

Our Child, Our Present from God

Pretty blue eyes and snow white skin,
A little blond hair standing on end.
Legs that wobble as they strain to stand,
Five fragile fingers she entrusts in my hand,
Trust and love, wonderment and joy,
The world is her plaything, her own giant toy.
There is something to be seen wherever she goes,
Whether spotting tall trees, or her own little toes.
She looks with amazement at all that she sees,
And with innocence abounding, tries to catch bees.
She demands your attention, no matter the time,
And hour upon hour her little legs grind.
And when she gets weary her eyes start to droop,
She holds up her arms and reaches for you.
She brings us hours of laughter and lifetimes of love,
And at the end of every day, I thank him above
For the great treasure of life he has given the world
And for our own little treasure, our own little girl.

— *Richard Wilson Fox*

A Baby's Precious First Steps

A baby's first steps, so precious, so few,
And each little step taken was once taken by you.
They crawl, then they stumble,
They struggle to get up, then they fumble.
You encourage them to try again.
You can see the twinkle in their eyes because they know they can.
They fall over once and then stand tall.
Then you say, *Just one more step, that's all.*
Finally they take that one tiny leap,
Then they are safe in your arms and soon fast asleep.
In that one precious moment was a memory that will last forever,
And you and your baby will always be together.

— *Connie Stevens*

Two Little Feet

Two little feet dancing with me
One goes left, and one goes right

Two little feet dancing with me
Now it is time to say good night.

We will dance and we will sing
You'll be queen and I'll be king
When we look up to the stars
We will wish the world were ours

Two little feet dancing with me
In the land of make believe
When the moon shines in the sky
Then it is time to close our eyes

We will dream the whole night through
And wake up when the day is new
Two little feet dancing with me
This is the end of our story

—*Susan Gombos*

My Mother

A queen to me she seems to be
This wonderful lady who is my mother.
Throughout the years her love's been there-
Her patience for me it seems no bother...

My love for Mom will never die.
I can count on her when times I cry-
My mom's the best as all would say-
But for real she is—she makes my day.

Thank God for Mother, my guide in life
For she was there through all my strife.
Thank you, Mom, for being there,
But most of all for the love we share.

— *Teddy R. Hill*

A Mother's Prayer

My beloved daughters, my beloved sons,
Come hold my hands, touch my cheek,
Sit beside me.
My heart bursts to tell you loving
thoughts that should be said.
Be wise, gentle, guard your speech;
use discipline in all things; desire
not what you cannot have.
Discipline a restless spirit;
Bring calmness to your heart.
Days grow short, eyes grow dim.
Heavenly father, hear my prayer.
Let not my children pass away
without seeking a path of
righteousness, keeping thy commandments.
Guide them, Bless them, see them worthy.
Christ Jesus our Savior, Amen.

—*Sophie Padilla*

Grow Up, Little One

To my sweet unborn child,
The pain I feel for you makes me wild
In this world you are to be born
Is full of hatred and scorn.

Grow up, little one,
And make this world a better place.

Now there is no one left to dry my tears,
No one left to silent my fears.
Daddy is gone far, far away.
You and I are the only ones who will pay.

Grow up, little one,
And make this world a better place.

I wish I could protect you
But what would that do
For someday, I will be gone
And you will have to face another dawn.

Grow up little one,
And make this world a better place.

—*Theresa Roy*

Despair

I see a young girl in the trees,
Her hair entwined in a lovely breeze.
She looks so sad and far away,
She is frightened, but she would not say.
My heart aches, as she weeps,
She looks more peaceful when she sleeps.
Help the person in despair,
She needs a life of love and care.

—*Coleen McKeown*

The Special Children

You walk into the classroom,
it's scary at first;
Your heart thrashing hard
like it's going to burst.
You don't know where to begin
or even what to say.
It is quite hard
on your very first day.
But the children you meet
are very unique.
Their actions, their emotions
are the language they speak.
A special relationship
you share with each other,
And later you'll see
you've learned from one another.
It's a grand experience
to see what you've done,
When you've made a special child
feel like they're number one!

— *Christie Francisci*

Remember the Child

Do not neglect the child who plays on the lawn
When she asks you to play with her.
When she plays alone, watch her.
In her games are hidden the answers to all questions.
In her dreams are the realities of future worlds.
If you become distracted and turn away,
When you return your gaze, you will find her gone.
The lawn will be empty except for the deserted doll.
Every so often her laughter will echo distantly in your halls
And when you catch your reflection
you will see a glimmer of her innocent eyes in your own,
But she will never return to play.
The sun has set on those days.

— *Zdena C. Quinn*

Someone Like You

It is a special privilege to know
Someone as special as you.
Someone who opens my heart and
Lets me give to you all I can,
Someone who knows me completely
From the inside,
Someone who knows my fears,
Insecurities and my dreams,
Someone like you understands my
Needs and desires.

You make me realize how special love can truly be.
When I think of love, I think
Of you and your gentle touch,
Your deep kisses and sweet embrace,
And how happy I feel when I am near you.
Just you being you, is the most precious
Gift I could ever receive from anyone.

—*Kendra Pandalis*

To Our World...Our Great Nation

The sky has turned to a world of wonder,
Filled each day with the grace of the wind.
Silenced by the imaculent thunder,
While bolts of lightening twist and bend.
A sword of sunshine slices the clouds.
In search of light to capture.
Rain which once soaked the crowds,
Now leaves the earth great rapture.
As sunlight smiles upon our earth,
I notice, in admiration.
The sky and sun give love and birth,
To our world...our great nation.

— *Lisa Tinsley*

Who Will He Be?

Who do I love?
Why isn't it clear?
Won't I ever feel,
Like I am near to the one I will love?
Who do I need?
Why don't I see?
When will I know I have found him?
Who rules my world?
Won't I ever see, won't I ever know?
Why can't life be a friend to me?
Who is near to my heart?
Who is dear to my life?
Won't I ever know the feeling so free?
Won't I ever know how it would be,
To love him, love him, love him

— *Linda B. Platt*

Shattered Dreams

I turn to look for your face,
I see only the world pass by,
There is just an empty space
For you, my friend, have died.
I don't understand why it happened to you
You seemed so happy and carefree.
I still cannot believe what you've done is true.
You know you could have come to me.
The last few days you seemed so faraway,
So down and so blue,
I really wish I could have helped you to stay
Why couldn't I see the clues?
It's time to say goodbye, my friend
But I'll always wonder why
You had to end your life so suddenly
And why...why...you had to die?

—*Cindy Johnson*

Love's Kiss

Fill my thoughts
Drain my heart
Cause my tears
Catch my pain
Hold my hand
Break my love
Drink my trust
Kill my need
Take my laughter
Possess my soul
Rip my words
Crush my mind
But always kiss my lips

— *Lorey Gelb*

A Concept

Fact,
Function,
End,
Means...
Creating
Concepts,
Living
Dreams...
Proposed
Purpose,
Itself
It seems...
Minimum
Method,
Remains
Unseen.

—*Karl Schaeffer*

Love

Three kinds
You for yourself,
For others,
And for all.

You for yourself
We all possess.
You for others
Is possible.

You for all, here's the rub
Altruistic love,
The all knowing love
And God's love.

Some day...
Ah yes, some day
When I know myself.

—*Dale A. Sinclair*

The Swing

The swing was joy.
Freedom of flight
Friendly breeze
Magical lift
Swoosh of braids.
Her favorite playmate.
A fatal friendship.
Her mother's hatred
Of the broken rope
The fall
The struggle
The death.
Bitter despise of
The swing.

— *K. B. Milek*

The Nightmare

Darkness;
Fear attacks all inner systems
Nerves are on edge;
As the nightmare comes.
Not one of death, or evil,
But of fear itself-
Fear of being unloved,
Of losing you.
In the silence my hands reach
For something to grasp
And hold onto; something
With which I might finally
Pull you closer and keep you with me
Forever; but all I touch is darkness,
And the nightmare goes on. I am afraid;
Afraid of being unloved-of losing you.

—*Leslie Collins*

An Old Man's Memories

The old man sat quietly down
He made a crude, somewhat frown.
Life could not be all that bad,
So why then, did he feel so sad?

Thinking back to so many years past
Of memories that would always last.
He recalled a time when he had fought
For all the truths that he had taught

Remembering also, the time he lost
All his close family at a high cost.
The pain, the teras, the final touch,
Brought back, oh, so very, very much.

Reflecting back some eighty years
Of a life filled with little fears.
Dreaming away of the love he had known,
Realizing that he was not on his own.

The old man stood to go
Time was quickly running out, I know.
No more frowns to make a crease
He had finally found his peace.

—*Linda Anzaldua*

Remembering

I may not see you with my eyes,
But in my heart you shine.
You made each day a special one,
The world was yours and mine.

You always did the sweetest things
With a smile upon your face.
No one will forget you, dear one,
And no one can take your place.

Now I will close with a tear on my cheek,
I am crying and in sorrow.
But I will smile again for you, dear one,
I will smile again...tomorrow.

— *Cathy Cummings*

Friends

We've never had the chance to be
The best of friends, you and me.
There aren't many friends that will be true
But, I know I can count on you.

You've been with me through good and bad
You were always there when I was sad.
Our ups and downs will never end
As long as we are true best friends.

—*Christina Jo Lane*

My Mother, My Friend

I often wonder how life would be
If I were alone, sentimental and free.
I'm my own person, that will always be
Though I'll never forget who first loved me.
She opened the doors and led the way,
Yet why is it now she's being pushed so far away?
My youngest years I needed her most.
I gave her my love while in return she molded me into my very best.
Now I've matured and my life is my peers'.
Why couldn't I stop to see her silent tears?
Have I neglected her love right before my eyes?
Deep within my flesh my heart begins to cry.
Teenage years are such a sudden change
Why couldn't I stop to heal her pain?
Now I realize what I've done; I've left both our lives unfair.
But I came out shining bright because I know she'll always care.

   —*Kelli Dippo*

Between Friends

Perfection you said you saw in me
Disappointment was surely your destiny
A friend was all I claimed to be, Compromising my own identity.
Circles of madness we all engaged;
Emotions and trust, we felt enraged
Words and thoughts we held inside, daring not to risk our pride
I ask what's wrong, you turn away.
What did I do? You will not say.
How can friendship be based on this? Communication must exist.
Arguments pass and anguish may fade,
But the memories I have
Will always remain.

   — *Kelli A. Fasano*

Teddy Bear

I am of many colors because I was made of scrap material. I'm
Lonely; no one plays with me. She has outgrown her childhood, now
She's a young woman. The only company I get is the tabby, old cat,
At naptime. At night I no longer sleep on the bed with her; she just
Throws me on the floor. And in the morning, as soon as the bed is made
Back on the bed I go to await my company. *One day,* she tells me sometimes
When she is sad. *You will belong to my little girl.* I just think,
If you throw me on the floor one more night and let your new puppy dog
Get ahold of me I won't be around that long.
But one good thing I do know, she still cares for me cause I'm her one
And only best friend. How do I know, well because she told me so.
I've listened to every word she's ever said, through the good times
And the bad. I've kept her safe through the rain and thunder of the
Stormy nights.

   — *Kim Gardner*

Wee Ones

God's greatest wonder, deep inside, flares at first, then burns bright.
A tiny candle deep inside, eternal light of God's own might.
Question not nor try to explain the wind at night, dew stead of rain,
For that within can only be felt, for in His presence, all words melt.
Learn whilst young to temper your sword and accept the toll
That chastisement brings within thy soul,
Soon to be in that heavenly row in His presence all things grow.
Feel this now and grow without pain; chastise thyself and Heaven remains.
Abiding within, God's love abounds, spiraling higher with every round.
Trust thry heart to chastise thy soul.
First nature 'twill be as ye grow old.
Cast off human nature, overcome the toll;
Rise free of the world, God's grace secured in thy soul.
Cling to Him now, redeem thee He may, sanctified now and in latter day.
Chastising redemption from day to day; close to himm thy will always stay.

   —*Linda D. Dunnaway*

Memories of Yesterday

The old plantation stands deserted now, through the shadow dimly cast
Mice and memories hover in the corners, of a civilization long since past
Memories made in gardens of flowers and fountains, parties, charm and
Social grace women in beautiful gowns and jewels.

Children running with laughter and joy, happy wonderful days of play
Growing up in a land of magic, never worrying about another day
The rumors began of a war to come, to make all men equal and free
Thousands would die so needlessly, as the civil war came to be.

One of the bloodiest wars to be fought in history
As the south lost the battle, with Sherman's march to the sea
Those days are long since gone, on the winds of yesterday
They are no more than a dream remembered, that we read about today.

   —*Keli Pinkston*

Alone

You are my future, I must forget my past.
Grief, anger, love turned hate; I hold to those memories fast.
I can care; I can feel. Dead emotions rise from dust.
I can give you my laughter, soul or heart; yet I cannot give you my trust.
Don't leave me just yet, darling. hold on to me a little longer.
I can forget, I promise this; for you are what makes me stronger.
You ask for my caring, my affection. for you, this I change.
You ask me for unlimited trust; It stays just out of range.
You asked me to let you have me; to open up, let feelings flow.
This I did, then started loving; yet just how much I did not know.
You asked me to let you touch me; This would be my fresh new start.
I held you, needed you next to me, then handed you my heart.
But nothing good lasts forever, as I did not need to be told.
For tonight I need to hold you; and you are not mine to hold.

   — *Jody Thompson*

Image

I imagine a room.
I enter the room.
The room is huge and as I looked around the room,
I think white walls, soft, white colored walls.
Then, there's a window, an open window to space and time
And on the window hung curtains, sheer curtains that moved softly
But briskly to the melody the wind played
   while through the window passing.
Next appeared columns of great height that reached from the ceiling
To the floor and between them sat a baby grand piano that I sat to
And began to play softly but briskly like the wind
   blowing through the window.
And with this composition of sight and sound, there was harmony
Between the room, the window and me.

   — *LaTrall Simon*

Autumn Tears

The autumn leaves gracefully fall from the trees.
Shadowing them are the patterns of my falling tears.
The leaves seem to fall with no feeling, not realizing that they are dying.
My tears, however, seem to flow knowing that the end is soon to come..
As the leaves fall, the tree becomes bare, alone
   and with nothing to protect it from the harsh realities of the world.
Also, as my tears fall, I begin to feel alone and unprotected
   from the hardships that I must face.
When all the leaves have fallen and have been blown away
   by the wind, the memory of what the tree once looked like
   is still remembered by those who cared enough to glance
   at it while they passed.
When all of my tears are wiped away, the memory of an emotionally
   disturbed girl can still be noticed by those who care to look deep
   enough to see the truth.
As visible to se as the names of sweethearts carved into the trunk of the tree
   are the hurt and pain that is etched into my heart.

   — *Cheryl Tremblay*

Growing Up

You are really tall and fast growing
You are so tall, it is really showing
Oh no, there is a pimple on your face
You cannot cover it up, oh what a disgrace
You are a teenager now, you grow up so fast
When you were little is all in the past.

    —Jodi Biaso

Alone

She sits alone,
The little grown up child.
As she thinks
They are thoughts of sadness.
Why?
She is alone, all alone.
No where to turn.
Friends really?
Parents, maybe.
Alone
Forever...

    —Kristen Jelormine

Tell Me

The tears in my eyes
Are hard to disguise
That after all these years
There is something to hear

When you told me you loved me
It was the greatest thing to hear
Only to go out on me
Was enough to bear

Now I see you with her
Is it only for a day?
Tell me, do you love her
Did she steal your heart away?

I am finally getting over
Of what I thought was love
To find someone new
And to think of

Tell me, does it hurt you
Like it hurt me once before
To find that special someone
Who has helped me reach the shore

    —Kathleen Bracy

Ode to Childhood

How long ago it was,
When small dirty hands
Chased the bumble bees buzz.
When cheeks were round and tanned.
Feet ran through the grass bare,
Warm and fuzzy puppies
All had innocent stares.
Oh, childhood was happy.
Winter playing in barn straw,
The ground covered with snow.
'Thought my nose would never thaw.
Frost bite on my toes!
Childhood quickly came and went.
I survived, somehow.
Wonderful times were spent.
Those days are gone now.

    — Dawn Adair Burger

Lost

See the boy in the dark over there,
Eyes big and blue, his skin color fair?
Do you know why he stands there and cries?
He can't stand to watch as his puppy dies.
Tears streaming freely across his sad face,
Some from each eye as though in a race.
He still loves that puppy with all of his heart
But 'cause of this tragedy, they now have to part.

The above story is somewhat true.
The boy there is me, the puppy is you.
I lay in my bed as many tears flow.
The above tragedy is that you have to go.

    — Lisa Luznar

Future's Past

As I rippled across old washboard trails
To distnt channels my mind now sails
Of future's past and dreams cleansed clear,
Of forgotten friends and infant tears.

The American pie has soured with time
As baseball and Grandma simply decline.
All that is seen of life's future reverie
Are fragments of our shattered memories.

    — Stuart J. Scott

Acceptance

Spring is over and her petals are dry.
He for whom she waited never stopped by
And now she knows that he never will,
So all of her hopes are dead and still.

When the autumn wind blows hard and strong,
When her petals have dropped and she is gone,
He will walk by so strong and so tall
And never remember she was there at all.

And this she knows,
So quietly she goes.

    —Deirdre S. Gough

As It Seems

I see the creature running swiftly
Through the mellow dawn,
The build is smaller than a mare,
Yet greater than a fawn;
Projecting skyward from its head
There seems to be a horn,
It is no devil from the woods,
But a lovely unicorn.

    —C. Eric Apple

Insane Children

Psychiatric ward this world.
Insane children
Of alcoholic father,
Opiated by misery;
Of home we lost memory.

Strolling in the yard
By the psychiatric ward
We often find Dad
Outside the railing
Numb, drunk and damned,
A bottle in hand,
Profusely, profanely raving.

Threatens,
Would drag us home and smack
If he finds us passing the gates.
Home...the mansion...he states.
Who knows it is not a shack!

    —Kuttikkattu

Abyss Abode

I sit
In my old mind's abyss
Reflecting, pondering
What needs to be done?
The dirt brown walls
Are crumbling,
The only picture
Is upside down.
The floor is a wet muddy mess
With dirty brown water
Circling silently around me.
The only sound
Is of the grandfather clock
Spookily ticking away noon;
And my old rickety cot
Sinking into the muddy floor
And my own mind's cries
Matching the silently loud sound.

    — Lori Schaeffer

Tumultuous Vision

In the midst of
the blackest of nights
A seizure from below
terra bella
Pulls me from my holy aura
Hasten to evasion
Still lost in my own obscurity
A provident utterance
Confirms my very subsistence
Anchor my person
Within my whitewashed channel
Awaiting a cognate convulsion
Rest a throbbing head
Against my withered post
Retire me to sober repose.

    — Cynthia Maudlin

I Dance the God

I dance the god,
The winds swirl in time,
Wrapping 'round my spirit
With echoes of forever.
Together, we spin through today,
Creating eternity for now
And myself for all time
Like clouds leaping across the moon,
Laughing.

    — S. Hale Abbot

Don't Ever Change

Baby, baby,
When I look into your eyes
I see magic
As incredible as the path
We walk
In this world of rock 'n' roll
Faces look the same
Young and innocent
Ready to explore
An open heart
But you can't look
Back to yesterday
For I feel I can have the
Earth and the sky
With you by my side
Forever the world will
Look brighter so
Don't ever change...

—*Joy Laplume*

skipping stones
 rippling a pond-
lazy day
— *Charles B. Rodning*

Spirit Love

Lay back and let me love you
Let my soul caress you
You are wounded and hurting
From other lovers
Lie still as I draw back the covers
My God, how beautiful you are
Though others have left heart scars
Lay back and let me love you
Let my soul caress you
Gently, softly, let my fingers
Of love be pleasing
Lie still now, As I begin
Loving and kissing
My God, how beautiful you are
As our love comes together
I will savor this moment forever,
Lay back and let me love you,
Let my soul caress you.

—*Joyce Petty*

Death So Close

Death so close
Life let go
A body froze
From hand to toe.

Death so close
Inner fight
To live to choose
Life kept in sight.

Death to approach
Weakness to feel
To lie on the coach
From such an ordeal.

Death must wait
Not time yet
Must end the hate
Then die to let.

—*Charlotte Moriggia Fantry*

Destiny

Inspires our paths
Guiding life's fate
Directs many dreams
Daring to wait
Searches depths
And alarming heights
Manifesting visions
Relentless to fight
Travels near and far
Oftentimes, in harm's way
Never ceasing pursuit
Of rewards it must pay
When the quest is achieved
To conclude, it would seem
But rather, to follow another dream...

— *Joseph H. Canady*

Lost Friend

We said that we would never part
Together forever in our hearts
The laughs that were shared
The deep secrets that we spared
Now time has gone by
You are you
I am me
We couldn't change one another
Now we can't accept each other
You are in your world
I am in mine
We are not far apart
Because there is still
    love together in our hearts.

—*Leslie Edens*

We Are One

We are one.
I come as a bud
And reach full blossom.
Even through three days of rain
I have ripened.
I so delicate a thing
Survived the raging night wind.
I am only a flower
You are man.
Yet, such a mere thing
As maturity
Takes thee so long
To comprehend.
The right to fully blossom
Is given each of us,
It is just
A natural thing.

—*Zellie Rainey Orr*

Friends Are Forever

Friends go here,
And friends will go there
But you'll always know
A friend will care.

You'll tell a friend something
Special to you
And know they'll keep it
A secret, too.

Remember when you're alone
Or when you're together,
Friends are friends
And friends are forever.

— *Joy Traxler*

An Unknown Thief

She does not know it, but she steals,
Not goods or loot,
But from us to which our heart appeals.
She does not know it but she is a thief.
She takes them away and then drops them.
Like the first needle to fall on the Christmas reif.
Have pity because she is one of the nicest people you will meet.
But soon to your eyes she will deceit.
Have pity for this unknown thief.

—*Lauren Gilligan*

The Temptress

You can tempt man with but a smile.
I was one of those young men who passed
Through the gates of your Hell,
Clothed and armed with only love and innocense of youth.
How very easy it must have been for you to undress my
Heart and mind leaving me naked to my understanding of
Myself and weaponless in the war between good and evil.
Oh, destroyer of flesh and soul, yes I know you, yes indeed.
I must tell all my brethern of your trechary.
Death and damnation are your only true lovers.
The grave is your home and the pits of Hell your bedroom.
Many enter but few are able to leave.
Woe, oh woman of darkness. Your judgement will be severe.
Doesn't the shepherd take total blame for the loss of his sheep?

— *Lester R. Gayton Jr.*

The Long Winding Road

I see a path through the hands that cover my eyes.
These hands won't let go, for they want to feel my tears and cries.
I don't understand, but I heard a voice,
There are two paths and you must make the choice.
Now I was not blind for I could see
The many lost souls that were staring at me.
Fright filled my soul; I was never so scared.
I didn't look at them, for they didn't care.
Forward I walked down the chosen path.
It was long, dark and I heard the souls laugh.
The hands, they touched me while tears fell from my eyes.
I was lost in myself; I had no disguise.
I saw frowns, smiles above at the ceiling.
Somehow they knew how I was feeling.
I proceeded to follow the path of winding trails.
I had no faith in myself; I knew I would fail.
I came to the end and saw a bright light;
Being so strong, I lost my sight.
I was blinded in darkness but I heard someone exclaim,
That is the loser; she is to blame!
I felt the light pass me by, but a gust of wind lifted me high.
I felt those hands one more time; I wondered whose they were, but they
    were mine.

—*Lauren Esposito*

Mirrors

People, sometimes too often than welcome, are difficult to understand.
We all have thoughts and unwanted worries that often at underhand.
Although God created us as whole individuals; we are the same.
We all try desperately to fit in, we all play the game.
Each and every human being created by God should love.
Yet at times we are all arrogant, and instead we push and shove.
In many ways we are all relatives of very close relation.
Our family links are selfishness, and the greed that runs our nations.
Yet there are still some individuals that thrive on love and attention.
Love and attention not for themselves, but us, who give neglection.
If all humanity would come together in peace to strengthen our bonds,
Our planet would evolve into an ocean of love.
Which before was the likes of a pond.

— *Cheryl Herback*

Scared

The down has broken into death
They gave the living a shiboleth.
The life in everyone had died
Only the living deride.
As they haunt
Everyone is taunt.
The free will go on living.
Only if the dead keep giving.

—Diane Steele

Repose

Stretched out on a plain of grass,
Beneath a crystal sky,
Curtained by sunlight all around,
Just to lie, just to lie.

Thoughts pushed aside for a moment,
Worries lightened by and by,
The breeze softly lifts my hair,
Just to lie, just to lie.

Let the world go slipping past,
Let me float up high,
Above the wars of time and place,
Oh, just to lie, just to lie.

With closed eyes I see anew,
With this spirit I can fly,
The promises and peace of nature,
Under God's gentle eye.

— Jennifer E. Briggs

My Emperor

Your body...decorative...as juniper...
painted on a collapsible lantern...
which...lit...at my touch.

In my mind there is a jade palace
and a Jade Emperor...
where life is translucent without focus...

We walk to music...of a silent lute...
sharing love...extended in space...
cinnamon scents from the yam vine
shine on my Emperor's body...
beneath the plum blossoms...
his raven hair...reflects my image...
through dark eyes...
cups of sweet tea...and you
My beloved Emperor...are there
with me...
in my mind...

—Jay Son

Princess

The silky gray cat
Shimmers in the sun
On a stool which she sits upon.
She is soft
Like the silky smooth skin of a baby.
She looks as if she were misted with dew.
Her tail is like
A wilted yet soft rose petal
That is if she sits just right.
Her eyes
Are like a full moon with a drop of minty green.
When she walks she is like a princess
With gray locks of curl.
The crowd spreads as she walks
Like the gathering at a wedding
When the bride enters.

—Jennifer Ganer

Love's Light

Love's blinding forecast
Is fading fast,
Can it ever last?

Flowing through with ignorant bliss,
Fading slightly with every kiss,
The loving times all do miss!

Thoughts go floating far away
Some thoughts come, but never stay
There are so many they go astray

They shed a tear for goodness sake,
For all the sadness they are sure to take.
The sadness pounds and sets its stake.

The time will come to reconcile,
But how come now it seems so vile?
So, now love searches mile through mile.

—Jennifer Dolph

Sometimes...

Sometimes during our
Lives of sorrow and happiness
We come across certain people.
These certain people have this
Certain something within
Themselves that we ourselves,
Can relate to. This something
Cannot be seen, touched,
Nor heard, but can be
Felt deep in the heart of both.
Once this something is emerged
In both persons, a life-time
Friendship can be made. Once Found
If its broken, everything is then
Lost and the pain is everlasting.

— Jennifer Epperson

Death of the Sea

Beneath the waves life's secrets lie,
Oh, such mystery makes me sigh,
Above we hear the sea birds cry,
They swoop and glide across the sky.

The wind blows fresh, the currents cold,
The ancient mysteries eons old,
It makes me wonder why so bold,
The marching wavelets endless stroll.

I see the future by and by,
The sea, the sea may someday die,
So I must surely ask you why,
The sea must suffer from up high.

Oh God, oh God, oh why, oh why,
Does acid rain come from the sky,
Must man's cities make me cry,
The sea, the sea must never die.

— Don Scarborough

Hearts of Pleasure

The color of a shell could be soft and pure,
That's the kind of heart I want for sure.
The kind of shell that can make a gentle noise,
The kind of heart to feel all the joys.
The kind of shell that is for me,
The one for all hearts to see.
The kind of shell that could feel a touch,
The kind of heart that I want so much.
The whispers inside it that I could hear
Just makes me wish that you were near.

— Jennifer Schleper

The Lonely Ones

The ocean waves crashed against the shore,
Like the breaking of my heart,
The gentle silence smothers me,
I'm drawn back,
Away from the world,
A stranger,
In a foreign place, I've lived all my life
A world that doesn't understand,
Could care less about the feelings of many,
Only a select few,
The society high,
The rest of us are to follow them,
And only them,
The lonely ones,
Are the people,
That think,
For themselves

—Jennifer L. Pownall

When I am Ninety

Do you suppose when I am ninety
I will cut locks of hair
When they get too long
And stash Christmas cookies
In the parlor all year
For relatives who never come.
Will I wear my old gingham dress
Cotton stockings, and buyon shoes
To Church and say
If they don't like it,
They can look the other way!
And when it is time for Church pictures
Will I balk and say
I am not going, I am too wrinkled
Then when someone says,
How nice, a party when you are ninety!
Will I say, Who needs a party,
I have mobile meals!

—Jeri Evans

The Traveler

I remember a traveler of many years ago,
Who stopped by my home for shade,
He did not sit, just stood and sighed,
And expressed how he was so dismayed.
He mentioned of his travels to many lands,
And talked of the deeds that he'd seen,
He seemed convinced that of all earth's creatures,
It is man who plots to be mean.
He thanked me for sharing the shade of my eave,
And he said he must be along his way,
That he was trying to reach by his last sundown,
The end of a perfect day.

— Howard H. Mackey Jr.

George Michael

Your dramatic actions and vibrant eyes.
They are so mysterious it's hard to hide.
You're everywhere I look this is true.
Oh how the people want to meet you.
To touch and look at this man
Of course they want to hold your hand.
The sad part is they don't want to talk.
Your appearance is all they want.
The price of fame has its precious cost.
To give up everything and hope to never get lost.

— Jennifer Large

The Squirrel

While walking thru the woods one day,
I chanced to turn around;
And there I saw, to my dismay,
A squirrel upon the ground.
I picked him up and said, *Hi, there,*
Let's you and me be friendly.
I can't, he said, *it won't be fair;*
It would cost too much to tend me.
You wait right here, I'll call my mom;
She'll have you earn your keep.
You'll scare the cats and chase them from
Our house so we can sleep.
Wake up, my son, it's time for school,
And you'll be late, young man!
Aw, mom, gee whiz, don't be so cruel;
You spoiled my dream again!

— *Carl Scheffel*

Building Again

The tornado dipped dangerously,
Taking its toll,
Demolishing buildings,
Both new and old.
Before the wind ceased,
Or the falling rain,
The writing spider started weaving
A webb again.
Man emerged from his shelter
In a state of shock,
Begain building his home again,
Block upon block.
Oblivious to disaster,
Defiant to fate,
Exhibiting the spirit
That makes America great.

— *Willie May Anderson*

Silent Cry

I weep and weep but nobody sees.
I scream and scream but nobody hears.
My father beats me but nobody suspects.
My body is black and blue
But I am too ashamed to reveal the truth.
I feel such pain.
Some beatings have become so sore
While others are just *there.*
My emotional scars
Have become all but unforgettable.
Those days of odium still linger
To remind me of what has been
And what will be.
I tell you my troubled story
But you too will not hear
Enmity between my father and I.

— *Evelyn Peters*

The Shadow

An image of yourself.
Someone who has the same values,
The same hopes, dreams, ambitions as you
Only if he could talk as he listens.
He knows your secrets, fantasies, dreams.
If only he'd speak.
You know you would get along.
But when you turn around, he is gone
Until he is needed again.

— *Jennifer Holtz*

Life

Heaven's gate is open wide,
Wishing I were on His side.
Lying down, but not asleep.
Wondering if my dreams I can keep.
Take me now, love my soul.
Caress me please, you, Lord hold the key.
I do not like it here.
I don't have to live for tomorrow.
I do not have the will.

— *Hope Hahn*

Reverie

I felt your eyes caressing me,
Exploring, searching;
A prelude to love
Sang in my heart,
A love that was pure, unspoiled
By conventions, deepened
By understanding and trust.
Such ecstasy when first your kiss
Did with rapture enthrall me.
As we entwined in passion lost,
Knew this our destiny to be.
But all loves die
That lie unkindled, unnourished.
Only my mind now fondles
The memories that did enslave
My soul to thee.

— *Jim McHeffey*

My Everything

As I sit here with memories
of my life pressed upon my mind
I realize that the most precious ones
are the ones spent with you.
You are not only a memory
but a significance in my future.
You are the answer to my prayers.

You were my yesterdays, you are my todays
and definitely my tomorrows,
In which I look forward to that day
when we exchange vows,
To become not two separate individuals,
but as one—a whole:
Ready and willing to seek out
a new life and greet each day with a smile.
Let's face it, you are my everything!
You are my world!

— *Joan Zebraski*

I Know the Deal

For the past years we've been as one.
But something new has just begun.
Somehow along the way we lost what we had,
And now our love is turning bad.
I know there's a song *No Pain, No Gain.*
But does love have to cause a strain?
I love you with all my heart.
Maybe love was too much for you to handle.
And because of this I must dangle.
But in my heart love will stay,
Even if you want to sway.
Just remember the days and the hours,
When love was our only tower,
Even through the showers.
Maybe someday you'll see,
That we were always meant to be.

— *Evonne L. Owens*

Lost

I spend my life searching
But I am not sure what for.
I keep reaching for something
But it slips through my grasp
Before I know what it is.
I am forever heading toward a destination
Yet I never arrive there.
I am surrounded by people
But I feel so alone.

— *Dorothy S. Rothschild*

Hope

In the shadows of the world's conscience,
another ghostly, tired,
old weather-beaten ship,
packed with men, women and children
is sinking off the coast of Florida.

Twenty more desperate souls,
find rest
in dark watery depths.

Dawn will bring a better life,
the next horizon, the distant shore.
The human spirit like the hungry gulls
must soar—.

— *Audrey Emery Childs*

Dedicated to John & Genevieve Jackson

Everyone so silent, so sad,
A tide of blacks and grays.
I am uncomfortable, angry; with
No one to be angry with.
You're being lowered now
Inch by inch/ Grain by grain.
The dirt claims you,
The earth takes you in.
and you're gone,
and I'm alone,
and it's over.
The room is dark, oddly scented,
A tide of shadows.
I am weary, unfocused,
I have no energy, left for pain
The gilded cage faintly rocks
I approach bit by bit.
The dedicated body
Becomes visible on the bottom
and you're gone
and I'm alone
and it's over...

— *Genisa Jennings*

Reflections on a Tune

Fragments of a dream I thought I heard.
A solitary note whose presence only heralded
A melody so true should cause my heart to break.
Delicate—
Spun as a spider's web,
Equisite intricate Belgian lace,
Woven silver strands upon the air.
Sit here I in wonderment and awe
And accept the gift you bring.
Wrap myself in the fine-spun lacework warmth
Of sound.

— *Deborah Lee*

Remember

The sky grows dark,
The stars come out,
And, yet, I sit
Brooding over days
Long forgotten.
Remembering simplicity,
Times without worry,
Wishing things would go my way,
As it did so long ago.

Yet knowing
The past is past
And the future is near,
Knowing the sun
Will rise
To greet a new morning,
Wishing today
Goodbye.

—*Wendy Sprague*

Celebration

If you would do for me anything,
I would ask of you but one thing,
To drown me not in your sorrows.
For I have know enough of pain,
And life it promises no gain,
For postponing all of our tomorrows.
So come and share my celebration,
Know I need no complications,
As I seek the answers I must find.
And when the show is over,
We will need not run for cover,
And I shall be unafraid to die.

— *Nancy Lynn Ross*

Never

Even though we've been apart,
Thoughts of you still fill my heart.
I trusted and believed in you,
You were my guiding star,
But now whenever I look your way,
You seem so very far.
Every time I see you
I almost start to cry
Knowing down in my heart
We'll never get another try.
But that was very long ago
And now I do see
Maybe our love was
Never really meant to be.

— *Nicole Lea Keeler*

Oh To Be Free

A wild bird is flying high
The mountains down below
The lakes and streams intertwine
The meadows bright and green.

A cold and scary place in this
A fish without the sea.
A cloud is covering everything
The sun will shine no more.

The sky is just a fleeting thought
The lakes have long since dried
The meadows bright and green are gone
The feelings just pushed aside.

—*Barbara C. Donnelly*

Accepted

A member
But not a part
Of the group

A figure
With qualities
Of a true member

An entity
That is yet foreign
To the body

Trying to fit in
Adopting
The insignia of the group

Now rebels
As the true light shines
To show shadows

—*Yasmin Y. Rigby*

Starting Anew

Broken records upon the floor,
Broken dreams that play no more.
Yesterday lost, filling the past.
Memories gone taken at last.

A day, a time, so people say.
Starting new dreams as of today.

—*Beth Roeder*

Paths of Gray

Some roads go on
Some roads end,
Ours is a road
I can't comprehend.

It started out smooth,
But turned rocky more so,
What actually happened,
I don't really know.

What I do know is,
We took off and ran,
But one was too slow
To hold the other's hand.

Our grasp came apart,
And you kept your pace,
I guess that was the end
Of our long, drawn out race.

— *Amy Johnson*

Time

I feel the press of time
as a white hot brand inside.
Filling heart and soul with urgency,
a deep burning need to be.
Sand flows in the hour glass,
like life it runs too fast.
How swiftly life does flow away,
years seem to be but days.
Like wine, age holds no bitterness,
the taste of it is sweet.
But I cannot make time cease,
Nor slow its steady onward beat.
One day it seems you're young,
the next day you are old.
Life is like a precious jewel,
but oh so hard to hold.

—*Carl E. Edwards*

Blending of Eons

And the Lord said, *Let there be light!*
The future's past is led beyond present sight!
Whoever set our pace is not here to finish the race!
The chartered course is in space!

The recharged batteries carry us to the lasting stars-
From launches of a parkway of missles instead of cars!
Up and coming roadside vehicles,
Are transportation miracles!

Projected visibilities of today-
Forsee our future's array!
Thank God always, and let U.S. of A. pray-
May our defensive-star wars be here to stay!

—*Pierre A. LeBlanc III*

Lucid Windows

When I look thru my window, I see past the outside view
To places where my mind can think of thoughts bright, clear and new
By my window I spend time, which seems to quickly pass,
While I watch the sunshine as it sparkles on the glass.

My window brings in soft breezes, and shelters out the rain,
Brings starlight in a dark room, and sunlight thru the pane
And gives me inspiration, to look at things with optimism
Giving color to gray skies, like white light thru a prism

My window is truly lucid, it's frame strong and fine
Not meant to be fogged or clouded, but simply meant to shine
Outside, pure snow and calm winds, reflect my contented feeling
While the afternoon comes in and cast shadows on the ceiling

So let light beam thru your window, never let the brightness fade
Open up the curtains, and don't pull down the shade
And when you go looking thru them, I hope the outside shows
Happiness and radiance, thru your lucid windows.

—*Dawn J. A. Cook*

Stupidity

The perfect person, beautiful, intelligent and innocent,
is present in my dreams.
This person is one of a kind. This person is you.
I remember your face; I hear your voice as if it were yesterday.
Thinking day after day of my foolish refusal
and missing my one and only chance to be with you.
A few words, that is all you asked,
but the mind of a child was unleashed which prevented this simple request.
Now, full of regret and sorrow, the pain burns in my heart.
The perfect person, time and surroundings all thrown away pitifully,
All of this due to one simple thing.
This thing is stupidity.

— *Vanessa Johnson*

Thoughts

Confused thoughts in my mind,
Do I like him? Do I not?
Wondering what happens next,
Still wondering and it has already passed.
So caught up in my emotions,
Not realizing that if I would just forget somethings
I would have more fun.
Then again, how do you just forget? You can't on purpose.
At least I don't know how.
There is always something out there, good or bad.
The thoughts in my mind are of everything:
Love, hate, peace, and war. There are times you shouldn't forget
And those are the times that slip your mind. But you always
Remember the bad times. When you recall them, they bring you down.
Making you look at everything only to see the bad side.
It's hard to see the bright side.

—*Amy Smith*

It Is Here, It Is Now

The sunset splinters like goldleaf between the firs,
Splendid, soundless sentinels by the Santiam.
The evening song of the meadowlark all that stirs,
The valley at twilight sadness's embers fans.

As if painted by a giant, celestial hands,
The silver highway of light, broader and broader,
Comes trapsing down the swiftly darkening band,
Streaming behind the speck of ghostlike marauder.

The long line appears, deepens, etches its finite mark
Like the path of life passing before the eye.
It makes the present vital; it sets this moment apart,
And, imperceptively, it fades into the evening sky.

—*Betty J. Luellen*

Night Dew

The sweet breath of summer
Comes through my window
Laying a peace on my mind
That nothing else can
A slight chill as midnight dew
Falls on my face
You lower your head to kiss me goodnight
And as sweet honeysuckle and lilac
Laces your warm breath
As the red moon rises on the trees
Night dew falls on me.

—*Betty Jo Morgan*

The Season of Blue and Gray

The season came and the battle raged,
Some wore blue and others gray.
Each one would fight for what was right
As shots rang long into the night.
A fire in the town burning out of control,
As prayers were given for each man's soul.
With frosted beards, climbing mountains cold,
Some men knew facts that were never told.
Sickness and death were the enemy, too,
For men both in the gray and blue.
As the season changed and all was still,
A void left never to be filled.
Escape the pain of days gone by.
Be still the sounds of battle cry.
And God bless each and every one
In the battle lost and the battle won,
As we remember each one upon this day
From the season past of blue and gray.

—*Barbara Richards Decker*

Rain

Rain fell
The earth drank it in
It washed the ground
And danced through the puddles.
Clouds lowered
With the rain
And quietly looked down
Patiently and kindly.
Lightning flashed with distant enthiusiasm
And rushed to meet us with thunder's crescendo
Rain fell
It scented the air clean and sweet.
I knew it filled you
With healing memories,
And gave you all the promises
You see in your heart.

—*Nancy Hopper*

Plant Dance

I tell my children
As we water our plants,
If you watch very closely
You might see them dance.

They'll do the dance of life for us
If we are patient and we trust,
If we believe in plants you see
Then they'll believe in you and me.

And let us see the dance of love
that they show us, because because,
The plants they love us
For taking care
Not to break them not to tear
Away their lovely bodies bare.
We let them live.
We show we care.

— *Bobbie J. Pemberton*

Squirrels

Spring is leaving.
Fall is coming.
Squirrels are scurrying about
Getting lots of nuts
In the cool green grass that's been cut
Under their home, the big oak trees,
Which is losing lots of its colored leaves.

— *Amy Stevenson*

Creation

I am past, present,
I am future
The essence of my soul is
Creation

I am beginning, middle
And end
I am infinity and ad infinitum
I am all of everything and exclusively
None of nothing

I am dawn, evening,
I am midnight
I will clothe myself in armour,
And charge into the sunset
For my beloved cause

Should death come claim me
Before my chase is done
Then let it be known
That I am creation
The essence of my soul is
Creation

—*Peggy Perry Hooper*

Old Hickory Tree

The strong old tall hickory tree
Stretches prudly up to Heaven
Curving and twisting up toward
The golden spiral staircase of Heaven
Stars light the path...followed by the milky way
And the moon encircles its roots as a halo,
As shimmering spray
When dawn creeps up he is down on his knotted knees
With his leafy branches spreading up toward
The Gates of Heaven
A silent whisper dimly heard,
Is the echo through the leaf
And a little voice talking to God,
Down on his gnarled knees.

—*Beverly Jenkins*

Woodland Bird

The calling cadence of the woodland bird,
Again the sound, and yet again it comes,
About its primal way without discord,
In rhythmic motion, plays on nature's drum.
And so—I pause to hear it from the ground,
Tapping out its beat staccato time.
Gentler then, and gentler yet it comes around,
Acting out its part as though a mime.
I hear not one, but two—not two, but three that fall-
Then rise into crescendo beats.
As God conducts the forest symphony,
The walnut woodsong falls to cedar seats.
It leaves its worthy echo in my ear,
Drumming tunes to keep me ever near.

— *Noel Bleu*

Wintertime

Gently falls the pure white snow
Down to the frozen ground,
Each flake is different, yet the same,
They make a heaping mound.

All of this is done at night
And when the daylight comes,
The children then go out to play
Beneath the glowing sun.

Snowmen soon stand smiling
On the clean white earth,
And when the children go inside,
The sun shines for all it's worth.

All the snow then melts away
Within a day or two,
But then one night in deepest dark
There falls a snow that's new.

— *Niki Patterson*

Our Life

Is there a tomorrow, or eternity of tomorrows,
For us to gain a peace we cannot comprehend?
This life with its sadness, bitterness, woe and strife,
The hell for sins we know.

Then the dawn of spring.
The sweetness of flowers, rain and joys,
The bit of heaven we shall attain.

Creation is possible through God alone.
He grants us this life to own.
Not eternal tomorrows of lifelessness...
But this, our todays of living breaths of heaven and hell.

— *Betty Berlin Byrne*

Love Spirits

The incense of body fragrances
beyond human expectations;
formulates a scream of joy.
Unity of ecstacy intertwines uncontrollable desires.
The force of melodic rhythms will soon fade
beneath an azure horizon;
never to die,
at intervals invades a serenity-magnetic heartbeat.

Fleshy frictions intercede a fantastic climax.
Cries of jubilant passion roar like a devastating hurricane
leaving behind a path of inner-peace;
surrounded by a sensational moment of tranquility.

— *Thelma (Tapp) Wiley*

The Dying Rose

White is the rose of first true love,
Pure and simple a blessing from above.
Ever so clean, ever so true,
Without any thorns it could never hurt you.

Then evil arrived and brought its thorns,
Sorrow and pain and mistrust were born.
The sacred white rose its beauty which fled,
Now turns the color of deep blood red.

Its petals which held a place to hide,
A fortress of comfort and security inside.
Now bleeds its poison to all who come near,
Killing everything precious and held most dear.

Black turns the rose of a lover's dream,
Draining its spirit of life so serene.
Restless and searching, never to be whole,
Only loneliness and death will satisfy its soul.

— *Dana Johnson*

All My Sweet Apples

The appls hung on my grandmother's trees
Like ornaments clinging long after the Christmas festivity.
Wolf Rivers lay in the grass, their one-pound
Immensity lost by the frosts of November.
Five Greenings puckered and shrank from the cold
Awaiting the winter to pluck them for burial.
Lovely the MacIntosh deep in the meadow-
All my sweet apples, why are you growing still?
None but the deer come to gather the harvest,
None but the whip-poor-wills call in the orchard at evening.

— *Josephine Breen*

My Mother

I know a person I'd like you to meet,
She's kind, nice, and really sweet.
She's always been a friend to me,
Even when everyone else was my enemy.
I can count on her anytime,
Even if it's just tomorrow a dime.
She listens to me when I speak,
And lifts me from the ground when I'm weak.
She's always there when I'm scared at night,
And she tells me what's wrong from right.
When in my eye there is a tear,
    she's the one who would be there.
This person I want you to know,
    is a person who has watched me grow.
I'll always know she'll be there,
And that she'll always care.
It's not a friend, sister or brother,
In fact this person is my mother.

—*Laura Hicho*

Friends Forever

The time has come to say
Good-bye, forever, never.
The times we spent together
while growing closer as friends
will always be one of my fondest memories.
Knowing you as my friend has meant
many things to me like knowing
that I will always have someone
to rely on, confide in and trust.
As I stand at the doorway and watch
you leave, the tears roll silently
down my face knowing that the greatest
friend I've ever known is leaving
forever. Never.

—*Tracey Slayton*

Another Day Is Done; Another Day Is Won

The sun is going down so quickly,
My senses catch up.
Another day is done,
Another day is won.

I look again to see the brilliance
And vermillion of this, one of the
Greatest wonders of this universe.
Another day is done, another day is won.

Surely, the light of that celestial
Body shines straightforward to the
Gates of heaven
Another day is done, another day is won.

Someday, the glory and graciousness
Of God's heavenly light will shine
On all of us, as we find;
Our final day is done,
Our final day is won.

—*Joel L. Avery*

Equals

You say you are better than I,
But on who's account?
You may have more money than I
And you may live in a bigger house.
But that doesn't mean you are better
For what if you and I and everyone and everything
Were just an image, just a dream
Dreamt up by some dreamer in the night?
And when that dreamer awoke
We will be no more.
You will no longer have more money
You will no longer live in a bigger house.
For you will have nothing, but neither will I,
For you shall be nothing and so shall I
And in the end we shall be equals.

— *Cheryl Bates*

Daddy

Sitting in my classroom, oblivious to everyone around,
Not hearing the teacher speak, for that a single sound.
Wondering what I'm doing here wondering who am I?
Having a deep unexplained feeling to crawl into a corner and cry.
Needing your strong voice to be there at my side,
I thought we had a knot that could not be untied.
How could you leave me without a single warning,
Leaving me to awake to a cold and empty morning?
You called me your baby, your little girl,
You made your heart an oyster and you made me the pearl.
I miss you, Daddy, how I miss you so.
When will I see you again, will I ever know?

— *Tracey McSwigin*

The Wild Ones

Have you ever seen the beauty of wild horses on the run,
With their manes and tails flying, backs and sides
Shining the in early morning sun?

Thre are bays and roans and pintos, blacks and yes some sorrels too
Though some say they are a nuisance,
I do not see their point of view.

They are a living part of our great west
As other creatures are
Must man take over all the land and from
It all wildlife bar?

In days gone by the horse was all the
Transportation that man had,
Now with machines they run they down and brand them all as bad.

If man would only take the time
To see the beauty of this land,
He would treasure all the wildlife including
The wild stallion and his band.

   —Olive G. Plock

Just A Short Flight Away

Just a flight away from Miami's shores
Through pristine, white clouds the huge airplane soars.
On to Batista's beautiful Cuban isle
Where hordes of tourists are greeted with a smile.

They enjoy all of Havana's Cuban delights.
Gambling is popular—just view the cock fights.
And a Vegas style show high up in the sky
Is so great you don't notice time passing by.

Then on to the forbidding prison Moro
Where men were thrown to the sharks not long ago.
A change of scene is easily in their reach.
It's all so different at Vero Dero Beach.

They lounge and play at that fine resort
It's a great place for the young people to court.
They leave that island sporting fine coats of tan
It's an awesome trip for every island fan.

   —Elaine Peterson

Memories

As we sat in the swing, looking back through the years
We watched the sunset, as our eyes filled with tears
How fast the time went, from then until now
But the memories we shared, only few are allowed

   —Apryll S. Kannard

Time Is Of the Essence

You only have five hundred days to really live your life.
Very little time is left after necesseties and strife.
In the next thirty six years, you will have the equivalent of 550 days.
So you better spend it wisely living fuller days.

For when the hours are gone each day to never return again.
We wonder when the day is past, where have we really been.
Live each day, one at a time and make it special too.
Twenty four hours in the day, there is so much to do.

Much time is spent in sleeping and whatever more the day brings.
Then we have to eat and work and take care of other things.
So spend your time to its best use, live each day full at most.
Include some laughter and some joy, then time will not be lost.

Each one is called to weave unique, his own tapestry of time.
Is he spending his days doing what is most sublime?
Each night erases what you fail to use, no time is yet reclaimed.
Life passes by so fast, no day is ever the same.

   —Jeannie Urban

Lullaby of the Rain

A gust of wind blew
And shook the tall palm trees,
The waves crashed violently
Against the jagged, black rocks
And the seagulls cried frantically.

Warm, golden sand clung to the bottom
Of our wet feet,
As the tide came upon the sand
Robbing it of its sparkling, burnished color,
Leaving it dull and brown.

Tiny drops of rain fell
Like cool refreshing tears
Splattering our heated bodies
And cooling the steamy air.

The boisterous waves lay silent
The seagulls listened intently,
And the breeze whistled in tune
To the lullaby of the rain.

   —Fawzia Chowdhury

The Skylark

Smell the heather as you walk amongst it
On a clear warm summer's day
It will uplift you as you enjoy it
And help you on your way.

To hear again the song of the skylark
As from the earth he doth start
Is to hear one of nature's wonders
For he sings from a pure heart.

Yes he sings his song to his maiden
To the one that he loves most dear
To the life that he is enjoying
And that message comes through most clear.

As he rises high he will tell you
Open your heart up to love
And God is high in His Heaven
As true as there're clouds above.

With the beautiful country around you
And the warm summer sun on your brow
You can take courage from the skylark
And face all your problems now.

   —Henry J. Howley

Unicorns

I am an imaginative girl who likes unicorns
I wonder if there were unicorns
I hear them crying out for help
I see the unicorns dancing through the forest
I want them to live again
I am an imaginative girl who likes unicorns.

I pretend often that I have one as a pet
I feel comforted when they are near and happy
I touch their silky soft mane and spiraled horn
I worry that people could be so wreckless
   and harmful to such beautiful creatures
I cry when people harm them out of lust and money
I am an imaginative girl who likes unicorns.

I understand the hurt they must feel
I say to myself, *How could they?*
I dream that someday they will roam the earth again
I try to love and wish for them enough to hear them
I hope they had a happy life
I am an imaginative girl who likes unicorns.

   —Dawn Grey

Family

When life is at its worse
When you have nowhere else to turn
There's family
To love without family
Is to live without love
To live without love
Is to live without family
Of all the things in life
That I could have
I would rather have family
Because family is life greatest treasure.

— *Herman Ray*

Untitled

When troubles will surround you,
And God seems far away.
Forget about your worries,
Just bow your head and pray.
When your feeling low,
Seems no friend is to be found,
Tell it all in prayer.
Soon peace will come around.
When you've got a problem,
Send a plea of request
With love you will be sent
Help from the very best.
No matter what occasion.
Or what time of day
He will always hear you.
And answer in someway.

— *Heidi L. Zschach*

Self Analysis

Look inside yourself
And those qualities you like
Look for in your fellow man
And those you do not understand
Search for the knowledge
And if you find virtues
That you desire changed
Work at them until suitable
And be not ashamed
Of the flaws you have
For before you can love another
Peace must exist within you
And you must be comfortable
With whom you find

—*George Clabon*

Forgotten Almost

Most of my friends are gone now,
Not from my mind or heart.
There they are still remembered.
They are gone physically.
They don't write, but I do.
I receive nothing but emptiness and tears.
There's a place in my heart
That is filled with tears.
They lie where happiness used to live.
I cry a lot now.
I miss them so much.
Life just isn't the same.
A large piece of my life seems missing,
Forgotten almost.

— *Heather Hunnewell*

Hope

Forty days man can live without food.
Eight minutes he will last without air.
Three days he will survive without water...
One second without hope, just despair.

The need for hope accelerates
With every passing day!
Loneliness, nothingness, destruction
Seems to be the modern way...

Art is the picture of our world today.
Music is the voice that he hear.
The movies are the earth's imitation...
The newspapers echo our fear.

Hope is the silver lining,
The castles we build in the air.
Hope is the rainbow, the anchor
That gives us a reason to care.

With hope, our battle is half won...
With God's grace we can win the rest...
In complete surrender admitting
God surely and always knows best!

—*Helen Burchfield*

Michael

I heard your heart beat before I saw your face.
I was the first to see your face,
Big, blue eyes, a precious face of an angel.

I've watched you grow,
Waiting for the first steps, the first words,
Waiting to hear you say my name.
You have so many things to see and learn.

You've taught my heart to beat with joy.
You've given meaning to my life
In less than two years of your life.

Michael, one who is like God,
You're a precious, beautiful angel;
A gift from God to love and care for.

— *Gina M. Porter*

Expressed Feelings

I couldn't put my feelings for you in words.
Nor could I find the courage to express them.
Just how much you liked me I wish I knew,
Since it would make it easier for me to say
What I'm feeling too.
For now I'll just hold on to what we've got
And try to add on to what we have not.
If you read this, I want you to know
My heart is there for you
Wherever you go.

— *Heather Karwoski*

The Patient

Slowly I walked over to her.
She was lying there, so painfully weak
Her face ashen like chalky paste
The years had been cruel, her face masked with fear.
Yet the eyes were still the same
And the fire stirring in those brown hollow windows
Motioned me to come closer.
I held her hand, scrawny and aged
From years of sacrifice and I prayed
For a better ending.

—*Howard Wiener*

In My Dreams

There is a dream I dream every night,
I will never let you out of my sight.
In my dreams our love is still strong.
In my dreams nothing went wrong.
You have changed my life forever,
I will never let you go, never.
In my dreams we are still together,
Heather and Corey, Corey and Heather
In my dreams that look is still in your eyes,
And the things you said were not just lies.
In my dreams I am still in your heart,
In my dreams we will never part.
In my dreams you still say, I love you,
And in my dreams I say I love you too.
I wake up and wish I could go back to sleep,
Because in my dreams you are mine to keep.

—*Heather Lynn Thomae*

The Dance of Deceit

Deceit, foul deceit,
you wrap your evanscent arms around me,
and we dance,
so lovingly, so tenderly,
as you caress my balloon soul
with your delicate pincered fingers.
I am enveloped by your sweet incense,
as we mesh together silently,
and you taunt me, and tease me,
and you consume my naivete with your subtlety
then with one razorlike stroke
I am felled,
and like a graceful tree I fall,
ruined,
as my world dissipates into silent abandon.

—*Valerie Miles Aznar*

Untitled

glittering jewel eyes of the city
perceive all
except where dusky shadows drive them back
night creatures crawl
about like ants, have pity

they appear to be going nowhere
running in circles of destruction
finding no new ways to commit slow suicide
death's construction
semblence of a dream evaporates in misty air

the new day balances on the verge of explosion
first warning shot
no time for sentimental farewells
scatter the festering rot
and run like an oil painting in motion

— *Jennifer Davidson*

State of Being

The density of mist blocking inner sight
Unproving eyes taught to see
Loneliness, a mindful essence of directed energy not
Suppressed desires, happiness hard to find
Despair, shared by few, pained by crying
  heart, inner laughter heard afar
Righteous reasons, pressured by
  nonunderstanding, knowledge expressed
Choice of will, a truth, sought by others
  of disbelief
Path of destiny, thyself

— *Gerard Maurier Merchant*

Anytime, Forever

When you need a helping hand
Just to hold or fix a favorite item
Call on me. Anytime, forever.

When you need an ear
To listen for you or hear your whispers
I'll be there. Anytime, forever.

When you need a set of eyes
To keep open or to look into,
I'll look for you. Anytime, forever.

When you need a heart
To love you more than you can ever love
Come find me. Anytime, forever.

When I want you and you are not there,
I'll remember you to bring my spirits up.
I'll see you all the time, forever.

When I think of your face,
My eyes are blinded by immense beauty.
I can imagine anytime forever.

Whether my spirits be up or down,
Whether you are loving me or not
I will and have loved you forever.

—*Steven W. Dyer*

Today You Became a Man

Today you became a man
Your responsibilities are all your own
We want you to understand
If ever you need us, you're not alone.
Always stand on your own two feet
Set your goals and standards high
Whatever they may be
Won't be accomplished if you don't try.
We have faith in you
To do the best you can
We feel proud in raising you
To be your own man.
Stand up for justice and truth
Show your courage and pride
Let no one misuse you
Be heard, never let your feelings hide.

—*Anthony R. Bradley*

Lord, I Am Your Clay

Lord, I have sinned, my burdens I can't bear.
Draw near and let me know You're still there.
Lift my heavy load, take my hand
And lift me from the sinking sand.
Bring me back into your fold
And warm me from the bitter cold.
Lead me down the path in the way I should go.
When I am weak, help me to stand and be strong.
Give me a new song each day
To help me along the way.
With each new step I take,
Mold me, for I am your clay.

— *Gwen A. Bisterfeldt*

Untitled

Sorrow, so intense a river once cried;
Deeper, raging, flourishing on grief,
Carried out was one, lost in a whirling tide.

A spark, formed sudden out of dismay;
Struggling, gasping in a search for destiny,
A flame roared its birth and carried a way.

Calm set in and only a tear lay on the ground;
A destiny sought, a strength was found.

—*Kimberly Abraham*

Far Away Friend

Far away and lost forever,
Not forever, but seemingly so.
Love's sweet song sings airily
Through the trees,
Whispering remembrance.
Yes, a time of peace,
Hearts wound intricately together.
Woven by tenderness,
Sometimes strained,
But never broken.
Never.
Then,
A sickening thud.
Fear and violent winds rip through
That supposedly stable adherence.
And to never,
Say never,
Again.

—*Chris St. John*

Emptiness

I feel this emptiness
Deep down inside,
Like a hunger
Needing to be filled.
The more my life
Goes on,
The more I try to fill it
And the emptier it becomes.
I believe there is someone
Out there
Who will fill me up
So overflowing
That I will never have
Another hungry day
For the rest of my life.

—*Karen R. Navagh*

Tiger

The jungle,
So hushed, stagnant,
until the shrill roar.

Then slowly, suddenly,
It runs out of hiding.

It roams freely, but
In captivity of man.

Fierce tiger.

—*Laura Lansink*

Gumball Machine

An innocent child
Clutches an ordinary penny,
But through his eyes
This penny
Opens a world of adventure.
As his little feet slowly step
Toward that big glass ball,
He realizes
That it is time
To say
Goodbye.
The plump hand opens.
And the warm coin
Is placed in the cold slot.
The crank is turned
And out tumbles
A new friend.

—*Becky Ortinau*

Forever Love

Blossoms blooming, waking, sighing
Silent eagle, soaring, flying
He said their love would last forever

Showers bringing rainbows after
Children playing, merry laughter
She couldn't stand to leave him ever

Summer beaches, ocean spraying
Mellow music, couples swaying
The ties between them broken never

Summer ending, slowly dying
Together lovers, silent crying
In his arms she died forever

Winter snowing, breezing, blowing
Nature dormant, no life showing
He knows he won't forget her ever

Spring awakens, new life starting
Quickening the winter's parting
His love for her could weaken never
Loving, caring, feeling, sharing
Grieving, sorrow overbearing
A year is gone, and now together.
Now at last they're joined forever.

—*Lisa Emond*

Neckties and Memories

Now that I am handicapped and old
There is something I have never told.
Because I have never thought of it,
It is about my neckties, some knit.
A wide one that is white and blue.
Reminds me of friends, I once knew.

I got a colorful tie for Christmas
It is green, white, brown and thus.
I have forgotten who gave it to me.
It reminds me of bygone events, see.
There are lots more ties on the rack.
Provoking memories that take me back.

There is a good fortune for them I say.
For when I die, they will be given away.
New experiences they will surely see.
As far as I know, they will not miss me.
I will wear the one that suits me best.
Still, I have memories of all the rest.

—*Reese M. Denniston*

My Friend

You were there when I was sad.
You were there when I was glad.
You did things others wouldn't.
You did things others couldn't.
You were there when I needed a friend.
You were there when I needed care.
Now that you have passed the test,
I can call you my true friend!

— *Judy Gutierrez*

The Bank

I went to a bank once.
I took nothing to deposit.
Nothing that is
But time and thoughts.
No one else was there.
But I didn't mind.
I had come to withdraw.
Rivers are such beautiful places.

— *Ronald Bernard Avington*

All for Love

His massive hoofs trod the ground
A rhythmic nimble touch
Mighty tusks, slash through silence
Trumpeting, shatters calm

A call of rage, to disengage
To save his clan from slaughter
Shots ring round, he falls to ground
It's all for love of ivory!

His face cut away, his tusks are weighed
Life is just a measure
For two hundred pounds, they shot him down
All for love of money!

His carcass spared, it stinks the air
Vultures leave their droppings
The suicide of humankind
Leaves a shadow in the falling
　—*Arden Heller*

Love

There once was a love,
That I thought would last forever
But one day it all just faded away
He told me that he loved me
And that nothing or nobody could change that.
But what happened that made him stop,
I will never know.
Yet I will remember what we shared,
All those long summer nights,
And cold winter days.
We do not see much of each other anymore.
But one day he will remember
This special thing we shared together,
And may this special thing be called love,
The kind that was supposed to last forever.
But was destroyed by his hope and unloving heart.
　—*Angela England*

Day By Day

Love is supposed to be so special, one of a kind.
Then why is there so much hate that I must find.
Every time I think that he is the one of my dreams,
I find out he is not all he seems to be.
My mind is so confused and my heart has been used.
Now I can only wish and dream of the day
That my Prince Charming will carry me away!
Until that day comes, I must go on and live my life day by day.
　— *Nicole Christian*

You Never Know

I only met you yesterday, but the length of time doesn't matter, you see.
I have these strong feelings that I want you to share with me.
I have this vision that you're my dream come true.
How nice it would be if I could be the same for you.
My heart is lonely; it needs what you have to give.
Deep down in your soul, I know it's a place for us to live.
You want to tke it slow because you don't know what tomorrow is about.
What you don't know is that the future is already here holding no doubts.
You have to learn to take a chance because time isn't fair.
Try jumping in with your eyes closed and grab on to what's there.
Just trust the feeling and let it flow; don't worry about finding the keys.
Then open your eyes and see your surprise; now your mind's at ease.
　—*Boutikaa Williams*

Your Touch

When in the darkness of the night I search in quite despair
For answers and times soothing balm
I find you're always there,
To offer me love's healing touch and understanding rare.

When in the fullness of the day, I walk the sunlit path
I know I have your love to share each step along the way.
In sunlight or in darkness our fates are interwined
And naught can overcome our love, that touch says you are mine.

It matters not if I am glad or if my heart is torn and bleak
It matters not if I am sad or if I am strong or weak
You are always standing by my side to lend a helping hand
And touch me with your priceless love, you make my life complete.
　—*Barbara N. Best*

Friends

A friend is someone you can call and tell your troubles to.
A friend is someone you can say *I love you,*
and they reply by saying *I love you, too.*
A friend is someone you can turn to when you think your heart will break.
A friend is someone who will look in your eyes and say,
Don't worry. There is no problem too big for us to undertake.
A friend is someone you can call any hour of the day.
A friend is someone who will help you unselfishly in each and every way.
A friend is someone we can tell our deepest secrets to.
A friend is someone who in turn will confide in you.
A friend is someone that no matter how near or how far,
they remain within our heart.
A friend is someone that only death can break that bond apart.
　— *Carole L. Rucki*

Just Friends

Friends: Just two people sharing each others' lives together, at times.
Friends: Loving each other for being our own individuals. Sharing only
with each other our intimate fantacies and feelings. Hugged together with
an energetic force called friendship.
Friends: Having the same likeness from clothes to sex and from that to the
deep feelings we feel for our own privacy and space.
Friends only telling each other we are just friends, saying that we are only
　　two separate people,
with only the time we share in common. However, sharing
in too intimate moods and each time rekindling the real feelings we have
for each other. Also, saying that we can let go with a kiss, a wave and
good-bye. But who are we really fooling?

Can we really let go? Can we lock the door to our special friendship?
Can we only remember the love we used to make without feeling and
remembering the warmth, security and passion we used to embrace each
　　other with,
when we did make love to each other.
Or can we not be afraid and accept the fact that we are in love with each
other but choose to stay *just friends...*
　—*Bartola L. Dick*

Holding On, Letting Go

The new year comes
And the old year is past
It seem to me to go too fast
If only I could hold onto it
Forever and ever.
Reliving it and letting go of it never
Thinking of the days
Of this wonderful year
Trying to remember, without a tear
Well, I can't make it stay
With anything I might say
But the memories will carry on with me.

　　　—Juanita Jerzak

True Love

I hope the flowers of love
Can bring us closer together
So we can float together
On the immortal waves of happiness.
Only true contentment
Can be found for me in your arms.
I realize now that you are my destiny
And with this knowledge
My love for you grows even stronger.
I know that I shall cherish
All the time we spend together
In good or bad.
I know I shall wait for you
Now and forever.

　　　—Christie Basler

Waiting in the Dark

It is about that time of night again;
When he usually comes,
No warning is given; he does not call.

He always seems to know when I am home.
My mind tells me I am being taken for granted.
My heart tells me that I do not care.

I want so much to see him.
I think I hear his car coming up the drive.
I look but my eyes see nothing.
My ears tell me I am hearing things.

I try to occupy myself;
So as not to expect his arrival.
I pick up a book, the clock tells me it is getting late.

The hum of an engine soon distracts my reading;
I need not look.
I have memorized the sound of his car.
My heart tells me he is here.

　　　—Teri Ardia

Friendship

Going to movies on friday nights,
Or going to see big, gang fights
We were always together wherever we went,
When we were apart you know what that meant!
The day that she left, my life turned around
And it seemed to be heading straight for the ground.
After that day I thought our friendship was over,
The feelings I felt could not be covered.
One week later, she wrote me a letter
And told me things that made me feel better.
She told me that there is absolutely no way
That any other friend could ever take my place.
There is no doubt in my mind that our friendship
Is one of a kind.

　　　—Tanya Kalle

Vanishing Tears

I cried myself to sleep tonight,
I fought my tears with all my fright.
I layed in bed to stop the fall,
Hoping maybe the water would stall.

I called out your name, I saw your
Face,
They now slow down and begin to
Pace.

I reach for you and I feel your touch,
My tears now vanish, I don't hurt so much
The night has ended my tears now dry,
I reach for you as I begin to cry.

　　　—Laurie Walsh

He Loves Me Not

Here I sit all alone in my room
Filling my day with sorrow and gloom.
He said that he loved me; I guess that he lied.
When I saw them together I sat down and cried.
He broke my heart and doesn't care,
Just walked away and left me there.
He doesn't even look at me.
If he did then he would see
A sad little girl with a tear in her eye
Looking at him and saying good-bye.

　　　— Lisa Watland

Sunshine

I remember you saying that my sun would shine.
It put a smile on my face, and a tear in my eye.
But now that I can see my sunshine through the storm;
You want to make me cry, it is not shining on you.

Well, I do not know how to carry this load.
I follow the sun and I am on the right road.

Do not make it hard on me now,
Because I am living for the first time.
Do not make it so hard for me, babe.
Now that I am feeling the sunshine.

Do not shine so bright on me.
Darkness overcomes the light.
I have seen my love like this before,
And I have watched it slip away.

　　　—Karen F. Smialek

Good-Bye

Good-bye...
isn't a word I thought I'd ever have to say to you.
I loved you so much
and when they told me you were gone
I didn't thing that it was true.
We had so many good times
and although I thought we'd have more to come,
I guess I should be thankful
because the few memories I carry are better than none.
I can only hope you're happy
up in your new home.
I don't want you to be sad
because through all of this we have grown,
grown to be better people
because when you left us,
you left an important part behind.
You left your memories and the lessons
that life brings for us to find.

　　　—Karen Ledermann

A Teardrop

A teardrop on my cheek
Is all it seems to be.
A teardrop on my cheek
Shed for you and me.
A teardrop lost and lonely
Lonely as I am for you.
A teardrop slowly sliding
Falling, as I fell for you.
A teardrop being wiped away
As easy as I was from you.

　　　— Tonya L. Horton

Our Love Belongs

As I sit and watch the
　ocean waves
Memories of our love, in my
　mind I save
The precious moments our
　love did share
The laughs, the cries, the ways we
　showed we cared
When I sit alone, my heart
　feels you near
I reach for your hand, concealing
　my tear
Like the roar of the ocean, our
　love is strong
Where sea meets the sky, like us
　they belong

　　　— Terri Scrogham

Tell Me

I love you;
Can't you see?
Just give me a clue
To let me know if you love me.

Your friends say you do,
But you don't reply.
One day you seem to,
But the next, you just walk by.

If you'd only give me a chance
To prove my love for you,
Then maybe, if we got together,
You would love me, too.

Tell me before it's too late,
The way you really feel inside.
Whatever you decide to do,
Remember, I'll love you always!

　　　— Kim Osada

Is This It

Why are you leaving me?
Where will you go?
You know that I love you,
And care for you so.

I need you right now
During this struggling time;
I need your arms around me
To show me you're mine.

Now that you're leaving
And going far away,
There is something before
You leave that I would like to say.

I will love you forever,
And you will always be mine,
And I wish we could have
Spent our lives together,
Until the end of time.

　　　—Bobbi Jo Bogold

Going to Florida

We all packed the car,
We were ready to go,
My parents, myself
And sisters Kelley, Scottie and Mo.
We got in the car
And started the motor,
Dad speeding down the highway,
Mom saying, *Go slower.*
We stopped at McDonalds
For something to eat,
Filling our hungrily awaiting mouths,
And stretching out our feet.
We're tired and very hot
From sitting in one spot.
Eleven hours in the car—
But Florida, here we are!

— *Mandy Mobley*

Outward Bound

Why do they not see
the beauty inside;
does it not show?
where does it hide?
Pushing and pushing, trying
to break free,
But the only one who knows it
and sees it is me.
Will there be a day for me
when the sun will rise,
Come out of the clouds
to brighten their eyes?
For that day, they will know
and see the profound
beauty within that is
outward bound.

— *Magdale Labbe*

Untitled

I am floating by
In the sky so high
Looking for adventure.
My friends back home
Think of me
With envy.
I travel the world on a
Nice, warm breeze,
My friends on the block still
Thinking of me.
I hope to go back
One of these days
If I can find my home,
My friends
In this great
Big
Maze.

—*Melyssa Rolfs*

As the Rose

As the rose
of the rose
Petal red as blood the rose
Budded, bloomed and shattered
Into a million—To give birth
To as many—As it was
Just as we are—As the rose
Of the rose and
The blood of the rose.

— *Melissa Steineck*

Journey

I journeyed to where I saw God standing
And arrived to find only me there.
I turned away in diappointment;
And I thought He did not care.

I looked behind to where I saw God standing
And all had grown dark.
I looked around to find me standing
In the center of my heart.
I almost gave up when I thought...

When I believe I can light my darkness
When I would believe He is in my soul;
And my own smile drove away my darkness,
And then I came to know...

This is where God's world has gone to...

—*Michelle Ruggles*

Little Red Dress In My Hand

With the little red dress in my hand
It is something I just cannot understand
How could someone be so very cruel
Take away, something as precious as a mother's jewel.

With tears falling from my eye
All I seem to do is sit here and cry
For she is no longer here you see
This is what you have done to me.

I am no longer happy as I used to be
Have not been since you took her from me
There is no longer a smile on my face
Seems as if, tears has took its place.

But way down deep in my heart
There is a love, no one can depart
For no one can ever take my baby's place
Through out eternity, that love cannot be erased.

—*Louise Birckhead Hopkins*

Crying

The days go by one by one
While the lambs in the pasture begin to run.
The days are long and the nights even longer,
All are spent crying on my dear Johnny's shoulder.
You must ask yourself, *Why is she always crying?*
I'd like to tell you; it's not easy to say,
But my baby is dying...fading away.

— *Michelle Moran*

Confusion

I pretend I don't care for you
And really it's not pretending at all.
But there are feelings I can't bury quite so easily
It confuses me.
Maybe your past loves treated you wrong...
But for you to turn around
And treat me the same way?
It confuses me.
Although you left me hanging on,
And then just dropped me into space
I'll never cry over you.
Does that confuse you?
And although you hurt me
And left a scar on my heart...
I'll never admit it.
Does that confuse you?
But love...
That's the most confusing thing of all...

—*Shareon Myers*

You

Wishing you were here with me
Holding me near to you,
Only if this would come true,
I know you could come to love me, too!
Because I need and love you so much,
All the time I long for your touch.
I know in my head these are only dreams
But in my heart this is so real
The way I feel for you,
Because I honestly love you!

— *Talli Davis*

Lost Souls

People living every day
Coming and going, searching for their way.
Some give up before they find
That precious state called peace of mind.

Some are living in a dream,
A life of fantasy, so it seems.
Our souls are alive; they hunger, too,
But lost souls don't know what to do.

Sometimes up and sometimes down,
Good and bad are all around.
Love and you will find your way.
Hate will lead your heart astray.

Faith alone will see you through,
But lost souls don't know what to do.

—*Joseph A. Kenner*

That One Thing

The one thing that we all have,
The one thing that we all cherish,
The one thing that we hold dear to our hearts
Is fear.

It is fear from our past,
It is fear of the crossroads,
The fear of ourselves.

Ultimately, it is the fear of intimacy,
Of standing naked to the world,
Of being seen through.

It is the fear of love
And the infinite powers of soul
Love is capable of reaching.

— *Tim Erickson*

Just a Peep

If I peeped out of my little world,
Would I like what I see?
Would there be love and caring there,
Would anyone notice me?
If I come out of my little world,
Would I be as safe as I am in here?
Would I have to live through love and pain,
Would I have to shed a tear?
If I went back to my little world,
Would I love it again?
Or would I miss the scary lives,
That haunt the realm of men?
No! I will just stay in my little world,
Left in the quiet and peace.
Hidden from the noise that I would not look at...
Well...maybe just a peep!

—*Roan Bryan*

Rose Within a Bed of Thorns

There is a pureness, an innocent gracefulness.
It is a shame that this unblemished seed would fall within a bed of thorns.
Still, its beauty remains, though the thorns twine themselves around it,
For this beautiful flower is losing sight because of the thorns' invigorous bite.
Though the thorns try to distort its graceful beauty, this rose stands alone.
Now the thorns choke at its life sustaining roots; its beauty, still it stands.
God, I wish that I could have this rose, but if not I,
Who will penetrate the thorns to retrieve this precious rose?
God? Please don't let this rose perish amongst the thorns,
But send a gentle breeze to transplant its seed in the pure grassy prairie
For this rose has suffered enough amongst the thorns.
Oh God, why is it not that I could have been that gentle breeze?
    —*Stanley Mitchell James*

Reflection of Life

When I look in the mirror I know what I see,
A face that is unique, a face I call me.
Then I take a good look, it scares me to death.
I want to jump up and down and crawl under the bed.
When I see my reflection, it reminds me of me,
Someone I've got to live with; someone who has got to please me.
No one is perfect, but we all try real hard
To be everyone else, that's how fashions get started.
It may be what is outside that catches the eye,
But once you look inside your heart, you will find
Life is really tough, but you must have know that.
So if you want to make it, you've got to know
That you cannot make it on looks all alone.
Beauty's not everything; there is more to control,
But as life goes on, you will learn how to love
That face in the mirror you once wanted to get rid of
And maybe one day you'll be able to say,
I coped with the world without giving up.
    —*Charity H. Bracy*

Crying Child

To the sad child lost inside having never known happiness,
Crying in the middle of the night for the love and comfort that never came.
Still wandering desolate streets in an apathetic and sometimes cruel place,
Where being kicked while you are down is a way of life.
Lost in a place called Nowhere.
Reaching out with expectations and being told you have nothing coming.
Giving your innocence in hope of receiving kindness and coming away bereaved.
Being told you are nothing, when you are nobody.
Knowing your time will have come and gone and no one will have noticed.
Weary with the tears of your own misery, hanging on to the tenuous threads of life.
God, why have You forsaken the crying child?
    — *Cynthia Hall Stanciel*

Suffer Not the Children

Who are you Lassiter waiting for me, your brown bag of Ripple held tight,
Your Cutty Pipe cigarette held in your lips rolled up in a paper of white?
The grey in your hair and the grey of your eyes held by a mixture of dirt
That sat in the wrinkles lining your face so deep that I know they must hurt.
The hands were all caloused with dirt in the nails and yellow with nicotine stain
And from the tall grass by the side of the road you called me up into your lane.
You tell me I'm naughty and no one must know or no one will ever like me
And if you should hurt me I dare not cry out, for someone would come and they'd see.
You pull me down quickly to sit on your lap and tell me how much that you care
While you push your large hands up under my clothes, your breath coming fast in my hair.
You rub and you push and you probe over me while you pull yourself free from your clothes.
You want me to touch you as you have touched me in ways that I don't even know.
And then your wet lips are all over my face as your eyes take a glassy-like haze.
Yes this was the first of many long years I carry through all of my days.
    — *Sheila D. Bloom*

Eyes Open

Through the doors of life I came,
Not knowing fear, guilt, hate or shame.
Yet as my years did slowly grow,
All these things I've come to know.
The feeling when one man hates another,
The shame of a child to an unwed mother.
The loss of having loved in vain,
The art of how to hide the pain.
But who's to blame for what takes place,
Those lines that form across our face.
No one...
No one...
No one.
    —*Jordan Williams*

Forty Years

Is forty years too late for youthful dreams?
Is forty years too late for all that's yearned?
Is forty years too late for love and laughter?
Is forty years too late, just too late?
Are youthful dreams mere figments of one's imagination?
Are youthful thoughts of love mere abstract delight?
Are youthful hopes and aspirations
Gone out like last night's lights?
When time has passed and youth has waned
Are then the dreams gone too?
Are dreams to youth as reality is to age
Or are they intertwined?
It seems at times the two can't mix,
That life gets in the way.
The efforts set forth to materialize the dreams
Are the causes that chase them away.
    — *A. Rudolph Rehrig*

Life's View

A life can be told by looking in one's eyes,
Their thoughts determines where their future lies.
To think of our endeavors, we have huge thoughts,
To think of others, we find many faults.

Looking beyond tomorrow we see a clear view,
But in the midst of it all, exist clouds of dew.
Even when spacious...but full of decisions,
Sometimes it appears as only visions.

Our mind sometime entangles as wire.
Yet we dream what our hearts desire.
Though sometimes rough, but smooth moments are their
The importance of it all is somebody care.
    — *Sandra Cardona*

Sybil

Sybil's love was sweet and gentle
Spiritual and mental
Not sullied—sordid or sensual.

Sybil's love was tender and true
Her faith in me, she tried to renew
But my dragon, she never slew.

Sybil's love was innocent and selfless
Before passion's assualt it was helpless
I was humbled and made worthless.

Sybil's love was steadfast and strong
It warred against wrong
it left its echo as a fleeting shepherd's pipe song.

Sybil was fey—I was satyr
I could not hate her.
If ever she sacrificed herself on my altar;
I could not consecrate bread and wine into flesh and blood.
    — *J. Pierritz*

Looking Out to the Sea

The night had fallen on a hot day
As I sat on my balcony.
I watched the sun set in.
The sun was bright orange
As it was falling into the sea
And the sky had turned into
A deep pink.
The waves roared in
As they hit the shore hard.
Looking out to the sea,
It was so huge and wide.
I had never seen the sea before,
But I will always remember
The time when I sat
Looking out to the sea...

    — Cecelia Castillon

Free as a Bird

As I stand here by the window,
Taking into account for the first time
The beautiful sight before me,
That feels just like magic.

The trees are full of blossoms,
The ground rich and green
The flowers out in full color.
The birds around in force.

While I look on in amazement,
I can't help but wonder what it's like
To be a bird able to roam freely,
Wondering only but to myself
How they are able to know exactly,
When it's time to fly south.

Before we are even aware,
Another day has gone past
But the scene is always there,
I just wish it would never change.

    —Cathy Lucescu

Birthday Gift

Love is a soft whisper
That wakens the sleeping heart;
Breath sweet upon the cheek;
Honey of a thousand blooms;
A prayer from heaven;
A stream of crystal water;
A sun within a sun.
Love dries tears of sadness;
Wraps the soul in hope.
Love is the end of the rainbow
Of every day living.
Love is my life, I place
Tenderly into your hands
Treat it gently.
Anoint it with prayer.

    —Cecilia G. Haupt

Jesus

I got Jesus when I walk
I got Jesus when I talk
I got Jesus when I sing
I got Jesus when I'm ashamed
Because Jesus is no game
He has the power flames.
All you got to do, is call Jesus name
If you not save Jesus not the blame

    —Cedrick B. Jackson

God's Blessings

Words of love,
I want to hear.
Close to my heart,
Forever dear.
For your words,
Have found a home.
Never again,
Will you be alone.
God has kept you,
Just for me.
Our heart beats as one,
So all will see.
That only He,
Holds the key.

    —Lois Henderson

Few Men

Every man has a song,
But only a few can sing.
Every man is rich,
But only a few have money.
Every man is a success,
But only a few make it big.
Every man has failures,
But only a few learn from them.
Every man needs help,
But only a few know how to ask.
Every man needs love,
But only a few can give it.
Every man has opportunities
Every man has choices to make.
It depends on how you make them,
Whether you will be one of the few.

    —Luanne Woods

Great Sea

The sea is noisy tonight
I hear it
Crashing, exploding
Rushing with white foam
Pounding the shore
Sweeping the sand
Like a huge broom
Carrying debris out into its depths
The sound echoes
In the wind
Into my ears
Magnificent calmness
Forever

    —Christie Johnson

Lightening of Spirit

Standing in the rain of time.
Rippling colors of like kind,
Dry waters soothing
Quicking (quick-en-ing) moving.
Sourceing salvation
Linking celebration
Ending's beginnings
Light rhythming.
Rolling squares infinite softly
Lowering where rising cares
Bareing questions
Brighten a countenance
A moments quest
Joyful living zest
Reaching believing feeling
Through anothers eyes seeing.

    — Cathleen Chesrow

Security Wall

Once upon a time ago
I could not bear to let you go
You cast your spell upon my heart
And told me we would never part
Now you are gone; there is nothing more
On my heart you closed the door
But I am still here standing tall
I have built it up again...
My security wall

    —Kristin Marie Galuppi

You and Me

Time has grown long,
like the distance between us.
The letters and phone calls are fewer,
The *I love you*'s rarely spoken,
But my love is still there.
My voice now goes unrecalled,
my face but vaguely remembered.
The deep feelings and emotions have shortened,
But my heart still belongs to you.
I cannot change the situation.
I cannot promise our love will always be.
And though time has changed us,
I still believe in you and me.

    —Kristin White

Reflection

Through the glass
I saw a familiar young woman.
We shamelessly stared at one another.
In her eyes I saw confusion,
Misunderstanding,
And the innocent cry of a child punished without cause.

In her expression I found disappointment,
Exhaustion
And a cynical old fool, disillusioned after all.

I tried to reach out.
Inside I felt beauty, strength and survival.
Just as I wanted to cry,
A tear streamed down her cheek.
We took a deep breath.
I turned from the glass,
And she turned from me,
And we both walked away.

    —Kristin Stewart

Together

You don't know how much I miss you,
Without you I don't know what I would do.
I sit and think of you day after day,
And how much I love you in every way.

I've made many wishes but the one I want has come true,
The wonderful wish of being loved by you.
I wish we could only sit and watch the sunset,
But I'm just so glad we really met.

I've waited so long to have someone like you come along,
The feeling is special to feel like you belong.
When everything goes wrong I just think of you and smile,
I just want to be with you again for awhile.

I think of all the moments we've shared,
And I want you to know I'll always care.
I hope this love lasts eternally,
In your arms is where I'll always want to be.

    —Kim Boone

A Secret Moment During a Lull in Battle

His rifle was balanced firmly between two solid sandbags,
pointing its ready-made death toward the foe;
his mud-daubed helmet standing sentinel one side of it,
he rested during the lull.
With head on outstretched arm and eyelids tightly closed
debarring the debacle of dreadful destruction
blatantly bare in the blazing sun-glare,
nostrils numbed against the pungent, death-wrought, sweetly putrid stench;
gently, very gently he reached out and touched
the vibrant chords of memory and, at his touch,
blissful pleasure resonated through his questing thoughts
and a peaceful quiet descended on him, relaxing his very soul:
for she was there,
radiant with the beauty of their love.
— *Thomas G. Winslow*

Man and War

The people scream and guns fire free.
The leaders push and watch with glee.
I feel unsafe where once no fear.
I told her *I'll see you my dear.*

Her tears I wiped, they fell, all fear.
I reassured her, drew her near.
My ego faltered, now unsure,
The man inside became a blurr.
My mind went back to happy days

When all I felt was love and praise.
My wife and I, so young,
So free I knew a war was not for me.
The train stops. Off to war I go.
The men on board are hard I know
They stare me down, all feeling gone.

Their sense of loss is but a yawn.
I find myself in shock, the crime. I now see but a thin
Red line, the blood that trickles from a gash
I turn and feel my head, it's slashed.
—*Susan Sanders*

Fugitive

Cast off
Among old maid mutters
And yesterday's hungover dreams,

I'm lost
Like the history of a sigh
And the unsung utterances of dead men,

A fugitive
Impaled on a fleeting wish,
Still shivering with consciousness.
— *Kathy L. Krafka*

Warrior's Lament

Crying in the night,
Only the wind hears me.
Tears of blood blind my sight,
Leaving me in the dark, I cannot see.

How long must I bear this pain?
Alone and afraid, I cry.
Scarlet tears fall like bloody rain
And in the wind, one hears a sigh.

Cannot dry bloody tears,
Tears that must be shed.
Pain and death are our fears.
Spilt blood from bodies bled.

Seek the answers in life
Nothing to find, there are none.
So I cry blood red tears of strife
Heavy hearts, we are done.
— *Sandie Morehead*

Rupert's Funeral

Comrades, you are now gathered
To hear my final words being read
Grant my one last wish of no tears
No flowers, no music, or good words said
I have smelled the flowers day by day
I danced to the music when I heard it play
I did a few good deeds along the way
Life has been my funeral;
There is nothing left to say.
The funeral wagon rolled away
On rusty wheels, squeaky and dry
Stiff backs followed in their chariots
With not a tear in an eye
Moss covered trees; leaning old tombstones
In a graveyard of many years
Where a well known departed body
Was placed among his peers.
—*Willard Lee Skelton*

The Veteran's War

It was such a needless war.
Many people are still sore.
Why did so many young men die?
Why did so many young girls cry?
Many people still mourn
Over the death of their first born.
And even though they are our pride.
All the country continues to cry.
Someday it might happen again.
Though nobody wants it to begin.
How many more will die?
How many more will cry?
How many of us will mourn
Over the death of our first born?
— *Stephanie Renee Duncan*

Veterans Remembered

Stand proud,
And hold your head up high,
For you changed a grey sky
Into a peaceful blue.
And somehow your memories
Of pain and sorrow,
Will make a soldier
Out of you.

Pain dies hard,
And friends are hard to lose.
But, always stand proud,
And remember...
War made a veteran of you.
—*Terri Lea Murray*

The Army Man

There I was
Watching as he left;
A tear fell
As I felt the cleft.
He kept repeating
That we had to part;
Though he still loved me
With all his heart.
This was very choatic
In my eyes;
I was younger then and didn't realize.
He was very adroit in this type of field;
But I was afraid of him being killed.
I'm talking of someone fighting as
Hard as he can; my brother the army man.
— *Celeste*

Night

You drape me in a veil of darkness;
Are you protector or predator?
Your presence unleashes a strange and mystical transformation;
A metamorphosis to which I am uncontrollably drawn.
Yet, I face you with fear in my heart;
Fear of your intrinsic power over me.
But is it you I fear; *your* power;
Or, is it I who invoke this power I accredit to you?
As I lie here, clothed only in the velvety folds of your cloak, as I feel you
    envelope my entire being, I no longer fear for you;
I am captivated by you.
My mind, my body are awakened by your gentle touch;
As you caress my skin, my pulse quickens;
I become intensely aware of my existence.

— *Kathy S. Moussette*

The Rivulet

Among the fearful lights which escape from green dimness,
hidden among foliages and roots,
playing with little flowers and colorful stones,
descends,
crystalline,
silent child of the forest,
guarded by old trees,
the rivulet.

Among the fearful lights which escape from your spiritual dimness,
hidden among sufferings and remembrances,
playing with little happinesses and colorful images,
descends,
transparent,
silent child of your soul,
guarded by deep ideas,
your faith.

—*Ignacio M. Albarracin*

The Protector

The gate is locked, the key retained with the gatemaster.
No one enters in these strong doors of emotions.
The shield of fear protects the contents
    which are hidden behind the gates of safety.
Yet another presence is in the midst of the one called fear.
One which is much greater and powerful in its own being.
Love, the only master key which exists,
    yet opens all closed and protected gates.
Yet, it seems minute against the strong barrier of fear.
However, with the passing of time, it matures much stronger
    and all-powerful than fear itself.
Love, which overtakes all emotions, like a spirit it opens the locked gate
and enters in beyond where no one has ever entered.
As it glides in slowly, the gates close, embracing the emotion
which causes another force to enter tranquility.

— *Karen Tays*

Money

Wealth, high society. Snobbery status
All revolving around a single piece of paper: the dollar bill.
Such a small token can control the lives of so many,
Can control the world.

A mansion built by the rich
Made out of the same wood used to create money,
So the upper class are surrounded by riches.

A Mercedes Benz...
Accommodated with genuine wooden paneling,
More wealth.

A heavily wooded forest still damp from a recent rain;
The wildlife scurrying from tree to tree...branch to branch.
Innocent to the pain, pressure and grief its home causes
Naive of the real world.

—*Signe Freiberg*

A Perfect Year

From my inner naked pools a rippling begins,
I was startled awake by the words of the wind
And a quake becoming ready, a rumble at its birth
Out of the womb of the stars;

The quake gathers strength from all the four directions
It's powerful hand molds the vessel, breathing out
It will encompass even it's Mother. Her household
Will tremble and shake, the lot will fall where it may
Nothing stands, no fences with their gates can
Stop our coming to the feast, the celebration

Moves us into a quiet awe of the vastness come
On the open side of the gate, from the center of the storm.
Our trembling gives rise above the common vessel,

Spilling forth an exquisite, sparkling wine mingled
With light and warmth, inviting flavor from each fruit
Mature and full, shaken by the tremor's echo, falls
The richness of the vine, freely into the gathering basket.

—*Teresa E. Sanchez-Daynorowicz*

A Dream

I saw myself clearly—so squat-
A sturdy, powerful oak tree;
Massive of trunk and roots.
I am safe, I said; *And impervious.*

The crackling thunder, it screeched
Through the battering wind. Such screeching!
My branches were severed, quite cleanly,
Twigs strewn and vulnerable.

If only I'd seen myself ideally:
A willow taller, more supple,
Why, then, a happier ending—
The wind could only but bend me.

— *Sherron Lee Sexton Cook*

Winter dreams now...

Winter dreams now,
That summer has layed to rest.
Still the birds are singing, practicing to be the springs best.

Snow falls and hot coffee,
Apple and pumpkin pie.
So much warmth and hospitality,
From such a cold and wayward mime.

Winter dreams now,
That summer has layed to rest.
Everyone wears jackets and smiles,
Dust off that old flannel vest.

Snowmen and Santa Claus.
Mistletoe, the Mardi Gras.
Even the scrooge found sunshine
Amidst winter's gloominess.

Winter dreams now,
That summer has layed to rest.

—*Kevin Dollins*

Does Nature?

Does the night cry silently?
Do the trees have tears?
Does the grass die of pain?
Do the trees look down on us with pain or sympathy?
Do the branches feel sorrow for simple human life?
Is rain nature's tears of pain, or death?
Are we killing all of nature for no reasonable answer?
Or is there a reasonable answer for killing?

—*Kandi Jenkins*

Heither and Yon

'Tis a tale of two children, of laughter and of song
of a blue-eyed girl called Heither
and a fair-haired boy named Yon

Together they were inseparable—friendship that binds so strong
and later they became lovers, of laughter and of song

On a hillside they pledged and vowed, together to be as one
this lovely girl called Heither
and this fair-haired young man named Yon

Through the years they became wise—the bind oh, so strong
and the children, they were many
the laughter and the songs

On that hillside they gathered, blessed offspring all
that place oh, so sacred and echoed with love so strong
with voices pure and lovely they filled the valley below
this tale of two lovers with God they now go

They came to rejoice, not mourn, this passing of two souls
for their love lives on inside them
strengthened a dozenfold

—*John M. Blankenship*

Cocaine

The people he would hurt, the hearts he would break,
It wasn't really him, but the drug he had to take.
They call it the big lie and this was no joke;
He was highly addicted and my heart was broke.
He hurt me deeply, I never thought he would,
But doing this to me, I realized that he could.
Now he acts as if everything is fine,
Like I don't care and shouldn't mind.
But I never know if I could trust him, for I can't be sure his habit is broke.
His habit of an addicting drug, a drug called coke.

— *J. Richardson*

I Can

I can dream dreams until my visions go black
And I can read your letters over again, but that won't bring you back.
I can hang onto our phone calls, but that won't bring me closer to you
And there are times when I know everything
and times that I don't know what to do.
I can wish one thousand wishes and I can watch them fade away.
I can watch the clouds in the sky hide the brightness of day.
But I can't bear to live life alone without you by my side.
And I can't bury the hurt or live without you in my life.
I can see a beauty on the inside that people usually don't see
And I can do anything in the world and be just what I want to be.
But I can only do these things if I can believe you care
And the things I value most are you and the life we might share!

— *Tammy Shoemaker*

For Francis

You have been everything to me: confidant, lover, mentor
No one else could take your place, once you've returned to her
Yet she has waited long enough, having lent or
Shared you knowingly—graciously—these years a lonely blur.
My heart has ached to think of this, but things will soon be as they should.
From the warmth and safety of your arms, with each embrace, each borrowed kiss
Still I knew I'd lose you, too, but I for good.

I wanted to make you a parting gift of my tearless face, my regal carriage
I wanted to be as brave as she seems.
But I find I cannot, at the thought of your marriage
To sleep would be sweet, albeit minus the dreams...
My life has value, now, only to you—so this I will give you, my soul-mate, my man
Take it, and know that for you I will live it
Accept this, and go while you can.

—*Lisa Carolyn Calhoun*

Acceptance

What is life?
A series of troughs, winding up and down through life's midstreams;
Once on the plateau, high as a bird, nothing can touch,
The heart preserved;
Then spiralling down the path so deep, fall to the bottom, the ravine
Is steep; now far below the earth's crust entwines, shadowing light,
Darkess surrounds; climb back above till the land lies flat, search
Far and wide for the pain to subside; feel no embrace, nor any
Distaste, surroundings are calmer, steady and stronger;
Realize, accept, no delusions expect,
Will never climb further or submerge thru terror;
Fulfillment awaits, though hardly content, wiser we are,
Disguised by life's scar;
Comprehension complete, we accept what we meet,
Though never quite receiving, life's broader meaning!

— *Karen R. Koppelman*

Kormi the Cat

I have a cat who loves to eat
Squirrels, spaghetti, fish or meat.
He is black and white and extremely bright,
And only I can see him in the night,
Which seems right.

—*Andor Meszaros*

Ode to a Friend

How far you have travelled once loved and now ignored
Deviated from the path how far shall you stray,
how long shall you go unloving and unloved,
How long before the path is left too far behind?
For loved you were by one and many all left
in the stranded path behind
How far shall you wander through woods unknown,
How far before the path is gone,
how far before all love is through?

Oh foolish pride thou dost rejoice
Once proven right does not retract
Oh blind pride you hinder thought
Fie! Fie! a battle won does not a victor make
A lesson learned rejects defeat!
We shall meet once more
in a battlefield 'tween the woods and path
Deprived of foolish pride to make amends
To find some day the friendship gone.

— *Sandra Rubio*

I'll Be There

No matter where, when or how, I'll be there.
If you need a helping hand, or just someone to talk to,
That's what I'm here for.
I don't want you to ever think you're not loved,
Or that no one cares for you, because I do.
I'll be the support you need, to help you through those tough times.
I'll be the friend you think you don't have.
I hope you never feel lonely, or like you just can't take it anymore,
Because I'll be there.
Suicide is not the answer, it never was, is or will be.
So please, come to me in your time of need.
I'll be there.

— *Darlene M. Homer*

Powerful, but Turbulent

Here is the story never told, but felt by many.
What is that powerful as an industrial revolution?
What is the most turbulent? Again...industrial revolutions!
Nobody ever stopped them. Electronic one all of that.
Powerful, turbulent, and irresistable!
The daybreak of electronic age did nopt lead to uprooting of poverty
And that daybreak lasts somewhat too long.
The pressure groups are lobbying rather for old than new.
Speculations are flourishing, but many technical opportunities neglected.

Look at what is happening in the world:
Higher concentration of wealth than ever,
More misery than ever! Oh destiny.

Oh, vision! When the men will learn what should be done
In these turbulent times, when...investments are falling,
Debts and deficits growing, markets crashing,
And warning signals are flashing, so often.

Oh heaven, stop ligthening and thundering!
The men need peace and time to reflect and judge.
Don't disturb them to understand the simple truth
That industrial revolutions require a new approach in education
Technical and other, in behavior, social and political, and attitudes...
The philospher said: They represent discontinuation in history.

    —Dan Branko

I Pray the Drops Will Stop

The tears of God come rolling down,
I pray the drops will stop.
The weeping seems to never end, one falls,
Another, then plop.

Lightening strikes, God is so angry.
Will he stop? Will his tears go on eternally?
I pray the drops will stop. I am scared now, the earth is shaking.
The tremors, they call it thunder, but I know better.
Could it be God is saying to the world
Be patient, my children, while I cleanse your souls.
Dear Lord, we pray we will be good, just please take the drops away.
He stops, He hears; He sees, He knows we will forget our promise.
He will look upon us and knowing our sins, smiles in spite of us.

A spectrum of color comes over us, each color dark and real
Because for the moment God is probably saying, *I love them.*
Dear God, my sweet Lord, my love, my life, my all
The same God who knows these sins and forgives them,
My Almighty Creator
My heavenly King, my earthly guider and my loving protector
I love you also.
Oh! And thank you for stopping the drops.

    —Sushana Austin

Daddy's Gone

Suddenly, after ten years of marriage he just got up and walked away.
Everyone was crying and pleading, but he still left that very same day.
Nobody has heard from him, don't even know if he's dead or alive.
I wish he would just call; we miss him so much, I was only five.
Then one day, when I turned eighteen, the doorbell rang about three o'clock.
There stood a man I didn't know; he was full of muscles, a regular jock.
He said, *Hi, how are you?* I looked at him from afar.
That's when my mother came by and I asked her who you are.
Her faced dropped to the ground; she said his name was Frank.
Then she invited him in; I kept looking at him, but I just drew a blank.
Then suddenly I realized who he was; I was so angry I could have killed him,
But I controlled myself and left the room; my memories of this man were very dim.
He said he was sorry for leaving us, but I could care less.
That was thirteen years ago; our life was a mess.
Now all of a sudden he wanted back in; my mother and I had just straightened out our life.
She married a wonderful man and in another six months I was to become a wife.
He said he'll keep in touch; I don't care if he does, my life will go on.
Then he stood up and walked out the door; as far as I'm concerned, my daddy's gone!

    —Lisa Ann Bagnasco

True Love

When the sun is shining,
Life just seems so grand,
Just like when a true love of yours,
Takes you by the hand.
They help you thru the hard times.
They always seem to care.
And as you walk down life's rocky road,
You know their love you share.
When the sun is shining.
And life seems so grand,
Remember how good a true love is,
And be glad that he is your man.

    —Ruth Simpson

Nuclear War

Oh my, the world seems grey today,
The world seems grey and cast away
Oh my, the world seems grey today.

Oh my, today the world seems sad,
Today the world seems sad, unhappy, mad,
Oh my, today the world seems sad.

Yesterday the world was glad,
Until they bombed Trinidad,
Yesterday the world was glad

The flowers died, the children cried,
They dropped the bombs amongst their liess,
The flowers died, the children cried.

Oh my, the world seems grey today,
The world seems grey and cast away,
Oh my, the world seems grey today.

    —Teva Harrison

I Dream...

I dream of a time when
  the world is fair
When confusion, complexity
  melts into air
I dream of a time when
  happiness shines
When the art of loving
  need not be defined
I dream of a time when
  the bad lays to rest
When the good finds itself
  a most permanent nest
I dream of a time when
  all fears go away
When faith in love
  is the thing of the day
I dream of a place where the pressure of time
Can't interrupt love's beautiful rhyme.

    —Lauren Heller

Together in Time

Thank you, dear friend, for sharing that
Sweet slice of life with me.
Our paths crossed, and we continued on our
Journey together as one.
Today our paths split, and we go our own
Separate ways;
You go your way, I go mine
But I have no doubt, dear friend,
We'll be together in time.

    — Lynne Schutter

All It Kills

All the pills
All it kills
Is the past
When we start
To release the fears
And cry all those tears.

I, too like you
Never wore
Someone else's shoes
But now I see
I have to be
Me.

—*Lisa E. West*

Heart Dance

Gaunt and straight,
he walks alone.
His face and hands
scarred by work.
A vision of duty
with few rainbows,
no dream words
fill his mouth.
Yet, his footfall
makes my heart dance.

— *Shirley B. Kostka*

Within

Always a smile
Never a frown
With that sparkle in her eye
She could never bring you down

But deep in her heart
Is where the pain hides
Noboby knows
How's she's feeling inside

Hidden within
Never to show
Is the pain that makes her cry
No one will ever know.

— *Kathleen Forcier*

Island Sky

Ancient angels
In a dance of love.
Pure
Truth
Adored
Waltz across
a midnight sky.
A playful leap
from star to star.
The song of ancients.
Of years gone by.
Beneath the throne of God.
Ancient angels,
In a dance of love.

— *Joshua Murry*

Nature

Breeze rustling tree tops
Water sheltering the fish
Grass growing in the spring
Clouds giving us some rain
Nature
Nature

—*Liisa Alto*

Lost Love

Some hearts never soared on love's wing,
To deeply loved and lost.
Not knowing what love can bring.
Never paying the painful cost.

No mortal should brush heaven's gate;
Nor feel its pleasures,
Blind to their tormenting fate,
For stealing of its treasures.

Dreams bring no peace.
Will the heartache never end?
Does the longing never cease?
Please time, will I ever mend?

—*K. R. Garrison*

Super Nova

Soaring towards your gravitational pull
I tumble into pure blind orbit,
Heart over head over heel
Queasy bliss, bilious ecstacy.

The center of a universe, a silent sun
You glow...you, the sweet spoiled cynosure
With surface flares, superficial explosions
Angry skin deep infernos
Dear star, I can see
I can see through the flame
I can see through the heat,
Your flaming drag queen incandescence.

And still I burn
Still I burn.

—*Virginia Kamouneh*

The Sun Will Rise

She looks upon herself in tears
Tears of anger, of bitterness
Her face reflects, reveals all fears
Only to shatter, only to break.
One last glimpse she must gaze
One last fear she must face
Before the end of all her days
There it lays, there the end.
Oh so near, yet oh so far
The night crawls forth, lurks behind
But there beyond, there they are
Rays of light, those of dawn.
She looks up, toward the light
Light that's warm, melts all fears
Her face reflects, yet is bright.
The sun will rise.

—*Teena Kim*

Me

Make silent the world,
    my own heart to hear.
Make gone the strings,
        others thoughts to disappear.
Let me listen, let me know,
        that I am.
Expections, molded purpose,
        let me dim.
Let me feel, let me do,
        let me be.
A soul awake, a mind that's free,
        I must be me.

—*Trudy Sue Clark*

Deep Winter's Night

Stars standing alone, flaming crystals on
Heaven's midnight palette.
Reflected light, from ethereal worlds, illuminating
silver velvet soft ground.
Snowflakes fluttering in mindless grace in the
face of the pale, liquid moon.
Hours pass, the wind dances in lonely
solitude through winter slumber.
The grey fox slips obscurely home as dawn
arrives.
Darkness has gone.

— *Richard A. Bechtold*

The Fat Rap

I worry, I eat,
I even dream that I am eating in my sleep.
I am overweight, who cares!
I find it very difficult to jog or run,
Without gasping for some air.
I paint myself a clown, to disguise my true disgust,
Yes, deep inside, it hurts!
I categorize myself as being obese,
Yet deep inside I know that I'm just fat.
I am so jolly that I can cry.
Doughnuts, chocolate and vanilla ice cream,
The dieting war, but the ultimate dream.
Fat,
Yes, this is me,
And if I don't lose some weight, the doctors make facts,
My obesity will be the end of that.

— *Kervin Fondren*

Genealogy—Truth or Speculation

What dreams drew you to this obscure place,
Of quiet solitude? Where towering pines,
And sun splotch shadows, interlace,
Reflect in waters, clear as crystaline.
Was it preordained you come alone,
To mine rich gold, found in this paradise?
Cornerstone of family life, did gold atone,
For deserting children, home and wife?
In time, *branch of your root,* discovered,
You were living with a lover. Did he kill two,
For the gold, or to avenge his Mother?
Under name carved rock, leave both to dust, of 1882.
Shrouded family secrets, secrets will remain.
They said, *great grandfather,* died adventuring.

— *Flossie F. Gregory*

I Love You, Rick

As I think of what you're doing to yourself,
I wonder if you really know how much I care for you.
As you hurt yourself,
You hurt me badly inside, too.
It's like we feel the hurt for each other.
I can feel my stomach pull
And I hear myself crying out for help for you.
I love you more than life.
You are my life;
You are my brother
Who I care about.
Please don't hurt yourself or me.
I know how I express myself sometimes;
It's as if I don't care,
But I do.
So always remember that I love you
And will always be here for you.

—*Monica J. Kallas*

The Dream

Sitting on the sand,
All smiles and sunshine
Writing about sea shells, pelicans, and seagulls.
Looking up at the sky,
Seeing only rainbows,
Lying down and closing eyes,
Painting the storms that created them.
Running into the sea,
All jeers and laughter,
Creating reefs and mermaids
That live below an azure surface.
Sleeping under a sheet of stars
Dreaming of winged horses,
And majestic powerful unicorns,
But then when morning arrived,
The tear that was shed
Wet the sand and the sun.

   —Ricardo J. Estevez

Teddy

You remind me of my teddy.
I carried through my childhood days,
I would hold him tight in my arms
And never lead him astray.

There was never a waking moment
That we would be apart,
I shared all my secretes with him
That I held dearly to my heart.

One day when I came home from school
My teddy was no longer there,
Someone took him away from me.
Someone did not care.

You are just like my teddy.
And I will always miss you so,
But there comes a time in life
When the things you love must go.

   — Renee Navarro

Beach Clock of Time

Sandy beaches, sifting through time
As seagulls cries sound out like chimes
My mind is ticking, thinking through
What could have happen between
Me and you.
The sun goes down as hours pass
Being engulfed by the blue, rippled mass
But I know our problems will pass
Soon.
Because I know time will reunite us
And it always heals wounds.

   — Dawn Bruce

The Dream

Last night I had a dream
I will never forget,
And I will tell it to you,
If you do not get upset:

I dreamt of an elephant
That sold ice cream cones
That instead of having ice cream,
Were filled up with stones.

I also remember clearly
A beautiful baby unicorn
That carried a magical mermaid
On it's only golden horn.

I also recall a flower
That flew from bee to bee;
And while dreaming impossibilities
I dreamt you belonged to me.

   —Claudia Rosani

First Child

A tiny nose, a dimpled chin
Two eyes so shiny bright
Sweet rosy cheeks, a toothless grin
A bundle of delight.

For many months you waited
To have this child to keep
And now you walk the floor and pray
For just one good night's sleep

The years go by so quickly
You have managed to survive
Just when you start to feel at ease
This child learns how to drive!

   —Sharon Kamman

The Eyes of a Child

There is nothing quite so wonderful
As the seeing the world
Through the eyes of a child.
Everything we know and have forgotten
Comes alive again
Through the seeking mind of a child.
The colorless images
Become bright and vivid
When touched by a child's imagination.
Nothing is old and dull,
But novel and exciting
With a child's insistent questions.
All the lonely and lifeless spaces
Become fulfilled and warm
Because of this new life,
The miracle of the child
You cradle in your arms
And behold in your heart.

   —Serena Folkerds

Friendship

Friendship is a glorious sign,
Friendship can be rare,
Friendship includes two or more people
Who are ready and willing to care.
Friendship is a special bond,
Friendship shows such love,
Friendship flies and touches people
Like the symbol of a dove.
Friendship is a sign of nature,
Friendship is only true,
Friendship is a wonderful thing
That I'm glad I share with you.

   — Susan Armstrong

Dreamers' Dreams

Dreamers often dream dreams that
Can never be,
They are impossible dreams, you see.
Far reaching and outstretched dreams,
But they keep dreaming, it seems.
Why do you suppose that's so?
Surely they must know,
That dreamers often dream dreams
That can never be,
They are impossible dreams, you see.
Perhaps that's what makes them dreams,
And not what reality deems.
It keeps them going,
But also from knowing
That dreamers often dream dreams
That can never be,
They are impossible dreams, you see.

   —Christine D. Hays

Remember

If you left because of love
To bring me to my senses,
You forgot to come again
When I awoke.

If you left because of thoughts
That you were not good enough,
You forgot that love judges nothing
But the heart.

If you left because of anger
To hurt me only for a season,
You forgot that friendship is forever
And you are gone.

Remember.

   —Steve Abelli

The Walls are Talking About Me

The walls are talking about me.
The walls are looking at me.
What are they saying?
What are they seeing?
Am I nice?
Am I mean?
Am I pretty?
Am I ugly?
I hope I am nice.
I hope I am pretty.

Will I ever know?

   —Joelle Belanger

The Ring

Throw a pebble in the lake,
And a ring at once is born,
Reaching for the distant shore,
From the spot where it was torn,

It seems to grow forever,
But dies upon the shore,
Reminding us that life must end,
Be you rich or poor.

Our ring of life begins at birth,
Torn from love's embrace,
Ever reaching for that shore,
Dressed in rags or lace,

You cannot cheat the hands of time,
No wealth upon this earth
As the ring began, so shall it end,
And begin again with birth.

   —Robert C. Larson

Adolescence

Why are feelings so mixed up.
And to be joyous times so unfun
It just may be the teenage years
Troubles for the lonely one.
No drink, nor drug can help these times
A constant fight with evil divines
The good may survive
And the bad may crumble, leaving all minds
In a mixed up jungle
Friends may be there when in need
This fact is indeed
Adolescence

—*Lollita VanderGriend*

The Expedition

Old men have many tales
As they look back on all the trails
An paths
They took along the way,
Some so nice, but others nay.
In this crusade, where they've always beens
Living there in leathered skin
An hide
From pain along the way.
As they grow old, and turn to gray.
Ancient veins inside no gold
With armored breast that age turns cold
An distant
Thunder sounds retreat
An they must charge with swollen feet.

— *Kenneth Whitley*

The Prairie Winds

Winter
    The winter winds, January cold,
    whip the white shrouded land with
    sculptured drifts of powdered snow,
    across a thousand flat miles.

Spring
    The gentle wind of warming May
    brushes the greening land of rounded
    hills and scented with vibrant life,
    stirs a meadowlark to song.

Summer
    The hot dry winds of summer give birth
    to dust devils with dirty skirts
    that dance with shimmering heat
    waves over the sun-baked land.

Fall
    The playful winds of late September
    pull golden leaves from sleepy trees
    and send them prancing and dancing
    through the smoke scented air.

—*R. Simpson*

A New Leaf

Sow thoughts among the stubborn few
Who seem to deny anything new.
To infiltrate the introverted;
An ancient idea, but
Not yet deserted.

Capricious cliches
Now out of phase,
Frequently fail sans fruition.
Hate the hackneyed same,
Go against the grain!
Break from mindless tradition.

— *Daniel Tobin*

The Last Man

The dust has finally settled,
I can see the sun.
Standing tall in the stilled sand,
I am the only one.

I'm the challenge of the GOD,
He knows that He has lost.
I've replaced His trees and grass,
And it was at His cost.

Earth shall always wear the fruit,
Of my arkitekchur skill.
They perpetuate the 'man',
To quote a phrase, 'my kill'.

I stand alone in the stilled sand,
Beneath the hostile sun.
The earth is now a mausoleum,
Oh, GOD!...What have I done?

—*Rose Cromer*

Dancing Leaves

Gentle autumn winds blowing
Tossing leaves to the ground
Do I hear sounds of music,
As they dance around?

They scamper, and twirl
What a sight to behold!
The dance of the leaves
In their recital so bold.

They once were so colorful,
But now they've grown old
They're weary from dancing
To and fro in the cold.

By the roadside they falter
Never more to appear
It's time for the finale
Of their dancing career.

— *Ruby B. Crocker*

When

When I think of you
I think of a sweet
Young man; loving,
Kind and gentle.

When I see you,
I see a good looking man
Filled with a lot of love
And affection.

When I remember you,
I am reminded of
A troublesome period of time.
Nothing but times
Of pain and agony.

—*Teresa Willard*

Untitled

You held me close
(Like a friend)
Wiped my tears
Shared my pain
Went to bed alone
(Like a friend)
The clown of my past present
And future
Smiles and says
Deja vu, baby,
Deja vu.

— *Susanne Justice*

Our Life Together

One day as I sat here thinking of you,
Your company filled my soul.
Your heart, mind, and love were all there too,
And filled my life with something more than *dull.*
Our love is more than just an infatuation.
It's a relationship of trust and honorship.
It holds the heavy key to our continuation;
And someday, will be unlocked by our courtship
The day that we as partners become one,
Will be the first day of our newly begun life
It's that day that our teenage love will be gone;
And that day will come as I'm wedded as your wife.
All parts of our hearts will be bonded together,
As we start our new world on our own.
Cherishing and remembering all our memories forever,
And recalling how our love had grown.

—*Samantha Betzold*

Music

Music is soothing and music is stirring
Music is life and its values concurring
It lifts you up high and it drags you down low
Taking you places you so love to go
It tickles your conscience and plays with your heart
Or rips through your body and tears you apart
The notes seem to float in the air as you snatch
But your fingers go right through your light airy catch
Watch them diffuse as you note in a daze
Your body is floating on some kind of haze
Then the more that you notice, the more that you lose
Then your mind and the music just simply unfuse
And you scream in your soul for the least little thing
To keep in the true world and help you to sing

—*Dawn Lisowski*

Friendships Lost

Friends are supposed to go on and on
Just laughing together, out on the lawn.
That's why it hurts deep down in your heart,
When you and your friend simply drift apart.
It might be because she's found other friends,
And can't stand the thought of making amends.
Maybe the friendship just disappears
And leaves your heart shedding silent tears.
Maybe it's you that shunned a good friend.
You said you'd stick with her 'til the end.
Imagine the sorrow that she must feel.
She thought she had a pal that was real.
There is no excuse for hurting this girl,
And wrecking a friendship that glowed like a pearl.
If you've pained her, apologize.
Make certain she sees it in your eyes.
Friends are precious and should not be lost.
Just like diamonds, friends are worth the cost.

—*Roberta Moberg*

A Great Friend

You are always there for me
Whenever I need someone to listen to my problems.
You hear my cries.
You always help me
And sometimes I think you're the only one
Who really understands me.
You've always been there
When I needed a shoulder to cry on.
To you I will always be grateful.
I just want you to know if you ever need someone,
I'm here for you!
You're a great friend
Who will always be special to me.

— *Chris Angelini*

The Path of a Loner

There was no place for pain
Unless
I searched for some.

I knew
How to shed tears
Whose salt mastered all other tastes...

What human incompatibility I
What disturbance of man my complexities.

I can not make light conversation
Nor deliberate in a worldly fashion
Over the chances
I take upon the path of a loner.

—*Leah Bernstein*

Girls

If ever you contemplate suicide
And consider Russian Roulette
Wait, for there is a better way
Redhead, blonde or brunette.

Death is as certain
And much more fun
Than an uncertain death
Attained with a gun.

If you are looking for sorrow, perfidy and joy
And you happen to be a teenage boy
Then look no farther, find you a Miss
That cute little mixture of sorrow and bliss!

— *J. Marthijohni*

Death

A small breath of life, a miracle new,
Is how we were born,
Me and you.
Some come and some go;
Some die and some grow.
Death is something we all have to face,
Every color, every race.
It is usually a sad moment of mourning and lamentation,
As everyone attends the funeral-
The town, the congregation.
Maybe we're just selfish
Or it is hard to face the fact,
That the one we love so dearly is never coming back;
But when we are put through all that pain,
Do not think that person's life was in vain.
Instead rememeber:
It is our loss...heaven's gain.

—*Lisa Huddleston*

The Old Man

His hands were large and boney, gnarled with age.
Those hands were once little hands,
Clutching his mother's skirts,
Laughing,patting her face in delight
When she lifted him up.

Boys hands happily holding a fishing pole,
Grubby from doing the things boys love to do.
A young man's hands strong
And steady, soothing, calming his horse.

Calloused, forceful hands, brown from the sun.
A man grown as he puts his hand to the plow.
Caressing, passionate, gentle hands
That tell his woman he loves her.

Clumsy, awkward hands too big
As he holds a tiny child, his first-born.
Reverent hands, folded in deference to his God.
My father's hands.

—*Mary Scroggins Crow*

Caught Between Cultures

A product of love
Some may say
A form of defiance
Others may say

Set aside
Alone
I often felt,
Alone
For I am

A breed apart
Hoppy, hoppy
Half breed
Words to describe
Who I am

Not Asian
Nor white

Dust to some.

—*Genevieve*

Beauty, Love, Life; You

Beauty is not a word,
Nor just a phrase or picture.
Beauty is you.
Beauty is our love.
Love is not a thing,
Nor just a feeling or emotion.
Love is you.
Love is us.
Life is not a moment
Nor just a presence or existence.
Life is beauty.
Life is love.
You are not a girl
Nor just a woman or lady.
You are my beauty.
You are my love.
You are my life.

—*Karl Yost*

Untitled

I remember those words
You said to me
That we weren't meant to be.
No one is made exactly for you
Or for me.
I wish you could see
Just what I see,
What could have happened
Between you and me.

— *Yvonne Devora*

Caution

Aids is a dangerous disease,
It's nothing to joke about
So you shouldn't tease
Many people around the world
Are dying;
The doctors haven't found a
Cure, but they're still trying.
Present or past abusers of illicit
Intravenous drugs;
Is just like getting aids by
Sharing drug needles with
Junkies and thugs.
So be more careful while
Doctors are trying;
If you don't, you'll be
The next one dying.

—*Nakya McDaniels*

My Dream

As I lie here and think of him,
I see his beautiful eyes and soft skin.
I hear him say how he loves me,
That we'll be together forever,
Just wait and see.
He knows we'll make a terrific team;
But as he says it,
I awake from my dream.

— *Misi Burrus*

Love Speaks

Love speaks—
    Green mountains show their
    everlasting jealousy for the
    pure white snow that has
    just fallen in the glenn.

Love speaks—
    The torn red roses cry for
    the attention of the cowardly
    yellow dandelions that
    dare not speak from fear.

Love speaks—
    The saddened blue sky weeps
    over the filth of brown roads
    that people mistake for the
    golden paths they wished for.

Love speaks—
    All colors—jealous of each other-
    as we are when all is not
    as we wish it to be.

—*Crystal Cochran*

Seeing Sights

While flying West to East into the dusk,
I saw a brilliant panoramic husk:
Ten thousand lights ten thousand feet below;
I saw them laid out in a velvet bow
As night encompassed me and planet Earth
Within her vastly omnipresent girth.

My fellow trav'lers pointedly ignored
That wond'ous stunning sight that I adored;
Sophisticated, sojourners, no doubt,
Declined to even cast a glance without.

Oh, Master Artist, You alone create
So many works to glorify our state
Of being here twixt tree and sky and sea,
But, in the end, the seeing's up to me.

— *Gus Wentz*

Mrs. Retiree

Can hear him up there honkin', thumpin'
Floor. Lost specs, I 'spect. I've hollered twice
It's served: green-onioned fries, coffee
Gettin' cold, homemade toast, new stepped-up
Datebran bowled to slow de-gripe the bowels.
Claims he aches, so snores away past
Breakfast. Wish he'd fast, not break it;
He's so blame mid-flabbed since he quit work,
No wonder paunch stays compact, even.
Come and get, it's gettin' cold! Two bits
He's huntin' pants I've tossed in tub, so
Filthy in and out, I'm half-minded
Throw them total out, let him grump, stomp
About without...Give new-moved neighbors
Glary shock to eyeball shriveled tool
Hang prinkled gaunt. That shirt he swears by's
So bad torn outworn not even Vets
Disabled would drive a foot to foul haul it off...

—*Lee Garner*

Rich White and Blue

For a good twenty years, the media pounds,
At my psyche with moral complaints.
White males are devils,
As *females seek levels*
And the *people of color are saints.*
For the pride of being caucasion,
Where getting on top is a sin,
For the pride of being caucasion,
Struck down from around and within.
We'll let you be white, we'll let you be male,
Just don't let it all go to your head,
For it's unpatriotic for you to be wealthy
We'd rather be sing you dead.
Though sadly I reach the *American Dream,*
How sadly, how guilty, how true? *Shamefully* hanging, my head
Will I scream, I'm glad to be rich white and blue!

—*Harvey E. Reese III*

Woman 'Neath the Vine

Her countenance of gloom 'neath the shadows I discern.
A woman of so many men...behold. Her eyes so stern!
Her jaw is that of ironstone, her brow reveals despair,
How many tales her face does tell of torrid love affairs.

She lives in isolation, no one enters, no one leaves.
She lends her faith to none for so many have deceived.
She appears but once a year at the window 'neath the vine
And tossing down a tarnished rose, utters Thou art mine.

Her eyes blaze for a heartbeat as the flower does descend
Yet he comes not to claim it and her visage grays again.
Now turning from her viewpoint, she draws the sashes closed
And does not see the hand that reaches for the withered rose.

—*Lesia Johnson Powell*

Where Do They Go?

While on a bench in Peaceful Park I watched with mellow eyes,
As man and child squirrels fed beneath the calming skies.
And as I viewed these many meals I thoughtfully surmised,
That no one knows where squirrels go when it is their turn to die.

You often see them on the road all squashed from tire tracks,
But what about the ones who suffer massive heart attacks.
And surely there are those who from old age at last expire,
But there is no place for them to go when it is time to retire.

And what about the broken bones from climbing limbs too fast,
I have never seen a squirrel in a little plaster cast.
And how about a simple scrape from falling after racing,
I doubt that squirrels carry tiny tubes of Bacitracin.

I think I know the answer now, I have studied and observed,
And it must be that every park one special tree reserves,
And in this sturdy, hollow tree are little rooms with beds,
Where sick and troubled squirrels go to rest their little heads.

—*Michael J. Scharf*

Grandfather

Grandfather sits in his rocking chair
Faced away from a day he can't see
And I sit at his feet, transfixed by his stare
As he whispers strange mem'ries to me.
He remembers the time he ate a sour cherry
From old Miz MacGuire's tree
But he can't remember where Grandma's buried
Or the games he's played with me
For hours he talks of the old summer fair
Where he went every day as a child
But then he'll think he's expected there
And when Mom stops him, he gets very wild.
Sometimes he scares me, when he's mean or unstrung
Or when he cries 'cause his bones are cold,
But what scares me most is
If he was young does that mean I'll get old?

—*Jeanne M. Stauffer*

Romance

Gazing out the castle window to the gates
She waits for her handsome prince to come.
In a carriage laced with gold, drawn by six white horses.

Her gown is long and beautiful.
But it is no match for her golden hair.
Deep brown eyes perfect his splendor.

The horn honks of the arriving limousine.
Within must be the man of her dreams.
He is waiting with champagne, perhaps a night on the town.

The girl next door steps out to meet him.
Her evening gown is soft silk and lace.
His greet is a kiss on the cheek and his arm for a stroll in the park.

Another sweet someone walks up to the door
Carrying a bouquet of fragrant daisies.
His shirt is untucked and his hightops unlaced.

Down the hall she races,
Grabs her jacket, and throws open the door.
There she greets him with her warm embrace.

—*Christy Halverson*

Collage of Love

The cupidlike bow that unleashes its unsolicited arrow
toward an unworthy object
The magnanimous magnet of affection that gathers the shattered fragments
of a life once sliced by the knife of hatred
The glowing offspring of emanating personal pulchritude
The magic mirror that reflects its innocent image to another's face
The plush, pleasant pillow of memorable, warm compassion
The gentle hand that rocks the cradle of beneficent care
The generous garment in which anonymous philanthropy is wrapped
The flickering candle that dispels the enveloping darkness of a dreary night
The burning brand that distinguishes enduring fact from fleeting fantasy
The badge of bravery for a friend or foe caught in the mesh of no return
The sheltering shadow for an injured, staggering fellow pilgrim
The secure staff on which the weary finds repose
The rope of rescue for the soul sinking in deep despair
The towering torch that signals triumph over struggle, tragedy and pain
The limitless extension of life for life

— *Wendell K. Babcock*

The Forgotten Bookcase

Lacy cobwebs decorate the corners of the heavy wooden shelves,
Upon which sit the works of the greatest authors of our time.
The phraseology of Shakespeare buried beneath;
Layers of old newspapers and candy wrappers.
The sensous sonnets of Elizabeth Barrett Browning
Caught between the Farmers Almanac of years ago,
And this year's Christmas wish book.
Bits and pieces of family history.
Tossed together in a beribboned box
Takes time to sort through yesteryears talent;
You may find your own literary genius.

— *Elizabeth E. Clark*

Highway of Love

Down the highway of love we walk, we walk apart but not alone.
On one side of the highway lies dreams and hope.
Dreams of making it, dreams of a life that could be ours.
Hope that we will make it no matter what stands in our way.
On the other side of the highway lies fears and doubt.
Fears that someone will interfere, fears of being too afraid to go on.
Doubt that we really don't love each other.
As we walk down this highway, a highway that everyone walks down
at least once in their life.
We only look to the side of dreams and hope and try to avoid
the side of fears and doubt.
For those who look to the side of fears and doubt
are the ones who never make it.

— *Victoria D. Jenkins*

Faith

Faith is the eye that sees God
No matter how dark the night.
Faith is the hand that leads and guides us
On the steep and rugged way.
Faith is the heart rejoicing,
Accepting God's promise true.
Faith is the ear that listens
To the voice that speaks to you.
Faith refuses to doubt Him
Though others are filled with fear.
Faith is believing the word
And knowing that God is near.

— *Carl Kent*

Black-N-Blue

I could always win
When you started
Emotional wars.
I was just as strong
As you with my words.
But when you began
Physical wars
I couldn't fight you
Not fairly anyway
Your strength left dark colors
On my peach skin.
In the original wars
The colors you left
Were only the circles under my eyes.
Now you leave colors in places
I can't correct with makeup.

—*Kristie Wright*

Intoxication

This pledge I sign
to drink no wine
Nor whiskey hot
to make a sot
No fiery rum
to turn my home
into a Hell
whence none could dwell

Where peace would fly
and hope would die
and love expire amid such a fire
So here I pledge
perpetual hate
to all that can
intoxicate

— *Moi C. Thompson*

Prophecy

One night came the raven, and said he
I bring you words of prophecy.
Your time is short, the world's not long,
Til all shall hear the banshie's song.
Ice shall burn, sun shall freeze,
And fish shall boil in the seas.
All answers shall at last be clear,
But questions shall be lost, I fear.
With the breaking of the seventh seal,
All that you see shall cease to be real.
The works of man shall fall to rust
And man himself shall be as dust.
Into the Cosmic his soul shall flee,
Free to explore for all eternity.
The raven turned, then was gone
But his last words lingered on...
Free for all eternity...

— *D. Thomas Lang*

Winter

The snow in shadow
Is gray and the ground is beige
As a sea of ice

— *Jason Craig*

Meeting

In the air we met
There was you, a hat and me
Through the hat our hearts met.
There was you, some words and me
Through the words our minds met.
There is you
There is me
In the land of nowhere we meet.

—*Limakatso*

For Jill

A single rose
of pristine white
waits in a vase
of crystal blue
A perfect rose
without a flaw
stands
in splendid solitude
Yet it cannot survive
the ravages of time
and willl not remain
one week hence
For beauty wasted
spare a sigh
Alas, the death
of Innocence

— *Lisa Martin*

Willow Breasted

Winged and velvet sighs
Aspect never to be
A willow breast...
Yearn ages gone
A willow breast beckons
A call deep from within
Draws near to my breast
A pulling
The presence-oh, my soul
Canter within
A willow breasted

— *Michael Owens*

He

He sits behind his dull, brown desk
Before the crowded room.
He reads aloud his ancient notes,
His voice reflects the gloom.

The students wriggle in their seats,
This man is such a bore.
The bell has rung, the man's alone,
Just like he was before.

His satchel he pries open,
Inserting notes and all,
And putting on his weathered hat,
He shuffles down the hall.

His career, once so exciting,
Is now so commonplace.
He's trapped inside his own routine,
He just keeps up the pace.

—*Sandra Clutter*

Here in Viet Nam

Young men walking, no one talking,
Waiting for the bomb.
Hearts like thunder, off to plunder,
Here in Viet Nam
Deadly quiet, now a riot,
A cry is heard—it's Tom.
Bullets flying, all are dying,
Here in Viet Nam
Medics running, Charlie gunning,
Fly-boys in from Guam.
Rotors turning, young men burning,
Here in Viet Nam.
Dust off rising, men are crying,
Body-bag for Tom.
No one's winning, world is spinning,
Here in Viet Nam

— *Roger J. Monigold*

Untitled

When I turn to look at you
And catch you looking back,
I get butterflies in my stomach
And my knees grow weak.
No other woman could ever love you more
But you don't seem to want what I have to give,
For your heart and mind are too full of her
As you live off the pain she gives.

—*Teresa D. Rankin*

Hatred Erased

Those men with slanted eyes
Killed my son for whom I cry
One more time I had to see
His cross at Punch Bowl, Hawaii
I flew in and got a room
Asked that a cab be there soon
The driver asked, *Where to, please?*
I read his name, he's Japanese
The cemetry! I bade him go
Angrily—so he would know
My hurt, my longing just to see
The son his people took from me
'Twas he who found the grave I sought
With his hand upon my arm he brought
Me to the site that held my son
Left me alone till visit done
He saw my heartbreak easily
And said, *Sit up here with me.*

—*Mary Holm*

Broken Hearted

I once had a heart that was untouched,
But then you came along and took clutch.
I felt really happy around you,
We were like two people from a crew.
You were always at my side,
And then suddenly you made me unshy.
I thought that I had it all, but little did I know,
That soon I would be feeling so low.
Then someone else came along,
And then you threw me away
Like there was something wrong.
You left me along the side,
Like I was on a roller coaster ride.
You now have my friends heart,
I guess I was just another name on your chart.
I am feeling empty and sad,
But more like mad.
I had so much faith in you,
But then I realized, I was such a fool.

—*Kerry Ann Presinzano*

Mother

You've always been there,
When I needed you most.
Even when I was scared of the, dark and
Thought I saw a ghost.

You'd give me a hug,
And make things better.
Whenever I was away you'd
Write *I love you* in my letters.

All those times that I'd cry,
And all of those lost tears.
You'd always wipe them off my face,
And make me forget all my fears.

All I ever really needed,
Was that sense of motherly touch.
I guess that's what makes me,
Love you so very very much!

    —*Rebecca Heaslett*

Mother

I am your creation,
An unfinished painting on the canvas of life,
And it is I who is able to display
The hard work and love that you have exerted
In painting my life.
My only hope is that I have reflected brilliant colors
To show the world the bonds between us and
How well we work together.
For when the world sees me
It sees my creator, my artist;
It sees you.
So, when you look upon me and are proud,
Be proud of yourself.
Because
What you see in me is merely
A reflection of yourself.

    —*Shaun Rawls*

Mother

One day while I was browsing along the shopper's way,
I viewed a true rare beauty in a case where it did lay.
Its price was well a fortune for many diamonds it did hold,
Yet it brought to me a vision of a treasure yet untold.

To memory came my mother who could enhance a stately throne,
But she chose instead to take a house and make of it a home.
A diamond must be sold away to give what it is able,
But mother served up daily love, so freely round our table.

A jewel can never ever know if you fear at night,
Nor using gentle soothing words put end to such a plight.
Giving comfort by touch and good cheer with a smile,
She was present when needed for that was her style.

Like rays from a diamond she lighted my life,
A beacon of safety through hardship and strife.
God knew she was needed like blue in the sky,
No science can match her, nor dare do they try.

She believed in the Lord, yes that above all,
She studied His Word and answered the call.
I will love her forever, this child-of-the-King
And praise God hallelujah for this human being.

    —*Thomas Koch*

To My Mom

To a special person, I love you dearly.
You have brightened my life ever so clearly.
These words come from a heart sincere.
Although I will be apart from you, my voice will be near.
When I think of the many sacrifices you have made just for me.
I know I am gently loved now, the same love I sensed when I was a baby.
For then, as now, there is a bond unbroken
Love can be sensed between us...yet unspoken.
God is love as I have recently experienced
Because of the things you have done, Mom
Among many, he must love you dearest.
I know there's a beautiful place for you in Heaven.
You have helped many lives with a heart made for caring.
From this poem, I hope you can see a little of how much you truly mean to me.
Maybe it'll give you a small clue, that I, your daughter Rachel, adore you.

    — *Rachel Caine*

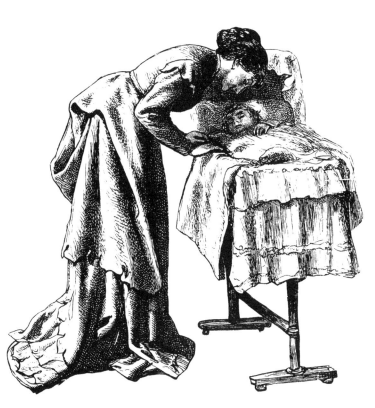

Mom Is a Legend

A lady that loves a child through good and bad times is a lady with class.
A mother that gives a smile through her tears; who is she?
She is a legend.

She's a hero who saves others from harm,
    from town to town and she cares for me.
When it rains, she brings the sun.
When I cry—she gives me a smile.
Who is she?
She's a mother that lives within a legend.

This lady is my mom!
And nobody can ever fill her shoes.
Although Mother's Day is near, she'll always be very dear
    all through the year.

So stand up and cheer! 'Cause there is no room for tears.
Yes, Mother's Day is coming.
My love for her is very dear.
Yes, my mom is a legend.

    — *Kenny Barrows*

Counterpane

Remember the unique counterpane
That gramma made so long ago?
A coverlet made of snips of cloth
From family clothing she did sew?
Yesterday I experienced a view
Of a gorgeous coverlet given to me.
I traversed a curve and rounded a bend
And a magnificent counterpane did see.
Tall slivers of yellow, olive green.
Rounds of brown and orange and jade,
Spots of gray against brick red dirt,
Fifteen greens in light and shade.
Bits and pieces fit together,
Not by chance, indeed by plan.
I stand in awe, am greatly blessed
God's counterpane—a gift to man.

— *Mary Funderberg*

Untitled

buds turning into flowers
winter turns to spring
rain falls
gently from the sky,
leaving a rainbow
that soon will fade to gray,
for all that lives is born to die
and however hard you try,
time cannot be traced
but once again the sun shines
and I try to reach above the clouds
for a silver lining to hold on to
before once again
the light melts away.

— *Lisa Ekiner*

A Dance of Love

The beautiful gown
We worn not a frown
The delicate roses, all in white.
The tears of happiness blurring my sight
The breathtaking dance,
And the way it revealed a wonderful romance
The wishes made on thousands of stars
For a love that can only be ours.
Oh, the happiness I have know since
I have found my very own Prince.

— *Regina Smith*

Faithfully

Faithfully,
I will be here for you
My friendship is always true
In no matter what you do
Truthfully,
I will be here, can't you see
Take my hand, and come with me
Where there's love constantly
And my friendship of honesty
Honestly, I won't leave, if you call
Or when your backs against the wall
I'll catch you if you fall
Patiently, I will be here can't you see
My love will set you free
Can't you see the friend you have in me.
I will be here faithfully.

— *Mary Helen*

Choosing Between Friends

A tug of war
Fighting for and between friends,
Hoping to win in a draw.
Holding on to memories,
Guessing what the other wants.
Fantasizing and or dreaming
Of things to do to win.
Sowing wild oats to anger the other
With which he was to begin.
This splits it up forever and ever
And only regrets have won.
For now I know never, to never
Fight to loose lost love.

— *Darlene Jones*

Together, Apart

Once we were together
Now we are not.
Once we were as close as friends could be...
Now we are strangers.
Why did you change?
Why not I?
I don't understand what happened to us
Nor do I know if I want it back.
All I know is you've changed.
Ex-friend.
Where did the real you go?
Find him and bring him back to me,
My dear best friend.
What we had is hidden,
Not gone.
Now let's find it together.

— *Michele J. Sacco*

Liberty Still Holds Her Torch

Someone shot an eagle
and our nation should weep
A change of dreams
and no one came home
The wind no longer lifts her wings
and spreads the message of freedom
We have lost a friend
but hold a memory in our hearts
Her grace cannot be forgotten
nor touched
Our loss will serve only
if her honor still flies

— *Lynette Sauter*

Accelerated Mind

The accelerated mind
Does not have time to think about fear.
The accelerated mind
Does not have time to hold someone dear.

The accelerated mind,
Trying to make a mark.
The accelerated mind,
Shooting out sparks.

Accelerated mind, in full bloom.
An accelerated mind
Made the clouds shaped like a mushroom.

The accelerated mind,
Reaching to infinity.
The accelerated mind,
Its own enemy.

— *Leo Reid Jr.*

A Journey to the Stars

After days filled with complications
There are times you have to get away.
That's why I must take a journey,
A journey to the stars.

On my journey to the stars,
I will live my life the way I want to live it.
There will be nothing I don't want.
Everything will be perfect.
Nothing dare go wrong.

Of course my trip could never take place,
But oh, what I wouldn't give
For a journey to the stars.

— *Janice Mesaric*

Look Around

Look at the things around you
There's so much to see and do
Be thankful for what God gave you.
His blessings are not few.

The beautiful sun that lights the day
All of the things that pass by your way
The trees in the forest, the sand and the sea
The high trailing mountains, the honeybee.

The deep blue ocean, the deep blue sky
The birds of the air, the baby's cry.
The crystal clear raindrop, the morning dew.
It was all put here especially for you.

So take some time to look around
To feel the love and hear the sound.
And thank God for what you've got
I'm sure you'll find you've got a lot.

— *Sharon Jastrzebski*

A True Best Friend

A true best friend is your
Friend no matter how hard
The times get.
A true best friend will be there
For you if you ever need
Someone to talk to.
A true best friend will always
Be your best friend no matter
What she gains or loses.
A true best friend won't leave
You in the cold when she
Finds a guy to love.
A true best friend won't ever get
Jealous of you, and she
Won't compete with you,
A true best friend is hard to find.

— *Misti Weedman*

Untitled

I was so taken by your eyes
And the heat that ignited
When they met mine,
That I did not feel the flames
Melting my heart to your soul.
Amidst the sounds of our burning passion,
I also did not hear you
Say
Goodbye.

— *Lori L. Sawyer*

When Two Become One

Twice as much happiness,
Twice as much fun
Twice as many good times,
And twice as much sun.

Only half of the grief,
And half of the pain
Half of the sorrow,
And half of the rain.

Someone to share with,
A new life begun
Your joy can only double
When two become one!
—*Kimberly Quigley*

Corporation Earth

After the cradles of security
And youths evaporation
Comes the unveiling
Of societies work order
Goals are awakened
Ambition is ignited
After the struggle
For conquest
Destinations are covered
With dreams dressed
And futures crisp
Profits are sliced
As bankbooks sprout
And mountain tops are crowned
—*Thomas M. Lo Castro*

Passing Time

The days get longer
But they go by.
We get stronger
Then we die.
Time is precious
And we must live
And learn something.
We have to give.
Our hearts are young,
Our souls are free.
There are so many things
We have to be.
— *Kim Haye*

Running

Running from life,
Wanting to hide,
Losing the confidence
Kept deep inside.
Like a flower,
Buried deep beneath
Heavy snow
I feel sad and lonely
Not wanting to grow.
Letting out tears
That were stored,
Praying deeply through them,
To the Lord.
Wishing to hide behind
A closed shield
I let life pass by me
While I sit and yield.

—*Karen Weiser*

The Fly

A saucy little house fly
With teeth all green and white
Flew on my lovely layer cake
And anon! he took a bite.
He sloshed around the icing,
Got stuck in the strawberry jam,
And took big bites of fluffy cake
So I swat him biff-bam.
— *Margaret R. Bergman*

Season's in Genesis

Mirrors shine out voices
Echoes from her past
Season's gone
Now as dusty patterns in her fast
Crisp morning reflections
Stretched her days along.
March winds blew amid
Earth's new growth
While summer's sun gave warmth
To days and evenings,
Shifting into autumn winds,
Leaves falling on the ground
Making room for winter's bed,
Cold and wet and dark
Racing back to springtime
To the doorstep of an Ark.
—*Judith Tucker*

On a Rainy Day

On a rainy day, the skies turn
Black and grey
Then there comes a loud thunder
Like the sky had to shout
Leaving the people in wonder
What the yelling's all about
It rains so hard like dogs and cats
Some people put on hoods, others put on hats
Some are running for shelter
Some are running away
And this is what happens on a rainy day.
— *Theresa Wright*

Whittier's Game

Cap tight on his sunlit hair,
Ready to pitch, he was right there.
Bases loaded, the crowd roared, go Whittier!
The score was tied, the winner will be either,
He pitched that ball, right or left it was neither,
The catcher fumbled, the ball hit a chair,
Time was up, the score was tied, unfair,
Still all left happy, including little Whittier.
— *Mary Lynn Winkel*

Drought of Love

The drought of love is a terrible thing,
It can make you dumb, it can make you sing.
I thirst for love as once before,
As when we ran along the shore.
That shore out west reminds me true,
Of the love I had which was for you.
Our love was deep, so beautiful,
But now no light, just dim and dull. I still carry your
Beautiful ring, for the dought of love is a terrible thing.
— *Eric Denner*

Dreams

Dreams are interesting
Dreams are fun
Dreams can happen to anyone.
Just close your eyes
And count to ten
Then you can dream again
When you open your eyes
Your dream goes away
Then you wish you could do it someday.
—*Stacy Neubauer*

The Quest

So the feeling slowly rises
To my elucid, lonely mind
The tears flow forever
Hoping it will find—
A place of rambling rivers
A fragrance in the air
Where you can sleep rest assured
Without a worry or a care.
But this land that never is
I've searched for many miles
Gone through every emotion
Suffered frowns and many smiles
Yet this land is never found
It seems so far away
But onward I will journey
To find this place someday.
—*Sarah Stith*

Verdict: Innocent; Sentence: Death

Lonely candle, wick burned off
All lit you to save their souls.
The flame's heat melted your flesh,
Vibrant! though you cry your tears,
Pink as shattered porcelain,
You'd rather be remolded,
So you could rekindle their
Hope of your light's salvation
But cath'lics just don't believe
In cremation to warrant
One's own reincarnation.
They believe when convenient.
They pray, fast and put on fronts...
While they abandon their God.
— *Michelle Obuhanick*

The Sparrow's Song

In the light of the stars,
Through a break in the trees,
Sat a child in prayer,
Alone on bent knees.
Dear God, if my words you hear,
End our suffering, pain and fear.
We need a sign, from you above,
A sign that in this world there is love.
These words, echoing loud and long,
Were answered by the pleasant song
Of a sparrow, who on impulse sings
To God, rising up on feathered wings,
Just as our very souls do soar
When we open up our minds before
The Lord.
— *R. David Schiffer Jr.*

A Corner of my Mind

I have tried to block your memory
To protect me from the pain,
Pretend I never knew you
And never heard your name.

But the walls I built are not strong enough,
And though I fight my tears in vain,
The feelings still come creeping through
And the hurt is still the same.

I wish that I could forget you,
Or make you see me now.
I thought you really cared
But it seems you do not know how.

The pain will ease with time
And the tears will subside.
And though I know it is over,
That what we had is gone,
The memories will live forever
In a corner of my mind.

—*Mary Eschinger*

Tomorrow

Tomorrow never seems to come.
Today will never pass.
The pain, it comes and makes you numb,
A piece of shattered glass.

There are other places
You know you'd like to be.
Being secluded from everything,
You dream once again of being wild and free.

If this day would ever get here,
Your troubles and worries would dissolve.
Until that day comes, nothing seems too dear.

Today seems to be here forever.
Tomorrow is just an illusion.
Keep calm and hold yourself together.

Your dreams tomorrow will come true.
Hold onto that end of the rope.
Tomorrow will come and pass
And become another memory.

—*Tina Brockman*

Shadow in the Night

She is a vision, she is a dream,
She is a woman
You have never seen.
She moves like a cat
With a gleam in her eye,
Like a shinning star
Within the night sky.
Her voice is a whisper
She is like a light,
For she is only a
Shadow in the night
When the night arrives
She will always be near, for she is a shadow
With nothing to fear.
She is a legend she is a light, for she is
Only a shadow in the night.

—*Michelle Drake*

Choices

The wind...
God bless it for being alive!
All I want is wind.
My friends, inside their houses, have closed doors.
Damn that savage wind!
And yet, God bless it for being alive...

— *Tom Troxel*

City Sky

Over the University
An inkwell sky
An incandescent orange cloud
A flaming streak across the heavens
The yellow-red stripe
On the ambulance parked beneath its glow
City soot and taxi flux
Shatter
The moon's light
Police sirens, neon billboards,
Penthouse gardens
Electrify
The passing nimbus
Like a Christmas show.

—*Katherine Roberts*

The Angry Sea

Roaring like a lion,
the sea foams upon the shore.
Darkness shields the giant waves
that toss and turn and swirl.
Lightning strikes across the sky,
the sound of thunder grips the land
like strong, cold fingers.
The storm urges on the sea,
screaming, as it urges on the sea.
The sea becomes a monster,
thrashing wildly, stretching to touch the heavens,
Icy fingers of water grab at the midnight sky.
After one last deafening cry,
the sea plunges into itself.
Then at dawn,
The sun, a ball of fire, rises
to shine upon a slow and sleepy sea.

— *Amy Lines*

A Myth to Me

I, as Odysseus, beckoned to Calyptic hire.
Though tied to the mast, it's Sirens I desire.
Her seduction, her beauty, so soon to expire.

Aphrodite, the antiquarian lover of the smile,
A golden beauty, a master crafter of beguile.
That I, as fated Anchise, so soon must defile.

The ivory maiden, once I did carve.
The Pygmalion in me begged the goddess above.
Venus, the immortal, sanctioned my love.

A choice of Apollonian or Dionysian I must preach.
That mere promise or beauty or ivory cannot reach.
Yet so simple, to believe in her, that I beseech.

But, nay, the finale lies on the horizon.
The waves are high and the sky is brazen.
For me, it's the Icarian raisin in the sun.

— *Tom Scullin*

The Rain

It danced;
It drummed.
It danced playfully;
It drummed rhythmically.
It danced playfully on sidewalks;
It drummed rhythmically on rooftops.
It danced playfully;
It drummed rhythmically.
It danced.
It drummed.
It rained.

— *Amy Hendrickson*

Melting Blood

The shores overflow
with my love as I walk
within the sand.
My sparks of desire
linger near as I hold
his melting hand.
To hold him tight
is to feel his touch for
the flow of his blood
is a flame.
We spread apart, go
our separate ways and
no one is to blame.

— *Melissa Adrienne Neill*

Karen

You remind me so much
Of a beautiful, fragrant rose.
Sweet, tender and glowing with beauty,
But different from other roses.
When they're all standing up
Straight and proud and happy,
You're wilting slightly
From both pain and sadness,
But no matter how different you are,
I'll always love you best.

— *Christine E. Mraz*

Inside A Dream

When I fall asleep, there I go,
So far away, no one will know.
There it all comes true,
Yes, I can be with you.
The passion we hold,
It must be true, it must be bold.
I wrap my arms tightly around you,
This isn't a dream, this must be true.
I must awake
Yes 'tis fake
Our love isn't true, inside a dream
It's me, not you.

— *Mikey Perez*

Dreams

Dreams are a dime a dozen
When you're ten years old.
High ambitions entrance the mind
Driving personalities to be bold.

A fireman saving lives
Policeman with sirens blaring
Halting crooks on the fly
Even adored by Doubleday's offsprings.

Life gets cruel as we grow old
Reality fashions our mold.
Dream vanish with old age
Banality creeps in on every page.

— *Winfred Partin*

Wonder

Whirled by your passions
Your eyes go blind.
Closed to the world of things
They see the wonder.

In dreams and in life
Hug those moments
In remembrance of your self.

— *Marak Moisis*

Relief for those Who Stay Behind

My heart is feeling old again today
Each hour brings a weak and gentle page
Subjected to an ancient flowing way
Eyes dim and seeking past the end of age

Betrayed by limbs too weak to stand alone
By hair that's lost its darkly shining sheen
Tired flesh has dwindled down to skin and bone
And left old hands to gesture lank and lean

A trail of tales once true remains untold
Experience unshared by younger lives
A furtive smile of love now growing old
A greeting for the end as it arrives

A hope for welcome
To a land that's warm and kind
Relief for me
And all who stay behind
— *Thomas Michael Trimble*

Together as Us

Sometimes I feel you standing close beside me here.
It makes my heart beat faster to know that you are near.
I see a fear in your eyes of all that we could share
But please always remember that I love you and I care.
When our special time comes and we meet face to face,
The tenderness your heart holds puts our love in its place.
After our brief moment is gone and we must part,
You leave me sad and lonely with a very empty heart.
Well, sometimes I think I know you and sometimes you're far away
But no matter what will happen, our love will always stay.
— *Melissa N. Maye*

The Face We Show

A frowning face, for the one we love,
A smile for a passing friend.
A forgiving word for the one who cheats.
For a loved one, sweet revenge.

What is the quirk that makes us shirk
When a kind word should be said?
Why will we wait until it's too late
And the ones that we loved are dead?

Why don't we strive, while they are alive
To bring them sweet content?
Why do we seem to enjoy being mean
Saying things that we never meant?

A pleasant surprise would light up the eyes,
The resentful heart would unbend
If only we'd show the one we love
The same face that we show to a friend.
— *Zola C. Beebe*

Daddy's Pride and Joy

Early every morning, he stands beside my bed
And wakes me up by dropping something on my head
He'll hide behind the door, not knowing what I'll do
Then innocently say, *Daddy, I love you.*
He'll watch his favorite TV show while sitting on my lap
And has to have a story read before he takes his nap
I could sit for hours watching him run and play
Knowing he'll grow up in time and then he'll move away
I hope all daddies in the world have a little boy
Someone they'll be proud to call their little pride and joy
I am thankful to the Lord that D.J. is my son
In daddy's heart he'll always be considered number one
My life would be empty without little David James,
He'll turn a frown into a smile with his little games,
He makes me glad that I'm his dad and he's my little boy
He may be mommy's angel, but he's daddy's pride and joy.
— *Mark J. Drury*

Reluctant Poet

To be a poet,
Writing witty words,
And recording wonderous thoughts
For amusement, reflection, posterity
Is the aim for whcih I constantly strive.
But, alas, my lines continue on without rhyme
And my rapid, wandering mind does abruptly change,
After each line, short sentences seem to grow longer
Which is a never ending and annoying, confusing drift.
— *Joseph D. Poulin*

Searching

Wish that I had insight to answers
That pierce my mind
Like where do broken dreams go
When its life has declined
Do they go with unfinished melodies
Or stories never told
Are they recylced and etched in molten gold
If dreams are tossed away
And never get fulfilled
Are they taken from the weakest
And given to the strong willed
Where does all the hope go
For those who are in despair
Did some more greedy take more than their share
If this black hole absorbs all the mystery
Such as that in space
Then how can the human spirit
Find its secret hiding place.
— *Inez Marie Smith*

The Fiddler

At the end of the platform there stands an old man,
With a fiddle under his chin and a bow in his hand.
His tattered fiddle case lies opened on the ground,
Just waiting for those nickels and dimes to be found.

With his right hand he draws the bow across the strings,
The fingers on his left hand make the fiddle sing.
I reached in my pocket and pulled out a dime,
Threw it in his case, and I saw a twinkle in his eye.

People passing by are entranced by the sounds,
In this small train station, the music echoes all around.
He stands bent but proud, and has drawn a small crowd,
Of nameless people from nameless towns.

He plays his fiddle for nickels and dimes,
I guess everybody has to do something to survive.
And me, I'm just a stranger killing some time,
Waiting for my train, I throw the fiddler another dime.
— *Kenneth F. Leck*

Tatiana-of-my heart

I watched you moving through the house last night
leotard pulling softly over young breasts
blue-jeans, *guess* of course, covering curves
that last week I did not notice.

Caught in the moment of your pre-teen reality
you danced across the living room
Walkman covering your sound reception
Def Leppard blasting in a space I could not enter.
We laughed, at breakfast, over friends follies
Toasted your journey and your lifes' successes
Drove to the airport and parted quickly
before hot tears could descend my cheeks
embarrassing you in public spaces.
My eyes followed you to the plane
Watched you board, hampered,
by self consciousness and the bags you carried
Good bye Tatiana-of-my-heart, I love you, Mom.
— *Joanie Junqueira*

Ancient Dreams

High in alpine tenderness
Lies the sparkling bejeweled
City of ancient dreams
Winds of memories breath
Life into this nestled town.
Muffled in cold silence yet
Its arms reach even now to
One more lingering caress.
Let us return again to this
Impassioned bastion of past
Delights, vibrant and beckoning
So coy beyond our reach.
Now before it lights be dimmed
And shrouded lay in frozen glacier arms
So cold beyond our reach.

— *Corrine Tsiaperas*

Untitled

O cool crisp autumn sky hold your wrath and anger
And let not Zeus hurl thunder and lightning
From Mount Olympus, but allow Aphrodite to grace us
With beauty and love to replenish the earth
With Demeter and Persephone.
O solemn winter sky cold and harsh
Send Apollo with his protective powers
To enlighten us with music and medicine
To comfort us from the cold, white wrath
You will send upon us.
And in the spring.
Send Dionysus with vegetation
So that we may prosper
In health and warmth

— *E. Andrews*

Contemplating

Carried away upon the wind
Have gone the days that once I lived
Fading memories, broken dreams
My box of thoughts to the clouds I give

I linger in the hallways of my mind
Which represent that span of time
Choosing which doors that I should lock
And which I should leave open behind

So that on those days I talk with him
And he says, remember when...
I will be able to say, Yes, I remember
But why should we return again?

— *Claudia J. Conger*

Night Lovers

The sun hid her warmth behind the mountains
and the moon slowly rose, bringing her chilling light.
The wind blew harder and his partner the clouds danced faster
Trying to escape the icy glare of the moonbeams.
Playing hide and seek, tempting, teasing, the moon would
Find the lovers, bring them out of hiding and chase them again
And again until finally the sun would take pity and send
Her warming rays and the wind would whisper to his lover,
Stay, stay, and the clouds would once again be lost forever
In the gentle arms of the wind and warmth of their friend.

— *Charlotte Keith*

The Hippocrat

Healer of others, when God allows,
Who will heal your wounds?
You, who vowed those sacred vows
Of morality. And immortality.
Do you, by reason of your trade,
Fell less of pain and suffering
Than lesser mortals made?
Healer of others you did choose to be
To play God, or pray God
Heal those who worship at your shrine.
Healer of all, healer of none,
The choice is not thine.
Physician, heal thyself.
But, you cannot, only God can heal
You are but a faker; an illusion maker,
To pretend you know what pain others feel.
False healer of others, heal thine own disease
You, so smug behind your white facade, as if you were God.

— *Beverly Hewitt Lowers*

Imagine

Imagine a support point in the precipice of your mind
Imagine that you have wings to cross the ocean of your doubts
Imagine that you can attempt it
When the angle of focus seems to be inaccesible

Imagine that there are no reefs
That we all have possibilities that no one is better than anyone else
And that no one is less than anyone else

Imagine that you can
That adversity is only a phantom, unreal and mocking

Imagine that you are not afraid
That everything has its deduction, even the polyhedron in its rotation

Imagine that you can transcend the horizon of your fugatious dreams
And start with the providence
To have a little faith in your imagination

— *David Irigoyen*

Follow What's Inside

People are always going to put you down
No matter what you're trying to do
But don't you listen to a word that they say
Just keep right on believing in you.

Don't ever let them change what you desire
They only want to see you fail
Because a man that is without belief and faith
Is just like a ship without a sail

So now go and climb up to the top
And never let anyone lead you astray
And if you keep persisting and never give up
Then you are bound to find your way.

Because everyone of us has a place
Where we are meant to be in life
So all you need is to take a look within
And then to follow what's inside.

  —Ronald S. Curazzato

It Burns

Love is but a challenge,
A do or die mirage that appears then fades into dust.
Love is a game of give and fake.
Never accept it, always object to the pain.
Love is fire burning us all:
 Surrounding our thoughts,
 Feeding us poison,
 Leaving us dry.
Love is a human's race
Making us run the distance from here to there.
Love is but a reflected image.

  — Lesley Garretson

Untitled

Slowly you get up as if not to disturb me,
But I'm awake.
I knew your leaving was just a matter of time.
I lay still not to ruin your plan to leave,
But all the time silently pleading you to stay.
You stumble against the bed and see if I awoke.
Carefully you put your hand on my cheek
And softly say goodbye,
As you walk out the door,
I begin to cry.

  — Michelle M. Kellogg

An Angel Cried

An angel cried,
her hair dampened by the mist.
A tear is formed,
a reminder of a lover she once held.
A memory of hands that once cradled
her soft face, as a mother with her newborn.
A memory of a promise to return one day
and take her away, away to a place where
the water flows through peaceful valleys,
there love renewed.
Awakened suddenly, she looks to the horizon.
He returns for me, she thinks, *on
a gleaming white charger,* but it is
only a cloud pushed on by the wind.
He will not return, the battle has taken its toll.
Left lifeless, he clutches a reminder of their love,
a locket of hair dampened by the mist,
when an angel cried.

  —Mike D. Barber

Defeat

I stand on my own two feet,
Only to face defeat.
Defeat, what a ugly name
No victory, but only shame.
Shame of the mind,
Shame of the soul,
Defeat gives you both,
And leaves you in the cold.
What I didn't understand
Till I was old was that
Defeat is actually a test.
A test of the mind,
And a test of the soul,
Now I stand on
My own two feet,
But I don't meet defeat,
I never met it again!

  —Lorie A. Forchia

The Days of Future's Past

Grandma cooked the finest foods
On a wood burning stove
That made me glad when time to eat
To the table we all strove
I can still hear her saying,
Don't forget your Bible verse,
If we started talking
She told us all to hush
We all knew to mind
The things she said and fast
Those were the good old days
Of future's past
Though, sometimes I got mad
And wished that I were grown
And sit around a table
With a family of my own
I do now and know at last
There is no more days like
The days of future's past

  —Mable Williams

Remembrance Now and Past

A tiny dog with eyes so bright,
Left her home an October night.
Wore a coat of gold and brown,
From friend's house, was found.
Nose like an olive, pads for feet,
To her home a special treat.
Came our way to stay awhile,
Brightened-all, with canine smile.
Twany body smaller than human baby,
Was in every sense, a little lady.
She's gone to pet's resting place,
It's very sad, but that's the case.
In memory now, she lives so long,
It hardly seems she has really gone.

  — King Gentry

Untitled

She was all alone
in the chill of the night.
Tears sparkled in her emerald eyes.
Her face was the color of sadness
as loneliness surrounded her
and the quiet whisper of the winds
echoed in the darkness.

  — Sarah Macy

A Little Bit of Right

You stand near her, the one I think you love.
You gently touch her smooth hair,
As you would the petal soft wings of a dove.
She looks up and motions toward me.
You lift your eyes,
My tears falling is what you see.

I've wronged you my love.
So how can it be that you'd ever want me?
I hear you say it's only her you see.

So tonight I'll sit in my room and cry.
But slowly you enter in by my side.
You take my chin and look in my eyes
And you softly say to me:
*You've done the best you could do, there
is a little bit of right in every wrong.*
There's a little bit of me in you.

  — Chrissy McPherson

Agony

They say that a soul does not grieve!
Mine hurts from loving you as I have
My soul weeps in silence
And the pain reaches deep
Like thorns that rip.
I feel cold, and sadness replaces
The illusions that loved you.
My soul is overwhelmingly sad.
Tired and alone I am.
They say that a soul does not grieve!
The soul agonizes when it feels
A furtive kiss that's not meant for it.
I have felt this agony within.
I weep...and they say that a
Soul does not grieve!

  — Regina T. Cabrera

Look

Look not into my eyes and judge me,
But look and see me as I really am
Look not into my soul and tell me that
I am different from you, look deeper
Then into the mirror my friend. For we
Were destined...you and I to touch
Each others lives and in this time to
Know each other's pain.

I have held you in my arms, cradled in a
Warm cocoon of love, safe and warm,
Protecting you from those who offer
Harm. I lifted you up and saw your
Spirit touch the sky, courageous and
Unafraid, and I will hold you there
Forever in my heart, as I give mine to
You

  —Ronna Warshaw

I Will Not Ever Forget Him

The first day I saw him
My knight in shining armor
I knew he was for me
He had golden hair
Almost as bright as the sun
The prettiest blue eyes
Almost as blue as the sea
Oh, what a thief he was
For he stole my heart in a matter of seconds
In a matter of days he disappeared
With a part of my heart
I cannot forget him
I will not ever forget him

  —Cindy Vasquez

The Future

Young and engaged, two women we talked.
She said, *Don't you wish you could see
And know now where we will have walked?*
No, because if I knew what would be,
I might not want to take the road.

Best we have our own *great expectations*
That help us carry our daily load.
Thus we weave complex interrelations
Each day with dreams that might never be
Into a surprise-filled tapestry.

— *Ruth A. Hall*

Friendship

F is for the forgiveness that she always seems to give.
R is for the rumors that we've always seemed to have spread.
I is for the independence that we love to share.
E is for the eagerness that we're always sure to have.
N is for the neverendless fun we have.
D is for the dependability, that which she always gives.
S is for the special times we have had together.
H is for all the help she's given me.
I is for how important she is to me.
P is how precious this all means to me.

— *Misty Memmer*

A Life It Can Take

It can snatch a soul in less than a second
It can be carried almost anywhere
It even comes smaller than a deck of cards
It can be purchased in any town

It's made of steel and will last a lifetime
It has one long eye that sees nothing but death
Its operations are simple,
Load
and
Kill

It can take six lives without a reload
It's not used for hunting
Or very seldom for fun
It is however all over the world in most everyone's home
This machine has mastered the art of killing
There is however one thing that it does lack; a warning sticker:
Caution: Completely harmless unless accompanied by a human.

—*Barry Griffith*

Just a Little Too Late

Our grandson was three years old or so
When he threw the ball up high-
Stuck on the roof of the house it did go.
Grandpa, will you get it down for me?
After I haul these bales to the cows, said he.
When Gramps was done and turned around twice,
Our five year old grandson was skating on the ice.
Please, Grandpa, come see my carnival show.
I will, my son, when my work is all done;
I'll come to see it then.
But when he got there, the arena was bare
And our grandson was going on ten.
The computer machine was then the in thing;
Our grandson was punching it in.
Please, Gramps, come see this neat thing and what it can do.
I will, my son, I certainly will, I'll come to see it soon.
But when he got there, he felt much despair,
Our grandson to college had gone.

—*Lorene Benkie*

The Puzzle Piece

Life is like a puzzle
That's slowly put together.
It grows and grows and grows
And it doesn't matter, whether
The pieces are all jagged,
Or smooth, and black, or red,
There's a picture in the making
That says everything about you
Everything you've ever done and ever said.

— *Monica Gries*

A Heart Full of Tears

Touch me with thy eyes, for I am forever lonely without thee.
Let thy arms keep me safe and warm and thy love light my way...
The darkness no longer will surround me.

My foolish heart longs to live those treasured moments within my life.
The beautiful memories held deep within my heart,
that time cannot take away...
A love greater than any words spoken in time.

Through time and space, my love shall be with thee, for I am within you.
I shall see through thy eyes, the birth of spring, the April rains
and the golden glow of the August moon...
The magic of moonlight.

Time passes as each day is gone with the wind forever.
Every night of my loneliness brings only images of my love, my life.
Fading in time through death and darkness we are torn apart,
leaving a broken heart, a handful of tears...
The last farewell.

—*Mary E. Kinzie*

I Feel

I feel like no one cares; like I have been betrayed
as my heart is shattered inside.
Everyone says don't look back; live your life. But I can't help but hurt.
What have I done?
I've never hurt you or anyone.
I gave, never expecting to receive.
You never cared; you never even looked back.
You cared only for yourself and what you could take from others.
There's nothing left to take, you've got it all.
I've never loved another, but still you said you loved and left.
I've cried for you again, and again, until my shouts were dry.
No sound remains; only my silent screams
grow louder and my pain deeper.
I can't starve myself for your love any longer.
I love too much.
I must leave my dream of hoping to ever get you back.
I love, but I hurt; so please take your knife from my heart,
go away and stop the pain.

— *Michelle Averett*

A Few Lines Written to a Friend Slowly Dying in Viet Nam

For you, the year is a quaint apologetic figure;
Thinned by fevers writhing through the greenblade hell
You tread. Monsoons offer, lean palms to your throat.
You lie helpless rotting under the ochre glare of flares;
By the time this note arrives, you may be dead.
At home, Careme has begun to parch your brown dirt;
Your red seeds dotting the hills, remind us of that red
Hell you forage in foreign lands: Fear muzzled
By your side, yet you fight on with the same zeal
That drags this pen. You are not afraid to die,
Where the echo of boots on dry twigs trigger
Despair. Already, your mother has bought your black
Shroud: When you die your soul flies home to God.
To that green shore where pink shells mourn; Where
Soft waves drum your lamentations to the land.
It is so useless rotting in alien sand.

—*Mc. D. Dixon*

Home Again?

Prisoners of war,
what are their names?
Is there a person responsible,
Is there someone to blame?

Will they ever come home,
come home to stay?
No one seems to know,
no one can say.

If I knew it would help,
I would surely say:
I'd be willing to go;
I'd be willing to stay.

Prisoners of war,
what did they do
to deserve such punishment
unknown to me and you?

—*Melodie Willis*

Here I Sit

So here I have to sit,
Covering up my tears.
Having to be strong again,
So other pains can disappear.
So here I have to sit,
Holding back the tears.
Having to forget the past,
To remember how to live.
So here I have to sit,
Wishing away the tears.
Having to be by myself,
To conquer all these fears.
So here I have to sit,
Cursing at the tears.
Having not to think twice,
About why they have appeared.

—*Kimberlee D. Brown*

Life

A meaning unknown
Perspective unclear
Perception disturbed
My voice no one hears.
A distorted dream sequence
A path left unshown
My voice unheard
My spirit alone.
Roaming thru unbeaten woods
A cry in the vast amount of black
Can't you hear me calling
Calling you back?
I'm at the end
The end of my rope
My feet are suspended
And lost are my hopes.

— *Shana Sides*

Christmas Is Beautiful

Christmas is beautiful
With the freshly fallen snow
And the gift of love
And the bright stars above
Where the angels sing
And everlasting peace begins.
The Christmas spirit never ends.

— *Karen Jordan*

Kaleidoscope

Watch it rain with hands upheld;
See angels sing in the rainbow.
Rays of rose shine and colors meld,
Blood to water, sorrow to snow.

Droplets cling to clusters of grapes
As distant clouds now fade from view.
Fields alive with budding lilacs
Flourish in a wave of ocean blue.

By an ancient tree with a secret to tell,
In a forest where infants run wild,
Sits a lonely man in a wishing well,
Clasping a coin thrown in by a child.

See the old man trudge a crooked path
Forever searching for a peaceful place.
He pauses to hear the doubting brook laugh,
Then resumes the same practiced pace.

— *Samuel T. Martin*

The Respite

I watched the cadence of the shadows
as they moved capriciously
Pregnant with impressions of
intriguing prophecy.
Light, an executioner, stealing 'cross
the lawn
And muting to the darkness
was welcomed as the dawn.

I listened to the shadows' whispers,
to the daring in their play,
But clever, these deceptive creatures
lithely slipped away.
Lost to some invention of the mind,
it seems to me
They weren't phantoms in the making
but clowns of mystery.

Billowy reflections, elusive as the breeze,
Dauntless their maneuvers, delicious revelry.

—*Rosalie Marlowe*

Untitled

To feel nothing, is pain.
To feel something, is nothing.
To see something, is to behold
To feel something, is to hold
To lose is something lost!
To have lost, you at least had to have tried.
To want, is to need
To need, is useless.
To love means pain
To know pain you've had to have loved.

— *Nina Shoe*

They Said

They said they could read me like a book,
But they didn't read all the words.
They said they knew how I felt,
But they felt different than I.
They said they knew the real me,
But they knew a me I didn't.
They said they would be with me forever,
But now they're gone.
I said I wouldn't let them get to me,
But now I'm gone, too.

—*Kitti Haynes*

Escape

In this hectic world of ours
There are times when there
Is a need to escape from reality.
A time to escape from the harsh
Ways of mankind and to discover
One's self. When I escape,
I can become whatever I want to be.
No time. No place. No one to
Judge me or accuse me of my actions.
I am lost, drifting between
Two different worlds or flying
Over distant hills.
A pencil and sheet of paper
Are my escape route.
From the depths of my mind,
I pour out my soul, my thoughts and creations.
I place myself in the perfect Utopia,
In a dream from which I
Will never want to awaken.

—*Melissa Anderson*

Wonder

You watch the tears run down his face.
You wish they were something you could erase.
You know you could not, so you let them be.
You wish you could open up for him to see.
You wonder why it is so hard to say goodbye
You wonder if you are always going to cry
You will always wonder why people change
Why does life have to be so strange.

—*Ronna Beland*

standing at my window on this
autumn-winded summer night,
i idly wish on stars
and think of you.
(visions that are memories
    fill my mind with the distance of dreams. i
    all at once hate and love you.
    affection for remembrances
    soft and (like innocence) warm collides with
    disdain for confusions that spiral
    through my brain, whirl bang crashing
    into sides that only slow them (momentarily) down.)
diving in these waters
between Friendship and Enmity
i come up breathless
to face an empty shore.

i walk alone through june's october.

—*Stephanie Cook*

The Death of a Salesman

Creakingly
The door opened creakingly
And there were of course cobwebs
Bespectacled young or not
so a young man's face peers
into

Dustily floating must fills
the barren parlour the (a wire here and there)
void (a coathanger)
Bashfully he makes his way cautiously (vacuum cleaner in hand)
on tiptoe door always open politely (derby in other hand)
clenched jaw (a trickle of sweat?)
set in determined
determinism

But the house is empty

— *Chris Kapsaroff*

Blowin' By

I'm a feather in the wind
However fleet
It's a message of love I send.
If the breeze blows fair
I'll light in your cap.
Then you may pluck me down.
Make a wish you can keep.
The effect will make you laugh
If you don't weep.
For much sorrow can be had
For those who wish lies.
Yet much joy
For those who are mine.

— *Marc Paine*

10:00 PM, Jacksonville

Rain spills unrestrained down
The grimy face of night,
Like the sudden, savage
Tears of lunacy,
and,
I wonder what mindless
Rage spends itself in an
Incandescent city's night storm.

— *Michalanne Newlin*

Together

You're my one and only love
And this I want you to know.
You mean more to me than anything;
I don't ever want you to go.

Loving you gives me happiness,
The kind I need each day
And if sometimes I don't show it,
I love you in each and every way.

If sometimes I get jealous,
It's only because I care.
The love I feel for you
Is ever so rare.

If I could have one wish,
Do you know what it would be?
For us to betogether
For all eternity.

—*Penny Cole*

Falling in Love

Although I know that it is a fact
That we have nearly met;
Your friendly smile is something
Sweet that I cannot forget;
I gazed into your eyes and saw
The answer to my prayers
That somebody would come
Along who seemed to care;
I know you only gave a glance,
And spoke a word or two;
And yet that was enough for me,
To fall in love with you;
I may have been mistaken,
When I looked at you that night
I have never seen the world so
Beautiful and bright.

—*Michelle Gates*

Misty to Slash

I hope, when death does retro down,
To blast me from earth-space,
The living find me tightly locked,
Within your hot embrace!
Like Beaver said, our legs entwined,
Though it would seem disgrace,
Our lips involved, in fiery mass,
Our hearts, a raging race.
Your laser touch, that burns a path,
Right to my very soul,
Let death be swiftly nuclear,
Super-colliding our love, whole.

— *Mary Jean Plantner*

Fleeting Youth

Sitting there
On the beach
In front of the waves,
I listen, I watch;
It's nighttime,
The waves seem strong and angry,
Yet peaceful and proud.
I'm ready to believe anything.
I think of the past, the present, the future.
There are so many questions;
I know my life will change.
I'm growing up.
I feel like everything safe
Has been turned upside-down.
Does everyone feel like this?
I wish I could stay here forever,
Watching, listening, thinking, caring.

—*Laura McCay*

Do Unto Others

Old men, old women, the unwanted seeds
thrown from the garden of dignity.
Hands that shake, hair turned dull
existing in silence, no one calls.

When they were 30 did they ever think
reaching maturity makes *importance* extinct.
What will be the choice of Young Society
when it's harvest time for you and me?

—*Madelyn K. Pellerito*

Alive in Love

O my God, I love you.
You are the reason
for my existence.
You are my king
my gentle ruler
my protector
my guide
my hope
my assurance
my wisdom
my forgiver.
You are the One
for whom I live
and with whom I desire to live forever
together with all whom you love
and who love you wholeheartedly.

—*Mary Frances*

Conspiracy

There is a conspiracy against me
It started in my home
Just who thought it up I don't know
But they are not working on their own

I'm convinced their trying to drive me crazy
Each one in his own way
And it's getting worse
Day after day after day

I can't pinpoint when it started
I can only estimate
I'd say around the time I got married
To the man I call my mate

Now there's three against one
And I'm trying to stay one step ahead
But what I really ought to do
Is change my name to Rose Red

— *Laura A. Fitte*

Are You All Right?

It is raining with the overtones of Bach.
The whole night is insisting to be heard.
Lightning quivers, a restless sleep
walker. Cars hiss on roads
like agitated snakes. Every now and then
a siren wakes from its nightmare.
Are you all right? I haven't heard
from you
since dawn, that oh-so-brittle promise
of another day.

— *Thomas A. West Jr.*

The Mystical River Flows

As I sit, I sit by the river
And dream many wonderful things
And a quick wind rushes down my spine,
And I begin to quiver.
I dream of this boy
His sensitivity brings me warmth and joy.
I dream of this boy becoming a man.
Oh River, I'm your number one fan.
There is so many sides to this mystical river,
He is not a taker in life, he's a giver.
As I sit by the river
The cool wind makes me quiver.
As I watch this mystical river flow,
I go where he goes.

— *Christine Smith*

I Love Snow

I look out my window and what do I see.
Snow and ice decorating my tree.
Reminds me of salvation pure and free.
God in heaven and a crystal sea.

I'm a child at heart I still love the snow.
Jesus goes with me wherever I go.
I remember a winter a few years ago.
Jesus found me I was lost in the snow.

Snow flakes are falling gently down.
Purity from heaven now covers the ground.
Happy children out there running around
Their laughter to me is a heavenly sound.

I love the snow it fills me with cheer.
I feel my savior so very near.
Winter is the best time of the year.
Makes me think of Jesus so very dear.

—*Katherine Keyser*

Negative Dog

We had a mascot, really, more, a crew,
A pitch black fuzzy dog, always glad to see us,
Excited, not an animal, a little girl,
Running, jumping, hopping, talking.
She acted so much like people,
We named her Negative Dog.

Negative Dog was afraid of everything,
Except her people. Bombs and rockets,
Other dogs, enemy attacks, all terrified her.
Bust she was warm and happy when we would
Come back from a cold and lonely patrol.

She withdrew with us during the hard
And bitter retreat back to Saigon.
Somewhere on Highway One we lost her.
So much meat for some Vietnamese dinner.

— *David H. Minton*

Beldame

Old age comes not as you
Naive did fancy.
A quiet grace mellowed in slow time,
A patined charm delightful.

Old age comes bete noire abrupt.
One day as out of your mirror,
A visage like unto that of Hecate
Looms. A wizened hag, a wicked witch!

Her cheek is toothless hollow;
Her hair, gray fallow, waxen thin;
Her throat, turkey buzzard's folded crepe;
Her eye, dark shadowed, fading candle dim.

But don't scare! Kink her hair!
Make it blue! Her eyelids, too!
Paint her lips and hollows!
Hide that awful sight!

— *Juanita Stroud Phillips*

Tangled Web

There is a love in me that must possess,
Must take by giving, kill by jest.
I tangle you in filament of fear and need,
A fragile, finely woven web
Of hope and dream
And expectation rarely met.

There is a love, a savage push and pull
And painful wriggling;
It wraps us round like spider's silk,
Knots us neatly up in fear and guilt.

Nothing is unraveled yet
Save this one thing:
There is a love
Painful, sweet, enveloping,
With sharp and sudden sting.

—*Karen Kowalski Singer*

The Dragon

Twinkling of an eye, shake of a tail
Lickity split, fish for a whale
Enter the Dragon breathing fire,
Nostrils flared, eyes of ire.

Journey inward to the promised land
I go alone, let go of my hand.
Sediment settled covered with dew
Placate, permeate, one of the two.

Exit the Dragon tail between legs;
Eyes filled with tears, back to the dregs.

—*James Karr*

Death of a Pet

The animal
that was once a part of you is gone
up into the clouds
where they lay and weep.
Those four paws
once heard at the door are now gone.
The sweet purr,
the rough bark
have flown into another world.

— *Stacy Girasuolo*

Short Love

I like to remember
How you loved me.
What happened next
Is what I'd like to see.
Looking at it from
My point of view
It's you who doesn't love me
But I still love you.
It seemed to be
Such short love.
The love that seemed
To fit like a glove.
It was that short love
That brought me such pain.
Your love, I wish, would
Start up again.

—*Kris Owen*

Faded Rose

Nature has a way
Of arousing your inner soul.
You can choose to see
A faded rose
And let that beauty
Revive and cure
Your roaming, wandering heart.
When you detect
The ruins of the next
Dark day,
Remember the beauty
Of a faded rose.

— *Jenny Pinette*

The Pet

A cat or a dog can become a part
Of his owners soul and heart
You treat him like a human being
As you watch it's a miracle you're seeing

You pamper your pet everyday
You watch him eat, you watch him play
You treat him right and show him caring
You realize that this life you're sharing

And then one day you lose your friend
You feel your life has come to an end
You spend the time to cry and mourn
Wishing he had never been born

Things no longer seem the same
Nobody runs in when you call his name
But you know the time will also come
That soon again there will be someone

You will love and tend and need
To help you share the life you lead

—*Lora Coslet*

Dudley's Demise

The sorrow and pain you have today,
In time, my dear, will fade away.
It's proper to cry for your wonderful pet,
Remember it fondly and never forget
All living things have a time to die
And are never replaced no matter how we try.
But our hearts and minds will hold others dear
Who help us heal and wash away our tears.

— *Teddy Tarr*

Spring Time

A little cow of spring time
Bawls to the dandelions
And their white parachutes
That tickle her nose.

A spotted fawn of morning
Nibbles on a green blade
And its weedy neighbors
That cover her cloven hooves.

A gray bunny of brush
Smells spring's fresh air
And the warm breeze
That ruffles her fur.

Hidden in forest shadows
Young miracles are born.
Listen to their hearts
That beat with the hands of spring time.

— *Christy A. Dargitz*

My Friend Brian

My friend died today
Yes, it is hard to believe
That just last week
I was talking to him
About how much I hated school
My friend died today
And as much as I want to
I cannot bring him back
Because he is somewhere friendly
And beautiful
Because that is the way Brian was
We all love you Brian
Wherever you are
Thanks for being a good friend

—*Kerry Smith*

I Don't Take Many Chances

I do not take many chances in life;
But you seem worth the gamble.
I do not usually open myself up so soon,
But your understanding, makes it hard for me to keep
To myself.
I have a fear of being hurt,
But you somehow erase the worry.
I do not usually smile so often,
Yet, with you it is hard to frown.
I am not usually this relaxed with someone new,
But with you, my tensions are low.
I do not usually see the sunny side of things in life,
Yet with you, there is very little that does not seem bright.
I am having a hard time believing that all this is true,
Whatever it is that is happening,
I am glad my world has changed
I give all my thanks to you!

—*Cindy Schuetrumpf*

Introspection

And the snow was falling for the first time since the last, it came this day.
When I went to get another glass of brew to begin this play.
All the while; down, down...and down it came!
It is snow—so very pretty and white...you know!
It stays always in the past.

And while it was here, a while it was, long enough it was-
It fell upon my memory with sadness,
      the kind I had longed for. I had to bear.
In the cold depths of winter has the glass eye
      of your mind perceived the white and black there?
How it was in the good-old—days of good.
When in winter—the dead of winter, crystal falling from the sky;
      and I remember it was. Oh! yes it was.
On an unknown street where I thought I belonged. I could see joy;
Just a streetlamp—but with omnifarious light.
But now, what words could describe it, love?
It was so long ago, young love that I lost—don't end, must begin again.

And so the silence was not golden, and the trees were not green,
But all without color—the essence of black and white.
How gentle it played on my imagining—the sounds
      of a winters love at night.
Even in the morning-day, when her light was bright,
      and her smile was gay.

—*Karl S. Zeller*

You Are a Part of Me

Every moment that we are together, I am learning something,
and that knowledge becomes a permanent part of me.
Though my feelings will be different a year from now
or ten years from now, part of the difference is you!
Because of you, I am a different person,
and the person I will grow to become,
with or without you by my side, will have gotten there
partly because of you.
If you were not in my life right now, I could not be who I am right now.
Nor would I be growing in exactly the same way.
Much of what I grow toward and change within myself has to do with
what I respond to in you, what I learn from you, what I understand
about myself through you and what I learn about my feelings
in the dynamics of our relationship.
I do not worry about our future together,
since we have already touched each other
and affected each other's lives on so many levels that we can
never be totally removed from each other's thoughts.
A part of me will always be you, and a part of you will always be me.
That much is certain, no matter what else happens.
I love you and always will.

— *Tammy Baldwin*

Take Liberty

In repose, the night salutes the early morn.
Traces of ellusive thought, fly by forlorn.
In silent moments, quaking ideas are born,
To those who wish to listen, their worlds are torn.
Thought is but a gift, if you hold the key.
Conviction tears the ropes of hypocrisy.
Bound, and tied, you cannot be found free,
To see truths in shambles of mediocrity.
We suffer from the heart, our love delusions.
Live by strange, long held, bent up illusions.
Stumble amidst the ensuing, patterned confusions.
Why not abandon, with pride, this world's intrusions?

— *Heike C. Strand*

Beauty Is

Beauty can be anything
That makes the heart within you sing.
It may be children at their play,
Or just a bright and sunny day.
It may be mountains, cliff or plains,
It may be soft and gentle rains.
It may be sunsets out at sea.
But this is what it is to me:
You smile, you hair, the way you walk;
Your eyes, you lips, the way you talk;
The way you sit, your little hand;
Your nose, your ears, the way you stand;
Your teeth, your laugh, you little feet;
The way you always dress so neat.
Your kindness and your thoughtful ways
That brighten up so many days.
I look at you and then I see
The things most beautiful to me.

—*J. O. Hillhouse*

Certificate of Appreciation

Through the storm and through the toil
You have been a faithful friend to us all
Through thick and thin, hard and rough.
You have been an inspiration to everyone.
You have denied your own personal ambitions
To yield to others.
The love and care you have shown
Has been overwhelming.
Your thoughtfulness and ceaseless working
Has been a great asset to those in need
For someone to care.
We love you a thousand times and
We couldn't say it enough.
May God bless you and forever
Keep you in His care.

— *Rose Mary Anderson*

Ab Ova Ad Finem

God! Your daylight is far too bright
Relentlessly by fate, at each new dawn
The incrassate curtain of life is drawn
Return to us inviolate, our halcyon night
Helplessly we liberate toward the lambent light.
Arrogant humanity is nature's expendable pawn.
And destiny treats man with vitating scorn.
While Olympian Gods laugh at his wretched plight.

God! Why tear us screaming from the maternal womb?
Callous priests, lusty harlots, virtuous maidens
Are sped through a futile life to the Eternal Tomb.
Reluctantly we are forced, at a present cadence
To hasten through this cycle of years, only to loom
Forsaken in history, our spirit lost in silence.

—*Theodore Femmel*

Life

Life can be full of obstacles that sometimes you can't overcome.
Life can be a cinch without ever being told, *No,* for some.
Life can be very meaningful with lessons always to be learned.
Life can be a joke as some of us are concerned.

Life can be filled with its ups and downs that have been witnessed by some
But you can always pick out the ones who can never get the job done.
The struggle in life is the victory and the win is the prize,
But others could care less if their dream lives or if it dies.

To me, I am happy to give the best that I can be.
Nobody can make me the best except for good old me.
Some may think I am just a dreamer with a head full of thoughts,
But someday, yes someday, I will be up at the top.

To win is to succeed, to succeed is to lose at first, then cry.
To lose is to stop trying, to stop trying is to die.
To live life to the fullest and give your very best,
You shall come to realize that God will take care of the rest!

— *Kristyn Cook*

My Return to School

The late August sun trickled through open windows
Mingling with aromas of fresh cut grass
I grabbed a desk; a large one
For room to spread my paraphernalia.
Will she look the same? I thought,
Like all my thoughts these past three months,
her eyes river blue and honest?
WIll her voice ring like last May?
I perceived me shy, out of place among
Years younger ones but felt inside: younger still.
I remained quiet, anticipating, while voices echoed.
And then...she was there...just the same
Three months was yesterday. Her energy frolicking
As I watched and listened to chalk tap-dancing across the board.
Ever so slowly, like a blossom swaying gently on air
She turned to us. Her smile lifted the weight from
My world and opened my heart once again.

—*Rita McClellan*

Imagine a World All Pure and Sweet

Imagine a world all pure and sweet, that's full of passion, desire,
And heat. Streams of wine flow through the land, with deserts of
Sugar instead of sand. Angels flying all around, ecstasy has finally
Been found. Bodies meet and join as one, together until the morning sun.
Making love on a cloud soft and white, feelings of happiness and delight.
Soft caresses and glowing eyes, as heart beats slowly begin to rise.
Motions quicken, the bodies are tense, Feelings of pleasure are immense.
Suddenly, flaming red fire burns free.
Chastity and pureness no longer will be.
All senses are lost as if in a dream.
Through the deafening silence there is a scream.
The bodies are still now as if asleep, but the love they share will
Always keep. Their arms reach out to hold and embrace; a smile will form
Upon each face. And then back they will go to their fantasy land.
Never straying apart, always hand in hand.

— *Tasha Lynn Kranz*

America, We Are Thankful

Thanksgiving Day, we are thankful as can be
For homeland America and our flag and for democracy.
Christmas Day, we are thankful as can be.
The reason for this season: Christ was born to give us Christianity.
New Year's Day, we are thankful as can be
For a happy new year, world peace and love with humanity.
Easter Day, we are thankful as can be.
Jesus arose to God in Heaven; He died for you and me.
Fourth of July, we are thankful as can be
For Independence Day and our freedom of justice and liberty.

— *June B. Clay*

Goodbye

Everytime I think of you my heart leaps.
I knew you would leave, you were not mine for keeps.
You knew everything about me and still cared.
You gave me love and knowledge when I was scared.

What will I ever do without you?
I find myself dreaming of what to do...
Someday I will find you wherever you are;
Wish upon a shooting star...

I will look at you and start to cry;
I will stare at you and ask you why.
Why did you leave me all alone here;
Not a word from you while you were there?

I would rush into your arms and hold you tight,
Your feelings give up without a fight.
I look at you wondering and you start to cry.
Because I love you and do not believe in goodbye.

—*Shannon Cripps*

Window Wooing

When sod's busy steps have no ends,
Never look up, windows remain blind,
Blank holes have no airy opening to the sun,
Love sits alone waiting for passing feet.
Travelers slowly turn around on their heels,
Forget the path up away; grunting molecules
Conceal their head-down posture, smell terrain,
Get lost in a circular constitution—self.
In a tiny absent corner, locomotion's private parts
Look down at hairy critters, confused, berserk.
They forget their eyes—there's someone blowing
Kisses on the balcony, waiting to be touched.
Sallow traffic keeps up its buzzing all night long,
Between the windows and the street, feet find no entry.
Lady at the window, your paint's chipping, wooing.
Pants, Beaux ride on, sirens call, all is off course.

— *Thomas Braga*

Bitterness

Sinking back to my primal origins,
Burning bridges left and right
Without a thought to any comfort
I may need, would want from you.
Fool that you are,
Perhaps someday you will realize
And return to my voided soul,
Swirling in masses of
Unforgiving, bleeding bastards,
Bastards of war who died to save a county where so much
Pain exists but, maybe only in my mind with the confines
that constrict me and my ability to swallow you up and
Spit you out like an unwanted bone and then feed you
To the dogs while I watch, smirking, as they rip you to
Pieces and castrate your soul upon the earth.

— *Deborah Nichols*

Erosion

The water is piled up against the shore.
White foam like whipped cream, covers the rocks,
Where the sandy beach is no more.
And strangers are fishing from our docks.
Our curly haired children have all gone away,
Along with my youth, that time could not stay.
The erosion of life takes place, in much the same way.
As ones' mind, body and face, succumb to the fray.
Soon only the water, the wind and the rain,
And our children's children will remain.
While away down the lake a new beach will form,
Built of the sand brought by our storm.

—*Nada Wager*

The King

The angry king,
He sits and gloats.
While his peasants,
Drown in the moat.
Tax the people, take their cattle.
Take their food,
And the baby's rattle.
Bring it here for me to see,
Take it all, and give it to me.
The people hear and see what is said,
So they kill the king,
And take his head.
A new king is appointed?,
And they are glad,
They think he is better than the one they had.
The new king comes forth,
And gives his decree,
He says, *Tax the people and bring it to me.*

—*Jon B. Parker*

Sometimes When I See Him

Sometimes when I see him
Walking down the street,
Walking right on by,
It makes me want to run
Right over to him and ask him why.
He probably won't give me an answer.
Or if he does it'll be a lie.
But I only want to know the
Real reason why.
He said he loved me and that
I was the only one
But while I was waiting for him
He was out having fun.
I know now it had to end.
Only time our hearts will
Have to mend.
I hope he learned something
Out of all this.
I know I did. And now
I leave him with a kiss.

—*Lynn Ney*

Winter Fights a Rear-Guard Action

Winter fights a rear-guard action
Marshalling its forces for its final onslaught.
Icy winds bugle their battle cry,
Shivering flakes spin in the wind,
Arthritic branches lash snowy trunks.

The old snow huddles in the corner,
Weary and spent and ready to yield
To the crocuses, daffodils and dogwood
Marching forward jauntily
Under the billowing banner of spring.

—*Sophie C. Aksel*

Working the Fields, 7 A.M.

Smoke rises silently above the wounded hearts
They lie awake at night, wishing and wondering
As tears run slowly down their faces
The morning brings healing to their hungry hearts
The yearning to be free, now become reality
For the sun has shown.
Giving them hope in their troubled lives.
Working the fields, they strive, for hope is their friend
And the Lord, their healer.

—*R.D. Staton*

The Challenger Crew

Sailing away
to Heaven's door
as only eagles dare,
I touch the wind
where sunlight shines,
with stardust everywhere.
I feel the warmth
of solar rays
in a universe so grand.

Beyond this world
my freedom's won
as eternity takes my hand.

—*Charles D. Meserole*

A Daughter's Note

There is no need
for alarm

No explanations I
could give

But Mathew does
love me

And from this is
my plague

My God given injury
we flee

I know what is best
I think

Do not worry.

—*Steven Schwarzkopf*

Pretty Boys All in a Row

Pretty boys all in a row,
Lined up against the wall,
Looking luscious and loose,
Yet hard to swallow...

Pretty boys, pretty boys,
Lined up in chairs,
Sitting out time,
Sober time.

Pretty boys,
do they grow up,
And become men,
Or do they stay pretty?

—*Lawrence Michael Dickson*

Illogical Conclusion

In this flame of passion,
Philosophies are burned.
In the sway of this emotion,
Restraint is overturned.

With this crazy feeling,
Sensation severs sense
And in this wave of wonder,
We drown in circumstance.

Other lives are in suspension,
But love is living too.
And if I must hand for their suspense
It is worth it holding you.

So while we practice dying,
Lying lusty in our bed,
We may be guilty of the murder
Of the lives that we have fled.

—*C. C. Howerton*

Once...

a single white petal
clinging tightly to a weak, lifeless
stem
is all that remains of a once perfect daisy.
he loves me not.

— *Sandra Kaye Nunley*

The Written Word

A sea of Emotions Drowning me Quickly
Ideas spoiled by thought of Hungry Public
Teeth Rotting out of their heads
By the Sugary Sensationalism
They've devoured.

scared and inhibited my pen hits
the paper and scrawls out
thoughts restrained by words
nothing planned, nothing analyzed,
just raw thoughts that I can
no longer repress but find hard
to express.

Emotion: hatred, love, greed, sickness.
where does it all come from?
and where does it all go?
It derives and accumulates from the
same source that preys upon it later.

—*Kati Johnson*

What is Life?

As I sit here alone,
In this silent room
Only one question passes through my mind.
What is life?
Is it a game,
To find the winner and loser?
Is it a test,
To see who is the best?
Is it a joke,
That we could laugh at our right and wrong?
Is it a charade,
Where everyone acts out their part?
Is it a serious matter,
That everything should be taken at heart?
All these questions
And still no answers.
So one question still remains.
What is life?

—*Teresa Caceres*

Resting Confidence on a Glass

Mother of two, sick in her shoe,
Doesn't know where to find them.
Selfish and high, won't even try,
Hoping to slip right by them.
Drunk for kicks, pickled by six,
Forgetting the promise she made,
Uncaring, so daring,
In debt and beginning to fade.
Never there, pretending to care,
Should she dress in the red or not?
Only worries—clothes and follies,
Thinking herself so hot.
Thought she'd be rich, professional bitch,
Watching her six year old lie.
Used to be sweet, now he fights, drags his feet,
My God, I wonder why?

—*Katherine A. Smith*

You

You came into my life like a blossoming rose,
Turning all the world into a beautiful array.
You taught me to love the ones around me
Yet not to put others ahead of myself in time of need.
You taught me to take what I want in life and hold on
And never let a stranger take it away.
You showed me honesty and respect in a way no other could,
And with that respect, I grew to love you as no other would,
But now you're gone and won't be back, and with your strength I will survive,
But never will I ever forget you, as what I am is all from you.

—*Gwen Fitzpatrick*

Miles Between

Even though we live in separate worlds, miles cannot take what we have.
The feelings, the bond between us is ever so strong;
I know with your love, nothing could go wrong.

Our love will wait for us, I know. The miles between bring tears
TO my eyes and make me feel sad. No one could share what we both had.

We had our whole lives ahead of us and this we should be glad,
But now we only have memories of what we had.
So hang on to every memory, yet dream every dream.

Parting, we will endeavor many different roads.
Some may be short, while others may last somewhat longer.
No, I do not think this will come between us, I only hope it makes us stronger.

Don't stop living life, for I know our roads will cross again.
Go on holding our memories in a tiny space in your heart,
Until someday we will be ever so near and never far apart.

—*Elizabeth Buckley*

Momma Mia Momma

I have searched the whole universe of the decades comparing relationships
Reminders of you are everywhere without a stone unturned a voice deep within
Cries like a child despite the passing of time or was it a dream reverie
Visions of you transpires in every thought word or deed yes I care
For the fruit does not fall far from the tree yes a clone
A facsimile of yours truly we have strolled the same avenues
Rolled and tumbled down the ravines the same streams and dales
Begotten and lost in the sea of humanity one sweet aria creates joy
Another stresses the woe where oh where did all the years go
Reproduction it goes on and one generation followed by another
And another and then it all came to pass, you momma stood out at the head
Of the class though some would say you were the prima donna sort
Oh you were unique the mother of all time from the womb to the shrouded grave
Santa madona momma mia momma what's in a name, momma mia momma

—*Grace Napolitano Cornish*

Stand By Me

When the pains of life subside my inner spirit and it seems I cannot hold on; don't leave me.
When my strength begins to whither and my confidence turns into reproach; adore me.
When the obscenities and injustices of this world shackle themselves around my heart
and my dreams are torn to shreds; stand by me.
When my spirit fades into emptiness and life feels like a waste of time; hold me.
When my heart seems cold towards you and I can no longer feel your love; be kind to me.
When my heavenly Father cannot reach me because I fear His secure embrace; pray for me.
When the lies of trust outweigh its honest appeal and I can no longer differentiate; liberate me.
When tears of bitterness and anger become my closest friends and a broken heart my support; praise me.
And when I've gone through this bitter-sweet life of roses and thorns;
When the sunlight no longer greets my awakening;
When the thin shadows of death embrace my soul and I am thrust into the arrival of my final destination;
Do not weep, for this is life.
Yet, as I live, only, stand by me.

— *Carman Suzanne Clark*

I Miss You

I miss you
How was I to know
The night's so empty
The day's so cold
Our love was like a flower at bloom
So sweet
So bold
So everlasting with promises
When pressed between the pages of a book
Would I ever be able to look in your eyes again
Could our love still be like a flower
Pressed together with the years
Sealed forever with my tears

—*Angie Buchanan*

Farewell and Good-Bye

I know it has come
As I see the water on the shore
The foam of the ocean
Washes around the rocks
And slowly I step up to the ledge
Far below, the water splashes against the rocks
Although looking very peaceful
The jagged edges of the rocks cut the water in half
I step closer to the edge
I feel as if I have become one with the water
As though I also must reach my destiny
As that destiny of water
I take my last step forward
I slip at that last step
All I can say is *God forgive me* then I collide
With the rocks, I have finally died and reached
My destiny, farewell and good-bye.

—*Angela Hubble*

Motions

At night we park on hilltops and gaze sleepily
At the transparent blue-ocean sky dotted with
Flourescent frecklesof city lights.
As we search pointlessly for our houses
And hope we can stretch the morning
(At least until always or tomorrow.)

I reach for your hands; my moment ripples
The stillness and we are reverently silent
As if we were in church or in a library.

Cautiously, we try not to disturb
Our serenity while we glow inside.
My feelings like the vibrant, misted-over colors
That shimmer within our hearts as one.

— *Victoria Bruce*

The Boardwalk In March

A lone gull cries
From atop a swaying sign.
Mourning the loss of discarded fries
And cold pizza crusts.
A snowflake falls
Like caramel corn
Without a hint of sugar
On his chilled beak.
He bleats again
For the rusty carousel.
And the boardwalk creaks
Under the tremendous pressure
Of emptiness.
        —*Pam Hawley*

Anniversary

A year of time together, hopefully it will last forever.
I love you more and more everyday, remembering the wonderful
Things you say. I hope we never have to part. I wouldn't be able
To make a new start. We went thru great trials. You always
Brought me out with a smile. You stayed with me even when I
Was almost dead. Always with strength holding up your proud head.
Treating me with love all the time. I get the feeling of the
Sound of a beautiful chime. You always get a top rate. When you
Take me out on your terrific dates. I hope we can keep God first, and
Not just once in awhile in little bursts. When I'm alone I think
And miss your wonderful kiss. I know I don't treat you good all the
Time, but you still treat me innocent of no crime. I love the gentle
Touch of your arm, always using your delightful charm.
Arm in arm we'll always be, looking to God we can always see
A year to time together, hopefully it will last forever.

        — *Wendy Loney*

Making Love

Here we lie with our bodies intertwined
Feeling your heart pound against mine.
As we stare into each other's eyes and knowing each other's wants, needs and desires,
You gently caress my face and lift my chin; my whole body and soul gives in.
Your lips sought to find mine; they willingly part in exact time.
As we kiss we feel the fire burn; to be closer we so yearn.
Our hands explore each other's bodies; we know them as well as our own.
You move your weight upon me; I smooth my hands down your back.
There's now no turning back!
We move together almost as one.
And then with a cry, it's all done.
We lay atop of each other, each body still.
Talking of sweet nothings we whisper, *I love you. I love you, too.*
Our hearts pound faster now as we gaze into each other's eyes
Knowing our love is never stronger than after we make love.

        — *Dionne Akkerhuis*

The Dream

Dusk had settled on my heart, emotions drained to an empty gaze.
The dream that raged like a fire in my eyes, guarded from all so that even the dreamer
Did not know if it was real or a lie, was now a flicker.
I would let it die out, or would I? I could, yes, I knew I could and even wanted to.
I must not look back, not at the dream or mirage that seemed ever before me in my waking moments.
I could face the mirage if I had to, knowing it was not real.
But even this, I could not look upon too long before being drawn into its warmth and depth.
I looked long and hard I looked, the dream and mirage were now one and standing there before me.
My heart pounded as though it would burst.
My hand reached out to touch the dream, trepadation swept thru my mind.
The thought of the dream fading to ashes was too much, my hand shrank back.
For the moment my mind was cautiously content to keep the dream alive, as only that, a dream.
My eyes, however, had rekindled the raging fire that now burned in my heart.
I must wake up, the dream will be real or not at all.

        —*Jeff Sorensen*

Beneath a Saucer Moon

I'll close my eyes and dream,
I'll dream of foaming seas and apple blossom tarts
In winter's eve.
I'll walk in forests low,
And stalk in mountains high and roam the southern plains
With eagle's eyes.
When petals fall on lakes,
And roses close and break,
Then will the summer's day begin.
When leaves in rivers run,
And all life has begun,
Then will whispering willows fall again.
But 'til that day so soon,
Back in the month of June, I'll sit here waiting
Beneath a saucer moon.

        — *Brenda Palmer*

Wisdoms of the Mind

When you face each new day with nothing to do,
How dreadfully boring it can be for you.
Cause a day with no purpose is painful indeed,
As a year with no sunshine, when a farmer plants seeds.

So be thankful each morning to have something to do;
To keep your mind busy, and your body busy, too.
It's a terrific feeling to have something planned;
To never be idle, mind—body—or hand.

And as you retire at the end of each day,
Think of something to do the next, and say,
I will do my best at each necessary task.
Then thank the Lord, it won't be your last.

You don't have to like it, or even to care;
But force yourself to do it, to make you aware-
The more you cultivate the Wisdoms of the Mind,
The better the yield of the Wisdoms of Time.

        — *Florence A. Klabunde*

The Dove

As I lie here thinking about our love
An image appears, it's that of a dove.
It seems so peaceful, so calm at heart
Like the way I've felt from the very start.

I long to be with you every minute of the day
Just to see you smile and hear you say
That you care for me the way I care for you
And want each day for us to start anew.

I think of you constantly, hardly a second goes by
Then I see your face and all over feel high
The love you've shown me has helped me, you know
To give you the love I've wanted to show

The love that says I'll be with you here
Now and forever without any fear
And each day I pray to the Lord above
That our love stay as pure as that snow white dove

        —*Gary Boehnlein*

Heart of Woe

Hear the wind call my name
Asking if I'll love again
Look into the shadows
Loneliness lives there
Desperation, heartache
Sorrow and despair
A heart of woe
Filled with pain
I know I'll never
Love again

        — *Christine A. Walton*

A Faded Memory

You told me how much you loved me,
You told me how much you cared.
You told me that the times that were special
Were the times we'd shared.
You made me feel like no one else had before
And when I needed you, you didn't seem to want me anymore.
Now you're gone and all that's left behind is a memory,
A memory that's slowly fading, fading,
So much I've almost forgotten your face.
The worst part is the waiting,
waiting for someone to take your place.

— *Julie Smith*

Burgular of My Heart

You came into my life
In a strange and mysterious way.
And like a thief of the night,
You stole my heart away.
You chose me as if I were the most valuable of all
You made me feel so beautiful, I stood up straight and tall.
Soon you removed those famous gloves that leave no fingerprints
And showered me with expressions of love, of which I'll never forget.
But now just like a thief of the night,
Why? I cannot understand.
You were gone with the turn of the light
And the gloves returned to your hands.
Without a word you picked up your things and turned towards the door
As soon as it closed behind you, I knew we'd love no more.

—*Tammy Oberst*

If...Then...

If humans could fly
Then I would make wonderful dances for the butterflies.
If I could catch moonbeams in a jar and lock them up tight
Then life would be short.
If there weren't any bugs
Then what would happen to the tiny creatures living in the sink?
If I could fly and see my grandfather before he dies
Then I would open all the windows and let the caged birds out.
If books had no words
Then animals could become humans.
If pink elephants danced around a shinig carousel
Then the world would be at peace.
If soda had no bubbles
Then the earth would shrink to nothing.

—*Lynette Ortiz*

Chasm

There's a chasm in my heart
To be forever empty of your love.
A decrepit bridge bonds both sides
Forged from forgotten sins.
Remembering your red wine lips
And our flesh-soaked dreams.
I'm on a razor's edge from heartbreak
Without you near me.
The serpent has found a place in Eden
Wrapped tightly about your heart.
I had a place in your life once but it is forever lost.
Drawing your face away from my window, those are tear drops not rain.
It's the bittersweet memory of you that causes all the pain.
I'm shading the sun from my eyes, when I watch the chasm crumble.
Dead dreams and lost secrets resurface as the chasm crumble.

— *Kara Renee Parlin*

In Search of Me

Where are you going? sighed the tall oak tree,
As I climbed up the mountain in search of *me.*
Who, who, who are you? screeched the wise old owl,
But try as I might, I could not tell.
You'll not find me here, came an echo within,
As I searched through the caverns and caves so dim.
I continued my search to the top of the hill,
Where the wind whispered softly, *search farther still.*
I hurried back home hoping to see a glimpse of that phantom
Who's supposed to be *me.*
For what are you searching? queried my ancestors old
As I searched through the albums, for what, my soul?
There is one place that you haven't tried,
Said the sad-faced photos, as if to chide.
Oh please, tell me where! I urgently cried.
The one place so obvious, dear child, look inside.

—*Rachel Sidebottom*

Love of My Life

You say sweet things to me. It makes me think of you and me.
I remember how our past is gone and think if we'll last for long.
I sit and wonder if we'll stay together,
Spending our lives with one another,
Hoping that some day we won't be apart
'Cause you will always be in my heart.
You're the one I really want. You're the one I will always love.
Each day that goes by, I pray that some day it will go our way.
We have each other forever to hold,
Leading each other to our rainbow of gold.
We know our feelings will never be wrong;
Between you and me, our love will be strong.
We think of the future and our lives we will live,
Hoping you'll share those moments with me.
Sometimes I say things to you that will never be true,
But deep down inside, I really love you.

—*Rita K. Schmidt*

Last Step

You left me lifeless lying on the shore
Never to return for my body once more
You came viciously at me, I could not even see
It was dark and the night was deep, those horrible memeroies,
    I will forever keep,
You came staggering at me with knives, tearing at my skin
Wondering why me it had to have been
For a split second, I was not even afraid of what they call death
For at that moment you took my last breath

—*Kathy D. Brown Johnson*

Untitled

I believe that I shall never touch the hand of God,
nor shall my soul know comfort
in the silence of the days remaining. I stand apart,
as one denounced,
amidst the sterile borders of my unbelief, and searching through my memory
I retrace the winding patterns and designs of grief.
We are but empty dreams;
the shapeless,
fateless phantoms
at the edge of light. Desiring a tenderness
denied the realm of night,
I fell in love with the deception of my heart;
and here within this hidden vale
I await the final anguish-
the true, unyielding knowledge that our love will not survive
the cold.
The season of the blossom is at end, and I am vanquished
like a flame before the wind.

—*Christine A. Pitt*

Dusk to Dawn

Work roughened hands caress her ivory curves.
Bearded lips kiss the length of her body.
The flame of her tresses mirrors the passion
that ignites between their bodies.
Hazel eyes send their message of desire
to his mistress with ocean-coloured eyes.
Held within the strength of his arms,
they consummate the hunger that burns deep within.
Their union is like the birth of a star
that sends them on an endless voyage of emotions.
Limbs entwined as their bodies lie spent.
Images of the night flash through her mind
as she awakens with the dawn.
Was it a dream or reality?

— *Robin Lorrainne Everett*

My Soul Mate

Deep, deep in the inner heart of Me
There is a love that knows no end...
A love that shines throughout Infinity...
A love that only the Father God could send.
And there astraddle of Heaven's
Two day door to ineffable Divinity's goal
Beckons to me my Beloved Linda's soul
My beloved Linda's soul.

Light...light...light...so white...so white!
That I have climbed Jacob's Ladder
And transcended the highest astral height
Into Realms Causal, Immeasurable, beyond
Coarse matter.
And there no longer astraddle of Heaven's
Two day door to ineffable Divinity's goal
Awaits therein my love...my Beloved Linda's Soul
In endless bliss serene...
Dissolving a Dream into Reality.

—*Robijan J. Gove*

Lack of Self Reliance

Modern man has built a car
But has lost the use of his feet.
He is supported by words
But lacks so much of their meaning.
Many fine watches he has
But fails to understand the
importance of time.
He has built an airplane which can
Cover much distance in little time
But has failed to see the beauty of
The land in that distance.
He has ventured far out in space
But has forgotten about the earth.
He has freedom, but does not appreciate it,
For he has never been deprived of it.
In every war there is a soldier
But in peace...where is the peacemaker?

—*Monica Slowick*

Scars

Old woman sunk into her rocking chair,
Banjo in her lap.
Creviced wrinkles, folded face,
Blotched skin and bald patches
Showing through thin silvered hair.

Arthritic claws hammering down,
Sliding, frailing, choking the rosewood neck
Eyes moisten, glistening as she pauses...
On this day 68 years ago,
Little William passed away.

—*Robert E. Hirsch*

The Chosen Kind

The rooster crowed today in a most peculiar way.
Early edge of dawn's haze, creeping
All around nature's mores. Blackbird
silhouetted against blueish-grey sky.

Capacious, consistent quietude presides
Over mountains and plains. History on
the verge of repeating itself again.

Automatic instinct foretold in ages past.
By pairs they assemble in line. Soon to
clamber into golden cages of archaic design.

Noah's Ark, ship of sanctuary to protect,
From the Almighty's consecrated flood of death.
Armageddon's fate of time, has called upon
the chosen kind.

— *Renae Foran*

Mask

Covering all the sadness, hiding all the blues.
Smothering the laughter, emotions that you lose.
Drowning out the sorrow, it's nothing that you feel.
You hide behind the mask, the mask is thick as steel.
No one cares to notice, when you're feeling pain.
They only seem to care if they're the ones to gain.
You try to tell your story, of feeling love then none.
But no one wants to listen, they only want what's fun.
So back behind the mask, you hide from all that's true.
Go back to feeling lonely, back to feeling blue.
Masking all emotions, to a simple straight-like face.
Where no one sees your sadness, or hear your heart in a race.
They'll never know the closeness, of love and friendship true.
It goes both ways, please hear me, it helps to listen too.
When we are together, it would be nice to ask,
Do you have a smile or frown, hidden behind your mask?

— *Joy Fuller*

Worn Out Shoes

Here something for you to hang onto,
When you are out there with those worn out shoes
That so many people hang onto,
When their dreams do not fall through
In the late afternoon.
When the sun and moon pass through in that sky of blue,
Where all those stars fall through,
Just for you
To have something to hang onto,
When you're out there with those worn out shoes.

—*Harold W. Stiles*

There's Hope For You

Its good to know that I can tell the world a story,
About our calamities. Why should we ever worry?
Our people! They are suffering from AIDS to Cancer.
Would you consider and believe that Jesus has the answer?
We're searching for a remedy all over this world.
But Jesus can heal you, whether you're young or old.
I believe it's time that we open our very eyes,
Or else, we'll face the bottomless pit whenever we die.
Would you take the time and consider for a moment,
How! Our people they die, and the way in which we lament.
Remember, God made us in his own image and likeness.
He is our light, and can bring us out of all darkness.
Now! If there appears to be a problem with the human body,
And there seems to be no cure, then take the time and study,
About Jesus! Who can heal you, because he alone is worthy,
He will never fail you, just you begin to live a life that's holy.
Today, if you will begin to obey the laws of god,
Then there'll be a great revival, because he is our Lord.

—*Cyril Smith Jr.*

When I Look At...

When I look at a star
I think of you,
And how lucky I am
To be here with you.
When I look at a rainbow
I think of how happy I am
To share so much with you.
When I look at a flower
I think of you.
And how colorful my life has been
Since I met you.
When I look at the sky
I think of how simple my fears become
When you're there with me.
When I look at you
I think of many beautiful things,
But most of all, I see the love
That is in your heart
—*Anna Wroblewski*

Niagara Falls

Niagara Falls is a soft, blue dream,
Plunging,
Bursting into lacy foam,
Churning,
Currents rushing rapidly,
Fleet,
A waterfall with power as a giant's,
Flowing,
Becoming shining waters,
Majestic,
Overflowing with stateliness and grace,
Radiant,
With the regalness and dignity of a king,
Niagara Falls is a soft, blue dream.
— *Rachel Rusch*

Love Scene

A bird flies above the sea,
A wave slowly crashes to the shore,
Sand, silky as could be,
How could anyone want more?

A wave slowly crashes to the shore,
But, a walk along the beach
How could anyone want more?
Holding hands with your lover,

But, a walk along the beach
All the stars in your reach,
Holding hands with your lover,
Staying in love forever.

All the stars in your reach,
Sand, silky as could be,
Staying in love forever,
A bird flies above the sea.
— *Rayna Quinn*

Jesus Is The Key

Jesus is the key
To every broken dream
He can solve every problem
No matter how hard it seems
So give him your heart today
Let Him have your all and all
And I guarantee He will be there
To catch you on every fall.
—*Shirley Paul*

Reminiscence

Before we walk away
  we stand
We toast to the past
  the forgotten and the remembered
So many years to recall
  And *love*
Was never mentioned
  through it all.
— *Renata Kinney*

Life

A spark of life, a beat in time
A lonely light that longs to shine
An open road that knows no end
A ray of hope around the bend
I got a dream, I want to fly.
I got an urge, I can't deny
Within my heart I found a voice.
It's calling me to make the choice.
I may be right, I can be wrong
I find the strength to carry on
I run a satellite, my star unknown
I chase the light that guides me home
I walk alone through rings of fire
I never lose my one desire
I look for the sight that is hard to see.
And know that we are meant to be.
—*Sheri Feuer*

About Life

When you are troubled with your life,
And everything looks blue,
Hold your head high, pick up your chin,
And look towards a brighter hue.

When you are outcast by your friends,
And hope looks out of sight,
Straighten your shoulders, look life in the eye,
And everything will turn our right.

No one goes through life
Without some small problems,
And also some big ones, too.
But life is worth living,
Don't throw it away,
Never, whatever you do.
—*Rachel Sellarole*

Slush

The class of kids had lunchroom dined
And now obediently were lined
To saunter down the mile-long hall
That rivaled any shopping mall.
One wee, small lad, *the leader*, led
His classmates with a trail of red.
He's leaking! someone loudly said.
His pocket's bleeding! Oh, what dread!

Calm and cool, *teach* stopped to see
What caused the class cacophony.
Jimmy-John, his lips a-quiver,
Shifted feet, began to shiver.
What's in your pocket? teach inquired.
My popsicle! he coldly cried.
*Don't waste food's my momma's rule,
So I saved dessert 'til after school!*

Poor Jimmy hasn't much to lick.
His popsicle's a wet, red stick.
—*Karen N. Sanders*

Gone

It seems like only yesterday,
You were picking on me
With that smile that lights up the room.
I didn't worry when you were around,
But then, BOOM.
You were gone.
Gone from my life like a stranger,
Just passing by.
You were gone.
Not really there,
But still, there in disguise.
You'll be always in my heart,
And in my memories.
I'll never forget the days when you were
Like a playful breeze,
But now, you're gone.
— *Monica Pase*

Sandcastles

A lone runner on a deserted beach
Happened upon the ruins of a sandcastle
Left by children not so long ago
Surely it must have been a wonderous structure
The fruit of hours of labor wrought by many little hands
How sad it shall fall to ruin, were his first thoughts
But then again,
They dreamed their dream
And made it real
Left it exquisitely satisfied
And went on to dream other dreams
—*John Cavendish*

I Wonder, What Is a Friend?

Sometimes I sit all alone and I simply wonder,
What is a friend?
A person that sticks with you through thick and thin,
A person who will stand by you till the very end.
Is this *friend* going to be reliable and true?
Will this person stick to you like glue?
Or will they find your deepest emotions?
Or will they set lying rumors in motion?
I don't know, but whatever it could be,
I know that a friend will see
When a friend comes along,
For they will stick together oh so strong!
— *Glennette White*

Untitled

I look around me,
And despise what I see.
So many people, homeless and hungry,
Dying from disease, wishing they were free.
Trying to be brave, trying not to cry
Trying to keep their heads up for just one more try.

What is this world ocming to?
That no one tries to help these people through
Everyone worried about themselves only
Not caring about the sick and lonely.
The abused didn't ask to be beat,
The homeless didn't ask to be left on the street.

If only someone cared, this world would be a better place,
For every color, religion and race.
So tonight in bed, before you drift into dreamland,
Ask the Lord to give them a helping hand.
I wonder who that someone is going to be,
I hope someday that someone will be me.
—*Karyn Georgaros*

The Wind Lords

Each rides high, carrying aloft the dreams and prayers of his children.
The East carries forth with fury, the South with tenderness,
The West sways as a gentle breeze, the North holds a touch of ice.
Each carries forth the hearts and hopes of the Wicca.

Together they form the four quarters of the Universe
And in so doing, the four reaches of the mind.
Fury and anger, tenderness and warmth, serenity and peace, chill and despair
All are carried by the Mighty Ones to a place afar.

Where spirits of loved ones lost and souls yet unborn
Repose in the cradle of the Gracious Goddess,
Awaiting the clarion call which will give them life anew.
Wiccans all, carrying the truth of her love.

The Great God, lord of death and resurrection, sighs.
His time is spent and his love Habondia returns.
The earth breathes her warmth and grows fertile.
Pregnant and swollen with new hope.

    —*George A. Baker*

Planet Earth

Countless lifetimes I have loved you.
The gentle fingers of your sunrise have touched my eyes to wakefulness.
My days have been a constant garden of your delights.

Enthralled by your mountains, deserts, seasons,
I have been uplifted by the ecstacy of your waterways,
    your wildlife, your skies.

Your scents, the ribbons of your sunsets trailing in the winds
    have overwhelmed me with their perfection
And I have slept, cradled in the softness of your evenings.

I see you now with great clarity, my old love,
    never more precious than in this leaving.
Hold me close, then let me go.

Ancient, vaguely remembered music drifts to me across the Universe,
Stirring my heart with an agony of longing to be gone;
Streaking across other Galaxies, a mote of cosmic glitter
    seeking unknown worlds.

    — *Ellen M. Crane*

Full Moon

I am sitting here under this full moon. It is quiet.
I am thinking about how some of us are able to cope under pressure.
I am wondering about those of us who are not. Strange, isn't it?
I wonder why that is. I guess I am just not strong enough.
They never told me living would be easy.
They never told me wanting to would be hard.
Maybe they just never told me at all.
I have tried so hard to make everyone happy and proud.
But, things are closing in on me now, and I have to get out.
I have searched my heart to find something new
    but my world is messed up and I cannot face you.
I have to do it, I have to do it soon. I must find somewhere
    that is quiet under this full moon.
I do not want to hurt you or make you cry. But things are too heavy for me.
I cannot explain why.
I just need it quiet so I can think. I have to be alone.
This is why I must find quiet...in a world of my own.

    —*Pamela Jean Owen*

A Silence

A silence sometimes speaks, so much louder than words,
Great things can be spoken, and nothing can be heard,
A will to live screams out in a troubled man's eyes,
Please don't kill me, pleads a deer, before you watch it die,
The hunger of a child can be heard in a silent cry,
A question can be asked, never saying why.
So the next time I say nothing, and you think that I don't care,
Look into my eyes so deep, I may say it in a stare.

    —*Autumn Clark*

To a Femal Unicorn

Oh nymph, with phalic spike upon your head,
Is it an outgrowth of what's on your mind?
Or did you crack your pate, a hurt unkind,
On kitchen sink or railing of your bed?

Nay, fabliaux and prose that we have read
Claim Unicorns are real but hard to find.
You see, romance to this brief life you bind
And your lone horn no symbol of sick dread.

But practical cold science claims you are false;
An entity propitious for the blind
Who dwell in dreams; impractically inclined,
They taste starlight and dance love's heady waltz.

Oh stay awhile...youth's fevered span is short.
Then, take my kisses back to your queen's court.

    —*Paul B. Anderson*

Forever Sand

Centuries come and go.
Our traditional sand lays,
Covering the earth like a thin blanket.
Only when the wind blows its triumphant song,
It silently runs along like a sudden quiver.
Then the wind dies and the sand falls
Covering the earth.

    — *Nicole Saville*

Upon the Hills

Beyond the hills are places to hide,
And tall mountains standing side by side.
The hills are my kind of place
With flowing water, reflecting your face.
While the night forms overhead
The hills are quiet like the dead.
The moon flies to the sky
And stars hand from the high
Sky through the dark
As sounds appear from a lark.
Upon the hills, there is a cave too
I sleep there until the day is blue.
And again I share,
My time in the wilderness and care;
For the hills...
That stand so peaceful and still.

    —*Caroline Szakacs*

The Crystal Tear

Sparkling tear drops, contain much of you and me.
If we could read this crystle ball,
We would become fairest of them all.

Crystal tears are kin to rain.
They flavor in beauty as though they were the same.
God made the rain to cleanse the earth, sky and sea.
God made the crystle tears to cleanse you and me.
Their work and their beauty are almost the same.

Rain comes from the heavens, tears come from the soul.
They are both from the family, where God is the Father
And there in His control.

Tears dry up as rain, and oh, what they contain.
From each little child and king that has reigned.

What the crystle teardrops has cleansed and washed away.
May make up the river of water of life in heaven.
Crystle clear and beautiful to behold.
But only God knows what the crystle tear holds.
   —*Melba Hayes*

The Road

The war was over, yet nobody had won.
The people came out of their shelters,
The red people on their side and the green people on their side.
The little red boy met the little green boy on the road.
It was a long dirt road stretching over the horizon on the right
and over the horizon on the left.
It separated the red and green lands.
The two boys sat down and played together
in the ditch on the side of the road.
Neither said a word.
They ran, laughed and showed each other how to make new
kinds of mud pies.
Soon the red mother came to call her son for dinner
and the green mother came to call her son.
When the red mother saw who her son was playing with,
she scolded her son and made nasty looks at the green mother.
When the green mother saw that her son had been playing,
she picked him up and asked if he had had a nice time.
And each mother and son walked off on their side of the road.
   — *Miriam Hoffman*

If There Were Roses

If there were roses as in her crown, I'd wear it
For this divine halo I could be proud
Draining myself out like some liquid, stripping my roots, stems, -unbound
In hope to hold/nurutre/love your shoots and limbs
That swell and bleed form the womb of my wild

Like a cobweb's cocoon, I weave
Between our vines to find the Golden Tree that yields your sweet Fruit-
So lush, yet and uncropped, in any season, dusk or dawn:

This seed in my will to bear still spawns; reaping to sow
 Though nothing lasts forever
Should your gold dust journey's end, and blow your branches down
Unlace yourself from these vines, you might find
Me to play Mother Hen, since you can be vulnerable as I am innocent...

If there were roses to valley my meadow,
 Would they still bloom in our jungle?
Amid those thorns, splitting and shedding their stalks-
From honeyed-milk saps that seep through veins,
and unveil but one's shame
To naked the mask I carve—conceived by fear beyond this shadow.
   —*Mimi Nguyen*

The Warning of Happiness

Happiness, that bit of joy in everyone's life.
That thing that comes like the day and leaves like the night.
It is the rarest of treasures, that are truly ever found.
The most beautiful place ever created.

But my dear friends, there is a price to pay.
Since when in this world has anything ever been free?
For all this love, joy and bliss
There must be some times of sorrow and despair,
A place so cold and barren no person should have to see it.

So be careful.
I have given my warning.
Cherish and protect that piece of happiness,
That comes your way.
Be cautious,
Things might not always stay so joyous.
   —*Melissa Anderson*

Relate to the Radio

Throw your books on your bed
Sit in your favorite chair, your smoking chair
Pull one out, light it up.
Hit the tunes, hit the volume, good song.
What? Come on Mom, it is not that loud.
Alright, alright, hit the volume, down this time.
Music, freedom of expression, expression of frustration
Frustration, from what?
School, peers, social demands, pressure from mom and dad.
Get a job! What do you want to do with your life?
Isn't that part of a song? Back to the radio.
Love this song. Feeling a little more relaxed.
Don't let things get you down. Listen to the radio.
Relax. Then think about tomorrow. It will all work out.
Mom and Dad aren't trying to be mean.
They're just trying to help. It will all work out.
Meanwhile, hit the volume, but just a little, Mom might yell.
   —*Molly Kaufman*

My Past and my Future

As i sit and recall all the people I cared about,
All of those in my past,
I wonder where they all have gone, and if they'll ever come back.
These are people who made my past,
Those who made me what I am today.
People come and people go, from these people
You learn to live, Learn to cope with problems and fears.
Listen to what they say and use it.
Each one different from the other.
Some meant more than others, and some meant nothing.
You leave your mark with people and they theirs on you.
Some you will never forget; While others you wish you never met.
Can everyone deal with these changes as I have?
Yet another question goes unanswered
I often wonder that when I speak,
Does anyone listen and have the answers?
Life is a game, complex and short, play it wisely.
   —*Michelle Hayes*

Peace and Tranquility

It is a land not far away and time has no hold.
It is a land where love is born and hate exists no more.
Planes, nor cars nor trains can take you to my land.
For this land lies over a rainbow and beyond the Gates of Heaven.
The ways unto my land are few and small for they exist only in a person's heart.
So look deep inside yourself when you want a way to my land.
Look beyond the hate and jealousy.
Look until you find your heart and it will tell you the way.
The way to Peace and Tranquility.
   — *Melissa Jayleene Smith*

A Feeling

Have you ever felt like there's
No where you can turn
To talk to someone
Or try to learn?
Have you ever felt like crying,
Hoping it would go away,
But the pain
Was there to stay?
Have you ever felt like dying,
Because where you turn
Problems are what you face,
and you wish you wouldn't leave a trace?
If you ever fell in love before,
You know what I mean.
It beats anything
I've ever seen.
So don't give your heart right away,
'Cause you never know if your love is going to stay.

—*Sheena Snow*

On the Other Side

On the other side of this door is liberty.
I yearn to be in that world
Where the birds sing gaily,
Where there is no one to protect you from danger,
Where the people live happily.
On the other side of this door is liberty.
I'm gonna live in that world.

Some day I will be happy.
Some day I will love again.
On the other side of this door is vitality.
On this side of the door is Jordan's bank.
I fear Jordan's bank, so I must leave.
On the other side of this door is liberty.
It's not my parents' world,
It's mine.

— *Sheryl Lynn Walker*

Fate

Black ice on the concrete surface,
Slippery and unseen,
Placed there by a *playful* demon
From somewhere in between.
A car at a high speed
Misses the spot by an inch.
More cars continue on
Missing, pinch by pinch.
The fragile webs of fate
Tangle in a rush.
A car starts to spin
Sliding in the slush.
Two cars meet, head to head.
Two threads snap, two souls dead.
All this unfortunate fate, for the pleasure of one.
Isn't it better to live your life,
Than to be killed for a night of fun?

—*Lori Gill*

Lonely Days

Lonely days and lonely nights
Because you're not here to hold me tight.
You're all I want; you're all I need.
Look deep into my eyes and that is what you'll see.
Look into my heart and there you'll find it, too.
I'll say it again, *All I want is you!*

— *Laura Kay Ward*

My Grave

do not stand by my grave and cry,
for I am not there.
I am a whisper in the wind,
My spirit is free.
So not stand by my grave and mourn,
for I am not there,
I am sitting in the highest tree,
Watching over you now.
So not put flowers by my grave,
For their beauty will die.
Leave them where they are,
And when I go by I can touch them,
And know you were there.
Do not stand by my grave and cry.
But remind yourself,
That I will always be with you.

—*Tammy Kidwell*

By His Hand

By His hand, I was created
By His hand, He made me see.
By His hand, I fell in love.
Now His hand is holding me.

By His love, He gave us freedom
When He died on calvary
By His promise of everlasting life
If thou believed in me

By His side I am standing
And His hand is holding me
While the other reaches out,
Just for someone else to see.

By His hand, we walk together
By His side, I am going to be
By His power, these words were written
By the hand that rescued me.

—*Joseph E. Borda*

Season's Change

Summer is almost done
Now fall is coming on
The pretty flowers and green grass
Are captives now of fall's harass
Soon green will turn to brown
The trees will shed their gowns
But a pure, white sheet will fall
Upon everything, short and tall
There's nothing that can hinder
That wonder we call winter.

—*Karin Lassel*

Aborted Dream

Memory splashes red in the mind,
Recalling cycles of you,
Planted in the early spring,
This fall you would turn two.
Fed by love but not by flesh,
You grew to be so small,
I prayed and cried, grew still inside,
My precious baby doll.
If God is good and God is kind I'd
Hold you in my arms,
I'd warm, caress and love you,
Protect you from all harm.
The pain inside has slowly ebbed,
Your absence left its mark,
I think about you in my sleep
And rock you in the dark.

— *Joni White*

Say Goodbye

If I am so happy all day
Then why do I cry all night
I am too tired to put up a fight
Doesn't it matter anymore worrying
Won't it make things right
Seems like I will never find what I am looking for
So I just sit down and cry somemore
The tears on my face
Do they have some meaning to fall
Someplace
I put on a good act, a good show
Everyone thinks I am happy but why
Shouldn't they know
I want to leave to say goodbye
And I will never have to make another decision
And I will never have to cry
If only I could forever say goodbye.

—*Kaye Vingerhoet*

Real Freedom

He strolls about the land so free
No friends nor wealth has he
Merely sky above and road below
To comfort him from woe.

His food is found from others trash
His clothes are rags; alas.
But he is free, as freedom goes,
A freedom few ever knows.

Some may call him but a tramp
And many refer to him as scamp
To others he is just a plain hobo
But what at all, do they really know?

Why do they put him down so bad
What is it about him that makes them mad
If they would be honest, maybe they would see
That he is what they long and wish to be;
He is free

—*Pamela Garrison*

A Hymn to Kim

It was just a little snow in 1985
That came two days before spring would arrive
And left before spring came
While calling only Kim by name.
The snow melted from the earth's face
But Kim returned to the sky in it's place.
Will she return with some other pre-spring snow?
We'll never know! We'll never know!
But we'll keep looking at the March sky
And wonder why! Why? Why?

—*T. Alton Jordan*

With a Vision

As writers with a vision...
We can hope
To capture
The beauty
In the rapture
Of a moment
As it is willed
Much as can the camera man
With an action shot of something vibrant
Or a set scene that has been stilled.

— *Connie Goodman*

Untitled

Love is what we are.
Love is what we say.
I'm so in love with you.
I'll tell you every day.
I've never felt this love
Until I looked at you.
That's when it all began
And today it still holds true.

— *Monica Begeman*

I Love Him

I Love him
I love him
For all that he is,
I miss him
I miss him
To hug and to kiss
I need him
I need him
To hold me so tight,
I want him
I want him
To cling to tonight.
I love him, I love him
I wish he would see.
I hate him, I hate him
He doesn't love me.

—*Meredith Villatore*

The Waves of Life

The ocean is my life.
I watch the waves play
my part.
They slowly gather up
force
and come crashing on the sand.
Then
with all unity gone
they retreat
to the source,
where they rise once more
to
try
again.

—*Melissa Haldeman*

A Friendship

A friendship that survives
the worst of a bad
situation
    Is worth keeping

A friendship that can grow
despite one's differences
    Is worth the love

A friendship that passes
the test of time
    Is worth one's effort
    to keep it alive

A friendship that is broken
yet starts anew
    Is worth the joy it brings
    the second time around

A friendship that carries on
into generations to come
    Will last forever

—*Michael D. Craig*

Weaver's Plan

Life is a pattern
In the Weaver's thread.
Live it, we must,
It has been said.
We all have a part
And a place to fit,
What we have now
Is all we may get.
A fantastic plan
He has for us,
To follow it through
Is an absolute must.
All we need
Is to believe in Him,
Because in the Weaver's plan
Our souls will never dim.

— *Michelle Thiessen*

Forgiveness

Your heart is torn
The feelings are gone.
I gave you pain,
You took it unwillingly.
Here I lie in this dark
Empty space
Searching for the right
To live at my own
Simple pace.
Do I have the right?
What did you ever do to me?
I am strong, yet you stand
And weep.
I took a part of you,
A part I can't give back
And yet the love you give
Allows me to live.

—*Melissa Moore*

Untitled

Struggling for identity
Inside a massive world
Wondering, searching,
Can I be any good?
Who can give me comfort?
Am I good for anyone?
Will my questions find some answers,
Or is my time almost gone?

— *Meribeth Waltman*

Feeling free
of care
loving love
picking dandelions
throwing kisses
to every old man in green I see
running down a street
shoes in hand
I dash into *21*
slap the maitre'd
on his butt
demand a table
get it
drink a whole goblet
of crystal water
eat the lemon slice
spit the seeds.

—*Rebekah Englishbee*

Farewell Eighty-Seven

It was a fast year full of memories,
Good and bad, hours of joys and sorrows,
There was death and desolation, without victory.
Young americans who's only reward, was a coffin with a flag.
Mothers and wives, with their families crying silently.
All the world is on distress, because drugs and wars
Unselfish is indispensable, give to others, because we have plenty.
We shall learn, to help without arrogance, they need nice words.
We are blessed here, but people from under developed places,
Are not too lucky, because of differences between them.
The power was abused by the grands, blaming americans without base
But the way of thinking never change, our soldiers suffer yes, the same.
I am a soldier mother, who pray for him and the others.
I used to cry, but my eyes became dry. No tears to shed.
In my heart, I hope the world is changing for the better.
No more negative feelings, we must keep faith and love instead.

— *Maria H. Perez*

An Unforgetable Tale

The moon was full and the stars were shining bright.
All was quiet, for it was a beautiful night.
I was young and still just a child.
My life was peaceful till all turned wild.
I stood with friends, but it was like we were in another dimension of time
And I searched about, but it was myself I could not find.
What is it that's happening to me? I cried.
But yet no one heard me and soon their voices died.
And so there I was just him and me
And the sky began to darken and those sparkling stars I could no longer see.
He took my hand and led the way
And I didn't even question him,
for I was too speechless, I didn't know what to say.
Then we stopped under a tall, dark, gloomy tree,
And as I stood there, I thought of what would soon become of me.
I wasn't yet frightened, for I still had no idea of what was going on,
For everything went so fast and soon the horrible nightmare was gone.
But was it gone? I asked. *Will it ever end?*
My life could never be the same, so why should I even pretend?
So who's to blame, him or me?
It doesn't make a difference, for I'll never forget
the night under the tall, dark, gloomy tree.

—*Michele Gargiulo*

Memory of 3rd Avenue El

wotta town! wot'n el! oh el! herculean structured—steel fashioned to
robust symmetry to guide and haste the *speed* of a jerky clink and clanky
noisy-neighed iron *steed*—faithful charger bearer of a plenitude of rider
readers lookers peepers sleepers (forgot *pushers* too)—you're now gone...
your city fabulous of 100 and one babelian tongues was degothamized when
blowtorch surgeons cut away your shoulders and saw you die. those goggled
surgeons who stole my high fleeting *view* of many facades gazing on the
avenue who with a sigh hid all wash apparel on each line swaying in the
sunless wind like a ballet at a world's fair dancing for a peace of skylit
cerulean *blue* to dry their daily washday tears from each *face* before dark
hungry clouds swallowed the sun lolled in slow *pace* over the bustled hurry
scurry multitude. oh el! oh el! why did goggle-surgeons send hustled rider
thinkers and etceteras to that roaring rolling rumbling graffiti-dappled
iron *steed* (of such envious *breed*) *below* to *grumble* in the bloated belly
mumble of the biggest wotta town i *know*?...no screed i need to write or say
oh el! oh el! to your epitaph:*may only rest dwell in your desecrated chaff
and memory's word extol each day you served me well.*

—*Marion Joseph Beauregard-Bezou*

The Tree

Family growing roots in different soils,
Brings fertilization of various types of nutrients.
Branches overlap to create a mosaic, intricate pattern of forests.
Embryonic thought lost within the microcosm of the roots.
Established through confrontation from others,
The seed germinates into a beautiful seedling.
Seedling nourished from the family unit,
Grows strong with re-enforcing fibers.
Continuous input of energy creates
Differentiation of growth within the maturing; strong, natural system.
Utilization of its functional purpose;
The seedling develops the specialization of character.
Life persists with the determining
Factor of conversion-love.

    — *Christopher C. Smith*

The Old Willow Tree

The old willow tree was always there for me in my time of desperate need.
It was a place where I could sit and grieve.
When hate filled my lungs, the big willow was standing right over me.
I always felt it could protect me. That tree was my comfort deep inside.

Some days I could just sit and swing on that old willow tree.
Other days I'd sit in my cozy old spot and just fall into an endless dream.
I could dream wonderous dreams right beneath the old willow tree.

One unfortunate night a terrible wind storm blew my tree right down.
I could have died at that very spot because that tree was always there for me.
I could no longer dream wonderous dreams.
My nights became sleepless, my bones started to ache with sorrow.

I cried and cried because now I felt completely lost.
There is no other tree like my special willow tree.
I'm telling you it might have only been a tree, but it was always there for me!

    — *Danielle Cohen*

Trip Down the Street

I was walking down the street one day,
A street corroded by whiskey bottles and drug paraphernalia,
A street I have spent my whole life affectionately trying to avoid.
The pavement was filled with drug-crazed lunacy and foul-smelling derelicts
And as I walked down it, I began to wonder what on earth possessed me to go there.
As I walked down this street, dodging animal excretion products and dirty old men
Being recharged (like a Duracell battery) intravenously with their imaginary
Happiness, I wasn't sure if I wanted to cry for them because they're society's downfall,
Or to laugh at them for placing all their trust in a needle.
Incidentally, I'm not going to walk down that street anymore.
It's a journey I can stomach only once in person.
If by chance I am about to walk down that street again,
I'll just watch the eleven o'clock news.
I'll see the exact same thing anyway.

    —*Kenya McCullum*

Eric

Watching the handsome man waiting to perform on the stage
Impressed by his presence, he seems an indeterminable age.
He lifts his horn, it seems to become a part of him;
smiling, he nods slightly and the music begins.
Putting the horn to his lips and looking relaxed
he closes his eyes, tilting his head back.
Transported by the beauty of his distinct sound,
I listen intently, sitting spellbound.
I sense him reaching inward to his secret core
interweaving outstanding talent, self discipline and more.
I'm aware of myriad of emotions this man has always concealed
and his vulnerability; only in his music are they revealed.
It's as if he was born with a predisposition
Solely to be a professional musician
His accomplished performance evoked admiration for all he has done.
Filled with love and pride, I watch this child of my heart, my son.

    —*Cherie Stone Stephens*

A Mere Twig

I am a broken branch on a weary tree,
Fearful of falling,
And wanting so very badly to hold on to the strong trunk, my security
Concealed by bark, I hide shyly from the world,
Afraid to show myself,
Afraid to share myself,
Yet loving all around me so very much.
In a world of forests, what am I but a mere twig?

    —*Kerry Goodwin*

Mirror Image

I look in the mirror and what I see is two reflections that puzzle me,
One is a child, scared and afraid,
the other an adult saying grow up and be brave.
The child feels the need for love and protection,
the adult needs her freedom without total rejection.
I see a child wanting to have fun and play, but the adult
Is wondering what the cost of enjoyment will make her pay.
The child gets injured and runs home to mom,
But the adult has no where to run so she must face the problem alone.
The child is energetic and full of smiles,
But the adult wishes only to rest for a while.
Again in the mirror the two reflecions I see
And I think to myself, which reflection is me.

    —*Karen Glogowski*

Days of the Hukilau

Watch the canoes! There they go, bobbing up and down.
Pulling the nets and ropes, with t-leaves tied around.
Quickly they go, not too far out; rowing, rowing, rowing.
Then slowly the ropes are dropped as the nets go gently floating.
Down, down, they sink; swishing to and fro,
Ready for the biggest catch, but not the tiny minnow.
The nets surround many a fish and the t-leaves make shadows scary,
So the fish they dare not swim away for fear of such imagery
Huki! yells a big Hawaiian. Huki, yells his brother
Many people run to shore, helping one another.
Pulling, laughing, singing: oh, the fun they shared.
Always working together, showed how much they cared.
Everyone shared the fish; no one was left without
Kind hearted Hawaiians they were, to me there is no doubt.
But where are the days of the hukilau? Only memories linger on,
For Hawaii has become commercialized and those hukilau days are gone
How I long for those days gone by...and my Isle of Paradise
For there is no place like Hawaii, through my sad and lonely eyes.

    —*Dorothy M. Decker*

On This You Can Depend

I've known you now for many years.
I've seen your strengths, heard your fears.
I will always be the one who cares.
I wonder how much you're aware
On this you can depend.

The world is full of changing scenes.
No two days will ever be the same.
Floods wash away entire towns;
Madmen maime great works of art,
On this you can depend.

This truth remains inside men's hearts:
One day we love, the next we part.
This kind of world, it can destroy
Your simple, loving child-like heart
On this you can depend.

I'm here to let you know, my love,
Your heart that longs to rise above
This uncertain world can now be free!
On this you can depend.

You have your truth, what you perceive
The kind of place this world should be.
Kindness, patience, courage, trust,
Faithfulness to those you love
On this you can depend.

I have my truth, simple and clear
Unchanging love removes all fear.
You now can rest because you've found
A powerful force to which you're bound
On which you can depend.

    —Michele Maupai

Juvenile Offender

Dear Mom and Dad,
I'm sorry to make you so sad.
I know I've been more than bad.
Say, *Hi!* to little sis
And if it is not too difficult, give her a kiss.
Tell her not to end up like this.
Let her play with her toys
So that she will enjoy just being a kid
And not a wisecracker like me.
Incarceration is a terrible sin,
Especially for us who are in.
Sunday Mass to keep us straight,
To soften hearts filled with hate.
Working out on prison grounds
Trying to adjust to ups and downs.
In winter outdoors can be Hell.
It's hard, oh God, it's hard to keep well.
Dear Mom and Dad, don't blame yourself.
I was reared in luxury and wealth.
Even thought I know I'm bad,
You're still the best family a kid could want and love.

    —Mattie Dobey

Our Perpetual Love

Admiring the stars above,
I think of our perpetual love.
An endless intimacy, full of adoration and spark;
A Flawless connection between two hearts.
An enchanting beautitude that is shared by two;
A unity of sweetness among me and you.
Two stars that have fallen into each other gentle hands;
A harmony so unblemished, no one else can understand.
It is this bond of sympanty, this immaculate love,
That the stars in the sky remind me of.

    —Lisa Laho

Fist Fight

Whatever happened to
A good old fashioned
Fist fight.

A knock me down,
Talk of the town,
Settle the score...and no more
Fist fight.

No sticks or stones,
No broken bones,
A *we'll still be friends*
As soon as this ends,
Fist fight.

    —Miriam Miller

And They Sit

And she sits
with her gray hair

And she sits
in her overstuffed chair

And she sits

And he sits
on his couch bed

And he sits

And the minutes

And the hours

...and they sit

And as the ending years date
the old man and woman

find

they can't

relate.

    — Margaret Klein

High School

High school is a place
Where a teenager belongs.
He/she belongs in a place
Where he/she can get an education.
Why be out on the streets
When you can be in the seats of school?
Looking into a teacher's eyes
Which are looking at you,
The eyes that are telling you,
After school, 30 minutes!

    — Francis Carmona

Icy Leaves

Filigree leaves upon the pane
Frosty morning wonders.
Snow white background glistening,
Winter's joys abundant.
The woodpeckers and chickadees
I watch, unnoticed as they eat.
The lacy leaves my curtain
Dissipating with the sun's heat.
What tiny drops of condensation,
That make my decor so Dresden.
Tomorrow morning—another view,
The window's frost will beckon.
Untold mysteries, peace and calm,
Descend each day upon me.
As I see the Artist's work
That he daily paints for me.

    —Rosena Fornaro

Untitled

Sometimes I look up there
And I wonder
What I want
What I think
Who I am
I feel helpless and lonely
I love,
But I'm not loved
And there is nobody I can talk to.
I just look at the stars
And dream that this all will change
That I'll find out
What I want
What I think
Who I am
That I'll find somebody who loves me,
sombody I can talk to
I wish it could be you, I really do...

    —Stefania Lucchetti

My Family

I pray to the Lord above-
that my family will always have
peace and love;
That our hearts will be full
of sweet tenderness
and that the Lord
will always bless;
If something were ever
to happen to me-
at least I would know how much
love there is in my fmily.

    — Colleen Sheerin

My Sun

As I sit on my porch
I can see the sun peeking over the hill,
Looking bright-eyed as usual
Putting glares on the window sill.

His smile reflects warmth
Making me want to smile back,
And his arms reach out to me
As my face begins to crack.

I wonder if the world has
Ever seen his smiling face?
Or have they just ignored him
Making him feel out of place?

As long as I can sit on my porch
And feel his beaming rays,
Forever in my heart
He will have a place to stay.

    — Tammy Childress

A Gallant Stand

Silent tears in the dark
A fierce and lonely knight rides out from
The dark
Mounted on a stead of wind
A blue gray sword in his hand
A brave and gallant lad
A gallant and noble stand
But alas he struck you down and your
Wishes became just like the sand
Like the sea that comes to take the sand
...Such a brave and gallant lad.

    — Anita Gutierrez

Untitled

Reflections...
Mist off water.
Faces in a mirror, with their backs turned...
Dust in the wind... soon to be real.
Clouds of anxiety—anxiously waiting
Laughter in a crowded room.
Where is the truth, where is your life?
You can't find it; can you?
Somewhere along the way you've lost it.
You feel alone and deserted... empty...
The ripples in the water, footprints in the sand...
Where did they come from, did you put them there?
There is no way to tell... no one knows.
You're waiting to be rescued—saved from lonliness.
Come back to me, love me again...
Let me be your savior,
Let me fulfill your needs...
Let me be your life...

   —Alison Meilinger

Patient Victim

Waiting in a wheelchair,
tearing at a monster devouring her almost living being.
In extended silence looking into space, eyes search
for touching hands to comfort and to heal.
Only a floral print
and rain swept window,
remind of a day left outside.
Antiseptic surroundings,
colorless boxes in rows with typed labels,
Offices ringing with telephones,
doctor's names on doors,
and a white clad nurse enters folder in hand
proclaiming
You're next.

   —Vincent Cannella

The Meaning of Christmas

Christmas is almost here at last,
The years they seem to go so fast;
It brings cards of joy over the miles,
Togetherness to families and to children smiles.

The meaning of Christmas has gone so far,
From snowmen to Santa when it first was a star;
A savior was born in a manger one night,
And took men out of darkness and showed them great light.

As we remember each other at this time every year,
Let's also remember that a savior lived here.
He brought to us love, we must all agree,
But if it wasn't for Him, Christmas wouldn't be.

   — Jo Ellen Nye

Sand Castle Dreams

He who can happily spend his days building castles in the sand,
Only to have them washed away with the tide...
He who can return the next day and begin anew...
He who can hold the sand in his hands without letting a single grain
   slip through his yielding fingers...
He who can watch his own creation being crushed and carried away
   by the forceful tide
Without a single regret...
He who can look at the new empty shore not as an end,
But as a beginning...
He who has the strength to do these things
   holds the key to a happiness unknown to most,
For they let it slip through their fingers like grains of sand.

   — Donna Norton

Nature's Niche

Nature speaks each morning as we watch the morning sun,
It calls upon us to greet the day, to meet a task undone.
Dedication summons us calling peaceful thoughts within,
Inspiration awakens the soul, as a new day is about to begin.

Listen to the sounds of the day as it greets you,
hear the voice of its call;
reply as you awaken to see the light
of a crisp clear morning of fall.

Nature lays its blanket of dew, feel the splendor of the morn,
Touch the soul of its gentle ways, experience as today is born.
Caress the challenge of yet another tomorrow,
Take a moment with nature to ponder,
The mystery of nature's niche,
Is truly God's place of wonder.

   —Jean C. Weeks

Man's Love

In this world it seems the thing that hurts the most is to love.
It hurts to care. Why? Should we all hate each other?
Would that make everyone happy? Is hatred the way we should live?
Maybe it wouldn't hurt as much. Love always ends in heartache.
You love your boyfriend, he leaves you.
You love your friends, they disappoint you.
You love your parents and their love just isn't there.
To live in this world you have to be hard and cold
Or your whole life will be filled with pain.
But yet there is still one way out, the love of Christ,
The one and only everlasting love.

   — Nicole McDonald

Return of a Pathfinder

He set astride his horse,
Suspended in time and space,
His dusty clothes hung loose,
His black hat pulled low over his face.

Unmindful of traffic on the interstate,
Or the airplanes high in the sky,
This Wyoming cowboy plodded,
As if he wished civilization would pass him by.

I watched as this horseman rode from the city pavement
Toward the open land,
A symbol of the past, passing through the present,
With the reins of the future in his hands.

   — Elizabeth McKinney

Shay

Miniscule cherub, alabaster and gold
Yearning to break free, yet longing to hold
The mother, the earth
The heart of her birth.
Spinning unhindered...silver threads follow her
Around dark Goliath, in whom longings stir.
But 'tis only wonder that draws him to try
To capture the fairy who's learning to fly.

She flits and she twirls,
Tiny fingers and toes
Unfettered by teachers.
Just one perfect rose...

Clad all in yellow, hair wispy and pale.
Delight and abandon won't lead her to fail
In finding the gladness that spills from her spree.
Her pleasure's unbridled.
After all...she's just three.

   —Jenny Harrison West

Time to Let Go

It seems like waves sweep over me.
Memories of you were controlled.
Then the longing would win over,
You've been gone long enough,
Now get yourself on home.
Time to let go.

Sometimes we wish to gain more space,
Our life's journey requires room.
Above space that you once occupied
Has now been moved below;
No more requests are heard.
Time to let go.

Oh, but joy comes in the morning.
God in His comforting mercy;
Newborn have come to fill that space,
Lauren, Christen, Taylor
Grandchildren, blessings three.
Time to let go.

—*Ida Marie Montgomery*

The Canadians on Vimy Ridge

They enlisted as determined men
Willing to die and to defend
The country that bore and gave them strength,
To fight throughout the country's length.

They were a breed of men apart,
Men possessed with the killing art.
Some left the safety of their farms,
To march beside their brothers-in-arms.

They were the troops of the Dominion
Who had bought our freedom from Great Britian.
The price of freedom they had paid
On the ridge where three thousand laid.

The divisions of Canadians
Were the bravest of all fighting men.
They rushed the entrenched German lines
With only victory in their minds.

Upon the highest point of Vimy
Stands the monument and the sea
Of countless crosses that marked the dead.
The bloody ridge, forever red.

—*Pete Wong Jr.*

I Cry

I live in distress when I'm alone.
For in the darkness of the nite
The secrecy controls.
I close my eyes to conceal the tears.
I pray for courage in hope to conquer
My human fear.
My emotions are confused by this touch
They call affection.
For my childhood is now moving in
The wrong direction.
My exposed body trembles from the pain
Felt so deep inside.
The suffering prolongs within my mind.
A cry for help if I must stay alive
Freedom come!
For I must survive!

—*Jacqueline Strickland*

Future Behold

You're the yellow grass,
which turns all green.
You're the window,
that will bare no screen.
You're the door,
that has no lock.
You're the bird,
leader of the flock.
You're the four-leaf clover,
in which you stand alone.
You're the first star,
how bright it shone.
You're the sun above the ocean,
will fill my heart with every emotion.
You're my future,
which will be bright.
You're my love,
at first sight.

—*Marie Poirier*

Mirror of Dreams

Again, the yield to unshakable sleep
demands of night its promises keep...
The slowly dawning hour of lead...
Gable, Power, Flynn are dead.

Slippers shuffle to a shrine
where arms of Buddha bear the wine
of soft anointing, proffered bliss;
faceless face—impervious.

And through the eyes of then and now;
still marcelled wave,
still pencilled brow;
reflections mock in mute aplomb
Ah, sweet romance, the hours's gone.

In timeless stare
she heaves a sigh
to silent
waiting
faithful
I.

—*Joan Matlaga*

The Irish in Me

I was Irish from
the day I was born.
I'm confused. I'm married
and changed my name.
I'm full of laughter
and fun and games.
Every St. Patrick's Day
I wear something green.
I tease him about
his nationality and
that's mean.
We met at a
St. Patrick's Party
a long time ago.
Doesn't matter
to me. He's *Polish*
and I love him so.

—*Marjorie Garwacki*

Ode to Legs

The female gender
Have legs that are long and slender
And when they're wrapped in white silk,
They can be as smooth and creamy as warm milk!

— *John Painter*

Mama's Love

Quite often my mind drifts back in time
Into my childhood days
Of life on the mountain
In the bright sunshine
Of mama's loving ways
All through the years
From tot to teen
I felt how lucky I was
Because never did a day go by
That I didn't feel mama's love
And even now that she is gone
To a home of another kind
I still see her smile
I still feel her love
For she left much behind

—*Judy Rathbone Skinner*

Remember

Remember those long
summer talks
and the days of growing up
to have a big sis
is what I really miss

For it seemed all the
problems I had
were never really bad

The weather changes
and the wind blows
in another direction

But as the tides roll in
upon the summer sets
I can always gaze
at the memories

— *Shaun Patrick*

Lost Love

I thought you loved me,
I guess I was wrong.
You took me to the valley,
And you sang me a song.
You said you loved me,
And I thought it was true
But when I turned around,
Something was missing, you!
Now my tears must fall again,
Because I thought you were my friend
With you gone there's nothing left,
But memories that I have kept.

— *Wendy Nakoff*

Once Again

My mind drifts back to yesteryears.
I try so hard to stop the tears.
Just for once I'd like to win.
But as on cue, they fall again.
Through my tears, I see your face.
Another time, another place.
Happy thoughts run through my mind.
As I go drifting back in time.
I see you there, you look so real.
I brace myself from the pain I feel.
But all to soon you drift away.
And once again, I'm forced to stay.
God saw fit to call you home.
And left me here, so all alone.
But soon I know, he'll call me to.
And once again, I'll be with you.

—*Darlene Green*

Rainbow of Dreams

Open your heart and begin to dream.
Hope and believe and it will soon seem
That the rainbow ends at your door.
You step into that spectrum
And your doubts or troubles are no more.
When life's got you down and you're feelin' blue,
Dance into red and the spotlight's on you!
Life in the fast lane is driving you mad.
It takes a green summer day and golden sunset
To show everything's not bad.
Unicorns, fairy tales, a merry-go-round;
Back away from the reality to which you seem bound.
A Broadway play and you have the lead part;
It can all be yours
If you begin to dream and open your heart.

—*Jennifer S. Steadman*

Father

Is this my father, sitting here?
I look again and see,
That he looks more like a skeleton.
He's so thin and wasted.
His skin, has a slight tinge to it.
His hair, almost white and strange looking.
My eyes saw him,
But my mind denied it was him.

— *Paula M. Eady*

The Winds of Autumn

As I sit and watch the wind
Toss the light clouds across the sky
And to watch the wild gulls wheeling
And to hear their wild cries.

The leaves are tumbling in the autumn winds
And some are flying high
As if to join the dancing clouds
As they prance across the sky.

As I watch this brand new dawn
To see the sun shining on those wispy clouds
Clouds of every color white, yellow, gold and grey
This is the beginning of a beautiful autumn day.

The Canadian geese are going south in formation
Being pushed by the playful winds
Ah, listen to their haunting cries.
And another era is coming to an end.

— *Helen Brown Burton*

Cheyenne Heartbeat

By the campfire sits a wizened old man
Gathering the young, the future of his clan
Lessons and stories he must begin to relay
Tribal prayers begin, he teaches the old ways
Customs and laws, formed in the beginning of time
His Cheyenne heart beats proudly with drums pounding rhyme
Gone is the past with rich lands unspoiled
Now smokestacks from skyscrapers, spew soot from their toils
Today's youth must carry on the long ago historic past
Heritage proud they stand tall at last
Knowing greatness will once more be theirs
In respect for land and ancestors, they dare to lay claim
Heads held high with purpose of mind
Cheyenne pride going forward, never following behind
Strength forged from learning, knowledge and wisdom
Implanted in their minds, now knowing where they belong
Banding together, tempering strength with tribal allies
One heartbeat for all, chant famillial Cheyenne ties

—*Joan Savage*

Eagles

Soar over the skies,
With wings outstretched,
Looking upon the Earth below.
Over flies an eagle
Pretty as it is.

Free as can be
With nothing to hold them back,
Over the landscape they go;
No worries at all.

The skies are scarce
Of these flying beauties,
But the place they go
Can only be;
Where the eagles fly.

—*Kathy Hinkle*

Wonders

I watch the day turn to twilight
Stars to brighten the night,
Soft falling dew kiss a rose
Whispering wind caress a posey,
Whip-poor-will calls to its mate
Together fly to an unknown fate,
Others search world for wonders
While I stand in awe and ponder,
Simple ones touched by the
　　Master's Hand!

— *Margaret Stanton*

First Crisis of Youth

I hear my mom and dad again,
But this time quiet, not like when
They yelled and fought and scared me bad,
And mom tried hard to hurt my dad.
This time it's nice and I'm so glad
That dad's OK and mom's not mad.
And I'm much better now I see
That they're no longer hating me.
I heard them talk a lot last night,
But couldn't seem to grasp their plight;
'Cause I'm just not enough along
To understand the right and wrong.
Now I'm relieved by how they touch;
Each one is warm, with love so much.
They worked it out, no longer torn...
I won't be killed before I'm born.

—*Robert Allan Ross*

Back Home

I went back home in my dream.
My mother, my father, sisters and brothers
all came together in my dream.
Home is where Mom's kitchen was always neat,
all kinds of good food to eat.
Summer flowers growing all around,
yard so clean, you could sit right down.
Sunday was the best.
We would all dress-up, Dad would even
wear his vest.
To school we walked two miles everyday,
when we got home we were too tired to play.
At night Dad would put us to bed,
Mom would come in to say goodnight
and kiss us on the head.
When I woke up, I was all alone.
In my dream, I was glad I went back home.

— *Eddie Mae Bennett*

Paean of Love

I was dead and you gave me life,
I was blind and you gave me eyes,
I was mute and you gave me voice,
I was weak and you gave me strength,
I was an outcast and you gave me friends,
I was hopeless and you gave me hope.
I was insane and you gave me sanity.
I was immersed in self-pity and you gave me the 12th step.
I was without laughter and you made me laugh.
I was without God and you gave me a higher power.
I was a prisoner and you gave me freedom.
I was full of hate and you gave me love.
I was so afraid and you gave me courage.
I could not walk and you gave me legs.
I cried because I had lost my children and you gave them back to me.
I was in turmoil and you gave me serenity.
I broke every law and you gave me responsibility.
Thank you AA, I am eternally grateful to you for my life.

—*Pauline Browne*

One You Never Knew

I wanted you to remember me because I knew you were forgetful,
So I scratched my name into sand, but when I returned the next day,
It was gone, not a trace left. The waters had washed me away.

I wanted you to remember me because I knew you were forgetful,
So I carved my name into the flesh of an old tree.
A year later there was new bark on top of my name,
Suffocating me out of existence.

I wanted you to remember me because I knew you were forgetful,
So I hired a plane to write my name in the sky above so when you looked up,
I'd be there, but hours later, the wind had blown me far away.

I wanted you to remember me because I knew you were forgetful,
So I engraved my name on a slab of stone and buried it in the earth.
Now you remember my name once a year and I wish you wouldn't remember me
Because it is not me you remember, but the name of one you never knew.

— *Ester Elena Peterson*

The Magic Lamp

If I were granted a million wishes from a geni in a lamp, I wouldn't waste them on worldly things,
But I'd trade some to have your everlasting love, and all the joyous bliss that your love brings.
I wouldn't wish to be a wealthy king that sits on a gold laden, bejeweled throne,
and daily watch my loyal subjects genuflect low at my feet, and sometimes lie prone.
No my love, my fluttery turtle dove, that's not my style, but if so, I'd rule you with all my love,
that will forever be strong and true, and sprinkled with blessings from above.

I would spend wished galore for your sweet love and devotion,
that will one day be higher than the blue sky and deeper than a turbulent ocean.
Should a royal proclamation be issued, dubbing me as Czar, I'd shock each third world nation,
by taking you for my wife, and forfeiting the extravagant, ceremonial coronation.
I would swap many wishes each day, for some special, tender-loving care from you.
I'd shout out my love daily, and will never-ever do a thing to make you unhappy or blue.

I'd swap many wishes if you could but lie beside me all through the cold, wintery nite.
My lips would cover your shivering body with a blanket of warm kisses, proving our love right.
I'd willingly give up the wishes, if I could only hear you say,
I love you now and will forever, dear Joe, then one more day.
When I come to the last wish, I'd use it to wish for a million more,
but I'll use them only to strengthen our love. *Ain't that what wishes are for?*

—*Joe Dovich*

Moon Dance

In the moonlight
Soft music cascades
Down earthly heights
I see the moon goddess
Dance over silvery seas
Her long hair full of
Lustery light
And in her hands
She hold for me
Stones of sapphire, sharp
And bright
Hands extended to godly gifts
Mortal hands cut dear and deep
Bright blood red on azure seas
And my soul is forever free.

— *Anh Pham*

Biographies of Poets

ABBOTT, KAREN
Pen name: Karen L. Abbott; *Born:* January 23, 1973, Philadelphia, Pennsylvania; *Education:* Kenrick High School; *Occupation:* Student; *Memberships:* Varsity cheerleader, softball player, Community Service Corp; *Honors:* Daughters of the American Revolution essay contest and Immaculata College Creative Writing, award winner; *Other writings:* I have written many poems and short stories that have recently been submitted for publication; *Personal note:* I enjoy writing poetry on a variety of topics but my short stories are most often murder mysteries, I especially admire and am influenced by the works of Stephen King and Edgar Allan Poe; *Address:* 1016 Bunting Road, Norristown, PA.

ADAMS, ANGEL
Pen name: Blondie and AJ; *Born:* August 4, 1972; *Parents:*Eldon Adams and Jackie Adams; *Education:* Valley High School; *Other writings:* I've written other poems, but I've never done anything with them; *Personal note:* I hope to write more good poems and achieve the goals I've set; *Address:* Box 375, Eden, ID.

AKSEL, SOPHIE C.
Born: March 3, 1909, New York, NY; *Parents:*Joseph Nudelman, Yette Nudelman; *Spouse:* Edward Aksel, March 1, 1934; *Children:* David Aksel; *Education:* Brooklyn College, Pratt Institute, MS (Psychology); *Occupation:* Teacher, Librarian; *Memberships:* Brooklyn Ethical Culture Society, Photographic Society of America, International Center, Institute of Retired Professionals and Executives, Friends of Pen, National Writer's Union; *Honors:* Salmagundi Club Honorable Mention for Photography; Photographer's Forum Magazine, Award of Excellence for Photography; World of Poetry-Honorable Mention for Poetry (two awards); *Other writings:* Written articles entitled, "Sophie's Revenge Reform Judaism"; "Focusing on a New Career After 70", "December Rose"; *Personal note:* I strive to reflect my commitment to social and political harmony through my documentation of other cultures and environments in the fields of writing and photography; *Address:* 911 East 58th Street, Brooklyn, NY.

ALLISON, MARGARET
Born: June 15, 1919, Mound Valley, Kansas; *Parents:*Dennis Wallingford & Margaret Wallingford; *Spouse:* Paul Allison, August 16, 1959; *Children:* Betty Jo; *Education:* Cherryvale High School; Kansas State University, Pittsburg, KS, BS; University of Illinois, MS; *Other writings:* Has written many poems and articles; *Personal note:* I had polio on my right side when I was two. It left my right hand useless, but my parents taught me to use my left hand. It made me a very determined and independent individual. I love God, people, and life in general;

ALSBROOKS, SHARHON
Pen name: Charmin, Nay Nay, Renee; *Born:* July 4, 1973, Cheraw, SC; *Parents:*Berthel Alsbrooks, Tommy Lee Alsbrooks; *Education:* Cheraw High School; *Memberships:* Girl Scouts; *Personal note:* I shall continue with my Lord's blessing to write more poems and short stories in my future time; *Address:* Rt. 3 Box 300, Cheraw, SC.

ANDEREGG, AMY BERNICE HELEN EMMA
Born: October 3, 1971, La Cross, Wisconsin; *Parents:*Marsha Bernice and Casper Anderegg; *Education:* Central High School; *Occupation:* Student; *Memberships:* YWCA; *Honors:* The Golden Poet Award of 1986; *Other writings:* Has written several poems; *Personal note:* I try to show love, honesty, sincerity, and gentleness in my writing. Robert Frost is one of my favorite authors; *Address:* 400 Monitor, Apt 35, LaCrosse, WI.

ANDERSON, INGRID
Born: February 4, 1989, Louisvile, Kentucky; *Parents:*Joy Anderson, Jim Leggett; *Occupation:* Student; *Memberships:* Literary staff, Drama Club, Thespian Society; *Honors:* 1st place in the poetry contest at school; Editor's Choice Award from the National Library of Poetry; *Other writings:* I have had other works published in local newspaper. Have a collection of poems that are unpublished; *Personal note:* Writing is a funny thing, you may desert it, but it will never desert you. Just when I fear that I have no words left I remember it was I who somehow had abandoned writing. It did not abandon me; *Address:* 8200 Speerlane, Crestwood, KY.

ANIBALLI, SHEILA
Born: September, 19, 1958, Sterling, Illinois; *Parents:*Howard & Mary Shaw; *Spouse:* Don Aninalli, August 20, 1983; *Education:* Aztec Municipal High School; *Occupation:* Truck Driver; *Personal note:* To let others know there is hope in any situation, there's a way to love, care and to live. Also the only way to God is through Jesus; *Address:* P.O. Box 81, Bluford, IL.

ARMSTRONG, MARY AILEEN
Born: November 18, 1922, Alliance, Ohio; *Parents:*James Leighton and Aileen Anderson; *Spouse:* Gerald Gordon Armstrong, August 25, 1943; *Other writings:* A bicentenary salute to "The People in Their Time"; Second book with same title is forthcoming; *Personal note:* Look where you stand and then do what you can; *Address:* Box 13, Lernaville, OH.

ATIYEH, STARR
Born: October 22, 1973, Arcadia, California; *Parents:*Heidi Borchers and George Atieyh; *Education:* Rosemead High School; *Occupation:* Student; *Other writings:* A poem published in school newspaper; *Personal note:* I write what I feel, I have over 100 poems on love, happiness, drugs (drinking and driving) and everyday events; *Address:* 6014 Bartlett, San Gabriel, CA.

AUTREY, STACI DIANNE
Born: December 4, 1972, Oakland, CA.; *Parents:*Thomas Robert Autrey and Sharon Mae Autrey; *Occupation:* Student; *Address:* 5384 Old Carriage Road, Northampton, PA.

BAKER, MICHELLE
Born: May 24, 1971, Camden, NJ; *Parents:*Sherry Baker & Harry W. Baker, Jr.; *Education:* West Deptford High School; *Occupation:* Student; *Other writings:* Has Written several poems; *Personal note:* I write about the way I feel about love; *Address:* West Deptford, NJ.

BAKER, PAM
Pen name: Pamela Baker; *Born:* June 27, 1955, Toledo, Ohio; *Parents:*Harold Bachtel, Mildred Eisenmann; *Spouse:* Mildred Eisenmann, June 5, 1982; *Education:* Mason Senior High School; Manatee Community College; *Occupation:* Data Entry Operator; *Other writings:* Has written poetry and short stories, publication pending in college anthology, article on government issue in local newspaper; *Personal note:* I desire to convey life vicariously in my writings in hopes of perhaps, unlocking someone's emotional isloation; *Address:* 10904 Country River Drive, Parrish, FL.

BALNIS-MEAGHER, TRACY LYNN
Pen name: Tracy Vincent; *Born:* December 21, 1969, Chicago, Illinois; *Parents:*Sylvia Meagher, John S. Meagher; *Spouse:* Michael D. Balnis, August 6, 1988; *Education:* Kelly High School; *Occupation:* Homemaker; *Honors:* Young Authors' Conference, 1986; *Personal note:* My poem is dedicated in the loving memory of Juan Madrigal. He was taken in the prime of his life, may he rest in peace; *Address:* 5515 S. Francisco, Chicago, IL.

BARBER, BARBARA
Pen name: Smyli; *Born:* February 2, 1955, Savannah, Georgia; *Parents:*Margaret and Edwin Phoenix; *Spouse:* Virgil Barber Jr., February 26; *Children:* Shameka and Joaquin Phoenix, Vernae and Versha Barber; *Education:* Quincy Diclerman Elementary, St. Jerimiah Burke High, Massasoit College; *Occupation:* I write poetry, but not for a profession; *Other writings:* "Razzle Dazzle," "Baby Babe," "1981," "Punk Rock Birth," "Risk," "I'm in Love But Without My Man," etc. These have not been published; *Personal note:* I strive to be successful in life if it takes me the rest of my life; *Address:* 53 Williams Avenue, Brockton, Massachusetts.

BARRERA, ANEL P.
Born: December 3, 1975, Beliz Central America; *Parents:*Hilma E. Barrera and Marco A. Barrera; *Education:* John Muir Junior High School; *Occupation:* Student; *Honors:* Service Award, Attendance Awards, Award of Honor, Achievement Awards, Musical Achievement; *Address:* 8707 Baring Cross Street, Los Angeles, CA.

BARROWS, KENNY
Pen name: Ken Barrows; *Born:* April 29, 1964, Olympia, Washington; *Parents:*George J. Barrows and Louise Barrows; *Occupation:* Self Employed *Memberships:* Elk's Lodge; *Honors:* Participant in essay contest sponsored by Knights of Columbus; *Other writings:* Has written Poems entitled, "Winter"; "Mom is a Legend"; *Personal note:* This poem is done in dedication to my mother Louise Barrows; *Address:* Rt 2, Box 192-A, Grayland, WA.

BATHER, KAREN
Pen name: Jade; *Born:* December 28, 1962, Bermuda; *Parents:*Neville and Elaine Whitecross; *Spouse:* Jose Bather, September 10, 1983; *Children:* Kassie Jade Bather; *Education:* Somerset Primary, Warwick Secondary, Bermuda College; *Occupation:* Accounts Payable; *Honors:* Editor's Choice Award; *Other writings:* Poem published in local magazine "The Bermudian"; *Personal note:* I strive to encourage all mankind to look to their creator to solve all their problems. Jer 10:23, Prov. 3:5,6; *Address:* P. O. Box SN 247, Southampton SNBX.

BATIZY, JULIANNA
Born: October 25, 1970, Arkron, Ohio; *Parents:*Levente and Patricia Batizy; *Education:* Akron Firestore High School; Ohio State University (with honor); *Occupation:* Student; *Honors:* National Honor Society; *Other writings:* Published in school literary magazine; *Personal note:* I would like to dedicate this poem to my late cousin and godchild Arpad Andras, from whom my inspiration came; *Address:* Akron, OH.

BENDER, MARTHA
Pen name: Martha; *Born:* April 14, 1932, Atwood, Illinois; *Parents:*Victor Heinzelmann and Caddie Fisher Heinzelmann; *Spouse:* Kenneth Bender, May 29, 1950; *Children:* Paul Edward; *Education:* Atwood School System; *Memberships:* Poetry Club of America; *Honors:* Golden Poet Award, Honorable Mention from the World of Poetry; *Other writings:* Numerous published articles; *Personal note:* As a poet, I write in rhyme about now and other times, all I want to do, is for you to have a smile or two; *Address:* 2711 Clayton Blvd, Champaign, IL.

BENNETT, ROBIN S.
Born: September 20, 1960, Pittsburg, Kansas; *Parents:*John and Pat Williams; *Children:* Jerrod Clayton; *Education:* Mulvane High School; *Occupation:* Bag Packer; *Other writings:* Has written "Mama Why"; *Personal note:* I hope through my poetry I can make someone smile or let someone know that others feel their pain; *Address:* 510 W. 6th, Pittsburg, KS.

BERARD NICOLE SUZANNE
Born: December 21, 1974, Framingham, MA; *Parents:*Susann Berard, Robert Goldberg; *Education:* Midway High School; *Occupation:* Student; *Memberships:* Medway Drama Club; *Honors:* Marietta Breakey Memorial Award for outstanding Scholarship, National Science Olympiad; *Other writings:* Unpublished Novel, "Le Drapeau Rouge"; *Personal note:* My life has been greatly influenced by Victor Hugo's Les Miserables. The future is in our grasp, it is our responsibility to right the present injustices and move forward to better horizons; *Address:* Medway, MA.

BEST, BARBARA N.
Born: January 27, 1931, Deville, Louisiana; *Parents:*Sam Parson Paul and Essie Dale Olive Paul; *Spouse:* John L. Best, January 19, 1975; *Children:* Allen Paul Dobson, Robert L. Dobson, James Andrew Dobson; *Education:* Springhill U.S. Army's Practical Nursing School High School; *Occupation:* Practical Nurse, Retired; *Memberships:* AARP, North Shore Animal League Salesian Missions; *Honors:* Best New Poet, World of Poetry 1988; Best New Poet, American Poetry Association, 1988; Placed 4th in poetry contest; *Other writings:* Two poems pending publication; Has published in several anthologies; *Personal note:* I strive to show my love of nature, mankind and country in my poems, and also reflect my concern for conservation; *Address:* 2027 Shannon Road, Alexandria, LA.

BIBBINS, MILDRED
Born: February 6, 1951, Stokes County, NC; *Parents:*Lillie Shuff and Gaither Shuff; *Spouse:* Anthony P. Bibbins, May 29, 1971; *Children:* Zandra, Anthony; *Education:* Hartford Connecticut Greater Hartford College; *Occupation:* Blue Collar Worker; *Personal note:* I enjoy writing, it brings me a sense of fulfillment and accomplishment of my ideas and dreams; *Address:* Hartford, CT.

BISHOP, BERNICE COUEY
Born: June 3, 1927, Floyd County, Georgia; *Parents:*Clara Sanders Couey, Bernard Couey; *Spouse:* Furman R. Bishop, July 7, 1946; *Children:* Furman Ralph, Ronald Eugene, Cmdr. Gene E. Carnicom; *Education:* Dallas High School, University of Georgia, Off Campus Center, Yeoman Training School, Iowa State Teacher's College; *Occupation:* Retired Office Manager-Secretary and Bookkeeper; *Memberships:* AARP, Epilepsy Assoc. of America, Floyd County Geneological Assoc., various other associations too numerous to list; *Honors:* Awarded 1988 Golden Poet Award by World of Poetry and invited to attend the poetry award convention in Anaheim, California; *Other writings:* Poems published in *The Golden Treasury of Great Poems, The National American Poetry Anthology, American Poetry Anthology, Treasured Book of Poems of America 1989* and *Many Voices, Many Lands*; Short story published in *Fate* magazine, article *Atlanta Journal Constitution*; *Personal note:* I tell everyone God gives me the words of the poems, songs and other things that I write; I am only His servant and faithfully write them down to share with others; *Address:* 5 Carrington Place Northeast, Rome, Georgia.

BLEU, NOEL
Born: November 3, 1953, Steubenville, Ohio; *Parents:*Ralph and Lois Morris; *Children:* Vicki Lee Walter; *Education:* Richmond Elementary, Jefferson Union High School; *Occupation:* Freelance Writer, Youth Advocate; *Memberships:* National Assn for Female Executives, Concerned Women for America, World Harvest Church; *Honors:* Nominated for Who's Who of American Women; *Other writings:* Feature articles in local newspaper including poems, poems appeared in approximately 15 anthologies 1976-89; *Personal note:* My early work reflects the romantic poets, while my recent work

shadows 20th century contemporaries. I strive for clarity, unity of thought and sharpness of imagery; *Address:* 7808 Worth-Galena Road, Worthington, OH.

BOAZ, DIANE

Pen name: Diane Bergstrom Boaz; *Born:* August 17, 1942, Waterloo, Iowa; *Parents:*Robert and Margaret Bergstrom; *Spouse:* Dennis Boaz, November 30, 1963; *Children:* Zachary, Jason, Jessica; *Education:* Teacher's College High School; School of Nursing, Cedar Rapids, Iowa; *Occupation:* Registered Nurse; *Personal note:* The Poem "Reflections" is dedicated to my teenage daughter, Jessica; *Address:* 1207 Independence Avenue, Waterloo, IA.

BONNICI, PAULINE

Born: November 18, 1974, Toronto, Ontario; *Parents:*Emmanuela Bonnici and John Bonnici; *Education:* St. Augustine High School; *Occupation:* Student; *Honors:* Poetry Award, Cardinal Newman Elementary, 1987; *Other writings:* Published poems; *Personal note:* The trees are my guide for as they grow twisting turning so must mankind; *Address:* Brampton, ONTARIO.

BORJA, DOINES M.

Pen name: Donnes Raelynn, "Fanciface"; *Born:* November 25, 1971; Talofofo, GU; *Parents:*George C. Borja and Amelia M. Borja; *Education:* St. Francis School; Notre Dame High School; *Memberships:* Honor Choir; *Honors:* Ms Personality, Liberation Day 1988; *Other writings:* Several articles in Pacific Voice and Royal Express Newspapers, poetry entries in the Royal Express, other unpublished creative writings, wrote the lyrics to a song entitled Beyond the Sun; *Personal note:* Writing is my self express, and you are my inspiration, when bonded together, a work of art is created, an art that I never want to loose; *Address:* 19 Mata Street, Talofofo, GU.

BOTELHO, EUGENE G.E.

Pen name: Eugene E.E. Botelho; Anonymous; *Born:* April 7, 1916, Yokohama, Japan; *Parents:*Francis Martin Botelho, Emily Yates Evans Botelho; *Education:* Radnor High School; Haverford College; *Occupation:* Retired; *Memberships:* Various national and internation Assn; *Honors:* Jane Addams Centennial Award for Community Service; State of California Legislature, San Diego County Board of Supervisors; Presidential Citation; *Other writings:* Have written articles, stories, brochures, booklets, etc; *Personal note:* To let the spiritual, unhidden and unconscious, grow up through the common and to share what I have in skills and wealth for the benefit of others; *Address:* P.O. Box 925, Eagle Pass, TX.

BOTTORFF, DEBORAH A.

Born: May 29, 1953, Connersville, Indiana; *Parents:*Charles and Laura Bottorff; *Education:* Indiana University, BS; Ball State University, MA; *Occupation:* President Pleasant Beginnings Day Care Inc; *Memberships:* A.D.O.U, Tri Kappa, DAR; *Other writings:* Various other poems published; *Personal note:* My poetry expresses feelings associated with everyday life; *Address:* RR #1, Box 448, Connersville, IN.

BOUDREAU, NICHOLE K.

Pen name: Nichole K. Boudreau; *Born:* January 10, 1974, Portland, Maine;*Parents:*Jean L. Boudreau & Richard J. Boudeau; *Education:* High School; *Occupation:* Student; *Honors:* Have won several poetry and art contests in school; *Personal note:* Always believe in yourself; *Address:* R.R. 1 Box 2305, Kenn, ME.

BOWERS, KAREN A.

Pen name: Emma Pendragon; *Born:* February 15, 1954, Bonham, Texas; *Parents:*Kenneth A. and Ednafae Bowers; *Education:* Proviso West High School; Triton College; *Occupation:* Assistant Office Manager; *Other writings:* Poems published in the Amherst Society Anthology, the Cambridge Collection and the National Library of Poetry's on the Threshold of a Dream; *Personal note:* Miracles do happen! They begin with a dream and culminate with an accomplishment; *Address:* 315 Marengo 3B, Forest Park, IL.

BRAIDIS, SUSAN RENE

Born: Seoul, Korea, August 13, 1970; *Parents:*Mary Ellen Braidis, Raymond P. Braidis; *Education:* Haddon Township High School; *Honors:* Choral Awards, Athletic Awards; *Other writings:* Have written many poems for private collection; *Personal note:* Poetry is my way of expressing the ways of how I see life through my eyes alone do I experience the beauty and the darkness that engulfs my thoughts; *Address:* Devereux Box 654, Chester, NJ.

BRANKEY, JOSEPH J.

Born: July 30, 1920, Chicago, Illinois; *Spouse:* Fern T. Brankey, November 26, 1949; *Education:* University of Wisconsin, AB; University of Illinois, MS; University of North Carolina; *Occupation:* Counselor; *Other writings:* Have written a book of poetry, two novels, several short stories; *Personal note:* I write what I feel, I recognize the fact that each individual lives a personal life and that there is pain and trauma; *Address:* POB-117, Kooskia, ID.

BRANKOVIC, SLOBODAN

Pen name: Dan Branko; *Spouse:* Vesna Butier-Brankovic; *Children:* Dejan, Nelly; *Education:* BA, PHD; *Occupation:* Former Senior Advisor; *Honors:* A prize at the World Contest of the Information Center of the United Nations; *Other writings:* Has written poems and songs; *Personal note:* Promotes the view that the society needs more scientists among poets, as well as poets with keen interest in social sciences and essential technological achievements; *Address:* 440 Arbor Road, Menlo Park, CA.

BRANSON, BENNIE MASON

Born: August 30, 1955, Wilspoint, Texas; *Parents:*Thelma and Sherwood Mason; *Spouse:* John F. Branson; *Children:* Ryland, Jeannette; *Education:* La Tourneau College, Tyler Junior College, Mt. Pleasant, Northeast Community College; *Occupation:* Entrepreneur; *Other writings:* Has written numerous poems and songs, currently writing first novel; *Personal note:* Writing is very personal to me, I share very intimate thoughts and memories. The lord blessed me with this gift. My father also was an outstanding writer; *Address:* Rt 3, Box 34G, Atlanta, TX.

BRILLANTES, GLADYS

Born: July 1, 1973, San Francisco, California; *Parents:*Jesse Brillantes, Violeta Brillantes; *Education:* Goose Creek High School; *Memberships:* Spanish Club, Video Club, Volleyball Club; *Personal note:* To my family: I love you and I want to thank you for always being there for me, and for influencing me to use my talents for such things as my poems, art and singing, I plan to have a career in music or businesss law; *Address:* 3516 Faraday Lane, Virginia Beach, VA.

BROOKS, JEANNE F.

Pen name: Jeanne Dykstra-Brooks, Janjse DeBroeks; *Born:* October 23, 1954, Everett, Washington; *Parents:*Richard and Evelyn Dykstra; *Spouse:* Stanton M. Brooks, August 17, 1973; *Children:* Fabian Stanton Mahon, Stanton Maconivan, Serena Megan; *Education:* Everett High School; Leo's College, Spokane Community College; The University of The State of New York; *Occupation:* Nurse; *Other writings:* Contributer to "Celebration!" Magazine, wirter of several children's books, authoring book on interracial marriage entitled, "Ebony and Ivory"; *Personal note:* To communicate is a gift from God, to write is a privilege, to be published a joy! to God be the glory! *Address:* 619 N. Monroe, Lebanon, IL.

BROWN-YOUNG, JOYICE BERNICE

Born: January 12, 1953, Richmond, VA; *Parents:*Thomas Nelson Young and Lute Mary Bernice Burnett-Young; *Spouse:* Raymond G. Brown, July 31, 1971; *Children:* P.J. Ramon; *Education:* Cambridge Academy; *Occupation:* Homemaker, Artist, Poet; *Memberships:* Art Committee, Video Drama Club; *Honors:* Numerous Awards, Honorable Mention; *Other writings:* Published author, published several poems; *Personal note:* We all have talent that is locked up which the Lord has given us to use in his glory for salvation for mankind, writing poetry is like painting a picture only in words; *Address:* Pennsauken, NJ.

BROWNING, JUDITH S.

Born: April 9, 1954, Cincinnati, Ohio; *Parents:*Richard J. Welz, Sr., Vincenza Panzeca Welz; *Spouse:* James P. Browning, Sr.; *Children:* Jim, David; *Education:* Seton High School; *Occupation:* Private Duty Nurses Assistant; *Personal note:* I try to reflect what's in my heart when I write. My only hope is that my poetry will make a difference to someone! *Address:* 3368 Niagara Street, Cincinnati, OH.

BRUCE, GORDON

Born: September 10, 1963, Toledo, Ohio; *Parents:*Jade Juven eau and Ampliss Walker; *Occupation:* Machinist; *Other writings:* Published author; *Personal note:* We flow from creativity, godliness, and our true self, we relish our true meaning because after our pact is done, we have left a piece of us to ponder; *Address:* 374 Lake Park, Bay Village, OH.

BRUNDAGE, BONNIE

Pen name: BBB; *Born:* August 20, 1943, Salinas, California; *Other writings:* Has written numerous poems;

BRUNER, JOHN DOUGLAS

Pen name: Doug Brunner; *Born:* November 6, 1943, San Antonio, Texas; *Parents:*John H. and Catherine Brunner; *Children:* Patrick Eugene Brunner; *Education:* San Antonio College; *Occupation:* Retail sales; *Honors:* Golden Poet Award, World of Poetry, 1985 and 1986; Numerous Merit Certificates; *Other writings:* Poems: "The Encounter", "Drunks' Luck", "Music Flutter", "Fumbles O'Toole", "Thoughts of Life", "The World Outside"; *Personal note:* To understand oneself helps us understand others, to understand others helps us understand the universe, to understand the universe give us a closeness with God; *Address:* P.O. Box 680671, San Antonio, TX.

BRYAN, ROAN

Born: May 2, 1973, Mobile, Alabama; *Parents:*Mary Helen Hill; *Occupation:* Student; *Honors:* Honor roll, Busy Bee Award; *Other writings:* Many books and poems; *Personal note:* I want to be greater than Steve King, and help everyone who needs help! *Address:* 310 W. Alabama, Vivian, LA.

RYANT, GLENDA

lorn: February 11, 1951, Washington, DC; *Parents:*William Whittington, Ilegn Whittington; *Children:* Angela, Misti, Germaine; *Education:* Springarn High School; *Occupation:* Former child care provider; *Memberships:* Parent Teachers Association; Full Gospel CHristian Center Child Care Committee; *Other writings:* Has written poem entitled, "Expression of the Heart"; *Personal note:* I live my life for my children's happiness, I feel great about others that try to live a joyful life also; *Address:* P.O. Box 637322, Washington, DC.

BUCHHOLTZ, JENNIFER M.

Born: December 18, 1973, Mineola, New York; *Parents:* Maurian and Henry Buchholtz; *Education:* St. Mary's Girls High School; *Occupation:* Student; *Memberships:* Student Against Drunk Driving; *Personal note:* The long trip isn't important, it's who you meet and what you achieve along the way that counts; *Address:* 358 Beebe Road, Mineola, NY.

BUFFKIN, BONITA CLAIRE

Born: August 12, 1960; *Parents:*Clerance Steele Holt, Patricia Joyce Gabbert; *Spouse:* Rickey Lynn Buffkin, June 1, 1982; *Children:* Colt Steele; *Occupation:* Song Writer; *Personal note:* I was raised in Alaska where beauty isn't taken for granted, where, it seems, poetry comes naturally to everyone; *Address:* HHC 11th AVN BDE, Box 193, APO NY;

BURCH, JERRY

Born: August 31, 1972, Fieldon, Illinois; *Parents:*Gerald F. and Sonia A. Burch; *Education:* Jersey Community High School; *Occupation:* Stockman; *Memberships:* JCHS Student Council, National Honor Society, SADD, French CLub; *Honors:* Jersey County Historical Society Writing Award, Who's Who Among American High School Student; *Other writings:* Numerous poems written for both personal enjoyment and as gifts to friends on certain occasions; *Personal note:* In my writings I try to reflect the bitter and disappointing aspects of modern society and human nature as seen through the eyes of a teenager. Influenced by Thoreau, Masters, E.A. Robinson; *Address:* 112 Rosewood Drive, Jerseyville, IL.

BURGOYNE, MICHELLE LYNN

Born: April 4, 1970, Lansing, Michigan; *Parents:*Eleanor Burgoyne; *Education:* Dewitt College; *Occupation:* Express Technician; *Memberships:* International Order of Jobes Daughter; *Other writings:* Has written 138 poems; *Personal note:* A special thanks to the people that pushed me to keep writing; *Address:* Lansing, MI.

BURNS, JOHN H.

Born: March 15, 1953, Baytown, Texas; *Spouse:* Brenda Burns; *Occupation:* Gospel Minister; *Other writings:* Has written gospel tracts in English and Spanish called the "60 Second Tract"; Phamplet entitled, "Is Church Necessary?"; Poetry book Entitled, "From the Heart"; *Personal note:* Whether you believe in the almighty God or not, the christain way is the best way. Only through God's inspiration do I write and that's only to help others up when they fall and to walk worthy of God; *Address:* P.O. Box 670484, Houston TX.

BURTON, HELEN

Pen name: Helen Brown Burton; *Born:* October 27, 1925, Mansonville, P. Que Canada; *Parents:*Mr. Harley Brown and Victoria Brown; *Spouse:* Herman Burton; *Occupation:* Housewife; *Honors:* Editor's Choice Award from the National Library of Poetry; *Other writings:* Have written over 100 poems published in local newspaper; *Personal note:* I try to make old people happy, if I get a smile, I feel as if I am well paid; *Address:* P.O. Box 339, Ayers Cliff, P.Quebec, CANADA.

BUSENDORFER, ALBERT P.

Born: October 9, 1932, Rochester, NY; *Education:* Los Angeles City College, Long Beach City College; *Occupation:* Transportation Analyst; *Memberships:* Independent Writers of Southern California; Romance Writers of America; *Other writings:* Several poems published in anthologies issued by the New York Poetry Association and the American Poetry Association, personal articles in pioneer Magazine; *Personal note:* Through my poetry I attempt to depict the strength in emotional experience; *Address:* 545 Chestnut Avenue #316, Long Beach, CA.

BYFIELD, MARLON ANTHONY

Pen name: M.A.B. *Born:* May 28, 1953, West Indies; *Other writings:* Recent acceptance for publication in several anthologies; *Address:* Worcester, MA.

CABRERA, REGINA T.

Born: July 29, 1952, Havana, Cuba; *Parents:*Mario Cabrera Saqui and Luisa Rodriquez Faxas; *Education:* Miami Dade

Community College; *Occupation:* Service Representative; *Memberships:* President and founder Future Telephone Pioneers Philatelic Club; *Honors:* Outstanding Academic Achievement; Miami Dade Community College, third place poetry contest; *Other writings:* Has written several prayers, paraphrase on love from scripture, book on St. Francis prayer, many poems in Spanish and one in French; *Personal note:* Writing is the music of the soul and a gift of God; *Address:* 7620 SW 82 Street J-103, Miami, FL.

CALHOUN, JENNIFER A.

Pen name: Jen Calhoun; *Born:* June 19, 1972, Hershey, Pennsylvania; *Parents:*Barry Calhoun, Patricia Calhoun; *Education:* Bishop McDevitt High School; *Occupation:* Student; *Memberships:* Peer Counselor, Vice President of Future Business Leaders of America, Drama Club, Softball; *Personal note:* I feel students should put their talents into something positive like writing rather than wasting talents on drugs and alcohol; *Address:* 445 Douglas Road, Hummelstown, PA.

CAMPION, CHRISTINE

Born: April 7, 1972, Janesville, Wisconsin; *Parents:*Dr. William and Sue Campion; *Education:* Janesville Craig High School; *Occupation:* Student; *Memberships:* Religious Organization, History and Spanish Clubs; *Honors:* Honor Roll, Forensic Speech Honors, Regional Oration Contest Placement, National Science Merit Award, Commendation for Outstanding History Grades and Knowledge; *Other writings:* Several other poems, published in various anthologies, and Has written speeches for school; *Personal note:* I feel the best way to learn is to experience first hand life outside of the community and area in which a person lives their own life. *Address:* 3140 Danbury Dr., Janesville, WI.

CANGIALOSE, WILLIAM T.

Pen name: Bill Thomas; *Born:* November 13, 1927, Lodi, New Jersey; *Parents:*Charles and Josephine Cangialose; *Spouse:* Josephine Cangialose, December 27, 1953; *Children:* Jeanne Marie, William Danial; *Education:* University of Miami, BED; *Occupation:* Phsyical Education Teacher (retired); *Memberships:* NJEA, NEA; *Honors:* All bergen football, all state football; *Other writings:* "High Up On a Mountain Top", "The Brother of Caine", "What's Left of Tomorrow?", "All I Need is You"; *Personal note:* If I can follow a straight path; If can avoid your terrible wrath; If I can avoid the face of sin; If I can take Life with a grin; Then I'll see you the day idle"; *Address:* 76 Washington Street, Lodi, NJ.

CARDENAS, VALERIE A.

Born: February 27, 1973, San Antonio, Texas; *Parents:*Tony and Lupe Cardenas; *Education:* McArthur High School; *Memberships:* AFS, Kiwonettes, Sunday school teacher; *Other writings:* Has written other poems and short stories; *Personal note:* Believe in yourself and your abilities and you will always succeed; *Address:* 9403 Lantana, San Antonio, TX.

CARTER, CUE JOHNSON

Born: May 10, 1970, Spartanburg, SC; *Parents:*Prentice W. Johnson, Martha C. Johnson; *Education:* University of Carolina; *Personal note:* Know the difference between what you can and cannot change and always try to reach beyond your grasp. *Address:* Shelby, NC.

CASH, SUSAN S.

Pen name: SUSAN CASH; *Born:* June 7, 1978, Westminister, California; *Parents:* Donna and Thomas Cash; *Children:* Andy and Susan Cash; *Education:* Tanque Verde Elementary; *Occupation:* Student; *Memberships:* Girl Scouts of America, Chorus, Dar Jrs; *Other writings:* Have written numerous poems and short stories; *Personal note:* Life is a big, red, juicy apple so take a big bite; *Address:* 4581 N. Sugarbush Place, Tucson, AZ.

CASSITY, MARTIN M.

Pen name: Mae Cassity; *Born:* July 20, 1944, Altus, Oklahoma; *Parents:* Martin M. Cassity and June Cassity; *Children:* Roybn, Gretchen, Scott; *Education:* USMA, West Point; Massachusetts Institute of Technology, MS, 1969; *Occupation:* Meteorologist, Pastor; *Honors:* Graduated 2nd in class at West Point; *Other writings:* I have published a few scientific articles in meteorological journals and some religious papers associated with my ministry, also in 1988 I published several poems in various poetry publications; *Personal note:* My hope as well as the hope of my small ministry is for the genuine gathering of human hearts in the oneness of love; My poetry reflects this hope and pain of alienation that usually prevails; *Address:* 139 Sandy Pond Road, Ayer, MA.

CHESROW, CATHLEEN GWEN

Born: January 16, 1947, Chicago, Illinois; *Parents:* Marguerite and Vernon Gras; *Children:* Albert John, Alexis Marie; *Education:* Art Institute of Chicago, BFA; *Occupation:* Writer, Horsewoman; *Memberships:* New York Academy of Science; American Association for the Advancement of Science; Chicago Council on Foreign Relations, Indiana Sheriff's Association; *Honors:* Best New Poet, 1987 and 1988; Golden Poet Award, Honorable Mention and Fourth Place, World of Poetry; *Other writings:* Has published several poems; *Personal note:* To me the essence of American education is to give everyone the ability to recognize and respect quality in living where ever; whenever it occurs; this quality in living transcends arbitrary boundaries of time, race and even sex; *Address:* P.O. Box 1675, La Porte, IN.

CLABON, GEORGE D.

Born: July 26, 1952, Saint Louis, Missouri; *Parents:* Lillie Ann Clabon; *Education:* Vashon High School, Carleton College; *Occupation:* Supervisor, Prudential Insurance Company of America; *Other writings:* Several Poems published in anthologies by Guild Press, Robbinsdale, Minnesota; *Personal note:* There are positives within the negatives of life. By examining the negatives, I strive to have my readers reflect on the positives and adapt those to our lifestyle; *Address:* 3401 Colfax South #311, Minneapolis, Minnesota.

CLARK, CARMAN SUZANNE

Pen name: C.S. Clark-Suzanne; *Born:* January 31, 1964, Alexandria, Louisiana; *Parents:* Frances M. Washington, Larry E. Washington; *Spouse:* Harold S. Clark II, November 26, 1983; *Children:* Harold Shelby, Alexander Clark, Jennifer B'rion Clark; *Education:* Ville Platte High School; Community College of the Air Force Midwestern; Midwestern State University, Solano Community College California; *Occupation:* U.S. Air Force Medial Laboratory Technologist; *Memberships:* American Society of Clinical Pathologists; Stephen Ministries Counselor; *Honors:* Trophy Recognition of Poetic Achievement; *Other writings:* Has written several poems, short stories, and plays pending publication; *Personal note:* The need to show love, sensitivity and appreciation for each other is above necessity, it is essential for the stability of human life. I try to reflect those qualities in all of my writings, my inspiration: The bible and person of the Lord Jesus Christ; *Address:* 123 David Street, Travis AFB, CA.

CLARK, HEATHER CHRISTINE

Born: August 20, 1970, Mobile, Alabama; *Parents:* Mr. and Mrs. Bill Knick; *Education:* Faulkner State Junior College; *Memberships:* College Choir; *Honors:* College scholarship for music, chosen for college ensemble; *Other writings:* Several poems, editorals and reporting news published in high school newspaper; *Personal note:* In our lives today we take so much for granted, If we would just stop and count our many blessings God gives us, our lives would become so much more meaningful; *Address:* 9720 Pleasant Road, Daphne, AL.

CLARK, JACKIE NEWSOM

Born: Eldorado, Arkansas; *Spouse:* Dr. Howard Clark, May 10, 1968; *Education:* Mississippi College, BA, 1989; *Other writings:* Have written many poems and a few short stories that I have never had published. *Personal note:* I mainly write of my own impressions and not of a particular event or place, but of feelings that result from the exposure of certain events or places. *Address:* 841 E. 4th Avenue, Morton, MS.

CLARK, MARIE

Pen name: c. clark *Born:* December 6, 1952, Longview, Washington; *Parents:* Darrell Clark; *Education:* Toutle Lake High School; Lower Columbia College; *Occupation:* Retail Security Officer; *Honors:* Citizenship Award, Dean's List, Employee of the Month, Loss Prevention Agent of the Quarter; *Other writings:* Has written numerous poems; *Personal note:* I believe one must become best friends with the one they love before becoming lovers. I thank my best friend for the encouragement to put my thoughts in poetic form to share with others; *Address:* Yuma, AZ.

CLARK, NICOLE D.

Pen name: Nicky; *Born:* May 25, 1976, Saddlebrook, NJ; *Parents:* James & Fran Clark; *Occupation:* Student; *Memberships:* Boy's Swim Team, Girl's Softball Team, Jr. Boilermaker cheerleader; *Honors:* Academic Achievement; *Personal note:* I like to write now that I see what I can do. I believe anyone could write if they try. *Address:* 262 Semel Avenue, Garfield, NJ.

CLARKE, JAKKI

Pen name: Jakki; *Born:* June 30, 1977, Woodbury, NJ.; *Parents:* Robert and Sandra Clarke; *Occupation:* Student; *Personal note:* Only write what you feel is right not what others think; *Address:* 715 Golfview Dr., Moorestown, NJ.

CLIFTON, RACHEL

Pen name: Ebodina; *Born:* December 1, 1974, Pekin, Illinois; *Parents:* Michael Clifton, Terri Cole; *Education:* Pekin High School; *Occupation:* Assistant in Cosmetology Center; *Other writings:* Has written numerous poems; *Personal note:* When I'm clicked into a certain mood, that 's what I write about, I believe poetry is a state of mind, when you feel depressed, your poems are sure to be sad. When you are happy your poems are ecstatic. *Address:* 1012 Hamilton Street, Pekin, IL.

CLINTON, DOROTHY LOUISE

Pen name: Dorothy Randle Clinton; *Born:* Des Moines, Iowa; *Parents:* Gilbert and Carrie Randle; *Spouse:* Moses S. Clinton, June 17, 1950; *Children:* Jerome Boyd; *Education:* Drake University, BFA; *Occupation:* Writer; *Honors:* Listed in numerous publication; *Other writings:* Has published numerous writings; *Personal note:* Never let another put a limit on your goals or the value of your ideas; *Address:* 1530 Maples, Des Moines, IA.

COLELLO, CAROL D.

Pen name: C.D. Colello; *Born:* November 7, 1954, Corbin, Kentucky; *Parents:* Mr and Mrs. Steeley G. Hubbs; *Spouse:* A.E. Colello, June 9, 1985; *Children:* Nadine, Christopher J.; *Education:* Kentucky State University; *Occupation:* Legal Secretary-Writer; *Honors:* 3rd Place in National Anthology Contest; *Other writings:* Collection of short stories; publications include poetry contest; poetry anthologies; *Personal note:* It's a known fact that love changes people and situations; My idea of succeeding is to reflect this love and show how to make that difference in the lives of others; *Address:* 5132 Conroy Road, #911, Orlando, FL.

COLEMAN, GREGORY

Pen name: Rita, Kenya, April, Dorothy; *Born:* January 27, 1966, New York, NY; *Parents:* Cathy Coleman; *Education:* Magna Dental School; John Robert Power Modeling School; *Occupation:* Dental Lab Technology; *Honors:* 1988 International Modeling Cover Guy; *Other writings:* Has written poem entitled, "Love and Commitment"; and song entitled, "Loving You Forever"; *Personal note:* Be all you can be in whatever you do and that will make your life much better; *Address:* Queens, NY.

COLLYER, DAVID LEE

Pen name: Waryock; *Born:* November 26, 1954, Miami, Florida; *Parents:* D.W. Curry and Mimi LeMay; *Education:* BS; *Memberships:* Universal Order of Continuity; *Other writings:* "Ramblings of an Isolated Man Who Refuse to Bite the Dust"; *Personal note:* I would that I be worthy of being an example of honor, strength, gentleness, solitude and open mindedness, save our children from the dark; *Address:* Miami, FL.

COMFORT, RALPH

Pen name: Maverick St. James; *Born:* May 23, 1957, Philadelphia, Pennsylvania; *Parents:* Ralph and Barbara Comfort; *Education:* Institute of Applied Science; Global School of Investigator; *Occupation:* Private Investigator, Inventory Control Specialist; *Honors:* 1988 Golden Poet Award, Award of Merit, Certificate of Merit; *Other writings:* Several poems and short stories printed in various newspapers and books; *Personal note:* To strive for greater achievements where love can be found, for God can give what no man will surrender; *Address:* 704 Main Street, Croydon, PA.

COOK, DIXIE RUTH

Born: November 10, 1926, Vian, OK; *Parents:* Charles Clinton and Clara Brockman Roark; *Spouse:* John Edward Cook, October 16, 1942; *Children:* Doris Ruth and Lewis Owen Cook; *Education:* Fresno State, BA, Fresno California; Northeastern State, Tahlequah Oklahoma, MA; *Occupation:* Retired Teacher; *Memberships:* Oklahoma Education Assn; National Education Assn; Oklahoma Retired Teacher Assn; *Other writings:* Several poems published in local newspaper, article for Tulsa world "Round the Clock"; Two family histories for Sequeyah Country History Book; *Personal note:* Writing has been the love of my life since I was a small child. Now that I'm retired, I plan to get serious about it; *Address:* Rt 1 Box 212-3, Vian, OK.

COOK, GRACE E.

Born: July 25, 1939, Fairbury, Illinois; *Parents:* George E. Calkin and Edyth Calkin; *Spouse:* Rev. Frederick S. Cook, Sr.; December 14, 1957; *Children:* Frederick, K. Mitzi, Andrew, John, Elizabeth, Hannah, Alma, Abbey; *Education:* Davenport Business College; *Occupation:* Homemaker, Volunteer School Librarian, Sunday School Teacher, Writer; *Memberships:* Lutheran High Guild; *Personal note:* 33 years ago, I was told I had a natural talent to write, since then, I have been writing for free on a part time as needs arose basis. I still have a strong desire to be a writer and have so many stories to tell; *Address:* 23 S. Central Avenue, Young America, MN.

COOK, SHERRON LEE SEXTON

Born: July 6, 1934, Laramie, Wyoming; *Parents:* Stephen M. Sexton, Mabel Sexton; *Children:* Donald Lee, David Brooks, Tina Marie, Anthony Stephen, Nancy, Robert, Oliver; *Education:* University of Wyoming; University of Metaphysics, Los Angeles California; U.C. Seminary, Los Angeles California; *Occupation:* Inspection Supervisor; *Memberships:* American Society Research and Clinical Hypnotists, American Parapsychological Research Fellowship, International Metaphysical Teachers Counselors Association; *Other writings:* Several articles in various small church magazines, poem in "Treasured Poems of American 1989", monthly column "Murphy's Log in Employers' Newsletter; *Personal note:* In my poems I attempts to grasp and express those elusive aspects of beauty and mystery most often lost in our day-to-day scuttle with time; *Address:* 2 Capitol Road, Apt 1, Milford, MA.

CORNELIUS, JEFF
Born: March 26, 1963, Brockton, MA; *Personal note:* I am hoping that this contest will give me the confidence to publish more of my work in the near future; *Address:* 108 Sunset Avenue, Brockton, MA.

CORSI, JILL DENISE
Born: April 15, 1971, Dunkirk, New York; *Education:* Dunkirk High School; *Occupation:* Student; *Memberships:* National Honor Society; *Honors:* Empire Girls' State; *Personal note:* To me, a piece of paper acts like a sponge, it's always there to absorb the overflow of my emotions; *Address:* 5 Gratiot Court, Dunkirk, NY.

COSTELLO, REBECCA
Born: December 31, 1974, San Jose, California; *Parents:* Cali Vrooman & Gordon Costello; *Occupation:* Student; *Address:* 2967 Mount View Ct., Cameron Park, CA.

COUCH, DEANNE
Pen name: Deanne Marie *Born:* August 17, 1972, Whittier, CA; *Parents:* David Couch and Becky Couch; *Education:* Estancia High School; *Address:* 1775 Pitcairn Drive, Costa Mesa, CA.

COURNOYER, RACHEL
Born: November 28, 1973, Holyoke, MA.; *Parents:* Raymond and Elizabeth Cournoyer; *Education:* Holyoke Catholic High School; *Personal note:* I have a passion for the romantic and spiritual side of life and I like my poetry to reflect that; *Address:* 75 St. James Avenue, Holyoke, MA.

CRISTOBAL, MARIO G.
Pen name: Stranger in America; *Born:* August 24, 1955, Olongago City Philippines; *Parents:* Pedro Cristobal and Adoracion Galapati; *Spouse:* Jimena Ruiz, April 26, 1988; *Children:* Robert Hector, Joy Khristine, Emerson; *Occupation:* Environmental Services; *Honors:* Best Worker of the Year, 1988; *Other writings:* Poems and Songs; *Personal note:* I like music because music is free, I can sing the blues in me, I could cry when nobody sees me, I can't do any harm to someone, especially to my love ones; *Address:* 129 Caldwell Avenue, Forked River, NJ.

CURAZZATO, RONALD S.
Born: September 12, 1955, Rochester, New York; *Parents:* Grace Curazzato and Joseph Curazzato; *Spouse:* Judith Ann Curazzato, March 30, 1979; *Children:* Anthony Michael; Arthur Joseph; *Education:* Clark County Community College, Las Vegas Nevada; Monroe Community College, Rochester New York; *Occupation:* Mailman; *Other writings:* Other poems published-1989 edition of Treasured Poems of American, National Poetry Anthology, Many Voices, Many Lands, The American Poetry Anthology; *Personal note:* It is my goal and hope that my poetry might help somebody to see a better day, brighter future, and motivate them to find success and happiness in their life, I would also like to become a songwriter one day and have been greatly influenced by the message in the lyrics of the musical group Earth, Wind, and Fire; *Address:* P.O. Box 24968, Rochester, NY.

CURRIE, MELISSA
Pen name: Missy Currie *Born:* November 8, 1974, Williamsburg, VA.; *Parents:* Terry & Franny Currie; *Education:* St. Pauls Schools; *Occupation:* Student; *Honors:* Poets Award, Awards for sports; *Other writings:* Has written several poem, published in school paper; *Personal note:* When I am writing I put all my heart and soul into it. I was influenced by romantic poets and songwriters; *Address:* 240 Wedgewood Drive, Spartanburg, SC.

CURRY, LONNIE
Born: January 29, 1969; *Parents:* Terence A. Curry & Jean Curry; *Education:* Iowa State University; *Occupation:* Electronic countermeasures specialist; *Memberships:* Air Force Association; *Other writings:* This is War, Heaven; *Personal note:* I enjoy putting my thoughts, feelings, and observations on paper so that other may enjoy them; *Address:* 725-38th Street, Sioux City, IA.

CURRY, PATSY J.
Born: November 23, 1939, Seven Pines, Texas; *Parents:* Elizabeth L. Bice, James N. Rose; *Spouse:* Thane Curry, March 10, 1987; *Children:* Donald, Phillip, Nila, Kenneth, Jason; *Education:* West Anchorage High School; *Occupation:* Library Assistant; *Memberships:* Professional and Business Christian Womens After Five Club; Soldotna Bible Chapel; *Other writings:* Poem published in the fall of 1986, New York Poetry Foundation Anthology; *Personal note:* I've found writing a excellent way to be able to express my emotions. I have to a strong faith that God can bless us even in the middle of crisis and sorrow. He's done it for me! *Address:* 304 Riverside Drive, Soldatna, AK.

DALEY, SHARON M.
Other writings: Authored numerous poems and songs; *Personal note:* My poetry and songs are interspersed with scriptural readings. Friends and I presented them in dramatic programs to small group gatherings as a means of raising money and consciousness for world hunger; *Address:* Spencer Street, EXT, Dolgeville, NY.

DARGITZ, CHRISTY A.
Born: March 14, 1973, Big Rapids, MI; *Parents:* Mickey and Darlene Dargitz; *Occupation:* Student; *Memberships:* Honor Society, Big Rapids Area Civic Orchestra, CMV Honors Orchestra, Blue Lake International Exchange Orchestra; *Honors:* Earns high ratings at solo and ensemble festival for violin, clarinet, and piano; *Personal note:* I write poems that will touch the minds and hearts of people everywhere; *Address:* Remus, MI.

DAVENPORT, GERALDINE
Pen name: Tiny; *Born:* October 29, 1950, Chicago, Illinois; *Parents:* Earnest Lee (deceased) and Annie Mae Davenport; *Children:* Lashone, Leotis, Willie; *Education:* Attended Crane Technical in Chicago, never finished, returned to get GED; *Occupation:* Professional assembler; *Memberships:* Holiday Project, Learning Exchange, Red Cross Blood Mobile; *Honors:* Honorable Mention for "The Silvery, Glistening Light"; *Other writings:* Many letters to the editor, song "One Stop for Love," many poems; "Common Sense and Logic," "Birds Sing" were published; *Personal note:* I feel everyone has a natural born talent that never needs a lot of training. If we pursue those talents, we will do our best; *Address:* Rockford, Illinois.

DAVIS, DEBORAH
Born: February 1, 1955, Bowling Green, Kentucky; *Parents:* James W. Neal and Sedell J. Neal; *Children:* Joshua Beal Davis; *Education:* Greenville High School, Western Kentucky; *Occupation:* Special Education Teacher; *Honors:* Dean's List; *Other writings:* Poems published in church bulletins, Sanctuary Inc. Newsletter, Ky. Domestic Violence Assn Newsletter, Merlin's Magic; *Personal note:* Writing allows me an opportunity to catch my emotions and to preserve them. I write as I live, with all of the sincerity I possess; *Address:* 214 Fairview, Greenville, KY.

DAVIS, WENDI JANELL
Born: April 29, 1968, Kingsburg, California; *Parents:* Patti P. Smeltzer, Norman Davis; *Education:* Kingsburg Joint Union High; College of Sequoias; Kings River Community College; *Occupation:* Child Development student; *Memberships:* California Girls State Alumni Foundation; *Honors:* Presidents List, Certificate Child Development; *Other writings:* Have written several other poems; *Personal Note:* Each of my poems reflect a part of me. It is through expression that one finds hope and understanding; *Address:* 1536 21st, Kingsburg, CA.

DAWN, SHAROLYN
Born: Spetember 25, 1937, Ennis, Texas; *Parents:* J.D. Farmer and Sybil Farmer; *Children:* Sharon Deline, Keith L. and Ricky; *Education:* Waxahachie High School; *Occupation:* Writer-Artist; *Memberships:* South Park Assembly of God Church; Writer and photographer Affiliate of City News Service; *Other writings:* Have written a collection of private poetry; *Personal note:* Absolutes are basic need in every human spirit; The written word is one way of both finding and sharing them; *Address:* 305 Lake Park Waxahachie, TX.

DECHAYNE, LAUREN K.
Born: February 12, 1971, Salem, MA; *Parents:* Gerald Dechayne, Maryanne Dechayne; *Education:* Peabody Veterans Memorial High School; *Occupation:* Student; *Memberships:* Vice President of Key Club, Captain Girls Varsity Tennis; *Honors:* National Honor Society, Inclusion in Who's Who Among American High School Students; *Personal note:* Life is neither the rough draft nor the final copy, it is the process between the two; *Address:* Peabody, MA.

DELGADO, ROSA JUDITH
Born: April 19, 1973, Bronx, New York; *Parents:* Ana Iris Delgado and Jose Luis Delgado; *Education:* St. Anselm's School, River Dell High School; *Occupation:* Student; *Memberships:* Track team, SADD Committee; *Honors:* Honor Roll, General Excellence Award; *Other writings:* Published numerous stories and poems; *Personal note:* I see poetry as a way of expressing my inner beauty and present experiences. I am inspired by the writings of Robert Frost; *Address:* 257 Wales Avenue, River Edge, NJ.

DEMERS, DENNIS G.
Born: September 8, 1945, Worcester, MA.; *Parents:* Richard O. Demers and Annette T. Demers; *Spouse:* Michele S. Demers, June 1, 1986; *Children:* Denise Marie, Deborah Anne, Sheri Lynn, Joseph, Shawn, Dennis; *Education:* St. Stephen's High School; David Hale Fanning School of Nursing; *Occupation:* Licensed Practical Nurse; *Other writings:* Other poems published in three other national anthologies;

Personal note: I strive to show the vast range of emotion in this fragile thing we call love; *Address:* P.O. Box 1056, Highland City, FL.

DENKINS, BEVERLY
Born: May 2, 1937, White Plains, NY; *Parents:* Woodrow and Helena Wilson; *Spouse:* Ed Denkins, April 13, 1988; *Children:* Edward, Marie; *Education:* White Plains High School; *Occupation:* Poet and Songwriter; *Honors:* Entered numerous poetry contest; *Other writings:* Has written several poems; *Personal note:* Dedicated to my family and friends, without their encouragement I would never have been a poet; *Address:* 213 N. Broad Street, Peekskill, NY.

DEVARY, KRISTINA LYNN
Born: November 1, 1973, Dover, Delaware; *Parents:* William and Linda DeVary; *Education:* Milford High School; *Other writings:* Has written several short stories and poems; *Personal note:* I just like to write; *Address:* 609 Woodmere Road, Milford, DE.

DIXON, MCDONALD
Born: October 1, 1945, Castries, St. Lucia, West Indies; *Education:* St. Mary's College, Castries St. Lucia, West Indies; afterwards, self-taught; *Occupation:* Banker, poet; *Honors:* Several small local awards, not very well known outside the Caribbean; *Other writings:* "On My Blackness" (1969), "Pebbles" (1974), "The Poet Speaks" (1979)—all small collections of 25 to 30 poems; *Personal note:* Through my work I seek to discover truth; to mirror this age for future generations; *Address:* Bronx, New York.

DOAN, KELLY
Born: February 13, 1973, Woodbury, New Jersey; *Parents:* William Doan Jr. and Mary Lou Doan; *Occupation:* Student; *Honors:* Honor Roll, French Award; *Personal note:* If you turn your back on life, you will never know what you have missed. The greatest things in life are not always noticeable; *Address:* Cape May Court House, NJ.

DONNELLY, BARBARA C.
Pen name: Lauren Gill; *Born:* November 2, 1967, Long Branch, New Jersey; *Parents:* Barbara May 31, 1986; *Children:* Shaun Ryan; *Education:* Long Branch High School; Marine Academy of Science and Technology; *Occupation:* Housewife; *Other writings:* Has written several unpublished poems for personal collection; *Personal note:* I believe that everyone and all things are created equal until proven otherwise; *Address:* 17 Airsdale Avenue, Long Branch, NJ.

DOUCETTE, CHRISTINE M.
Born: June 11, 1965, Falmouth, MA.; *Parents:* James and Cheryl Doucette; *Education:* Wilmington High School, Bridgewater State College; *Occupation:* Lead Sales Clerk; *Memberships:* The American Society for the Prevention of Cruelty to Animals; *Other writings:* Several poems published in Anthologies, many unpublished poems; *Address:* 13 Phillips Avenue, Wilmington, MA.

DRAKE, MICHELLE
Born: January 27, 1971, Villa Rica, Georgia; *Parents:* Wallace Drake and Fredda Drake; *Education:* Senior at Alexander High School; *Occupation:* File Clerk; *Honors:* First runner up in beauty pageant, 3rd place in talent show, honorable mention in art show; *Other writings:* Has written numerous poems; *Personal note:* My emotions are reflected through my poetry, I have been greatly influenced by Stevie Nicks; *Address:* 4694 Woods Valley Dr. Douglasville, GA.

DRUMHELLER, LINDA JO
Born: April 1, 1951, Mountain Home, Arkansas; *Parents:* Joe W. and Hazel R. Hill; *Spouse:* Gene B. Drumheller, August 5, 1971; *Children:* Timothy G. Drumheller; *Education:* Atlantic Airline School; *Occupation:* Administrative Secretary; *Other writings:* Poem to be published in upcoming volume II, No. 2 of Many Voices-Many Lands; *Personal note:* As the quote goes: "there is no such thing as defeat; only respectful submission until the next battle." That has become my philosophy in life; *Address:* Falls Church, VA.

DUNCAN, ELVIN J.
Born: August 4, 1944, Alum Ridge, Virginia; *Parents:* Hasker E. Duncan and Laura Cox Duncan; *Children:* Lisa Duncan Williams, Monica Duncan Wallace, Sonia R. Duncan; *Education:* Willis High, New River Community College (Magna Cum Laude); *Occupation:* Salesman; *Memberships:* Lions Club; *Honors:* Certificate of Recognition for Outstanding Community Service, several sales award; *Other writings:* Published in The National Library of Poetry's on The Threshold of a Dream. *Personal note:* Although we, as human beings, may vary in our perspectives, abilities, and social standings our basic needs, feelings, and emotions are the same; *Address:* P.O. Box 14061, Roanoke, VA.

DUNN, DOROTHY J.
Born: May 13, 1933, Hinsdale, Illinois; *Children:* Julie Bellura, Lawrence Allen Dunn, Terrence Henry Dunn, Timothy

Kenneth Dunn; *Education:* Broward Community College, AS; *Occupation:* City Official, City Clerk; *Memberships:* Board of Directors, Florida Assn of City Clerks; Int'l Institute of Municipal Clerks, Business and Professional Women, Sierra Club, Amnesty International, Freelance Writers Assn; *Other writings:* Articles and Poems published in local newspapers, co-writer of several songs; *Personal note:* I turn negatives into positives, enemies into friends and lemons into lemonade, all the while savoring each of life's precious moments; *Address:* 511 SE 13th Court Deerfield Beach, FL.

DVORAK, JULIA LOUISE

Pen name: Julie L. Dvorak *Born:* June 28, 1937, Chicago, Illinois; *Parents:* Percival Reginal Turner & Marianne V. Chavez; *Spouse:* October 12, 1956, Myron M. Dvorak; *Children:* Michael C., Julianne B., Kathleen M. Chodor, David M., Daniel P.; *Education:* McCord High School, Columbia College, Chicago, Illinois; *Occupation:* Self Employed; *Memberships:* YWCA; *Honors:* Award from YWCA; *Other writings:* Editor and Publisher for the Ceramic Gazette Newspaper; *Personal note:* Would like my poetry to express life's feelings and to bring joy into one's mine with my writings; *Address:* 5536 S. Fairfield Avenue, Chicago, IL.

ELKINS, APRIL

Pen name: Ape; *Born:* April 21, 1971, Danville, Virginia; *Parents:* Ronald and Alice Pressley; *Education:* West Grand High School; *Occupation:* Student; *Memberships:* FBLA; *Other writings:* Poem published in local newspaper; *Personal note:* I would like to dedicate this poem to my cloest friends, my Mother, Alice, Sheila, Clint, Bryan, Gina, Vicki, Crissy, and My Father, Rickie; You are worth everything to me; *Address:* P.O. Box 119, Kremmling, CO.

ELLIOTT, ELIZABETH

Born: October 2, 1973, Oxnard California; *Parents:* Terrance and Dianne Elliott; *Education:* Santa Clara High School; *Occupation:* Student; *Memberships:* Te Deum Bell Ringers; *Honors:* Academic Achievement Award, 1988; Perfect Attendance Award, 1988, Certificate, Completion of all modeling; *Personal note:* I like to write about nature and people, I would like my writing to reflect God's blessing; *Address:* 1315 El Portal Way, Oxnard, CA.

ENTWISLE, KELLIE

Born: April 27, 1969, Virginia Beach, Virginia; *Parents:* Brooke Entwisle, Peggy Entwisle; *Address:* Weaver Mill Road, Rector, PA.

EPSKAMP, YOLCINDA

Born: April 14, 1976, Soest, Holland; *Parents:* Wilhemus and Cheryl Epskamp; *Occupation:* Student; *Honors:* Spelling, language and athletics awards; *Other writings:* Has written poems and songs; *Personal note:* I enjoy expressing my thoughts and feelings in my poems that I write. I also enjoy listening to music; to get ideas for lyrics; *Address:* 716 Donner Court, Lodi, CA.

ESCHINGER, MARY

Born: August 8, 1973, Washington, DC; *Parents:* Kenneth & Frances Eschinger; *Education:* Frederick Douglas High School; *Occupation:* Student; *Memberships:* National Committee for Animal Rights; *Other writings:* Several short stories; *Personal note:* Long you live and high you fly. Smiles you'll give tears you'll cry. All you touch and all you see, is all your life will ever be. *Address:* 8701 Duvall Road, Upper Marlboro, MD.

ESTLE, LISA D.

Born: June 6, 1969, Topeka, Kansas; *Parents:* Ole and Harla Estle; *Education:* Hesston High School; *Occupation:* Secretary; *Other writings:* I have been writing poetry, short stories and have kept journals for the past three years. None of my writings have been published until now; *Personal note:* I would rather be a "could be" if I could not be an "are" for a "could be" is a "maybe" with the chance of going far... *Address:* Rt 4, Box 214, Sabetha, KS.

EVANS, CORNELIA LOUISE

Born: Wilson, North Carolina, December 11, 1940; *Parents:* Woodrow Mercer and thelma Mercer; *Children:* Frederick Steven, Curtis Clyde, Donna Louise; *Occupation:* Bookeeper, Waitress; *Personal note:* My writing was inspired by my late father who had a love for words and a unique way of expressing them; *Address:* Rt 4, Box 286A, Greenville, NC.

EVANS FRANCES A.

Pen name: Frances Avera Evans; *Born:* Mart, Texas; *Parents:* Hardy Richard Avera and Inez Watford Avera; *Children:* Gayle Evans-Steinman and Gary Williams Evans; *Education:* Palestine High School; University of Houston, BS, MED; *Occupation:* Teacher; *Memberships:* Texas State Council of International Reading Assn; Texas Secondary Reading Council; *Honors:* Certificate, Houston-Harris Country Writing Workshop, Honor Roll Student; *Other writings:* Has written several poems and newspaper article; *Personal note:* If poetry reflects the soul of the poet, then poetry must be the soul of mankind; *Address:* 14300 Tandem Blvd, Apt 116, Austin, TX.

EVANS, PERRY VAN

Pen name: Perry Evans; *Born:* October 31, 1948, Pineville, Kentucky; *Parents:* Sil Evans and Beulah Evans; *Spouse:* Nancy Evans, March 2, 1968; *Children:* Perry Van Evans, Jr.; *Education:* Morristown Hamlen High Cumberland College; *Occupation:* Mining Industry; *Honors:* Kentucky Colonel, Colonel Aide de Camp, Governor's Staff, State of Tennessee; *Other writings:* Several poems of various subjects for future publication; Past editor of a company magazine; *Address:* P.O. Box 772, Middlesboro, KY.

FALLOS, WILLIAM

Born: October 23, 1963, Milwaukee; *Occupation:* Machine Operator; *Personal note:* I love poetry because it says so much in so few words, It allows a reader if he can follow the poem to link up with his own personal muse. There is something magical about how this happens, a contrast to the techniques of short story writing; *Address:* W244 N6586 Grogan Drive, Sussex, WI.

FEINLAND, STEPHEN

Pen name: Chairman Steve; *Born:* March 18, 1943, Brooklyn, New York; *Parents:* Irving, Ernestine; *Honors:* Greenwich Village Poet Laurente; *Other writings:* "People's Gospel", "King of the Lions"; *Personal note:* Most I write upon the ground where it says, here your happiness cannot be found, but some write upon the skies where it says, here your soul to meet the Lord may rise; *Address:* 113 Monroe Street, Lawrence, NY.

FELICIANO, CANDID

Born: January 10, 1921, Aguada, Puerto Rico; *Parents:* Francisca Jimenez, Candido Feliciano; *Occupation:* Seamstress, Homemaker; *Honors:* Honorable Mention for Poetry; *Other writings:* Has written four poems; *Personal note:* We should learn as much as we can, respect the rights of others, don't leave for tomorrow what we can do today;

FIELDS, MARY

Born: August 3, 1950, Chicago, Illinois; *Parents:* Emily and Frank Porter; *Spouse:* Frank Fields, June 15, 1973; *Children:* Jim, Bob, Kim; *Occupation:* Instructor, Nurse; *Honors:* Award for Poetic Achievement, Certificate for Exceptional Artistry and Creativity and Certificate of Merit; *Other writings:* I have had poems published by Wide Open Magazine, Odessa Poetry Review, Yes Press, Poetry Press, Fine Arts Press, The American Poetry Association, Sparrograss Poetry Forum, The Poetry Center, The Pet Gazette and the Amherst Society; *Personal note:* I have written a book of poetry called "All my Best", I am working on volume II, but someday I hope to write a novel; *Address:* 10205 S. California Avenue, Chicago, IL.

FLESHMAN, KEVIN DELONG

Born: February 29, 1960, Columbus, Ohio; *Parents:* Hobert & Mae Fleshman; *Education:* Columbus North Sr. High School; Purdue University; *Occupation:* Retail Management; *Other writings:* Wrote a poem that was published by the Amherst Society, 1988; Working on a trilogy for which the poem *Reflections* is the title poem; *Personal note:* Magic is...The power of love through the eyes of an owl; *Address:* 1713 Geraldine Avenue, Columbus, OH.

FLYNN, SHARON W.

Born: January 14. 1949, Winchester, Massachusetts; *Parents:* Ruth Murray and Robert Washburn; *Spouse:* William E. Flynn, December 10, 1977; *Children:* Daniel Matthew, Sean Michael, Rebecca Lynn, Dawn Kimberly; *Education:* Technical High School, Institue of Children's Literature; *Occupation:* Secretary; *Honors:* Golden Poet's Award; *Other writings:* Published in the Springfield Journal and in other anthologies of poetry; *Personal note:* Success, without God, is empty; for the only true measure of success is to please God by using the talents he bestowed on us to bless someone else; *Address:* 106 Lang Street, Springfield, MA.

FORD, ERICKA

Born: December 5, 1971, Cherry Point, NC; *Parents:* Bobby and Nancy Ford; *Education:* Springbrook High School; *Occupation:* Student; *Honors:* Certificate of Merit-World of Poetry; MCPC Honoree; *Other writings:* Two other poems published in a book and the school newspaper; articles published in school newspaper; *Personal note:* Through family and friends I have found my ability to write; *Address:* 11700 Old Columbia Pike, Apt 919, Silver Spring, MD.

FOULKES, ROLAND ALEXANDER

Born: February 6, 1956, Fort Lauderdale, Florida; *Parents:* Arthur A. Foulkes, Jr. and Clemonteese J.L. Foulkes; *Education:* Cornell University, BA, 1982; Boston University, Cert., 1984; University of California, MA, 1985; PhD (antic.); *Occupation:* Medical Anthropologist; *Memberships:* African Studies Assn., International Peace Academy, World Future Society; *Honors:* Fulbright Fellowship, Outstanding Senior Award; *Other writings:* "My Proposals for a Peaceful World in the 1980s"; "Call for a National Association of Student Anthropologists"; *Personal note:* I write from personal experience; and, I live fully so as to have enough experience(s) from which to write. *Address:* P.O. Box 40217, Berkeley, CA.

FRANCISCI, CHRISTIE

Pen name: Christie Keeth; *Born:* March 17, 1974, Brooklyn, NY.; *Education:* St. Francis Preparatory High School; *Honors:* All Star Award, 2CD Honors, Award for an essay written in the 8th grade; *Other writings:* Several unpublished poems and short stories; *Personal note:* I like to write about true feelings and life itself.

FRANK, JENNIFER ROBIN

Pen name: Jennifer R. Van Duzer; *Born:* July 28, 1972, Sun Valley, California; *Parents:* Linda Van Duzer and Joseph Van Duzer; *Children:* Maxwell Andrew, Eugene; *Education:* Monterey High School; *Occupation:* Student; *Honors:* Youth Board, City Council representing Monterey High School; *Other writings:* Articles and poetry published in the Panther Pause; *Personal note:* I pray every day that God will show himself through my writing. I know that with help the oppression of men, women, and children will be defeated and it will truly be on earth as it is in heaven; *Address:* 268 W. Verdugo #205, Burbank, CA.

FRAZIER, GLORIA WILSON

Born: May 31, 1937, New York, NY; *Parents:* Roy and Kate Wilson; *Spouse:* Bennie Frazier, March 16, 1973; *Children:* Carlton, Eric, Malinda; *Education:* Manhattan Community College, College of New Rochelle; *Occupation:* Executive Director; *Memberships:* Winston-Salem Urban League; *Honors:* Hundred Year Assn; Career Civil Service Award; *Personal note:* My poetry reflects the feelings of the black people who come in may hues but are still proud to be called black until we are called by the master; *Address:* P.O. Box 361, Walkertown, NC.

FRIEDLAND, CHRISTINE

Pen name: C.A.F., CA, Friedland; *Born:* July 20, 1960, Alameda, California; *Parents:* Bryan and Anne Holmes; *Spouse:* David, March 10, 1981; *Education:* Mt. Diablo High School; *Occupation:* Marketing-Customer Service Representative; *Other writings:* "Explorer Prayer", "Dark Creation"; *Personal note:* I strive to reflect sociological change and my own experiences in life. Writing has been great therapy for me by forcing me to face the mirror which is my past; *Address:* 10174 Fairbanks NE, Albequerque, NM.

FROHLICH, LINDA

Born: December 23, 1950, Anniston, Alabama; *Parents:* Norris and Bettie Hall; *Spouse:* Herb Frohlich, October 25, 1980; *Children:* Melinda, Laura, Cindy; *Education:* College Graduate; *Memberships:* A.R.E.; *Other writings:* Currently working on a book of poetry and inspirational writing; *Personal note:* After many personal hardships I started to realize the power of the human spirit to create a new life and awareness; *Address:* 11305 Taylor, West Olive, MI.

FUKUMOTO, JANICE Y.

Born: January 5, 1953, Honolulu, Hawaii; *Education:* Farrington High School; University of Hawaii; The Institute of Childrne's Literature; *Occupation:* Career Educational Assistant; *Other writings:* "Awesome is the Lord" in Poetic Voices of America, 1988; "The Choice" in On the Threshold of a Dream; "The Lamb of God", in American Poetry Anthology, 1988; *Personal note:* I write to glorify God; *Address:* 1677 Ala Amoamo Street, Honolulu, HI.

GALLO, HEATHER

Born: August 25, 1974; New Brunswick, NJ; *Parents:* Robert and Catherine Gallo; *Education:* Mt. Carmel High School; *Memberships:* MEND; *Address:* San Diego, CA.

GALOZO, PETE G.

Born: Candon, Ilocos Sur, Phil., August 30, 1917; *Parents:* Florentino Galozo and Pia Garuneta Galozo; *Spouse:* Petronila Pagaduan Galozo, January 25, 1947; *Children:* Carmencita, Rudy, Rogelio, Danilo, Angelito, Evelyn, Jocelyn; *Education:* BSED; *Occupation:* Teacher; *Memberships:* AARP; *Honors:* 2nd Lt. Presidential Award in recognition of military service; *Other writings:* Several articles published; *Personal note:* I always strive to be honest and truthful to work for quality and perfection to begin and finish to see the result of performance; *Address:* 647 Albany Avenue, Apt. 3-G, Brooklyn, NY.

GARAMELLA, TRINITY

Born: December 17, 1973, St. Louis, Missouri; *Parents:* Andre and Karen Garamella; *Education:* Oakville Senior High School; *Occupation:* Poet; *Other writings:* Several poems not yet published; *Personal note:* I write poetry to express my feelings or fears. My interest in poetry was influenced greatly by the works of Edgar Allan Poe; *Address:* 2960 Meramar, St. Louis, MO.

GARDNER, W. LEE
Born: November 17, 1920, St. Marys, PA.; *Parents:* Karl J. and Verna L; *Spouse:* Helen Hamill, March 6, 1964; *Children:* Grant, Georgia; *Education:* State University of Iowa, PHD; *Occupation:* Technical Writer; *Memberships:* National STC; *Other writings:* Has written numerous articles, poems, and a 2-act play; *Personal note:* I am trying to bring back Browning's dramatic monologue style; *Address:* Albuquerque, NM.

GARNER, CECELIA LOUIS
Born: February 1, 1952, Washington, DC; *Parents:* William and Elizabeth Russell; *Spouse:* Curby Dean Garner, November 12, 1973; *Children:* Michael, William, Mary Jeannetee, Dawn, Daniel; *Occupation:* Wood Finisher; *Honors:* Honorable Mention for poem "Feelings", Golden Award for 1988, from World of Poetry; *Other writings:* Has written a poem entitled, "Feelings"; *Personal note:* I love to write poems for the people I love and care about and about beautiful things in life; *Address:* 12 Leonard Street, Thomasville, NC.

GAUVIN, DEBBIE
Born: April 13, 1956; *Parents:* Francis and Eileen Moran; *Education:* Mattatuck Community College; *Occupation:* Kitchen Aide, Hostess; *Honors:* Outstanding work in English; Service on Student Action Staff; *Other writings:* Poems published in other anthologies; *Address:* 48 Grand Street, Seymour, CT.

GEBEL, WILLIAM R.
Born: August 1, 1956, Chicago Illinois; *Parents:* William R. Gebel and Mary F. Gebel; *Spouse:* Donna L. Gebel, December 22, 1978; *Children:* William, Kitty L., Michelle F.; *Education:* Proviso West High School; *Other writings:* Has written 137 Poem and short stories "Passion" was the first I've published; *Personal note:* I love to write about my personal experiences, also I love to create my work through my imagination; writing is creating and communication, it's a wonderful gift from God; *Address:* 30 S. Lavergne, North Lake, IL.

GEESLIN, LORETTA NICOLE
Born: January 26, 1973, Van Nuys, California; *Parents:* James E. Geeslin and Paula F. Geeslin; *Education:* Cleveland High School; *Occupation:* Student, Model; *Memberships:* Northridge Library; *Honors:* Award of merit for personal accomplishment in steering committee, mini class award for drawing; *Personal note:* What I feel, I write; a person doesn't have to try to be something that he/she isn't, just be yourself and tell the truth; *Address:* 8213 White Oak Avenue, Reseda, CA.

GENTRY, M.M.
Pen name: King Gentry; *Born:* September 12, 1913, Decatur, Texas; *Parents:* Charles Boone and Ora Mary Gentry; *Spouse:* Zoe M. Gentry, February 1, 1942; *Children:* Mary Ann Veselka, Betty Zoe Bunce; *Education:* Decatur Baptist College; Rutgers University; Mary Hardin Baylor University; *Occupation:* Retired; *Other writings:* Published a novel and numerous poems; *Personal note:* Live, work and play each day in such a way that you will be proud of the future-past; *Address:* 508 Alexander Street, Killeen, TX.

GETZELMAN, HEATHER L.
Pen name: T.M. Scott; *Born:* March 27, 1970, Elgin, Illinois; *Parents:* John M. Nancy J. Getzelman; *Education:* Clear Creeh Secondary School, Institute of Children's; *Occupation:* Student; *Memberships:* Thespian; *Other writings:* Has written articles for high school newspaper; *Personal note:* The best times of the day are the sunrise and the sunset, the best things in life are what God put here, and your family; *Address:* R.R. 1 Box 388, Greenbrier, AR.

GODBURN, KAREN CHARLENE
Born: August 20, 1962; Waterbury, Connecticut; *Education:* Indian River Community College; *Occupation:* Preschool Teacher; *Other writings:* Has written short stories and poems; *Personal note:* For the most part I enjoy writing for children as I am always fascinated and entertained by them; writing has also worked as a release for me, I find I can express myself more effectively and creatively while writing; my father is a writer and he is a great encouragment to me; *Address:* Jensen Beach, FL.

GOLDMAN, SHIRLEY L.
Born: April 26, 1916, Chicago, Illinois; *Parents:* Belle and Elias Tanenbaum; *Education:* BEd, MSED; *Occupation:* Teacher; *Memberships:* Lincolnwood Apple User's Group; *Honors:* Phi Delta Kappa; *Other writings:* "Math is Fun" in Chicago Sun Times; *Personal note:* Education of future generation is top priority;

GOODMAN, CONSTANCE BETH
Pen name: Connie Goodman; *Born:* September 3, 1963, Philadelphia, PA; *Parents:* Marvin J. and Linda S; *Education:* George Washington University School of Medicine, Washington DC, BA (with Distinction); *Occupation:* Freelance Writer; *Memberships:* American Medical Writers Assn; Philadelphia Writers Organization; *Honors:* Who's Who in US Writers, Editors and Poets, 1989; Communications Award of the Student Academy of the American Academy of Physicaian Assistants; Alpha Epsilon Delta, Psi Chi; Phi Eta Sigma; *Other writings:* Has written numerous poems and essays; *Personal note:* As a writer with a vision, I hope to illuminate the paths of those who may wish ever to see the more luminous light of life; *Address:* 4 Park Avenue, Apt. 18H, New York, NY.

GRABER, CARYN ROSE
Pen name: Caryn Rose; *Born:* December 26, 1975, New Brunswick, NJ; *Parents:* Sandra Ray and Bruce Graber; *Occupation:* Student; *Honors:* Student of the Month Awards, Spelling Bee Certificate; *Other writings:* Writer for the School Newspaper; *Personal note:* I admire fellow poets and their writings; *Address:* P.O. Box 456, Blakeslee, PA.

GREEN, BRENDA
Born: November 18, 1943, Baltimore, Maryland; *Parents:* Alfred and Doris Bellamy; *Education:* College of Notre Dame; *Occupation:* Student; *Personal note:* It doesn't matter a great deal how one starts out in life, if in the end one finds joy and inner peace; *Address:* 106 Summar Ct, Apt 2C, Baltimore, MD.

GREY, DAWN
Born: May 3, 1975, Belvidere, Illinois; *Parents:* Lawrence O. Grey, Jr. & Ruth E. Grey; *Occupation:* Mid Western Christian Academy, Sedalia Middle School; *Memberships:* Salvation Army; *Honors:* Honor Jr. Soldier, Commissioner Sunbeam, Presidential Academic Award; *Personal note:* Special thanks to God and my teacher, Mrs. Underhill, who made me write it; *Address:* 3401 S. Stewart, Sedalia, MO.

GRILL, NAN E.
Born: May 28, 1914, Petrolia Ontario, Canada; *Parents:* Ben J. Miles Rogers and Hannah Cecelia Foxall; *Spouse:* Raymond J. Grill, August 28, 1934; *Children:* Nannette Louise Grill, Diane Mary, Charonne, Leigh Wali, Raymond; *Education:* UCLA; *Occupation:* Real Estate Broker, Securities Broker; *Memberships:* Beverly Hills-Toastmistress; *Honors:* Numerous outstanding awards; *Other writings:* Have written stories and poetry; *Personal note:* I am a medium and do some writing automatically, my father taught me poetry before I attended school; *Address:* 18011 NE 196 Street, Woodinville, WA.

GROSS, BETTY JO HAMMONS
Pen name: Betty J. Gross; *Born:* Skeggs, Virginia; *Parents:* Roy Hammons and Ida Hammons; *Spouse:* John Allen Gross, August 9, 1959; *Children:* Beth Ann, Allen Paul, Laura Ann, Rachel Ann; *Education:* Akron University, BSED; Webster University, MA; *Occupation:* Writer; *Memberships:* S.C. Poetry Society, Charleston Area Arts Council, Events Unique, Inc.; *Honors:* Touch of Frost Award, 1972; Writer in Residence for Charleston County PRT; National Endowment of the Arts Grant; *Other writings:* Authored two books, environmental poems and many articles; *Personal note:* Family life education a flower learning continues to struggle for power. I have been greatly influenced by Richard Eberhart, Linda Pasten, Roy Ivan Johnson, and my mother who enjoyed reading poetry aloud; *Address:* 3502 N.W. 10th Avenue, Gainesville, FL.

GUERRIERO, JESSICA J.
Born: December 20, 1969, Oneonta, NY; *Parents:* Joseph and Andrea Guerriero; *Education:* Morris Central School; State University College, Oneonta, NY; *Occupation:* Student; *Memberships:* EF Educational Tours, American Film Institute, 4-H, Amnesty International; *Honors:* Music Participation in chorus received awards and letters; *Other writings:* Authored "Willows of Jessica"; *Personal note:* It only takes one great mind to change the world; *Address:* Morris, NY.

GUSTAW, ELEANOR LEE
Born: August 20, 1958, Beausejour, Manitoba; *Parents:* Bernice and Frank Gustaw; *Other writings:* Has written nonfiction book entitled, "A Patience Beloved", poetry published in The American Poetry Anthology, several poems and short stories published in the Interlake Spectator and The Messenger; *Personal note:* I believe that writing is one of the most beautifully delicate and facilitated doors by which all hearts can receive the fullness and joy of life's manifold kaleidoscopic seasons of our earthly journeys; *Address:* Box 302, Riverton Manitoba, Canada.

HALL, SONIA KAY
Born: December 10, 1963, Portsmouth, VA.; *Parents:* Nancy V. Williams, Roosevelt Williams; *Spouse:* Odell Hall, Jr., October 2, 1982; *Children:* Kaye Nicole, Monica Renee, Odell; *Education:* Barbizon School of Modeling, Norfolk

State University; *Other writings:* "Father Please Enter Into My Life"; *Personal note:* I love the Lord my God which is in heaven. He is worthy to be praised and is my inspiration and my guide; *Address:* 21st TAACOM ACS Log, AER, Lo-TA, NY, NY.

HAMER, THOMAS R.
Pen name: Tom Hamer; *Born:* May 7, 1926, Logan, WV.; *Parents:* Robert W. & Edda B. Hamer; *Spouse:* Judith H. Hamer, July 6, 1986; *Occupation:* Writer; *Memberships:* Florida Free Lance Writers Association; *Other writings:* Weekly Columnist for the Huntington West Virginia Herald Dispatch; *Personal note:* An incurable idealist, I always have and always will expect more from human nature than it is realistically capable of providing; *Address:* 3201 Minnesota Avenue, Winter Park, FL.

HAMILTON, NORMA
Pen name: Farika Birhan; *Born:* Kingston, Jamaica; *Parents:* Aubrey and Ruby Hamilton; *Children:* Ashley, Sahai, Marcus, Gize; *Education:* University of West Indies; *Occupation:* Writer, Researcher, Peforming Poet, Cultural Consultant; *Memberships:* Women's Institute for the Freedom of the Press, National Alliance for Third World Journalist; *Honors:* Fellowship Creative Writing Instituto Allende, Gto Mexico, Prize Winner International Black Writers Contest, London; Winner of several medals in Jamaica Literary Contests; *Other writings:* Short stories publis hed, England, USA and Jamaica; Articles published Jamaica, News Media, syndicated Pafica, News Service; Poetry published, California Raggae Magazine and Caribbean Anthology; *Personal note:* My writing is rooted in my island experience, focused on the theme of the universality of the human race and the rainbow dawning; *Address:* 3300 Ross Place, NW, Washington, DC.

HANLEY, BETTYE L.
Born: March 14, 1935, Kentucky; *Parents:* Robert W. and Lucy L. Hager; *Spouse:* Daryl R. Hanley, July 13, 1957; *Children:* Daryl Jr., Cathy, Mary, Patty, Robert and Michael; *Education:* Barry University; *Occupation:* Crisis Nurse, College Instructor; *Memberships:* Belong to a 12 step self help, support group at present; *Honors:* Community service award, Indian River Community College; *Other writings:* I am in the process of writing a short story, I have written several poems concerning my discoveries in life; *Personal note:* You can take charge of your life, take a look within, honor the light and the dark side, honor the feminine and masculine side, honor all of you; *Address:* 1479 S.W. Sea Hawk Way, Palm City, FL.

HARRIS, MARY S.
Pen name: Suzy Harris; *Born:* December 3, 1968, Springfield, Ohio; *Parents:* James and Yvonna Harris; *Education:* Springfield South High School; *Occupation:* Dental Assistant; *Memberships:* YMCA; *Honors:* Choir and Ensemble Awards; *Other writings:* Have written several poems; *Personal note:* I write about people and feelings who have touched my life; *Address:* 413 Gruen Drive, Springfield, OH.

HARRIS, VALERIE L.
Born: July 14, 1956, Houston, TX.; *Parents:* Willard J. Young, Sr., Charlotte G. Young; *Spouse:* March 17, 1978, Willie E. Harris; *Children:* Matthew, Charlotte, Sondra, John; *Education:* Prairie View A&M University, (Dean's List); *Occupation:* Engineer, Electrical; *Honors:* Eta Kappa Nu, Tau Beta Pi, Delta Sigma Theta; *Other writings:* Poem published in "On The Threshold of a Dream"; Several songs recorded on LPs; *Personal note:* Poetry is the language of the heart and soul. I would like to extend to the world a part of myself that radiates a love for humanity and zest for life; *Address:* 8025 Hickok Lane, Houston, TX.

HART, HEATHER
Born: November 11, 1974, Dearborn, Michigan; *Parents:* Patricia Hart; *Education:* Bryant Junior High School; *Occupation:* Student; *Memberships:* FOA; *Honors:* Cheerleading, Soccer, Basketball, Volleyball, Track, Softball, Honor Roll; *Personal note:* When I write my poems, I usually write about past experiences of my friends, or myself. I like my poems to be real; *Address:* 22682 Beech, Dearborn, MI.

HATFIELD, ELOISE
Born: April 20, 1947, St. Louis, Missouri; *Parents:* Basil and Dorothy Hatifield; *Education:* Pattonville High School; University of Missouri, Columbia, Missouri; *Memberships:* University of Missouri Alumni Association, Health Club; *Other writings:* Articles and poems published by World wide Challenge Magazine; His People News Magazine, Christian Single Magazine, Sunday Digest, Decision; *Personal note:* My interest in writing has always been more than a hobby, I want to use my degree in journalism to uplift and inspire others and whenever possible to share spiritual insights creatively; *Address:* 3145 Parkwood Lane, Maryland Height, MO.

HAUPT, CECILIA G.
Born: January 5, 1919, Los Angeles, CA; *Parents:* Joseph Jedofsky, Reinhard F. Gudeman; *Spouse:* William Dean Haupt Jr., December 27, 1942; *Children:* Cecilia, William

III, Maria Christine, Kevin, Teresa, Monica, Bridget; *Education:* Romana Convent; Occidental College, Los Angeles; Laval University, Quebec, Canada; Continuing Education: Psychology, Languages; *Occupation:* Retired Psychological Market Research Interviewer; *Memberships:* Catholic Press Council, Media Communication Mass and Breakfast Pacific Pioneer Broadcasters, Pasadena Crime Prevention, Women's Parish Council, SCRC, Renewal of Catholic Church, AlAnon; *Honors:* Silver and Golden Poet Awards from World of Poetry; *Other writings:* Poems in newspapers, critiques on articles, church renewal process, personal and observed psychological materials; *Personal note:* I attempt to incorporate into my writings the fantasies as well as sorrows of love, spiritual and human. My work has been influenced by predominent liberal Catholic writers; *Address:* 3300 Florecita Drive, Altadena, CA.

HAWES, DONNA KAYE
Born: August 20, 1952, Maywood, California; *Parents:* James and Helen Russell; *Spouse:* Michael R. Hawes, August 22, 1981; *Children:* Deanna, Darren, Beth, Melissa, Deena and Brigette; *Education:* St. Bernard Catholic School; *Occupation:* Homemaker; *Other writings:* Poems published in the American Poetry Anthology, National Poetry Anthology and Best New Poets of 1988; *Personal note:* I enjoy a wide variety of the great poet's style. A particular favorite is the style of Lord Byron, I also appreciate the love, support and encouragement of my family; *Address:* Rowland Heights, CA.

HAWKINS, CINDY
Pen name: Cynthia Anne Hawkins; *Born:* May 17, 1974, Fairfax, Virginia; *Parents:* Melinda L. Hawkins and Charles R. Hawkins; *Education:* Manteo High School; *Personal note:* I wrote this for my family, but most of all, in appreciation of my grandparents, Bea and Thomas A. Hawkins, who have helped me to eliminate my boundaries and now it is time to reach for the sky; *Address:* Kill Devil Hills, NC.

HAYDEN, JUDY
Pen name: Judy Van Osdell; *Born:* August 20, 1946, Baton Rouge Louisiana; *Education:* Florida College of Nursing; *Occupation:* Partime Writer and Nurse; *Other writings:* Several poems published in other anthologies; *Personal note:* Poetry is my self expression reaching out to connect with others; *Address:* Jacksonville, FL.

HENDRICKSON-JONES, S. B.
Born: June 3, 1945, Sandy Point, St. Kitts, West Indies; *Parents:* Emily Jones-James, Ernest Hendrickson; *Spouse:* Cora L.E. Christian, October 23, 1976; *Children:* Nesha Rosita, Marcus Benjamin; *Education:* Illinois State University, AA, CVI; University of Exeter England, BS, MS; *Occupation:* Associate Professor of Economic; *Memberships:* National Writer Club, American Economic Association, Carib Studies Assn. *Honors:* Omicron Delta Epsilon, Three times faculty of the year; *Other writings:* Have written three books, one volume of poetry, one cultural volume; *Personal note:* Be a creator of circumstances, not a creature of circumstances; *Address:* Box 1338, Frederiksted, VI.

HENINGTON, KRISTINA LYNN
Born: October 14, 1971, Fayettville, Arkansas; *Parents:*-Bobbi Henington and Jim Henington; *Education:* West Fork High School; *Occupation:* Student; *Memberships:* National Honor Society, Future Business Leaders of America, Teens for Christ, Business Executive Team; *Other writings:* Collection of Poems; *Personal note:* My poetry is the reflection of inner feelings and thoughts that cannot otherwise be expressed; *Address:* P.O. Box 107, West Fork, AR.

HERICKS, RHONDA KELLY
Born: August 27, 1972, Cincinnati, Ohio; *Parents:* Lawrence & Sally Hericks; *Education:* Oakhall High School; *Personal note:* By working part time and writing I am hoping to earn enough money for my first year of college. *Address:* 5771 North Glen Road, Cincinnati, OH.

HERKEL, DEBBIE
Born: March 22, 1975, Berwyn, Illinois; *Parents:* Sharon Hostetler and Robert Hostetler; *Education:* Orland Junior High School; *Occupation:* Student; *Personal note:* When I write poetry, I think of a topic and then I express my feelings; *Address:* 15733 Orland Brook Drive #65, Orland Park, IL.

HERMAN, TRACEY MICHELLE
Pen name: Angel, Tracella, Tra; *Born:* December 18, 1974, Manhattan, New York; *Parents:* Gary Herman, Dee Laff; *Education:* Portledge Academy, Locust Valley High School, Pinehenge School; *Occupation:* Student; *Honors:* Honors at school, swimming trophies, horseback riding awards; *Other writings:* Other poetry; *Personal note:* I am 14 years old; this is my first competition I have entered with my poetry. I am a student at Elan School for Drug Abuse and Family Problems. I am helping myself to return home as an asset to society, self and family. I hope and wish other young people will take what they have and use it to be helpful instead of destroying themselves; *Address:* E-1 Corp. RR 1 Box 370, Poland Springs, Maine.

HERRING, JAMES BARTON
Born: March 8, 1963, Boonville, Missouri; *Parents:* Jimmy and Ruth Herring; *Education:* Kemper Military School, University of Missouri; *Other writings:* Published numerous poems in anthologies; *Personal note:* We should all be so lucky to remember our past. That way, when it comes back to haunt us, we're not caught napping; *Address:* Rt 2, Box 150, Glasgow, MO.

HICKEY, RUTH ANN BURRELL
Born: April 13, 1933, Havre de Grace, Maryland; *Parents:*-William Cleaver Burrell and Ruth Lear Burrell; *Spouse:* James Ezra Hickey, March 16, 1977; *Children:* Akram William K. Moore, Ahmad Paul K. Moore; *Education:* Santa Monica College, Santa Monica California, AA; George Washington University, Washington DC; *Occupation:* Retired; *Memberships:* American Motorcycle Assn; *Other writings:* Has written occasional essays and world travel personal journals *Personal note:* Thanks to my mother for giving me 10 little volumes of old classic poetry; *Address:* Star Route, NM.

HILL, TEDDY R.
Born: January 18, 1938, Coalinga, California; *Parents:* Jesse L. Hill and Edith Lawrence; *Spouse:* Carolyn J. Hill, November 20, 1982; *Children:* Cindy, Mark, Larry, Nancy, Rene, Tricia, Debby, Vincent, Scott, Tammy, Vicky; *Education:* Fresno City College, AA; *Occupation:* Maintenance Mechanic; *Memberships:* AARP; *Other writings:* Several poems published in newsletter, also published in On the Threshold of a Dream; *Personal note:* If something I write can help someone or please someone, then it makes me happy. I don't know where it comes from, but I enjoy writing and reading; *Address:* 1615 Scott Court, Clovis, CA.

HILLHOUSE, JAMES O.
Born: September 16, 1926, Clearwater, Florida; *Parents:* Horace M. & Susie O. Hillhouse; *Children:* Carol Lee, Debra Lou, Patti Joh; *Education:* Clearwater High School; *Occupation:* Retired; *Memberships:* F & AM Lodge; *Honors:* Editors Choice Award, 1988; *Other writings:* "You'll Know Her When You See Her", "This Tear", Loneliness", "Forbidden Dreams", "Soon", "To A Friend", "The Lonely Man", "Week End Leisure"; *Address:* 16031 Sacramento Avenue, Brooksville, FL.

HOLTZ, JENNIFER
Born: May 27, 1974, Washington, DC; *Parents:* Raeleen Komendar Holtz and John Holtz; *Occupation:* Student; *Memberships:* School Newspaper, Junior Achievement, Young Lawyers of America; *Honors:* First Honors Honor Roll, Placed first in science fairs and county science fairs, a finalist in the Miss Teen Pennsylvania Pageant; *Other writings:* Authored many poem, some have been published; *Personal note:* I try to write my poems according to what I feel and to try and describe what other people feel at different times; *Address:* 102 Crosswind Drive, Shrewsbury, PA.

HOPKINS, SHIRLEY
Born: May 16, 1970, Fairfax, Virginia; *Parents:* Dennis and Evelyn Hopkins; *Education:* Osbourn Park High School, Lee College; *Occupation:* Student; *Memberships:* Acts of God; *Other writings:* Several personal poems; *Personal note:* The poem "Mr. Doll" is dedicated to my loving friend Andy Cookson; *Address:* 8919 June St. Manassas, VA.

HOUDE, JODIE
Born: March 8, 1973, Newport Beach, California; *Parents:* Mr and Mrs Alan Houde; *Occupation:* Key Club and French Club; *Honors:* Graduate of John Robert Powers Modeling School, received a certificate of graduation; *Other writings:* Poem published in Threshold of a Dream; *Address:* 31675 NE Canter Lane, Sherwood, OR.

HOWARD, SYLVIA D.
Pen name: Syl; *Born:* March 2, 1938, Portsmouth, VA.; *Parents:* Columbus and Julia Bynum; *Children:* Andre, Lamar, Tino Lamonte; *Education:* McClymonds High School, College of Alameda, Merritt College, Laney College; *Occupation:* Management Analyst (retired); *Memberships:* AARP, USNE, NAACP, Assn for professional Business Women; *Honors:* Dean's List, numerous letters and certificates; *Other writings:* Have written over 100 poems, User Manuels for Computer Software, Novels, Songs excepted for recording; *Personal note:* Life is a broad spectrum of living and experiencing, thru my expressions of poetry I would like to leave with mankind a part of my uniqueness; *Address:* 623-59th Street, Oakland, CA.

HRANEK, STEPHEN G.
Pen name: Stephen Gee; *Born:* North Kingstown, Rhode Island; *Parents:* Stephen Hranek and Theresa M. Bradshaw; *Spouse:* Levia L. Keyes, August 16, 1973; *Other writings:* Has written several poems: "Warlords", "Psy the Dog Star"; *Personal note:* Heavens is dedicated to the memory of my brother and fellow astronomer, David John Hranek who travels effortlessly throughout the universe as was his greatest wish; *Address:* 3325 W. Aster Dr., Phoenix, AZ.

HUCK, CHRISTINA
Born: December 20, 1972, Chicago, Illinois; *Parents:* Josef Huck and Therea Huck; *Occupation:* Student; *Other writings:* Personal collection of my own; *Personal note:* Believe in faith, hope, and your future, and one day it shall find you, disbelieve in it and it shall pass you by; *Address:* 108 Ann St. Delhi, Ontario, NE.

HUDSON, PAMELA J.
Pen name: Lady Janelle Peverel; *Born:* September 8, 1958, Macon, Georgia; *Parents:* Marilyn Jean, Coney Herschel Johnson; *Spouse:* Don Allen Hudson, January 3, 1975; *Children:* David Allen, Nathan Lee; *Education:* Fayette County High School; Clayton Junior College, Griffin Technical School; *Occupation:* Computer Data Entry, Musician, Lyricist; *Memberships:* Society for Creative Anachronism, Fayetteville Church of Christ; *Honors:* AOA, Society of Creative Anachronism; *Other writings:* Has written three poems for American Poetry Anthology; *Personal note:* "Go placidly amid the noise and haste, and seek what peace there may be in silence..." Excerpt from Desiderata; *Address:* 142 Scogin Road, Newnan, GA.

HUMMONS, MARION T.
Pen name: The Passerby" or KionJeki Yi; *Born:* January 6, New Orleans, Louisiana; *Parents:* Alexander Taylor, Octavia Pierre Taylor; *Spouse:* John Hummons, September 3, 1942; *Children:* Adrian, Nellifern, Carol, Marilyn; *Education:* Chicago Roosevelt University, Chicago, Illinois; *Occupation:* Retired; *Memberships:* Du Sable Museum of African American History; the Culture Fund; *Honors:* Federal Employee of the Year; *Other writings:* "Soul Brotha Motha's" and several poems and articles published in newspapers and periodicals; *Personal note:* I write exactly and I talk and for self expression, most of which is semi-satirical wherein I attempt to get messages across to my people and other ethnic groups; *Address:* 5 East Carriage Way, Apt 205, Hazel Crest, IL.

HUOT, TAMMIE PATRICIA
Born: December 31, 1968, Rhode Island; *Parents:* Roger N. Huot, Judith A. Huot; *Education:* Charles County Community College; *Occupation:* Residential Supervisor; *Memberships:* St. Mary's County for the Association for retarded citizens; *Other writings:* Has written several unpublished poems; *Personal note:* Thanks to my sister, Robyn, for the encouragement she gave me at graduation. To Mark for always standing by me. *Address:* 127 Essex Drive, Lexington Park, MD.

IRISH, ALVA
Born: January 2, 1950, Liberty, Texas; *Spouse:* Joseph J. Baumgarter, May 25, 1966; *Education:* Broward Community College, AA; Washburn University, BFA; Rice University; *Occupation:* Animal Sculptor, Artist, Poet, Songwriter; *Memberships:* MENSA; *Honors:* Third Place in 1978, Poet's Anthology published in the World of Poetry; *Other writings:* Has published several poems; *Personal note:* I try to give an uplifting hidden message in my work. I try to move a person, to touch them deeply...to help somehow; *Address:* 7811 E. 67th Street, Kansas City, MO.

IRRGANG, MARILYN J.
Pen name: Mary Jean; *Born:* July 4, 1935, Indianapolis, Indiana; *Parents:* Mr and Mrs George Irrgang; *Occupation:* Psychiatric Technician; *Honors:* Award for working over 20 years for the state of Indiana; *Other writings:* Has written several poems entitled, "Freedom!", "First Priorities", "The Easter Story", "The Ressurrection"; *Personal note:* The more moral a man is the more masculine he be, the more masculine a man be the more moral he is; *Address:* 4445 W. Jackson Street, Indianapolis, IN.

ISARDAS, GEETA J.
Born: March 3, 1973, Queens, New York; *Parents:* Lal T. Isardas, Miriam A. Isardas; *Education:* Fiorello H. Laguardia High School of the Performing Arts; *Honors:* Young Writers Contest; *Personal note:* I enjoy writing about deep or complicated emotion and putting them in a different perspective; *Address:* 83-26 Lefferts Blvd., Kew Gardens, NY.

JACKSON, CEDRICK B.
Pen name: Dr. C; *Born:* January 21, 1965, Monroe, Georgia; *Parents:* Revis Jackson, Clara S. Jackson; *Spouse:* Ethel G. Jackson, June 14, 1987; *Children:* Allie Sierra Jackson; *Education:* Monroe Area Comprehensive High School; *Occupation:* Carpenter; *Memberships:* NAACP; *Personal note:* I hope that you read my poetry and understand that Jesus is the answer to your prayer; *Address:* P.O. Box 1506, Loganville, GA.

JACKSON, SHELLIE MARIE
Born: April 9, 1976, Clarksville, Tennessee; *Parents:* Willard W. Jackson, Jr. and Terry F. Jackson; *Occupation:* Student; *Honors:* Won two talent contest for piano solo; *Address:* 1089 Cal Suddeath Road, Allensville, KY.

JELORMINE, KRISTEN
Born: February 13, 1975, Bridgeport, Connecticut; *Parents:*-JoAnn and Michael Jelormine; *Occupation:* Student; *Memberships:* Dance, Cheerleading, Scuba Diving; *Honors:* Cheeringleading trophy, 4th place; *Other writings:* Two articles in the Bridgeport Post and two other poems in a contest; *Personal note:* I will achieve all my dreams; *Address:* 93 E. Medson Drive, Stratford, CT.

JENKINS, KANDI
Born: May 1, 1974, Muncie, Indiana; *Parents:*Ann and Jake Jenkins; *Education:* Parchment High School; *Other writings:* Published author; *Personal note:* I believe teens can make a difference; *Address:* 147 Hay Mac, Parchment, MI.

JENKINSON, GRACE GARCIA
Pen name: Grace Jenkinson; *Born:* June 10, 1961, Bacolod City, Philippines; *Parents:*Ernesto & Imelda Garcia; *Spouse:* John Jenkinson, June 6, 1987; *Education:* La Concolacion College, University of Negros Occidental-Recoletos, La Salle College; *Occupation:* Homemaker; *Personal note:* A great love for my husband has convinced me to get into this world of writing, fulled with beauty and imagination; *Address:* 198 North Bryce Lane, Fallbrook, CA.

JESSIE, JEFFERY
Born: March 11, 1960, Opp, Alabama; *Parents:*Freddie and Mollie Jessie; *Spouse:* Lisa Banks Jessie, August 23, 1986; *Children:* Maurice Skanes, David Jessie; *Education:* Contral Data Institute; *Occupation:* Team supervisor; *Honors:* Beta Club, Math Club, Science Fair Award; *Other writings:* "Someone Hard to Find" is one of a collection of forty poems in a group entitled, "Reality"; Each poem deals with a certain matter of day to day living; *Personal note:* All of my poems are meant to make the reader recognize what their faults are, if they can relate to the situation, possibly they will be persuaded to change and to improve their lives and themselves making it a better place for all of us; *Address:* 2308 Dauphine Street, East Point, GA.

JEUDY, NOEMIE MARIE
Born: September 11, 1975, New York, NY; *Parents:*Marie Jeudy, Wilmer Jeudy; *Occupation:* Student; *Honors:* A physical education award; *Personal note:* I express my feelings of the unforgetable days when I write my poems. My mind has been caught up by the beauty of nature; *Address:* 2508 Broadway #7D, New York, NY.

JOHNS, JENNI
Born: February 8, 1974, San Clemente, California; *Parents:*Herb Johns, Susan Johns; *Education:* Temeculd Valley High School; *Memberships:* Polar Bear Ski Club; *Honors:* Award for most creative book written at Murrieta School, 1988; *Other writings:* "The Mystical Forest"; *Personal note:* A poem I think is made up of yesterdays memories and tomorrows experiences. I'm greatly influenced by passion and romance; *Address:* Murrieta, CA.

JOHNSON, BESSIE FRANCES
Born: Crab Orchard, Kentucky; *Parents:*Charlie Leavell and Florence Webster Leavell; *Children:* Kathenia Carol, Michael Anthony, Sheryl Melaine, Stephen Mathon; *Education:* Waukegan Business College; *Occupation:* Clerical Worker; *Honors:* High School Honor Roll; *Other writings:* Several other poems and limericks not published; *Personal note:* Beginning at a very young age, I have always loved poetry and enjoy writing it, I feel that poetry should not be just a conglomeration of words that rhyme, but should have meaning and make sense; *Address:* Waukegan, IL.

JOHNSON, CYNTHIA L.
Pen name: Cyndi Johnson; *Born:* March 10, 1952, Baytown, Texas; *Parents:*Brainard Johnson, Martha Havard Johnson; *Education:* Robert E. Lea High School, Baytown Texas; *Occupation:* Legal Secretary; *Other writings:* Poems published in Hearland, Poetic Voices of America, The National Poetry Anthology; *Personal note:* Poetry is my form of release, and generally embodies my particular emotions at the time of writing each poem; *Address:* 6306 Stones Mill, San Antonio, TX.

JOHNSON, JENNIFER ANNE
Pen name: Madaline; *Born:* July 9, 1973, McKees Rocks, Pennsylvania; *Parents:*Keith George Johnson & Monica Anne Johnson *Education:* Upper Merion Senior High School; *Occupation:* Student; *Other writings:* Have written a collection of poetry and short stories in my own personal collection; *Personal note:* Life is only what you make it, so live it up; *Address:* 1134 Pugh Road, Wayne, PA.

JOHNSON, KATI
Born: May 31, 1971, Beloit, Wisconsin; *Education:* Beloit Catholic High School; *Personal note:* I am inspired by the warmth of the sun, motivated by my restless pen, and curious as to what's above the clouds; *Address:* 11504 W. Brandherm, Beloit, WI.

JOHNSON, TINA
Born: March 31, 1974, Augsburg Germany; *Parents:*Deborah Heckman and Chartie Johnson; *Occupation:* Student; *Honors:* Junior Womens Club, 2 first place prizes; Honorable Mention; *Personal note:* Through the canvas of my mind I wander, ponder the past, looking for the future and as you read these words you also walk through the canvas of my mind; *Address:* 112 Oakview Drive, Leesburg, VA.

JOHNSON, TOMMY
Pen name: T.J. *Born:* February 18, 1984, Natchez, Mississippi; *Parents:*Isaac and Julia Johnson; *Education:* Jackson State University; *Occupation:* Instructor; *Memberships:* Mississippi Delta Arts Council; *Honors:* Kappa Alpha Psi; *Other writings:* Has written the "Clashing of the Worlds", "Future Shock 2020, and a book of poems; *Personal note:* I feel that poetry is feelings expressed in words only when one captures the essence of the creative juices can he be called a writer; *Address:* Rt. 1 Box 616, Clarksdale, MS.

JONES, KATHERINE
Born: June 29, 1977, Tuskegee, Alabama; *Parents:*Mara S. Jones; *Other writings:* "The Tuskegee News"; *Personal note:* I try to reflect awareness to man kind in my writings. Man must bare the burden of past and present. Where are we without the knowledges of them both; *Address:* 607 East Oak Street, Tuskegee, AL.

JOYCE, MICHELLE R.
Born: December 23, 1974, Omaha, Nebraska; *Parents:*David and Carol S. Joyce; *Occupation:* Student; *Memberships:* American Red Cross; *Honors:* Placed 2nd in state wide essay competition, placed 1st in state-wide piano competition, several awards for superior scholastic achievement; *Personal note:* I would like to encourage young people such as myself to express their feelings and ideas whether it be through poetry, stories, song or whatever appeals to them, I believe it is important for the young voices of America to be heard; *Address:* P.O. Box 364, Goshen, OH.

JUNQUEIRA, JOAN
Pen name: Joanie Junqueira; *Born:* May 19, 1950, Minneapolis, Minnesota; *Parents:*John Merton Dobbin and Tonei L. Sackey; *Spouse:* Celso Luiz Junqueira, July 7, 1977; *Children:* Marisol, Victor, Tatiana; *Education:* University of Minnesota, BA; *Occupation:* Technical Editor-Writer; *Memberships:* Survivors Network incorporated, Laadan Women's Language Network, Tomyris, Social Cybernetics; *Honors:* Who's Who, Students in America; *Other writings:* "Midwives of Winter", Anthology of women's writings, many lands, many voices; an anthology of poetry, the american poetry anthology; *Personal note:* Writing poetry allows me to see my soul, feel my emotions and express my subconscious throughts, it is a healing act of love of self; *Address:* 147 Sutphen Street, Santa Cruz, CA.

KANGAS, JUANITA HUTSON
Pen name: J.K.; *Born:* April 23, 1933, Urbana, Illinois; *Parents:*William Hutson and Eva Collins Hutson; *Spouse:* Marvin Raymond Kangas, December 3, 1987; *Children:* Brenda Ann Lott, Robert Wayne Richardson; *Education:* Grant Pass High School; *Occupation:* Writer and Housewife; *Other writings:* Has written several poems; Written articles for Schnook Observer Newspaper; *Personal note:* I am thankful that my poems have been published, and I dedicate them to my children in memory of my mother; *Address:* P.O. Box 263, Ocean Park, WA.

KARR, JAMES
Born: March 16, 1956, Cleveland, Ohio; *Parents:*Norman Karr, Melania Karr; *Education:* Ohio University, Athens Ohio, BS; *Occupation:* Assistant Operations Manager; *Other writings:* The Gallery, to be published by the Amherst Society; *Personal note:* I have a lantern called intuition, and if I listen carefully keeping my mind and my eyes open, a light will shine upon a clear path to follow; *Address:* 3822 Memphis Avenue, Cleveland, OH.

KEITH, CHARLOTTE DEAN
Born: December 10, 1948, Dayton, Tennessee; *Parents:*Samuel Cox and Inex Cox; *Spouse:* Charles L. Keith, September 27, 1964; *Children:* Doug, Lisa, Brian Keith; *Education:* Rhea Central High School; *Occupation:* Director of Sales and Marketing; *Other writings:* Have written several poems, currently writing a novel; *Personal note:* As a dear friend once suggested I should like to bring people's hurried lives to a more tranquil and softer plane by offering them my dreams by way of my poems; *Address:* Manchester, TN.

KELLAR, MARY R.
Born: November 22, 1935, Montreal Canada; *Parents:*Albert Mount; *Children:* Rosemary, Robert, Christine, Heather; *Education:* Mount Allison University, BED; University of Montreal, MA; *Occupation:* Teacher; *Memberships:* Metis Assn of Saskatchewan; Saskatehewan Writers' Guild, St. Michael's and All Angels Anglican Church; *Other writings:* Writes regularly for Native paper New Breed; *Personal note:* My poems reflects my prayer for mankind, I try to live to love God and my neighbor; *Address:* 153 227 Saquenay Drive, Saskatoon, Canada;

KENUL, MARILYN T.
Born: Yonker, New York; *Parents:*Filippo Spina and Rosa Bello Spina; *Spouse:* Remo; *Children:* John, Phil, Paul and Robert; *Education:* Yonkers High School of Commerce; *Occupation:* Realtor; *Memberships:* Adrenal Metabolic Research Society; *Honors:* Golden Poet Award; *Other writings:* Has written "Soliloguy", "Discovery", "Apology", "Changing Time", "Only an Illusion", "Salute To Life" and "What Happened to Tomorrow?" *Personal note:* Has not published song, but has written for night club entertainers; So many others have said, "it's much easier to smile and spread warmth". *Address:* 22 Lane Avenue, Plainview, NY.

KERNS, CATHERINE
Born: January 1, 1945, Fauquier County; *Parents:*Mr and Mrs Frank Berkely Owens; *Spouse:* Ernest T. Kerns, May 31, 1975; *Children:* Elizabeth Ann Weaver; *Occupation:* Poet, Author, Songwriter, Housewife; *Memberships:* Songwriter Club of America; *Honors:* 4 Golden Poet Awards; Awarded 26 Merit Awards; *Other writings:* Poems published in 54 anthology books; *Personal note:* I strive to reflect beauty and widsom in my poems; *Address:* Rt 3 Box 228, Warrenton, VA.

KILE, SUSAN
Born: July 20, 1972, Bethesda, Maryland; *Parents:*Bryan Z., Carol L. Kile; *Education:* Casda Grande Union High School; *Occupation:* Student; *Honors:* 2nd Place Optimist Oratorical Contest; *Other writings:* I am currently writing a play entitled, "Starving for Love"; *Personal note:* My goal is to write and star in a made for television movie; *Address:* 1121 Avenida Grande, Casa Grande, AZ.

KINZIE, MARY E.
Pen name: Lace; *Born:* November 11, 1940, Painesville, Ohio; *Parents:*Mary Toth, Joseph S. Toth; *Education:* Harvey High School; *Occupation:* Bookeeper-Assistant; *Other writings:* "To My Little Girl". "Inspiration"; *Personal note:* Poetry is very much a personal part of the poet himself, and I strive to leave the readers of my poetry with a good impression of both my poems and myself; *Address:* 515 North Oakland Avenue, Mishawake, IN.

KIRKPATRICK, MARY SUSAN
Born: April 13, 1971, Richmond, Virginia; *Parents:*Mary Ann N. and Thomas McGuffin Kirkpatrick, Jr.; *Education:* Marymount High School; *Occupation:* Student; *Memberships:* Marymount Art Club, International Club, Sewing Club; *Other writings:* Two poems printed in my high schools literary magazine; *Personal note:* I write about how I see the world through my eyes; *Address:* Richmond, VA.

KOPPELMAN, RACHEL KAREN
Born: March 1, 1959, Liverpool, England; *Parents:*Max and Arline Nieman; *Spouse:* Jay Koppelman, March 23, 1986; *Education:* Childwall Hall College of Further Education; *Occupation:* Executive Administrative Assistant to Land Developers; *Memberships:* National Notary Assn., American Society of Notaries, London Pro Arte Choir; *Personal note:* I have written poetry since I was eight years old. I enjoy creating poems. My work is based upon my life's experiences and my view of the world. *Address:* 8423 Kingsland Road, San Diego, CA.

KOSTER, KERRY
Pen name: June 30, 1955, San Gabriel, California; *Born:* Jeannie Mae and Richard A. Hankins; *Children:* Gary Flewell, Ryan, Chastine; *Occupation:* Homemaker, Poet; *Honors:* Writers Institute, 5 Beauty Contest, VIP Badge for outstanding work in schools; *Other writings:* Has written "The Comfort", Treasured Poems of America; "If I Only Knew"; *Personal note:* I write poetry as I find it a release for emotions I have that I can't express orally, and have found everyone who reads them is touched; *Address:* 193 River Road, Chehalis, WA.

KRZYWICKI, JOHN W. JR.
Pen name: Swiki; *Born:* March 3, 1966, Nanticoke, PA; *Parents:*John W. Krzywicki, Sr., Gloria Gerchak; *Spouse:* Kimberly Szymaszek, May 10, 1986; *Education:* John S. Fine High School, ICS College, Lowry Technical, Luzerne County Community College; *Occupation:* Accountant, self-employed; *Memberships:* Student Association, ICS, US Air Force Veteran, Advisory Council for local radio station; *Honors:* High school honor student, USAF Outstanding Airman Awards, Commander's Certificate of Appreciation, Jr. High Award Winner (Science-Math), ICS Honor Roll; *Other writings:* Several other poems published with other associations. Correspondence with President Reagan, articles with local newspapers; *Personal note:* Where would we be without dreams? Only one horizon is left, the mind. And is there a better platform than love? *Address:* Rd #1 Lot #18, Lakeview Terrace, Harveys Lake, Pennsylvania.

KYLE, ROSEMARY H.
Born: Crockett Texas; *Parents:*Willie B and Maudie L. Hamilton; *Spouse:* SHerman Kyle, May 22; *Children:* Christopher Shermein, Shannon Andre; *Education:* Jarvis Christian, BSED; Prairie View A & M University, MSED; *Occupation:* Teacher; *Memberships:* North Forest Federation of Teachers; *Other writings:* "Freeway Madness" and "Solitude" published in American Anthology of Poetry; *Address:* 1339 Stevenage, Channelview, TX.

LAABS, THEODORE R.
Pen name: Ted Laabs; Rodney; *Born:* March 27, 1938, Milwaukee, Wisconsin; *Parents:*Theodore F. and Selma Laabs; *Children:* Robert Theodore; *Education:* University of Wisconsin; University of North Texas; *Occupation:* Eductor, Writer; *Other writings:* Wrote "Play After the Wall", has written articles, chapters, and scripts; *Personal note:* Cognitive aesthetic, illustrated by the following dyads: apparent-reality, universal-meaning, precise-language, simple-syntax, economy-expression; Influenced by Donne, T.S. Eliot, W. Stevens; *Address:* Trophy Club, TX.

LAGASSE, HARVEY L.
Born: January 23 1921, Bristol, CT; *Parents:*Harvey and Maude Lagasse; *Spouse:* Carol Lagasse, August 8, 1969; *Occupation:* Professional Soldier, currently retired Lt Colonel; *Memberships:* Ex POW Assn: Air Force Assn: AARP; *Honors:* Air Medal, Prisoner of War Medal, Various theater of operations medals; *Other writings:* Novel "The Distant Bugle", Song-"You Don't Have to be a Star", "Follow Me", "The Gold Balloon"; *Personal note:* I consider my poetry as a "Walk Through Life". Some reflect my feeling about God's creatures. Others from experience as a flyer on a bomber combat and prisoner of war; *Address:* 203 Yoakum Pkwy, Apt 1120, Alexandria, VA.

LAMBERT, KATIE
Pen name: A. K. Penn-Lambert; *Born:* March 21, 1944, Albertville, Alabama; *Parents:*Marjorie Davis; *Children:* Gregory Alanson, Jason Andrew; *Education:* High School; *Occupation:* Former Editor, *Outstanding Young Men of the Year, Encyclopedia of Space,* and various marketing group publications for Fuller and Dees Publishing Company, Montgomery, Alabama; Professional artist working in etched and stained glass medias; *Honors:* Editor's Choice Award, The National Library of Poetry, 1988; *Other writings: Footsteps of the Prophet,* a philosophical tribute to Kahlil Gilbrian; numerous poems; four unpublished science fiction novels; currently workingon a science fantasy novel, *The Shydom of the Dwee*; *Personal note:* Man's future lies in his imagination. My wish for us all is a fruitful fantasy. *Address:* 1108 Glenwood Street, Dothan, Alabama.

LANE, CHRISTINA JO
Pen name: Christy Lane, *Born:* August 20, 1973, Buffalo, Oklahoma; *Parents:*Leroy Lane & Ellen Lane; *Education:* Ft. Supply Public School; *Memberships:* FHA; *Honors:* 8th Grade Salutatorian; *Personal note:* Poetry to me demolishes stress and shows true emotion. This poem is dedicated to Teresa Hayes of Ft. Supply Oklahoma; *Address:* Rt. 1 Box 63, Ft. Supply, OK.

LARSON, ROBERT C.
Born: March 13, 1942, Belmond, Iowa; *Parents:*A.E. & Anna Mae Larson; *Children:* Robert Charles Larson II; *Education:* High School; *Occupation:* Machinist, Carpenter; *Memberships:* FOE, VFW; *Other writings:* Made 2 Records (country and western); *Personal note:* I write mainly about life since I worry constantly about world conditions. I just wish people would wake up and smell the roses; *Address:* P.O. Box 37, Pearce, AZ.

LASSEL, KARIN
Born: July 22, 1972, Warren, Michigan; *Parents:*Ewald Lassel, Ruth Lassel; *Education:* Northfield Junior Academy; *Other writings:* Poems have been published in school booklet "Bit of Lit"; *Personal note:* I'd like to say that I write all my poems with the Lord in mind, and I thank him for all of his blessings; *Address:* 7271 E. 46 ½ Road, Cadillac, MI.

LASSEN, TIFFANY ANNE
Pen name: Tiffany Lassen; *Born:* November 7, 1974, Chico, California; *Parents:*Chris and Bonnie Lassen; *Education:* Currently 8th grade student, Stidwell Jr. High; *Occupation:* Student and poet; *Memberships:* Ohana Volleyball Association, President of Student Body; *Honors:* Natural Helper, MVP trophy for track, gymnastics awards; *Other writings:* "Fairies," "The Great Fall," "Love," "Roses," "Seagulls," "Freedom," "Tears," "Popularity"; *Address:* 1700 Glen Gary Road, Sagle Idaho.

LATORRE, KATHY
Pen name: Kathy Jo; *Born:* October 18, 1942, Roscoe, Illinois; *Parents:*Mary Raaymakers & Herbert Hinde; *Spouse:* Lawson Latorre, December 31, 1963; *Children:* Bill, Gina, Lisa; *Education:* San Lorenzo High School; Sierra Community College; *Occupation:* Independent Contractor; *Memberships:* Box Project, Grant-A-Wish, Friends of KM Hospital; *Honors:* Al Collins Award, Volunteer of the Year; *Other writings:* Has written numerous poems published in various anthologies; *Personal note:* I write for my own personal enjoyment, I am often surprised at what I have written; *Address:* 140 Mulberry Lane, Auburn, CA.

LATOUCHE, EMMANUEL
Born: July 25, 1955, Port-au-Prince, Haiti; *Parents:*Emanuel Latouche and Sylvia Latouche; *Spouse:* Irmine B. Latouche; December 24, 1983; *Children:* Ted Emmanuel Latouche, David Latouche; *Education:* Hume Business School; *Occupation:* Working in Law Firm; *Memberships:* American Museum of National History; *Other writings:* Several poems published in Paris, Haiti, and in New York in local newspapers; *Personal note:* Day after day I feeling great about my writing, I want to tell everyone, thanks for reading my poems; *Address:* P.O. Box 070265, Brooklyn, NY.

LAWRIMORE, DORIS LOUISE
Born: October 11, 1935, Georgetown, South Carolina; *Parents:*David Lester Lawrimore and Bessie Louise Moore Rogers; *Children:* Carl Julius, Teresa, Ruth Elizabeth, Doris April; *Education:* John Dela Howe School; *Occupation:* Health Aid; *Memberships:* WIBC; *Other writings:* Has published a poem entitled, "Don't Do It"; *Personal note:* A united and cooperative world is our only key to survival. Now is the time to understand, the fatherhood of God, the brotherhood of man; *Address:* 4440 Abbott Avenue, Titusville, FL.

LEBLANC, PIERRE A.
Pen name: Pete Armstrong, April 21, 1921; *Born:* Providence Quebec, Canada; *Children:* Amber Nicole, Kathryne Ann, Beverly; *Memberships:* American Forestry Association; *Honors:* Certificate of Merit, Commemorative Awards, Certificate of Recognition by NY Governor Mario Cuomo; *Other writings:* Has written a collection of primitive poetry; *Personal note:* Born again with recaptured optimism keep us tame as we reach for fame! My admiration goes out to all poets and friends who acclaim, may you have the same with health and happiness; *Address:* 24 Main Street Apt #2, Tupper Lake, NY.

LEDOUX, DENISE LAVERNE
Born: September 21, 1971, Prince Albert Sask; *Parents:*-Norman Ledoux and Lorna Bird; *Education:* Leask High School; *Occupation:* Student; *Memberships:* Mistawasis Youth Group *Honors:* Certificate for scholastic achievement; *Other writings:* Has written a collection of personal poetry; *Personal note:* Share your love with others today as they may be gone tomorrow. The poems I have written are based on my own personal experiences and feelings; *Address:* Leask, CANADA.

LEE, IMOGENE
Born: 1911, Illinois; *Education:* High School; College; *Occupation:* Retired; *Memberships:* Songwriter's Guild and National Academy of Song Writers; *Personal note:* Only since retirement have I developed an interest in writing; favorite poet is Ralph Waldo Emerson; *Address:* 140 Forest Lake Blvd., Daytona Beach, FL.

LEE, YVONNE
Born: October 19, 1935, West Branch, Michigan; *Occupation:* Nurse Aide; *Memberships:* Patient's Advisory Board; *Other writings:* Has written book entitled, "Life's Candle Light"; *Personal note:* I like people to read my writings to give them a chance to see and reflect their own inner beauty; *Address:* P.O. Box 48015, Seattle, WA.

LEMBO, MARIE
Pen name: Marie Sue Lembo; *Born:* July 9, 1904, Mary Lebone, England; *Parents:*Joseph & Angelamakie Deluca; *Spouse:* James R. Lembo, February 3, 1945; *Children:* 1 Daughter; *Education:* St. Mary's School; *Occupation:* Housewife; *Honors:* 4 awards in writing; *Other writings:* Several poems in Haven Press, 1945; A book of poems by Paebar Co. 1945, and World of Poetry, Poems by Ted Rosen; *Personal note:* I'm interested in music, art and lyric writing; *Address:* P.O. Box 3305, Pawtucket, RI.

LICHOTA, ANNA MARIA
Born: September 21, 1972, Buffalo, NY.; *Parents:*Edward Lichota, Mary Lichota; *Education:* Immaculata Academy; *Memberships:* Student Council; *Honors:* Honor Roll; *Other writings:* Written articles for school newsletter; *Address:* 208 Heritage Farm Road, West Seneca, NY.

LINDQUIST, JENNIFER
Born: April 17, 1974, Arcadia, California; *Parents:*Larry and Charleen Lindquist *Occupation:* Student; *Personal note:* Poetry is my one special hobby, which is different from most of my friends and family; *Address:* 627 Hampton Road, Arcadia, CA.

LINDSEY, FALLA
Born: October 13, 1972, Lancanster, SC; *Education:* Attala Christian School; *Personal note:* Poetry is the way I express my feelings. I gave God all the tribute for my talent. *Address:* Rt. 5, Box 866, Kosciusko, MS.

LINZEY, STANFORD E.
Born: October 13, 1920, Houston, Texas; *Parents:*Stanford Linzey, Eva Faye Westphal; *Spouse:* July 13, 1941, Verna May Linzey; *Children:* Gena May, Janice Ellen, Stanford E., Virginia Darnella, Sharon Faye, George W., Vera Evelyn, Paul, David, James; *Education:* Linda Vista Baptist College, BA; ThB; American Baptist Seminary, MDIV; Fuller Theological Seminary, Pasadena California, DMIN; *Occupation:* Captain (retired); *Memberships:* Retired Officefs Assn, National Geographic Society, Biblical Archaelogical Society; *Other writings:* Has written "Pentacost in the Pentagon", "Why I believe in the Baptism with the Holy Spirit", "Filling Your Boots"; *Personal note:* I believe God is concerned for all men everywhere. I have been influenced by the great heroes at the church; *Address:* 1641 Kenora Drive, Escondido, CA.

LOBECK, LISA
Born: July 3, 1970, Minneapolis, Minnesota; *Parents:*Ron and Joy Lobeck; *Education:* Washburn High School; *Occupation:* Sales Associate; *Other writings:* Portfolio of lyrics and poetry; *Personal note:* Peace; *Address:* 522S Park Avenue Minneapolis, MN.

LOGAN, HOWARD TAYLOR
Born: Crestline, Ohio; *Parents:*Frank & Viola Taylor Logan; *Spouse:* Susie Frances; *Children:* E. Diann Denshoff, Nancy J.; *Education:* Galion High School; Ohio State University, Mansfield Business College; *Occupation:* Auctioneer, Real Estate; *Memberships:* National Storytellers Association, Ohio Auctioner Association, Graphoanalysis; *Other writings:* Words of Love for Those Who Care, Green River Murder Case, Jake the Super Star, Julie; *Personal note:* A good memory, clear communication, a creative soul, and you will do well! *Address:* P.O. Box 1095, Galion, OH.

LORENZETTI, REGINA ANNE
Born: August 15, 1948, Los Nanos, California; *Parents:*Don and Pat Estep; *Children:* Stephanie, Freddie; *Education:* Junior College; *Occupation:* Investor; *Honors:* Nominated to Marquis Who's Who; *Other writings:* Published author of "Love is Like Snow"; *Personal note:* Listen to your instincts and go for it. A dream is only as far as that first step; *Address:* 1037 Dos Palos Avenue, Dos Palos, CA.

LOWERS, HEWITT BEVERLY
Born: January 14, 1942, Monroe County, WV; *Parents:*Caroline and Roy Hewitt; *Spouse:* Martin Lowers; October 14, 1958; *Children:* Julia, Virgil, Sarah, Randall, Laura, Marta, Kendall; *Education:* Garrett Community College; *Occupation:* Administrative Assistant; *Memberships:* Fellowship of Christ; *Other writings:* Have been writing poems, compositions, and short stories since junior high school, some have appeared in local publications; *Personal note:* I believe it is the responsibility of all people, but particularly of those possessing talent-means of attracting the public, to uphold-encourage high moral standards by word and deed; *Address:* P.O. Box 96, Liberty Street, Oakland, MD.

LUCESCU, MARY CATHERINE
Pen name: Kathleen Wilcox; *Born:* January 26, 1958, Welland, Ontario; *Parents:* David and Gloria Lucescu; *Education:* Westbrook Secondary School; *Occupation:* Student; *Honors:* Coached girls' atom and bantam house league teams to league and playoff championships in 1983-84; *Other writings:* Course with Institute of Children's Literature; entering writing (short story) contests; presently working on a novel and submitting short stories to various children's magazines; *Personal note:* I personally believe to be a good writer, anything you write about is all due to personal feeling or experience. I hope to fulfill "my grandmother's dream" of being a writer. I love writing; *Address:* 2190 Ellesmere Road #701, Scarborough, Ontario, Canada.

LYONS, MARK ERIC
Pen name: Mel; *Born:* August 15, 1957, Milwaukee, Wisconsin; *Parents:* Willie Lyons, Jr. and Vera Mae; *Spouse:* Patricia Ann Mallett, January 1, 1977; *Children:* Nicole M., Joseph W., Erike A.; *Education:* North Division High School; *Occupation:* General Laborer; *Memberships:* Songwriters Club of America; President, Mel's Traveling Threater and founder; *Honors:* Best Actors Award, 1974-75; High School Scholarship; *Other writings:* Sixteen plays, anthology of contemporary poetry, song, published for the "Sake of our Children", "I'm Moving On", Twelve other songs unpublished and over 50 greeting cards; *Personal note:* It's plain enough for a blind man to see, we do possess a great land, and oh how much better it could be by lending those less fortunate a hand; *Address:* Milwaukee, WI.

MAHONEY, ROBERT W.
Pen name: Bob Mahoney; *Born:* September 12, 1950, Concord, MA. *Parents:* William D. & Jean E. Mahoney; *Occupation:* Retired; *Memberships:* DAV; *Other writings: Drill Sergeant, Bridge, Candles*; *Address:* P.O. Box 354, Ridgway, CO.

MARAZZANI, SANTA A. LALLI
Born: January 1, 1946, Bonefro (CB) Italy; *Parents:* Professor Luigi Lalli, Anna M. Aloia Lalli; *Spouse:* Count Leopoldo Marazzani, Captain, September 16, 1981; *Children:* Albert Anthony, Michael Phillip; *Education:* University of Rome, Magistero Faculty, Rome, Italy; *Occupation:* Italian teacher, psychosocial counselor; *Memberships:* The Vizcayans, the Metropolitan Museum, YWCA; *Honors:* Diploma of Merit with silver medal from the Papal Organization of Assistance; Golden Poet Award for 1988 World of Poetry; Scholarship from the Embassy of France in Italy; Scholarship from the Institute of French of the University of Rome; *Other writings:* Other poems published, have written articles for *Il Direttore Commericale*, Milano, Italy; *Personal note:* What I cannot express with my loud voice I hope to do with the words of my poems. I want my children to have something to remember me for; *Address:* 2121 North Bayshore Drive, Apt. 915, Miami, Florida.

MARCHESE, BRIDGET
Born: October 6, 1973, Rock Island, Illinois; *Parents:* Bill and Margo Marchese; *Education:* Geneseo High School; *Personal note:* I have always enjoyed reading poetry; I hope now you will enjoy reading mine; *Address:* 38 Genesco Hills, Geneseo, IL.

MARLOWE, ROSALIE
Born: June 9, 1951, Dallas, Texas; *Parents:* Alton F. Marlowe, Sr., and Elenor Painter-Marlows; *Education:* North Texas State University, BA; Columbia University Teachers College, MA; *Occupation:* Special Education Teacher; *Memberships:* Assn of Returned Peace Corps Volunteers, Modern Poetry Assn; *Honors:* Kappa Delta Phi, Dean's List, Peach Corps Fellows Award; *Other writings:* Poems Published in Kuman Ju, Clover Book of Verse; *Personal note:* There are no ordinary people, only extra ordinary wonderous lives, each an essence worthy of celebration; *Address:* 34 Hillside Avenue Apt 3H, New York, NY.

MARTIN, ELYSE
Pen name: Ginger; *Born:* October 16, 1917, New York, New York; *Spouse:* Ted Martin, December 2, 1952; *Occupation:* Housewife; *Memberships:* Sacred Heart Alter Society, Merced Atwater Bowling Assn; *Honors:* Citation from American Cancer Society for Volunteer Service, *Other writings:* Has written poems and essays; *Personal note:* I am quick to anger, when I see or hear of injustices to the underdog, and I like to help people in need; *Address:* Merced, CA.

MARTINSON, DENISE
Born: April 14, Detroit, Michigan; *Parents:* Florence and Daniel Gallik; *Spouse:* Michael Ray; *Children:* Danielle Syzanne, Michael Daniel; *Education:* Institute of Children's Literature and NIA; *Occupation:* Free Lance Writer; *Memberships:* National Writer's Club; Who's Who in US Writers, Editors, and Poets; *Honors:* Numerous Awards for Poetry; *Other writings:* Published in local newspaper, church paper, have two chapter books published, and numerous poetry publications; *Personal note:* If a person persists, rewards can abound. I believe a writer should never give up. Sooner or later an editor will take notice. I am fortunate to have won awards and have widely published because of this; *Address:* Madison Heights, MI.

MASFERRER, MARGARET
Born: January 5, 1968, Jersey City, NJ; *Parents:* Jose Antonio Masferrer and Carmen Masferrer; *Education:* Emerson High School; St. Peter's College, Jersey City New Jersey; *Occupation:* Student; *Honors:* Dean's List, Distinguished Scholar Award, Jersey Girls State; *Personal note:* I believe that through God's love anything may be achieved. This achievement I owe to my Emmaus brothers and sister at SPC in which God's love continues to grow; *Address:* 1411 Summit Avenue, Union City, NJ.

MATHIESEN, DANA
Born: December 25, 1971, New Jersey; *Parents:* Diana & Hal Mathiesen; *Occupation:* Student; *Memberships:* Varsity Soccer Team, Student Government; *Honors:* Honor Roll; *Personal note:* When you let go of you dream, you die; *Address:* 3 New Hampshire Avenue, Cherry Hill, NJ.

MAU, JASMIN
Pen name: Jasmin Laura Lei Mau; *Born:* March 9, 1974, Honlulu, HI; *Parents:* Kathleen Osmond and Jacob P. Mau; *Occupation:* Student; *Personal note:* Life is only what you make it, learn to ignore something you consider distasteful and learn to find a meaning for everything you see; *Address:* 94-509 Palai Street, Waipahu, HI.

MAXWELL, STACIE LEEAN
Born: December 23, 1970, Knoxville, Tennessee; *Parents:* Karen Cash; *Education:* Campbell High, Smyrna Tennessee; Young Harris College; *Occupation:* Student; *Other writings:* Writer for college newspaper and literary magazine published on campus; *Personal note:* My writing reflects the events of the world on a personal level. *Address:* 3086 Farmington Lane, Atlanta, GA.

MCCALL, SHIRLEY DEAN
Pen name: Sandy James McCall; *Born:* December 27, 1939, Oklahoma City, Oklahoma; *Parents:* Timothy and Beaulah McCoy; *Spouse:* Jim D. McCall, November 9, 1983; *Children:* Debra Kay, Phillip Darryl, Linda Michael; *Education:* Capital Hill High School, SOuthwestern Jr. College, Rose State College, Columbus College; *Occupation:* Graduate Student, Columbus College, Columbus, Georgia; *Memberships:* Edgewood Baptist Church Choir; *Honors:* Dean's List; *Other writings:* American Anthology of Poetry, Southwestern Jr. College Book of Poetry, Rose State College Newspaper, Columbus College—poetry; *Personal note:* I strive to reflect the truth of our time in my writing. "Truth is the eternal key that opens all doors"; *Address:* Columbus, Georgia.

MCCARVER, SHIREE
Born: September 1, 1964, Scottsboro, Alabama; *Parents:* Mildred and Willie LaFleur; *Education:* S.R. Butler High School; *Memberships:* Modern Music Masters; *Honors:* Most outstanding 1st soprano, section leader, choir student; *Other writings:* Has written a novel entitled, "Loving Lavina"; *Personal note:* To those I love; my family. my motto is: to achieve the impossible is as easy as believing in yourself; *Address:* 3917 Sparkman Dr., Huntsville, AL.

MCCONNELL, JOHN ROBERT
Born: April 15, 1958, Dickinson, North Dakota; *Parents:* Charles and Vivian McConnell; *Education:* Boise Bible College, Boise Idaho; *Occupation:* Logger, Caretaker, carpenter, advertising sales; *Honors:* Creative writing award, Interpretation award for interpreting and portraying character in a high school drama; *Other writings:* "Living Gem" Magazine of Boise Idaho published poem entitled, "I know Who God is", Has also written short stories; *Personal note:* I have written for years as a hobby with the hope of writing professionally; I have an unpublished collection of poetry which may be published soon; *Address:* Box 81, Ione, OR.

MCCUTCHEN, MARGARET SAWYER
Pen name: William H. Sawyer; *Born:* South Carolina; *Parents:* Sarah Lane Harrelson Sawyer; *Spouse:* Joe Cunningham McCutchen; *Occupation:* Public School Music Teacher, Choir Director; *Memberships:* Dramatic Club, Choral Society Sunday School Teacher, Music Chairman of C.W. Club, Adult Choir Singer; *Honors:* Merit Certificate, Honorable Mention, Golden Poet Award, 1988, Best New Poet of 1988; *Personal note:* Poetry is an outlet for me emotionally; *Address:* 106 W. Shepard Lane, Summerville, SC.

MCDANIELS, NAKYA
Born: October 12, 1974, South Carolina; *Parents:* Albert and Annette Felder; *Education:* Eau Claire High School; *Occupation:* Student; *Other writings:* Several poems and stories for school contests; *Address:* 100 Lorick Avenue Apt. 12-7, Columbia, South Carolina.

MCDONALD, NICOLE
Born: December 18. 1973, Boston, MA; *Parents:* Linda and Richard McDonald; *Occupation:* Student; *Personal note:* In my poem I try to express the love of Christ, because even as a teen I can see people need to feel loved and I want them to be aware that Jesus always does; *Address:* 27 Dunloggin Road, Nashu, NH.

MCKELVEY, GERALD H.
Born: August 6, 1939, Rochester, New York; *Parents:* Doris Crapp, Geraldine H. McKelvey; *Children:* Adam & Jessica; *Occupation:* Licensed Vocational Nurse, Private Investigator; *Other writings:* "The World Around Us." *Personal note:* Most of my poems reflect my religious background, my love of nature and the fact that I am a romantic. I love that which is good in life and detest that which is bad; *Address:* 7111 Waite Dr., La Mesa, CA.

MCKINLEY, DELAYNE
Born: October 8, 1948, Lake City, Minnesota; *Parents:* Ed and Helen Walters; *Spouse:* Gary Mckinley; *Education:* Ann Arundle County College; *Honors:* National Dean's List; *Personal note:* Life is the gift we are given, with love and compassion we should live it; *Address:* 201 Ave A. Plattsmouth, NE.

MCKITTRICK, OPAL
Born: January 11, 1920, West Salem, Illinois; *Parents:* Thomas and Emma Gawthorp; *Spouse:* Edwin McKittrick, February 24, 1944; *Children:* Thomas, Peggy, Kathy, and Cheryl; *Education:* University of Illinois, Eastern Illinois State Teacher's College; *Occupation:* Teacher; *Memberships:* Swedish Medical Center Auxiliary; *Honors:* Mile High Poetry Society; *Other writings:* Has written several poems for family and friends; *Personal note:* I was influenced by my maternal grandfather, Kahlil Gibran and contemporary poets; *Address:* 3 Glenview Drive, Littleton, CO.

MCLAUGHLIN, BRIAN MICHAEL
Pen name: Brian Michael; *Born:* June 29, 1968, Fairfax, Virginia; *Other writings:* Has written books of poetry; *Personal note:* I try to write with words from my heart instead of my mind. Seeing what is true in life through my heart, with visions in life of realism reflected in poetry of love and truth; words struggling for peace in love and truth in life through the eyes of a poet; *Address:* 6701 Mallards Cove Raod 12-H, Jupiter, FL.

MCMILLIAN, FRANCES MILLS
Born: September 17, 1937, Thomasville, Georgia; *Parents:* George Cornelius Mills and Ada Ruth Capps Mills; *Children:* Kim, Charles, Mark D.; *Education:* Taylor County High School, Perry Florida; *Occupation:* Assistant to Nursing; *Other writings:* I have written many poems since 1972; *Personal note:* I desire to expand my God given talent to being happiness and a glimpse of hope to others through publication, greetings cards and songwriting; *Address:* P.O. Box 764 Selma Al.

MCNAMARA, CHARLENE MARIE
Pen name: C.J. Gordon; *Born:* July 24, 1971, Amsterdam, NY; *Parents:* William McNamara and Catherine McNamara; *Education:* St. Stanislaus Amsterdam High School; *Occupation:* Student; *Memberships:* Montgomery County Council; *Honors:* Centry Club (2nd Place), SADD; *Other writings:* Published Perished and Mirror Image, Creative Collection V; *Personal note:* Always reach for that unreachable star. Keep faith, hope and your dreams alive. For you'll get there no matter who you are for as long as you strive.-..reach to that star; *Address:* RD #1, Fonda, NY;

MCVAY, SHIRLEY ANNE
Born: April 7, 1938, Jackson, Alabama; *Parents:* W.D. & Jimmie FInch; *Spouse:* Gene G. McVay, April 25, 1959; *Children:* Paul Frank McVay; *Education:* Jackson High School; Springhill College; *Occupation:* Title Researcher; *Memberships:* McCann's United Methodist Church, Titles Unlimited; *Honors:* Won Honorable Mention for numerous works; *Other writings:* Poem published in the Sparrowgrass Poetry Forum, Inc.; *Personal note:* I feel that my skills for writing poems comes from a greater power; *Address:* Jackson, AL.

MEADOWS, KATHRYN
Pen Name: Katie Em; *Born:* December 17, 1963, Hanover, Pennsylvania; *Parents:* Phyllis and Bob Meadows; *Education:* Hanover Sr. High School, Villa Julie College; *Occupation:* Manager of daycare center; *Memberships:* Church Scolarship committee, Board member of Country Club Association; *Other writings:* Various poems and short stories published in local magazines and newletters; *Personal note:* I have always enjoyed the search for just the right words to express my thoughts. Without the right words, the thoughts are diminished in the telling; *Address:* 431 Church Rd, Reisterstown, Maryland.

MERCHANT, GERARD MAURIER
Born: December 3, 1959, Lynchburg, VA. *Parents:* Williams Leroy Merchant and Julia Elizabeth Rucker; *Spouse:* Marie Starr LePiano, February 28, 1987; *Occupation:* Carpenter; *Personal note:* My poems are for people to reach into their insight and see the positive self; *Address:* 101 E. Geneva Drive, Temep, AZ.

MESELEY, JOHN ALLEN
Pen name: Lucius Drake; *Born:* December 14, 1965, Winchester, Tennessee; *Parents:* Lanny and Jennifer Moseley; *Education:* Motlow State Community College, Tullahoma Tennessee; *Occupation:* Soldier, Carpenter, Musician; *Honors:* Good Conduct Medal, Army Commendation Medal; *Other writings:* Sundry of unsubmitted poems, novels and self help articles; *Personal note:* The greatest power this world offers is the ability to love beyond the hurt beyond the needs of yourself to love life because love and hatred are all we own; *Address:* Rte 2, Box 269, Winchester, TN.

MESEROLE, CHARLES D.
Born: December 28, 1936, Wayne County, Illinois; *Parents:* Embree and Hattie Meserole; *Spouse:* Diann L. Meserole, September 25, 1962; *Children:* Daniel, Rita, Duane, Douglas and Regina; *Occupation:* Mental Health Therapist; *Honors:* 5 golden poet awards, Ursus Press Book award, several honorable mentions; *Other writings:* Published in Action News, Inclusion in numerous anthologies and wide open magazine; *Personal note:* I would like, through poetry, to give someone a view they haven't seen or a feeling they haven't experienced. Moving them, much as I have been moved by poets of old; *Address:* 9537 Los Coches Road, Lakeside, CA.

MILARDO, PHYLLIS WALKER
Born: December 20, 1934, Middletown, CT; *Education:* Phoenix College, AA, (With Distinction); *Occupation:* Geriatrics; *Memberships:* Masque and Dagger, The National Writers Club; *Honors:* Delta Psi Omega, Phi Theta Kappa, Masonic Order of the Eastern Star, Honorable Mention,

World of Poetry, 1988; 4th Place in "Win a Bundle" Poetry Contest: *Other writings: The River*, Kivel News, *Searching Souls*, World Treasury of Great Poems, *My Mother's Passing*, Summerfield Journal; *Personal note:* Writing is my way of expressing inner growth, that goes beyond the superficialities of life in search of truth. I have a deep affinity for nature and the universe in all its forms, which is the main theme for most of my poetry; *Address:* 389 Pine Street, Middletown, CT.

MILLER, CARY

Born: August 31, 1954, Independence, Missouri; *Parents:* Rev. and Mrs. William S. Miller; *Education:* Universityof-Kentucky, BA; Southwestern School of Law, (Dean's List), Los Angeles California; *Occupation:* Artist and Freelance Writer; *Memberships:* Sierra Club; *Honors:* Phi Beta Kappa, National Dean's List, Special Achievement (In legal writing and research); *Other writings:* Writes for the Lexington Leader, Feature stories, Movie and ALbum Reviews; *Personal note:* This is my first poem; it was adapted from my unpublished essay, written about my attempts to rescue my step nephew from a "Moonie" like religion; *Address:* 410 E. 41st Apt. 1E, Kansas City, MO.

MILLER, FLORENCE

Born: March 24, 1919, Twillingate, NFLD; *Parents:* James Adey and Crolyn Adey; *Spouse:* George Miller, July 21, 1944; *Children:* Joan, Blanche, Leaburn, Rosemary; *Education:* Teacher's Training; *Occupation:* Retired teacher; *Memberships:* St. John's Ambulance Dorcas Society, Women's Institution; *Honors:* Bronze Quill Creative Enterprises; Award of Appreciation; *Other writings:* Written novel entitled, "Private Thoughts", Published two poems in local newspaper; *Address:* P.O. Box 684, Botwood, NFLD, AOH IEO,

MIROCHA, ANGELENE

Pen name: Angie Mirocha; *Born:* April 10, 1973; *Parents:* Richard and Kay Mirocha; *Occupation:* Student; *Other writings: Nothing But You On My Mind, Enchanting Dream, Baby, Two, Corry, Goodbye, Silent Dreams*; *Personal note:* The poems I write are reflections of how I feel inside, through my writing I bring out true and inspirational emotions;

MITCHELL, ENID

Born: September 21, 1919, Shawnee, Ohio; *Parents:* Hazel Robertson Mitchell and Charles T. Mitchell; *Education:* North High School; Ohio State University; *Occupation:* Writer-Poet; *Memberships:* The American Biographical Institute Research Assn; Writer's International Alliance; *Honors:* Golden Poet Award, 1988; Who's Who in U.S. Writers; Editor and Poets, 1988 and 1989; The International Directory of Distinguished Leadership Personalities of America; *Other writings:* Poetry published in American Poetry Association Anthologies, Scimitar and Song, Poetry Center, Sparrowgrass Poetry Forum and the World of Poetry; *Personal note:* Poetry is metaphysical and is greatly inspired by my mother's writings and philosophy as found in the Religion of spiritualism which presents the proof of the continuity of life after death; *Address:* 1665 Summit Street, Columbus, OH.

MOBERG, ROBERTA

Pen name: Bert; *Born:* April 29, 1974, St. Paul, Minnesota; *Parents:* Nancy Moberg, Donald Moberg; *Education:* Mounds View High School; *Occupation:* Aspiring Model; *Memberships:* S.A.D.D; *Honors:* Honor Roll, Dance Competitions; *Other writings:* Have written several poems; *Personal note:* My poem was written for an old friend of mine, Shilo; *Address:* 1629 Glenview Court, Arden Hills, MN.

MOBLEY, MANDY

Born: October 6, 1976, Atlanta Georgia; *Parents:* David T. and Cathy H. Mobley; *Occupation:* Student; *Memberships:* Student Council; *Honors:* Discovery Program, Honor Certificates; *Address:* 2613 Cosmos Ct. Atlanta, GA.

MONESSON, HARRY S.

Pen name: He-Who-Peeks-Into-Earth; *Born:* March 1, 1935, New Jersey; *Parents:* Marian B. Selbin, Louis Monesson; *Occupation:* Blueberry-cranberry grower, writer and author; *Memberships:* Archaeological Society of New Jersey; *Honors:* The Alumni Association, Author Award; *Other writings:* Writes children's and adult fiction books; author of "Knibblers in the Sands", "Sand Sharks in the Pines"; published a collection of Native American poems; *Personal note:* All things inspired; themes go in all direction... everything from the enigmas of time, destiny, and universe to poetic humor and political satire. Tales and poems of the New Jersey Pinelands are a special joy; *Address:* 315 Magnolia Road, Pemberton, NJ.

MOORE, VICKIE SUE

Pen name: Vickie Pollitt Moore; *Born:* November 13, 1942, Vanceburg, Kentucky; *Parents:* William and Grace Kennedy Pollitt; *Spouse:* Leo Louis Moore, December 12, 1964; *Children:* Faith Ann, Steven Leo, Stacy Rena, Larry; *Education:* Lewis County School Systems; *Occupation:* Writer; *Honors:* 9 Merit Awards, Golden Poet Award; *Other writings:* Poetry published in Lewis Co. Herald, Poems published in nine anthologies. Chapbook titled "Love, Wisdon, and Emotions in Poetry", just completed a nonfiction prose and a short story ready for publication; *Personal note:* I love good poetry, I love to read it, I love to write it, I love the beautiful world of knowledge, I want to grasp all I can in this lifetime; *Address:* HC73 Box 674, Vanceburg, KY.

MORIN, ANNETTE

Born: November 1, 1964, North Bay, Ontario, Canada; *Parents:* Ronald Morin and Theresa Morin; *Education:* Ecole Secondaire, Algonquin; *Occupation:* Bookkeeper; *Other writings:* Has written several poems; *Personal note:* Life has its up and downs as we all know; however, we must believe that eventually things will go our way. We must have faith in ourselves; *Address:* 12 Judge Avenue, Apt #2, North Bay, Ontario, CANADA.

MOSQUERA, ANA MARIA

Pen name: Mamina; *Born:* January 26, 1973, New York, New York; *Parents:* Raul & Ana Mosquera; *Education:* Elizabeth High School; *Occupation:* Student; *Honors:* Awarded medal for poetry for writing; *Other writings:* Won a volleyball trophy, published a poem that was published in school newspaper; *Personal note:* My dream is to one day become a writer or an English literature teacher; *Address:* Elizabeth, NJ.

MOYLE, TROY

Born: September 20, 1968, Des Moines, Iowa; *Parents:* Ronald and Jackie Moyle; *Education:* Lincoln High School; *Occupation:* Computer Operator; *Personal note:* Many of my poems are written about the pain caused by love, or as my friend would say, for me to be happy I have to be sad; *Address:* 500 S.W. Gray, Des Moines, IA.

MUSA, MELINDAH

Born: May 4, 1974, Edmonton, Alberta Canada; *Parents:* Dr. and Mrs. Bakri Musa; *Education:* Gilroy High School; *Occupation:* School; *Memberships:* Junior Statesmen of America, Math Engineering and Science Achievement, California Scholarship Federation; *Honors:* Presidential Academic Fitness Award, Gilroy Elks Lodge, Merit Award, CMEA Honor Choir; *Other writings:* Various poems published at young authors' conference; *Personal note:* I would like to thank my parents and friends, Sabrina and Katrina, for their everlasting support; *Address:* 7190 Harvard Place, Gilroy, CA.

NADON, RENE

Born: January 31, 1952, Detroit, Michigan; *Parents:* Melvin Nadon, Evelyn Nadon; *Spouse:* Denise Nadon, February 3, 1973; *Children:* Kimerly, Timothy John; *Education:* Cerritos Junior College; *Occupation:* Assistant Manager; *Memberships:* Mt. Whitney High School Music Boosters; *Other writings:* Has written several poems; *Personal note:* This poem was written for my daughter for an oral interpretation in school; *Address:* Visalia, CA.

NAPOLITANO-CORNISH, GRACE

Born: September 12, 1924, Toronto, Ontario; *Parents:* Paulo and Mattea Napolitano; *Spouse:* Ralph Victor Cornish (deceased), October 8, 1970; *Children:* Four by previous marriages, seven grandchildren, three great grandchildren; *Education:* Elementary—dropped out during the Hungry Thirties—a slow learner who has bloomed into a late bloomer; *Honors:* Two videos on a local community cabel channel called "The Readings of a Grandmama of the Eighties"; *Other writings:* In the Canadian and American Anthology, "Graziell the Bad Seed," "He and She," "Nostalgic Kahshe Lake," "Sex Is Here to Stay," "Reflections," "Confessions of a Cigarette Girl"; *Personal note:* A doctor prescribed some memoribilia therapy when he thought I was losing it when I was suddenly widowed and was left all alone to cope. It was great advice and I have never looked back. I have fallen in love with the written word with the full realization that "Love is Blind"; *Address:* 273 Crawford Street, Orillia, Ontario, Canada.

NASH, SHARON LEE

Pen name: Sharon Crooks Nash; *Born:* March 10, 1940, Hamilton, Montana; *Parents:* Sammy Crooks and Evelyn Crooks Daniel; *Spouse:* Harold Lee Roy Nash, September 4, 1974; *Children:* Gerald Lee, Gene Allen, Gordon Ray; *Education:* Stevensville High School; *Occupation:* Artist, Photographer, Pharmacy A-Tech; *Memberships:* Washington State Pharmacy Tech Assn, Washington State Art Society, WSU Cougar Club; *Honors:* Editor's Choice Award; *Other writings:* Has written poems and short stories with illustration: "Adventures of Jacob McNaughton", "Joshu McTavish Finds A Home"; *Personal note:* I strive to reflect the beauty of the world through my poetry as in my art, I try to write for the working class person that deals with same every day problems I do, to creatively spark a memory can add joy to their day; *Address:* N. 6105 Stone Street, Spokane, WA.

NELSON-GRIER, GLORIA EMBER

Pen name: Embernal; *Born:* February 17, 1956, Witchita, KS.; *Parents:* Moses Nelson, Gloria Nelson; *Spouse:* Alexander S. Grier, II; August 30, 1986; *Children:* Ramapo College; *Education:* Entrepreneur; *Other writings:* "Ember's Eternity", "The Nightingale", "Peace Please" "The Emerald City"; *Personal note:* It's not enough to say "I think, therefore, I am". You must contemplate before you say, "I think". *Address:* 304 North Street, Middletown, NY.

NELSON, THERESA LYNN

Born: October 24, 1975, Park Ridge, Illinois; *Parents:* William E. and Diane J. Nelson; *Education:* Hopewell Junior School; *Occupation:* Student; *Personal note:* Attending many different schools in different parts of the country provided experience background for my poems; *Address:* 7827 Bennington drive, Cincinnati, OH.

NEVAREZ, MELISSA

Born: April 11, 1975, Monteray Park, California; *Parents:* Rebecca Garrido and Oscar Nevarez; *Other writings:* "In the Dark"; *Personal note:* Trust and believe in the Lord with all your heart and you will never be let down; *Address:* W. Covina, CA.

NIEVES-SANTANA, MAGDALENA

Pen name: Magdalena Nieves; *Born:* February 11, 1968, St. Thomas, Virgin Island; *Parents:* Evelyn Danet-Santana, Carolos Juan Santana; *Spouse:* Richardo Nieves, July 16, 1986; *Children:* Richard Matthew Nieves; *Education:* University of the Virgin Islands; *Occupation:* Pharmaceutical Technician; *Other writings:* "My Sweet Husband"; *Personal note:* I write what comes out of my heart and mind. I try to express my deepest feelings and emotions in whatever I write, I am a hopeless romantic but can also differentiate it from reality. My dead son and my husband are my greatest inspirations; *Address:* P.O. Box 5444, Sunny Isles, St. Croix, VI.

NOBLE, ILENE

Born: January 5, 1913, Sarepta, Missisippi; *Parents:* Lucian and Daisy Poynor; *Spouse:* Duncan Noble, Sr., September 29, 1946; *Children:* Duncan Jr., Dwight, Nathan; *Education:* Nursing Degree; *Occupation:* Nursing, Homemaker, Poet and Song Writer; *Honors:* Editors Choice Award from National Library of Poetry; *Other writings:* Poems published in three poetry books; has written two songs that were recorded; *Personal note:* I am happy every time anyone succeeds for good. God owns all people and everything. We should praise him; *Address:* 1301 Hastings Road, Gautier, MS.

NULTY, MONICA KATHERINE

Born: January 19, 1976, Detroit, Michigan; *Parents:* Timothy Edward, Leslie Ellen Nulty; *Education:* Takoma Park Junior High School; *Occupation:* Student; *Memberships:* Montgomery Swim Club, Wheaton Figure Skating Club; *Honors:* Superintendent's Writing Award, 1988-89; *Other writings:* I have written about 25 other poems and several short stories; *Personal note:* Life is not always sunny and happy, and I try to convey sadness through a point of view that will make people stand up and listen; *Address:* 8107 Roanoke Avenue, Takoma Park, MD.

OAKWOOD, TRACY

Born: April 3, 1967, Oak Ridge, Tennessee; *Education:* S.D. Bishop State Jr. College, (With Honors), Mobile, AL; *Other writings:* Has written 3 poems published in the Alabama Poets Reunion; Book published in Phenix City Alabama; *Address:* Rt. 1 Box 684, Irvington, AL.

OBED, LEONORA RITA

Born: May 22, 1971, Manila, Philippines; *Parents:* Reynaldo Nera and Josefina Villegas; *Education:* Notre Dame High School; *Occupation:* Student; *Memberships:* National Honor Society, Spanish Honor Society; *Honors:* Outstanding High School student of America, 1985, National Honor Roll; *Other writings:* "Taciture Azure"; *Personal note:* "A thing of beauty is a joy forever." John Keats is my favorite poet. I admire his honesty, artistry and determination to overcome obstacles court; *Address:* 10 Michelle Court, Trenton, NJ.

OBERLEE, JEFFREY SCOTT

Born: August 16, 1968, Grand Rapids, Michigan; *Parents:* Lawrence Edward, Mary Diane; *Education:* Owosso High School, Michigan State University; *Occupation:* Student-Writer; *Personal note:* One can only sympathize for those who fall prey to social injustices; *Address:* 541 E. Exchange Street, Owosso, MI.

O'BRIEN, KATIE

Born: April 3, 1948, Glendale, CA.; *Parents:* Mary and Gene LaRue; *Spouse:* Pat O'Brien, October 10, 1981; *Children:* Kelly, Shannon; *Education:* Glendale College, 1968; *Occupation:* Free-lance community correspondenant; *Memberships:* VFW Auxiliary; *Honors:* Pin Award; *Other writings:* Poems and articles published in local news paperss, newsletters, anthologies; *Personal note:* I believe in the personal enlightment of all souls and in the universal consciousness of love and peace. What you conceive and believe can be achieved. *Address:* 10414 Fernglen Avenue, Tujunga, CA.

O'BRIEN, MARY ELLEN

Born: Manhattan, New York; *Education:* Bachelor of Science, Teaching Certification; *Occupation:* Writer; *Honors:* Alpha Psi Omega; *Other writings:* Has written children's stories and science fiction; *Personal note:* I write words that stay; words in print come from one person's imagination and goes to another person's imagination, that's incredible;

OLSON, MILDRED E.

Born: August 18, 1912, South Haven, MN.; *Parents:* August Erickson; *Spouse:* Carl H. Olson, June 6, 1934; *Children:* Sharon, Karen, Charles; *Education:* St. Cloud State University, BS, (withhonors); MacPhail School of Drama, University of Utah, University of Minnesota; *Occupation:* Retired Teacher; *Memberships:* SDA, Church of Litchfield, MN; *Honors:* Merit Mother of MN, 1981; 2 Trophies from World of Poetry; *Other writings:* Book of Poetry, "Tender Thoughts for Quiet Moments", 1981; *Personal note:* I am handicapped due to a fall while teaching, I thank the Lord for giving me the opportunity to write; *Address:* Rt. 1 Box 256, South Haven, MN.

OVISSI, MARYAM

Born: October 7, 1973, Tehran, Iran; *Parents:* Nasser Ovissi and Susan Samily; *Education:* Herndon High School; *Memberships:* North Shore Animal League; *Honors:* 1st Place School Art Competition, 1st Place County Art Competition, 2nd State Art Competition, 7th in National French Examination; *Personal note:* I believe no matter how bad things may appear to be there is always hope; *Address:* Reston, VA.

OWENS, EVONNE LOUISE

Born: October 24, 1967, Orangeburg, SC; *Parents:* Richard Owens and Pernetha Riley Owens; *Education:* University of South Carolina; *Occupation:* Student; *Memberships:* Mount Olive Baptist Church, International Thespian Society; *Honors:* Phi Beta Lambda; *Personal note:* "Aim high, remembering that all things are possible if you believe in yourself and the Creator"; *Address:* 2112 Mays SE, Orangeburg, SC.

OZBURN, DIANE

Born: February 2, 1968; *Parents:* Adam Louis, Patricia Ann Ozburn; *Occupation:* Restaurant Manager; *Address:* 245 Fleetwood Lane, Elk Grove, IL.

PADILLA, SOPHIE JANE

Born: July 5, 1930, Oved, Colorado; *Parents:* Margret and Manuel Bon Padilla; *Spouse:* Archie Gonzales, January 20, 1948; *Children:* Dolline and Julie; *Education:* High School graduate and Barber School; *Occupation:* Health care attendant; *Memberships:* Poetry center-Drama club; *Honors:* Honorable Mention Poet, Golden Poet Award; *Other writings:* I enjoy writing children's stories and poems for my grandchildren; *Personal note:* I grew up during the depression, I recall the struggles, the sad things, but now I have only begun to discover, to touch, to feel and see fragile humanity's new horizons. There is so much beauty to write about in this great blue universe, from the mind's eye to prayer, I go in flight of new discoveries; *Address:* P. O. Box 61361, Sacramento, California.

PANNULLO-PARNOFIELLO, LOUISE

Pen name: Louise Parnell; *Born:* Passaic, NJ; *Parents:* Vincenzo Pannullo, Giovannina Anzovino; *Spouse:* January 11, 1942, Frank J. Parnofiello; *Education:* Paterson State Teacher's College; New York University; Fairleigh Dickinson University; *Occupation:* Free Lance writer and translator; *Memberships:* NJ Press Club, NJ Professional women; *Honors:* Phi Zeta Kappa, Italian American authors and their contribution to American Literature; *Other writings:* Written a volume of poetry entitled, "Stolen Moments", "Change the World", "We Sing Our Praise to Mary"; *Personal note:* I attempt to exemplify, in my life, the compassionate depth of an understanding heart; a warm friendliness; quick sympathy; keen appreciation of beauty; and a strong feeling for life's little things; *Address:* 18 Fair Hill Road, Clifton, NJ.

PARDALLIS, VICKI

Born: December 12, 1970, Athens, Greece; *Parents:* Alexis John Pardallis and Dr. Maria Papanicolaou-Pardallis; *Education:* Boston University; *Occupation:* Student; *Honors:* British Literature Award; *Other writings:* I have written many poems, essays, and short stories in my spare time; *Personal note:* One cannot reach what he cannot dream but he can dream what he cannot reach, or what he thinks he cannot reach; *Address:* Medford, MA.

PARKER, EDNA MAE

Born: March 17, 1910, Leith, North Dakota; *Parents:* Jacob W. Good and Erma Meyers Good; *Spouse:* Laurence Yale Parker, August 19, 1938; *Children:* Mary Ann, Elisabeth; *Education:* Newspaper Institute of America; *Occupation:* Retire postmaster; *Memberships:* NAPUS, Cedarville Area Historical Society, Illinois Sheriffs Association, Assn of Chiefs of Police; *Honors:* Published author; *Other writings:* Published several books: "Every Memory Precious", "My Backyard Jungle", "My Unforgettable ABC"; *Personal note:* Writing from personal experience, to people of all ages, showing how God will help us, gives more true happiness than money can buy! *Address:* 125 W. Cherry Street, Cedarville, Il.

PARKINS, SILVIA

Born: July 15, 1925, Germany; *Spouse:* Will Parkins; *Children:* Will, Silvy; *Education:* High School Graduate; *Occupation:* Retired Teacher; *Honors:* Editor's Choice Award; *Other writings:* Has written children's stories and poems; *Personal note:* I like to focus on that which is good, honorable and beautiful around us, God made this world perfect, it is mankind who fails; *Address:* Box 104, Wauna, WA.

PARKS, RACHEL ANN

Born: April 19, 1976, Wingham, Ontario, Canada; *Parents:* Ray Parks and Ellen Parks; *Education:* Wellington St. Public School, Homedale Senior Elementary School; *Occupation:* Student; *Honors:* Academic honors in math, french, english, environmental studies; *Personal note:* Poetry helps me feel good about myself, it gives me a different perspective on life and the world; *Address:* 4 Isabel Street, St. thomas, Ontario, Canada.

PARRIS, ANGELA R.

Pen name: Angela Rousseve Parris *Born:* January 25, 1935, New Orleans, Louisiana; *Parents:* Dr. Ferdinand L. Rousseve and Elise Mirault Rousseve; *Spouse:* Joseph F. Parris, June 4, 1955; *Children:* Joseph F. Parris, Jr., Renee Parris, Mark A; *Education:* Thomas Secretarial School, Hesser College, Institute of Arts and Sciences, New Hampshire Technical Institute; *Memberships:* Postal Comemorative Society's U.S. First Day Cover Service; *Other writings:* "As a Child" published by the National Library of Poetry: Anthology 1988; "A Special Love" Published by American Poetry: Anthology 1988, Vol VIII No. 3; *Personal note:* It is my hope that all of our children will have support to excel to their potential. That they all will be seen as special people, each individual will sparkle with lights of many shades, to fill our world with new incentives, new ideas and new dreams; *Address:* P.O. Box 242, Henniker, NH.

PASQUARIELLO, LAURA ANNE

Born: July 13, 1972, Bellmore, New York; *Parents:* Maria Pasquariello and Joseph Pasquariello; *Education:* Norte Dame High School; *Occupation:* Student; *Memberships:* Drama Club, Dandy Striper, Italian Catholic Federation; *Honors:* Citizenship Award; *Personal note:* I would like people who read my poetry to enjoy it and be inspired by it; *Address:* 8685 Muir Drive, Gilroy, CA.

PATEL, ESTELA

Pen name: Estela Aboyme-Patel; *Born:* Manila, Philippines; *Parents:* Manuel Aboyme and Ving Aboyme; *Spouse:* Hemendra H. Patel, December 10, 1971; *Children:* Rikha, Sheila, Nina; *Education:* University of Santo Tomas; *Occupation:* Window Clerk; *Honors:* Dean's List; *Other writings:* Poems published in local Schaumburg APWU newsletter, World of Poetry, New American Poetry Anthology; *Personal note:* Treat others the way you want others to treat you; *Address:* Streamwood, IL.

PAYNE, LILLIAN WELLS

Born: September 20, 1910, Sumter, South Carolina; *Parents:* Pauline and James Richard Wells; *Education:* Duke Hospital; *Occupation:* Operating Room Supervisor; *Memberships:* Nurses State Association; *Honors:* Golden Poet Awards; Best New Poet, 1986; *Other writings:* Has published several poem entitled, "A Hurting World", "It Could have Been You", "Be Still"; *Address:* 3650 Hazarerre Church Road, Sumter, SC.

PEELER, ANITA JEANETTE

Pen name: Neat; *Born:* April 12, 1973, Spartanburg, SC; *Parents:* Debbie and Danny Peeler; *Education:* Landrum High School; *Occupation:* Student; *Memberships:* FCA, The Just Say No Club, The Pep Club, Science Club; *Honors:* MVP of Basketball Team, Penmanship Award, Outstanding Academic Achievement Award; *Other writings:* Write copy for the cardinal yearbook; *Personal note:* In my writing I like to reflect the issues of the current world concerning my friends and I; *Address:* 105 Edwards Road, Landrum, SC.

PENA, ALBA H. DELA

Born: April 24, 1942, Havana, Cuba; *Parents:* Alcibades De La Pena and Zoila Dela Pena; *Education:* Assumption Academy, Miami Florida; Sam Houston State University, BA; *Occupation:* Independent Marketing Representative; *Honors:* Kappa Delta Pi, Sigma Delta Pi; *Other writings:* Written other poems that have been published in church newsletter; Authored an unpublished short story and several children's books; *Personal note:* A writer's life should not be judged by his personal life; but by the fruits of the works he or she leaves behind; *Address:* Miami, FL.

PEREZ, MARIA H.

Pen name: Maria Hermintia Santana; *Born:* Chiloe' Chile, July 29, 1917; *Parents:* Ricardo Santana and Lavinia; *Spouse:* Jose R. Perez Sr., Mary 4, 1957; *Children:* Rick; *Education:* Liceo of Anoud High School, University of Chile School of Nurses, Henry Ford Community College; *Occupation:* Retired Register Nurse; *Memberships:* AARP; *Honors:*-Three Awards of Merit; *Other Writings;*Authored a novel and several articles and poems; *Personal note:* I am a Chilean American, retired register nurse, I have been always been inspired by poetry from the being of my school years; the classics have been a fascination for me. *Address:* 278 Sandpiper Avenue, Royal Palm Beach, FL.

PETERSON, DARRELL M.

Born: February 6, 1947, Sioux City, Iowa; *Parents:* Arnold and Agnes Peterson; *Occupation:* Electronic Assembler; *Honors:* 1988 Golden Poet Award, four honorable mentions; *Personal note:* I strive to reflect God's love in my writing I hope to encourage others to see the Glory to God; *Address:* 8668 Eastern Avenue, Byron, MI.

PETERSON, ELAINE

Born: December 22, 1920, Chicago, Illinois; *Parents:* Axel and Viola Meyer; *Spouse:* Harry E. Peterson, May 26, 1944; *Education:* Wright Junior College, Bryant and Stratton Business College; *Occupation:* Homemaker; *Memberships:* Danville Art League, Danville Symphony Orchestra Guild, Women in the Arts; *Honors:* National Library of Poetry-Editors, Choice Award, Honorable Mention, Ford Times, Famous Artists Finalist in Design Competition; *Other writings:* Poem published in the National Library of Poetry, American Anthology of poetry, published book entitled, "The Aerosal Game"; *Address:* 1311 N. Vermilion Street, Danville, IL.

PHILLIPS, NANCY A.

Born: March 30, 1955, Danville, IL.; *Parents:* Carl & Irene Makemson; *Spouse:* Bill J. Phillips, May 11, 1982; *Children:* Donald Ray, Carol Jean, Craig Shane; *Education:* Brainerd High School, McKenzie College, (with honors); *Occupation:* Clerical Secretary; *Other writings:* Has written several poems; *Personal note:* My first poem came to me in a dream, since then I have been inspired to write many more of my thoughts and feelings into words and rhythms, with God in my heart and hand there will be more; *Address:* 3207 Old Ringgold Road, East Ridge, TN.

PINKSTON, KELI

Pen name: KELI; *Born:* May 16, 1940, Ft. Collins. Colorado; *Parents:* W.A. Bowling-Edna Irene Minnick; *Children:* Kevin Allan, Keith Aaron, Kristin Michelle, Kyle Dean; *Education:* Missouri Valley College; *Occupation:* Writer and Artist; *Memberships:* Associate Member of the Academy of American Poets, ALDS Club; *Honors:* 4 Golden Poets Awards, 19 Merit Awards; *Other writings:* Several poems published in newspaper, 20 published in books of poetry one book published by myself; *Personal note:* If I am able to convey my feelings in poetry for other people to enjoy, then I know I have been chosen for a special reason, it is my hope that whoever reads my poems will receive all the feelings I feel when I put them down on paper; *Address:* 500 E. College Marshall, MO.

PITTMAN, NANETTE DORENE

Pen name: Nanny; *Born:* September 29, 1969, Frankfurt, Germany; *Parents:* Larry & Martha Pittman; *Spouse:* Carter Mitchell, May 6, 1989; *Education:* Loganville High School; *Occupation:* Self Employed; *Memberships:* YWCA; *Honors:* Senior Superlative; *Other writings: Making Love-it's Nothing at all, Yes, and they Are Gone*; *Personal note:* I write all my poems on personal experiencesl I love to write and hope that one day I will shine through at just the right time; *Address:* Rt 5, Old Zion Cemetary Road, Loganville, GA.

PLUNKETT, ROBERT BUTLER

Pen name: Robert Butler Lee; *Born:* June 7, 1965, Deer Park, Texas; *Parents:* Cecil E. Plunkett and Mildred Hope Plunkett; *Education:* Deer Park High School; *Occupation:* Marine; *Other writings:* Published in "On The Threshold of a Dream"; *Personal note:* One must sit down and discover his or her talents and then use them and know them like your best friend because they can be your greatest comfort; *Address:* 4410 Pasadena Blvd, Deer Park, TX.

POIRIER, MARIE-EVE

Born: December 24, 1973, Nova Scotia, Canada; *Parents:* Michel and Mimi Poirier; *Education:* 9th Grade, Dwight Ross School, Nova Scotia; *Occupation:* Student; *Honors:* Public Speaking Award, 3 Citizenship Awards, 2 Consistent Effort Awards; *Personal note:* I believe writing poetry is a way of putting thoughts into words, and a way to relieve my problems. *Address:* P. O. Box 864, Greenwood, Nova Scotia, Canada.

POLLWORTH, KAREN JOY

Pen name: The BRANCH; *Born:* April 4, 1947, Medina, New York; *Parents:* Viola Lindke and Norman Lindke;

Children: Kyle Alexander, Brian Richard, Jennifer Alicia; *Education:* NY State High School Regents; LPN Diploma; *Occupation:* Factory Worker; *Memberships:* Time Analmaly Research Assn; Citizen Organization to protect the Environment; *Honors:* Golden Poet Award, 1987 from World of Poetry; *Personal note:* Sisterly love was divinely inspired is dedicated to the memory of my brother-in-law; Douglas Donald Burdick, Sr.; *Address:* 24 Park Avenue, Middleport, NY.

PORTULAS, KIMBERLY
Born: March 12, 1973, Brunswick, Georgia; *Parents:* Barbara Gibbs, Guy Portulas; *Education:* Brantley County High School; *Other writings:* "His Eyes", "Lost in the Clouds", "Memories of Us", "Waiting", "Out with the Old, in with the New"; *Address:* P.O. Box 398, Waynesville, GA.

POWER, ANN MARIE
Education: MS, Psychology; PhD (antic.); *Occupation:* Student; *Other writings:* Written numerous poems and short articles; *Address:* West Los Angeles, CA.

PRICE, TAUNYA
Born: February 5, 1959, Baton Rouge, Louisiana; *Parents:* Howard and Mittie Yates; *Spouse:* Dale Stevenson Price, September 19 1982; *Children:* Julie LaFaye, Steve Jr., Lawanda Shauneen; *Education:* Enterrpise High School, Shasta College; *Occupation:* Carpenter; *Memberships:* Save the Animals Foundation; *Personal note:* Through my writing, I hope that everyone finds fulfillment of an empty time and place in their life "we all have endured". *Address:* Orangevale, CA.

PUDELSKI, JOHN
Pen name: JJ Pudelski; *Born:* March 6, 1969, Cleveland, Ohio; *Parents:* Dolores Pudelski, John Pudelski; *Education:* Saint Joseph High School; John Carroll University; *Occupation:* Student; *Memberships:* The Cleveland Free-net; *Other writings:* Several fantasy novels that have yet to be published, countless poems; *Personal note:* Fantasy at the limit of complexity is reality; Friends are a commodity only fools speculate on; *Address:* 1220 E. 175, Cleveland, OH.

PULLEY, ROBIN R.
Born: July 1, 1943, Murray, Utah; *Parents:* R.L. and Esther Robison; *Spouse:* Jerral R. Pulley, APril 2, 1987; *Children:* Deborah Dianne, Randy, Leon, Ryan Reed; *Education:* Jerome High School; Brigham Young University, Boise State University; *Occupation:* Stockbroker, Writer, Photography; *Memberships:* Photographic Society of America; National Assn Security Dealers; *Honors:* Idaho's outstanding young woman of the year, NAMPA's outstanding young woman of the year; photographs published nationally; *Other writings:* I am a lyricist working with a well know composer, my writings have had regional exposure, currently writing a book that is a combination of my writings and photograph; *Personal note:* Being able to express thoughts and feelings that strike the cords of common, human responsiveness gives me a great sense of joy in illuminating those feelings; *Address:* 2964 Sheffield Drive, Emmaus, PA.

PYLES, JENNIFER
Born: November 10, 1972, Everett, Washington; *Parents:* Bill and Mary Pyles; *Education:* Everett High; *Occupation:* Student; *Memberships:* Several Book Clubs, Girls Club, Tennis Team; *Honors:* Track ribbons, marching ribbons; *Other writings:* I've written other poems but have never turned them in for publication; *Personal note:* I strive to do the best in everything I do. Never give up when times get hard; *Address:* Everett, Washington.

QUIGLEY, KIMBERLY
Born: July 18, 1966, Salem, New Hampshire; *Parents:* Charlene and David Burke; *Spouse:* Herb Quigley, August 25, 1984; *Children:* Elyssa Brooke Quigley; *Education:* Timberlane High; Northern Essex College, (Dean's List); *Occupation:* Medical Transcriptionist; *Other writings:* Several poems which have not yet been published, songs and childrens stories which have not yet been published; *Personal note:* Follow your dreams for someday you will catch up to them; *Address:* P.O. Box 616, Epping, NH.

RACKLEY, KELLY
Born: July 31, 1973, Santa Barbara, California; *Parents:* Jay and Janet Rackley; *Education:* Irvine High School; *Occupation:* Student; *Personal note:* Always appreciate your best friend; *Address:* 49 Columbus Drive, Irvine, CA.

RAGERBEER, KHALONTIE
Pen name: Leana; *Born:* February 22, 1953, Guyana, South American; *Occupation:* Cashier; *Other Writings:* Unpublished copywrited lyric "My Tears Have Fallen"; *Personal note:* I thank Mother Durga and all the devas for guiding me on earth; *Address:* 5 Garden of Eden, East Bak Demerara, Guyana, SC.

RAYNOR, MONIQUE
Born: September 29, 1975, Bermuda; *Parents:* Willard and Carol Raynor; *Education:* Bermuda High School for Girls; *Honors:* The Emily Gray Memorial Prize; *Other writings:* Several poems published in the the school paper, "The BHS Voice"; *Personal note:* I hope that one day I will have a book published with just my poems in it; *Address:* Car-Wil, 212 Middle Road, Southampton SN04, Bermuda.

REAM, THERESE A.
Born: March 24, 1955, Altoona, Pennsylvania; *Parents:* Verneda A. & Leo J. Wachter, Sr.; *Spouse:* David Marion D. Ream, August 26, 1978; *Education:* St. Francis College; *Occupation:* Instructor of of Education; *Memberships:* Secular Franciscan Order, National Catholic Catechists Society, Assn for Supervision and Curriculum Development; *Honors:* SFC Education Department Award, 1977; *Personal note:* I intend for my writing to reflect my deep seated Franciscan spirituality which is profoundly incarnational yet utterly simple in nature. To everyone I wish the Lord's peace! *Address:* 1105 Robin Lane, Duncanscille, PA.

REED, LEANE H.
Born: August 17, 1947, Gardiner, Maine; *Parents:* Arand Hasselbrock, Adeline K. Hasselbrock; *Spouse:* D. Richard Reed, Sr., November 25, 1966; *Children:* D. Richard, Sheila L. Reed; *Education:* Hall-Dale High School, Husson College; *Occupation:* Secretary, Central Maine; *Other writings:* "A Query?", Published in Rhyme and Reason, Vol. I, Poetry Press; Migration, Published in American Poetry Anthology, Vol. VI, No. 5, American Poetry Assn; *Personal note:* Try to call everyone you meet "friend". *Address:* RFD #1, Box 733, Readfield, ME.

REIMERS, AMBER DAWN
Pen name: Bambi Dawn; *Born:* October 19, 1973, Iowa City, Iowa; *Parents:* Richard L. Reimers Sr. and Louise Reimers; *Education:* Muscatine High School; *Occupation:* Student; *Honors:* Honored student, has received many sports award; *Other writings:* Has written several poems; *Personal note:* Don't worry, be happy!; *Address:* 219 Pond Street, Muscatine, IA.

RENFRO, APRIL
Born: July 17, 1975, Madisonville, KY; *Parents:* Roger Renfro and Vanita Renfro; *Occupation:* Student; *Memberships:* Junior Beta Club; *Honors:* Talent Identification Program, Duke University; *Other writings:* Poem Published in local newspaper; *Personal note:* I greatly enjoy exploring the endless and boundless possibilities of writing; *Address:* P.O. Box 376, Mortons Gap, KY.

REYNALDO, ERAINA Q.
Pen name: Rainey Day; *Born:* June 23, 1945, Los Angeles, California; *Parents:* Glenn and Lillian Reynaldo; *Children:* Eraina, Leijuana, Stephani and Little Jimi; *Education:* Tocoma Community College; *Occupation:* Journeyman Barber; *Memberships:* NAACP; *Other writings:* "The Moon was Once Our Sun", "Grandeur Pettiness", "Paleozistorics"; *Personal note:* Science is fun, science should be shared, its assumptions discussed and written about by all peoples. I had more fun writing "Trop" then I ever had at the 'Whiskey A-go go' back in the sixties; *Address:* 112 Santa Barbara Plaza, Los Angeles, CA.

RICHARD, KATHY
Pen name: The Kat; *Born:* February 28, 1971, Abbeville, LA; *Parents:* Ella and Hulin Richard; *Occupation:* Student; *Personal note:* I Love poetry! I am just beginning to write and enjoy writing short stories and photography; *Address:* P.O. Box 52832, Lafayette, LA.

RICHARDS, MARY
Born: May 30, 1938, Lamar, Colorado; *Parents:* William Brown and Dora Brown; *Spouse:* Donald R. Richards, November 10, 1979; *Children:* Linda Irene; Alvin Eugene; Diane Renee; *Education:* Lamar Union High School; *Occupation:* Bookkeeping; *Memberships:* Unity of the High Plains; *Honors:* Editor's Choice Award; *Other writings:* A few articles of prose and numerous poems of which several are published in hardbound books; *Personal note:* "Our Minds are instrument of God's mind" to express my mind through poetry, knowing it is a gift from God, just gives me such an exhilarating feeling of reward; *Address:* 2026 Hawk Lane, Amarillo, TX.

RICHARDSON, JESSICA
Born: July 16, 1974, Oceanside, NY.; *Parents:* Bruce E. Richardson and Lynn C. Radtke; *Occupation:* Student; *Honors:* Science Recognition from Congressman; *Address:* Ronkonkoma, NY.

RICKMAN, PEGGY SUE
Pen name: Penny R. Kade; *Born:* May 5, 1957, Abilene, Kansas; *Parents:* Bruce and Karen Reiner; *Spouse:* Gary DS. Rickman, July 5, 1975; *Children:* Travis Robert, Nathan Gary, Amanda Dean; *Education:* Absarokee High School; *Occupation:* Writer; *Memberships:* Organzing member of local writer's group; *Other writings:* Written over 40 poems, working on poetry book to be published in 1989; Twice published in GRIT and local newspapers; *Personal note:* Speaking words of wisdom and writing your life through rhyme, doesn't make you insensitive but puts you in better step with time; *Address:* HC 55, Box 420, Fishtail, MT.

ROBITAILLE, PRISCILLA A.
Born: October 20, 1952, East Derry, New Hamsphire; *Parents:* Dana and Alice Rockwell; *Children:* Wendy; *Education:* Hood Junior High School; *Occupation:* Housewife; *Memberships:* Top Records, CRC Records; *Honors:* Golden Poet Award and numerous other commendation; *Other writings:* Has two songs up for a trial session entitled, "Your Loving Arms" and "Short Time Love"; *Personal note:* I am proud to mention that I just had a song released by Rainbow Records entitled, "Happy Birthday"; *Address:* Derry, NH.

RODGERS, KARALEIGH
Born: August 24, 1973, Casper, Wyoming; *Parents:* Harry and Lynda Rodgers; *Occupation:* Student; *Other writings:* Has published in World of Poetry; *Personal note:* I hope to encourage other young people to begin writing; *Address:* Evansville, WY.

ROLFS, MELYSSA
Born: May 9, 1970, Tuscaloosa, Alabama; *Parents:* Benne Rolfs, Sheryl Rolfs; *Education:* Washington High School; *Personal note:* My family and friends have been supportive and I hope to accomplish more in the future; *Address:* 816 30 Street, N.E., Cedar Rapids, IA.

ROPER, ERMA
Born: April 29, 1912, Coalville, Utah; *Parents:* Edward and Artrimesia Powell; *Spouse:* Russel Roper, January 7, 1946; *Children:* Jeanie Ricks, Paul D. Roper; *Education:* Brigham Young University; *Occupation:* Office worker; *Honors:* 1st prize awarded for quilts at county fairs; *Other writings:* Has written numerous poems; *Personal note:* Eluded predicted death at age 29, had to heart operations, I am thankfully living each day to the best of my ability, achieves contentment and peace; *Address:* 711 Beechwood Avenue, Vallejo, CA.

ROSASCO, SHARI LEE
Born: August 8, 1964, Rahway, NJ; *Parents:* John and Linda Shamus; *Spouse:* Robert Anthony Rosasco, April 4, 1987; *Education:* Charlotte High School, Real Estate School, Travel Agency School; *Occupation:* General Restaurant Manager, Real Estate Saleswoman; *Honors:* National Junior Honor Society; *Other writings:* Authored several poems and short stories; *Personal note:* Being able to see your poem in print and sharing it with the world is one of the most satisfying feelings a writer can have; *Address:* 223 Porto Velho Street, Port Charlotte, FL.

ROSIER, JOYCE
Pen name: Joy; *Born:* December 8, 1965, Brooklyn, NY; *Education:* Far Rockaway High School; *Personal note:* In God we trust, during the good times, as well as the bad. He comes through;

RYLANDER, AMALIA L.
Pen name: Sabina Cacho; *Born:* May 4, 1944, Belize, Central America; *Parents:* Zoilo Blanco, Francisca Blanco; *Spouse:* Herbert Rylander, December 10, 1977; *Children:* Christianne Joy Rylander, Zoilo Rylander; *Education:* St. Catherine Academy; California State University, BA; Hartford Seminary, MA; *Occupation:* Minister-Pastor; *Memberships:* Hartford Conference of Churches, Hartford Ministerial Alliance; *Honors:* Dean's List; *Other writings:* Has written "Two Widows"; "Maria Stewart: Hope Lady", "Jesus the Wine Maker", "Family Image"; *Personal note:* I like to write about the hidden strengths people possess; I am greatly influenced by biblical themes; *Address:* 870 Prospect Avenue, Hartford, CT.

SALTER, EVELYN SAPP
Born: May 10, 1929, Pace, Florida; *Parents:* John and Thelma Sapp; *Spouse:* Hughston Salter, August 16, 1952; *Children:* James, Hughston Jr., Betty, Bobbie, Judy; *Education:* Milton High School; *Occupation:* Retired; *Memberships:* AARP; *Honors:* Golden Poet Award, for 1985, 1986, 1988; Song Writers Award, 16 Awards of Merit, Editor Choice Award; *Other writings:* Has published numerous poems; *Personal note:* Happiness is only a state of mind, real happiness comes from within and we have to look within our own selves to find it, I was influenced a great deal by Edgar Allan Poe; *Address:* 3807 Rolf Drive, Tallahassee, FL.

SALTZ, ELIZABETH
Born: June 15, 1930, Brooklyn, New York; *Parents:* Arthur and Minnie Saltz; *Spouse:* David Klinick, September 1963; *Children:* Bob, Lisa; *Education:* Queens College, BA; *Occupation:* Social Caseworker; *Memberships:* Queens College Alumni Assn; *Honors:* 35 Award of Merit Certificate; *Other*

writings: "Dreams to Dream", "Loves Greatest Treasures"; *Personal note:* Poetry is a source of inspiration when it flows from the heart, once a hobby it presents ideas of philosophy, it is the moving spirit that guides one, great poets speak words or wisdom; *Address:* 88-178th Street, Jamaica, NY.

SANDERS, KAREN NORDBERG

Born: March 14, 1939, Washington, DC; *Parents:* John and Lydia Nordberg; *Spouse:* Donald Wilson Sanders; June 11, 1960; *Children:* Kathleen Annette, David Mark, Scott Allen; *Education:* Hood College, BA; Texas Woman's University, MED; North Texas University, PHD; *Occupation:* Teacher; *Memberships:* Assn of Supervision and Curriculum Development, Richardson Educator's Assn, Kindergarten Teacher of Texas; *Honors:* Delta Kappa Gamma; Phi Delta Kappa; Bill Grey Award for Excellence in Teaching Free Enterprise, 1st and 2nd Prize in Elementary Division; *Other writings:* Has written numerous poems, Curriculum in Elementary Economist, Phonics Songs; *Personal note:* My verse reflects the turmoil and humor I find in everyday life. This poem is one of a collection about children entitled "Pockets of Innocents"; *Address:* 25 Shady Core, Richardson, TX.

SANTUCCI, RITA

Born: May 15, 1970, Pittsburgh, PA.; *Parents:* Maria Santucci; *Education:* River High School, 1988, School of Business; *Occupation:* Student, Cashier; *Other writings:* Has written numerous poems; *Personal note:* This poem has helped me finally deal with the death of my father at the age of 4. Whenever it's read I feel him in my heart. I'm glad I could share it with others; *Address:* 436 Parker Street, Verona, PA.

SAUNDERS, JULIE DEANN

Born: July 28, 1972, Henryetta, Oklahoma; *Parents:* Phyllis Davis and Toby Davis; *Education:* Henryetta High School; *Occupation:* Student; *Memberships:* Muscogee Creek Nation; Henryetta High School Band, Drill Team; *Honors:* 1st place in Alexander Posey Poetry Contest, Lettered in high school band; *Personal note:* I have been influenced by great poets, encouraged by family, peers; my goal is not only to be a successful writer, but also a more developed one; *Address:* P.O. Box 41, Henryetta, OK.

SCHAEFFER, KARL

Born: August 15, 1959, Howell, Michigan; *Occupation:* Graphic Artist; *Memberships:* Publisher's Clearing House President's Club; *Other writings:* Two collections of poetry-lyrics, currently co-writing a collection of short stories; *Personal note:* Inspired writing can be fun, especially when done for profit; *Address:* 1902 Hussion, Houston, TX.

SCHIFFER, RICHARD DAVID

Born: September 1, 1969, Abington, Pennsylvania; *Parents:* Richard Schiffer and Jane Wolvington; *Education:* The Academy of the New Church Boys School, 1988; *Occupation:* Student; *Memberships:* Boys Scouts of America, Bryn Athyn Fire Company, Festerville Fire Company; *Honors:* Nat'l Honor Society, White Horse Chapter, Union League of Philadelphia's Boys Citizenship Award; *Other writings:* Several poems published in school newspaper, poem for "New Church Home"; *Personal note:* My poems seek to make the reader aware of the presence of the Lord in everything around us. The writings of Emanuel Swendenborg have strongly influenced me; *Address:* P.O. Box 212, Huntingdon Valley, PA.

SCHMIDT, RITA KRISTINE

Pen name: Kristie Schmidt; *Born:* August 14, 1970, Philadelphia, PA; *Parents:* Joseph Schmidt and Rita Schmidt; *Education:* Buck County Community College; *Occupation:* Student; *Memberships:* Dance Association, Alumni Association High School, Community Service Corps, French Club; *Honors:* Dance Awards, Perfect Attendance, Hemisphere pageant title winner; *Other writings:* Several Poems published in the high school newspaper; *Personal note:* I enjoy writing poems for my family and friends. I want to accomplish something for myself and to show my talent to other people. I was greatly influenced by my sister and brother-in-law, who showed me how to express my feelings; *Address:* 9 Maureen Road, Holland, PA.

SCHNEIDER, MARC S.

Born: October 29, 1957, Kansas City, Missouri; *Parents:* Gerald and Marjorie Schneider; *Education:* Bear Creek High School; *Occupation:* Cook/Chef, Chauffer and Clerk; *Memberships:* National Trust/Beer Drinkers of America; *Other writings:* Several poems, writing a manuscript; *Personal note:* Trust in God work the best you can and respect and honor your parents but also remember that when it's time to go don't be afraid to go with someone you trust; *Address:* P.O. Box 94, Sedalia, CO.

SCHNEIDER, SOREN

Born: December 26, 1942, Germany; *Education:* PDP, BGS; *Occupation:* Teacher; *Memberships:* BC Teachers Federation; *Other writings:* Has written numerous poems: "Nature Summer", "A Prayer", "A Winter Scene", "The Approach of Winter", "The Snowman"; *Personal note:* In my poetry, I try to express my feelings and thoughts in such a way, that it gives the reader a vivid portrait of what I am writing about, this particular poem goes out to my family and to the students I have taughts;

SCHOFIELD, JEN

Born: July 1, 1972, Clinton, MA.; *Parents:* Dale and Debra Schofield; *Education:* Orford High School; *Honors:* Art and Science Award; *Other writings:* Have written several other poems; *Personal note:* My poetry reflects upon my thoughts and creates an important way of thinking for people, in a manner which one will stop and think about what can be seen not only with the eyes but with the heart; *Address:* Rt. 118, Box 70E, Warren, NH.

SENAN, DINESH

Born: June 3, 1962, Singapore; *Parents:* G. S. and Shiva Senan; *Spouse:* Sugidha Nithiananthan (fiance); *Education:* National University of Singapore; *Occupation:* Lawyer; *Memberships:* International Law Association (Australian Branch); *Other writings:* Several poems published in the Straits Times, Singapore; A number of poems published in a local anthology of Singapore poetry; *Personal note:* I believe that poetry is a most enjoyable thing, and I hope that writers and publishers will continue to assume the collective responsibility to make this art form available to the people of the world; *Address:* 44 Jalan Terubok, Singapore 2057, Republic of Singapore.

SETTLE, HEATHER DIONNE

Pen name: Dionne; *Born:* September 24, 1974, Lubbock, Texas; *Parents:* Darlene and Larry Settle; *Education:* Crockett Jr. High, W. T. Hanes Elementary; *Occupation:* Student; *Honors:* Solo and Ensemble first place medals, 800m dash first place in city, 8th grade favorite, All Region Choir; *Personal note:* I write the words of my life and the feelings of my heart in my poems. *Address:* 4129 Highcrest Drive, Irving, Texas.

SHAHIJANIAN, ADRINEH

Born: February 23, 1974, Tehran, Iran; *Parents:* Madis Shahijanian, Knarit Shahijanian; *Occupation:* Student; *Honors:* Valedictorian in Junior High School; *Personal note:* I try to show the human need for love. I've been influenced by all kinds of novel authors from Charles Dickens to S.E. Hinton. If one person improved their life because of me, then I've been rewarded ten folds; *Address:* 2136 18th Avenue, San Francisco, CA.

SHAW, EDWIN L.

Born: September 29, 1949, San Jose, California; *Parents:* Paul F. Shaw and Betty J. Shaw; *Spouse:* Lota T. Shaw, November 4, 1979; *Children:* Erwyn Teseoro, Abinadi Rafael, Joseph Morain Cumer; *Education:* New Plymouth High; *Occupation:* Sailor; *Personal note:* The mind is full of thoughts that can help anyone on earth, but if not used will stop the growth of many nations, but it must be used for good not evil to be a help; *Address:* USS Midway CV-41, FPO, SF, CA.

SHAW, JILL JOSETTE

Born: June 7, 1961, St Joseph, Missouri; *Parents:* George Shaw and Joanna Noonan; *Education:* AAS, BS; *Occupation:* Social Worker; *Memberships:* St. Peter Lutheran Church, Planetary Society, Unknown Writer's Grapevine; *Honors:* Excellence in Journalistic Writing, Excellence as an Editor; *Other writings:* Poetry published in various anthology books; Currenting a novel about a woman's frustrating search for the right man; *Personal note:* My poetry reflects upon the shortness of life and the neverending quest to fulfill one's destiny; *Address:* 311 ½ North 16 Street, St. Joseph MO.

SHERMAN, JOSEPH JOHN

Pen name: J.J., Dr. Joseph J. Sherman, Joseph J. Sherman; *Born:* July 10, 1927, Yonkers, New York; *Parents:* Roland E. Sherman Sr. and Leona B. Sherman; *Spouse:* Frankie C. Sherman; *Children:* Linda Guthrie; *Education:* Cazenovia Junior College, Hobart College, Valparaiso Law School, JD; *Occupation:* Lapidarist, Instructor; *Memberships:* Founder of Macon Co. Gem and Mineral Society, President; *Honors:* Phi Alpha Delta; *Other writings:* Authored three books: "Secrets of Gem Stone Cutting", "Gems in the Rough", "Augulations"; Published poems and songs: "Tell Me", wrote for Glasford Gazette and Pulitzer Prize Newspaper; *Personal note:* To leave a footprints in "Lifes" Span of Time; *Address:* P.O. Box 527, Franklin, NC.

SIDES, TAMERA

Born: March 15, 1971, Houston, Texas; *Parents:* Barry Sides, Lynda Sides; *Education:* University of Texas; *Occupation:* Student; *Memberships:* Greenpeace Amnesty International, International Thespian Society, The Living Bank, Whale Adoption Project, Earth Island Institute, Center for Environmental Education; *Honors:* Who's Who Among American High School Students, Literary Magazine Editor, Honor Bar Thespain; *Other writings:* Written several poems in school literary Magazine; *Personal note:* I lay the things that mean the most beside my heart so they will never go away. *Address:* Houston, TX.

SIMMONS, SHIRLEY J.

Born: July 24; *Education:* Pace University; *Occupation:* Teacher; *Memberships:* Poets and Writers; *Honors:* Published Author; *Other writings:* "Song of Circe"; *Personal note:* Poetry is a wonderful way of arriving at an understanding of all the philosophies of life and as such has served as my "religion". It permitted me to consort with the greatest minds that civilization has produced. It can serve the purpose for all that think and love beauty and understanding; *Address:* P.O. Box 7496, APO NY.

SIMPSON, MARSHALL P.

Born: Edenton, North Carolina, July 15, 1929; *Parents:* Edward J. Simpson, J. Evelyn Welch Simpson; *Spouse:* Glenda Jordan Simpson, December 21, 1957; *Children:* Mark Lee, Elizabeth Elaine; *Education:* Old Dominion University, BS; *Occupation:* Procurement Analyst; *Memberships:* Disabled American Veterans; *Address:* 2160 Armada Drive, Chesapeake, VA.

SIZEMORE, JENNIFER

Born: October 27, 1973, Portales, New Mexico; *Parents:* Paula Sizemore and Darrell Sizemore; *Education:* Smithfield Junior High School; *Occupation:* Student; *Memberships:* International Rainbow for Girls, Girls Softball Association; *Honors:* Various awards in rainbow, several softball trophies, medals in target shooting; *Other writings:* I've written several poems but I've never tried to publish them; *Personal note:* Poetry helps me to escape from the real world and enter a fantasy land; I'm influenced greatly by my encounters as a growing woman; *Address:* 7723 West Cliff, N. Richaland Hills, TX.

SLOSSER, SHEPPARD, BETTY JANE

Pen name: Betty Jane Sheppard; *Born:* November 29, 1932, Trenton, NJ; *Parents:* Florence Leona Spafford and Thomas Allen Sheppard; *Spouse:* George Slosser, Jr., February 9, 1952; *Children:* Mark, Florence Ann; *Education:* Trenton Central High School; *Occupation:* Housewife; *Honors:* Commendations awarded in high school; *Other writings:* Has written a private collection of poetry; *Personal note:* I like people, we're really all the same yet quite different. We all laugh and cry the same, but have different personalities; *Address:* 1099 S. Broad Street, Trenton, NJ.

SMITH, KATHERINE A.

Pen name: Katherine A Smith-Kathy Amber; *Born:* October 18, 1967, Melbourne, Australia; *Parents:* Anne and Brian; *Education:* BS; *Occupation:* Writer, Nanny, Boarding School Supervisor; *Memberships:* Christian Workcamps *Honors:* Awards for Poetry, Dog Training, Guitar Playing; *Other writings:* Several books in the melting pot, countless poems, most are unpublished; *Personal note:* I am not afraid of tomorrow, for I have have seen yesterday and I love today; Also to Mum and Dad-Cheers!; *Address:* 2 Avenue Road, Glebe, Sydney NSW, 2037 AUSTRALIA.

SMITH, SARA MICHELLE

Pen name: Erin Smith; *Born:* August 20, 1976, Flint, Michigan; *Parents:* Janice Kay Smith and Gary Fredrick Smith; *Occupation:* Student; *Honors:* AWANA Award, Spring Hill Camps Certificate of Tennis Achievement; *Personal note:* I never expected any work of mine to be published; *Address:* 409 River Bend Drive, Flushing, MI.

SMITH, THOMAS F.

Born: February 15, 1941, New York, NY; *Parents:* Thomas and Margaret Smith; *Education:* MA; *Occupation:* Writer, Investor; *Memberships:* American Foreign Polcy, American Poetry Association, AUSA; *Other writings:* Published in New Voices in American Poetry, 1985, 1988; American Poetry Association; *Personal note:* I began writing after a "Born Again" experience, it was God's gift to me; *Address:* 1560 Unionport Road, NY, NY;

SNYDER, JENNIFER M.

Born: August 10, 1973, Denver, Colorado; *Education:* Lakewood High School; *Occupation:* Student; *Other writings:* Written numerous poems; *Personal note:* I adore nature because it's so beautiful and free. I am also a sixties fanatic. My greatest influence and idol is a talented musician and poet-Dovonan Leitch; *Address:* 2545 Allison, Lakewood, CO.

SONKSEN, COLETTE FAITH

Born: August 23, 1972, Grand Rapids, Michigan; *Parents:* Raymond E and Faith H. Sonksen; *Occupation:* Student; *Personal note:* My poems reflect my own feelings. I would like to say, my teachers, family and friends help me feel good about what I write and to write more; *Address:* 1264 Northey, Waterloo, IA.

SPARKS, SANDRA B.

Born: March 7, 1955, Bryan, Texas; *Parents:* L.C. Sparks & Ella Mae Sparks; *Children:* LaShay, Tracey, Jamie, Charity, Bobby, James; *Occupation:* Student; *Other writings:* Has written several poems, several songs; *Personal note:* I try to do my best in all that I do, God has inspired me greatly, I give thanks and love to him; *Address:* 2209 W. 30th Street, Bryan, TX.

SPAULDING, CARISSA ANN
Born: July 30, 1969, Fort Smith, Arkansas; *Parents:* Gary Spaulding and Penny Spaulding; *Education:* Northside High School; *Occupation:* Salesperson; *Personal note:* I enjoy writing as a form of relaxation, self expression and education; *Address:* Rt 1, Box 124-10, Alma, AR.

SPOTTS, S.L.
Born: June 28, Ashland, Ohio; *Children:* Paul Douglas; *Education:* Kent State University; *Occupation:* Teacher; *Memberships:* NEA; *Personal note:* To be of service and share my insights with others; *Address:* 1265 Beach Avenue, Rochester, NY.

ST PETERS, JOAN
Born: May 9. 1972, Alton, Illinois; *Parents:* Rodger and Kathy St. Peters; *Education:* Jersey Community High School; *Memberships:* Spanish Club, Swing Choir; *Honors:* National Library of Poetry, World of Poetry, 4 Awards; *Other writings:* US-and many yet unpublished works; *Personal note:* Sometimes it snows in April, sometime I feel so bad, sometimes I wish, that life was neverending, but all good things, they say, never last; *Address:* RR #3, Box 193D, Jerseyville, IL.

STANCIEL, CYNTHIA HALL
Born: Detroit, Michigan; *Parents:* Eugene & Dorothy Hall; *Children:* Rachel Gabriel; *Education:* Eastern Michigan University; *Occupation:* Writer-Poet; *Address:* Detroit, MI.

STAUFFER, PATRICIA IRENE COLE
Born: February 11, 1957, Hillsdale, Michigan; *Parents:* Kenneth Cole, Ruby Cole; *Spouse:* Martin L. Stauffer, July 15, 1978; *Children:* Timothy Dale, Jonathan Phillip; *Education:* Hillsdale High School; Manchester College; *Occupation:* Dairy Wife, Author; *Memberships:* MADD, Polo Arts Council, Cab Scouts Committee Member, CBN; *Honors:* Honorable Mention, Writer's Digest Competition, Short Story "Captured"; *Other writings:* Has written numerous poems and song lyrics; *Personal note:* I write for escape and enjoyment, I hope those who read my writing learn something valuable as well. To share a thought with another person is one of the greatest things in the world; *Address:* 106 N. Evergreen Road, Polo, IL.

STEFANAC, LEANNE
Honors: Published in "On The Threshold of a Dream"; *Other writings:* Authored published writings; *Address:* 41 Judith Avenue, Cabramatta, NSW, Australia.

STONE, LAURA BARNHART
Pen name: Laura Bristain Stone; *Born:* April 17, 1941, Panama, Republica de Panama; *Parents:* Walter Lloyd Barnhart and Isabel Coco Bristan; *Spouse:* John Eaton Stone, Jr.; *Children:* Teresa, Laura, Camille, Gerald, Leonard, Alessandra; *Education:* Cochise College; *Occupation:* Housewife; *Honors:* Appeared in the Register of Outstanding Junior and Community College Students; Winner of several awards; *Other writings:* Unpublished poem; wrote for the Apache, Cochise College Newspaper; *Personal note:* My childhood was filled with the sounds of music and poetry as my grandmother trained and coached my aunts who sang and recited poetry on their own radio programs; *Address:* 125 Carl Hayden Drive, Sierra Vista, AZ.

STRAIN, LIAH
Born: September 7, 1976, Orlando, Florida; *Parents:* Ed & Cecilia Strain; *Personal note:* Loves to write about humor and other things that will make people laugh; *Address:* P.O. Box 520666, Longwood, FL.

STRICKLAND, LOLA
Born: October 31, 1971, Savannah, Georgia; *Parents:* Judy and Ed Strickland; *Education:* Windsor Forest High School; *Memberships:* Amnesty International; *Personal note:* Although I am young, I think I tend to write about more complex subjects then those my age, which can be both good and bad; *Address:* 117 Wilshire Blvd, Savannah, GA.

STUART, JOHN T.
Education: University of Wisconsin, BA; *Occupation:* Student; *Memberships:* Wet Ink; *Other writings:* Several poems and one short story published in the Muse, campus literary paper; *Personal note:* I view my writing as a means of self exploration. I have been influenced by my mother, by some of my former English professors, and by the work of William Wordsworth; *Address:* Deerfield, IL.

STYER, SHARON
Born: November 30, 1972, West Chester, PA; *Parents:* Kathy Styer and J. Penrose Styer; *Education:* East High School; *Other writings:* Several unpublished poems; *Personal note:* The poem "Always a Friend" was inspired by three of

my close friends, I was mainly influenced to write poetry by my ninth grade English teacher; *Address:* 1210 Sylvan Road, West Chester, PA.

SULLIVAN, ANN MARIE
Born: April 2, 1952, Chicago, Illinois; *Parents:* John and Betty Cologna; *Children:* Ann Marie; *Occupation:* Insurance Agent; *Memberships:* CAIW, NAFE; *Personal note:* We are here to learn;

SUMMER, CLODAH G.
Born: January 23, 1918, Hudson, Ohio; *Education:* San Antonio College; *Occupation:* Freelance Writer, Poet, Photographer, Ham Artist; *Memberships:* International On-The-Beam Club; The Bulverde Area Human Society; *Honors:* Won many honorable mentions and the Golden Poet's Award, 1986, 1987, 1988; *Other writings:* Has written poems entitled, "Courage to Tackle", "Many a Mile", "Query Yourself", "Twilight Years", "Rain Predictions", "Night Owe's 7 AM Reluctance", "Even Without Skin", "Santa Speaks Intelligence"; *Personal note:* Poetry helped relax my mind after high school and gave me self expression. My interests in psychology science and metaphysics show up in my poetry. I try to teach important lessons in life; *Address:* 950 Redcloud Drive, San Antonio, TX.

TALLMAN, PERRY VANCE
Pen name: Thet Wood; *Born:* January 7, 1967; Montpelier, Vermont; *Parents:* Maxine Tallman and Gilbert Tallman; *Education:* Harwood Union High School; *Honors:* Editor's Choice Award, 1988; *Other writings:* Published in Poetic Voices of American Anthology, 1988; also the American Poetry Anthology Volume VIII, No. 2, 1988 Poem "Maple Sugaring"; *Personal note:* Lessons we learn are like candles that burn, to light a darkened hallway...I have very diverse tastes when it comes to writing poetry, but I hope everyone finds enjoyment in my writings; *Address:* RD #2, Box 1485, Waterbury, VT.

TAYLOR, CAROL L.
Born: June 7, 1969, Fairless Hills, PA.; *Parents:* James and Dolores Taylor; *Education:* Bishop Conwell High, Bucks County Community College, Centenary College; *Occupation:* Secretary; *Memberships:* Catholic Youth Organization; *Other writings:* Has written numerous poem and speeches; *Personal note:* Thing are really hectic here in the land of make believe; *Address:* Failess Hills, PA.

TEMME, MARK E.
Born: April 10, 1955, Fond du Lac, Wisconsin; *Education:* High School; *Occupation:* Security Officer *Honors:* Editor's Choice Award, 1988; *Other writings:* Minstrel Poet, 1980; Deiter Hess, 1985; *Personal note:* Influence by the writings of Baruch Spimoza and Marcus Aurelius; *Address:* Stockton, CA.

THOMAS, PENELOPE TRIER
Pen name: Penne T. Thomas; *Born:* July 4, 1946, Akron, Ohio; *Parents:* Wayne and Bette Dillinger; *Spouse:* Adam Thomas; *Education:* University of Virginia; *Occupation:* Writer, Homemaker, Editor; *Memberships:* Vineyard Christian Fellowship, Christian Writer's Group *Honors:* College Scholarship, 1988 Editor's Award; *Other writings:* Publish a bimonthly Christian newsletter/study; several poems published in anthologies. Have previously had booklets on leadership, motivation and public speaking published, allegorical novel in progress; *Personal note:* I love the Lord Jesus and strive to bring glory to God through the writing gift he has given me, whatever the subject matter; *Address:* P.O. Box 4263, Anaheim, CA.

TOLLISON, ROBYN M.
Born: January 7, 1974, Augusta, Georgia; *Parents:* Robert Lynn and Patricia Ann Tollison; *Education:* 9th grade, Hephzibah High School, Augusta, Georgia; *Occupation:* Student; *Memberships:* High School Student Council, Drama Club, French Club, School Band, Cheerleader; *Honors:* Have had several musical awards (flute), modeling titles and scholastic honors; *Other writings:* I write poetry of all types for a hobby. To me it's an easy way to express my thoughts. I see literature as a challenge and when people can relate to my work I feel satisfied; *Personal note:* I have one motto which is: Having no goals is like a plane with no wings...you never make it off the ground; *Address:* P. O. Box 58, Hephzibah, Georgia.

TRAXLER, JOY ELEXAL
Born: September 28, 1975, Vicksburg, MS. *Parents:* Ed Douglas & Glenda Faye Traxler; *Education:* Warren Central Junior High School; *Occupation:* Student; *Address:* 199 Clear Creek Road, Vicksburg, MS.

TREND-TROUERN, KATHERINE
Born: October 5, 1970, Hartford, CT; *Parents:* John B.G. Trouern-Trend and Violet M. Trovern-Trend; *Education:* Simsbury High School, University of Maine; *Occupation:* Student; *Memberships:* Circle K International; *Other writings:* One poem published in local newspaper another published in the American Poetry Anthology; *Personal note:*

With my writing I am extending myself to the world, a helping hand does not have physical limitations, the more you give the more you learn; *Address:* Simsbury, CT.

TRIBBLE, FREDERIC D.
Pen name: Duste; *Born:* November 5, 1912, Franklin, Kentucky; *Children:* Ron, Al, Larry, Fred, Mike, Donna Jean; *Occupation:* Retired Musician; *Memberships:* American Legion, ASCAP, American Society of Composers, Authors and Publishers; *Honors:* Numerous military awards and commendations; *Other writings:* Has written music and poems; *Personal note:* To meet people and do my best to make others happy, especially the elderly and disabled, people from all walks of life, this has brought me great happeness; *Address:* P.O. Box 382, Salem, OR.

TUTTLE, LARRY L.
Born: December 5, 1942, Newberg, Oregon; *Parents:* Lawrence J and Bernice Tuttle; *Occupation:* Poet; *Other writings:* Has written numerous poems; *Personal note:* Have faith in God, for all things are possible; *Address:* P.O. Box 1654, Fernely, NV.

UHLMANN, KATE
Born: June 6, 1974, Kansas City, Missouri; *Parents:* John Uhlmann, Patricia Werthan Whlmann; *Honors:* Headmasters List; *Personal note:* I express my feelings and private thoughts in my writings, so they will always be preserved. *Address:* 8221 Nall Avenue, Prairie Village, KS.

UNIACKE, JENNIFER BRONTE
Born: October 5, 1962, Oakland California; *Parents:* Anne Stephens, Stan Stephens; *Spouse:* Thomas Uniacke, October 24, 1987; *Children:* Stephanie Anne Uniacke; *Education:* High School; *Occupation:* Freelance; *Memberships:* National Writers Union, Writers Connection, Media Alliance, National Writer Club; *Other writings:* "Love is a blanket", "Sweet Dreams to Sidney", "I Do, "Death of a Love Judge and Jury"; *Address:* #2 Geneva Apt 10, San Francisco, CA.

VAN MEER, DAVID J.
Born: August 10, 1950, San Deigo, California; *Parents:* Marvin R. & Lillian C. Van Meer; *Education:* Concrete High School, Skagit Valley Community College, Western Washington University; *Occupation:* Business Manager, Computer Operator; *Memberships:* Self Realization Fellowship, North West Gamers Guild; *Honors:* Dean's List, 1st KSVR Radio Award; *Other writings:* Written poems that have been published in Beacon Review; *Personal note:* In my work I strive to catch the essence of a moment, the strength of an emotion as it slips into eternity, I am influenced by Chinese and Japanese poets; *Address:* 310 Myrtle-#402, Mount Vernon, WA.

VENTALORO, JESSIE
Pen name: Rusty; *Born:* December 11, 1934, Smiths' Grove, Kentucky; *Parents:* Alice Williams Prudich & Rusten Castellanos; *Spouse:* Vincent Ventaloro, February 12, 1956; *Children:* Michele Lillian, Paul, Mary Alice; *Other writings:* Currently working on non-fiction book about the homeless; *Address:* 823 NE High School Road, Bainbridge Island, WA.

VILARDI, ANDREA
Born: December 31, 1965, Queens, New York; *Parents:* John and Joanne Vilardi; *Education:* Farmingdale High School; *Occupation:* Receptionist; *Other writings:* 15 other poems, plus I wrote a story that was published in a christian magazine; *Personal notes:* I believe that through my poems I can reflect how the lord loves his people; my inspiration to writing is given to me by God; *Address:* 109 Henry Street, North Massapequa, NY.

WADDELL, WENDY
Born: February 20, 1974, Patuxent River, Maryland; *Parents:* Linda Cooper and Ray Waddell; *Education:* Coronado High School; *Occupation:* Student; *Memberships:* Drama Club, Youth to Youth Club; *Honors:* Language Arts Award, Presidential Academic Fitness Award, Voted Most Talented in 8th Grade; *Other writings:* Several poems and short stories which are unpublished; *Personal note:* I want all of my poems to have some sort of personal message to the reader, I want my poems to arouse the thinking of all who read them; *Address:* 549 F Avenue, Coronado, CA.

WALCH, PHILLIP O.
Pen name: Phil Walch; *Born:* March 16, 1944, Seattle, Washington; *Parents:* Ozzie and Ruth Walch; *Education:* North Idaho College, AA; University of Idaho, BS; *Occupation:* Factory Expeditor; *Memberships:* World Vision, World of Poetry; *Honors:* Silver Poet Award, 1986; Golden Poet Awards, 1987 and 1988; 14 Honorable Mentions; *Other writings:* The News Press, 1986 and 1987, Kellogg, Idaho 2 poems published, Eye on Cherry-Cherry Textron, 1983; and 1986, 2 poems published; several times published by American Poetry Association, Poetry Center and World of Poetry;

Personal note: Preparing book of poems to be titled, "Testimony of Hope, Tears", and "Prayers"; Themes: Nature, childred, Spiritual Growth; *Address:* Santa Ana, CA.

WALLS, EDWIN E.

Born: May 22, 1968, Manassas, Virginia; *Parents:* Albert C. Walls and Jacqueline B. Walls; *Education:* Northern Virginia Community College; *Occupation:* Graphic Artist; *Memberships:* World Tae Kwon Do Federation; *Honors:* 1st Degree Black Belt, Who's Who American High School Student; *Other writings:* Articles published in Journal Messenger, American Poetry Assn, Anthology Vol VIII, No. 5 "In Her"; *Personal note:* In my poetry I strive to touch the heart and enlighten the mind. My life has been influenced by Edgar Allen Poe and Henry David thoreau; *Address:* 9700 Dean Drive, Manassas, VA.

WALTER, JULIE ANN

Born: June 28, 1965, Taft, California; *Parents:* Ruth Elaine MacIntyre, James Deland Walter; *Education:* South Broward High School; *Occupation:* Travel Consultant; *Memberships:* East Coast Academy of Poets; *Other writings:* "The Other Brother Glass Windows", Still Beautiful Around me"; *Personal note:* You're my best friends, advisors and directors. Through your love, expression blossoms freely, thanks Mom and dad; *Address:* 52 S.W. 5th Street, Dania, FL.

WARD, MORRIS E.

Pen name: Morris Eldon Ward *Born:* October 10, 1923, Los Angeles California; *Parents:* M.L. and Flossie Ward; *Spouse:* Geri Ward, July 31, 1943; *Children:* Roger A., Lynn Ellyn, Mark E.; *Occupation:* Mait. Welder (Retired); *Memberships:* Masonic Fraternity, Shrine, Scottish Rite, York Rite; *Honors:* World of Poetry Award and 3 Certificates, Several Anthologies; *Other writings:* Newspaper and an upcoming quarterly; *Personal note:* I have been writing verse or poems to my wife and daughter for years and finally decided to see if anyone else would like them. A great feeling and enjoyment; *Address:* P.O. Box 1126 Chester, CA.

WASHINGTON, GLORIA J.

Born: December 30, 1955, Cook County, Chicago, IL; *Parents:* Walter and Winnie Moore; *Children:* Latrisha, Samuel Jr., Samantha and Anecia; *Education:* Jackson Central High, Hinds Junior College, Mississippi College; *Occupation:* Graphics Specialist; *Memberships:* American Society for professional and Executive Women; *Honors:* Phi Theta Kappa, PE Award, Bibical Counselor; *Other writings:* Editor of "Household of Faith:, Church's Newsletter; Letter published in Essence Magazine, also has written other poems for various occasions; *Personal note:* I am inspired by God when I write and my work reflects his divine inspiration. To God be the glory! *Address:* 6501 Lake Forest Drive, Jackson, MS.

WEHR, JUNE L.

Born: December 11, 1933, Duquesne, Pennsylvania; *Parents:* Mr and Mrs Albert Larson; *Spouse:* Robert Wehr, November 29, 1953; *Children:* Keith Leroy, Todd Larson, Craig Gordon; *Education:* Zelienople High School; Pinkerton Business; *Occupation:* Owner and Manager; *Memberships:* Zelienople Historical Society, Butler County Visitor Bureau, Aglow Fellowship; *Other writings:* Song published with Singspiration, Articles published in Christian Life; *Personal note:* I write of feelings within and trust it will touch hearts in a positive way; *Address:* RD #1 Box 241, Portersville, PA.

WEISENBERGER, MARY BETH

Born: February 15, 1872, Cincinnati, Ohio; *Parents:* Cliff & Sally Weisenberger; *Education:* Diamond Oaks Vocational School; *Memberships:* Business Professionals of America; *Honors:* Citizenship Awards, Volunteering Awards, Writers Awards, Band Awards, President of the Word Processing Class of 1990 Award; *Other writings:* Several Poems and Short Stories; *Personal note:* To Always have a good time and live one day at a time. To always try your best no matter what it is; *Address:* 2665 Tobermory, Cincinnati, OH.

WELSH, JENNIFER NATASHIA

Pen name: Jenny, Jen, Unique, Pru; *Born:* May 8, 1972, Manhattan; *Parents:* Lovendora & Vincent Welsh; *Education:* High School; *Occupation:* Student; *Honors:* Literature Awards, Spelling Award; *Other writings:* Haswritten: *Who Can You Talk To?, The Lost Boys, The Flying Unicorns, Love Songs, Knight on a Dark Horse, The Little Boy in the Park*; *Personal note:* Good things come to those who wait; *Address:* 3665 Willett Avenue, Bronx, NY.

WETHERBEE, GLADYS

Pen name: Renee; *Born:* September 24, 1971, Lexington, NC; *Other writings:* "What is a Cousin?" "What is a Sister?" "What is a Mother?" *Personal note:* I like to write poems to express my feelings that I couldn't say in words; *Address:* Rt 1 Box 19, Stantonsburg, NC.

WHEELERS, STEPHANIE IRENE

Pen name: Steffani; *Born:* March 21, 1973, Fort Polk, Louisiana; *Parents:* Charles F. Wheeler and Bonnie S. Wheeler; *Education:* Spring Hill High School; *Occupation:* Student; *Honors:* Honor Society, Many Scholastic Literary Awards, Citizenship Award, Excellence in Language Arts Award; *Other writings:* Various Poems and short stories printed in school literary magazines; *Personal note:* My writings are dedicated to those who like me, who have a longing to see the world with their hearts rather than their eyes; *Address:* 1921 Osage Circle, Olatha, KS.

WHITE, JANET DARLENE

Born: May 2, 1972, Sweetwater, Tennessee; *Parents:* William and Nancy White; *Education:* Vonore High School; *Memberships:* SADD, FHA, Annual Staff, School Newspaper; *Personal note:* I praise God that he has given me the talents to write, writing is an important part of my life; *Address:* Rt 4, Box 42865, Madisonville, TN.

WIESNER, WAYNE

Born: July 5, 1916, Silverton, Oregon; *Parents:* Archie and Helen Wiesner; *Spouse:* Janet Wiesner, August 30, 1941; *Children:* Sue, Don, Richard; *Education:* Oregon State University, New York University; *Occupation:* Consulting Engineer; *Memberships:* AHER Helicopter Society, AHA; American Inst. of Aeron and Astron., AIAA; *Honors:* Honorary Fellow, Klemin Award, AHS; *Other writings:* 20 Papers on Helicopter and Wind Turbine Design; Helicopter Design Book; *Personal note:* Goal of my writing, to document people and events so that coming generations will have a better understanding of days gone by; *Address:* 13403 SE 243 PL, Kent, WA.

WILEY, THELMA

Pen name: Sister "Tapp", "Little Tapp"; *Born:* January 20, 1944, Little Rock, Arkansas; *Parents:* Leola Jones, Mr. James W. Wiley Sr.; *Education:* Horace Mann High School; Philander Smith College; *Occupation:* Social Worker and Social Activist; *Memberships:* American Cancer Society, Annie Malone Children Home; United Black Community Association; *Honors:* Honors and commendation for civic contribution; *Other writings:* "A Love Affair"; *Personal note:* While I'm fighting for a cause, there's always somebody trying to defeat it; also charity is for the needy and not the greedy; the homeless, needy and loveless people inspire my writing; *Address:* 4531 Park Apt C., Berkeley, MD.

WILLIAMS, EDDIE G.

Born: October 20, 1970, Griffin Georgia; *Parents:* Sally Williams and Eddie Williams; *Education:* Jones Sr. High School; *Occupation:* Writer; *Other writings:* Song publishing with Hollywood Record Company, I am currently working on a novel; *Personal note:* Reality is a sudden, clash with imagination: Edgar was just too wrapped up in his own world, expand; *Address:* 732 James Street, Gainesville, GA.

WILLIAMS, MABLE L.

Born: April 26, 1933, Georgetown, GA; *Parents:* Catherine Lewis & Timothy Lewis; *Spouse:* Elbert Williams, January 8, 1952; *Children:* Jackie, Rayford, Ben, Freddy, Mac, Harvery; *Education:* Glenville High School, Columbus Technical; *Occupation:* Janitor; *Honors:* Awarded Merits Certificates and Golden Poet Award from World of Poetry; *Other writings:* Published several poems and two songs; *Personal note:* Wish to share my writing with everyone, Hope someday everyone will be able to read a book of poems and enjoy them as much as I have; *Address:* 3705 Stratford Dr., Columbus, GA.

WILLIAMS, SUSAN

Born: September 26, 1972, Pittsburgh, PA; *Parents:* John Williams and Donna Williams; *Education:* Sacred Heart High School; *Occupation:* Student; *Other writings:* Several poems that have been published; *Personal note:* My goal is to make people aware of all that is precious and created by God through poetry; *Address:* 1308 Franklin Avenue, Pittsburgh, PA.

WILLIS, JOYCE

Born: April 23, 1932, England; *Parents:* Ernest Walter Willis, and Maysie Irene Ellen Willis; *Occupation:* Nurse; *Honors:* Golden Poet Award, 1988; 3 honorable mentions; *Other writings:* Writing a story of nursing; *Personal note:* I enjoy writing as I am very imaginative and I find writing an expression of thinking; *Address:* 1665 Chestnut Street #103, San Francisco, CA.

WILLIS, VIVIAN E.M.

Born: July 7, 1948, Los Angeles, CA; *Parents:* Odea B. Meek and Emma G. Meek; *Children:* Jeffrey Michael; *Education:* Paducah Community College, AS; Murray State University, BS; *Occupation:* Restaurant Manager; *Other writings:* Has written poem entitled, "God's of the Night"; "The Winter Sea"; *Personal note:* Only through the encouragement of close friends have I made my first step into print. May this first step lead to many, many more; *Address:* 5801 Altama Avenue 4E, Brunswick, GA.

WISE, AMELIA

Pen name: A.A. Wise *Born:* May 30, 1954, Honolulu,Hawaii; *Parents:* Mr and Mrs. Robert Lee; *Spouse:* Donald K. Wise, February 14, 1976; *Education:* Kalami High School; *Occupation:* Recreation Aide; *Personal note:* My goal in life is to achieve the highest state of spiritual and earthly perfection to give of my light in hopes that others may be lifted also; *Address:* 123 David Street, Travis AFB, CA.

WOLLACK, CARRIE

Born: May 25, 1975, Miami, Florida; *Parents:*Richard & Sue Wollack; *Occupation:* Student; *Other writings:* School Anthology; *Personal note:* I believe in being nice to everybody and helping my society as much as possible; *Address:* 3464 Clay St., San Francisco, CA.

WOOD, SAM E.

Born: January 20, 1933, Williamsburg County, South Carolina; *Parents:*Sam E. Woods and Lottie Carol Woods; *Occupation:* Custodian; *Memberships:* Community Help Mission; *Honors:* Employee of the Year, 1987; *Other writings:* Has written poems entitled, "Thank You Lord", "Oh Precious Lord", "Situations Can be Better Honey", Attitudes to SUccess", "The Victorious March"; *Personal note:* Writing is something I enjoy doing, I feel it is a God given gift, given to me to help uplift people's spirits; *Address:* Rt 2 Box 425, Lillington, NC;

WRIGHT, RON

Born: April 15, 1948, Monticello, Iowa; *Parents:*John V. Wright, Mildred Mae Wright; *Children:* Alicia Rae, Paul David; *Education:* Monticello High School, Northwestern College, University of Oregon; *Occupation:* Theatre Director, Teacher; *Memberships:* National Right to Life, Oregon Right to Life, Bible-a-month Club, Christian Broadcasting Newwork, Christians in the Arts Networking; *Other writings:* Written numerous poems, lyrics, religious essays and plays; *Personal note:* Jesus serves no champagne brunch but blood and guts for lunch; *Address:* 3435 Canterbury Circle, Corvallis, OR.

WYCHE-HAMILTON, ELIZABETH

Pen name: Elizabeth Hamilton; *Born:* January 2, 1952, Pasco, Washington; *Parents:*Bessie and Elmer Hamilton; *Spouse:* Stuart W. Wyche, July 18, 1987; *Occupation:* Label operator; *Memberships:* Audobon Society, National Wildlife Federation; *Honors:* Won several awards; *Other writings:* Wrote "A Crystal Lake"; *Personal note:* Am currently writing music, in the process of publishing several books, I also write poetry;

WYLLIE, MARION J.E.

Pen name: Marion Fields Wyllie; *Born:* October 26, 1906, Collingwood Twp. Grey County; *Parents:*Wellington Herbert Fields, Christina Isobel Campbell Fields; *Spouse:* Victor Fleming Wyllie, June 17, 1939; *Children:* George, Douglas and Robert; *Occupation:* Later Country Correspondent; *Memberships:* Grey-Bruce Writers, Women's Institute Association for the Retarded; *Honors:* Five year Ontario Volunteer pin, first at W.I. County level for centennial poem, second place laureate award, certificates from the United Amateur Press;; *Other writings:* Self-published poems, "Pebbles on the Beach and Spring Onions", "The Smawls of Shoobawks; One book length manuscrip awaiting publication. Also published and edit soft voices, a small amateur journal for United Amateur Press; *Personal note:* I derive much pleasure and satisfaction from several correspondence clubs of writers. I like writing nostalgia, but it is hard to market; My unpublished book is a religious work; *Address:* 788 Fifth Street, Owen Sound, Ontario.

YOUNGBLOOD, SKY EARTH

Born: November 8, 1974, Colorado; *Parents:*Jacalyn Youngblood, Carlos Cueller; *Education:* Creighton Junior High School; *Occupation:* Student; *Memberships:* Odyssey of the Mind; Rocky Mountain Karate Assn; *Honors:* Honor Roll; *Personal note:* I write to learn about myself and to help others understand me; *Address:* 911 S. Pierson Way, Lakewood, CO.

YUN, CATHY

Born: September 21, 1976, Washington, DC; *Parents:*Kang W. Yun, Hans S. Yun; *Honors:* Board of Education Scholar, Numerous awards in the academic areas; *Other writings:* Have written short novels; *Personal note:* Put love and feelings into everything you do, especially writing; *Address:* 1324 Juneau Court, Tucker, GA.

ZELLER, KARL S.

Born: October 9, 1957, Kent, Ohio; *Personal note:* I like music; My favorite writer is Edgar A. Poe; *Address:* 20 Wickliffe Circle, Austintown, OH;

ZERILLO, JOHN P.
Pen name: The forked River Poet; *Born:* February 8, 1914, New Jersey; *Spouse:* Genevieve, May 24, 1941; *Children:* John, Sam;M *Education:* Fawcet Art Schook, Newark NJ; *Occupation:* Air Craft Worker, UF Forestry Firefighter, Boxer; *Memberships:* UAW, VFW, DAV, International Racing Pigeon Organizations; *Honors:* Many trophys in sports, race car and restoration.

ZIPUSCH, MIKA EVE
Born: November 19, 1976, Granada Hills, California; *Parents:*Walter and Yoko Zipusch; *Occupation:* Student; *Honors:* Musical certificates of merit for piano and Japanese school; *Personal note:* I think happiness is important for success; *Address:* 18419 Blackhawk Street, Northridge, CA.

ZYSSET, JEFF A.
Born: February 1, 1969, Holdrege, Nebraska; *Parents:*Eldon and Irene Zysset; *Education:* Farnam High School; *Occupation:* Sailor; *Honors:* Who's Who Among High School Students, Valdictorian "I Dare You"; *Other writings:* "The Rose", "Mother's Day", "Father's Day Poem", "The Journey of a Snow Flake", "The Way of Life"; *Personal note:* I write from personal feelings I write mostly about my friends and family because my family is my entire life; *Address:* HC 70, Farnam, NE.

Index

ABAD, ABIGAIL 26
ABBAZIA, MICHELE 135
ABBOT, S. HALE 260
ABBOTT, KAREN 86
ABBOTT, RENEE 242
ABEJON, MICHELLE 58
ABEL, VALERIE JO 11
ABELLI, STEVE 280
ABOYME-PATEL, ESTELA 184
ABRAHAM, KIMBERLY 269
ABRAMS, REGINA R. 232
ACORN, AMY 242
ADA, PENNE 85
ADAIR, SUSAN L. 209
ADAM, MONIQUE 110
ADAMS, ANGEL 169
ADAMS, GLENN 91
ADAMS, JENNY 189
ADAMS, MICHELLE 65
ADAMS, TIFFANY 189
AGOTESKU, VIVIAN M. 154
AGUSTIN, CHARLENE 194
AIKEN, JENNA 25
AKKERHUIS, DIONNE 300
AKL, AIDA 199
AKSEL, SOPHIE C. 298
ALBARRACIN, IGNACIO 276
ALBERS, CARLLY 187
ALBINDER, STACY 222
ALESSANDRO, JERI 192
ALESSO, SUZI 45
ALEXANDER, ASHLEE 139
ALFORD, ERIN 21
ALFORD, KENNETH 3
ALFORD, OLIVIA 97
ALI, AUNDREA 19
ALLEN, MELONIE D. 236
ALLISON, MARGARET 60
ALLIX, HEREWARD 5
ALONZO, THERESA Z. 256
ALSBROOKS, SHARON 247
ALTMAN, KRISTINE V. 248
ALTO, LIISA 279
AMANDA, 199
AMBRISCO, PEGGY 203
AMBRISCO, PEGGY 54
AMBROSE, KATHLEEN C. 124
AMODEI, ALMA 148
AMUNDSEN, EARL 187
ANDELMO, MARGARET 112
ANDEREGG, AMY B.H. 85
ANDEROS, ALICIA M. 188
ANDERSON, B.J. 155
ANDERSON, DANIELLE 154
ANDERSON, ELIZABETH 180
ANDERSON, INGRID 176
ANDERSON, KATHY JONES 44
ANDERSON, LISA K. 244
ANDERSON, MARGARET ANN 87
ANDERSON, MARY E. 222
ANDERSON, MELISSA 293
ANDERSON, MELISSA 305
ANDERSON, PAUL B. 304
ANDERSON, ROSE M. 296
ANDERSON, WILLIE MAY 263
ANDREW, L. SHANNON 57
ANDREWS, BILLY F. 173
ANDREWS, E. 290
ANDREWS, KATHRYN 211
ANGELINI, CHRIS 281
ANGERSTEIN, MYRA 66
ANIBALLI, SHEILA 59
ANNESE, DREW 214
ANZALDUA, LINDA 258
APPLE, C. ERIE 260
APPLEBY, AMY 21
APPLEBY, DONNA 255
ARAKAS, NIKI YULISSA 179
ARBLASTER, PAUL 222
ARCHETT, LIZ 131
ARDIA, TERI 271
ARDRY, DAWN 4
ARMSTRONG, FRAN 24
ARMSTRONG, MARY AILEEN 65
ARMSTRONG, SUSAN 280
ARNETT, FRANK 172
ARNETT, TINA 232

ARREDONDO, MIROSLAVA 65
ASBURY, CAROL 27
ASHLEY, ARTHUR 216
ASKEW, DANA 100
ASKEW, KEVIN 135
ASTOR, ADINA 167
ATIYEH, STARR 119
ATKISSON, MELISSA 46
AUSTIN, GAIL D. 22
AUSTIN, SUSHANA 278
AUTREY, STACI 76
AVERETT, MICHELLE 292
AVERSON, CONNIE 193
AVERY, GALE E. 19
AVERY, JOEL L. 266
AVEY, BOB 23
AVILA, SARAH E. 233
AVINGTON, RONALD B. 269
AYRES, DEBRA 173
AZNAR, VALERIE M. 268
B.J. 217
BABBIDGE, L. E. 194
BABCOCK, WENDELL K. 20
BABCOCK, WENDELL K. 283
BACHELIER, ALBERT A. 47
BAGNASCO, LISA 278
BAGNASCO, MICHELLE 113
BAHM, CONNIE 78
BAILEY, ANGELA 86
BAILEY, BERNADINE 38
BAILEY, LUCILLE S. 230
BAILEY, SHELLEY LYNN 47
BAINS, JOHN 51
BAJOVICH, ANN 183
BAKER, DORSEY 145
BAKER, GEORGE A. 304
BAKER, JAMES B. 163
BAKER, JENNIFER 162
BAKER, JOANN 45
BAKER, MICHELLE 229
BAKER, PAMELA 199
BAKER, WALTER H. 222
BALDRIDGE, PETRA G. 196
BALDWIN, TAMMY 296
BALEY, GENEVE 81
BALKO, JULEE 84
BALL, AIMEE 41
BANAYNAL, FRANCIS M. 29
BANKOFF, GEORGE 11
BANKS, RAYMOND 247
BANNING, AMANDA 137
BARB, CAROL 8
BARB, DORIS 230
BARBER, BARBARA 141
BARBER, MIKE D. 291
BARBER, THERESA 34
BARBOSA, ANTOINETTE 36
BARFIELD, DAVID 156
BARNARD, F. ESTHER 27
BARNES, NICOLE 220
BARNES, SHEERAN 87
BARNES, TAMMY F. 153
BARNHART, JOHN 108
BARNUM, AMBER C. 199
BARREN, JAMIE 138
BARRERA, ANEL P. 10
BARRETT, SANDRA LYNN 121
BARROWS, KENNY 285
BARTON, BONNIE 98
BARTON, CHRISTOPHER 115
BASIOS, ALEXIA 140
BASLER, CHRISTIE 271
BASS, JENNIFER 4
BASS, KAREN 50
BASSETT, D. 6
BATES, CHERYL 266
BATHER, KAREN 77
BATIZY, JULIANNA 62
BAVERSO, KATHERINE S. 239
BEARDSLEY, HEATHER 70
BEATTY, JODI L. 154
BECHTOLD, RICHARD A. 279
BECKER, ARNOLD S. 29
BECKLEY, MARGUERITE 87
BECKMAN, BRIGETTE 220
BEEBE, ZOLA C. 289
BEECH, CARRIE 134

BEGEMAN, MONICA 307
BELAND, RONNA 293
BELANGER, JOELLE 280
BELL, CONSTANCE W. 126
BELL, RICHARD A. 70
BELL, TAMMY 42
BELOFF, EVAN 182
BELUE, RUSOUN 18
BEN-DOR, MIRIAM 228
BENDER, MARTHA 114
BENKIE, LORENE 292
BENNA, TIFFANY 53
BENNERMAN, INEZ 108
BENNETT, AMY 91
BENNETT, ARLINE 250
BENNETT, EDDIE MAE 312
BENNETT, ISABELLE 73
BENNETT, MAURINA 223
BENNETT, ROBIN S. 73
BENSON, CHRIS 18
BERARD, NICOLE SUZANNE 98
BERARDI, STEPHANIE 255
BERARDINO, MARK 78
BERGMAN, MARGARET R. 287
BERGMAN, STEFFI 72
BERGUM, CHRISTA 123
BERMAN, ZACHARY 168
BERNARD, JAMES M. 89
BERNARD, REGINA 116
BERNDT, ANGELA 21
BERNING, RENEE F. 234
BERNSTEIN, LEAH 282
BERRY, AMY 125
BERRY, BUSTER 14
BERRY, SHIRLEY 243
BERTEAUX, SHIRLEY 122
BERYL, BENITA 176
BESS, TONYA 45
BEST, BARBARA N. 270
BEST, DEBBIE 189
BEST, JOHANNA 45
BETANCOURT, ERIC 77
BETHANY, (KERENSA E) 195
BETZOLD, SAMANTHA 281
BEZOU, MARION J. B. 307
BIA, REGINA 211
BIASO, JODI 260
BIBBINS, MILDRED 233
BIELEFELD, DAWNE C. 94
BIGGS, KAREN 222
BIMPONG, ERIC 55
BIRHAN, FARIKA F. 146
BISCOTTI, LAURA 35
BISHOP, BERNICE COUEY 167
BISTERFELDT, GWEN A. 269
BIVANS, MICHAELA 68
BIZYAK, LESLEY A. 246
BJORNSEN, ROBERT J. 70
BLACK, SARAH C. 218
BLACK, SHELLEY ANN 219
BLAIR, CATHERINE 186
BLANCH, EMMA J. 46
BLANK, B.J. 16
BLANKE, DANIELLE 52
BLANKENBAKER, M. 127
BLANKENSHIP, DEBBIE 177
BLANKENSHIP, JOHN M. 277
BLASKA, AMY 152
BLECHA, JUDY ATWELL 62
BLEDSOE, MARK LANE 79
BLEU, NOEL 265
BLOCKER, SUSAN BONNY 34
BLOOM, SHELIA D. 273
BLUM, GAIL 201
BOAZ, DIANE B. 252
BOEHNLEIN, GARY 300
BOGAN, ERIC 196
BOGGS, BEV 35
BOGGS, BOBETTE 40
BOGOLD, BOBBI JO 271
BOIVIN, LYNN J. 130
BOLDEN, KENNETH D. 30
BOLINGER, NICOLE 220
BOLTON, CYNTHIA G. 115
BONEKEMPER, WENDY 148
BONNETTE, JENNIFER 93
BONNICI, PAULINE 167

BOON, NATALIE 134
BOONE, JACKI J. 4
BOONE, KIM 274
BOOTH, JAIMIE 91
BOOTHE, HEATHER 80
BORDA, JOSEPH E. 306
BORDEN, LUCILLE FIELDS 51
BORJA, DOINES 37
BORSUM, JENNIFER 177
BOSWELL, FRANCEILIA 150
BOTELHO, EUGENE G.E. 13
BOTTORFF, DEBORAH A. 107
BOUCHER, JACQUELINE 163
BOUDREAU, NICHOLE K. 40
BOULINEAU, JUDSON JR. 158
BOUNDS, MARK T.C. 249
BOURQUE, JEAN 201
BOWERS, KAREN A. 50
BOWLING, KRISTIN 43
BOWMAKER, SANDRA 244
BOWMAN, AMY 223
BOWN, JEANETTE C. 38
BOYCE, KATHLEEN A. 208
BOYD, DENA 92
BOYD, HOLLY 92
BOYINGTON, ELIZABETH 85
BOYNTON, HEATHER W.A. 145
BOZSAN, KATHY ABERTH 133
BRACKEN, WANDA 97
BRACY, CHARITY H. 273
BRACY, KATHLEEN 260
BRADFORD, MARILYN 87
BRADLEY, ANTHONY R. 269
BRADLEY, SHIRLEY ANN 55
BRAGA, THOMAS 297
BRAHM, PATRICIA A. 41
BRAIDIS, SUSAN 45
BRAIN, MARNIE 231
BRANDEMUHL, ALISSA 134
BRANKEY, JOSEPH J. 30
BRANKO, DAN 278
BRANSON, BENNIE 167
BREEN, JOSEPHINE 266
BREIKSS, JURIS 194
BRENDA, SABRA 126
BRESLAU, CHARLES 48
BREWSTER, YOULANDA 235
BRICE, KELLIE 215
BRICKMAN, PARTICIA A. 202
BRIDGER, ASHLYN 27
BRIGGS, JENNIFER E. 262
BRIGHT, CHRISTINE 55
BRIGHT, CHUCK 48
BRILEY, CHARLES B. 74
BRILLANTES, GLADYS 218
BRITTON, CAROL ANN 10
BROADWELL, WILLIAM E. 137
BROAKER, LESLIE WEHLE 52
BROCK, EVELYN R. 152
BROCK, VIRGINIA A. 214
BROCKMAN, TINA 288
BRODIN, TAMERA 90
BROMLEY, STACIE 128
BRONK, DANA 32
BROOKS, SHANNON 219
BROSIUS, ALYS C. 176
BROWER, DAWN 145
BROWN, AMIE 178
BROWN, BOB 167
BROWN, CAROL 41
BROWN, DOROTHY C. 255
BROWN, JOYICE YOUNG 88
BROWN, JULI 110
BROWN, KIMBERLEE D. 293
BROWN, LORI 35
BROWN, LYNELL A. 142
BROWN, NEWTON 245
BROWN, PAULA L. 42
BROWN, RHONDA 47
BROWNE, GRETCHEN 152
BROWNE, PAULINE 313
BROWNING, JUDY 230
BROWNING, MARY LOREE 68
BRUCE, DAWN 280
BRUCE, GORDON 176
BRUCE, VICTORIA 299
BRUDER, BETTY V. 29
BRUNDAGE, BONNIE 167

BRUNELL, LISA M. 210
BRUNER, DOUG 179
BRYAN, ROAN 272
BRYANT, GLENDA 10
BRYANT, K. 216
BRYANT, MARNA 112
BUAK, KAREN 238
BUCHANAN, ANGIE 299
BUCHHOLTZ, JENNIFER M. 89
BUCHHOLZ, MISSY 133
BUCK, KRISTEN 207
BUCKLEY, EDITH 139
BUCKLEY, ELIZAETH 299
BUCKLEY, TARA 131
BUCKMILLER, ROBIN 121
BUDGETTS, BRIDGET D. 22
BUENO, ANNABEL 198
BUETTNERR, DEBI 25
BUFFKIN, BONITA 140
BUGLIONE, VICTORIA 181
BUIE, ALI 184
BUJOK, HEIDI LYNN 251
BULLARD, ANGELA 253
BUNONO, FRANCO 186
BUNYAN, MICKIE 213
BURBRIDGE, JENNIFER 179
BURCH, HOWARD R. 94
BURCH, JERRY 43
BURCHFIELD, HELEN 268
BURFORD, TAMARA D. 246
BURGER, DAWN ADAIR 260
BURGER, HOPE 254
BURGESS, BEKAH 13
BURGHARD, SHARON L. 57
BURGHER, C.J. 21
BURGOYNE, MICHELLE 231
BURKE, CONNIE M. 105
BURKE, DONNA GILL 4
BURKES, LORETTA ANNE 31
BURKHAMER, KERI 75
BURKHART, SYLVIA 244
BURKHART, VITA 19
BURKITT, TRACIE 257
BURKS, KAY 157
BURNES, KIMBERELY 63
BURNETTE, VICTOR C. 253
BURNS, DAWN 33
BURNS, JOHN H. 131
BURNS, RUBY 237
BURRUS, MISI 282
BURTON, HELEN BROWN 312
BURTON, JESSICA 69
BUSENDORFER, ALBERT P. 90
BUSSE, HEIDI 134
BUTCH, MARLA COLLEEN 96
BUTTERFIELD, BECKY 98
BUTTON, PATRICIA L. 143
BUTTREY, TRISHA 153
BUYLE, JEFFREY S. 94
BUZAN, LURENA 60
BUZZO, ALBERT L. 183
BYFIELD, MARLON A. 229
BYOUS, MELISSA 213
BYRNE, JBETTY BERLIN 265
BYWATER, RICHARD L. 78
CABRERA, REGINA T. 291
CACERES, TERESA 298
CAHILL, VERNA 36
CAINE, RACHEL 285
CALDER, WESLEY L. 5
CALDWELL, DONALD JR. 97
CALDWELL, ROZELL 248
CALHOUN, JENNIFER A. 255
CALHOUN, LISA C. 277
CAMDEN, BEKKI 252
CAMILLERI, ALLEN 187
CAMPBELL, H. DOYLE 109
CAMPBELL, KIMBERLY E. 240
CAMPBELL, KRISI 234
CAMPBELL, THERESA 59
CAMPION, CHRISTINE 158
CAMPOS, ELIZABETH 16
CANADY, JOSEPH H. 261
CANGIALOSE, WILLIAM 201
CANNELLA, VINCENT 310
CANNON, JAMES M. 13
CAPONE, MARIE A. 66

CAPONIGRO, CHERYL 45
CAPPY, TRACEY 133
CAPUTO, TONI ANN 217
CARDENAS, VALERIE 49
CARDINAL, SUE E. 34
CARDONA, SANDRA 273
CAREY, EVANGELINE 235
CARGILL, STEPHANIE 79
CARLSON, JESSIE 159
CARLSON, LILLA 158
CARLSON, LUANNE M. 129
CARMONA, FRANCIS 309
CARNEVALE, LORENE H. 31
CAROLLA, HEATHER 81
CARPANZANO, MARY BETH 64
CARPENTER, TERESA 227
CARR, TRACI 226
CARROLL, AMRJORIE J. 77
CARRULBA, JENNIFER 25
CARRUTH, WENDI 178
CARSON, GWEN 98
CARTER, JACKIE 176
CARVO, CAROLYN 147
CASADO, EDWARD 169
CASANTA, ISABELLE 203
CASCONE, MARIA E. 232
CASH, SUSAN 77
CASO, PATRICIA 23
CASSITY, MARTIN M. 232
CASSON, HEATHER 225
CASTANEDA, MICHELLE A. 76
CASTELLANOS, MARIA 166
CASTELLO, FREDDIE III 190
CASTIGLIONE, TANYA 122
CASTILLON, CECELIA 274
CASTLE, KATHRYN 78
CASTLE, PAT 36
CASTRO, CARLOS 187
CATALO, MARIANNE N. 119
CAUM, NICOLE 97
CAUSEY, MARY SEWELL 135
CAUSLEY, JENNIFER 90
CAVENDISH, JOHN 303
CELESTE, 275
CELIBERTI, ALLISON M. 170
CEMBRANO, JENNIFER 144
CERVANTES, ALOUETTE 7
CHAMBERLAIN, CLEO 65
CHAMPION, TOM 54
CHAMPNEY, NATAHSA T. 107
CHAPMAN, SONIA 124
CHATTIN, MARCY 127
CHAVEZ, JOHN A. 30
CHENOWETH, MARIANNE S. 63
CHESROW, CATHLEEN 274
CHESSMORE, SANDRA 224
CHEZAR, ARIELLA 184
CHILDRESS, TAMMY 309
CHILDS, AUDREY 263
CHILDS, ERIC 136
CHIVIS, THELMA D. 170
CHO, JAN 80
CHORNYJ, ALEX 81
CHOWDHURY, FAWZIA 267
CHRISMAN, BECKY 92
CHRISTIAN, NICOLE 270
CHRISTIAN, SHELIA 106
CHRISTOPHER, LEE 18
CIEMNIECKI, JEAN 228
CIONI, MARLA 112
CIPOLLA, CHESLEY 228
CISNEROS, ANGELO 188
CLABON, GEORGE 268
CLAEYS, KERRY 114
CLAIBORNE, RONALD 211
CLARK, AUTUMN 304
CLARK, BRANDON 82
CLARK, C. 120
CLARK, CARMAN S. 299
CLARK, CARRIE 172
CLARK, ELIZABETH E. 283
CLARK, HEATHER C.172
CLARK, JACKIE NEWSOM 90
CLARK, NICOLE D. 20
CLARK, SUSAN A. 34
CLARK, TRUDY SUE 279
CLARKE, JAKKI 138

CLARKE, PIA ALTHEA 8
CLARKE, ROBERT E. 243
CLARKE, SUSAN 45
CLAY, JUNE B. 297
CLEMENTSON, LISA 217
CLEMONS, ANDREW F. 83
CLEVERINGA, HELEN M. 190
CLIFTON, AMY 94
CLIFTON, RACHEL 204
CLINTON, DOROTHY R. 228
CLOTHIER, DONNA 41
CLOUD, KELLY 232
CLUTTER, SANDRA 284
COATES, DIANE C. 93
COATS, KENICA RAHN 205
COCHRAN, CRYSTAL 282
COCHRAN, TITUS 78
COCIVERA, GINA MARIE 39
COFFYN, MARLENA 96
COGAR, SAMUAL N. 211
COHEN, DANIELLE 308
COKER, JULIETT 159
COLE, PENNY 294
COLE, TRACIE L. 130
COLELLO, CAROL D. 99
COLEMAN, GREGORY 172
COLLIE, ANNA 90
COLLIER DAVID L. 19
COLLIER, MELANIE 213
COLLINS, ALEX 146
COLLINS, LADETTE 122
COLLINS, LESLIE 258
COLLINS, LOU B. 254
COLLINS, MAREN M. 57
COLLINS, MARIA E. 78
COLLINS, SANDYE R. 74
COLLSON, JOHN 215
COLON, CHRISTINE E. 228
COMA, CAROL 220
COMALANDER, PEGGY M. 171
COMFORT, RALPH 243
COMSTOCK, MARY 60
CONGER, CLAUDIA J. 290
CONNER, DOVA B. 143
CONNORS, CARY 172
CONTI, SHELBY 242
CONTINO, ROSALIE H. 126
COOK, ANA167
COOK, DAWN J.A. 264
COOK, DIXIE RUTH 161
COOK, GRACE E. 147
COOK, KRISTYN 297
COOK, PAULA 169
COOK, SANDRA 61
COOK, SHERRON LEE 276
COOK, STEPHANIE 293
COOKIS, HOLLY 177
COOLEY, GLADYS 81
COONS, KELLY 233
COOPER, TESS 166
CORBETT, S. 51
CORDS, NAOMI 81
CORGLIANO, FRANCINE 188
CORNELIUS, JEFF 39
CORNELL, ANN 94
CORNETT, CHRISTINE K. 48
CORNISH, GRACE N. 299
CORRIGAN, DORIETTA 22
CORSI, JILL DENISE 4
CORTEZ, DANIEL A. 218
CORY, JENNIFER 252
COSKI, R. CHRISTOPHER 74
COSLET, LORA 295
COSTELLO, BRANDY 40
COSTELLO, REBECCA 129
COTTRELL, MISSY 114
COUNTRYMAN, DONYLL 102
COURNOYER, RACHEL 204
COURT, BERNADETTE 222
COVALT, JENNY 178
COVINGTON, CHERRON 229
COWIN, TAMMY 78
COWLES, JENNIFER 41
COX, CINDY 119
COX, DANIEL G. 69
COX, JENNIFER 143
CRADDOCK, HAZE 203

CRAIG, JASON 284
CRAIG, MICHAEL D. 307
CRAIG, MICHEL 234
CRANE, ELLEN M. 304
CRANER, GAIL L. 197
CRANMER, PAMELA 138
CRAWFORD, ARDEN YALE 146
CRAWFORD, VIRGINIA 253
CREECH, GEORGANNA 184
CRESCENZO, MENA 166
CRINITI, MARY P 217
CRIPPS, SHANNON 297
CRISP, AUTUMN S. 187
CRISP, TINA LOUISE 214
CRISTOBAL, MARIO 79
CROBAUGH, EMMA 29
CROCKER, RUBY B. 281
CROMER, ROSE 281
CROSSAN, CARIN E. 190
CROUCH, SALLY F. 233
CROW, MARY S. 282
CROWDER, MELANIE 65
CRUICE, KELLY A. 158
CRUZ, GINA MARIE 20
CULL, JOHN 121
CULLEY, SHELIA 244
CUMMINGS, CATHY 258
CUMMINS, ABIGAIL G. 20
CURAZZATO, RONALD S. 291
CURLISS, CLAUDE E. 232
CURRIE, MISSY 247
CURRY, LONNIE V. 158
CURRY, PATSY J. 117
CURTIS, JACK 21
CUTCHER, JUSTINE 62
CUTLER, SHANE 115
CUTTER, BARBARA 233
D'AGOSTINO, DEBRA 94
D'AOUST, NICOLE 122
DAHLSTROM, QUINN E. 33
DALEY, SHARON M. 52
DALY, DEBRA L. 144
DAMON, CHRISTIE 121
DANIELS, CALVIN E. 99
DARBE, NEVA F. 98
DARDE, CLAUDIA 48
DARGITZ, CHRISTY A. 295
DARNIELLE, MARY LOU 234
DARR, TAMMY 239
DAUGHERTY, ELIZAbeth 235
DAUKSHUS, MICHELLE 112
DAVENPORT, GERALDINE 251
DAVIDSON, C.J. 12
DAVIDSON, CORTNEY 123
DAVIDSON, JENNIFER 268
DAVIDSON, JaNELL 162
DAVIDSON, MEGAN 206
DAVIES, HEATHER L. 172
DAVIS, CARRIE LYNN 190
DAVIS, CLIFFORD A. III 77
DAVIS, DALE W. 120
DAVIS, DEBORAH 4
DAVIS, DONELLA L.S. 143
DAVIS, LARRY S. 193
DAVIS, ROBERT 69
DAVIS, SHANNON B. 119
DAVIS, STACEY L. 218
DAVIS, TALLI 272
DAVIS, WENDY JANELL 41
DAVIS-KING, MICHAEL 166
DAWN, SHAROLYN 217
DAWSON, AMIE 251
DAY, KATHLEEN 225
DAYNOIROWICZ, TERESA 276
DAZEY, BILLY M. 36
DE FIORI, ALLAN J. 223
DE LA PENA, ALBA H. 183
DE LEON, ROWENA 128
DEAN, ANNE W. 181
DEAVERS, ANGIE 174
DECHAYNE, LAUREN K. 156
DECKER, BARBARA R. 265
DECKER, BECKIE 132
DECKER, DOROTHY M. 308
DECKER, ROBIN KAYE 53
DEES, DOLLY 236
DEETS, TRACEY 123

DEHART, MELISSA 229
DEHRER, NANCY 89
DEISHER, NORMA 91
DEITZ, JAMES NELSON 177
DEJARNETTE, SARAH 115
DEL PALACIO, MARGARET 78
DELAVERGNE, PEGGY 107
DELGADO, ROSA 68
DELMORAL, CHASTITY ANN 48
DELUCIA, JOSEPH A. 52
DEMARCO, CHRISSY 105
DEMATIO, ANTHONY 137
DEMERS, DENNIS G. 4
DEMPSEY, BARBARA 134
DENNER, ERIC 287
DENNEY, WILLIAM L. 95
DENNIS, DUSTY 39
DENNISTON, REESE M. 269
DENOFIO, NANCY 41
DERIFIELD, GWENDOLYN 157
DES RE'MAUX, AMANDA 132
DESIREY, TONJA 204
DESMOND, MARGARET 76
DETRY, DENISE M. 168
DEVARY, KRISTINA 193
DEVILLERES, DAVID L. 129
DEVINE, TIFFANY 69
DEVITO, JOSEPH 230
DEVORA, YVONNE 282
DEVRIES, CONNIE 111
DEWTLINGER, ROXANN 129
DIAMOND, KARRISSA 121
DIAZ, AMANDA 255
DIAZ, MAYRA C. 224
DIAZ, MAYRA C. 58
DIBLASI, HEATHER 132
DICK, BARTOLA L. 270
DICK, CAROL A. 17
DICK, CLARA S. 75
DICKENS, APRIL 19
DICKSON, LAWRENCE M. 298
DICKSON, VIVAN REY 14
DIENER, MARY 236
DIETRICH, AUBREY 86
DIETTERICH, SUSAN M. 45
DILL, SHELIA 129
DILLINGHAM, DON 4
DILLON, KIM 205
DINARDO, STEPHANIE 44
DIPPO, KELLI 259
DIXON, MC. D. 292
DIXON, REBECCA L. 207
DOAN, KELLY 229
DOBEY, MATTIE 309
DODGE, ELEANOR 180
DODGE, LAURA 68
DODSON, O. RAY 73
DOLLINS, KEVIN 276
DOLPH, JENNIFER 262
DOMENICHINI, SANDRA 121
DONNELL, DENICE 142
DONNELLY, BARBARA C. 264
DONYUO, MBA SUNG 224
DOREN, JANE VAN 139
DOSS, TINA 193
DOUCET, RAMONA 207
DOUCETTE, CHRISTINE 207
DOUGHERTY, RON 206
DOUGHERTY, STEPHANIE 28
DOVICH, JOE 32
DOWER, ANNE MULCAHY 26
DOWNING, MAXINE CHOATE 75
DOWNING, TAMMY 46
DOWSETT, DANIELLE 119
DRAEHN, CATHY 228
DRAKE, MICHELLE 288
DRAN, JENNA 222
DRENNAN, JOHN W. 196
DRENNEN, KRISTINE 60
DRUMHELLER, LINDA JO 254
DRURY, GARY A. 5
DRURY, MARK J. 289
DRUST, JENNIFER L. 33
DU MONT, DANIEL J. 215
DUBE, J. MICHAEL 10
DUBIN, ALICE 199
DUDLEY, PEGGY L. 12

DUKE, KARRIE 60
DUNCAN, ANGELA 24
DUNCAN, ELVIN J. 200
DUNCAN, MICHELLE 116
DUNCAN, STEPHANIE R. 275
DUNGHE, KRISTI 156
DUNHAM, CHELCEY 123
DUNHAM, LAURA 38
DUNLAP, JENNIFER L. 9
DUNN, ANGIE 28
DUNN, DOROTHY J. 163
DUNNAWAY, LINDA D. 259
DUVALL, REBECCA 72
DVORAK, JULIE L. 154
DYAL, DONNA 91
DYE, PAULA 213
DYER, STEVEN W. 269
DYKINS, VI 188
DYKSTRA, JEANNE B. 141
DYKSTRA, NANCY J. 194
EADY, PAULA M. 312
EAGLE, SASHA 218
EARP, HELEN L. 214
EARP, TERRY 225
EBEL, JoDEE G. 232
EBERHARTER, LISA 42
ECO, REGINA 135
EDENS, LESLIE 261
EDMONDS, JERRY L. 151
EDWARDS, ANASTASIA N. 10
EDWARDS, BERTIE 235
EDWARDS, CARL E. 264
EDWARDS, IRVIN 136
EFFLAND, CHERYL 68
EGGERT, KIM 72
EHRLICHER, EDWARD 186
EICHACKER, MICHELLE 56
EKINER, LISA 286
ELDRIDGE, MICHELLE 232
ELKINS, APRIL M. 4
ELKINS, CAROL 187
ELKINS, ReDONN 213
ELKUN, DANA 77
ELLIN, GEORGIA 185
ELLIOOT, RON 55
ELLIOTT, ELIZABETH 255
EMERY, DEB 19
EMERY, JAN 111
EMERY, WANETA V. 81
EMISON, MARY SUE 224
EMOND, LISA 269
EMORY, AMY 149
EMRICH, CASEY 91
ENDRES, SANDRA J. 47
ENGELMAN, LISA 121
ENGLAND, ANGELA 270
ENGLE, AMRY BETH 59
ENGLISH, DONNA LYNN 141
ENGLISHBEE, REBEKAH 307
ENTWISLE, KELLIE 61
EPPERSON, JENNIFER 262
EPSKAMP, YOLANDA 20
ERBE, PAMELA S. 97
ERICKSON, TIM 272
ERNST, KRISTA 211
ERNST, SHELLEY 236
ERSEVIM, ISMAIL 97
ESCHINGER, MARY 288
ESCOFFIER, SUSAN 34
ESPERICUETA, MELISSA 114
ESPOSITO, LAUREN 261
ESTELLE. TANYA KAY 164
ESTEP, WILLIAM L. 171
ESTEVEZ, RICARDO J. 280
ESTLE, LISA 105
ESTRADA, PHYLISS 245
ETHERTON, CHRISTINE 241
EVANS, FRANCES A. 253
EVANS, JERI 262
EVANS, LOUISE 54
EVANS, PERRY 144
EVERETT, ROBIN L. 302
FAHRNKOPF, SUSANNE K. 193
FAIRBANKS, SARA 243
FALLOS, WILLIAM III 134
FANTRY, CHARLOTTE M. 261
FARLEY, DAYTON JR. 180

FARMER, ERIC J. 139
FARRAR, HOPE 14
FARRELL, EVA J. 7
FARRIOR, EVAN B. 16
FASANO, KELLI A. 259
FASCO, KELLY A. 3
FASTEAU, MINDY A. 213
FAVOR, DENNIS 25
FAY, DI ANN 139
FEATHERLY, AMITY 91
FEINGOLD, KEVIN 216
FEINLAND, LEWIS 118
FEINLAND, STEPHEN 71
FELICIANO, CANDID 109
FELICIANO, REGINA 53
FEMMEL, THEODORE 296
FENIMORE, JENIFER 25
FERRARO, DANA 240
FERRAZZA, JOSETTE S. 224
FERREE, DEVON 80
FERRON, D.R. 136
FESTA, JANINE C. 66
FETHERSTON, LAURA 209
FETTY, SCARLET 67
FEUER, SHERI 303
FIELD, NORMA 238
FIELDS, MARY 18
FIORUCCI, ADRIEN 99
FIRST, MARCI 113
FISCHER, ANGIE 17
FISCHER, HELEN 123
FISHER, DAVID O. 46
FITTE, LAURA A. 294
FITZ-PATRECK, SHIRLEY 202
FITZGERALD, ANNE 225
FITZPATRICK, GWEN 299
FITZPATRICK, MIKE 57
FLESHMAN, KEVIN DELONG 42
FLETCHER, PHILIP GAY 214
FLICKLINGER, SUSAN R. 149
FLORINDO, SHERLLYN 52
FLYNN, CARA L.V. 145
FLYNN, DORRY R. 252
FLYNN, MISTY LEE 224
FLYNN, SHARON W. 106
FOLKERDS, SERENA 280
FONDA, SHARIDAN 100
FONDREN, KERVIN 279
FONTAINE, JENNFER LEE 138
FONTENAT, MELONIE 166
FORAN, RENAE 302
FORCHIA, LORIE A. 291
FORCIER, KATHLEEN 279
FORD, ERICKA 24
FORDE, JAY HUGO 228
FORNARO, ROSENA 309
FORRESTER, MARY E. 118
FORSTER, PEGGYE F. 141
FOSTER, BRIGID L. 182
FOSTER, DAVID L. 53
FOSTER, PATRICIA HART 104
FOSTER, SUZANNE 175
FOULKES, ROLAND A. 47
FOWLER, CAROL 82
FOX, MARY CAROLYN 118
FOX, RICHARD W. 257
FOXHALL, LESLEY 52
FRANCES, MARY 294
FRANCIS, TAMMYE J. 206
FRANCISCI, CHRISTIE 257
FRANKLIN, ALISA 82
FRANKS, MARSHA 65
FRAZIER, GLORIA 22
FRECHETTE, WENDY M. 19
FREEMAN, AMANDA 23
FREEMAN, DEBBIE 177
FREUDENBERGER, NELL 194
FRIEBERG, SIGNE 276
FRIEDLAND, C.A. 225
FRIEDLAND, DEBBIE 216
FRIEDLAND, LILAH 30
FRITSCHE, PATRICIA A. 149
FROHLICH, LINDA 232
FRYE, MICHEALE 248
FUKUMOTO, JANICE Y. 238
FULK, JAMES A. 5
FULLER, JOY 302

FUNDERBERG, MARY 286
FUREY, EVELYN 198
FUSTING, DARLENE 209
GAETZ, GINA 152
GAGE, DONALD M. 213
GAGNELIUS, GENNA 251
GALLIVAN, JEANNETTE 180
GALLO, HEATHER 24
GALOZO, PETE G. 99
GALUPPI, KRISTIN M. 274
GANER, JENNIFER 262
GARAMELLA, TRINITY 67
GARDNER, KIM 259
GARDNER, LEOLA C. 66
GARDNER, STACIE 242
GARGIULO, MICHELE
GARNER, CECELIA L. 229
GARNER, LEE 282
GARRETSON, LESLEY 291
GARRETT, JANET 68
GARRETT, LAURA B. 158
GARRISON, K.R. 279
GARRISON, PAMELA 306
GARRITY, SARAH K. 207
GARWACKI, MARJORIE 311
GARY, MICHAEL 166
GATES, MICHELLE 294
GATEWOOD, LORI 78
GAUTHIER, MONA JEAN 112
GAUVIN, DEBBIE 92
GAY, HEATHER LYNN 181
GAYTON, LESTER R. JR. 261
GEBBIE, SHARON 241
GEBEL, WILLIAM R. JR. 126
GEE, STEPHEN 193
GEISINGER, GEORGE S. 202
GELB, LOREY 258
GENEVIEVE, 282
GENOVESI, PAUL M. 168
GENTRY, KING 291
GEORGAROS, KARYN 303
GEORGE, TAMILIA 153
GERO, MELISSA 231
GESSLIN, LORETTE N. 240
GETZELMAN, HEATHER L. 14
GETZINGER, JENNIFER 181
GIANNAMORE, CHRISTINA 215
GIBBONS, AMY 17
GIBBONS, RANDALL C. 71
GIBLOCK, DANA 108
GIDNEY, HEATHER 202
GIL, RACHEL 96
GILBERT, PATTI 41
GILEWSKI, AMBER 172
GILGEN, KIMBERLY I. 67
GILL, DIANNE 25
GILL, LORI 3306
GILLESPIE, MICHELE 217
GILLESPIE, W.H. 26
GILLIAN, LAUREN 261
GILLISSIE, KIM 47
GILSAN, BRENDA 36
GINGERICH, JESSIE 73
GIRASUOLO, STACY 295
GIVENS, E. GENE 235
GLASER, RIVKA 137
GLASGOW, WILLARD M. 9
GLASS, JANE 4
GLEASON, LAURA T. 130
GLEBUS, SHERRI LYNN 75
GLENDENNING, RUSSELL 249
GLENN, RHONDA 229
GLOGOWSKI, KAREN 308
GLUCK, P.J. 139
GODBURN, KAREN 215
GODDEN, KIMBERLY 30
GOEBEL, JULIE M. 154
GOELLER, CHRIS 30
GOFFAUX, LYN 130
GOLDMAN, CAROL 16
GOLDMAN, SHIRLEY L. 48
GOMBOS, SUSAN 257
GOMES, STACEY 75
GONZALEZ, ALBERT 85
GONZALEZ, CAROLINE 49
GONZALEZ, JEANNE M. 162
GOODMAN, CONNIE 306

GOODWIN, KERRY 308
GOPEE, TONI 58
GORDON, HERMAN 221
GORDON, JEAN CREA 92
GORECKI, G. 221
GORZELSKY, ALLEGRA 11
GOSIZK, DONNA MARIE 144
GOSNAY, VELMA 86
GOUGH, DEIRDRE S. 260
GOULD, DEBORAH 203
GOVE, ROBIJAN J. 302
GRABER, CARYN R. 134
GRAEF, THOMAS T. 175
GRAHAM, AVA 8
GRAHAM, SARA 48
GRAM, GEORGE 54
GRANT, CARRIE JOANN 253
GRASER, HOLLY 12
GRAVES, JULIE 59
GRAY, ELAINE 250
GRAY, JOHN MORRISSEY 54
GRAY, SHERRY LYNN 219
GREAYER, HANNAH I.R. 143
GREEN, BRENDA 171
GREEN, DARLEEN 212
GREEN, DARLENE 311
GREEN, MICHAEL LEWIS 65
GREENBERG, TONYA 193
GREENE, ERIN 10
GREENE, WENDY 167
GREENING, RUTH M. 219
GREENLUN, AARON 225
GREENWOOD, CATHERINE 49
GREGERSEN, ERA 147
GREGOR, LISA I. 191
GREGORY, FLOSSIE F. 279
GREGORY, SAMANTHA L. 211
GRENIER, PAT 199
GRESCHLER, MICHAEL 103
GRESE, DARLA 44
GREY, DAWN 267
GRIES, MONICA 292
GRIEVESON, KAREN 156
GRIFFITH, BARRY 292
GRIFFITH, BRENDA 19
GRIFFITH, SHELLEY 95
GRILHO, FRANCIS D. 190
GRILL, NAN E. 225
GRIZZLE, AUTUMN 7
GROAT, CAROLYN L. 198
GROSS, BETTY J. 198
GROSS, DEANA 90
GROSS, NELLIE 5
GROSSI, LUCY 44
GROVE, BEVERLY J. 169
GRUBB, PEGGY A. 198
GRUNERT, HOLLY 63
GUERRA, RAECHEL R. 68
GUERRIERO, JESSICA J. 75
GUETENS, DEBBIE 90
GUILBEAU, EMILY 172
GUILLIAMS, JANET 9
GUNTER, MARY C. 133
GUSTAW, ELEANOR LEE 8
GUTIERREZ, ANITA 309
GUTIERREZ, JUDY 269
GUTSHE, HENRY W. 136
GUTWILLIG, MARTA 110
HAAS, DWIGHT 255
HAGA, DEBBIE 89
HAHN, HOPE 263
HAIG, DIANE MICHELLE 179
HAILEY, V. R. 250
HAINES, KATIE 122
HALASZ, KAT 230
HALCOMB, MARGARET 127
HALDEMAN, MELISSA 307
HALEY, COURTNEY 230
HALKYARD, JEFFREY 153
HALL, B. WASHBOURNE 98
HALL, JANICE 161
HALL, RUTH A. 292
HALL, SONIA K. 237
HALL-KELLER, MOLLIE 249
HALLOCK, MICHAEL J. 114
HALVERSON, CHRISTY 283
HAMBY, LEE ANN 131

HAMER, TOM 207
HAMILTON, KARLA 196
HAMILTON, LUCY C. 109
HAMMEL, COLLEEN 218
HAMMER, PATRICIA 41
HAMMETT, CHARLES SR. 100
HAMMOND, CYNDI 234
HANCOCK, GEORGE A. 202
HANCOCK, JEANETTE 38
HANCOCK, STEPHANIE 242
HANDY, BARBARA 195
HANLEY, BETTYE L. 22
HANNAN, NANCY 49
HANSON, BARBARA A. 86
HANSON, COLEEN 113
HARDY, MYRONN E. 106
HARICH, W.G. 155
HARRINGTON, LINDA 126
HARRIS, ANNE BURWELL, 143
HARRIS, JUDY 196
HARRIS, MARY S. 206
HARRIS, VALERIE L. 82
HARRISON, PATRICIA C. 22
HARRISON, TEVA 278
HART, DONNA 94
HART, HEATHER 20
HART, NORA 220
HARTLAND, MICHAEL C. 249
HARTMAN, RALPH 73
HARTZELL, JOHN 158
HARVEY, KRISS 129
HARWELL, AMY 62
HARWELL, PAT 20
HASENAUER, CARLA 94
HASH, CATHERRINE 200
HASTINGS, ANGEL N. 132
HATFIELD, ELOISE 97
HAUPT, CECILIA G. 274
HAWES, DONNA KAYE 89
HAWKINS, CYNTHIA A. 206
HAWKINS, WANDA 13
HAWLEY, PAM 300
HAYDEN, AMANDA 6
HAYDEN, JANA 101
HAYDEN, JUDY 205
HAYE, KIM 287
HAYES, ALIX 15
HAYES, JENNIE 168
HAYES, MELBA 305
HAYES, MICHELLE 305
HAYNES, KITTI 293
HAYS, CHRISTINE D. 280
HAZELBAKER, ANGELA 83
HEAP, ANDREA167
HEAPS, BARBARA W. 235
HEARN, SANDY 48
HEASLETT, REBECCA 285
HEASLEY, SANDY 238
HECHAVARRIA, BARBARA 176
HEDENLAND, DEE 174
HEEP, AMY LYNN 220
HEFFERNAN, LAURA 234
HEIBEL, CHERYLL 66
HEINZE, DAVIE M. 233
HELEN, MARY 286
HELIER, MICHELLE 232
HELLER, ARDEN 270
HELLERR, LAUREN 278
HELLWIG, KHELLEY 170
HEMEYER, MARIANN E. 118
HEMMERS, KATHLEEN 247
HEMRY, TRACY 256
HENDERICKSON, AMY 288
HENDERSON, LOIS 274
HENDRIX, ALICE E. 27
HENINGTON, KRISTIE 87
HENRIKSON, TRACEY 72
HENRY, DEBBIE 41
HENSHAW, DEBORAH 101
HERBACK, CHERYL 261
HERBERT, SHARON 233
HERICKS, RHONDA K. 227
HERKEL, DEBBIE 136
HERMAN, KATIE 74
HERMAN, TRACEY 64
HERNANDEZ, NORMA I. 255
HERRING, JAMES 4

HERRIOTT, STACY 207
HERRON, CARRIE 68
HERST, BARBARA N. 10
HERWOOD, CAROL 14
HESTER, JULIE 54
HIBSHMAN, KRYSTAL 69
HICHO, LAURA 266
HICKEY, RUTH ANN 67
HICKMAN, JANI 177
HICKS, BRANDY 23
HICKS, LORRAINE 213
HIGGINS, DAWN 101
HILL, DARLENE M. 120
HILL, GLENNA 36
HILL, LOUISE R. 191
HILL, TEDDY R. 257
HILLHOUSE, J. O . 296
HILLIARD, MILDRED 249
HINKLE, KATHY 312
HIRSCH, JULIE 47
HIRSCH, ROBERT E. 302
HISS, BEATRICE 81
HLYWA, LISA 124
HO, SONG 48
HODGES, JAMIE 145
HOEFER, DEVON D. 4
HOEKSTRA, NANCY 115
HOEY, CAROLYN 186
HOFACKER, AMANDA M. 255
HOFER, KATHLEEN 229
HOFFMAN, DALE P. 159
HOFFMAN, MIRIAM 305
HOFFMAN, MOLLIE 248
HOFMAN, ABIGAIL 184
HOGSETT, MATT 58
HOISINGTO, KENDRA 240
HOLBROOK, BRAIN 239
HOLCOMBE, R.G. JR. 130
HOLDEN, J. PRESTON 151
HOLDEN, SONIA 208
HOLLAND, BRIDGETT 98
HOLLINSHED, GENOULIA 7
HOLLMAN, DEBRA M. 179
HOLM, MARY 284
HOLMAN, PATHENIA W. 255
HOLMBERG, MARY E. 246
HOLMES, CAROL IVES 92
HOLMES, MELANIE 232
HOLTZ, JENNIFER 263
HOMER, DARLENE M. 277
HOOD, KELLI 194
HOOPER, PEGGY P. 265
HOPKINS, ANNIE P. 149
HOPKINS, FRANK J. 29
HOPKINS, LOUISE B. 272
HOPKINS, SHIRLEY 214
HOPKINS, THERESA J. 256
HOPPER, NANCY 265
HORN, LARISSA 215
HORST, MINDI 248
HORTON, TONYA L. 271
HOTHAM, DOUG 102
HOUDE, FREDERICK JR. 52
HOUDE, JODIE 130
HOUGHTEN, MICHELE 131
HOUSTON, SARAH 108
HOVANEC, PAM 167
HOVANEC, PAM 98
HOWARD, BETH 11
HOWARD, CHRISTINE 244
HOWARD, LEANNA 55
HOWARD, SYLVIA 52
HOWELL, KELLY 122
HOWERTON, C.C. 298
HOWLEY, HENRY J. 267
HOYOS, ANGELA C. 6
HUBBARD, CALVIN E. 86
HUBBARD, TRACEY 156
HUBBLE, ANGELA 299
HUCK, CHRISTINA 70
HUCKABEE, SAMANTHA 211
HUDDLESTON, LISA 282
HUDSON, PAMELA J. 139
HUFF, JOYCE 120
HUFNAGLE, DARCEY 70
HUGHART, ROBERTA LEIGH 70
HUGHES, BRIAN 143

HUMMONS, MARION T. 110
HUNDLEY, TRACY 3
HUNNEWELL, HEATHER 268
HUNTER, AMBER 216
HUNTER, MARISA 66
HUNTING, HARRY S. 85
HUOT, TAMMIE P. 124
HUPP, KATHRYN 154
HURILLA, DIANE C. 80
HUSMAN, LEIF 158
HUSTON, MARCI 114
HUTCHERSON, THERESA 88
HUTCHINSON, CALVIN 52
HUTCHINSON, VERNA 146
HUTSON, PATRICIA FAIN 55
HUTTO, J. WESLEY 26
HYMAN, JENNIFER 12
ICKLER, JOANNE 48
IGHILE, GABRIEL O. 125
INGLIS, RAYE 129
INGRAM, DANA 191
INOUYE, LEWIS 131
IRIGOYEN, DAVID 290
IRISH, ALVA 183
IRRGANG, MARILYN J. 127
IRVING, AMY M. 104
IRVING, CARMEN187
ISARDAS, GEETA J. 100
ISBELL, CORA LYONS 32
ISLEY, SANDRA 227
ITUARTE, ANA 134
IVY, LAUREN 221
JACKSON, ANGELA 253
JACKSON, BECKY 178
JACKSON, BETH 149
JACKSON, CEDRICK B. 274
JACKSON, SHELLIE M. 106
JACKSON, TAMMY 189
JACOBS, HOPE 140
JACOBS, MICHELLE 133
JAMES, GENE 251
JAMES, SHIRLEY 95
JAMES, STANLEY M. 273
JAMES, TAMMY 114
JANOWSKI, RONDA 100
JARRET, GLORIA B. 93
JASTRZEBSKI, SHARON 286
JAUSSI, JACKIE 107
JAY, ADELE 102
JELORMINE, KRISTEN 260
JELSMA, TERRIE 214
JENKINS, BEVERLY 265
JENKINS, KANDI 276
JENKINS, MILLARD 113
JENKINS, MYRA 231
JENKINS, VICTORIA D. 283
JENKINS, ZERETHA L. 120
JENKINSON, GRACE 150
JENNINGS, GENISA 263
JENNINGS, JENI 252
JENSEN, BOBBI 97
JENSEN, DONELLE 39
JERINA, JULIANNE 62
JERZAK, JUANITA 271
JERZAKOWSKI, LEESA 35
JESSIE, JEFFERY 142
JETLAND, LORRAINE 165
JEUDY, NOEMI MARIE 149
JEWETT, HALEY 78
JIRIK, TAMMY 71
JOBE, GENEVA N. 160
JODI LYNN BLASCO 65
JOEL, ISSAAC BEN 21
JOHANSEN, STACIE 73
JOHNS, JENNI 203
JOHNSON, B.F. 21
JOHNSON, CARRRIE R. 186
JOHNSON, CARTER CUE 154
JOHNSON, CHRISTIE 274
JOHNSON, CINDY 258
JOHNSON, CYNDI 128
JOHNSON, DANA 266
JOHNSON, HOLLIE 252
JOHNSON, JENNIFER 97
JOHNSON, JENNIFER A. 143
JOHNSON, JOYCE 158
JOHNSON, KATHY D.B. 301

JOHNSON, KATHY W. 170
JOHNSON, KATI 298
JOHNSON, LISA E. 239
JOHNSON, MELINDA 103
JOHNSON, MICHELE 18
JOHNSON, NICOLLE M. 198
JOHNSON, ONYX L. 221
JOHNSON, S.E. 229
JOHNSON, SARAH 110
JOHNSON, SUNSHINE 212
JOHNSON, THOMAS JR. 189
JOHNSON, TINA M. 231
JOHNSON, TOMMY 66
JOHNSON, VANESSA 264
JOHNSON. AMY 264
JOHNSTON, KAREN 110
JOHNSTON, VIRGINIA 190
JONAS, LEONARD A. 157
JONES, ALDEN E. 183
JONES, BLAINE A 92
JONES, CINDY 109
JONES, CYNDI 113
JONES, DARLENE 286
JONES, ERIN K. 104
JONES, KATHERINE 64
JONES, MEGAN 248
JONES, NICHOLLE 201
JONES, SAMANTHA 211
JONES, SHERRY 44
JONES, SOLOMON 106
JONES-HENDRICKSON, S. 100
JORDAN, KAREN 293
JORDAN, SUSAN 88
JORDAN, T. ALTON 306
JOSEPH, MARIYLN 231
JOTEN, DOROTHY J. 109
JOYCE, MICHELLE 58
JOZWIAK, THERESA 45
JUDGE, ALICE 150
JUMPER, KATHY WATSON 69
JUNQUEIRA, JOANIE 289
JUSTICE, SUSANNE 281
KAAPUNI, REBECCA A. 243
KACZKOWSKI, WALTER 132
KADDASH, MARY E. 226
KAG, T. AILEEN 208
KAHLER, LEE W. 159
KAINE, DOLORES 145
KALBUNDE, FLORENCE A. 300
KALLAS, MONICA J. 279
KALLE, TANYA 271
KAMMAN. SHARON 280
KAMOUNEH, VIRGINIA 279
KANGAS, JUANITA H. 109
KANICS, JYOTHI 175
KANNARD, APRYLL S. 267
KANTZ, FLOYD J. 167
KAPSAROFF, CHRIS 293
KAR, JAMES J295
KARWOSKI, HEATHER 268
KASSNER, ED 183
KATO, LES 164
KAUFMAN, MOLLY 305
KAVANAUGH, LISA 74
KAYE, LAURIE 112
KEELER, NICOLE LEA 264
KEELING, SHONDA D. 126
KEEN, STANLEY E. 23
KEENE, DEBORAH A. 25
KEITH, CHARLOTTE 290
KELLAR, MARY R. 164
KELLEY, JOAN E. 157
KELLOGG, MICHELLE M. 291
KELLY, APRIL D. 25
KELSO, JILL 23
KEMP, INEZ SIMPSON 83
KEMPER, JENNIFER 162
KENNDEY, JOHN R. 254
KENNEDY, KYLE 77
KENNER, JOSEPH A. 272
KENNEY, ALICE GRANT 173
KENT. CARL 284
KENTNER, AIMEE 202
KENUL, AMRILYN T. 114
KERN, DAVID A. 64
KERN, SHERI 115
KERNS, CATHERINE 46

KERSEY, ELAINE 6
KESSLER, AMALIA 29
KEUCHER, WILLIAM F. 33
KEYSER, KATHERINE 294
KHEEDO, SARGON 52
KHOSHABA, NATALIE 83
KIBER, SARA 61
KIDA, JESSICA VICTORIA 57
KIDWELL, LORNA T. 111
KIDWELL, TAMMY 306
KIGER, STEPHANIE K. 105
KILBOURNE, DIANA M. 101
KILE, SUSAN 204
KILGORE, LESLIE 156
KIM, JEAN 139
KIM, TEENA 279
KIMBERLYNN, ANN 187
KIMBROUGH, BETTY SUE 173
KIMMEL, CATHE 188
KIMMEL, KEVIN J. 28
KING, DENISE 101
KING, EMERY 92
KING, LESLIE E. 124
KING, STEPHEN D. 206
KING, WALTER MAE 140
KINGETER, KATHLEEN 52
KINGSTON, THOMAS P. 46
KINNEY, RENATA 303
KINSEY, AMY 220
KINYON, STACY 165
KINZIE, MARY E. 292
KIRKHOFF, JOHN L. 218
KIRKPATRICK, SUSAN 51
KISE, JIM 162
KLEIN, MARGARET 309
KLIMSAK, KAREN 256
KLINE, MISSY 114
KLOMP, DEANNA M. 92
KNIFFEN, SHANNON 248
KNIGHT, BOB 240
KNIGHT, DEBBY 89
KNIGHT, LORRAINE V. 35
KNOBBE, LYNNE C. 42
KNOWLES, SIMONE 243
KNOWLES, VIOLET 250
KNOX, DANICA 32
KOBERSTINE, LORI 66
KOCH, THOMAS 285
KOCHUYT, SHERRY 95
KOEHN, SUZANA M. 212
KOEPPEL, BECKY 199
KOHN, SILVA M. 102
KOLLIN, CYNTHIA 57
KOMNINOS, ALEXIA 202
KOPPLEMAN, KAREN R. 277
KOREN, JENNIFER 9
KOSTER, KERRY L. 43
KOSTKA, SHIRLEY B. 279
KOTESKEY, FREDERICK 101
KOTTER, JAMES I. 155
KOVACS, DEBORAH A. 162
KOZAK, ELIZABETH T. 132
KRAFKA, KATHY L. 275
KRAFT, KATHY 196
KRAJEWSKI, TARA 193
KRANZ, TASHA LYNN 297
KRASSNER, APRIL IVY 197
KRAUSE, ANNE-MARIE 55
KREBS, DEBORA R. 180
KROLL, KIMBERLY J. 133
KRONER, LUCILLE M. 192
KRULL, F. A. 104
KRYWUCKI, KAREN P. 215
KRYZYWICKI, JOHN W. 221
KUAFMAN, MAXWELL C. 224
KUEHN, ALAN DUANE 139
KUMPF, AMY 150
KUNG, PANG JEN 181
KUSKE, JENNIFER 178
KUTTIKKATTU 260
KUZMICK, MICHELE 112
KYLE, ROSEMARY H. 236
LAABS, TED 218
LABBE, MAGDALE 272
LACAYO, DEBORAH J. 94
LACEBY, JOE 45
LACY, ANN M. 125

LADEN, TANYA 77
LADUKE, AMY 190
LAGASSE, HARVEY 29
LAHO, LISA 309
LAHO, ROBERT O. 72
LAHR, AMY 46
LAI, KAREN 52
LAJOIE, DENISE M. 142
LAMB, ELVA R. 117
LAMB, PAUL M. 23
LAMBERT, KATHLEEN M. 157
LAMONT, JENNIFER 40
LAMPE, ANNACAROL 80
LANDMARK, WENDY 220
LANDRETH, NORTH 23
LANE, CHRISTINA JO 258
LANG, D. THOMAS 284
LANGLEY, JAMES T. JR. 80
LANITIS, MICHAEL 248
LANSINK, LAURA 269
LANZAROTTO, SHERYL B. 122
LAPHAM, KATHERINE D. 254
LAPLUME, JOY 261
LAPORTE, DANIEL 116
LARMAN, ALLEN 56
LARSEN, JACKIE A. 198
LARSON, CAMI 187
LARSON, KALAI T. 63
LARSON, ROBERT C. 280
LASSEL, KARIN 306
LASSEN, TIFFANY 238
LATALLADE, MARY A. 246
LATIMORE, WILLIE MAE 185
LATORRE, KATHY 233
LATOUCHE, EMMANUEL 174
LATRALL, SIMON 259
LAVEGLIA, GERI 177
LAWRIMORE, DORIS L. 111
LAWSON, HELEN 29
LAWSON, JAN P. 180
LAWSON, KIM 84
LAWTHER, RICH 243
LAYCOCK, ROBIN MARIE 96
LE ROUX, THOMAS J. 156
LEANDRO, CLAUDETTE 124
LEBLANC, PIERRE III 264
LECK, KENNETH F. 289
LEDERMANN, KAREN 271
LEDOUX, DENISE 15
LEE, ADRIENNE 24
LEE, DEBORAH 263
LEE, DEBRA J. 151
LEE, IMOGENE V. 93
LEE, MARILYN 127
LEE, MIYUNG SUSAN 56
LEE, PENG ENG 19
LEE, SABRINA M. 109
LEE, TANIA 189
LEE, TIFFANY AMBER 74
LEE, YVONNE 20
LEES, CHRISTIAN 210
LEGER, REBECCA 207
LEIGH, SANDY 100
LEISTIKO, KERI 120
LEITL, DEBRA J. 203
LEKSA, BRUCE J. 174
LEMBO, MARIE S. 59
LEMMONS, C. CHERYL 182
LEMONS, BRONSON 213
LEMPERLE, VIRGINIA 29
LENKER, STACIE 227
LENY, JANICE ARTHUR 13
LENZIE, BRIDGET 192
LEON, ELVIRA M. 254
LEON, ELVIRA M. 33
LEON, GONZALO 144
LEROW, SARAH 170
LESTER, DARLENE 189
LETTERMAN, CINDY 103
LEVASSEUR, CARMEN 183
LEVINE, JENNIFER 37
LEVINSKY, JENNIFER K. 59
LEWIS, HEATHER 7
LEWIS, SHARON L. 229
LEWIS, SHERI 122
LEWIS, TERESA 244
LEYBA, CHRISTINA 100

LI, SHARI 228
LICHOTA, ANNA MARIA 99
LILES, JENNIFER ANN 56
LILLIE, SHERRI 105
LIMAKATSO, 284
LIN, SONDRA 133
LINCOLN, ANNA 92
LINDER, JESSICA 178
LINDQUIST, JENNIFER 37
LINDSEY, FALLA 13
LINDSTROM, SANDRA 239
LINEHAN, MICOLE 79
LINES, AMY 288
LINGER, MARILYN 77
LINIMON, AMY 242
LINK, CAROL B. 150
LINK, EMILY 251
LINVILLE, RAINA 207
LINZEY, STANFORD JR. 207
LIPFORD, TANIKA 63
LISOWSKI, DAWN 281
LITCHFIELD, KATHY 115
LITTLE, AMY BETH 99
LIVERNOIS, CONSTANCE 128
LO CASTRO, THOMAS M. 287
LOBECK, LISA 233
LOCKHART, ANGELIC 5
LOCKWOOD, NORMA R. 250
LOESER, AMY 22
LOGAN, HOWARD T. 171
LOGSDON, LOIS 193
LOMBARDO, DEANNA 73
LONEY, WENDY 300
LONG, BESSIE 235
LOOMIS, CHERYL 43
LORENZ, MELANIE 130
LORENZ, VALERIE N. 49
LOSEY, JEANNE 191
LOTZ, JACQUELYNE A. 174
LOUIS, VINCENT DE PAUL 5
LOVELESS, PATRICK 250
LOVELL, MICHAEL 75
LOWDEN, JOHN L. 135
LOWERS, BEVERLY H. 290
LOWRY, VERONICA 253
LOZIER, ELISABETH A. 146
LUCAS, JULIA 196
LUCCHETTI, 309
LUCER, ANITA R. 36
LUCESCU, CATHY 274
LUELLEN, BETTY J. 265
LUFFMAN, EMMERSON172
LUGINBILL, TRACI 128
LUNDBERG, CHRISTA R. 100
LUNDEEN, BRANDY 21
LUZNAR, LISA 260
LYLE, DENIS 144
LYNCH, JAMES 80
LYNCH, LINDA E. 120
LYON, DIANE 136
LYON, SARAH 121
LYONS, MARK ERIC 79
LYSENG, CHRISTINE 42
MACIORSKI, VINNIE 92
MACK, KELLY S. 52
MACK, ROBIN 239
MACKENZIE, DEENA 252
MACKEY, HOWARD JR. 262
MACMULLEN, HEATHER 85
MACNEILLE, ELIZABETH 24
MACY, SARAH 291
MAGRUDER, RAY 238
MAHON, PATRICIA 223
MAHONEY, BOB 101
MAHONEY, LINDA L 227
MAIETTA, DIANE 174
MAKELIN, JAMIE 255
MALARD, ALICIA 202
MALONE, PHYLLIS 179
MALONEY, CAHTERINE 33
MANCINELLI, ASHLEY 91
MANGUS, AMY 149
MANKOWITZ, RACHEL 219
MANN, DEBBIE 252
MANNING, MARY A 170
MAPLE, MARCI 224
MAPP, CATHY R. 133

MARAZZANI, SANTA A. 74
MARCHESE, BRIDGET 182
MARGOSIAN, JENNI 144
MARGY, GRANDMA 253
MARIE, VAL 92
MARION, BECKY 199
MARION, SHARYN E. 46
MARKLE, JAMES R. SR. 12
MARLOWE, ROASLIE 293
MARSHALL, ANITA 250
MARTHIJOHNI, J. 282
MARTIN, DAWN 5
MARTIN, DEBRA L. 136
MARTIN, ELYSE 203
MARTIN, FRAN 147
MARTIN, HEATHER A. 91
MARTIN, R. TROY 44
MARTIN, SAMUEL T. 293
MARTIN, VICTORIA R. 54
MARTINEAU, JENNY 30
MARTINELLI, CARLA 90
MARTINEZ, MELISSA 249
MARTINSON, DENISE 80
MARTISH, MONICA E. 131
MARX, NADINE 165
MASARAKI, MONICA 165
MASFERRER, MARGARET 246
MASON, REX 74
MASSEY, GAYLE 14
MATHIESEN, DANA 239
MATLAGA, JOAN 311
MATTHEWS, BARBARA 208
MATTHEWS, TANYA 63
MATTIO, ALETHIA E. 148
MAU, JASMIN L. 30
MAUDLIN, CYNTHIA 260
MAUPAI, MICHELE 309
MAXIE, CHARLES THOMAS 18
MAXWELL, LEANNE 191
MAY, CHERYL 52
MAY, EDITH E. 75
MAYE, MELISSA N. 289
MAYS, JENNIFER 89
MAZOLA, BELLE 199
MCARTHUR, JACKI 199
MCBRATNEY, JOSEPH C. 128
MCCALL, SANDY J. 244
MCCALL, TAMMY 100
MCCANN, TINA 87
MCCARVER, SHIREE 122
MCCAY, LAURA 294
MCCLAIN, HAZEL M. 164
MCCLELLAN, RITA 297
MCCLELLAND, GENEVIEVE 117
MCCOLLUM, GARY 24
MCCONNELL, JOHN R. 240
MCCONNELL, SCOTT 61
MCCONNELL, WENDY 6
MCCORD, SHANNON 57
MCCOY, KARYN 121
MCCOY, MELODY 170
MCCRACKEN, MICHAEL D. 64
MCCRAY, FRED 33
MCCREA, SCOTT 69
MCCULLOUGH, MARY L. 131
MCCULLUM, KENYA 308
MCCURN, PATRICIA 139
MCCUTCHEN, MARGARET 103
MCCUTCHEON, HEATHER 83
MCCUTCHEON, HELEN 6
MCDANIEL, JEANNETTE A. 71
MCDANIELS, NAKYA 282
MCDONALD, ALISHA 197
MCDONALD, NICOLE 310
MCFARLAND, CHARLOTTE 230
MCGEE, ANGIE 6
MCGILL, AMANDA 150
MCGILL, LINDA JEANNE 54
MCGONEGAL, BOBBI 197
MCGOWAN, ELIZABETH M. 200
MCGUIRE, KEISHA 119
MCGUIRE, STEPHANIE 208
MCHEFFEY, JIM 263
MCINERNEY, JENNY MARIE 89
MCINTYRE, BRIAN 98
MCINTYRE, JUANITA 192
MCKAY, CYNTHIA 122

MCKELVEY, GERALD H. 91
MCKENNA, TIMOTHY 28
MCKEOWN, COLEEN 257
MCKINLEY, DELAYNE 181
MCKINNEY, ELIZABETH 310
MCKITTRICK, OPAL 195
MCLAIN, ALTA R. 150
MCLAMB, AMY 72
MCLEMORE, ANN 138
MCLLWAINE, BECKY 168
MCMANUS, LISA 158
MCMILLIAN, FRANCES M. 86
MCNAMARA, CHARLENE 118
MCNAUGHTON, HELEN 63
MCPETERS, SHARON 52
MCPHAIL, LOUISE 30
MCPHERSON, CHRISSY 291
MCREE, GIORGETTA 152
MCSWIGIN, TRACEY 266
MCVAY, SHIRLEY A. 243
MCWATTERS, EDD DAVID 16
MEACHER, STELLA 217
MEADOWS, SHANNON 69
MEAHGER, TRACY 72
MEDDAUGH, CORRIE 28
MEDEI, KERI 230
MEFFORD, JESSICA 181
MEHL, SHANNON 61
MEILINGER, ALISON 310
MEINEN, MARYANN 234
MEINERS, BRIDGETTE 168
MELBY, JUSTINE 224
MELENDEZ, SANDRA 67
MELLINGER, ANN MARIE 178
MELOS, R.A. 164
MELTON, EDEN L. 147
MELTZER, AMBER C. 75
MEMMER, MISTY 292
MENDEL, KATHLEEN LEE 45
MENDOZA, KATHERINE 71
MENG, SHANNON 228
MENNINGER, KATHY L. 115
MERCER, BETTY D. 225
MERCHANT, GERAD M. 268
MERCIER, MARA E. 233
MERRILL, JULIA W. 62
MERTEN, JULIE 218
MESARIC, JANICE 286
MESEROLE, CHARLES D. 298
MESERVY, JANIE 144
MESMER, LESLIE 123
MESSNER, MARY GARNETT 65
MESTRE, HENRY M. JR. 17
MESZAROS, ANDOR 277
METCALF, MISSY 116
METRAS, NICOLE 195
MEYER, ANGIE 10
MICELI, ANTONINA M. 250
MICHAEL, BRIAN 23
MICHAEL, PAT 36
MICKENS, DARRYL BRUCE 71
MILARDO, PHYLLIS W. 13
MILBURY, HEATHER 235
MILEK, K. B. 258
MILLER, ALICE M. 188
MILLER, AMY 194
MILLER, CARY 137
MILLER, DOUG 177
MILLER, FLORENCE 199
MILLER, LISA 247
MILLER, MARSHA ANN 65
MILLER, MIRIAM 309
MILLER, ROGER MAX 108
MILLER, STEVE 153
MILLER, YVONNE LEE 169
MILLETTE, STEPHANIE 74
MILLS, DALE A. 123
MILLS, DAVID A. 88
MILLWOOD, PAMELA E. 104
MILO, GENNARO 12
MIMM, HEIEI 173
MINOR, MICHELLE 65
MINTON, DAVID H. 295
MIROCHA, ANGIE 178
MISIAK, JENNY M. 80
MISTERKA, ADAM F. 184
MITCHELL, ENID 238

MITCHELL, KENA M. 239
MIXON, AUDRE J. 141
MIYAKE, LYNN 218
MJOEN, CRYSTAL 131
MOBERG, ROBERTA 281
MOBLEY, MANDY 272
MOELLER, ELLEN 90
MOELLERS, DEBRA R. 93
MOFFATT, MONIQUE 46
MOGLE, JUDY 194
MOHRBACHER, TRACY 63
MOIRE, CHRISTINE 75
MOISIS, MARAK 288
MOLLANDER, JULIE 55
MOMINEE, GRETCHEN 152
MONESSON, HARRY S. 151
MONIGOLD, ROGER J. 284
MONK, THELMA G. 219
MONTERO, NATASHA E.M. 151
MONTERO, NATASHA MAYES 98
MONTGOMERY, IDA MARIE 311
MONTGOMERY, MICHELLE 58
MONTGOMERY, SHANNON 108
MOONEY, EILEEN 186
MOONEY, LANA 32
MOORE, ADRIENNE C. 201
MOORE, BETHE 148
MOORE, GRIN 253
MOORE, JULIE A. 196
MOORE, MELISSA 307
MOORE, NICOLE 178
MOORE, TERI 66
MOORE, VICKIE POLLITT 152
MOORHEAD, RACHEL 120
MORAIS, MARIE E. 87
MORAN, HEATHER 185
MORAN, MICHELLE 272
MOREHEAD, SANDIE 275
MORELOCK, MARSHA 113
MORGAN, BETTY JO 265
MORGAN, JOHNNY R. III 131
MORGENSEN, BRITTNEY 90
MORIARITY, AMY 206
MORIARTY, CHRIS 42
MORIN, ANNETTE 227
MORRIS, LEONARD J. JR. 34
MORRIS, LISA 53
MORRIS, MARCIA R. 76
MORRIS, RUFUS VARKER 53
MORRISON, BETTY G. 13
MORSE, BETH 149
MORSE, PAM 140
MOSELEY, JOHN ALLEN 78
MOSIER, LISA D. 243
MOSLEY, BARBARA F. 39
MOSQUERA, ANA MARIA 125
MOTA, GINA 152
MOULTON, LAURA 56
MOUSSETTE, KATHY S. 276
MOYLE, TROY 175
MRAZ, CHRISTINE E. 288
MUELLER, LYNNETTE 165
MUIR, TOBIN LYNN 87
MULLANEY, CORINNE 165
MULLINS, JANET 161
MURPHY, COLLEEN LYNN 62
MURPHY, ERIN 83
MURPHY, I. C. 181
MURPHY, MARGARET 118
MURRAY, GWENDOLYN 179
MURRAY, THOMAS P. 18
MURRELL, ANN MARIE 183
MURRY, JOSHUA 279
MUSA, T. MELINDAH 72
MUSGRAVE, FLORENCE M. 24
MUSSER, JULIE 105
MUSSMAN, HEATHER 12
MUZATKO, EDWARD J. 146
MUZYCHKA, CHRISTINE 193
MYERS, DAWN BRYAN 56
MYERS, SHAREON 272
MYKYTA, MARY A. 206
MYRONES, GINA 200
NACCARI, ROBIN 122
NADON, RENE M. 244
NAKOFF, WENDY 311
NANSTAD, LISA 154

NAPOLI, MICHELLE 58
NASH, SHARON CROOKS 244
NASON, MARDI D. 224
NAU, LARRY 238
NAVAGH, KAREN R. 269
NAVARRO, RENEE 280
NEELEY, JACQUIE 178
NEILL, MALISSA A. 288
NEILLAND, SEAN K. II 106
NELSON, J. JOSEPH 252
NELSON, THERESA 246
NELSON, WENDY 6
NELSON-GRIER, GLORIA 163
NESBITT, ROSE 43
NEUBAUER, STACY 287
NEVAREZ, MELISSA 130
NEWKIRK, ANNA MARIE 102
NEWLIN, MICHALANNE 294
NEWMAN, TRICIA 35
NEWTON, LAUREL 56
NEY, LYNN 298
NGUYEN, MIMI 305
NGUYEN, NHUNG 21
NICE, ANGELA 85
NICHOLS, DEBORAH 297
NICHOLS, DONNA 26
NICK, GINA 195
NICK, STACY 128
NICKELL, ANN 245
NICKERSON, DOROTHY 162
NIELSEN, KAREN 79
NIELSEN, LYNNEA R. 194
NIEVES, MAGDALENA 234
NIKOSEY, STEVEN 256
NINO, DIANE 107
NIX, THOMAS E. 236
NOBLE, ILENE 15
NOECKER, SUZETTE 104
NOEL, CHERYL A. 239
NOGUERIRA, MARIA D.C. 127
NOLAND, JENNIFER 201
NORMAN, DONNA 91
NORMAN, JENNIFER 89
NORRIS, ASHLEIGH 253
NORTON, DONNA 310
NORTON, MS. 113
NOTO, CARLA 186
NOVOTNY, EMILY 36
NOWAK, MARIE T. 213
NOYES, LAUREANE 205
NULTY, MONICA 228
NUNLEY, SANDRA KAYE 298
NYE, JO ELLEN 310
O'BRIEN, ALICE 11
O'BRIEN, DONNA 177
O'BRIEN, KARIN 76
O'BRIEN, KATIE 227
O'BRIEN, MARY ELLEN 232
O'BRIEN, RITA 56
O'BRIEN, TIMOTHY 248
O'CONNOR, BRENDA 148
O'DONNELL, KATHERINE 210
O'LEARY, KAREN 216
O'MARA, JESSICA 123
O'MARA, MICHAEL 112
O'NEIL, KATHLEEN 62
O'NEIL, KERRI 230
OAKWOOD, TRACY 256
OBED, LENORA RITA 246
OBERLEE, JEFFREY 88
OBERMAN, CAROLYN 198
OBERST, TAMMY 301
OBUHANICK, MICHELLE 287
OEHLEY, BERTA 220
OGDEN, CELESTE 47
OGDEN, TINA 244
OKORIE, SAMUEL O. 211
OLSON, MILDRED E. 226
ORR, ZELLIE RAINEY 261
ORSOL, HENRIETTA 138
ORTINAU, BECKY 269
ORTIZ, LYNETTE 301
ORTIZ, REYLVIE E. 241
ORZADA, RANDY 43
OSADA, KIM 271
OSBORN, JENNIFER 161
OSTER, JANE 139

OSURA, DOROTHY 93
OUELLETTE, TIM 34
OVISSI, MARYANN 231
OWEN, KRIS 295
OWEN, NANCY 235
OWEN, PAMELA J. 304
OWENS, EVONNE L. 263
OWENS, JANICE M. 32
OWENS, MICHAEL 284
OWINGS, AMY L. 24
OZBURN, DIANE 168
PACHOCKA, BARBARA F. 107
PADILLA, SOPHIE 257
PAFFRATH, KENNETH F. 73
PAGE, ANNE 7
PAINE, MARC 294
PAINTER, JOHN 311
PALMER, BRENDA 300
PALMER, NICOLE 167
PALMIERI, ROCCO 70
PANAGAKOS, ANASTASIA 172
PANDALIS, KENDRA 258
PANDYA, SAMPURNA 211
PAPPA, RUTH 120
PARADIS, JENNIFER 124
PARDALLIS, VICKI 146
PARHAMOVICH, JOHN 109
PARKER, EDNA M. 186
PARKER, HAYLEY 176
PARKER, JON B. 298
PARKINS, SILVIA 243
PARKS, RACHEL ANN 108
PARLETTE, JULIE 215
PARLIER, KEITH ALLEN 35
PARLIN, KARA RENEE 301
PARNELL, WENDY SUE 160
PARNOFIELLO, LOUISE P. 31
PARRIS, ANGELA R. 11
PARRY, LYNETTE 158
PARSLEY, JAMIE ALLEN 145
PARSONS, JACQUE 173
PARTIN, WINFRED 288
PASE, MONICA 303
PASK, MARY 217
PASKETT, MARNAE 87
PASQUARIELLO, LAURA 205
PASSANISI, KATIE 133
PATRICK, SHAUN 311
PATRONITE, ANETA 40
PATTEN, TAMERA 229
PATTERSON, ANDY J. 114
PATTERSON, NIKI 265
PATTON, KATHLEEN 3
PAUL, SHIRLEY 303
PAULACHOK, AMI 146
PAVLICEK, SUSAN 254
PAYNE, LILLAN WELLS 226
PAZ, REINA 73
PEARSON, GRACE 55
PECORA, THOMAS 241
PEED, COLBY 213
PEELER, ANITA 36
PEIFER, COURTNAY 73
PEIRSON, MARGARET E. 79
PELLEGRINO, ROBIN 61
PELLERITO, MADELYN K. 294
PEMBERTON, BOBBIE J. 265
PENNELL, KIM 44
PENNES, WENDY S. 55
PENNINGTON, KIMBERLY 31
PEREZ, MARIA H. 307
PEREZ, MIKEY 288
PERGA, SUZANNE 222
PERKINS, HOLLY 19
PESCE, CHARLENE 159
PESOLA, DAWN 161
PESTER, MARY MARGARET 59
PETERS, EVELYN 263
PETERS, MISTY 58
PETERSON, AMY 72
PETERSON, DARRELL M. 135
PETERSON, ELAINE 267
PETERSON, ESTER ELENA 313
PETERSON, LEAH 130
PETERSON, MICHELLE 105
PETERSON, PAUL 245
PETERSON, PEGGY 197
PETIT, CARLETON F. 210

PETRO, RAMONA S. 106
PETTY, JOYCE 261
PEYER, DON 92
PEZZANO, MARIE 105
PFAFF, JULIE 50
PFISTER, JOHN A. 254
PHAM, ANH 313
PHEIL, CONNI 42
PHELAN, THOMAS A. 123
PHELPS, PAT 193
PHIFER, MICHELLE D. 170
PHILLIPS, DEAN 80
PHILLIPS, JUANITA S. 295
PHILLIPS, KATHRINE R. 196
PHILLIPS, MIKE 102
PHILLIPS, NANCY 141
PHILLIPS, OLIE H. 39
PHILPOTT, JENNI 178
PIERCE, BERNARD H. 14
PIERRITZ, J. 273
PIERSON, DENISE 94
PIESKAS, TONI 34
PINCH, CHRISTINA 242
PINE, ANA 38
PINEDA, RHONDA M. 237
PINETTE, JENNY 295
PINKSTON, KELI 259
PINTAR, FRANCINE E. 152
PIPPIN, JANE 102
PITMAN, RODNEY E. 228
PITT, CHRISTINE A. 301
PITTERSON, HOWARD A. 149
PITTMAN, NANETTE 23
PITTS, JOHN 194
PLACE, REGINA A. 68
PLANTNER, MARY JEAN 294
PLATT, LINDA B. 258
PLOCK, OLIVE G. 267
PLUNKETT, DONNA 145
POIRIER, MARIE 311
POISSOT, SHANA D. 106
POLES, ALESSANDRA A. 203
POLIZZI, LUCY 131
POLK, AMY 99
POLLOCK, JENNIFER 162
POLLWORTH, KAREN J. 209
PONTING, JEAN 210
PONTON, ELEANOR 140
POOLE, JACINDA 26
POOLE, STEPHANIE 115
POPOVIC, ALEXSANDRA 27
PORTER, GINA M. 268
PORTER, WAYNE 94
PORTULAS, KIMBERLY 159
POSEY, KIMBERELY M. 74
POULIN, JODIE 218
POULIN, JOSEPH D. 289
POWELL, LESIA J. 283
POWER, ANN MARIE 180
POWNALL, JENNIFER L. 262
PRATT, DEBBY 181
PRELL, CHRISTINE 243
PRELL, LAMONT 72
PRESINZANO, KERRY A. 284
PRESTA, DIANE M. 177
PRETTYMAN, DON A. 214
PRICE, AMBEL A. 66
PRICE, NORMA L. 144
PRICE, STACY 50
PRICE, TAUNYA 133
PRITCHETT, ELVEDA O. 27
PROBASCO, APRIL 182
PROCALAMOS, ELLEN 153
PROCTOR, STARR 154
PROFUMO, DENISE 197
PROPHET, KATHLEEN S. 52
PROVANCE, CHERYL 210
PRUETT, SHANE 106
PRYSTAUK, WILLIAM D. 90
PUCKETT, SHIRLEY M. 129
PUDELSKI, JOHN 254
PUGH, BOBBIE J. 21
PUGH, ROBERT O. 50
PULLEY, ROBIN R. 124
PURVIS, DANIELLE 52
PYLES, JENNIFER 163
QUAID, R.L. 44
QUALE, ERICKA 15

QUERRY, CONNIE 45
QUERRY, HEATHER 73
QUIGGLE, BRUCE JR. 33
QUIGLEY, KIMBERLY 287
QUINN, JUDY 159
QUINN, RAYNA 303
QUINN, ZALENA C. 257
RABB, ANN M. 150
RACHELS, ALICE MARY 136
RACKLEY, KELLY 31
RADER, JENNIFER 162
RADIN, BEN 136
RADOY, GINA 152
RAFIQUE, JOYCE 205
RAGUBEER, KHALOUTIE 110
RAHBARI, CAROL J. 104
RALEY, CARINA 235
RAMIREZ, MELAENA 79
RAMOS, ELYSON 202
RAMSEY, TIFFANIE 126
RAMSOUR, JENNIFER 161
RANEY, JENNIFER 161
RANKIN, TERESA D. 284
RAREY, PATRICIA A. 26
RASMUSSEN, VIRGINIA 190
RAUPP, EDWARD ROBERT 162
RAWLS, SHAUN 285
RAWLSTON, VALERIE 13
RAY, GAY E. 160
RAY, HERMAN 268
RAY, JENNIFER 162
RAYMOND, SHARON L. 165
RAYNOR, MONIQUE 216
REAM, THERSE' A. 224
RECALDE, L.S. 124
REDDICK, BLONDINE L. 22
REDHEAD, ANDREA M. 92
REDLING, KRISTINE 78
REDNER, SHARON 135
REED, BERNICE ANITA 98
REED, CONNIE 230
REED, CYNTHIA M. 32
REED, ELIZABETH 25
REED, LEANE H. 130
REED, MYRTLE FROST 71
REED, W.W. 17
REEDER, HUBERT 22
REEDY, BEVERLY 138
REEF, KATRINA 56
REES, CHRISTY 191
REES, JULIE 239
REESE, HARVEY E. III 283
REESE, HEATHER 182
REEVES, DIANE MARIE 101
REHRIG, A. RUDOLPH 273
REICHEL, KATHY 62
REID, A. K. 195
REID, LEO JR. 286
REIMERS, AMBER D. 85
REINHART, INGRE 14
REITER, DEANNA 38
RENAUD, MICHELLE 56
RENFRO, APRIL 118
RENNER, JENNIFER 30
RESCZENKO, PAUL 195
REVECKY, RUTH M. 219
REXRODE, KELLI 215
REYBURN, STANLEY S. 106
REYNALDO, ERAINA Q. 176
REYNOLDS, ANNE 104
REYNOLDS, CAROLE 108
REYNOLDS, KELLY 256
REYNOLDS, SANDRA 206
RHYNE, KEVIN 242
RIBNICK, RACHEL 170
RICE, TRACY 238
RICHARD, KATHY 50
RICHARDS, AIMEE L. 17
RICHARDS, ASHLY 188
RICHARDS, HELEN 202
RICHARDS, MARY 231
RICHARDS, PAULINE J. 97
RICHARDS, TAMMY 254
RICHARDSON, ELLA W. 151
RICHARDSON, J. 277
RICHARDSON, R.G. 129
RICHEY, APRIL 198

RICKMAN, PEGGY SUE 197
RIDDLE, LOIS 50
RIDENOUR, KIMBERLY 103
RIDGLEY, TERISA 156
RIGBY, YASMIN Y. 264
RIGGINS, CATHY 71
RINARD, JUDY 55
RINCON, DEBORAH 80
RIORDAN, PATRICIA 104
RITENOUR, GLADYS 64
ROASNI, CLAUDIA 280
ROBBINS, DEBORA 202
ROBERTS, CHRISTOPHER 241
ROBERTS, JESSIE R. 240
ROBERTS, JO ANN 95
ROBERTS, KATHERINE 288
ROBERTS, LOU 194
ROBICHAUD, DICK 198
ROBIN, TONIJOY 28
ROBINS, DAVID 191
ROBINSON, ELIZABETH 175
ROBINSON, KELLEY 194
ROBINSON, MICHELLE 233
ROBINSON, PATRICIA A. 98
ROBINSON, RICHARD 237
ROBINSON, SUSAN A. 68
ROBINSON, VELMA 251
ROBITAILLE, PRISCILLA 16
ROBRECHT, JOANNE 66
ROCKWELL, AMY 10
ROCKYVICH, CHARLES 242
RODGERS, KARALEIGH 108
RODIGUEZ, LOURDES 240
RODLI, NORA 22
RODNING, CHARLES B. 261
RODRIGUES, SUSAN 124
RODRIGUEZ, CELESTE 206
ROE, CAROL R. 187
ROEDER, BETH 264
ROGERS, LORALIE R. 204
ROGERS, TRACY 154
ROLBAND, WARREN 64
ROLFS, MELYSSA 272
ROLLF, MALYSSA 248
RONK, AMY LYNN 217
ROOKS, LOREI 71
ROPER, ERMA 140
ROPER, KELLI 236
ROSASCO, SHARI LEE 212
ROSE, ANGELA LEA 24
ROSE, DAPHNE 87
ROSE, DAVID R. 66
ROSE, LISA 119
ROSE, NADINE 139
ROSE, RHONDA J. 227
ROSE, ROBIN M. 76
ROSEBOOM, DEWAYNE K. 71
ROSEBORO, WILLIAM 16
ROSEN, KEITH 207
ROSENBERRY, JENNIFER 37
ROSIER, JOYCE 62
ROSS, JACQUETTA M. 136
ROSS, KAREN J. 60
ROSS, NANCY LYNN 264
ROSS, ROBERT ALLAN 312
ROSSEAU, SHANTELE 57
ROSSI, MARK ANTONY 55
ROTHSCHILD, DOROTHY 263
ROUNTREE, MELISSA 247
ROWE, ED 107
ROWLAND, JENNIFER 123
ROY, THERESA 257
RUBIN, AMY 220
RUBIN, ELAINE 152
RUBIO, SANDRA 277
RUCKI, CAROLE L. 270
RUDD, KIMBERLY 32
RUDER, MARGARET K. 127
RUDOLPH, DEANE 107
RUGGLES, MICHELLE 272
RUIZ, REGINA 96
RUMMEL, LYNETTE 193
RUOCCHIO, PATRICIA 142
RUPPERT, ELFRIEDE E. 168
RUSCH, ALYCIA 198
RUSCH, RACHEL 303
RUSSELL, CAMIE 255

RUSSELL, DONNA L. 25
RUSSELL, HELEN D. 83
RUSSELL, LOUISE 175
RUSSELL, SARAH 57
RUSSELL, SHERRI 17
RUSSIE, DEBBIE 145
RUTH, CAROL L. 187
RYAN, MICHAEL 66
RYAN, THOMAS M. 244
RYLANDER, AMALIA L. 195
SACCO, MICHELE J. 286
SALERNO, LAURA ANN 95
SALITSKY, ANNETTE 132
SALRIN, CHRISTINE ANN 194
SALTER, EVELYN SAPP 29
SALTZ, ELIZABETH 200
SALUSTRI, CATHY 164
SALVATI, VINCENT 15
SAMMONS, DAYNA 25
SAMMONS, VIRGIE MCCOY 140
SAMPLE, BECKY 15
SAMS, JUNE E. 226
SAMUELSON, ANNA M. 132
SANARAS, JENNY 162
SANDEE D. MORTVEDT 119
SANDERS, DARRAH 164
SANDERS, KAREN N. 303
SANDERS, SUSAN 275
SANDILAND, STACIE 204
SANDOVAL, BARBARA 220
SANDOVAL, YVONNE 12
SANIFER, JENNIFER 59
SANTOLOCI, DONNA 88
SANTUCCI, RITA 228
SAPOZNIK, MARC 65
SARC, THOMAS H. 156
SARMIENTO, ALLISON 200
SARTO, JOSEPH KENNETH 63
SATTERFIELD, MERNA 77
SAUNDERS, JULIE DEANN 109
SAUTER, LYNETTE 286
SAVAGE, JOAN 312
SAVARESE, JEN 94
SAVILLE, NICOLE 304
SAVINO, ANN 85
SAWICKI, CARLEEN M. 147
SAWREY, KATHRYN 120
SAWYER, LORI L. 286
SAYESS, LISA 68
SCADDEN, DEANNA 203
SCARBOROUGH, DON 262
SCHAEFER, KEELY D. 109
SCHAEFFER, KARL 258
SCHAEFFER, LORI 260
SCHAFF, BILLIE JO 13
SCHAFFER, MISHA T. 96
SCHAFFER, STEPHANIE 216
SCHARF, MICHAEL J. 283
SCHEFFEL, CARL 263
SCHIFFER, R. DAVIE 287
SCHILL, ANN 41
SCHLENKER, HAROLD II 9
SCHLEPER, JENNIFER 262
SCHLIENTZ, CARMEN M. 6
SCHMIDT, ANDREA LEE 184
SCHMIDT, BEVERLY 85
SCHMIDT, LLOYD 239
SCHMIDT, PAUL F. 142
SCHMIDT, RITA K. 301
SCHMIEDSKAMP, KARSON 48
SCHNEIDER, D. G. 213
SCHNEIDER, MARC S. 241
SCHNEIDER, SOREN 60
SCHNEIDER, VAL 168
SCHNEIDERLOCHNER, S. 84
SCHOCKEY, SHAWANA 204
SCHOEN, TONI L. 51
SCHOFIELD, JEN 180
SCHOLL, PAUL V. 225
SCHOPEN, DAYLE 151
SCHRADER, HENRY C. 251
SCHROEDER, SARA 209
SCHUETRUMPF, CINDY 296
SCHULDT, MICHELLE H. 248
SCHULTE, MARY J. 60
SCHUTTER, LYNNE 278
SCHWARZKOPF, STEVEN 298

SCHWINN, PATRICIA ANN 23
SCIACCA, ROSE ANN 119
SCOFIELD, HOLLY 26
SCOGNAMILLO, JOHN 45
SCOTT, BARBARA S. 108
SCOTT, LORI 237
SCOTT, STURAT J. 260
SCROGHAM, TERRI 271
SCRUGGS, ANDREW 148
SCULL, MICHELLE 217
SCULLIN, TOM 288
SEABERG, E.C. JR. 148
SEAL, CHASTITY 238
SEGVIC, IVANA 132
SEIGEL, JAY 252
SELBY, JENNIFER 144
SELLITTI, STACY 88
SELVAGGIO, DENISE L. 141
SEMEL, SYLVIA 42
SEMEL, SYLVIA 48
SENAN, DINESH 221
SENSENIG, LAURA 133
SEQUERIA, AYRON 167
SEREDA, DEBBY 55
SETTLE, HEATHER 85
SEVERANCE, COLLEEN 240
SEVERY, MICHELLE 63
SEXTON, JENNIFER 212
SHAHIJANIAN, ADRINEH 184
SHALLENBERGER, ANGELA 186
SHANK, SUSAN 111
SHAW, EDWIN L. 17
SHAW, JILL JOSETTE 115
SHAW, MOLLY 246
SHAYNE, VICTORIA 140
SHEALY, JEFFREY M. 9
SHEERIN, COLLEEN 309
SHEMWELL, DAN 212
SHERMAN, JENNIFER 178
SHERMAN, JOSEPH J. 26
SHERR, KIVA 32
SHERRIFF, SHARON 70
SHERZEY, TERESA 84
SHIKO, CRYSTAL LEA 256
SHOCKLEY, BRENDA 82
SHOE, NINA 293
SHOEMAKER, TAMMY 277
SHUMAN, GEOFFREY RAY 81
SHUPE, AMY MARIE 21
SIBERT, CINDY 30
SICHMELLER, EVA 23
SIDEBOTTOM, RACHEL 301
SIDELINGER, KATHY 70
SIDES, SHANA 293
SIDES, TAMERA 123
SILANSKIS, C. 202
SILVA, KATHLEEN 209
SIM, VALERIE 132
SIMOES, KRISTEN 156
SIMPSON, MARSHALL P. 217
SIMPSON, R. 281
SIMPSON. RUTH 278
SINCLAIR, AMY 40
SINCLAIR, DALE A. 258
SINCLAIR, WILLIAM C.182
SINGER, KAREN K. 295
SIZEMORE, JENNIFER 40
SJM 56
SKAGGS, MELISSA 87
SKALABRIN, LORI 116
SKAMANGAS, ANNA LYNN 125
SKELLEY, KEVIN 31
SKELTON, WILLARD LEE 275
SKIDMORE, AMANDA 60
SKINNER, JUDY R. 311
SKINNER, SARAH 242
SLATE, ANTONIA 169
SLATER, DELLA 94
SLAYTON, TRACEY 266
SLEDGE, PAM 22
SLOBODIAN, ROSEMARY 218
SLOKE, CARLA 174
SLOSSER, BETTYJANE 236
SLOTKIN, CHANDRA 244
SLOWICK, MONICA 302
SMALLWOOD, JANICE P. 37
SMART, ANGELA 173

SMATHERS, JENN 173
SMIALEK, KAREN F. 271
SMITH, AMY 264
SMITH, APRIL D. 40
SMITH, ASHLEY 168
SMITH, AUTUMN M. 145
SMITH, CHRISTINE 294
SMITH, CHRISTOPHER C. 308
SMITH, CONSTANCE 124
SMITH, CRYIL JR. 302
SMITH, ERIKA 203
SMITH, ESTHER M.G. 172
SMITH, FRED W.A. 184
SMITH, INEZ MARIE 289
SMITH, J. ELMO 168
SMITH, JENNY 144
SMITH, JESSICA 226
SMITH, JODI 42
SMITH, JULIE 301
SMITH, KANOA 189
SMITH, KATHERINE A. 298
SMITH, KATHRYN 230
SMITH, KENNETH 175
SMITH, KERRY 295
SMITH, LAURA LEE 212
SMITH, LESLIE A. 110
SMITH, MELISSA J. 305
SMITH, MITZIE 58
SMITH, REGINA 286
SMITH, SANDRA 204
SMITH, SARA 108
SMITH, SHANNEN 115
SMITH, THOMAS F. 129
SMOKE, AMY K. 180
SNODGRASS, SHERRI 105
SNOW, MARY 75
SNOW, SHEENA 306
SNOWBALL, EMMA 180
SNYDER, HEIDI 252
SNYDER, JENNA 145
SODA, STELLA A. 44
SODEN, EMILY 26
SODY, TARA 130
SOLANDER, TARA 103
SON, JAY 262
SONKSEN, COLETTE 111
SORENSEN, DEBORAH 142
SORENSEN, JEFF 300
SORENSON, MIKE 247
SOWERS, FLORENCE J. 171
SPANGLE, AMY 146
SPARKS, ERIC 63
SPARKS, RACHEL M. 212
SPARKS, SANDRA 208
SPAULDING, CARISSA A. 187
SPECE, JOANNE 60
SPEED, LYNNE OCONE 95
SPENCE, D. LESLIE 95
SPENCER, BETH 178
SPICER, CHRISTINA 84
SPOFFORD, SERENA 74
SPOTTS, BONNIE WALP 9
SPOTTS, S.L. 70
SPRAGUE, WENDY 264
SQUIRES, MEREDITH 223
ST. LAURENT, NANCY 245
ST. PETERS, JOAN 51
ST. JOHN, CHRIS 269
STAFFORD, JAN 145
STAFFORD, ROSE 103
STAFFORD, VANESSA ANN 155
STALLWORTH, NATASHA 198
STANCIEL, CYNTHIA H. 273
STANDLEY, EUNICE I. 80
STANFORD, LAWANNA L. 110
STANSELL, SHEILA 118
STANTON, MARGARET 312
STAR, ALIEN 245
STATEN, KRISTA 122
STATON, R.D. 298
STAUFFER, JEANNE M. 283
STAUFFER, PATRICIA 199
STEADMAN, JENNIFER S. 312
STEADMAN, LISA 105
STEAGER, MARTINA 233
STEARNS, CAROL D. 25
STEELE, DIANE 262

STEFANAC, L. 34
STEGEMEIER, RUTH 46
STEINECK, MELISSA 272
STEPHEND, EDWIN L. 183
STEPHENS, CHERIE S. 308
STEPHENSON, DOROTHY 94
STERRANTINO, JOY 61
STEVENS, CONNIE 257
STEVENS, JADENE F. 223
STEVENS, LINDA 192
STEVENS, MARLENE 166
STEVENS, PATRICIA A. 15
STEVENSON, AMY 265
STEWART, ALEX 222
STEWART, ANGELA 253
STEWART, KRISTIN 274
STICKLE, CHARLES E. 159
STIEBER, RENEE 121
STILES, HAROLD W. 302
STILL, SUSAN 254
STITH, SARAH 287
STODDART, NICOLE 174
STOGNER, LINDA S. 157
STONE, JAMES D. 13
STONE, LAURA B. 209
STONE, RICHARD 71
STOWE, ROBERT L. 72
STRAIN, LIAH 156
STRAND, HEIKE C. 296
STRANGE, ELENA 172
STRATTON, JOSEPH F. 105
STRELETZ, MICHELE 111
STRICKLAND, J. 311
STRICKLAND, LOLA 72
STRINGER, JANE 102
STRONG, GABRIELLE J. 13
STROUP, SUSANNE B. 60
STUART, JOHN T. 121
STUCKY, NICOLE 220
STURM, HEATHER 104
STUTLER, BECKY 36
STYER, SHARON L. 241
STYLES, D. EDWARD JR. 230
SUBRAMANI, KAVITA 30
SULEJMAN, ENVER 86
SULLIVAN, ANN MARIE 8
SULLIVAN, ERICA 24
SUMERA, DENISE M. 136
SUMMER, CLODAH G. 133
SUMMERS, SCOTT T. 106
SUNDERLAND, MICHELE 166
SURINA, E. 6
SUTCLIFFE, STEVE 31
SUTHERLIN, ALLISON J. 163
SWAB, LESLIE 73
SWALLOW, AMY 251
SWAN, FRANCES 188
SWARTZ, MICHELLE R. 58
SWERDLOW, NANCY ELLYNE 49
SWICKLAS, JEANNE 161
SWIFT, ELIZABETH 203
SYBIL, ERMA J. 160
SZAKACS, CAROLINE 304
SZMIOT, SHAYNA 43
TABB, SUSIE 31
TAIT, BOYD J. 221
TALBOT, BRIDGET 149
TALBOTT, EUNICE 150
TALIK, TAMARA 153
TALLMAN, PERRY 104
TANKARD, KATHY 84
TANKERSLEY, RESSIE238
TARANTO, BRIDGETT O. 17
TARKOUSKI, LYNDA 156
TARR, TEDDY 295
TAVITAS, LAURA 240
TAYLOR, CAROL L. 183
TAYLOR, DENISE 181
TAYLOR, JOHN C. 63
TAYLOR, MARIE ANNE L. 96
TAYLOR, MARY ANN 221
TAYS, KAREN 276
TEBO, CINDY E. 44
TEEHAN, JOHN T. 88
TEEVAN, VIRGINIA 152
TELESCO, ANGEL 82
TEMME, MARK E. 105

TENG, MONIQUE LOWI 126
TENHAEFF, HOPE 41
TERESKY, E.A. 38
TERRILL, RAE ANN 43
TERRY, LAURA 100
TERWILLEGER, TAMMI 170
TERWILLIGER, LUCINDA 237
TESCHER, ERICA 252
TESSIERI, ENRIQUE 178
THATCHER, BECKY 203
THIELE, MARGO MASE 246
THIESSEN, MICHELLE 307
THIESZEN, JENNA 178
THOMAE, HEATHER LYNN 268
THOMAS, AGNES W. 222
THOMAS, DIANE H. 36
THOMAS, JENNIFER 38
THOMAS, LORIE 226
THOMAS, MICHELLE D. 236
THOMAS, PAULA C.J. 136
THOMAS, PENELOPE T. 137
THOMASON, VIRGINIA W. 185
THOMPSON, ALLEN 150
THOMPSON, CAROLINE 210
THOMPSON, DAWN161
THOMPSON, DESOREE 179
THOMPSON, JODY 259
THOMPSON, JUDY 205
THOMPSON, M.H. 113
THOMPSON, MOI C. 284
THOMPSON, WILLIAM G. 180
THOMSON, L.W. 210
THOMTON, DANI 153
THORP, DEBIE 89
THRONEBERRY, MARY R. 112
THWAITES, KATHY ANNE 196
TIDMORE, KENNETH W. 63
TIFFANY, SHERYL L. 120
TILLMAN, ALISHIA 150
TIMMERMAN, MICHELLE 68
TINIO, CLAUDINE 191
TINSELY, LISA 258
TOBIN, DANIEL 281
TODD, ORIEN 17
TODD, TABBATHA 229
TOKATYAN, JENNIFER 33
TOLLEFSON, MARGARET 114
TOLLISON, ROBYN208
TOOLEY, PAUL E. JR. 171
TOOMEY, ANN M. 186
TOPPER, JENNY 37
TORRO, LAUREN-MICHELE 28
TOVANI, AMY 89
TOWNES, VIVIANNE HARDY 6
TRACY, LORI 133
TRAIL, TAMMIE R. 170
TRAINOR, KATHLEEN ANN 69
TRAINOR, KRISTEN 158
TRAPANESE, JOANNE R. 109
TRASK, BEVERLY 140
TRAXLER, JOY 261
TREECE, TERRI 74
TREES, JODI 165
TREMBLAY, CHERYL 259
TREND, KATHERINE T. 121
TREUMUTH, MARJORY A 226
TRIBBLE, DUSTE 90
TRIMBLE, THOMAS M. 289
TROXEL, TOM 288
TRUAX, CARLTON W. 184
TRUETT, LINDA 70
TRUMAN, JO 56
TRUTH 69
TSIAPERAS, CORRINE 290
TUCKER, JUDITH 287
TUNSTALL, TRACEY 84
TURANO, DEBBIE 80
TURNER, SARAH 115
TUTTLE, LARRY L. 192
TYNER, MATT 224
UCHIMURA, GABRIELA 190
UHER, AMY 190
UHLMANN, KATE 45
UNGER, PAULINE 198
UNIACKE, JENNIFER B. 171
URBAN, ADRIANNA 190
URBAN, JEANNIE 267
UTELL, JANINE M. 158

VALLEJO, ADA IVETTE 169
VAN BALEN, MAUREEN E. 114
VAN DUZER, JENNIFER R 163
VAN MEER, DAVID J. 68
VAN ORSDALE, ROSALETA 206
VAN VACTER, WILLIAM A. 33
VAN VALKENBURG, AMY 186
VAN VLEET, TINA 3
VAN WOERT, LOUISE 44
VANCAMP, KELLY 247
VANCE, SANDY 124
VANDERGRIEND, LOLLITA 281
VANDERHOEF, DOROTHY 38
VANDERLINDEN, CARIE 225
VANDYKE, KATHLEEN W. 214
VANGSNESS, KRISTEN 215
VARGA, BOZSI D. 177
VASQUEZ, CINDY 291
VAUGHN, JENNIFER 33
VAUGHN, PEGGY 143
VELDRAN, CAROL 160
VELEZ, LAURA 157
VENTALORO, RUSTY J. 219
VERCIGLIO, BETH 16
VERDU, ALYSSA 250
VERGA, APRIL 40
VERNER, DANENE 204
VIEIRA, BRENDA S. 81
VILARDI, ANDREA 107
VILLATORE, MEREDITH 307
VINCENT, C.L. 56
VINGERHOET, KAYE 306
VITALOS, ROBERT F. 70
VLACICH, JENNIFER 37
VNABUREN, DORIS 138
VOGEL, MARNIE L. 76
VOLK, STEPHEN 222
VRANISKOSKI, HELEN 141
WAARD, LAURA KAY 306
WACK, J.W. 15
WADDELL, WENDY 84
WADE, HEATHER 206
WADE, YVONNE KATHLEEN 51
WAGER, NADA 297
WAGER, RICHARD C. 100
WAKEMAN, JEAN ANN 181
WALCH, PHIL 198
WALCZAK, TARA 106
WALDRON, NICOLE 149
WALKER, DORIS M. 177
WALKER, HENRI EMERSON 251
WALKER, JEANETTE M. 201
WALKER, JENNIFER LYNN 192
WALKER, KRISTINA 223
WALKER, SHERYL LYNN 306
WALKER, TONYA 154
WALL, TRACI 237
WALLACE, JUDI 159
WALLICK, JENNIFER LEE 144
WALLS, EDWIN E. 97
WALSH, LAURIE 271
WALSH, S. BRENDA 120
WALTER, BERNICE 143
WALTER, HUGO 193
WALTER, JULIE ANN 69
WALTERS, LYNN D. 254
WALTERS, ROY E. 223
WALTMAN, MERIBETH 307
WALTON, CHRISTINE A. 300
WANG, KATH 119
WARD, ARTHUR F. 17
WARD, DOROTHY MILLER 89
WARDLAW, VANESSA A. 86
WARNER, LYNN 211
WARREN, CHRIS 159
WARREN, ELIZABETH A. 27
WARRNEBURG, WANDA 39
WARSHAW, RONNA 291
WASHINGTON, GLORIA J. 185
WAT, PAM 137
WATKINS, BRUCE W. 17
WATKINS, CARRIE M. 150
WATKINS, JODI 109
WATLAND, LISA 271
WATSON, BETTY 132
WATTS, BETH JOELLE 26
WEAVER, BUFFY 181
WEBB, JENNY 248

WEBB, NICKI 9
WEBER, MICHELLE 87
WEBER, REBECCA 204
WEBSTER, J. DERRICK 199
WEEDMAN, MISTI 286
WEEKS, JEAN C. 310
WEETMAN, ROBERT 53
WEHNER, SHANNON 242
WEHR, JUNE L. 62
WEIKEL, BONNIE 235
WEINLICK, AMY 7
WEISENBERGER, MARY 222
WEISER, KAREN 287
WELIEVER, KATHY 96
WELLS, D. BURNETT 164
WELLS, DANIEL E. 157
WELLS, GRETCHEN 86
WELLS, KERRY 48
WELLS, WENDY 123
WELSH, JENNIFER JENNA 40
WENTZ, GUS 282
WENZEL, EVELYN M. 149
WERFELMAN, KRIS TINA 34
WESLEY, MONICA 257
WEST, CYNTHIA L. 211
WEST, GABRIEL A. 104
WEST, HEATHER 22
WEST, JENNY HARRISON 310
WEST, LISA E. 279
WEST, THOMAS A. JR. 294
WETHERBEE, GLADYS 111
WHEAT, MARTI L. 58
WHEATLEY, TAMMY 42
WHEELER, STEPHANIE 3
WHELAN, JACKIE 40
WHELLER, ILONA 23
WHELPLEY, JAN C. 237
WHIPPLE, JENNI 168
WHISNANT, JULIE 44
WHITE, CHERYL 57
WHITE, CRYSTAL 78
WHITE, DARLENE JANET 161
WHITE, GLENNETTE 303
WHITE, HOLLY F. 117
WHITE, JAIME R. 143
WHITE, JONI 306
WHITE, KEITH L. 119
WHITE, KRISTIN 274
WHITE, LORI 129
WHITE, NICOLE 85
WHITEHEAD, JANET 161
WHITESEL, PATRICIA 40
WHITFIELD, AMY 184
WHITFIELD, VALERIE 11
WHITLEY, KENNETH 281
WHITMARSH, JOHN III 240
WHITTAKER, WILLIAM R. 21
WICKSTROM, JULIE 46
WIENER, HOWARD 268
WIESE, SHELLEY 243
WIESNER, WAYNE 195
WIGET, EDWARD D. 27
WILBUR, DONNA M. 90
WILEY, THELMA TAPP 266
WILHELM, MICHAEL D. 249
WILHITE, LORI A. 159
WILLARD, JULIE 196
WILLARD, TERESA 281
WILLEY, MICHAEL R. 133
WILLHELM, AUDRYE 38
WILLIAMS, ALAN 17
WILLIAMS, ALI 89
WILLIAMS, BARBARA L. 132
WILLIAMS, BEVERLY J. 215
WILLIAMS, BONNIE 143
WILLIAMS, BOUTIKAA 270
WILLIAMS, CARA 186
WILLIAMS, EDDIE 39
WILLIAMS, JORDAN 273
WILLIAMS, KRISTI 210
WILLIAMS, LISA 42
WILLIAMS, M. 222
WILLIAMS, MABLE 291
WILLIAMS, MARCIA 204
WILLIAMS, MARY L. 164
WILLIAMS, NATHAN 149
WILLIAMS, SUSAN L. 193

WILLIAMS, TAMILA A. 116
WILLIAMS, TINA 116
WILLIAMS, WALTER E. 169
WILLIS, JESSICA 163
WILLIS, JOYCE 50
WILLIS, MELODIE 293
WILLIS, VIVIAN E.M. 250
WILLOUGHBY, DEANN 91
WILLS, MARIE 164
WILLS, VIRGINIA 251
WILSON, ERICA 102
WILSON, M. V. 207
WILSON, REBECCA 129
WILSON, STACY 67
WILSON, STEPHANIE 154
WINDHAM, REVISH 64
WINEBRENNER, BRENDA 155
WINKEL, MARY LYNN 287
WINSLOW, ARTHUR E. 183
WINSLOW, THOMAS G. 275
WINSOR, DON 97
WINSTON, TONYA LYNN 72
WINTER, LAINIE 131
WIRICK, ANNE 137
WISE, AMELIA A. 37
WISNIEWSKI, MELANIE 77
WISOR, LYNN 108
WISSE, DENISE B. 151
WODRICH, RONALD P. 211
WOHL, ABBY 69
WOHLERT, BEVERLY 23
WOLDAHL, WANDA 23
WOLF, ANDREW M. 125
WOLFE, JENNA 158
WOLFE, VICKY 145
WOLFSON, STEVEN ALAN 28
WOLLACK, CARRIE 7
WOLTER, MELISSA D. 58
WOMACK, A.M. 182
WONG, PETE JR. 311
WOO, ANDREA 169
WOODALL, RAYFORD SR.204
WOODARD, JAMIE 197
WOODRUFF, MISSI 135
WOODS, LUANNE 274
WOODS, SAM E. 51
WOOLDRIDGE, DOOTHY H. 171
WORDSWORTH, ANNETTE 99
WRIGHT, CAROLE M. 140
WRIGHT, JOYCE 62
WRIGHT, KRISTIE 284
WRIGHT, MARGARET E. 57
WRIGHT, PAIGE 83
WRIGHT, RON 57
WRIGHT, THERESA 287
WROBLEWSKI, ANNA 303
WURZBACHER, JENNI 52
WYBLE, KATHRYN E. 192
WYCHE, ELIZABETH H. 11
XANDRIA 19
YAKOUBIAN, WILLIAM K. 80
YARVIS, JOEL 239
YEAGER, ROBERT G. 164
YOST, KARL 282
YOUNG, ELIZABETH 13
YOUNG, LUCY M. 175
YOUNGBLOOD, SKY EARTH 67
YOUSHAH, LARRY 158
YU, JUDY 116
YUN, CATHY 210
YUND, TED 67
ZACCHINA, ANNA B. 130
ZAGOREC, SHIRLEY D. 76
ZANONE, MARIBETH 164
ZARLENGO, DANIELLE 46
ZEAPHEY, PEGGY 208
ZEBRASKI, JOAN 263
ZELLER, KARL S. 296
ZERILLO, JOHN P. SR. 128
ZETTLER, TAMMY 34
ZIEGELMANN, VICKIE 86
ZIMMER, JENNIFER 33
ZIMMERMAN, AMANDA 222
ZINSMEISTER, PAMELA 38
ZIPUSCH, MIKA EVE 217
ZITZELBERGER, PATTI 8
ZSCHACH, HEDI L. 268
ZYSSET, JEFF A. 161